WELCOME TO THE CARIBBEAN

Yes, the Caribbean is famous for gorgeous beaches, but that's not all that lures travelers back year after year. The string of islands that arcs from Turks and Caicos to Aruba includes dozens of individual nations, each with a unique history, cuisine, and way of life. If you want to do more than soak up the sun on a white-sand beach, the Caribbean offers an abundance of sea and shore experiences, from snorkeling off remote cays to sipping cocktails under a palm tree. Whatever you choose, the tropical warmth and relaxed pace guarantee an enchanting vacation.

TOP REASONS TO GO

★ **Beaches:** Nearly every island has a beach that ranks among the world's best.

★ **Resorts:** There's everything from luxurious beachfront hideaways to simple inns.

★ **Water Sports:** Diving, sailing, snorkeling, and kayaking can be enjoyed year-round.

★ **Island Culture:** History and folklore give each island a unique identity.

★ **Nature:** Lush rain forests and mountains make for great hiking and bird-watching.

★ **Parties:** Beach bars, carnivals, and celebrations galore enliven the scene.

Fodor's CARIBBEAN 2015

Publisher: Amanda D'Acierno, *Senior Vice President*

Editorial: Arabella Bowen, *Editor in Chief*; Linda Cabasin, *Editorial Director*

Design: Fabrizio La Rocca, *Vice President, Creative Director*; Tina Malaney, *Associate Art Director*; Chie Ushio, *Senior Designer*; Ann McBride, *Production Designer*

Photography: Melanie Marin, *Associate Director of Photography*; Jessica Parkhill and Jennifer Romains, *Researchers*

Maps: Rebecca Baer, *Senior Map Editor*; David Lindroth; Mark Stroud, Moon Street Cartography *Cartographers*

Production: Linda Schmidt, *Managing Editor*; Evangelos Vasilakis, *Associate Managing Editor*; Angela L. McLean, *Senior Production Manager*

Sales: Jacqueline Lebow, *Sales Director*

Marketing & Publicity: Heather Dalton, *Marketing Director*; Katherine Punia, *Senior Publicist*

Business & Operations: Susan Livingston, *Vice President, Strategic Business Planning*; Sue Daulton, *Vice President, Operations*

Fodors.com: Megan Bell, *Executive Director, Revenue & Business Development*; Yasmin Marinaro, *Senior Director, Marketing & Partnerships*

Writers: Carol M. Bareuther, Jonique Gaynor, Steve Larese, Lynda Lohr, Elise Meyer, Susan MacCallum-Whitcomb, Catherine MacGillivray, Marie Elena Martinez, Vernon O'Reilly-Ramesar, Jody Rathgeb, Paulina Salach, Ramona Settle, Richard Sitler, Eileen Robinson Smith, Roberta Sotonoff, Julie Schwietert Collazo, Jordan Simon, Susan Zaluski, Jane E. Zarem

Editors: Eric B. Wechter (lead editor), Perrie Hartz
Editorial Contributors: Bob Fagan, Alexis Kelly, Steven Montero, Douglas Stallings
Production Editor: Elyse Rozelle

ISBN 978-0-8041-4262-5

ISSN 1524–9174

All details in this book are based on information supplied to us at press time. Always confirm information when it matters, especially if you're making a detour to visit a specific place. Fodor's expressly disclaims any liability, loss, or risk, personal or otherwise, that is incurred as a consequence of the use of any of the contents of this book.

SPECIAL SALES

This book is available at special discounts for bulk purchases for sales promotions or premiums. For more information, e-mail specialmarkets@randomhouse.com

PRINTED IN THE UNITED STATES OF AMERICA

10 9 8 7 6 5 4 3 2 1

Fodor's 2015

CARIBBEAN

CONTENTS

MAPS

ABOUT THIS GUIDE

Fodor's Recommendations

Everything in this guide is worth doing—we don't cover what isn't—but exceptional sights, hotels, and restaurants are recognized with additional accolades. Fodor's Choice★ indicates our top recommendations; and **Best Bets** call attention to notable hotels and restaurants in various categories. Care to nominate a new place? Visit Fodors.com/contact-us.

Trip Costs

We list prices wherever possible to help you budget well. Hotel and restaurant price categories from **$** to **$$$$** are noted alongside each recommendation. For hotels, we include the lowest cost of a standard double room in high season. For restaurants, we cite the average price of a main course at dinner or, if dinner isn't served, at lunch. For attractions, we always list adult admission fees; discounts are usually available for children, students, and senior citizens.

Hotels

Our local writers vet every hotel to recommend the best overnights in each price category, from budget to expensive. Unless otherwise specified, you can expect private bath, phone, and TV in your room. For expanded hotel reviews, facilities, and deals visit Fodors.com.

Restaurants

Unless we state otherwise, restaurants are open for lunch and dinner daily. We mention dress code only when there's a specific requirement and reservations only when they're essential or not accepted. To make restaurant reservations, visit Fodors.com.

Credit Cards

The hotels and restaurants in this guide typically accept credit cards. If not, we'll say so.

Top Picks	Hotels & Restaurants
★ Fodor'sChoice	
	🏨 Hotel
Listings	⤵ Number of rooms
⊠ Address	🍽️ Meal plans
⊠ Branch address	✕ Restaurant
☎ Telephone	⚓ Reservations
🖷 Fax	👔 Dress code
⊕ Website	⊟ No credit cards
✉ E-mail	Ⓢ Price
⊞ Admission fee	
☉ Open/closed times	**Other**
Ⓜ Subway	⇨ See also
⊹ Directions or Map coordinates	☞ Take note
	🏌️ Golf facilities

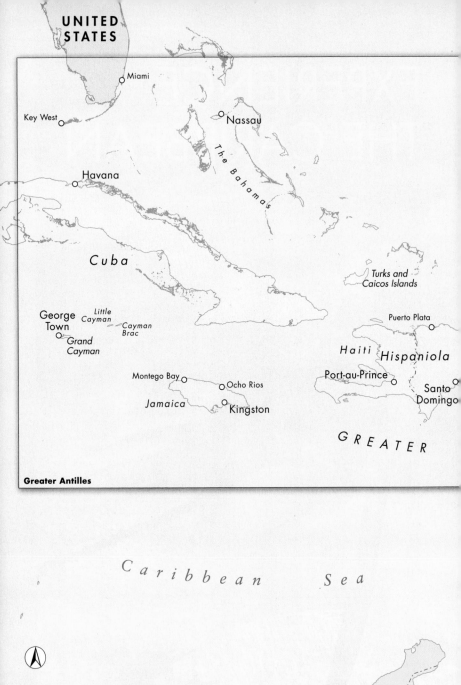

UNITED
STATES

Miami

Key West

Nassau

The Bahamas

Havana

Cuba

Turks and
Caicos Islands

George
Town
*Little
Cayman*
*Cayman
Brac*

*Grand
Cayman*

Puerto Plata

Haiti *Hispaniola*

Montego Bay
Ocho Rios
Port-au-Prince

Santo
Domingo

Jamaica
Kingston

G R E A T E R

Greater Antilles

C a r i b b e a n   S e a

0   200 mi
0   200 km

Cartagena   **COLOMBIA**   Maracaibo

The Caribbean

ATLANTIC OCEAN

Dominican Republic

San Juan

Puerto Rico

St. Thomas

St. John

Tortola

Virgin Gorda

LEEWARD ISLANDS

Anguilla

St. Barthélemy

St. Maarten/ St. Martin

Saba

Barbuda

St. Eustatius

St. Croix

St. Kitts

Nevis

Antigua

Montserrat

Guadeloupe

Marie Galante

ANTILLES

Dominica

Martinique
Fort-de-France

WINDWARD ISLANDS

Leeward Islands

St. Lucia

Barbados

St. Vincent

Bridgetown

Bequia

The Grenadines

Carriacou

St. George's

Grenada

Tobago

Aruba

Curaçao

Bonaire

Willemstad

LESSER ANTILLES

Islas Los Roques

Port of Spain

Trinidad

La Guaira

Windward Islands

Caracas

VENEZUELA

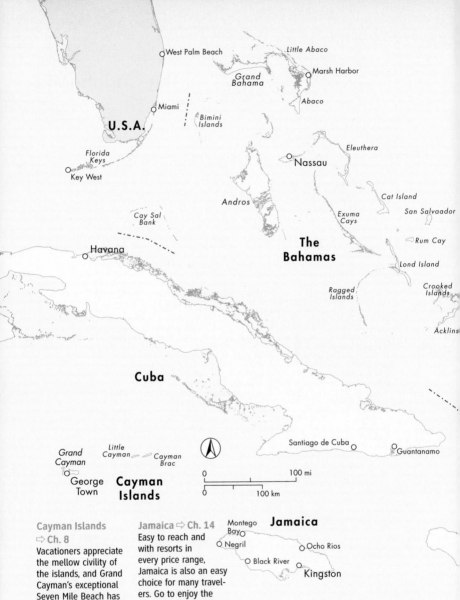

West Palm Beach

Little Abaco

Grand
Bahama

Marsh Harbor

Miami

Abaco

U.S.A.

Bimini
Islands

Eleuthera

Nassau

Florida
Keys

Key West

Cat Island

Andros

San Salvaador

Cay Sal
Bank

Exuma
Cays

Rum Cay

Havana

The
Bahamas

Lond Island

Ragged
Islands

Crooked
Islands

Acklins

Cuba

Santiago de Cuba

Guantanamo

Little
Cayman

Cayman
Brac

Grand
Cayman

George
Town

Cayman
Islands

0   100 mi

0   100 km

Cayman Islands
⇨ Ch. 8
Vacationers appreciate
the mellow civility of
the islands, and Grand
Cayman's exceptional
Seven Mile Beach has
its share of fans. Divers
come to explore the
pristine reefs or perhaps
to swim with friendly
stingrays. Go if you
want a safe, family-
friendly vacation spot.
Don't go if you're trying
to save money, because
there are few real
bargains here.

Jamaica ⇨ Ch. 14
Easy to reach and
with resorts in
every price range,
Jamaica is also an easy
choice for many travel-
ers. Go to enjoy the
music, food, beaches,
and sense of hospitality
that's made it one of
the Caribbean's most
popular destinations.
Don't go if you can't
deal with the idea that
a Caribbean paradise
still has problems of
its own to solve.

Montego
Bay

Jamaica

Negril

Ocho Rios

Black River

Kingston

G R E A T E R

Caribbean

THE GREATER ANTILLES

The islands closest to the United States mainland—composed of Cuba, Jamaica, Haiti, the Dominican Republic, and Puerto Rico—are also the largest in the chain that stretches in an arc from the southern coast of Florida down to Venezuela. Haiti and Cuba aren't covered in this book. The Cayman Islands, just south of Cuba, are usually included in this group.

Dominican Republic ⇨ Ch. 11

Dominicans have beautiful smiles and warm hearts and are proud of their island, which is blessed with pearl-white beaches and a vibrant, Latin culture. Go for the best-priced resorts in the Caribbean and a wide range of activities that will keep you moving day and night. Don't go if you can't go with the flow. Things don't always work here, and not everyone speaks English.

Turks and Caicos Islands ⇨ Ch. 26

Miles of white-sand beaches surround this tiny island chain, only eight of which are inhabited. The smaller islands seem to come from some long-forgotten era of Caribbean life. Go for deserted beaches and excellent diving on one of the world's largest coral reefs. Don't go for nightlife and a fast pace. And don't forget your wallet. This isn't a budget destination.

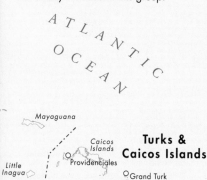

Puerto Rico ⇨ Ch. 17

San Juan is hopping day and night; beyond the city, you'll find a sunny escape and slower pace. Party in San Juan, relax on the beach, hike the rain forest, or play some of the Caribbean's best golf courses. You have the best of both worlds here, with natural and urban thrills alike. So go for both. Just don't expect to do it in utter seclusion.

WHAT'S WHERE

LESSER ANTILLES: THE EASTERN CARIBBEAN

The Lesser Antilles are larger in number but smaller in size than the Greater Antilles, and they make up the bulk of the Caribbean arc. Beginning with the Virgin Islands but going all the way to Grenada, the islands of the Eastern Caribbean form a barrier between the Atlantic Ocean and the Caribbean Sea. The best beaches are usually on the Caribbean side.

U.S. Virgin Islands ⇨ Ch. 27

A perfect combination of the familiar and the exotic, the U.S. Virgin Islands are a little bit of America set in an azure sea. Go to St. Croix if you like history and interesting restaurants. Go to St. John if you crave a back-to-nature experience. Go to St. Thomas if you want a shop-'til-you-drop experience and a big selection of resorts, activities, and nightlife.

British Virgin Islands ⇨ Ch. 7

The lure of the British Virgins is exclusivity and personal attention, not lavish luxury. Even the most expensive resorts are selling a state of mind rather than state-of-the-art. So go with an open mind, and your stress may very well melt away. Don't go if you expect glitz or stateside efficiency. These islands are about getting away, not getting it all.

Montserrat ⇨ Ch. 16

Montserrat has staged one of the best comebacks of the new century, returning to the tourism scene after a disastrous volcanic eruption in 1995. Go for exciting volcano ecotourism and great diving or just to taste what the Caribbean used to be like. Don't go for splashy resorts or nightlife. You'll be happier here if you can appreciate simpler pleasures.

Anguilla ⇨ Ch. 2

With miles of brilliant beaches and a range of luxurious resorts (even a few that mere mortals can afford), Anguilla is where the rich, powerful, and famous go to chill out. Go for the fine cuisine in elegant surroundings, great snorkeling, and funky late-night music scene. Don't go for shopping and sightseeing. This island is all about relaxing and reviving.

St. Maarten/ St. Martin ⇨ Ch. 23

Two nations (Dutch and French), many nationalities, one small island, a lot of development. But there are also more white, sandy beaches than days in a month. Go for the awesome restaurants, excellent shopping, and wide range of activities. Don't go if you're not willing to get out and search for the really good stuff.

St. Barthélemy ⇨ Ch. 19

If you come to St. Barth for a taste of European village life, not for a conventional full-service resort experience, you will be richly rewarded. Go for excellent dining and wine, great boutiques with the latest hip fashions, and an active, on-the-go vacation. Don't go for big resorts, and make sure your credit card is platinum-plated.

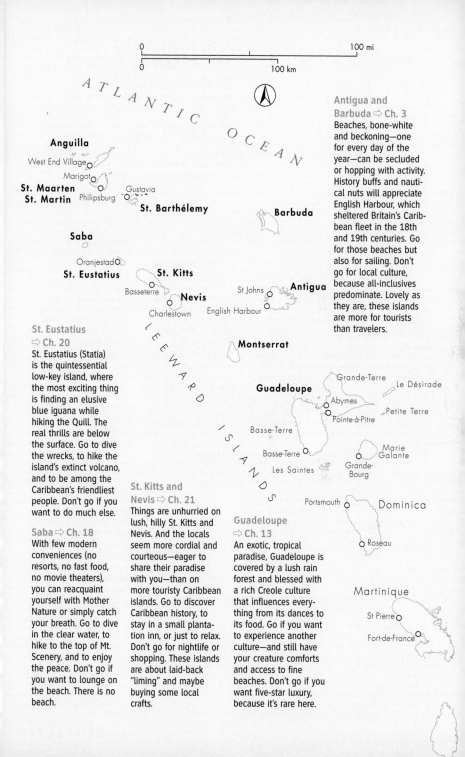

Antigua and Barbuda ⇨ Ch. 3
Beaches, bone-white and beckoning—one for every day of the year—can be secluded or hopping with activity. History buffs and nautical nuts will appreciate English Harbour, which sheltered Britain's Caribbean fleet in the 18th and 19th centuries. Go for those beaches but also for sailing. Don't go for local culture, because all-inclusives predominate. Lovely as they are, these islands are more for tourists than travelers.

St. Eustatius ⇨ Ch. 20
St. Eustatius (Statia) is the quintessential low-key island, where the most exciting thing is finding an elusive blue iguana while hiking the Quill. The real thrills are below the surface. Go to dive the wrecks, to hike the island's extinct volcano, and to be among the Caribbean's friendliest people. Don't go if you want to do much else.

Saba ⇨ Ch. 18
With few modern conveniences (no resorts, no fast food, no movie theaters), you can reacquaint yourself with Mother Nature or simply catch your breath. Go to dive in the clear water, to hike to the top of Mt. Scenery, and to enjoy the peace. Don't go if you want to lounge on the beach. There is no beach.

St. Kitts and Nevis ⇨ Ch. 21
Things are unhurried on lush, hilly St. Kitts and Nevis. And the locals seem more cordial and courteous—eager to share their paradise with you—than on more touristy Caribbean islands. Go to discover Caribbean history, to stay in a small plantation inn, or just to relax. Don't go for nightlife or shopping. These islands are about laid-back "liming" and maybe buying some local crafts.

Guadeloupe ⇨ Ch. 13
An exotic, tropical paradise, Guadeloupe is covered by a lush rain forest and blessed with a rich Creole culture that influences everything from its dances to its food. Go if you want to experience another culture—and still have your creature comforts and access to fine beaches. Don't go if you want five-star luxury, because it's rare here.

WHAT'S WHERE

THE WINDWARD AND SOUTHERN ISLANDS

The Windward Islands—Dominica, Martinique, St. Lucia, St. Vincent, and Grenada—complete the main Caribbean arc. These dramatically scenic southern islands face the trade winds head-on. The Grenadines—a string of small islands between Grenada and St. Vincent—are heaven for sailors. The Southern Caribbean islands—Trinidad, Tobago, Aruba, Bonaire, and Curaçao—are rarely bothered by hurricanes.

Aruba ⇨ Ch. 4
Some Caribbean travelers seek an undiscovered paradise, some seek the familiar and safe: Aruba is for the latter. On the smallest of the ABC islands, the waters are peacock blue, and the white beaches are beautiful and powdery soft. For Americans, Aruba offers all the comforts of home: English is spoken universally, and the U.S. dollar is accepted everywhere.

Bonaire ⇨ Ch. 6
With only 15,000 year-round citizens and huge numbers of visiting divers, Bonaire still seems largely untouched by tourism. Divers come for the clear water, profusion of marine life, and great dive shops. With a surreal, arid landscape, immense flamingo population, and gorgeous turquoise vistas Bonaire also offers a wonderful land-based holiday.

Curaçao ⇨ Ch. 9
Rich in heritage and history, Curaçao offers a blend of island life and city savvy, wonderful weather, spectacular diving, and charming beaches. Dutch and Caribbean influences are everywhere, but there's also an infusion of touches from around the world, particularly noteworthy in the great food. Willemstad, the picturesque capital, is a treat for pedestrians, with shopping clustered in areas around the waterfront.

Dominica ⇨ Ch. 10
Dominica is the island to find your bliss exploring nature's bounty, not in the sun and surf. Go to be active, either diving under the sea or hiking on land. Don't go for great beaches or a big-resort experience. This is one island that's delightfully behind the times.

Martinique ⇨ Ch. 15
Excellent cuisine, fine service, highly touted rum, and lilting Franco-Caribbean music are the main draws in Martinique. Go if you're a Francophile drawn to fine food, wine, and sophisticated style. Don't go if you are looking for a bargain and don't have patience. Getting here is a chore, but there are definitely rewards for the persistent.

Caribbean

Aruba
Oranjestad

Bonaire
Kralendijk

Curaçao Willemstad

Sea

Islas Los Roques

La Guaira

Isla La Tortuga

Caracas

| 0 | | 100 mi |
| 0 | 100 km | |

VENEZUELA

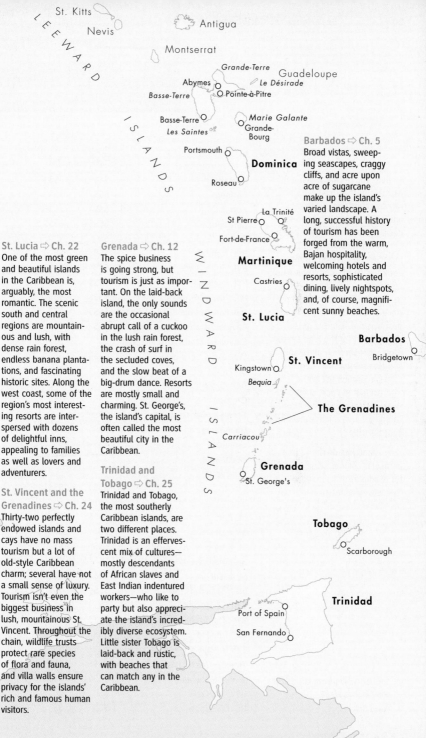

St. Kitts
Nevis

L E E W A R D

Antigua

Montserrat

I S L A N D S

Grande-Terre
Abymes ○
Basse-Terre
Le Désirade
○ Pointe-à-Pitre

Guadeloupe

Basse-Terre ○
Les Saintes

Marie Galante
○ Grande-Bourg

Portsmouth ○

Dominica

Roseau ○

La Trinité
St Pierre ○ ○
Fort-de-France ○

Barbados ⇨ Ch. 5
Broad vistas, sweeping seascapes, craggy cliffs, and acre upon acre of sugarcane make up the island's varied landscape. A long, successful history of tourism has been forged from the warm, Bajan hospitality, welcoming hotels and resorts, sophisticated dining, lively nightspots, and, of course, magnificent sunny beaches.

Martinique

Castries ○

St. Lucia ⇨ Ch. 22
One of the most green and beautiful islands in the Caribbean is, arguably, the most romantic. The scenic south and central regions are mountainous and lush, with dense rain forest, endless banana plantations, and fascinating historic sites. Along the west coast, some of the region's most interesting resorts are interspersed with dozens of delightful inns, appealing to families as well as lovers and adventurers.

St. Vincent and the Grenadines ⇨ Ch. 24
Thirty-two perfectly endowed islands and cays have no mass tourism but a lot of old-style Caribbean charm; several have not a small sense of luxury. Tourism isn't even the biggest business in lush, mountainous St. Vincent. Throughout the chain, wildlife trusts protect rare species of flora and fauna, and villa walls ensure privacy for the islands' rich and famous human visitors.

Grenada ⇨ Ch. 12
The spice business is going strong, but tourism is just as important. On the laid-back island, the only sounds are the occasional abrupt call of a cuckoo in the lush rain forest, the crash of surf in the secluded coves, and the slow beat of a big-drum dance. Resorts are mostly small and charming. St. George's, the island's capital, is often called the most beautiful city in the Caribbean.

Trinidad and Tobago ⇨ Ch. 25
Trinidad and Tobago, the most southerly Caribbean islands, are two different places. Trinidad is an effervescent mix of cultures—mostly descendants of African slaves and East Indian indentured workers—who like to party but also appreciate the island's incredibly diverse ecosystem. Little sister Tobago is laid-back and rustic, with beaches that can match any in the Caribbean.

W I N D W A R D

I S L A N D S

St. Lucia

Barbados
○ Bridgetown

St. Vincent
Kingstown ○
Bequia

The Grenadines

Carriacou

Grenada
St. George's ○

Tobago
○ Scarborough

Trinidad
Port of Spain ○
San Fernando ○

ISLAND FINDER

To help you decide which island is best for you, we've rated each island in several areas that might influence your decision on choosing the perfect Caribbean vacation spot. Each major island covered in this book has been rated in terms of cost from $ (very inexpensive) to $$$$$ (very expensive), and since prices often vary a great deal by season, we've given you a rating for the high season (December through mid-April) and low season (mid-April through November). We've also compared each island's relative strength in several other categories that might influence your decision.

If an island has no marks in a particular column (under "Golf" for example), it means that the activity is not available on the island.

	Cost High Season	Cost Low Season
Anguilla	$$$$	$$$
Antigua	$$$	$$
Aruba	$$$	$$
Barbados	$$$$	$$$$
Bonaire	$$	$$
BVI: Tortola	$$$	$$
BVI: Virgin Gorda	$$$$$	$$$$
BVI: Anegada	$$$$	$$$
BVI: Jost Van Dyke	$$$$	$$$
Cayman Islands: Grand Cayman	$$$$	$$$
Cayman Islands: Little Cayman	$$$	$$$
Cayman Islands: Cayman Brac	$$	$$
Curaçao	$$$$	$$$
Dominica	$$	$
Dominican Republic	$$	$
Grenada	$$$	$$$
Grenada: Carriacou	$$	$
Guadeloupe	$$	$$
Jamaica	$$$	$$
Martinique	$$$	$$
Montserrat	$	$
Puerto Rico	$$$	$$
Saba	$$	$
St. Barthélemy	$$$$$	$$$$
St. Eustatius	$$	$
St. Kitts & Nevis: St. Kitts	$$$	$$
St. Kitts & Nevis: Nevis	$$$$	$$$
St. Lucia	$$$$	$$$
St. Maarten/St. Martin	$$$	$$$
SVG: St. Vincent	$$	$$
SVG: The Grenadines	$$$$	$$$
T&T: Trinidad	$$$	$$
T&T: Tobago	$$$	$$
Turks & Caicos Islands	$$$$*	$$$*
USVI: St. Thomas	$$$$	$$$
USVI: St. Croix	$$	$
USVI: St. John	$$$	$$

*   *Cost for Provo (Parrot Cay $$$$$, other islands $$)*

**   *Provo Only*

	Beautiful Beaches	Fine Dining	Shopping	Casinos	Nightlife	Diving	Golf	Eco-tourism	Good for Families
	▲▲▲▲	▲▲▲▲	▲▲		▲▲	▲	▲▲▲	▲	▲▲
	▲▲▲▲▲	▲▲▲▲▲	▲▲▲▲	▲▲▲	▲▲▲	▲▲	▲▲▲	▲▲▲	▲▲▲
	▲▲▲▲	▲▲▲▲	▲▲▲▲	▲▲▲▲	▲▲▲▲▲	▲▲▲	▲▲	▲▲	▲▲▲▲
	▲▲▲	▲▲▲▲▲	▲▲▲		▲▲▲	▲	▲▲▲▲▲	▲▲	▲▲▲▲
	▲▲▲	▲▲▲	▲▲	▲	▲	▲▲▲▲▲		▲▲▲▲	▲▲▲▲
	▲▲	▲▲▲	▲▲		▲▲	▲▲▲		▲▲▲	▲▲▲
	▲▲▲▲▲	▲▲▲	▲		▲	▲▲▲		▲▲▲▲	▲▲▲
	▲▲▲▲▲	▲▲▲			▲	▲▲▲▲		▲▲▲▲	▲▲▲
	▲▲▲▲	▲▲▲▲	▲			▲▲▲		▲▲▲	▲▲▲
	▲▲▲▲▲	▲▲▲▲	▲▲▲▲▲		▲▲	▲▲▲▲	▲▲▲	▲▲	▲▲▲▲
						▲▲▲▲	▲▲▲▲▲	▲▲▲▲	▲▲▲
	▲▲					▲▲▲▲		▲▲▲	▲▲▲
	▲▲▲▲	▲▲▲▲	▲▲▲		▲▲▲▲	▲▲▲	▲▲▲	▲▲▲	▲▲▲
	▲	▲▲▲	▲▲▲		▲▲	▲▲▲▲▲		▲▲▲▲	▲▲▲
	▲▲▲▲▲	▲▲▲	▲▲	▲▲▲	▲▲▲▲	▲▲▲	▲▲▲▲▲	▲▲▲	▲▲▲
	▲▲▲▲	▲▲▲	▲		▲	▲▲▲	▲	▲▲▲▲	▲▲▲
	▲▲▲	▲	▲					▲▲▲▲	▲▲
	▲▲▲▲	▲▲	▲▲▲	▲▲▲	▲▲▲	▲▲▲	▲▲▲	▲▲▲▲	▲▲▲
	▲▲▲	▲▲▲	▲▲	▲	▲▲▲▲	▲▲▲	▲▲▲▲▲	▲▲▲▲▲	▲▲▲▲▲
	▲▲▲▲	▲▲▲▲	▲▲▲	▲	▲▲▲	▲▲▲	▲▲▲	▲▲▲	▲▲
	▲	▲	▲		▲	▲▲▲▲		▲▲▲▲	▲▲
	▲▲▲	▲▲▲▲	▲▲▲	▲▲▲▲	▲▲▲▲▲	▲▲▲	▲▲▲	▲▲▲▲▲	▲▲▲▲▲
		▲▲▲▲	▲▲		▲	▲▲▲▲▲		▲▲▲▲▲	▲
	▲▲▲▲	▲▲▲▲▲	▲▲▲▲▲		▲▲	▲▲▲			▲
	▲	▲	▲▲		▲	▲▲▲▲▲		▲▲▲▲▲	▲▲▲
	▲▲▲	▲▲▲	▲▲▲	▲▲▲▲	▲▲▲	▲▲▲▲	▲▲▲▲	▲▲▲▲▲	▲▲▲▲▲
	▲▲▲	▲▲▲▲	▲▲		▲▲▲	▲▲▲▲	▲▲▲▲▲	▲▲▲▲▲	▲▲▲▲▲
	▲▲▲	▲▲▲	▲▲▲		▲▲▲	▲▲▲	▲	▲▲▲▲▲	▲▲▲
	▲▲▲▲	▲▲▲▲▲	▲▲▲▲	▲▲▲	▲▲▲▲	▲▲▲	▲	▲▲	▲▲▲
	▲	▲▲	▲	▲	▲	▲▲▲▲		▲▲▲▲▲	▲▲▲
	▲▲▲▲▲	▲▲▲▲	▲		▲	▲▲▲▲▲	▲▲▲▲▲	▲▲▲	▲▲▲▲
	▲▲▲	▲▲▲	▲▲	▲▲▲	▲▲▲▲▲	▲▲▲▲	▲▲▲	▲▲▲▲	▲▲▲▲
	▲▲▲▲	▲▲▲	▲▲	▲▲▲	▲▲▲	▲▲▲▲	▲▲▲▲	▲▲▲▲	▲▲▲
	▲▲▲▲▲	▲▲**	▲	▲	▲	▲▲▲▲▲	▲▲▲▲**	▲▲▲▲	▲▲▲**
	▲▲▲▲	▲▲▲▲	▲▲▲▲▲		▲▲	▲▲▲	▲▲▲▲	▲▲	▲▲▲▲
	▲▲▲	▲▲▲	▲▲	▲▲	▲▲	▲▲▲	▲▲▲	▲▲▲	▲▲▲
	▲▲▲▲▲	▲▲▲	▲▲		▲	▲▲▲	▲▲▲	▲▲▲▲	▲▲▲▲▲

CARIBBEAN LODGING

When to Reserve

School vacation periods, especially in high season, generally require advance booking at most hotels. The most popular properties book as much as a year in advance because of their high numbers of repeat clientele, many of whom request the same room every year. Many respected chain resorts, such as the Ritz-Carlton and the Four Seasons, also book well in advance during peak periods. The most difficult time to find a well-priced room is typically around the Christmas holidays and New Year's, when minimum-stay requirements of one to two weeks may be common and room rates typically double.

But for the typical Caribbean resort, two months is usually sufficient notice. In popular mass-market destinations such as Punta Cana or Negril, you could probably find something even a couple of weeks in advance. Paradoxically, it's easier to find an acceptable room in the busiest destinations by sheer virtue of the number of rooms available at any given time. Although waiting until the last minute doesn't net as many bargains as cruises, flexibility can pay off either in a deep discount (usually at a larger resort) or a room category upgrade.

Fees and Add-Ons

Every island charges an accommodations tax, whether on private villa rentals, bed-and-breakfast stays, or mega-resorts. This ranges from 7% to 15%, depending on the destination (you can find the exact surcharge listed in the individual chapters' hotel and restaurant price chart). In addition, most Caribbean hotels and resorts tack on a service fee, usually around 10%. The service fee isn't quite the same as a tip for service, and it is customary at most non-all-inclusive resorts to tip the staff. Generally, expect to pay at least 20% above and beyond the base rate for a Caribbean resort room. The latest growing trend—though it's hardly unique to the Caribbean—is the "resort fee." You can encounter this almost anywhere, though resort fees are almost universal in San Juan, Puerto Rico. The fee presumably covers costs such as housekeeping (though you might sometimes see this on your bill, too, especially for villa rentals), utilities, and use of resort facilities. Figure $5 to $50 per night, but know that this is generally restricted to larger hotels and defies generalization because it depends more on the individual resort or hotel chain than the island itself. These additional costs aren't always mentioned when you book, so be sure to inquire.

Picking the Best Room

On virtually every island, especially at beachfront lodgings, the better the beach access or ocean view, the higher the price. If you're the active type who really uses a room only to sleep, then you can save $100 or more per night by choosing a garden-, mountain-, or town-view room. But regardless of view, be sure to ask about the property's layout. For example, if you want to be close to the "action" at many larger resorts, whether you have mobility concerns or just need to satisfy your gambling or beach-gamboling itch, the trade-off might be noise, whether from screaming kids jumping in the pool or DJs pumping and thumping reggae in the bar. Likewise, saving that $100 may not be worth it if your room faces a busy thoroughfare. This is your vacation, so if you have any specific desires or dislikes, discuss them thoroughly with the reservations staff.

Types of Lodgings	Inclusive or Not?

Most islands offer the gamut of glitzy resorts, boutique-chic hotels, historic hostelries, family-run B&Bs, condo resorts, self-catering apartments, and private villas that are typical throughout the Caribbean.

Condos and Time-Shares Condo resorts are increasingly popular and can offer both extra space and superior savings for families, with kitchens, sofa beds, and more. In fact, they dominate the sensuous sweeps of Grand Cayman's Seven-Mile Beach and Provo's amazing Grace Bay in the Turks and Caicos. Some of these are time-share properties, but not all time-shares require you to sit through a sales pitch.

Inns and B&Bs Historic inns come in all shapes and sizes. The old Spanish colonial capitals of Santo Domingo and San Juan have converted monasteries. Puerto Rico also offers affordable lodgings in its paradors, patterned after the Spanish system, most of them historically and/or culturally significant buildings such as old-time thermal baths or working coffee plantations. Longtime sailing and whaling destinations such as Antigua or Bequia in the Grenadines offer their own pieces of history adapted to modern comfort, and Guadeloupe and Martinique feature converted sugar plantations. St. Kitts and Nevis are also prized by Caribbean connoisseurs for their restored greathouse plantation inns, often with a resident eccentric expat owner who lives on-site and enhances your experience with amusing anecdotes and insider insights.

Private Villas Another increasingly popular option for families or those seeking a surprising bargain: private villas. Self-catering means saving on dining out on more expensive islands, such as St. Barth (where villas usually cost much less than hotels), though a car is usually necessary except in mini-villages such as Cayman Kai on Grand Cayman. Many villas have private pools with stunning sea views and/or beachfront access. Montserrat offers exceptional value for anyone.

Resorts Most prevalent are large resorts, including all-inclusives, usually strategically positioned on the beach. These include golf/spa resorts and name-brand chain hotels in various price categories from Ritz-Carlton to Comfort Suites. Jamaica and the Dominican Republic specialize in the all-inclusive experience. Some islands abound in cookie-cutter tour-group hotels that look like they could be plonked down anywhere, including Aruba (along one of the Caribbean's most alluring beaches) and Guadeloupe, though both also offer distinctive properties as well.

The AI (which stands for "all-inclusive") concept is especially prominent on islands such as Jamaica, the Dominican Republic, Antigua, and St. Lucia. For those who have only a week for vacation, the allure is obvious: a hassle-free, pay-one-price vacation including accommodations, meals, unlimited drinks, entertainment, and most activities. And you tend to get what you pay for: AIs range from hedonistic high-tech luxury to barebones beachfront bang-for-the-buck, with prices to match. Some of these resorts are intimate romantic hideaways, some emphasize sporting options, others cater to families, and still others cater to singles ready to mingle in a nonstop frat-party atmosphere.

But there are caveats. Few AIs offer *everything* for free. That sybaritic spa treatment, the scuba trip (and instruction), the sunset cruise, or the tour of the nearby plantation generally won't be included. Moreover, there can be surcharges for dining in some restaurants (which must be reserved).

AI resorts appeal most to travelers who just need to get away and bask in the sun, piña colada within easy reach. They're not for more adventuresome types who seek genuine interaction with the locals and immersion in their culture, nor are they good for people who want to eat local food, since most AI travelers rarely leave their resort boundaries.

CARIBBEAN LOGISTICS

Time

The Cayman Islands, Cuba, Haiti, Jamaica, and the Turks and Caicos Islands are all in the Eastern Standard Time zone. All other Caribbean islands are in the Atlantic Standard Time zone, which is one hour later than Eastern Standard. Caribbean islands don't observe daylight saving time, so during that period (March through October) Eastern Standard is one hour behind, and Atlantic Standard is the same time as Eastern Daylight Time.

Driving

Your own valid driver's license works in some countries. However, temporary local driving permits are required in several Caribbean destinations (Anguilla, Antigua, Barbados, the British Virgin Islands, Cayman Islands, Dominica, Grenada, Nevis, St. Kitts, St. Lucia, and St. Vincent and the Grenadines), which you can get at rental agencies or local police offices on presentation of a valid license and a small fee. St. Lucia and St. Vincent and the Grenadines require a temporary permit only if you don't have an International Driving Permit (available from AAA).

Flights

Many carriers fly nonstop or direct routes to the Caribbean from major international airports in the United States, including Atlanta, Boston, Charlotte, Chicago, Dallas, Fort Lauderdale, Houston, Miami, New York (JFK), Newark, Philadelphia, Phoenix, and Washington (Dulles). If you live somewhere else in the United States, you'll probably have to make a connection to get to your Caribbean destination. It's also not uncommon to make a connection in the Caribbean, most often in San Juan, Montego Bay, Barbados, or St. Maarten.

Some flights will be on small planes operated by local or regional carriers, which may have code-share arrangements with major airlines from the United States. Or you can confidently book directly with the local carrier, using a major credit card, sometimes online but more often by phone.

Some smaller airlines may make multiple stops, accepting and discharging passengers and/or cargo at each small airport or airstrip along the way. This is not unusual. What is also not unusual is the sometimes erratic schedules these smaller airlines can have. Be sure to confirm your flights on interisland carriers, and make sure that the carrier has a local contact telephone number for you, as you may be subject to a small carrier's whims: if no other passengers are booked on your flight, particularly if the carrier operates "scheduled charters," you'll be rescheduled on another flight or at a different departure time (earlier or later than your original reservation) that is more convenient for the airline. If you're connecting from an interisland flight to a major airline, be sure to include a substantial buffer of time for these kinds of delays.

TYPICAL TRAVEL TIMES BY AIR		
	NEW YORK	**MIAMI**
Puerto Rico	3½ hours	2½ hours
Jamaica	4½ hours	1½ hours
St. Lucia	4½ hours	3½ hours
Trinidad	5 hours	3½ hours
Aruba	4¾ hours	2½ hours

Airlines

Major Airlines Air Jamaica (📞 800/920–4225 ⊕ www.airjamaica.com). **American Airlines** (📞 800/433–7300 ⊕ www.aa.com). **Caribbean Airlines** (📞 800/920–4225 ⊕ www.caribbean-airlines.com). **Delta Airlines** (📞 800/241–4141 ⊕ www.delta.com). **JetBlue** (📞 800/538–2583 ⊕ www.jetblue.com). **Spirit Airlines** (📞 801/401–2200 [new reservations, fees apply], 801/400–2222 [existing reservations] ⊕ www.spirit.com). **United Airlines** (📞 800/864–8331 ⊕ www.united.com). **US Airways** (📞 800/428–4322 ⊕ www.usairways.com).

Smaller/Regional Airlines Air Antilles Express (📞 0890/648–648 in Guadeloupe ⊕ www.airantilles.com). **Air Caraïbes** (📞 0820/835–835 in Guyana ⊕ www.aircaraibes.com). **Air Sunshine** (📞 800/327–8900, 800/435–8900 in Florida ⊕ www.airsunshine.com). **Air Turks & Caicos** (📞 888/957–3223 in U.S., 649/946–4999 in the Turks and Caicos ⊕ www.airturksandcaicos.com). **Bahamas Air** (📞 242/702–4140 in Nassau, 800/222–4262 in U.S. ⊕ bahamasair.com). **Caicos Express** (📞 649/941–5730 in the Turks and Caicos, 305/677–3116 in U.S. ⊕ caicosexpressairways.com). **Cape Air** (📞 866/227–3247, 508/771–6944 outside U.S. ⊕ www.capeair.com). **Cayman Airways** (📞 345/949–2311 in the Cayman Islands, 800/422–9626 in U.S. ⊕ www.caymanairways.com). **InselAir** (📞 (599) 9/737–0444 in Curaçao, 855/493–6004 in U.S. ⊕ www.fly-inselair.com). **LIAT** (📞 480–5582 in Antigua, 888/844–5428 within the Caribbean ⊕ www.liatairline.com). **Mustique Airways** (📞 718/618–4492 in U.S., 784/458–4380 in St. Vincent ⊕ www.mustique.com). **Seaborne Airlines** (📞 340/773–6442 in St. Thomas, 866/359–8784 in U.S. ⊕ www.seaborneairlines.com). **St. Barth Commuter** (📞 590/27–54–54 in St. Barth ⊕ www.stbarthcommuter.com). **SVG Air** (📞 784/457–5124 in St. Vincent ⊕ www.svgair.com). **Winair** (Windward Islands Airways 📞 866/466–0410 ⊕ www.fly-winair.com). **Windward Express Airways** (📞 599/545–2001 in St. Maarten ⊕ www.windwardexpress.com).

Ferries

Interisland ferries are an interesting and often less expensive way to travel around certain areas of the Caribbean, but they are not offered everywhere. A few destinations are reached only by ferry (St. John, for example). In most cases, where service is offered it is frequent (either daily or several times daily).

MAJOR FERRY ROUTES

Ferries connect Puerto Rico with the outlying islands of Vieques and Culebra; St. Thomas with Water Island, St. John, St. Croix, and the British Virgin Islands; the various islands of the British Virgin Islands with each other and with the U.S. Virgin Islands; St. Martin/St. Maarten with Anguilla, St. Barth, and Saba; St. Kitts with Nevis; Antigua with Barbuda and Montserrat; Guadeloupe with La Désirade, Marie-Galante, and Les Saintes, as well as Dominica, Martinique, and St. Lucia; St. Lucia with Guadeloupe, Martinique, Dominica, and Barbados; St. Vincent with Bequia and the other islands of the Grenadines; Grenada with Carriacou and Petite Martinique; and Trinidad with Tobago; there's limited ferry service in the Turks and Caicos Islands (Provo and North Caicos, Grand Turk and Salt Cay). In most cases, service is frequent—either daily or several times daily.

RENTING A VILLA

In the Caribbean the term villa can be used to describe anything from a traditional cottage to a luxurious architectural wonder, but what it almost always means is a stand-alone accommodation, often privately owned. Villa rentals provide some of the region's most desirable accommodations, both from a comfort and an economic point of view. We recommend considering this option, especially if you're a group of friends or a family: you get a lot more space, much more privacy, and a better sense of the island than you would get at a hotel, usually at a fraction of the cost.

Factor in the ability to fix simple meals, snacks, and drinks, and the savings really add up. An additional advantage to Americans is that villa rates are generally negotiated in dollars, thus bypassing unfavorable euro fluctuations in St. Martin, St. Barth, and Martinique.

What Does It Cost?

Rental rates vary widely by island and by season. In-season rates range anywhere from $1,200 for a simple one-bedroom cottage to more than $40,000 a week for a multiroom luxury home. Many full-service resorts also offer villas of varying sizes on their property, and although pricey, these can be an excellent choice if you want the best of both worlds—full service and facilities but also space and privacy. In many cases, renting a villa at a resort will cost less than renting three or four "normal" rooms, and you can still have a waiter deliver your 'ti punch to a beach chair or enjoy access to a high-tech fitness room.

What's Included?

Units are generally furnished nicely and have updated bathrooms and usable kitchens. They are equipped with linens, kitchen utensils, CD and DVD players, a phone, satellite TV, and, increasingly, Wi-Fi access to the Internet. The sophistication of all of the above is factored into the price, so the more luxurious the digs, the higher the price.

Upscale rental villas generally have small, private swimming pools (rather few are beachfront), and housekeeping service a few hours daily except Sunday included in the quoted price. On some islands, including the Dominican Republic, Jamaica, and Barbados, two or even three staff members are common. Inquire about the villa's staff, and specify particular needs or expectations right from the start, including start times and specific duties such as laundry, cooking, or child care.

How Do You Rent?

Some owners rent their properties directly (⊕ *www.vrbo.com*), but in general, we recommend renting a villa through a reputable local agency that both manages and maintains the properties and has an office with local staff to facilitate and troubleshoot on your behalf if something goes wrong. Lavish catalogs or websites with detailed descriptions and photographs of each villa can help to assuage your fears about what to expect. The agent will meet you at the airport, bring you to the villa, explain and demonstrate the household systems, and even stock the kitchen with starter groceries (for a fee). Some agencies provide comprehensive concierge services and will arrange or recommend car rentals and help you find additional staff such as chefs or babysitters or yoga instructors. Some of the larger companies even host a weekly cocktail party so renters can meet each other and form a community to share local information or socialize. Specific villa-rental companies are listed and recommended throughout this guide.

Choosing a Villa

These days, your hunt will no doubt start on the Internet. A simple search for "villa rental [island name]" will get you started, and the tourist board of each island can provide a list of reputable local rental agents.

Villa-rental websites allow you to see pictures of the places you may wish to rent. And, via the website, you can talk to a knowledgeable representative who can help you sort through the listings according to your requirements. But use caution, warns Peg Walsh of St. Barths Properties: "There are a lot of websites and listings [from] people who say they do villa rentals, but in many cases, they don't actually know the villa they are renting." Instead, they consolidate listings from other sources. It pays to seek out reputable companies, especially if you are a first-time renter.

Things to Think About When Searching for a Villa

How many people are you? How many bedrooms will you want? Do they have to be equal? Do they all have to be attached to the house? If you are two couples, you might want to specify that there be two master suites. If you are traveling with young children, you might not want them in a separate bedroom pavilion. Definitely confirm what types of beds are in each room; couples may prefer queens or kings, whereas kids would be better in single beds. Those looking for a bit more privacy might prefer to be in a guesthouse or small cottage that's separate from the main house.

What location do you prefer? Do you need to be right on a beach? Do you want to walk to town? Will proximity to a particular activity such as golf or scuba diving enhance your vacation? Are you willing to rent a car to get around?

What are your requirements for electronics and appliances? Do you require satellite TV? Internet service (and if so, does it need to be Wi-Fi)? Or would you be okay with something less connected? Do you need a dishwasher? A microwave? How about an outdoor gas grill, or is charcoal sufficient?

Is the villa child-friendly? Ask whether rooms have direct access to the pool area; this might not be a safe choice for younger kids who could open a sliding door and enter the pool area unsupervised. Are you comfortable at all having a pool? Most Caribbean villas don't have childproof security gates around pools, or pool alarms. If the villa has two floors, are the rooms best suited for kids on a floor separate from the master suite?

What specific issues about your destination will affect your villa choice? There are realities about personal security in many areas of the Caribbean. Evaluate the location of potential rentals in relation to known problem areas, and ask if the villa has an alarm system. A surprisingly low rental rate on an otherwise expensive island might be a red flag.

Will you really be comfortable on your own? The final thing to consider is your relative hardiness and that of your traveling companions. Is this your first time in the destination? Do you relish or dread the idea of navigating local markets? Will you miss having a concierge to help arrange things for you? Do you really want to be faced with a sink full of dishes a few times a day? Will your kids be happy without a hotel full of peers? What about you?

CARIBBEAN TOP EXPERIENCES

Diving in Bonaire

(A) Nautical nuts love Bonaire for the kaleidoscopic profusion of marine life, dramatic underwater-scape, excellent environmental stewardship, and accessibility of its pyrotechnic reefs: the majority explode with color just 5–25 minutes from shore in currents mild enough for snorkeling, too.

Hiking in Dominica

(B) Morne Trois Pitons National Park, a UNESCO World Heritage Site, explains Dominica's nickname "The Nature Isle." The island is so green that you can practically see plants grow during rainfall, with mountains filigreed by waterfalls, crater lakes, and natural pools—contrasted with the blast furnace Valley of Desolation, including the world's second-largest fumerole, Boiling Lake, which belches sulfurously.

Snorkeling the Cayman Islands

(C) Swimming at Stingray City, even wading at the adjacent sandbar, you can interact with gracefully balletic stingrays, so tame you can feed them as they nuzzle you, practically begging petlike for handouts. Numerous boats take you out for the ray-diant experience. Shore diving and snorkeling excels throughout all three islands.

Shopping St. Thomas

(D) The Caribbean has colorful historic capitals known for duty-free shopping, including Curaçao's Willemstad and St. Maarten's Philipsburg, but Charlotte Amalie on St. Thomas is like an elegant bazaar, with name-brand luxury boutiques tucked away in its charming arcaded Danish alleys.

Birding in Trinidad

(E) Trinidad is noted for Carnival, calypso, oil, and asphalt production—and bountiful birdlife. More than 200 species

flutter flirtatiously through the Asa Wright Nature Centre, a glorious old plantation also home to bats and giant lizards. Flocks of scarlet ibis turn the mangroves at Caroni Bird Sanctuary into a Christmas decoration come sunset.

Whale-Watching in the Dominican Republic

(F) Samaná in the northeast D.R. is revered for shimmering water, champagne-hue strands, and superior sportfishing. But its signature aquatic activity is world-class whale-watching in season (January through March) as pods of humpbacks mate and calve, the male's signature song echoing across the water.

Dining in St. Martin

(G) Few places rival the French West Indies for fine food and exotic ambience. One small St. Martin fishing village, Grand Case, has become the Caribbean's Restaurant Row. More than 40 eateries line the main beachfront drag, from humble lolos (shacks serving heaping helpings of creole fare at fair prices) to Michelin-worthy haute kitchens.

Boating in the Grenadines

(H) Yachties forever debate the merits of the British Virgin Islands versus the Grenadines for calm waters, exquisite anchorages, warm islanders, boisterous beach bars (such as Basil's on Mustique), and splendid diving and snorkeling (and beachcombing) at such spots as the deserted Tobago Cays.

Viewing Colonial Architecture in Puerto Rico

(I) Old San Juan is a majestic maze of narrow cobblestone alleys opening into broad tree-shaded plazas; beautifully preserved 18th-century Spanish buildings range from stone mansions with wrought-iron balconies (now housing chic boutiques and restaurants) to the UNESCO World Heritage El Morro fortress guarding the bay.

IF YOU LIKE

Great Beaches

What makes a great beach can depend on personal preference. You might dream of sifting your toes in soft white sand with just a hint of warmth. You may love to walk along a virgin beach with nothing but the occasional palm tree. You may be charmed by that cute little crescent that's reachable by a precipitous climb down an almost-sheer rock cliff. You may want to be surrounded by a hundred pairs of beautiful limbs, all smelling slightly of coconut oil. The Caribbean can give you all these. Part of the fun of taking a tropical vacation is discovering your own favorites, which are sometimes the ones you'd least suspect. Here are a few of the beaches we like:

■ **Baie Orientale, St. Maarten/St. Martin.** Often crowded, but considered by many to be the island's most beautiful beach.

■ **The Baths, Virgin Gorda, British Virgin Islands.** Giant boulders form grottoes filled with seawater that you can explore.

■ **Eagle Beach, Aruba.** Once undeveloped, this beach on Aruba's southwestern coast is now hopping and happening.

■ **Half Moon Bay, Providenciales, Turks and Caicos Islands.** A natural ribbon of ivory sand joins two tiny, uninhabited cays.

■ **Macaroni Beach, Mustique, St. Vincent and the Grenadines.** The most famous beach on the most famous Grenadine.

■ **Negril Beach, Jamaica.** Seven miles of sand lined by bars, restaurants, and hotels in westernmost Jamaica.

■ **Seven Mile Beach, Grand Cayman, Cayman Islands.** Free of litter and peddlers, the best northern sections are a sight to behold.

■ **Shoal Bay, Anguilla.** Sand or talcum powder? You decide.

Diving and Snorkeling

Many people would rather spend their days under the sea than on the beach. Generally, the best conditions for diving—clear water and lots of marine life—are also good for snorkelers, though you won't see as much from the surface looking down. If you haven't been certified yet, take a resort course. After learning the basics in a pool, you can often do a short dive from shore. Here are some of the Caribbean's best dive destinations:

■ **Anegada, British Virgin Islands.** The reefs surrounding this flat coral-and-limestone atoll are a sailor's nightmare but a scuba diver's dream.

■ **Bonaire.** The current is mild, the reefs often begin just offshore, visibility is generally 60 feet to 100 feet, and the marine life is magnificent.

■ **Dominica.** Serious divers know that the pristine, bubbly waters around Dominica's submerged volcanic crater are among the best in the world.

■ **Little Cayman, Cayman Islands.** The drop-off at Bloody Bay Wall goes from 18 feet to more than 1,000 feet—diving doesn't get much better than this.

■ **Saba.** Beside one of the lively Caribbean reefs, the diving on Saba is some of the best in the world.

■ **St. Eustatius.** The waters here are tops for wreck diving.

■ **Tobago Cays, St. Vincent and the Grenadines.** A group of five uninhabited islands surrounds a beautiful lagoon studded with sponges, coral formations, and countless colorful fish.

■ **Turks and Caicos Islands.** The world's third-largest coral reef is visible from the air and packed with exotic marine life, dramatic wall drop-offs, colorful fans, and pristine coral formations.

Shopping

Almost as many people go to the Caribbean to shop as to lie on the beach. Whether it's jewelry in St. Maarten, fragrant spices in Grenada, high-end designer fashions in St. Barth, or island crafts almost anywhere, you're likely to come home with a bag full of treasures.

■ **Grenada.** Visit a historic spice plantation, tour a nutmeg-processing plant, and replenish your spice rack with nutmeg, cinnamon sticks, cocoa, and cloves at an outdoor market.

■ **Puerto Rico.** From the boutiques of Old San Juan to ateliers of the young designers elsewhere in metro San Juan to galleries scattered all over the island, there's plenty to see and buy. You may also consider picking up some of the santos created in San Germán.

■ **St. Barthélemy.** Without a doubt, the shopping here for luxury goods and fashion is the best in the Caribbean. The variety and quality are astounding. The unfavorable exchange rates mean fewer bargains for Americans, but the prices here—all duty-free—are still less than what you'd pay in Paris or St.-Tropez.

■ **St. Maarten/St. Martin.** Hundreds of duty-free shops in Philipsburg make the island the best in the Caribbean for bargain hunters, especially for high-quality jewelry and perfumes. Marigot has its fair share of nice boutiques.

■ **St. Thomas, U.S. Virgin Islands.** Main Street in Charlotte Amalie is well known for numerous duty-free shops, selling everything from rum to designer fashions and gems. The Caribbean's biggest cruise port also has several malls.

Staying Active

There's much more to do in the Caribbean than simply lie on the beach, sip rum punches, or play a round of golf. Try hiking through rain forests, kayaking through mangroves, or sailing on a board through a windswept bay.

■ **Bird-Watching, Trinidad and Tobago.** So the watching part isn't so active, but hiking through the rain forests and savannas on these sister islands will give you the opportunity to see more bird species than any other place in the Caribbean.

■ **Hiking the Quill, St. Eustatius.** The crater of Statia's extinct volcano is filled with a primeval rain forest and is a top hiking destination.

■ **Horseback Riding at Chukka Cove, Jamaica.** Headquartered at the Ocho Rios polo fields, Chukka Caribbean Adventures is now Jamaica's top soft-adventure outfitter, having added canopy tours, river rafting, and more to its excellent horseback-riding program.

■ **Kayaking Through Bahía Mosquito, Puerto Rico.** Vieques's bioluminescent bay is best experienced on a kayak tour on a moonless night, when every stroke makes the water light up.

■ **Tennis at Casa de Campo, Dominican Republic.** Casa de Campo isn't just for golfers. With 13 courts (10 lighted for night play) and a staff of more than 25 pros and instructors, this is one place where you can enjoy your game, whether you're an experienced player or a beginner.

■ **Trekking to Boiling Lake, Dominica.** This bubbly, brackish cauldron is actually a flooded fumarole. A trek here is an unforgettable trip into an otherworldly place.

IF YOU WANT

To Take It Easy on Your Wallet

The Caribbean isn't all about five-star resorts. Often, you may want to save a bit of your vacation cash to eat in elegant restaurants or to shop for the perfect gift. Saving money in the Caribbean doesn't have to mean sacrificing comfort. Sometimes it just means going to a cheaper island, such as the Dominican Republic, Saba, or Dominica. But there are some unique inns and resorts in the Caribbean where you can sleep for much less and still have a great time.

■ **Bayaleau Point Cottages, Carriacou.** Owner Dave Goldhill built four colorful gingerbread guest cottages on this peaceful Windward hillside overlooking the Grenadines, as well as a 28-foot boat to take his guests on snorkeling trips.

■ **Bay Gardens Beach Resort, St. Lucia.** One of three Bay Gardens properties in Rodney Bay known for their friendly hospitality, this family-friendly hotel has a prime location on beautiful Reduit Beach.

■ **Beachcombers Hotel, St. Vincent.** Cheryl Hornsey's family home, once a tiny B&B, has morphed into a popular, 31-room beachfront hotel overlooking the sea at Villa Beach.

■ **Bellafonte Chateau de la Mer, Bonaire.** An oceanfront room at this chic, palazzo-style hotel will remind you why you came to the Caribbean.

■ **Carringtons Inn, St. Croix, U.S. Virgin Islands.** A stay at this spacious B&B harks back to a gentler time, when people spent the winter, rather than a week, in the Caribbean.

■ **Coco Palm, St. Lucia.** Rodney Bay is a beehive of activity, and this stylish boutique hotel is definitely the honey—beautiful rooms, amenities you'd expect at pricier resorts, a great restaurant, and nightly entertainment.

■ **Frangipani Hotel, Bequia.** Luxurious guest rooms, built of local stone and hardwoods, are tucked into a gentle slope filled with fragrant frangipani trees and overlook Admiralty Bay.

■ **The Horny Toad, St. Maarten/St. Martin.** A marvelous little oceanfront guesthouse with a funky name offers the island's best value for those who want to keep costs down.

■ **La Sagesse, Grenada.** At this secluded country inn on La Sagesse Bay, 10 miles from town, guest rooms are 30 feet from the beach and a hop, skip, and jump from surrounding nature trails.

■ **Rockhouse Hotel, Jamaica.** Perched on the cliffs of Negril's West End, unique bungalows blend comfort and rustic style. Regular rooms keep costs down, but if you want to spend a bit more, the dramatic villas are worth every penny.

■ **Siboney Beach Club, Antigua.** This beachfront oasis is nestled in a tranquil corner of Dickenson Bay. Service is warm and friendly, and the surroundings are natural and secluded.

To Have the Perfect Honeymoon

Swaying palms, moonlight strolls on the beach, candlelit dinners: no wonder the Caribbean is a favorite honeymoon destination. Whatever you are looking for in a honeymoon—seclusion, privacy, or more active fun—you can certainly find it, and it will usually be on a perfect beach. You can be pampered or just left alone, stay up late or get up with the sun, get out and stay active or simply rest and relax. Our favorites run the gamut; from easy access to remote, we have the perfect spot.

■ **Horned Dorset Primavera, Puerto Rico.** Whisk your beloved to this sunset-kissed hotel and just disappear. You may never

leave your elegant oceanfront room. When you do, the restaurant is one of the best in Puerto Rico.

■ **Palm Island, Grenadines.** Enjoy five dazzling beaches for water sports, nature trails for quiet walks, a pool with waterfall, sophisticated dining, impeccable service, exquisite accommodations—and privacy.

■ **Sandals Grande St. Lucian Spa & Beach Resort, St. Lucia.** Big, busy, and all-inclusive, this resort is a favorite of young honeymooners—particularly for its complimentary weddings.

■ **The Somerset, Turks and Caicos Islands.** Provo's most beautiful resort is more focused on your comfort than on attracting a celebrity clientele, so regular folks will still feel at home.

■ **Spice Island Beach Resort, Grenada.** Grenada's best resort has impeccable service, placing it among the Caribbean's finest small resorts.

To Eat Well

Caribbean food is a complex blend of indigenous, African, and colonial influences. Native tubers such as yuca and taro, leafy vegetables like callaloo, and herbs such as cilantro recur in most island cuisines. Africans brought plantains, yams, pigeon peas, and assorted peppers. The Spanish introduced rice, and the British brought breadfruit from the South Pacific. Here are some of our favorite Caribbean restaurants:

■ **Banana Tree Grille, St. Thomas, U.S. Virgin Islands.** The eagle's-eye view of the Charlotte Amalie harbor from this breeze-cooled restaurant is as fantastic as the food.

■ **Blue by Eric Ripert, Cayman Islands.** Grand Cayman's best restaurant is brought to you by one of New York's finest chefs.

■ **Boston Jerk Centre, Port Antonio, Jamaica.** To enjoy the best Jamaican jerk in the place where it was invented, these simple beach huts are the place to head.

■ **The Cliff, Barbados.** Chef Paul Owens's mastery is the foundation of one of the finest dining experiences in the Caribbean, with prices to match.

■ **Coral Grill, Nevis, St. Kitts and Nevis.** The steak house at the Four Seasons Nevis is stunning and wildly successful—and a memorable place to eat.

■ **Coyaba Restaurant, Providenciales, Turks and Caicos Islands.** This posh eatery is one of the island's most romantic and inviting places to dine.

■ **Iguane Café, Guadeloupe.** Unquestionably original cuisine with influences from around the world is daring and dramatic, not to mention delicious.

■ **Le Tastevin, St. Martin.** In the heart of Grand Case, Le Tastevin is on everyone's list of favorites.

■ **Le Ti St. Barth Caribbean Tavern, St. Barthélemy.** Chef-owner Carole Gruson captures the funky, sexy spirit of the island in her wildly popular hilltop hot spot.

■ **Marmalade, Puerto Rico.** Old San Juan's hippest and finest restaurant, Marmalade's inventive menu is California-French.

WHEN TO GO

The Caribbean high season is traditionally winter—from December 15 to April 14. During this season you're guaranteed the most entertainment at resorts and the most people with whom to enjoy it. It's also the most fashionable, the most expensive, and the most popular time to visit—and most hotels are heavily booked. You must make reservations at least two or three months in advance for the very best places (sometimes a year in advance for the most exclusive spots). Hotel prices drop 20% to 50% after April 15; airfares and cruise prices also fall. Saving money isn't the only reason to visit the Caribbean during the off-season. Temperatures are only a few degrees warmer than at other times of the year, and many islands now schedule their carnivals, music festivals, and other events during the off-season. Late August, September, October, and early November are the least crowded.

Climate

The Caribbean climate is fairly constant. The average year-round temperatures for the region are 78°F to 88°F. The temperature extremes are 65°F low, 95°F high; but, as everyone knows, it's the humidity, not the heat, that makes you suffer, especially when the two go hand in hand.

As part of the late-fall rainy season, hurricanes occasionally sweep through the Caribbean. Check the news daily and keep abreast of brewing tropical storms. The southernmost Caribbean islands are generally spared the threat of hurricanes. The rainy season consists mostly of brief showers interspersed with sunshine. You can watch the clouds thicken, feel the rain, then have brilliant sunshine dry you off, all while remaining on your lounge chair. A spell of overcast days or heavy rainfall is unusual.

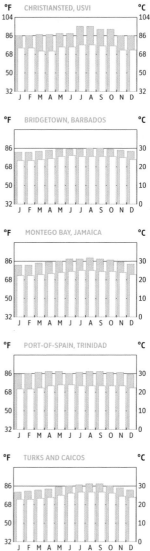

HURRICANE SEASON

The Atlantic hurricane season lasts from June 1 through November 30, but it's fairly rare to see a large storm in either June or November. Most major hurricanes occur between August and October, with the peak season in September.

Avoiding the Storms: Keep in mind that hurricanes are rarer the farther south you go. The ABC Islands (Aruba, Bonaire, and Curaçao) as well as Trinidad and Tobago are the least likely to see a direct hit by a hurricane, but all these islands have had their run-ins, so it's not a certainty that you'll avoid storms by going south. Similarly, Barbados is less likely to be adversely affected by a strong storm because it lies 100 miles farther east than the rest of the Antilles.

Airlines: Airports are usually closed during hurricanes and many flights canceled, which results in a disruption of the steady flow of tourists in and out of affected islands. If you are scheduled to fly into an area where a hurricane is expected, check with your airline regularly and often. If flights are disrupted, airlines will usually allow you to rebook at a later date, but you will not get a refund if you have booked a nonrefundable ticket, nor in most cases will you be allowed to change your ticket to a different destination; rather, you will be expected to reschedule your trip for a later date.

Hotels and Resorts: If a hurricane warning is issued and flights to your destination are disrupted, virtually every Caribbean resort will waive cancellation and change penalties and allow you to rebook your trip for a later date; some will allow you to cancel even if a hurricane threatens to strike, even if flights aren't canceled. Some will give you a refund if you have prepaid for your stay; others will expect you to rebook your trip for a later date. Some large resort companies—including Sandals and SuperClubs—have "hurricane guarantees," but they apply only when flights have been canceled or when a hurricane is sure to strike.

Travel Insurance: If you plan to travel to the Caribbean during the hurricane season, it is wise to buy travel insurance that allows you to cancel for any reason. This kind of coverage can be expensive (up to 10% of the value of the trip), but if you have to prepay far in advance for an expensive vacation package, the peace of mind may be worth it. Just be sure to read the fine print; some policies don't kick in unless flights are canceled and the hurricane strikes, something you may not be assured of until the day you plan to travel. To get a complete cancellation policy, you must usually buy your insurance within a week of booking your trip. If you wait until after the hurricane warning is issued to purchase insurance, it will be too late.

Track Those Hurricanes: The obsessive and naturally curious keep a close eye on the Caribbean during hurricane season. You can, too. Several websites track hurricanes during the season, including ⊕ *www. weather.com*, ⊕ *hurricanetrack.com*, and ⊕ *www.accuweather.com*.

WEDDINGS

Destination weddings, once the exclusive domain of celebs and the superrich, are becoming more affordable in the Caribbean. Many resorts offer attractive packages that couples are taking advantage of to create their ultimate island-paradise wedding. As an added bonus, many islands and resorts provide a plethora of experienced wedding planners. So whether you picture an intimate beachfront ceremony for two or a full-blown affair, you can confidently leave the details to a professional and simply concentrate on exchanging your vows.

Finding a Wedding Planner

Hiring a planner to handle all of the logistics—from the preliminary paperwork right down to final toast—allows you to relax and truly enjoy your big day. The best of the bunch will advise you about legalities (like any residency requirements), help organize the marriage license, and hire the officiant, plus arrange for venues, flowers, music, refreshments, or anything else your heart desires. Planners typically have established relationships with local vendors and can bundle packages with them—which can save you money. Most resorts have on-site coordinators. But there are also many independents available, including those who specialize in certain types of ceremonies—by locale, size, religious affiliation, and so on. Island tourism boards often maintain an online list of names, and a simple "Caribbean weddings" Google search will yield scores more. What's important is that you feel comfortable with your coordinator. Ask for references—and call them. Share your budget. Ask how long they've been in business, how much they charge, how often you'll meet with them, and how they select vendors. Above all, request a detailed, written list of what they'll provide. If your vision of the dream wedding doesn't match their services, try someone else. If you can afford it, you might even want to schedule a preliminary trip to meet the planner in person.

Making It Legal

Your goal is to tie the knot, not get tied up in red tape. So it is important to be mindful of the legalities involved. Specifics vary widely, depending on the type of ceremony you want (civil ones are invariably less complicated than religious services) and the island where you choose to wed. In the Dominican Republic, for example, key documents must be submitted in Spanish: unless you enlist a translator, your wedding will be conducted in Spanish, too. On the French-speaking islands (Guadeloupe, Martinique, St. Barth, and St. Martin) language issues are further compounded by stringent residency requirements, which can make marrying there untenable.

There are, however, **standard rules** that apply throughout the islands:

■ Most places will expect you to produce a valid passport as proof of identification when applying for a marriage license (the exceptions being Puerto Rico and the U.S. Virgin Islands, where official government-issued picture ID will suffice for American citizens).

■ If you are under 18 years old, parental consent is also needed unless otherwise stated in the chart that follows.

■ If you are divorced, the original divorce or annulment decree is required.

■ If you are a widow or widower, original marriage and death certificates are required. (In certain locales, an apostille stamp confirming the authenticity of such documents must be attached.)

ISLAND	COSTS	WAITING PERIOD	GOOD TO KNOW
Anguilla http://ivisitanguilla.com/weddings	License $284	At least 2 business days to process license	Special rules apply here for religious weddings. Couples marrying in church must allow extra time; some churches require prenuptial consultation and extra documentation.
Antigua www.antigua-barbuda.org/agmarr01.htm	License $150; marriage officer's fee $50; registration $40	None	Couples landing in Antigua after 3 pm won't have enough time to get a license from the Ministry of Justice and wed the same day. If you're really in a rush, catch an earlier flight.
Aruba www.aruba.com/aruba-vacations/weddings-honeymoons	License $80 during office hours; $200 on Sat. or after hours	None, provided all documents are submitted at least one month in advance	Civil ceremonies may take place in Oranjestad's historic City Hall, on the beach, or at your venue of choice.
Barbados www.visitbarbados.org/weddings	License $50 plus $13 stamp fee. Separate magistrate and court fees for civil ceremonies at the court, $63; at alternative venues $175	None	All fees must be paid in cash. Couples may wait at the Ministry of Home Affairs in Wildey, St. Michael, for the license to be processed, but both parties must be present to take the oath.
Bonaire www.tourismbonaire.com/en/vacation-planner/specialized-vacations/wedding-honeymoons	License $150	One partner must be on-island 7 days to establish residency; license takes 4 business days to process.	One partner must get a temporary residency permit before applying for a license. Official witnesses must do the same, but most wedding coordinators can arrange for local ones.
British Virgin Islands www.bvitourism.com/rules-requirements	Registrar's fee $340 for weddings in the office and $220 at other locations	One business day	It is standard practice to have 2 witnesses at your ceremony. In BVI you also need 2 witnesses present when you sign your license application.

ISLAND	COSTS	WAITING PERIOD	GOOD TO KNOW
Cayman Islands www.cayman-vows.ky	License $250	None	When applying for a license, you must present a letter from the marriage officer who will be officiating (a list can be obtained from the deputy chief secretary's office).
Curaçao www.curacao.com/plan-your-trip/get-married-a-true-caribbean-wedding	License $320, excluding extra stamp and translation fees.	Must be on the island 3 days before applying for license; no other waiting period.	Curaçao is a stickler for paperwork, so hiring a wedding pro helps. Documents, which must be original, recent, and apostille-stamped, are to be with your planner at least 2 months in advance.
Dominica www.dominica.dm	License $112; statutory declaration fee $187; registrar's fee $11 for weddings at the office and $37 at other locations	One partner must be on-island 2 days before the wedding.	Couples must sign a statutory declaration of marital status in the presence of a local lawyer. You must also complete an application form and have it witnessed by a magistrate.
Dominican Republic www.godomin-icanrepublic.com/en	Combined fees $400 for civil ceremonies in the registry office; $600 elsewhere	Notice of intended marriage must be published before ceremony.	Both partners must provide proof of single status that has been translated into Spanish at a Dominican Consulate. All paperwork should be submitted at least 6 months in advance.
Grenada www.grenadag-renadines.com/explore/wedding	License and stamps $14	Couples must be on-island 3 days before applying for a license; 2 business days needed for processing.	Processing your license may take a bit longer if you've been married before.
Jamaica www.visitja-maica.com/weddings-and-honeymoons	License $55; marriage officer's fee $50–$250	24 hours	Accommodating laws and upscale couples-only resorts make Jamaica a top pick. Some all-inclusives even offer complimentary weddings, complete with officiant and license.
Nevis www.nevisis-land.com/weddings.htm	License $80 if on-island for a minimum of 2 business days; $20 if on-island for 15 days beforehand	None	You'll pay $20 to complete your application before a justice of the peace. If you've never been married, also be prepared to pop $20 for a notarized affidavit of single status.
Puerto Rico www.seepuer-torico.com/romance	License and stamp fees $20	None	You must submit a medical certification indicating that you met all the required tests for marriage back in your place of residence to the Demographic Registry Office. The certification is good for 10 days.

ISLAND	COSTS	WAITING PERIOD	GOOD TO KNOW
St. Eustatius www.statiatourism.com/weddings.htm	License, stamp fees, and marriage book $300	14 days after document registration	Marriages performed outside the marriage hall require 6 witnesses.
St. Kitts www.stkittstourism.kn/weddings/tying_knot.asp	License EC $200	Both parties must be on-island a minimum of 2 business days.	Thinking of a casual sunrise or sunset ceremony on the beach? Consider this: Civil weddings are performed only from 8 to 6. Church weddings may be held 6 to 6.
St. Lucia www.stlucia.org/planner/weddings.asp	License $125 for special, $200 for special; registrar fee $160; marriage certificate $8	None with a special license, 3 days with a standard license	St. Lucia, a leader in the destination wedding biz, has a streamlined process that makes marrying easy. Most lodgings have enticing packages and on-site planners.
St. Maarten www.st-maarten.com/index.php/weddings2 or www.stmartin-island.com	Combined cost of civil ceremony, marriage book, certificate, and stamps is about $400, depending on day and location of wedding.	Couples must submit requests 14 days before the wedding.	It is somewhat easier to marry in St. Maarten than in St. Martin. The French side of the island requires translated documents and different requirements, depending on the citizenships of the couple.
St. Vincent and the Grenadines www.discoversvg.com/index.php/en/whattodo/weddingshoneymoons	License $185 plus approximately $8 for stamp fees	24 hours on-island	Blessed with postcard-pretty beaches, gorgeous gardens, private island resorts, and historic buildings, this archipelago of 32 islands boasts a range of likely venues.
Trinidad and Tobago www.gotrinidadandtobago.com/tobago/weddings.php	License $55	3 days	To obtain a license both partners must be nonresidents. Documents, such as airline tickets, are required to confirm your dates of entry and onward passage.
Turks and Caicos www.turksandcaicostourism.com/tci-weddings.html	License $150; $250 if you marry on cruise ship; application fee $250	Couples must be on the island 48 hours before submitting application.	The marriage is registered here. To have it registered in your home country, you must make special arrangements. Parental consent needed if under 21.
U.S. Virgin Islands www.visitusvi.com/plan_events/weddings_honeymoons/stcroix	Marriage application and license fee $200; officiating fee $200 if not married in court by a judge.	8 days from receipt of application	Licenses must be picked up in person on weekdays, but you can shorten the wait by applying from home.

KIDS AND FAMILIES

Traveling with kids to the Caribbean is fun and easy. Many resorts, except for those that are exclusively couples-only, offer kids free promotions, special restaurant menus, and programs for tots on up to teens.

Choosing a Place to Stay

Everything from brand-name resorts to independent hotels, condominiums, and even campgrounds can offer a great family vacation. It just depends what you're looking for.

Let them entertain you. If you prefer to relax while the kids are entertained, choose a major resort with all-inclusive meal plan and kids' program. A few best bets are **Beaches Resorts** (Beaches Turks and Caicos and Beaches Ocho Rios in Jamaica). The **Sandals**-owned chain (Antigua, Jamaica, St. Lucia) has kids' programs to match all ages, outdoor playgrounds, gaming centers, trips for ages 12 and up such as snorkeling and scuba diving, and *Sesame Street* character appearances. **Hyatt Regency Aruba Beach Resort & Casino** features Camp Hyatt, where kids ages 3 to 12 can participate in a variety of activities and adventures. **Club Med Punta Cana,** in the Dominican Republic, offers a baby gym, Crayola arts-and-crafts programs, hip-hop dance instruction, Petite Chef (ages 3 to 7) cooking classes, and The Ramp, an interactive club for 14- to 17-year-olds.

DIY. If you'd prefer more of a home base from which to explore the island on your own, choose a hotel, condo, or villa near the attractions you'd most like to visit. Condos and villas provide more of an at-home atmosphere with full kitchens and separate bedrooms, and many include home entertainment systems. **Maho Bay Camps** on St. John, in the U.S. Virgin Islands, is a great kid-friendly option.

You stay in screened cottages or canvas tents. There are cooking facilities in each unit, and a cafeteria-style restaurant gives Mom the night off. Lifeguards are on duty, there are water-sports rentals, and there's plenty of white-sand beach for sand castles and swimming.

Top Attractions

The Caribbean offers an abundance of family attractions. Museums, forts, caves, zoos, and aquariums are sure to keep tots, teens, adults, and seniors happy when it's time to take a break from the sun, sand, and sea.

Museums. Many kids have read about Christopher Columbus in history books, but at **El Faro a Colón** (Columbus Lighthouse), just outside Santa Domingo in the Dominican Republic, they can visit his tomb. The huge pyramid-shape complex has six museums that trace the history of the area from the ancient Indian days to the construction of this modern, multimillion-dollar structure. Kids will marvel over ancient maps, jewelry-studded royal crowns, and replicas of dugout canoes. For a real treat, visit at night when the 688-foot-tall lighthouse projects a cross-shape beam of light some 44 miles into the sky. In Jamaica, teenagers may enjoy the **Bob Marley Museum**. This former home of the late great king of reggae music—painted Rastafarian red, yellow, and green—is filled with Marley's personal memorabilia. A 15-minute video presents the life story of Marley along with familiar music clips. Kids will also love the **Kool Runnings Adventure Park** in Negril, Jamaica. This park has 10 waterslides and a ¼-mile lazy-river float ride, as well as a go-kart track and kayaking. There's also outdoor laser combat games, bungee jumping, a "kool kanoe" adventure, a wave pool, and paintball.

Fortresses. A long grassy walk leads up to the 500-year-old **Castillo del Morro** (El Morro) Castle, an imposing structure in Puerto Rico's Old San Juan that looks like the Wicked Witch's scary fortress. Venture inside the thick walls and cruise the ramparts, tunnels, and dungeons. Wax mannequins model historic battle uniforms, and a video shows the history of building and defending this stronghold. Equally imposing is St. Kitts's **Brimstone Hill**, known as the Gibraltar of the West Indies. Ft. George, which sits atop the hill, is built of 7-foot-thick walls of black volcanic stone. Kids can woefully imagine being imprisoned here during a "time-out." From high atop the fort's cannon ways, kids can search the horizon for the islands of Nevis, Montserrat, Saba, St. Maarten/St. Martin, and St. Barth. It's also fun to try spotting the scampering green monkeys that play along the nature trails that wind around this 38-acre site.

Caves. Don a bright yellow hard hat and ride a tramcar into Barbados's **Harrison's Cave.** Specially lighted caverns illuminate the stalactites, stalagmites, and underground waterfalls so the caves don't seem too spooky. The **Hato Caves** in Curaçao were made during the Ice Age, but today the inhabitants are not cavemen but long-nosed bats. Puerto Rico's **Rio Camuy Cave Park** tour begins with a short video and then a trolley ride right to the mouth of the cave. Though 200 feet high, the cave is only half a mile long. The walking tour is level and flat, allowing kids' eyes to roam all over without fear of stumbling.

Zoos. Roam freely with the animals at the **Barbados Wildlife Reserve.** This outdoor zoo keeps kids engaged as they walk along shady pathways and spot exotic animals, reptiles, and birds in their natural habitat. There are land turtles, fine-feathered peacocks, green monkeys, parrots, and even an otter. Some species here are threatened with extinction. After exploring outside, kids can check out the walk-in aviary and the many natural-history exhibits. The **Emperor Valley Zoo**, named for Trinidad's native blue butterflies, is one of the best in the Caribbean. The island's president and prime minister have houses on this site, but most intriguing for kids is the 8-acre zoo that is filled with birds and other wildlife from the region, ranging from blue-and-gold macaws and small red brocket deer to giant anacondas.

Aquariums. Curaçao Sea Aquarium boasts more than 400 species of sea life. Some of the most fascinating creatures are the sharks—hand-fed daily, to the delight of kids of all ages. This interactive **Coral World Ocean Park,** on St. Thomas, is an aquarium and water-sports center that has a 2-acre dolphin habitat, as well as several outdoor pools where you can pet baby sharks, feed stingrays, touch starfish, and view endangered sea turtles. You can also Snuba, swim with a sea lion, and view an 80,000-gallon coral reef exhibit (one of the largest in the world).

THE ISLANDS' GLOBAL FLAVORS

Island cuisine developed through waves of wars, immigration, and natives' innovations from the 15th century through the mid-19th century. Early Amerindian native peoples, the Arawaks and the Caribs, are said to have introduced the concept of spicing food with chili peppers, a preparation that remains a hallmark of Caribbean cuisine. Pepper pot stew was a staple for the Caribs, who would make the dish with *cassareep*, a savory sauce made from cassava. The stew featured wild meats (possum, wild pig, or armadillo), squash, beans, and peanuts, which were added to the cassareep and simmered in a clay pot. The dish was traditionally served to guests as a gesture of hospitality. Today's recipes substitute meats like pig trotters, cow heel, or oxtail.

Caribbean-style curried goat

After Columbus' discovery of the New World, European traders and settlers brought new fruits, vegetables, and meats. Their arrival coincided with that of African slaves en route to the Americas. Every explorer, settler, trader, and slave brought something to expand the palette of flavors. Although Caribbean cooking varies from island to island, trademark techniques and spices unite the cuisine.

SPANISH INFLUENCES

The Caribbean islands were discovered by Christopher Columbus in 1492, while he was working for the Spanish crown. When he returned to colonize the islands a year later, he brought ships laden with coconut, chickpeas, cilantro, eggplant, onions, and garlic. The Bahamas, Hispaniola, and Cuba were among Columbus' first findings, and as a result, Cuba and nearby Puerto Rico have distinctly Spanish-accented cuisine, including *paella* (a seafood- or meat-studded rice dish), *arroz con pollo* or *pilau* (chicken cooked with yellow rice), and white-bean Spanish stews.

FRENCH TECHNIQUE

As tobacco and sugar crops flourished and the Caribbean became a center of European trade and colonization, the French settled Martinique and Guadeloupe in 1635 and later expanded to St. Barthélemy, St. Martin, Grenada, St. Lucia, and western Hispaniola. French culinary technique meets the natural resources of the islands to create dishes like whelk (sea snail) grilled in garlic butter, fish cooked *en papillote* (baked in parchment paper), and *crabs farcis*, land crab meat that is steamed, mixed with butter, breadcrumbs, ham, chilis, and garlic, then stuffed back into the crab shells and grilled.

DUTCH INGENUITY

Beginning in the 1620s, traders from the Dutch East India Company brought Southeast Asian ingredients like soy sauce to the islands of Curaçao and St. Maarten. Dutch influence is also evident throughout Aruba and Bonaire (all have been under Dutch rule since the early 19th century), where dishes like *keshi yeni*, or "stuffed cheese," evolved from stuffing discarded rinds of Edam cheese with minced meat, olives, and capers. Another Dutch-influenced dish is *boka dushi* (Indonesian-style chicken satay), which translates to "sweet mouth" in the islands' Papiamento dialect.

Arroz con Pollo

Paella

Boka dushi

Jerk meat

Roti

Whelk

ENGLISH IMPORTS

British settlers brought pickles, preserves, and chutneys to the Caribbean, and current-day chefs take advantage of the islands' indigenous fruits to produce these items. British influence also is evidenced by the Indian and Chinese contributions to Caribbean cuisine. British (and Dutch) colonists brought over indentured laborers from India and China to work on sugar plantations, resulting in the introduction of popular dishes like curry goat and *roti,* an Indian flatbread stuffed with vegetables or chicken curry.

AFRICAN INGREDIENTS

The African slave trade that began in the early 1600s brought foods from West Africa, including yams, okra, plantains, breadfruit, pigeon peas, and oxtail to the islands. Slave cooks often had to make do with plantation leftovers and scraps, yielding dishes like cow heel soup and pig-foot souse (a cool soup with pickled cucumber and meat), both of which are still popular today. One of the most significant African contributions to the Caribbean table is "jerking," the process of dry-rubbing meat with allspice, Scotch bonnet peppers, and other spices. Although the cooking technique originated with native Amerindians, it

was the Jamaican Maroons, a population of runaway African slaves living in the island's mountains during the years of slavery, who developed and perfected it, resulting in the style of jerk meat familiar in restaurants today.

CARIBBEAN'S NATURAL BOUNTY

Soursop

Despite its spicy reputation, Caribbean food isn't always fiery; the focus is on enhancing and intensifying flavors with herbs and spices.

Food plays a major role in island culture, family life, and traditions, and no holiday would be complete without traditional dishes prepared from the island's natural products.

TANTALIZING TROPICAL FRUIT

Breadfruit, a versatile starch with potato-like flavor, can be served solo—baked or grilled—or added to soups and stews.

With its rich, refreshing milk, **coconut** frequently appears in soups, stews, sauces, and drinks to help temper hot, spicy flavors with its rich, refreshing milk.

The bright orange tropical fruit **guava** tastes somewhat like a tomato when it's not fully ripe, but is pleasantly sweet when mature. It is used in compotes, pastes, and jellies.

The pungent smell of **jackfruit** may be off-putting for some, but its sweet fleshy meat is popular in milkshakes.

Papaya is sweet and floral when ripe; unripe, it can be shredded and mixed with spices and citrus for a refreshing salad. It is often

used in fruit salsas that are served with seafood.

The brightly flavored **passion fruit** is commonly puréed and used in sauces, drinks, and desserts.

The dark-green skinned, creamy fleshed **soursop** is known for its sweet-tart juice used in drinks, sorbets, and ice creams.

The fibrous stalks of **sugarcane**, a giant grass native to India, are rich with sugar, which can be consumed in several forms, including freshly extracted juice and processed sugar.

Tamarind is the fruit of a large tree. The sticky pulp of its pod is used in chutneys and curries to impart a slightly sweet, refreshingly sour flavor.

FARM-FRESH VEGETABLES

Cassava (also called yucca) can be used much like a potato in purées, dumplings, soups, and stews. The flour of its roots is made into tapioca.

Chayote is a versatile member of the squash and melon family, often used raw in salads or stuffed with cheese and tomatoes and baked.

Dasheen (taro) is much like a potato, but creamier. It can be

Jackfruit

sliced thinly and fried like a potato chip.

Fitweed (or French thistle) is a tropical herb related to coriander (cilantro), and is popular in Caribbean seasonings.

Pod-like **okra** is commonly used in *callaloo*, the national dish of Trinidad and Tobago. The creamy, spicy stew is made of leafy greens, okra, and crabmeat.

Green plantain is a cooking staple across the Caribbean, often sliced, pounded, dipped in a seasoned batter, and deep-fried.

The leafy green **sorrel** is typically pureed in soups

Tamarind

Chayote

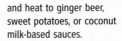
Curry powder

and stews, or used in salads.

SWEET AND SAVORY SPICES

Native **allspice**, also called Jamaican pepper, is commonly added to Caribbean curries. It is the dried unripe berry of the evergreen pimento tree. Native Jamaicans once used it to preserve meats. It is an essential ingredient in jerk preparations.

Curries are intensely seasoned gravy-based dishes originating from India—they are most prevalent on the islands of Jamaica, Trinidad, and Tobago.

Native Carib people pioneered the use of **chili peppers** in the islands for hot, spicy flavoring, using primarily habaneros and Scotch bonnet peppers.

Ginger can be used raw or dried and ground into a powder that adds flavor

and heat to ginger beer, sweet potatoes, or coconut milk-based sauces.

The mix of spices in **jerk** seasoning vary, but typically include scallions, thyme, allspice, onions, and garlic.

The tiny island of Grenada is the second largest exporter of **nutmeg** in the world. It often accents sweet dishes, and is frequently added to vegetables in Dutch preparations.

ISLAND FISH AND SEAFOOD

Bonito is a medium-sized fish in the mackerel family. Atlantic bonito is moderately fatty, with a firm texture and darker color. It is served blackened, grilled (sometimes with fruit-based salsas), or Jamaican jerk style.

On many islands, including the Bahamas, **conch**—a large shellfish—are made into conch fritters, a mix of conch meat, corn meal, and spices that are deep fried and make an excellent snack.

Cascadura fish is a small fish found in the freshwater swamps of Trinidad and Tobago. It is typically served in curry with a side of rice or dumplings.

Conch salad

Flying fish are named for the wing-like fins that enable them to glide or "fly" over water. Firm in texture, it is typically served steamed or fried. Flying fish is a staple in Bajan cuisine and is found in abundance off the coast of Barbados.

Kingfish is another word for wahoo, a delicate white fish commonly fished off the coasts of St. Croix and Barbados. It's served *escabeche* style, marinated in a vinegar mixture, then fried or poached.

Land crab is found throughout the islands. Delicate in flavor, its common preparations include curried crab stewed in coconut milk, stuffed crab, and crab soup.

Mahi mahi is fished off the coast of St. Croix. With a subtle, sweet flavor, its firm, dark flesh lends itself to soy sauce glazes and Asian preparations.

Salt fish is a dish made from dried cod, often seasoned with tomatoes, onions, and thyme. Stir-fried ackee (a tropical fruit with nutty-flavored flesh) and saltfish is Jamaica's national dish.

Allspice

Salt fish

THE RISE OF RUM

The Caribbean is the world center for rum production, with many islands making their own brands and styles of rum. Dozens of rum companies operate throughout the islands. Although larger, mainstream brands like Bacardi, Captain Morgan, and Mount Gay are available on every island, you may have to look harder for the smaller brands. The best-quality rums are dark, aged rums meant for sipping, priced from $30 to $700 a bottle. For excellent sipping rum at the lower end of the spectrum, try Appleton or Rhum Barbancourt. For mixed drinks, use clear or golden-colored rums that are less expensive and pair well with fruit juices or cola. Spiced and flavored rums are also popular in cocktails. Here are some of the best rums you'll encounter at an island bar:

Appleton Estate (Jamaica) The Estate VX is an amber-colored rum with subtle brown sugar aromas and a smooth, toasted honey finish. Excellent mixer for classic cocktails.

Bacardi (Bermuda, PR) Superior is a clear, mild rum with subtle hints of vanilla and fresh fruits. It is smooth and light on the palate. Best in mixed drinks.

Captain Morgan (PR) Its Black Label Jamaica Rum is dark, rich, and smooth, with strong notes of vanilla. Sip it iced, or with a splash of water.

Clarke's Court (Grenada) The Original White is clear with a touch of sweetness

and a hint of heat, best used as a mixer.

Cruzan (VI) Less strong and sweet than most rums, the White Rum is smooth, and best suited for mixing.

Havana Club (Cuba) The Añejo 3 Años is deceiving—light in color and body and delicate in flavor. It is a nice rum to sip neat.

Mount Gay Rum (Barbados) Eclipse, the brand's flagship rum, has a golden color with a butterscotch caramel nose and sweet taste on the palate with mouth-warming flavor.

Pusser's (BVI) Self-described as "the single malt of rum," the aged 15-year variety boasts notes of cinnamon, woody spice, and citrus. A good sipping rum.

Rhum Barbancourt (Haiti) Aged 15-years, this premium dark rum is distilled twice in copper pot stills and often called the "Cognac of Rum." Sip it neat.

Ron Barceló (DR) The Añejo is dark copper in color, with a rich flavor, while the aged Imperial boasts notes of toffee on the nose, and a buttery smooth finish.

Shillingford Estates (Dominica) Its most popular product, Macoucherie Spiced is a blend of rum, the bark of the Bois Bande tree, and spices.

(left) Pusser's Rum, (right) Havana Club

ISLANDS' BEST BREWS

Beer in the Caribbean was largely home-made for centuries, a tradition inherited from British colonial rulers. The first commercial brewery in the islands was founded in Trinidad and Tobago in 1947.

In the islands, do what the locals do: drink local beer. Whatever brand is brewed on-island is the one you'll find at every restaurant and bar. And no matter where you go in the Caribbean, there's a local island brew worth trying. Another plus: local brands are almost always cheaper than imports like Corona or Heineken. Most island beers are pale lagers, though you'll find a smattering of Dutch-style pilsners and English-style pale ales. The beers listed below are our top picks for beachside sipping:

Kalik

Carib Lager Beer

Banks Beer (Banks Breweries, Barbados) A straw-colored lager that is light tasting with a touch of maltiness on the nose and tongue.

Blackbeard Ale (Virgin Islands Brewing Co., Virgin Islands) This English pale ale-style beer is bright amber in color with a creamy white head. Well-crafted beer with a nice hoppy bite at the finish.

Balashi Beer (Brouwerij Nacional Balashi N.V., Aruba) Refreshingly light, this Dutch pilsner boasts mild flavor, slight sweetness, and subtle hop bitterness.

Legends Premium Lager (Banks Breweries, Barbados) One of the Caribbean's best brews, this golden yellow lager offers crisp hops and a clean finish. Distinctive toasty, malt character.

Carib Lager Beer (Carib Brewery, Trinidad and Tobago) This great beach refresher is pale yellow color with a foamy head. Fruity and sweet malty corn aromas, it is sometimes referred to as the "Corona of the Caribbean."

Kalik Gold (Commonwealth Brewery LTD., New Providence, Bahamas) Clear straw color with gentle hoppy, herbal notes, this is an easy drinking, warm weather lager.

Medalla Light (Puerto Rico) This bright gold lager is substantial for a light beer. It's a local favorite.

Red Stripe (Jamaica) The Jamaican lager pours golden yellow in color with lots of carbonation. Light bodied, crisp, and smooth.

Piton (St. Lucia) Light and sparkly with subtle sweetness, this pale yellow lager is pleasant enough, but barely flavored.

Presidente (Domincan Republic) Slight citrus aroma, light body, and fizziness, plus a clean finish make for easy drinking. Perfect pairing for barbecued meats.

Wadadli (Antigua Brewery Ltd., Antigua and Barbuda) A crisp, light-bodied American-style lager. Toasty malt on the nose.

Banks Beer

(left) Red Stripe,
(right) Presidente

WELCOME TO ANGUILLA

TRANQUIL AND UPSCALE

This dry limestone isle is the most northerly of the Leeward Islands, lying between the Caribbean Sea and the Atlantic. The low-lying island is only 16 miles (26 km) long and 3 miles (5 km) wide, and its highest spot is 213 feet above sea level. Since there are neither streams nor rivers—only saline ponds used for salt production—water comes from desalinization plants and cisterns that collect rainwater.

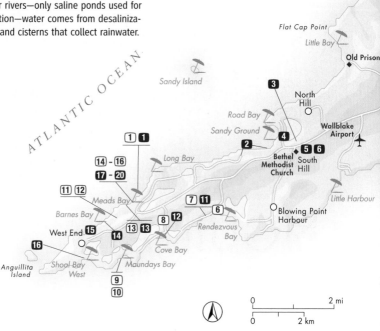

In tiny Anguilla, where fishermen have been heading out to sea for centuries in handmade boats, the beaches are some of the Caribbean's best and least crowded. Heavy development has not spoiled the island's atmospheric corners, and independent restaurants still thrive, as do a few quaint inns, which share the island with some genuinely over-the-top palaces.

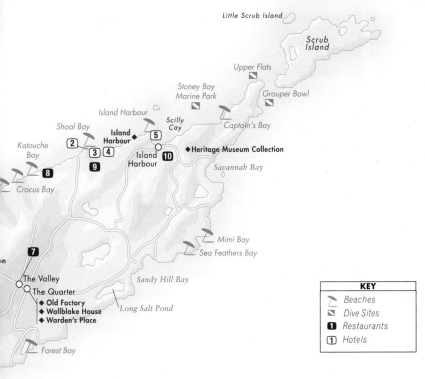

KEY

⟩	*Beaches*
◺	*Dive Sites*
❶	*Restaurants*
①	*Hotels*

Restaurants	▼			Hotels & Rentals	▼		
Blanchard's	**18**	Ocean Echo	**20**	Allamanda	**3**	Mead's Bay Beach Villas	**16**
Blanchard's Beach Shack	**17**	Picante	**15**	Anacaona	**13**	Paradise Cove	**8**
da'Vida	**8**	Roy's Bayside Grille	**4**	Anguilla Great House	**6**	Serenity Cottages	**4**
Dolce Vita	**3**	Smokey's	**12**	Arawak Beach Inn	**5**	Sheriva Villa Hotel	**10**
English Rose	**7**	Straw Hat	**1**	Cap Juluca	**9**	Shoal Bay Villas	**2**
Firefly	**13**	Tasty's	**6**	Caribella	**12**	Turtle's Nest Beach Resort	**15**
Geraud's Patisserie	**5**	Tokyo Bay	**11**	Carimar Beach Club	**14**	The Viceroy	**11**
Hibernia	**10**	Trattoria Tramonto	**16**	CuisinArt Golf Resort & Spa	**7**		
Jacala Beach Restaurant	**19**	Veya	**2**	Frangipani Beach Club	**1**		
Mango's	**14**	Zara's	**9**				

TOP REASONS TO VISIT ANGUILLA

1 Beautiful Beaches: Miles of brilliant beach ensure you have a high-quality spot in which to lounge.

2 Great Restaurants: The dining scene offers both fine dining and delicious casual food.

3 Fun, Low-Key Nightlife: A funky late-night local music scene features reggae and string bands.

4 Upscale Accommodations: Excellent luxury resorts coddle you in comfort.

5 Hidden Bargains: You'll find a few relative bargains if you look hard enough.

Updated by Elise Meyer

Peace, pampering, great food, and a wonderful local music scene are among the star attractions on Anguilla (pronounced ang-*gwill*-a). Beach lovers may become giddy when they first spot the island from the air; its blindingly white sand and lustrous blue-and-aquamarine waters are intoxicating. And if you like sophisticated cuisine served in casually elegant open-air settings, this may be your culinary Shangri-la.

The island's name, a reflection of its shape, is most likely a derivative of *anguille*, which is French for "eel." (French explorer Pierre Laudonnaire is credited with having given the island this name when he sailed past it in 1556.) In 1631 the Dutch built a fort here, but so far no one has been able to locate its site. English settlers from St. Kitts colonized the island in 1650, with plans to cultivate tobacco and, later, cotton and then sugar. But the thin soil and scarce water doomed these enterprises. Except for a brief period of independence, when it broke from its association with St. Kitts and Nevis in the 1960s, Anguilla has remained a British colony ever since.

From the early 1800s various island federations were formed and disbanded, with Anguilla all the while simmering over its subordinate status and forced union with St. Kitts. Anguillians twice petitioned for direct rule from Britain and twice were ignored. In 1967, when St. Kitts, Nevis, and Anguilla became an associated state, the mouse roared; citizens kicked out St. Kitts's policemen, held a self-rule referendum, and for two years conducted their own affairs. To what *Time* magazine called "a cascade of laughter around the world," a British "peacekeeping force" of 100 paratroopers from the Elite Red Devil unit parachuted onto the island, squelching Anguilla's designs for autonomy but helping a team of royal engineers stationed there to improve the port and build roads and schools. Today Anguilla elects a House of Assembly and its own leader to handle internal affairs, and a British governor is responsible for public service, the police, the judiciary, and external affairs.

The territory of Anguilla includes a few islets (or cays, pronounced "keys"), such as Scrub Island, Dog Island, Prickly Pear Cay, Sandy Island, and Sombrero Island. The 16,000 or so residents are predominantly of African descent, but there are also many of Irish background, whose ancestors came over from St. Kitts in the 1600s. Historically, because the limestone land was unfit for agriculture, attempts at enslavement never lasted long; consequently, Anguilla doesn't bear the scars of slavery found on so many other Caribbean islands. Instead, Anguillians became experts at making a living from the sea and are known for their boatbuilding and fishing skills. Tourism is the stable economy's growth industry, but the government carefully regulates expansion to protect the island's natural resources and beauty. New hotels are small, select, casino-free, and generally expensive; Anguilla emphasizes its high-quality service, serene surroundings, and friendly people.

PLANNING

WHEN TO GO

As in much of the Caribbean, high season runs from mid-December through mid-April, and some resorts in Anguilla still close from September through mid-December, though many remain open year-round. A few resorts require long minimum stays until after New Year's Day.

GETTING HERE AND AROUND

AIR TRAVEL

There are no nonstop flights to Anguilla from the United States. Trans-Anguilla Airways offers daily flights from Antigua, St. Thomas, and St. Kitts. Windward Islands Airways flies several times a day from St. Maarten (SXM). Anguilla Air Services flies from St. Maarten (SXM) and St. Barth (SBH). LIAT comes in from Antigua, Nevis, St. Kitts, St. Thomas, and Tortola. Cape Air has two daily flights from San Juan (three on peak travel days).

Airport **Clayton J. Lloyd Airport** ☎ *264/497–3510.*

Local Airline Contacts **Anguilla Air Services** ☎ *264/498–5922, 264/235–7122* ⊕ *www.anguillaairservices.com.* **Cape Air** ☎ *866/227–3247, 508/771–6944* ⊕ *www.capeair.com.* **LIAT** ☎ *264/497–5002* ⊕ *www.liatairline.com.* **TransAnguilla Airways** ☎ *264/497–8690* ⊕ *www.transanguilla.com.* **Windward Islands Airways** ☎ *866/466–0410* ⊕ *www.fly-winair.com.*

BOAT AND FERRY TRAVEL

Ferries run frequently between Anguilla and St. Martin. Boats leave from Blowing Point on Anguilla approximately every half hour from 7:30 am to 6:15 pm and from Marigot, St. Martin, every 45 minutes from 8 am to 7 pm. You pay a $20 departure tax before boarding ($5 for day-trippers—but be sure to make this clear at the window where you pay), in addition to the $15 one-way fare. Children under two years of age are free, children 2–5 are $10. On very windy days the 20-minute trip can be bouncy. The drive between the Marigot ferry terminal and the airport is vastly improved thanks to a new bridge across Simpson Bay. Transfers by speedboat to Anguilla are available

LOGISTICS

Getting to Anguilla: There are no nonstop flights to Anguilla (AXA) from the United States, so you will almost always have to fly through San Juan, St. Maarten, or some other Caribbean island. You'll ordinarily be making the hop on a smaller plane. You can also take a variety of boats and ferries from the airport in St. Maarten, or Marigot on the French side.

Hassle Factor: Medium.

On the Ground: Some hotels provide transfers from the airport or ferry pier, especially the more expensive ones. For everyone else, if you don't rent a car, the taxi ride from the airport to your hotel will be less than $25 even to the West End (and considerably less if you're going to Sandy Ground).

Getting Around the Island: It's possible to base yourself in Sandy Ground, Rendezvous Bay, Meads Bay, or Shoal Bay without a car, but restaurants and resorts are quite spread out, so for the sake of convenience you may wish to rent a car for a few days or for your entire stay. If you do, prepare to drive on the left. Taxis are fairly expensive on Anguilla, another reason to consider renting a car.

from a new terminal right at the airport, at a cost of about $75 per person (arranged directly with a company, or through your Anguilla hotel). Private ferry companies listed below run six or more round-trips a day, coinciding with major flights, between Blowing Point and the airport in St. Maarten. On the St. Maarten side they will bring you right to the terminal in a van, or you can just walk across the parking lot. These trips are $35 one-way or $60 round-trip (cash only), and usually include departure taxes. There are also private charters available.

A late-night sea shuttle service leaves St. Maarten for Anguilla at 10:30 pm. This sea shuttle meets the daily American flight from Miami, which arrives at 9:55 pm. It then takes you directly to Blowing Point in Anguilla. The trip costs $85 per person. Another sea shuttle, which departs at 7 pm, also goes from St. Maarten to Anguilla. This connects with JetBlue and InselAir flights originating in San Juan; the cost is $65 per person.

Contacts Funtime Ferry ☎ 866/334-0047 ⊕ www.funtime-charters.com. **GB Express** ☎ 264/584-6205 ⊕ www.anguillaferryandcharter.com. **Link Ferries** ☎ 264/497-2231 ⊕ www.link.ai. **Shauna Ferries** ☎ 264/476-6275.

CAR TRAVEL

Although most of the rental cars on-island have the driver's side on the left as in North America, Anguillian roads are like those in the United Kingdom—driving is on the left side of the road. It's easy to get the hang of, but the roads can be rough, so be cautious, and observe the 30 mph (48 kph) speed limit. Roundabouts are probably the biggest driving obstacle for most. As you approach, give way to the vehicle on your right; once you're in the rotary, you have the right of way.

Car Rentals: A temporary Anguilla driver's license is required to rent a car—you can get into real trouble if you're caught driving without one. You get it for $20 (good for three months) at any of the car-rental agencies at the time you pick up your car; you'll also need your valid driver's license from home. Rental rates start at about $45 to $55 per day, plus insurance.

Car-Rental Contacts Andy's Car Rental ☎ 264/235–7010 ⊕ www.andyrentals.com. **Apex/Avis** ✉ Airport Rd. ☎ 264/497–2642 ⊕ www.avisanguilla.com. **Bryans Car Rental** ✉ Blowing Point ☎ 264/497–6407 ⊕ www.bryanscarrentals.com. **Triple K Car Rental/Hertz** ✉ Airport Rd. ☎ 264/497–2934.

TAXI TRAVEL

Taxis are fairly expensive, so if you plan to explore the island's many beaches and restaurants, it may be more cost-effective to rent a car. Taxi rates are regulated by the government, and there are fixed fares from point to point, which are listed in brochures the drivers should have handy and are also published in the local guides. It's $26 from the airport or $22 from Blowing Point Ferry to West End hotels. Posted rates are for one or two people; each additional passenger adds $5 to the total, and there is a $1 charge for each piece of luggage beyond the allotted two. You can also hire a taxi for the hourly rate of $28. Surcharges of $4–$10 apply to trips after 6 pm. You'll always find taxis at the Blowing Point Ferry landing and at the airport. You'll need to call them to pick you up from hotels and restaurants, and arrange ahead with the driver who took you if you need a taxi late at night from one of the nightclubs or bars.

Taxi Contacts Blowing Point Ferry Taxi Stand ☎ 264/497–6089. **Maurice & Sons Exquisite Taxi Services** ☎ 264/235–2676.

ESSENTIALS

Banks and Exchange Services Legal tender is the Eastern Caribbean (EC) dollar, but U.S. dollars are widely accepted. ATMs dispense both U.S. and EC dollars. All prices quoted in this chapter are in U.S. dollars.

Electricity 110 volts, just as in the United States; no adapter required for American electronics.

Passport Requirements All visitors must carry a valid passport and have a return or ongoing ticket.

Phones Most hotels will arrange with a local provider for a cell phone to use during your stay (or you can rent one). A prepaid, local cell gives you the best rates. Some U.S. GSM phones will work in Anguilla, some will not. To call Anguilla from the United States, dial 1 plus the area code 264, then the local seven-digit number. To call the United States and Canada, dial 1, the area code, and the seven-digit number.

Safety Anguilla is a quiet, relatively safe island, but crime has been on the rise, and there's no sense in tempting fate by leaving your valuables unattended in your hotel room, on the beach, or in your car. Avoid remote beaches, and lock your car, hotel room, and villa. Most hotel rooms are equipped with a safe for stashing your valuables.

2

Taxes The departure tax is $20 for adults and $10 for children, payable in cash, at the airport at Blowing Point Ferry Terminal. If you are staying in Anguilla but day-tripping to St. Martin, be sure to mention it, and the rate will be only $5. A 10% accommodations tax is added to hotel bills along with a $1-per-night marketing tax, plus whatever service charge the hotel adds (can be up to 10%).

Tipping Despite any service charge, it's usually expected that you will tip more—$5 per day for housekeeping, $20 for a helpful concierge, and $10 per day to beach attendants. Many restaurants include a service charge of 10% to 15% on the bill; if there's no surcharge, tip about 15%. Taxi drivers should receive 10% of the fare.

ACCOMMODATIONS

Anguilla is known for its luxurious resorts and villas, but there are also some places that mere mortals can afford (and a few that are downright bargains).

HOTEL AND RESTAURANT PRICES

Prices in the restaurant reviews are the average cost of a main course at dinner or, if dinner is not served, at lunch; taxes and service charges are generally included. Prices in the hotel reviews are the lowest cost of a standard double room in high season, excluding taxes, service charges, and meal plans (except at all-inclusives). Prices for rentals are the lowest per-night cost for a one-bedroom unit in high season.

For expanded lodging reviews and current deals, visit Fodors.com.

VISITOR INFORMATION

Contacts Anguilla Tourist Office ⊠ *Coronation Ave., The Valley* ☎ *264/497–2759, 800/553–4939 from U.S.* ⊕ *ivisitanguilla.com.*

WEDDINGS

Weddings are common, but there's a huge $241.80 (EC$650) fee for a license. Visit Anguilla's government website for more information:

Contacts Government of Anguilla Judicial Department ☎ *264/497–2377* ⊕ *gov.ai/marriage.php.*

EXPLORING

Exploring on Anguilla is mostly about checking out the spectacular beaches and resorts. The island has only a few roads. Locals are happy to provide directions, but using the readily available tourist map is the best idea. Visit the Anguilla Tourist Board, centrally located on Coronation Avenue in The Valley.

The Anguilla Heritage Trail is a free, self-guided tour of 10 important historical sights that can be explored independently in any order. Wallblake House, in The Valley, is the main information center for the trail, or you can just look for the large boulders with descriptive plaques.

Bethel Methodist Church. Not far from Sandy Ground, this charming little church is an excellent example of skillful island stonework. It also has some colorful stained-glass windows. ⊠ *South Hill.*

Heritage Museum Collection. Don't miss this remarkable opportunity to learn about Anguilla. Old photographs and local records and artifacts trace the island's history over four millennia, from the days of the Arawaks. The tiny museum (complete with gift shop) is painstakingly curated by Colville Petty. High points include the historical documents of the Anguilla Revolution and the albums of photographs chronicling island life, from devastating hurricanes to a visit from Queen Elizabeth in 1964. You can see examples of ancient pottery shards and stone tools along with fascinating photographs of the island in the early 20th century—many depicting the heaping and exporting of salt and the christening of schooners—and a complete set of beautiful postage stamps issued by Anguilla since 1967. ⊠ *East End at Pond Ground* ☎ *264/235–7440* ✉ *$5* ☉ *Mon.–Sat. 10–5.*

Island Harbour. Anguillians have been fishing for centuries in the brightly painted, simple, handcrafted fishing boats that line the shore of the harbor. It's hard to believe, but skillful pilots take these little boats out to sea as far as 50 miles or 60 miles (80 km or 100 km). Late afternoon is the best time to see the day's catch. ■ **TIP→** **Hail the free boat to Gorgeous Scilly Cay, a classic little restaurant offering sublime lobster and Eudoxie Wallace's knockout rum punches on Wednesday and Sunday.** ⊠ *Island Harbor Rd.* ⊕ *www.scillycayanguilla.com.*

Old Factory. For many years the cotton grown on Anguilla and exported to England was processed in this beautiful historic building. Later it was a General Store, and now it's the home of Sotheby's Real Estate. There is a small art gallery on the lower level in an old stone cellar. ⊠ *Government Corner, The Valley* ☎ *264/497–2759* ⊕ *www.oldfactory-anguilla. ai* ✉ *Free* ☉ *Weekdays 10–noon and 1–4.*

Old Prison. The ruins of this historic jail on Anguilla's highest point—213 feet above sea level—have outstanding views. ⊠ *Valley Rd. at Crocus Hill.*

Sandy Ground. Almost everyone who comes to Anguilla stops by this central beach, home to several popular open-air bars and restaurants, as well as boat-rental operations. This is where you catch the ferry for tiny Sandy Island, 2 miles (3 km) offshore.

Wallblake House. The only surviving plantation house in Anguilla, Wallblake House was built in 1787 by Will Blake (Wallblake is probably a corruption of his name). The place is associated with many a tale involving murder, high living, and the French invasion in 1796. On the grounds are an ancient vaulted stone cistern and an outbuilding called the Bakery (which wasn't used for making bread at all but for baking turkeys and hams). Tours of the thoroughly and thoughtfully restored house and grounds are usually offered three days a week, and you can only visit on a guided tour. It's also the information center for the Anguilla Heritage Tour. ⊠ *Wallblake Rd., The Valley* ☎ *264/497–6613* ⊕ *www.wallblake.ai* ✉ *Free* ☉ *Tours Mon., Wed., and Fri. at 10 and 2.*

BEACHES

Anguilla's beaches are among the best and most beautiful in the Caribbean. You can find long, deserted stretches suitable for sunset walks, or beaches lined with lively bars and restaurants—all surrounded by crystal clear warm waters in several shades of turquoise. The sea is calmest at 2½-mile-long Rendezvous Bay, where gentle breezes tempt sailors. But Shoal Bay (East) is the quintessential Caribbean beach. The white sand is so soft and abundant that it pools around your ankles. Cove Bay and Maundays Bay, both on the southeast coast, must also rank among the island's best beaches. Maundays is the location of the island's famous resort, Cap Juluca, Meads Bay's arc is dominated by the tony Viceroy Resort, and smaller Cove Bay is just a walk away. In contrast to the French islands, Anguilla doesn't permit topless sunbathing.

NORTHEAST COAST

Captain's Bay. On the north coast just before the eastern tip of the island, this quarter-mile stretch of perfect white sand is bounded on the left by a rocky shoreline where Atlantic waves crash. If you make the tough, four-wheel-drive-only trip along the dirt road that leads to the northeastern end of the island toward Junk's Hole, you'll be rewarded with peaceful isolation. The surf here slaps the sands with a vengeance, and the undertow is strong—so wading is the safest water sport. **Amenities:** none. **Best for:** solitude.

Island Harbour. These mostly calm waters are surrounded by a slender beach. For centuries Anguillians have ventured from these sands in colorful handmade fishing boats. It's not much of a beach for swimming or lounging, but there a several restaurants (Hibernia, Arawak Café, and Smitty's), and this is the departure point for the three-minute boat ride to Scilly Cay, where a thatched beach bar serves seafood. Just hail the restaurant's free boat and plan to spend most of the day (the all-inclusive lunch starts at $40 and is worth the price—Wednesday and Sunday only). **Amenities:** food and drink. **Best for:** partiers.

NORTHWEST COAST

Little Bay. Little Bay is on the north coast between Crocus Bay and Shoal Bay, not far from the Valley. Sheer cliffs lined with agave and creeping vines rise behind a small gray-sand beach, usually accessible only by water (it's a favored spot for snorkeling and night dives). The easiest way to get here is a five-minute boat ride from Crocus Bay (about $10 round-trip). The young and agile can clamber down the cliffs by rope to explore the caves and surrounding reef; this is the only way to access the beach from the road and is not recommended to the inexperienced climber. Do not leave personal items in cars parked here, because theft can be a problem. **Amenities:** none. **Best for:** snorkeling.

Road Bay (*Sandy Ground*). The big pier here is where the cargo ships dock, but so do some pretty sweet yachts, sailboats, and fishing boats. The brown-sugar sand is home to terrific restaurants that hop from day through dawn, including Veya, Roy's Bayside Grille, Ripples, Barrel Stay, the Pumphouse, and Elvis', the quintessential beach bar. There are all kinds of boat charters available here. The snorkeling isn't very good, but the sunset vistas are glorious, especially with a rum punch in your hand. **Amenities:** food and drink. **Best for:** sunset.

Sandy Island. A popular day trip for Anguilla visitors, tiny Sandy Island shelters a pretty lagoon nestled in coral reefs about 2 miles (3 km) from Road Bay, with a restaurant that serves lunch and great islandy cocktails. From November through August you can take the "Happiness" sea shuttle from Sandy Ground ($10). ■TIP→ The reef is great for snorkeling. **Amenities:** food and drink. **Best for:** partiers; snorkeling; swimming. ⊕ *www.mysandyisland.com.*

FAMILY **Shoal Bay.** Anchored by sea grape and coconut trees, the 2-mile (3-km)
Fodor'sChoice powdered-sugar strand at Shoal Bay (not to be confused with Shoal
★ Bay West at the other end of the island) is one of the world's prettiest beaches. You can park free at any of the restaurants, including Elodia's, Uncle Ernie's, or Gwen's Reggae Grill, most of which either rent or provide chairs and umbrellas for patrons for about $20 a day per person. There is plenty of room to stretch out in relative privacy, or you can barhop or take a ride on Junior's Glass Bottom Boat. The relatively broad beach has shallow water that is usually gentle, making this a great family beach; a coral reef not far from the shore is a wonderful snorkeling spot. Sunsets over the water are spectacular. **Amenities:** food and drink. **Best for:** sunset; swimming; walking.

SOUTHEAST COAST

Sandy Hill. You can park anywhere along the dirt road to Sea Feathers Bay to visit this popular fishing center. What's good for the fishermen is also good for snorkelers. But the beach here is not much of a lounging spot. The sand is too narrow and rocky for that. However, it's a great place to buy lobsters and fish fresh out of the water in the afternoon. **Amenities:** food and drink. **Best for:** walking.

SOUTHWEST COAST

Fodor'sChoice **Cove Bay.** Follow the signs to Smokey's at the end of Cove Road, and
★ you will find water that is brilliantly blue and sand that's as soft as sifted flour. It's just as spectacular as its neighbors Rendezvous Bay and Maundays Bay. You can walk here from Cap Juluca for a change of pace, or you can arrange a horseback ride along the beach. Weekend barbecues with terrific local bands at Smokey's are an Anguillian must. **Amenities:** food and drink. **Best for:** partiers; swimming; walking.

Fodor'sChoice **Maundays Bay.** The dazzling, mile-long platinum-white beach is espe-
★ cially great for swimming and long beach walks. It's no wonder that Cap Juluca, one of Anguilla's premier resorts, chose this as its location. Public parking is straight ahead at the end of the road near Cap Juluca's Pimms restaurant. You can have lunch or dinner at Cap Juluca (just be prepared for the cost). Depending on the season you can book a massage in one of the beachside tents. **Amenities:** food and drink; parking; toilets. **Best for:** partiers; swimming; walking.

Rendezvous Bay. Follow the signs to Anguilla Great House for public parking at this broad swath of pearl-white sand that is some 1½ mile (2½ km) long. The beach is lapped by calm, bluer-than-blue water and a postcard-worthy view of St. Martin. The expansive crescent is home to three resorts; stop in for a drink or a meal at one, or rent a chair and umbrella at one of the kiosks. Don't miss the daylong party at the tree-house Dune Preserve, where Bankie Banx, Anguilla's most famous musician, presides. **Amenities:** food and drink; parking; toilets. **Best for:** partiers; swimming; walking.

Shoal Bay West. This glittering bay bordered by mangroves and sea grapes is a lovely place to spend the day. The mile-long beach is home to Covecastles villas. The tranquility is sublime, with coral reefs for snorkeling not too far from shore. Punctuate your day with a meal at beachside Trattoria Tramonto. Reach the beach by taking the main road to the West End and bearing left at the fork, then continuing to the end. Note that similarly named Shoal Bay is a separate beach on a different part of the island. **Amenities:** food and drink; parking; toilets. **Best for:** solitude; swimming; walking.

WHERE TO EAT

Despite its small size, Anguilla has around 70 restaurants: stylish temples of haute cuisine; classic, barefoot beachfront grills; roadside barbecue stands; food carts; and casual cafés. Many have breeze-swept terraces for dining under the stars. Call ahead—in winter to make a reservation and in late summer and fall to confirm whether the place you've chosen is even open at that time. Anguillian restaurant meals are leisurely events, and service is often at a relaxed pace, so settle in and enjoy. Most restaurant owners are actively and conspicuously present, especially at dinner.

What to Wear: During the day, casual clothes are widely accepted: shorts will be fine, but don't wear bathing suits and cover-ups unless you're at a beach bar. In the evening, shorts are okay at the extremely casual eateries. Elsewhere, women wear sundresses or nice casual slacks; men will be fine in short-sleeve shirts and casual pants. Some hotel restaurants are slightly more formal, but that just means long pants for men.

$$$$
ITALIAN
✕ **AXA Seafood.** New on the Anguilla dining scene in 2013 is this lively seafood restaurant. Longtime visitors will remember Luna Rosa, formerly in this location, and Axa Seafood brings Abi and Sylvestro back together. There is a lively bar, frequent live music, and a menu full of tasty fresh seafood (and meat) choices including a crowd-pleasing paella, a signature lobster mac-and-cheese, and several daily specials according to the day's "catch." The desserts are a standout, especially the espresso-mascarpone mousse garnished with white chocolate. $ *Average main:* $38 ⊠ *South Hill* ☎ 264/497–7979 ⊕ *www.axaseafoodhouse.com.*

$$$$
ECLECTIC
Fodor'sChoice
★
✕ **Blanchard's.** This absolutely delightful restaurant is one of the best in the Caribbean. Proprietors Bob and Melinda Blanchard moved to Anguilla from Vermont in 1994 to fulfill their culinary dreams. A festive atmosphere pervades the handsome, airy white room, which is accented with floor-to-ceiling teal-blue shutters to let in the breezes, and colorful artwork by the Blanchards' son Jesse on the walls. A masterful combination of creative cuisine, an upscale atmosphere,

attentive service, and an excellent wine cellar (including a selection of aged spirits) pleases the star-studded crowd. The nuanced contemporary menu is ever changing but always good; house classics like corn chowder, lobster and shrimp cakes, and a Caribbean sampler are crowd-pleasers, and vegetarians will find ample choices. For dessert, you'll remember concoctions like the key lime "pie-in-a-glass" or the justly famous "cracked coconut" long after your suntan has faded. $ *Average main: $49* ⊠ *Meads Bay* ☎ *264/497–6100* ⊕ *www. blanchardsrestaurant.com* ⊛ *Reservations essential* ⊙ *Closed Sun. No lunch. Closed Mon. May–mid-Dec. Closed Sept. 1–Oct. 17.*

$$
AMERICAN
FAMILY
✕ **Blanchards Beach Shack.** You'll find the perfect antidote to high restaurant prices at this spinoff, right on the sands of Meads Bay Beach. Opened in late 2011 right next to Blanchards, this chartreuse-and-turquoise cottage serves yummy lunches and dinners of lobster rolls, all-natural burgers, tacos, and terrific salads and sandwiches—you can dine at nearby picnic tables or rent a beach chair. Frozen drinks like mango coladas and icy mojitos please grown-ups, while kids dig into the fresh-made frozen yogurt concoctions. Organic produce and happy smiles are always on offer. Lots of choices for kids and vegetarians, too. ■TIP➔ **Diners are welcome to hang around on the beach.** $ *Average main: $12* ⊠ *Meads Bay* ☎ *264/498–6100* ⊕ *www. blanchardsrestaurant.com* ⊙ *Closed Sun. Closed Sept. 1–Oct. 17.*

$$$$
CARIBBEAN
FAMILY
✕ **da'Vida.** Sometimes you really can have it all. Right on exquisite Crocus Bay, this beautifully designed resort, restaurant, and club is a place where you could spend the whole day dining, drinking, and lounging under umbrellas on the comfortable chairs. Snorkeling equipment and kayaks are available for rent, and there's a boutique as well as a beachside spa. You can picnic at the Beach Grill (burgers, hot dogs, wraps, salads) or head inside the main building for dumplings, soups, pastas, and pizzas. Lunch starts at 11, and you can get tapas and sunset drinks from about 3. At dinner, the stylish wood interior (built by craftspeople from St. Vincent) is accented by candlelight. On the menu are such dishes as tasty seared snapper with gingered kale, coconut-crusted scallops, and Angus steaks. Go for the music on Friday and Saturday nights. ■TIP➔ **Call for information about their nightly shuttle service.** $ *Average main: $33* ⊠ *Crocus Bay* ☎ *264/498–5433* ⊕ *www.davidaanguilla.com* ⊙ *Closed Mon.*

$$$$
ITALIAN
✕ **Dolce Vita Italian Beach Restaurant & Bar.** Serious Italian cuisine and warm and attentive service are provided here, in a romantic beachside pavilion in Sandy Ground for lunch and dinner. Freshly made pasta stars in classic lasagna, fettuccini bolognese, pappardelle with duck sauce, and a meatless eggplant parmigiana. A carniverous quartet can preorder suckling pig, or a sample first-quality chops and steaks. Pizza is offered only at lunch. Italian wine fans will discover new favorites from the cellar. What's for dessert? How about Nutella cheesecake? $ *Average main: $34* ⊠ *Sandy Ground* ☎ *264/497–8668* ⊕ *www. dolcevitasandyground.com* ⊛ *Reservations essential* ⊙ *Closed Sun. No lunch Sat. Closed Sept. 1–Oct. 15.*

$$ CARIBBEAN 🍴 **English Rose Bar and Restaurant.** Lunchtime finds this neighborhood hangout packed with locals: cops flirting with sassy waitresses, entrepreneurs brokering deals with politicos, schoolgirls in lime-green outfits doing their homework. The decor is nothing to speak of, but this is a great place to eavesdrop or people-watch while enjoying island-tinged specialties like beer-battered shrimp, jerk-chicken Caesar salad, snapper creole, and buffalo wings. There is karaoke on Friday. [$] *Average main: $12* ✉ *Carter Rey Blvd., The Valley* ☎ *264/497–5353* ⏲ *Closed Sun.*

$$$ CARIBBEAN FAMILY 🍴 **Firefly Restaurant.** Set on a breezy poolside patio, Firefly—the restaurant at Anacaona Boutique Hotel—serves huge portions of tasty Caribbean fare by a longtime Anguillian chef. The pumpkin-coconut soup is a winner, as are the local snapper, mahimahi, and crayfish. Breakfast and lunch are also served. Lunch and drinks delivered to the beach is also a possibility here. ■ TIP→ **For great value, and terrific fun, book a table at the Thursday night buffet, with a lively performance by the folkloric theater company, Mayoumba, or the Tuesday night Chinese feast.** Friday night is Latin night: great food and music for practicing your salsa and your merengue with a professional dancer. [$] *Average main: $28* ✉ *Meads Bay* ☎ *264/497–6827* 🌐 *anacaonahotel.com.*

$$ FRENCH 🍴 **Geraud's Patisserie.** A stunning array of absolutely delicious French pastries and breads—and universal favorites like cookies, brownies, and muffins—are produced by Le Cordon Bleu dynamo Geraud Lavest in this well-located shop. Come in the early morning for cappuccino and croissants, or healthy fresh juices and smoothies, and pick up fixings for a wonderful and thrifty lunch later (or choose from among the list of tempting daily lunch specials). The little shop carries a small selection of interesting condiments, teas, and gourmet goodies. During the high season (December through May), a terrific Sunday brunch is available. Geraud also does a large amount of off-site catering, from intimate villa and yacht dinners to weddings. His sophisticated wedding cakes are an island wonder. [$] *Average main: $13* ✉ *South Hill Plaza* ☎ *264/497–5559* 🌐 *www.anguillacakesandcatering.com* ⏲ *Closed Mon. No dinner. Weekends 5:30 am– noon.*

$$$$ ECLECTIC Fodor's Choice ★ 🍴 **Hibernia Restaurant and Art Gallery.** Some of the island's most creative dishes are served in this wood-beam cottage restaurant overlooking the water at the far eastern end of Anguilla. Unorthodox yet delectable culinary pairings—inspired by chef-owners Raoul Rodriguez and Mary Pat's annual travels to Asia—bring new tastes and energy to the tables. The restaurant uses local organic products whenever possible. Long-line fish is served with a gratin of local pumpkin, shiitake mushrooms, and an essence of bitter oranges grown beside the front gate. Every visit here is an opportunity to share the owners' passion for life, expressed through the vibrant combination of setting, art, food, unique tableware, beautiful gardens, and thoughtful hospitality. There is a shuttle service available for dinner, call for details. ■ TIP→ **Mary Pat stocks the tiny art gallery here with amazing, and reasonable, finds from her roaming around the globe.** [$] *Average main: $36* ✉ *Harbor Ridge Dr., Island Harbour* ☎ *264/497–4290* 🌐 *www.hiberniarestaurant.com* ⏲ *Closed mid-July–Nov. Call for seasonal hrs.*

Straw Hat's outdoor patio on Forest Bay

$$$ FRENCH Fodor's Choice ★ 🍴 **Jacala Beach Restaurant.** Right on beautiful Meads Bay, this restaurant opened to raves in 2010. Alain the chef and Jacques the maître d' (from Malliouhana) have joined forces, and the happy result is carefully prepared and nicely presented French food served with care in a lovely open-air restaurant, accompanied by good wines and a lot of personal attention. A delicious starter terrine of feta and grilled vegetables is infused with pesto. For an entrée, you must try hand-chopped steak tartare, or seared and marinated sushi-grade tuna on a bed of delightful mashed plantain. Lighter lunchtime options include a tart cucumber-yogurt soup garnished with piquant tomato sorbet. After lunch you can digest on the beach in one of the "Fatboy" loungers. In any case, save room for the chocolate *pot de crème.* [$] *Average main: $30* ✉ *Meads Bay* ☎ *264/498–5888* ✍ *Reservations essential* 🕑 *Closed Mon. and Tues. and Aug. and Sept.*

$$$$ SEAFOOD FAMILY 🍴 **Mango's.** Sparkling-fresh fish specialties have starring roles on the menu here. Light and healthy choices include spicy grilled whole snapper, and Cruzan Rum barbecued chicken. Save room for dessert—the warm apple tart and the coconut cheesecake are worth the splurge. Come at lunch for sandwiches and burgers. There's an extensive wine list, and the Cuban cigar humidor is a luxurious touch. [$] *Average main: $36* ✉ *Barnes Bay* ☎ *264/497–6479* 🌐 *www.mangosseasidegrill.com* ✍ *Reservations essential* 🕑 *Closed Tues. and Aug.–Oct.*

$$ CARIBBEAN FAMILY 🍴 **Ocean Echo.** Newly opened in 2012, this relaxed and friendly restaurant is great for salads, burgers, grills, pasta and fresh fish. Heartier appetites will enjoy the ribs and steaks. It's every day, nonstop, from lunch until late. Sunday, Friday, and Wednesday there is live music as well as the enticing possibility of a bit of dancing with an

islandy cocktail in hand. $\boxed{\$}$ *Average main: $31* ✉ *Mead's Bay, West End* ☎ *264/498–5454* ⊕ *www.oceanechoanguilla.com.*

$$$
MEXICAN
FAMILY
✕ **Picante.** This casual, wildly popular bright-red roadside Caribbean *taquería*, opened by a young California couple, serves huge, tasty burritos with a choice of fillings, fresh warm tortilla chips with first-rate guacamole, huge (and fresh) taco salads, seafood enchiladas, and tequila-lime chicken grilled under a brick. Passion-fruit margaritas are a must, and the creamy Mexican chocolate pudding makes a great choice for dessert. Seating is at picnic tables; the friendly proprietors cheerfully supply pillows on request. Reservations are recommended. $\boxed{\$}$ *Average main: $21* ✉ *West End Rd., West End* ☎ *264/498–1616* ⊕ *www.picante-restaurant-anguilla.com* ⊘ *No lunch. Dec.–May, closed Tues. May–Aug., closed Mon. and Tues.*

$$$
CARIBBEAN
FAMILY
✕ **Roy's Bayside Grille.** Some of the best grilled lobster on the island is served here, along with burgers, great fish-and-chips, and good home-style cooking. On Friday from 5 to 7 there's a happy hour with a special menu. On Sunday you can get roast beef and Yorkshire pudding, and there's free Wi-Fi. The $35 prix fixe here is a good deal with lots of choices, and Ray's is very accommodating toward kids and people with food allergies. $\boxed{\$}$ *Average main: $27* ✉ *Road Bay, Sandy Ground* ☎ *264/497–2470* ⊕ *www.roysbaysidegrill.com.*

$$$
CARIBBEAN
FAMILY
✕ **Smokey's.** This quintessential Anguillian beach barbecue, part of the Gumbs family mini-empire of authentic and delicious eateries, is on pretty Cove Bay. On the beach, lounges with umbrellas welcome guests. Hot wings, honey-coated smoked ribs, curry goat, smoked chicken salad, and grilled lobsters are paired with local staple side dishes such as spiced-mayonnaise coleslaw, hand-cut sweet-potato strings, and crunchy onion rings. If your idea of the perfect summer lunch is a roadside lobster roll, be sure to try the version here, served on a home-baked roll with a hearty kick of hot sauce. The dinner menu includes lobster fritters, grilled tuna with lemon-caper butter, and rum chicken. On Saturday afternoon, a popular local band enlivens the casual, laid-back atmosphere, and on Sunday the restaurant is party central for locals and visitors alike. $\boxed{\$}$ *Average main: $25* ✉ *Cove Rd., Cove Bay* ☎ *264/497–6582* ⊕ *www.smokeysatthecove.com.*

$$$$
ECLECTIC
FAMILY
Fodor's Choice
★
✕ **Straw Hat.** Charming owners, a gorgeous oceanfront location, sophisticated and original food, and friendly service are the main reasons this stylish restaurant has been in business since the late 1990s. Whether for breakfast, lunch, or dinner, you will find appealing, tasty, and fresh choices to mix up or share for the perfect meal. Try Anguilla's only "real" bagel, tuna flatbread, jerk-braised pork belly, lobster spring rolls, or curried goat. "Fish of the day" truly means fish caught that day. Vegetarians and kids will find many options. A small garden out in the back is the source for the super-fresh greens. $\boxed{\$}$ *Average main: $39* ✉ *Frangipani Beach Club, Meads Bay* ☎ *264/497–8300* ⊕ *www.strawhat.com* ⌂ *Reservations essential* ⊘ *Closed Sept. and Oct.*

$$$
CARIBBEAN
✕ **Tasty's.** Once your eyes adjust to the quirky kiwi, lilac, and coral color scheme, you'll find that breakfast, lunch, or dinner at Tasty's is, well, very tasty. It's open all day long, so if you come off a midafternoon plane starving, head directly here—it's near the airport and the ferry

terminal. Chef-owner Dale Carty trained at Malliouhana, and his careful, confident preparation bears the mark of French culinary training, but the menu is classic Caribbean with a creole edge. It's worth leaving the beach at lunch for the lobster salad here. A velvety pumpkin soup garnished with roasted coconut shards is superb, as are the seared jerk tuna and the garlic-infused marinated conch salad. Don't be stuffy—try the goat stew. Yummy desserts end meals on a high note. This is one of the few restaurants that don't allow smoking, so take your Cubans elsewhere for an after-dinner puff. The popular Sunday brunch buffet features island specialties like salt-fish cakes. There is live music on Saturday night. $ *Average main: $23* ⊠ *Main Rd., South Hill Village, South Hill* ☎ *264/497–2737* ⊕ *www.tastysrestaurant.com* ⚠ *Reservations essential* ⊘ *Closed Thurs.*

$$$$ ✕ **Tokyo Bay.** This chic sushi and teppanyaki restaurant, dramatically lit
SUSHI and perched at the top of CuisinArt's spa building, opened to raves in
FAMILY 2012. Chances are that this is where you will find many local chefs and other restaurant people on their night out. The sake bar features terrific cocktails with names like Eager Ninja and Saketini, and Japanese chefs slice up ocean-fresh fish for sushi both traditional and otherwise. Hot pots, rice dishes, wagyu beef, and yakitori skewers round out the menu. "Chocolate Sushi" is an amusing finale to dinner. $ *Average main: $42* ⊠ *CuisinArt Resort and Spa, Rendevous Bay* ☎ *264/498–2000* ⊕ *www. cuisinartresort.com* ⊘ *No lunch. Closed Tues.*

$$$ ✕ **Trattoria Tramonto and Oasis Beach Bar.** The island's only beachfront Ital-
ITALIAN ian restaurant features a dual (or dueling) serenade of Andrea Bocelli on
FAMILY the sound system and gently lapping waves a few feet away. Chef Valter Belli artfully adapts recipes from his home in Emilia-Romagna. Try the delicate lobster ravioli in truffle-cream sauce. For dessert, don't miss the tiramisu. Though you might wander in here for lunch after a swim, when casual dress is OK, you'll still be treated to the same impressive menu. You can also choose from a luscious selection of champagne fruit drinks, a small and fairly priced Italian wine list, and homemade grappa. Hang out on chairs on the spectacular beach before or after your meal. $ *Average main: $28* ⊠ *Shoal Bay West* ☎ *264/497–8819* ⊕ *www.trattoriatramonto.com* ⚠ *Reservations essential* ⊘ *Closed Mon. and Aug.–Oct.*

$$$$ ✕ **Veya.** On the suavely minimalist four-sided verandah, the stylishly
ECLECTIC appointed tables glow with flickering candlelight (in white-matte, sea
Fodor's Choice urchin–shape votive holders made of porcelain). A lively lounge where
★ chic patrons mingle and sip mojitos to the purr of soft jazz anchors the room. Inventive, sophisticated, and downright delicious, Carrie Bogar's "Cuisine of the Sun" features ingenious preparations of first-rate provisions. Ample portions are sharable works of art—sample Moroccan-spiced shrimp "cigars" with roast tomato–apricot chutney or Vietnamese-spiced calamari. Jerk-spiced tuna is served with a rum-coffee glaze on a juicy slab of grilled pineapple with curls of plantain crisps, and crayfish in beurre blanc is divine. $ *Average main: $38* ⊠ *Sandy Ground* ☎ *264/498–8392* ⊕ *www.veya-axa.com/* ⚠ *Reservations essential* ⊘ *Closed Sun., June–Aug., and weekends June–Oct. Restaurant Closed Sept. 1–Oct. 16.*

$$$ ECLECTIC 🍴 **Zara's.** Chef Shamash Brooks presides at this under-the-radar but cozy restaurant with beamed ceilings, terra-cotta floors, and colorful artwork. His kitchen turns out tasty fare that combines Caribbean and Italian flavors with panache (Rasta Pasta is a specialty). Standouts include a velvety pumpkin soup with coconut milk, crunchy calamari, lemon pasta scented with garlic, herbed rack of lamb served with a roasted applesauce, and spicy fish fillet steamed in banana leaf. Follow the signs to Allamanda. [$] *Average main: $25* ✉ *Allamanda Beach Club, Upper Shoal Bay* ☎ *264/497–3229* ⏲ *No lunch.*

WHERE TO STAY

Tourism on Anguilla is a fairly recent phenomenon—most development didn't begin until the early 1980s. The lack of native topography and, indeed, vegetation, and the blindingly white expanses of beach have inspired building designs of some interest; architecture buffs might have fun trying to name some of the most surprising examples. Inspiration largely comes from the Mediterranean: the Greek Islands, Morocco, and Spain, with some Miami-style art deco thrown into the mixture.

Anguilla accommodations basically fall into two categories: grand resorts and luxury resort-villas, or low-key, simple, locally owned inns and small beachfront complexes. The former can be surprisingly expensive, the latter surprisingly reasonable. In the middle are some condo-type options, with full kitchens and multiple bedrooms, which are great for families or for longer stays. Private villa rentals are becoming more common and are increasing in number and quality every season as development on the island accelerates.

A good phone chat or email exchange with the management of any property is a good idea, as units within the same complex can vary greatly in layout, accessibility, distance to the beach, and view. When calling to reserve a room, ask about special discount packages, especially in spring and summer. Most hotels include continental breakfast in the price, and many have meal-plan options. But keep in mind that Anguilla is home to dozens of excellent restaurants before you lock yourself into an expensive meal plan that you may not be able to change. All hotels charge a 10% tax, a $1 per room/per day tourism marketing levy, and—in most cases—an additional 10% service charge. A few properties include these charges in the published rates, so check carefully when you are evaluating prices.

PRIVATE VILLAS AND CONDOS

The tourist office publishes an annual *Anguilla Travel Planner* with informative listings of available vacation apartment rentals.

Anguilla Luxury Collection. This operator also manages the Anguilla Affordable Collection, another group of less-expensive villas. ☎ *264/497–6049* 🌐 *www.anguillaluxurycollection.com.*

Ani Villas. Two stunning cliffside villas for up to 24 guests offer breathtaking views and total luxury to families or groups looking for total pampering. Included in the rental rate are private boat transfers from St. Martin, rental car, a full service team: concierge, butler, chef, housekeepers, breakfasts, dinner chef service, and all beverages. Tennis pros, spa services, trainers and guides are all available on demand. There is room for 100 guests for a party or a wedding; and a dramatic and romantic promontory for the ceremony. A tennis court, bikes, fitness room, pool, cliffside hot-tubs, and playrooms mean that except for beach going, you never have to leave. Check for promotions that include unlimited golf at the CuisinArt Golf Course. ☎ *264/497–7888* ⊕ *www.anivillas.com.*

myCaribbean. Gayle Gurvey and her staff manage and rent more than 100 local villas, and have been in business since 2000; it's the largest local company for private villa rentals. The "last minute" deals on the website offer good deals for the impulsive. ☎ *321/392–0828* ⊕ *www. mycaribbean.com.*

RECOMMENDED HOTELS AND RESORTS

$
RENTAL
FAMILY
Allamanda Beach Club. Youthful, active couples from around the globe happily fill this casual, three-story, white-stucco building hidden in a palm grove just off the beach, opting for location and price over luxury. **Pros:** front row for all Shoal Bay's action; young crowd; good restaurant. **Cons:** location requires a car; rooms are pleasant, but not at all fancy. $ *Rooms from: $175* ⊠ *The Valley* ☎ *264/497–5217, 305/396–4472* ⊕ *www.allamanda.ai* ⤳ *20 units* ۞ *Closed Sept.* ۞ *No meals.*

$
RESORT
FAMILY
Anacaona Boutique Hotel. Imbued with the culture and traditions of the island, this resort makes low-key yet chic hideaway (its name is pronounced "an-nah-cah-*oh*-na"). **Pros:** friendly clientele, sensitive to local culture; modern and good value; nice high-tech amenities. **Cons:** bit of a walk to beach; smallish rooms. $ *Rooms from: $265* ⊠ *Meads Bay* ☎ *264/497–6827, 877/647–4736* ⊕ *www.anacaonahotel.com* ⤳ *27 rooms and suites* ۞ *Multiple meal plans.*

$$
RESORT
FAMILY
Anguilla Great House Beach Resort. These traditional West Indian–style bungalows are strung along one of Anguilla's longest beaches. **Pros:** real, old-school Caribbean; right on the gorgeous beach, young crowd; good prices. **Cons:** rooms are very simple; internet access is spotty. $ *Rooms from: $310* ⊠ *Rendezvous Bay* ☎ *264/497–6061, 800/583–9247* ⊕ *www. anguillagreathouse.com* ⤳ *31 rooms* ۞ *Multiple meal plans.*

$
B&B/INN
Arawak Beach Inn. These hexagonal two-story villas are a good choice for a funky, budget-friendly, low-key guesthouse experience. **Pros:** funky, casual crowd; friendly owners; very competitive rates. **Cons:** not on the beach; air-conditioning included only in premium rooms; isolated location makes a car a must. $ *Rooms from: $265* ⊠ *The Valley, Island Harbour* ☎ *264/497–4888, 877/427–2925 reservations* ⊕ *www. arawakbeach.com* ⤳ *17 rooms* ۞ *Multiple meal plans.*

$$$$
RESORT
Cap Juluca. Strung along 179-acres of breathtaking Maundays Bay, the romantic, domed, Moorish-style villas have been an Anguilla favorite for 25 years, thanks to caring staff, great sports facilities, and plenty of room for privacy and comfort. **Pros:** lots of space to stretch out on miles of talcum-soft sand; warm service; romantic atmosphere. **Cons:** ongoing renovations, comparatively high rates, some of the units are currently closed. $ *Rooms from: $995* ⊠ *Maundays Bay* ☎ *264/497–6779, 888/858–5822 in U.S.* ⊕ *www.capjuluca.com* ⤳ *69 rooms, 7 patio suites, 6 pool villas* ۞ *Some meals.*

CuisinArt Resort and Spa, Rendezvous Bay

$$$ RENTAL 🏨 **Caribella.** These spacious Mediterranean-style villas on the broad sands of Barnes Bay are a good deal at the much-discounted weekly rate. **Pros:** huge amount of space for the cost; beautiful views from huge balconies. **Cons:** basic decor. [$] *Rooms from: $450* ✉ *Barnes Bay* ☎ *264/497–6045* 🌐 *www.lambertventures.com* 🛏 *6 units* 🍴 *No meals.*

$$$ RENTAL FAMILY 🏨 **Carimar Beach Club.** This horseshoe of bougainvillea-draped Mediterranean-style buildings on beautiful Meads Bay has the look of a Sun Belt condo. **Pros:** tennis courts; easy walk to restaurants and spa; great beach location; laundry facilities. **Cons:** no pool or restaurant. [$] *Rooms from: $435* ✉ *Meads Bay* ☎ *264/497–6881, 866/270–3764* 🌐 *www.carimar.com* 🛏 *24 apartments* 🕒 *Closed Sept.–mid-Oct.* 🍴 *Multiple meal plans.*

$$$$ RESORT FAMILY Fodor's Choice ★ 🏨 **CuisinArt Golf Resort and Spa.** Anguilla's only family-friendly full-service resort has it all: miles of stunning beach, world-class golf, a gorgeous spa and health club, top dining, and sports galore. **Pros:** family-friendly; great spa and sports; gorgeous beach and gardens. **Cons:** food service can be slow; pool area is noisy, beach lounges need replacement. [$] *Rooms from: $800* ✉ *Rendezvous Bay* ☎ *264/498–2000, 800/943–3210* 🌐 *www.cuisinartresort.com* 🛏 *100 rooms, 2 penthouses, 6 villas* 🕒 *Closed Sept. and Oct.* 🍴 *Multiple meal plans.*

$$$ RESORT FAMILY 🏨 **Frangipani Beach Club.** This flamingo-pink Mediterranean-style property perches on the beautiful champagne sands of Meads Bay. **Pros:** great beach; good location for restaurants and resort-hopping; first-rate on-site restaurant; helpful staff. **Cons:** some rooms lack a view, so be sure to ask if you care. [$] *Rooms from: $400* ✉ *Meads Bay* ☎ *264/497–6442, 877/593–8988* 🌐 *www.frangipaniresort.com* 🛏 *19 rooms* 🕒 *Closed Sept. and Oct.* 🍴 *Breakfast.*

$$$$ RENTAL FAMILY **Mead's Bay Beach Villas.** These gorgeous one-, two-, and three-bedroom villas set right on Mead's Bay have a cult following, so it's sometimes hard to book them. **Pros:** big private apartments; beautiful beach location; private plunge pools; free phone calls to the U.S. **Cons:** more condo than hotel in terms of service. [$] *Rooms from: $550* ✉ *Mead's Bay Rd.* ☎ *264/497–0271* 🌐 *www.meadsbaybeachvillas.com* 🛏 *4 villas* 🍴 *No meals.*

$$ RENTAL FAMILY **Paradise Cove.** Located 500 yards away from Cove Beach, this simple complex of huge, reasonably priced studios, one- and two-bedroom apartments has two whirlpools, a large pool, and tranquil tropical gardens where you can pluck fresh guavas for breakfast. **Pros:** reasonable rates; great pool; lovely gardens. **Cons:** a bit far from the beach; bland decor. [$] *Rooms from: $320* ✉ *The Cove* ☎ *264/497–6959, 264/497–6603* 🌐 *www.paradise.ai* 🛏 *12 studio suites, 17 1- and 2-bedroom apartments* 🍴 *No meals.*

$$ RENTAL FAMILY **Serenity Cottages.** Despite the name, these aren't cottages but rather large, fully equipped, and relatively affordable one- and two-bedroom apartments (and studios created from them) in a small complex set in a lush garden at the farthest end of glorious Shoal Bay Beach. **Pros:** big apartments; quiet end of beach; snorkeling right outside the door; very reasonable rates for weeklong packages. **Cons:** no pool; more condo than hotel in terms of staff; location at the end of Shoal Bay pretty much requires a car and some extra time to drive to the West End. [$] *Rooms from: $325* ✉ *Shoal Bay East* ☎ *264/497–3328* 🌐 *www.serenity.ai* 🛏 *2 1-bedroom suites, 8 2-bedroom apartments* 🕒 *Closed Sept.* 🍴 *No meals.*

$$$$ RENTAL FAMILY **Sheriva Villa Hotel.** This intimate, luxury-villa hotel is made up of three cavernous villas with a total of 20 guest rooms and seven private swimming pools, which overlook a broad swath of turquoise sea. **Pros:** incredible staff; all the comforts of home and more; good value for large family groups. **Cons:** not on the beach; you risk being spoiled for life by the staff's attentions; expensive. [$] *Rooms from: $1500* ✉ *Maundays Bay Rd., West End* ☎ *264/498–9898* 🌐 *www.sheriva.com* 🛏 *20 rooms* 🍴 *Multiple meal plans.*

$$ RENTAL FAMILY **Shoal Bay Villas.** This old-style property well located right on Shoal Bay's incredible 2-mile beach. **Pros:** friendly; casual; full kitchens; beachfront. **Cons:** not fancy; you'll want a car to get around; there's construction going on in the area, so check on progress before booking. [$] *Rooms from: $410* ✉ *Shoal Bay* ☎ *264/497–2051* 🌐 *sbvillas.ai* 🛏 *12 units* 🍴 *No meals.*

$$ RENTAL FAMILY **Turtle's Nest Beach Resort.** This collection of studios and one- to three-bedroom oceanfront condos is right on Meads Bay beach, with some of the island's best restaurants a sandy stroll away. **Pros:** beachfront; huge apartments; well-kept grounds and pool. **Cons:** no elevator, so avoid booking a fourth floor unit if you don't want to climb a lot of stairs, despite the great views. [$] *Rooms from: $340* ✉ *Meads Bay* ☎ *264/462–6378* 🌐 *www.turtlesnestbeachresort.com* 🛏 *29 units* 🍴 *No meals.*

Viceroy Anguilla, Meads Bay

$$$$ 🏨 **The Viceroy.** On a promontory over 3,200 feet of the gorgeous pearly sand on Meads Bay, Kelly Wurstler's haute-hip showpiece wows international sophisticates, especially those lucky enough to stay in one of the spacious two- to five-bedroom villas, complete with private infinity pools and hot tubs, indoor-outdoor showers, electronics galore, and a gourmet professional kitchen stuffed with high-end equipment, not to mention a house manager to keep it all running smoothly. **Pros:** state-of-the-art luxury; cutting-edge contemporary design; flexible, spacious rooms. **Cons:** international rather than Caribbean in feel; very large resort; kind of a see-and-be-seen scene; really expensive. [$] *Rooms from: $795* ✉ *Barnes Bay, West End* ☎ *264/497–7000, 866/270–7798 in U.S.* 🌐 *www.viceroyhotelsandresorts.com* 🛏 *163 suites, 3 villas* 🕒 *Closed Sept.* 🍴 *Breakfast.*

RESORT
FAMILY
Fodor's Choice ★

NIGHTLIFE

In late February or early March, on the first full moon before Easter, reggae star and impresario Bankie Banx stages Moonsplash, a three-day music festival that showcases local and imported talent. The boat races on Anguilla Day in May is the most important island sporting event of the year. At the end of July is the Anguilla Summer Festival, with boat races by day and Carnival parades, calypso competitions and parties at night. Some years there is a Jazz Festival, check the Tourist Board website for information.

The nightlife scene here runs late into the night—the action doesn't really start until after 11 pm. If you do not rent a car, be aware that taxis are not readily available at night. If you plan to take a taxi back to your hotel or villa at the end of the night, be sure to make arrangements in advance with the driver who brings you or with your hotel concierge.

Dune Preserve. The funky Dune Preserve is the driftwood-fabricated home of Bankie Banx, Anguilla's famous reggae star. He performs here weekends and during the full moon. There's a dance floor and a beach bar, and sometimes you can find a sunset beach barbecue in progress. In high season there's a $15 cover charge. ⊠ *Rendezvous Bay* ☎ *264/497–6219* ⊕ *www.bankiebanx.net.*

Fodor'sChoice **Elvis' Beach Bar.** This is the perfect locale (it's actually a boat) to hear
★ great music and sip the best rum punch on earth. The bar is open every day but Tuesday, and there's live music on Wednesday through Sunday nights during the high season—as well as food until 1 am. Check to see if there's a full-moon LunaSea party. You won't be disappointed. ⊠ *Sandy Ground* ☎ *264/772–0637.*

Johnno's Beach Stop. Things are lively at Johnno's, where there is live music and alfresco dancing every night and on Sunday afternoon, when just about everybody drops by (on Sunday night, there's live jazz). This is *the* classic Caribbean beach bar, attracting a funky eclectic mix, from locals to movie stars. It's open Tuesday–Sunday from 11 to 9. ⊠ *Sandy Ground* ☎ *264/497–2728* ◷ *Closed Mon.*

Fodor'sChoice **Pumphouse.** At the Pumphouse, in the old rock-salt factory, you can find
★ live music most nights—plus surprisingly good food from snacks like wings and calvados-flamed Camembert to burgers and steaks. Check out the mini-museum of artifacts and equipment from 19th-century salt factories. There's entertainment every night: Tuesday is Lady's night, and trivia is Sunday. ⊠ *Sandy Ground* ☎ *264/497–5154* ⊕ *www. pumphouse-anguilla.com.*

SHOPPING

Anguilla is by no means a shopping destination. In fact, if your suitcase is lost, you will be hard-pressed to secure even the basics on-island. If you're a hard-core shopping enthusiast, a day trip to nearby St. Martin will satisfy. The island's tourist publication, *What We Do in Anguilla,* has shopping tips and is available free at the airport and in shops. For upscale designer sportswear, check out the small boutiques in hotels (some are branches of larger stores in Marigot on St. Martin). Outstanding local artists sell their work in galleries, which often arrange studio tours (you can also check with the Anguilla Tourist Office).

Cheddie's Carving Studio. Cheddie's showcases Cheddie Richardson's fanciful wood carvings and coral and stone sculptures. ⊠ *Driftwood Haven, The Cove* ☎ *264/497–6027* ⊕ *news.ai/web/cheddie/* ◷ *Closed Sun.*

Devonish Art Gallery. This gallery purveys the wood, stone, and clay creations of Courtney Devonish, an internationally known potter and sculptor, plus creations by his wife, Carolle, a bead artist. Also available are works by other Caribbean artists and regional antique maps. ⊠ *West End Rd., George Hill* ☎ *264/497–2949* ⊕ *devonishart.com/.*

The Galleria at World Art and Antiques. The peripatetic proprietor of World Arts, Christy Douglas, displays a veritable United Nations of antiquities: exquisite Indonesian ikat hangings to Thai teak furnishings, Aboriginal didgeridoos to Dogon tribal masks, Yuan Dynasty jade pottery to Uzbeki rugs. There is also handcrafted jewelry and handbags, and Anguilla souvenirs also. ⊠ *West End Rd, West End* ☎ *264/497–5950, 264/497–2767* ⊕ *www.worldartandantiques.com.*

Hibernia Restaurant and Gallery. Hibernia has striking pieces culled from the owners' travels, from contemporary Eastern European artworks to traditional Indo-Chinese crafts. ⊠ *Island Harbour* ☎ *264/497–4290* ⊕ *www.hiberniarestaurant.com/.*

Savannah Gallery. Here you'll find works by local Anguillian artists as well as other Caribbean and Central American art, including oil paintings by Marge Morani. You'll also find works by artists of the renowned Haitian St. Soleil school, as well as Guatemalan textiles, Mexican pottery, and brightly painted metalwork. ⊠ *Coronation St., Lower Valley* ☎ *264/497–2263* ⊕ *www.savannahgallery.com.*

CLOTHING

Irie Life. This popular boutique sells vividly hued beach- and resort wear and flip-flops, as well as attractive handcrafts, jewelry, and collectibles from all over the Caribbean. ⊠ *South Hill* ☎ *264/497–6526* ⊕ *www.irielife.com/.*

ZaZaa. Sue Ricketts, the first lady of Anguilla marketing, owns ZaZaa boutiques in South Hill on the Main Road, and near the entrance of Anacaona Resort, on Meads Bay. Buy Anguillian crafts as well as wonderful ethnic jewelry and beachwear from around the globe, such as sexy Brazilian bikinis and chic St. Barth goodies. There are beach sundries and souvenirs as well. ⊠ *Lower South Hill, South Hill* ☎ *264/235–8878* ⊕ *www.anguillaluxurycollection.com.*

SPORTS AND ACTIVITIES

Anguilla's expanding sports options are enhanced by its beautiful first golf course, designed by Greg Norman, and part of the CuisinArt Resort, to accentuate the natural terrain and maximize the stunning ocean views over Rendezvous Bay. The Anguilla Tennis Academy, designed by noted architect Myron Goldfinger, operates in the Blowing Point area. The 1,000-seat stadium, equipped with pro shop and seven lighted courts, was created to attract major international matches and to provide a first-class playing option for tourists and locals.

A Day at the Boat Races

If you want a different kind of trip to Anguilla, try for a visit during Carnival, which starts on the first Monday in August and continues for about 10 days. Colorful parades, beauty pageants, music, delicious food, arts-and-crafts shows, fireworks, and nonstop partying are just the beginning. The music starts with sunrise jam sessions—as early as 4 am—and continues well into the night. The high point? The boat races. They are the national passion and the official national sport of Anguilla.

Anguillians from around the world return home to race old-fashioned, made-on-the-island wooden boats that have been in use on the island since the early 1800s. Similar to some of today's fastest sailboats, these are 15 to 28 feet in length and sport only a mainsail and jib on a single 25-foot mast. The sailboats have no deck, so heavy bags of sand, boulders, and sometimes even people are used as ballast. As the boats reach the finish line, the ballast—including some of the sailors—gets thrown into the water in a furious effort to win the race. Spectators line the beaches and follow the boats on foot, by car, and from even more boats. You'll have almost as much fun watching the fans as you will the races.

BOATING AND SAILING

FAMILY **Sandy Island Enterprises.** Take a day trip to the tiny island for a romantic barbecue lunch with your toes in the sand and a rum punch in your hand—"The Bachelor" did. The sea shuttle Happiness departs from the Sandy Ground Beach. The boat costs $10 per person round-trip. While reservations are preferred, you can come on a lark. ■TIP→ **This is one of the best snorkeling spots on the island.** ⊠ *Sandy Ground* 🕾 *264/476–6534* ⊕ *www.mysandyisland.com* ☉ *Closed after 4 pm; Aug. and Sept. by special arrangement.*

DIVING

Sunken wrecks; a long barrier reef; terrain encompassing walls, canyons, and hulking boulders; varied marine life, including greenback turtles and nurse sharks; and exceptionally clear water—all of these make for excellent diving. Prickly Pear Cay is a favorite spot. **Stoney Bay Marine Park,** off the northeast end of Anguilla, showcases the late-18th-century *El Buen Consejo,* a 960-ton Spanish galleon that sank here in 1772. Other good dive sites include **Grouper Bowl,** with exceptional hard-coral formations; **Ram's Head,** with caves, chutes, and tunnels; and **Upper Flats,** where you are sure to see stingrays.

Anguillian Divers. This is a full-service dive operator with a PADI five-star training center. The five-dive packages are a good deal, and they offer open-water certifications, too. ⊠ *Meads Bay* 🕾 *264/497–4750* ⊕ *www.anguilliandiver.com.*

FAMILY **Shoal Bay Scuba and Watersports.** Single-tank dives start at $50 and two-tank dives at $90 at this highly rated Padi Dive Center. They run up to six different dives daily from their two locations, one at Sandy Ground at Roy's, and one in West End. Daily snorkeling trips at 1 pm are $25 per person. The shop sells a full range of masks, snorkels, fins, T-shirts, hats, shorts and SPF 50 water shirts. There are also private Fishing Charters, private dives, snorkel and sightseeing charters, and sunset cruises on offer. ⊠ *West End, The Valley* ☏ *264/235–1482* ⊕ *www.shoalbayscuba.com.*

FISHING

Johnno's Beach Stop. Albacore, wahoo, marlin, barracuda, and kingfish are among the fish found off Anguilla's shores. You can strike up a conversation with almost any fisherman you see on the beach, and chances are, you'll be a welcome addition on his next excursion. If you'd rather make more formal arrangements, Johnno's Beach Stop in Sandy Ground has a boat and can help you plan a trip. ⊠ *Sandy Ground Village, Sandy Ground* ☏ *264/497–2728.*

GOLF

Fodor's Choice **CuisinArt Golf Club.** This Greg Norman course, a $50 million wonder,
★ qualifies as one of the best golf courses in the Caribbean. Thirteen of its 18 holes are directly on the water. The course features sweeping sea vistas, elevation changes, and an ecologically responsible watering system of ponds and lagoons that snake through the grounds. Players including President Bill Clinton have thrilled to the spectacular vistas of St. Maarten and blue sea at the tee box of the 390-yard starting hole—the Caribbean's answer to Pebble Beach. There is an attractive Italian restaurant for lunch. Course typically closes for the second half of October for maintenance. ■ TIP→ Dress requirements include long shorts or slacks and a collared shirt. ⊠ *Long Bay* ☏ *264/498–5602* ⊕ *www.cuisinartresort.com* ⚑ *18 holes, 7200 yards, par 72* ⛳ *$170 for 9 holes, $270 for 18 holes, $145 for guests 9 holes, $225 for guests 18 holes.*

GUIDED TOURS

A round-the-island tour by taxi takes about 2½ hours and costs $55 for one or two people, $5 for each additional passenger.

Anguilla Access Tours. Take a three-hour tour of Anguilla for a comprehensive introduction to Island heritage, food, nightlife, arts and crafts, or just beaches. Sign up online, get picked up at your hotel or villa. ⊠ *Government Center, The Valley* ☏ *267/772-9827* ⊕ *anguillaaccess.com.*

Anguilla Tourist Office. Contact the Anguilla Tourist Office to arrange the tour by Sir Emile Gumbs, the island's former chief minister, of the Sandy Ground area. This tour, which highlights historic and ecological sites, is held Tuesday at 10 am. The $20 fee benefits the Anguilla Archaeological Historical Society. Gumbs also organizes bird-watching expeditions that show you everything from frigate birds to turtledoves. Other tours include a visit to Sea Turtle nesting sites, the Heritage Collection, and Wallblake House. ⊠ *Coronation Ave., The Valley* ☎ *264/497–2759, 800/553–4939* ⊕ *ivisitanguilla.com.*

Bennie's Travel & Tours. This is one of the island's more reliable tour operators. ⊠ *Blowing Point* ☎ *264/497–2788.*

HORSEBACK RIDING

Seaside Stables. If a sunset gallop (or slow clomp) has always been your fantasy, contact this company. Private rides on very gentle horses at any time of the day are $90 per hour, group rides in the morning or afternoon are $70; or try a bareback ocean romp or full-moon ride for $120; prior riding experience is not required. Choose from English, Western, or Australian saddles. ⊠ *Paradise Dr., Cove Bay* ☎ *264/497–3667* ⊕ *www.seaside-stables.com.*

SEA EXCURSIONS

Chocolat. This 35-foot catamaran is available for private charter or scheduled excursions to nearby cays. Captain Rollins is a knowledgeable, affable guide. Rates for day sails with lunch (prepared by the captain's wife, Jacquie, of Ripples Restaurant) are about $80 per person. ⊠ *Sandy Ground* ☎ *264/497–3394.*

Funtime Charters. This charter and shuttle service operates five powerboats ranging in size from 32 to 38 feet. They will arrange private boat transport to the airport ($65 per person), day trips to St. Barth, or other boat excursions. A new, fully air-conditioned 42-seat boat, *The Sunshine Express,* runs late-night and early morning direct to SXM, and also has inter-island excursions. ⊠ *The Cove* ☎ *264/497–6511, 866/334–0047* ⊕ *www.funtimechartersanguilla.com.*

FAMILY **Junior's Glass Bottom Boat.** For an underwater peek at sea turtles and stingrays without getting wet, catch a ride ($20 per person) on Junior's Glass Bottom Boat. Snorkeling trips and instruction are available, too. Just show up at Shoal Bay Beach and look for the boat or ask for Junior at the Dive Shop. ⊠ *Sandy Ground* ☎ *264/497–4456* ⊕ *www.junior.ai.*

Sandy Island Enterprises. Picnic, swimming, and diving excursions to Prickly Pear Cay, Sandy Island, and Scilly Cay are available through Sandy Island Enterprises, which also rents Sunfish and Windsurfers and arranges fishing charters. Fans of TV's *The Bachelor* might recall the Valentine's Day picnic date here in 2011. You, too, can enjoy some rum punch and lobster. The Sandy Island sea shuttle leaves from the small pier in Sandy Ground daily November–July, and by reservation August–October. ⊠ *The Valley* ☎ *264/476–6534* ⊕ *mysandyisland.com.*

ANTIGUA AND BARBUDA

WELCOME TO ANTIGUA AND BARBUDA

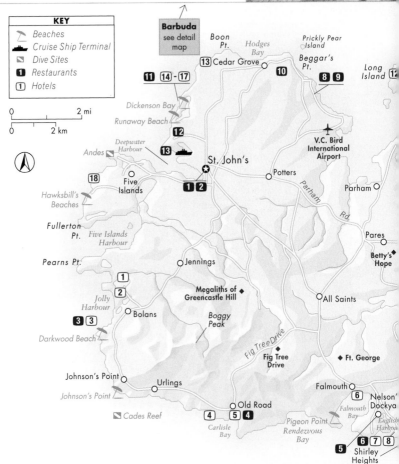

KEY

- ➤ Beaches
- ⚓ Cruise Ship Terminal
- ◣ Dive Sites
- **1** Restaurants
- ① Hotels

| 0 | | 2 mi |
| 0 | 2 km | |

Barbuda
see detail map

Boon Pt.

Hodges Bay

Prickly Pear Island

Beggar's Pt.

13 Cedar Grove

10

8 9

Long Island **12**

11 **14** - **17**

Dickenson Bay

Runaway Beach

12

Deepwater Harbour

V.C. Bird International Airport

Andes ◣

13 ⚓

St. John's

18

Five Islands

1 2

Potters

Parham

Hawksbill's Beaches

Parham Rd.

Fullerton Pt.

Five Islands Harbour

Pares

Pearns Pt.

Jennings

Betty's Hope

1

2

Megaliths of Greencastle Hill ◆

All Saints

Jolly Harbour

3 ③

Bolans

Boggy Peak

Darkwood Beach

Fig Tree Drive

Fig Tree Drive ◆

◆ Ft. George

Johnson's Point

Johnson's Point

Urlings

Falmouth

6 Nelson's Dockya

◣ Cades Reef

4 **5** **4**

Old Road

Falmouth Bay

English Harbou

Carlisle Bay

Pigeon Point

Rendezvous Bay

6 **7** **8**

5 Shirley Heights

Excellent beaches—365 of them—might make you think that the island has never busied itself with anything more pressing than the pursuit of pleasure. But for much of the 18th and 19th centuries English Harbour sheltered Britain's Caribbean fleet. These days, pleasure yachts bob where galleons once anchored.

A BEACH FOR EVERY DAY

At 108 square miles (280 square km), Antigua is the largest of the British Leeward Islands. Its much smaller sister island, Barbuda, is 26 miles (42 km) to the north. Together, they are an independent nation and part of the British Commonwealth. The island was under British control from 1667 until it achieved independence in 1981.

3

ANTIGUA AND BARBUDA

Restaurants ▼	
Admiral's Inn	6
The Bay @ Nonsuch	7
Big Banana	2
Cecilia's High Point	8
Coconut Grove	11
East	4
La Bussola	12
Le Bistro	10
Le Cap Horn	5
Papa Zouk	1
Russell's	13
Sheer Rocks	3
The Tides	9

Hotels ▼	
Admiral's Inn	7
Blue Waters Hotel	13
Buccaneer Beach Club	17
Carlisle Bay	5
Catamaran Hotel	6
CocoBay	3
Curtain Bluff	4
Dickenson Bay Cottages	15
Galley Bay	18
Jolly Beach Resort	2
Jolly Harbour Villas	1
Jumby Bay	12
Nonsuch Bay Resort	10
Ocean Inn	8
St. James's Club	9
Sandals Grande	14
Siboney Beach Club	16
Verandah Resort & Spa	11

TOP REASONS TO VISIT ANTIGUA AND BARBUDA

1 Beaches Galore: So many paradisiacal beaches of every size provide a tremendous selection for an island its size.

2 Nelson's Dockyard: One of the Caribbean's best examples of historic preservation.

3 Sailing Away: With several natural anchorages and tiny islets to explore, Antigua is a major sailing center.

4 Activities Galore: Land and water sports, sights to see, and nightlife.

5 Shopping Options: A nice selection of shopping options, from duty-free goods to local artists and craftspeople (especially distinctive ceramics).

Updated by
Jordan Simon

The wonder of Antigua, and especially its astonishingly undeveloped sister island, Barbuda, is that you can still play Robinson Crusoe here. Travel brochures trumpet the 365 sensuous beaches, "one for every day of the year," as locals love saying, though when the island was first developed for tourism, the unofficial count was 52 ("one for every weekend"). Either way, even longtime residents haven't combed every stretch of sand.

The island's extensive archipelago of cays and islets is what attracted the original Amerindian settlers—the Ciboney—at least 4,000 years ago. The natural environment, which is rich in marine life, flora, and fauna, has been likened to a "natural supermarket." Antigua's superior anchorages and strategic location naturally caught the attention of the colonial powers. The Dutch, French, and English waged numerous bloody battles throughout the 17th century (eradicating the remaining Arawaks and Caribs in the process), with England finally prevailing in 1667. Antigua remained under English control until achieving full independence on November 1, 1981, along with Barbuda, 26 miles (42 km) to the north.

Boats and beaches go hand in hand with hotel development, and Antigua's tourist infrastructure has mushroomed since the 1950s. Though many of its grandes dames such as Curtain Bluff remain anchors, today all types of resorts line the sand, and the island offers something for everyone, from gamboling on the sand to gambling in casinos. Environmental activists have become increasingly vocal about preservation and limiting development, and not just because green travel rakes in the green. Antigua's allure is precisely that precarious balance and subliminal tension between its unspoiled, natural beauty and its sun-sand-surf megadevelopment. And the British heritage persists, from teatime (and tee times) to fiercely contested cricket matches.

LOGISTICS

Getting to Antigua and Barbuda: Antigua is a Caribbean base, and several airlines fly there nonstop. There is ferry service to Barbuda several days a week, though it's geared for day-trippers. Antigua Barbuda Montserrat Air provides flights between the two islands. Good package deals are often available from resorts.

Hassle Factor: Low for Antigua, medium for Barbuda.

On the Ground: Taxis meet every flight, and drivers will offer to guide you around the island. Taxis are unmetered, but rates are posted at the airport. Drivers must carry a rate card with them. The fixed rate from the airport to St. John's is $12 (although drivers have been known to quote in Eastern Caribbean dollars), to Dickenson Bay $16, and to English Harbour $31.

If you are staying at an isolated resort or wish to sample the island's many fine restaurants, a car is a necessity, less so if you are staying at an all-inclusive with limited island excursions. It's possible to get by without a car if you are staying near St. John's or English Harbour, but taxi rates mount up quickly. A temporary driving permit is required on the island ($20), and you drive on the left.

PLANNING

WHEN TO GO

The high season runs from mid-December through April; after that time, you can find real bargains, as much as 40% off the regular rates, particularly if you book an air-hotel package. A fair number of the restaurants and properties close most of the time between August and October, especially around English Harbour.

GETTING HERE AND AROUND

AIR TRAVEL

Nonstop flights are available from Atlanta (Delta, twice weekly in season), Charlotte (US Airways), Miami (American, Caribbean Airlines, Continental), New York–JFK (American, Caribbean), and Newark (Continental).

Airport Contact V. C. Bird International Airport (ANU). ☏ 268/462–4672, 268/462–0358, 268/562–6798.

Airline Contacts American Airlines ☏ 268/462–0950 ⊕ www.aa.com. **Antigua Barbuda Montserrat Air** ☏ 268/562–8033, 268/562–7183 ⊕ www.abm-air.com. **Caribbean Airlines** ☏ 268/480–2900, 800/744–2225 ⊕ www.caribbean-airlines.com. **Continental Airlines** ☏ 268/462–5355 ⊕ www.continental.com. **Delta Airlines** ☏ 800/532–4777, 268/562–5951 ⊕ www.delta.com. **LIAT.** In addition to many nonstop flights from the United States, LIAT has daily flights to and from many other Caribbean islands. ☏ 268/480–5600 ⊕ www.liatairline.com. **US Airways** ☏ 268/480–5601, 268/562–5901 ⊕ www.usairways.com.

Taxes and Service Charges The departure tax is $37.50, which should be included in your airfare; if not, your carrier's airport check-in agent will request payment in cash only—either U.S. or EC currency. Hotels collect an 8.5%–10.5% government room tax; some restaurants will add a 7% tax. Hotels and restaurants also usually add a 10% service charge to your bill.

Tipping Restaurants, 5% beyond the regular service charge added to your bill; taxi drivers 10%; porters and bellmen about $1 per bag; maids $2 to $3 per night. Staff at all-inclusives aren't supposed to be tipped unless they've truly gone out of their way.

ACCOMMODATIONS

In Antigua you're almost certain to have an excellent beach regardless of where you stay. Dickenson Bay and Five Islands Peninsula suit beachcombers who want proximity to St. John's, and Jolly Harbour offers affordable options and activities galore. English Harbour and the southwest coast have the best inns and several excellent restaurants—although many close from August well into October; it's also the yachting crowd's hangout. Resorts elsewhere on the island are ideal for those seeking seclusion; some are so remote that all-inclusive packages or rental cars are mandatory. Barbuda has one posh resort, one fairly upscale hotel, and several guesthouses.

All-Inclusive Resorts: Most of the all-inclusives aim for a mainstream, package-tour kind of crowd—with varying degrees of success—though offerings such as Galley Bay and Curtain Bluff are more upscale.

Luxury Resorts: A fair number of luxury resorts cater to the well-heeled in varying degrees of formality on both Antigua and Barbuda.

Small Inns: A few small inns, some historic, can be found around Antigua, mostly concentrated in or near English Harbour.

HOTEL AND RESTAURANT PRICES

Prices in the restaurant reviews are the average cost of a main course at dinner or, if dinner is not served, at lunch; taxes and service charges are generally included. Prices in the hotel reviews are the lowest cost of a standard double room in high season, excluding taxes, service charges, and meal plans (except at all-inclusives). Prices for rentals are the lowest per-night cost for a one-bedroom unit in high season.

For expanded lodging reviews and current deals, visit Fodors.com.

VISITOR INFORMATION

Antigua & Barbuda Department of Tourism ⊠ *Government Complex, Queen Elizabeth Hwy., St. John's* ☎ *268/462–0480, 268/462–0651* ⊕ *www.antigua-barbuda.org.*

Antigua and Barbuda Tourism Authority ⊠ *ACB Financial Centre, High St., St. John's* ☎ *268/562–7600.*

Antigua & Barbuda Tourist Offices ☎ *212/541–4117 in New York City, 305/381–6762 in Miami, 888/268–4227* ⊕ *www.antigua-barbuda.org.*

Antigua Hotels & Tourist Association ⊠ *Island House, Newgate St., St. John's* ☎ *268/462–0374, 268/462–3703* ⊕ *www.antiguahotels.org.*

Barbudaful.net ⊕ *www.barbudaful.net.*

WEDDINGS

No minimum residency or blood test is required. A license application fee is $150. You must have valid passports as proof of citizenship and, in the case of previous marriages, the original divorce or annulment decree. A marriage certificate registration fee is $40. The marriage officer receives $50.

EXPLORING

ANTIGUA

Hotels provide free island maps, but you should get your bearings before heading out on the road. Street names aren't listed (except in St. John's), though *some* easy-to-spot signs lead the way to major restaurants and resorts. Locals generally give directions in terms of landmarks (turn left at the yellow house, or right at the big tree). Wear a swimsuit under your clothes—one of the sights to strike your fancy might be a secluded beach.

ST. JOHN'S

Antigua's capital, with some 45,000 inhabitants (approximately half the island's population), lies at sea level at the inland end of a sheltered northwestern bay. Although it has seen better days, a couple of notable historic sights and some good waterfront shopping areas make it worth a visit.

At the far south end of town, where Market Street forks into Valley and All Saints roads, haggling goes on every Friday and Saturday, when locals jam the **Public Market** to buy and sell fruits, vegetables, fish, and spices. Ask before you aim a camera; your subject may expect a tip. This is old-time Caribbean shopping, a jambalaya of sights, sounds, and smells.

TOP ATTRACTIONS

Fodor'sChoice
★
Redcliffe Quay. Redcliffe Quay, at the water's edge just south of Heritage Quay, is the most appealing part of St. John's. Attractively restored (and superbly re-created) 19th-century buildings in a riot of cotton-candy colors house shops, restaurants, galleries, and boutiques and are linked by courtyards and landscaped walkways. ⊠ *Redcliff St., St. John's* ⊕ *www.historicredcliffequay.com.*

WORTH NOTING

Anglican Cathedral of St. John the Divine. At the south gate of the Anglican Cathedral of St. John the Divine are figures of St. John the Baptist and St. John the Divine, said to have been taken from one of Napóleon's ships ànd brought to Antigua. The original church was built in 1681, replaced by a stone building in 1745, and destroyed by an earthquake in 1843. The present neo-baroque building dates from 1845; the parishioners had the interior completely encased in pitch pine, hoping to forestall future earthquake damage. Tombstones bear eerily eloquent testament to the colonial days. ⊠ *Between Long and Newgate Sts., St. John's* ☎ *268/461–0082.*

Heritage Quay. Shopaholics head directly for Heritage Quay, an ugly multimillion-dollar complex. The two-story buildings contain stores that sell duty-free goods, sportswear, down-island imports (paintings, T-shirts, straw baskets), and local crafts. There are also restaurants, a bandstand, and a casino. Cruise-ship passengers disembark here from the 500-foot-long pier. Expect heavy shilling. ⊠ *High and Thames Sts., St. John's.*

Museum of Antigua and Barbuda. Signs at the Museum of Antigua and Barbuda say "Please touch," encouraging you to explore Antigua's past. Try your hand at the educational video games or squeeze a cassava through a *matapi* (grass sieve). Exhibits interpret the nation's history, from its geological birth to its political independence in 1981. There are fossil and coral remains from some 34 million years ago; models of a sugar plantation and a wattle-and-daub house; an Arawak canoe; and a wildly eclectic assortment of objects from cannonballs to 1920s telephone exchanges. The museum occupies the former courthouse, which dates from 1750. The superlative museum gift shop carries such unusual items as calabash purses, seed earrings, warri boards (warri being an African game brought to the Caribbean), and lignum vitae pipes, as well as historic maps and local books (including engrossing monographs on varied subjects by the late Desmond Nicholson, a longtime resident). ⊠ *Long and Market Sts., St. John's* ☎ *268/462–1469* ⊕ *antiguahistory.net/Museum* ⊠ *$3; children under 12 free* ☉ *Weekdays 8:30–4, Sat. 10–2. Closed Sun.*

ELSEWHERE ON ANTIGUA
TOP ATTRACTIONS

Fodor'sChoice **Nelson's Dockyard.** Antigua's most famous attraction is the world's only ★ Georgian-era dockyard still in use, a treasure trove for history buffs and nautical nuts alike. In 1671 the governor of the Leeward Islands wrote to the Council for Foreign Plantations in London, pointing out the advantages of this landlocked harbor. By 1704 English Harbour was in regular use as a garrisoned station.

In 1784, 26-year-old Horatio Nelson sailed in on the HMS *Boreas* to serve as captain and second-in-command of the Leeward Island Station. Under him was the captain of the HMS *Pegasus*, Prince William Henry, duke of Clarence, who was later crowned King William IV. The prince acted as best man when Nelson married Fannie Nisbet on Nevis in 1787.

When the Royal Navy abandoned the station at English Harbour in 1889, it fell into a state of decay, though adventuresome yachties still lived there in near-primitive conditions. The Society of the Friends of English Harbour began restoring it in 1951; it reopened with great fanfare as Nelson's Dockyard on November 14, 1961. Within the compound are crafts shops, restaurants, and two splendidly restored 18th-century hotels, the Admiral's Inn and the Copper & Lumber Store Hotel, worth peeking into. (The latter, occupying a supply store for Nelson's Caribbean fleet, is a particularly fine example of Georgian architecture, its interior courtyard evoking Old England.) The Dockyard is a hub for oceangoing yachts and serves as headquarters for the annual Boat Show in early December and the Sailing Week Regatta in late April and early May. Water taxis will ferry you between points for EC$5. The Dockyard National Park also

Nelson's Dockyard at English Harbour

includes serene nature trails accessing beaches, rock pools, and crumbling plantation ruins and hilltop forts.

The **Dockyard Museum,** in the original Naval Officer's House, presents ship models, mock-ups of English Harbour, displays on the people who worked there and typical ships that docked, silver regatta trophies, maps, prints, antique navigational instruments, and Nelson's very own telescope and tea caddy. ⊠ *Dockyard Dr., English Harbour* ☏ *268/481–5027 for Dockyard Museum, 268/481–5028 for National Parks Authority, 268/460–1379 also for Dockyard Museum* ⊕ *www.nationalparksantigua. com, www.dockyardmuseum.org* ☑ *$2 suggested donation* ☺ *Daily 9–5.*

Shirley Heights. This bluff affords a spectacular view of English Harbour and Falmouth Harbour. The heights are named for Sir Thomas Shirley, the governor who fortified the harbor in 1781. At the top is Shirley Heights Lookout, a restaurant built into the remnants of the 18th-century fortifications. Most notable for its boisterous Sunday barbecues that continue into the night with live music and dancing, it serves dependable burgers, pumpkin soup, grilled meats, and rum punches. ⊠ *Dockyard Dr., Shirley Heights* ☏ *268/481–5021* ⊕ *www.nationalparksantigua.com.*

Dows Hill Interpretation Centre. Not far from Shirley Heights is the Dows Hill Interpretation Centre, where observation platforms provide still more sensational vistas of the English Harbour area. A multimedia sound-and-light presentation on island history and culture, spotlighting lifelike figures and colorful tableaux accompanied by running commentary and music, results in a cheery, if bland, portrait of Antiguan life from Amerindian times to the present. ⊠ *Shirley Heights* ☏ *268/481–5045* ⊕ *www.nationalparksantigua.com* ☑ *EC$15* ☺ *Daily 9–5.*

WORTH NOTING

Betty's Hope. Just outside the village of Pares, a marked dirt road leads to Antigua's first sugar plantation, founded in the 1670s. You can tour the twin windmills, various ruins, still-functional crushing machinery, and the visitor center's exhibits (often closed) on the island's sugar era. The private trust overseeing the restoration has yet to realize its ambitious, environmentally aware plans to replant indigenous crops destroyed by the extensive sugarcane plantings. Indeed, the site is somewhat neglected, with goats grazing the grounds. ⊠ *Pares Village Main Rd., Pares* ☎ *268/462–1469* ⊡ *$2* ⊙ *Tues.–Sat. 10–4.*

Devil's Bridge. This limestone arch formation, sculpted by the crashing breakers of the Atlantic at Indian Town, is a national park. Blowholes have been carved by the hissing, spitting surf. The park also encompasses some archaeological excavations of Carib artifacts. ⊠ *Dockyard Dr., Long Bay* ⊕ *www.nationalparksantigua.com.*

Falmouth. This town sits on a lovely bay backed by former sugar plantations and sugar mills. The most important historic site here is St. Paul's Church, which was rebuilt on the site of a church once used by troops during the Horatio Nelson period.

Fig Tree Drive. This often muddy, rutted, steep road takes you through the rain forest, which is rich in mangoes, pineapples, and banana trees (*fig* is the Antiguan word for "banana"). The rain forest is the island's hilliest area—1,319-foot Boggy Peak (renamed Mt. Obama), to the west, is the highest point. At its crest, Elaine Francis sells seasonal local fruit juices—ginger, guava, sorrel, passion fruit—and homemade jams at a stall she dubs the Culture Shop. A few houses down (look for the orange windows) is the atelier of noted island artist Sallie Harker (shimmering seascapes and vividly hued fish incorporating gold leaf). You'll also pass several tranquil villages with charming churches and Antigua Rainforest Canopy Tours here (⇨ *Zip-Lining under Sports and Activities later in this chapter).* ⊠ *Fig Tree Dr.*

Ft. George. East of Liberta—one of the first settlements founded by freed slaves—on Monk's Hill, this fort was built from 1689 to 1720. Among the ruins are the sites for 32 cannons, water cisterns, the base of the old flagstaff, and some of the original buildings. ⊠ *Great Fort George Monk's Hill Trail, Saint Paul.*

Harmony Hall. Northeast of Freetown (follow the signs), this art gallery/restaurant is built on the foundation of a 17th-century sugar-plantation greathouse. No longer affiliated with the original Jamaican outpost, the Antigua facility is run by enterprising Italians who operate a fine restaurant and six spare but chic cottage suites (with a villa development planned). Its remote location is a headache, but you can allot the whole afternoon to enjoy lunch (dinner Wednesday through Saturday), soak in the historic ambience and panoramic ocean views, browse through the exhibits, comb the beach, and perhaps even snorkel at nearby Green Island via the property's dragon boat, *Luna.* ⊠ *Brown's Bay Mill, Dockyard Dr., Brown's Mill* ☎ *268/460–4120* ⊕ *www.harmonyhallantigua. com* ⊙ *June–mid-Nov., daily 10–6, later Wed., Fri., and Sat.*

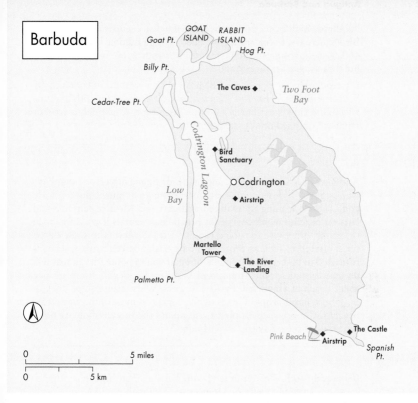

Parham. This sleepy village is a splendid example of a traditional colonial settlement. St. Peter's Church, built in 1840 by English architect Thomas Weekes, is an octagonal Italianate building with unusual ribbed wooden ceiling, whose facade is richly decorated with stucco and keystone work, though it suffered considerable damage during an 1843 earthquake.

BARBUDA

This flat, 62-square-mile (161-square-km) coral atoll—with 17 miles (27 km) of gleaming white-sand beaches (sand is the island's main export)—is 26 miles (42 km) north of Antigua. Most of Barbuda's 1,200 people live in Codrington. Nesting terns, turtles, and frigate birds outnumber residents at least 10 to 1. Goats, guinea fowl, deer, and wild boar roam the roads, all fair game for local kitchens. There are a few very basic efficiencies and guesthouses, but most visitors stay overnight at the deluxe Coco Point Lodge or Lighthouse Bay (two other glam properties have closed). Pink Beach lures beachcombers, a bird sanctuary attracts ornithologists, caves and sinkholes filled with rain forest or underground pools (containing rare, even unique crustacean species) attract spelunkers, and reefs and roughly 200 offshore wrecks draw divers and snorkelers. Barbuda's sole historic ruin is the 18th-century, cylindrical, 56-foot-tall **Martello Tower,** which was probably a lighthouse built by the Spaniards before English occupation. The **Frigate Bird Sanctuary,** a wide mangrove-filled lagoon, is home to an estimated 400 species of birds, including frigate birds with 8-foot wingspans. Your hotel can make arrangements.

It's reachable by plane on ABM Air (⊕ *www.abm-air.com*)and by boat, the *Barbuda Express* (⊕ *www.antiguaferries.com*), although the 95-minute ride is extremely bumpy ("a chiropractor's nightmare—or fantasy," quipped one passenger).

BEACHES

Antigua's beaches are public, and many are lined with resorts that have water-sports outfitters and beach bars. The government does a fairly good job of cleaning up seaweed and garbage. Most restaurants and bars on beaches won't charge for beach-chair rentals if you buy lunch or drinks; otherwise the going rate is $3 to $5. Access to some of the finest stretches, such as those at the Five Islands Peninsula resorts, is restricted to hotel guests (though, often, if you're polite, the guards will let you through). Sunbathing topless is strictly illegal except on one small beach at Hawksbill by Rex Resorts. When cruise ships dock in St. John's, buses drop off loads of passengers on most of the west-coast beaches. Choose such a time to visit one of the more remote east-end beaches or take a day trip to Barbuda.

ANTIGUA

Darkwood Beach. This ½-mile (1-km) beige ribbon on the southwest coast has stunning views of Montserrat. Although popular with locals and cruise ship passengers on weekends, it's virtually deserted during the week. Waters are generally calm, but there's scant shade, little maintenance, no development other than Darkwood Beach Bar (and Admiral's Bar across the coastal road), and little to do other than bask in solitude. **Amenities:** food and drink. **Best for:** solitude; swimming. ⊠ *2 miles (3 km) south of Jolly Harbour and roughly ½ mile (1 km) southwest of Valley Church, off Valley Rd.*

Dickenson Bay. Along a lengthy stretch of well-kept powder-soft white sand and exceptionally calm water you can find small and large hotels (including Siboney Beach Club, Sandals, and Rex Halcyon Cove), water sports, concessions, and beachfront restaurants. There's decent snorkeling at either point. **Amenities:** food and drink; water sports. **Best for:** partiers; snorkeling; swimming; walking. ⊠ *2 miles (3 km) northeast of St. John's, along main coast road.*

Half Moon Bay. This ½-mile (1-km) ivory crescent is a prime snorkeling and windsurfing area. On the Atlantic side, the water can be rough at times, attracting intrepid hard-core surfers and wake-boarders. The northeastern end, where a protective reef offers spectacular snorkeling, is much calmer. A tiny bar has restrooms, snacks, and beach chairs. Half Moon is a real trek, but one of Antigua's showcase beaches. **Amenities:** food and drink. **Best for:** snorkeling; sunrise; surfing; windsurfing. ⊠ *On southeast coast, 1½ miles (2½ km) from Freetown, Dockyard Dr.*

Johnson's Point/Crabbe Hill. This series of connected, deserted beaches on the southwest coast looks out toward Montserrat, Guadeloupe, and St. Kitts. Notable beach bar–restaurants include OJ's, Jacqui O's Beach House, and Turner's. The water is generally placid, though not good for snorkeling. **Amenities:** food and drink. **Best for:** swimming; sunset; walking. ⊠ *3 miles (5 km) south of Jolly Harbour complex, on main west-coast road.*

Pigeon Point. Near Falmouth Harbour lie two fine white-sand beaches reasonably free of seaweed and driftwood. The leeward side is calmer, the windward side is rockier, and there are sensational views and snorkeling around the point. Several restaurants and bars are nearby, though Bumpkin's (and its potent banana coladas) satisfies most on-site needs. **Amenities:** food and drink. **Best for:** snorkeling; swimming; walking. ⊠ *Off main south-coast road, southwest of Falmouth.*

Runaway Beach. An often unoccupied stretch of bone-white sand, this beach is still rebuilding after years of hurricane erosion, with just enough palms left for shelter. Both the water and the scene are relatively calm, the sand reasonably well-maintained, and beach restaurants such as Sandhaven and La Bussola offer cool shade and cold beer. Hug the lagoon past the entrance to Siboney Beach Club to get here; the Buccaneer Beach Club is the unofficial demarcation point between Dickenson and Runaway Bays. **Amenities:** food and drink. **Best for:** snorkeling; swimming; walking. ⊠ *Approximately 2 miles (3 km) northwest of St. John's, down main north-coast road from Dickenson Bay, St. John's.*

BARBUDA

Fodor'sChoice
★
Pink Beach. You can sometimes walk miles of this classic strand without encountering another footprint. It has a champagne hue, with sand soft as silk; crushed coral often imparts a rosy glint in the sun, hence its unofficial name (officially the part in front of the exclusive former K Club has been renamed Princess Diana Beach). The water can be rough with a strong-ish undertow in spots, though it's mainly protected by the reefs that make the island a diving mecca. Hire a taxi to take you here, since none of the roads are well marked. **Amenities:** none. **Best for:** solitude; snorkeling; walking. ⊠ *1 mile (2 km) from ferry and airstrip along unmarked roads.*

WHERE TO EAT

Antigua's restaurants are almost a dying breed since the advent of all-inclusives. But several worthwhile hotel dining rooms and nightspots remain, especially in the English/Falmouth Harbour and Dickenson Bay areas. Virtually every chef incorporates local ingredients and elements of West Indian cuisine.

Most menus list prices in both EC and U.S. dollars; if not, ask which currency the menu is using. Always double-check whether credit cards are accepted and service is included. Dinner reservations are needed during high season.

What to Wear: Perhaps because of the island's British heritage, Antiguans tend to dress more formally for dinner than dwellers on many other Caribbean islands. Wraps and shorts (no beach attire) are de rigueur for lunch, except at local hangouts.

$$$$
ECLECTIC

× **Admiral's Inn.** The restaurant at the Admiral's Inn is a must for Anglophiles and mariners. Soak up the centuries at the inside bar, where 18th-century sailors reputedly carved their ships' names on the dark timbers. Most diners sit on the flagstone terrace under shady Australian gums to enjoy the views of the harbor complex and trendy exhibition kitchen; yachts seem close enough to eavesdrop. The menu is limited but expertly prepared; consider ordering two or three appetizers tapas-style. Specialties include ceviche, lobster toast, and the pulled pork open sandwich with chipotle mayo and red onion marmalade. $ *Average main: $35* ⊠ *Dockyard Dr., Nelson's Dockyard, English Harbour* ☎ *268/460–1027* ⊕ *www.admiralsantigua.com* ⟋ *Reservations essential.*

$$$$
ECLECTIC

× **The Bay @ Nonsuch.** This restaurant's tiered wooden decks, swaddled in billowing white curtains, wrap around the bluff fronting Nonsuch Bay. Chef Mitchell Husbands deftly marries local ingredients to international techniques. His presentation alone is appetizing, the plates painted with swirls of red pepper coulis or basil reduction. The stellar starters are sometimes superior to the fine entrées. For lunch order several, tapas-style: perhaps the chunky yet silken crab cakes perfectly counterpointed by arugula aioli. Or try such creative wraps and paninis as pulled pork and jerk mahimahi. For dinner, enjoy cocktails in the refined lounge with the lively mix of yachties and expats, then order soft-shell crab with pink peppercorn marmalade over sweet corn-flavored blini, segueing into coco-spiced mahimahi with a sautéed spinach-and-potato napoleon and *chimichurri* sauce. The small, savvy wine list is admirably suited to the menu and climate, with selections like Eden Valley Rieslings and Albariños. Or look for the frequent four-course pairing menus. Finish with the dense, decadent banoffee (banana toffee) pie drowning in warm brandy sauce. $ *Average main: $33* ⊠ *Nonsuch Bay Resort, Hughes Point, Nonsuch Bay, St. Philips* ☎ *268/562–8000, 888/844–2480* ⊕ *www.nonsuchbayresort.com* ⟋ *Reservations essential* ⊗ *Closed Sept.*

$$
PIZZA

× **Big Banana—Pizzas in Paradise.** This tiny, often crowded spot is tucked into one side of a restored 18th-century rum warehouse with broad plank floors, wood-beam ceiling, and stone archways. Cool, Benetton-style photos of locals and musicians jamming adorn the brick walls. Big Banana serves some of the island's best pizza—try the lobster or the seafood variety—as well as fresh fruit crushes, classic pastas, wraps, burgers, and sub sandwiches bursting at the seams. There's live entertainment some nights, and a large-screen TV for sports fans. $ *Average main: $18* ⊠ *Redcliffe Quay, Redcliffe St., St. John's* ☎ *268/480–6985* ⊕ *www.bigbanana-antigua.com* ⊗ *Closed Sun.*

$$$
ECLECTIC

× **Cecilia's High Point Café.** The eponymous owner, a vivacious, striking Swedish ex-model, floats (and once in a while flirts) about the tables in this cozy beachfront Creole cottage. An equally animated cross section of Antiguan life usually packs the coveted patio tables (it's a terrific spot to eavesdrop on island gossip), as well as the lounges on the point. The day's selections, including wine specials, are written on a blackboard.

Stellar standbys run from goat cheese and caramelized apples in puff pastry to homemade gravlax on potato pancake to mushroom ravioli nestled in spinach with a gossamer creamy pesto, but the high points are the setting and Cecilia herself. As a bonus, Wi-Fi access is free. $ *Average main: $27* ✉ *Dutchman's Bay, Texaco Dock Rd.* ☎ *268/562–7070* ⊕ *www.highpointantigua.com* ⏴ *Reservations essential* ⊗ *Closed Tues. and Wed. No dinner Fri.–Sun.*

$$$$ ✕ **Coconut Grove.** Coconut palms grow through the roof of this open-
ECLECTIC air thatched restaurant, flickering candlelight illuminates colorful local murals, waves lap the white sand, and the waitstaff provides just the right level of service. Jean-François Bellanger's artfully presented dishes fuse French culinary preparations with island ingredients. Top choices include pan-seared mahimahi served over cauliflower puree with finger-ling potatoes and mango-pineapple chutney; and sautéed shrimp with roasted plantain and hickory bacon finished with champagne-Parmesan sauce. The kitchen can be uneven, the wine list is unimaginative and overpriced, and the buzzing happy-hour bar crowd lingering well into dinnertime can detract from the otherwise romantic atmosphere. None-theless, Coconut Grove straddles the line between casual beachfront boîte and elegant eatery with aplomb. $ *Average main: $30* ✉ *Siboney Beach Club, Marina Bay Rd., Dickenson Bay* ☎ *268/462–1538* ⊕ *www. coconutgroveantigua.com* ⏴ *Reservations essential.*

$$$ ✕ **East.** Imposing Indonesian carved doors usher you into this bold and
ASIAN FUSION sexy Asian fusion spot. Flames flicker in the outdoor lily pond while can-dles illuminate lacquered dark-wood tables with blood-red napery and oversize fuchsia-color chairs. Exquisite pan-Pacific fare (with delicious detours to the Indian subcontinent) courts perfection through simplicity and precision: prawn spring rolls with hoisin–sweet chili sauce; superla-tive sashimi; entrées from Thai lobster curry to tandoori chicken; and green tea crème brûlée. The small main courses mandate tapas-style din-ing; the comprehensive wine list is pricey but offers values from intriguing lesser-known regions. Families appreciate the extensive, comparatively inexpensive children's menu. $ *Average main: $32* ✉ *Carlisle Bay, Old Road* ☎ *268/484–0000* ⏴ *Reservations essential* ⊗ *No lunch.*

$$$$ ✕ **La Bussola.** Blend a genuinely *simpatico* welcome with lapping waves,
ITALIAN the murmur of jazz, and expert Italian fare and you have Omar Taglia-
Fodor's Choice venti and family's recipe for the perfect beachfront bistro. Bleached-
★ wood ceilings, old island photos of Antigua, boating paraphernalia, and brightly painted plates enhance the relaxed, romantic mood. The presentation is invariably pretty and Omar has a particularly facile touch with seafood; try the artichoke-shrimp pie in satiny garlic sauce, lobster-asparagus risotto, shark tartare with grapefruit nestling on a bed of arugula, mahimahi with olive "pâté" in filo, or the "fishermen's" spaghetti. Or savor the "true Italian-style" thin-crust pizzas. The care-fully considered, affordable wine list showcases lesser-known Italian regions. Your evening ends with a complimentary grappa, Frangelico, or *limoncello* (lemon liqueur), representing northern, central, and southern Italy. La Bussola means "the compass" in Italian, and it certainly takes the right gastronomic direction. $ *Average main: $28* ✉ *Rush Night Club Rd., Runaway Bay* ☎ *268/562–1545* ⊕ *www.labussolarestaurant. net* ⏴ *Reservations essential* ⊗ *Closed Tues.*

3

$$$$ ✕ **Le Bistro.** This Antiguan institution's peach, periwinkle, and pistachio
FRENCH accents subtly match the tile work, jade chairs, mint china, and painted
lighting fixtures. Trellises divide the large space into intimate sections.
Chef Patrick Gauducheau delights in blending classic regional fare with
indigenous ingredients, displaying an especially deft hand with delicate
sauces. The kitchen now runs smoothly after bouts of inconsistency. Opt
for daily specials, such as smoked marlin carpaccio with pink peppercorns,
prawns in a gossamer ginger white wine sauce laced with leeks, lobster
medallions in roasted red bell pepper-lime sauce flamed with grappa,
and almost anything swaddled in puff pastry. The fine wine list hits all
the right spots, geographically and varietally, without outrageous mark-
ups. Co-owner Phillipa Esposito doubles as hostess and pastry chef; her
passion-fruit mousse and chocolate confections are sublime. $ *Average
main: $34* ⊠ *Hodges Bay Rd., Hodges Bay* ☎ *268/462–3881* ⊕ *www.
antigualebistro.com* ⚑ *Reservations essential* ⊙ *Closed Mon. No lunch.*

$$$$ ✕ **Le Cap Horn.** As Piaf and Aznavour compete with croaking tree frogs in
FRENCH a trellised, plant-filled room lighted by straw lamps, it's easy to imagine
yourself in a tropical St. Tropez. Begin with escargots in tomato, onion,
and pepper sauce (sop it up with the marvelous home-baked bread) or the
ultimate in hedonism (and expense), lobster–foie gras millefeuille; then
segue into tiger shrimp swimming in gossamer vanilla-lobster sauce or
duck breast wrapped with mango in rice sheet floating in rum-tamarind
sauce. Or cook your own seafood and/or beef on a hot volcanic stone at
your table. Gustavo Belaunde (he's Peruvian of Catalan extraction) elicits
delicate, almost ethereal flavors from his ingredients; his versatility is displayed in the restaurant's other half, a pizzeria replete with wood-burning
oven (with much lower prices and rowdier ambience). Finish with wife
Hélène's divine desserts or a cognac and cigar. $ *Average main: $43*
⊠ *English Harbour* ☎ *268/460–1194* ⊙ *Closed Aug., Sept., and Thurs.
Closed Wed. in low season (May–July, Oct. and Nov.). No lunch.*

$$$ ✕ **Papa Zouk.** Who would have thought that two jovial globe-trotting
CARIBBEAN German gents could create a classic Caribbean hangout? But the madras
tablecloths, straw lamps, fishnets festooned with Christmas lights,
painted bottles of homemade hot sauces, art naif, colorful island cli-
entele, and lilting rhythms on the sound system justify the name (*zouk*
is a sultry musical stew of soul and calypso). Seafood is king, from
butterfish to Barbudan snapper, served either deep-fried or steamed
with a choice of such sauces as guava-pepper teriyaki or tomato-basil-
coriander. Tangy Caribbean bouillabaisse with garlicky Parmesan may-
onnaise and the tapas platter are specialties, as are the knockout rum
punches. Finish dinner with a snifter of aged rum: the tiny, Pollock-style
handpainted bar holds 250 varieties from around the globe. $ *Average
main: $24* ⊠ *Hilda Davis Dr., Gambles Terrace, St. John's* ☎ *268/464–
0795, 268/464–6044* ⊟ *No credit cards* ⊙ *Closed May–Oct. and Sun.
No lunch sometimes; call ahead for hrs.*

$$ ✕ **Russell's.** By restoring part of Ft. James, with its glorious views of
CARIBBEAN the bay and headlands, and converting it into a semi-alfresco eatery,
Russell's delivers a delightful dining experience. Jazz and reggae on the
sound system (live music Friday and Sunday, with open mike Monday),
beamed ceilings, cool canvases of musical instruments in fevered Fauvist

hues, and red or black hurricane lamps lend a romantic aura to the stone-and-wood terrace. The limited menu—local specialties emphasizing seafood—includes fabulous chunky conch fritters and whelks in garlic butter. Danielle Russell maintains the tradition her father established at this restaurant. Russell's sister Faye co-owns Papa Zouk, and sister Valerie runs Shirley Heights Lookout; the Hodges might well be Antigua's first family of food. [$] *Average main: $20* ✉ *Fort James* ☎ *268/462–5479* 🕒 *Closed Tues. No lunch Sun.*

3

$$$ ECLECTIC Fodor's Choice ★ 🍴 **Sheer Rocks.** This sensuous eatery, a series of tiered wood decks carved into a sheer cliff side, showcases the setting sun from the staggered, thatched dining nooks, many separated by billowing white-gauze curtains. White four-poster beds surround infinity pools, making it equally sybaritic for daytime lounging. The menu encompasses a tapestry of creative tapas, many of which can be served in larger portions. Chef Alex Grimley's philosophy emphasizes simplicity, detail, and only the freshest ingredients to create a symphonic counterpoint of flavors and textures—subtle to lusty, crispy to creamy. Witness foie gras parfait with onion puree, lentil vinaigrette and seven-grain toast; decadent truffle mac-'n'-cheese infused with porcini stock; or slow-cooked mahimahi with bok choy, black olives and saffron sauce. Add a dash of sultry music, season with smashing views, complement with an admirable wine list (not to mention inventive cocktails), and you have the recipe for a tropical St. Tropez experience. It closes more often in low season; call ahead. [$] *Average main: $28* ✉ *CocoBay Resort, Valley Rd.* ☎ *268/562–4510, 268/464–5283* 🌐 *www.cocobayresort.com* ✍ *Reservations essential* 🕒 *Closed Tues. No dinner Sun.*

$$$ SEAFOOD 🍴 **The Tides.** The look of this seaside eatery suggests a yacht: decks on either side, steering wheels, oars hung as artwork, and petrified-driftwood mobiles, as well as antique Asian doors and lovely local ceramics for color. Although the kitchen isn't quite shipshape, it isn't shipwrecked, making visits to several gastronomic ports of call from the Mediterranean to the Pacific Rim. Start with beetroot-goat cheese tart drizzled with honey in puff pastry, or the almost-by-the-book bouillabaisse, then segue to the mixed vegetable crepe in lemongrass-infused red curry or mahimahi with black olive tapenade. More affordable, lunch emphasizes sushi, grilled items and foccacia; opt for the poolside seating. Management also runs several affordable beachfront cottages next door. [$] *Average main: $31* ✉ *Dutchman's Bay Dr.* ☎ *268/462–8433* 🌐 *www.thetidesantigua.com* 🕒 *Closed Aug. No dinner Sun.–Tues.*

WHERE TO STAY

Scattered along Antigua's beaches and hillsides are exclusive, elegant hideaways; romantic restored inns; and all-inclusive hot spots for couples. Check individual lodgings for restrictions (many have minimum stays during certain high-season periods). Look also for specials on the Web or from tour packagers, since hotels' quoted rack rates are often negotiable (up to 45% off in season). There are several new condo and villa developments; although not reviewed in this edition, Sugar Ridge opened in 2009 in the Jolly Harbour area. (Despite its nice if smallish units, elegant setting, Aveda Spa, and fine upscale restaurant, it suffers from the lack of beachfront.) At this writing, Tamarind Hills and South Point Resort are among several other major developments slated to open by late 2014.

$
B&B/INN
Fodor's Choice
★

▦ **Admiral's Inn.** This Georgian brick edifice, originally the shipwright's offices in what is now Nelson's Dockyard, has withstood acts of God and war since 1788. **Pros:** historic ambience yet contemporary boutique style; central English Harbour location; fine value; free Wi-Fi; charming restaurant setting. **Cons:** occasionally noisy when yachties take over the bar; recently remodeled bathrooms are still cramped; no beach; no air-conditioning in some units. $ *Rooms from: $175* ✉ *Dockyard Dr., English Harbour* ☎ *268/460–1027, 268/460–1153* ⊕ *www.admiralsantigua.com* ⤷ *14 rooms, 4 suites, 1 2-bedroom apartment* ◉| *No meals.*

$$$$
RESORT

▦ **Blue Waters Hotel.** A well-heeled Brit crowd goes barefoot at this swank yet understated seaside retreat. **Pros:** pomp without pretension; exquisite setting; huge savings on week-long packages. **Cons:** small beachfront; little steps along the hillside make it less accessible for the physically challenged; difficult to obtain reservations at Bartley's at peak times. $ *Rooms from: $399* ✉ *Boon Point, Atlantic Ave., Soldier's Bay* ☎ *268/462–0290, 800/557–6536 reservations only* ⊕ *www.bluewaters.net* ⤷ *67 rooms, 32 suites, 3 villas, 4 penthouses* ☾ *Closed Sept.* ◉| *Multiple meal plans.*

$$
RENTAL

▦ **Buccaneer Beach Club.** This stylish compound opens onto the quieter part of Dickenson Bay, yet it's merely steps away from the rollicking restaurants and nightlife. **Pros:** free Wi-Fi; quieter part of beach; well-equipped units with flat-screen TVs in the living room and every bedroom; complimentary laundry facilities (individual washer/dryers in the cottages). **Cons:** few facilities on-site; hotel's section of beach sometimes eroded. $ *Rooms from: $229* ✉ *Marina Bay Rd., Dickenson Bay* ☎ *268/562–6785* ⊕ *www.buccaneerbeach.com* ⤷ *15 1-bedroom suites, 2 2-bedroom cottages* ◉| *No meals.*

$$$$
RESORT
Fodor's Choice
★

▦ **Carlisle Bay.** This cosmopolitan, boutique sister property of London's trendy One Aldwych hotel daringly eschews everything faux colonial and Creole. **Pros:** luxury resort; attentive service; family-friendly. **Cons:** aggressively hip; lovely beach but often murky water; pricey restaurants; no elevators. $ *Rooms from: $920* ✉ *Old Rd., Carlisle Bay* ☎ *268/484–0000, 866/502–2855 reservations only* ⊕ *www.carlislebay.com* ⤷ *82 suites* ☾ *Closed late Aug.–early Oct.* ◉| *Breakfast.*

$
HOTEL

▦ **Catamaran Hotel.** The main building at the congenial cozy harborfront "Cat Club" evokes a plantation greathouse with verandahs, white columns, and hand-carved doors. **Pros:** intimacy; central location; friendly staff; children under 12 stay free; free sailing lessons. **Cons:** small beach (swimming not advised); smallish rooms; surrounding area has limited dining and nightlife options during off-season (May–November). $ *Rooms from: $170* ✉ *Great Fort George Monks Hill Trail, Falmouth Harbour* ☎ *268/460–1036* ⊕ *www.catamaranantigua.com* ⤷ *12 rooms, 2 suites* ◉| *No meals.*

One of the beaches at Curtain Bluff resort

$$$ ALL-INCLUSIVE **CocoBay.** This healing, hillside hideaway aims to "eliminate all potential worries" by emphasizing simple natural beauty and West Indian warmth. **Pros:** emphasis on local nature and culture, including no room TVs; beautiful views; free Wi-Fi; nice main pool and bar; generally pleasant staff. **Cons:** mediocre food; stifling on breezeless days; difficult climb for those with mobility problems; smallish beaches; bar closes early; poor bedroom lighting. [$] *Rooms from: $480* ✉ *Valley Rd., Valley Church* ☎ *268/562–2400, 877/385–6516, 508/506–1006 toll-free U.S.* 🌐 *www.cocobayresort.com* 🛏 *49 rooms, 4 2-bedroom houses* 🍴 *All-inclusive.*

$$$$ ALL-INCLUSIVE Fodor's Choice ★ **Curtain Bluff.** An incomparable beachfront setting, impeccable service, superb extras (free scuba diving and deep-sea fishing), effortless elegance: Curtain Bluff is that rare retreat that stays modern while exuding a magical timelessness. **Pros:** luxury lodging; sublime food, including the new Italian eatery on the beach; beautiful beaches; incredible extras. **Cons:** some find clientele standoffish; lodgings atop bluff not ideal for those with mobility problems; despite offering value, pricey by most standards. [$] *Rooms from: $1195* ✉ *Old Rd., Morris Bay* ☎ *268/462–8400, 888/289–9898 for reservations* 🌐 *www.curtainbluff.com* 🛏 *18 rooms, 54 suites* ⏲ *Closed late July–Oct.* 🍴 *All-inclusive.*

$ RENTAL **Dickenson Bay Cottages.** Lush landscaping snakes around the two-story buildings and pool at this small hillside complex, which offers excellent value for families. **Pros:** relatively upscale comfort at down-home prices; walking distance to Dickenson Bay dining and activities. **Cons:** hike from beach; lacks cross-breeze in many units. [$] *Rooms from: $170* ✉ *Anchorage Rd., Marble Hill* ☎ *268/462–4940* 🌐 *www.dickensonbaycottages.com* 🛏 *11 units* 🍴 *No meals.*

$$$$ ALL-INCLUSIVE Fodor's Choice ★ **Galley Bay.** This posh, adult-only all-inclusive channels the fictional Bali H'ai (with colonial architectural flourishes) on 40 lush acres. **Pros:** luxury lodging; gorgeous beach and grounds; impeccable maintenance; fine food by all-inclusive standards. **Cons:** some lodgings are small and lack a view; outdoor spa can get hot; surf is often too strong for weaker swimmers; only suites have tubs. [$] *Rooms from: $990* ✉ *Grays Farm Rd., Five Islands* ☎ *268/462–0302, 866/237–1644, 800/858–4618 reservations only* 🌐 *www.galleybayresort.com* 🛏 *98 rooms* 🕐 *Closed mid-Aug.–early Sept.* 🍴 *All-inclusive.*

$$ RESORT **Jolly Beach Resort.** If you're looking for basic sun-sand-surf fun, this active resort—Antigua's largest—fits the bill luring a gregarious blend of honeymooners, families, and singles. **Pros:** inexpensive; great range of activities for the price; nice beach; good food for a cheaper all-inclusive; incredible online specials. **Cons:** many cramped, ugly rooms; overrun by tour groups; often impersonal service; lack of elevators and rambling layout make it difficult for the physically challenged. [$] *Rooms from: $388* ✉ *Valley Rd., Jolly Harbour* ☎ *268/462–0061, 866/905–6559* 🌐 *www.jollybeachresort.com* 🛏 *461 units, 2 2-bedroom cottages, 1 1-bedroom cottage* 🍴 *Multiple meal plans.*

$ RENTAL **Jolly Harbour Villas.** These duplex, two-bedroom villas ring the marina of a sprawling, 500-acre compound offering every conceivable facility from restaurants and shops to a golf course. **Pros:** nice beach; good value; plentiful recreational, dining, and nightlife choices nearby. **Cons:** mosquito problems; reports of hidden surcharges; inability to charge most restaurants and activities to your villa; some units have 220-volt outlets requiring adapters. [$] *Rooms from: $170* ✉ *Jolly Harbour* ☎ *268/462–6166, 268/484–6100* 🌐 *www.hbkvillas.com* 🛏 *150 villas* 🍴 *No meals.*

$$$$ ALL-INCLUSIVE FAMILY Fodor's Choice ★ **Jumby Bay.** This refined resort proffers all the makings of a classic Caribbean private island hideaway, right from the stylish airport sedan pickup, private launch, dockside greeting, and registration at your leisure. **Pros:** isolated private island location; sterling cuisine; free bicycles; inventive, complimentary children's programs; thoughtful extras upon request such as cooking classes and wireless baby monitors; the lovely Sense by Rosewood spa. **Cons:** isolated private island location; jet noise occasionally disturbs the main beach. [$] *Rooms from: $1595* ✉ *Burma Rd., Long Island* ☎ *268/462–6000, 888/767–3966* 🌐 *www.jumbybayresort.com* 🛏 *40 suites, 14 villas* 🍴 *All-inclusive.*

$$$ RESORT FAMILY Fodor's Choice ★ **Nonsuch Bay Resort.** This exclusive 40-acre compound's handsome, gabled Georgian-style buildings cascade down the lushly landscaped hillside to the eponymous bay, flecked with sails. **Pros:** contemporary luxury; fully equipped units; standout cuisine; lovely beach and setting; superlative sailing fleet and lessons; free Wi-Fi. **Cons:** remote setting mandates a car; pretty but poky beach; hilly layout presents mobility challenges. [$] *Rooms from: $276* ✉ *Hughes Point, Nonsuch Bay, St. Philips* ☎ *268/562–8000, 888/844–2480* 🌐 *www.nonsuchbayresort.com* 🛏 *13 1-bedroom apartments, 16 2-bedroom apartments, 8 3-bedroom apartments, 7 2-bedroom cottages, 7 3-bedroom residences, 4 villas* 🕐 *Closed Sept.* 🍴 *Some meals.*

CLOSE UP

Other Lodgings to Consider on Antigua

We can't include every property deserving mention without creating an encyclopedia. Consider the following accommodations, many of which are popular with tour operators.

Antigua Yacht Club Marina & Resort. Antigua Yacht Club Marina & Resort is a handsome collection of 19 hotel rooms and 30 studio and one-bedroom condos (for rent when owners are off-island), climbing a hill with stunning marina views. Accommodations are stylish if spare, with island crafts and the occasional high-tech amenity; the adjacent marina is a center of nautical hubbub with several restaurants, pubs, and shops. ⊠ *Falmouth Harbour* ☎ *268/562–3030, 888/790–5264, 268/460–1544* ⊕ *www.aycmarina.com.*

Grand Pineapple Beach Resort. Grand Pineapple Beach Resort is a Sandals-owned, Sandals-branded all-inclusive (formerly Allegro/ Occidental) on a tranquil beach and hillside amid lush landscaping. It's in the midst of ongoing renovations, restoring its sheen. Buildings containing 180 rooms feature almost edible pastel hues inside and out; the beachfront units and 500 block offer smashing east-coast views. ⊠ *Long*

Bay ☎ *268/463–2006, 800/327–1991* ⊕ *www.grandpineapple.com.*

Hermitage Bay. Hermitage Bay is a deluxe enclave of 30 beachfront and hillside cottages on a secluded, hard-to-reach but pretty stretch of sand. Affecting a look and ambience that borrow from both Carlisle Bay and Curtain Bluff, the enormous minimalist-chic lodgings include a garden shower and private plunge pool. The kitchen turns out admirable organic fare, much of it sourced from its gardens; the creative mixologists and the spa also utilize local ingredients where possible. ⊠ *Hermitage Bay* ☎ *268/562–5500, 855/562–8080 toll-free* ⊕ *www.hermitagebay.com.*

Rex Halcyon Cove Beach Resort. Rex Halcyon Cove Beach Resort is a large, impersonal but admirably outfitted resort (from dive shop to car rental) on one of Antigua's top beaches. The Warri Pier restaurant, jutting into the Caribbean on stilts, is a romantic destination. Buildings are a bit institutional-looking, and you'll have to watch out for stampeding tour groups; however, you can usually find good package deals here. ⊠ *Dickenson Bay* ☎ *268/462–0256, 305/471–6170* ⊕ *www.rexresorts.com.*

$
B&B/INN

Ocean Inn. Views of English Harbour, affable management, and affordability distinguish this homey inn. **Pros:** fabulous views; affable staff; inexpensive. **Cons:** rickety paths down a steep hill linking cottages; worn rooms need updating; Wi-Fi dodgy; gym is basic and public. $ *Rooms from: $110* ⊠ *English Harbour* ☎ *268/463–7950* ⊕ *www. theoceaninn.com* ⤴ *6 rooms, 4 with bath; 4 cottages* �‖ *Breakfast.*

$$$$
ALL-INCLUSIVE

St. James's Club. Management has diligently smartened the public spaces and exquisite landscaping here, taking full advantage of the peerless location straddling 100 acres on Mamora Bay. **Pros:** splendid remote location; beautiful beaches and landscaping; complimentary Wi-Fi in public areas and Royal Suites; plentiful activities; additional adult pools offer more privacy. **Cons:** remote location makes a car a necessity for non-all-inclusive guests; tour groups can overrun the resort; uneven food and service; sprawling hilly layout not ideal for physically challenged. $ *Rooms from: $740* ⊠ *Dockyard Dr., Mamora Bay* 🕾 *268/460–5000, 800/858–4618 reservations only, 866/237–2071* ⊕ *www.stjamesclubantigua.com* 🛏 *215 rooms, 72 villas (usually 40 in rental pool)* ⏶ *All-inclusive.*

$$$$
ALL-INCLUSIVE
🏨 **Sandals Grande Antigua Resort & Spa.** The sumptuous public spaces, lovely beach, glorious gardens, and plethora of facilities almost mask this resort's impersonal atmosphere. **Pros:** lively atmosphere; excellent spa; good dining options; huge online advance booking savings. **Cons:** sprawling layout; too bustling; uneven service. $ *Rooms from: $624* ⊠ *Dickenson Bay* 🕾 *888/726–3257 reservations only, 268/484–0100* ⊕ *www.sandals.com* 🛏 *100 rooms, 257 suites, 16 rondavels* ⏶ *All-inclusive* 🛏 *3-night minimum.*

$$
HOTEL
Fodor's Choice
★
🏨 **Siboney Beach Club.** This affordable beachfront oasis nestled in a tranquil corner of Dickenson Bay delights with intimacy and warmth, and knowledgeable Aussie owner Tony Johnson gladly acts as a de facto tourist board. **Pros:** friendly service; superb location; great value; well maintained with rooms smartly refurbished regularly. **Cons:** no TV in bedrooms; patios lack screens, thus forcing a choice between sweltering and swatting pests on rare still days; no elevator; inconsistent Wi-Fi signal. $ *Rooms from: $315* ⊠ *Dickenson Bay* 🕾 *268/462–0806, 800/533–0234* ⊕ *www.siboneybeachclub.com* 🛏 *12 suites* ⏶ *No meals.*

$$$$
ALL-INCLUSIVE
FAMILY
🏨 **Verandah Resort & Spa.** Verandah's splendid hillside setting overlooks calm, reef-protected Dian Bay, and hiking trails snake around the property to Devil's Bridge National Park. **Pros:** gorgeous remote location; sprawling but cleverly centralized; good kids' club and facilities with own pool; frequent discounted packages. **Cons:** smallish beaches; noise carries between adjoining units; inconsistent service; though shuttles ply the resort, its hilly layout is problematic for the physically challenged. $ *Rooms from: $690* ⊠ *Long Bay* 🕾 *268/562–6848, 800/858–4618, 866/237–1785 reservations only* ⊕ *www.verandahresortandspa.com* 🛏 *200 suites* ⏶ *All-inclusive.*

NIGHTLIFE

Most of Antigua's evening entertainment takes place at the resorts, which occasionally present calypso singers, steel bands, limbo dancers, and folkloric groups. Check with the tourist office for up-to-date information. In addition, a cluster of clubs and bars pulsate into the night in season around English and Falmouth Harbours.

BARS

Abracadabra. It's always a party at busy, bright trattoria Abracadabra. Late nights often turn into a disco with live music from jazz to soca or DJs spinning reggae and 1980s dance music, while special events run from art exhibits to masquerades to fashion shows to fire-eating performances. There's even a fine late-night Italian snack menu and a fun, funky boutique. ⊠ *Nelson's Dockyard, English Harbour* 🕾 *268/460–2701* ⊕ *www.theabracadabra.com.*

Carmichael's. Carmichael's is the fine-dining hilltop aerie at the Sugar Ridge residential complex. Nestle into a banquette or lounge in the infinity pool while sipping luscious libations that match the setting sun's colorful display. It's also a splendid spot for a postprandial cigar and port or single malt. You can always head downhill to sister nightspot, the bustling, buzzing **Sugar Club** (by the resort entrance) for live music (jazz to funk) and DJ disco evenings. ⊠ *Tottenham Park, across from Jolly Harbour* ☎ *268/562–7700* ⊕ *www.sugarridgeantigua.com.*

Indigo on the Beach. Indigo on the Beach is a soigné spot, yet it's relaxed and great any time of day for creative tapas, salads, grills, and burgers, but the beautiful people turn out in force come evening to pose at the fiber-optically lighted bar, or on white lounges scattered with throw pillows. ⊠ *Carlisle Bay, Old Road* ☎ *268/480–0000.*

Inn at English Harbour Bar. The Inn at English Harbour Bar, with its green leather, wood beams, fieldstone walls, 19th-century maps, steering-wheel chandeliers, petit point upholstery, and maritime prints, is uncommonly refined. ⊠ *English Harbour* ☎ *268/460–1014.*

Mad Mongoose. The Mad Mongoose is a wildly popular yachty (and singles') joint, splashed in vivid Rasta colors, with tapas and martini menus, live music Fridays (and some Tuesdays), joyous happy hours, a game room with pool tables, and satellite TV. ⊠ *Falmouth Harbour* ☎ *268/463–7900* ⊕ *www.madmongooseantigua.com.*

Mainbrace Pub. The Mainbrace Pub has a historic ambience, right down to its warm brick walls and hardwood accents, and is known as a beer, darts, and fish-and-chips kind of hangout for the boating set. ⊠ *Copper & Lumber Store Hotel, English Harbour* ☎ *268/460–1058.*

Fodor'sChoice
★ **Shirley Heights Lookout.** Sunday-afternoon barbecues continue into the night with reggae, soca, and steel-band music and dancing that sizzles like the ribs on the grill. Residents and visitors gather for boisterous fun, the latest gossip, and great sunsets. Most tourist groups vanish by 7 pm, when the real partying begins. Admission is EC$20. There's occasionally another, less frenetic party Thursday evenings called Made in Pride in Antigua, which in addition to barbecue serves up traditional food, drink, crafts and music. ⊠ *Shirley Heights* ☎ *268/460–1785, 268/728–0636, 268/764–0389* ⊕ *www.shirleyheightslookout.com.*

Trappa's. Trappa's is a hipster hangout set in a bamboo-walled courtyard hung with huge hibiscus paintings. It serves delectable, sizable tapas (tuna sashimi, deep-fried Brie with blackcurrant jelly, Thai mango chicken curry, beer-batter shrimp with garlic dip) for reasonable prices (EC$25–EC$50) into the wee hours. Live music is often on the menu. ⊠ *Main Rd., English Harbour* ☎ *268/562–3534.*

CASINOS

There are two full casinos on Antigua, as well as several holes-in-the-wall that have mostly one-armed bandits. Hours depend on the season, so it's best to inquire upon your arrival.

King's Casino. You can find abundant slots and gaming tables at the somewhat dilapidated, unintentionally retro (icicle chandeliers, Naugahyde seats, and 1970s soul crooners on the sound system) King's Casino. The best time to go is Friday night, which jumps with energetic karaoke competitions, live bands, and dancing. ⊠ *Heritage Quay, St. John's* ☎ *268/462–1727* ⊕ *www.kingscasino.com.*

SHOPPING

Antigua's duty-free shops are at Heritage Quay, one reason so many cruise ships call here. Bargains can be found on perfumes, liqueurs, and liquor (including English Harbour Antiguan rum), jewelry, china, and crystal. As for other local items, check out straw hats, baskets, batik, pottery, Susie's hot sauce, and hand-printed cotton clothing. Fine artists to look for include Gilly Gobinet (neo-postimpressionist island-scapes), Heather Doram (exquisite, intricately woven collage wall hangings), Jan Farara, Jennifer Meranto (incomparable hand-painted black-and-white photos of Caribbean scenes), and Heike Petersen (delightful dolls and quilts). Several artists and craftspeople have banded together to form ⊕ *www.antiguanartists.com,* which lists their information, including whether they accept atelier visits by appointment.

SHOPPING AREAS

Fodor's Choice ★ **Heritage Quay,** in St. John's, has 35 shops—including many that are duty-free—that cater to the cruise-ship crowd, which docks almost at its doorstep. Outlets here include Benetton, the Body Shop, Sunglass Hut, Dolce & Gabbana, and Oshkosh B'Gosh. There are also shops along **St. John's, St. Mary's, High,** and **Long streets.** The tangerine-and-lilac-hue four-story **Vendor's Mall** at the intersection of Redcliffe and Thames streets gathers the pushy, pesky vendors who once clogged the narrow streets. It's jammed with stalls; air-conditioned indoor shops sell some higher-price, if not higher-quality, merchandise. On the west coast the Mediterranean-style, arcaded **Jolly Harbour Marina** holds some interesting galleries and shops, as do the marinas and the main road snaking around English and Falmouth Harbours.

Redcliffe Quay, on the waterfront at the south edge of St. John's, is by far the most appealing shopping area. Several restaurants and more than 30 boutiques, many with one-of-a-kind wares, are set around landscaped courtyards shaded by colorful trees.

ALCOHOL AND TOBACCO

Manuel Dias Liquor Store. Head to Manuel Dias Liquor Store for a wide selection of Caribbean rums and liqueurs. ⊠ *Long and Market Sts., St. John's* ☎ *268/462–0490.*

Quin Farara. You'll find terrific deals on both liquor and wines as well as cigars at Quin Farara. ⊠ *Long St. and Corn Alley, St. John's* ☎ *268/462–3869* ⊠ *Heritage Quay, St. John's* ☎ *268/462–1737, 268/462–3197* ⊠ *Jolly Harbour* ☎ *268/462–6245.*

ART

Harmony Hall. This is Antigua's top exhibition venue. A large space is used for one-person shows; other rooms display works in various media, from Aussie aboriginal carvings to Antillean pottery. The sublime historic ambience, sweeping vistas, and fine Italian fare compensate for the remote location. ⊠ *Brown's Mill Bay, Brown's Mill* ☎ *268/460–4120* ⊕ *www.harmonyhallantigua.com.*

BOOKS AND MAGAZINES

Best of Books. This bookstore is an excellent, extensive source for everything from local cookbooks and nature guides to international newspapers. Check out the works of Jamaica Kincaid, whose writing about her native Antigua has won international acclaim. You'll also find an intriguing selection of crafts and artworks. ⊠ *Lower St. Mary's St., St. John's* ☎ *268/562–3198.*

CLOTHING

Exotic Antigua. This shop sells everything from antique Indonesian ikat throws to crepe de chine caftans to Tommy Bahama resort wear. ⊠ *Redcliffe Quay, St. John's* ☎ *268/562–1288.*

Galley Boutique. At Galley Boutique, Janey Easton personally seeks out exclusive creations from both international (Calvin Klein, Adrienne Vittadini) and local Caribbean designers, ranging from swimwear to evening garb. She also sells handicrafts and lovely hammocks. ⊠ *Nelson's Dockyard, English Harbour* ☎ *268/460–1525.*

Jacaranda. This shop sells batik, sarongs, and swimwear as well as Caribbean food, perfumes, soaps, and artwork. ⊠ *Redcliffe Quay, St. John's* ☎ *268/462–1888.*

New Gates. For duty-free threads, head to New Gates, an authorized dealer for such name brands as Ralph Lauren, Calvin Klein, and Tommy Hilfiger. ⊠ *Redcliffe Quay, St. John's* ☎ *268/562–1627.*

Noreen Phillips. Glitzy appliquéd and beaded evening wear—inspired by the colors of the sea and sunset—in sensuous fabrics ranging from chiffon and silk to Italian lace and Indian brocade are created at Noreen Phillips. ⊠ *Redcliffe Quay, St. John's* ☎ *268/462–3127.*

Sunseakers. At Sunseakers, you'll find every conceivable bathing suit and cover-up—from bikini thongs to sarongs—by top designers. ⊠ *Heritage Quay, St. John's* ☎ *268/462–3618.*

DUTY-FREE GOODS

Abbott's. You'll find luxury items from Breitling watches to Belleek china to Kosta Boda art glass in a luxurious, air-conditioned showroom at Abbott's. ⊠ *Heritage Quay, St. John's* ☎ *268/462–3107* ⊕ *www. abbottsjewellery.com.*

Lipstick. You'll find high-priced imported scents and cosmetics—from Clarins to Clinique and Gucci to Guerlain—at Lipstick. ⊠ *Heritage Quay, St. John's* ☎ *268/562–1130.*

Passions. This shop gives Abbott's a run for its (and your) considerable money on luxury brands like Chanel, Hermès, and Lalique. ⊠ *Heritage Quay, St. John's* ☎ *268/562–5295.*

HANDICRAFTS

Cedars Pottery. The airy studio of Michael and Imogen Hunt is Cedars Pottery. Michael produces a vivid line of domestic ware and Zen-simple teapots, vases, and water fountains featuring rich earth hues and sensuous lines. Imogen fashions ethereal paper-clay fish sculptures, and mask-shaped, intricately laced light fixtures and candelabras. ⊠ *St. Clare Estate, Buckleys Rd., Buckleys* ☎ *268/460–5293* ⊕ *www.cedarspottery.com.*

Eureka. The offerings at Eureka span the globe, from Azerbaijani hand-blown glass to Zambian weavings and carvings. ⊠ *Thames St., St. John's* ☎ *268/560–3654.*

Isis. Island and international baubles and bric-a-brac, such as antique jewelry, hand-carved walking sticks, elaborate chess sets, and glazed pottery, are available at Isis. ⊠ *Redcliffe Quay, St. John's* ☎ *268/462–4602.*

Pottery Shop. This shop sells the work of gifted potter Sarah Fuller, whose hand-painted tiles, wind chimes, and plates and cobalt-blue glazes are striking (as are her driftwood hangings mixed with clay and copper). You can also visit her studio–gallery on Dutchman's Bay. ⊠ *Redcliffe Quay, St. John's* ☎ *268/562–1264 studio-gallery, 268/462–5503 shop* ⊕ *www.sarahfullerpottery.com.*

Rhythm of Blue Gallery. Nancy Nicholson co-owns Rhythm of Blue Gallery; she's renowned for her exquisite glazed and matte-finish ceramics, featuring Caribbean-pure shades, as well as her black-and-white yachting photos. You'll also find exhibitions showcasing leading regional artists working in media from batik to copper. ⊠ *Dockyard Dr., English Harbour* ☎ *268/562–2230* ⊕ *www.rhythmofblue.com.*

JEWELRY

Colombian Emeralds. The Antiguan branch of the largest retailer of Colombian emeralds in the world also carries a wide variety of other gems. ⊠ *Heritage Quay, St. John's* ☎ *268/462–3462* ⊕ *www. colombianemeralds.com/OurStores/Antigua.*

Diamonds International. You'll find a huge selection of loose diamonds as well as a variety of watches, rings, brooches, bracelets, and pendants at Diamonds International. Several resorts have branches. ⊠ *Heritage Quay, St. John's* ☎ *268/481–1880.*

Goldsmitty. Hans Smit is the Goldsmitty, an expert goldsmith who turns gold, black coral, petrified coral (which he dubs Antiguanite), and precious and semiprecious stones into one-of-a-kind works of art. ✉ *Redcliffe Quay, St. John's* ☎ *268/462–4601* ⊕ *www.goldsmitty.com.*

SPORTS AND ACTIVITIES

Several all-inclusives offer day passes that permit use of all sporting facilities, from tennis courts to water-sports concessions, as well as free drinks and meals. The cost begins at $50 for singles (but can be as much as $200 for couples at Sandals), and hours generally run from 8 am to 6 pm, with extensions available until 2 am. Antigua has long been famed for its cricketers (such as Viv Richards and Richie Richardson); aficionados will find one of the Caribbean's finest cricket grounds right by the airport, with major test matches running January through June.

ADVENTURE TOURS

Antigua is developing its ecotourist opportunities, and several memorable offshore experiences involve more than just snorkeling. The archipelago of islets coupled with a full mangrove swamp off the northeast coast is unique in the Caribbean.

Adventure Antigua. The enthusiastic Eli Fuller, who is knowledgeable not only about the ecosystem and geography of Antigua but also about its history and politics (his grandfather was the American consul), runs Adventure Antigua. His thorough seven-hour excursion (Eli dubs it "recreating my childhood explorations") includes stops at Guiana Island (for lunch and guided snorkeling; turtles, barracuda, and stingrays are common sightings), Pelican Island (more snorkeling), Bird Island (hiking to vantage points to admire the soaring ospreys and frigate and red-billed tropic birds), and Hell's Gate (a striking limestone rock formation where the more intrepid may hike and swim through sunken caves and tide pools painted with pink and maroon algae). The company also offers a fun "Xtreme Circumnavigation" variation on a racing boat catering to adrenaline junkies who "feel the need for speed" that also visits Stingray City and Nelson's Dockyard, as well as a more sedate Antigua Classic Yacht sail-and-snorkel experience that explains the rich West Indian history of boatbuilding. ☎ *268/727–3261, 268/726–6355* ⊕ *www.adventureantigua.com.*

"Paddles" Kayak Eco Adventure. "Paddles" Kayak Eco Adventure takes you on a 3½-hour tour of serene mangroves and inlets with informative narrative about the fragile ecosystem of the swamp and reefs and the rich diversity of flora and fauna. The tour ends with a hike to sunken caves and snorkeling in the North Sound Marine Park, capped by a rum punch at the fun Creole-style clubhouse nestled amid botanic gardens. Experienced guides double as kayaking and snorkeling instructors, making this an excellent opportunity for novices. Conrad and Jennie's brainchild is one of Antigua's better bargains. ✉ *Seaton's Village* ☎ *268/463–1944* ⊕ *www.antiguapaddles.com.*

FAMILY **Stingray City Antigua.** Stingray City Antigua is a carefully reproduced "natural" environment nicknamed by staffers the "retirement home," though the 30-plus stingrays, ranging from infants to seniors, are frisky. You can stroke, feed, even hold the striking gliders ("they're like puppy dogs," one guide swears), as well as snorkel in deeper, protected waters. The tour guides do a marvelous job of explaining the animals' habits, from feeding to breeding, and their predators (including man). ⊠ *Seaton's Village* ☎ *268/562–7297* ⊕ *www.stingraycityantigua.com.*

BOATING

Antigua's circular geographic configuration makes boating easy, and its many lovely harbors and coves provide splendid anchorages. Experienced boaters will particularly enjoy Antigua's east coast, which is far more rugged and has several islets; be sure to get a good nautical map, as there are numerous minireefs that can be treacherous. If you're just looking for a couple of hours of wave-hopping, stick to the Dickenson Bay or Jolly Harbour area.

Nicholson Yacht Charters. Nicholson Yacht Charters are real professionals, true pioneers in Caribbean sailing, with three generations spanning 60 years of experience. A long-established island family, they can offer you anything from a 20-foot ketch to a giant schooner. ⊠ *English Harbour* ☎ *268/460–1530, 305/433–5533* ⊕ *www.nicholson-charters.com.*

Ondeck. Ondeck runs skippered charters on the likes of Farr and Beneteau out of the Antigua Yacht Club Marina in Falmouth Harbour, terrific one- and two-day sailing workshops, and eco-adventure trips to Montserrat on a racing yacht. You can even participate in official regattas. Instructors and crew are all seasoned racers. Bareboating options and sunset cruises are also available. ☎ *268/562–6696* ⊕ *www.ondeckoceanracing.com.*

Sunsail. Sunsail has an extensive modern fleet of dinghies and 32-foot day-sailers starting at $25 per half day, $50 for a full day (always call in advance as the Nelson's Dockyard office is open sporadically). But its primary focus is bareboat yachting, often in conjunction with hotel stays. ☎ *268/460–2615, 888/350–3568* ⊕ *www.sunsail.com.*

DIVING

Antigua is an unsung diving destination, with plentiful undersea sights to explore, from coral canyons to sea caves. Barbuda alone features roughly 200 wrecks on its treacherous reefs. The most accessible wreck is the 1890s bark *Andes,* not far out in Deep Bay, off Five Islands Peninsula. Among the favorite sites are **Green Island, Cades Reef,** and **Bird Island** (a national park). Memorable sightings include turtles, stingrays, and barracuda darting amid basalt walls, hulking boulders, and stray 17th-century anchors and cannon. One advantage is accessibility in many spots for shore divers and snorkelers. Double-tank dives run about $90.

Dockyard Divers. Owned by British ex-merchant seaman Captain A.G. "Tony" Fincham, Dockyard Divers is one of the island's most established outfits and offers diving and snorkeling trips, PADI courses, and dive packages with accommodations. They're geared to seasoned divers, but staff work patiently with novices. Tony is a wonderful source of information on the island; ask him about the "Fincham's Follies" musical extravaganza he produces for charity. ⊠ *Nelson's Dockyard, English Harbour* ☎ *268/460–1178* ⊕ *www.dockyard-divers.com.*

FISHING

Antigua's waters teem with game fish such as marlin, wahoo, and tuna. Most boat trips include equipment, lunch, and drinks. Figure at least $495 for a half day, $790 for a full day, for up to six people.

Obsession. The 45-foot Hatteras Convertible Sportfisherman *Obsession* has top-of-the-line equipment, including an international-standard fighting chair, Rupp outriggers, and handcrafted rods. Also available is the new 55-foot Hatteras Sportfisherman, the *Double Header.* ⊕ *www. charternet.com/charters/obsession.*

Overdraft. Frankie Hart, a professional fisherman who knows the waters intimately and regales clients with stories of his trade, operates *Overdraft,* a spacious, fiberglass 40-footer outfitted with the latest techno-gadgetry. He also rents the 26-foot *H2O,* a ProKat versatile enough to accommodate fly-fishing and deeper-water bay bait fishing. ☎ *268/464– 4954, 268/463–3112* ⊕ *www.antiguafishing.com.*

GOLF

Though Antigua hardly qualifies as a duffer's delight, its two 18-hole courses offer varied layouts.

Cedar Valley Golf Club. Northeast of St. John's, Cedar Valley Golf Club has a driving range and par-70, 6157-yard, 18-hole course. Finished as Antigua's first 18-hole golf course in 1977, it is not particularly well-maintained terrain nonetheless offers some attractive vistas and challenges with narrow hilly fairways and numerous doglegs (Hole 7 is a perfect example). The 5th hole has exceptional ocean vistas from the top of the tee, and the par-5 9th offers the trickiest design with steep slopes and swales. Carts are $42 ($22 for 9 holes). The Spinach! Cafe offers free Wi-Fi. ⊠ *Friar's Hill* ☎ *268/462–0161* ⊕ *www.cedarvalleygolf.ag* ⚑ *18 holes, 6157 yards, par 70* ⛳ *$49 ($25 for 9 holes).*

Jolly Harbour Golf Course. Jolly Harbour Golf Course is a par-71, 5587-yard 18-hole course designed by Karl Litten. The flat Florida-style layout is lushly tropical with the trade winds a challenge. Seven lakes add to the challenge, but the facility struggles with conditioning. The 15th is the signature hole, with a sharp dogleg and long carry over two hazards. Unfortunately, fairways are often dry and patchy, drainage is poor, and the pro shop and "19th hole" are barely adequate. Visitors can participate in regular tournaments and "meet-and-greet" events. ⊠ *Jolly Harbour* ☎ *268/462–7771* ⊕ *www.jollyharbourantigua.com/ golf* ⚑ *18 holes, 5587 yards, par 71* ⛳ *$57.50 ($97.75 including cart); $23 for 9 holes.*

GUIDED TOURS

Almost all taxi drivers double as guides; an island tour with one costs about $25 an hour. Every major hotel has a cabbie on call and may be able to negotiate a discount, particularly off-season. Several operators specialize in off-road four-wheel-drive adventures that provide a taste of island history and topography.

Island Safaris. Four-wheel off-road adventures by Island Safaris, which also runs other land- and water-based excursions, enables you to fully appreciate the island's natural beauty, history, folklore, and cultural heritage as you zoom about the southwest part of Antigua. Hiking is involved, though it's not strenuous. Lunch and snorkeling are also included. Active adventurers will particularly enjoy the combo Land Rover–kayak outback ecotour. Prices start at $99 per adult, $60–$75 children 7–12. ☎ 268/480–1225 ⊕ www.tropicaladventures-antigua.com.

Scenic Tours. Scenic Tours gives affordable half- and full-day island tours, geared toward cruise passengers, that focus on such highlights as Devil's Bridge, Shirley Heights, and English Harbour, as well as soft adventure hikes. ⊠ Woods Mall, St. John's ☎ 268/764–3060, 888/271–4004 ⊕ www.scenictoursantigua.com.

HORSEBACK RIDING

Comparatively dry Antigua is best for beach rides, though you won't find anything wildly romantic and deserted à la *Black Stallion*.

Antigua Equestrian Center. The former Spring Hill Riding Club specializes in equestrian lessons in show jumping and dressage but also offers $65 hour-long trail rides on the beach or through the bush past ruined forts, $125 for two hours (bareback riding in the ocean is an additional $45); half-hour private lessons from a British Horse Society instructor are $35. ⊠ Falmouth Harbour ☎ 268/460–7787, 268/773–3139 ⊕ www. antiguaequestrian.com.

SAILING AND SNORKELING

Not a sailor yourself? Consider signing up for one of the following boat tours. Each tour provides a great opportunity to enjoy the seafaring life while someone else captains the ship.

Miguel's Holiday Adventures. Miguel's Holiday Adventures leaves every Tuesday, Thursday, and Saturday morning at 10 am from the Hodges Bay jetty for snorkeling, rum punches, and lunch at Prickly Pear Island, which offers both shallow- and deepwater snorkeling, as well as hiking. In this comfortable family operation, Miguel's wife, Josephine, prepares an authentic, lavish West Indian buffet including lobster, and Miguel and his son Terrence are caring instructors. ☎ 268/460–9978, 268/772–3213, 268/723–7418 mobile ⊕ www.pricklypearisland.com.

Tropical Adventures. Barbuda day trips on the catamaran *Excellence* overflow with rum and high spirits, as do circumnavigations of Antigua. Tropical Adventures also operates ecokayaking tours and slightly more sedate, intimate catamaran cruises from sunset to snorkeling on the *Mystic*. Most tours cost $99–$115, with discounts for children 12 and under. ☎ *268/480–1225* ⊕ *www.tropicaladventures-antigua.com.*

Wadadli Cats. Wadadli Cats offers several cruises, including a circumnavigation of the island and snorkeling at Bird Island or Cades Reef, on its five sleek catamarans, including the handsome, fully outfitted *Spirit of Antigua*. Prices are fair ($95–$110), and advance direct bookers get a free T-shirt. ☎ *268/462–4792* ⊕ *www.wadadlicats.com.*

WINDSURFING AND KITEBOARDING

Most major hotels offer windsurfing equipment. The best areas are Nonsuch Bay and the east coast (notably Half Moon and Willoughby bays), which is slightly less protected and has a challenging juxtaposition of sudden calms and gusts.

KiteAntigua. KiteAntigua offers lessons in the Caribbean's hot new sport, kiteboarding, where a futuristic surfboard with harness is propelled only by an inflated kite; kite-board rentals (for the certified) are also available at $30 per hour, $50 half day, $70 full day. The varied multiday lesson packages are expensive but thorough; a four-hour private beginners course is $280. KiteAntigua closes from September through November, when winds aren't optimal. The center is on a stretch near the airport, but road trips to secret spots are arranged for experienced kitesurfers seeking that sometimes harrowing "high." ⊠ *Jabberwock Beach* ☎ *268/720–5483, 268/727–3983* ⊕ *www.kitesurfantigua.com.*

Windsurfing Antigua. Patrick Scales of Windsurfing Antigua has long been one of Antigua's, if not the Caribbean's, finest instructors; he now offers a mobile service in high season. He provides top-flight equipment for $30 per hour (first hour; $25 subsequent hours, $70 per half-day, and $80 per day), two-hour beginner lessons for $90, and specialty tours to Half Moon Bay and other favorite spots for experienced surfers. ⊠ *Jabberwock Beach* ☎ *268/461–9463, 268/773–9463* ⊕ *www. windsurfantigua.net.*

ZIP-LINING

Antigua Rainforest Canopy Tours. Release your inner Tarzan at Antigua Rainforest Canopy Tours. You should be in fairly good condition for the ropes challenges, which require upper-body strength and stamina; there are height and weight restrictions. But anyone (vertigo or acrophobia sufferers, beware) can navigate the intentionally rickety "Indiana Jones–inspired" suspension bridges, then fly (in secure harnesses) 200–300 feet above a rain-forest-filled valley from one towering turpentine tree to the next on lines with names like "Screamer" and "Leap of Faith." There are 21 stations, as well as a bar–café and interpretive signage. First-timers, fear not: the "rangers" are affable, amusing, and accomplished. Admission varies slightly, but is usually $85 and up. It's open Monday–Saturday from 8 to 6, with two scheduled tours at 9 and 11 (other times by appointment). ⊠ *Fig Tree Dr., Wallings* ☎ *268/562–6363* ⊕ *www. antiguarainforest.com.*

ARUBA

WELCOME TO ARUBA

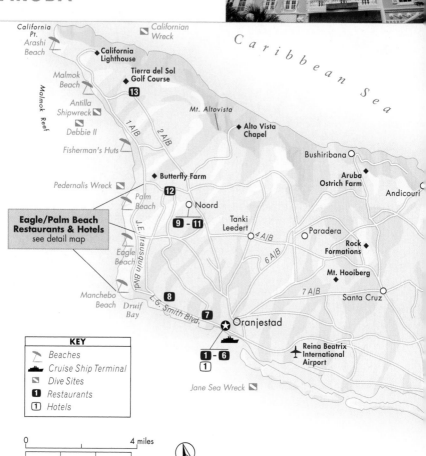

California Pt.
California Wreck
Arashi Beach
California Lighthouse
Malmok Beach
Tierra del Sol Golf Course
13
Malmok Reef
Antilla Shipwreck
Debbie II
Fisherman's Huts
1 A/B
2 A/B
Mt. Altovista
Alto Vista Chapel
Caribbean Sea
Bushiribana
Aruba Ostrich Farm
Andicouri
Pedernalis Wreck
Butterfly Farm
12
Palm Beach
Noord
Tanki Leedert
4 A/B
Paradera
Rock Formations
9 - 11
Mt. Hooiberg
6 A/B
Eagle/Palm Beach Restaurants & Hotels
see detail map
J.E. Irausquin Blvd.
Eagle Beach
Manchebo Beach
Druif Bay
L.G. Smith Blvd.
8
7 A/B
Santa Cruz
7
Oranjestad
Reina Beatrix International Airport
1 - 6
1
Jane Sea Wreck

KEY
- Beaches
- Cruise Ship Terminal
- Dive Sites
- **1** Restaurants
- **1** Hotels

0 — 4 miles
0 — 6 km

The pastel-color houses of Dutch settlers still grace the waterfront in the capital city of Oranjestad. Winds are fierce, even savage, on the north coast, where you'll find a landscape of cacti, rocky desert, and wind-bent divi-divi trees. On the west coast the steady breezes attract windsurfers to the shallow, richly colored waters.

THE A IN THE ABC ISLANDS

The A in the ABC Islands (followed by Bonaire and Curaçao), Aruba is small—only 19½ miles (31½ km) long and 6 miles (9½ km) across at its widest point. It became an independent entity within the Netherlands in 1986. The official language is Dutch, but almost every native speaks English and Spanish as well. The island's population is 108,000.

4

ARUBA

Restaurants ▼

2 Fools and a Bull **12**
Bucaneer **10**
Carpe Diem **7**
Deli France **8**
El Gaucho
Argentine Grill **2**
Flying Fishbone **14**
Gasparito Restaurant
& Art Gallery **11**
Gostoso **4**
L. G. Smith's
Steak & Chop House **1**
Marandi **3**
Papiamento **9**
Pinchos Grill & Bar **6**
Qué Pasa? **5**
Ventanas del Mar **13**

Hotels ▼

Renaissance
Aruba Resort & Casino .. **1**

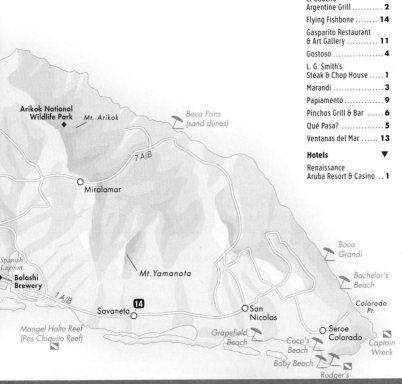

TOP REASONS TO VISIT ARUBA

1 The Nightlife: Some of the best in the Caribbean. The colorful Kukoo Kunuku party bus picks you up and pours you out at your hotel.

2 The Beaches: Powder-soft beaches and turquoise waters are legendary.

3 The Restaurants: Great restaurants offer a wide range of cuisine as good as any in the Caribbean.

4 The Casinos: Aruba's casinos will please both casual and serious gamblers.

5 The Welcome: A friendly population devoted to tourism guarantees welcoming smiles throughout the island.

Updated
by Vernon
O'Reilly-
Ramesar

Cruise ships gleam in Oranjestad Harbour, and thousands of eager tourists scavenge through souvenir stalls looking for the perfect memento. The mile-long stretch of L.G. Smith Boulevard is lined with cafés, designer stores, and signs for the latest Vegas-style shows. The countryside is dotted with colorful *cunucu* (country-style houses) and small neighborhood shops. Suddenly, the rocky desert landscape is startlingly austere.

Aruba offers a lot of variety in a small package. Tourists flock here for the sunny climate, perfect waters, and excellent beaches—so much so that the area around beautiful Eagle Beach is an almost unbroken line of hotels, restaurants, and bars. Here on the south coast, the action is nonstop both day and night, whereas the fiercely rugged north coast is a desolate and rocky landscape that has so far resisted development.

As with Bonaire and Curaçao, the island was originally populated by the Caquetio, an Amerindian people related to the Arawak. After the Spanish conquered the island in 1499, Aruba was basically left alone, since it held little in the way of agricultural or mineral wealth. The Dutch took charge of the island in 1636, and things remained relatively quiet until gold was discovered in the 1800s.

Like the trademark *watapana* (divi-divi) trees that have been forced into bonsailike angles by the constant trade winds, Aruba has always adjusted to changes in the economic climate. Mining dominated the economy until the early part of the 20th century, when the mines became unprofitable. Shortly thereafter, Aruba became home to a major oil-refining operation, which was the economic mainstay until the early 1990s, when its contribution to the local economy was eclipsed by tourism. Today, after being so resolutely dedicated to attracting visitors for so many years, Aruba's national culture and tourism industry are inextricably intertwined.

LOGISTICS

Getting to Aruba: Many airlines fly nonstop to Aruba from several cities in North America; connections will usually be at a U.S. airport. Smaller airlines connect the Dutch islands in the Caribbean, often using Aruba as a hub. Travelers to the United States clear U.S. Customs and Immigration before leaving Aruba.

Hassle Factor: Low.

On the Ground: A taxi from the airport to most hotels takes about 20 minutes. An hour-long island taxi tour costs about $45, with up to four people. Rides into town from Eagle Beach run about $10; from Palm Beach, about $11. If you want to explore the countryside at your leisure and try different beaches, then you should rent a car, but for just getting to and around town, taxis are preferable, and you can use tour companies to arrange your activities. If you rent a car, try to make reservations before arriving, and rent a four-wheel-drive vehicle if you plan to explore the island's natural sights. Some companies have minimum ages for renting a car.

4

With more than a million visitors a year, Aruba is not a destination that will appeal to those trying to avoid the beaten path—but you should visit Aruba if you're looking for a pleasant climate, excellent facilities, lots of nightlife, and no unpleasant surprises. The U.S. dollar is accepted everywhere, and English is spoken universally, which makes Aruba a popular spot for Americans who want an overseas trip to a place that doesn't feel foreign. In fact, Americans go through U.S. customs right at the airport in Aruba, so there are no formalities upon landing in the United States.

PLANNING

WHEN TO GO
Aruba's popularity means that hotels are usually booked solid during the high season, from mid-December through mid-April or early May, so early booking is essential. During other times of the year, rate reductions can be dramatic.

Aruba doesn't really have a rainy season and hardly ever sees a hurricane, so you take fewer chances by coming here in late summer and fall. However, if you travel at this time, remember that hurricanes and tropical storms are not unheard of—just rare.

February or March witnesses a spectacular **Carnival,** a riot of color whirling to the tunes of steel bands and culminating in the Grand Parade, where some of the floats rival the extravagance of those in the Big Easy's Mardi Gras.

GETTING HERE AND AROUND
AIR TRAVEL
Many airlines fly nonstop to Aruba from several cities in North America; connections will usually be at a U.S. airport.

Nonstop Flights There are nonstop flights from Atlanta (Delta), Boston (American, JetBlue, US Airways), Charlotte (US Airways), Chicago (United—weekly), Fort Lauderdale (Spirit—weekly), Houston (United), Miami (American), Newark (United), New York–JFK (American, Delta, JetBlue), Philadelphia (US Airways—twice weekly), and Washington, D.C.–Dulles (United).

The island's **Reina Beatrix International Airport** (AUA) is equipped with thorough security, lots of flight displays, and state-of-the-art baggage-handling systems.

Airline Contacts American Airlines ☎ *297/582–2700 on Aruba, 800/433–7300* ⊕ *www.aa.com.* **Delta Airlines** ☎ *297/800–1555 on Aruba, 800/221–1212 for U.S. reservations, 800/241–4141 for international reservations* ⊕ *www.delta.com.* **JetBlue** ☎ *800/538–2583* ⊕ *www.jetblue.com.* **KLM** ☎ *5999/868–0195 on Aruba, 31/20–4–747–747 in Amsterdam* ⊕ *www.klm. com.* **Spirit Airlines** ☎ *800/772–7117* ⊕ *www.spiritair.com.* **United Airlines** ☎ *297/562–9592 on Aruba, 800/538–2929 in North America* ⊕ *www. united.com.* **US Airways** ☎ *800/455–0123 for U.S. and Canada reservations, 001–800/622–1015 for international reservations* ⊕ *www.usairways.com.*

BUS TRAVEL

Buses run hourly trips between the beach hotels and Oranjestad. The one-way fare is $1.25 ($2.25 round-trip), and exact change is preferred (so be sure to keep some U.S. change handy if you plan to pay in U.S. currency). There are also minibuses that will pick you up at the same stops for the same price; just be sure to look for the "ATA approved" sign. Buses also run down the coast from Oranjestad to San Nicolas for the same fare.

Contact Arubus ⊕ *www.arubus.com.*

CAR TRAVEL

If you want to explore the countryside and try different beaches, then you should rent a car. Try to make reservations before arriving, and rent a four-wheel drive if you plan to explore the island's natural sights. For just getting to and around town, taxis are preferable, and you can use tour companies to arrange your activities.

To rent a car you'll need a driver's license, and you must meet the minimum age requirements of the company (Budget, for example, requires drivers to be over 25; Avis, between 23 and 70; and Hertz, over 21). A deposit of $500 (or a signed credit-card slip) is required. Rates are between $47 and $75 a day (local agencies generally have lower rates).

Contacts Avis ✉ *330 J.E. Irausquin Blvd., Oranjestad* ☎ *297/586–2181, 800/522–9696* ⊕ *www.avis.com* ✉ *Airport* ☎ *297/582–5496.* **Budget** ✉ *Camacuri 10, Oranjestad* ☎ *297/582–8600, 800/472–3325* ⊕ *www.budget.com.* **Dollar** ✉ *Queen Beatrix Airport, Oranjestad* ☎ *297/583–0101* ⊕ *www.dollar.com.* **Economy** ✉ *Bushiri 27, Oranjestad* ☎ *297/582–0009* ⊕ *www.economyaruba.com.* **Hertz** ✉ *Sabana Blanco 35, near airport, Oranjestad* ☎ *297/582–1845* ⊕ *www.arubarentcar.com.* **Thrifty** ✉ *Wayaca 33-F, Oranjestad* ☎ *297/583–4042* ⊕ *www.thriftycarrentalaruba.com* ✉ *Airport* ☎ *297/583–4902.*

TAXI TRAVEL

There's a dispatch office at the airport; you can also flag down taxis on the street (look for license plates with a "TX" tag). Rates are fixed (i.e., there are no meters; the rates are set by the government and displayed on a chart), though you and the driver should agree on the fare before your ride begins. Add $2 to the fare after midnight and $3 on Sunday and holidays. An hour-long island tour costs about $45, with up to four people. Rides into town from Eagle Beach run about $10; from Palm Beach, about $11.

Contact Airport Taxi Dispatch
☏ *297/582–2116.*

ARUBA DRIVING TIPS

International traffic signs and Dutch-style traffic signals (with an extra light for a turning lane) can be misleading if you're not used to them; use extreme caution, especially at intersections, until you grasp the rules of the road. Speed limits are rarely posted but are usually 50 mph (80 kph) in the countryside. Aside from the major highways, the island's winding roads are poorly marked. Gas prices average about $1.63 a liter (roughly $6.20 a gallon), which is reasonable by Caribbean standards.

ESSENTIALS

Banks and Exchange Services The local currency is the Aruban florin (AFl 1.79 to US$1). The florin is pegged to the U.S. dollar, and Arubans accept U.S. dollars readily, so you need acquire local currency only for pocket change. Note that the Netherlands Antilles florin used on Curaçao is not accepted on Aruba. ATMs are easy to find.

Electricity 110 volts, 50 cycles.

Emergency Services Dr. Horacio Oduber Hospital ✉ *L.G. Smith Blvd. 47, Manchebo Beach* ☏ *297/587–4300.*

Language Everyone on the island speaks English, but the official languages are Dutch and Papiamento. Most locals speak Papiamento—a rapid-fire mix of Spanish, Dutch, English, French, and Portuguese—in normal conversation. Here are a few helpful phrases: *bon dia* (good day), *bon nochi* (good night), *masha danki* (thank you very much).

Taxes The airport departure tax is a hefty $37 for departures to the United States and $33.50 to other international destinations (including Bonaire and Curaçao), but the fee is usually included in your ticket price. Hotels collect 9.5% in taxes (2% of which goes to marketing to tourists) on top of a typical 11% service charge, for a total of 20.5%. A 3% B.B.O. tax (turnover tax) is included in the price charged in most shops.

Tipping Restaurants generally include a 10% to 15% service charge. If service isn't included, a 10% tip is standard; if it is included, it's customary to add something extra at your discretion. Taxi drivers, 10% to 15%; porters and bellhops, about $2 per bag; housekeeping, about $2 a day.

ARUBA ACCOMMODATIONS

Almost all of the resorts are along the island's southwest coast, along L.G. Smith and J.E. Irausquin boulevards, with the larger high-rise properties being farther away from Oranjestad. A few budget places are in Oranjestad itself. Since most hotel beaches are equally fabulous, it's the resort, rather than its location, that's going to be a bigger factor in how you enjoy your vacation.

Boutique Resorts: You'll find a few small resorts that offer more personal service, though not always the same level of luxury as the larger places. But smaller resorts are better suited to the natural sense of Aruban hospitality you'll find all over the island.

Large Resorts: These all-encompassing vacation destinations offer myriad dining options, casinos, shops, water-sports centers, health clubs, and car-rental desks. The island has only a handful of all-inclusives, though these are gaining in popularity.

Time-shares: Large time-share properties are cropping up in greater numbers, luring visitors who prefer to prepare some of their own meals and have a bit more living space than in a typical resort hotel room.

HOTEL AND RESTAURANT PRICES

Prices in the restaurant reviews are the average cost of a main course at dinner or, if dinner is not served, at lunch; taxes and service charges are generally included. Prices in the hotel reviews are the lowest cost of a standard double room in high season, excluding taxes, service charges, and meal plans (except at all-inclusives). Prices for rentals are the lowest per-night cost for a one-bedroom unit in high season.

For expanded lodging reviews and current deals, visit Fodors.com.

VISITOR INFORMATION

Aruba Tourism Authority ⊠ *L.G. Smith Blvd. 172, Eagle Beach* ☎ *800/862–7822 in U.S./International, 297/582–3777 in Aruba* ⊕ *www.aruba.com.*

WEDDINGS

You must be over 18 and submit the appropriate documents one month in advance. Couples are required to submit birth certificates with raised seals, through the mail or in person, to Aruba's Office of the Civil Registry. They also need an apostille—a document proving they are free to marry—from their country of residence. Most major hotels have wedding coordinators, and there are other independent wedding planners on the island.

Contacts Aruba Fairy Tales ☎ *297/583–8000* ⊕ *www.arubafairytales.com.* **Dream Weddings Aruba** ⊠ *Catiri 29G, Oranjestad* ☎ *297/564–3289* ⊕ *www.dreamweddingsaruba.com.*

EXPLORING

Aruba's wildly sculpted landscape is replete with rocky deserts, cactus clusters, secluded coves, blue vistas, and the trademark divi-divi tree. To see the island's wild, untamed beauty, you can rent a car, take a sightseeing tour, or hire a cab for $45 an hour (for up to four people). The main highways are well paved, but on the windward side (the north- and east-facing side) some roads are still a mixture of compacted dirt and stones. Although a car is fine, a four-wheel-drive vehicle will allow you to explore the unpaved interior.

Traffic is sparse, but signs leading to sights are often small and hand-lettered (this is slowly changing as the government puts up official road signs), so watch closely. Route 1A travels southbound along the western coast, and 1B is simply northbound along the same road. If you lose your way, just look to the divi-divi trees, which always lean southwest.

ORANJESTAD AND ENVIRONS

Aruba's charming capital is best explored on foot. L.G. Smith Boulevard, the palm-lined thoroughfare in the center of town, runs between pastel-painted buildings, old and new, of typical Dutch design. You'll find many malls with boutiques and shops here.

WORTH NOTING

FAMILY **Archaeological Museum of Aruba.** This small museum has two rooms chock-full of fascinating artifacts from the indigenous Arawak people, including farm and domestic utensils dating back hundreds of years. ⊠ *J.E. Irausquin Blvd. 2A, Oranjestad* ☎ *297/582–8979* ⊒ *Free* ⊙ *Tues.–Fri. 10–5, weekends 10–2.*

Aruba Aloe. Learn all about aloe—its cultivation, processing, and production—at this farm and factory. Guided tours lasting about a half hour will show you how the gel—revered for its skin-soothing properties—is extracted from the aloe vera plant and used in a variety of products, including after-sun creams, soaps, and shampoos. Though not the most exciting tour on the island—and unlikely to keeps kids entertained—it is free and might be a good option on a rainy day. You can purchase the finished goods in the gift shop where the tour ends. ⊠ *Pitastraat 115, Oranjestad* ☎ *297/588–3222* ⊒ *Free* ⊙ *Weekdays 8:30–4, Sat. 9–noon.*

Balashi Brewery. The factory that manufactures the excellent local beer, Balashi, offers daily tours to the public that will take you through every stage of the brewing process. It makes for a fascinating hour, and the price of the tour includes a free drink at the end. Note that closed shoes are required for the tour. Those more interested in beer drinking than beer making might want to visit the factory beer garden Friday evening from 6 to 9 for happy hour, where there's live music. ⊠ *Balashi 75, Balashi* ☎ *297/592–2544* ⊒ *$6.*

Ft. Zoutman. One of the island's oldest edifices, Aruba's historic fort was built in 1796 and played an important role in skirmishes between British and Curaçao troops in 1803. The Willem III Tower, named for the Dutch monarch of that time, was added in 1868 to serve as a lighthouse. Over time the fort has been a government office building, a police station, and a prison; now its historical museum displays Aruban artifacts in an 18th-century house. ⊠ *Zoutmanstraat, Oranjestad* ☎ *297/582–6099* ⊒ *$5* ⊙ *Weekdays 8–noon and 1–4.*

4

MANCHEBO AND DRUIF BEACHES

One beach seamlessly merges with another resulting in a miles-long stretch of powdery sand peppered with a few low-rise resorts. This part of the island is much less crowded than Palm Beach and great for a morning or evening stroll.

EAGLE BEACH

This area is often referred to as Aruba's low-rise hotel area. It's lined with smaller boutique resorts and time-share resorts. Eagle Beach is considered one of the best beaches in the Caribbean, the white sand here seems to stretch on forever. The water is great for swimming and there are numerous refreshment spots along the beach. Although the beach can get busy during the day there's never a problem finding a spot, but if you're looking for shade, it's best to stick near one of the hotel bar huts along the beach.

PALM BEACH AND NOORD

The district of Noord is home to the strip of high-rise hotels and casinos that line Palm Beach. The hotels and restaurants, ranging from haute cuisine to fast food, are densely packed into a few miles running along the beachfront. When other areas of Aruba are shutting down for the night, this area is guaranteed to still be buzzing with activity. Here you can also find the beautiful **St. Ann's Church,** known for its ornate 19th-century altar. In this area Aruban-style homes are scattered amid clusters of cacti.

FAMILY   **Butterfly Farm.** Hundreds of butterflies from around the world flutter about this spectacular garden. Guided 30- to 45-minute tours (included in the price of admission) provide an entertaining look into the life cycle of these insects, from egg to caterpillar to chrysalis to butterfly. After your initial visit, you can return as often as you like for free during your vacation. ⊠ *J.E. Irausquin Blvd., Palm Beach* ☎ *297/586–3656* ⊕ *www. thebutterflyfarm.com* ☜ *$15* ☉ *Daily 9–4:30; last tour at 4.*

WESTERN TIP (CALIFORNIA DUNES)

No trip to Aruba is complete without a visit to the California Lighthouse and it's also worth exploring the rugged area of the Island's Western tip. This is the transition point between Aruba's calmer and rougher coasts. Malmok Beach and Arashi Beach are popular for windsurfing and are excellent for grabbing dramatic sunset photos.

WORTH NOTING

Alto Vista Chapel. Alone near the island's northwest corner sits this scenic little chapel. The wind whistles through the simple mustard-color walls, eerie boulders, and looming cacti. Along the side of the road back to civilization are miniature crosses with depictions of the stations of the cross and hand-lettered signs with "Pray for us Sinners" and other heartfelt evocations of faith. ⊠ *Alto Vista Rd., Oranjestad* ✛ *Follow the rough, winding dirt road that loops around the island's* *northern tip, or from the hotel strip, take Palm Beach Road through three intersections and watch for the asphalt road to the left just past the Alto Vista Rum Shop.*

California Lighthouse. The lighthouse, built by a French architect in 1910, stands at the island's far northern end. Although you can't go inside, you can climb the hill to the lighthouse base for some great views. It's surrounded by huge boulders and sand dunes; in this stark landscape you might feel as though you've just landed on the moon. ⊠ *Arashi, Oranjestad.*

SANTA CRUZ

Though not a tourist hot spot (by Aruba standards) this town in the center of the island offers a good taste of how the locals live. It's not architecturally interesting, but there are many restaurants and local shops offering something a bit different from the usual tourist fare (and at reasonable prices).

Mt. Hooiberg. Named for its shape (*hooiberg* means "haystack" in Dutch), this 541-foot peak lies inland just past the airport. If you have the energy, you can climb the 562 steps to the top for an impressive view of Oranjestad (and Venezuela on clear days). ⊠ *Oranjestad.*

SAVANETA

The Dutch settled here after retaking the island in 1816, and it served as Aruba's first capital. Today it's a bustling fishing village with a 150-year-old *cas di torto* (mud hut), the oldest dwelling still standing on the island.

SAN NICOLAS

During the oil refinery heyday, Aruba's oldest village was a bustling port; now its primary purpose is tourism. The major institution in town is Charlie's Restaurant & Bar. Stop in for a drink and advice on what to see and do in this little town. Aruba's main red-light district is here and will be fairly apparent to even casual observers.

SEROE COLORADO

What was originally built as a community for oil workers is known for its intriguing 1939 chapel. The site is surreal, as organ-pipe cacti form the backdrop for sedate whitewashed cottages. The real reason to come here is a **natural bridge.** Keep bearing east past the community, continuing uphill until you run out of road. You can then hike down to the cathedral-like formation. It's not too strenuous, but watch your footing as you descend. Be sure to follow the white arrows painted on the rocks, as there are no other directional signs. Although this bridge isn't as spectacular as its more celebrated sibling (which collapsed in 2005), the raw elemental power of the sea that created it, replete with hissing blowholes, certainly is.

ARIKOK NATIONAL PARK AND ENVIRONS

Nearly 20% of Aruba has been designated part of Arikok National Park, which sprawls across the eastern interior and the northeast coast. The park is the keystone of the government's long-term ecotourism plan to preserve Aruba's resources and showcases the island's flora and fauna as well as ancient Arawak petroglyphs, the ruins of a gold-mining operation at Miralmar, and the remnants of Dutch peasant settlements at Masiduri. Within the confines of the park are Mt. Arikok and the 620-foot Mt. Yamanota, Aruba's highest peak.

Anyone looking for geological exotica should head for the park's caves, found on the northeastern coast. Baranca Sunu, the so-called Tunnel of Love, has a heart-shape entrance and naturally sculpted rocks farther inside that look like the Madonna, Abraham Lincoln, and even a jaguar. Fontein Cave, which was used by indigenous peoples centuries ago, is marked with ancient drawings (rangers are on hand to offer explanations). Bats are known to make appearances—don't worry, they won't bother you. Although you don't need a flashlight because the paths are well lighted, it's best to wear sneakers.

WORTH NOTING

Arikok Visitor Center. At the park's main entrance, Arikok Visitor Center houses offices, restrooms, and food facilities. All visitors must stop here upon entering so that officials can manage the traffic flow and hand out information on park rules and features. ☎ 297/585–1234 ⊕ www. arubanationalpark.org ✉ $10 ⊗ 8–5.

Aruba Ostrich Farm. Everything you ever wanted to know about the world's largest living birds can be found at this farm. A large *palapa* (palm-thatched roof) houses a gift shop and restaurant that draws large bus tours, and tours of the farm are available every half hour. This operation is virtually identical to the facility in Curaçao; it's owned by the same company. ⊠ *Makividiri Rd., Paradera* ☎ 297/585–9630 ⊕ *www.arubaostrichfarm.com* ✉ *Adults $12, children under 12 $6* ⊗ *Daily 9–4.*

Rock Formations. The massive boulders at Ayo and Casibari are a mystery, as they don't match the island's geological makeup. You can climb to the top for fine views of the arid countryside. On the way you'll doubtless pass Aruba whiptail lizards—the males are cobalt blue, and the females are blue-gray with light-blue dots. The main path to Casibari has steps and handrails, and you must move through tunnels and along narrow steps and ledges to reach the top. At Ayo you can find ancient pictographs in a small cave (the entrance has iron bars to protect the drawings from vandalism). You may also encounter boulder climbers, who are increasingly drawn to Ayo's smooth surfaces. There's a café at the base for those who prefer to look at others do the climbing. ⊠ *Paradera* ⚐ *Access to the rock formations at Casibari is via Tanki Hwy. 4A; you can reach Ayo via Rte. 6A. Watch carefully for the turnoff signs near the center of the island on the way to the windward side.*

BEACHES

There are few destinations that can match the glorious beach vistas of Aruba. There's white sand, turquoise waters, and constant breezes that are a lovely cool counterpoint to the intense sunshine.

There's also virtually no litter—everyone takes the "no tira sushi" (no littering) signs very seriously, which is fortunate given the island's $280 fine. Virtually every popular beach has a resort attached, but because nearly all beaches are public, there is never a problem with access.

The major beaches, which back up to the hotels along the southwestern strip, are usually crowded. You can make the hour-long hike from the Holiday Inn to the Tamarijn without ever leaving sand. Make sure you're well protected from the sun—scorching happens fast here. Luckily, there's at least one covered bar (and often an ice-cream stand) at virtually every hotel. On the island's northeastern side, stronger winds make the waters too choppy for swimming, but the vistas are great, and the terrain is wonderful for exploring.

Arashi Beach. This is a 1-km (½-mile) stretch of gleaming white sand. Although it was once rocky, nature—with a little help from humans—has turned it into an excellent place for sunbathing and swimming. Despite calm waters, the rocky reputation keeps most people away, making it relatively uncrowded. **Amenities:** parking. **Best for:** swimming; walking. ⊠ *West of Malmok Beach, on west end.*

FAMILY **Baby Beach.** On the island's eastern tip (near the now closed refinery), this semicircular beach borders a placid bay of turquoise water that's just about as shallow as a wading pool—perfect for tots, shore divers, and terrible swimmers. Thatched shaded areas are good places to cool off. Down the road is the island's rather unusual pet cemetery. Stop by the nearby snack trucks for burgers, hot dogs, beer, and soda. The road to this beach (and several others) is through San Nicolas and along the road toward Seroe Colorado. Just before reaching the beach, keep an eye out for a strange 300-foot natural seawall made of coral and rock that was thrown up overnight when Hurricane Ivan swept by the island in 2004. **Amenities:** food and drink. **Best for:** snorkeling; swimming; walking. ⊠ *Near Seroe Colorado, on east end.*

Boca Grandi. This is a great spot for windsurfers, but swimming is not advisable as the water is rough and there are no lifeguards. It's near Seagrape Grove and the Aruba Golf Club, toward the island's eastern tip. **Amenities:** none. **Best for:** walking; windsurfing. ⊠ *Near Seagrape Grove, on east end.*

Druif Beach. Fine white sand and calm water make this beach a fine choice for sunbathing and swimming. Convenience is a highlight, too: the many Divi hotels are close at hand, and the beach is accessible by bus, rental car, or taxi. **Amenities:** parking. **Best for:** swimming, sunbathing. ⊠ *Parallel to J.E. Irausquin Blvd., near Divi resorts, south of Punta Brabo.*

Fodor's Choice ★ **Eagle Beach.** On the southwestern coast, across the highway from what is quickly becoming known as Time-Share Lane, is one of the Caribbean's—if not the world's—best beaches. With all the resorts here, this mile-plus-long beach is always hopping. The white sand is literally

Cunucu Houses

Pastel houses surrounded by cacti fences adorn Aruba's flat, rugged *cunucu* ("country" in Papiamento). The features of these traditional houses were developed in response to the environment. Early settlers discovered that slanting roofs allowed the heat to rise and that small windows helped to keep in the cool air. Among the earliest building materials was *caliche*, a durable calcium carbonate substance found in the island's southeastern hills.

Many houses were also built using interlocking coral rocks that didn't require mortar (this technique is no longer used, thanks to concrete). Contemporary design combines some of the basic principles of the earlier homes with touches of modernization: windows, though still narrow, have been elongated; roofs are constructed of bright tiles; pretty patios have been added; and doorways and balconies present an ornamental face to the world beyond.

dazzling, and sunglasses are essential. Many of the hotels have facilities on or near the beach, and refreshments are never far away. **Amenities:** food and drink; toilets. **Best for:** swimming; walking; sunset. ⊠ *J.E. Irausquin Blvd., north of Manchebo Beach.*

Fisherman's Huts (*Hadicurari*). North of the Marriott is a windsurfer's haven with good swimming conditions and a decent, slightly rocky, white-sand beach. Take a picnic lunch (tables are available) and watch the elegant purple, aqua, and orange sails struggle in the wind. **Amenities:** none. **Best for:** swimming; windsurfing. ⊠ *North of Aruba Marriott Resort, Palm Beach.*

Grapefield Beach. Just North of Boca Grandi on the Eastern coast, a sweep of blinding-white sand in the shadow of cliffs and boulders is marked by an anchor-shape memorial dedicated to seamen. Pick sea grapes from January to June. Swim at your own risk; the waves here can be rough. This is not a popular tourist beach, so finding a quiet spot is almost guaranteed, but the downside of this is a complete lack of facilities or nearby refreshments. **Amenities:** none. **Best for:** solitude. ⊠ *Southwest of San Nicolas, on east end.*

Malmok Beach (*Boca Catalina*). On the northwestern shore, this small, nondescript beach borders shallow waters that stretch 300 yards from shore. There are no snack or refreshment stands here, but shade is available under the thatched umbrellas. It's the perfect place to learn to windsurf. Right off the coast here is a favorite haunt for divers and snorkelers—the wreck of the German ship *Antilla*, scuttled in 1940. **Amenities:** none. **Best for:** solitude; snorkeling. ⊠ *At end of J.E. Irausquin Blvd., Malmokweg.*

Manchebo Beach (*Punta Brabo*). Impressively wide, the white-sand shoreline in front of the Manchebo Beach Resort is where officials turn a blind eye to the occasional topless sunbather. This beach merges with Druif Beach, and most locals use the name Manchebo to refer to both. **Amenities:** food and drink; toilets. **Best for:** swimming. ⊠ *J.E. Irausquin Blvd., at Manchebo Beach Resort.*

Palm Beach. This stretch runs from the Westin Aruba Resort, Spa & Casino to the Marriott's Aruba Ocean Club. It's the center of Aruban tourism, offering good swimming, sailing, and other water sports. In some spots you might find a variety of shells that are great to collect, but not as much fun to step on barefoot—bring sandals. **Amenities:** food and drink; toilets; water sports. **Best for:** swimming; walking. ⊠ *J.E. Irausquin Blvd., between Westin Aruba Resort and Marriott's Aruba Ocean Club.*

FAMILY **Rodger's Beach.** Near Baby Beach on the island's eastern tip, this beautiful curving stretch of sand is only slightly marred by its proximity to the tanks and towers of the now defunct oil refinery at the bay's far side. Swimming conditions are excellent here. The snack bar at the water's edge has beach-equipment rentals and a shop. Drive around the refinery perimeter to get here. **Amenities:** food and drink; water sports. **Best for:** swimming. ⊠ *Next to Baby Beach, on east end, San Nicolas.*

4

WHERE TO EAT

Arubans tend to eat their main meal at lunchtime, so feel free to follow suit and save money by trying the lunch menus at the better restaurants. Be sure to try such Aruban specialties as *pan bati* (a mildly sweet bread that resembles a pancake) and *keshi yena* (a baked concoction of Gouda or Edam cheese, spices, and meat or seafood in a rich brown sauce). On Sunday you may have a hard time finding a restaurant outside a hotel that's open for lunch, and many restaurants are closed for dinner on Sunday or Monday. Reservations are essential for dinner in high season.

Aruba Gastronomic Association (*AGA*). To give visitors an affordable way to sample the island's eclectic cuisine, the Aruba Gastronomic Association has created a Dine-Around program involving more than 20 island restaurants. Here's how it works: you can buy tickets for three dinners ($120 per person), five dinners ($200), seven dinners ($276), or five breakfasts or lunches plus four dinners ($236). Dinners include an appetizer, an entrée, dessert, coffee or tea, and a service charge (except when a restaurant is a "VIP member," in which case $38 will be deducted from your final bill instead). Other programs, such as gift certificates and coupons for dinners at the association's VIP member restaurants, are also available. You can buy Dine-Around tickets using the association's online order form, through travel agents, or at the De Palm Tours sales desk in many hotels. Participating restaurants and conditions change frequently; the AGA website has the latest information. ⊠ *Rooi Santo 21, Noord* 🕾 *297/586–1266, 914/595–4788 in U.S.* ⊕ *www.arubadining.com.*

What to Wear. Even the finest restaurants require at most a jacket for men and a sundress for women. If you plan to eat in the open air, remember to bring along insect repellent—the mosquitoes sometimes get unruly.

$$$$ ╳ **2 Fools and a Bull.** Friends Paul and Fred have teamed up to offer an
INTERNATIONAL evening of culinary entertainment that's more like a fun dinner party than a mere dining experience. Guests are assembled and introduced to one another. Then the evening's meal is explained before everyone

sits down at the U-shape communal dinner table for a five-course culinary adventure. The menu changes daily and there's a selection of suggested wine pairings available by the glass. This isn't a cheap eating-out experience, but it'll certainly be a cherished memory of Aruba. This is one of the few restaurants on the island where reservations are advisable at least a few weeks in advance. ■ TIP → Be sure to state any dietary restrictions in advance. $ *Average main: $90* ✉ *Palm Beach 17, Noord* ☎ *297/586–7177* ⊕ *www.2foolsandabull. com* ⌖ *Reservations essential* ☉ *Closed weekends.*

$$$ ✕ **Aqua Grill.** Aficionados flock here to enjoy a wide selection of seafood
SEAFOOD and the largest raw bar on the island. The atmosphere is casual, with a distinctly New England feel. Things can get a little noisy in the open dining room, especially when kids are underfoot (which is often), but a few sips of wine from the extensive list should help numb the effect. Maine lobster and Alaskan king crab legs are available, but why try the usual fare when you can order the Fisherman's Pot, which is filled with scallops, monkfish, and other seafood? The wood grill serves up great low-cal dishes, including mahimahi. There are cheaper restaurants that serve better-prepared seafood meals on the island, but the variety of offerings here sets it apart. The restaurant is an AGA VIP member. $ *Average main: $32* ✉ *J.E. Irausquin Blvd. 374, Palm Beach* ☎ *297/586–5900* ⊕ *www.aqua-grill.com* ☉ *No lunch.*

$$$ ✕ **Buccaneer.** Imagine you're in a sunken ship where sharks, barracudas,
ECLECTIC and grouper swim past the (rectangular) portholes. That's what you can
FAMILY find at Buccaneer, a restaurant dominated by a 10,000 gallon aquarium and where each table has its own individual aquarium. The chefs prepare passable but not especially noteworthy fare. The catch of the day is usually a safe bet. The interior and exterior theme park feel and kitsch makes this place great for those with kids but may prove to be a bit too much for those without. The restaurant has been operating for over 30 years and participates in AGA's Dine-Around program. $ *Average main: $29* ✉ *Gasparito 11 C, Noord* ☎ *297/586–6172* ⊕ *www. buccaneeraruba.com* ☉ *Closed Sun. No lunch.*

$$ ✕ **Carpe Diem.** Beautifully presented food, great service and wonderful
ECLECTIC ocean views all make this establishment a worthwhile dining choice.
Fodor's Choice Even though the large dining space is open to the ocean, the whimsical
★ interior design provides an equally smile-inducing distraction. The tuna and salmon tartare is an appetizer worth ordering, and the catch of the day in a lemon herb sauce never disappoints. Instagramers should have their camera phones as the courses arrive. The restaurant is on the marina opposite the Renaissance. $ *Average main: $28* ✉ *L.G. Smith Blvd 11, Oranjestad* ☎ *297/562–3499* ⊕ *www.carpediem.aw* ☉ *Closed Sun.*

$ ✕ **DeliFrance.** If there's a breakfast haven in Aruba, this is it. Skip the
DELI usual hotel routine, and head over to this popular deli for a selection of freshly baked bagels and egg dishes galore. DeliFrance is also an excellent choice for lunch, when you can choose from dozens of sandwiches—fillings ranging from the comforting (ham and cheese) to the downright unusual (steak tartare). Save room for one of the hearty desserts, such as sugar waffles with whipped cream and strawberries or a French apple turnover. For java lovers, the coffee alone may be worth

the trip. Takeaway sandwiches are a great idea for a hotel room snack later in the day. $ *Average main: $11* ✉ *Certified Mega Mall, L.G. Smith Blvd. 150, Druif Beach* ☎ *297/588–6006* ⊕ *www.delifrance-aruba.com* ⊗ *No dinner.*

$$$$
STEAKHOUSE
FAMILY

✕ **El Gaucho Argentine Grill.** Faux-leather-bound books, tulip-top lamps, wooden chairs, and tile floors decorate this Argentina-style steak house, which has been in business since 1977. The key here is meat served in mammoth portions (think 16-ounce steaks) with a range of sides. A welcome feature is a children's playroom, which allows adults to dine while the kids are entertained with videos and games. Be warned, though: even with the kids out of sight, the noise level can still be a bit high in this busy restaurant. $ *Average main: $40* ✉ *Wilhelminastraat 80, Oranjestad* ☎ *297/582–3677* ⊕ *www. elgaucho-aruba.com* ⊗ *No lunch Sun.*

$$$$
SEAFOOD
Fodor'sChoice
★

✕ **Flying Fishbone.** This friendly, relaxed beach restaurant is well off the beaten path in Savaneta, so be sure to have a map in the car. You can dine with your toes in the water or enjoy your meal on the wooden deck. The emphasis here is on fresh seafood—beautifully presented on colorful beds of vegetables—but there are good choices for landlubbers, too. The shrimp, shiitake, and blue-cheese casserole is a tried-and-true favorite kept on the menu to keep the regulars happy. This place pulls a crowd year-round. ■ TIP➔ **Arrive early for dinner to get a good table nearer the water.** $ *Average main: $34* ✉ *Savaneta 344, Savaneta* ☎ *297/584–2506* ⊕ *www.flyingfishbone.com* ⚓ *Reservations essential.*

$$$
STEAKHOUSE

✕ **French Steakhouse.** You can hear someone say "ooh-la-la" whenever a sizzling steak is served here. People come from all over the island, which means the lines are often out the door. Classical music plays in the background as the friendly staff serves hearty meat entrées, fresh tuna or grouper, and some vegetarian dishes. A five-course prix-fixe option is available seven nights a week. This eatery participates in AGA's Dine-Around program. $ *Average main: $30* ✉ *Manchebo Beach Resort, J.E. Irausquin Blvd. 55, Manchebo Beach* ☎ *297/582–3444* ⊕ *www. manchebo.com/steakhouse* ⊗ *No lunch.*

$$$
CARIBBEAN
Fodor'sChoice
★

✕ **Gasparito Restaurant & Art Gallery.** You can find this enchanting hideaway in a *cunucu* (country) house in Noord, not far from the hotels. Dine indoors, where works by local artists are showcased on softly lighted walls, or on the outdoor patio. Either way, the service is excellent. The Aruban specialties—pan bati, keshi yena—are feasts for the eye as well as the palate. The standout dish is the Gasparito chicken; the sauce recipe was passed down from the owner's ancestors and features seven special ingredients, including brandy, white wine, and pineapple juice. (The rest, they say, are secret.) Gasparito is an AGA Dine-Around member. $ *Average main: $25* ✉ *Gasparito 3, Noord* ☎ *297/586–7044* ⊕ *www.gasparito.com* ⊗ *Closed Sun. No lunch.*

$$
CARIBBEAN
Fodor'sChoice
★

✕ **Gostoso.** Locals adore the magical mixture of Portuguese, Aruban, and international dishes on offer at this consistently excellent establishment. The decor walks a fine line between kitschy and cozy, but the atmosphere is relaxed and informal and outdoor seating is available. The *bacalhau* vinaigrette (dressed salted cod) is a delightful Portuguese appetizer and pairs nicely with most of the Aruban dishes on the menu. Meat lovers are

4

sure to enjoy the Venezuelan mixed grill, which includes a 14-ounce steak and chorizo accompanied by local sides like fried plantain. $ *Average main: $23* ⊠ *Caya Ing Roland H. Lacle 12, Oranjestad* ☏ *297/588–0053* ⊕ *www.gostosoaruba.com* ⬧ *Reservations essential* ☽ *Closed Mon.*

$$$$
STEAKHOUSE
Fodor'sChoice
★

✕ **L.G. Smith's Steak & Chop House.** A study in teak, cream, and black, this fine steak house offers some of the best beef on the island. Subdued lighting and cascading water create a pleasant atmosphere, and the view over L.G. Smith Boulevard to the harbor makes for an exceptional dining experience. The menu features high-quality cuts of meat, all superbly prepared. The casino is steps away if you fancy some slots after dinner. $ *Average main: $37* ⊠ *Renaissance Aruba Beach Resort & Casino, L.G. Smith Blvd. 82, Oranjestad* ☏ *297/523–6195* ⊕ *www. lgsmiths.com* ☽ *No lunch.*

$$$
EUROPEAN
Fodor'sChoice
★

✕ **Madame Janette.** Named after a local chili pepper (and not a local temptress), this restaurant seems haunted by the spirit of Auguste Escoffier. Large portions and cream sauces are well represented on the menu, and hollandaise and cheese sauces abound. Presentation is an essential part of the dining experience here, and entrées rise majestically off their plates. The best part is that everything tastes as good as it looks, so those looking for a more traditional but exquisite meal will be very pleased. Try the lamb or beef rotisseries with one of the special sauces; if you're in the mood for something lighter, there are tasty salads. For an overwhelming finish, top off your meal with a sundae that billows over the edges of a massive champagne glass. Savor each course in the outdoor pebble garden, where tabletop candles cast a soft glow. Note that you may feel a bit hot in the outdoor area given the relative lack of breezes. $ *Average main: $33* ⊠ *Cunucu Abao 37, Cunucu Abao* ☏ *297/587–0184* ⊕ *www. madamejanette.info* ⬧ *Reservations essential* ☽ *No lunch. Closed Sun.*

$$$
ECLECTIC
Fodor'sChoice
★

✕ **Marandi.** This seaside restaurant is simultaneously cozy and chic. Tables are tucked under a giant thatched roof by the water's edge. The emphasis here is on Caribbean-influenced dishes using only fresh fish. Popular options include mushroom risotto and the fresh catch of the day. There's a good selection of wines on offer and the waiter will happily suggest the perfect pairing for every course. This is a popular place for romantic occasions and deservedly so. If possible book an early dinner and have sunset cocktails while watching the sun go down and the neighborhood fish swimming about right next to your table. The location is a bit out of the way but worth it for the view and excellent food. Mosquitoes can be a problem depending on the time of year, so bring repellent with you or ask the server. $ *Average main: $26* ⊠ *Bucutiweg 50, Oranjestad* ☏ *297/582–0157* ⊕ *www.marandi-aruba. com* ⬧ *Reservations essential* ☽ *No lunch.*

$$$$
ECLECTIC

✕ **Papiamento.** The Ellis family converted its 126-year-old manor into a bistro with an atmosphere that is elegant, intimate, and always romantic. You can feast in the dining room, which is filled with antiques, or outdoors on the terrace by the pool (sitting on plastic patio chairs covered in fabric). The chefs mix continental and Caribbean cuisines to produce sumptuous seafood and meat dishes. Those seeking a bit of novelty can order one of the hot stone dishes, which come to the table sizzling. Service is unhurried, so don't come here if you're in a rush.

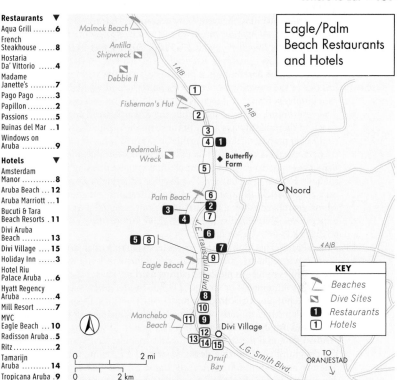

Eagle/Palm
Beach Restaurants
and Hotels

4

Noord

KEY

⟋	*Beaches*
◥	*Dive Sites*
1	*Restaurants*
①	*Hotels*

Malmok Beach

Antilla
Shipwreck

Debbie II

Fisherman's Hut

Pedernalis
Wreck

◆ Butterfly
Farm

Palm Beach

Eagle Beach

Manchebo
Beach

Divi Village

Druif
Bay

TO
ORANJESTAD

0   2 mi

0   2 km

$ *Average main: $32* ✉ *Washington 61, Noord* ☎ *297/586–4544* ⊕ *pa-piamentoaruba.com* ⌖ *Reservations essential* ⊘ *Closed Mon. No lunch.*

$$$$
FRENCH
Fodor'sChoice
★

✕ **Papillon.** Despite being inspired by Henri Charrière's escape from Devil's Island, the food here couldn't be more removed from bread and water. The owners use the famous story as a metaphor for a culinary journey to freedom as classic French cuisine is transformed with Caribbean flair. There are whimsical prison touches throughout the restaurant and especially in the washrooms. The menu includes classics like beef bourguignon but isn't afraid to offer more adventurous dishes such as a standout crispy duck breast served with passion fruit and chocolate. Whatever you order, you'll find the presentation is always impeccable. $ *Average main: $32* ✉ *Irausquin Blvd. 348A, The Village, Palm Beach* ☎ *297/586–5400* ⊕ *www.papillonaruba.com* ⌖ *Reservations essential.*

$$$$
CARIBBEAN
Fodor'sChoice
★

✕ **Passions on the Beach.** Every night the Amsterdam Manor Beach Resort (⇨ *Where to Stay*) transforms the area of Eagle Beach in front of the hotel into a magical and romantic beach dining room. Tiki torches illuminate the white sand, and the linen-covered tables are within inches of the lapping water. Dine on imaginative dishes that are as beautiful as they are delicious. The huge tropical watermelon salad presented in a watermelon half is refreshing and whets the appetite with a slight chili heat. In this "reef cuisine," the main courses lean toward seafood, though meat lovers also are indulged. After dinner, relax with your toes in the sand and enjoy the best show that nature has to offer over signature cocktails. $ *Average main: $32 ⊠ J.E. Irausquin Blvd. 252, Eagle Beach, Eagle Beach ☎ 297/527–1100 ⊕ www.passions-restaurant-aruba.com ⩘ Reservations essential.*

$$$
ECLECTIC
Fodor'sChoice
★

✕ **Pinchos Grill & Bar.** Built on a pier, this casual spot with only 16 tables has one of the most romantic settings on the island. At night the restaurant glimmers from a distance as hundreds of lights reflect off the water. The restaurant's name comes from the Spanish word for a skewered snack so there are always a few of those on the menu. Guests can watch as the chef prepares delectable meals on the grill in his tiny kitchen while owners, Anabela and Robby, keeps diners comfortable and happy. The fish-cakes appetizer with a pineapple-mayonnaise dressing is a marriage made in heaven. The bar area is great for enjoying ocean breezes over an evening cocktail, and there is live entertainment every weekend. Many visitors consider a visit to Pinchos an essential part of the Aruba experience. $ *Average main: $24 ⊠ L.G. Smith Blvd. 7, Oranjestad ☎ 297/583–2666 ⊗ No lunch.*

$$
ECLECTIC

✕ **Qué Pasa?.** This funky eatery serves as something of an art gallery–restaurant where diners can appreciate the colorful, eclectic works of local artists while enjoying a meal or savoring a drink. The terra-cotta outdoor spaces are illuminated by strings of lights. Inside, jewel-color walls serve as an eye-popping backdrop for numerous paintings. Despite the name, there isn't a Mexican dish on the menu, which includes sashimi, rack of lamb, and fish dishes (they are especially good). Everything is done with Aruban flair, and the staff is helpful and friendly. Save room for one of the delightfully comforting desserts, such as a brownie with ice cream. The bar area is fun, too. $ *Average main: $22 ⊠ Wilhelminastraat 18, Oranjestad ☎ 297/583–4888 ⊕ www.quepasaaruba.com ⊗ No lunch.*

$$$$
CARIBBEAN

✕ **Ruinas del Mar.** Locally cut limestone walls, lush gardens, black swans and falling water make this one of the most stylish restaurants on the island. Try to get a seat near the torch-lit koi pond. The food is good, not exceptional, but the surroundings make this establishment well worth a visit. The Sunday champagne brunch buffet is a wonder and may be the best bet in terms of price. A 15% service charge is added to your check. $ *Average main: $39 ⊠ Hyatt Regency Aruba Beach Resort & Casino, J.E. Irausquin Blvd. 85, Palm Beach ☎ 297/586–1234 ⊗ No lunch. No dinner Sun.*

$$$$
ECLECTIC

✕ **Ventanas del Mar.** Floor-to-ceiling windows provide ample views across the lovely Tierra del Sol golf course and beyond to rolling sand dunes and the sea off the island's western tip. Dining on the intimate terrace amid flickering candles inspires romance. Sandwiches, salads, conch fritters, nachos, and quesadillas fill the midday menu; at night the emphasis is on seafood and meat. Crispy whole red snapper in a sweet-and-sour sauce and crab-and-corn chowder are specialties. The restaurant is an Aruba Gastronomic Association VIP member. $ *Average main: $32 ⊠ Tierra del Sol Resort, Malmokweg ☎ 297/586–7800 ⊕ www.tierradelsol.com/en ⊗ Closed Sun. Apr.–Nov.*

$$$$
INTERNATIONAL

✕ **Windows on Aruba.** Sunset views over the greens to the ocean beyond, live music, and impeccable service make this restaurant in the clubhouse of the Divi golf course one of the most romantic spots on the island.

Menu items include the usual seafood and meat assortment but are exquisitely prepared and beautifully presented. The cauliflower and truffle soup—an excellent starter—reveals an understanding of turning simple ingredients into a complex taste experience. This is one of the better choices for a special evening out on the island. [$] *Average main: $36* ✉ *Divi Village Golf Resort, J.E. Irausquin Blvd. 41, Druif Beach* ☎ *297/730–5017* 🌐 *www.windowsonaruba.com* ✍ *Reservations essential* ⊗ *No lunch weekends.*

WHERE TO STAY

4

Hotels on the island are categorized as low-rise or high-rise and are grouped in two distinct areas along L.G. Smith and J.E. Irausquin boulevards north of Oranjestad. The low-rise properties are closer to the capital, the high-rises in a swath a little farther north. Hotel rates, with the exception of those at a few all-inclusives, generally do not include meals or even breakfast. The larger resorts are destinations unto themselves, with shopping, entertainment, and casinos.

$$ HOTEL FAMILY Fodor's Choice ★

🏨 **Amsterdam Manor Beach Resort.** For an excellent value check out this intimate, family-run hotel with a genuinely friendly staff and an authentic Dutch-Caribbean atmosphere. **Pros:** feels like a European village; very good family restaurant; friendly and helpful staff; minigrocery on-site; modern and airy rooms; public bus stop in front of hotel for easy access to downtown and the high-rise area. **Cons:** across the road from the beach; lacks the boutiques and attractions of a larger hotel; small pool. [$] *Rooms from: $305* ✉ *J.E. Irausquin Blvd. 252, Eagle Beach* ☎ *297/527–1100, 800/932–6509* 🌐 *www.amsterdammanor.com* 🛏 *68 rooms, 4 suites* 🍴 *No meals.*

$ HOTEL FAMILY

🏨 **Aruba Beach Club.** The colonial charm and Dutch hospitality both help keep families coming back year after year. **Pros:** fun, family-friendly atmosphere; great beach; numerous activities; excellent value; lively bars. **Cons:** pool area can be very busy; on-site restaurant is good but a bit pricey; hard to find a quiet spot on the grounds. [$] *Rooms from: $200* ✉ *J.E. Irausquin Blvd. 51–53, Punta Brabo Beach* ☎ *297/582–3000* 🌐 *www.arubabeachclub.net* 🛏 *89 rooms, 42 suites* 🍴 *No meals.*

$$$$ RESORT Fodor's Choice ★

🏨 **Aruba Marriott Resort & Stellaris Casino.** The gentle sound of the surf and splashing waterfalls create the backdrop of this sprawling compound, where everything seems to run smoothly. **Pros:** large rooms; variety of excellent restaurants; great shopping; every imaginable service is conveniently on-site. **Cons:** large, impersonal resort; reception can become gridlocked in peak season. [$] *Rooms from: $569* ✉ *L.G. Smith Blvd. 101, Palm Beach* ☎ *297/586–9000, 800/223–6388* 🌐 *www.marriott.com* 🛏 *388 rooms, 23 suites* 🍴 *No meals.*

$$$ RESORT Fodor's Choice ★

🏨 **Bucuti & Tara Beach Resorts.** An extraordinary beach setting, impeccably understated service, and attention to detail help this elegant Green Globe resort easily outclass anything else on the island. **Pros:** great atmosphere; impeccable service; luxurious without insulating guests from island life; free Wi-Fi throughout; free use of netbooks during stay; no kids means a bit more peace and quiet. **Cons:** beach can get busy, because other hotels share it; little to buy at hotel; no room service. $ *Rooms from: $451* ⊠ *L.G. Smith Blvd. 55B, Eagle Beach* ☎ *297/583–1100* ⊕ *www.bucuti.com* ⇌ *63 rooms, 38 suites, 3 bungalows* ⦿ *Breakfast.*

$$$ ⚀ **Divi Aruba Beach Resort All Inclusive.** The free food and drinks here and
ALL-INCLUSIVE the ability to use the facilities of the adjoining Tamarijn Resort *(⇨ below)*
FAMILY mean you have very little reason to wander far from the idyllic beach location. **Pros:** on wonderful stretch of beach; margarita machines in lobby; common areas feel light and airy; live nightly entertainment. **Cons:** poolside area can get pretty noisy; restaurants are acceptable but not great; rooms could use updating. $ *Rooms from: $638* ⊠ *L.G. Smith Blvd. 93, Manchebo Beach* ☎ *297/582–3300, 800/554–2008* ⊕ *www.diviaruba. com* ⇌ *203 rooms* ⦿ *All-inclusive* ⇱ *5-night minimum.*

$$ ⚀ **Divi Aruba Phoenix Beach Resort.** A breathtaking location, a lively atmo-
RESORT sphere, and relatively reasonable rates make this hotel justifiably popular. **Pros:** great beach; small grocery store on premises; lively crowd at the beach bar. **Cons:** beach can get crowded during peak times; not near major shopping areas. $ *Rooms from: $414* ⊠ *J.E. Irausquin Blvd. 75, Palm Beach* ☎ *297/586–1170* ⊕ *www.diviarubaphoenix.com* ⇌ *60 rooms, 151 1-bedroom suites, 21 2-bedroom suites, 8 3-bedroom suites* ⦿ *No meals.*

$$ ⚀ **Divi Village Golf & Beach Resort.** Although it's just across the road
RESORT from its sister Divi properties, this all-suites version is quieter and more refined. **Pros:** excellent golf course; spacious rooms; lushly landscaped grounds; great savings for being a mere 20 yards from the beach. **Cons:** bit of a hike from some rooms to the lobby; you must cross a busy road to get to the beach; it might be a bit too quiet for some. $ *Rooms from: $309* ⊠ *J.E. Irausquin Blvd. 93, Oranjestad* ☎ *297/583–5000, 297/583–5000* ⊕ *www.divivillage.com* ⇌ *250 suites* ⦿ *Multiple meal plans* ⇱ *3-night minimum.*

$ ⚀ **Holiday Inn Resort Aruba.** This popular, family-oriented package-tour
RESORT resort has three seven-story buildings filled with spacious rooms lining a
FAMILY sugary, palm-dotted shore. **Pros:** affordable; great beachfront location; lots of activities for the kids; hotel was renovated in 2013. **Cons:** lines at reception can make you feel you are back at the airport; restaurants are mediocre at best and service can be a problem. $ *Rooms from: $204* ⊠ *J.E. Irausquin Blvd. 230, Palm Beach* ☎ *297/586–3600, 800/465–4329* ⊕ *www.holidayarubaresort.com* ⇌ *600 rooms, 7 suites* ⦿ *No meals.*

$$$$ ⚀ **Hotel Riu Palace Aruba.** This white wedding cake of a resort tow-
ALL-INCLUSIVE ers over Palm Beach with one 8-story and two 10-story towers. **Pros:** beautiful vistas; drink dispensers in all rooms; large and lively pool area. **Cons:** pool area is always crowded and loud; unimpressive à la carte restaurants; standard Riu interior decor is a bit out of place for an island destination. $ *Rooms from: $674* ⊠ *J.E. Irausquin Blvd. 79, Palm Beach* ☎ *297/586–3900, 800/345–2782* ⊕ *www.riuaruba.com* ⇌ *450 rooms* ⦿ *All-inclusive.*

$$$$ ⚀ **Hyatt Regency Aruba Beach Resort & Casino.** This 12-acre property is
RESORT popular with families, but honeymooners head here, too, because the resort
FAMILY is big enough to provide quiet, romantic corners. **Pros:** beautiful grounds;
Fodor's Choice great for kids; excellent restaurants. **Cons:** small balconies for a luxury
★ hotel; some rooms are quite a stretch from the beach. $ *Rooms from: $585* ⊠ *J.E. Irausquin Blvd. 85, Palm Beach* ☎ *297/586–1234, 800/554–9288* ⊕ *www.aruba.hyatt.com* ⇌ *342 rooms, 18 suites* ⦿ *No meals.*

Amsterdam Manor Beach Resort

$$$$ RENTAL FAMILY 🏨 **Marriott's Aruba Ocean Club.** First-rate amenities and lavishly decorated villas have made this time-share the talk of the island. **Pros:** relaxed atmosphere; feels more like a home than a hotel room; excellent beach. **Cons:** bit of a hike to restaurants at hotel next door; pricey; attracts large families, so kids are everywhere. [$] *Rooms from: $675* ✉ *L.G. Smith Blvd. 99, Palm Beach* ☎ *297/586–2641* 🌐 *www.marriott.com* 🛏 *93 rooms, 213 suites* 🍴 *No meals.*

$ RESORT FAMILY 🏨 **Mill Resort & Suites.** A short walk from the beach, this low-rise resort is laid out around a busy pool and bar area, and the open-air Mediterranean-style lobby has free coffee day and night. **Pros:** entire compound has an intimate feel; lively bar area; theme nights are fun; numerous activities to keep kids amused. **Cons:** not on the beach; pool area can be busy and noisy; rates are not the steal they used to be; staff could be friendlier. [$] *Rooms from: $258* ✉ *J.E. Irausquin Blvd. 330, Palm Beach* ☎ *297/586–7700* 🌐 *www.millresort.com* 🛏 *64 studios, 121 suites* 🍴 *Multiple meal plans.*

$ HOTEL FAMILY Fodor's Choice ★ 🏨 **MVC Eagle Beach.** What started as a vacation facility for the visiting families of Dutch marines is now a great bargain hotel across from Eagle Beach. **Pros:** unbeatable price; popular restaurant with food at affordable prices; since the main language is Dutch, you feel that you're someplace other than South Florida here; very short walk to beach; friendly and helpful staff; attentive staff. **Cons:** lacks all the amenities of larger resorts; not for those who want to be away from kids. [$] *Rooms from: $205* ✉ *J.E. Irausquin Blvd. 240, Eagle Beach* ☎ *297/587–0110* 🌐 *www.mvceaglebeach.com* 🛏 *16 rooms, 3 suites* 🍴 *No meals.*

$$$$
RESORT
FAMILY
Fodor's Choice
★

🏨 **Radisson Aruba Resort & Casino.** The lavish rooms at this 14-acre resort are appointed with colonial West Indian–style furniture, and their large balconies overlook the ocean or tropical gardens. **Pros:** rooms feel homey; top-notch fitness center; one of the best spas on the island; free high-speed Internet in rooms. **Cons:** restaurants are good but not great; some rooms are on the small side and don't seem worth the cost. $ *Rooms from: $661* ⊠ *J.E. Irausquin Blvd. 81, Palm Beach* ☎ *297/586–6555* ⊕ *www.radisson.com* ⇲ *321 rooms, 34 suites* ⊙ *No meals.*

$$$
RESORT
Fodor's Choice
★

🏨 **Renaissance Aruba Resort & Casino.** This landmark property right on the port offers guests the best of both worlds—a short walk to the best shopping on the island and access to a beautiful private beach via a short boat ride from the hotel lobby. **Pros:** in the heart of the downtown shopping district; lobby and shopping areas are always lively; pool area offers an unmatched view of the port; free access to private island with beaches and tame flamingos. **Cons:** rooms overlooking the atrium can be a bit claustrophobic; beach is off-site; hard to find a quiet spot; no hotel grounds; no balconies in downtown section. $ *Rooms from: $397* ⊠ *L.G. Smith Blvd. 82, Oranjestad* ☎ *297/583–6000, 800/421–8188* ⊕ *www.renaissancearuba.com* ⇲ *287 rooms, 269 suites* ⊙ *No meals.*

$$$$
RESORT

🏨 **Ritz-Carlton Aruba.** Aruba's newest resort provides all the luxuries associated with the Ritz-Carlton brand. **Pros:** absolute luxury; two pools so they never feel crowded; 24-hour room service; excellent restaurants on-site. **Cons:** far from downtown shopping at the end of Palm Beach; beach is off-site; lacks the intimate feel of smaller properties. $ *Rooms from: $650* ⊠ *107 L.G. Smith Blvd., Palm Beach* ☎ *297/527–2222* ⊕ *www.ritzcarlton.com/en/properties/aruba* ⇲ *265 rooms, 55 suites* ⊙ *No meals.*

$$$
ALL-INCLUSIVE

🏨 **Tamarijn Aruba All-Inclusive Beach Resort.** An upscale alternative to its sister property, the Divi Aruba (⇨ *above*), this resort is pleasantly laid-back for an all-inclusive. **Pros:** stunning beach; access to the Divi Aruba All Inclusive next door; perfect for families. **Cons:** being right on the beach can mean noise during busy periods; the linear layout means some rooms are quite far from the lobby; Wi-Fi is an additional charge. $ *Rooms from: $614* ⊠ *J.E. Irausquin Blvd. 41, Punta Brabo* ☎ *297/525–5200, 800/554–2008* ⊕ *www.tamarijnaruba.com* ⇲ *216 rooms, 20 suites* ⊙ *All-inclusive* ⊙ *3-night minimum.*

$
RESORT
FAMILY

🏨 **Tropicana Aruba Resort & Casino.** An excellent waterslide, fast-food options, and a nearby supermarket make this complex of self-contained time-share units right across from Eagle Beach a popular choice for families. **Pros:** self-catering can be great for families; Dunkin' Donuts and pizza restaurant on the compound; new supermarket right across the street; price is hard to beat for a hotel so close to the beach. **Cons:** feels like an apartment complex; public areas are noisy and crowded; beach is across a road; despite the attractions for children there are no kids programs available. $ *Rooms from: $191* ⊠ *J.E. Irausquin Blvd. 250, Eagle Beach* ☎ *297/587–9000, 800/835–7193* ⊕ *www.troparuba. com* ⇲ *362 suites* ⊙ *No meals.*

NIGHTLIFE AND THE ARTS

NIGHTLIFE

Unlike many islands, Aruba's nightlife isn't confined to the touristy folkloric shows at hotels. Arubans like to party. They usually start celebrating late, and the action doesn't pick up until around midnight.

BARS

Charlie's Bar. An Aruba institution since 1941, Charlie's is far from most hotels but worth the trip if only for the experience. Expect a raucous and considerably soused crowd of good-natured folks. The food here is good but basic, all the better for padding your stomach before the margaritas, but keep in mind that you may want to arrange a cab ride to this place if you're staying at a distant hotel. ⊠ *Zeppenfeldstraat 56, San Nicolas* ☎ *297/584–5086.*

Iguana Joe's. The reptilian-themed decor is as colorful and creative as the specialty cocktails served here. It's a favorite hangout for those who want to enjoy the view of the port from the second floor balcony. The crowd is primarily tourists during the early evening, and many locals enjoy the laid back vibe on Friday and Saturday nights. ⊠ *Royal Plaza Mall, L.G. Smith Blvd. 94, Oranjestad* ☎ *297/583–9373* ⊕ *www.iguanajoesaruba.com.*

Fodor'sChoice
★ **MooMba Beach Bar.** If you're looking to enjoy a cocktail with your toes in the cool sand, MooMba is your place. Enjoy tropical cocktails under a giant, thatched-roof that shades couches, lounges, and a circular bar. ⊠ *Between Holiday Inn and Marriott Surf Club, J.E. Irausquin Blvd. 230, Palm Beach* ☎ *297/586–5365* ⊕ *www.moombabeach.com.*

Palms Restaurant. With front-row seats to view the green flash—that ray of light that supposedly flicks through the sky as the sun sinks into the ocean—the Palms Restaurant is the perfect spot to enjoy the sunset with a cocktail or two. ⊠ *Hyatt Regency Aruba Beach Resort & Casino, J.E. Irausquin Blvd. 85, Palm Beach* ☎ *297/586–1234.*

Pelican Terrace. Sip creative cocktails, dance around the pool, and grab a late-night snack—perhaps a pizza that's piping hot from the wood-burning oven. Live music every evening makes this a popular nightspot. A busy scene is guaranteed, as most of the other patrons are resort guests enjoying all-inclusive drinks. ⊠ *Divi Aruba Beach Resort, J.E. Irausquin Blvd. 45, Druif Beach* ☎ *297/582–3300* ⊕ *www.diviaruba.com/bars-lounges.*

CASINOS

Aruban casinos offer something for both high and low rollers, as well as live, nightly entertainment in their lounges. Die-hard gamblers may want to look for the largest or the most active casinos, but many simply visit the casino closest to their hotel.

Alhambra Casino. Amid the Spanish-style arches and leaded glass, you can try your luck at blackjack, Caribbean stud poker, three-card poker, roulette, craps, or one of the 300 slot machines that accept American nickels, quarters, and dollars. A casual atmosphere and $5 tables further the welcoming feel. Head to one of the novelty touch-screen machines, each of which has a variety of games. There's also bingo every Saturday, Monday, and Thursday beginning at 1 pm. If you fill your card, you can collect the grand prize of a few hundred dollars—not bad for a $5 investment. Be sure to sign up for the Alhambra Advantage Card, which gives you a point for each dollar you spend—even if you lose at the tables, you can still go home with prizes. Of course, winners can spend their earnings immediately at the many on-site shops. The casino is owned by the Divi Divi resorts, and golf carts run to and from nearby hotels every 15 minutes or so. The slots here open daily at 10 am; gaming tables operate from 6 pm until 4 am. It can get quite smoky sometimes. ⊠ *L.G. Smith Blvd. 47, Oranjestad* ☎ *297/583–5000* ⊕ *www.casinoalhambra.com.*

Crystal Casino. Adorned with Austrian crystal chandeliers and gold-leaf columns, the Renaissance Aruba's glittering casino evokes Monaco's grand establishments. The Salon Privé offers serious gamblers a private room for baccarat, roulette, and high-stakes blackjack. This casino is popular among cruise-ship passengers, who stroll over from the port to watch and play in slot tournaments and bet on sporting events. The Crystal Lounge, which overlooks the betting floor, offers live music along with cocktails. ⊠ *Renaissance Aruba Resort & Casino, L.G. Smith Blvd. 82, Oranjestad* ☎ *297/583–6000.*

Hyatt Regency Casino. Ablaze with neon, this hotel casino is an enormous complex with a Carnival-in-Rio theme. The most popular games here are slots, blackjack, craps, and baccarat. Slots and some other games are available at noon, the dice start rolling at 6 pm, and all other pursuits are open by 8 pm. From 9 pm to 2 am there's live music at the stage near the bar—you'll find it hard to steal away from the pulsating mix of Latin and American tunes. You can register for free dinners and brunches and hotel discounts at the hostess station. The casino is open until 4 am. ⊠ *Hyatt Regency Aruba Beach Resort & Casino, J.E. Irausquin Blvd. 85, Palm Beach* ☎ *297/586–1234* ⊕ *www.aruba.hyatt.com.*

Stellaris Casino. Mirrors on the ceilings reflect the glamorous chandeliers at this 24-hour facility. Take your pick between craps, roulette, Caribbean stud poker, minibaccarat, and superbuck (like blackjack with suits). Every night except Sunday there's a performance by musician Cesar Olarta that may boost your luck. Check in with the casino when you arrive at the hotel and you can get a membership card. If you play high enough stakes at the tables, you can win free meals and other prizes. If not, you can at least get a postcard in the mail offering a special rate on future stays. The hotel offers a 30% discount to those who play at least four hours each day. This is the largest casino on the island. ⊠ *Aruba Marriott Resort, L.G. Smith Blvd. 101, Palm Beach* ☎ *297/586–9000.*

DANCE AND MUSIC CLUBS

Club Hipsz Aruba. Latin flavor and a lively crowd make this slightly out-of-the-way club a new favorite on the island. Thursday night is the time for displaying your karaoke skills, whether real or perceived. The club is nonsmoking. ⊠ *Near Eagle Bowling, Pos Abao* ☎ *297/587–2444.*

Gilligan's. The Radisson's beachside bar puts local bands in the spotlight. The decor and view will make you feel as if you've been shipwrecked on an uncharted tropical isle, albeit one with a fully stocked bar. ⊠ *Radisson Aruba Caribbean Resort, J.E. Irausquin Blvd. 81, Palm Beach* ☏ *297/586–6555.*

Nikky Beach. This upscale hot spot is party central on Friday night. Local bands perform on Sunday. The venue is often booked for special events so call ahead. ⊠ *L.G. Smith Blvd. 2, Oranjestad* ☏ *297/582–0153* ⊕ *www.nikkybeacharuba.com.*

NIGHTLIFE TOURS

Banana Bus. For $45-per-person, you can enjoy a ride in a bus with a 20-foot banana mounted on the roof! But the real fun is that this party bus makes its way to a number of lively, local bars, and five drinks are included in the price. Reservations can be made at your hotel front desk. The bus will pick you up there as well. ⊕ *www.bananabusaruba.com.*

Kukoo Kunuku. To many repeat visitors, this wandering party bus is an integral part of the Aruba experience. Every night except Sunday you can find as many as 40 passengers traveling among three bars from sundown to around midnight. The $65 fee per passenger includes a so-so dinner, some drinks, and pickup at your hotel. The main point is the nonstop entertainment and the chance to make friends with a fun-loving crowd. ☏ *297/586–2010* ⊕ *www.kukookunuku.com.*

THE ARTS

ART GALLERIES

Gasparito Restaurant & Art Gallery. A permanent exhibition by a variety of Aruban artists is featured here ranging from colorful landscapes to more abstract offerings. ⊠ *Gasparito 3, Noord* ☏ *297/586–7044.*

Insight Art Studio. Owner Alida Martinez, a Venezuelan-born artist, likes more-avant-garde displays, so don't expect to find the usual paintings of pastel-color skies here. Inventive works by local and international artists are featured. Martinez's own mixed-media creations juxtapose erotic and religious themes. The space, which includes a studio, is a magnet for the island's art community. Viewing is by appointment only. ⊠ *Paradera Park 215, Paradera* ☏ *297/582–5882.*

ISLAND FESTIVALS

Fodor'sChoice
★

Bon Bini Festival. This year-round folklore event (the name means "welcome" in Papiamento), is held every Tuesday from 6:30 pm to 8:30 pm at Ft. Zoutman in Oranjestad. In the inner courtyard you can check out the Antillean dancers in resplendent costumes, feel the rhythms of the steel drums, browse among the stands displaying local artwork, and sample local food and drink. Admission is usually around $3, but can be as high as $10, depending on what is on offer. ⊠ *Oranjestad.*

Carubbian Festival. Held most Thursdays from 6 to 10 pm, this family-friendly festival turns San Nicolas's Main Street into a party full of Aruban music, street food, culture, and booths selling handicrafts. Hotel packages to the festival, which include round-trip bus transportation, cost about $50. ⊠ *Main St., San Nicolas.*

SHOPS AND SPAS

Duty-free *is* a magical term in the Caribbean—but it's not always accurate. The duty-free shopping zone in Aruba closed several years ago, so the only true duty-free shopping is in the departure area of the airport. (Passengers bound for the United States should be sure to shop before proceeding through U.S. customs in Aruba.) Downtown stores often advertise "duty-free prices," with markdowns of up to 25%, but that doesn't mean comparison shopping should go out the window. Major credit cards are welcome virtually everywhere, U.S. dollars are accepted almost as readily as the local currency, and traveler's checks can be cashed with proof of identity.

Aruba's souvenir and crafts stores are full of Dutch porcelains and figurines, as befits the island's heritage. Dutch cheese is a good buy, as are hand-embroidered linens and any products made from the native aloe vera plant—sunburn cream, face masks, or skin refreshers. Local arts and crafts run toward wood carvings and earthenware emblazoned with "Aruba: One Happy Island" and the like. Since there's no sales tax, the price you see on the tag is usually what you pay. (Large stores in town and at hotels include the value-added tax of 3%, but tiny shops and studios may add it separately.) Don't try to bargain. Arubans consider it rude to haggle, despite what you may hear to the contrary.

AREAS AND MALLS

Alhambra Casino Shopping Arcade. Souvenir shops, boutiques, and fast-food outlets fill the arcade, which is open until midnight. It's attached to the popular casino. ⊠ *L.G. Smith Blvd. 47, Manchebo Beach.*

Caya G.F. Betico Croes. Aruba's chief shopping street, Caya G.F. Betico Croes is a busy thoroughfare and is lined with several shops advertising "duty-free prices" (again, these are not truly duty-free), boutiques, and jewelry stores noted for the aggressiveness of their vendors on cruise-ship days. ⊠ *Oranjestad.*

Dutch Crown Center. This tiny shopping center sandwiched between the major malls is easy to miss, but you shouldn't. You can find good swimwear and jewelry inside. ⊠ *L.G. Smith Blvd. 150(some shops face Havenstraat), Oranjestad.*

Holland Aruba Mall. You'll find a collection of stylish shops such as Kenneth Cole and Perfume Palace, several souvenir shops and decent eateries including an outdoor café here. ⊠ *Havenstraat 6, Oranjestad.*

Palm Beach Plaza. Aruba's newest and largest mall caters to shoppers with an eye for luxury. Stores include Mont Blanc, Ferragamo, Swarovski, and other high-end brands. Dining options range from burgers to sushi, and those seeking entertainment can enjoy a movie at the the mall's megaplex. ⊠ *Palm Beach ⊕ www.palmbeachplaza.com.*

Paseo Herencia. It's all about style at this shopping center, which is just minutes away from the high-rise hotel area. The great bell tower, the nightly dancing-waters shows, and the selection of restaurants pull in shoppers. Offerings include Cuban cigars, the sportswear of Lacoste, Italian denim goods at Moda & Stile, perfumes, cosmetics, and lots of souvenir shops. ⊠ *L.G. Smith Blvd., Palm Beach* ☎ *297/586–6533.*

Port of Call Marketplace. Stores here sell fine jewelry, perfumes, low-priced liquor, batiks, crystal, leather goods, and fashionable clothing. ⊠ *L.G. Smith Blvd. 17, Oranjestad.*

Renaissance Mall. The upscale stores here, which include Guess, Lacoste, and Calvin Klein, have prices that are about the same or more than in the United States. ⊠ *Renaissance Hotel, L.G. Smith Blvd. 82, Oranjestad.*

Renaissance Marketplace. Five minutes from the cruise-ship terminal, the Renaissance Marketplace, also known as Seaport Mall, has more than 120 stores selling merchandise to meet every taste and budget; the Seaport Casino is also here. ⊠ *L.G. Smith Blvd. 82, Oranjestad.*

Royal Plaza Mall. Across from the cruise-ship terminal, the Royal Plaza Mall's pink, gabled building has cafés, a post office (open weekdays 8 to 3:30), and such stores as Nautica, Benetton, and Tommy Hilfiger. There's also a cybercafé. ⊠ *L.G. Smith Blvd. 94, Oranjestad.*

Strada I and Strada II. These pastel-color shopping complexes are in Dutch-style buildings. There are a variety of clothing shops including the ubiquitous Benetton and a branch of the phone company SETAR. ⊠ *Klipstraat and Rifstraat, Oranjestad.*

SPECIALTY STORES

CIGARS

Cigar Emporium. The Cubans come straight from the climate-controlled humidor at Cigar Emporium. Choose from Cohiba, Montecristo, Romeo y Julieta, Partagas, and more. ⊠ *Renaissance Mall, L.G. Smith Blvd. 82, Oranjestad* ☎ *297/582–5479.*

CLOTHING

Alivio. Whether you're seeking something for just walking around town or for dressing up for dinner, you can find the right shoe in this Oranjestad shop. Look for Birkenstock from Germany, Piedro and Wolky from Holland, and Mephisto from France. Men's, women's, and children's shoes are all available. ⊠ *Steenweg 12-1, Oranjestad.*

Colombia Moda. The lingerie sold here is made of high-quality microfiber fabrics. ⊠ *Wilhelminastraat 19, Oranjestad* ☎ *297/582–3460.*

Extreme Sports. Invest in a set of in-line skates or a boogie board, or pick up a backpack, bathing suit, or pair of reef walkers in funky shades at this hip sports shop. ⊠ *Royal Plaza Mall, L.G. Smith Blvd. 94, Oranjestad* ☎ *297/583–7105.*

Fodor'sChoice **Wulfsen & Wulfsen.** One of the most highly regarded clothing stores in
★ Aruba and the Netherlands Antilles, Wulfsen & Wulfsen carries elegant suits for men and linen cocktail dresses for women. It's also a great place to buy Bermuda shorts. ⊠ *Caya G.F. Betico Croes 52, Oranjestad* ☎ *297/582–3823.*

HANDICRAFTS

Artistic Boutique. This boutique is known for its Giuseppe Armani figurines from Italy, usually sold at a 20% discount; Aruban hand-embroidered linens; gold and silver jewelry; and porcelain and pottery from Spain. ⊠ *L.G. Smith Blvd. 90–92, Oranjestad* ☎ *297/588–2468* ⊠ *Holiday Inn Resort Aruba, J.E. Irausquin Blvd. 230, Palm Beach* ☎ *297/583–3383.*

Creative Hands. There's an interesting selection of porcelain and ceramic miniatures of *cunucu* (country) houses and divi-divi trees, but the store's real draw is its exquisite Japanese dolls. ⊠ *Socotorolaan 5, Oranjestad* ☎ *297/583–5665.*

El Bohio. You'll be charmed by El Bohio's wooden-hut displays holding Arawak-style pottery, Dutch shoes, and wind chimes. You can also find classic leather handbags. ⊠ *Port of Call Marketplace, L.G. Smith Blvd. 17, Oranjestad* ☎ *297/582–9178.*

Fodor'sChoice ★ **The Mask.** Come here for intriguing souvenirs. Buds from the *mopa mopa* tree are boiled to form a resin, which is colored using vegetable dyes, then stretched by hand and mouth. Tiny pieces are cut and layered to form intricate designs—these are truly unusual gifts. ⊠ *Paseo Herencia, J.E. Irausquin Blvd. 382-A, Local C017, Palm Beach* ☎ *297/596–2900.*

Tropical Wave. Clothes from Aruba and Indonesia, hand-painted mobiles, and bamboo wind chimes are among the goodies at Tropical Wave. ⊠ *Port of Call Marketplace, L.G. Smith Blvd. 17, Oranjestad* ☎ *297/582–1905.*

JEWELRY

Colombian Emeralds. If green fire is your passion, Colombian Emeralds has a dazzling array. There are also fine European watches. ⊠ *Renaissance Mall, L.G. Smith Blvd. 82, Oranjestad* ☎ *297/583–6238.*

Diamonds International. For all that glitters, head to Diamonds International. ⊠ *Port of Call Marketplace, L.G. Smith Blvd. 17, Oranjestad* ☎ *800/515–3935* ⊕ *www.diamondsinternational.com.*

Kenro Jewelers. An island institution, the company has restructured and opened a new large store. On offer are bracelets and necklaces from Ramon Leopard; jewelry by Arando, Micheletto, and Blumei; and various watches. ⊠ *St. Cruz 115-B, Santa Cruz* ☎ *297/585–8909.*

PERFUMES

Aruba Trading Company. For perfumes, cosmetics, men's and women's clothing, and leather goods (including Bally shoes), stop in at Aruba Trading Company, which has been in business since the 1930s. ⊠ *Caya G.F. Betico Croes 12, Oranjestad* ☎ *297/582–2602.*

J.L. Penha & Sons. A venerated name in Aruba, J.L. Penha sells high-end perfumes and cosmetics. It stocks such brands as Boucheron, Cartier, Dior, and Givenchy. ⊠ *Caya G.F. Betico Croes 11/13, Oranjestad* ☎ *297/582–4160, 297/582–4161.*

Little Switzerland. This Caribbean retail giant is the place to go for brand-name men's and women's fragrances, as well as china, crystal, and fine tableware. ⊠ *Royal Plaza Mall, L.G. Smith Blvd. 94, Oranjestad* ☎ *297/583–4057.*

Weitnauer. You can find specialty Lenox items as well as a wide range of fragrances here. ⊠ *Caya G.F. Betico Croes 29, Oranjestad* ☎ *297/582–2790.*

SPAS

Intermezzo Spa. This full-service spa offers a range of treatments at some of the best prices on the island—almost all 60-minute treatments are under $100. Earth tones and a vaguely Asian feel set the stage for pure relaxation. The aromatherapy, deep-tissue, and acupressure massages are especially popular. In cases where couples can't be accommodated because of space or staffing limitations, a shuttle will whisk them off to the spa's branch at the nearby Mill Resort. When the intense Aruba sun plays havoc with delicate skin there's a "nourishing wrap," which promises to return suppleness and moisture using locally grown aloe and a custom blend of ingredients. ⊠ *Bucuti & Tara Beach Resorts, L.G. Smith Blvd. 55B, Eagle Beach* ☎ *297/583–1100* ☞ *$85, 60-min massage. $260 half-day spa packages. Hair salon, hot tub. Gym with: Cardiovascular machines, free weights. Services: Aromatherapy, body wraps, facials, massage.*

Larimar Spa and Salon. The expansive oceanfront spa at the Radisson offers possibly the most complete spa experience on the island. The bamboo and pastel interior has everything from hydrotherapy to a full workout and an almost limitless list of pampering options. The rum-and-aloe massage uses two of the island's most loved products to create 80 minutes of pure bliss. All the usual massage options are here as well as some unique offerings such as the tiger clam–shell and mango massage. The "I Deserve It!" package offers four hours of treatments and a delicious spa lunch. ⊠ *Radisson Aruba Resort & Casino, J.E. Irausquin Blvd. 81, Palm Beach* ☎ *297/526–6053* ☞ *$125, 50-min massage. $352 half-day spa packages. Hair salon, hot tub, sauna, steam room. Gym with: Cardiovascular machines, free weights, weight-training equipment. Services: Aromatherapy, body wraps, facials, hydrotherapy, massage, Vichy shower. Classes and programs: Aqua-aerobics, cycling, Pilates, spinning, yoga.*

Nafanny Spa. Massage therapist Fanny Lampe's home and yard in Alto Vista provide a peaceful and picturesque backdrop for the pure relaxation to come. Thai, Swedish, bamboo, and hot-stone massages are all on offer as are various treatments including a 90-minute wine-therapy session and numerous facial treatments using soothing botanicals designed to ease away impurities and stress lines. The location is a bit remote but the tranquil setting makes that something of an advantage. Fanny will often pick up clients at their resort. Daily yoga classes are also offered. Though not offered as a package, customized half- and full-day spa bundles can be created. Nafanny Spa isn't the fanciest on the island, but the individual attention is unbeatable and so are the prices. ⊠ *Alto Vista 39F, Noord* ☎ *297/586–3007* ⊕ *www. nafanny.com* ☞ *$70, 50-min Swedish massage. Services: Aromatherapy, body wraps, facials, massage, yoga.*

Okeanos. The ocean provides the backdrop for this spa in the Renaissance, which has its own massage cove that seems a world apart from the rest of the resort. Outdoor massages and showers help to bring the calming effects of nature into the treatments. In addition to the usual assortment of massages and wraps, the spa also offers both anti-cellulite and anti-aging treatments. There are a huge number of packages available including one that combines Swedish massage with a meal served by your own butler. Pampering doesn't get much better than this. There are also optional packages to use the spa services at the Cove Spa located on the resort's private island. ⊠ *Renaissance Aruba Resort & Casino, L.G. Smith Blvd. 82, Palm Beach* ☏ *297/583–6000* ⊕ *www. renaissancearubaspa.com* ⌁ *$140, 75-min massage. $525 day-spa packages. Hair salon, hot tub, sauna, steam room. Gym with: Cardiovascular machines, free weights, weight-training equipment. Services: Aromatherapy, body wraps, facials, hydrotherapy, massage.*

ZoiA Spa. It's all about indulgence at the Hyatt's upscale spa. Gentle music and the scent of botanicals make the world back home fade into the background. Newly arrived visitors to the island can opt for the jet lag massage that combines reflexology and aromatherapy, before getting into the swing of things. Those with the budget and time for a full day of relaxation can opt for the Serene package, and there's even a mother-to-be package available. Island brides can avail themselves of a full menu of beauty services ranging from botanical facials (using local ingredients) to a full makeup job for the big day. The Pure High Tea package offers a delicious assortment of snacks and teas along with an hour of treatments. ⊠ *Hyatt Regency Aruba Beach Resort & Casino, J.E. Irausquin Blvd. 85, Palm Beach* ☏ *297/586–1234* ⊕ *www. aruba.hyatt.com* ⌁ *$145, 60-min massage. $575 day-spa packages. Hair salon, hot tub, sauna, steam room. Services: Aromatherapy, body wraps, facials, hydrotherapy, massage.*

SPORTS AND ACTIVITIES

On Aruba you can participate in every conceivable water sport, as well as play tennis and golf or go on a fine hike through Arikok National Wildlife Park.

BIKING

Rancho Notorious. Exciting mountain-biking tours are available here. The 2.5-hour tour to the Alto Vista Chapel and the California Lighthouse are $50 ($75 with bike rental). ⊠ *Boroncana, Noord* ☏ *297/586–0508* ⊕ *www.ranchonotorious.com.*

DAY SAILS

If you plan to take a cruise around the island, keep in mind that the trade winds can make the waters choppy and that catamaran rides are much smoother than those on single-hull boats. Sucking on a peppermint or ginger candy may soothe your queasy stomach; avoid boating

A bouquet of colorful reefs can be explored in the waters of Aruba.

with an empty or overly full stomach. Moonlight cruises cost about $40 per person. There is also a variety of snorkeling, dinner and dancing, and sunset party cruises to choose from, priced from $30 to $60 per person. Many of the smaller operators work out of their homes; they often offer to pick you up (and drop you off) at your hotel or meet you at a particular hotel pier.

Mi Dushi. This romantic, two-masted ship ("My Sweetheart") offers daytime snorkeling trips that include breakfast, lunch, and drinks for $59 per person. It also offers popular sunset happy-hour cruises. ✉ *Turibana Plaza, Noord 124, Noord* ☎ *297/586–2010* ⊕ *www.midushi.com.*

Octopus Sailing Charters. The drinks flow freely on Octopus's trimaran. It holds about 20 people for a three-hour afternoon sail, which costs $35. ✉ *Pelican Pier, Palm Beach* ☎ *297/586–4281* ⊕ *www.octopusaruba.com.*

Red Sail Sports. Red Sail can arrange everything for your fishing trip. Choose between four catamarans, including the 70-foot *Rumba.* They offer a popular sunset sail, including drinks and a lively atmosphere for $49 per person; the dinner cruise package includes a three-course meal and open bar for $99. Red Sail Sports also has locations at the Hyatt and Marriott hotels. And though it's best known for its diving trips, Red Sail will also take you parasailing, and they offer courses for children and others new to scuba diving. An introductory class costs about $95. ✉ *J.E. Irausquin Blvd. 348-A, Palm Beach* ☎ *297/586–1603, 305/454–2538 in U.S.* ⊕ *www.redsailaruba.com.*

Tranquilo Charters Aruba. Operated by Captain Hagedoorn, Tranquilo offers entertaining cruises, including a six-hour tour to the south side of the island for $75. Snorkeling equipment and free lessons are included in the package, and so is the very good "mom's Dutch pea soup" served with lunch (also included). The owner's little dog scampering about the deck with a life jacket on is an added bonus. ⊠ *Renaissance Marina, Oranjestad* ☎ *297/586–1418* ⊕ *www.tranquiloaruba.com.*

DIVING AND SNORKELING

With visibility of up to 90 feet, the waters around Aruba are excellent for snorkeling and diving. Advanced and novice divers alike will find plenty to occupy their time, as many of the most popular sites—including some interesting shipwrecks—are found in shallow waters ranging from 30 to 60 feet. Coral reefs covered with sensuously waving sea fans and eerie giant sponge tubes attract a colorful menagerie of sea life, including gliding manta rays, curious sea turtles, shy octopuses, and grunts, groupers, and other fish. Marine preservation is a priority on Aruba, and regulations by the Conference on International Trade in Endangered Species make it unlawful to remove coral, conch, and other marine life from the water.

Expect snorkel gear to rent for about $20 per day and trips to cost around $45. Scuba rates are around $50 for a one-tank reef or wreck dive, $75 for a two-tank dive, and $55 for a night dive. Resort courses, which offer an introduction to scuba diving, average $65 to $80. If you want to go all the way, complete open-water certification costs around $450.

Aruba Pro Dive. Experienced divers head here for good deals. ⊠ *Ponton 90, Noord* ☎ *297/582–5520* ⊕ *www.arubaprodive.com.*

Dive Aruba. Resort courses, certification courses, and trips to interesting shipwrecks make Dive Aruba worth checking out. ⊠ *Wilhelminastraat 8, Oranjestad* ☎ *297/582–7337* ⊕ *www.divearuba.com.*

Native Divers Aruba. Underwater naturalist courses are taught by PADI-certified instructors here, and the company has legions of return customers. ⊠ *Marriott Surf Club, Palm Beach* ☎ *297/586–4763* ⊕ *www. nativedivers.com.*

FISHING

Deep-sea catches here include barracuda, kingfish, wahoo, bonito, and tuna. November to April is the catch-and-release season for sailfish and marlin. Many skippered charter boats are available for half- or full-day sails. Packages include tackle, bait, and refreshments. Prices range from $300 to $500 for a half-day charter and from $550 to $700 for a full day.

Teaser Charters. The expertise of the Teaser crew is matched by a commitment to sensible fishing practices, which include catch and release and avoiding ecologically sensitive areas. The company's two boats are fully equipped, and the crew seem to have an uncanny ability to locate the best fishing spots. Captain Kenny runs a thrilling expedition. ⊠ *Renaissance Marina, Oranjestad* ☎ *297/582–5088* ⊕ *www. teasercharters.com.*

GOLF

The Links at Divi Aruba. This 9-hole course was designed by Karl Litten and Lorie Viola. The par-36 flat layout stretches to 2952 yards and features paspalum grass (best for seaside courses) and takes you past beautiful lagoons. It is a testy little course with water abounding, making accuracy more important than distance. Amenities include a golf school with professional instruction, a swing-analysis station, a driving range, and a two-story golf clubhouse with a pro shop. Two restaurants are available: Windows on Aruba for fine dining and Mulligan's for a casual and quick lunch. ⊠ *Divi Aruba Resort, J.E. Irausquin Blvd. 93, Oranjestad* ☎ *297/581–4653* ⚑ *9 holes, 2952 yards, par 36* ⚐ *$90 for 9 holes, $129 for 18 holes, Dec.–Apr.* ⊕ *www.divilinks.com.*

Fodor'sChoice **Tierra del Sol.** Stretching out to 6811 yards, this stunning course is sit-
★ uated on the northwest coast near the California Lighthouse and is Aruba's only 18-hole course. Designed by Robert Trent Jones Jr., Tierra del Sol combines Aruba's native beauty—cacti and rock formations, stunning views, and good conditioning. Wind can also be a factor here on the rolling terrain as are the abundant bunkers and water hazards. Greens fees include a golf cart equipped with GPS and a communications system that allows you to order drinks for your return to the clubhouse. The fully stocked golf shop is one of the Caribbean's most elegant, with an extremely attentive staff. ⊠ *Malmokweg* ☎ *297/586–0978* ⊕ *www.tierradelsol.com* ⚑ *18 holes, 6811 yards, par 71* ⚐ *$159 in morning, $129 from 1 pm; 3- and 5-day packages also available.*

HIKING

Hiking Aruba's arid and rugged countryside will give you the best opportunities to see the island's wildlife and flora. Arikok National Wildlife Park is an excellent place to glimpse the real Aruba, free of the trappings of tourism. The heat can be oppressive, so be sure to take it easy, wear a hat, and have a bottle of water handy.

FAMILY **Nature Sensitive Tours.** Eddy Croes, a former park ranger whose passion for the area is seemingly unbounded, runs this outfitter with care. Groups are never larger than eight people, so you'll see as much detail as you can handle. Expect frequent stops, when Eddy asks for silence so that you can hear the sounds of the park. The hikes are done at an easy pace and are suitable for basically anyone. A moonlight walk is available for those looking to avoid the heat. ⊠ *Pos Chiquito 13E, Savaneta* ☎ *297/585–1594* ⊕ *www.naturesensitivetours.com.*

HORSEBACK RIDING

Ranches offer short jaunts along the beach or longer rides along trails passing through countryside flanked by cacti, divi-divi trees, and aloe vera plants. Ask if you can stop off at Cura di Tortuga, a natural pool that's reputed to have restorative powers. Rides are also possible in Arikok National Wildlife Park. Rates run from $35 for an hour-long trip to $65 for a three-hour tour; private rides cost slightly more.

Rancho Daimari. Rancho Daimari will lead your horse to water—either at Natural Bridge or Natural Pool—in the morning or afternoon for $80 per person. The "Junior Dudes" program is tailored to young riders. There are even ATV trips. ⊠ *Palm Beach 33B, Noord* ☎ *297/586–6284.*

Rancho Notorious. The one- to three-hour tours here include one to the countryside for $55 and a trip to the beach for $100. All skill levels are welcome. The company also organizes ATV and mountain-biking trips. ⊠ *Boroncana, Noord* ☎ *297/586–0508* ⊕ *www.ranchonotorious.com.*

KAYAKING

Aruba Watersport Center. Operating since 1960, Aruba Watersport offers both single and double kayaks. ⊠ *L. G. Smith Blvd. 81B, Noord* ☎ *297/586–6613.*

WINDSURFING

The southwestern coast's tranquil waters make windsurfing conditions ideal for both beginners and intermediates, as the winds are steady but sudden gusts are rare. Experts will find the Atlantic coast, especially around Grapefield and Boca Grandi beaches, more challenging; winds are fierce and often shift course without warning. Most operators offer complete windsurfing vacation packages.

Aruba Active Vacations. Aruba Active Vacations is a major windsurfing center on the island. ⊠ *Near Fisherman's Huts, Malmok Beach* ☎ *297/586–0989* ⊕ *www.aruba-active-vacations.com.*

Sailboard Vacations. Complete windsurfing packages, including accommodations, can be arranged with Sailboard Vacations. Equipment can be rented for $60 a day. ⊠ *L.G. Smith Blvd. 462, Malmok Beach* ☎ *297/586–2527* ⊕ *www.sailboardvacations.com.*

BARBADOS

WELCOME TO BARBADOS

Broad vistas, sweeping seascapes, craggy cliffs, and acre upon acre of sugarcane—that's Barbados. Beyond that, what draws visitors to the island is the Bajan hospitality, the welcoming hotels and resorts, the sophisticated dining, the never-ending things to see and do, the exciting nightspots, and, of course, the sunny beaches.

Restaurants ▼	Hotels ▼
The Atlantis 9	Accra Beach Hotel & Spa 2
Bellini's Trattoria 5	The Atlantis Hotel 15
Brown Sugar 1	Bougainvillea Beach Resort 9
Café Luna 8	Cobblers Cove Hotel ..17
Café Sol 6	Sandal's Barbados 7
Champers 3	Courtyard Bridgetown by Marriott 3
Fish Pot 12	The Crane 14
L'Azure at the Crane ..10	Divi Southwinds Beach Resort 8
Naniki Restaurant 11	Hilton Barbados 1
Shakers 2	Island Inn Hotel 4
Sweet Potatoes 4	Little Arches Hotel 12
Waterside Restaurant 7	Little Good Harbour ...16
	Ocean Two 10
	Radisson Aquatica 5
	Silver Point Hotel 13
	SoCo Hotel 6
	Turtle Beach Resort ...11

TOP REASONS TO VISIT BARBADOS

1 Great Resorts: They run the gamut—from unpretentious to knock-your-socks-off.

2 Great Golf: Golfers can tee off at some of the best championship courses in the Caribbean.

3 Restaurants Galore: Great food includes everything from street-party barbecue to world-class dining.

4 Wide Range of Activities: With plenty of land and water sports, sightseeing options, and nightlife, there's always plenty to do.

5 Welcoming Locals: Bajans are friendly, welcoming, helpful, and hospitable. You'll like them; they'll like you.

BARBADOS BASICS

Barbados stands apart—both geographically and geologically—from its Caribbean neighbors; it's a full 100 miles (161 km) east of the Lesser Antilles chain. The top of a single submerged mountain of coral and limestone, Barbados is 21 miles (34 km) long, 14 miles (22½ km) wide, and relatively flat. The population is about 300,000, and the capital city is Bridgetown.

5

BARBADOS

KEY
- Beaches
- Cruise Ship Terminal
- Dive Sites
- **1** Restaurants
- ① Hotels

Updated by
Jane E. Zarem

Barbados stands apart from its neighbors in the Lesser Antilles archipelago, the chain of islands that stretches in a graceful arc from the Virgin Islands to Trinidad. Barbados is isolated in the Atlantic Ocean, 100 miles (160 km) due east of its nearest neighbor, St. Lucia.

Geologically, most of the Lesser Antilles are the peaks of a volcanic mountain range, whereas Barbados is the top of a single, relatively flat protuberance of coral and limestone—the source of building blocks for many a plantation manor. Several of those historic "greathouses," in fact, have been carefully restored. Two are open to visitors.

Bridgetown, both capital city and commercial center, is on the southwest coast of pear-shape Barbados. Most of the 300,000 Bajans (*Bay*-juns, which derives from the British pronunciation of *Barbadian*) live and work in and around Bridgetown, elsewhere in St. Michael Parish, or along the idyllic west coast or busy south coast. Others reside in tiny villages that dot the interior landscape. Broad sandy beaches, craggy cliffs, and numerous coves make up the coastline, and the interior is consumed by forested hills and gullies and acre upon acre of sugarcane.

Without question, Barbados is the "most British" island in the Caribbean. In contrast to the turbulent colonial past experienced by neighboring islands, which included repeated conflicts between France and Britain for dominance and control, British rule in Barbados carried on uninterrupted for 340 years—from the first established British settlement in 1627 until independence was granted in 1966. That's not to say, of course, that there weren't significant struggles in Barbados, as elsewhere in the Caribbean, between the British landowners and their African-born slaves and other indentured servants.

With that unfortunate period of slavery relegated to the history books, the British influence on Barbados remains strong today in local manners, attitudes, customs, and politics—tempered, of course, by the characteristically warm nature of the Bajan people. In keeping with British-born traditions, many Bajans worship at the Anglican church, afternoon tea is a ritual, cricket is the national pastime (a passion, most admit), dressing for dinner is a firmly entrenched tradition, and patrons at some bars are

LOGISTICS

Getting to Barbados: Several airlines fly nonstop to Barbados, or you may have to connect in Miami. Grantley Adams International Airport (BGI) is in Christ Church Parish on the south coast; the airport is about 15 minutes from hotels situated along the south coast, 45 minutes from the west coast, and 30 minutes from Bridgetown.

Hassle Factor: Low.

On the Ground: Ground transportation is available immediately outside the customs area. Airport taxis aren't metered, but fares are regulated ($38–$40 to Speightstown, $30–$35 to west-coast hotels, $16–$22 to south-coast hotels). Be sure, however, to establish the fare before getting into the taxi and confirm whether the price quoted is in U.S. or Barbadian dollars.

Getting Around the Island: If you are staying in an isolated area, you may want to rent a car, but bus service is good, especially between Bridgetown and stops along the west and south coasts. Taxis, of course, are always an option.

as likely to order a Pimm's Cup or a shandy as a rum and Coke. And yet, Barbados is hardly stuffy—this is still the Caribbean, after all.

Tourist facilities are concentrated on the west coast in St. James and St. Peter parishes (appropriately dubbed the Platinum Coast) and on the south coast in Christ Church Parish. Traveling north along the west coast to historic Holetown, the site of the first British settlement, and continuing to the city of Speightstown, you can find posh beachfront resorts, luxurious private villas, and fine restaurants enveloped by lush gardens and tropical foliage. The trendier, more commercial south coast offers competitively priced hotels and beach resorts, and its St. Lawrence Gap area is known for its restaurants and nightlife. The relatively wide-open spaces along the southeast coast are proving ripe for development, and some wonderful inns and hotels already take advantage of those intoxicatingly beautiful ocean vistas. For their own vacations, though, Bajans escape to the rugged east coast, where the Atlantic surf pounds the dramatic shoreline with unrelenting force.

All in all, Barbados is a sophisticated tropical island with a rich history, lodgings to suit every taste and pocketbook, and plenty to pique your interest both day and night—whether you're British or not.

PLANNING

WHEN TO GO

Barbados is busiest in the high season, which extends from December 15 through April 15. Off-season hotel rates can be half of those charged during the busy period. During the high season, too, a few hotels may require you to buy a meal plan, which is usually not required in the low season. As noted in the listings, some hotels close in September and October, the slowest months of the off-season, for annual renovations. Some restaurants may close for brief periods within that time frame as well.

GETTING HERE AND AROUND

AIR TRAVEL

Nonstop Flights: You can fly nonstop to Barbados from Atlanta (Delta), Charlotte (US Airways), Dallas–Ft. Worth (American), Miami (American), and New York–JFK (JetBlue).

Other Flights: Caribbean Airlines offers connecting service from Fort Lauderdale, Miami, and New York via Port of Spain, Trinidad, but this adds at least two hours to your flight time even in the best of circumstances and may not be the best option for most Americans. Barbados is also well connected to other Caribbean islands via LIAT. Mustique Airways and SVG Air connect Barbados to St. Vincent and the Grenadines. Many passengers use Barbados as a transit hub, sometimes spending the night each way.

Airline Contacts: Not all airlines flying into Barbados have local numbers. If your airline doesn't have a local contact number on the island, you will have to pay for the call.

Airline Contacts American Airlines ☎ *800/744–0006 in Barbados only* ⊕ *www.aa.com.* **Caribbean Airlines** ☎ *246/429–5929, 800/744–2225* ⊕ *www.caribbean-airlines.com.* **JetBlue** ☎ *877/596–2413 in Barbados, landline only* ⊕ *www.jetblue.com.* **LIAT** ☎ *246/434–5428, 888/844–5428* ⊕ *www.liat.com.* **Mustique Airways** ☎ *246/428–1638* ⊕ *www.mustique.com.* **SVG Air** ☎ *246/247–3712* ⊕ *www.svgair.com.* **US Airways** ☎ *800/622–1015* ⊕ *www.usairways.com.*

Airport Grantley Adams International Airport (*BGI*). ⊠ *Christ Church* ☎ *246/428–7101.*

BUS TRAVEL

Bus service is efficient and inexpensive. Public buses are blue with a yellow stripe; yellow buses with a blue stripe are privately owned and operated; and "Zed-R" vans (so called for their ZR license plate designation) are white with a maroon stripe and also privately owned and operated. All buses travel frequently along Highway 1 (St. James Road) and Highway 7 (South Coast Main Road), as well as inland routes. The fare is Bds$2 for any one destination; exact change in either local or U.S. currency ($1) is appreciated. Buses run about every 20 minutes. Small signs on roadside poles that say "To City" or "Out of City," meaning the direction relative to Bridgetown, mark the bus stops. Flag down the bus with your hand, even if you're standing at the stop. Bridgetown terminals are at Fairchild Street for buses to the south and east and at Lower Green for buses to Speightstown via the west coast.

CAR TRAVEL

Barbados has good roads, but traffic can be heavy on main roads, particularly around Bridgetown. Be sure to keep a map handy, as the road system in the countryside can be very confusing—although the friendly Bajans are always happy to help you find your way. Drive on the left, British-style. When someone flashes headlights at you at an intersection, it means "after you." Be especially careful negotiating roundabouts (traffic circles). The speed limit is 55 mph (90 kph) on highways, 37 mph (60 kph) on minor roads in the countryside, and 20 mph (30 kph) in town. Bridgetown actually has rush hours: 7 to 9 a.m. and 4 to 6 p.m. Park only in approved parking areas; downtown parking costs Bds75¢ to Bds$1 per hour.

Car Rentals: Most car-rental agencies require renters to be between 21 and either 70 or 75 years of age. Dozens of agencies rent cars, jeeps, or minimokes (small, open-sided vehicles). Rates range from about $50 per day for a minimoke to $65 per day for a four-wheel-drive vehicle and $85 or more for a luxury car (or $225 to $400 or more per week) in high season. Most firms also offer discounted three-day rates, and many require at least a two-day rental in high season.

Car-Rental Agencies Coconut Car Rentals ⊠ *Bayside, Bay St., Bridgetown, St. Michael* ☎ *246/437–0297* ⊕ *www.coconutcars.com.* **Courtesy Rent-A-Car** ⊠ *Grantley Adams International Airport, Christ Church* ☎ *246/431–4160* ⊕ *www.courtesyrentacar.com.* **Drive-a-Matic Car Rental** ⊠ *CWTS Complex, Lower Estate, St. Michael* ☎ *246/422–3000, 800/581–8773* ⊕ *www.carhire.tv.*

TAXI TRAVEL

Taxis operate 24 hours a day. They aren't metered but rates are fixed by the government. They carry up to three passengers, and the fare may be shared. Sample one-way fares from Bridgetown are $20 to Holetown, $25 to Speightstown, $20 to St. Lawrence Gap, and $30 to Bathsheba. Drivers can also be hired for an hourly rate of about $35–$40 for up to three people.

ESSENTIALS

Banks and Exchange Services The Barbados dollar is pegged to the U.S. dollar at the rate of Bds$1.98 to $1. The U.S. dollar is widely accepted, although you will receive your change in local currency. Barbados National Bank has a branch at Grantley Adams International Airport open daily from 8 am until the last plane lands or departs. ATMs are available 24 hours a day throughout the island. *All prices quoted in this chapter are in U.S. dollars.*

Electricity The electric current throughout Barbados is 110 volts, 50 cycles, U.S. standard.

Emergency Services Ambulance ☎ *511.* **Divers' Alert Network** ☎ *246/684–8111, 246/684–2948.* **Fire** ☎ *311.* **Hyperbaric Chamber in Barbados** ☎ *246/436–5483 to treat decompression illness in divers, 246/436–6185 for nonemergencies.* **Police** ☎ *211 emergencies, 246/430–7100 nonemergencies.*

Passport Requirements To enter Barbados, all visitors must have a valid passport and a return or ongoing ticket.

Phones The area code for Barbados is 246. Local calls from private phones are free; some hotels charge a small fee. For directory assistance, dial 411. U.S. visitors can dial 1-800 CALL USA (225–5872) to call home from any phone; it's less expensive than using a calling card, a credit card, or calling collect. Calls from pay phones cost Bds25¢ for five minutes. Prepaid phone cards, which can be used throughout Barbados and other Caribbean islands, are sold at shops, attractions, transportation centers, and other convenient outlets. Most U.S. cell phones will work in Barbados, though roaming charges can be expensive. Renting a cell phone or buying a local SIM card for your own unlocked phone may be a less expensive alternative if you're planning an extended stay or expect to make a lot of local calls. Top-off services are available at several locations throughout the island.

Taxes and Service Charges A 7.5% government tax is added to all hotel bills. A 7.5% V.A.T. is imposed on restaurant meals, admissions to attractions, and merchandise sales (other than those that are duty-free). Prices are often tax-inclusive; if not, the V.A.T. will be added to your bill. A 10% service charge is often added to hotel bills and restaurant checks.

Tipping If no service charge is added to your bill, tip waiters 10% to 15% and maids $2 per room per day. Tip bellhops and airport porters $1 per bag. Taxi drivers and tour guides appreciate a 10% tip.

ACCOMMODATIONS

Most people stay either in luxurious enclaves on the fashionable west coast—north of Bridgetown—or on the action-packed south coast with easy access to small, independent restaurants, bars, and nightclubs. A few inns on the remote southeast and east coasts offer ocean views and tranquility, but those on the east coast don't have good swimming beaches nearby. Prices in Barbados are sometimes twice as high in season as during the quieter months. Most hotels include no meals in their rates; some include breakfast, many offer a meal plan, some require you to purchase the meal plan in the high season, and a few offer all-inclusive packages.

Resorts: Great resorts run the gamut—from unpretentious to knock-your-socks-off—in terms of size, intimacy, amenities, and price. Many are well suited to families.

Small Inns: A few small, cozy inns may be found in the east and southeast regions of the island.

Villas and Condos: Families and long-term visitors may choose from a wide variety of condos (everything from busy time-share resorts to more sedate vacation complexes). Villas and villa complexes can be luxurious, simple, or something in between.

HOTEL AND RESTAURANT PRICES

Prices in the restaurant reviews are the average cost of a main course at dinner or, if dinner is not served, at lunch; taxes and service charges are generally included. Prices in the hotel reviews are the lowest cost of a standard double room in high season, excluding taxes, service charges, and meal plans (except at all-inclusives). Prices for rentals are the lowest per-night cost for a one-bedroom unit in high season.

For expanded lodging reviews and current deals, visit Fodors.com.

VISITOR INFORMATION

Contacts **Barbados Tourism Authority** ⊠ *Harbour Rd., Bridgetown, St. Michael* ☎ *246/427–2623* ⊕ *www.visitbarbados.org* ⊠ *Grantley Adams International Airport, Christ Church* ☎ *246/428–5570* ⊠ *Cruise-Ship Terminal, Deep Water Harbour, Bridgetown, St. Michael* ☎ *246/426–1718.*

WEDDINGS

There are no minimum residency requirements to get married; however, you need to obtain a marriage license from the Ministry of Home Affairs (☎ *246/228–8950*). The license fee is Bds$100 plus Bds$13 for a stamp. For a civil marriage, a separate fee of Bds$125 is payable to the Court; for an alternative venue, Bds$350. All fees must be paid in cash. If either person was divorced or widowed, appropriate paperwork must be presented to obtain the license.

EXPLORING

The terrain changes dramatically from each of the island's 11 parishes to the next, and so does the pace. Bridgetown, the capital, is a somewhat sophisticated city. West-coast resorts and private estates ooze luxury, whereas the small villages and vast sugar plantations found throughout central Barbados reflect the island's history. The relentless Atlantic surf shaped the cliffs of the dramatic east coast, and the northeast is called Scotland because of its hilly landscape and broad vistas. Along the lively south coast, the daytime hustle and bustle produce a palpable energy that continues well into the night at restaurants, dance clubs, and nightspots.

BRIDGETOWN

This bustling capital city is a major duty-free port with a compact shopping area. The principal thoroughfare is Broad Street, which leads west from National Heroes Square.

TOP ATTRACTIONS

The Careenage. In the early days, Bridgetown's natural harbor was where schooners were turned on their sides (careened) to be scraped of barnacles and repainted. Today, the Careenage serves as a marina for pleasure yachts and excursion boats, as well as a gathering place for locals and tourists alike. A boardwalk skirts the north side of the Careenage; on the south side, a lovely esplanade has pathways and benches for pedestrians and a statue of Errol Barrow, the first prime minister of Barbados. The Chamberlain Bridge and the Charles Duncan O'Neal Bridge cross the Careenage.

Nidhe Israel Synagogue. Providing for the spiritual needs of one of the oldest Jewish congregations in the Western Hemisphere, this synagogue was formed by Jews who left Brazil in the 1620s and introduced sugarcane to Barbados. The adjoining cemetery has tombstones dating from the 1630s. The original house of worship, built in 1654, was destroyed in an 1831 hurricane, rebuilt in 1833, and restored with the assistance of the Barbados National Trust in 1987. Friday-night services are held during the winter months, but the building is open to the public year-round. Shorts are not acceptable during services but may be worn at other times. ⊠ *Synagogue La.* ☎ *246/436–6869* ✉ *Donation requested* ◷ *Weekdays 9–4.*

Queen's Park. Northeast of Bridgetown, Queen's Park contains one of the island's two immense baobab trees. Brought to Barbados from Guinea, West Africa around 1738, this tree has a girth of more than 60 feet. Queen's Park Art Gallery, managed by the National Culture Foundation, is the island's largest gallery; exhibits change monthly. Queen's Park House, built in 1783 and the historic home of the British troop commander, has been converted into a theater, with an exhibition room on the lower floor and a restaurant. Originally called King's House, the name was changed upon Queen Victoria's succession to the throne. ⊠ *Constitution Rd.* ☎ *246/427–2345 gallery* ✉ *Free* ◷ *Daily 9–5.*

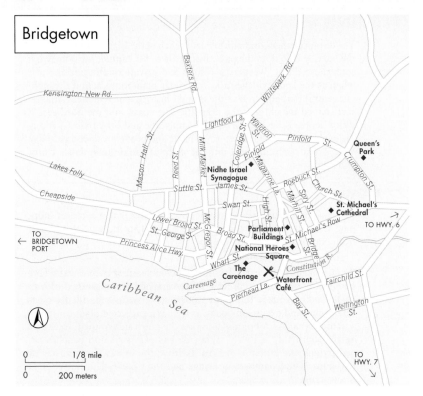

Bridgetown

Kensington New Rd.

Baxter's Rd.

Whitepark Rd.

Lightfoot La.

Waldron St.

Coleridge St.

Pinfold

Pinfold St.

Queen's Park

Crumpton St.

Lakes Folly

Mason Hall St.

Reed St.

Milk Market

Magazine La.

Roebuck St.

Church St.

Spry St.

Cheapside

Suttle St.

Nidhe Israel Synagogue

James St.

High St.

Marhill St.

St. Michael's Row

Bridge St.

St. Michael's Cathedral

TO HWY. 6

Swan St.

Lower Broad St.

St. George St.

McGregor St.

Broad St.

Parliament Buildings

National Heroes Square

TO ← BRIDGETOWN PORT

Princess Alice Hwy.

Wharf St.

Constitution R.

Fairchild St.

Caribbean Sea

Careenage

The Careenage

Pierhead La.

Waterfront Café

Bay St.

Wellington St.

0   1/8 mile

0   200 meters

TO HWY. 7

WORTH NOTING

National Heroes Square. Across Broad Street from the Parliament Buildings and bordered by High and Trafalgar streets, this triangular plaza marks the center of town. Its monument to Lord Horatio Nelson, who was in Barbados only briefly in 1777 as a 19-year-old navy lieutenant, predates Nelson's Column in London's Trafalgar Square by 30 years (1813 vs. 1843). There's also a war memorial and a fountain that commemorates the advent of running water on Barbados in 1865. ⊠ *Broad St., across from Parliament.*

Parliament Buildings. Overlooking National Heroes Square in the center of town, these Victorian buildings were constructed around 1870 to house the British Commonwealth's third-oldest parliament. A series of stained-glass windows depicts British monarchs from James I to Victoria. The National Heroes Gallery & Museum is located in the West Wing. ⊠ *National Heroes Sq., Trafalgar St.* 📠 *246/427–2019* 💳 *Donations welcome* ☉ *Tours weekdays at 11 and 2, when parliament isn't in session.*

St. Michael's Cathedral. Although no one has proved it, George Washington is said to have worshipped here in 1751 during his only trip outside the United States. By then, the original structure was already nearly a century old. Destroyed twice by hurricanes, it was rebuilt in 1784 and again in 1831. ⊠ *Spry St., east of National Heroes Sq.*

SOUTH COAST

Christ Church Parish, which is far busier and more developed than the west coast, is chockablock with condos, high- and low-rise hotels, and beach parks. It is also the location of St. Lawrence Gap, with its many places to eat, drink, shop, and party. As you move southeast, the broad, flat terrain comprises acre upon acre of cane fields, interrupted only by an occasional oil rig and a few tiny villages. Along the byways are colorful chattel houses, which were the traditional homes of tenant farmers. Historically, these typically Barbadian, ever-expandable small buildings were built so they could be dismantled and moved, as required.

TOP ATTRACTIONS

FAMILY **Barbados Concorde Experience.** Opened to the public since 2007, the Concorde Experience focuses on the British Airways Concorde G-BOAE (Alpha Echo, for short) that for many years flew between London and Barbados. The retired supersonic jet has made its permanent home here. Besides boarding the sleek aircraft itself, you'll learn about how the technology was developed and how this plane differed from other jets. You may or may not have been able to fly the Concorde when it was still plying the Atlantic, but this is your chance to experience some unique modern history—up close and personal. ⊠ *Grantley Adams International Airport, adjacent to terminal bldg., Christ Church* ☎ *246/420–7738* ⊕ *www.barbadosconcorde.com* 🖃 *$20* ⊗ *Daily 9–5.*

FAMILY **Barbados Museum.** This intriguing museum, established in 1933 in the Fodor'sChoice former British Military Prison (1815) in the historic St. Ann's Garrison area, has artifacts from Arawak days (around 400 BC) along with galleries that depict 19th-century military history and everyday social history. You can see cane-harvesting tools, wedding dresses, ancient (and frightening) dentistry instruments, and slave sale accounts noted in spidery copperplate handwriting. The museum's Harewood Gallery showcases the island's natural environment, its Cunard Gallery has a permanent collection of West Indian prints bequeathed to the museum by Sir Edward Cunard, and its Warmington Gallery showcases decorative arts that depict the planter's lifestyle in Barbados. Additional galleries include one with exhibits targeted to children. The Shilstone Memorial Library houses rare West Indian documentation—archival documents, genealogical records, photos, books, and maps—dating back to the 17th century. The museum also has a gift shop and a café. ⊠ *St. Ann's Garrison, Hwy. 7, Garrison, St. Michael* ☎ *246/427–0201* ⊕ *www.barbmuse.org.bb* 🖃 *$7.50* ⊗ *Mon.–Sat. 9–5, Sun. 2–6.*

Fodor'sChoice **Sunbury Plantation House and Museum.** Lovingly rebuilt after a 1995 fire destroyed everything but the thick flint-and-stone walls of this 300-year-old greathouse, Sunbury offers an elegant glimpse of the 18th and 19th centuries on a Barbadian sugar estate. Period furniture, old prints, and a collection of horse-drawn carriages lend an air of authenticity. A buffet luncheon is served daily in the courtyard for $32.50 per person. A five-course candlelight dinner is served ($100 per person, reservations required) two nights a week at the 200-year-old mahogany dining table in the Sunbury dining room. ⊠ *Off Hwy. 4B, Six Cross Roads, St. Philip* ☎ *246/423–6270* ⊕ *www.barbadosgreathouse.com* 🖃 *$7.50* ⊗ *Daily 9–5; last tour at 4:30.*

WORTH NOTING

Codrington Theological College. An impressive stand of royal palms lines the road leading to the coral-stone buildings and serene grounds of Codrington College, an Anglican theological seminary opened in 1745 on a cliff overlooking Conset Bay. The benefactor of the college was Christopher Codrington III (1668–1710), a former governor-general of the Leeward Islands whose antislavery views were unpopular in the plantocracy of the times. In an effort to "Christianize" the slaves and provide them with a general education, Codrington's will established that "300 negroes at least" would always be allowed to study at the institution; the planters who acted as trustees, however, were loath to teach the slaves how to read and write. You're welcome to tour the buildings, explore the grounds, and walk the nature trails. Keep in mind, though, that beachwear is not appropriate here. ⊠ *Sargeant St., Conset Bay, St. John* ☎ *246/423–1140* ⊕ *www.codrington.org* ▨ *Donations welcome* ⊙ *Daily 10–4.*

Emancipation Statue. This powerful statue of a slave—whose raised hands, broken chains hanging from each wrist, evoke both contempt and victory—is commonly referred to as the Bussa Statue. Bussa was the man who, in 1816, led the first slave rebellion on Barbados. The work of Barbadian sculptor Karl Brodhagen, the statue was erected in 1985 to commemorate the emancipation of the slaves in 1834. ⊠ *St. Barnabas Roundabout, intersection of ABC Hwy. and Hwy. 5, Haggatt Hall, St. Michael.*

FAMILY **George Washington House.** George Washington slept here! This carefully restored and refurbished 18th-century plantation house in Bush Hill was the only place where the future first president of the United States actually slept outside North America. Teenage George and his older half-brother Lawrence, who was suffering from tuberculosis and seeking treatment on the island, rented this house overlooking Carlisle Bay for two months in 1751. Opened to the public in 2007, the lower floor of the house and the kitchen have period furnishings; the upper floor is a museum with both permanent and temporary exhibits that display artifacts of 18th-century Barbadian life. The site includes an original 1719 windmill and bathhouse, along with a stable added to the property in the 1800s. Guided tours begin with an informative 15-minute film appropriately called *George Washington in Barbados*. ⊠ *Bush Hill, Garrison, St. Michael* ☎ *246/228–5461* ⊕ *www. georgewashingtonbarbados.org* ▨ *$10* ⊙ *Weekdays 9–4:30.*

Ragged Point. The easternmost point of Barbados is the location of East Coast Light, one of four strategically placed lighthouses on the island. Although civilization in the form of new homes is encroaching on this once-remote location, the view of the entire Atlantic coastline of Barbados is still spectacular—and the cool ocean breeze is beautifully refreshing on a hot, sunny day. ⊠ *Marley Vale, St. Philip.*

Tyrol Cot Heritage Village. This coral-stone cottage just south of Bridgetown, constructed in 1854, is preserved as an example of period architecture. In 1929, it became the home of Sir Grantley Adams, the first premier of Barbados and the namesake of the island's international

Sunbury Plantation House

airport. Part of the Barbados National Trust, the cottage is filled with antiques and memorabilia that belonged to the late Sir Grantley and Lady Adams. It's also the centerpiece of an outdoor "living museum," where artisans and craftsmen have their workshops in a cluster of traditional chattel houses. Workshops are open, crafts are for sale, and refreshments are available at the "rum shop" primarily during the winter season and when cruise ships are in port. ⊠ *Rte. 2, Codrington Hill, St. Michael* ☎ *246/424–2074* ⬜ *$9* ⊙ *Weekdays 8–4:30; last tour 4 pm.*

CENTRAL BARBADOS

On the west coast, in St. James Parish, Holetown marks the center of the Platinum Coast—so called for the vast number of luxurious resorts and mansions that face the sea. Holetown is also where Captain John Powell and the crew of the British ship *Olive Blossom* landed on May 14, 1625, to claim the island for King James I (who had actually died of a stroke seven weeks earlier). On the east coast, the crashing Atlantic surf has eroded the shoreline, forming steep cliffs and exposing prehistoric rocks that look like giant mushrooms. Bathsheba and Cattlewash are favorite seacoast destinations for local folks on weekends and holidays. In the interior, narrow roads weave through tiny villages and along and between the ridges. The landscape is covered with tropical vegetation and is rife with fascinating caves and gullies.

TOP ATTRACTIONS

Fodor's Choice ★ **Andromeda Botanic Gardens.** More than 600 beautiful and unusual plant specimens from around the world are cultivated in 6 acres of gardens nestled among streams, ponds, and rocky outcroppings overlooking the sea above the Bathsheba coastline. The gardens were created in 1954 with flowering plants collected by the late horticulturist Iris Bannochie. They're now administered by the Barbados National Trust. The Hibiscus Café serves snacks and drinks. ⊠ *Foster Hall, Bathsheba, St. Joseph* ☎ *246/433–9384* ⊕ *andromeda.cavehill.uwi.edu* ✉ *$10* ⊙ *Daily 9–5.*

Fodor'sChoice   **Flower Forest.** It's a treat to meander among fragrant flowering bushes,
★   canna and ginger lilies, puffball trees, and more than 100 other species of tropical flora in a cool, tranquil forest of flowers and other plants. A ½-mile-long (1-km-long) path winds through the 53.6-acre grounds, a former sugar plantation; it takes about 30 to 45 minutes to follow the path, or you can wander freely for as long as you wish. Benches throughout the forest give you a place to pause and reflect. There's also a snack bar, a gift shop, and a beautiful view of Mt. Hillaby, at 1,100 feet the highest point of land on Barbados. ⊠ *Hwy. 2, Richmond, St. Joseph* ☎ *246/433–8152* ⊕ *www.flowerforestbarbados.com* ✉ *$10* ⊙ *Daily 8–4.*

FAMILY   **Gun Hill Signal Station.** The 360-degree view from Gun Hill, 700 feet
Fodor'sChoice   above sea level, gave this location strategic importance to the 18th-
★   century British army. Using lanterns and semaphore, soldiers based here could communicate with their counterparts at the Garrison on the south coast and at Grenade Hill in the north. Time moved slowly in 1868, and Captain Henry Wilkinson whiled away his off-duty hours by carving a huge lion from a single rock—which is on the hillside just below the tower. Come for a short history lesson but mainly for the view; it's so gorgeous, military invalids were once sent here to convalesce. ⊠ *Gun Hill, St. George* ☎ *246/429–1358* ✉ *$5* ⊙ *Weekdays 9–5.*

FAMILY   **Harrison's Cave.** This limestone cavern, complete with stalactites, stalag-
Fodor'sChoice   mites, subterranean streams, and a 40-foot waterfall, is a rare find in
★   the Caribbean—and one of Barbados's most popular attractions. Tours include a nine-minute video presentation and an hour-long underground journey through the cavern via electric tram. The visitor center has interactive displays, life-size models and sculptures, a souvenir shop, restaurant facilities, and elevator access to the tram for people with disabilities. Tours fill up fast, so book a reservation. ⊠ *Hwy. 2, Welchman Hall, St. Thomas* ☎ *246/417–3700* ⊕ *www.harrisonscave.com* ✉ *$30* ⊙ *Daily 8:45–3:45.*

Fodor'sChoice   **Hunte's Gardens.** Horticulturist Anthony Hunte spent two years convert-
★   ing an overgrown sinkhole (caused by the collapse of a limestone cave) into an extraordinary garden environment. Trails lead up, down, and around 10 acres of dense foliage—everything from pots of flowering plants and great swaths of thick ground cover to robust vines, exotic tropical flowers, and majestic 100-year-old cabbage palms reaching for the sun. Benches and chairs, strategically placed among the greenery, afford perfect (and fairly private) vantage points, while classical music plays overhead. Hunte lives on the property and welcomes visitors to his verandah for a glass of juice or rum punch. Just ask, and he'll be happy to tell you the fascinating story of how the gardens evolved. ⊠ *Castle Grant, St. Joseph* ☎ *246/433–3333* ⊕ *www.huntesgardensbarbados. com* ✉ *$15* ⊙ *Daily, 9–4.*

Mount Gay Rum Visitors Centre. On this popular tour, you learn the colorful story behind the world's oldest rum—made in Barbados since 1703. Although the modern distillery is in the far north, in St. Lucy Parish, tour guides at the Visitors Centre here in St. Michael explain the rum-making procedure. Equipment, both historic and modern, is on display, and rows and rows of barrels are stored in this location. The 45-minute tour runs hourly (last tour begins at 3:30 weekdays, 2:30 on Saturday) and concludes with a tasting and an opportunity to buy bottles of rum and gift items—and even have lunch or cocktails, depending on the time of day. ⊠ *Spring Garden Hwy., Brandons, St. Michael* ☎ *246/425–8757* ⊕ *www.mountgayrum.com* ✉ *$7, $50 with lunch; $35 with cocktails* ⊙ *Weekdays 9–5, Sat. 10–4.*

WORTH NOTING

Chalky Mount. This tiny east-coast village is perched high in the clay-yielding hills that have supplied local potters for about 300 years. A few working potteries are open daily to visitors, who can watch as artisans create bowls, vases, candleholders, and decorative objects—which are for sale. ⊠ *Chalky Mount, St. Andrew.*

FAMILY **Cockspur Beach Club.** Just north of Bridgetown, the fun-loving folks at West Indies Rum Distillery, makers of Cockspur and Malibu rums, invite visitors to enjoy a day at the beach, a variety of water-sports, and a complimentary rum punch. Changing rooms with lockers and showers are available for beachgoers to use, along with beach umbrellas and chairs. Snorkeling equipment can be rented for the day ($5). The beachside grill serves lunch and drinks. This is a very popular outing for cruise-ship passengers. ⊠ *Brighton Beach, Black Rock, Brighton, St. Michael* ☎ *246/425–9393* ✉ *$10* ⊙ *Daily 8:30–4:30.*

FAMILY **Folkestone Marine Park and Visitor Centre.** The mission of family-oriented Folkestone Marine Park, a marine protected area just north of Holetown, is to provide high-quality recreational activities in a sustainable way that will educate and entertain Barbadians and visitors alike. Facilities include a playground, basketball court, picnic area, museum, and beach with lifeguards. The museum (two rooms with artifacts and photos of how the sea is used for various purposes) illuminates some of the island's marine life. For some firsthand viewing, there's an underwater snorkeling trail (equipment rental, $10 for the day) around Dottins Reef, just off the beach in the protected marine reserve area; nonswimmers can enjoy a glass-bottom boat tour. A barge sunk in shallow water is home to myriad fish, making it a popular dive site. The park is open around the clock, with full security; lifeguards are on duty at the beach from 9 to 5:30 every day. A canteen serves snacks and drinks. ⊠ *Hwy. 1, Church Point, Holetown, St. James* ☎ *246/425–2871* ✉ *Free; 60 cents to view exhibits* ⊙ *Park daily 24 hrs; museum weekdays 9:30–5.*

Orchid World. Follow meandering pathways through tropical gardens filled with thousands of colorful orchids. You'll see Vandaceous orchids attached to fences or wire frames, Schomburgkia and Oncidiums stuck on mahogany trees, Aranda and Spathoglottis orchids growing in a grotto, and Ascocendas suspended from netting in shady enclosures. You'll find seasonal orchids, scented orchids, multicolor Vanda orchids, and more. Benches are well placed to stop for a little rest, admire the flowers, or simply take in the expansive view of the surrounding cane fields and distant hills of Sweet Vale. Snacks, cold beverages, and other refreshments are served in the café. ⊠ *Hwy. 3B, Groves, St. George* ☎ *246/433–0774* ⊕ *www.orchidworldbarbados.com* ✉ *$10* ⊙ *Daily 9–5.*

Welchman Hall Gully. This 1½-mile-long (2-km-long) natural gully is really a collapsed limestone cavern, once part of the same underground network as Harrison's Cave. The Barbados National Trust protects the peace and quiet here, making it a beautiful place to hike past acres of labeled flowers and stands of trees. You can see and hear some interesting birds—and, with luck, a native green monkey. The tour is self-guided (although a guide can be arranged with 24 hours' notice) and takes about 30 to 45 minutes; the last tour begins at 4 pm. ⊠ *Welchman Hall, St. Thomas* ☎ *246/438–6671* ⊕ *www.welchmanhallgullybarbados.com* ✉ *$12* ⊙ *Daily 9–4:30.*

NORTHERN BARBADOS

Speightstown, the north's commercial center and once a thriving port city, now boasts appealing local shops and informal restaurants. Many of Speightstown's 19th-century buildings, with traditional overhanging balconies, have been restored. The island's northernmost reaches, St. Peter and St. Lucy parishes, have a varied topography and are lovely to explore. Between the tiny fishing towns along the northwestern coast and the sweeping views out over the Atlantic to the east are forest and farm, moor and mountain. Most guides include a loop through this area on a daylong island tour—it's a beautiful drive.

TOP ATTRACTIONS

FAMILY **Animal Flower Cave.** Small sea anemones, or sea worms (resembling flowers when they open their tiny tentacles), live in small pools in this sea cave at the island's very northern tip. The cave itself, discovered in 1780, has a coral floor that ranges from 126,000 to 500,000 years old, according to geological estimates. The view of breaking waves from inside the cave is magnificent. Steep stairs, uneven surfaces, and rocks make this an unwise choice for anyone with walking difficulties. ⊠ *North Point, St. Lucy* ☎ *246/439–8797* ✉ *$10* ⊙ *Daily 9–4.*

FAMILY **Barbados Wildlife Reserve.** The reserve is the habitat of herons, innumerable land turtles, screeching peacocks, shy deer, elusive green monkeys, brilliantly colored parrots (in a large walk-in aviary), a snake, and a caiman. Except for the snake and the caiman, the animals run or fly freely—so step carefully and keep your hands to yourself. Late afternoon is your best chance to catch a glimpse of a green monkey. ⊠ *Farley Hill, St. Peter* ☎ *246/422–8826* ✉ *$12.50* ⊙ *Daily 10–5.*

Fodor'sChoice **St. Nicholas Abbey.** The island's oldest greathouse (circa 1650) was
★ named after the original British owner's hometown, St. Nicholas Parish near Bristol, and Bath Abbey nearby. Its stone-and-wood architecture makes it one of only three original Jacobean-style houses still standing in the Western Hemisphere. It has Dutch gables, finials of coral stone, and beautiful grounds that include an "avenue" of mahogany trees, a

St. Nicholas Abbey

"gully" filled with tropical trees and plantings, formal gardens, and an old sugar mill. The first floor, fully furnished with period furniture and portraits of family members, is open to the public. A fascinating home movie, shot by a previous owner's father, records Bajan life in the 1930s. Behind the greathouse is a rum distillery with a 19th-century steam press. Visitors can purchase artisanal plantation rum produced nearby (the Abbey's production will become fully aged about 2018), browse the gift shop, and enjoy light refreshments at the Terrace Café. ⊠ *Cherry Tree Hill, St. Peter* ☎ *246/422–5357* ⊕ *www.stnicholasabbey. com* ▱ *$17.50* ☉ *Sun.–Fri. 10–3:30.*

WORTH NOTING

Cherry Tree Hill. Be sure to stop at the crest of Cherry Tree Hill, just east of St. Nicholas Abbey, for a panoramic view of the entire eastern coast of Barbados and the Atlantic surf. It's absolutely stunning. ⊠ *Cherry Hill Rd., St. Andrew.*

Farley Hill. At this national park in northern St. Peter, across the road from the Barbados Wildlife Reserve, gardens and lawns—along with an avenue of towering royal palms and gigantic mahogany, whitewood, and casuarina trees—surround the imposing ruins of a plantation greathouse built by Sir Graham Briggs in 1861 to entertain royal visitors from England. Partially rebuilt for the filming of *Island in the Sun,* the classic 1957 film starring Harry Belafonte and Dorothy Dandridge, the structure was destroyed by fire in 1965. Behind the estate, there's a sweeping view of the region called Scotland for its rugged landscape. The park is also the site of various festivals and musical events during the year. ⊠ *Farley Hill, St. Peter* ▱ *$2 per car, pedestrians free* ☉ *Daily 8:30–6.*

FAMILY **Morgan Lewis Sugar Mill.** Built in 1727, the mill was operational until 1945. Today it's the only remaining windmill in Barbados with its wheelhouse and sails intact. No longer used to grind sugarcane, except for occasional demonstrations, it was donated to the Barbados National Trust in 1962 and eventually restored to its original working specifications in 1998 by millwrights from the United Kingdom. The surrounding acres are now used for dairy farming. ⊠ *Southeast of Cherry Tree Hill, Morgan Lewis, St. Andrew* ☎ *246/422–7429* ⌨ *$5* ⊙ *Weekdays 9–5.*

BEACHES

Geologically, Barbados is a coral-and-limestone island (not volcanic) with few rivers and, as a result, beautiful beaches, particularly along the island's southern and southeastern coastlines.

The west coast has some lovely beaches as well, but they're more susceptible to erosion after major autumn storms, if any, have taken their toll. When the surf is too high and swimming becomes dangerous, a red flag will be hoisted on the beach. A yellow flag—or a red flag at half-staff—means swim with caution. Topless sunbathing—on the beach or at the pool—is not allowed anywhere in Barbados.

SOUTH COAST

A young, energetic crowd favors the south-coast beaches, which are broad and breezy, blessed with powdery white sand, and dotted with tall palms. The reef-protected areas with crystal clear water are safe for swimming and snorkeling. The surf is medium to high, and the waves get bigger and the winds stronger (windsurfers, take note) the farther southeast you go.

FAMILY **Accra Beach.** This popular beach, also known as Rockley Beach, is next to the Accra Beach Hotel. You'll find a broad swath of white sand with gentle surf and a lifeguard, plenty of nearby restaurants for refreshments, a children's playground, and beach stalls for renting chairs and equipment for snorkeling and other water sports. **Amenities:** food and drink; lifeguards; parking (free); water sports. **Best for:** snorkeling; swimming. ⊠ *Hwy. 7, Rockley, Christ Church.*

Fodor's Choice ⋆ **Bottom Bay Beach.** Popular for fashion and travel-industry photo shoots, Bottom Bay is the quintessential Caribbean beach. Secluded, surrounded by a coral cliff, studded with a stand of palms, and blessed with an endless ocean view, this dreamy enclave is near the southeasternmost point of the island. The Atlantic Ocean waves can be too strong for swimming, but it's the picture-perfect place for a day at the beach and a picnic lunch. Park at the top of the cliff and follow the steps down to the beach. **Amenities:** none. **Best for:** solitude; swimming; walking. ⊠ *Hwy. 5, Apple Hall, St. Philip.*

Fodor's Choice ⋆ **Crane Beach.** This exquisite crescent of pink sand on the southeast coast was named not for the elegant long-legged wading bird but for the crane used to haul and load cargo when this area served as a busy port. Crane Beach usually has a steady breeze and lightly rolling surf that varies in color from aqua to turquoise to lapis and is great for bodysurfing. Access to the beach is either down 98 steps or via a cliff-side, glass-walled elevator on The Crane resort property. **Amenities:** food and drink; lifeguards; parking (free); toilets. **Best for:** swimming; walking. ⊠ *Crane Bay, St. Philip.*

Fodor'sChoice ★ **Miami Beach.** Also called Enterprise Beach, this lovely spot on the coast road, just east of Oistins, is a slice of pure white sand with shallow and calm crystal-clear water on one side, deeper water with small waves on the other, and cliffs on either side. Located in a mainly upscale residential area, the beach is mostly deserted except for weekends, when folks who live nearby come for a swim. You can find a palm-shaded parking area, snack carts, and chair rentals. It's also a hop, skip, and jump from Little Arches Hotel. **Amenities:** food and drink; parking (free). **Best for:** solitude; swimming. ⊠ *Enterprise Beach Rd., Enterprise, Christ Church.*

Fodor'sChoice ★ **Pebbles Beach.** On the southern side of Carlisle Bay, just south of Bridgetown, this broad half circle of white sand is one of the island's best beaches—and it can become crowded on weekends and holidays. The southern end of the beach wraps around the Hilton Barbados; the northern end is adjacent to the Radisson Grand Barbados Hotel and a block away from Island Inn. Park at Harbour Lights or at the Boatyard Bar and Bayshore Complex, both on Bay Street, where you can also rent umbrellas and beach chairs and buy refreshments. **Amenities:** food and drink. **Best for:** snorkeling; swimming; walking. ⊠ *Off Bay St., south of Bridgetown, Needham's Point, St. Michael.*

FAMILY **Sandy Beach** (*Dover Beach*). This beach has shallow, calm waters and a picturesque lagoon, making it an ideal location for families with small kids. Park right on the main road. You can rent beach chairs and umbrellas, and plenty of places nearby sell food and drinks. **Amenities:** food and drink; parking (free). **Best for:** swimming; walking. ⊠ *Hwy. 7, Worthing, Christ Church.*

Silver Sands–Silver Rock Beach. Nestled between South Point, the southernmost tip of the island, and Inch Marlow Point, Silver Point Hotel overlooks this broad strand of beautiful white sand that always has a strong breeze. That makes this beach the best in Barbados for intermediate and advanced windsurfers and, more recently, kiteboarders. There's a small playground for children and shaded picnic tables. **Amenities:** parking (free); water sports. **Best for:** solitude; swimming; walking; windsurfing. ⊠ *Off Hwy. 7, Christ Church.*

Turtle Beach. Stretched from Turtle Beach Resort and Sandals Barbados at the eastern end of St. Lawrence Gap to Bougainvillea Beach Resort on Maxwell Coast Road, this broad strand of powdery white sand is great for sunbathing, strolling, and—with low to medium surf—swimming and boogie boarding. This beach is a favorite nesting place for turtles; if you're lucky, you may see hundreds of tiny hatchlings emerge from the sand and make their way to the sea—nature at its best! Find public access and parking on Maxwell Coast Road, near the Bougainvillea Beach Resort. **Amenities:** food and drink; parking (free). **Best for:** swimming; walking. ⊠ *Maxwell Coast Rd., Dover, Christ Church.*

EAST COAST

Be cautioned: swimming at east-coast beaches is treacherous, even for strong swimmers, and is *not* recommended. Waves are high, the bottom tends to be rocky, the currents are unpredictable, and the undertow is dangerously strong.

Bathsheba Beach. Although not safe for swimming, the miles of untouched sand along the East Coast Road in St. Joseph Parish are great for beachcombing and wading. As you approach Bathsheba Soup Bowl, the southernmost stretch just below Tent Bay, the enormous mushroom-shape boulders and rolling surf are uniquely impressive. The Soup Bowl is where expert surfers from around the world converge each November for the Independence Classic Surfing Championship. **Amenities:** none. **Best for:** solitude; sunrise; surfing; walking. ⊠ *East Coast Rd., Bathsheba, St. Joseph.*

Cattlewash Beach. Swimming is unwise at this windswept beach with pounding surf, which follows the Atlantic Ocean coastline in St. Andrew, but you can take a dip, wade, and play in the tide pools. Barclays Park, a 50-acre public park directly across the road, has a shaded picnic area. **Amenities:** none. **Best for:** solitude; sunrise; walking. ⊠ *Ermy Bourne Hwy., Cattlewash, St. Andrew.*

WEST COAST

Gentle Caribbean waves lap the west coast, and leafy mahogany trees shade its stunning coves and sandy beaches. The water is perfect for swimming and water sports. An almost unbroken chain of beaches runs between Bridgetown and Speightstown. Elegant homes and luxury hotels face much of the beachfront property in this area, dubbed Barbados's "Platinum Coast."

West-coast beaches are considerably smaller and narrower than those on the south coast. Also, prolonged stormy weather in September and October may cause sand erosion, temporarily making the beach even narrower. Even so, west-coast beaches are seldom crowded. Vendors stroll by with handmade baskets, hats, dolls, jewelry, even original watercolors; owners of private boats offer waterskiing, parasailing, and snorkeling excursions. Hotels and beachside restaurants welcome nonguests for terrace lunches (wear a cover-up), and you can buy picnic items at supermarkets in Holetown.

Brighton Beach. Calm as a lake, this is where you can find locals taking a quick dip on hot days. Just north of Bridgetown, Brighton Beach is also home to the Cockspur Beach Club. **Amenities:** food and drink; parking (free). **Best for:** swimming; walking. ⊠ *Spring Garden Hwy., Brighton, St. Michael.*

Fodor's Choice ★ **Mullins Beach.** This lovely beach just south of Speightstown is a perfect place to spend the day. The water is safe for swimming and snorkeling, there's easy parking on the main road, and Mullins Restaurant serves snacks, meals, and drinks—and rents chairs and umbrellas. **Amenities:** food and drink; parking (free); toilets. **Best for:** sunset; swimming; walking. ⊠ *Hwy. 1, Mullins Bay, St. Peter.*

Paynes Bay Beach. The stretch of beach just south of Sandy Lane is lined with luxury hotels—Tamarind, The House, and Treasure Beach among them. It's a very pretty area, with plenty of beach to go around, calm water, and good snorkeling. Public access is available at several locations along Highway 1, though parking is limited. **Amenities:** food and drink. **Best for:** snorkeling; sunset; swimming; walking. ⊠ *Hwy. 1, Paynes Bay, St. James.*

WHERE TO EAT

First-class restaurants and hotel dining rooms serve quite sophisticated cuisine—often prepared by chefs with international experience and rivaling the dishes served in the world's best restaurants. Most menus include seafood: dolphin (mahimahi), kingfish, snapper, and flying fish prepared every way imaginable. Flying fish is so popular that it has officially become a national symbol. Shellfish also abounds, as do steak, pork, and local black-belly lamb.

Local specialty dishes include *buljol* (a cold salad of pickled codfish, tomatoes, onions, sweet peppers, and celery) and *conkies* (cornmeal, coconut, pumpkin, raisins, sweet potatoes, and spices, mixed together, wrapped in a banana leaf, and steamed). *Cou-cou,* often served with steamed flying fish, is a mixture of cornmeal and okra, usually topped with a spicy creole sauce made from tomatoes, onions, and sweet peppers. Bajan-style pepper pot is a hearty stew of oxtail, beef, and other meats in a rich, spicy gravy and simmered overnight.

For lunch, restaurants often offer a traditional Bajan buffet of fried fish, baked chicken, salads, macaroni pie (macaroni and cheese), and a selection of steamed or stewed provisions (local roots and vegetables). Be cautious with the West Indian condiments—like the sun, they're hotter than you think. Typical Bajan drinks—in addition to Banks Beer and Mount Gay, Cockspur, or Malibu rum—are *falernum* (a liqueur concocted of rum, sugar, lime juice, and almond essence) and *mauby* (a nonalcoholic drink made by boiling bitter bark and spices, straining the mixture, and sweetening it). You're sure to enjoy the fresh fruit or rum punch, as well.

What to Wear: The dress code for dinner in Barbados is conservative, casually elegant, and, occasionally, formal—a jacket and tie for gentlemen and a cocktail dress for ladies in the fanciest restaurants and hotel dining rooms, particularly during the winter holiday season. Jeans, shorts, and T-shirts (either sleeveless or with slogans) are always frowned upon at dinner. Beach attire is appropriate only at the beach.

BRIDGETOWN

$$$ ✕ **Waterfront Café.** This friendly bistro alongside the Careenage is the
CARIBBEAN perfect place to enjoy a drink, snack, or meal—and to people-watch. Locals and tourists alike gather for alfresco all-day dining on sandwiches, salads, fish, pasta, pepper-pot stew, and tasty Bajan snacks such as buljol, fish cakes, or plantation pork (plantains stuffed with spicy minced pork). The panfried flying-fish sandwich is an especially

popular lunchtime treat. Dinner is served only Thursday, Friday, and Saturday nights; the menu is more extensive, and diners are treated to live jazz. [$] *Average main: $25* ✉ *The Careenage, Bridgetown, St. Michael* ☎ *246/427–0093* 🌐 *www.waterfrontcafe.com.bb* 🕑 *No dinner Mon.–Wed. Closed Sun.*

SOUTH COAST

$$$ ITALIAN FAMILY 🍴 **Bellini's Trattoria.** Classic northern Italian cuisine is the specialty at Bellini's, on the main floor of the Little Bay Hotel. Toast the evening with a Bellini cocktail (ice-cold sparkling wine with a splash of fruit nectar) and start your meal with bruschetta, an individual gourmet pizza, or perhaps a homemade pasta dish with fresh herbs and a rich sauce. Move on to the signature garlic shrimp entrée or the popular chicken parmigiana—then top it all off with a sweet extravagance such as chocolate mousse cake. We recommend making your reservations early; request a table on the Mediterranean-style veranda to enjoy one of the most appealing dining settings on the south coast. [$] *Average main: $32* ✉ *Little Bay Hotel, St. Lawrence Gap, Dover, Christ Church* ☎ *246/420–7587* 🌐 *www.bellinisbarbados.com* ✍ *Reservations essential.*

$$$ CARIBBEAN FAMILY 🍴 **Brown Sugar.** Set back from the road in a traditional Bajan home, the lattice-trimmed dining patios here are filled with ferns, flowers, and water features. Brown Sugar is a popular lunch spot for local businesspeople, who come for the nearly 30 delicious local and creole dishes spread out at the all-you-can-eat, four-course Bajan buffet. Here's your chance to try local specialties such as flying fish, cou-cou, buljol, *souse* (pickled pork, stewed for hours in broth), fish cakes, and pepper pot. In the evening, the à la carte menu has dishes such as fried flying fish, coconut shrimp, and plantain-crusted mahimahi; curried lamb, filet mignon, and broiled pepper chicken; and seafood or pesto pasta. Bring the kids—there's a special children's menu with fried chicken, fried flying-fish fingers, and pasta dishes. Save room for the warm pawpaw (papaya) pie or Bajan rum pudding with rum sauce. [$] *Average main: $28* ✉ *Bay St., Aquatic Gap, St. Michael* ☎ *246/426–7684* 🌐 *www.brownsugarbarbados.com* 🕑 *No lunch Sat. No dinner Oct.*

$$$$ ECLECTIC 🍴 **Café Luna.** With a sweeping view of pretty Miami (Enterprise) Beach, the alfresco dining deck on top of the Mediterranean-style Little Arches Hotel is spectacular at lunchtime and magical in the moonlight. At lunch (for hotel guests only), sip on crisp white wine or a fruity cocktail while you await your freshly made salad, pasta, or sandwich. At dinner, the expertise of executive chef (and co-owner) Mark de Gruchy is displayed through contemporary dishes from around the world, including fresh Scottish salmon grilled to perfection, oven-roasted New Zealand rack of lamb, fresh seafood bouillabaisse, and local chicken breast with mango chutney. Their special three-course menu is a good deal; sushi is a specialty on Thursday and Friday night. [$] *Average main: $33* ✉ *Little Arches Hotel, Enterprise Beach Rd., Oistins, Christ Church* ☎ *246/420–4689* 🌐 *www.littlearches.com* ✍ *Reservations essential.*

$$ MEXICAN FAMILY 🍴 **Café Sol.** Have a hankerin' for good Tex-Mex food? Enjoy nachos, tacos, burritos, empanadas, fajitas, and tostadas in this Mexican bar and grill at the entrance to busy St. Lawrence Gap. Or choose a

burger, honey-barbecue chicken, or flame-grilled steak from the gringo menu. Helpings of rice and beans, a Corona, and plenty of jalapeño peppers, guacamole, and salsa give everything a Mexican touch. Some people come just for the margaritas—15 fruity varieties rimmed with Bajan sugar instead of salt. With two happy hours every night, this place gets really busy, and reservations are accepted only for parties of four or more. $ *Average main: $20* ✉ *St. Lawrence Gap, Dover, Christ Church* ☎ *246/420–7655* 🌐 *www.cafesolbarbados.com* ✍ *Reservations not accepted* 🕘 *No lunch Mon.*

BEST BETS FOR DINING

Fodor's Choice ★
The Atlantis, Champers, The Cliff, Daphne's, The Tides, Waterside

BEST VIEW
L'Azure at the Crane, The Atlantis, Champers, The Tides

BEST FOR FAMILIES
Bellini's Trattoria

MOST ROMANTIC
The Mews, Lone Star, Waterside

BEST FOR LOCAL BAJAN CUISINE
Brown Sugar, Naniki, Waterfront Café

$$$$ ECLECTIC FAMILY Fodor's Choice ★

🍴 **Champers.** Chiryl Newman's snazzy seaside restaurant is in an old Bajan home just off the main road in Rockley. Luncheon guests—about 75% local businesspeople—enjoy repasts such as char-grilled beef salad, Champers fish pie, or grilled barracuda. Dinner guests swoon over dishes such as the herb-crusted rack of lamb with spring vegetables and mint-infused jus, the grilled sea scallops with risotto primavera, and the parmesan-crusted barracuda with wholegrain mustard sauce. The portions are hearty and the food is well seasoned with Caribbean flavors, "just the way the locals like it," says Newman. Dining out with the family? There's a kid's menu, too. The cliff-top setting overlooking the eastern end of Accra Beach offers diners a panoramic view of the sea and a relaxing atmosphere for daytime dining. Nearly all the artwork gracing the walls is by Barbadian artists and may be purchased through the on-site gallery. $ *Average main: $35* ✉ *Skeetes Hill, off Hwy. 7, Rockley, Christ Church* ☎ *246/434–3463* 🌐 *www.champersbarbados.com* ✍ *Reservations essential.*

$$$$ SEAFOOD FAMILY Fodor's Choice ★

🍴 **L'Azure at the Crane.** Perched on an oceanfront cliff, L'Azure is an informal breakfast and luncheon spot by day that becomes elegant after dark. Enjoy seafood chowder or a light salad or sandwich while absorbing the breathtaking panoramic view of Crane Beach and the sea beyond. At dinner, candlelight and soft guitar music enhance tamarind-glazed snapper or a fabulous Caribbean lobster seasoned with herbs, lime juice, and garlic butter and served in its shell; if you're not in the mood for seafood, try the crusted rack of lamb or herb-infused pork tenderloin. Sunday is really special, with a Gospel Brunch ($26) at 9 or 10 am and a Bajan Buffet ($40) at 12:30 pm. $ *Average main: $35* ✉ *The Crane, Crane Bay, St. Philip* ☎ *246/423–6220* 🌐 *www.thecrane.com* ✍ *Reservations essential* 🕘 *No dinner Wed.*

$$ CARIBBEAN

🍴 **Shaker's.** Locals and visitors alike gather at this "upscale rum shop" for a variety of drinks—a Banks beer or two, a Margarita, a pitcher of Sangria, or whatever wets their whistle—and delicious local food.

Simple dishes like beer-battered flying fish, grilled catch of the day, barbecued chicken, grilled steak, or a solid cheeseburger deliver the goods. All main dishes include crisp green salad, coleslaw, and either grilled or french-fried potatoes. It's a colorful, convivial place, full of laughter and chatter—partly because the tables are so close together and partly because of the rum shop atmosphere. Arrive early or make a reservation if you want an outside table, as it fills up quickly; and be prepared to pay in cash. [$] *Average main: $15* ✉ *Browne's Gap, Rockley, Christ Church* ☎ *246/228–8855* 🌐 *www.shakersbarbados.com* ✍ *Reservations essential* 💳 *No credit cards* 🕒 *Closed Sun. and Mon. No lunch.*

$$ CARIBBEAN 🍴 **Sweet Potatoes.** "Good Old Bajan Cooking" is the slogan at this popular restaurant in the Gap, and that's what you can expect. Of course, you'll want to start everything off with a chilled rum punch. Then whet your appetite with some favorite local appetizers such as buljol (marinated codfish seasoned with herbs and onions), sweet plantains stuffed with minced beef, pumpkin-and-spinach fritters, or deep-fried fish cakes. A selection of Bajan appetizers will make a filling lunch as well. The dinner menu includes flying fish stuffed with local vegetables, grilled chicken breast in a Malibu Rum sauce, catch of the day bathed in a creole sauce, and jerk pork. Rum cake, flambéed bananas, and bread pudding with rum sauce are traditional desserts. [$] *Average main: $20* ✉ *St. Lawrence Gap, Dover, Christ Church* ☎ *246/420–7668.*

$$$$ CONTEMPORARY Fodor's Choice ★ 🍴 **Waterside Restaurant.** You won't get much closer to dining on the water without being on a boat. Tables here are set on a broad porch suspended over the beachfront and spaced generously to allow for pleasant and private conversation; all the bustle of vibrant St. Lawrence Gap is left at the door. Once inside, the setting becomes sophisticated, tranquil, and definitely picturesque; the mood, quiet and intimate. And then there's the food. Chef Michael Hinds's truly elegant cuisine features dishes such as seared and crusted red snapper with tarragon emulsion, fire-roasted tiger prawns on bamboo and lemon-scented basmati rice with cashews, five-spice braised short rib with garlic mashed potatoes, and more. For dessert, don't miss the spiced banana spring rolls with coconut ice cream and brandy caramel coulis. [$] *Average main: $34* ✉ *St. Lawrence Gap, Dover, Christ Church* ☎ *203/418–9750* 🌐 *www.watersiderest.com* ✍ *Reservations essential* 🕒 *Closed Mon. No lunch.*

EAST COAST

$$$ CARIBBEAN Fodor's Choice ★ 🍴 **The Atlantis.** For decades, an alfresco lunch on the Atlantis deck overlooking the ocean has been a favorite of visitors and Bajans alike. Pleasant atmosphere and good food have always been the draw, with an elegant dining room and a top-notch menu that focuses on local produce, seafood, and meats. The Bajan buffet lunch on Wednesday and Sunday is particularly popular. At dinner, entrées include fresh fish, lobster (seasonal), roasted black-belly lamb or free-range chicken, fricassee of rabbit, and more. Or choose more traditional pepper pot, saltfish, or chicken stew with peas and rice, cou-cou, yam pie, or breadfruit mash, all of which are available at the Bajan buffet. [$] *Average main: $25* ✉ *The Atlantis Hotel, Tent Bay, St. Joseph* ☎ *246/433–9445* 🌐 *www.atlantishotelbarbados.com* ✍ *Reservations essential* 🕒 *No dinner Sun.*

$$$ ✕**Naniki Restaurant.** Rich wooden beams and stone tiles, clay pottery,
CARIBBEAN   straw mats, and colorful dinnerware set the style at Naniki (an Arawak
word meaning "full of life"). Huge picture windows and outdoor porch
seating allow you to enjoy the exhilarating view of surrounding hills
and gardens along with your lunch of exquisitely prepared Caribbean
standards. Seared flying fish, grilled dorado, stewed lambi (conch), and
jerk chicken or pork are accompanied by cou-cou, peas and rice, or
salad. For dinner (by special request only), start with conch fritters or
Caribbean fish soup; then try roasted Bajan black-belly lamb or shrimp
garnished with tarragon. Sunday brunch is a Caribbean buffet often
featuring great jazz music by some of the Caribbean's best musicians.
Vegetarian dishes are always available. $ *Average main: $28* ⊠ *Lush
Life Nature Resort, Suriname, St. Joseph* ☎ *246/433–1300* ⊕ *www.
lushlife.bb/naniki* ⋈ *Reservations essential.*

WEST COAST

5

$$$$ ✕**The Cliff.** Chef Paul Owens's mastery is the foundation of one of the
ECLECTIC   finest dining experiences in the Caribbean, with prices to match. Steep
Fodor'sChoice   steps hug the cliff on which the restaurant sits to accommodate those
★   arriving by yacht, and every candlelit table has a sea view. Starter sug-
gestions include smoked salmon ravioli with garlic sauce or grilled
portobello mushroom on greens with truffle vinaigrette; for the main
course, try char-grilled swordfish with Thai yellow curry sauce, seared
tuna with saffron caper sauce and tomato coulis, or Cajun salmon with
pesto cream sauce. Dessert falls into the sinful category, and service is
impeccable. The prix-fixe menu will set you back $125 per person for
a two-course meal or $145 per person for a three-course meal. Reserve
days or even weeks in advance to snag a table at the front of the ter-
race for the best view. $ *Average main: $125* ⊠ *Hwy. 1, Derricks, St.
James* ☎ *246/432–1922* ⊕ *www.thecliffbarbados.com* ⋈ *Reservations
essential* ⊘ *Closed Sun. Apr. 15–Dec. 15. No lunch.*

$$$$ ✕**Daphne's.** The beachfront restaurant at the House, Daphne's is the
ITALIAN   chic Caribbean outpost of the famed London eatery of the same name,
Fodor'sChoice   with chef Marco Festini Cromer whipping up contemporary Italian cui-
★   sine. Grilled mahimahi, for example, becomes "modern Italian" when
combined with marsala wine, *peperonata* (stewed peppers, tomatoes,
onions, and garlic), and zucchini. Perfectly prepared *melanzane* (egg-
plant) and zucchini alla parmigiana is a delicious starter, and a half por-
tion of risotto with porcini mushrooms, green beans, and Parma ham is
fabulously rich. Pappardelle with braised duck, red wine, and oregano
is a sublime pasta choice. There's even a gluten-free dinner menu. The
extensive wine list features both regional Italian and fine French selec-
tions. $ *Average main: $40* ⊠ *The House, Hwy. 1, Paynes Bay, St.
James* ☎ *246/432–2731* ⊕ *www.daphnesbarbados.com* ⋈ *Reservations
essential* ⊘ *Closed Mon. June–Nov.*

$$$$ ✕**Fish Pot.** Just north of the little fishing village of Six Men's Bay, on
MEDITERRANEAN   the northwestern coast of Barbados, this attractive seaside restau-
Fodor'sChoice   rant serves excellent Mediterranean cuisine and some of the island's
★   freshest fish. Gaze seaward through windows framed with pale-green
louvered shutters while lunching on a seafood crepe, a grilled panini,

snow-crab salad, or perhaps pasta with seafood or roasted-pepper-and-chili tomato sauce; in the evening, the menu may include seafood bouillabaisse; seared, herb-crusted tuna on garlic-and-spinach polenta; sun-dried-tomato risotto tossed with vegetables; or braised lamb shank with pan gravy. Bright and cheery by day and relaxed and cozy by night, the Fish Pot offers a tasty dining experience in a setting that's classier than its name might suggest. [$] *Average main: $35* ✉ *Little Good Harbour Hotel, Shermans, St. Peter* ☎ *246/439–3000* 🌐 *www.littlegoodharbourbarbados.com* ✍ *Reservations essential.*

$$ CARIBBEAN 🍴 **Fisherman's Pub.** This is as local as local gets. Fisherman's Pub is an open-air, waterfront restaurant built on stilts just a stone's throw from the Speightstown fish market. For years fishermen and other locals have come here daily for the inexpensive, authentic Bajan buffet served at lunchtime. For $10 or so you can soak up the atmosphere and fill your plate with fried flying fish, stewed chicken or pork, curried goat or lamb, macaroni pie, fried plantain, cou-cou, and crisp green salad. On Wednesday nights, fill your plate from the buffet and dance—or simply listen—to catchy steel pan or calypso music. (Whether dinner is served varies from season to season, so call ahead.) [$] *Average main: $20* ✉ *Queen St., Speightstown, St. Peter* ☎ *246/422–2703* ✍ *Reservations not accepted.*

$$$$ EUROPEAN 🍴 **Lone Star.** Top chefs in the snazzy restaurant at the tiny but chic Lone Star Hotel turn the finest local ingredients into gastronomic delights. All day, tasty dishes like fish soup with rouille, Caesar or Thai chicken salad, and linguine with tomato-basil sauce and feta cheese are served in the oceanfront beach bar. At sunset the casual daytime atmosphere turns trendy. You might start with tuna tartare with mango or Thai crab cakes with peppers and lemongrass dip, followed by crispy Peking duckling, grilled fish of the day, or lamb shank with basil mashed potatoes—or choose from dozens of other tasty land, sea, and vegetarian dishes. [$] *Average main: $36* ✉ *Lone Star Hotel, Hwy. 1, Mount Standfast, St. James* ☎ *246/419–0599* 🌐 *www.thelonestar.com.*

$$$$ EUROPEAN 🍴 **The Mews.** Dining at the Mews is like being invited to a friend's very chic home for dinner. Once a private home, the front room is now an inviting bar and an interior courtyard is an intimate, open-air dining area. The second floor is a maze of small dining rooms and balconies, but it's the food, mostly international cuisine with a contemporary flair, that draws the visitors. A plump chicken breast, for example, will be stuffed with cream cheese, smoked salmon, and herb pâté and served on a garlic-and-chive sauce and a braised lamb shank is presented on a bed of cabbage with a port-thyme jus and creamed potatoes. Some call the atmosphere avant-garde; others call it quaint. Everyone calls the food delicious. But don't stop at dinner; by about 10 pm, the bar begins to bustle. [$] *Average main: $38* ✉ *2nd St., Holetown, St. James* ☎ *246/432–1122* 🌐 *themewsbarbados.com* ✍ *Reservations essential* 🕑 *No lunch.*

$$$ ECLECTIC 🍴 **Scarlet.** Movers and groovers come to this bright-red building on the side of the road to chill over a martini and share nibbles, such as a plate of flying-fish lollipops, or to settle in after cocktails for a burger with sophisticated toppings, Bajan ham with corn pancakes,

or perhaps Baxter's Road chicken. Enjoy your meal sitting at the large bar—the centerpiece of this casual but stylish watering hole—or at a nearby table. Specialty of the house: Scarlet Rocks (vodka, raspberry schnapps, strawberries, cranberry juice, basil, and black pepper!). $ *Average main: $28* ✉ *Hwy. 1, Paynes Bay, St. James* ☎ *246/432–3663* ⊕ *www.scarletbarbados.com* ⌿ *Reservations essential* ⊙ *Closed Sun. and Mon. No lunch.*

$$$$
EUROPEAN
Fodor'sChoice
★

✕ **The Tides.** Local residents and repeat visitors agree that the Tides is one of the island's best restaurants. Enter the courtyard of what was once a private mansion and have a cocktail at the cozy bar or visit the on-site art gallery before proceeding to your seaside table. Perhaps the most intriguing feature of this stunning setting—besides the sound of waves crashing onto the shore just feet away—is the row of huge tree trunks growing right through the dining room. The food is equally dramatic. Chef Guy Beasley and his team give a contemporary twist to fresh seafood, filet of beef, rack of lamb, and other top-of-the-line main courses by adding inspired sauces and delicate vegetables and garnishes. A full vegetarian menu is also available. Save room for the sticky toffee pudding—definitely worth the calories. $ *Average main: $50* ✉ *Balmore House, Hwy. 1, Holetown, St. James* ☎ *246/432–8356* ⊕ *www. tidesbarbados.com* ⌿ *Reservations essential* ⊙ *No lunch weekends.*

WHERE TO STAY

Most visitors stay either on the fashionable west coast, north of Bridgetown, or on the action-packed south coast. On the west coast, the beachfront resorts in St. Peter and St. James parishes are mostly luxurious, self-contained enclaves. Highway 1, a two-lane road with considerable traffic, runs past these resorts; strolling to a nearby bar or restaurant can be a bit difficult. Along the south coast in Christ Church Parish, several hotels are clustered near the busy strip known as St. Lawrence Gap, convenient to dozens of small restaurants, bars, and nightclubs. On the much more remote east coast, a few small inns offer oceanfront views and get-away-from-it-all tranquillity.

In keeping with the smoke-free policy enforced throughout Barbados, smoking is restricted to open outdoor areas such as the beach. It is not permitted in hotels (neither rooms nor public areas) or in restaurants.

Prices in Barbados may be twice as high in season (December 15–April 15) compared with the quieter months; special promotions and vacation packages are often available throughout the year. Most hotels include no meals in their rates, but some include breakfast and many offer a meal plan. Some require you to purchase a meal plan in the high season, and a few offer all-inclusive packages.

Resorts run the gamut—from unpretentious to exceedingly formal—in terms of size, intimacy, amenities, and price. Families and long-term visitors may choose from a wide variety of villas and condos. A few small, cozy inns are found along the east and southeast coasts, as well as the northwest. They can be ultraluxurious, fairly simple, or something in between.

5

Villa and condo complexes, which are continually cropping up along the south and west coasts of Barbados, may be the most economical option for families, groups, or couples vacationing together. Non-owner vacationers rent individual units directly from the property managers, the same as reserving hotel accommodations. Apartments are available for vacation rentals in buildings or complexes with as few as three or four units or as many as 30 to 40 units—or even more.

PRIVATE VILLAS AND CONDOS

Local real-estate agencies will arrange vacation rentals of privately owned villas and condos along the west coast in St. James and St. Peter. All villas and condos are fully furnished and equipped—including appropriate staff depending on the size of the villa or unit, which can range from one to eight bedrooms; the staff usually works six days a week. Most villas have TVs and other entertainment devices; all properties have telephones, and some have Internet access. International telephone calls are usually blocked; plan on using your own mobile phone or a phone card or calling card. Vehicles generally are not included in the rates, but rental cars can be arranged for and delivered to the villa upon request. Linens and basic supplies (such as bath soap, toilet tissue, and dishwashing detergent) are normally included.

Villas or condos with one to eight bedrooms and as many baths run $200 to $2,500 per night in summer, and double that in winter. Rates include utilities and government taxes. The only additional cost is for groceries and staff gratuities. A security deposit is required upon booking and refunded seven days after departure less any damages or unpaid miscellaneous charges.

Villa Rental Contacts Altman Real Estate ⊠ *Hwy. 1, Derricks, St. James* ☎ *246/432–0840, 866/360–5292 in the U.S.* ⊕ *www.aaaltman.com.* **Bajan Services** ⊠ *Newton House, Battaleys, St. Peter* ☎ *246/422–2618* ⊕ *www.bajanservices.com.* **Island Villas** ⊠ *Trents Bldg., Holetown, St. James* ☎ *246/432–4627, 866/978–8499 in the U.S.* ⊕ *www.island-villas.com.*

Apartment Rental Contacts Barbados Tourism Authority. The Barbados Tourism Authority on Harbour Road in Bridgetown has a listing of apartments in prime resort areas on both the south and west coasts, complete with facilities offered and current rates. ⊠ *Harbour Rd., Bridgetown, St. Michael* ☎ *246/427–2623* ⊕ *www.visitbarbados.org* ⊟ *No credit cards.*

BEST BETS FOR LODGING

Fodor's Choice ★

The Atlantis Hotel, Cobblers Cove Hotel, Coral Reef Club, Fairmont Royal Pavilion, Hilton Barbados, The Sandpiper, Sandy Lane, Sweetfield Manor

BEST FOR HONEYMOONERS

Cobblers Cove Hotel, Couples Barbados, Fairmont Royal Pavilion, The House, Treasure Beach, Sweetfield Manor

BEST FOR FAMILIES

Bougainvillea, Divi Southwinds, Hilton Barbados, Tamarind, Turtle Beach Resort

SOUTH COAST

$ RESORT 🏨 **Accra Beach Hotel and Spa.** A full-service resort in the middle of the busy south coast, Accra is large, it's modern, it faces a great beach, and it's competitively priced. **Pros:** on a great beach and, on the street side, near shopping, restaurants, and nightspots; good value; complimentary Wi-Fi. **Cons:** rooms facing the street are inexpensive but have a lousy view; a/c in some rooms needs upgrading. [$] *Rooms from: $230* ✉ *Hwy. 7, Rockley, Christ Church* ☎ *246/435–8920, 888/712–2272 in the U.S.* 🌐 *www.accrabeachhotel.com* 🛏 *190 rooms, 34 suites* 🍴 *Multiple meal plans.*

$$$$ RESORT FAMILY 🏨 **Bougainvillea Beach Resort.** Attractive seaside townhouses, each with a separate entrance, wrap around the pool or face the beachfront; the suites are huge compared with hotel suites elsewhere in this price range, are decorated in appealing Caribbean pastels, and have full kitchens. **Pros:** great for families but also appeals to honeymooners; popular wedding venue; easy stroll to St. Lawrence Gap or to Oistins; complimentary Wi-Fi. **Cons:** rooms are on four levels with no elevator; sea can be a little rough for swimming. [$] *Rooms from: $480* ✉ *Maxwell Coast Rd., Maxwell, Christ Church* ☎ *246/418–0990, 800/495–1858 in the U.S.* 🌐 *www.bougainvillearesort.com* 🛏 *138 suites* 🍴 *Multiple meal plans.*

$ HOTEL 🏨 **Courtyard Bridgetown by Marriott.** Comfortable, contemporary, convenient, and economical, this place is pleasant and the rooms are well appointed. **Pros:** good value; especially suited to business travelers; modern, attractive accommodations. **Cons:** walk to beach and restaurants; comparatively little "Caribbean resort" atmosphere; limited on-site dining options. [$] *Rooms from: $239* ✉ *Hwy. 7, Hastings Main Rd., set back a block from road, the Garrison Historic Area, Hastings, Christ Church* ☎ *246/625–0000* 🌐 *www.marriott.com* 🛏 *118 rooms* 🍴 *No meals.*

$$ RESORT 🏨 **The Crane.** Hugging a seaside bluff on the southeast coast, The Crane incorporates the island's oldest hotel in continuous operation; the original coral-stone hotel building (1887) is the centerpiece of a luxurious, 40-acre villa complex. **Pros:** enchanting view; lovely beach; fabulous suites; great restaurants. **Cons:** remote location; rental car recommended; villas are considerably more expensive than historic rooms. [$] *Rooms from: $320* ✉ *Crane Bay, St. Philip* ☎ *246/423–6220* 🌐 *www.thecrane.com* 🛏 *4 rooms, 14 suites, 202 villas* 🍴 *Multiple meal plans.*

$ RESORT FAMILY 🏨 **Divi Southwinds Beach Resort.** The all-suites Divi Southwinds is situated on 20 acres of lawn and gardens bisected by action-packed St. Lawrence Gap. **Pros:** beautiful beach; beach villas are the best value; close to shopping, restaurants, and nightspots. **Cons:** few water sports available and none included; some rooms aching for renovations. [$] *Rooms from: $139* ✉ *St. Lawrence Main Rd., Dover, Christ Church* ☎ *246/428–7181* 🌐 *www.divisouthwinds.com* 🛏 *121 1-bedroom suites, 12 2-bedroom suites* 🍴 *Multiple meal plans.*

$$$ HOTEL FAMILY Fodor's Choice ★ 🏨 **Hilton Barbados.** Beautifully situated on the sandy Needham's Point peninsula, all 350 rooms and suites in this high-rise resort hotel have private balconies overlooking either the ocean or Carlisle Bay; 77 rooms on executive floors offer a private lounge and concierge services. **Pros:** great location near town and on a beautiful beach; excellent accommodations; lots of services and amenities; frequent promotional deals provide real value. **Cons:** huge convention hotel; attracts groups; lacks

"island" ambience. $ *Rooms from: $399* ✉ *Needham's Point, St. Michael* ☎ *246/426–0200* ⊕ *www.hiltonbarbadoshotel.com* ✈ *317 rooms, 33 suites* ⦿ *Multiple meal plans.*

$$$
ALL-INCLUSIVE

⌖ **Island Inn Hotel.** Originally constructed in 1804 as a rum storage facility for the British Regiment, this quaint, all-inclusive boutique hotel—less than a mile from Bridgetown and steps away from beautiful Pebbles Beach on Carlisle Bay—appeals to singles, couples, and families. **Pros:** friendly, accommodating atmosphere; smartly decorated rooms; excellent value. **Cons:** small pool; request a room near the pool, as rooms near the front can be noisy and don't have a patio. $ *Rooms from: $415* ✉ *Garrison Historic Area, Aquatic Gap, St. Michael* ☎ *246/436–6393* ⊕ *www.islandinnbarbados.com* ✈ *20 rooms, 4 suites* ⦿ *All-inclusive.*

$$$
HOTEL

⌖ **Little Arches Hotel.** Just east of the fishing village of Oistins, this classy boutique hotel has a distinctly Mediterranean ambience and a perfect vantage point overlooking the sea. **Pros:** stylish accommodations; good restaurant; across from fabulous Miami Beach. **Cons:** fairly remote; rental car advised. $ *Rooms from: $310* ✉ *Enterprise Beach Rd., Oistins, Christ Church* ☎ *246/420–4689* ⊕ *www.littlearches.com* ✈ *8 rooms, 2 suites* ⦿ *Multiple meal plans.*

$$$
RESORT

⌖ **Ocean Two.** Couples and families alike are drawn to this sophisticated beachfront resort right in the midst of lively St. Lawrence Gap. **Pros:** large, luxurious accommodations; beautiful beach; planned children's activities during summer and holiday season. **Cons:** showers only, no tubs; meals at Taste could be more tasty, but plenty of dining options are nearby. $ *Rooms from: $471* ✉ *St. Lawrence Gap, Dover, Christ Church* ☎ *246/418–1800* ⊕ *www.oceantwobarbados.com* ✈ *18 rooms, 68 1- and 2-bedroom suites* ⦿ *Some meals.*

$$
HOTEL

⌖ **Radisson Aquatica Resort Barbados.** Radisson invested $50 million to refurbish the former Grand Barbados Beach Resort and in 2013 reopened the renamed high-rise hotel overlooking pretty Carlisle Bay, just south of Bridgetown. **Pros:** lovely beach; comfortable rooms, all with an ocean view; complimentary Wi-Fi. **Cons:** skip the Pier Restaurant and opt, instead, for neighboring Brown Sugar. $ *Rooms from: $329* ✉ *Aquatic Gap, Carlisle Bay, St. Michael* ☎ *246/426–6000* ⊕ *www.radisson.com/barbados* ✈ *124 rooms* ⦿ *Breakfast.*

$$$$
ALL-INCLUSIVE

⌖ **Sandals Barbados.** Purchased by Sandals in November 2013, the former Casuarina Hotel is one of just two adults-only, all-inclusive resorts on the island and the only one on the south coast. **Pros:** great beach and beautiful garden; lots of included activities, including scuba diving; a magnet for weddings, honeymoons, and vow renewals. **Cons:** lots of good restaurants to try in nearby St. Lawrence Gap, but you've paid for an all-inclusive; ocean-facing building (Block 1) has elevators, but other buildings are four-story walkups. $ *Rooms from: $580* ✉ *St. Lawrence Gap, at Maxwell Coast Rd., Dover, Christ Church* ☎ *246/428–3600* ⊕ *www.sandals.com* ✈ *280 rooms* ⦿ *All-inclusive.*

$
HOTEL

⌖ **Silver Point Hotel.** This gated community of modern condos at Silver Sands–Silver Rock Beach is operated as a trendy boutique hotel that appeals to singles, couples, and families—but especially to windsurfers and kitesurfers. **Pros:** stylish suites; perfect location for windsurfers and

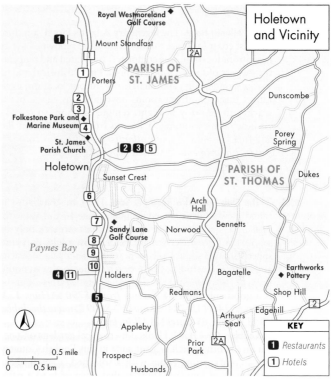

Holetown
and Vicinity

kitesurfers; gated community. **Cons:** very remote; not within walking distance of anything except the beach; sea can be rough for swimming; rental car recommended. [$] *Rooms from: $230* ⊠ *Silver Sands, Christ Church* ☎ *246/420–4416* ⊕ *www.silverpointhotel.com* ⇆ *58 suites* ⦿ *Multiple meal plans.*

$$$$ ⚏ **The SoCo Hotel.** Sophisticated couples love this ultramodern boutique
ALL-INCLUSIVE hotel strategically poised on the beachfront in Hastings Well-respected Bajan hotelier Ralph Taylor opened the property in mid-2013. **Pros:** stylish rooms; personalized service; excellent restaurant; lovely beach with long boardwalk; complimentary Wi-Fi. **Cons:** showers only, no tubs, for those who care; very expensive. [$] *Rooms from: $800* ⊠ *Hastings Main Rd., Hastings, Christ Church* ☎ *246/228–6955* ⊕ *www. thesocohotel.com* ⇆ *24 rooms* ⦿ *All-inclusive.*

$$$$ ⚏ **Turtle Beach Resort.** Families flock to Turtle Beach Resort because it
ALL-INCLUSIVE offers large, bright suites and enough all-included activities for everyone
FAMILY to enjoy. **Pros:** perfect for family vacations; nice pools; roomy accommodations; lots of services and amenities. **Cons:** beach is relatively narrow; open vent between bedroom and hallway can be noisy at night. [$] *Rooms from: $845* ⊠ *St. Lawrence Gap, Dover, Christ Church* ☎ *246/428–7131* ⊕ *www.turtlebeachresortbarbados.com* ⇆ *164 suites* ⦿ *All-inclusive.*

Harbour Lights. This open-air, beachfront club claims to be the "home of the party animal." Wednesday and Friday nights are the hottest with dancing under the stars to reggae and soca music. ⊠ *Marine Villa, Bay St., south of town, Carlisle Bay* ☎ *246/436–7225* ⊕ *www. harbourlightsbarbados.com.*

Waterfront Café. From November through April, there's live jazz Thursday, Friday, and Saturday evenings at Waterfront Café, which also has a small dance floor. The location alongside the wharf is also a draw. ⊠ *The Careenage* ☎ *246/427–0093* ⊕ *www.waterfrontcafe.com.bb* ☉ *Closed Sun.–Wed.*

SOUTH COAST

Bubba's Sports Bar. On the south coast, Bubba's offers merrymakers and sports lovers live action on three 10-foot video screens and a dozen TVs, along with a Bajan à la carte menu and drinks at the bar. ⊠ *Main Rd., Rockley, Christ Church* ☎ *246/435–6217.*

FAMILY
Fodor'sChoice
★

Oistins Fish Fry. Oistins is the place to be on Friday evenings, when the south-coast fishing village becomes a lively and convivial outdoor street party. Barbecued chicken and a variety of fish, along with all the traditional sides (rice and peas, yams, fries, macaroni pie, salad, etc.), are served fresh from the grill and consumed at roadside picnic tables; servings are huge, and prices are inexpensive—about $10 per plate. Drinks, music, and dancing add to the fun. ⊠ *Oistins, Christ Church.*

Reggae Lounge. This is a popular nightspot in the Gap, where live bands or DJs play the latest Jamaican hits and old reggae favorites every night until the wee hours. ⊠ *St. Lawrence Gap, Dover, Christ Church* ☎ *246/435–6462.*

Sugar Ultra Lounge. Sugar Ultra Lounge is a chic, upscale, techno nightspot—complete with a light show wall—that attracts international talent in addition to the usual DJ and occasional local band. The club is open Tuesday, Thursday, and Saturday nights from 10 pm to 3 or 4 am. Rush Restaurant is adjacent to the club for casual dining. ⊠ *St. Lawrence Gap, Dover, Christ Church* ☎ *246/420–7662.*

WEST COAST

Fodor'sChoice
★

Lexy Piano Bar. Lexy's is a cool, trendy club named for owner Alex Santoriello, a transplanted Broadway singer and actor. A changing roster of singer-pianists play sing-along standards, classic rock, R&B, and Broadway tunes—and you can also enjoy a treat from the sushi bar. While it's open earlier, the fun really starts at 10 or 11 pm. And most any night you'll find Santoriello there. ⊠ *2nd St., Holetown, St. James* ☎ *246/432–5399* ⊕ *www.lexypianobar.com* ☉ *Closed Mon.*

A local chef cooks up a fish fry at the Oistins fish market in Bridgetown.

SHOPPING

WHAT TO BUY

One of the most long-lasting souvenirs to bring home from Barbados is a piece of authentic Caribbean art. The colorful flowers, quaint villages, mesmerizing seascapes, and fascinating cultural experiences and activities that are endemic to the region and familiar to visitors have been translated by local artists onto canvas and into photographs, sculpture, and other media. Gift shops and even some restaurants display local artwork for sale, but the broadest array of artwork will be found in a gallery. Typical Bajan crafts include pottery, shell and glass art, wood carvings, handmade dolls, watercolors, and other artwork (both originals and prints).

Although many of the private homes, greathouses, and museums in Barbados are filled with priceless antiques, you'll find few for sale—mainly British antiques and some local pieces, particularly mahogany furniture. Look especially for planters' chairs and the classic Barbadian rocking chair, as well as old prints and paintings.

DUTY-FREE SHOPPING

Duty-free luxury goods—china, crystal, cameras, porcelain, leather items, electronics, jewelry, perfume, and clothing—are found in Bridgetown's Broad Street department stores and their branches, at the high-end Limegrove Lifestyle Centre in Holetown, at the Bridgetown Cruise Terminal (for passengers only), and in the departure lounge at Grantley Adams International Airport. Prices are often 30% to 40% less than full retail. To buy goods at duty-free prices, you must produce

Where de Rum Come From

For more than 300 years (from 1655 through "Black Tot Day," July 31, 1970), a daily "tot" of rum (2 ounces) was duly administered to each sailor in the British navy—as a health ration. At times, rum has also played a less appetizing—but equally important— role. When Admiral Horatio Nelson died in 1805 aboard ship during the Battle of Trafalgar, his body was preserved in a cask of his favorite rum until he could be properly buried.

Hardly a Caribbean island doesn't have its own locally made rum, but Barbados is truly "where de rum come from." Mount Gay, the world's oldest rum distillery, has continuously operated on Barbados since 1703, according to the original deed for the Mount Gay Estate, which itemized two stone windmills, a boiling house, seven copper pots, and a still house. The presence of rum-making

equipment on the plantation at the time suggests that the previous owners were actually producing rum in Barbados long before 1703.

Today, much of the island's interior is still planted with sugarcane—where the rum really does come from—and several greathouses on historic sugar planta- tions have been restored with period furniture and are open to the public.

To really fathom rum, however, you need to delve a little deeper than the bottom of a glass of rum punch. Mount Gay offers an interesting 45-minute tour of its main plant, followed by a tasting. You can learn about the rum-making process from cane to cocktail, hear more rum-inspired anecdotes, and have an opportunity to buy bottles of its famous Eclipse or Extra Old rum at duty-free prices. Bottoms up!

your passport, immigration form, or driver's license, along with depar- ture information (such as flight number and date) at the time of pur- chase—or you can have your purchases delivered free to the airport or harbor for pickup; duty-free alcohol, tobacco products, and some electronic equipment *must* be delivered to you at the airport or harbor.

GROCERIES

If you've chosen self-catering lodgings, are looking for snacks, or just want to explore a local grocery store, you'll find large, modern super- markets at Sunset Crest in Holetown on the west coast; in Oistins, at Sargeant's Village (Sheraton Mall), and in Worthing on the south coast; and at Warrens (Highway 2, north of Bridgetown) in St. Michael.

BRIDGETOWN

Bridgetown's **Broad Street** is the primary downtown shopping area. **DaCosta Manning Mall,** in the historic Colonnade Building on Broad Street, has more than 25 shops that sell everything from Piaget watches to postcards; across the street, **Mall 34** has 22 shops where you can buy duty-free goods, souvenirs, and snacks. At the **cruise-ship terminal** shopping arcade, passengers can buy both duty-free goods and Barbadian-made crafts at more than 30 boutiques and a dozen vendor carts and stalls.

DEPARTMENT STORES

Cave Shepherd. Cave Shepherd offers a wide selection of clothing and luxury goods; branch stores are at the Sunset Crest and West Coast malls in Holetown and the Vista shopping complex in Worthing. Boutiques are located at the airport departure lounge and cruise-ship terminal. ⊠ *Broad St.* ☎ *246/431–2121.*

Harrison's. Harrison's is a department store with several locations, including three large stores on Broad Street, one at the Sheraton Centre Mall on the South Coast, and boutiques in the airport departure lounge mall and cruise-ship terminal. ⊠ *Broad St.* ☎ *246/431–5500.*

HANDICRAFTS

Island Crafts. This store offers locally made pottery, wood carvings, straw items, glass art, batik, and wire sculptures. Additional shops are at Harrison's Cave, the airport courtyard, and the airport departure lounge. ⊠ *5 Pelican Craft Centre* ☎ *246/435–0542.*

Pelican Village Craft Centre. Pelican Village is a cluster of workshops located halfway between the cruise-ship terminal and downtown Bridgetown where craftspeople create and sell locally made leather goods, batik, basketry, carvings, jewelry, glass art, paintings, pottery, and other items. It's open weekdays 9 to 5 and Saturday 9 to 2; things here are most active when cruise ships are in port. ⊠ *Princess Alice Hwy.* ☎ *246/426–2300.*

WEST COAST

Holetown has the upscale **Limegrove Lifestyle Centre,** a stylish shopping mall with high-end designer boutiques, as well as **Chattel House Village,** small shops selling local products, fashions, beachwear, and souvenirs. Also in Holetown, **Sunset Crest Mall** has two branches of the Cave Shepherd department store, a bank, a pharmacy, and several small shops; at **West Coast Mall** you can buy duty-free goods, island wear, and groceries.

Fodor's Choice ★ **Earthworks Pottery.** Earthworks is a family-owned and -operated pottery workshop, where you can purchase anything from a dish or knickknack to a complete dinner service or one-of-a-kind art piece. You'll find the characteristically blue or green pottery—and, more recently, peach and brown hues—decorating hotel rooms and for sale in gift shops throughout the island; but the biggest selection (including "seconds") is at Earthworks, where you also can watch the potters at work. ⊠ *Edgehill Heights, St. Thomas* ☎ *246/425–0223* ⊕ *www.earthworks-pottery.com* ⊘ *Closed Sun.*

Gallery of Caribbean Art. This gallery is committed to promoting Caribbean art from Haiti and Cuba in the north to Curaçao and Guyana in the south—and, particularly, the works of Barbadian artists. ⊠ *Northern Business Centre, Queen St., Speightstown, St. Peter* ☎ *246/419–0858* ⊕ *www.artgallerycaribbean.com* ⊘ *Closed Sun.*

On the Wall Art Gallery. Artist and gallery owner Vanita Comissiong offers an array of original paintings by Barbadian artists, along with handmade arts and crafts and jewelry products. An additional gallery is located in a dedicated space at Champers restaurant on the south coast. ⊠ *Earthworks Pottery, Edgehill Heights, St. Thomas* ☎ *246/234–9145* ⊕ *www.onthewallartgallery.com* ⊘ *Closed Sun.*

SPORTS AND ACTIVITIES

Cricket, football (soccer), polo, and rugby are extremely popular sports in Barbados for participants and spectators alike, with local, regional, and international matches held throughout the year. Contact the Barbados Tourism Authority or check local newspapers for information about schedules and tickets.

DIVING AND SNORKELING

More than two dozen dive sites lie along the west coast between Maycocks Bay and Bridgetown and off the south coast as far as the St. Lawrence Gap. Certified divers can explore flat coral reefs and see dramatic sea fans, huge barrel sponges, and more than 50 varieties of fish. Nine sunken wrecks are dived regularly, and at least 10 more are accessible to experts. Underwater visibility is generally 80 to 90 feet. The calm waters along the west coast are also ideal for snorkeling. The marine reserve, a stretch of protected reef between Sandy Lane and the Colony Club, contains beautiful coral formations accessible from the beach.

On the west coast, **Bell Buoy** is a large, dome-shape reef where huge brown coral tree forests and schools of fish delight all categories of divers at depths ranging from 20 to 60 feet. At **Dottins Reef,** off Holetown, you can see schooling fish, barracudas, and turtles at depths of 40 to 60 feet. **Maycocks Bay,** on the northwest coast, is a particularly enticing site; large coral reefs are separated by corridors of white sand, and visibility is often 100 feet or more. The 165-foot freighter *Pamir* lies in 60 feet of water off Six Men's Bay; it's still intact, and you can peer through its portholes and view dozens of varieties of tropical fish. **Silver Bank** is a healthy coral reef with beautiful fish and sea fans; you may get a glimpse of the *Atlantis* submarine at 60 to 80 feet. Not to be missed is the *Stavronikita,* a scuttled Greek freighter at about 135 feet; hundreds of butterfly fish hang out around its mast, and the thin rays of sunlight filtering down through the water make fully exploring the huge ship a wonderfully eerie experience.

Farther south, **Carlisle Bay** is a natural harbor and marine park just below Bridgetown. Here you can retrieve empty bottles thrown overboard by generations of sailors and see cannons and cannonballs, anchors, and six unique shipwrecks (*Berwyn, Fox, CTrek, Eilon,* the barge *Cornwallis,* and *Bajan Queen*) lying in 25 to 60 feet of water, all close enough to visit on the same dive. The *Bajan Queen,* a cruise vessel that sank in 2002, is the island's newest wreck.

Dive shops provide a two-hour beginner's "resort" course ($85 to $100) followed by a shallow dive, or a weeklong certification course (about $425). Once you're certified, a one-tank dive runs about $70 to $80; a two-tank dive is $120 to $125. All equipment is supplied, and you can purchase multidive packages. Gear for snorkeling is available (free or for a small rental fee) from most hotels. Snorkelers can usually accompany dive trips for $25 for a one- or two-hour trip. Most dive shops have relationships with several hotels and offer special dive packages, with transportation, to hotel guests.

Dive Shop, Ltd. Near the Carlisle Bay marine park just south of Bridgetown, the island's oldest dive shop offers daily reef and wreck dives, plus beginner classes, certification courses, and underwater photography instruction. Underwater cameras are available for rent. Free transfers are provided between your hotel and the dive shop. ✉ *Amey's Alley, Upper Bay St., next to Nautilus Beach Apts., Bridgetown, St. Michael* ☎ *246/426–9947, 866/978–6683 in the U.S.* ⊕ *www.divebds.com.*

Hightide Watersports. On the west coast, Hightide Watersports offers three dive trips daily—one- and two-tank dives and night reef–wreck–drift dives—for up to eight divers, along with PADI instruction, equipment rental, and free transportation. ✉ *Coral Reef Club, Hwy. 1, Holetown, St. James* ☎ *246/432–0931, 800/970–0016, 800/513–5763* ⊕ *www.divehightide.com.*

Reefers & Wreckers Dive Shop. In Speightstown, the most northerly dive shop allows easy access to the unspoiled reefs in the north but also offers regular trips to the dive sites and wrecks along the west coast and in Carlisle Bay. ✉ *Queen St., Speightstown, St. Peter* ☎ *246/422–5450* ⊕ *www.scubadiving.bb.*

FISHING

Fishing is a year-round activity in Barbados, but prime time is January through April when game fish are in season. Whether you're a serious deep-sea fisher looking for marlin, sailfish, tuna, and other billfish or you prefer angling in calm coastal waters where wahoo, barracuda, and other small fish reside, you can choose from a variety of half- or full-day charter trips departing from the Careenage in Bridgetown. Expect to pay $175 per person for a shared half-day charter; for a private charter, expect to pay $500 to $600 per boat for a four-hour half-day or $950 to $1,000 for an eight-hour full-day charter. Spectators who don't fish are welcome for $50 per person.

Billfisher II. *Billfisher II,* a 40-foot Pacemaker, accommodates up to six passengers with three fishing chairs and five rods. Captain Winston ("The Colonel") White has been fishing these waters since 1975. His full-day charters include a full lunch and guaranteed fish (or a 25% refund); all trips include drinks and transportation to and from the boat. ✉ *Bridge House Wharf, The Careenage, Bridgetown, St. Michael* ☎ *246/431–0741.*

Cannon II. *Cannon II,* a 42-foot Hatteras Sport Fisherman, has three chairs and five rods and accommodates six passengers; drinks and snacks are complimentary, and lunch is served on full-day charters. ✉ *Cannon Charters, The Careenage, Bridgetown, St. Michael* ☎ *246/424–6107* ⊕ *www.fishingbarbados.com.*

High Seas Charters. *Ocean Hunter,* a 42-foot custom-built sportfishing boat, has an extended cockpit that easily accommodates six people. Choose a four-, six-, or eight-hour charter. All tackle and bait are supplied, as well as drinks and snacks. Charter rates include hotel transfers. ✉ *The Careenage, St. Michael* ☎ *246/233–2598* ⊕ *www. sportfishingbarbados.com.*

GOLF

Barbadians love golf, and golfers love Barbados. Courses open to visitors are listed below.

Barbados Golf Club. The first public golf course on Barbados is an 18-hole championship course redesigned in 2000 by golf course architect Ron Kirby. The course has hosted numerous competitions including the European Senior tour in 2003. Several hotels offer preferential tee-time reservations and reduced rates. Club and shoe rentals are available. ⊠ *Hwy. 7, Durants, Christ Church* ☎ *246/428–8463* ⊕ *www. barbadosgolfclub.com* ⚐ *18 holes, 6805 yards, par 72* ⚑ *$105 for 18 holes; $65 for 9 holes (carts not included). Unlimited 3-day, 5-day, and 7-day golf passes are available ($255, $400, $525 respectively).*

Fodor'sChoice **Country Club at Sandy Lane.** At the prestigious Country Club at Sandy
★ Lane, golfers can play on the Old Nine or on either of two 18-hole championship courses: the Tom Fazio–designed Country Club Course or the spectacular Green Monkey Course, which is reserved for hotel guests and club members only. The three layouts offer everything from a limestone quarry setting (Green Monkey), a modern-style with lakes (Country Club) or traditional small greens and narrow fairways (Old Nine). Golfers have complimentary use of the club's driving range. The Country Club Restaurant and Bar, which overlooks the 18th hole, is open to the public. Golf carts with GPS, caddies, or trolleys are available for hire, as are clubs and shoes. Carts are equipped with GPS, which alerts you to upcoming traps and hazards, provides tips on how to play the hole, and allows you to order refreshments! ⊠ *Sandy La., Hwy. 1, Paynes Bay, St. James* ☎ *246/444–2500* ⊕ *www. sandylane.com/golf* ⚐ *Green Monkey Course: 18 holes, 7343 yards, par 72; Country Club Course: 18 holes, 7060 yards, par 72; Old Nine: 9 holes, 3345 yards, par 36* ⚑ *$240 for 18 holes ($205 for hotel guests); $155 for 9 holes ($135 for hotel guests).*

Royal Westmoreland Golf Club. The Royal Westmoreland Golf Club has a well-regarded Robert Trent Jones Jr.–designed,18-hole championship course that meanders through the 500-acre property. This challenging course is highlighted by challenging greens. A great set of par-three holes, and ocean views from every hole is primarily for members and villa renters, with a few midmorning tee times (no Saturdays) for visitors, subject to availability. Greens fees include use of an electric cart (required); club rental is available. ⊠ *Royal Westmoreland Resort, Westmoreland, St. James* ☎ *246/419–0394* ⊕ *www.royal-westmoreland.com* ⚐ *18 holes, 7045 yards, par 72* ⚑ *For villa renters or guests at hotels with golf privileges at the club: $215 for 18 holes, $108 for 9 holes; for visitors (10 am to 11 am tee times only) $260.*

Continued on page 196

SPORT FISHING

Marlise Kast

With its abundance of marlin, sailfish, tuna, and Mahi Mahi, the Caribbean has enough catch to beckon any angler. Crystal-blue waters, white-sand beaches, and tropical weather make this the perfect place to set sail. From Barbados and the Bahamas to Puerto Rico and the Virgin Islands, there is plenty of opportunity to cast your line.

Fishing on sailing boat, Grenadines Islands.

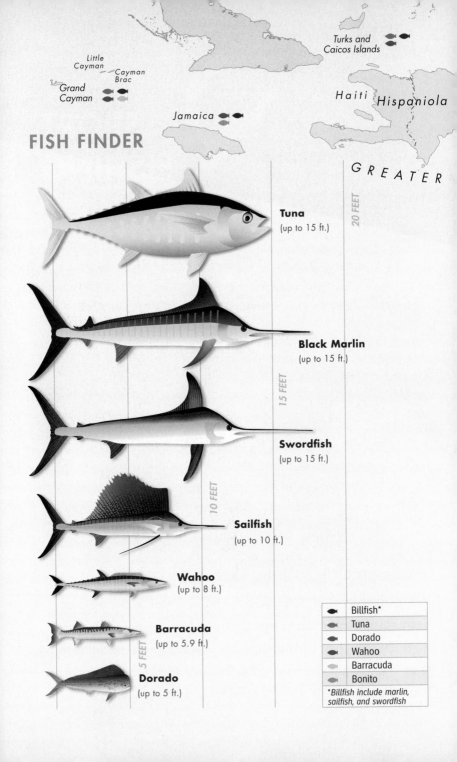

Turks and
Caicos Islands

Little
Cayman
Cayman
Brac
Grand
Cayman

Jamaica

Haiti Hispaniola

FISH FINDER

G R E A T E R

20 FEET

Tuna
(up to 15 ft.)

Black Marlin
(up to 15 ft.)

15 FEET

Swordfish
(up to 15 ft.)

10 FEET

Sailfish
(up to 10 ft.)

Wahoo
(up to 8 ft.)

Barracuda
(up to 5.9 ft.)

5 FEET

Dorado
(up to 5 ft.)

	Billfish*
	Tuna
	Dorado
	Wahoo
	Barracuda
	Bonito
Billfish include marlin, sailfish, and swordfish	

ominican
Republic

LEEWARD ISLANDS

St. John   Tortola
St.
Thomas   Virgin
Gorda

Anguilla
St. Barthélemy
St. Maarten/
St. Martin   Saba   Barbuda

ANTILLES   Puerto   St.   St. Eustatius
Rico   Croix   St. Kitts   Antigua
Nevis
Montserrat   Marie
Guadeloupe   Galante

Dominica

Martinique

0   200 mi
0   200 km

St. Lucia   Barbados

WINDWARD ISLANDS

St. Vincent
Bequia

The Grenadines
Carriacou

Aruba

Curaçao   Bonaire

LESSER ANTILLES

Islas Los
Roques

Grenada

Tobago

Trinidad

So many islands, so little time. Among anglers' favorites are the **Virgin Islands**, known for bluefish, wahoo, swordfish, and shark. These deep-sea fishing waters host annual tournaments where eight world records for blue marlin have been set. Equally attractive to deep-sea fishermen are the **Cayman Islands**, home to tuna, wahoo, and marlin. Bottom dwellers, such as grouper and snapper are always an easy hook in this area.

For great bonefishing, head to nearby Little Cayman at Bloody Bay. Between January and June, the **Dominican Republic** is popular with sport fishermen in search of sailfish, bonito, marlin, and wahoo. Although the bonefish-laden **Bahamas** cater to fly-fishermen, **Barbados** is a paradise for both deep-sea anglers reeling in billfish, and for coastal catchers forging for wahoo, barracuda, and smaller fish. Luring fishermen from afar, **Puerto Rico's** coast has reeled in 30+ world records, making it the fishing capital of the Caribbean.

DEEP SEA VS. SHALLOW WATERS

Swordfish

Too deep or not too deep? That is the question!

From fly-fishing at the river mouth to sport fishing in the open waters, the Caribbean can satisfy any angler's longing to reel one in. It's a question of what type of experience you're looking for. How active vs. passive of an experience do you want?

If you're feeling strong head for the deep. Any quest for catch below 30 meters (98 ft) is considered deep-sea fishing. The massive sport fish that frequent the deeper waters are magnificent specimens, and it's a thrilling experience to wrestle one from the deep. Albacore, marlin, barracuda, and tuna are the common catch, and it requires a tremendous amount of patience, strength, and effort to properly hook and land these mighty creatures.

For a more tranquil way to enjoy the Caribbean waters, try shallow-water fishing over reefs and shipwrecks. Tarpon, permit, pompano, wahoo, and small barracuda are the primary catch. Casting your line inshore is both convenient and affordable because chartering a large boat is unnecessary.

TAKE THE BAIT

In the Caribbean, it is best to use natural bait such as ballyhoo, tuna strips, or flying fish. Because a variety of big game fish feed on ballyhoo, they are considered ideal enticers when trolling the open waters. Live bait will also help lure larger fish, which are attracted to the blood and movement on the line. Depending on the type of catch you are after, almost any baitfish can be used including squid, shrimp, conch, and sardines. Aiding in the hunt are digital fishfinders, commonly utilized by sport fishermen to detect schools of fish. Bait is the same for both inshore and deep-sea fishing, and rarely are artificial lures used in the Caribbean.

A golden catch from shallow waters.

PRACTICAL INFORMATION

TYPE OF FISHING	COSTS	CHARACTERISTICS
OFFSHORE TRIPS	Start at $325 for a half-day, $625 for a full day.	Many packages include roundtrip transportation to and from your hotel, a boat crew, food, beverages, bait, gear, taxes and licenses. Tips are not included.
REEF FISHING	$300 to $600 per day; or cut the fee in half by opting for a 4-hour trip. A bonefishing guide is $250 for a half-day.	An experienced captain to steady the boat directly over the reefs is recommended. Most reefs are home to large schools of fish, but some areas are barren. Use a braided line, which is more abrasion resistant than monofiliament lines, to keep your line from snapping between the crevices.
DEEP-SEA FISHING	From $500 for a half-day to $1,500 for a full day.	The open waters are where you'll find the big catch. Most operators offer half-day and full-day charters with an experienced crew that knows where to find that trophy fish. Packages generally include your captain, crew, fishing tackle, bait, license and fees.

Private boat owners who plan on fishing for tuna, shark, swordfish and billfish in the Atlantic Ocean, (including the Gulf of Mexico and Caribbean Sea), must obtain an **Atlantic Highly Migratory Species** (HMS) permit for $20.00. Valid from the date of issue through December of that same year, permits can be ordered online through the **National Marine Fisheries Service** (⊕ www.hmspermits.noaa.gov).

MAN OVERBOARD: RULES/REGULATIONS

Although guidelines vary from island to island, it is safe to assume that a permit is required for fishing in the Caribbean. These licenses are usually included in sport fishing tours and packages, but it is best to inquire prior to booking. Because hundreds of fish can be hooked in a single day in the Caribbean waters, the catch-and-release method is vital for conservation. Throughout the entire region, spear fishing is illegal as is fishing within the boundaries of any marine park. It's advisable to utilize the services of licensed professionals.

Many of the Caribbean territories do not require a saltwater fishing license. One definite exception is the British Virgin Islands, where visitors must obtain permits, valid up to one month. Fishing permits are available from the Department of Conservation and Fisheries ☎284/494–5681 ⊕ www.bvidef.org.

Deep-sea fishing boats.

STAYING AFLOAT: SAFETY

Before setting sail, be sure to inform someone of your intended whereabouts as well as the time of your scheduled return. If you're fishing solo, double check all safety equipment including your means of communication, life jackets, and emergency supplies. Above all, inquire about local weather conditions and policies before booking your charter.

GUIDED TOURS

Taxi drivers will give you a personalized tour of Barbados for about $35 to $40 per hour for up to three people. Or you can choose an overland mountain-bike journey, a 4x4 safari expedition, or a full-day bus excursion. The prices vary according to the mode of travel and the number and kind of attractions included. Ask guest services at your hotel to help you make arrangements.

Highland Adventure Centre. Highland Adventure Centre offers mountain-bike tours for $60 per person, including transportation, guides, and refreshments. The trip is an exhilarating 7½-mile (12-km) ride (15% uphill) through the heart of northern Barbados, ending up at Barclays Park on the east coast. ⊠ *Cane Field, St. Thomas* ☎ *246/438–8069.*

Island Safari. Island Safari will take you to all the popular spots via a 4x4 Land Rover—including some gullies, forests, and remote areas that are inaccessible by conventional cars and buses. The cost for half-day or full-day tours ranges from $50 to $92.50 per person, including snacks or lunch. ⊠ *CWTS Complex, Salters Rd., Lower Estate, St. George* ☎ *246/429–5337* ⊕ *www.islandsafari.bb.*

HIKING

Hilly but not mountainous, the northern interior and the east coast are ideal for hiking.

Arbib Heritage and Nature Trail. The Arbib Heritage and Nature Trail, maintained by the Barbados National Trust, is actually two trails—one offers a rigorous hike (3.5 hours) through gullies and plantations to old ruins and remote north-country areas; the other is a shorter, easier "Round-de-Town Stroll" (2 hours) through Speightstown's side streets and past an ancient church and chattel houses. Guided hikes take place from 9 am to 2 pm on Wednesday, Thursday, and Saturday and cost $25 per person; group rates are available. Book ahead, preferably four days in advance. Not recommended for children under 5. ⊠ *Speightstown, St. Peter* ☎ *246/234–9010* ⊕ *www.barbadosnationaltrust.org.*

Hike Barbados. A program of free walks sponsored by the Barbados National Trust, Hike Barbados treks take place year-round on Sundays from 6 am to about 9 am and from 3:30 pm to 6 pm; once a month, a moonlight hike substitutes for the afternoon hike and begins at 5:30 pm (bring a flashlight). Experienced guides group you with others of similar levels of ability. Stop and Stare hikes go 5 to 6 miles (8 to 10 km); Here and There, 8 to 10 miles (13 to 16 km); and Grin and Bear, 12 to 14 miles (19 to 23 km). Wear loose clothes, sensible shoes, sunscreen, and a hat, and bring your camera and a bottle of water. Routes and locations change, but each hike is a loop, finishing in the same spot where it began. Check local newspapers, call the Trust, or check online for the full hike schedule or the scheduled meeting place on a particular Sunday. ⊠ *Wildey House, Wildey, St. Michael* ☎ *246/436–9033, 246/426–2421* ⊕ *www.barbadosnationaltrust.org.*

SEA EXCURSIONS

Mini-submarine voyages are enormously popular with families and those who enjoy watching fish but don't wish to get wet. Party boats depart from Bridgetown's Deep Water Harbour for sightseeing and snorkeling or romantic sunset cruises. Prices are $70 to $125 per person for four- or five-hour daytime cruises and $60 to $85 for three- or four-hour sunset cruises, depending on the type of refreshments and entertainment included; transportation to and from the dock is provided. For an excursion that may be less splashy in terms of a party atmosphere—but is definitely splashier in terms of the actual experience—turtle tours allow participants to feed and swim with a resident group of hawksbill and leatherback sea turtles.

FAMILY **Atlantis Submarine.** The 48-passenger *Atlantis* Submarine turns the Caribbean into a giant aquarium. The 45-minute underwater voyage aboard the 50-foot submarine ($104 per person, including hotel transfers) takes you to wrecks and reefs as deep as 150 feet. Children love the adventure, but they must be at least 3 feet tall to go aboard. ⊠ *The Shallow Draught, Bridgetown, St. Michael* ☎ *246/436–8929* ⊕ *www. barbados.atlantissubmarines.com.*

Cool Runnings. On the catamaran *Cool Runnings*, owner Captain Robert Povey skippers a five-hour lunch cruise ($90) with stops to swim with the fishes, snorkel with sea turtles, and explore a shallow shipwreck. A four-hour sunset cruise ($80) includes swimming, snorkeling, and exploring underwater as the sun sinks below the horizon. Delicious meals with wine, along with an open bar, are part of all cruises. ⊠ *Carlisle House, Carlisle Wharf, Hincks St., Bridgetown, St. Michael* ☎ *246/436–0911* ⊕ *www.coolrunningsbarbados.com.*

Jolly Roger 1. The whole family will get a kick out of a "pirate" ship sailing adventure on *Jolly Roger 1.* The four-hour day and sunset cruises along the island's west coast include a barbecue lunch or dinner, freeflowing drinks, lively music, swimming with turtles, and "pirate" activities such as walking the plank and rope swinging. ⊠ *The Shallow Draught, Bridgetown, St. Michael* ☎ *246/436–2885, 246/826–7245* ⊕ *www.barbadosblackpearl-jollyroger1.com.*

Tiami Catamaran Cruises. Tiami operates five catamaran party boats for luncheon cruises to a secluded bay for swimming with turtles or for romantic sunset and moonlight cruises with special catering and live music. ⊠ *Shallow Draught Harbour, Bridgetown, St. Michael* ☎ *246/430–0900* ⊕ *www.tiamicatamarancruises.com.*

SURFING

The best surfing is at Bathsheba Soup Bowl on the east coast, but the water on the windward (Atlantic Ocean) side of the island is safe only for the most experienced surfers. Surfers also congregate at Surfer's Point, at the southern tip of Barbados near Inch Marlow, where the Atlantic Ocean meets the Caribbean Sea.

Dread or Dead Surf Shop. Dread or Dead Surf Shop promises to get beginners from "zero to standing up and surfing" in a single afternoon. The three-hour course—"or until you stand up or give up"—costs $75 per person and includes a board, wax, a rash guard (if necessary), a ride to and from the surf break, and instruction; additional lessons cost $50 for 2½ hours of water time and continual instruction. Intermediate or experienced surfers can rent boards for $50 per day. ⊠ *Hastings Main Rd., Hastings, Christ Church* ☎ *246/228–4785* ⊕ *www. dreadordead.com.*

Zed's Surfing Adventures. Zed's Surfing Adventures rents surfboards, provides lessons, and offers surf tours—which include equipment, a guide, and transportation to surf breaks appropriate for your experience. ⊠ *Surfer's Point, Inch Marlow, Christ Church* ☎ *246/428–7873* ⊕ *www.zedssurftravel.com.*

WINDSURFING AND KITEBOARDING

Part of the World Cup Windsurfing Circuit, Barbados is one of the prime locations in the world for windsurfing. Winds are strongest November through April at the island's southern tip, at Silver Sands–Silver Rock Beach, which is where the Barbados Windsurfing Championships are held in mid-January. Use of windsurfing boards and equipment, as well as instruction, is often among the amenities included at larger hotels and sometimes can be rented by nonguests. Kiteboarding is a more difficult sport that requires several hours of instruction to reach proficiency; Silver Sands is about the only location in Barbados where you'll find kiteboarding equipment and instruction.

deAction Surf Shop. At his shop, directly on Silver Sands–Silver Rock Beach, Brian "Irie Man" Talma stocks a range of rental surfing equipment and offers beginner windsurfing, kiteboarding, and surfing lessons taught by professional instructors. All equipment is provided. ⊠ *Silver Sands–Silver Rock Beach, Silver Sands, Christ Church* ☎ *246/428–2027* ⊕ *www.briantalma.com.*

BONAIRE

WELCOME TO BONAIRE

At the market in Kralendijk, hagglers vie for produce brought in by boat from lusher islands. But nature holds sway over human pursuits on this scrubby, cactus-covered landfall. Divers come to explore some of the best sites this side of Australia's Great Barrier Reef. Above the water are more than 15,000 flamingos—the biggest flock in the Western Hemisphere.

TOP REASONS TO VISIT BONAIRE

1 The Diving: As locals say, you come here to dive, eat, dive, sleep, and dive.

2 The Snorkeling: You don't have to be a certified diver to appreciate Bonaire's reefs; snorkelers can see a lot of the beauty just below the surface of the water.

3 The Quiet: Visitors came to enjoy the tranquillity of the island long before they started exploring offshore.

4 The Dining: Dining is surprisingly good and varied for such a small island.

5 The Smiles: Bonaireans are genuinely friendly without a hint of the phoniness sometimes found on other tourist-dependent islands.

DIVER'S PARADISE

With just over 16,000 people, this little island (112 square miles [290 square km]) has a real small-town atmosphere. Kralendijk, the capital, has just 3,000 inhabitants. The entire coastline—from the high-water tidemark to a depth of 200 feet—is protected as part of the Bonaire Marine Park, making it one of the best diving destinations in the Western Hemisphere.

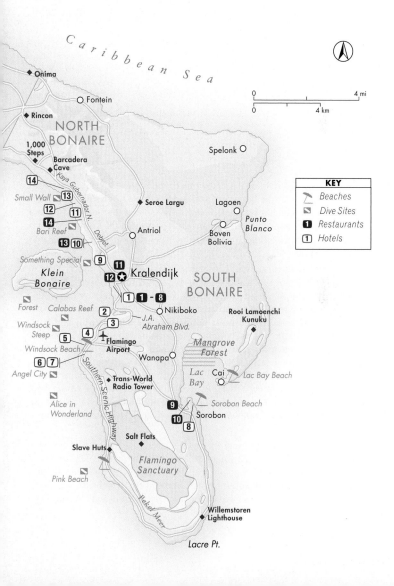

Caribbean Sea

◆ Onima

○ Fontein

◆ Rincon

NORTH BONAIRE

1,000 Steps

Barcadera Cave

Kaya Gubernador N.

14

Small Wall 13

12 11

14

Bari Reef

13 10

Something Special 9

Klein Bonaire

11

12 ★ **Kralendijk**

SOUTH BONAIRE

1 1 - 8

Forest

Calabas Reef 2

○ Nikiboko

Rooi Lamoenchi Kunuku ◆

Windsock Steep 3

J.A. Abraham Blvd.

5 4 ✈ **Flamingo Airport**

Windsock Beach

Wanapa ○

Mangrove Forest

6 7

Angel City

Southern Scenic Highway

Lac Bay Cai ○ *Lac Bay Beach*

Alice in Wonderland

Trans-World Radio Tower ◆

9 ⟩ *Sorobon Beach*

10 Sorobon

8

Salt Flats ◆

Slave Huts ◆

Flamingo Sanctuary

Pink Beach

Pekel Meer

Willemstoren Lighthouse ◆

Lacre Pt.

◆ **Spelonk** ○

◆ **Seroe Largu** Lagoen ○

Antriol ○ ○ *Punto Blanco*

○ Boven Bolivia

KEY	
⟩	*Beaches*
◨	*Dive Sites*
1	*Restaurants*
1	*Hotels*

0   4 mi
0   4 km

6

BONAIRE

Updated
by Vernon
O'Reilly
Ramesar

Bonaire is widely regarded as one of the best destinations in the Caribbean for shore diving, and with good reason. The dry climate and coral composition of the island mean that there's little soil runoff, allowing near-perfect visibility in the coastal waters. The islanders have exploited this advantage, and you can find local businesses that cater to virtually every diving need.

Even though tourism is the backbone of the economy here, authorities try to ensure that the booming hotel industry does not damage the environment on which it is based. Thankfully, the fact that most visitors to Bonaire come for the natural beauty has prevented the kind of tourism that has turned neighboring islands such as Aruba into commercialized tourist magnets.

Islanders are serious about conserving Bonaire's natural beauty. All the coastal waters of the island were turned into a national park in 1979, and in 1999 Bonaire purchased the 1,500-acre privately owned outlying island of Klein Bonaire to prevent unwanted development. Anyone diving around the island must purchase a one-year permit, and park rangers patrol the waters, handing out hefty fines to people who violate park rules. Spearfishing, removing coral, and even walking on coral are just some of the restricted activities. Rather than restricting legitimate divers, these rules have resulted in a pristine marine environment that makes for a supremely satisfying dive experience. Damage to the reefs caused by rare passing hurricanes is usually quickly repaired by the healthy ecosystem. Small wonder that even the license plates in Bonaire declare it a diver's paradise.

Bonaire also offers a variety of experiences above the surface to those willing to explore its 112 square miles (290 square km). The southern salt flats give an interesting glimpse into the island's economic history. Washington–Slagbaai National Park, in the north, has the island's highest peak (784 feet) and is a haven for some of the thousands of flamingos

LOGISTICS

Getting to Bonaire: Most flights from the United States connect in San Juan or Aruba. If you want to connect through Aruba, you'll more likely than not have to book your flight directly with an island-based airline. Bonaire's Flamingo Airport (BON) is tiny but welcoming (the KLM 747 almost dwarfs the airport when it lands).

Hassle Factor: Medium to high.

On the Ground: Rental cars and taxis are available, but try to arrange for pickup through your hotel. A taxi will run between $11 and $15 (for up to four people) to most hotels; $26 to the Sorobon Beach Resort. Fares are 25% extra from 7 pm to midnight and 50% extra from midnight to 6 am. If you anticipate having to change your flight details while on Bonaire, be mindful that some airline counters may close at 5 pm. Many folks just use bicycles to get around, unless they are going more than a few miles.

that make Bonaire their home. The near-perfect climate also makes Bonaire the ideal destination for soaking in some sun.

Although many islanders claim that the name Bonaire comes from the French for "good air," this explanation is unlikely, particularly because the island was never colonized by the French. The island was first inhabited by an Amerindian people (related to the Arawaks) called the Caquetios. Alonso de Ojeda and Amerigo Vespucci landed here in 1499 and claimed it for Spain. It seems likely that they adopted the Amerindian name for the island, which probably sounded very much like Bonaire and meant "low country." Because the Spanish found little use for the island except as a penal colony, the original inhabitants were shipped off to work on the plantations of Hispaniola, and Bonaire remained largely undeveloped. When the Dutch seized the islands of Aruba, Bonaire, and Curaçao in 1633, they started building the salt industry in Bonaire, which fueled the economy then and remains an important industry today.

The majority of the 16,000 inhabitants live in and around the capital, Kralendijk. The word almost universally applied to this diminutive city with a downtown area that can be traversed in less than three minutes is cute. Part of the BES Islands, Bonaire, St. Eustatius, and Saba were made special municipalities of the Netherlands in 2010. Before this change Bonaire was governed from neighboring Curaçao.

PLANNING

WHEN TO GO

High season in Bonaire mirrors that in much of the Caribbean: basically from mid-December through mid-April. In the off-season, rates will be reduced at least 25% and often more. Hurricanes and severe tropical storms are rare—though still possible—in Bonaire, which means the island has good weather almost year-round.

GETTING HERE AND AROUND

AIR TRAVEL

Canadians and Americans will usually have to change planes in Curaçao or Aruba. Dutch Antilles Express provides connecting service. KLM offers daily direct flights from Amsterdam. The only nonstops from the United States are from New York–Newark, New York–JFK, Houston, Miami, and Atlanta.

Airline Contacts Delta ☎ 800/221–1212 ⊕ www.delta.com.
Insel Air ☎ 599/737–0444 ⊕ www.fly-inselair.com. **KLM** ☎ 599/717–5600
⊕ www.klm.com. **United Airlines** ☎ 800/864–8331 ⊕ www.united.com.

Airport Flamingo Airport. United Airlines offers once-weekly direct service to Flamingo Airport from Houston and Newark, Insel Air offers once-weekly direct service from Miami (via Curaçao on other days), and Delta offers once-weekly service from Atlanta. ✉ BON ☎ 599/717–3800.

BIKE AND MOPED TRAVEL

Scooters are a great way to get around the island. Rates are about $25 per day for a one-seater and up to $35 for a deluxe two-seater. A valid driver's license and cash deposit or credit card are required.

Contacts Bonaire Motorcycle Shop. Rent Harley-Davidson motorcycles at this shop. ✉ Kaya Grandi 64, Kralendijk ☎ 599/717–7790. **Macho Scooter Rental.** The folks at Macho Scooter Rental will have you zipping about. ✉ J.A. Abraham-boulevard 80, Plaza Resort Bonaire, Kralendijk ☎ 599/701–1232.

CAR TRAVEL

Minimum and maximum age to rent a car are 21 and 70. There's a government tax of 5% per rental; no cash deposit is needed if you pay by credit card.

Gas prices are about double those of the United States. Main roads are well paved, but during the rainy season (October and November), mud—called Bonairean snow—can be difficult to navigate. Traffic is to the right, and there's not a single traffic light.

Contacts Avis ✉ Flamingo Airport, Kralendijk ☎ 599/717–5795 ⊕ www.avis.com. **Bonaire Rent a Car** ✉ Kaya International 1, Kralendijk ☎ 599/786–6090. **Budget** ✉ Kaya Industria 10, Kralendijk ☎ 599/717–4700 ⊕ www.budget.com. **Hertz** ✉ Flamingo Airport, Kralendijk ☎ 599/717–7221 ⊕ www.hertz.com. **Island Rentals** ✉ Opposite Flamingo Airport, Kaya Internationaal 130, Kralendijk ☎ 599/717–2100.

TAXI TRAVEL

Taxis are unmetered; fixed rates are controlled by the government. From most hotels into town it costs between $10 and $17. Fares increase from 7 pm to midnight by 25% and from midnight to 6 am by 50%. Drivers will conduct half-day tours; they charge about $28 per hour for up to four passengers.

Contacts Airport Taxi Stand. Fare to your hotel with Airport Taxi Stand is $9 to $22 for up to four passengers. ☎ 599/717–8100. **Taxi Central Dispatch** ☎ 599/717–8100.

ESSENTIALS

Banks and Exchange Services In 2011 the U.S. dollar became the official currency, replacing the NAf guilder. You can find ATMs at the airport, in Kralendijk, and at Hato branches of MCB, as well as at the Sand Dollar Condominium Resort and the Plaza Resort; at the Tourism Corporation Bonaire; and at Banco di Caribe on Kaya Grandi.

Electricity 120 AC/50 cycles. A transformer and occasionally a two-prong adapter are required. Some appliances may work slowly; hair dryers may overheat, and sensitive equipment may be damaged.

Emergency Services Ambulance ☎ *599/717–8900.* **Fire** ☎ *599/717–8000.* **Police emergencies** ☎ *599/717–8000.* **Scuba-diving emergencies** ☎ *599/717–8187.*

Language The official language is Dutch, but the everyday language is Papiamento, a mix of Spanish, Portuguese, Dutch, English, and French, as well as African tongues. You can light up your waiter's eyes if you can say *masha danki* (thank you very much) and *pasa un bon dia* (have a nice day). English is spoken by almost everyone on the island.

Passport Requirements U.S. citizens must carry valid passports. In addition, everyone must have a return or ongoing ticket, and you are advised to confirm reservations 48 hours before departure. The maximum stay is 90 days.

Phones The country code for Bonaire is 599; 717 is the exchange for every four-digit number on the island. Phone cards from home rarely work on Bonaire. You can try AT&T by dialing 001–800/872–2881 from public phones. To call Bonaire from the United States, dial 011–599/717 plus the local four-digit number.

Taxes The departure tax when going to Curaçao, St. Maarten, St. Eustatius, Saba, or Aruba is $9. For all other destinations it's $35. This tax is supposed to be included in the ticket price. Hotels charge a room tax of $6.50 per person, per night in addition to the V.A.T. (value-added tax). Many hotels add a 10% to 15% service charge to your bill. A V.A.T. of 6% is tacked on to dining and lodging costs. The V.A.T. may or may not be included in your quoted room rates, so be sure to ask. It's almost always included in restaurant prices.

ACCOMMODATIONS

Alongside the numerous lodges that offer only the basics (mostly catering to divers), you can now find some real resorts. Families can find self-catering accommodations, and many smaller inns will appeal to budget travelers. The best resorts are often on decent beaches, but these are mostly man-made. Almost all the island's resorts are clustered around Kralendijk.

HOTEL AND RESTAURANT PRICES

Prices in the restaurant reviews are the average cost of a main course at dinner or, if dinner is not served, at lunch; taxes and service charges are generally included. Prices in the hotel reviews are the lowest cost of a standard double room in high season, excluding taxes, service charges, and meal plans (except at all-inclusives). Prices for rentals are the lowest per-night cost for a one-bedroom unit in high season.

For expanded lodging reviews and current deals, visit Fodors.com.

WEDDINGS

One person must apply for temporary residency. Official witnesses must also apply for residency, but most wedding coordinators can arrange for local witnesses. After the marriage, an apostille (official seal) must be placed on the marriage license and certificate. Blood tests are not required.

EXPLORING

Two routes, north and south from Kralendijk, the island's small capital, are possible on the 24-mile-long (39-km-long) island; either route will take from a few hours to a full day, depending on whether you stop to snorkel, swim, dive, or lounge. Those pressed for time will find that it's easy to explore the entire island in a day if stops are kept to a minimum.

KRALENDIJK

Bonaire's small, tidy capital city (population 3,000) is five minutes from the airport. The main drag, J.A. Abraham Boulevard, turns into **Kaya Grandi** in the center of town. Along it are most of the island's major stores, boutiques, and restaurants. Across Kaya Grandi, opposite the Littman jewelry store, is Kaya L.D. Gerharts, with several small supermarkets, a handful of snack shops, and some of the better restaurants. Walk down the narrow waterfront avenue called Kaya C.E.B. Hellmund, which leads straight to the **North and South piers.** In the center of town, the Harbourside Mall has chic boutiques. Along this route is **Ft. Oranje,** with its cannons. From December through April, cruise ships dock in the harbor once or twice a week. The diminutive ocher-and-white structure that looks like a tiny Greek temple is the **fish market;** local anglers no longer bring their catches here (they sell out of their homes these days), but you can find plenty of fresh produce brought over from Colombia and Venezuela. Pick up the brochure *Walking and Shopping in Kralendijk* from the tourist office to get a map and complete list of all the monuments and sights in the town.

SOUTH BONAIRE

The trail south from Kralendijk is chock-full of icons—both natural and man-made—that tell Bonaire's minisaga. Rent a four-wheel-drive vehicle (a car will do, but during the rainy season of October through November the roads can become muddy) and head out along the Southern Scenic Route. The roads wind through dramatic desert terrain, full of organ-pipe cacti and spiny-trunk mangroves—huge stumps of saltwater trees that rise from the marshes like witches. Watch for long-haired goats, wild donkeys, and lizards of all sizes.

WORTH NOTING

FAMILY **Rooi Lamoenchi Kunuku.** Owner Ellen Herrera restored her family's homestead north of Lac Bay, in the Bonairean *kadushi* (cactus) wilderness, to educate tourists and residents about the history and tradition of authentic kunuku living and show unspoiled terrain in two daily tours. You must make an appointment in advance and expect to spend a couple of hours. ⊠ *Kaya Suiza 23, Playa Baribe* ☎ *599/717–8489* ✈ *$21* ⏾ *By appointment only.*

Salt Flats. You can't miss the salt flats—voluptuous white drifts that look like mountains of snow. Harvested once a year, the "ponds" are owned by Cargill, Inc., which has reactivated the 19th-century salt industry with great success (one reason for that success is that the ocean on this part of the island is higher than the land—which makes irrigation a snap). Keep a lookout for the three 30-foot obelisks—white, blue, and red—that were used to guide the trade boats coming to pick up the salt. Look also in the distance across the pans to the abandoned solar saltworks that's now a designated **flamingo sanctuary.** With the naked eye you might be able to make out a pink-orange haze just on the horizon; with binoculars you will see a sea of bobbing pink bodies. The sanctuary is completely protected, and no entrance is allowed (flamingos are extremely sensitive to disturbances of any kind).

FAMILY **Slave Huts.** The salt industry's gritty history is revealed in Rode Pan, the site of two groups of tiny slave huts. The white grouping is on the right side of the road, opposite the salt flats; the second grouping, called the red slave huts (though they appear yellow), stretches across the road toward the island's southern tip. During the 19th century, slaves working the salt pans by day crawled into these huts to rest. Each Friday afternoon they walked seven hours to Rincon to weekend with their families, returning each Sunday. Only very small people will be able to enter, but walk around and poke your head in for a look.

Willemstoren Lighthouse. Bonaire's first lighthouse was built in 1837 and is now automated (but closed to visitors). Take some time to explore the beach and notice how the waves, driven by the trade winds, play a crashing symphony against the rocks. Locals stop here to collect pieces of driftwood in spectacular shapes and to build fanciful pyramids from objects that have washed ashore.

NORTH BONAIRE

The Northern Scenic Route takes you into the heart of Bonaire's natural wonders—desert gardens of towering cacti (kadushi, used to prepare soup, and the thornier *yatu*, used to build cactus fencing), tiny coastal coves, and plenty of fantastic panoramas. The road also weaves between eroded pink-and-black limestone walls and eerie rock formations with fanciful names such as the Devil's Mouth and Iguana Head (you'll need a vivid imagination and sharp eye to recognize them). Brazil trees growing along the route were used by Indians to make dye (pressed from a red ring in the trunk). Inscriptions still visible in several island caves were made with this dye.

A snappy excursion with the requisite photo stops will take about 2½ hours, but if you pack your swimsuit and a hefty picnic basket (forget about finding fast food), you could spend the entire day exploring this northern sector. Head out from Kralendijk on Kaya Gobernador N. Debrot until it turns into the Northern Scenic Route. Once you pass the Radio Nederland towers, you cannot turn back to Kralendijk. The narrow road becomes one way until you get to Landhuis Karpata, and you have to follow the cross-island road to Rincon and return via the main road through the center of the island.

TOP ATTRACTIONS

FAMILY **Washington–Slagbaai National Park.** Once a plantation producing divi-divi trees (the pods were used for tanning animal skins), aloe (used for medicinal lotions), charcoal, and goats, the park is now a model of conservation. It's easy to tour the 13,500-acre tropical desert terrain on the dirt roads. As befits a wilderness sanctuary, the well-marked, rugged routes force you to drive slowly enough to appreciate the animal life and the terrain. (Think twice about coming here if it has rained recently—the mud you may encounter will be more than inconvenient.) If you're planning to hike, bring a picnic lunch, camera, sunscreen, and plenty of water. There are two routes: the long one (22 miles [35½ km]) is marked by yellow arrows, the short one (15 miles [24 km]) by green arrows. Goats and donkeys may dart across the road, and if you keep your eyes peeled, you may catch sight of large iguanas camouflaged in the shrubbery.

Bird-watchers are really in their element here. Right inside the park's gate, flamingos roost on the salt pad known as **Salina Mathijs,** and exotic parakeets dot the foot of **Mt. Brandaris,** Bonaire's highest peak, at 784 feet. Some 130 species of birds fly in and out of the shrubbery in the park. Keep your eyes open and your binoculars at hand. Swimming, snorkeling, and scuba diving are permitted, but you're asked not to frighten the animals or remove anything from the grounds. Absolutely no hunting, fishing, or camping is allowed. A useful guide to the park is available at the entrance for about $6. To get here, take the secondary road north from the town of Rincon. The Nature Fee for swimming and snorkeling also grants you free admission to this park—simply present proof of payment and some form of photo ID. ☎ *599/717–8444* ⊕ *www.washingtonparkbonaire.org* ✉ *Free with payment of scuba diving nature fee ($25) or $15 with nonscuba Nature Fee ($10). Otherwise $25 for 1 calendar yr of entry* ☉ *Daily 8–5; you must enter before 3.*

WORTH NOTING

1,000 Steps. Directly across the road from the Radio Nederland towers on the main road north, you'll see a short yellow marker that points to the location of these limestone stairs carved right out of the cliff. If you trek down the stairs, you can discover a lovely coral beach and protected cove where you can snorkel and scuba dive. Actually, you'll count only 67 steps, but it feels like 1,000 when you walk back up carrying scuba gear. ⊠ *Queen's Hwy.*

Barcadera Cave. Once used to trap goats, this cave is one of the oldest in Bonaire; there's even a tunnel that looks intriguingly spooky. It's the first sight along the northern route; watch closely for a yellow marker on your left before you reach the towering Radio Nederland antennas. Pull off across from the entrance to the Bonaire Caribbean Club, and you can discover some stone steps that lead down into a cave full of stalactites and vegetation.

FAMILY **Gotomeer.** This saltwater lagoon near the island's northern end is a popular flamingo hangout. Bonaire is one of the few places in the world where pink flamingos nest. The shy, spindly leg creatures—affectionately called "pink clouds"—are magnificent birds to observe, and there are about 15,000 of them in Bonaire (more than the number of human residents). The best time to catch them at home is January to June, when they tend to their gray-plumed young. For the best view take the paved access road alongside the lagoon through the jungle of cacti to the parking and observation area on the rise overlooking the lagoon and Washington–Slagbaai National Park beyond.

Landhuis Karpata. This mustard-color building was the manor house of an aloe plantation in the 19th century. The site was named for the *karpata* (castor bean) plants that are abundant in the area—you can see them along the sides of the road as you approach. Notice the rounded outdoor oven where aloe was boiled down before the juice was exported. Although the government has built a shaded rest stop at Karpata, there's still no drink stand.

FAMILY **Mangazina di Rei.** Built around the second-oldest stone structure on Bonaire, this cultural park a few miles before Rincon provides a fascinating insight into the island's history. The museum commands an excellent view of the surrounding countryside and contains artifacts tracing the often hard lives of the early settlers. There are numerous traditional structures built around the museum illustrating how living conditions have changed over the years. The park is usually filled with local school kids learning how to use traditional musical instruments and how to cook local foods. ⊠ *Kaya Rincon z/n, Rincon* ☎ *599/786–2101* ⊕ *www.mangazinadirei.org* ⊒ *$10 adults, $5 children under 12* ☉ *Tues.–Sat. 10–5.*

Onima. Small signposts direct the way to the Indian inscriptions found on a 3-foot limestone ledge that juts out like a partially formed cave entrance. Look up to see the red-stained designs and symbols inscribed on the limestone, said to have been the handiwork of the Arawak Indians when they inhabited the island centuries ago. The pictographs date back at least to the 15th century, and nobody has a clue what they mean. To reach Onima, pass through Rincon on the road that heads back to Kralendijk, but take the left-hand turn before Fontein.

Rincon. The island's original Spanish settlement, Rincon is where slaves brought from Africa to work the plantations and salt fields lived. Superstition and voodoo lore still have a powerful impact here, more so than in Kralendijk, where the townspeople work hard at suppressing old ways. Rincon is now a well-kept cluster of pastel cottages and 19th-century buildings that constitute Bonaire's oldest village. Watch your driving here—goats and dogs often sit right in the middle of the main drag.

Seroe Largu. Just off the main road, this spot, at 394 feet, is one of the highest on the island. A paved but narrow and twisting road leads to a magnificent daytime view of Kralendijk's rooftops and the island of Klein Bonaire. A large cross and figure of Christ stand guard at the peak, with an inscription reading *ayera* (yesterday), *awe* (today), and *semper* (always).

BEACHES

Although most of Bonaire's charms are underwater, there are a few excellent beaches. Even those beaches that are unsuitable for sunbathing can be worth a visit if only to view the intense turquoise waters that surround this little desert island. Don't expect long stretches of glorious powdery sand. Bonaire's beaches are small, and though the water is blue (several shades of it, in fact), the sand isn't always white. Bonaire's National Parks Foundation requires all nondivers to pay a $10 annual Nature Fee to enter the water anywhere around the island (divers pay $25). The fee can be paid at most dive shops, and the receipt will also allow access to Washington–Slagbaai National Park.

Boca Slagbaai. Inside Washington–Slagbaai Park is this beach of coral fossils and rocks with interesting offshore coral gardens that are good for snorkeling. Bring scuba boots or canvas sandals to walk into the water, because the beach is rough on bare feet. The gentle surf makes it an ideal place for swimming and picnicking. **Amenities:** parking; water sports. **Best for:** solitude; snorkeling; swimming; walking. ⊠ *Off main park road, in Washington–Slagbaai National Park.*

Klein Bonaire. Just a water-taxi hop across from Kralendijk, this little island offers picture-perfect white-sand beaches. The area is protected, so absolutely no development has been allowed. Make sure to pack everything before heading to the island, including water and an umbrella to hide under, because there are no refreshment stands or changing facilities, and there's almost no shade to be found. Boats leave from the Town Pier, across from the City Café, and the round-trip water-taxi ride costs roughly $20 per person. **Amenities:** none. **Best for:** solitude; snorkeling; swimming; walking.

Lac Bay Beach. Known for its festive music on Sunday nights, this open bay area with pink-tinted sand is equally dazzling by day. It's a bumpy drive (10 to 15 minutes on a dirt road) to get here, but you'll be glad when you arrive. It's a good spot for diving, snorkeling, and kayaking (as long as you bring your own), and there are public restrooms and a restaurant for your convenience. **Amenities:** food and drink; parking; showers; toilets. **Best for:** partiers; surfing; swimming; windsurfing. ⊠ *Off Kaminda Sorobon, Lac Cai.*

Playa Funchi. This Washington–Slagbaai National Park beach is notable for the lagoon on one side, where flamingos nest, and the superb snorkeling on the other, where iridescent green parrot fish swim right up to shore. **Amenities:** none. **Best for:** solitude; snorkeling; swimming. ⊠ *Off main park road, in Washington–Slagbaai National Park.*

Sorobon Beach. This is *the* windsurfing beach on Bonaire and one of the most beautiful beaches on the island, with a wide swath of soft white sand sloping gently into the intense blue waters of the sheltered cove. You can find a restaurant-bar next to the resort and windsurfing outfitters on the beach. The public beach area has restrooms and huts for shade. Take E.E.G. Boulevard south from Kralendijk to Kaya I.R. Randolf Statuuis Van Eps, and then follow this route straight on to Sorobon Beach. **Amenities:** food and drink; parking; showers; toilets;

water sports. **Best for:** snorkeling; surfing; windsurfing. ✉ *Kaya I.R. Randolf Statuuis Van Eps, Sorobon Beach.*

Windsock Beach (*aka Mangrove Beach*). Near the airport (just off E.E.G. Boulevard), this pretty little spot looks out toward the north side of the island and has about 200 yards of white sand along a rocky shoreline. It's a popular dive site, and swimming conditions are good. **Amenities:** none. **Best for:** snorkeling; swimming. ✉ *Off E.E.G. Blvd., near Flamingo Airport.*

WHERE TO EAT

Dining on Bonaire is far less expensive than on Aruba or Curaçao, and you can find everything from Continental to Tex-Mex to Asian fare. Many restaurants serve only dinner—only a few establishments not affiliated with hotels are open for breakfast, so check ahead.

$$ EUROPEAN

🍴 **Appetite.** This delightful establishment is an oasis of chic. The historic house offers cozy private rooms and a large courtyard, which always seems to be buzzing. The menu encourages diners to forget the main course and order a series of starters, but such items as stewed veal cheek with crispy sweetbreads are worth the splurge. A four-course chef's menu is available as well. The restaurant is just a few steps away from the Tourism Corporation Bonaire office. [$] *Average main: $28* ✉ *Kaya Grandi 12* ☎ *599/717–3595* ⏲ *Closed Sun.*

$$ FRENCH Fodor's Choice ★

🍴 **Bistro de Paris.** Any restaurant that welcomes you with a free glass of Kir and a personal greeting from the owner should be taken very seriously. Patrice Rannou has transformed an unassuming house into a lovely bistro serving the best French food on the island. The low-key decor (complete with Perrier-bottle vases) belies the extraordinary food on offer. Lamb lovers will fall to pieces over the char-grilled chops served with haricots verts and asparagus. The dinner menu is very reasonably priced, but those on an extremely tight budget should at least explore the lunch offerings or even order sandwiches to take along on a day of exploring. Those with kids and a lot of patience may want to try the novelty of the grill stone, which lets diners cook their own meal at the table. Many patrons choose to dine on the outdoor patio. [$] *Average main: $23* ✉ *Kaya Gobernador N. Debrot 46* ☎ *599/717–7070* ⏲ *Closed Sun. No lunch Sat.*

$$ ECLECTIC Fodor's Choice ★

🍴 **Boudoir.** Despite the nighttime-bedroom connotation this excellent patio eatery at the Royal Palm Mall is only open for breakfast, lunch, and late-afternoon snacks. Besides having some of the best coffee on the island, Boudoir offers a range of soups, salads, sandwiches, and burgers that should please even the most discerning of diners. It's the perfect place to relax with an iced coffee and a smoked-salmon-and-capers sandwich after a day of exploring Kralendijk. [$] *Average main: $9* ✉ *Kaya Grandi 26 F/G, Royal Palm Mall* ☎ *599/717–4321.*

$$ ITALIAN Fodor's Choice ★

🍴 **Capriccio.** This splendid, family-run Italian eatery has plenty to boast about. The pastas are handmade daily, and fresh mozzarella is imported from Italy once a week. The wine cellar includes hundreds of labels and thousands of bottles. You can opt for casual à la carte dining on the terrace or a romantic meal in the tonier, air-conditioned dining room. If your appetite is hearty, go for the five-course prix-fixe menu.

Otherwise, choose from 50 regular offerings. $ *Average main: $25* ✉ *Kaya Hellmund 5* 🕾 *599/717–7230* ⊕ *www.capricciobonaire.com* ⌂ *Reservations essential* ☾ *Closed Tues. No lunch weekends.*

$$
ECLECTIC
Fodor's Choice
★

✕ **City Café/City Restaurant.** This busy waterfront eatery is also one of the most reliable nightspots on the island, so it's always hopping day or night. Breakfast, lunch, and dinner are served daily at reasonable prices. Seafood is always featured, as are a variety of sandwiches and salads. The pita sandwich platters are a good lunchtime choice for the budget challenged. Weekends, there's always live entertainment and dancing. This is the place to people-watch on Bonaire, as it seems everyone ends up at City Café eventually. $ *Average main: $15* ✉ *Hotel Rochaline, Kaya Grandi 7* 🕾 *599/717–6050* ⊕ *www.citybonaire.com.*

$$$
ITALIAN

✕ **Donna & Giorgio.** Donna and her Sardinian-born husband, Giorgio, serve delicious home-style meals in this charming restaurant on the Kralendijk waterfront. With Giorgio in the kitchen, Donna and her daughter greet diners and make them feel at home. You may choose to sit in the cozy interior near the bar or outside at one of the tables on the terrace, which is lovely on a cloudless night and has a nice view of the ocean. You can always find a selection of pizzas and pastas, as well as daily specials displayed on a blackboard outside. Live music on weekends attracts a large crowd. $ *Average main: $18* ✉ *Kaya Grandi 52* 🕾 *599/717–3799* ☾ *Closed Wed., Sun., and Sept.*

$$
ECLECTIC

✕ **It Rains Fishes.** Those seeking upscale urban chic flock to this waterfront establishment where beautiful people serve beautiful food. The grilled seafood platter is superb, and the ambience is unbeatable. Despite its popularity and large size, by Bonaire standards, service is impeccable and efficient. The funky bar is a popular hangout until late in the night, and live entertainment is sometimes featured. $ *Average main: $28* ✉ *Kaya Jan N.E. Craane 24* 🕾 *599/717–8780* ⊕ *www.itrainsfishesbonaire.com* ⌂ *Reservations essential* ☾ *Closed Sun. No lunch Sat.*

$$
ECLECTIC
FAMILY

✕ **Kontiki Beach Club.** The dining room is a harmonious blend of terra-cotta tile floors and rattan furnishings around a limestone half-moon bar. There's also a brick terrace for alfresco dining. Chef-owners Miriam and Martin are especially proud of their Dutch *kibbeling* (fish in a beer batter served with chili sauce). Those in the know order the Antillean fish soup, a delightful blend of fresh seafood and finely diced carrots and cucumber. The display of local art on the walls changes constantly. It's quite far from downtown, but the view of the lagoon and intimate ambience mean it is definitely worth the drive. $ *Average main: $18* ✉ *Kaminda Sorobon 64, Lac Bay* 🕾 *599/717–5369* ⊕ *www.kontikibonaire.com.*

$$$
TAPAS

✕ **La Guernica.** This trendy eatery overlooking the boardwalk and the harbor is great for people-watching; there's outdoor seating as well as a couch-and-pillow-filled lounge area. The interior is done in hacienda style, with terra-cotta tiles, clay decorations, and comfy lounge chairs. Though many come here for the excellent tapas, those with heartier appetites can choose from a variety of seafood and meat main courses, including an excellent beef tenderloin with a blue-cheese sauce. The lunch menu offers a range of sandwiches and salads. This is *the* place to sip a cocktail and be seen. $ *Average main: $27* ✉ *Kaya Bonaire 4C* 🕾 *599/717–5022* ⊕ *www.laguernica.com.*

$$ EUROPEAN Fodor's Choice ★

🍴 **Mona Lisa Bar & Restaurant.** Here you can find Continental, Caribbean, and Indonesian fare as well as throngs of regulars who would not dream of visiting Bonaire without a meal here. Popular bar dishes include Wiener schnitzel and fresh fish with curry sauce. The intimate stucco-and-brick dining room, presided over by a copy of the famous painting of the lady with the mystic smile, is decorated with Dutch artwork, lace curtains, and whirring ceiling fans. The colorful bar adorned with baseball-style caps is a great place for late-night schmoozing and noshing on light snacks or the catch of the day, which is served until 10 pm. [$] *Average main: $38* ✉ *Kaya Grandi 15* ☎ *599/717–8718* ✍ *Reservations essential* ⏲ *Closed Sun. No lunch.*

$$ SOUTHWESTERN

🍴 **Paradise Moon.** The menu at this Texan-owned waterfront eatery favors Tex-Mex, but there are also Asian and Continental choices. The food is reasonably priced by Bonaire standards, and portions are huge by any definition. The lion fish ceviche is a popular favorite and with good reason. Fans of throwing calorie caution to the wind will appreciate such Texan touches as deep-fried cheesecake and homemade apple pie floating in a sea of melted butter infused with rum. [$] *Average main: $19* ✉ *Kaya Korsou 1* ☎ *599/717–5025* 🌐 *www.paradisebonaire.com* ⏲ *Closed Sat. No lunch.*

$$ STEAKHOUSE

🍴 **Patagonia Argentinean Steakhouse.** Meat lovers pack this 60-seat waterfront establishment. Though it caters largely to steak lovers with everything from top sirloin to prime rib, there's a respectable selection of seafood and other meats, too. The quality of some of the lower-price steaks can be a bit erratic. Portions are huge, and the quality of the high-end cuts is consistently good. The restaurant's popularity can lead to lengthy wait times and the noise level can be a bit distracting. The restaurant has relocated from its previous location at the Harbour Village Marina lighthouse. [$] *Average main: $32* ✉ *Gob. N. Deprot 67* ☎ *599/717–7725* ✍ *Reservations essential* ⏲ *Closed Mon. No lunch weekends.*

$ CARIBBEAN

🍴 **Wind & Surf Beach Hut Bar.** Part of Bonaire Windsurf Place—and located right on the beach—this fun eatery is one of the most casual dining experiences on the island. Tables and chairs are set directly in the sand under a straw-roof structure so that cooling winds sweep through the space. The food is simple but very good; the main offerings are sandwiches, salads, and burgers. The experience of dining with your toes in the sand is sure to leave lingering pleasant memories. The weekly barbecue on Wednesday nights with live entertainment is well worth the drive. [$] *Average main: $10* ✉ *Sorobon Beach* ☎ *599/717–2288* 💳 *No credit cards.*

$$ ECLECTIC

🍴 **Zeezicht Bar & Restaurant.** Zeezicht (pronounced zay-*zeekt* and meaning "sea view") serves three meals a day and is a Kralendijk institution. At breakfast and lunch you get basic American fare with an Antillean touch, such as a fish omelet; dinner is more Caribbean and mostly seafood, served either on the terrace overlooking the harbor or in the nautically themed, homey, rough-hewn main room. Locals are dedicated to this hangout, especially for the ceviche, conch sandwiches, and the Zeezicht special soup with conch, fish, and shrimp. The location makes it a popular spot for sunset watchers. [$] *Average main: $21* ✉ *Kaya J.N.E. Craane 12* ☎ *599/717–8434.*

6

WHERE TO STAY

Although meal plans are available at most hotels, the island has many excellent—and often inexpensive—restaurants. If you're planning a dive vacation, look into the many attractive dive packages.

RENTAL APARTMENTS

If you prefer do-it-yourself home-style comfort over the pampering and other services offered by a hotel, you can rent a fully furnished apartment.

Bonaire Hotel & Tourism Association. The tourism association has information on a variety of properties ranging from budget to upscale. ☎ 599/717–5134 ⊕ www.bonhata.org.

Sun Rentals. A range of accommodations are available through Sun Rentals. Offerings include private ocean-view villas in luxurious areas like Sabadeco, furnished oceanfront apartments (with a pool) in town, or bungalows in Lagoenhill, an inland community. The Sun Oceanfront Apartments are an excellent budget choice for families. ☎ 599/717–6130 ⊕ www.sunrentalsbonaire.com.

RECOMMENDED HOTELS AND RESORTS

$$
HOTEL
Fodor's Choice
★
Bellafonte Chateau de la Mer. Although it lacks the amenities of a large resort—including a pool—the intimacy and exclusivity of this elegant palazzo-style hotel near Kralendijk more than compensate. **Pros:** well-designed rooms; diving straight from hotel pier; upper rooms have excellent views; free Wi-Fi; groceries can be ordered online before arrival. **Cons:** no restaurant or bar; not close to downtown or shopping; no pool. $ *Rooms from:* $145 ⊠ E.E.G. Blvd. 10, Belnem ☎ 599/717–3333 ⊕ www.bellafontebonaire.com ➼ 4 studios, 8 1-bedroom suites, 8 2-bedroom suites, 2 penthouses ⏐⏐ No meals.

$$
B&B/INN
Bruce Bowker's Carib Inn. The cozy rooms and owner–dive-instructor Bruce Bowker's personal touch have given his inn the highest return-visitor ratio on the island. **Pros:** intimate and friendly; excellent dive courses; Wi-Fi throughout. **Cons:** smaller size means fewer amenities such as shopping; nondivers will find little to entertain them. $ *Rooms from:* $119 ⊠ J.A. Abraham Blvd. 46 ☎ 599/717–8819 ⊕ www.caribinn.com ➼ 10 units ⏐⏐ No meals.

$$
RESORT
FAMILY
Buddy Dive Resort. Well-equipped rooms, a nicely landscaped compound, and excellent dive packages keep guests coming back to this large resort. **Pros:** excellent dive shop; rooms are spacious; open-air restaurant has one of the best ocean views on the island; excellent value for money. **Cons:** complex can feel like a maze; room amenities vary, depending on location. $ *Rooms from:* $147 ⊠ Kaya Gobernador N. Debrot 85 ☎ 599/717–5080, 866/462–8339 ⊕ www.buddydive.com ➼ 6 rooms, 72 apartments ⏐⏐ No meals.

$$
HOTEL
Captain Don's Habitat. Bonaire's first hotel catering to divers remains a favorite, with a PADI five-star dive center offering more than 20 specialty courses. **Pros:** variety of accommodation types; pizzeria with wood-burning oven; excellent diving facilities. **Cons:** little to entertain

Pool at the Harbour Village Beach Club

nondivers; Wi-Fi coverage is spotty. $ *Rooms from: $221* ⊠ *Kaya Gobernador N. Debrot 113* ☎ *599/717–8290, 800/327–6709* ⊕ *www. habitatbonaire.com* ⟿ *24 rooms, 12 junior suites, 5 villas, 19 cottages* ⦿*No meals.*

$ 🏠**Coco Palm Garden & Casa Oleander.** Friends and neighbors operate this
RENTAL series of cozy cottages and villas, each fully equipped and individually
FAMILY decorated. **Pros:** charming and quirky with no two rooms alike; friendly staff; quiet pool area. **Cons:** not close to downtown; limited on-site dining options; long walk from the villas to the common areas and office; charge for using the a/c. $ *Rooms from: $86* ⊠ *Kaya I.R. Randolf Statuuis van Eps 9, Belnem* ☎ *599/717–2108, 599/790–9080* ⊕ *www. cocopalmgarden.org* ⟿ *19 rooms, 6 villas* ⦿*No meals.*

$$ 🏠**Den Laman Condominiums.** Though the exterior of this property will
RENTAL not win any design awards, the location and beautifully finished interiors are definitely first-class. **Pros:** rooms are chicly appointed; convenient to downtown. **Cons:** no elevator; common areas feel a little sterile; spotty Wi-Fi coverage. $ *Rooms from: $170* ⊠ *Kaya Gobernador N. Debrot 77* ☎ *599/717–1700* ⊕ *www.denlaman.com* ⟿ *16 condos* ⦿*No meals.*

$$ 🏠**Divi Flamingo Resort.** The brightly colored buildings of this resort are
RESORT a two-minute stroll from downtown, but the main draw is the combi-
FAMILY nation of a top-notch dive program and the only casino on Bonaire.
Fodor'sChoice **Pros:** beautifully landscaped grounds; steps from downtown and restau-
★ rants; on-site casino. **Cons:** pool can get crowded; beach is quite small. $ *Rooms from: $165* ⊠ *J.A. Abraham Blvd. 40* ☎ *599/717–8285, 800/367–3484* ⊕ *www.diviflamingo.com* ⟿ *129 rooms* ⦿*No meals.*

$$$ HOTEL FAMILY Fodor's Choice ★ 🏨 **Harbour Village Beach Club.** This snazzy enclave of ocher-color buildings is the benchmark for luxury accommodations on the island. **Pros:** great for a secluded getaway; not awash with budget tourists; convenient to downtown. **Cons:** some rooms are quite far from the beach; grounds can feel a bit deserted. [$] *Rooms from: $390* ✉ *Kaya Gobernador N. Debrot 71* ☎ *599/717–7500, 800/424–0004* 🌐 *www.harbourvillage.com* 🛏 *40 rooms, 14 1-bedroom suites, 6 2-bedroom suites* 🍴 *No meals.*

$$ RESORT 🏨 **Plaza Resort Bonaire.** No other property in Bonaire can match the range of activities offered here, with everything from tennis to water sports, not to mention a gorgeous beach. **Pros:** every imaginable recreational activity is available; good shopping in hotel; beautiful grounds; most rooms are huge. **Cons:** size of the compound can make getting around a chore; not an easy walk to downtown; Wi-Fi reception is spotty except in lobby. [$] *Rooms from: $292* ✉ *J.A. Abraham Blvd. 80* ☎ *599/717–2500, 800/766–6016* 🌐 *www.plazaresortbonaire.com* 🛏 *174 rooms, 48 villas* 🍴 *No meals.*

$$ HOTEL FAMILY 🏨 **Roomer.** This excellent, economically priced family hotel has small rooms, but they are individually decorated with tasteful splashes of color. **Pros:** very family-oriented; excellent for budget travelers; kid-friendly pool area; free Wi-Fi. **Cons:** not on the ocean; miles from downtown. [$] *Rooms from: $100* ✉ *E.E.G. Blvd. 97, Belnem* ☎ *599/717–7488* 🌐 *www.roomerbonaire.com* 🛏 *10 rooms* 🍴 *No meals.*

$$ RENTAL FAMILY 🏨 **Sand Dollar Condominium Resort.** This condo complex has family-friendly apartments ranging from studios to three-bedrooms, each of which is individually owned and decorated for a comfortable, lived-in feeling. **Pros:** all rooms have great ocean views; well equipped for families; grocery and ATM on property; during peak season stay six nights and get one for free. **Cons:** few rooms have phones; no beach bar; air-conditioning in living room costs an extra $10 per day. [$] *Rooms from: $187* ✉ *Kaya Gobernador N. Debrot 79* ☎ *599/717–8738, 800/288–4773* 🌐 *www.sanddollarbonaire.com* 🛏 *50 condos* 🍴 *No meals.*

$$ RESORT FAMILY 🏨 **Sorobon Beach Resort.** This basic, family-oriented property on Lac Bay is all about the beach. **Pros:** stunning beachfront; Wi-Fi throughout; next to one of the island's most popular windsurfing centers. **Cons:** miles from shopping and restaurants; no radios or TVs in rooms; rooms are a bit sparse. [$] *Rooms from: $175* ✉ *Sorobon Beach, Lac Bay* ☎ *599/717–8080* 🌐 *www.sorobonbeachresort.com* 🛏 *28 1-bedroom chalets, 1 2-bedroom chalet, 1 3-bedroom house* 🍴 *No meals.*

$$ RENTAL FAMILY Fodor's Choice ★ 🏨 **Waterlands Village.** These individually owned, roomy cottages offer all the comforts of home and feature thoughtful touches such as canopy beds and the option of a private outdoor shower. **Pros:** great price for relatively upscale accommodations; lovely pool area. **Cons:** no ocean view; airport noise can be an issue at times; bit of a walk to downtown; hefty $95 cleaning charge per stay. [$] *Rooms from: $146* ✉ *Kaya International* ☎ *599/701–5540* 🌐 *www.bonairecomfortrentals.com* 🛏 *24 cottages (18 for rent)* 🍴 *No meals.*

$$ 🏨 **Yachtclub Apartments.** Across from Harbour Village, these apartments
RENTAL offer some of the best budget lodging on the island. **Pros:** reasonable
price for excellent accommodations; expansive pool area is great for
sunbathing; close to several good restaurants, and the on-site restau-
rant is excellent; very friendly staff. **Cons:** no ocean view from some
rooms; hotel is on the main road to Kralendijk and can get dusty;
stays less than seven days incur a 25% rate surcharge. $ *Rooms from:*
$101 ⊠ *Kaya Gobernador N. Debrot 52* 📞 *599/717–7424* ⊕ *www.*
yachtclubapartmentsbonaire.com ⬎*13 apartments* ❌*No meals*
⌒ *2-night minimum.*

NIGHTLIFE

Most of Bonaire's nightlife consists of sitting on a quiet beach and sip-
ping a local Amstel Bright beer. Top island performers, including the
Foyan Boys, migrate from one resort to another throughout the week.
You can find information in the free magazines (published once a year)
Bonaire Affair and *Bonaire Nights*. The twice-monthly *Bonaire Update
Events and Activities* pamphlet is available at most restaurants.

6

BARS

City Café. Downtown, City Café is a wacky hangout splashed in magenta,
banana, and electric blue. Here you can find cocktails, snack food,
live music on weekends, and karaoke on Wednesday nights. ⊠ *Hotel
Rochaline, Kaya Grandi 7* 📞 *599/717–8286.*

Deco Stop Bar. The Thursday-night happy hour at Deco Stop Bar is
popular. ⊠ *Captain Don's Habitat, Kaya Gobernador N. Debrot 113*
📞 *599/717–8286.*

Karel's. Perched on stilts above the sea, Karel's is *the* place for min-
gling—especially on Friday and Saturday nights, when there's live
island and pop music 'til the wee hours. ⊠ *Kaya J.N.E. Craane 12*
📞 *599/717–8434.*

La Guernica. With an ultrachic bar and a comfy couch-lined terrace fac-
ing the ocean, La Guernica is the place to be seen on weekend nights.
⊠ *Kaya Bonaire 4C* 📞 *599/717–5022.*

DANCE CLUBS

City Café. This is the island's closest thing to a dance club. On weekend
nights the restaurant moves the tables aside to create an instant dance
floor. ⊠ *Kaya Grandi 7* 📞 *599/717–8286.*

Sunday Party at Lac Cai. On Sunday afternoon at Lac Cai enjoy the festive
Sunday Party, where locals celebrate the day with live music, dancing,
and local food from 3 to 11. Take a taxi, especially if you plan to imbibe
a few rum punches. ⊠ *Lac Cai.*

SHOPPING

You can get to know all the shops in Kralendijk in an hour or so. Almost all the shops are on the Kaya Grandi and adjacent streets and in tiny malls. Harbourside Mall is a pleasant, open-air mall with several fine air-conditioned shops. The most distinctive local crafts are fanciful, painted pieces of driftwood and hand-painted *kunuku*, or little wilderness houses. ■TIP➔ Don't take home items made of goatskin or tortoiseshell; they aren't allowed into the United States. Remember, too, that it's forbidden to take sea fans, coral, conch shells, and all other forms of marine life off the island.

CLOTHING

Benetton. This Benetton outpost claims that its prices for men's, women's, and children's clothes are 30% lower than in New York. ⊠ *Kaya Grandi 29* ☏ *599/717–5107.*

Best Buddies & Pearls. You'll find a good selection of Indonesian batik shirts, pareus, and T-shirts at Best Buddies. ⊠ *Kaya Grandi 32* ☏ *599/796–7451.*

Island Fashions & Gifts. Buy swimsuits, sunglasses, T-shirts, and costume jewelry at this stylish shop. ⊠ *Kaya Grandi 5* ☏ *599/717–7071.*

DUTY-FREE GOODS

Flamingo Airport Duty Free. Perfumes and cigarettes are available at Flamingo Airport Duty Free. ⊠ *Flamingo Airport* ☏ *599/717–5563.*

Perfume Palace. This shop sells perfumes and makeup from Lancôme, Estée Lauder, Chanel, Ralph Lauren, and Clinique. ⊠ *Harbourside Mall, Kaya Grandi 31* ☏ *599/717–5288.*

HANDICRAFTS

JanArt Gallery. On the outskirts of town, JanArt Gallery sells unique paintings, prints, and art supplies; artist Janice Huckaby also hosts art classes. ⊠ *Kaya Gloria 7* ☏ *599/717–5246.*

Kas di Arte. The works of local and international artists—including such notables as Ronald Verhoeven—are featured at Kas di Arte. ⊠ *Kaya J.N.E. Craane 34* ☺ *Closed Sun.*

Maharaj Gifthouse. If you're searching for gifts, check out the hand-painted delft blue china, local artwork, and stainless-steel and crystal items at Maharaj Gifthouse. ⊠ *Kaya Grandi 11* ☏ *599/717–4402.*

Richter Art Gallery. This dedicated fine art gallery run by Linda Richter features a range of work from local artists including paintings by Linda and her late husband. In addition to paintings the gallery also features prints and handmade jewelry. ⊠ *Kaya Statius van Eps 17, Belnem* ☏ *599/717–4112* ⊕ *www.richterart.com.*

Yenny's Art. Every visitor should make a point of visiting Yenny's Art. Roam around her house, which is a replica of a traditional Bonaire town complete with her handmade life-size dolls and the skeletons of all her dead pets. Fun (and sometimes kitschy) souvenirs made out of driftwood, clay, and shells are all handmade by Jenny Rijna. ⊠ *Kaya Betico Croes 6, near post office* ☎ *599/717–5004.*

JEWELRY

Atlantis. This shop carries a large range of precious and semiprecious gems; the tanzanite collection is especially beautiful. You will also find Sector, Raymond Weil, and Citizen watches, among others, all at great savings. Since gold jewelry is sold by weight here, it's an especially good buy. ⊠ *Kaya Grandi 32B* ☎ *599/717–7730.*

Littman's. Owner Steven Littman handpicks many of the items available in this upscale jewelry and gift shop during his regular trips to Europe. Look for Rolex, Omega, Cartier, and Tag Heuer watches; fine gold jewelry; antique coins; nautical sculptures; resort clothing; and accessories. ⊠ *Kaya Grandi 33* ☎ *599/717–8160* ⊠ *Harbourside Mall, Kaya Grandi 31* ☎ *599/717–2130.*

SPORTS AND ACTIVITIES

6

BICYCLING

Bonaire is generally flat, so bicycles are an easy way to get around. Because of the heat it's essential to carry water if you're planning to cycle for any distance and especially if your plans involve exploring the deserted interior. There are more than 180 miles (290 km) of unpaved routes (as well as the many paved roads) on the island.

Bike Rental Delivery Bonaire. Opened in 2012, this service offers bike delivery to your door in their trademark yellow van. Rental prices start at $14 a day or $60 a week and tours can be arranged. Prices vary depending on duration of rental, size of group, and route. ☎ *599/786–1166.*

Tropical Travel. This tour operator offers bikes for $14 per day or $60 per week (a $300 deposit is required). ⊠ *Plaza Resort Bonaire, J.A. Abraham Blvd. 80* ☎ *599/701–1232* ⊕ *www.tropicaltravelbonaire.com.*

DAY SAILS AND SNORKELING TRIPS

Regularly scheduled sunset sails and snorkeling trips are popular (prices range from $35 to $50 per person), as are private or group sails (expect to pay about $500 per day for a party of four).

Kantika de Amor Watertaxi. This company provides daily rides to Klein Bonaire and drift snorkel and evening cruises with complimentary cocktails. ⊠ *Kaya J.N.E. Craane 24, opposite restaurant It Rains Fishes* ☎ *599/796–7254.*

Mushi Mushi. The *Mushi Mushi* is a catamaran offering a variety of two- and three-hour cruises starting at $55 per person. It departs from the Bonaire Nautico Marina in downtown Kralendijk (opposite the restaurant It Rains Fishes). ☎ *599/790–5399.*

Tropical Travel. If you want to do some sailing on your own, Tropical Travel offers a variety of cruise packages, with prices available on request. ✉ *Plaza Resort Bonaire, J.A. Abraham Blvd. 80* ☎ *599/701–1232* ⊕ *www.tropicaltravelbonaire.com.*

Woodwind. The *Woodwind* is a 37-foot trimaran that offers regular sailing and snorkeling trips as well as charters. It leaves from the dock at Divi Flamingo and offers a sail-snorkel–sunset cruise for $55 per person. ☎ *599/786–7055* ⊕ *www.woodwindbonaire.com.*

DIVING AND SNORKELING

Bonaire has some of the best reef diving this side of Australia's Great Barrier Reef. It takes only 5 to 25 minutes to reach many sites, the current is usually mild, and although some reefs have sudden, steep drops, most begin just offshore and slope gently downward at a 45-degree angle. General visibility runs 60 to 100 feet, except during surges in October and November. You can see several varieties of coral: knobby-brain, giant-brain, elkhorn, staghorn, mountainous star, gorgonian, and black. You can also encounter schools of parrot fish, surgeonfish, angelfish, eel, snapper, and grouper. Beach diving is excellent just about everywhere on the leeward side, so night diving is popular. There are sites here suitable for every skill level; they're clearly marked by yellow stones on the roadside.

Bonaire, in conjunction with *Skin Diver* magazine, has also developed the **Guided Snorkeling Program.** The highly educational and entertaining program begins with a slide show on important topics, from a beginner's look at reef fish, coral, and sponges to advanced fish identification and night snorkeling. Guided snorkeling for all skill levels can be arranged through most resort dive shops. The best snorkeling spots are on the island's leeward side, where you have shore access to the reefs, and along the west side of Klein Bonaire, where the reef is better developed. All snorkelers and swimmers must pay a $10 Nature Fee, which allows access to the waters around the island and Washington–Slagbaai National Park for one calendar year. The fee can be paid at most dive shops.

Fodor'sChoice
★
Bonaire Marine Park. In the well-policed Bonaire Marine Park, which encompasses the entire coastline around Bonaire and Klein Bonaire, divers take the rules seriously. Don't even *think* about (1) spearfishing; (2) dropping anchor; or (3) touching, stepping on, or collecting coral. In order to dive (as opposed to simply swim and enter the water), you must pay a fee of $25 (used to maintain the park), for which you receive a colored plastic tag (to attach to an item of scuba gear) entitling you to one calendar year of unlimited diving. Checkout dives—dives you do first with a master before going out on your own—are required, and you can arrange them through any dive shop. All dive operations offer classes in free buoyancy control, advanced buoyancy control, and photographic buoyancy control. Tags are available at all scuba facilities and from the Marine Park Headquarters. ✉ *Karpata* ☎ *599/717–8444* ⊕ *www.bmp.org.*

A Bonaire diver shows off her photographic buoyancy control.

DIVE SITES

The *Guide to the Bonaire Marine Park* lists 86 dive sites (including 16 shore-dive-only and 35 boat-dive-only sites). Another fine reference book is the *Diving and Snorkeling Guide to Bonaire,* by Jerry Schnabel and Suzi Swygert. Guides associated with the various dive centers can give you more complete directions. It's difficult to recommend one site over another; to whet your appetite, here are a few of the popular sites.

Angel City. Take the trail down to the shore adjacent to the Radio Nederland tower station; dive in and swim south to Angel City, one of the shallowest and most popular sites in a two-reef complex that includes Alice in Wonderland. The boulder-size green-and-tan coral heads are home to black margates, Spanish hogfish, gray snappers, stingrays, and large purple tube sponges.

Bari Reef. Catch a glimpse of the elkhorn and fire coral, queen angelfish, and other wonders of Bari Reef, just off the Sand Dollar Condominium Resort's pier.

Calabas Reef. Off the coast of the Divi Flamingo Resort, this is the island's busiest dive site. It's replete with Christmas-tree worms, sponges, and fire coral adhering to a ship's hull. Fish life is frenzied, with the occasional octopus putting in an appearance.

Forest. You need to catch a boat to reach Forest, a dive site off the southwest coast of Klein Bonaire. Named for the abundant black-coral forests found in it, the site gets a lot of fish action, including a resident spotted eel that lives in a cave.

Rappel. This spectacular site is near the Karpata Ecological Center. The shore is a sheer cliff, and the lush coral growth is the habitat of some unusual varieties of marine life, including occasional orange sea horses, squid, spiny lobsters, and spotted trunkfish.

Small Wall. One of Bonaire's three complete vertical wall dives (and one of its most popular night-diving spots), Small Wall is in front of the Black Durgon Inn, near Barcadera Beach. Because the access to this site is on private property, this is usually a boat-diving site. The 60-foot wall is frequented by squid, turtles, tarpon, and barracuda and has dense hard and soft coral formations; it also allows for excellent snorkeling.

Something Special. South of the marina entrance at Harbour Village Beach Club, this spot is famous for its garden eels. They wave about from the relatively shallow sand terrace looking like long grass in a breeze.

Town Pier. Known for shielding one of Bonaire's best night dives, the pier is right in town, across from the City Café. Divers need permission from the harbormaster and must be accompanied by a local guide.

Windsock Steep. This excellent shore-dive site (from 20 to 80 feet) is in front of the small beach opposite the airport runway. It's a popular place for snorkeling. The current is moderate, the elkhorn coral profuse; you may also see angelfish and rays.

DIVE OPERATORS

Many of the dive shops listed *below* offer PADI and NAUI certification courses and SSI, as well as underwater photography and videography courses. Some shops are also qualified to certify dive instructors. Full certification courses cost approximately $385; open-water refresher courses run about $240; a one-tank boat dive with unlimited shore diving costs about $40; a two-tank boat dive with unlimited shore diving is about $65. As for equipment, renting a mask, fin, and snorkel costs about $12 altogether; for a BC (buoyancy compensator) and regulator, expect to pay about $20. Check out children's programs such as Aquakids and Ocean Classroom—or inquire about their equivalents.

Most dive shops on Bonaire offer a complete range of snorkel gear for rent and will provide beginner training; some dive operations also offer guided snorkeling and night snorkeling. The cost for a guided snorkel session is about $50 and includes slide presentations, transportation to the site, and a tour. Gear rental is approximately $10 per 24-hour period.

FAMILY **Bonaire Dive & Adventure.** For first-timers who want a stress-free introduction to the sport, Bonaire Dive & Adventure is probably the best choice. ⊠ *Sand Dollar Condominium Resort, Kaya Gobernador N. Debrot 77A* ☎ *599/717–2229* ⊕ *www.bonairediveandadventure.com.*

Bonaire Scuba Center ⊠ *Black Durgon Inn, Kaya Gobernador N. Debrot 145* ☎ *599/717–5736.*

Bruce Bowker's Carib Inn Dive Center ⊠ *J.A. Abraham Blvd. 46* ☎ *599/717– 8819* ⊕ *www.caribinn.com.*

FAMILY **Buddy Dive Resort** ⊠ *Kaya Gobernador N. Debrot 85* ☎ *599/717–5080* ⊕ *www.buddydive.com.*

Captain Don's Habitat Dive Shop ⊠ *Kaya Gobernador N. Debrot 113* ☎ *599/717–8290* ⊕ *www.habitatbonaire.com.*

Dive Friends Bonaire ⊠ *Kaya Grandi 6* ☎ *599/717–3911* ⊕ *www.dive-friends-bonaire.com.*

Divi Dive Bonaire ⊠ *Divi Flamingo Resort & Casino, J.A. Abraham Blvd. 40* ☎ *599/717–8285* ⊕ *www.diviflamingo.com.*

FAMILY **Toucan Diving.** The Aquakids program—for children ages 5 to 12—is offered by Toucan Diving. ⊠ *Plaza Resort Bonaire, J.A. Abraham Blvd. 80* ☎ *599/717–2500* ⊕ *www.toucandiving.com.*

Touch the Sea with Dee Scarr ☎ *599/717–8529* ⊕ *www.touchthesea.com.*

Wannadive ⊠ *Eden Beach Resort, Kaya Gobernador N. Debrot 73, on the beach* ☎ *599/717–8884* ⊕ *www.wannadivebonaire.com.*

FISHING

Le Grand Bleu. You can rent the 44-foot *Striker* for $500 for a half day or $650 for a full day of deep-sea fishing. ☎ *599/795–1139* ⊕ *www.fishingbonaire.com.*

Piscatur Charters. This company offers light-tackle angler reef fishing for jackfish, barracuda, and snapper. You can charter the 42-foot Sport Fisherman *Piscatur*, which carries up to six people, for $450 for a half day or $600 for a full day. ⊠ *Kaya H.J. Pop 3* ☎ *599/717–8774* ⊕ *www.piscatur.com.*

GUIDED TOURS

Achie Tours. This tour operator offers several half- and full-day options. ⊠ *Kaya Nikiboko Noord 33* ☎ *599/717–8630.*

Bonaire Tours & Vacations. This tour company will chauffeur you around on two-hour tours of either the island's north or south sides. An all-day tour of Washington Park ($80), which includes lunch and a snorkel, is also offered. ⊠ *Kaya Gobernador N. Debrot 79* ☎ *599/717–8778* ⊕ *www.bonairetours.com.*

Or simply ask any taxi driver for an island tour (be sure to negotiate the price up front).

HORSEBACK RIDING

FAMILY **Horse Ranch Club.** You can take hour-long trail rides at the 166-acre Horse Ranch Club (formerly the Riding Academy Club) for $120. A guide takes you through groves of cacti where iguanas, wild goats, donkeys, and flamingos reside; there is even an opportunity to swim with the horses. Reserve one of the gentle pintos or Paso Finos a day in advance, and try to go early in the morning, when it's cool. Tours are available by reservation only and are limited to two people. ⊠ *Near airport, east of Kralendijk* ☎ *599/560–7949, 599/786–2094.*

KAYAKING

Divers and snorkelers can use kayaks to reach otherwise inaccessible dive sites and simply tow the craft along during their dive. Nondivers can take advantage of the calm waters around the island to explore the coastline and the fascinating stands of mangrove around the Lac Bay area. The mangrove harbors myriad wildlife and acts as a hatchery for marine life. Almost all of the kayaks used are of the sit-on-top variety, which are able to negotiate shallow waters better.

Bonaire Dive & Adventure. This operator rents kayaks and also leads guided trips. ⊠ *Kaya Gobernador N. Debrot 79* ☎ *599/717–2229* ⊕ *www.bonairediveandadventure.com.*

Jibe City. At Jibe City, which is primarily a windsurfing outfit, kayaks are free if you are renting surf equipment. Otherwise, they go for $10 (single) and $15 (double) for the first two hours; $25 and $30, respectively, per half day. ⊠ *Sorobon Beach* ☎ *599/717–5233* ⊕ *www.jibecity. com* ⊗ *Closed Sept.*

Mangrove Info & Kayak Center. This outfit offers guided kayak tours of the mangrove forest at 9 am and 11 am daily, for $27 an hour and $46 for two hours. The center houses a unique mangrove aquarium designed to study the Lac Bay mangroves' effect on the global ecosystem as well as a photo gallery showing underwater existence within the forest like never before. The tours are pleasant even for the exercise-challenged and usually provide a great way to work on your tan. The two-hour tour includes snorkeling and is a lot more fun. ⊠ *Kaminda Lac 141, on road to Lac Cai, Lac Bay* ☎ *599/780–5353* ⊕ *www.mangrovecenter.com.*

WINDSURFING

With near-constant breezes and calm waters, Bonaire is consistently ranked among the best places in the world for windsurfing. Lac Bay, a protected cove on the east coast, is ideal for windsurfing. The island's windsurfing companies are headquartered there on Sorobon Beach.

Bonaire Windsurf Place. Commonly referred to as "the Place," this shop rents the latest Hot Sails Maui, Starboard, and RRD equipment for $145 for a two-day rental. A one-hour group lesson costs $50; private lessons are $80 per hour (these rates do not include equipment, which adds at least $40 to the price). Groups are generally limited to four people. Owners Elvis, Roger, and Constantine are all former windsurfing champs. ⊠ *Sorobon Beach* ☎ *599/717–2288* ⊕ *www. bonairewindsurfplace.com.*

Jibe City. This company offers lessons for $50 (includes board and sail for beginners only); board rentals start at $30 an hour, $70 for a day. There are pickups at all the hotels at 9 am and 1 pm; ask your hotel to make arrangements. ⊠ *Sorobon Beach* ☎ *599/717–5233* ⊕ *www.jibecity.com.*

BRITISH VIRGIN
ISLANDS

7

Visit Fodors.com for advice, updates, and bookings

WELCOME TO BRITISH VIRGIN ISLANDS

NATURE'S LITTLE SECRETS

Most of the 60-some islands, islets, and cays that make up the British Virgin Islands (BVI) are remarkably hilly and volcanic in origin, having exploded from the depths of the sea some 25 million years ago. The exception is Anegada, which is a flat coral-limestone atoll. Tortola (about 10 square miles [26 square km]) is the largest member of the chain.

The British Virgin Islands are mostly quiet and casual, so don't expect to party until dawn, and definitely leave the tux at home. Luxury here means getting away from it all rather than getting the trendiest state-of-the-art amenities. And the jackpot is the chance to explore the many islets and cays by sailboat.

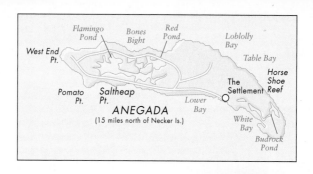

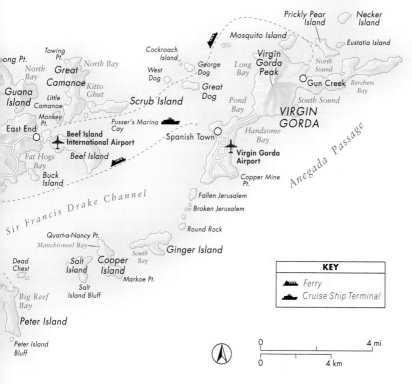

KEY

Ferry
Cruise Ship Terminal

0   4 mi
0   4 km

TOP REASONS TO VISIT BRITISH VIRGIN ISLANDS

1 The Perfect Place to Sail: With more than 60 islands in the chain, sailors can drop anchor at a different, perfect beach every day.

2 Low-Key Resorts: Laid-back (but luxurious) resorts offer a full-scale retreat from your everyday life.

3 Diving and Snorkeling: Both are great, and vibrant reefs are often just feet from the shore.

4 Jost Van Dyke: Your trip isn't complete until you've chilled at the casual beach bars here.

5 Few Crowds: There's no mass tourism; the farther you get from Tortola, the quieter things become.

Updated by
Susan Zaluski

Once a collection of about 60 sleepy islands and cays, the British Virgin Islands—particularly the main island of Tortola—now see huge cruise ships crowding the dock outside Road Town. Shoppers clog the downtown area, and traffic occasionally comes to a standstill. Even the second-largest island, Virgin Gorda, gets its share of smaller ships anchored off the main village of Spanish Town. Despite this explosive growth in the territory's tourism industry, it's still easy to escape the hubbub. Hotels outside Road Town usually provide a quiet oasis, and those on the other islands can be downright serene.

Each island has a different flavor. Want access to lots of restaurants and shopping? Make Tortola your choice. The largest of the BVIs, it covers 10 square miles (26 square km) and sits only a mile from St. John in the United States Virgin Islands (USVI). If you want to kick back at a small hotel or posh resort, try Virgin Gorda. Sitting nearly at the end of the chain, the 8-square-mile (21-square-km) island offers stellar beaches and a laid-back atmosphere. If you really want to get away from it all, the outermost islands, including Anegada and Jost Van Dyke, will fill the bill. Some of the smallest—Norman, Peter, Cooper, and Necker—are home to just one resort or restaurant. Others remain uninhabited specks on the horizon.

Visitors have long visited the BVI, starting with Christopher Columbus in 1493. He called the islands Las Once Mil Virgines—the 11,000 Virgins—in honor of the 11,000 virgin companions of St. Ursula, martyred in the 4th century AD. Pirates and buccaneers followed, and then came the British, who farmed the islands until slavery was abolished in 1834. The BVI are still politically tied to Britain, so the queen appoints a royal governor, but residents elect a local Legislative Council. Offshore banking and tourism share top billing in the territory's economy, but the majority of the islands' jobs are tourism-related. Despite the growth, you can usually find a welcoming smile.

LOGISTICS

Getting to the BVI: There are no nonstop flights to the BVI from the United States. Most travelers connect in San Juan or St. Thomas. You can fly to Tortola, Virgin Gorda, or Anegada, but only on a small plane. There are also ferries from St. Thomas, with regular service to Tortola, Jost Van Dyke, and Virgin Gorda.

Hassle Factor: Medium to high.

On the Ground: Although taxi service is good, you may wish to rent a car on Tortola or Virgin Gorda to explore farther afield or try many different beaches (you may need to if you are staying at an isolated resort). On Anegada it's possible to rent a car, but most people rely on taxis for transportation. Jost Van Dyke has a single road, and visitors travel on foot or by local taxi.

Getting Around the Islands: Most people take ferries to get from island to island, though flights are possible (some are regularly scheduled, or there are plenty of charter opportunities if you are traveling in a group).

PLANNING

WHEN TO GO

High season doesn't really get into full swing until Christmas and ends sooner (usually by April 1) than on most Caribbean islands. In the off-season, rates can be a third less. Locals and yachties gather at Foxy's bar on Jost Van Dyke for the annual Halloween party in October.

Glimpse the colorful spinnakers as sailing enthusiasts gather for the internationally known **BVI Spring Regatta and Sailing Festival,** which begins during the last week in March and continues until the first weekend in April. Tortola celebrates **Carnival** on and around August 1 to mark the anniversary of the end of slavery in 1834. A slew of activities culminating with a parade through the streets take place in Road Town. Hotels fill up fast, so make sure to reserve your room and rental car well in advance.

In August you can also try your hand at sportfishing, as anglers compete to land the largest catch at the **BVI Sportfishing Tournament**.

GETTING HERE AND AROUND

AIR TRAVEL

Several airlines have regularly scheduled service to either Tortola or Virgin Gorda. Although it may be cheaper to fly via Puerto Rico, the connections are better through St. Thomas. If you have seven or more people in your party, you can also charter a plane from St. Thomas or San Juan.

Airports Tortola (TOC), Virgin Gorda (VIJ), and Anegada (no code).

Airline Contacts Air Sunshine ☎ *800/327–8900, 800/435–8900 in Florida, 888/879–8900 in USVI, 284/495–8900 in BVI* ⊕ *www.airsunshine.com.*
American Airlines/American Eagle ☎ *800/433–7300 in Tortola, 340/776–2560 in St. Thomas, 340/778–2000 in St. Croix* ⊕ *www.aa.com.* **Cape Air** ☎ *866/227–3247, 284/495–1440 in Tortola* ⊕ *www.flycapeair.com.* **Fly BVI** ☎ *284/495–1747* ⊕ *www.bviaircharters.com.* **LIAT** ☎ *888/844–5428, 866/549–5428 in USVI, 284/495–1693 in Tortola* ⊕ *www.liat.com.*

Airport Transfers Mahogany Rentals and Taxi Service ⊠ *The Valley, Virgin Gorda* ☎ *284/495–5469* ⊕ *www.mahoganycarrentalsbvi.com.*

BOAT AND FERRY TRAVEL

Frequent daily ferries connect Tortola with St. Thomas (both Charlotte Amalie and Red Hook) and St. John. Ferries also link Tortola with Jost Van Dyke, Peter Island, and Virgin Gorda. Tortola has three ferry terminals—one at West End, one on Beef Island (at the airport), and one in Road Town. Schedules vary, and not all companies make daily trips. All Red Hook–bound ferries stop in Cruz Bay to clear customs and immigration.

Ferries also connect Virgin Gorda with St. Thomas (both Charlotte Amalie and Red Hook) and St. John, but not daily. All Red Hook–bound ferries stop in Cruz Bay to clear customs and immigration. Ferries to Virgin Gorda land in Spanish Town. Schedules vary by day, and not all companies make daily trips.

The BVI Tourist Board website ⊕ *www.bvitourism.com/inter-island-ferries* has links to all the ferry companies, and these sites are the best sources for ever-changing routes and schedules.

Boat and Ferry Contacts Dohm's Water Taxi ☎ *340/775–6501 in St. Thomas* ⊕ *www.watertaxi-vi.com.* **Inter-Island Boat Service** ☎ *340/776–6597 in St. John,* 284/495–4166 *in Tortola.* **Native Son** ☎ *340/774–8685 in St. Thomas,* 284/495–4617 *in Tortola* ⊕ *www.nativesonferry.com.* **New Horizon Ferry Service** ☎ *284/495–9278 in Tortola.* **North Sound Express** ☎ *284/495–2138 in Tortola.* **Peter Island Ferry** ☎ *284/495–2000 in Tortola* ⊕ *www.peterisland. com.* **Reefer** ☎ *340/776–8500 in St. Thomas* ⊕ *www.marriottfrenchmansreef. com.* **Smith's Ferry** ☎ *340/775–7292 in St. Thomas,* 284/494–4454 *in Tortola* ⊕ *www.bviferryservices.com.* **Speedy's Ferries** ☎ *284/495–5235 in Tortola* ⊕ *www.speedysbvi.com.* **Road Town Fast Ferry** ☎ *284/494–2323 in Tortola* ⊕ *www.tortolafastferry.com.*

CAR TRAVEL

Driving in the BVI is on the left, British-style, but your car will always have its steering wheel on the left, as in the United States. Your valid U.S. license will also do for driving in the BVI. The minimum age to rent a car is 25. Most agencies offer both four-wheel-drive vehicles and cars (often compacts). Both Tortola and Virgin Gorda have a number of car-rental agencies.

Tortola Car-Rental Contacts Avis ⊠ *Opposite police station, Road Town* ☎ *284/494–2193* ⊕ *www.avis.com* ⊠ *Towers, West End* ☎ *284/495–4973.* **D&D** ⊠ *West End Rd., West End* ☎ *284/495–4765.* **Itgo Car Rental** ⊠ *Wickham's Cay I, Road Town* ☎ *284/494–2639* ⊕ *www.itgobvi.com.* **National** ⊠ *Airport, Beef Island* ☎ *284/495–2626* ⊕ *www.national.com* ⊠ *Waterfront Dr., Duff's Bottom, Road Town* ☎ *284/494–3197* ⊠ *Long Bay Hotel, Long Bay Rd., Long Bay* ☎ *284/495–4877.*

Virgin Gorda Car-Rental Contacts L&S Jeep Rental ⊠ *The Valley, Virgin Gorda* ☎ *284/495–5297* ⊕ *www.landsjeeprental.com.* **Mahogany Rentals & Taxi Service** ⊠ *Spanish Town, Virgin Gorda* ☎ *284/495–5469* ⊕ *www.mahoganycarrentalsbvi.com.* **Speedy's Car Rentals** ⊠ *The Valley, Virgin Gorda* ☎ *284/495–5240* ⊕ *www.speedysbvi.com.*

TAXI TRAVEL

Taxi rates aren't set in the BVI, so you should negotiate the fare with your driver before you start your trip. Fares are per destination, not per person here, so it's cheaper to travel in groups. The taxi number is always on the license plate.

Tortola Taxi Contacts BVI Taxi Association ☎ *284/494-3942.* **Waterfront Taxi Association** ☎ *284/494-6362.* **West End Taxi Association** ☎ *284/495-4934.*

Virgin Gorda Taxi Contacts Andy's Taxi and Jeep Rental ✉ *The Valley, Virgin Gorda* ☎ *284/495-5252* ⊕ *www.virgingordatours.com.* **Mahogany Rentals and Taxi Service** ✉ *The Valley, Virgin Gorda* ☎ *284/495-5469* ⊕ *www.mahoganycrrentalsbvi.com.*

ESSENTIALS

Banks and Exchange Services The currency in the BVI is the U.S. dollar. ATMs are common in Road Town, Tortola, and around Virgin Gorda Yacht Harbour.

Electricity 110 volts, the same as in North America, so American appliances work just fine.

Passport Requirements All travelers going to the British Virgin Islands need to have a valid passport, even if they are traveling by private yacht.

Phones The area code for the BVI is 284; when you make calls from North America, you need to dial only the area code and the number. To call anywhere in the BVI once you've arrived, dial all seven digits. A local call from a pay phone costs 25¢, but such phones are sometimes on the blink. An alternative is a Caribbean phone card, available in $5, $10, and $20 denominations. They're sold at most major hotels and many stores and can be used to call within the BVI, as well as all over the Caribbean, and to access **USADirect** (☎ *800/872–2881, 111 from a pay phone*) from special phone-card phones. For credit-card or collect long-distance calls to the United States, use a phone-card telephone or look for special USADirect phones, which are linked directly to an AT&T operator. USADirect and pay phones can be found at most hotels and in towns.

Taxes The departure tax is $15 per person by boat and $20 per person by plane. There are separate booths at the airport and ferry terminals to collect this tax, which must be paid in cash in U.S. currency. Most hotels add a service charge ranging from 5% to 18% to the bill. A few restaurants and some shops tack on an additional 10% charge if you use a credit card. There's no sales tax in the BVI. However, there's a 7% government tax on hotel rooms.

ACCOMMODATIONS

Pick your island carefully, because each is different, as are the logistics of getting there. **Tortola** gives you a wider choice of restaurants, shopping, and resorts. **Virgin Gorda** has fewer off-resort places to eat and shop, but the resorts themselves are often better, and the beaches are wonderful. **Anegada** is remote and better suited for divers. **Jost Van Dyke** has some classic Caribbean beach bars, along with fairly basic accommodations.

When you want to be pampered and pampered some more, consider a remote, **private-island resort** reached only by ferry, or even one of the appealing outer-island resorts that are still somewhat affordable for mere mortals.

If you want to enjoy everything the BVI have to offer, **charter a sailboat** so you can drop anchor where and when you want.

The largest resort in the British Virgin Islands has 120-some rooms, and most have considerably fewer. Luxury here is more about personal service than over-the-top amenities. The best places are certainly comfortable, but they aren't showy. You'll find **villas and condos** in abundance, and they are a good option for families.

HOTEL AND RESTAURANT PRICES

Prices in the restaurant reviews are the average cost of a main course at dinner or, if dinner is not served, at lunch; taxes and service charges are generally included. Prices in the hotel reviews are the lowest cost of a standard double room in high season, excluding taxes, service charges, and meal plans (except at all-inclusives). Prices for rentals are the lowest per-night cost for a one-bedroom unit in high season.

For expanded lodging reviews and current deals, visit Fodors.com.

VISITOR INFORMATION

Contacts **BVI Tourist Board** ☎ 212/563–3117, 800/835–8530 in U.S. ⊕ www.bvitourism.com.

WEDDINGS

You must apply in person for your license ($110) weekdays at the attorney general's office in Road Town, Tortola. You must wait three days to pick it up at the registrar's office in Road Town. If you plan to be married in a church, announcements (called *banns* locally) must be published for three consecutive Sundays in the church bulletin. Only the registrar or clergy can perform ceremonies. The registrar charges $35 at the office and $100 at another location. No blood test is required.

Contacts **BVI Wedding Planners and Consultants** ☎ 284/494–5306 ⊕ www.bviweddings.com.

TORTOLA

Updated by Lynda Lohr

Once a sleepy backwater, Tortola is definitely busy these days, particularly when several cruise ships tie up at the Road Town dock. Passengers crowd the streets and shops, and open-air jitneys filled with cruise-ship passengers create bottlenecks on the island's byways. That said, most folks visit Tortola to relax on its deserted sands or linger over lunch at one of its many delightful restaurants. Beaches are never more than a few miles away, and the steep green hills that form Tortola's spine are fanned by gentle trade winds. The neighboring islands glimmer like emeralds in a sea of sapphire. It can be a world far removed from the hustle of modern life, but it simply doesn't compare to Virgin Gorda in terms of beautiful beaches—or even luxury resorts, for that matter.

Initially settled by Taíno Indians, Tortola saw a string of visitors over the years. Christopher Columbus sailed by in 1493 on his second voyage to the New World, and ships from Spain, Holland, and France made periodic visits about a century later. Sir Francis Drake arrived in 1595, leaving his name on the passage between Tortola and St. John. Pirates and buccaneers followed, with the British finally laying claim to the island in the late 1600s. In 1741 John Pickering became the first lieutenant governor of Tortola, and the seat of the British government moved from Virgin Gorda to Tortola. As the agrarian economy continued to grow, slaves were imported from Africa. The slave trade was abolished in 1807, but slaves in Tortola and the rest of the BVI did not gain their freedom until August 1, 1834, when the Emancipation Proclamation was read at Sunday Morning Well in Road Town. That date is celebrated every year with the island's annual Carnival.

> ### DRIVING ON TORTOLA
>
> Tortola's main roads are well paved, for the most part, but there are exceptionally steep hills and sharp curves. Road Town's traffic and parking can be horrific. Try to avoid driving along the Waterfront Drive at morning and afternoon rush hours. It's longer, but often quicker, to take a route through the hills above Road Town. Parking can be very difficult in Road Town, particularly during the busy winter season. There's parking along the waterfront and on the inland side on the eastern end of downtown.

Visitors have a choice of accommodations, but most fall into the small and smaller-still categories. Only Long Bay Resort on Tortola's North Shore qualifies as a resort, but even some of the smaller properties add an amenity or two. A couple of new hotel projects are in the works, so look for more growth in the island's hotel industry over the next decade.

EXPLORING

Tortola doesn't have many historic sights, but it does have lots of beautiful natural scenery. Although you could explore the island's 10 square miles (26 square km) in a few hours, opting for such a whirlwind tour would be a mistake. There's no need to live in the fast lane when you're surrounded by some of the Caribbean's most breathtaking panoramas. Also, the roads are extraordinarily steep and twisting, making driving demanding. The best strategy is to explore a bit of the island at a time. For example, you might try Road Town (the island's tiny metropolis) one morning and a drive to Cane Garden Bay and the little town of West End the next afternoon. Or consider a visit to East End, a *very* tiny town exactly where its name suggests. The North Shore is where all the best beaches are found. Sights are best seen when you stumble on them on your round-the-island drive.

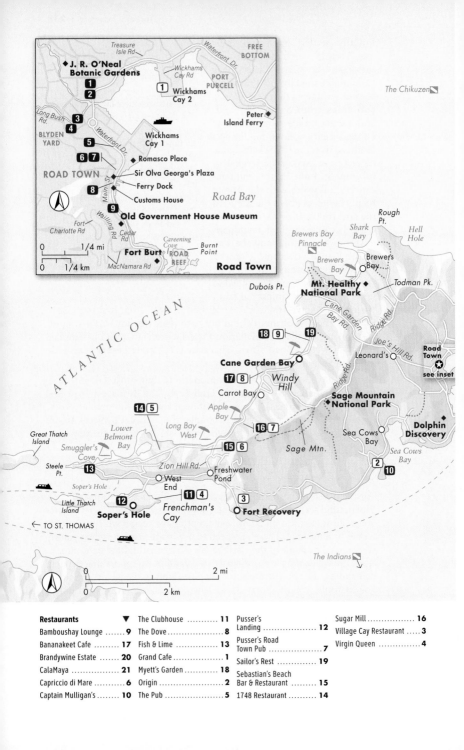

Road Town

J. R. O'Neal
Botanic Gardens

Treasure Isle Rd.

Wickhams Cay Rd

Waterfront Dr.

FREE BOTTOM

PORT PURCELL

Wickhams Cay 2

Peter Island Ferry

The Chikuzen

Long Bush Rd.

BLYDEN YARD

Waterfront Dr.

Wickhams Cay 1

ROAD TOWN

Romasco Place

Sir Olva Georga's Plaza

Ferry Dock

Customs House

Road Bay

Main St.

Old Government House Museum

Fort Charlotte Rd

Walling Rd.

Cedar Rd

Careening Cove

Burnt Point

Rough Pt.

Shark Bay

Hell Hole

Brewers Bay Pinnacle

Brewers Bay

Brewers Bay

Dubois Pt.

Mt. Healthy National Park

Todman Pk.

0   1/4 mi
0   1/4 km

MacNamara Rd.

Fort Burt

ROAD REEF

Road Town

ATLANTIC OCEAN

Cane Garden Bay Rd.

Ridge Rd.

Joe's Hill Rd.

Leonard's

Road Town
see inset

Cane Garden Bay

Windy Hill

Carrot Bay

Ridge Rd.

Sage Mountain National Park

Apple Bay

Great Thatch Island

Smuggler's Cove

Lower Belmont Bay

Long Bay West

Sage Mtn.

Sea Cows Bay

Dolphin Discovery

Steele Pt.

Zion Hill Rd.

Freshwater Pond

Sea Cows Bay

Soper's Hole

West End

Little Thatch Island

Soper's Hole

Frenchman's Cay

Fort Recovery

← TO ST. THOMAS

The Indians

0   2 mi
0   2 km

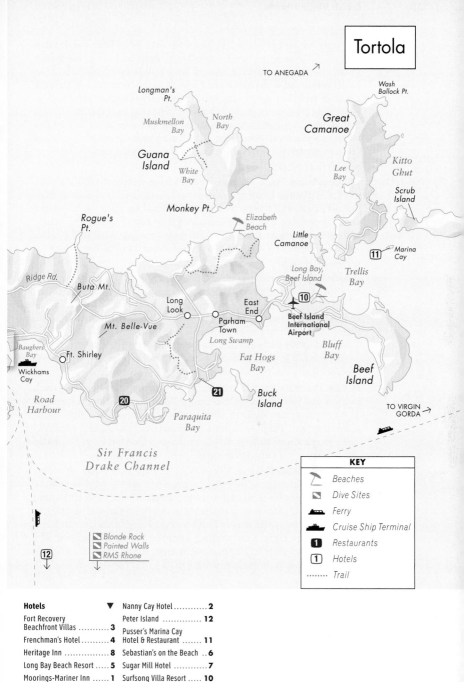

Tortola

TO ANEGADA

Wash
Ballock Pt.

Longman's
Pt.

Muskmellon
Bay

North
Bay

*Great
Camanoe*

*Guana
Island*

White
Bay

Lee
Bay

*Kitto
Ghut*

Scrub
Island

Monkey Pt.

Elizabeth
Beach

Little
Camanoe

11 Marina
Cay

*Rogue's
Pt.*

Long Bay,
Beef Island

Trellis
Bay

Ridge Rd.

Buta Mt.

Long
Look

East
End

10

Beef Island
International
Airport

Mt. Belle-Vue

Parham
Town

Long Swamp

*Bluff
Bay*

*Baughers
Bay*

Ft. Shirley

Fat Hogs
Bay

*Beef
Island*

Wickhams
Cay

20

21

Buck
Island

TO VIRGIN
GORDA

*Road
Harbour*

*Paraquita
Bay*

*Sir Francis
Drake Channel*

KEY

	Beaches
	Dive Sites
	Ferry
	Cruise Ship Terminal
1	Restaurants
1	Hotels
....	Trail

12

Blonde Rock
Painted Walls
RMS Rhone

AROUND ROAD TOWN

The bustling capital of the BVI looks out over Road Harbour. It takes only an hour or so to stroll down Main Street and along the waterfront, checking out the traditional West Indian buildings painted in pastel colors and with corrugated-tin roofs, bright shutters, and delicate fretwork trim. For sightseeing brochures and the latest information on everything from taxi rates to ferry schedules, stop in at the BVI Tourist Board office. Or just choose a seat on one of the benches in Sir Olva Georges Square, on Waterfront Drive, and watch the people come and go from the ferry dock and customs office across the street.

TOP ATTRACTIONS

Fodor's Choice
★

Old Government House Museum. The official government residence until 1997, this gracious building now displays a nice collection of artifacts from Tortola's past. The rooms are filled with period furniture, hand-painted china, books signed by Queen Elizabeth II on her 1966 and 1977 visits, and numerous items reflecting Tortola's seafaring legacy. ⊠ *Waterfront Dr., Road Town* ☎ *284/494–4091* ⊕ *www.oghm.org* ⊠ *$5* ⊗ *Weekdays 9–3.*

WORTH NOTING

FAMILY **Dolphin Discovery.** Get up close and personal with dolphins as they swim in a spacious seaside pen. There are three different programs. In the Royal Swim, dolphins tow participants around the pen. The less expensive Adventure and Discovery programs allow you to touch the dolphins. ⊠ *Waterfront Dr., Road Town* ☎ *284/494–7675, 888/393–5158* ⊕ *www.dolphindiscovery.com* ⊠ *Royal Swim $149, Adventure $99, Discovery $79* ⊗ *Royal Swim daily at 10, noon, 2, and 4. Adventure and Discovery daily at 11 and 1.*

Ft. Burt. The most intact historic ruin on Tortola was built by the Dutch in the early 17th century to safeguard Road Harbour. It sits on a hill at the western edge of Road Town and is now the site of a small hotel and restaurant. The foundations and magazine remain, and the structure offers a commanding view of the harbor. ⊠ *Waterfront Dr., Road Town* ⊠ *Free* ⊗ *Daily dawn–dusk.*

J.R. O'Neal Botanic Gardens. Take a walk through this 4-acre showcase of lush plant life. There are sections devoted to prickly cacti and succulents, hothouses for ferns and orchids, gardens of medicinal herbs, and plants and trees indigenous to the seashore. From the tourist office in Road Town, cross Waterfront Drive and walk one block over to Main Street and turn right. Keep walking until you see the high school. The gardens are on your left. ⊠ *Botanic Station, Road Town* ☎ *284/494–3650* ⊕ *www.bvinationalparkstrust.org* ⊠ *$3* ⊗ *Mon.–Sat. 8:30–4:30.*

WEST END
TOP ATTRACTIONS

Soper's Hole. On this little island connected by a causeway to Tortola's western end, you can find a marina and a captivating complex of pastel West Indian–style buildings with shady balconies, shuttered windows, and gingerbread trim that house art galleries, boutiques, and restaurants. Pusser's Landing is a lively place to stop for a cold drink (many are made with Pusser's famous rum) and a sandwich and to watch the boats in the harbor. ⊠ *Soper's Hole.*

Old Government House Museum, Road Town

WORTH NOTING

Ft. Recovery. The unrestored ruins of a 17th-century Dutch fort sit amid a profusion of tropical greenery on the grounds of Fort Recovery Beachfront Villas and Suites. There's not much to see here, and there are no guided tours, but you're welcome to stop by and poke around. ⊠ *Waterfront Dr., Pockwood Pond* ☎ *284/495–4467* 🖙 *Free.*

NORTH SHORE

TOP ATTRACTIONS

Fodor'sChoice
★

Cane Garden Bay. Once a sleepy village, Cane Garden Bay has become one of Tortola's most important destinations. Stay at a small hotel or guesthouse here, or stop by for lunch, dinner, or drinks at a seaside restaurant. You can find a few small stores selling clothing and basics such as suntan lotion, and one of Tortola's most popular beaches is at your feet. The roads in and out of this area are dauntingly steep, so use caution when driving. ⊠ *Cane Garden Bay.*

MID-ISLAND

WORTH NOTING

Mount Healthy National Park. The remains of an 18th-century sugar plantation can be seen here. The windmill structure has been restored, and you can see the ruins of a mill, a factory with boiling houses, storage areas, stables, a hospital, and many dwellings. It's a nice place to picnic. ⊠ *Ridge Rd., Todman Peak* ⊕ *www.bvinpt.org* 🖙 *Free* ☉ *Daily dawn–dusk.*

Sage Mountain National Park. At 1,716 feet, Sage Mountain is the highest peak in the BVI. From the parking area, a trail leads you in a loop not only to the peak itself (and extraordinary views) but also to a small rain forest that is sometimes shrouded in mist. Most of the forest was cut down over the centuries for timber, to create pastureland, or for growing sugarcane, cotton, and other crops. In 1964 this park was established to preserve what remained. Up here you can see mahogany trees, white cedars, mountain guavas, elephant-ear vines, mamey trees, and giant bullet woods, to say nothing of such birds as mountain doves and thrushes. Take a taxi from Road Town or drive up Joe's Hill Road and make a left onto Ridge Road toward Chalwell and Doty villages. The road dead-ends at the park. ⊠ *Ridge Rd., Sage Mountain* ☎ *284/852–3650* ⊕ *www.bvinpt.org* ⌨ *$3* ⊘ *Daily dawn–dusk.*

BEACHES

WEST END

Long Bay Beach West. This beach is a stunning, mile-long stretch of white sand; have your camera ready to snap the breathtaking approach. Although Long Bay Resort sprawls along part of it, the entire beach is open to the public. The water isn't as calm here as at Cane Garden or Brewers Bay, but it's still swimmable. Rent water-sports equipment and enjoy the beachfront restaurant at the resort. Turn left at Zion Hill Road; then travel about half a mile. **Amenities:** food and drink; toilets; water sports. **Best for:** swimming. ⊠ *Long Bay Rd., Long Bay.*

Smuggler's Cove Beach. A beautiful, palm-fringed beach, Smuggler's Cove is down a pothole-filled dirt road. After bouncing your way down, you'll feel as if you've found a hidden piece of the island. You probably won't be alone on weekends, though, when the beach fills with snorkelers and sunbathers. There's a fine view of Jost Van Dyke from the shore. The beach is popular with Long Bay Resort guests who want a change of scenery, but there are no amenities other than vendors selling food and drink during the winter season. Follow Long Bay Road past Long Bay Resort, keeping to the roads nearest the water until you reach the beach. It's about a mile past the resort. **Amenities:** food and drink (in winter season). **Best for:** snorkeling; swimming. ⊠ *Long Bay Rd., Long Bay.*

NORTH SHORE

Apple Bay Beach. Along with nearby Little Apple Bay and Capoon's Bay, this is your spot if you want to surf—although the white, sandy beach itself is narrow. Sebastian's, a casual hotel, caters to those in search of the perfect wave. The legendary Bomba's Surfside Shack—a landmark festooned with all manner of flotsam and jetsam—serves drinks and casual food. Otherwise, there's nothing else in the way of amenities. Good waves are never a sure thing, but you're more apt to find them in January and February. If you're swimming and the waves are up, take care not to get dashed on the rocks. **Amenities:** food and drink; toilets. **Best for:** surfing; swimming. ⊠ *North Shore Rd. at Zion Hill Rd., Apple Bay.*

Brewers Bay Beach. This beach is easy to find, but the steep, twisting paved roads leading down the hill to it can be a bit daunting. An old sugar mill and ruins of a rum distillery are off the beach along the road. You can actually reach the beach from either Brewers Bay Road East or Brewers Bay Road West. **Amenities:** none. **Best for:** snorkeling; swimming. ⊠ *Brewers Bay Rd. E, off Cane Garden Bay Rd., Brewers Bay.*

Cane Garden Bay Beach. A silky stretch of sand, Cane Garden Bay has exceptionally calm, crystal-line waters—except when storms at sea turn the water murky. Snorkeling is good along the edges. Casual guesthouses, restaurants, bars, and shops are steps from the beach in the growing village of the same name. The beach is a laid-back, even somewhat funky place to put down your towel. It's the closest beach to Road Town—one steep uphill and downhill drive—and one of the BVI's best-known anchorages (unfortunately, it can be very crowded). Water-sports shops rent equipment. **Amenities:** food and drink; toilets; water sports. **Best for:** snorkeling; swimming. ⊠ *Cane Garden Bay Rd., off Ridge Rd., Cane Garden Bay.*

BVI FERRIES

BVI ferries can be confusing for newcomers. Ferries depart from three different places in Tortola—Road Town, West End, and Beef Island—so make sure you get to the right place at the correct time. Sometimes boats bound for Jost Van Dyke, Virgin Gorda, Anegada, St. Thomas, and St. John depart minutes apart; other times the schedule is skimpy. Departures can be suddenly canceled, particularly in the summer season. To avoid being stranded, always call your ferry company on the morning of departure, and check with the locals catching a ferry if you're still not sure.

EAST END

Elizabeth Beach. Home to a small resort, Elizabeth Beach is a palm-lined, wide, and sandy beach with parking along its steep downhill access road. Other than at the hotel and its restaurant, which welcomes nonguests, there are no amenities aside from peace and quiet. Turn at the sign for Lambert Beach Resort. If you miss it, you wind up at Her Majesty's Prison. **Amenities:** food and drink; parking; toilets. **Best for:** solitude; swimming. ⊠ *Lambert Rd., off Ridge Rd., on eastern end of island, Lambert Bay.*

Long Bay Beach, Beef Island. Long Bay on Beef Island has superlative scenery: the beach stretches seemingly forever, and you can catch a glimpse of Little Camanoe and Great Camanoe islands. If you walk around the bend to the right, you can see little Marina Cay and Scrub Island. Long Bay is also a good place to search for seashells. Swim out to wherever you see a dark patch for some nice snorkeling. There are no amenities, so come prepared with your own drinks and snacks. Turn left shortly after crossing the bridge to Beef Island. **Amenities:** none. **Best for:** snorkeling; swimming; bird-watching. ⊠ *Beef Island Rd., Beef Island.*

WHERE TO EAT

Local seafood is plentiful on Tortola, and although other fresh ingredients are scarce, the island's chefs are a creative lot who apply their skills to whatever the boat delivers. Contemporary American dishes with Caribbean influences are very popular, but you can find French and Italian fare as well. The more expensive restaurants have dress codes: long pants and collared shirts for men and elegant but casual resort wear for women. Prices are often a bit higher than they are back home, and the service can be a tad on the slow side, but enjoy the chance to linger over the view.

AROUND ROAD TOWN

$$ ✕ **Bamboushay Lounge.** Attached to the Bamboushay pottery and bou-
CAFÉ tique on Main Street, newly opened Bamboushay Lounge on adjacent Waterfront Drive serves lunch options (weekdays) such as salads, pastas, rotis, and stuffed potatoes in an idyllic open-air garden-like setting. The free Wi-Fi seems to attract a lively mix of young local professionals, resident expats, visiting yachties, and tourists who have eagerly returned to lounge "after hours" on Thursday and Friday, helping Bamboushay Lounge gain itself a reputation as the new "it" spot. Call for dinner reservations; as of November 2013, the Lounge began offering dinner on Friday evenings and hopes to expand based on demand. $ *Average main: $16 ⊠ Waterfront Dr. ☎ 284/342–0303 ☉ Closed weekends.*

$$$$ ✕ **Brandywine Estate.** At this Brandywine Bay restaurant, candlelit out-
MEDITERRANEAN door tables have sweeping views of nearby islands. With a Mediterra-
Fodor's Choice nean flair, the menu changes often, but you might find a three-cheese
★ tortellini with garlic-and-truffle sauce or scallops in a saffron sauce. Finish your meal with a delightful cheese platter. $ *Average main: $32 ⊠ Sir Francis Drake Hwy., east of Road Town, Brandywine Bay ☎ 284/495–2301 ⊕ www.brandywinerestaurant.com ☉ Closed Tues.*

$$ ✕ **Capriccio di Mare.** Stop by this casual, authentic Italian outdoor café
ITALIAN for an espresso, a fresh pastry, a bowl of perfectly cooked penne, or a
Fodor's Choice crispy tomato-and-mozzarella pizza. Drink specialties include a mango
★ Bellini, an adaptation of the famous cocktail served at Harry's Bar in Venice. $ *Average main: $19 ⊠ Waterfront Dr. ☎ 284/494–5369 ⚋ Reservations not accepted ☉ Closed Sun.*

$$ ✕ **Captain Mulligan's.** Located at the entrance to Nanny Cay, this sports
AMERICAN bar self-proclaims that it has "the second-best burger on the island,"
FAMILY underlying the eatery's irreverent tone. (We never found out who has the best!) Hot wings, pizza, ribs, and burgers are on the menu, and most people come to watch the game on the big screen. A mini-golf course has also been established and provides an activity for children of all ages, along with a children's recreation area. $ *Average main: $15 ⊠ Nanny Cay ☎ 284/494–0602 ⊕ www.captainmulligans.com.*

$$$ ✕ **The Dove.** The food matches the romantic feeling at this Road Town
ECLECTIC restaurant. Start with jumbo prawns sautéed with a vanilla bean and almonds before moving on to the mushroom-and-Parmesan-crusted rib-eye steak. Desserts are often new twists on old standards, as with the soursop (the fruit of a Caribbean evergreen tree) crème brûlée. $ *Average main: $29 ⊠ Waterfront Dr. ☎ 284/494–0313 ⊕ www.thedovebvi.com ☉ Closed Sun. and Mon. No lunch.*

$$$ ✕ **Grand Cafe.** Birds and bougainvillea brighten the patio of this breezy
FRENCH French restaurant and bar, a popular gathering spot for locals and
visitors alike. French onion soup and smoked salmon salad are good
appetizer choices. From there, move on to the grilled tuna with wasabi
sauce, sole in a brown butter sauce, or beef tenderloin with green pep-
percorn sauce. Save room for such tasty desserts as chocolate cake and
crème brûlée, or opt for a platter of French cheeses. ⓈⒹ *Average main:
$23* ✉ *Waterfront Dr.* ☎ *284/494–8660* ☉ *Closed Sun.*

$ ✕ **Origin.** Located in the heart of Road Town across from the Ferry Ter-
SUSHI minal, this lively sushi restaurant and cocktail bar offers quality afford-
ably-priced sushi. The place jumps on Friday night and can be a noisy
dining experience; request a table on the rooftop for a more relaxed
setting. Ⓢ *Average main: $12* ☎ *284/494–8295* ⊕ *www.originbvi.com*
☉ *Closed Sun. and Mon.*

$$$ ✕ **The Pub.** At this lively waterfront spot, tables are arranged along a
ECLECTIC terrace facing a small marina and the harbor in Road Town. Ham-
burgers, salads, and sandwiches are typical lunch offerings, along with
classic British Fare such as Shepherd's Pie and Liver & Onions. In the
evening you can also choose grilled fish, sautéed conch, sizzling steaks,
or barbecued ribs. There's live entertainment Thursday and Friday, and
locals gather here nightly for spirited games at the pool table. Ⓢ *Average main: $23* ✉ *Waterfront Dr.* ☎ *284/494–2608* ☝ *Reservations not
accepted* ☉ *No lunch Sun.*

$$ ✕ **Pusser's Road Town Pub.** Almost everyone who visits Tortola stops
ECLECTIC here at least once to have a bite to eat and to sample the famous Puss-
FAMILY er's Rum Painkiller (fruit juices and rum). The nonthreatening menu
includes cheesy pizza, shepherd's pie, fish-and-chips, and hamburgers.
Dine inside in air-conditioned comfort or outside on the verandah,
which looks out on the harbor. Ⓢ *Average main: $15* ✉ *Waterfront Dr.*
☎ *284/494–3897* ⊕ *www.pussers.com.*

$$$$ ✕ **Village Cay Restaurant.** Docked sailboats stretch nearly as far as the
ECLECTIC eye can see at this busy Road Town restaurant. Its alfresco dining and
convivial atmosphere make it popular with both locals and visitors. For
lunch, try the grouper club sandwich with an ancho chili mayonnaise,
or their extensive lunch buffet, which is popular with local professionals
and yachties alike. Dinner offerings run to fish served a variety of ways,
including West Indian–style with okra, onions, and peppers, as well as
a seafood jambalaya with lobster, crayfish, shrimp, mussels, crab, and
fish in a mango-passion-fruit sauce. Ⓢ *Average main: $32* ✉ *Wickhams
Cay I* ☎ *284/494–2771.*

$$ ✕ **Virgin Queen.** The sailing and rugby crowds head here to play darts,
ECLECTIC drink beer, and eat Queen's Pizza—a crusty, cheesy pie topped with sau-
sage, onions, green peppers, and mushrooms. Also on the menu is excellent West Indian and English fare: barbecued ribs with beans and rice,
bangers and mash, shepherd's pie, and grilled sirloin steak. Ⓢ *Average
main: $17* ✉ *Flemming St.* ☎ *284/494–2310* ⊕ *www.virginqueenbvi.
com* ☉ *Closed Sun. No lunch Sat.*

WEST END

$$$ FRENCH 🍴 **The Clubhouse at Frenchman's Cay.** Nestled in the confines of the Frenchman's Hotel, the Clubhouse offers some of the best cuisine on the island. Chef Paul Mason's menu is a labor of love, incorporating fresh and unique Caribbean ingredients and spices, while using classical French preparation. Piña-colada drunken duckling, conch pasta carbonera, Bajan seasoned filet mignon, and grilled seafoods are a few of the stars on the dinner menu. The three-course fixed-price brunch on Sunday is a great value and excellent way to pass a Sunday relaxing by the pool or strolling the beach afterward. Brunch includes classic items such as eggs Benedict and rum-and-coconut-crusted French toast, as well as sirloin steaks, French country pâté, and yellowfin tuna. [$] *Average main: $30* ✉ *Frenchman's Cay* ☎ *284/494–8811* 🌐 *www.frenchmansbvi.com* ⏲ *Closed Mon.*

$$$ SEAFOOD 🍴 **Fish and Lime Inn.** In walking distance of the West End Ferry terminal, this pleasantly breezy, waterside restaurant delights daytime visitors with burger, salad, and sandwich offerings that are accompanied by hand-cut french fries. While many find their way here as a convenient stopover spot, it's worth the trip. After sunset, candles illuminate the picnic tables on the waterside deck and visiting yachties arrive by dinghy to enjoy menu items that include items such as grilled lobster, cornish game hen, Asian-marinated barbecue ribs, and a savory hot spinach and avocado cheesecake that will delight vegetarians. Occasional live music and happy hour specials also keep the bar lively, which fills will local expatriates on weekends. [$] *Average main: $26* ✉ *West End* ☎ *284/495–4276* 🌐 *www.fishnlime.com.*

$$$ AMERICAN FAMILY 🍴 **Pusser's Landing.** Yachters navigate their way to this waterfront restaurant. Downstairs, from late morning to well into the evening, you can belly up to the outdoor mahogany bar or sit downstairs for sandwiches, fish-and-chips, and pizzas. At dinnertime head upstairs for a harbor view and a quiet alfresco meal of grilled steak or fresh fish. [$] *Average main: $26* ✉ *Soper's Hole* ☎ *284/495–4554* 🌐 *www.pussers.com.*

NORTH SHORE

$$$ INTERNATIONAL 🍴 **1748 Restaurant.** Relax over dinner in this open-air eatery at Long Bay Beach Resort. Tables are well spaced, offering enough privacy for intimate conversations. The menu changes daily, but several dishes show up regularly. Start your meal with a seafood cocktail, creamy carrot soup, or a mixed green salad. Entrées include grilled London broil served with a rosemary mushroom sauce, roasted potatoes and vegetables, grilled tuna steak in a spicy cilantro coconut sauce, and a pesto-marinated grilled vegetable plate. There are always at least five desserts, and they might include Belgian chocolate mousse, strawberry cheesecake, or a fluffy lemon-and-coconut cake. [$] *Average main: $25* ✉ *Long Bay Beach Resort, Long Bay Rd., Long Bay* ☎ *284/495–4252* 🌐 *www.longbay.com.*

$$$ ECLECTIC 🍴 **Bananakeet Cafe.** The sunset sea-and-mountain views are stunning, so arrive early for the predinner happy hour. "Caribbean fusion" best describes the fare, with an emphasis on seafood, including local Anegada conch swimming in an herb-butter broth. Those without a taste for seafood won't go hungry—the menu also includes lamb, beef, and

chicken dishes. Locals and tourists alike come to enjoy the spectacular sunset- and enjoy a complimentary "sundowner" shot. [$] *Average main: $24* ✉ *North Coast Rd., Great Carrot Bay* ☎ *284/494–5842* 🌐 *www.bananakeetcafe.com* 🕒 *No lunch.*

$$$$ ECLECTIC 🍴 **Myett's Garden and Grille.** Partly because it's right on the beach, this bi-level restaurant and bar is hopping day and night for breakfast, lunch, and dinner. Chowder made with fresh conch is the specialty here, and the menu and includes vegetarian dishes as well as grilled shrimp, steak, and tuna. There's live entertainment every night in winter. [$] *Average main: $32* ✉ *Cane Garden Bay* ☎ *284/495–9649* 🌐 *www.myettent.com.*

$$$ CARIBBEAN 🍴 **Sailor's Rest.** Perched atop a rocky outcropping overlooking Cane Garden Bay and its bustling dinghy dock, this tiny eatery is open for breakfast, lunch, and dinner. The restaurant's artful interior is a unique tribute to the BVI's sailing and seafaring traditions: cutouts of wooden vessels, old articles on maritime heritage, and hand-painted signs are some of the unique touches. Menu offerings include a number of local Caribbean dishes and specials in addition to standard American fare. [$] *Average main: $25* ✉ *Cane Garden Bay* ☎ *284/495–9908* 🕒 *Closed Sun.*

$$$ ECLECTIC 🍴 **Sebastian's Seaside Grill.** The waves practically lap at your feet at this beachfront restaurant on Tortola's North Shore. The menu emphasizes seafood—especially lobster, conch, and local fish—but you can also find dishes such as ginger chicken and filet mignon. It's a perfect spot to stop for lunch on your around-the-island tour. Try the grilled dolphinfish (mahimahi) sandwich, served on a soft roll with an oniony tartar sauce. Finish off with a cup of Sebastian's coffee, spiked with home-brewed rum. [$] *Average main: $28* ✉ *Sebastian's on the Beach, North Coast Rd., Apple Bay* ☎ *284/495–4212* 🌐 *www.sebastiansbvi.com.*

$$$$ ECLECTIC Fodor's Choice ★ 🍴 **Sugar Mill Restaurant.** Candles gleam, and the background music is peaceful in this romantic restaurant inside a 17th-century sugar mill. Well-prepared selections on the à la carte menu, which changes nightly, include some pasta and vegetarian entrées. Lobster bisque with basil croutons and a creamy conch chowder are good starters. Favorite entrées include fresh fish with soba noodles, shiitake mushrooms, and a scallion broth; filet mignon topped with an herb-cream sauce; grilled shrimp and scallops with mango salsa; and pumpkin-and-black-bean lasagna. [$] *Average main: $32* ✉ *Sugar Mill Hotel, North Coast Rd., Apple Bay* ☎ *284/495–4355* 🌐 *www.sugarmillhotel.com* 🕒 *No lunch.*

EAST END

$$ ECLECTIC 🍴 **CalaMaya.** Casual fare is what you can find at this waterfront restaurant. You can always order a burger or Caesar salad; the chicken wrap with sweet-and-sour sauce is a tasty alternative. For dinner, try the mahimahi with sautéed vegetables and rice. [$] *Average main: $17* ✉ *Hodge's Creek Marina, Blackburn Hwy., Hodge's Creek* ☎ *284/495–2126.*

WHERE TO STAY

Luxury on Tortola is more about a certain state of mind—serenity, seclusion, gentility, and a bit of Britain in the Caribbean—than about state-of-the-art amenities and fabulous facilities. Some properties, especially the vacation villas, are catching up with current trends, but others seem stuck in the 1980s. But don't let a bit of rust on the screen door or a chip in the paint on the balcony railing mar your appreciation of the ambience. You will likely spend most of your time outside, so the location, size, or price of a hotel should be more of a factor to you than the decor.

Hotels in Road Town don't have beaches, but they do have pools and are within walking distance of restaurants, bars, and shops. Accommodations outside Road Town are relatively isolated, but most face the ocean. Tortola resorts are intimate—only a handful have more than 50 rooms. Guests are treated as more than just room numbers, and many return year after year. This can make booking a room at popular resorts difficult, even off-season, despite the fact that more than half the island's visitors stay aboard their own or chartered boats.

A few hotels lack air-conditioning, relying instead on ceiling fans to capture the almost constant trade winds. Nights are cool and breezy, even in midsummer, and never reach the temperatures or humidity levels that are common in much of the United States. Note that all accommodations listed here have air-conditioning unless we mention otherwise. Remember that some places may be closed during the peak of hurricane season—August through October—to give their owners a much-needed break.

PRIVATE VILLAS

Renting a villa is growing in popularity. Vacationers like the privacy, the space to spread out, and the opportunity to cook meals. As is true everywhere, the most important thing is location. If you want to be close to the beach, opt for a villa on the North Shore. If you want to dine out in Road Town every night, a villa closer to town may be a better bet. Prices per week during the winter season run from around $2,000 for a one- or two-bedroom villa up to $10,000 for a five-room beachfront villa. Rates in summer are substantially less. Most, but not all, villas accept credit cards.

VILLA RENTAL CONTACTS

Areana Villas. Areana Villas represents top-of-the-line properties. Pastel-color villas with one to five bedrooms can accommodate up to 10 guests. Many have pools, whirlpool tubs, and tiled courtyards. ☎ 284/494–5864 ⊕ www.areanavillas.com.

McLaughlin-Anderson Luxury Villas. The St. Thomas–based McLaughlin-Anderson Luxury Villas manages nearly two dozen properties around Tortola. Villas range from one to six bedrooms and come with full kitchens and stellar views. Most have pools. The company can hire a chef and stock your kitchen with groceries. ☎ 340/776–0635, 800/537–6246 ⊕ www.mclaughlinanderson.com.

CLOSE UP

American or British?

Yes, the Union Jack flutters overhead in the tropical breeze, schools operate on the British system, place-names have British spellings, Queen Elizabeth II appoints the governor—and the queen's picture hangs on many walls. Indeed, residents celebrate the queen's birthday every June with a public ceremony. You can overhear that charming English accent from a good handful of expats when you're lunching at Road Town restaurants, and you can buy "biscuits"—what Americans call cookies—in the supermarkets.

But you can pay for your lunch and the biscuits with American money, because the U.S. dollar is legal tender here. The unusual circumstance is a matter of geography. The practice started in the mid-20th century, when BVI residents went to work in the nearby USVI. On trips home, they brought their U.S. dollars with them. Soon they abandoned the barter system, and in 1959 the U.S. dollar became the official form of money. Interestingly, the government sells stamps (for use only in the BVI) that often carry pictures of Queen Elizabeth II and other royalty with the monetary value in U.S. dollars and cents.

The American influence continued to grow when Americans began to open businesses in the BVI because they preferred its quiet to the hustle and bustle of St. Thomas. Inevitably, cable and satellite TV's U.S.-based programming, along with Hollywood-made movies, further influenced life in the BVI. And most goods are shipped from St. Thomas in the USVI, meaning you can find more American products than British ones on the supermarket shelves.

7

Smiths Gore. Although Smiths Gore has properties all over the island, many are in the Smuggler's Cove area. They range from two to five to bedrooms: all have stellar views, lovely furnishings, and lush landscaping. ☎ *284/494–2446* 🌐 *www.smithsgore.com.*

AROUND ROAD TOWN

$ HOTEL 🏨 **Moorings-Mariner Inn.** If you enjoy the camaraderie of a busy marina, this inn on the edge of Road Town may appeal to you. **Pros:** good dining options; friendly guests; excellent spot to charter boats. **Cons:** busy location; long walk to Road Town; need car to get around. [$] *Rooms from: $220* ✉ *Waterfront Dr.* ☎ *284/494–2333, 800/535–7289* 🌐 *www.bvimarinerinnhotel.com* 🛏 *32 rooms, 7 suites* 🍴 *No meals.*

$ HOTEL 🏨 **Nanny Cay Hotel.** This quiet oasis is far enough from Road Town to give it a secluded feel but close enough to make shops and restaurants convenient. You're just steps from the hotel's restaurant, boat charters, and the chance to stroll the busy boatyard to gawk at the yachts under repair, but you still have to drive a good 20 minutes to get to the closest beach at Cane Garden Bay. **Pros:** nearby shops and restaurant; pleasant rooms; marina atmosphere. **Cons:** busy location; need car to get around. [$] *Rooms from: $150* ✉ *Waterfront Dr., Nanny Cay* ☎ *284/494–2512* 🌐 *www.nannycay.com* 🛏 *38 rooms* 🍴 *No meals.*

WEST END

$$ RESORT FAMILY
🏨 **Fort Recovery Beachfront Villas.** This is one of those small but special properties that stands out because its friendly service and the chance to get to know your fellow guests rather than the poshness of the rooms and the upscale amenities. **Pros:** beautiful beach; spacious units; historic site. **Cons:** need car to get around; isolated location. [$] *Rooms from: $310* ✉ *Waterfront Dr., West End, Tortola* ☎ *284/495–4354, 855/349–3355* 🌐 *www.fortrecovery.com* 🛏 *30 suites* 🍴 *No meals.*

NORTH SHORE

$$$ RESORT
🏨 **Frenchman's Hotel.** Small and tucked on a beautiful but often overlooked corner of Tortola (technically it's a separate island), Frenchman's Hotel is a quiet, intimate resort with stunning scenic vistas and beautifully landscaped, lush grounds. **Pros:** a tranquil spot. **Cons:** you need a car to get around. [$] *Rooms from: $365* ✉ *Frenchman's Cay, Tortola* ☎ *284/494–8811* 🌐 *www.frenchmansbvi.com* 🛏 *8 villas* 🍴 *Breakfast.*

$ B&B/INN
🏨 **Heritage Inn.** The gorgeous sea and mountain views are the stars at this small hotel perched on the edge of a cliff. **Pros:** stunning views; fun vibe, room has kitchenette. **Cons:** need car to get around; close to road. [$] *Rooms from: $225* ✉ *North Coast Rd., Great Carrot Bay, Tortola* ☎ *284/494–5842* 🌐 *www.bananakeetcafe.com* 🛏 *6 rooms* 🍴 *No meals.*

$ RESORT
🏨 **Long Bay Beach Resort.** If you want all the resort amenities, including a beach, scads of water sports, and tennis courts, then this is your only choice for Tortola. **Pros:** resort atmosphere; good restaurants; many activities. **Cons:** need car to get around; sometimes curt staff; uphill hike to some rooms. [$] *Rooms from: $403* ✉ *Long Bay Rd., Long Bay, Tortola* ☎ *284/495–4252, 800/858–4618* 🌐 *www.longbay.com* 🛏 *62 rooms, 10 cabanas,* 🍴 *Multiple meal plans.*

$ HOTEL
🏨 **Myett's.** Tucked away in a beachfront garden, this tiny hotel puts you right in the middle of Cane Garden Bay's busy hustle and bustle. **Pros:** beautiful beach; good restaurant; shops nearby. **Cons:** busy location; need car to get around. [$] *Rooms from: $200* ✉ *Cane Garden Bay, Tortola* ☎ *284/495–9649* 🌐 *www.myettent.com* 🛏 *6 rooms, 4 cottages, 1 villa* 🍴 *No meals.*

$ RESORT
🏨 **Sebastian's on the Beach.** Sitting on the island's north coast, Sebastian's definitely has a beachy feel, and that's its primary charm. **Pros:** nice beach; good restaurants; beachfront rooms. **Cons:** on busy road; some rooms nicer than others; need car to get around. [$] *Rooms from: $135* ✉ *North Coast Rd., Apple Bay, Tortola* ☎ *284/495–4212, 800/336–4870* 🌐 *www.sebastiansbvi.com* 🛏 *26 rooms, 9 villas* 🍴 *No meals.*

$$ RESORT Fodor's Choice ★
🏨 **Sugar Mill Hotel.** Though it's not a sprawling resort, the Sugar Mill Hotel has a Caribbean cachet that's hard to beat, and it's a favorite place to stay on Tortola. **Pros:** lovely rooms; excellent restaurant; nice views. **Cons:** on busy road; small beach; need car to get around. [$] *Rooms from: $350* ✉ *North Coast Rd., Apple Bay, Tortola* ☎ *284/495–4355, 800/462–8834* 🌐 *www.sugarmillhotel.com* 🛏 *19 rooms, 2 suites, 1 villa, 1 cottage* 🍴 *No meals.*

Surfsong Villa Resort

EAST END

$$$$ RESORT Fodor's Choice ★ **Surfsong Villa Resort.** Nestled in lush foliage right at the water's edge, this small resort on Beef Island provides a pleasant respite for vacationers who want a villa atmosphere with some hotel amenities. **Pros:** lovely rooms; beautiful beach; chef on call. **Cons:** need car to get around; no restaurants nearby. [$] *Rooms from: $465* ✉ *Off Beef Island Rd., Beef Island, Tortola* ☎ *284/495–1864* 🌐 *www.surfsong.net* 🛏 *1 suite, 7 villas* 🍴 *Multiple meal plans.*

NIGHTLIFE AND THE ARTS

NIGHTLIFE

Like any other good sailing destination, Tortola has watering holes that are popular with salty and not-so-salty dogs. Many offer entertainment; check the weekly *Limin' Times* (🌐 *www.limin-times.com*) for schedules and up-to-date information. Bands change like the weather, and what's hot today can be old news tomorrow. The local beverage is the Painkiller, an innocent-tasting mixture of fruit juices and rums. It goes down smoothly but packs quite a punch, so give yourself time to recover before you order another.

Bomba's Surfside Shack. By day, you can see that Bomba's, which is covered with everything from crepe-paper leis to ancient license plates to spicy graffiti, looks like a pile of junk; by night it's one of Tortola's liveliest spots. There's a fish fry and a live band every Wednesday and Sunday. People flock here from all over on the full moon, when bands play all night long. ✉ *North Coast Rd., Apple Bay, Tortola* ☎ *284/495–4148.*

Fodor'sChoice **Myett's.** Local bands play at this popular spot, which has live music
★   during happy hour, and there's usually a lively dance crowd. ⊠ *Cane
Garden Bay, Tortola* ☎ *284/495–9649* ⊕ *www.myettent.com.*

The New Quito's Restaurant and Bar. BVI recording star Quito Rhymer
sings island ballads and love songs at his rustic beachside bar–restaurant. Solo shows are on Tuesday and Thursday at 8:30; on Friday at
9:30 Quito performs with his band. ⊠ *Cane Garden Bay* ☎ *284/495–
4837* ⊕ *www.quitorymer.com.*

Pub. At this popular watering hole, there's a happy hour from 5 to 7
every day and live music on Thursday and Friday. ⊠ *Waterfront St.,
Road Town* ☎ *284/494–2608.*

Pusser's Road Town Pub. Courage is what people are seeking here—John
Courage beer by the pint. Or try Pusser's famous mixed drink, called
the Painkiller, and snack on the excellent pizza. ⊠ *Waterfront St., Road
Town, Tortola* ☎ *284/494–3897* ⊕ *www.pussers.com.*

Sebastian's. There's often live music at Sebastian's on Sunday evenings,
and you can dance under the stars. ⊠ *North Coast Rd., Apple Bay,
Tortola* ☎ *284/495–4212* ⊕ *www.sebastiansbvi.com.*

THE ARTS

Fodor'sChoice **BVI Music Festival.** Every May hordes of people head to Tortola for this
★   popular three-day festival to listen to reggae, gospel, blues, and salsa
music by musicians from around the Caribbean and the U.S. mainland.
⊠ *Cane Garden Bay, Tortola* ⊕ *www.bvimusicfestival.com.*

Performing Arts Series. Musicians from around the world take to the
stage during the island's Performing Arts Series, held annually October
through May. Past artists have included Latin jazz artist Tito Puente Jr.,
gospel singer Kim Burrell, and pianist Richard Ormond. ⊠ *H. Lavity
Stoutt Community College, Blackburn Hwy., Paraquita Bay, Tortola*
☎ *284/494–4994* ⊕ *www.hlscc.edu.vg.*

SHOPPING

The BVI aren't really a shopper's delight, but there are many shops
showcasing original wares, such as jams, spices, resort wear, and often-
excellent artwork.

SHOPPING AREAS

Many shops and boutiques are clustered along and just off Road Town's
Main Street. You can shop in Road Town's **Wickham's Cay I** adjacent to the
marina. The **Crafts Alive Market** on the Road Town waterfront is a collection of colorful West Indian–style buildings with shops that carry items
made in the BVI. You might find pretty baskets or interesting pottery or
perhaps a bottle of home-brewed hot sauce. A growing number of art
and clothing stores are opening at **Soper's Hole** in West End.

SPECIALTY STORES

ART

Allamanda Gallery. Photography by the gallery's owner, Amanda Baker, as well as books, gifts, and cards are on display and available to purchase. ⊠ *124 Main St., Road Town, Tortola* ☎ *284/494–6680* ⊕ *www. virginportraits.com.*

Sunny Caribbee. This gallery has many paintings, prints, and watercolors by artists from around the Caribbean, and is also known for its collection of spices, hot sauces and other food products. ⊠ *Main St., Road Town, Tortola* ☎ *284/494–2178* ⊕ *www.sunnycaribbee.com.*

CLOTHES AND TEXTILES

Arawak. This boutique carries batik sundresses, sportswear, and resort wear for men and women. There's also a selection of children's clothing. ⊠ *Nanny Cay Marina, Nanny Cay, Tortola* ☎ *284/494–3983.*

Latitude 18°. This store sells Maui Jim, Ray-Ban, and Oakley sunglasses; Freestyle watches; and a fine collection of beach towels, sandals, Crocs, sundresses, and sarongs. ⊠ *Waterfront Dr., Road Town, Tortola* ☎ *284/494–6196* ⊕ *www.latitude18.com.*

Pusser's Company Store. The Road Town Pusser's sells nautical memorabilia, ship models, and marine paintings. There's also an entire line of clothing for both men and women, handsome decorator bottles of Pusser's rum, and gift items bearing the Pusser's logo. ⊠ *Main St. at Waterfront Rd., Road Town, Tortola* ☎ *284/494–2467* ⊕ *www.pussers.com.*

Zenaida's of West End. Vivian Jenik Helm travels through South America, Africa, and India in search of batiks, hand-painted and hand-blocked fabrics, and interesting weaves that can be made into pareus (women's wraps) or wall hangings. The shop also sells unusual bags, belts, sarongs, scarves, and ethnic jewelry. ⊠ *Soper's Hole Marina, West End, Tortola* ☎ *284/495–4867.*

FOOD

Ample Hamper. Head here to stock your yacht or rental villa—or have the staff do it for you. It carries an outstanding collection of cheeses, wines, fresh fruits, and canned goods from the United Kingdom and the United States. ⊠ *Inner Harbour Marina, Road Town* ☎ *284/494–2494.*

Best of British. This boutique has lots of nifty British food you won't find elsewhere. Shop here for Marmite, Vegemite, shortbread, frozen meat pies, and delightful Christmas "crackers" filled with surprises. ⊠ *Wickham's Cay I, Road Town, Tortola* ☎ *284/494–3462.*

RiteWay. This market carries a good (but not massive) selection of the usual supplies. RiteWay will stock villas and yachts. ⊠ *Waterfront Dr. at Pasea Estate, Road Town, Tortola* ☎ *284/494–2263* ⊠ *Flemming St., Road Town, Tortola* ☎ *284/494–2263* ⊕ *www.rtwbvi.com.*

GIFTS

Fodor'sChoice
★ **Bamboushay.** Some of the handcrafted Tortola-made pottery sold here comes in beautiful blue shades that reflect the sea. ⊠ *Nanny Cay Marina, Waterfront Dr., Nanny Cay, Tortola* ☎ *284/494–0393* ⊕ *www.bamboushay.com* ⊠ *109 Main St., Road Town, Tortola* ☎ *294/ 494–7752.*

Sunny Caribbee. In a brightly painted West Indian house, this store packages its own herbs, teas, coffees, vinegars, hot sauces, soaps, skin and suntan lotions, and exotic concoctions—Arawak Love Potion and Island Hangover Cure, for example. ⊠ *Main St., Road Town, Tortola* ☎ *284/494–2178* ⊕ *www.sunnycaribbee.com.*

JEWELRY

Samarkand. The charming jewelry sold here includes gold-and-silver pendants, earrings, bracelets, and pins, many with island themes such as seashells, lizards, pelicans, and palm trees. There are also reproduction Spanish pieces of eight (old Spanish coins) similar to those found on sunken galleons. ⊠ *Main St., Road Town, Tortola* ☎ *284/494–6415* ⊗ *Closed Sun.*

STAMPS

BVI Post Office. The BVI's post office has a worldwide reputation for exquisite stamps in all sorts of designs. Although the stamps carry U.S. monetary designations, they can only be used for postage in the BVI. ⊠ *Blackburn Rd., Road Town, Tortola* ☎ *284/468–3701.*

SPORTS AND ACTIVITIES

DIVING AND SNORKELING

Clear waters and numerous reefs afford some wonderful opportunities for underwater exploration. In some spots visibility reaches 100 feet, but colorful reefs teeming with fish are often just a few feet below the sea surface. The BVI's system of marine parks means the underwater life visible through your mask will stay protected.

There are several popular dive spots around the islands. **Alice in Wonderland** is a deep dive south of Ginger Island with a wall that slopes gently from 15 feet to 100 feet. It's an area overrun with huge mushroom-shape coral, hence its name. Crabs, lobsters, and shimmering fan corals make their homes in the tunnels, ledges, and overhangs of **Blonde Rock,** a pinnacle that goes from 15 feet below the surface to 60 feet deep. It's between Dead Chest and Salt Island. When the currents aren't too strong, **Brewers Bay Pinnacle** (20 to 90 feet down) teems with sea life. At the **Indians,** near Pelican Island, colorful coral decorates canyons and grottoes created by four large, jagged pinnacles that rise 50 feet from the ocean floor. The **Painted Walls** is a shallow dive site where coral and sponges create a kaleidoscope of colors on the walls of four long gullies. It's northeast of Dead Chest.

The *Chikuzen,* sunk northwest of Brewers Bay in 1981, is a 246-foot vessel in 75 feet of water; it's home to thousands of fish, colorful corals, and big rays. In 1867 the **RMS *Rhone*,** a 310-foot royal mail steamer, split in two when it sank in a devastating hurricane. It's so well preserved that it was used as an underwater prop in the 1977 movie *The Deep.* You can see the crow's nest and bowsprit, the cargo hold in the bow, and the engine and enormous propeller shaft in the stern. Its four parts are at various depths, from 30 to 80 feet. Get yourself some snorkeling gear and hop aboard a dive boat to this wreck near Salt Island (across the channel from Road Town). Every dive outfit in the BVI runs scuba and snorkel tours to this part of the BVI National Parks Trust; if you have time for only one trip, make it this one. Rates start at around $70 for a one-tank dive and $100 for a two-tank dive.

Most of Tortola's shops are in Road Town.

Your hotel probably has a dive company right on the premises. If not, the staff can recommend one nearby. Using your hotel's dive company makes a trip to the offshore dive and snorkel sites a breeze. Just stroll down to the dock and hop aboard. All dive companies are certified by PADI, the Professional Association of Diving Instructors, which ensures that your instructors are qualified to safely take vacationers diving. The boats are also inspected to make sure they're seaworthy. If you've never dived, try a short introductory dive, often called a resort course, which teaches you enough to get you under water. In the unlikely event you get a case of the bends, a condition that can happen when you rise to the surface too fast, your dive team will take you to the decompression chamber at Roy L. Schneider Regional Medical Center in nearby St. Thomas.

Blue Waters Divers. If you're chartering a sailboat, Blue Waters Divers' boat will meet yours at Peter, Salt, Norman, or Cooper Island for a rendezvous dive. The company teaches resort, open-water, rescue, and advanced diving courses, and also makes daily dive trips. Rates include all equipment as well as instruction. Reserve two days in advance. ⊠ *Nanny Cay Marina, Nanny Cay, Tortola* ☎ *284/494–2847* ⊠ *Soper's Hole Marina, Soper's Hole, Tortola* ☎ *284/495–1200* ⊕ *www.bluewaterdiversbvi.com.*

FISHING

Most of the boats that take you deep-sea fishing for bluefish, wahoo, swordfish, and shark leave from nearby St. Thomas, but local anglers like to fish the shallower water for bonefish. A half day for two people runs about $480, a full day around $850. Wading trips are $325.

Caribbean Fly Fishing ⊠ *Nanny Cay Marina, Nanny Cay, Tortola* ☎ *284/ 494–4797* ⊕ *www.caribflyfishing.com.*

HIKING

FAMILY   Sage Mountain National Park attracts hikers who enjoy the quiet trails that crisscross the island's loftiest peak. There are some lovely views and the chance to see rare species that grow only at higher elevations.

SAILING

FAMILY

Fodor's Choice

★

The BVI are among the world's most popular sailing destinations. They're clustered together and surrounded by calm waters, so it's fairly easy to sail from one anchorage to the next. Most of the Caribbean's biggest sailboat charter companies have operations in Tortola. If you know how to sail, you can charter a bareboat (perhaps for your entire vacation); if you're unschooled, you can hire a boat with a captain. Prices vary depending on the type and size of the boat you wish to charter. In season, a weekly charter runs from $1,500 to $35,000. Book early to make sure you get the boat that fits you best. Most of Tortola's marinas have hotels, which give you a convenient place to spend the nights before and after your charter.

If a day sail to some secluded anchorage is more your cup of tea, the BVI have numerous boats of various sizes and styles that leave from many points around Tortola. Prices start at around $80 per person for a full-day sail, including lunch and snorkeling equipment.

Aristocat Charters. This company's 48-foot catamaran sets sail daily to Jost Van Dyke, Norman Island, and other small islands. ⊠ *West End, Tortola* ☎ *284/499–1249* ⊕ *www.aristocatcharters.com.*

BVI Yacht Charters. The 31- to 52-foot sailboats for charter here come with or without a captain and crew, whichever you prefer. ⊠ *Port Purcell, Road Town, Tortola* ☎ *284/494–4289, 888/615–4006* ⊕ *www.bviyachtcharters.com.*

The Catamaran Company. The catamarans here come with or without a captain. ⊠ *Maya Cove Marina, Fat Hog's Bay, Tortola* ☎ *284/494–6661, 800/262–0308* ⊕ *www.catamarans.com.*

The Moorings. One of the world's best bareboat operations, The Moorings has a large fleet of monohulls and catamarans. Hire a captain or sail the boat yourself. ⊠ *Wickham's Cay II, Road Town, Tortola* ☎ *284/494–2332, 800/535–7289* ⊕ *www.moorings.com.*

Regency Yacht Vacations. If you prefer a powerboat, call Regency Yacht Vacations. It handles both bareboat and captained sail and powerboat charters. ⊠ *Wickham's Cay I, Road Town, Tortola* ☎ *284/495–1970, 800/524–7676* ⊕ *www.regencyvacations.com.*

Sunsail. A full fleet of boats to charter with or without a captain is available here. ⊠ *Wickham's Cay II, Road Town, Tortola* ☎ *284/495–4740, 800/327–2276* ⊕ *www.sunsail.com.*

Voyage Charters. Voyage has a variety of sailboats for charter, with or without a captain and crew. ⊠ *Soper's Hole Marina, West End, Tortola* ☎ *284/494–0740, 888/869–2436* ⊕ *www.voyagecharters.com.*

White Squall II. This 80-foot schooner has regularly scheduled day sails to The Baths at Virgin Gorda, Cooper, the Indians, and the Caves at Norman Island. ⊠ *Village Cay Marina, Road Town, Tortola* ☎ *284/541–2222* ⊕ *www.whitesquall2.com.*

Continued on page 260

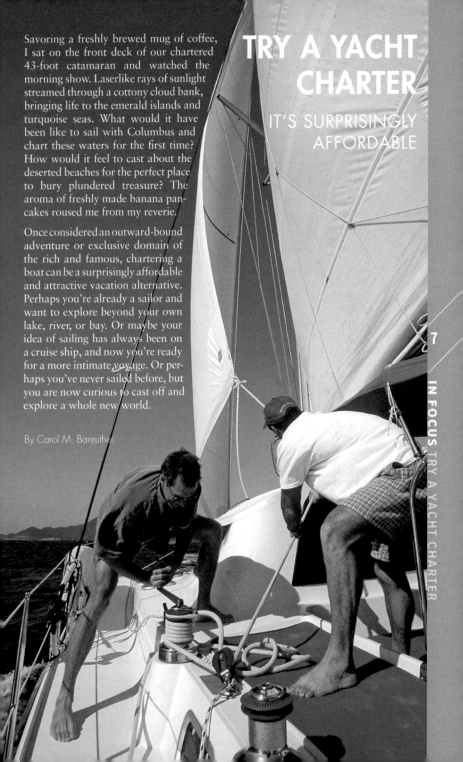

TRY A YACHT CHARTER

IT'S SURPRISINGLY AFFORDABLE

Savoring a freshly brewed mug of coffee, I sat on the front deck of our chartered 43-foot catamaran and watched the morning show. Laserlike rays of sunlight streamed through a cottony cloud bank, bringing life to the emerald islands and turquoise seas. What would it have been like to sail with Columbus and chart these waters for the first time? How would it feel to cast about the deserted beaches for the perfect place to bury plundered treasure? The aroma of freshly made banana pancakes roused me from my reverie.

Once considered an outward-bound adventure or exclusive domain of the rich and famous, chartering a boat can be a surprisingly affordable and attractive vacation alternative. Perhaps you're already a sailor and want to explore beyond your own lake, river, or bay. Or maybe your idea of sailing has always been on a cruise ship, and now you're ready for a more intimate voyage. Or perhaps you've never sailed before, but you are now curious to cast off and explore a whole new world.

By Carol M. Bareuther

CREWED CHARTER

On a crewed charter, you sit back and relax while the crew provides for your every want and need. Captains are licensed by the U.S. Coast Guard or the equivalent in the British maritime system. Cooks—preferring to be called chefs—have skills that go far beyond peanut butter and jelly sandwiches. There are four meals a day, and many chefs boast certificates from culinary schools ranging from the Culinary Institute of America in New York to the Cordon Bleu in Paris.

The advantage of a crewed yacht charter, with captain and cook, is that it takes every bit of stress out of the vacation. With a captain who knows the local waters, you get to see some of the coves and anchorages that are not necessarily in the guidebooks. Your meals are prepared, cabins cleaned, beds made up every day—and turned down at night, too. Plus, you can sail and take the helm as often as you like. But at the end of the day, the captain is the one who will take responsibility for anchoring safely for the night while the chef goes below and whips up a gourmet meal.

APPROXIMATE COSTS	PROS	CONS
From $4,300 for 2 people for 5 days	■ Passengers just have to lay back and relax (unless they want to help sail)	■ More expensive than a bareboat, especially if you get a catamaran
From $5,500 for 2 people for 7 days	■ Most are catamarans, offering more space than monohulls	■ Less privacy for your group than on a bareboat
From $8,600 for 6 people for 5 days	■ You have an experienced, local hand on board if something goes wrong	■ Captain makes ultimate decisions about the course
From $10,500 for 6 people for 7 days	■ Water toys and other extras are often included	■ Chance for personality conflicts: you have to get along with the captain and chef. This is where a charter yacht broker is helpful in determining what yachts and crews might be a good fit.
Prices are all-inclusive for a 50- to 55-foot yacht in high season except for 15%–20% gratuity.	■ Competively priced within an all-inclusive resort	

(top) Family sailing in the British Virgin Islands

BAREBOAT

If you'd like to bareboat, don't be intimidated. It's a myth that you must be a graduate of a sailing school in order to pilot your own charter boat. A bareboat company will ask you to fill out a resume. The company checks for prior boat-handling experience, the type of craft you've sailed (whether powerboat or sailboat), and in what type of waters. Real-life experience, meaning all those day and weekend trips close to home, count as valuable know-how. If you've done a bit of boating, you may be more qualified than you think to take out a bareboat.

Costs can be very similar for a bareboat and crewed charter, depending on the time of year and size of the boat. You'll pay the highest rates between Christmas and New Year's, when you may not be allowed to do a charter of less than a week. But there are more than 800 bareboats between the USVI and BVI, so regardless of your budget, you should be able to find something in your price range. Plus, you might save a bit by chartering an older boat from a smaller company instead of the most state-of-the-art yacht from a larger company.

APPROXIMATE COSTS	PROS	CONS
From $3,200 for a small monohull (2–3 cabins)	■ The ultimate freedom to set the yacht's course	■ Must be able to pass a sailing test
From $5,200 for a large monohull (4–5 cabins)	■ A chance to test your sailing skills	■ Those unfamiliar with the region may not find the best anchorages
From $5,500 for a small catamaran (2 cabins)	■ Usually a broader range of boats and prices to choose from	■ You have to cook for and clean up after yourself
From $7,500 for a large catamaran (4 cabins)	■ More flexibility for meals (you can always go ashore if you don't feel like cooking)	■ You have to do your own provisioning and planning for meals
Prices exclude food, beverages, fuel, and other supplies. Most bareboat rates do not include water toys, taxes, insurance, and permits.	■ You can always hire a captain for a few days	■ If something goes wrong, there isn't an experienced hand onboard

Three women rigging the sails.

PREPARING FOR YOUR CHARTER

British Virgin Islands—anchorage in a tropical sea with breakfast on board.

PROVISIONING

Bareboaters must do their own provisioning. It's a good idea to arrange provisioning at least a week in advance.

Bobby's Market Place ⌧ *Wickham's Cay I, Road Town, Tortola* ☎ *284/494–2189* ⊕ *www.bobbysmarketplace.com*) offers packages from $20 to $30 per person per day. **Ample Hamper** (⌧ *Inner Harbour Marina, Road Town, Tortola* ☎ *284/494–2494* ⌧ *Frenchmans Cay Marina, West End, Tortola* ☎ *284/495–4684* ⊕ *www.amplehamper.com*) offers more than 1,200 items but no pre-arranged packages.

Provisioning packages from the charter company are usually a bit more expensive, at $30 to $35 per person per day, but they save you the hassle of planning the details. You can also shop on arrival. Both St. Thomas and Tortola have markets, though larger grocery stores may require a taxi ride. If you shop carefully, this route can still save you money. Just be sure to allow yourself a few hours after arrival to get everything done.

PLANNING

For a crewed charter, your broker will send a preference sheet for both food and your wishes for the trip. Perhaps you'd like lazy days of sleeping late, sunning, and swimming. Or you might prefer active days of sailing with stops for snorkeling and exploring ashore. If there's a special spot you'd like to visit, list it so your captain can plan the itinerary accordingly.

PACKING TIPS

Pack light for any type of charter. Bring soft-sided luggage (preferably a duffle bag) since space is limited and storage spots are usually odd shapes. Shorts, T-shirts, and swimsuits are sufficient. Bring something a bit nicer if you plan to dine ashore. Shoes are seldom required except ashore, but you might want beach shoes to protect your feet in the water. Most boats provide snorkel equipment, but always ask. Bring sunscreen, but a type that will not stain cockpit cushions and decks.

WHAT YOU'LL SEE IN THE USBVI

Cruz Bay in St. John

MAIN CHARTER BASES

The U.S. and British Virgin Islands boast more than 100 stepping-stone islands and cays within a 50-nautical-mi radius. This means easy line-of-sight navigation and island-hopping in protected waters, and it's rare that you'll spend more than a few hours moving between islands.

Tortola, in the British Virgin Islands, is the crewed charter and bareboat mecca of the Caribbean. This fact is plainly apparent from the forest of masts rising out from any marina.

The U.S. Virgin Islands fleet is based in **St. Thomas.** Direct flights from the mainland, luxurious accommodations, and duty-free shopping are drawing cards for departures from the U.S. Virgin Islands, whereas the British Virgins are closer to the prime cruising grounds.

POPULAR ANCHORAGES

On a typical weeklong charter you could set sail from Red Hook, St. Thomas, then cross Pillsbury Sound to St. John, which offers popular north-shore anchorages in Honeymoon, Trunk, or Francis bays.

But the best sailing and snorkeling always includes the British Virgin Islands (which require a valid passport or passport card). After clearing customs in West End, Tortola, many yachts hop along a series of smaller islands that run along the south side of the Sir Francis Drake Channel. But some yachts will also visit Guana Island, Great Camanoe, or Marina Cay off Tortola's more isolated east end.

The islands south of Tortola include **Norman Island,** the rumored site of Robert Lewis Stevenson's *Treasure Island.* The next island over is **Peter Island,** famous for it's posh resort and a popular anchorage for yachters. Farther east, off Salt Island, is the wreck of the **RMS *Rhone***—the most magnificent dive site in the eastern Caribbean. Giant boulders form caves and grottos called The Baths at the southern end of **Virgin Gorda.**

A downwind run along Tortola's north shore ends at **Jost Van Dyke,** where that famous guitar-strumming calypsonian Foxy Callwood sings personalized ditties that make for a memorable finale.

SURFING

Surfing is big on Tortola's north shore, particularly when the winter swells come into Josiah's and Apple bays. Rent surfboards starting at $65 for a full day.

HIHO. Lots of good surfboards and standup paddleboards are available for rent as well as for sale. The staff will give you advice on the best spots to put in your board. ⊠ *Trellis Bay, Trellis Bay, Tortola* ☎ *284/494–7694* ⊕ *www.go-hiho.com.*

WINDSURFING

Steady trade winds make windsurfing a breeze. Three of the best spots for sailboarding are Nanny Cay, Slaney Point, and Trellis Bay on Beef Island. Rates for sailboards start at about $25 an hour or $100 for a two-hour lesson.

Boardsailing BVI Watersports. This company rents equipment and offers private and group lessons. ⊠ *Trellis Bay, Beef Island* ☎ *284/495–2447* ⊕ *www.adventures-bvi.com/.*

SIDE TRIPS FROM TORTOLA

There are several islands that make great side trips from Tortola, including lovely Marina Cay and tony Peter Island. Both have great accommodations, so you might want to spend the night.

MARINA CAY

FAMILY Beautiful little Marina Cay is in Trellis Bay, not far from Beef Island. Sometimes you can see it and its large J-shape coral reefs—a most dramatic sight—from the air soon after takeoff from the airport on Beef Island. Covering 8 acres, this islet is considered small even by BVI standards. On it there's a restaurant, Pusser's Store, and a six-unit hotel. Ferry service is free from the dock on Beef Island.

WHERE TO STAY

$ 🏨 **Pusser's Marina Cay Hotel and Restaurant.** If getting away from it all is
HOTEL your priority, this may be the place for you, because there's nothing to do on this beach-rimmed island other than swim, snorkel, and soak up the sun—there's not even a TV to distract you. **Pros:** lots of character; beautiful beaches; interesting guests. **Cons:** older property; ferry needed to get here. $ *Rooms from: $175* ⊠ *West side of Marina Cay* ☎ *284/494–2174* ⊕ *www.pussers.com/t-marina-cay.aspx* 🛏 *4 rooms, 2 2-bedroom villas* ⏹ *Breakfast.*

$$$$ 🏨 **Scrub Island Resort, Spa and Marina.** Part of Marriott's Autograph
RESORT Collection, this swanky resort is located on a 250-acre island near
Fodor'sChoice Tortola's Beef Island Airport. **Pros:** new property; lots of activities.
★ **Cons:** need ferry to get there; expensive. $ *Rooms from: $480* ⊠ *Scrub Island* ☎ *877/890–7444, 284/394–3440* ⊕ *www.scrubisland.com* 🛏 *52 rooms, 7 villas* ⏹ *No meals.*

PETER ISLAND

Although Peter Island is home to the resort of the same name, it's also a popular anchorage for charter boaters and a destination for Tortola vacationers. The scheduled ferry trip from Peter Island's shoreside base outside Road Town runs $15 round-trip for nonguests. The island is lush, with forested hillsides sloping seaward to meet white sandy beaches. There are no roads other than those at the resort, and there's nothing to do but relax at the lovely beach set aside for day-trippers. You're welcome to dine at the resort's restaurants.

WHERE TO STAY

$$$$
RESORT
Fodor's Choice
★

[⬚] **Peter Island Resort & Spa.** Total pampering and prices to match are the ticket at this luxury resort. **Pros:** lovely rooms; nice beach. **Cons:** need ferry to get here; pricey rates. [$] *Rooms from: $800* [☎] *284/495–2000, 800/346–4451* ⊕ *www.peterisland.com* ⬿ *52 rooms, 3 villas* [¶] *Multiple meal plans.*

> **VIRGIN GORDA FERRIES**
>
> The ferry service from the public dock in Spanish Town can be erratic. Call ahead to confirm the schedule, get there early to be sure it hasn't changed, and ask at the dock whether you're getting on the right boat. Thursday and Sunday service between Virgin Gorda and St. John is particularly prone to problems.

VIRGIN GORDA

Updated by
Susan Zaluski

Virgin Gorda, or "Fat Virgin," received its name from Christopher Columbus. The explorer envisioned the island as a pregnant woman in a languid recline, with Gorda Peak being her big belly and the boulders of The Baths her toes. Different in topography from Tortola, with its arid landscape covered with scrub brush and cactus, Virgin Gorda has a slower pace of life, too. Goats and cattle own the right-of-way, and the unpretentious friendliness of the people is winning.

EXPLORING

One of the most efficient ways to see Virgin Gorda is by sailboat. There are few roads, and most byways don't follow the scalloped shoreline. The main route sticks resolutely to the center of the island, linking The Baths on the southern tip with Gun Creek and Leverick Bay at North Sound. The craggy coast, cut through with grottoes and fringed by palms and boulders, has a primitive beauty. If you drive, you can hit all the sights in one day. The best plan is to explore the area near your hotel (either Spanish Town or North Sound) first, then take a day to drive to the other end. Stop to climb Gorda Peak, which is in the island's center. There are few signs, so come prepared with a map.

THE VALLEY

TOP ATTRACTIONS

FAMILY
Fodor's Choice
★

The Baths National Park. At Virgin Gorda's most celebrated sight, giant boulders are scattered about the beach and in the water. Some are almost as large as houses and form remarkable grottoes. Climb between these rocks to swim in the many placid pools. Early morning and late afternoon are the best times to visit if you want to avoid crowds. If it's privacy you crave, follow the shore northward to quieter bays—Spring Bay, the Crawl, Little Trunk, and Valley Trunk—or head south to Devil's Bay. ⊠ *Off Tower Rd., The Valley* ☎ *284/852–3650* ⊕ *www.bvinationalparkstrust.org* ⬿ *$3* ☉ *Daily dawn–dusk.*

WORTH NOTING

Copper Mine Point. A tall stone shaft silhouetted against the sky and a small stone structure that overlooks the sea are part of what was once a copper mine, now in ruins. Established 400 years ago, it was worked first by the Spanish, then by the English, until the early 20th century. The route is not well marked, so turn inland near LSL Restaurant and look for the hard-to-see sign pointing the way. ⊠ *Copper Mine Rd., The Valley* ⊕ *www.bvinpt.org* ✉ *Free.*

Spanish Town. Virgin Gorda's peaceful main settlement, on the island's southern wing, is so tiny that it barely qualifies as a town at all. Also known as The Valley, Spanish Town has a marina, some shops, and a couple of car-rental agencies. Just north of town is the ferry slip. At the Virgin Gorda Yacht Harbour you can stroll along the dock and do a little shopping. ⊠ *Spanish Town.*

NORTHWEST SHORE

TOP ATTRACTIONS

Coastal Islands. You can easily reach the quaintly named Fallen Jerusalem Island and the Dog Islands by a boat, which you can rent in either Tortola or Virgin Gorda. They're all part of the National Parks Trust of the Virgins Islands, and their seductive beaches and unparalleled snorkeling display the BVI at their beachcombing, hedonistic best. ⊕ *www.bvinpt.org* ✉ *Free.*

WORTH NOTING

Virgin Gorda Peak National Park. There are two trails at this 265-acre park, which contains the island's highest point, at 1,359 feet. Signs on North Sound Road mark both entrances. It's about a 15-minute hike from either entrance up to a small clearing, where you can climb a ladder to the platform of a wooden observation tower and a spectacular 360-degree view. ⊠ *North Sound Rd., Gorda Peak* ⊕ *www.bvinpt.org* ✉ *Free.*

BEACHES

THE VALLEY

The Baths Beach. This stunning maze of huge granite boulders extending into the sea is usually crowded midday with day-trippers. The snorkeling is good, and you're likely to see a wide variety of fish, but watch out for dinghies coming ashore from the numerous sailboats anchored offshore. Public bathrooms and a handful of bars and shops are close to the water and at the start of the path that leads to the beach. Lockers are available to keep belongings safe. **Amenities:** food and drink; parking; toilets. **Best for:** snorkeling; swimming. ⊠ *About 1 mile (1½ km) west of Spanish Town ferry dock on Tower Rd., The Valley* ☎ *284/852–3650* ⊕ *www.bvinpt.org* ✉ *$3* ⊙ *Daily dawn–dusk.*

Spring Bay Beach. This national-park beach that gets much less traffic than the nearby Baths, and has the similarly large, imposing boulders that create interesting grottoes for swimming. It also has no admission fee, unlike the more popular Baths. The snorkeling is excellent, and the grounds include swings and picnic tables. **Amenities:** none. **Best for:** snorkeling; swimming. ⊠ *Off Tower Rd., 1 mile (1½ km) west of Spanish Town ferry dock, The Valley* ☎ *284/852–3650* ⊕ *www.bvinpt. org* ✉ *Free* ⊙ *Daily dawn–dusk.*

The Baths

NORTHWEST SHORE

Nail Bay Beach. At the island's north tip, the three beaches at Nail Bay Resort are ideal for snorkeling. Mountain Trunk Bay is perfect for beginners, and Nail Bay and Long Bay beaches have coral caverns just offshore. The resort has a restaurant, which is an uphill walk but perfect for beach breaks. **Amenities:** food and drink; toilets. **Best for:** snorkeling; swimming. ⊠ *Nail Bay Resort, off Plum Tree Bay Rd., Nail Bay* 🖾 *Free* ⊙ *Daily dawn–dusk.*

Savannah Bay Beach. This is a wonderfully private beach close to Spanish Town. It may not always be completely deserted, but you can find a spot to yourself on this long stretch of soft, white sand. Bring your own mask, fins, and snorkel, as there are no facilities. The view from above is a photographer's delight. **Amenities:** none. **Best for:** solitude; snorkeling; swimming. ⊠ *Off N. Sound Rd., ¾ mile (1¼ km) east of Spanish Town ferry dock, Savannah Bay* 🖾 *Free* ⊙ *Daily dawn–dusk.*

WHERE TO EAT

Most folks opt to have dinner somewhere at or near their hotel to avoid driving on Virgin Gorda's twisting roads at night. The Valley does have a handful of restaurants if you're sleeping close to town.

THE VALLEY

$$
ECLECTIC
✕ **Bath and Turtle.** You can sit back and relax at this informal tavern with a friendly staff—although the noise from the television can sometimes be a bit much. Well-stuffed sandwiches, homemade pizzas, pasta dishes, and daily specials such as conch soup round out the casual menu. Local

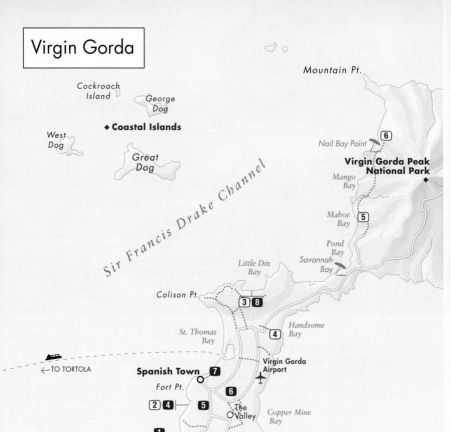

Virgin Gorda

Cockroach Island

George Dog

West Dog

◆ **Coastal Islands**

Great Dog

Sir Francis Drake Channel

Mountain Pt.

Nail Bay Point ⬙ **6**

Virgin Gorda Peak National Park ◆

Mango Bay

Mahoe Bay **5**

Pond Bay

Savannah Bay

Little Dix Bay

Colison Pt.

3 **8**

St. Thomas Bay

Handsome Bay

4

⬛ TO TORTOLA

Spanish Town **7**

Fort Pt.

Virgin Gorda Airport

6

2 **4** — **5**

The Valley

Copper Mine Bay

⬛**1**

1

Spring Bay Beach
Devil's Bay

The Baths ◆ **2**

Crook's Bay

3 ◆ **Copper Mine Point**

Stoney Bay

Fallen Jerusalem ◆ **Coastal Islands**

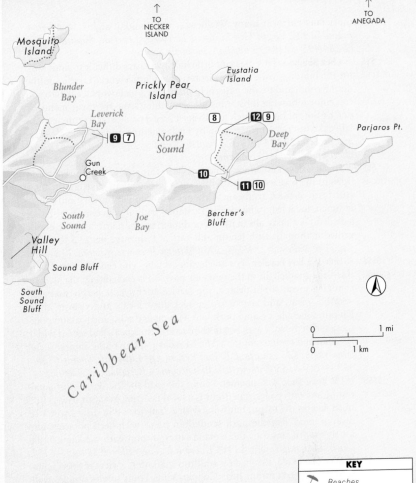

↑
TO NECKER ISLAND

↑
TO ANEGADA

Mosquito Island

Blunder Bay

Leverick Bay

Prickly Pear Island

Eustatia Island

Parjaros Pt.

North Sound

Deep Bay

Gun Creek

South Sound

Joe Bay

Bercher's Bluff

Valley Hill

Sound Bluff

South Sound Bluff

Caribbean Sea

0   1 mi
0   1 km

KEY
Beaches
Ferry
Cruise Ship Terminal
Restaurants
Hotels
Trail

musicians perform many Wednesday and Sunday nights. $ *Average main: $19* ⊠ *Virgin Gorda Yacht Harbour, Lee Rd., Spanish Town* ☎ *284/495–5239* ⊕ *www.bathandturtle.com.*

$$$
ECLECTIC

✕**Chez Bamboo.** This pleasant little hideaway isn't difficult to find; look for the building with the purple-and-green latticework. Candles in the dining room and on the patio help make this a mellow place where you can enjoy a bowl of lobster bisque, something from the tapas menu, or one of the specialties such as lobster curry. For dessert, try the chocolate cake or crème brûlée. Stop by Friday night for live music. $ *Average main: $29* ⊠ *Lee Rd., Spanish Town* ☎ *284/495–5752* ⊕ *www. chezbamboo.com* ⊘ *No lunch.*

$$$
ECLECTIC

✕**Fischer's Cove Restaurant.** Dine seaside at this alfresco restaurant that's open to the breezes. If pumpkin soup is on the menu, give it a try for a true taste of the Caribbean. Although you can get burgers and salads at lunch, local fish (whatever is available) and *fungi* (a cornmeal-based side dish) is a tasty alternative. For dinner, try the Caribbean lobster or grilled mahimahi with lemon and garlic. $ *Average main: $30* ⊠ *Lee Rd., The Valley* ☎ *284/495–5252* ⊕ *www.fischerscove.com.*

$$$$
INTERNATIONAL

✕**Little Dix Bay Pavilion.** For an elegant evening, you can't do better than this—the candlelight in the open-air pavilion is enchanting, the always-changing menu sophisticated, the service attentive. Superbly prepared seafood, meat, and vegetarian entrées draw locals and visitors alike. Favorites include a Cajun pork loin with mango salsa and scallion potatoes, and mahimahi with warm chorizo and chickpea salad served with a zucchini and tomato chutney. The Monday evening buffet shines. $ *Average main: $33* ⊠ *Little Dix Bay Resort, Off Little Rd., Spanish Town* ☎ *284/495–5555* ⊕ *www.littledixbay.com* ⌂ *Reservations essential.*

$$$$
ECLECTIC

✕**LSL Bake Shop & Restaurant.** Along the road to The Baths, this small restaurant with pedestrian decor is a local favorite. You can always find fresh fish on the menu, but folks with a taste for other dishes won't be disappointed. Try the pork tenderloin pesto with herb potatoes and a peppercorn sauce or the banana curry shrimp with a coconut milk sauce. $ *Average main: $33* ⊠ *Tower Rd., The Valley* ☎ *284/495–5151.*

$$
ECLECTIC

✕**Mine Shaft Café.** Perched on a hilltop that offers a view of spectacular sunsets, this restaurant near Copper Mine Point serves simple, well-prepared food, including grilled fish, steaks, and baby back ribs. Tuesday night features an all-you-can-eat Caribbean-style barbecue. The monthly full-moon parties draw a big local crowd. $ *Average main: $22* ⊠ *Near Copper Mine Point, The Valley* ☎ *284/495–5260.*

$$$$
ITALIAN

✕**The Rock Café.** Good Italian cuisine and seafood is served among the waterfalls and giant boulders that form the famous Baths. For dinner at this open-air eatery, feast on saffron lobster pasta or fresh red snapper with a creamy risotto. For dessert, don't miss the chocolate mousse. $ *Average main: $39* ⊠ *Lee Rd., The Valley* ☎ *284/495–5482* ⊕ *www. bvidining.com* ⊘ *No lunch.*

$$
ECLECTIC
FAMILY

✕**Top of the Baths.** At the entrance to The Baths, this popular restaurant has tables on an outdoor terrace or in an open-air pavilion; all have stunning views of the Sir Francis Drake Channel. The restaurant starts serving at starts serving at 8 am; for lunch, hamburgers, coconut chicken sandwiches, and fish-and-chips are among the offerings. For dessert, the key lime pie is excellent. The Sunday barbecue, served from noon until 3 pm, is an island event. [$] *Average main: $23* ✉ *The Valley* ☎ *284/495–5497* 🌐 *www.topofthebaths.com* ⏲ *No dinner Mon.*

$ ECLECTIC 🍴 **The Village Cafe and Restaurant.** Lunch is served poolside under the shade of umbrellas. The menu includes salads, wraps, and burgers, but the lobster-and-crab salad (yes, it contains both!) is a must-have. [$] *Average main: $15* ✉ *Virgin Gorda Village, North Sound Rd., The Valley* ☎ *284/495–5350* ⏲ *No dinner.*

WORD OF MOUTH

"The Baths are incredible, especially since you'll be able to go when the cruise ships aren't there. First thing in the morning or later in the day is just perfect! We really enjoyed taking the ferries to both Saba Rock and the Bitter End for lunches. We wanted to rent a little dinghy to do a little exploring on our own from Leverick, but it was always too windy in February. Your daughter might enjoy the Friday night barbecue buffet and dancing with the [Moko Jumbie stilt dancers] at Leverick Bay too!" —Jayneann

NORTH SOUND

$$$$ INTERNATIONAL 🍴 **Biras Creek Restaurant.** This hilltop restaurant at the Biras Creek Hotel has eye-popping views of North Sound. The four-course prix-fixe menu changes daily and includes several choices per course. For starters, there may be an artichoke, green bean, and wild mushroom salad topped with balsamic vinaigrette, or cream of sweet potato soup accompanied by potato straws. Entrées may include pan-seared snapper over horseradish pearl pasta. The desserts, including a lemon ricotta cheesecake with a spicy passion-fruit sauce, are stupendous. Dinner ends with Biras Creek's signature offering of cheese and port. Most days, lunch is a barbecue on the beach. [$] *Average main: $85* ✉ *Biras Creek Hotel, North Sound* ☎ *284/494–3555, 800/223–1108* 🌐 *www.biras.com* ✍ *Reservations essential.*

$$$ ECLECTIC 🍴 **The Clubhouse.** The Bitter End Yacht Club's open-air waterfront restaurant is a favorite rendezvous for sailors and their guests, so it's busy day and night. You can find lavish buffets for breakfast, lunch, and dinner, as well as an à la carte menu. Dinner selections include grilled mahimahi or tuna, local lobster, and porterhouse steak, as well as vegetarian dishes. [$] *Average main: $29* ✉ *Bitter End Yacht Club, North Sound* ☎ *284/494–2745* 🌐 *www.beyc.com* ✍ *Reservations essential.*

$$ ECLECTIC FAMILY 🍴 **Fat Virgin's Café.** This casual beachfront eatery offers a straightforward menu of baby back ribs, chicken roti, vegetable pasta, grouper sandwiches, and fresh fish specials for lunch and dinner. You can also find a good selection of Caribbean beer. [$] *Average main: $19* ✉ *Biras Creek Resort, North Sound* ☎ *284/495–7052* 🌐 *www.fatvirgin.com.*

$$$ ECLECTIC 🍴 **Restaurant at Leverick Bay.** The laid-back menu at this beach restaurant draws cruise ship passengers on tour as well as hotels guests and locals. The menu includes burgers, pizza, roti, chili, and fish and chips for lunch. Upstairs, there's an upscale restaurant that serves dinner with dishes that feature wild salmon and Kobe beef. [$] *Average main: $25* ✉ *Leverick Bay Resort & Marina, Leverick Bay Rd., Leverick Bay* ☎ *284/495–7154* 🌐 *www.leverickbay.com.*

7

WHERE TO STAY

Villas are scattered all over Virgin Gorda, but hotels are centered in and around The Valley, Nail Bay, and in the North Sound area. Except for Leverick Bay Resort, which is around the point from North Sound, all hotels in North Sound are reached only by ferry.

PRIVATE VILLAS

Those craving seclusion would do well at a villa. Most have full kitchens and maid service. Prices per week in winter run from around $2,000 for a one- or two-bedroom villa up to $10,000 for a five-room beachfront villa. Rates in summer are substantially less. On Virgin Gorda a villa in the North Sound area means you can pretty much stay put at night unless you want to make the drive on its narrow roads. If you opt for a spot near The Baths, it's an easier drive to town.

VILLA RENTAL AGENTS

McLaughlin-Anderson Luxury Villas. The St. Thomas–based McLaughlin-Anderson Luxury Villas represents about 17 properties all over Virgin Gorda. Villas range in size from two bedrooms to six bedrooms, and come with full kitchens, pools, stellar views, and other amenities. The company can hire a chef and stock your kitchen with groceries. A seven-night minimum is required during the winter season. ☎ *340/776–0635, 800/537–6246* 🌐 *www.mclaughlinanderson.com.*

Villas Virgin Gorda. This management company's dozen properties stretch from The Baths to the Nail Bay area. Several budget properties are included among the pricier offerings. Most houses have private pools, and a few are right on the beach. A sister company at the same number, Tropical Nannies, provides babysitting services. ☎ *284/495–6493* 🌐 *www.villasvirgingorda.com.*

Virgin Gorda Villa Rentals. This company's 40 or so properties are all near Leverick Bay Resort and Mahoe Bay, so they are perfect for those who want to be close to activities. Many of the accommodations—from studios to six or more bedrooms—have private swimming pools and air-conditioning, at least in the bedrooms. All have full kitchens, are well maintained, and have spectacular views. ☎ *284/495–7421, 800/848–7081* 🌐 *www.virgingordabvi.com.*

THE VALLEY

$ RESORT FAMILY 🏨 **Fischer's Cove Beach Hotel.** The rooms are modest, the furniture is discount-store-style, and the walls are thin, but you can't beat the location right on the beach and within walking distance of Spanish Town's shops and restaurants. **Pros:** beachfront location; budget price; good restaurant. **Cons:** very basic units; thin walls; no a/c in some rooms. [$] *Rooms from: $165* ✉ *Lee Rd., The Valley* ☎ *284/495–5252* 🌐 *www.fischerscove.com* 🛏 *12 rooms, 8 cottages* 🍴 *No meals.*

$ RENTAL 🏨 **Guavaberry Spring Bay Vacation Homes.** Rambling back from the beach, these hexagonal one- and two-bedroom villas give you all the comforts of home—and that striking boulder-fringed beach is just minutes away. **Pros:** short walk to The Baths (and excellent snorkeling); easy drive to town; great beaches nearby. **Cons:** few amenities; older property; basic decor. [$] *Rooms from: $250* ✉ *Tower Rd.,*

The Valley ☎ *284/495–5227* 🌐 *www.guavaberryspringbay.com* 🛏 *12 1-bedroom units, 6 2-bedroom units, 1 3-bedroom unit, 16 villas* 💳 *No credit cards* 🍴 *No meals.*

$$$$ RESORT FAMILY 🏨 **Rosewood Little Dix Bay.** This laid-back luxury resort offers a gorgeous crescent of sand, plenty of activities, and good restaurants. **Pros:** convenient location; lovely grounds; near many restaurants. **Cons:** expensive; very spread out; insular though not isolated. [$] *Rooms from: $405* ✉ *Off Little Rd., The Valley* ☎ *284/495–5555* 🌐 *www.littledixbay.com* 🛏 *78 rooms, 20 suites, 7 villas* 🍴 *No meals.*

$ RENTAL 🏨 **Virgin Gorda Village.** All the condos in this upscale complex a few minutes' drive from Spanish Town have at least partial ocean views. **Pros:** close to Spanish Town; lovely pool; recently built units. **Cons:** no beach; on a busy street; some noisy roosters nearby. [$] *Rooms from: $250* ✉ *North Sound Rd.* ☎ *284/495–5544* 🌐 *www.virgingordavillage.com* 🛏 *30 condos* 🍴 *No meals.*

NORTHWEST SHORE

$ RENTAL 🏨 **Mango Bay Resort.** Sitting seaside on Virgin Gorda's north coast, this collection of contemporary condos and villas will make you feel right at home. **Pros:** nice beach; lively location; easy drive to restaurants. **Cons:** drab decor; some units have lackluster views; need car to get around. [$] *Rooms from: $195* ✉ *Plum Tree Bay Rd., Pond Bay* ☎ *284/495–5672* 🌐 *www.mangobayresort.com* 🛏 *17 condos, 5 villas* 🍴 *No meals.*

$ RESORT 🏨 **Nail Bay Resort.** On a hill above the coast, this beachfront resort offers a wide selection of rooms and suites. **Pros:** full kitchens; lovely beach; close to town. **Cons:** busy neighborhood; bit of a drive from main road; uphill walk from beach. [$] *Rooms from: $240* ✉ *Off Nail Bay Rd., Nail Bay* ☎ *284/494–8000, 800/871–3551* 🌐 *www.nailbay.com* 🛏 *4 rooms, 4 suites, 7 villas* 🍴 *No meals.*

NORTH SOUND

$$$$ RESORT 🏨 **Biras Creek Resort.** Tucked out of the way on the island's North Sound, Biras Creek has a get-away-from-it-all feel that's a major draw for its well-heeled clientele. **Pros:** luxurious rooms; professional staff; good dining options; private, white-sand beach. **Cons:** very expensive; isolated; difficult for people with mobility problems. [$] *Rooms from: $530* ✉ *North Sound* ☎ *284/494–3555, 877/883–0756* 🌐 *www.biras.com* 🛏 *31 suites* 🍴 *Multiple meal plans.*

$$$$ ALL-INCLUSIVE FAMILY Fodor's Choice ★ 🏨 **Bitter End Yacht Club.** Sailing's the thing at this busy hotel and marina in the nautically inclined North Sound, and the use of everything from small sailboats to kayaks to windsurfers is included in the price. **Pros:** lots of water sports; good diving opportunities; friendly guests. **Cons:** expensive rates; isolated; lots of stairs. [$] *Rooms from: $646* ✉ *North Sound* ☎ *284/494–2746, 800/872–2392* 🌐 *www.beyc.com* 🛏 *85 rooms* 🍴 *All-inclusive.*

$ RESORT 🏨 **Leverick Bay Resort and Marina.** With its colorful buildings and bustling marina, Leverick Bay is a good choice for visitors who want easy access to water-sports activities. **Pros:** fun location; good restaurant; small grocery store. **Cons:** small beach; no laundry in units; 15-minute drive to town. [$] *Rooms from: $149* ✉ *Off Leverick Bay Rd., Leverick Bay* ☎ *284/495–7421, 800/848–7081* 🌐 *www.leverickbay.com* 🛏 *13 rooms, 4 apartments* 🍴 *No meals.*

$ ⛏ **Saba Rock Resort.** Reachable only by a free ferry or by private yacht,
RESORT   this resort on its own tiny cay is perfect for folks who want to mix
and mingle with the sailors who drop anchor for the night. **Pros:** party
atmosphere; convenient transportation; good diving nearby. **Cons:** tiny
beach; isolated location; on a very small island. Ⓢ *Rooms from: $150*
⊠ *North Sound* ☎ *284/495–7711, 284/495–9966* ⊕ *www.sabarock.
com* ⇨ *7 1-bedroom suites, 1 2-bedroom suites* ⏻ *Breakfast.*

NIGHTLIFE

Pick up a free copy of the *Limin' Times* (⊕ *www.limin-times.com*)—
available at most resorts and restaurants—for the most current local
entertainment schedule.

Bath and Turtle. During high season, the Bath and Turtle is one of the
liveliest spots on Virgin Gorda, hosting island bands Wednesday and
Sunday from 8 pm until midnight. ⊠ *Virgin Gorda Yacht Harbour,
Lee Rd., Spanish Town* ☎ *284/495–5239* ⊕ *www.bathandturtle.com.*

Chez Bamboo. This is the place for calypso and reggae on Tuesday and
Friday nights. ⊠ *Lee Rd., Spanish Town* ☎ *284/495–5752* ⊕ *www.
chezbamboo.com.*

Mine Shaft Café. The cafe has music on Tuesday and Friday. ⊠ *Near Copper Mine Point, The Valley* ☎ *284/495–5260* ⊕ *www.mineshaftbvi.com.*

Restaurant at Leverick Bay. This resort's main restaurant hosts music
on Tuesday and Friday in season. ⊠ *Leverick Bay Resort &
Marina, Leverick Bay Rd., Leverick Bay* ☎ *284/495–7154* ⊕ *www.
therestaurantatleverickbay.com.*

Rock Café. There's live piano music nearly every night during the Rock
Café's winter season. ⊠ *Lee Rd., The Valley* ☎ *284/495–5177* ⊕ *www.
bvidining.com.*

SHOPPING

Most boutiques are within hotel complexes or at Virgin Gorda Yacht
Harbour. Two of the best are at Biras Creek and Little Dix Bay. Other
properties—the Bitter End and Leverick Bay—have small but equally
good boutiques.

FOOD

Bitter End Emporium. This store at the Bitter End is the place for local
fruits, cheeses, baked goods, and gourmet prepared food. ⊠ *Bitter End
Yacht Harbor, North Sound* ☎ *284/494–2746* ⊕ *www.beyc.com.*

Buck's Food Market. This market is the closest the island offers to a full-
service supermarket, with an in-store bakery and deli as well as fresh
fish and produce departments. ⊠ *Virgin Gorda Yacht Harbour, Lee
Rd., Spanish Town* ☎ *284/495–5423* ⊠ *Gun Creek, North Sound*
☎ *284/495–7368* ⊕ *www.bucksmarketplace.com.*

Chef's Pantry. This store has the fixings for an impromptu party in your
villa or on your boat—fresh seafood, specialty meats, imported cheeses,
daily baked breads and pastries, and an impressive wine and spirit

selection. ⊠ *Leverick Bay Marina, Leverick Bay Rd., Leverick Bay* ☎ *284/495–7677.*

Rosy's Supermarket. This store carries the basics plus an interesting selection of ready-to-cook meals, such as a whole seasoned chicken. ⊠ *Coppermine Rd., The Valley* ☎ *284/495–5245* ⊕ *www.rosysenterprisesvg.com.*

Virgin Gorda Cash & Carry. The store isn't much to look at, inside or out, but it has the best wine prices on Virgin Gorda, along with the usual basic supermarket items. ⊠ *Lee Rd., Spanish Town* ☎ *284/347–1200.*

GIFTS

Allamanda Gallery. This shop showcases owner Amanda Baker's tropical photography, but it's also a good place to browse for cards, magnets, and other take-home gifts. ⊠ *The Baths, Tower Rd., The Valley* ☎ *284/495–5935* ⊕ *www.virginportraits.com.*

Caribbean Too. While this cozy store sells T-shirts and other vacation necessities, it's also a great place to shop for tropical wear in linen and other comfortable fabrics. ⊠ *The Baths, Tower Rd., The Valley* ☎ *284/495–6288.*

Reeftique. This store carries island crafts and jewelry, clothing, and nautical odds and ends with the Bitter End logo. ⊠ *Bitter End Yacht Harbor, North Sound* ☎ *284/494–2746* ⊕ *www.beyc.com.*

Thee Nautical Gallery. This boutique sells attractive handcrafted jewelry, paintings, and one-of-a-kind gift items, as well as books about the Caribbean. ⊠ *Leverick Bay Marina, Leverick Bay Rd., Leverick Bay* ☎ *284/495–7479.*

SPORTS AND ACTIVITIES

DIVING AND SNORKELING

Where you go snorkeling and what company you pick depends on where you're staying. Many hotels have on-site dive outfitters, but if they don't, one won't be far away. If your hotel does have a dive operation, just stroll down to the dock and hop aboard—no need to drive anywhere. The dive companies are all certified by PADI. Costs vary, but count on paying about $75 for a one-tank dive and $110 for a two-tank dive. All dive operators offer introductory courses as well as certification and advanced courses. Should you get an attack of the bends, which can happen when you ascend too rapidly, the nearest decompression chamber is at Roy L. Schneider Regional Medical Center in St. Thomas.

There are some terrific snorkel and dive sites off Virgin Gorda, including areas around The Baths, the North Sound, and the Dogs. The Chimney at Great Dog Island has a coral archway and canyon covered with a

You can learn to sail at the Bitter End Yacht Club.

wide variety of sponges. At Joe's Cave, an underwater cavern on West Dog Island, huge groupers, eagle rays, and other colorful fish accompany divers as they swim. At some sites you can see 100 feet down, but divers who don't want to go that deep and snorkelers will find plenty to look at just below the surface.

FAMILY **Bitter End Yacht Club.** The BEYC schedules two snorkeling trips a day. ⊠ *North Sound* ☎ *284/494–2746* ⊕ *www.beyc.com.*

Dive BVI. In addition to day trips, Dive BVI also offers expert instruction and certification. ⊠ *Virgin Gorda Yacht Harbour, Lee Rd., Spanish Town* ☎ *284/495–5513, 800/848–7078.* ⊠ *Leverick Bay Marina, Leverick Bay Rd., Leverick Bay* ☎ *284/495–7328, 800/848–7078* ⊕ *www.divebvi.com.*

Sunchaser Scuba. Resort, advanced, and rescue courses are all available here. ⊠ *Bitter End Yacht Club, North Sound* ☎ *284/495–9638, 800/932–4286* ⊕ *www.sunchaserscuba.com.*

SAILING AND BOATING
The BVI waters are calm, and terrific places to learn to sail. You can also rent sea kayaks, waterskiing equipment, dinghies, and powerboats, or take a parasailing trip.

Aristocat Charters. Set sail aboard the 48-foot catamaran *Lionheart* to snorkel Cooper, Salt, and Dog islands. ⊠ *Virgin Gorda Yacht Harbour, Lee Rd., Spanish Town* ☎ *284/499–1249* ⊕ *www.aristocatcharters.com.*

FAMILY **Bitter End Sailing School.** Classroom, dockside, and on-the-water lessons are available for sailors of all levels. Private lessons are $75 per hour. ⊠ *Bitter End Yacht Club, North Sound* ☎ *284/494–2746* ⊕ *www.beyc.com.*

Double "D" Charters. If you just want to sit back, relax, and let the captain take the helm, choose a sailing or power yacht from Double "D" Charters. Rates run from $89 for a day trip. Private full-day cruises or sails for up to eight people run from $950. ✉ *Virgin Gorda Yacht Harbour, Lee Rd., Spanish Town* 📞 *284/499–2479* 🌐 *www.doubledbvi.com.*

JOST VAN DYKE

Updated by
Susan Zaluski

Named after an early Dutch settler, Jost Van Dyke is a small island northwest of Tortola. It's also a place to *truly* get away from it all. Mountainous and lush, the 4-mile-long (6½-km-long) island—with fewer than 200 full-time residents—has one tiny resort, some rental houses and villas, a campground, a few shops, a handful of cars, and a single road. There are no banks or ATMs on the island, and many restaurants and shops accept only cash. It's a good idea to buy groceries on St. Thomas or Tortola before arriving if you're staying for a few days. Life definitely rolls along on "island time," especially during the off-season from August to November, when finding a restaurant open for dinner can be a challenge. Water conservation is encouraged, as the source is rainwater collected in basementlike cisterns. Many lodgings will ask you to follow the Caribbean golden rule: "In the land of sun and fun, we never flush for number one." Jost is one of the Caribbean's most popular anchorages, and there are a disproportionately large number of informal bars and restaurants, which have helped earn Jost its reputation as the "party island" of the BVI.

BEACHES

FAMILY **Great Harbour Beach.** Great Harbour has an authentic Caribbean feel that's not just for tourists. Small bars and restaurants line the sandy strip of beach that serves as the community's main street. While the island's main settlement may not have the unspoiled natural beauty of some popular beaches, it holds a quaint charm. Activity picks up after dark, but many of the restaurants also serve excellent lunches without huge crowds. There are a few areas suited to swimming, with calm, shallow water perfect for children. ⚠ **Bring your bug spray for sandflies in the early evenings. Amenities:** food and drink; toilets. **Best for:** swimming. ✉ *Great Harbour.*

Sandy Cay Beach. Just offshore, the little islet known as Sandy Cay is a gleaming sliver of white sand with marvelous snorkeling and an inland nature trail. Previously part of the private estate of the late philanthropist and conservationist Laurance Rockefeller, the cay recently became a protected area. You can hire any boatman on Jost Van Dyke to take you out; just be sure to agree on a price and a time to be picked up again. As this is a national park, visitors are asked to "take only photos and leave only footprints." Nevertheless, it's become an increasingly popular location for weddings, which require approval from the BVI National Parks Trust. ⚠ **Experienced boaters can rent a boat or dinghy to go here, but be aware that winter swells can make beach landings treacherous. Amenities:** none. **Best for:** snorkeling; swimming.

FAMILY Fodor's Choice ★ **White Bay Beach.** On the south shore, this long stretch of picturesque white sand is especially popular with boaters who come ashore for a libation at one of the many beach bars that offer refuge from the sun. Despite the sometimes rowdy bar scene, the beach is large enough to find a quiet spot, particularly late in the day when most of the day-trippers disappear and the beach becomes serene. Nearby accommodations include the Sandcastle Hotel, White Bay Villas, Perfect Pineapple, and the Pink House Villas. ⚠ **Swimmers and snorkelers should be cautious of boat traffic in the anchorage.** **Amenities:** food and drink; toilets. **Best for:** swimming; walking. ✉ *White Bay.*

WHERE TO EAT

Restaurants on Jost Van Dyke are informal (some serve meals family-style at long tables) and often charming. The island is a favorite charter-boat stop, and you're bound to hear people exchanging stories about the previous night's anchoring adventures. Most restaurants don't take reservations (but for those that do, they are usually required). In all cases, dress is casual.

$$$ ECLECTIC 🍴 **Abe's by the Sea.** Many sailors who cruise into this quiet bay come so they can dock right at this open-air eatery to enjoy the seafood, conch, lobster, and other fresh catches. Chicken and ribs round out the menu, and affable owners Abe Coakley and his wife, Eunicy, add a pinch and dash of hospitality that makes a meal into a memorable evening. Casual lunches are also served, and an adjoining market sells ice, canned goods, and other necessities. Dinner reservations are required by 5 pm. [$] *Average main: $31* ✉ *Little Harbour* ☎ *284/495–9329* ✍ *Reservations essential.*

$$$ SEAFOOD 🍴 **Ali Baba's.** Lobster is the main attraction at this beach bar with a sandy floor, which is just some 20 feet from the sea. Grilled local fish, including swordfish, kingfish, and wahoo, are specialties and caught fresh daily. There's also a pig roast on Monday nights in season. Beware: Ali Baba's special rum punch is as potent as it is delicious. Reservations aren't mandatory for dinner, but you'll probably find yourself waiting a long time without them. [$] *Average main: $29* ✉ *Great Harbour* ☎ *284/495–9280* 💳 *No credit cards.*

$$$ BARBECUE 🍴 **Cool's Breeze Bar & Restaurant.** This brightly colored eatery is often frequented by island locals, particularly late in the evening, when you can occasionally find DJ'd parties, karaoke, or a game of dominoes. The establishment added full dinner options in 2012, offering fresh grilled lobster, barbecue, and baby back ribs. [$] *Average main: $29* ✉ *Great Harbour* ☎ *284/496–0855* 💳 *No credit cards.*

$$$ ECLECTIC 🍴 **Corsairs Beach Bar and Restaurant.** On an island known for seafood, it's the pizza that draws raves at this friendly beach bar considered by some to be Jost's version of *Cheers.* If pizza doesn't appeal, the lunch and dinner menus have a wide variety of selections with an eclectic, Continental flare, and the owners brought a new chef on board in late 2013. Bring an appetite to breakfast, when the choices include hearty omelets and breakfast burritos. The bar is easily recognized by its signature pirate paraphernalia and a restored U.S. military M37 Dodge truck parked next to the steps-from-the-sea dining room. [$] *Average main: $32* ✉ *Great Harbour* ☎ *284/495–9294* 🌐 *www.corsairsbvi.com.*

Boaters docking at Jost Van Dyke

$$$$ ECLECTIC FAMILY 🍴 **Foxy's Taboo.** It's well worth the winding hilly drive or sometimes-rough sail to get to Taboo, where there's a sophisticated menu and a welcoming attitude. Located on Jost's mostly undeveloped East End, Taboo is less of a party bar than Foxy's in Great Harbour but usually has a great breeze and scenic views. You'll find specialties with a Mediterranean twist like eggplant cheesecake, kabobs, and hot-from-the-oven pizza. The lunch menu differs from the standard island fare. Even the burgers are a step up from average, and the salads are the best on the island. Coupled with a walk to the nearby Bubbly Pool (ask for a map at the bar), a visit to Taboo is a good way to while away a few hours. Dinner reservations are required by 4 pm. [$] *Average main: $33* ✉ *East End* ☎ *284/340–9258.*

$$$ ECLECTIC FAMILY 🍴 **Foxy's Tamarind Bar and Restaurant.** The big draw here is the owner, Foxy Callwood, a famed calypso singer who will serenade you with lewd and laugh-worthy songs as you fork into burgers, grilled chicken, barbecue ribs, and lobster. Check out the pennants, postcards, and weathered T-shirts that adorn every inch of the walls and ceiling of this large, two-story beach shack; they've been left by previous visitors. On Friday and Saturday nights in season Foxy hosts Caribbean-style barbecue with grilled fresh fish, chicken and ribs, peas and rice, salad, and more, followed by live music. Other nights choose from steak, fresh lobster, pork, or pasta; at lunch Foxy serves sandwiches and salads. Whether because of the sheer volume of diners or the experience of the management, Foxy's is one of the most reliable eating establishments on Jost. And it's also home to the only espresso on the island, and the only locally brewed beer in the BVI. You're unlikely to find Foxy performing at night, but he takes the mike many afternoons, and

takes time to mingle with guests, making this a popular happy-hour pit stop. $\boxed{\text{\$}}$ *Average main: $29* ✉ *Great Harbour* ☎ *284/495–9258* ⊕ *www.foxysbar.com.*

$$$ ✕ **Gertrude's Beach Bar.** A casual bar right on White Bay Beach, Ger-
CAFÉ   trude's will make you feel at home with burgers, conch fritters, and rotis. It's open for lunch and dinner, but it's a good idea to call ahead for dinner reservations. Sometimes Gertrude, and helpful staffer Olga, will let you pour your own drinks. $\boxed{\text{\$}}$ *Average main: $21* ✉ *White Bay* ☎ *284/495–9104.*

$$ ✕ **Harris' Place.** Owner Cynthia Harris is as famous for her friendli-
ECLECTIC   ness as she is for her food. Lobster in a garlic butter sauce, and other
FAMILY   freshly caught seafood, as well as pork, chicken, and ribs are on the menu. Homemade Key lime pie and expertly blended bushwackers are "to live for," as Cynthia would say, but diners also praise the fresh fish and lobster. Call for schedule of live music, which varies from season to season. Breakfast and lunch are served, too. $\boxed{\text{\$}}$ *Average main: $34* ✉ *Little Harbour* ☎ *284/495–9302.*

$$ ✕ **One Love Bar and Grill.** The Food Network's Alton Brown sought out
ECLECTIC   this beachfront eatery and featured its stewed conch on a 2008 flavor-finding trip. Menu items include freshly caught seafood, quesadillas, sandwiches and salads. Try their specialty drink, a Bushwhacker. Seddy built the bar himself and decorated it with the flotsam and jetsam he has collected over his years as a fisherman. $\boxed{\text{\$}}$ *Average main: $28* ✉ *White Bay* ⊕ *www.onelovebar.com.*

$$$$ ✕ **Soggy Dollar Bar.** While this spot is well-known for its liquid offerings,
ECLECTIC   it also offers up decent fare. For lunch, if you can find your way through the throngs ordering Painkillers at the bar, choose from burgers, rotis, sandwiches, and fish-and-chips. They offer a sit-down breakfast each morning and rotate choices like poached eggs, banana pancakes, and cinnamon-rum French toast throughout the week. At night, candles illuminate this tiny beachfront, palm-lined dining room, making it one of the most romantic settings on the island. Island-born chef Dwayne Donovan impresses guests with a variety of poultry, meat, and fish selections at dinner. Reservations aren't essential for dinner, but they're still a good idea. $\boxed{\text{\$}}$ *Average main: $33* ✉ *White Bay* ☎ *284/495–9888* ⊕ *www.soggydollar.com.*

$$$$ ✕ **Sydney's Peace and Love.** Here you can find great local lobster and
ECLECTIC   fish, as well as barbecue chicken and ribs with all the fixings, including peas and rice, corn, coleslaw, and potato salad. Book early for all-you-can-eat lobster on Monday and Thursday nights. Meals are served on an open-air terrace or in an air-conditioned dining room at the water's edge. The find here is a sensational (by BVI standards) jukebox. The cognoscenti sail here for dinner, since there's no beach—and therefore no annoying sand fleas. Breakfast and lunch are served, too, and guests help themselves at the honor bar. $\boxed{\text{\$}}$ *Average main: $33* ✉ *Little Harbour* ☎ *284/495–9271.*

WHERE TO STAY

$$ B&B/INN **Ali Baba's Heavenly Rooms.** Just above Ali Baba's restaurant, owner Wayson "Baba" Hatchett has added three simple but attractive rooms, each equipped with air-conditioning and a private bath. **Pros:** convenient location. **Cons:** noisy area of Great Harbour. [$] *Rooms from: $140* ✉ *Great Harbour* ☎ *284/495–9280* 🌐 *www.alibabasrestaurantandbarbvi.com* 🛏 *3 rooms.*

$$ B&B/INN **Perfect Pineapple Guest Houses.** One-bedroom suites, as well as one- and two-bedroom guesthouses, all come equipped with private bath, air-conditioning, stove, satellite TV, and refrigerator. **Pros:** located just steps from the popular White Bay beach; **Cons:** rooms have only basic furnishings; in need of updating. [$] *Rooms from: $160* ✉ *White Bay* ☎ *284/495–9401* 🌐 *www.perfectpineapple.com* 🛏 *6 rooms* 🍴 *No meals.*

$$$ HOTEL **Sandcastle.** Sleep steps from beautiful White Bay beach at this tiny beachfront hideaway, an island favorite for more than 40 years. **Pros:** beachfront rooms; near restaurants and bars; comfy hammocks. **Cons:** some rooms lack air-conditioning; beach sometimes clogged with day-trippers; no children allowed. [$] *Rooms from: $310* ✉ *White Bay* ☎ *284/495–9888* 🌐 *www.soggydollar.com* 🛏 *2 rooms, 4 1-bedroom cottages* 🍴 *Multiple meal plans.*

$ RENTAL FAMILY **White Bay Villas and Seaside Cottages.** Beautiful views and friendly staff keep guests coming back to these hilltop one- to three-bedroom villas and cottages. **Pros:** incredible views; full kitchens; friendly staff. **Cons:** 10- to 15-minute walk to White Bay and Great Harbour's restaurants and beaches; rental cars recommended. [$] *Rooms from: $220* ✉ *White Bay* ☎ *410/571–6692, 800/778–8066* 🌐 *www.jostvandyke.com* 🛏 *7 villas, 3 cottages* 🍴 *No meals.*

7

NIGHTLIFE

Jost Van Dyke is the most happening place to go barhopping in the BVI, so much so that it is an all-day enterprise for some. In fact, yachties will sail over just to have a few drinks. All the spots are easy to find, clustered in three general locations: Great Harbour, White Bay, and Little Harbour (⇨ *see Where to Eat, above*). On the Great Harbour side you can find Foxy's, Corsairs, and Ali Baba's; on the White Bay side are the One Love Bar and Grill and the Soggy Dollar Bar, where legend has it the famous Painkiller was first concocted; and in Little Harbour are Harris' Place, Sydney's Peace and Love, and Abe's by the Sea. If you can't make it to Jost Van Dyke, you can have a Painkiller at almost any bar in the BVI.

SPORTS AND ACTIVITIES

Abe and Eunicy Rentals. This company's two-door Suzukis ($65 a day), four-door Suzukis ($75 a day), and four-door Monteros ($80 a day) will help you explore by land. There's pick-up and drop-off service from anywhere on the island. ✉ *Little Harbour* ☎ *284/495–9329.*

Endeavour II Sailing. Built entirely from scratch on island with local high school students, this 32-foot traditionally-inspired sailing vessel was part of a maritime heritage project initiated by the Jost Van Dykes Preservation Society. Day sails aboard help fund dive and sail training for young Jost Van Dyke islanders. Two-hour sunset cruises are offered for $65. ✉ *Great Harbour* ☎ *284/540–0861* ⊕ *www.jvdps.org.*

JVD Scuba and BVI Eco-Tours. Check out the undersea world around the island with dive master Colin Aldridge. One of the most impressive dives in the area is off the north coast of Little Jost Van Dyke. Here you can find the Twin Towers: a pair of rock formations rising an impressive 90 feet. A one-tank dive costs $95, a two-tank dive $115, and a four-hour beginner course is $120 plus the cost of equipment. Colin also offers day-trips to Sandy Cay and Sandy Spit, Norman Island, Virgin Gorda (The Baths), and custom outings. You can also rent snorkel equipment or dive gear. ✉ *Great Harbour* ☎ *284/495–0271* ⊕ *www. bvi-ecotours.com* ☻ *Closed Sat.*

Paradise Jeep Rentals. Paradise Jeep Rentals offers the ideal vehicles to tackle Jost Van Dyke's steep, winding roads. Even though Jost is a relatively small island, you really need to be in shape to walk from one bay to the next. This outfit rents two-door Suzukis for $60 per day and four-door Grand Vitaras and Sportages for $70. Discounts are available for rentals of six or more days. It's next to the Fire Station in Great Harbour. ■TIP➔ **Reservations are a must.** ✉ *Great Harbour* ☎ *284/495–9477.*

Paradise Powerboat Rental. Franky Chinnery, who was born and raised on Jost Van Dyke, owns Paradise Powerboat Rental. The company offers day-trip boat tours to Sandy Cay, Sandy Spit, Normal Island, The Baths, and custom trips, along with dinghy rentals, sportfishing, and other services on board the *Betram* and *Renegade* powerboats. It also provides water-taxi service between Jost Van Dyke and Tortola or USVI (call for prices). ✉ *Great Harbour* ☎ *284/442–4651.*

ANEGADA

Updated by
Susan Zaluski

Anegada lies low on the horizon about 14 miles (22½ km) north of Virgin Gorda. Unlike the hilly volcanic islands in the chain, this is a flat coral-and-limestone atoll. Nine miles (14 km) long and 2 miles (3 km) wide, the island rises no more than 28 feet above sea level. In fact, by the time you're able to see it, you may have run your boat onto a reef. (More than 300 captains unfamiliar with the waters have done so since exploration days; note that bareboat charters don't allow their vessels to head here without a trained skipper.) Although the reefs are a sailor's nightmare, they (and the shipwrecks they've caused) are a scuba diver's dream. Snorkeling, especially in the waters around Loblolly Bay on the North Shore, is a transcendent experience. You can float in shallow, calm water just a few feet from shore and see one coral formation after another, each shimmering with a rainbow of colorful fish. Many local captains are happy to take visitors out fishing for bonefish. Such watery pleasures are complemented by ever-so-fine, ever-so-white sand (the northern and western shores have long stretches of the stuff) and the occasional beach bar (stop in for burgers, local lobster, or a frosty beer). The island's population of about 180 lives primarily in a small south-side village called the Settlement, which has two grocery stores, a bakery, and a general store. In 2009 Anegada got its first bank, but it's open only one day a week, and there's still no ATM. Many restaurants and shops take only cash.

WHERE TO EAT

There are between 6 and 10 restaurants open at any one time, depending on the season and on whim. Check when you're on the island. Fresh fish and lobster are the island's specialties. The going rate for a lobster dinner is $50, and it's always the most expensive thing on any restaurant menu.

$$$$ SEAFOOD Fodor's Choice ★ 🍴 **Anegada Reef Hotel Restaurant.** Seasoned yachters gather here nightly to share tales of the high seas; the open-air bar is the busiest on the island. Dinner is by candlelight under the stars and always includes famous Anegada lobster, steaks, and succulent baby back ribs—all prepared on the large grill by the little open-air bar. The ferry dock is right next door, so expect a crowd shortly after it arrives. Dinner reservations are required by 4 pm. Breakfast favorites include lobster omelets and rum-soaked French toast; at lunch the Reef serves salads and sandwiches. [$] *Average main: $37* ✉ *Setting Point* ☎ *284/495–8002* ✍ *Reservations essential.*

$$$ SEAFOOD FAMILY 🍴 **Big Bamboo.** This beachfront bar and restaurant tucked among sea grape trees at famous Loblolly Bay is the island's most popular destination for lunch. After you've polished off a plate of succulent Anegada lobster, barbeque chicken or fresh fish, you can spend the afternoon on the beach, where the snorkeling is excellent and the view close to perfection. Fruity drinks from the cabana bar and ice cream from the freezer will round out your day. Dinner is by request only. If your heart is set on lobster, it's a good idea to call in the morning or day before to put in your request. [$] *Average main: $29* ✉ *Loblolly Bay West* ☎ *284/495–2019* 🌐 *www.bigbamboo.vg.*

$$$$ SEAFOOD 🍴 **Cow Wreck Bar and Grill.** Named for the cow bones that once washed up on shore, this wiggle-your-toes-in-the-sand beachside eatery on the north shore is a fun place to watch the antics of surfers and kiteboarders skidding across the bay. Tuck into conch ceviche, lobster fritters, or the popular hot wings for lunch. The homemade coconut pie is a winner. Pack your snorkel gear and explore the pristine reef just a few strokes from the shore before you eat, or browse the on-site gift shop. Dinner is served by request; reservations required by 4 pm. [$] *Average main: $36* ✉ *Loblolly Bay East* ☎ *284/495–8047* 🌐 *www.cowwreckbeach.com* ✍ *Reservations essential.*

$$$$ SEAFOOD FAMILY Fodor's Choice ★ 🍴 **Neptune's Treasure.** The owners, the Soares family, have lived on the island for more than half a century, and the Soares men catch, cook, and serve the seafood at this homey bar and restaurant a short distance from Setting Point. The fresh lobster, swordfish, tuna and mahimahi are all delicious. In 2013, Pam's Kitchen, a small bakery to the exterior

Anegada has miles of beautiful white-sand beaches.

of the property was incorporated into the restaurant and rounds out offerings with freshly baked breads; sweet treats including made-from scratch desserts (including Key lime pie, chocolate brownies, and apple pie); and pizzas. Dinner is by candlelight at the water's edge, often with classic jazz playing softly in the background. If you've tired of seafood, Neptune's has a nice variety of alternatives, including vegetarian pasta, pork loin, and orange chicken. The view is spectacular at sunset. Breakfast and lunch are also served. Dinner reservations are essential by 4 pm. $ *Average main: $32* ✉ *Bender's Bay* ☎ *284/495–9439* ⊕ *www. neptunestreasure.com* ⌂ *Reservations essential.*

$$$$ ✕ **Pomato Point Restaurant.** This relaxed restaurant and bar sits on one
SEAFOOD of the best beaches on the island and enjoys Anegada's most dramatic sunset views. Entrées include lobster, stewed conch, and freshly caught seafood. It's open for lunch daily; call by 4 pm for dinner reservations. Be sure to take a look at owner Wilfred Creque's displays of island artifacts, including shards of Arawak pottery and 17th-century coins, cannonballs, and bottles. These are housed in a little one-room museum adjacent to the dining room. $ *Average main: $38* ✉ *Pomato Point* ☎ *284/495–9466* ⌂ *Reservations essential* ☾ *Closed Sept.*

$$$$ ✕ **Potter's By the Sea.** Owner Liston Potter, a great staff, and a lively
SEAFOOD atmosphere just a few steps from the dock complement freshly grilled lobster and other seafood selections such as snapper and grouper. Potter's also offers a beach shuttle, free Wi-Fi, pool tables, and live music (ask about schedule when you call ahead for dinner reservations). $ *Average main: $37* ✉ *Setting Point* ☎ *284/495–9182* ⌂ *Reservations essential.*

WHERE TO STAY

$$ | ⊡ **Anegada Beach Club.** Laid-back beach club setting where beach
RESORT | enthusiasts can enjoy beach volleyball and badminton. **Pros:** with the
option of adjoining king and "junior" suites (with two twin beds)
and plenty of outdoor activities, this is a great spot for families. **Cons:**
some find Anegada too remote. $ *Rooms from: $275* ⊠ *Keel Point*
☏ *800/871–3551* ⊕ *www.anegadabeachclub.com* ⤴ *4 rooms, 7 villas*
†○† *No meals.*

$ | ⊡ **Anegada Reef Hotel.** Head here if you want to bunk in comfortable
HOTEL | lodging near Anegada's most popular anchorage. **Pros:** everything
you need is nearby; nice sunsets. **Cons:** basic rooms; no beach; often
a party atmosphere at the bar. $ *Rooms from: $175* ⊠ *Setting Point*
☏ *284/495–8002* ⊕ *www.anegadareef.com* ⤴ *16 rooms* †○† *Multiple
meal plans.*

$$ | ⊡ **Cow Wreck Beach Resort.** The resort's best attribute is its location
RENTAL | Cow Wreck Beach. **Pros:** secluded location; great snorkeling. **Cons:**
the island's infamous, free-roaming livestock sometimes leave "presents" behind; location too remote for some. $ *Rooms from: $275*
⊠ *Cow Wreck Beach* ☏ *284/495–8047* ⊕ *www.cowwreckbeach.com*
⤴ *4 units.*

$ | ⊡ **Neptune's Treasure.** Basic waterfront rooms with simple furnishings
B&B/INN | and lovely views of the ocean are the hallmark of this family-owned
FAMILY | guesthouse. **Pros:** waterfront property; run by a family full of tales
of the island; nice sunset views. **Cons:** simple rooms; no kitchens;
no beach. $ *Rooms from: $150* ⊠ *Bender's Bay* ☏ *284/495–9439*
⊕ *www.neptunestreasure.com* ⤴ *9 rooms, 2 cottages* †○† *No meals.*

SPORTS AND ACTIVITIES

Anegada Reef Hotel. Call the hotel to arrange bonefishing and sportfishing outings with seasoned local guides. ⊠ *Setting Point* ☏ *284/495–
8002* ⊕ *www.anegadareef.com.*

Danny Vanterpool. Danny offers half-, three-quarter-, and full-day
bonefishing excursions around Anegada. The cost ranges from $350
for a half day to $550 for a full day. ☏ *284/441–6334* ⊕ *www.
dannysbonefishing.com.*

OTHER BRITISH VIRGIN ISLANDS

COOPER ISLAND

Updated by
Susan Zaluski

This small, hilly island on the south side of the Sir Francis Drake Channel, about 8 miles (13 km) from Road Town, Tortola, is popular with
the charter-boat crowd. There are no paved roads (which doesn't really
matter, as there aren't any cars), but you can find a beach restaurant,
a casual hotel, a few houses (some are available for rent), and great
snorkeling at the south end of Manchioneel Bay.

WHERE TO STAY

$$ ALL-INCLUSIVE Fodor's Choice ★ 🏨 **Cooper Island Beach Club.** Diving is the focus at this small resort, but folks who want to simply swim, snorkel, or relax can also feel right at home. **Pros:** lots of quiet; the Caribbean as it used to be. **Cons:** small rooms; island accessible only by ferry, and there is no nightlife. [$] *Rooms from: $225* ✉ *Manchioneel Bay* ☎ *284/495–9084, 800/542–4624* 🌐 *www.cooperislandbeachclub.com* 🛏 *9 rooms* 🍴 *All-inclusive.*

GUANA ISLAND

Guana Island sits off Tortola's northeast coast. Sailors often drop anchor at one of the island's bays for a day of snorkeling and sunning. The island is a designated wildlife sanctuary, and scientists often come here to study its flora and fauna. It's home to a back-to-nature resort that offers few activities other than relaxation. Unless you're a hotel guest or a sailor, there's no easy way to get here.

WHERE TO STAY

$$$$ RESORT Fodor's Choice ★ 🏨 **Guana Island Resort.** Here's a good resort if you want to stroll the hillsides, snorkel around the reefs, swim at its seven beaches, and still enjoy some degree of comfort. **Pros:** secluded feel; lovely grounds. **Cons:** very expensive; need boat to get here. [$] *Rooms from: $1250* ✉ *Guana Island* ☎ *284/494–2354, 800/544–8262* 🌐 *www.guana.com* 🛏 *15 rooms, 1 1-bedroom villa, 1 2-bedroom villa, 1 3-bedroom villa* 🍴 *All meals.*

CAYMAN ISLANDS

WELCOME TO CAYMAN ISLANDS

KEY

- Beaches
- Dive Sites

Caribbean Sea

LITTLE CAYMAN

Jacksons Pt.

Bloody Bay Wall

Anchorage Bay

Gov. Gore Bird Sanctuary

South Town

South Hole Sound

West End Point

Edward Bodden Airfield

Owen Island

Tarpoon Alley

Eagle Ray Pass

Head of Barkers

Stingray City

MARINE PARK
Rum Point

DISTANCE ON MAP IS COMPRESSED

Water Cay

Cayman Kai

Old Man Bay

A4

A3

West Bay

A1

North Sound

Booby Cay

HUTLAND

Malportas Pond

OLD MAN BAY

GRAND CAYMAN

PEASE BAY

BREAKERS

A4

HALF MOON BAY

A3

NORTH SOUND ESTATES

BELFORD ESTATES

A3

Pease Bay

Ironshore Point

NEWLANDS

SAVANNAH

A2

Bodden Bay

Southweat Point

A5

A2

Grand Cayman may be the world's largest offshore finance hub, but other offshore activities have put the Caymans on the map. Pristine waters, breathtaking coral formations, and plentiful and exotic marine creatures beckon divers from around the world. Other vacationers are drawn by the islands' mellow civility.

FUN ON AND OFF SHORE

Grand Cayman, which is 22 miles (36 km) long and 8 miles (13 km) wide, is the largest of the three low-lying islands that make up this British colony. Its sister islands (Little Cayman and Cayman Brac) are almost 90 miles (149 km) north and east. The Cayman Trough between the Cayman Islands and Jamaica is the deepest part of the Caribbean.

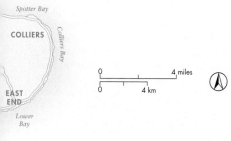

8

CAYMAN ISLANDS

TOP REASONS TO VISIT CAYMAN ISLANDS

1 **Diving:** Underwater visibility is among the best in the Caribbean, and nearby reefs are healthy.

2 **Safety and Comfort:** With no panhandlers, little crime, and top-notch accommodations, it's an easy place to vacation.

3 **Dining Scene:** The cosmopolitan population extends to the varied dining scene, from Italian to Indian.

4 **Fabulous Snorkeling:** A snorkeling trip to Stingray City is an experience you'll always remember.

5 **Beaches:** Grand Cayman's Seven Mile Beach is one of the Caribbean's best sandy beaches.

Updated by
Jordan Simon

This British Overseas Territory, which consists of Grand Cayman, smaller Cayman Brac, and Little Cayman, is one of the Caribbean's most popular destinations, particularly among Americans, who have become homeowners and constant visitors. The island's extensive array of banks also draws travelers.

Columbus is said to have sighted the islands in 1503 and dubbed them Las Tortugas after seeing so many turtles in the sea. The name was later changed to Cayman, referring to the caiman crocodiles that once roamed the islands. The Cayman Islands remained largely uninhabited until the late 1600s, when England seized them and Jamaica from Spain. Emigrants from England, Holland, Spain, and France arrived, as did refugees from the Spanish Inquisition and deserters from Oliver Cromwell's army in Jamaica; many brought slaves with them as well. The Cayman Islands' caves and coves were also perfect hideouts for the likes of Blackbeard, Sir Henry Morgan, and other pirates out to plunder Spanish galleons. Many ships fell afoul of the reefs surrounding the islands, often with the help of Caymanians, who lured vessels to shore with beacon fires.

Today's Cayman Islands are seasoned with suburban prosperity (particularly Grand Cayman, where residents joke that the national flower is the satellite dish) and stuffed with crowds (the hotels that line the famed Seven Mile Beach are often full, even in the slow summer season). Most of the 52,000 Cayman Islanders live on Grand Cayman, where the cost of living is at least 20% higher than in the United States, but you won't be hassled by panhandlers or fear walking around on a dark evening (the crime rate is very low). Add political and economic stability to the mix, and you have a fine island recipe indeed.

LOGISTICS

Getting to the Cayman Islands: There are plenty of nonstop flights to Grand Cayman (GCM) from the United States. Most people hop over to the Brac and Little Cayman (LYB) on a small plane from Grand Cayman; a weekly nonstop between the Brac and Miami was reinstated. Flights land at Owen Roberts Airport (Grand Cayman), Gerrard Smith Airport (Cayman Brac), or Edward Bodden Airstrip (Little Cayman).

Hassle Factor: Low for Grand Cayman; medium for Little Cayman and Cayman Brac.

On the Ground: In Grand Cayman you must take a taxi or rent a car at the airport, because most hotels are not permitted to offer airport shuttles. Hotel pickup is more readily available on Cayman Brac and Little Cayman.

Getting Around the Islands: It's possible to get by without a car on Grand Cayman if you are staying in the Seven Mile Beach area, where you could walk, take a local bus, or ride a bike. If you want to explore the rest of the island—or if you are staying elsewhere—you'll need a car. Though less necessary on Cayman Brac or Little Cayman, cars are available on both islands.

PLANNING

WHEN TO GO

High season begins in mid-December and continues through early to mid-April. During the low season you can often get a substantial discount of as much as 40%.

GETTING HERE AND AROUND

AIR TRAVEL

You can fly nonstop to Grand Cayman from Atlanta (Delta), Boston (US Airways, once weekly, JetBlue), Charlotte (US Airways), Chicago (Cayman Airways, twice weekly), Detroit (Delta, once weekly), Fort Lauderdale (Cayman Airways), Houston (Continental, once weekly), Miami (American, Cayman Airways), Minneapolis (Delta, once weekly), New York–JFK (Cayman Airways, JetBlue), New York–Newark (Continental, once weekly), Philadelphia (US Airways, once weekly), Tampa (Cayman Airways), and Washington, D.C. (Cayman Airways, twice weekly, and United).

Almost all nonstop air service is to Grand Cayman, with connecting flights on Cayman Airways Express to Cayman Brac and Little Cayman on a small propeller plane; there's also interisland charter-only service on Island Air. There is a once-weekly nonstop on Cayman Airways between Miami and Cayman Brac.

Airports Edward Bodden Airstrip (LYB). ✉ Little Cayman ☎ 345/948–0021. **Gerrard Smith International Airport** (CYB). ✉ Cayman Brac ☎ 345/948–1222. **Owen Roberts International Airport** (GCM). ✉ Grand Cayman ☎ 345/943–7070.

Airline Contacts American Airlines ☎ 345/949–0666. **Cayman Airways** ☎ 345/949–2311. **Delta** ☎ 345/945–8430. **JetBlue** ☎ 800/538–2583 ⊕ www.jetblue.com. **United** ☎ 345/916–5545. **US Airways** ☎ 345/949–7488.

8

BUS TRAVEL

On Grand Cayman, bus service—consisting of minivans marked "Omni Bus"—is efficient, inexpensive, and plentiful, running from 6 am to midnight (depending on route) roughly every 15 minutes in the Seven Mile Beach area and George Town with fares from CI$1.50 to CI$3.

CAR TRAVEL

Driving is easy on Grand Cayman, but there can be considerable traffic, especially during rush hour. One major road circumnavigates most of the island. Driving is on the left, British-style, and there are roundabouts. Speed limits are 30 mph (50 kph) in the country, 20 mph (30 kph) in town. There's much less traffic on Cayman Brac and even less on Little Cayman. Gas is expensive.

Car Rentals: You'll need a valid driver's license and a credit card to rent a car. Most agencies require renters to be between 21 and 70, though some require you to be 25. If you are over 75, you must have a certified doctor's note attesting to your ability. A local driver's permit, which costs $20, is obtained through the rental agencies. Rates can be expensive (from $45 to $95 per day), but usually include insurance.

Car-Rental Contacts (Grand Cayman) Ace Hertz ☎ 345/949–2280, 800/654–3131, 855/212–1713 toll-free. **Andy's Rent a Car** ☎ 345/949–8111, 855/691–3991 toll-free ⊕ www.andys.ky. **Avis** ☎ 345/949–2468 ⊕ www.aviscayman.com. **Budget** ☎ 345/949–5605 ⊕ www.budgetcayman.com. **Coconut Car Rentals** ☎ 345/949–7703, 800/941–4562 ⊕ www.coconut.ky. **Dollar** ☎ 345/949–4790 ⊕ www.dollarlac.com. **Economy** ☎ 345/949–9550 ⊕ www.economycarrental.com.ky. **Thrifty** ☎ 345/949–6640, 800/367–2277 ⊕ www.thrifty.com.

Car-Rental Contacts (Cayman Brac) B&S Motor Ventures ☎ 345/948–1646 ⊕ www.bandsmv.com. **CB Rent-a-Car** ☎ 345/948–2424, 345/948–2847 ⊕ www.cbrentacar.com. **Four D's Car Rental** ☎ 345/948–1599, 345/948–0459.

Car-Rental Contacts (Little Cayman) McLaughlin Rentals ☎ 345/948–1000 ✑ littlcay@candw.ky.

TAXI TRAVEL

On Grand Cayman, taxis operate 24 hours a day; if you anticipate a late night, however, make pickup arrangements in advance. You generally cannot hail a taxi on the street except occasionally in George Town. Fares are metered, and are not cheap, but basic fares include as many as three passengers. Taxis are scarcer on the Sister Islands; rates are fixed and fairly prohibitive. Your hotel will provide recommended drivers.

ESSENTIALS

Banks and Exchange Services You should not need to change money in Grand Cayman, since U.S. dollars are readily accepted. ATMs generally offer the option of U.S. or Cayman dollars. The Cayman dollar is pegged to the U.S. dollar at the rate of CI$1.25 to $1. Be sure you know which currency is being quoted when making a purchase.

Electricity Electricity is reliable and is the same as in the United States (110 volts/60 cycles).

Emergency Services Ambulance ☎ *911.* **Cayman Hyperbaric** ✉ *Hospital Rd., George Town, Grand Cayman* ☎ *345/949–2989.* **Fire** ☎ *911.* **Police** ☎ *911.*

Passport Requirements All visitors must have a valid passport and a return or ongoing ticket to enter the Cayman Islands. A birth certificate and photo ID are *not* sufficient proof of citizenship.

Phones The area code for the Cayman Islands is 345. To make local calls (on or between any of the three islands), dial the seven-digit number. Many international cell phones work in the Cayman Islands, though roaming charges can be significant. Mobile phone rental is available from LIME and Digicel, the two major providers; you can stay connected for as little as CI$5 per day plus the cost of a calling card (denominations range from CI$10 to CI$100). International per-minute rates usually range from CI35¢ to CI60¢.

Taxes At the airport, each adult passenger leaving Grand Cayman must pay a departure tax of $25 (CI$20), payable in cash. It's usually added to airfare—check with your carrier. A 10% government tax is added to all hotel bills. A 10% service charge is often added to hotel bills and restaurant checks in lieu of a tip.

Tipping At large hotels a service charge is generally included; smaller establishments and some villas and condos leave tipping up to you. Although tipping is customary at restaurants, note that some automatically include 15% on the bill—so check the tab carefully. Taxi drivers expect a 10% to 15% tip.

ACCOMMODATIONS

Grand Cayman draws the bulk of Cayman Island visitors. It's expensive during the high season but offers the widest range of resorts, restaurants, and activities both in and out of the water. Most resorts are on or near Seven Mile Beach, but a few are north in the West Bay Area, near Rum Point, or on the quiet East End. Both Little Cayman and Cayman Brac are more geared toward serving the needs of divers, who make up the majority of visitors. Beaches on the Sister Islands, as they are called, don't measure up (literally) to Grand Cayman's Seven Mile Beach. The smaller islands are cheaper than Grand Cayman, but with the extra cost of transportation, the overall savings are minimized.

HOTEL AND RESTAURANT PRICES

Prices in the restaurant reviews are the average cost of a main course at dinner or, if dinner is not served, at lunch; taxes and service charges are generally included. Prices in the hotel reviews are the lowest cost of a standard double room in high season, excluding taxes, service charges, and meal plans (except at all-inclusives). Prices for rentals are the lowest per-night cost for a one-bedroom unit in high season.

For expanded lodging reviews and current deals, visit Fodors.com.

VISITOR INFORMATION

Contacts Cayman Islands Department of Tourism ☎ *305/599–9033 in Miami, 847/678–6446 in Chicago, 212/889–9009 in New York City, 713/461–1317 in Houston, 877/422–9626, 345/949–0623* ⊕ *www.caymanislands.ky.*

8

WEDDINGS

Getting married in the Cayman Islands is a breeze. Documentation can be prepared ahead of time or in one day while on the island. There's no on-island waiting period. Larger resorts have on-site wedding coordinators.

GRAND CAYMAN

Grand Cayman has long been known for two offshore activities: banking (the new piracy, as locals joke) and scuba diving. With 296 banks, the capital, George Town, is relatively modern and usually bustles with activity, but never more so than when two to seven cruise ships are docked in the harbor, an increasingly common occurrence. Accountants in business clothes join thousands of vacationers in their tropical togs, jostling for tables at lunch. When they're not mingling in the myriad shops or getting pampered and pummeled in spas, vacationers delve into sparkling waters to snorkel and dive; increasingly, couples come to be married, or at least to enjoy their honeymoon.

The effects of recent devastating hurricanes such as Omar and Paloma, both in 2008, are visible only in the mangrove swamps and interior savanna. There is a lot of new construction and plenty of traffic, so check with a local to plan driving time. It can take 45 minutes during rush hours to go 8 miles (13 km).

EXPLORING

The historic capital of George Town, on the southwest corner of Grand Cayman, is easy to explore on foot. If you're a shopper, you can spend days here; otherwise, an hour will suffice for a tour of the downtown area. To see the rest of the island, rent a car or scooter or take a guided tour. The portion of the island called West Bay is noted for its jumble of neighborhoods and a few attractions. When traffic is heavy, it's about a half hour to West Bay from George Town, but the opening of a new bypass road that runs parallel to West Bay Road has made the journey easier. The less-developed East End has natural attractions from blowholes to botanical gardens, as well as the remains of the island's original settlements. Plan at least 45 minutes for the drive out from George Town (more during rush hours). You need a day to explore the entire island—including a stop at a beach for a picnic or swim.

GEORGE TOWN

Begin exploring the capital by strolling along the waterfront Harbour Drive to **Elmslie Memorial United Church,** named after the first Presbyterian missionary to serve in Cayman. Its vaulted ceiling, wooden arches, and sedate nave reflect the religious nature of island residents. In front of the court building, in the center of town, names of influential Caymanians are inscribed on the **Wall of History,** which commemorates the islands' quincentennial in 2003. Across the street is the **Cayman Islands Legislative Assembly Building,** next door to the **1919 Peace Memorial Building.** In the middle of the financial district is the **General Post Office,** built in 1939. Let the kids pet the big blue iguana statues.

Cayman Turtle Farm, Grand Cayman

WORTH NOTING

FAMILY
Fodor's Choice
★

Cayman Islands National Museum. Built in 1833, the historically significant clapboard home of the national museum has had several different
incarnations over the years, serving as courthouse, jail, post office, and
dance hall. It features an ongoing archaeological excavation of the Old
Gaol and excellent 3-D bathymetric displays, murals, dioramas, and
videos that illustrate local geology, flora and fauna, and island history.
The first floor focuses on natural history, including a microcosm of
Cayman ecosystems, from beaches to dry woodlands and swamps, and
offers such interactive elements as a simulated sub. Upstairs, the cultural
exhibit features renovated murals, video history reenactments, and 3-D
back panels in display cases holding thousands of artifacts ranging from
a 14-foot catboat with an animatronic captain to old coins and rare
documents painting a portrait of daily life and past industries such as
shipbuilding and turtling, stressing Caymanians' resilience when they
had little contact with the outside world. There are also temporary
exhibits focusing on aspects of Caymanian culture, a local art collection, and interactive displays for kids. ⊠ *Harbour Dr.* ☎ *345/949–8368*
⊕ *www.museum.ky* ☎ *$8, $5.60 Sat.* ☉ *Weekdays 9–5, Sat. 10–2.*

Fodor's Choice
★

National Gallery. A worthy nonprofit organization, this museum displays and promotes the range of Caymanian artists and craftspeople,
both established and grassroots. The gallery coordinates a wealth of
first-rate outreach programs for everyone from infants to inmates. It
usually mounts six major exhibitions a year, including three large-scale
retrospectives or thematic shows and multimedia installations. Director Natalie Urquhart also brings in international shows that somehow
relate to the island, often inviting local artists for stimulating dialogue.

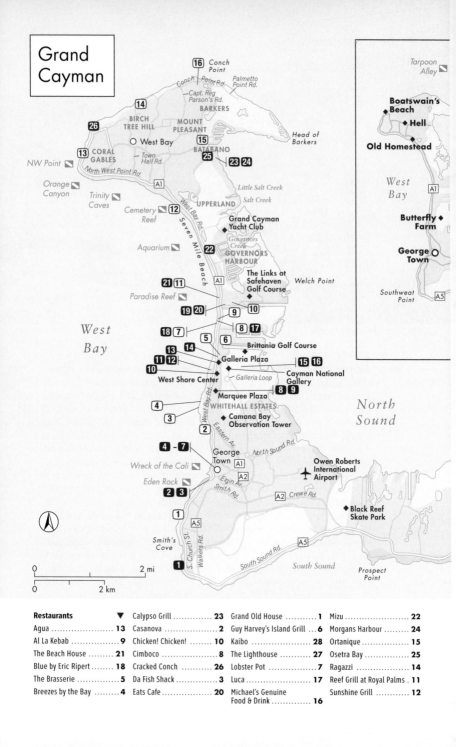

Grand Cayman

Conch Point

Palmetto Point Rd.

Conch Point Rd.

Capt. Reg Parson's Rd.

BARKERS

BIRCH TREE HILL

MOUNT PLEASANT

West Bay

BATABANO

Town Hall Rd.

CORAL GABLES

North West Point Rd.

NW Point

Orange Canyon

Trinity Caves

Cemetery Reef

UPPERLAND

Little Salt Creek

Salt Creek

Grand Cayman Yacht Club

Governors Creek

Aquarium

GOVERNORS HARBOUR

Seven Mile Beach

West Bay Rd.

The Links at Safehaven Golf Course

Welch Point

Paradise Reef

West Bay

Brittania Golf Course

Galleria Plaza

West Shore Center

Galleria Loop

Cayman National Gallery

North Sound

Marquee Plaza

WHITEHALL ESTATES

West Bay Rd.

Eastern Av.

Camana Bay Observation Tower

George Town

Wreck of the Cali

Eden Rock

North Sound Rd.

Owen Roberts International Airport

Elgin Av.

Smith Rd.

Crewe Rd.

Black Reef Skate Park

Smith's Cove

S. Church St.

Walkers Rd.

South Sound Rd.

South Sound

Prospect Point

Tarpoon Alley

Boatswain's Beach

Hell

Old Homestead

West Bay

Butterfly Farm

George Town

Southweat Point

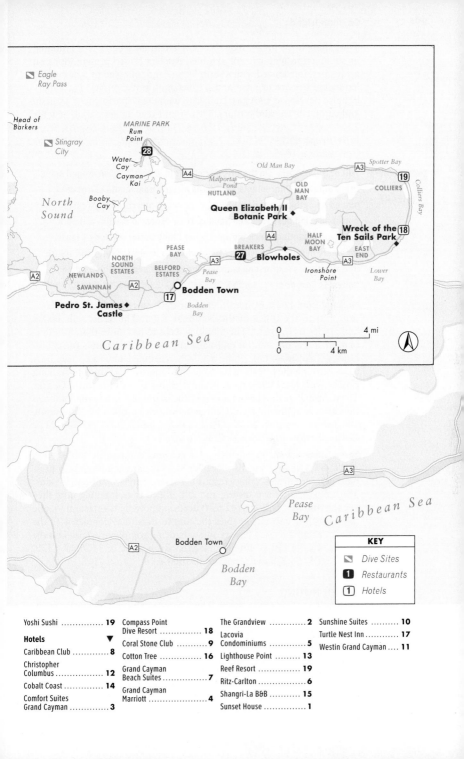

Eagle
Ray Pass

Head of
Barkers

Stingray
City

*North
Sound*

MARINE PARK
Rum
Point

28

Water
Cay
Cayman
Kai

Booby
Cay

A4

*Malportas
Pond*
HUTLAND

Old Man Bay

OLD
MAN
BAY

Spotter Bay

A3

19

COLLIERS

Colliers Bay

**Queen Elizabeth II
Botanic Park** ◆

**Wreck of the
Ten Sails Park**

18

NORTH
SOUND
ESTATES

PEASE
BAY

BELFORD
ESTATES

BREAKERS

27 **Blowholes** ◆

HALF
MOON
BAY

EAST
END

A3

A2

NEWLANDS

SAVANNAH

A2

A3

*Pease
Bay*

17

○ **Bodden Town**

*Ironshore
Point*

*Lower
Bay*

**Pedro St. James
Castle** ◆

*Bodden
Bay*

A4

Caribbean Sea

0   4 mi

0   4 km

A3

*Pease
Bay*

Caribbean Sea

A2

Bodden Town ○

*Bodden
Bay*

KEY

◣ *Dive Sites*

1 *Restaurants*

1 *Hotels*

The gallery hosts public slide shows, a lunchtime lecture series running in conjunction with current exhibits, Art Flix (video presentations on art history, introduced with a short lecture and followed by a discussion led by curators or artists), and a CineClub (movie night). The gallery has also developed an Artist Trail Map with the Department of Tourism and can facilitate studio tours. There's an excellent shop and, new for 2014, an Art Cafe. ⊠ *Esterly Tibbetts Hwy. at Harquail Bypass, Seven Mile Beach* ☎ *345/945–8111* ⊕ *www.nationalgallery.org.ky* ⊠ *Free* ⊙ *Weekdays 10–5, Sat. 10–3.*

NEED A BREAK?

Full of Beans Cafe. On the surprisingly large, eclectic, Asian-tinged menu using ultrafresh ingredients, standouts include homemade carrot cake, mango smoothies, cranberry-Brie-pecan salad, and rosemary-roasted portobello and pesto chicken paninis. Their espresso martini will perk up anyone wanting a pick-me-up. Owner Cindy Butler fashions a feast for weary eyes as well, with rotating artworks (many for sale) and stylish mosaic mirrors contrasting with faux-brick walls and vintage hardwood tables. ⊠ *Pasadora Pl., Smith Rd.* ☎ *345/943–2326, 345/814–0157.*

National Trust. For a wonderful map of the historic and natural attractions, go to the office of the National Trust. The Trust sells books and guides to Cayman. The fabulous website has more than 50 information sheets on cultural and natural topics from iguanas to schoolhouses. Take advantage of the regularly scheduled activities, from boat tours through the forests of the Central Mangrove Wetlands to cooking classes with local chefs to morning walking tours of historic George Town. Stop here first before you tour the island. Be forewarned: though the office is walkable from George Town, it's an often-hot 20-minute hike from downtown. ⊠ *Dart Park, 558 S. Church St.* ☎ *345/749–1121* ⊕ *www.nationaltrust.org.ky* ⊙ *Weekdays 9–5.*

Seven Fathoms Rum. Surprisingly, this growing company, established in 2008, is Cayman's first distillery. It's already garnered medals in prestigious international competitions for its artisanal small-batch rums. You can stop by for a tasting and self-guided tour, learning how they age the rum at 7 fathoms (42 feet) deep; supposedly the natural kinetic motion of the currents enables the rum to maximize contact with the oak, extracting its rich flavors and enhancing complexity. Based on the results, it's not just yo-ho-hokum. ⊠ *65 Bronze Rd.* ☎ *345/925–5379, 345/926–8186* ⊕ *www.sevenfathomsrum.com.*

SEVEN MILE BEACH

WORTH NOTING

FAMILY **Camana Bay Observation Tower.** This 75-foot structure provides striking 360-degree panoramas of otherwise flat Grand Cayman, sweeping from George Town and Seven Mile Beach to the North Sound. The double-helix staircase is impressive in its own right. Running alongside the steps (though an elevator is also available), a floor-to-ceiling mosaic replicates the look and feel of a dive from seabed to surface. Constructed of countless tiles in 114 different colors, it's one of the world's largest marine-themed mosaic installations. Benches and lookout points encourage you to take your time and take in the views as you ascend. Afterward you can enjoy 500-acre Camana Bay's gardens, waterfront boardwalk, and pedestrian paths lined with shops and restaurants, or frequent live entertainment. ⊠ *Extending between Seven Mile Beach and North Sound, 2 miles (3 km) north of George Town, Camana Bay* ☏ *345/640–3500* ⊕ *www.camanabay.com* ⊡ *Free* ☉ *Sunrise–10 pm.*

WEST BAY

WORTH NOTING

Cayman Motor Museum. This unexpected collection documents the magnificent obsession of one man, Norwegian magnate Andreas Ugland. More than 80 vehicles, preening like supermodels, gleam in ranks. "Holy hot-rod, Batman," it's one of the three original Batmobiles from the 1960's TV series. There's the world's first produced auto, an 1886 Benz! Tiers of classic Ferraris, Jags, Corvettes, BMWs, and more date back nearly a century, including such unique collectibles as Elton John's Bentley, the 1930 Phantom driven in the film *Yellow Rolls Royce*, and Queen Elizabeth II's first limo. You can go hog wild over Harleys and other bad-ass bikes. And well, just because, coffee grinders. This isn't actually mere kitchen kitsch: Peugeot started producing mills and grinders in the mid-19th century. An avid sailor, Mr. Ugland wants to start a boat museum as well. That might be fun but it likely won't capture the unlikely charm of this Cayman oddity. ⊠ *864 Northwest Point Rd., West Bay* ☏ *345/947–7741* ⊕ *www.caymanmotormuseum.com* ⊡ *$15* ☉ *Mon.–Sat. 9–5* ☉ *Closed Sun.*

FAMILY **Cayman Turtle Farm.** Cayman's premier attraction, the Turtle Farm, has been transformed into a marine theme park. The expanded complex now has several souvenir shops and restaurants. Still, the turtles remain a central attraction, and you can tour ponds in the original research–breeding facility with thousands in various stages of growth, some up to 600 pounds and more than 70 years old. Turtles can be picked up from the tanks, a real treat for children and adults as the little creatures flap their fins and splash the water. Four areas—three aquatic and one dry—cover 23 acres; different-color bracelets determine access (the steep full-pass admission includes snorkeling gear). The park helps promote conservation, encouraging interaction (a tidal pool houses invertebrates such as starfish and crabs) and observation. Animal Program events include Keeper Talks, where you might feed birds or iguanas, and biologists speaking about conservation and their importance to the ecosystem. The freshwater **Breaker's Lagoon,** replete with cascades plunging over moss-carpeted rocks evoking Cayman Brac, is the islands' largest pool. The saltwater **Boatswain's Lagoon,** replicating all the Cayman Islands and the Trench, teems with 14,000 denizens of the deep milling about a cannily designed synthetic reef. You can snorkel here (lessons and guided tours are available). Both lagoons have underwater 4-inch-thick acrylic panels that look directly into **Predator Reef,** home to six brown sharks, four nurse sharks, and other predatory fish such as tarpons, eels, and jacks. These predators can also be viewed from terra (or terror, as one guide jokes) firma. Make sure you check out feeding times! The free-flight

Aviary, designed by consultants from Disney's Animal Kingdom, is a riot of color and noise as feathered friends represent the entire Caribbean basin, doubling as a rehabilitation center for Cayman Wildlife and Rescue. A winding interpretive **nature trail** culminates in the Blue Hole, a collapsed cave once filled with water. Audio tours are available with different focuses, from butterflies to bush medicine. The last stop is the living museum, **Cayman Street**, complete with facades duplicating different types of vernacular architecture; an herb and fruit garden; porch-side artisans, musicians, and storytellers; model catboats; live cooking on an old-fashioned caboose (outside kitchen) oven; and interactive craft demonstrations from painting mahogany to thatch weaving. ⊠ *825 Northwest Point Rd., Box 812, West Bay* ☎ *345/949– 3894* ⊕ *www.turtle.ky, www.boatswainsbeach.ky* ⬛ *Comprehensive ticket $45 ($25 children under 12); Turtle Farm only, $30* ⊘ *Mon.– Sat. 8–4:30, Sun. 10–4. Lagoons close ½ hr to 2 hrs earlier.*

FAMILY **Dolphin Discovery.** If you ever dreamed of frolicking with Flipper, here's your (photo) opportunity, as the organizers of this global business promise a "touching experience." The well-maintained facility, certified by the Alliance of Marine Mammal Parks and Aquariums, offers three main options, essentially depending on time spent splashing in the enormous pool with the dolphins and stingrays. They range in price from $99 to $169 (kids receive a discount but must swim with an adult). The premium is the Royal Swim, which includes a dorsal tow and foot push, showcasing the amazing strength, speed, and agility of these majestic marine mammals. Other options offer a handshake, kiss, even a belly ride. All participants receive free entrance to their choice of Stingray City or the Turtle Farm across the street, taking some of the sting out of the high prices. ⊠ *Northwest Point Rd., West Bay* ☎ *345/769–7946, 866/393–5158 toll-free from U.S., 345/949–7946* ⊕ *www.dolphindiscovery.com/grand-cayman.*

Hell. Quite literally the tourist trap from Hell, especially when overrun by cruise-ship passengers, this attraction does offer free admission, fun photo ops, and sublime surrealism. Its name refers to the quarter-acre of menacing shards of charred brimstone thrusting up like vengeful spirits (actually blackened and "sculpted" by acid-secreting algae and fungi over millennia). The eerie lunarscape is now cordoned off, but you can prove you had a helluva time by taking a photo from the observation deck. The attractions are the small post office and a gift shop where you can get cards and letters postmarked from Hell, not to mention wonderfully silly postcards titled "When Hell Freezes Over" (depicting bathing beauties on the beach), "The Devil Made Me Do It" bumper stickers, Scotch bonnet–based Hell sauce, and "The coolest shop in Hell" T-shirts. Ivan Farrington, the owner of the Devil's Hang-Out store, cavorts in a devil's costume (horn, cape, and tails), regaling you with demonically bad jokes. ⊠ *Hell Rd., West Bay* ☎ *345/949–3358* ⬛ *Free* ⊘ *Daily 9–6.*

NORTH SIDE
WORTH NOTING

Fodor'sChoice
★

Queen Elizabeth II Botanic Park. This 65-acre wilderness preserve showcases a wide range of indigenous and nonindigenous tropical vegetation, approximately 2,000 species in total. Splendid sections include numerous water features from limpid lily ponds to cascades; a Heritage Garden with a traditional cottage and "caboose" (outside kitchen) that includes crops that might have been planted on Cayman a century ago; and a Floral Colour Garden arranged by color, the walkway wandering through sections of pink, red, orange, yellow, white, blue, mauve, lavender, and purple. A 2-acre lake and adjacent wetlands includes three islets that provide a habitat and breeding ground for native birds just as showy as the floral displays: green herons, black-necked stilts, American coots, blue-winged teal, cattle egrets, and rare West Indian whistling ducks. The nearly mile-long Woodland Trail encompasses every Cayman ecosystem from wetland to cactus thicket, buttonwood swamp to lofty woodland with imposing mahogany trees. You'll encounter birds, lizards, turtles, agoutis, and more, but the park's star residents are the protected endemic blue iguanas, found only in Grand Cayman. The world's most endangered iguana, they're the focus of the National Trust's Blue Iguana Recovery Program, a captive breeding and reintroduction facility. This section of the park is usually closed to the general public, though released "blue dragons" hang out in the vicinity. The Trust conducts 90-minute behind-the-scenes safaris Monday–Saturday at 11 am for $30. ⊠ *367 Botanic Rd.* ☎ *345/947–9462* ⊕ *www.botanic-park.ky* ⊠ *$10; ages 12 and under free with parent* ☉ *Daily 9–5:30; last admission 1 hr before closing.*

BODDEN TOWN
WORTH NOTING

In the island's original south-shore capital you can find an old cemetery on the shore side of the road. Graves with A-frame structures are said to contain the remains of pirates. There are also the ruins of a fort and a wall erected by slaves in the 19th century. The National Trust runs tours of the restored 1840s Mission House. A curio shop serves as the entrance to what's called the Pirate's Caves ($8), partially underground natural formations that are more hokey (decked out with fake treasure chests and mannequins in pirate garb, with an outdoor petting zoo) than spooky.

Fodor'sChoice
★

Pedro St. James Castle. Built in 1780, the greathouse is Cayman's oldest stone structure and the only remaining late-18th-century residence on the island. In its capacity as courthouse and jail, it was the birthplace of Caymanian democracy, where in December 1831 the first elected parliament was organized and in 1835 the Slavery Abolition Act signed. The structure still has original or historically accurate replicas of sweeping verandahs, mahogany floors, rough-hewn wide-beam ceilings, outside louvers, stone and oxblood- or mustard-color limewash-painted walls, brass fixtures, and Georgian furnishings (from tea caddies to canopy beds to commodes). Paying obsessive attention to detail, the curators even fill glasses with faux wine. The mini-museum also includes a hodgepodge of displays from slave emancipation to old stamps. The buildings are surrounded by 8 acres of natural parks and woodlands. You can stroll through landscaping of native Caymanian flora and experience one of the most spectacular views on the island from atop the dramatic Great Pedro Bluff. First watch the impressive multimedia theater show, complete with smoking pots, misting rains, and two film screens where the story of Pedro's Castle is presented on the hour. The poignant Hurricane Ivan Memorial outside uses text, images, and symbols to represent important aspects of that horrific 2004 natural disaster. ⊠ *Pedro Castle Rd., Savannah* ☎ *345/947–3329* ⊕ *www.pedrostjames.ky* ⊒ *$10* ⊙ *Daily 9–5.*

EAST END

WORTH NOTING

FAMILY **Blowholes.** When the easterly trade winds blow hard, crashing waves force water into caverns and send impressive geysers shooting up as much as 20 feet through the ironshore. The blowholes were partially filled during Hurricane Ivan in 2004, so the water must be rough to recapture their former elemental drama. ⊠ *Frank Sound Rd., roughly 10 miles (16 km) east of Bodden Town, near East End.*

Cayman Islands Brewery. This brewery occupies the former Stingray facility; free tours are available on the hour (weekdays from 9 to 4 by appointment only). The guide will explain the iconic imagery of the bottle and label, and the nearly three-week process: seven days' fermentation, 10 days' lagering (storage), and one day in the bottling tank. The brewery's ecofriendly features are also championed: local farmers receive the spent grains used to produce the beer to serve as cattle feed at no charge, while waste liquid is channeled into one of the Caribbean's most advanced water-treatment systems. Then enjoy your complimentary tasting with the knowledge that you're helping the local environment and economy. ⊠ *366 Shamrock Rd., Red Bay* ☎ *345/947–6699* ⊕ *www.cib.ky* ⊒ *Free* ⊙ *Weekdays 9–5.*

Wreck of the Ten Sails Park. This lonely, lovely park on Grand Cayman's windswept eastern tip commemorates the island's most (in)famous shipwreck. On February 8, 1794, the *Cordelia,* heading a convoy of 58 square-rigged merchant vessels en route from Jamaica to England, foundered on one of the treacherous East End reefs. Its warning cannon fire was tragically misconstrued as a call to band more closely together due to imminent pirate attack, and nine more ships ran aground. The local sailors, who knew those rough seas, demonstrated great bravery in rescuing all 400-odd seamen. Popular legend claims (romantically but inaccurately) that King George III granted the islands an eternal tax exemption. Queen Elizabeth II dedicated the park's plaque in 1994. Interpretive signs document the historic details. The ironically peaceful headland provides magnificent views of the reef (including more recent shipwrecks); bird-watching is superb from here half a mile south along the coast to the Lighthouse Park, perched on a craggy bluff. ⊠ *Gun Bay, East End* ☎ *345/949–0121 (National Trust)* ⊒ *Free* ⊙ *Daily.*

BEACHES

Limestone, coral, shells, water, and wind collaborated to fashion the Cayman Islands beaches. It's a classic example of the interaction between geology and marine biology. Most of the beaches in Cayman, especially on Grand and Little Cayman, resemble powdered ivory. A few, including those on Cayman Brac, are more dramatic, a mix of fine beige sand and rugged rocky "ironshore," which often signals the healthiest reefs and best snorkeling.

Barkers. A series of secluded, spectacular beaches are accessed via a dirt road just past Papagallo restaurant. There are no facilities (that's the point!), but some palms offer shade. Unfortunately, the shallow water and rocky bottom discourage swimming, and it can be cluttered at times with seaweed and debris. Kitesurfers occasionally come here for the gusts. **Amenities:** none. **Best for:** solitude; walking; windsurfing. ⊠ *Conch Point Rd., Barkers, West Bay.*

East End Beaches. Just drive along and look for any sandy beach, park your car, and enjoy a stroll. The vanilla-hue stretch at Colliers Bay, by the Reef and Morritt's resorts, is a good, clean one with superior snorkeling. **Amenities:** food and drink; water sports. **Best for:** snorkeling; solitude; sunrise; walking. ⊠ *Queen's Hwy., East End.*

Old Man Bay. The North Side features plenty of hidden coves and pristine stretches of perfect sand, where you'll be disturbed only by seabirds dive-bombing for lunch and the occasional lone fishers casting nets for sprats, then dumping them into buckets. This area is easily accessed off Frank Sound Road. Over the Edge restaurant is less than 1 mile (1½ km) west. Otherwise, it's fairly undeveloped for miles, save for the occasional private home. Snorkeling is spectacular when waters are calm. **Amenities:** food and drink. **Best for:** snorkeling; solitude; walking. ⊠ *Queen's Hwy., just off Frank Sound Rd., North Side.*

Rum Point. This North Sound beach has hammocks slung in towering casuarina trees, picnic tables, casual and "fancier" dining options, well-stocked shop for seaworthy sundries, and Red Sail Sports, which offers various water sports and boats to explore Stingray City. The barrier reef ensures safe snorkeling and soft sand. The bottom remains shallow for a long way from shore, but it's littered with small coral heads, so kids be careful. The Wreck is an ultracasual hangout serving outstanding pub grub from fish-and-chips to wings, as well as lethal Mudslide cocktails. Just around the bend, another quintessential beach hangout, Kaibo, rocks during the day. **Amenities:** food and drink; parking; toilets; showers; water sports. **Best for:** partiers; snorkeling. ⊠ *Rum Point, North Side.*

Fodor's Choice ★ **Seven Mile Beach.** Grand Cayman's west coast is dominated by the famous Seven Mile Beach—actually a 6½-mile-long (10-km-long) expanse of powdery white sand overseeing lapis water stippled with a rainbow of parasails and kayaks. Free of litter and pesky peddlers, it's an unspoiled (though often crowded) environment. Most of the island's resorts, restaurants, and shopping centers sit along this strip. The public beach toward the north end offers chairs for rent ($10 for the day, including a beverage), a playground, water toys aplenty, beach bars, restrooms,

8

and showers. The best snorkeling is at either end, by the Marriott and Treasure Island or off the northern section called Cemetery Reef Beach. **Amenities:** food and drink; parking; showers; toilets; water sports. **Best for:** partiers; snorkeling. ⊠ *West Bay Rd., Seven Mile Beach.*

Smith's Cove. South of the Grand Old House, this tiny but popular protected swimming and snorkeling spot makes a wonderful beach wedding location. The bottom drops off quickly enough to allow you to swim and play close to shore. Although slightly rocky (its pitted limestone boulders resemble Moore sculptures), there's little debris and few coral heads, plenty of shade, picnic tables, restrooms, and parking. Surfers will find decent swells just to the south. Note the curious obelisk cenotaph "In memory of James Samuel Webster and his wife Arabella Antoinette (née Eden)," with assorted quotes from Confucius to John Donne. **Amenities:** parking; toilets. **Best for:** snorkeling; sunset; swimming. ⊠ *Off S. Church St.*

South Sound Cemetery Beach. A narrow, sandy driveway takes you past the small cemetery to a perfect beach. The dock here is primarily used by dive boats during winter storms. You can walk in either direction; the sand is talcum-soft and clean, the water calm and clear (though local surfers take advantage of occasional small reef breaks; if wading, wear reef shoes, since the bottom is somewhat rocky and dotted with sea urchins). You'll definitely find fewer crowds. **Amenities:** none. **Best for:** solitude; surfing. ⊠ *S. Sound Rd., Prospect.*

WHERE TO EAT

Despite its small size, comparative geographic isolation, and British colonial trappings, Grand Cayman offers a smorgasbord of gastronomic goodies. With more than 100 eateries, something should suit and sate every palate and pocketbook (factoring in the fast-food franchises sweeping the islandscape like tumbleweed, and stands dispensing local specialties). The term *melting pot* describes both the majority of menus and the multicultural population. The sheer range of dining options from Middle Eastern to Mexican reflects the island's cosmopolitan clientele. Imported ingredients make up their own United Nations, with chefs sourcing salmon from Norway, foie gras from Périgord, and lamb from New Zealand. Wine lists can be equally global in scope. And don't be surprised to find both Czech and Chilean staffers at a remote East End restaurant. As one restaurateur quipped, "Cayman is the ultimate culture-shock absorber."

Prices are about 25% more than those in a major U.S. city. Many restaurants add a 10% to 15% service charge to the bill; be sure to check before leaving a tip. Alcohol with your meal can send the tab skyrocketing. Buy liquor duty-free before you leave the airport and enjoy a cocktail or nightcap from the comfort of your room or balcony. Cayman customs limits you to two bottles per person. You should make reservations at all but the most casual places, particularly during the high season. Note that many bars offer fine fare (and many eateries have hip, hopping bar scenes).

What to Wear: Grand Cayman dining is casual (shorts are okay, but *not* beachwear and tank tops). Mosquitoes can be pesky when you are dining outdoors, especially at sunset, so plan ahead or ask for repellent. Winter can be chilly enough to warrant a light sweater.

AROUND GEORGE TOWN

$$$

ECLECTIC

✕ **The Brasserie.** Actuaries, bankers, and CEOs frequent this contemporary throwback to a colonial country club for lunch and "attitude adjustment" happy hours for creative cocktails and complimentary canapés. Inviting fusion cuisine, emphasizing local ingredients whenever possible (the restaurant even has its own boat and garden), includes terrific bar tapas like chipotle-braised oxtail taco with pepper aioli and pickled vegetables, or melted Brie with white truffle–and-mango marmalade. Several evenings, you can get a five- or eight-course market-driven "Random Acts of Cooking" blind tasting. Dishes deftly balance flavors and textures without sensory overload: this is serious food with a sense of playfulness. Save room for desserts, from an artisanal cheese plate to an ice-cream-and-sorbet tasting menu to elaborate architectural confections. Lunch is more reasonably priced but equally creative; the adjacent Market excels at takeout, and the wine list is well considered. Ⓢ *Average main: $34* ✉ *171 Elgin Ave., Cricket Sq.* ☎ *345/945–1815* ⊕ *www.brasseriecayman.com* ⌲ *Reservations essential* ⊘ *Closed weekends.*

$$

CARIBBEAN

✕ **Breezes by the Bay.** There isn't a bad seat in the house at this nonstop fiesta festooned with tiny paper lanterns, Christmas lights, ship murals, model boats, and Mardi Gras beads (you're "lei'd" upon entering). Wraparound balconies take in a dazzling panorama from South Sound to Seven Mile Beach. It's happy hour all day every day, especially during Countdown to Sunset. Signs promise "the good kind of hurricanes," referring to the 23-ounce signature "category 15" cocktails with fresh garnishes. Chunky, velvety conch chowder served in a bread bowl or conch fritters are meals in themselves. Hefty sandwiches are slathered with jerk mayo or garlic aioli. Signature standouts include meltingly moist whole fish escoveitch, popcorn shrimp, sliders, and any pie from the pizza station. Ⓢ *Average main: $18* ✉ *Harbor Dr.* ☎ *345/943–8439* ⊕ *www.breezesbythebay.com.*

$$$

ITALIAN

✕ **Casanova Restaurant by the Sea.** Owner Tony Crescente and younger brother–maître d' Carlo offer a genuinely simpatico dining experience, practically exhorting you to *mangia,* and sending you off with a chorus of ciaos. The kitchen serves sterling Italian favorites like salmon marinated in citrus, olive oil, and basil; lemony veal piccata;

BEST BETS FOR DINING

Fodor's Choice ★

Agua, Blue by Eric Ripert, Grand Old House, Luca, Michael's Genuine Food and Drink, Ortanique, Ragazzi, Mizu

BEST VIEW

Cracked Conch, Reef Grill at Royal Palms

MOST ROMANTIC

Grand Old House

BEST FOR LOCAL CUISINE

Chicken! Chicken!, Cimboco, Over the Edge, Vivine's Kitchen

HOT SPOTS

Agua, Guy Harvey's Island Grill, Luca, Mizu, Ragazzi, Yoshi Sushi

8

gnocchetti in velvety four-cheese sauce with a blush of tomato; or seafood grill in parsley-garlic-lemon sauce. Enjoy grappa at the marble bar of Il Bacio lounge, which is lined with wooden wine racks (the impressive selection isn't overly Italian-centric). The patio juts over the harbor; the moonlight (abetted by a soundtrack of Bocelli to Bennett) would transform any amorous coward into a Casanova. [$] *Average main: $31* ✉ *65 N. Church St.* ☎ *345/949–7633* 🌐 *www.casanova.ky* ✍ *Reservations essential.*

$$ SEAFOOD 🍴 **Da Fish Shack.** This classic clapboard seaside shanty couldn't be homier: constructed from an old fishing vessel, the structure is an authentic representation of original Caymanian architecture. The deck couldn't be better placed to savor the breezes and water views, and the chill Caribbean vibe makes it feel like you're dining at a friend's home. The owners source fresh local ingredients wherever possible and developed relationships with Caymanian fishermen, who often cruise up to the dock with their catch. Savor jerk fish tacos, saltfish fritters, coconut shrimp with pineapple tomato salsa, and golden crunchy breadfruit fries. A wide array of nonseafood dishes are offered, from chicken schnitzel to a rib eye with sauce chasseur. The place hops on "Sundown Saturdays" with a CI$20 waterfront barbecue. Free Wi-Fi and occasional DJs are bonuses. [$] *Average main: $16* ✉ *127 N. Church St., George Town, Grand Cayman* ☎ *345/947–8126* 🌐 *www.dafishshack.com.*

$$$$ EUROPEAN Fodor's Choice ★ 🍴 **Grand Old House.** Built in 1908 as the Petra Plantation House and transformed into the island's first upscale establishment decades ago, this grande dame is that rare restaurant that evokes bygone grandeur sans pretension. The interior rooms, awash in crystal, recall its plantation-house origins. Outside, hundreds of sparkling lights adorn the gazebos to compete with the starry sky. Live nightly music and rumors of a charming blond ghost trailing white chiffon complete the picture: this is a place to propose. You'll find expertly executed classics such as pan-fried foie gras with ice wine raspberry compote, broiled lobster tail with smoked bell-pepper butter, or filet mignon with green peppercorn sauce. The subtle yet complex flavor interactions, stellar service, and encyclopedic if stratospherically priced wine list ensure legendary landmark status. Nightly happy hours with discounted tapas are a sensational bargain. [$] *Average main: $56* ✉ *648 S. Church St.* ☎ *345/949–9333* 🌐 *www.grandoldhouse.com* ✍ *Reservations essential* ⏲ *Closed Sept. Closed Sun. in low season. No lunch weekends.*

$$$ SEAFOOD 🍴 **Guy Harvey's Island Grill.** At this stylish, sporty, upstairs bistro you half expect to find Hemingway regaling fellow barflies in the clubby interior with mahogany furnishings, ship's lanterns, porthole windows, fishing rods, and Harvey's action-packed marine art. The cool blues echo the sea and sky on display from the balcony. Seafood is carefully chosen to exclude overexploited and threatened species. Seasonally changing dishes are peppered with Caribbean influences but pureed through the French chef's formal training. Hence, silken lobster bisque is served with puff pastry, scallops Rockefeller with spinach and béarnaise sauce, and the signature crab cakes with roasted-red-pepper aioli. You can select your fish baked, pan-sautéed, or grilled with any of eight sauces.

Carnivores needn't despair, with rack of lamb Provençal in balsamic glaze or an intensely flavored filet mignon Roquefort (frites optional). Many specialties are cheaper at lunch. Nightly specials for CI$9.99 and the four-course CI$30 dinner reel in savvy locals. $ *Average main: $40* ✉ *Aquaworld Duty-Free Mall, 55 S. Church St.* ☎ *345/946–9000* ⊕ *www.guyharveysgrill.com.*

$$$$
SEAFOOD ✕ **Lobster Pot.** The nondescript building belies the lovely marine-motif decor and luscious seafood at the intimate, second-story restaurant overlooking the harbor. Enjoy lobster prepared several ways along with reasonably priced wine, which you can sample by the glass in the cozy bar. The two musts are the Cayman Trio (lobster tail, grilled mahimahi, and garlic shrimp), and the Pot (lobster, giant prawns, and crab). The kitchen happily provides reduced-oil and -fat alternatives to most dishes; vegetarians love such flavorful selections as chili-lime polenta with grilled artichoke in mango cream and roasted pumpkin, garlic, and thyme risotto. The recently enlarged balcony offers a breathtaking view of the sunset tarpon feeding. Lobster is market price and can be as much as $60; other entrées are less expensive. $ *Average main: $45* ✉ *245 N. Church St.* ☎ *345/949–2736* ⊕ *www.lobsterpot. ky* ◷ *No lunch Sat.*

SEVEN MILE BEACH

$$$$
ITALIAN
Fodor's Choice
★
✕ **Agua.** This quietly hip spot plays up an aquatic theme with indigo glass fixtures, black-and-white nautical photos, and cobalt-and-white walls subtly recalling foamy waves. The team of young, international chefs emphasize seafood, preparing regional dishes from around the globe with a Caymanian slant. Thai ceviche with kaffir lime and coconut milk and tuna tiradito (similar to carpaccio) with avocado tamarind sauce burst with flavor. Superlative pastas include buffalo mozzarella tortelli in basil butter and lobster-shiitake ravioli with potato mascarpone sauce. Don't miss the authentic gelatos to cap your meal. Wine selections from lesser-known regions often represent good value, with 20 offered by the glass; the bartenders also creatively pair cocktails and food. Happy-hour free tapas and the CI$19.95 three-course lunch menu are steals. $ *Average main: $36* ✉ *Galleria Plaza, Seven Mile Beach* ☎ *345/949–2482* ⊕ *www.agua.ky* ⌚ *Reservations essential.*

$
MIDDLE EASTERN
✕ **Al La Kebab.** The Silvermans started by serving late-night kebabs and gyros, and now their eatery works miracles out of two makeshift lean-tos splashed in vibrant colors. They remain open until 4 am weeknights and 2 am weekends. Alan calls it a building-block menu, where you can modify the bread and sauce—a dozen varieties, including several curries, peanut satay, mango *raita* (yogurt, tomatoes, chutney), tahini, teriyaki, garlic cream, even gravy like Mom used to make. The menu romps from Malaysia through the Mediterranean to Mexico: spicy chicken tikka, Thai chicken-lemongrass soup, and tzatziki share the stage with unusual salads (try the fabulous Lebanese *fattoush*—toasted bread, mint, and parsley) and creative sides (addictive jalapeño-cheddar salsa for fries). $ *Average main: $9* ✉ *Marquee Plaza, West Bay Rd., Seven Mile Beach* ☎ *345/943–4343* ⊕ *www.kebab.ky* ⌚ *Reservations not accepted.*

8

$$
ASIAN
Fodor's Choice
★

✕ **Mizu.** It's a toss-up as to which is sexier at this pan-Pacific bistro: the sleek decor, the model-worthy waitstaff, or the glistening, artfully presented food. The former, courtesy of Hong Kong designer Kitty Chan, is as sensuous as a 21st-century opium den with a back-lit dragon, contemporary Buddhas, glowing granite bar, and enormous mirrors. The bartenders have developed a loyal local following for their flair in more ways than one. The latter trots effortlessly all over Asia for culinary inspiration: terrific tuna tartare, decadent duck gyoza, killer kung pao chicken, smashing Singapore fried noodles, heavenly honey-glazed ribs, beautifully crispy Okinawan-style pork belly, and two dozen ultrafresh maki (try the signature roll). An extensive tea selection and a sake and wine list are also offered. $ *Average main: $24* ✉ *Camana Bay* ☎ *345/640–0001* ⊕ *www.mizucayman.com.*

$$$$
ECLECTIC
Fodor's Choice
★

✕ **Ortanique.** The vibrant food at Ortanique lives up to its nickname, "Cuisine of the Sun." It's an outpost of chef Cindy Hutson and Delius Shirley's Miami Ortanique, which helped revolutionize Floribbean fusion fare. The interior gleams in rich yellows and oranges that subtly recall plantation living, though prize seating is on the patio, shaded by sea grape trees overlooking a small islet. There is an emphasis on Caribbean and South American cuisine infused with Asian inspirations. Executive Chef Sara Mair, a semifinalist on *Top Chef,* reinvents classics with an island twist: jerk-rubbed foie gras with burnt-orange marmalade, or the signature jerked double pork chop, fire-tamed by guava-spiced rum glaze. Save room for such decadent desserts as a deceptively airy Cloud of Coconut Joy or rum-soaked banana fritters. Best of all are almost nightly specials from Mojito Madness Monday to Tapas Thursday. $ *Average main: $42* ✉ *47 Forum La., The Crescent, Camana Bay* ☎ *345/640–7710* ⊕ *www.ortaniquerestaurants.com.*

$$$
ITALIAN
Fodor's Choice
★

✕ **Ragazzi.** The name means "good buddies," and this strip-mall jewel is always percolating with conversation and good strong espresso. The airy space is convivial: blond woods, periwinkle walls and columns, and handsome artworks of beach scenes, sailboats, and palm trees. Chef Adriano Usini turns out meticulously prepared standards. The antipasto alone is worth a visit, as are the homemade breadsticks and focaccia, and definitive carpaccio and insalata Caprese. The shellfish linguine in a light, silken tomato sauce, with cherry-tomato skins pulled back and crisped, and gnocchi in four-cheese sauce with brandy and pistachios will please any pasta perfectionist. Two dozen first-rate pizzas emerge from the wood-burning oven, and meat and seafood mains are beautifully done, never overcooked. The wine list is notable (400-odd choices) for a casual eatery, showcasing great range and affordability even on high-ticket, hard-to-find heavy hitters such as Biondi Santi Brunello, Jermann Pinot Grigio, and Giacosa Barbaresco; the knowledgeable staff will gladly suggest pairings. $ *Average main: $29* ✉ *Buckingham Sq., West Bay Rd., Seven Mile Beach* ☎ *345/945–3484* ⊕ *www.ragazzi.ky.*

$$$$
ECLECTIC

✕ **Reef Grill at Royal Palms.** This class act appeals to a casual, suave crowd, many of them regulars, who appreciate its consistent quality, efficient service, soothing seaside setting, top-notch entertainment, and surprisingly reasonable prices. The space is cannily divided into four areas, each with its own look and feel, including private beach cabanas (no extra charge). Co-owner–chef George Dahlstrom gives his perfectly prepared, familiar items just enough twist to satisfy jaded palates: calamari is fried in arborio rice batter with jalapeño aioli while sea scallops are pan-seared with a creamy roasted corn–smoked bacon mash. The Royal Palms menu offers more casual, inexpensive fare. Dance the calories off to the estimable reggae, calypso, and soca sounds of Coco Red or really sweat it out during Chill Wednesdays, and then adjourn to the cozy lounge for an aged rum or single malt. It's equally enticing at lunch, when it exudes a soigné beach bar ambience. [$] *Average main: $33* ✉ *537 West Bay Rd., Seven Mile Beach* ☎ *345/945–6358* 🌐 *www.reefgrill.com* 🕓 *No dinner Sun. May–Nov.*

$$$$ **STEAKHOUSE**
🍴 **Seven.** The Ritz-Carlton's all-purpose dining room transforms from a bustling breakfast buffet into an elegant eatery come evening. Tall potted palms, soaring ceilings, black and beige color scheme, twin wine walls bracketing a trendy family-style table, and the tiered pool just outside are lighted to strategically stylish effect. Sinatra and Ella keep the sultry beat while the kitchen jazzes standard meat-and-potatoes dishes with inventive seasonings and eye-catching presentations. Splendid aged Niman Ranch steaks come with five sauces and rubs, from five-peppercorn to béarnaise. Even such sides as truffled mac-and-cheese redefine divine decadence. The calorie- and cholesterol-conscious can savor melt-in-your-mouth ahi tuna poke or impeccably cooked Dover sole with hazelnut brown butter. Then just surrender to such confections as chocolate and sea salt caramel candy bar. [$] *Average main: $54* ✉ *Ritz-Carlton Grand Cayman, West Bay Rd., Seven Mile Beach* ☎ *345/943–9000* 🌐 *www.ritzcarlton.com.*

$$ **CARIBBEAN** **FAMILY**
🍴 **Sunshine Grill.** This cheerful, cherished locals' secret serves haute comfort food at bargain-basement prices. Even the chattel-style poolside building, painted a delectable lemon with lime shutters, whets the appetite. Sunshine ranks high in the island's greatest burger debate, while the chicken egg rolls with mango chutney and jerk mayo and fabulous fish tacos elevate pub grub to an art form. Wash it down with one of the many signature libations, like the Painkiller. Take advantage of affordably priced nightly dinner specials such as red snapper amandine in lemon butter caper sauce, and Cuban roast chicken marinated with sour orange, garlic, lime and olive oil. [$] *Average main: $18* ✉ *Sunshine Suites, 1465 Esterley Tibbetts Hwy., Seven Mile Beach* ☎ *345/949–3000, 345/946–5848.*

$$ **JAPANESE**
🍴 **Yoshi Sushi.** Superlative sushi is served at this modish, modern locals' lair. Scarlet cushions, cherry pendant blown-glass lamps, leather-and-bamboo accents, fresh orchids, and maroon walls help create a sensuous, even charged vibe in the main room. The backlit bar sees its share of carefree customers trying to manipulate their chopsticks after a few kamikaze sake bomber missions (plunging hot cups of sake into frosty Kirin beer). Savvy diners literally leave themselves in Yoshi's hands (the rolls and nightly special sushi "pizzas" are particularly creative), and the raw-phobic can choose from fine cooked items, from tuna tataki to tempura to teriyaki. The congenial staff recommends intriguing sake and beer pairings, though the wine list and martini selection are also admirable for an Asian eatery. [$] *Average main: $21* ✉ *Falls Plaza, West Bay Rd., Seven Mile Beach* ☎ *345/943–9674* 🌐 *www.eats.ky, www.legendz.ky* ✍ *Reservations essential.*

WEST BAY

$$$$ ECLECTIC 🍴 **Calypso Grill.** Shack chic describes this inviting split-level space splashed in Dr. Seuss primary colors that contrast with brick walls, hardwood furnishings, terra-cotta floors, trompe l'oeil shutters, and (real) French doors opening onto sweeping North Sound views. If the interior is like stepping into a Caribbean painting, the outdoor deck serenely surveying frigate birds watchfully circling fishing boats is a Winslow Homer canvas brought to life. George Fowler's menu rightly emphasizes fish hauled in at the adjacent dock, so fresh (and never overcooked) that it almost literally jumps from the plate. You'll never go wrong with the unvarnished catch of the day grilled, blackened, or sautéed. Though this is seafood turf, landlubbers can savor escargot bourguignon, beef carpaccio, or a proper rack of lamb. End with the sticky toffee pudding. [$] *Average main: $43* ✉ *Morgan's Harbour, West Bay* ☎ *345/949–3948* 🌐 *www.calypsogrillcayman.com* ✍ *Reservations essential* 🕓 *Closed Mon.*

$$$$ ECLECTIC 🍴 **Cracked Conch.** This island institution effortlessly blends upscale and down-home. The interior gleams from the elaborate light-and-water sculpture at the gorgeous mosaic-and-mahogany entrance bar to the plush booths with subtly embedded lighting. Take in the remarkable water views through large shutters, but for maximum impact, dine on the multitiered patio. Executive chef Gilbert Cavallaro reinvents familiar dishes to create such delectables as honey-jerk-glazed tuna tartar with tomato sorbet and crispy calamari with cardamom-marinated carrots and chipotle sauce. Stellar signature items include the conch chowder or ceviche, silken short rib ravioli with truffles and Parmesan foam, and mahimahi poached *sous vide* over cannellini emulsion drizzled with truffle oil. Locals flock to Sunday brunch, or they just hang out at the dockside Macabuca tiki bar (fab sunsets, sunset-hue libations), which lives up to its mellow name, indigenous Taíno for "What does it matter?" [$] *Average main: $44* ✉ *Northwest Point Rd., West Bay* ☎ *345/945–5217* 🌐 *www.crackedconch.com.ky* 🕓 *No lunch June–Nov. Closed Sept.–mid-Oct.*

$$$ ECLECTIC 🍴 **Morgans Harbour.** Energetic, effervescent Janie Schweiger patrols the front while husband Richard rules the kitchen at this simpatico seaside spot with smashing North Sound views. Locals and fishermen literally cruise into the adjacent dock for refueling of all sorts. You can sit in one of the cozy buildings decorated with Depression-era chandeliers and vivid aquatic artworks or admire the dexterous marine maneuverings from the interlocking decks. Richard's menu dances just as deftly from Asia to his Austrian home. Nimbly prepared nibbles include the wildly popular 10-ounce Brie-topped jerk burger and ceviche, but everything from chicken schnitzel to Thai seafood curry is expertly cooked to order. Lunch offers several of the restaurant's greatest hits at even more palatable prices. [$] *Average main: $32* ✉ *4 Morgan's La., Morgan's Harbour, West Bay* ☎ *345/946–7049* ✍ *Reservations essential.*

$$$$ ECLECTIC 🍴 **Osetra Bay.** Whether by day (when fishing boats as brightly colored as a child's finger painting trawl the tourmaline North Sound) or by night (when Cayman Kai's lights twinkle as the moon dapples the water with a thousand gold doubloons), the view alone guarantees a memorable

meal. The design is almost as appetizing, from glowing columns strategically placed to flatter diners to the intimate, billowingly draped dining cabanas to the Starck-ish white-on-white ultralounges. Every element infuses the casual Caribbean underpinnings with a chic South Beach sensibility, literally bringing caviar to Cayman. The ever-changing, seasonal menu (sourced locally wherever possible) emphasizes seafood: blackened mahi with corn pancetta cream sauce and thyme fingerlings or tuna with fruit chutney, local string beans and beet puree—though vegetarians delight in the pastas, and carnivores can stake out dishes like the classic beef tartare or dry-aged rib eye. $ *Average main: $45* ⊠ *Morgan's Harbour, West Bay* ☎ *345/325–5000, 345/623–5100* ⊕ *www. osetrabay.com* ⏃ *Reservations essential* ⊗ *Closed lunch Mon.–Sat. Closed Sun. dinner.*

EAST END

$$$$
SEAFOOD

✕ **The Lighthouse.** This lighthouse surrounded by fluttering flags serves as a beacon for hungry East End explorers. The interior replicates a yacht: polished hardwood floors, ship's lanterns, mosaic hurricane lamps, steering wheels, portholes, and waiters in crew's garb with chevrons. Most tables afford sweeping sea vistas, but prize romantic seating is on the little deck. Starters include Miss Nell's red conch chowder or flash-fried calamari with sweet chili dip. Entrées include a platter of seafood floating on linguine alfredo and a mustard/herb-crusted rack of lamb with Marsala-mint sauce. Vegetarian options include curries, tofu stir-fries, and pastas. Save room for desserts, including the Illy espresso crème brûlée. The comprehensive wine list extends to a superb postprandial selection of liqueurs, aged rums, ports, and grappas. There are inexpensive prix-fixe lunch and dinner specials (CI$9.95 and $15, respectively). $ *Average main: $35* ⊠ *Bodden Town Rd., Oceanside, Breakers, East End* ☎ *345/947–2047* ⊕ *www.lighthouse.ky.*

NORTH SIDE

$$$
CARIBBEAN

✕ **Kaibo Beach Bar and Grill.** Spectacularly overlooking the North Sound, this quintessential beach hangout rocks days (fantastic lunches that cost half the price of dinner, festive atmosphere including impromptu volleyball tourneys, and free Wi-Fi), but serves murderous margaritas and mudslides well into the evening to a boisterous bevy of yachties, locals, sports buffs, and expats. Enjoy New England–style conch chowder with a hint of heat, smoked mahimahi pâté, hefty burgers, and wondrous wraps, either on the multitiered deck garlanded with ships' rope and Christmas lights or in hammocks and thatched cabanas amid the palms. The handsome, nautically themed Upstairs dining room swaddled in white muslin, open Thursday through Sunday nights (reservations essential), serves more creative fare at higher prices; specialties include baked grouper with Kaffir lime–leaf crust in lemongrass velouté. The ultimate in romance is the catered "Luna del Mar" evening hosted every Friday closest to the full moon. Tuesday beach barbecues are highly popular (including limbo dancing, live music, half-price drinks, and discounted water taxi service to the "mainland"). $ *Average main: $30* ⊠ *585 Water Cay Rd., Cayman Kai, North Side* ☎ *345/947–9975* ⊕ *www.kaibo.ky.*

8

WHERE TO STAY

Brace yourself for resort prices—there are few accommodations in the lower price ranges. You'll find no big all-inclusive resorts on Grand Cayman (though the Reef Resort offers an optional AI plan to its guests), and very few offer a meal plan other than breakfast. Parking is always free at island hotels and resorts. Although the island has several resorts (mostly along Seven Mile Beach), the majority of accommodations are vacation rentals, and these are scattered throughout the island. Some of the condo complexes even offer resort-style amenities.

They may be some distance from the beach and short on style and facilities, but the island's guesthouses offer rock-bottom prices, a friendly atmosphere, and your best shot at getting to know the locals. Rooms are clean and simple, and most have private baths.

PRIVATE VILLAS AND CONDOMINIUMS

Most condo complexes are very similar, with telephones, satellite TV, air-conditioning, living and dining areas, patios, and parking. Differences are amenities, proximity to town and beach, and the views. As with resorts, rates are higher in winter, and there may be a three- or seven-night minimum. There are dozens of large private villas available on the beach, especially on the North Side near Cayman Kai. A growing trend: "green" condos. We no longer recommend individual private villas, especially since they frequently change agents. However, among the properties we've inspected worth looking for are Coral Reef, Venezia, Villa Habana, Great Escapes, Fishbones, and Pease Bay House. Several of the condo and villa rental companies have websites where you can see pictures of the privately owned units and villas they represent.

VILLA RENTAL AGENCIES

Cayman Island Vacations. Cayman Island Vacations was started by the affable couple Don and Linda Martin in 1989. Longtime Cayman homeowners, they represent more than 50 villas and condos (including their own). Extremely helpful with island suggestions, they can make arrangements for a rental car and extras. They arrange diving discounts, and Linda is one of Cayman's leading wedding coordinators. ☎ *813/854–1201, 888/208–8935* ⊕ *www.caymanvacation.com.*

Cayman Villas. The locally owned Cayman Villas represents top-notch villas and condos on Grand and Little Cayman. ⊠ *177 Owen Roberts Dr.* ☎ *800/235–5888, 345/945–4144* ⊕ *www.caymanvillas.com.*

Golden Sun/Le Soleil d'Or. Mirjana Mirjanic's company rents some of the Brac's newest, most luxurious homes but sets itself apart with the little extras (for a price): in-house spa treatments, personal training, and gourmet chefs, even cooking classes. The rental office also doubles as a delightful little shop, selling Mirjana's organic foodstuffs (sorrel flower jam, Meyer lemon marmalade), goat cheese soaps, and candles, all sourced from Golden Sun's own Garden Farm. ⊠ *403 Gerrard Smith Ave., Suite 4, Cayman Brac* ☎ *345/948–0555, 888/988–0521* ⊕ *www. goldensuncayman.com.*

BEST BETS FOR LODGING

Fodor's Choice ★
Caribbean Club, Lighthouse Point, Reef Resort, Ritz-Carlton Grand Cayman

BEST BEACHFRONT
Coral Stone Club, Lacovia Condominiums, Reef Resort, Southern Cross Club (Little Cayman), Westin Grand Cayman

BEST FOR AN ECOFRIENDLY TRIP
Cobalt Coast, Compass Point, Lighthouse Point, Pirate's Point (Little Cayman)

BEST FOR FAMILIES
Ritz-Carlton Grand Cayman

BEST SERVICE
The Alexander (Cayman Brac), Reef Resort, Ritz-Carlton Grand Cayman

BEST FOR ROMANCE
Caribbean Club, Cotton Tree, Shangri-La B&B, Turtle Nest Inn

Grand Cayman Villas. Grand Cayman Villas was started by Virginia resident Jim Leavitt, who carries listings for dozens of fine properties island-wide. He and his staff visit the island regularly to ensure quality and remain up-to-date with the latest development that might interest clients. ☎ 866/358–8455 ⊕ www.grandcaymanvillas.net.

Island Hideaways. Island Hideaways rents villas all over the Caribbean, including some in the Cayman Islands. ☎ 800/832–2302 ⊕ www. islandhideaways.com.

Wimco. Wimco, or the West Indies Management Company, is synonymous with quality throughout the world, especially the Caribbean. ☎ 866/850–6140, 800/449–1553 ⊕ www.wimco.com.

AROUND GEORGE TOWN

$$$
HOTEL
⬚ **Sunset House.** This amiable seaside dive-oriented resort is on the ironshore south of George Town, close enough for a short trip to stores and restaurants yet far enough to feel secluded. **Pros:** great shore diving and dive shop; lively bar scene; fun international clientele; great package rates. **Cons:** often indifferent service; somewhat run-down; no real swimming beach; spotty Wi-Fi signal. $ *Rooms from: $290* ⊠ *390 S. Church St.* ☎ *345/949–7111, 800/854–4767* ⊕ *www.sunsethouse.com* ⤴ *58 rooms, 2 suites* ⦿ *No meals.*

SEVEN MILE BEACH

$$$$
RENTAL
Fodor's Choice
★
⬚ **Caribbean Club.** This gleaming boutique facility includes a striking lobby filled with aquariums, a stunning infinity pool, and the contemporary trattoria, Luca. **Pros:** luxurious, high-tech facilities beyond the typical apartment complex; trendy Italian restaurant on-site; service on the beach. **Cons:** stratospheric prices; poor bedroom reading lights; though families are welcome, they may find it rather imposing; smaller balconies on top floor (albeit amazing views). $ *Rooms from: $1256* ⊠ *871 West Bay Rd., Seven Mile Beach* ☎ *345/623–4500, 800/941–1126* ⊕ *www.caribclub.com* ⤴ *37 3-bedroom condos* ⦿ *No meals.*

$$$$ RESORT FAMILY Fodor's Choice ★ **Westin Grand Cayman Seven Mile Beach Resort and Spa.** The Westin offers something for everyone, from conventioneers to honeymooners to families, not to mention what the hospitality industry calls "location location location." **Pros:** terrific children's programs; superb beach (the largest resort stretch at 800 feet); better than advertised ocean views. **Cons:** occasionally bustling and impersonal when large groups book; daily $35 resort fee. [$] *Rooms from: $559* ✉ *West Bay Rd., Seven Mile Beach* ☎ *345/945–3800, 800/937–8461* 🌐 *www.westingrandcayman.com* 🛏 *339 rooms, 8 suites* 🍴 *No meals.*

WEST BAY

$$$ RESORT **Cobalt Coast Resort and Suites.** This small ecofriendly hotel is perfect for divers who want a moderately priced spacious room or suite right on the ironshore far from the madding crowds. **Pros:** superb dive outfit; friendly service and clientele; free Wi-Fi; environmentally aware. **Cons:** poky golden-sand beach; unattractive concrete pool area; remote location, so a car (included in some packages) is necessary. [$] *Rooms from: $290* ✉ *18-A Sea Fan Dr., West Bay* ☎ *345/946–5656, 888/946–5656* 🌐 *www.cobaltcoast.com* 🛏 *7 rooms, 15 suites* 🍴 *Multiple meal plans.*

$$$$ RENTAL Fodor's Choice ★ **Cotton Tree.** Cayman-born owner Heather Lockington has created an authentic haven where guests can embrace Caymanian heritage and reconnect with nature without sacrificing comfort. **Pros:** peaceful and quiet setting; beautifully designed and outfitted accommodations; complimentary airport transfers; wonderful immersion in local culture. **Cons:** luxury comes with a price tag; remote location means a car is required; beach narrow and tangled with sea grape trees. [$] *Rooms from: $890* ✉ *375 Conch Point Rd., West Bay* ☎ *345/943–0700, 561/807–8566 in U.S.* 🌐 *www.caymancottontree.com* 🛏 *4 2-bedroom cottages* ⏲ *Closed Sept.* 🍴 *No meals.*

$$$$ RESORT Fodor's Choice ★ **Lighthouse Point.** Leading scuba operator DiveTech's stunning ecodevelopment features sustainable wood interiors and recycled concrete, an ecosensitive gray-water system, energy-saving appliances and lights, and Cayman's first wind turbine generator. **Pros:** ecofriendly; fantastic shore diving (and state-of-the-art dive shop); creative and often recycled upscale look; superb eatery. **Cons:** no real beach; car necessary; bit difficult for physically challenged to navigate. [$] *Rooms from: $450* ✉ *571 Northwest Point Rd., West Bay* ☎ *345/949–1700* 🌐 *www.lighthouse-point-cayman.com* 🛏 *9 2-bedroom apartments* 🍴 *No meals.*

$$ B&B/INN **Shangri-La B&B.** Accomplished pianist George Davidson and wife Eileen built this lavish lakeside retreat and truly make guests feel at home, along with dogs Roxie and Stella. **Pros:** use of kitchen; elegant decor; DVD players and Wi-Fi included. **Cons:** rental car necessary; not on the beach. [$] *Rooms from: $149* ✉ *1 Sticky Toffee La., West Bay* ☎ *345/526–1170* 🌐 *www.shangrilabandb.com* 🛏 *6 rooms, 1 apartment* 🍴 *Breakfast.*

EAST END

$$$ RESORT **Compass Point Dive Resort.** This tranquil, congenial little getaway run by the admirable Ocean Frontiers scuba operation would steer even nondivers in the right direction. **Pros:** top-notch dive operation; free bike and kayak use; good value especially with packages; affable international staff and clientele. **Cons:** isolated location requires

a car; "eco-green" conservation is admirable but a/c can't go too low. [$] *Rooms from: $295* ✉ *Austin Conolly Dr., East End* ☎ *345/947–7500, 800/348–6096, 345/947–0000* 🌐 *www.compasspoint.ky* 🛏 *17 1-bedroom, 9 2-bedroom, and 3 3-bedroom condos* 🍴 *No meals.*

$ RESORT Fodor's Choice ★ 🏨 **Reef Resort.** This exceedingly well-run time-share property seductively straddles a 600-foot beach on the less hectic East End. **Pros:** romantically remote; glorious beach; enthusiastic staff (including a crackerjack wedding coordinator); great packages. **Cons:** remote; few dining options within easy driving distance; sprawling layout. [$] *Rooms from: $270* ✉ *Queen's Hwy., East End* ☎ *345/947–3100, 888/232–0541* 🌐 *www.thereef.com* 🛏 *152 suites* 🍴 *Multiple meal plans.*

$$ RENTAL 🏨 **Turtle Nest Inn and Condos.** This affordable, intimate, Mediterranean-style seaside inn has roomy one-bedroom apartments and a pool overlooking a narrow beach with good snorkeling. **Pros:** wonderful snorkeling; thoughtful extras; caring staff; free Wi-Fi. **Cons:** car necessary; occasional rocks and debris on beach; ground-floor room views slightly obscured by palms; road noise in back rooms. [$] *Rooms from: $149* ✉ *166 Bodden Town Rd., Bodden Town* ☎ *345/947–8665* 🌐 *www.turtlenestinn.com, www.turtlenestcondos.com* 🛏 *8 apartments, 10 2-bedroom condos.*

NIGHTLIFE

Grand Cayman nightlife is surprisingly good for such a quiet-seeming island. Check the Friday edition of the *Caymanian Compass* for listings of music, movies, theater, and other entertainment. Bars are open during evening hours until 1 am, and clubs are generally open from 10 pm until 3 am, but none may serve liquor after midnight on Saturday and none can offer dancing on Sunday. Competition is fierce between Grand Cayman's many bars and restaurants. In addition to entertainment (fish feeding to fire-eating), even upscale joints host happy hours offering free hors d'oeuvres and/or drinks.

8

AROUND GEORGE TOWN

BARS AND MUSIC CLUBS

My Bar. This bar is optimally perched on the water's edge, looking almost due west with a perfect vantage point for watching the sunset. The leviathan open-sided cabana is drenched in vivid Rasta colors and crowned by an intricate South Seas–style thatched roof (containing approximately 36,000 palm fronds). Christmas lights and the occasional customer dangle from the rafters year-round. Great grub and a mischievous mix of locals, expats, and tourists from all walks of life prove that ecocentric Cayman offers wild life alongside the wildlife. ✉ *Sunset House, S. Church St.* ☎ *345/949–7111* 🌐 *www.sunsethouse.com.*

Rackam's Waterfront Pub and Restaurant. A Cayman mosaic of fishermen to Who's-the-Hugo-Boss financiers savors sensational sunsets followed by exuberantly pirouetting tarpon feeding at the open-air, marine-theme happenin' bar built on a jetty jutting into the harbor (boaters, even snorkelers cruise right up the ladder for drinks while anglers leave their catch on ice) that has complimentary snacks on Friday and serves pub fare at fair prices until midnight. ✉ *93 N. Church St.* ☎ *345/945–3860* 🌐 *www.rackams.com.*

BARS AND MUSIC CLUBS

The Attic. The Attic is a chic sports bar with three billiard tables, classic arcade games (Space Invaders, Donkey Kong), air hockey, and large-screen TVs (you can nab a private booth with its own flat-panel job). Events encompass daily happy hours, trivia nights, and the Caribbean's reputedly largest Bloody Mary bar on Sunday. Along with downstairs sister hot spot "O" Bar, it's ground zero for the Wednesday Night Drinking Club. For a $25 initiation fee (you get a T-shirt and personalized leather wristband, toga optional) and $10 weekly activity fee, you'll be shuttled by bus to several different bars, with free shots and drinks specials all night. ⊠ *Queen's Court, 2nd fl., West Bay Rd., Seven Mile Beach* ☎ *345/949–7665* ⊕ *www.obar.attic.ky.*

Calico Jack's. For a casual drink, visit this friendly outdoor beach bar at the north end of the public beach with a DJ on Saturday and open-mike night on Tuesday, bands many Friday nights, and riotous parties during the full moon when even Ritz-Carlton guests let their hair and inhibitions down. ⊠ *West Bay Rd., Seven Mile Beach* ☎ *345/945–7850.*

Deckers. Always bustling and bubbly, Deckers takes its name from the red English double-decker bus that forms the focal point of the main outdoor bar. You can luxuriate indoors on cushy sofas over a chess game and signature blood-orange mojito; hack your way through the 18-hole safari miniature-golf course; find a secluded nook in the garden terrace framed by towering palms, old-fashioned ornate streetlamps, and colonial columns; or groove Thursday through Saturday nights to the easy-listening potpourri of pop, reggae, blues, and country courtesy of the Hi-Tide duo. Worthy Carib-Mediterranean fusion cuisine is a bonus (try the Caribbean lobster mac 'n' cheese or the coconut shrimp with citrus marmalade and green papaya salad). ⊠ *West Bay Rd., Seven Mile Beach* ☎ *345/945–6600* ⊕ *www.deckers.ky.*

Duke's Seafood & Rib Shack. Duke's offers the ultimate in beach shack chic (albeit a half-block back from the sand), from the awesome surfing photos to the reclaimed driftwood patio bar to the statue of the big kahuna with shades and board atop a manta ray. Locals and visitors alike belly up to the raw and real bars, especially during nightly happy hours, to soak up "Cayman's endless summer." ⊠ *West Bay Rd. across from public beach, Seven Mile Beach* ☎ *345/640–0000* ⊕ *www.dukescayman.com.*

Fidel Murphy's Irish Pub. This pub has an unusual logo, a stogie-smoking Castro surrounded by shamrocks. Indeed, the congenial Irish wit and whimsy are so thick that you half expect to find Fidel and Gerry Adams harping on U.S. and U.K. policy over a Harp. The pub's Edwardian decor of etched glass, hardwood, and brass may be prefabricated (it was constructed in Ireland, disassembled, and shipped), but everything else is genuine, from the warm welcome to the ales and cider on tap to the proper Irish stew (though the kitchen also turns out conch fritters and chicken tandoori wraps). Sunday and Monday host all-you-can-eat extravaganzas (fish-and-chips, carvery) at rock-bottom prices. Trivia nights and live music lure regulars through the week. Weekends welcome live televised Gaelic soccer, rugby, and hurling, followed by karaoke and *craic* (if you go, you'll learn the definition soon enough). ⊠ *Queen's Court, West Bay Rd., Seven Mile Beach* ☎ *345/949–5189.*

Legendz. A sports bar with a clubby, retro feel (Marilyn Monroe and Frank Sinatra photos channel the glamour days, while scarlet booths and bubble chandeliers add oomph), it's the usual testosterone test drive with plentiful scoring of both types. Good luck wrestling a spot at the bar for Pay-Per-View and major live sporting events (though 10 TVs, including two 6-by-8 foot, high-resolution screens broadcast to every corner). It doubles as an entertainment venue, booking local bands, stand-up comics, and leading island DJs. You can also savor grilled fare at fair prices. ⊠ *Falls Centre, West Bay Rd., Seven Mile Beach.*

Lone Star Bar and Grill. The bar and restaurant proudly calls itself Cayman's top dive (and indeed, locals from dive masters to dentists get down and occasionally dirty over kick-ass margaritas). The noisy bar glorifies sports, Texas, T&A, and the boob tube, from murals of Cowboys cheerleaders to an amazing sports memorabilia collection (including items signed by both Bushes), and 17 big-screen TVs tuned to different events. ⊠ *686 West Bay Rd., Seven Mile Beach* ☎ *345/945– 5175* ⊕ *www.lonestarcayman.com.*

Stingers Resort and Pool Bar. Stingers Resort and Pool Bar offers tasty affordable food in an appealing setting (check out the stupendous "stinger" mosaic), with cover-free live music and dancing Thursday and Friday. Wednesday nights there's a very affordable all-you-can-eat Caribbean luau. The band Heat, a local institution, sizzles with energetic, emotionally delivered calypso, reggae, soca, salsa, and oldies; then the limbo dancers and fire-eaters keep the temperature rising. If you recoil from audience participation, stay far away. More exhibitionistic "spring break" sorts might find their photo adorning the "Wall of Shame," but the worst blackmail is persuading you to buy another blue-green Stingers punch. ⊠ *Comfort Suites, West Bay Rd., Seven Mile Beach* ☎ *345/945–3000* ⊕ *www.stingersrestaurantandbar.com.*

The Wharf. You can dance near the water to mellow music on Saturday evenings; when there's a wedding reception in the pavilion, the crashing surf and candles twinkling as if competing with the stars bathe the proceedings in an almost Gatsby-esque glow. For something less sedate, Roger and Sarah conduct sizzling salsa dancing and lessons on Tuesdays after dinner, while most Fridays morph into a wild 1970s disco night (after free hors d'oeuvres during the joyous happy hour). The stunning seaside setting on tiered decks compensates for often undistinguished food and service. The Ports of Call bar is a splendid place for sunset fanciers, and tarpon feeding off the deck is a nightly 9 pm spectacle. ⊠ *West Bay Rd.* ☎ *345/949–2231.*

Although you can find black-coral products in Grand Cayman, they're controversial. Most of the coral sold here comes from Belize and Honduras; Cayman Islands marine law prohibits the removal of live coral from its own sea (although most of it has been taken illegally). Black coral grows at a very slow rate (3 inches every 10 years) and is an endangered species. Consider buying other products instead.

AROUND GEORGE TOWN

ART GALLERIES

Al Ebanks Studio Gallery. This gallery shows the eponymous artist's versatile, always provocative work in various media. Since you're walking into his home as well as atelier, everything is on display. Clever movable panels maximize space "like Art Murphy beds." His work, while inspired by his home, could never be labeled traditional Caribbean art, exhibiting vigorous movement through abstract swirls of color and textural contrasts. Though nonrepresentational (save for his equally intriguing sculpture and ceramics), the focal subject from carnivals to iguanas is always subtly apparent. Ask him about the Native Sons art movement he co-founded. ⊠ *186B Shedden Rd.* ☎ *345/927–5365, 345/949–0693.*

Cathy Church's Underwater Photo Centre and Gallery. Come see a collection of the acclaimed underwater shutterbug's spectacular color and limited-edition black-and-white underwater photos. Have Cathy autograph her latest coffee-table book and regale you with anecdotes of her globe-trotting adventures. The store also carries the latest marine camera equipment, and she'll schedule private underwater photography instruction as well on her own dive boat outfitted with special graphics-oriented computers to critique your work. She also does wedding photography, both above and underwater. If you don't have time to stop in, check out the world's largest underwater photo installation, 9 feet high and 145 feet long, at Grand Cayman's Owen Roberts Airport Baggage Claim area, curated by Cathy and her team. ⊠ *S. Church St.* ☎ *345/949–7415* ⊕ *www.cathychurch.com.*

Guy Harvey's Gallery and Shoppe. This is where world-renowned marine biologist, conservationist, and artist Guy Harvey showcases his aquatic-inspired action-packed art in nearly every conceivable medium, branded tableware, and sportswear (even logo soccer balls and Zippos). The soaring, two-story 4,000-square-foot space is almost more theme park than store, with monitors playing his sportfishing videos, wood floors inlaid with tile duplicating rippling water, dangling catboats "attacked" by lifelike shark models, and life-size murals honoring such classics as Hemingway's *Old Man and the Sea.* Original paintings, sculpture, and drawings are expensive, but there's something (tile art, prints, lithographs, and photos) in most price ranges. ⊠ *49 S. Church St.* ☎ *345/943–4891* ⊕ *www.guyharvey.com.*

Pure Art. About 1½ miles (2½ km) south of George Town, Pure Art purveys wit, warmth, and whimsy right from the wildly colored front steps. Its warren of rooms resembles a garage sale run amok or a quirky grandmother's attic spilling over with unexpected finds, from foodstuffs to functional and wearable art. ⊠ *S. Church St. and Denham-Thompson Way* ☎ *345/949–9133* ⊕ *www.pureart.ky.*

CLOTHING

Blue Wave. Your adrenalin starts pumping as soon as you enter this so-called lifestyle wear-surf shop. All the accoutrements you need to play the Big Kahuna are handsomely displayed, from sandals to sunglasses, Billabong plaid shirts to Quicksilver shorts, surfboards to eco-sensitive Olukai footwear (talk to the clerks and you're ready to sign up for Greenpeace). ⊠ *10 Shedden Rd.* ☎ *345/949–8166.*

FOODSTUFFS

There are seven modern, U.S.-style supermarkets for groceries (three of them have full-service pharmacies) on Grand Cayman. The biggest difference you'll find between these and supermarkets on the mainland is in the prices, which are about 25% to 30% more than at home.

Foster's Food Fair-IGA. The island's biggest supermarket chain has five stores. The Airport Centre and Strand stores have full-service pharmacies. These stores are open from Monday through Saturday, 7 am to 11 pm. ⊠ *Airport Centre, 63 Dorcy Dr.* ☎ *345/949–5155, 345/945–3663* ⊕ *www.fosters-iga.com.*

Tortuga Rum Company. This company bakes, then vacuum-seals, more than 10,000 of its world-famous rum cakes daily, adhering to the original "secret" century-old recipe. There are eight flavors, from banana to Blue Mountain coffee. The 12-year-old rum, blended from private stock though actually distilled in Guyana, is a connoisseur's delight for after-dinner sipping. You can buy a fresh rum cake at the airport on the way home at the same prices as at the factory store. ⊠ *N. Sound Rd., Industrial Park* ☎ *345/943–7663* ⊕ *www.tortugarumcakes.com.*

MALLS AND SHOPPING CENTERS

Kirk Freeport Plaza. This downtown shopping center, home to the Kirk Freeport flagship department store, is ground zero for couture; it's also known for its boutiques selling fine watches and jewelry, china, crystal, leather, perfumes, and cosmetics, from Baccarat to Bulgari, Raymond Weil to Waterford and Wedgwood (the last two share their own autonomous boutique). Just keep walking—there's plenty of eye-catching, mind-boggling consumerism in all directions: Boucheron, Cartier (with its own mini-boutique), Chanel, Clinique, Christian Dior, Clarins, Estée Lauder, Fendi, Guerlain, Lancôme, Yves Saint Laurent, Issey Miyake, Jean Paul Gaultier, Nina Ricci, Rolex, Roberto Coin, Rosenthal and Royal Doulton china, and more. ⊠ *Cardinall Ave.*

SEVEN MILE BEACH

JEWELRY

24K-Mon Jewelers. This store sells works of art from many jewelers, including Wyland, Merry-Lee Rae, and Stephen Douglas, as well as designs courtesy of owner-goldsmith Gale Tibbetts and her friends, incorporating everything from Swarovski crystals to Spanish doubloons. Most pieces are inspired by the sea. The adjacent gallery is one of the few commercial outlets for local artists such as Miguel Powery. ⊠ *Buckingham Sq., Seven Mile Beach* ☎ *345/949–1499* ⊕ *www.24k-mon.com.*

8

MALLS AND SHOPPING CENTERS

The Strand Shopping Centre. This mall has branches of Tortuga Rum and Blackbeard's Liquor, and banks galore—the better to withdraw cash for shops with cachet like Polo Ralph Lauren and another Kirk Freeport (this branch particularly noteworthy for china and crystal, from Kosta Boda to Baccarat, as well as a second La Parfumerie). ⊠ *West Bay Rd., Seven Mile Beach.*

SPORTS AND ACTIVITIES

BIRD-WATCHING

Silver Thatch Tours. Silver Thatch Tours is run by Geddes Hislop, who knows his birds and his island (though he's Trinidadian by birth). He specializes in customizable five-hour natural and historic heritage tours that culminate at the Queen Elizabeth II Botanic Park's nature trail and lake or other prime birding spots. The cost is $60 per hour for one to four people. Serious birders leave at the crack of dawn, but you can choose the time and leave at the crack of noon instead. The cost includes guide service, pickup and return transport, and refreshments such as local drinks (a great excuse for discourse on herbal medicinal folklore); tours must be arranged in advance. ☎ *345/925–7401* ⊕ *www.earthfoot.org/places/ky001.htm.*

DIVING

One of the world's leading dive destinations, Grand Cayman's dramatic underwater topography features plunging walls, soaring skyscraper pinnacles, grottoes, arches, swim-throughs adorned with vibrant sponges, coral-encrusted caverns, and canyons patrolled by Lilliputian grunts to gargantuan groupers, hammerheads to hawksbill turtles.

There are more than 200 pristine dive sites, many less than half a mile from land and easily accessible, including wreck, wall, and shore options. Add exceptional visibility from 80 to 150 feet and calm, current-free water at a constant bathlike 80°F. Cayman is serious about conservation, with Marine Park, Replenishment, and Environmental Park Zones and stringently enforced laws to protect the fragile, endangered marine environment (fines of up to $500,000 and a year in prison are the price for damaging living coral, which can take years to regrow). Most boats use biodegradable cleansers and environmentally friendly drinking cups; moorings at popular sites prevent coral and sponge damage caused by continual anchoring, and diving with gloves is prohibited to reduce the temptation to touch.

Pristine clear water, breathtaking coral formations, and plentiful marine life mark the **North Wall**—a world-renowned dive area along the North Side of Grand Cayman. **Trinity Caves,** in West Bay, is a deep dive with numerous canyons starting at about 60 feet and sloping to the wall at 130 feet. The South Side is the deepest, its wall starting 80-feet deep before plummeting, though its shallows offer a lovely labyrinth of caverns and tunnels in such sites as Japanese Gardens. The less-visited, virgin East End is less varied geographically beyond the magnificent Ironshore Caves and Babylon Hanging Gardens ("trees" of black coral plunging 100 feet) but teems with "Swiss-cheese" swim-throughs and exotic life in such renowned gathering spots as the Maze.

CAYMAN DIVE DEVELOPMENTS

The Cayman Islands government acquired the 251-foot, decommissioned U.S. Navy ship **USS** *Kittiwake*. Sunk in 2011, it has already become an exciting new dive attraction (⊕ *www.kittiwakecayman.com*) while providing necessary relief for some of the most frequently visited dive sites. The top of the bridge is just 15 feet down, making it accessible to snorkelers. There's a single-use entry fee of $10 ($5 for snorkelers).

The **Cayman Dive 365** (⊕ *www.divecayman.ky/dive365*) initiative is part of a commitment to protect reefs from environmental overuse. New dive sites will be introduced while certain existing sites are "retired" to be rested and refreshed. Visitors are encouraged to sponsor and name a new dive site from the list of selected coordinates.

Other good shore-entry snorkeling spots include **West Bay Cemetery,** north of Seven Mile Beach, and the reef-protected shallows of the island's **north and south coasts.** Ask for directions to the shallow wreck of the *Cali* in the George Town harbor area; there are several places to enter the water, including a ladder at Rackam's Pub. Among the wreckage you'll recognize the winch and, of course, lots of friendly fish.

Fodor's Choice **Devil's Grotto.** Its neighbor, Devil's Grotto, resembles an abstract paint-
★ ing of anemones, tangs, parrotfish, and bright purple Pederson cleaner shrimp (nicknamed the dentists of the reef, as they gorge on whatever they scrape off fish teeth and gills). Extensive coral heads and fingers teem with blue wrasse, horse-eyed jacks, butterfly fish, Indigo hamlets, and more. The cathedral-like caves are phenomenal, but tunnel entries here aren't clearly marked, so you're best off with a dive master.

Fodor's Choice **Eden Rock.** If someone tells you that the silverside minnows are in at
★ Eden Rock, drop everything and dive here. The schools swarm around you as you glide through the grottoes, forming quivering curtains of liquid silver as shafts of sunlight pierce the sandy bottom. The grottoes themselves are safe—not complex caves—and the entries and exits are clearly visible at all times. Snorkelers can enjoy the outside of the grottoes as the reef rises and falls from 10 to 30 feet deep. Avoid carrying fish food unless you know how not to get bitten by eager yellowtail snappers. ⊠ *S. Church St., across from Harbour Place Mall by Paradise Restaurant.*

Fodor's Choice **Stingray City.** Most dive operators offer scuba trips to Stingray City in
★ the North Sound. Widely considered the best 12-foot dive in the world, it's a must-see for adventurous souls. Here dozens of stingrays congregate—tame enough to suction squid from your outstretched palm. You can stand in 3 feet of water at **Stingray City Sandbar** as the gentle stingrays glide around your legs looking for a handout. Don't worry—these stingrays are so acclimated to tourist encounters that they pose no danger; the experience is often a highlight of a Grand Cayman trip. ⊠ *Near West Bay, North Sound.*

8

Diving at one of the Cayman Islands' famous coral reefs

Turtle Reef. Turtle Reef begins 20 feet out and gradually descends to a 60-foot mini-wall pulsing with sea life and corals of every variety. From there it's just another 15 feet to the dramatic main wall. Ladders provide easy entrance to a shallow cover perfect for pre-dive checks, and since the area isn't buoyed for boats, it's quite pristine. ⊠ *West Bay.*

DIVE OPERATORS

As one of the Caribbean's top diving destinations, Grand Cayman is blessed with many top-notch dive operations offering diving, instruction, and equipment for sale and rent. A single-tank boat dive averages $80, a two-tank dive about $105 (discounts for multidive packages). Snorkel-equipment rental is about $15 a day. Divers are required to be certified and possess a C-card. If you're getting certified, to save time during your limited vacation, you can start the book and pool work at home and finish the open-water portion in warm, clear Cayman waters. Certifying agencies offer this referral service all around the world.

Strict marine-protection laws prohibit you from taking any marine life from many areas around the island.

Ambassador Divers. Ambassador Divers is an on-call, guided scuba-diving operation offering dive trips to parties of two to eight persons. Co-owner Jason Washington's favorite spots include the excellent dive sites on the West Side and South and North Wall. Ambassador offers three boats, a 28-foot custom Parker (maximum six divers), a 46-foot completely custom overhauled boat, and a 26-footer primarily for snorkeling. They are available around the clock, and interested divers can be picked up from their hotels or condos. The price for a two-tank boat dive is $105 ($90 for two or more days). ⊠ *Comfort Suites, 22 Piper Way, West Bay Rd., Seven Mile Beach* ☎ *345/743–5513, 345/949–4530* ⊕ *www.ambassadordivers.com.*

Cayman Aggressor IV. *Cayman Aggressor IV,* a 110-foot live-aboard dive boat, offers one-week cruises for divers who want to get serious bottom time, as many as five dives daily. Nine staterooms with en suite bathrooms sleep 18. The fresh food is basic but bountiful (three meals, two in-between snacks), and the crew offers a great mix of diving, especially when weather allows the crossing to Little Cayman. Digital photography and video courses are also offered (there's an E-6 film-processing lab aboard) as well as Nitrox certification. The price is $2,595 to $2,995 double occupancy for the week. ☎ *345/949–5551, 800/348–2628* ⊕ *www.aggressor.com.*

FAMILY
Fodor'sChoice
★

DiveTech. DiveTech has opportunities for shore diving at its two north-coast locations, which provide loads of interesting creatures, a mini-wall, and the North Wall. With quick access to West Bay, the boats are quite comfortable. Technical training (a specialty of owner Nancy Easterbrook) is unparalleled, and the company offers good, personable service as well as the latest gadgetry such as underwater DPV scooters and rebreathing equipment. They even mix their own gases, and there are multiple dive instructors for different specialties, with everything from extended cross-training Ranger packages to Dive and Art workshop weeks, popular photography–video seminars with Courtney Platt, deep diving, less disruptive free diving, search and recovery, stingray interaction, reef awareness, and underwater naturalist. Snorkel and diving programs are available year-round for children ages eight and up, SASY (supplied-air snorkeling, which keeps the unit on a personal flotation device) for five and up. Excellent multiday discounts are a bonus. ⊠ *Cobalt Coast Resort & Suites, 18-A Sea Fan Dr., West Bay* ☎ *345/946–5658, 888/946–5656* ⊕ *www.divetech. com* ⊠ *Lighthouse Point, near Boatswain's Beach, 571 N.W. Point Rd., West Bay* ☎ *345/949–1700.*

Don Foster's Dive Cayman Islands. Don Foster's Dive Cayman Islands has a pool with a shower as well as snorkeling along the ironshore at Casuarina Point, easily accessed starting at 20 feet, extending to depths of 55 feet. There's an underwater photo center, and there are night dives and Stingray City trips with divers and snorkelers in the same boat (perfect for families). Specialties include Nitrox, Wreck, and Peak Performance Buoyancy courses. Rates are competitive, and there's free shuttle pickup–drop-off along Seven Mile Beach. If you go out with Don, he might recount stories of his wild times as a drummer in the islands, but all the crews are personable and efficient. The drawback is larger boats and groups. ⊠ *218 S. Church St.* ☎ *345/949–5679, 345/945–5132* ⊕ *www.donfosters.com.*

Indigo Divers. Indigo Divers is a full-service, mobile PADI-teaching facility specializing in exclusive guided dives from its 28-foot Sea Ray Bow Rider or 32-foot Donzi Express Cruiser, the *Cats Meow* and the *Cats Pyjamas.* Comfort and safety are paramount, and the attention to detail is superior. Luxury transfers in a Chevy Avalanche are included, and

8

the boat is stocked with goodies like fresh fruit and homemade cookies. Captain Chris Alpers has impeccable credentials: a licensed U.S. Coast Guard captain, PADI master scuba diver trainer, and Cayman Islands Marine Park officer. Katie Alpers specializes in wreck, DPV, dry suit, boat, and deep diving, but her primary role is resident videographer, and she edits superlative DVDs of your adventures, complete with music and titles. They guarantee a maximum of six divers. The individual attention is a bit pricier, but the larger your group, the more you save. ⊠ *Seven Mile Beach* 🖀 *345/946–7279, 345/525–3932* ⊕ *www.indigodivers.com.*

Fodor's Choice
★

Ocean Frontiers. Ocean Frontiers is an excellent ecocentric operation, offering friendly small-group diving and a technical training facility, exploring the less trammeled, trafficked East End. The company provides valet service, personalized attention, a complimentary courtesy shuttle, and an emphasis on green initiatives and specialized diving, including unguided computer, Technical, Nitrox Instructor, underwater naturalist, and cave diving for advanced participants. You can even participate in lionfish culls. But even beginners and rusty divers (there's a wonderful Skills Review and Tune-Up course) won't feel over their heads. Special touches include hot chocolate and homemade muffins on night dives; the owner, Steve, will arrange for a minister to conduct weddings in full face masks. ⊠ *Compass Point, 346 Austin Connelly Dr., East End* 🖀 *345/640–7500, 800/348–6096, 345/947–0000* ⊕ *www.oceanfrontiers.com.*

FAMILY **Red Sail Sports.** Red Sail Sports offers daily trips from most of the major hotels. Dives are often run as guided tours, a perfect option for beginners. If you're experienced and your air lasts a long time, consult the boat captain to see if he requires that you come up with the group (determined by the first person who runs low on air). There is a full range of kids' dive options for ages 5 to 15, including SASY and Bubblemakers. The company also operates Stingray City tours, dinner and sunset sails, and just about every major water sport from Wave Runners to windsurfing. 🖀 *345/949–8745, 345/623–5965, 877/506–6368* ⊕ *www.redsailcayman.com.*

Sunset Divers. Sunset Divers, a full-service PADI-teaching facility at the George Town hostelry catering to the scuba set, has great shore diving and six dive boats to hit all sides of the island. Divers can be independent on their boats as long as they abide by the maximum time and depth standards. Instruction and packages are comparatively inexpensive. Though the company is not directly affiliated with acclaimed underwater shutterbug Cathy Church (whose shop is also at the hotel), she'll often work with the instructors on special courses. ⊠ *Sunset House, 390 S. Church St.* 🖀 *345/949–7111, 800/854–4767* ⊕ *www.sunsethouse.com.*

FISHING

If you enjoy action fishing, Cayman waters have plenty to offer. Experienced, knowledgeable local captains charter boats with top-of-the-line equipment, bait, ice, and often lunch included in the price (usually $550 to $750 per half day, $900 to $1,500 for a full day). Options include deep-sea, reef, bone, tarpon, light-tackle, and fly-fishing. June and July are good all-around months for fishing for blue marlin, yellow- and blackfin tuna, dolphinfish, and bonefish. Bonefish have a second season in the winter months, along with wahoo and skipjack tuna.

Black Princess Charters. Black Princess Charters, owned by Captain Chuckie Ebanks, is fully equipped for deep-sea and reef fishing as well as snorkel trips on his fully equipped and supplied eponymous 40-foot Sea Ray. His rates are comparatively reasonable, and he can arrange clean, inexpensive local accommodations. ☎ *345/916–6319, 345/949–0400* ⊕ *www.fishgrandcayman.com.*

Oh Boy Charters. Oh Boy Charters charters a 60-foot yacht with complete amenities for day (and overnight) trips, as well as sunset and dinner cruises, plus a 34-foot Crusader. Alvin Ebanks—son of Caymanian marine royalty, the indomitable Captain Marvin Ebanks—jokingly claims he's been playing in and plying the waters for a century and tells tales (tall and otherwise) of his father reeling him in for fishing expeditions. No more than eight passengers on the deep-sea boats ensures the personal touch (snorkeling on the 60-footer accommodates more people). Guests always receive a good selection of their catch; if you prefer others to do the cooking, go night fishing (including catch-and-release shark safaris), which includes dinner. ☎ *345/949–6341, 345/926–0898* ⊕ *www.ohboycharters.com.*

R&M Fly Shop and Charters. Captain Ronald Ebanks of R&M Fly Shop and Charters is arguably the island's most knowledgeable fly-fishing guide, with more than 10 years' experience in Cayman and Scotland. He also runs light-tackle trips on a 24-foot Robalo. Everyone from beginners—even children—to experienced casters will enjoy and learn from the trip (whether wading or poling from a 17-foot Stratos Flats boat); free transfers are included. Captain Ronald even ties his own flies (he'll show you how). ☎ *345/947–3146, 345/946–0214* ⊕ *www. flyfishgrandcayman.com.*

Sea Star Charters. Sea Star Charters, aka Captain Clinton's Watersports, is run by Clinton Ebanks, a fine and very friendly Caymanian who will do whatever it takes to make sure that you have a wonderful time on his two 27- and 28-foot cabin cruisers (and from the 35-foot trimaran used primarily for snorkeling cruises), enjoying light-tackle, bone-, and bottom-fishing. He's a good choice for beginners and offers a nice cultural experience as well as sailing charters and snorkeling with complimentary transportation and equipment. Only cash and traveler's checks are accepted. ☎ *345/949–1016 evenings, 345/916–5234.*

GOLF

Britannia. The Britannia golf course, next to the Grand Cayman Beach Suites, was designed by Jack Nicklaus. The course is really a 9-hole routing with two sets of different tees so as to provide an 18-hole experience when played twice. The courses feature artificial abrupt mounding and lots of water similar to what Nicklaus did early on in Florida. Signature tough holes include 3 and 10; beware tricky winds on 7 through 11. Amenities include a full pro shop and the Britannia Golf Grille (with particularly good breakfasts and local fare). ⊠ *West Bay Rd., Seven Mile Beach* ☎ *345/745–4653* ⊕ *www.britannia-golf.com* ⛳ *9-hole course with 2 tees for 18-hole equivalent, 5829 yards, par 70* 💲 *$100 for 9 holes, $150 for 18 ($75/$115 in off-season).*

North Sound Golf Club. Formerly the Links at Safehaven, the North Sound Golf is Cayman's only 18-hole golf course and infamous among duffers for its strong wind gusts. Roy Case factored the wind into his design, which incorporates lots of looming water and sand bunkers. The handsome setting features many mature mahogany and silver thatch trees where iguana lurk. Wear shorts at least 14 inches long (15 inches for women); no T-shirts are allowed, only collared shirts. Green fees change seasonally, and there are twilight and walking discounts (though carts are recommended), and there's a fine pro shop and an open-air bar with large-screen TVs. ⊠ *Off West Bay Rd., Seven Mile Beach* ☎ *345/947–4653* ⊕ *www.northsoundclub.com* ⸙ *18 holes, 6605 yards, par 71* ⊟ *$175 for 18 holes; $110 for 9 holes, including cart.*

GUIDED TOURS

Taxi drivers will give you a personalized tour of Grand Cayman for about $25 per hour for up to three people. Or you can choose a fascinating helicopter ride, a horseback or mountain-bike journey, a 4x4 safari expedition, or a full-day bus excursion. Ask your hotel to help you make arrangements.

Costs and itineraries for island tours are about the same regardless of the tour operator. Half-day tours average $40 to $50 a person and generally include a visit to Hell and the Turtle Farm at Boatswain's Beach aquatic park in West Bay, as well as shopping downtown. Full-day tours ($60 to $90 per person) add lunch, a visit to Bodden Town (the first settlement), and the East End, where you stop at the Queen Elizabeth II Botanic Park, blowholes (if the waves are high) on the ironshore, and the site of the wreck of the *Ten Sails* (not the wreck itself—just the site). The pirate graves in Bodden Town were destroyed during Hurricane Ivan in 2008, and the blowholes were partially filled. As you can tell, land tours here are low-key. Children under 12 often receive discounts.

A.A. Transportation Services. A.A. Transportation Services offers taxis and tour buses—ask for Burton Ebanks. ☎ *345/949–6598, 345/926–8294, 345/949–7222.*

Cayman Safari. Cayman Safari hits the usual sights but emphasizes interaction with locals, so you learn about craft traditions, folklore, and herbal medicines; careening along in Land Rovers is incidental fun. ☎ *345/925–3001, 866/211–4677* ⊕ *www.caymansafari.com.*

Majestic Tours. Majestic Tours caters mostly to cruise-ship and incentive groups but also offers similar options to individuals and can customize tours, starting at $45 per person; it's particularly good for West Bay, including the Cayman Turtle Farm and Hell. ☎ *345/949–7773* ⊕ *www. majestic-tours.com.*

McCurley Tours. McCurley Tours is owned by B.A. McCurley, a freespirited, freewheeling Midwesterner who's lived in Cayman since the mid-1980s and knows everything and everyone on the East End. Not only is she encyclopedic and flexible, but she also offers car rentals and transfers for travelers staying on the North Side or East End; don't be surprised if she tells you what to order at lunch, especially if it's off the menu. ☎ *345/947–9626, 345/916–0925.*

Tropicana Tours. Tropicana Tours offers several excellent Cayman highlights itineraries on its larger buses, including Stingray City stops, as well as reef runner adventures across the North Sound through the mangrove swamps. ☎ *345/949–0944* ⊕ *www.tropicana-tours.com.*

HIKING

Mastic Trail. The National Trust's internationally significant Mastic Trail, used in the 1800s as the only direct path to and from the North Side, is a rugged 2-mile (3-km) slash through 776 dense acres of woodlands, black mangrove swamps, savannah, agricultural remnants, and ancient rock formations. It embraces more than 700 species, including Cayman's largest remaining contiguous ancient forest (one of the heavily deforested Caribbean's last examples). A comfortable walk depends on weather—winter is better because it's drier, though flowering plants such as the banana orchid set the trail ablaze in summer. Call the National Trust to determine suitability and to book a guide for $30; tours are run daily from 9 to 5 by appointment only, regularly on Wednesday at 9 am (sometimes earlier in summer). Or walk on the wild side with a $5 guidebook that provides information on the ecosystems you traverse, the endemic wildlife you might encounter, seasonal changes, poisonous plants to avoid, and folkloric uses of various flora. The trip takes about three hours. ⊠ *Frank Sound Rd., entrance by fire station at botanic park, Breakers, East End* ☎ *345/749–1121, 345/749–1124 for guide reservations* ⊕ *www.nationaltrust.org.ky.*

HORSEBACK RIDING

Coral Stone Stables. Coral Stone Stables offers 90-minute leisurely horseback rides along the white-sand beaches at Barkers, and inland trails at Savannah; complimentary photos are included. Your guide is Nolan Stewart, whose ranch contains 20 horses, chickens, and "randy" roosters. Nolan offers a nonstop narrative on flora, fauna, and history. He's an entertaining, endless font of local information, some of it unprintable. Rides are $80; swim rides cost $120. ⊠ *Conch Point Rd., next to Restaurante Papagallo on left, West Bay* ☎ *345/916–4799* ⊕ *www.csstables.com.*

FAMILY **Pampered Ponies.** Pampered Ponies offers what is called "the ultimate tanning machine": horses walking, trotting, and cantering along the beaches. You can do either private tours or a variety of guided trips, including sunset, moonlight, and swim rides along the uninhabited beach from Conch Point to Morgan's Harbour on the north tip beyond West Bay. ⊠ *355 Conch Point Rd., Barkers, West Bay* ☎ *345/945–2262, 345/916–2540* ⊕ *www.ponies.ky.*

KAYAKING

FAMILY **Cayman Kayaks.** Cayman Kayaks explores Grand Cayman's protected mangrove wetlands, providing an absorbing discussion of the indigenous animals (including a mesmerizing stop at a gently pulsing, non-stinging Cassiopeia jellyfish pond) and plants, the effects of hurricanes, and conservation efforts. Even beginners will find the tours easy (the guides dub it low-impact aerobics), and the sit-on-top tandem kayaks are quite stable and comfortable. The Bio Bay tour involves more strenuous paddling, but the underwater light show is magical as millions of bio-luminescent microorganisms called dinoflagellates glow like fireflies when disturbed. It runs only on moonless nights for full effect and

8

books well in advance. This is a mobile operation, so tours depart from different locations, most from the public access jetty just to the left of Rum Point; costs run from $25 to $59 (some tours offer kids' and group discounts). ⊠ *Rum Point, Cayman Kai, North Side* ☎ *345/746–3249, 345/926–4467* ⊕ *www.caymankayaks.com.*

SEA EXCURSIONS

The most impressive sights in the Cayman Islands are on and underwater, and several submarines, semisubmersibles, glass-bottom boats, and Jules Verne–like contraptions allow you to see these wonders without getting your feet wet. Sunset sails, dinner cruises, and other theme (dance, booze, pirate) cruises are available from $30 to $90 per person.

FAMILY **Atlantis Submarines.** This submarine takes 48 passengers safely and comfortably along the Cayman Wall down to 100 feet. You peep through panoramic portholes as good-natured guides keep up a humorous but informative patter. A guide dons scuba gear to feed fish, who form a whirling frenzy of color rivaling anything by Picasso. At night, the 10,000-watt lights show the kaleidoscopic underwater colors and nocturnal stealth predators more brilliantly than during the day. Try to sit toward the front so you can watch the pilot's nimble maneuverings and the depth gauge. If that literally in-depth tour seems daunting, get up close and personal on the *Seaworld Observatory* semisubmersible (glorified glass-bottom boat), which just cruises the harbor (including glimpses of the *Cali* and *Balboa* shipwrecks). The cost is $89–$104 (children $49–$64) for the submarine, $39 (children $24) for the semisubmersible. There are frequent online booking discounts. ⊠ *30 S. Church St.* ☎ *345/949–7700, 800/887–8571* ⊕ *www.caymanislandssubmarines.com.*

FAMILY **Jolly Roger.** The *Jolly Roger* is a two-thirds-size replica of Christopher Columbus's 17th-century Spanish galleon *Niña*; the company also owns the *Anne Bonny*, a wooden Norwegian brig built in 1934 that holds more than 100 passengers. On the afternoon snorkel cruise, play Captain Jack Sparrow while experiencing swashbuckling pirate antics, including a trial, sword fight, and walking the plank; the kids can fire the cannon, help hoist the main sail, and scrub the decks (it's guaranteed that they will love it even if they loathe doing chores at home). The evening options (sunset and dinner sails) are more standard booze cruises, less appropriate for the kiddies. Food is more appropriate to the brig, and it's more yo-ho-hokum than remotely authentic, but it's fun. Prices range from $40 to $60. ⊠ *South Terminal, next to Atlantis Submarines* ☎ *345/945–7245* ⊕ *www.jollyrogercayman.com, www.piratesofthecaymans.com.*

FAMILY **Sea Trek.** Sea Trek offers helmet diving, permitting you to walk and breathe 26 feet underwater—without getting your hair wet—for an hour. No training or even swimming ability is required, and you can wear glasses. Guides give a thorough safety briefing, and a sophisticated system of compressors and cylinders provides triple the amount of air necessary for normal breathing while a safety diver program ensures four distinct levels of backup. The result at near-zero gravity resembles an exhilarating moonwalk. The minimum age is eight. The cost is $89 to $99 per person (the latter for an "Ultimate Stingray City" excursion). ⊠ *The Cabana, N. Church St.* ☎ *345/949–0008* ⊕ *www.seatrekcayman. com, www.snubacayman.com.*

A group of stingrays patrols the grassy shallows of Grand Cayman.

SNORKELING

Stingray City Sandbar is the most popular snorkeling destination by far, and dozens of boats head that way several times a day. It's a not-to-be-missed experience that you will remember for years to come. The area is always less crowded if you can go on a day when there aren't too many cruise ships in port.

SNORKELING SITES

Wreck of the Cali. You can still identify the engines and winches of the Wreck of the *Cali*, an old sailing freighter, which settled about 20 feet down. The sponges are particularly vivid, and tropical fish, shrimp, and lobster abound. Many operators based in George Town and Seven Mile Beach come here, as well as Eden Rock. ⊠ *About 50 yards out from Rackam's Waterfront Pub, 93 N. Church St.*

SNORKELING OPERATORS

Bayside Watersports. Bayside Watersports offers half-day snorkeling trips, North Sound beach lunch excursions, Stingray City and dinner cruises, and full-day deep-sea fishing. The company operates several popular boats out of West Bay's Morgan's Harbour. Full-day trips include lunch and conch diving in season (November–April). ⊠ *Morgan's Harbour, West Bay* ☏ *345/949–3200* ⊕ *www.baysidewatersports.com.*

FAMILY **Fantasea Tours.** Captain Dexter Ebanks runs Fantasea Tours on his 38-foot trimaran, *Don't Even Ask,* usually departing from the Cayman Islands Yacht Club. He doesn't pack you in like sardines (20 people max) and is particularly helpful with first-timers. Like many of the captains, he has his own pet names for the rays (ask him to find Lucy, whom he "adopted") and rattles off fascinating factoids during an

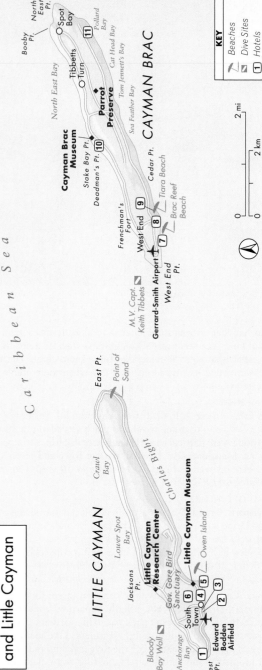

Cayman Brac and Little Cayman

LITTLE CAYMAN

Little Cayman Research Center

Little Cayman Museum

Caribbean Sea

West End Pt.
Edward Bodden Airfield
Anchorage Bay
Bloody Bay Wall
Jacksons Pt.
Louver Spot Bay
Gov. Gore Bird Sanctuary
South Town
Owen Island
Charles Bight
Crawl Bay
East Pt.
Point of Sand

CAYMAN BRAC

Cayman Brac Museum

North East Bay
Stake Bay Pt.
Deadman's Pt.
Frenchman's Fort
West End
West End Pt.
Gerrard-Smith Airport
M.V. Capt. Keith Tibbets
Cedar Pt.
Brac Reef Beach
Tiara Beach
Parrot Preserve
Tibbetts Turn
Sea Feather Bay
Tom Jennett's Bay
Cat Head Bay
Pollard Bay
Spot Bay
Booby Pt.
North East Pt.

KEY

Beaches
Dive Sites
1 Hotels

2 mi
2 km

entertaining, non-stop narration. It's a laid-back trip, with Bob Marley and Norah Jones on the sound system, and fresh fruit and rum punch on tap. ⊠ *West Bay Rd., Seven Mile Beach* ☎ *345/916–0754* ⊕ *www. dexters-fantaseatours.com.*

FAMILY **Red Sail Sports.** Red Sail Sports offers Stingray City, sunset, and evening sails (including dinner in winter) on its luxurious 62- and 65-foot catamarans, the *Spirits of Cayman, Poseidon, Calypso,* and *Ppalu.* It often carries large groups; although the service may not be personal, it will be efficient. In addition to the large cats, a glass-bottom boat takes passengers to Stingray City/Sandbar and nearby coral reefs. It operates from several hotels, including the Westin and Morritt's, in addition to its Rum Point headquarters. The cost ranges from $40 to $80 ($20 to $40 for children under 12). ☎ *345/949–8745, 345/623–5965, 877/506–6368* ⊕ *www.redsailcayman.com.*

CAYMAN BRAC

Cayman Brac is named for its most distinctive feature, a rugged limestone bluff ("brac" in Gaelic) that runs up the center of the 12-mile (19-km) island, pocked with caves and culminating in a sheer 140-foot cliff at its eastern end. The Brac, 89 miles (143 km) northeast of Grand Cayman, is accessible via Cayman Airways. It's a splendidly serene destination for eco-enthusiasts, offering world-class birding, scuba diving, bonefishing in the shallows or light-tackle and deep-sea angling, hiking, spelunking, and rock climbing. With only 1,800 residents—they call themselves Brackers—the island has the feel and easy pace of a small town. Brackers are known for their friendly attitude toward visitors, so it's easy to strike up a conversation. Locals wave at passing and might invite you home for a traditional rundown (a thick, sultry fish stew) and storytelling, usually about the sea, the turtle schooners, and the great hurricane of 1932 (when the caves offered shelter to islanders).

Brackers are as calm and peaceful as their island is rugged, having been violently sculpted by sea and wind, most recently by Hurricane Paloma, which leveled the island in 2008 (locals quip that all 18 churches sustained significant damage—but no bars).

EXPLORING

Cayman Brac Museum. Here you'll find a diverse, well-displayed collection of historic Bracker implements from scary dental pliers to pistols to pottery. A meticulously crafted scale model of the Caymanian catboat *Alsons* has pride of place. The front room faithfully reconstructs the Customs, Treasury, bank, and post office as they would have looked decades ago. Permanent exhibits include those on the 1932 hurricane, turtling, shipbuilding, and typical old-time home life, including a child's bedroom; the back room hosts rotating exhibits such as one on herbal folk medicine. ⊠ *Old Government Administration Bldg., Stake Bay* ☎ *345/948–2622, 345/244–4446* 🖾 *Free* ⊙ *Weekdays 9–4, Sat. 9–noon.*

Fodor'sChoice **Parrot Preserve.** The likeliest place to spot the endangered Cayman
★ Brac parrot—and other indigenous and migratory birds—is along this
National Trust hiking trail off Major Donald Drive, aka Lighthouse
Road. Prime time is early morning or late afternoon; most of the
day they're camouflaged by trees, earning them the moniker "stealth
parrot." The loop trail incorporates part of a path the Brackers used
in olden days to cross the bluff to reach their provision grounds on
the south shore or to gather coconuts, once a major export crop. It
passes through several types of terrain: old farmland under grass and
native trees from mango to mahogany unusually mixed with orchids
and cacti. Wear sturdy shoes, as the terrain is rocky, uneven, and
occasionally rough. The 6-mile (10-km) gravel road continues to the
lighthouse at the bluff's eastern end, where there's an astonishing
view from atop the cliff to the open ocean—the best place to watch
the sunrise. ⊠ *Lighthouse Rd., ½ mile (1 km) south of town, Tibbetts
Turn* ☎ *345/948–0319* ⌂ *Free* ⊗ *Daily sunrise–sunset.*

BEACHES

Much of the Brac's coastline is ironshore, though there are several
pretty sand beaches, mostly along the southwest coast (where swimmers will also find extensive beds of turtle grass, which creates less
than ideal conditions for snorkeling). In addition to the hotel beaches,
where everyone is welcome, there is a public beach with good access
to the reef; it's well marked on tourist maps. The north-coast beaches,
predominantly rocky ironshore, offer excellent snorkeling.

Pollard Bay. The beach by Cayman Breakers is fairly wide for this
eastern stretch of the island. You can start clambering east underneath the imposing Bluff, past the end of the paved road, to find
strikingly beautiful deserted stretches accessible only on foot, but the
water here starts churning like a washing machine. It becomes pro-
gressively rockier, littered with driftwood; you might stumble upon
locals searching for whelks here. There are also new steps by the
Breakers leading to shore dive sites. Flocks of seabirds darken the sun
for seconds at a time, while blowholes spout as if answering migrant
humpback whales. Don't go beyond the gargantuan rock called First
Cay—the sudden swells can be hazardous—unless you're a serious
rock climber. **Amenities:** none. **Best for:** solitude; walking. ⊠ *South
Side Rd. E, East End.*

Public Beach. Roughly 2 miles (3 km) east of the Brac Reef and Carib
Sands/Brac Caribbean resorts, just past the wetlands (the unsightly
gate is visible from the road; if you hit the Bat Cave you've passed
it), lie a series of strands culminating in this relatively deserted beach
(despite its name). The surf is calm and the crystalline water fairly
protected for swimming. There are picnic tables and showers in uncer-
tain condition. Snorkeling is quite good. **Amenities:** showers. **Best for:**
snorkeling. ⊠ *South Side Rd. W, South Side.*

Sea Feather Bay. The central section of the south coast features several
lengthy ribbons of soft ecru sand, only occasionally maintained, with
little shade aside from the occasional coconut palm, no facilities, and

blissful privacy (aside from the occasional villa). **Amenities:** none. **Best for:** solitude; swimming; walking. ⊠ *South Side Rd. just west of Ashton Reid Dr., Sea Feather Bay, South Side.*

WHERE TO STAY

Cayman Brac has a handful of hotels and resorts, as well as a decent bed-and-breakfast and several apartments. Several private villas on Cayman Brac can also be rented, most of them basic but well maintained, ranging from one to four bedrooms. Most resorts offer optional meal plans, but there are several restaurants, some of which provide free transport from your hotel. Most restaurants serve island fare (local seafood, chicken, and curries). On Friday and Saturday nights the spicy scent of jerk chicken fills the air; several roadside stands sell take-out dinners. This is a nature and outdoor island; if the weather is bad, there are no indoor activities, so bring a good book just in case.

$$ **Alexander Hotel.** This chic boutique business hotel elevates Brac
HOTEL lodging to a new level, though with no on-site activities to offer vacationers who make up the larger proportion of Brac travelers, its ultimate target audience is unclear. **Pros:** high-tech amenities; stylish yet affordable; next door to small shopping mall for sundries and food; delightful alfresco bar. **Cons:** two-minute walk to a pebbly beach; small pool; inadequate bedside and bathroom lighting; no on-site activities; Wi-Fi spotty in some rooms. Ⓢ *Rooms from: $179* ⊠ *Off South Side Rd., West End* ☎ *345/948–8222, 800/381–5094* ⊕ *www.alexanderhotelcayman.com* ⤸ *29 rooms, 2 2-bedroom suites* ⑪ *No meals.*

$$ **Brac Caribbean and Carib Sands.** These neighboring, beachfront, sister
RESORT complexes offer condos with one to four bedrooms, all individually owned and decorated beyond a "starter" design. **Pros:** lively restaurant-bar; excellent value for families, especially with weekly discounts. **Cons:** pretty but narrow, often unmaintained beach; limited staff; Wi-Fi dodgy. Ⓢ *Rooms from: $165* ⊠ *Bert Marson Dr.* ☎ *345/948–2265, 866/843–2722* ⊕ *www.caribsands.com, www.866thebrac.com* ⤸ *65 condos* ⑪ *No meals.*

$$ **Brac Reef Beach Resort.** Popular with divers, this well-run ecofriendly
RESORT resort features a beautiful sandy beach shaded by sea grape trees slung with hammocks. **Pros:** great dive outfit; friendly vibe; free Wi-Fi; good online packages; coin-operated laundry. **Cons:** noise from planes; view often obscured from ground-floor units; mandatory airport transfer of $20 per person. Ⓢ *Rooms from: $284* ⊠ *West End* ☎ *345/948–1323, 727/323–8727 for reservations in Florida, 800/594–0843* ⊕ *www. bracreef.com* ⤸ *40 rooms* ⑪ *Multiple meal plans.*

$ **Cayman Breakers.** This attractive, pink-brick, colonnaded condo
RENTAL development sitting between the bluff and the southeast coastal ironshore caters to climbers, who scale the bluff's sheer face, as well as divers, who appreciate the good shore diving right off the property. **Pros:** spectacular views; thoughtful extras like complimentary bikes, jigsaw puzzles, and climbing-route guides; very attentive managers who live

8

on-site. **Cons:** nearest grocery is a 15-minute drive; gorgeous beach is rocky with rough surf; some units slightly musty and faded. [$] *Rooms from: $150* ✉ *South Side Rd., near East End* ☎ *345/948–1463* 🌐 *www.caybreakers.com* 🛏 *26 2-bedroom condos* 🍴 *No meals.*

$ B&B/INN **Walton's Mango Manor.** This beautifully restored traditional West Indian home has five rooms (all with bath), accented with lovely antique furnishings, nautical gadgets, maps, model catboats, and bric-a-brac from the Waltons' world travels. **Pros:** true Caymanian hospitality; beautiful grounds; excellent snorkeling; free Wi-Fi access. **Cons:** poky beach across the street; car required. [$] *Rooms from: $120* ✉ *Stake Bay* ☎ *345/948–0518, 321/226–0440 from U.S., 888/866–5809* 🌐 *www.waltonsmangomanor.com* 🛏 *5 rooms, 1 2-bedroom cottage* 🍴 *Breakfast.*

SPORTS AND ACTIVITIES

DIVING AND SNORKELING

Cayman Brac's waters are celebrated for their rich diversity of sea life, from hammerhead and reef sharks to stingrays to sea horses. Divers and snorkelers alike will find towering coral heads, impressive walls, and fascinating wrecks. The snorkeling off the **north coast** is spectacular, particularly at West End, where coral formations close to shore attract all kinds of critters. The walls feature remarkable topography with natural gullies, caves, and fissures blanketed with Technicolor sponges, black coral, gorgonians, and sea fans. Some of the famed sites are the West Chute, Cemetery Wall, Airport Wall, and Garden Eel Wall. The South Wall is a wonderland of sheer drop-offs carved with a maze of vertical swim-throughs, tunnels, arches, and grottoes that divers nickname Cayman's Grand Canyon. Notable sites include Anchor Wall, Rock Monster Chimney, and the Wilderness. Many fish have colonized the 330-foot MV *Capt. Keith Tibbetts,* a Russian frigate—now broken in two—that was deliberately scuttled within swimming distance of the northwest shore. An artist named Foots has created an amazing underwater Atlantis off Radar Reef. The island's two dive operators offer scuba and snorkel training and PADI certification.

Brac Scuba Shack. Partners Martin van der Touw, his wife Liesel, and Steve Reese form a tremendous troika at this new PADI outfit, whose selling points include small groups (no more than 10 divers on the custom Newton 36 boat), flexible departures, valet service, and computer profiles. There's also the 30-foot smaller central console *Big Blue*, which escorts no more than five divers per trip, and does double-duty for deep-sea fishing charters. Courses range from Discover Scuba through Divemaster Training, as well as such specialties as wreck, Nitrox, and night diving. The rates are extremely competitive ($90 for two-tank dives). ✉ *West End* ☎ *345/948–8472* 🌐 *www.bracscubashack.com.*

Reef Divers. Pluses here include five Newton boats, valet service, and enthusiastic, experienced staff. Certified divers can purchase à la carte dive packages even if they aren't guests of the hotel. They also arrange snorkeling tours. ✉ *Brac Reef Beach Resort, West End* ☎ *345/948–1642, 345/948–1323* 🌐 *www.reefdiverscaymanbrac.com, www.bracreef.com.*

HIKING

Brac Tourism Office. Free printed guides to the Brac's many heritage and nature trails can be obtained from the Brac Tourism Office; you can also get the guides at the airport or at your hotel. Traditional routes across the bluff have been cleared and marked; trailheads are identified with signs along the road. It's safe to hike on your own, though some trails are fairly hard going (wear light hiking boots) and others could be better maintained. ⊠ *West End Community Park, west of airport* ☎ *345/948–1649* ⊕ *www.itsyourstoexplore.com, sita.ky.*

Christopher Columbus Gardens. For those who prefer less-strenuous walking, Christopher Columbus Gardens has easy trails and boardwalks. The park showcases the unique natural flora and features of the bluff, including two cave mouths. This is a peaceful spot dotted with gazebos and wooden bridges that traverses several ecosystems from cacti to mahogany trees. ⊠ *Ashton Reid Dr. (Bluff Rd.), just north of Ashton Rutty Centre.*

Sister Islands District Administration. The administration arranges free, government-sponsored, guided nature and cultural tours with trained local guides. Options include the Parrot Reserve, nature trails, wetlands, Lighthouse/Bluff View, caving, birding, and heritage sites. You just supply the wheels and spirit of adventure. ☎ *345/948–2222.*

SPELUNKING

If you plan to explore Cayman Brac's caves, wear good sneakers or hiking shoes, as some paths are steep and rocky and some cave entrances are reachable only by ladders. **Peter's Cave** offers a stunning aerial view of the northeastern community of Spot Bay. **Great Cave,** at the island's southeast end, has numerous chambers and photogenic ocean views. In **Bat Cave** you may see bats hanging from the ceiling (try not to disturb them). **Rebecca's Cave** houses the grave site of a 17-month-old child who died during the horrific hurricane of 1932.

8

NIGHTLIFE

Divers are notoriously early risers, but a few bars keep things hopping if not quite happening, especially on weekends, when local bands (or "imports" from Grand Cayman) often perform. Quaintly reminiscent of *Footloose* (without the hellfire and brimstone), watering holes are required to obtain music and dancing permits. Various community events including talent shows, recitals, concerts, and other stage presentations at the Aston Rutty Centre provide the rest of the island's nightlife.

Barracuda's Bar. New Yorker Terry Chesnard built his dream bar from scratch, endowing it with an almost 1960s Rat Pack ambience. Nearly everything is handcrafted, from the elegant bar itself to the blown-glass light fixtures to the shot specials (try the Barracuda "if you dare") and cocktails with *cojones* (though Terry takes greatest pride in his top-of-the-line espresso machine). The kitchen elevates pub grub to an art form, with reubens and French melts. Local flock here for free pasta Friday, karaoke Wednesday, and live music on Thursday. You might walk in on a hotly contested darts or dominos tournament, but the vibe is otherwise mellow at this charming time-warp hangout. ⊠ *West End* ☎ *345/948–8511* ⊕ *www.barracudas.ky.*

LITTLE CAYMAN

The smallest, most tranquil of the three Cayman Islands, Little Cayman has a full-time population of only 170, most of whom work in the tourism industry. This 12-square-mile (31-square-km) island is still unspoiled and has only a sand-sealed airstrip, no official terminal building, and few vehicles. The speed limit remains 25 mph (40 kph), as no one is in a hurry to go anywhere. In fact, the island's iguanas use roads more regularly than residents; signs created by local artists read "Iguanas Have the Right of Way." With little commercial development, the island beckons ecotourists who seek wildlife encounters, not urban wildlife. It's probably best known for its spectacular diving on world-renowned Bloody Bay Wall and adjacent Jackson Marine Park. The ravishing reefs and plummeting walls encircling the island teem with more than 500 different species of fish and more than 150 kinds of coral. Fly-, lake-, and deep-sea fishing are also popular, as well as snorkeling, kayaking, cycling, and hiking. And the island's certainly for the birds. The National Trust Booby Pond Nature Reserve is a designated wetland of international importance, which protects around 20,000 red-footed boobies, the Western Hemisphere's largest colony. It's just one of many superlative spots to witness avian aerial acrobatics. Pristine wetlands, secluded beaches, unspoiled tropical wilderness, mangrove swamps, lagoons, bejeweled coral reefs: Little Cayman practically redefines escape. Yet aficionados appreciate that the low-key lifestyle doesn't mean sacrificing the high-tech amenities, and some of the resorts cater to a quietly wealthy yet unpretentious crowd.

EXPLORING

Little Cayman Museum. This newly renovated museum displays relics and artifacts, including a wing devoted to maritime memorabilia, that provide a good overview of this tiny island's history and heritage. ⊠ *Across from Booby Pond Nature Reserve, Blossom Village* ☎ *345/948–1033 for Little Cayman Beach Resort* ⊠ *Free* ☉ *Thurs. and Fri. 3–5, by appointment only.*

Fodor'sChoice ★ **Little Cayman National Trust.** This traditional Caymanian cottage overlooks the Booby Pond Nature Reserve; telescopes on the breezy second-floor deck permit close-up views of their markings and nests, as well as the other feathered friends. Inside you'll find shell collections, panels and dioramas discussing endemic reptiles, models "in flight," and diagrams on the growth and life span of red-footed boobies, frigate birds, egrets, and other island "residents." The shop sells exquisite jewelry made from Caymanite and spider-crab shells, extraordinary duck decoys and driftwood carvings, and great books on history, ornithology, and geology. Mike Vallee holds an iguana information session and tour every Friday at 4 pm. The cheeky movie *Calendar Girls* inspired a local equivalent: Little Cayman women, mostly in full, ripe maturity, going topless for an important cause—raising awareness of the red-footed booby and funds to purchase the sanctuary's land. Nicknamed, appropriately, "Support the Boobies," the calendar is tasteful, not titillating: the lasses strategically hold conch shells, brochures, flippers, tree branches, and so on. ⊠ *Blossom Village* ⊕ *www.nationaltrust.org.ky* ☉ *Weekdays 3–5.*

Little Cayman Research Center. Near the Jackson Point Bloody Bay Marine Park reserve, this vital research center supports visiting students and researchers, with a long list of projects studying the biodiversity, human impact, reef health, and ocean ecosystem of Little Cayman. Its situation is unique in that reefs this unspoiled are usually far less accessible; the National Oceanic and Atmospheric Administration awarded it one of 16 monitoring stations worldwide. The center also solicits funding through the parent U.S. nonprofit organization Central Caribbean Marine Institute; if you value the health of our reefs, show your support on the Web site. Chairman Peter Hillenbrand proudly calls it the "Ritz-Carlton of marine research facilities, which often are little more than pitched tents on a beach." Tours explain the center's mission and ecosensitive design (including Peter's Potty, an off-the-grid bathroom facility using compostable toilets that recycle fertilizer into gray water for the gardens); sometimes you'll get a peek at the upstairs functional wet labs and dormitories. To make it layperson-friendlier, scientists occasionally give talks and presentations. The Dive with a Researcher program (where you actually help survey and assess environmental impact and ecosystem health, depending on that week's focus) is hugely popular. ⊠ *North Side* ☎ *345/948–1094* ⊕ *www. reefresearch.org* ☉ *By appointment only.*

BEACHES

The southwest part of the island seems like one giant beach; this is where virtually all the resorts sit, serenely facing Preston Bay and South Hole Sound. But there are several other unspoiled, usually deserted strands that beckon beachcombers, all the sand having the same delicate hue of Cristal champagne and just as apt to make you feel giddy.

Fodor's Choice ★ **Owen Island.** This private, forested island can be reached by rowboat, kayak, or an ambitious 200-yard swim. Anyone is welcome to come across and enjoy the deserted beaches and excellent snorkeling. Nudity is forbidden as "idle and disorderly" in the Cayman Islands, though that doesn't always stop skinny-dippers (who may not realize they can be seen quite easily from shore on the strands facing Little Cayman). **Amenities:** none. **Best for:** snorkeling; solitude; swimming.

Fodor's Choice ★ **Point of Sand.** Stretching over a mile on the easternmost point of the island, this secluded beach is great for wading, shell collecting, and snorkeling. On a clear day you can see 7 miles (11 km) across to Cayman Brac. It serves as a green- and loggerhead turtle nesting site in spring, and a marvelous mosaic of coral gardens blooms just offshore. It's magical, especially at moonrise, when it earns its nickname, Lovers' Beach. There's a palapa for shade but no facilities. The current can be strong, so watch the kids carefully. **Amenities:** none. **Best for:** snorkeling; solitude; sunset; walking.

WHERE TO STAY

Accommodations are mostly in small lodges, many of which offer meal and dive packages. The meal packages are a good idea; the chefs in most places create wonderful dishes with often limited resources.

$$$ RENTAL
🏨 **The Club.** These ultramodern, luxurious, three-bedroom condos are Little Cayman's nicest units, though only five are usually included in the rental pool. **Pros:** luxurious digs; lovely beach; hot tub. **Cons:** housekeeping not included; rear guest bedrooms dark and somewhat cramped; handsome but heavy old-fashioned decor. [$] *Rooms from: $311* ✉ *South Hole Sound* ☎ *345/948–1033, 727/323–8727, 800/327–3835* 🌐 *www.theclubatlittlecayman.com* 🛏 *8 condos* 🍴 *No meals.*

$$$ RENTAL FAMILY
🏨 **Conch Club.** The handsome oceanfront development grafts Caribbean-style gingerbread onto New England maritime architecture with gables and dormers. **Pros:** splendid views; gorgeous beach; complimentary airport transfers; beachfront hot tub; complimentary bicycles and kayaks. **Cons:** long walk to nearby restaurants; dated decor; housekeeping surcharge. [$] *Rooms from: $350* ✉ *Blossom Village* ☎ *345/948–1026, 561/283–1715 from U.S.* 🌐 *www.conchclubcondos.com* 🛏 *18 2-bedroom condos, 2 3-bedroom condos* 🍴 *No meals.*

$$$ RESORT FAMILY
🏨 **Little Cayman Beach Resort.** This two-story hotel, the island's largest, offers modern facilities in a boutique setting. **Pros:** extensive facilities; fun crowd; glorious LED-lighted pool; topnotch bone- and deep-sea fishing. **Cons:** less intimate feel than other island resorts; tiny patios; fee to rent bikes. [$] *Rooms from: $399* ✉ *Blossom Village* ☎ *345/948–1033, 800/327–3835* 🌐 *www.littlecayman.com* 🛏 *40 rooms* 🍴 *Multiple meal plans.*

$$ RENTAL
🏨 **Paradise Villas.** The cozy, sunny, one-bedroom units have beachfront terraces and hammocks and are simply but immaculately appointed with rattan furnishings, marine artwork, painted driftwood, and bright abstract fabrics. **Pros:** good value; friendly staff; frequent online-only deals in addition to good dive packages. **Cons:** noisy some weekend nights in season; poky beach; now a (minimal) charge for bike use; dive shop no longer on-site (though the contracted operation runs smoothly). [$] *Rooms from: $200* ✉ *South Hole Sound* ☎ *345/948–0001, 877/322–9626* 🌐 *www.paradisevillas.com* 🛏 *12 1-bedroom villas* 🕓 *Closed mid-Sept.–late Oct.* 🍴 *No meals.*

$$$$ RESORT Fodor's Choice ★
🏨 **Pirates Point Resort.** Comfortable, recently renovated rooms and fine cuisine make this hideaway nestled between sea grape and casuarina pines on a sweep of sand one of Little Cayman's best properties. **Pros:** fabulous food; fantastic beach; dynamic dive program; fun-loving staff and owner. **Cons:** everyone respects honeymooners' privacy, but this isn't a resort for antisocial types; tasteful rooms are fairly spare; occasional Internet problems. [$] *Rooms from: $484* ✉ *Pirates Point* ☎ *345/948–1010* 🌐 *www.piratespointresort.com* 🛏 *11 rooms* 🕓 *Closed Sept.–mid-Oct.* 🍴 *Multiple meal plans.*

$$$$ RESORT Fodor's Choice ★
🏨 **Southern Cross Club.** Little Cayman's first resort was cofounded in the 1950s as a private fishing club by the CEO of Sears-Roebuck and CFO of General Motors, and its focus is still on fishing and diving. **Pros:** barefoot luxury; complimentary use of kayaks and snorkel gear; splendiferous beach; international staff regales you with globe-trotting

exploits. **Cons:** not child-friendly (though families can rent a separate cottage); Wi-Fi promised but still not available in some rooms, with spotty signal otherwise. $ *Rooms from: $704* ⊠ *South Hole Sound* ☎ *345/948–1099, 800/899–2582* ⊕ *www.southerncrossclub. com* ➽ *12 suites, 1 2-bedroom cottage* ☉ *Closed mid-Sept.–mid-Oct.* �🍽 *All meals.*

SPORTS AND ACTIVITIES

BIRD-WATCHING

Little Cayman offers bountiful bird-watching, with more than 200 indigenous and migrant species on vibrant display, including red-footed boobies, frigate birds, and West Indian whistling ducks. Unspoiled wetland blankets more than 40% of the island, and elevated viewing platforms (carefully crafted from local wood to blend harmoniously with the environment) permit undisturbed observation—but then, it's hard to find an area that doesn't host flocks of warblers and waterfowl. Brochures with maps are available at the hotels for self-guided bird-watching tours.

Fodor's Choice ★ **Booby Pond Nature Reserve.** The reserve is home to 20,000 red-footed boobies (the largest colony in the Western Hemisphere) and Cayman's only breeding colony of magnificent frigate (or man-of-war) birds; other sightings include the near-threatened West Indian whistling duck and vitelline warbler. The RAMSAR Convention, an international treaty for wetland conservation, designated the reserve a wetland of global significance. Near the airport, the sanctuary is open to the public, and has a gift shop and reading library. ⊠ *Next to National Trust, Blossom Village.*

DIVING AND SNORKELING

Expect to pay around $105 for a two-tank boat dive and $25–$30 for a snorkeling trip. The island is small and susceptible to wind, so itineraries can change like a sudden gust.

Fodor's Choice ★ **Bloody Bay Wall.** This beach, named for having been the site of a spectacular 17th-century sea battle, has been declared one of the world's top three dive sites by no less than the *maîtres* Jacques and Philippe Cousteau and forms part of a protected marine reserve. It plunges dramatically from 18,000 to 6,000 feet, with a series of staggeringly beautiful drop-offs and remarkable visibility. Even snorkelers who are strong swimmers can access the edge from shore, gliding among shimmering silver curtains of minnows, jacks, bonefish, and more. The critters are amazingly friendly, including Jerry the Grouper, whom dive masters joke is a representative for the Cayman Islands Department of Tourism.

RECOMMENDED DIVE OPERATORS

Pirate's Point Dive Resort. This popular resort has fully outfitted 42-foot Newtons with dive masters who excel at finding odd and rare creatures, and encourage computer diving so you can stay down longer. ⊠ *Pirate's Point* ☎ *345/948–1010* ⊕ *www.piratespointresort.com.*

8

Reef Divers. Little Cayman Beach Resort's outfitter also offers valet service and a full complement of courses, with Nitrox one of the specialties; their custom boats' state-of-the-art outfitting includes AEDs (defibrillators). ⊠ *At Little Cayman Beach Resort, Blossom Village* ☎ *345/948–1033* ⊕ *www.littlecayman.com.*

Southern Cross Club. The Southern Cross Club limits each of its boats to 12 divers and has its own dock. It's particularly good with specialty courses and mandates computer diving. ⊠ *73 Guy Banks Rd., at Southern Cross Club, South Hole Sound* ☎ *345/948–1099, 800/899–2582* ⊕ *www.southerncrossclub.com.*

FISHING

Bloody Bay is equally celebrated for fishing and diving, and the flats and shallows including South Hole Sound Lagoon across from Owen Island, Tarpon Lake, and the Charles Bight Rosetta Flats offer phenomenal light-tackle and fly-fishing action: surprisingly large tarpon, small bonefish, and permit (a large fish related to pompano) weighing up to 35 pounds. Superior deep-sea fishing is available right offshore for game fish such as blue marlin, dolphinfish, wahoo, tuna, and barracuda.

Southern Cross Club. The Southern Cross Club offers light-tackle and deep-sea fishing trips. ⊠ *73 Guy Banks Dr., South Hole Sound* ☎ *345/ 948–1099, 800/899–2582* ⊕ *www.southerncrossclub.com.*

CURAÇAO

WELCOME TO CURAÇAO

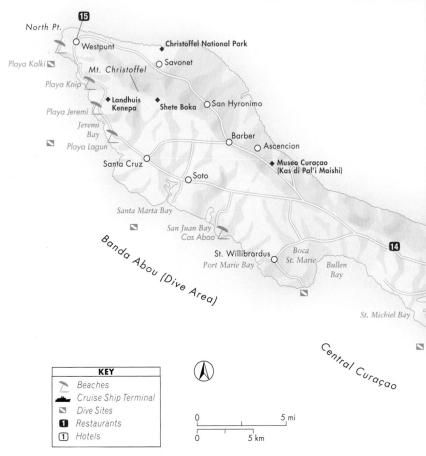

North Pt.

15

Westpunt

Playa Kalki

Christoffel National Park

Savonet

Mt. Christoffel

Playa Knip

Landhuis Kenepa

Shete Boka

San Hyronimo

Playa Jeremi

Jeremi Bay

Playa Lagun

Barber

Ascencion

Museo Curaçao (Kas di Pal'i Maishi)

Santa Cruz

Soto

Santa Marta Bay

San Juan Bay
Cas Abao

St. Willibrordus
Port Marie Bay

Boca St. Marie

Bullen Bay

Banda Abou (Dive Area)

14

St. Michiel Bay

Central Curaçao

KEY	
⚲	Beaches
⚓	Cruise Ship Terminal
◪	Dive Sites
1	Restaurants
①	Hotels

0 _____ 5 mi
0 _____ 5 km

Willemstad's fancifully hued, strikingly gabled town houses glimmer across Santa Anna Bay, and vendors at the Floating Market sell tropical fruit from their schooners. Curaçao's diverse population mixes Latin, European, and African ancestries. Religious tolerance is a hallmark here. All people are welcome in Curaçao, and even tourists feel the warmth.

AN ISLAND REBORN AND REDISCOVERED

The largest and most populous of the Netherlands Antilles is 38 miles (61 km) long and no more than 7½ miles (12 km) wide. Its capital, Willemstad, has been restored and revived over the past few years and is a recognized UNESCO World Heritage Site. The colorful waterfront town houses are unique to the island.

Restaurants ▼	Hotels ▼
Awa di Playa **4**	Avila Hotel **8**
Bistro Le Clochard **1**	Baoase **4**
Blues **9**	Blue Bay Village **13**
CRU Steak House **7**	Curaçao Marriott **11**
Dal Toro **8**	Floris Suite Hotel **12**
Fort Nassau Restaurant **11**	Hilton Curaçao **14**
Gouverneur de Rouville Restaurant & Café **2**	Hotel't Klooster **1**
Jaanchies **15**	Howard Johnson Plaza Hotel **2**
La Bahia **3**	Lagun Blou Dive & Beach Resort **7**
L'aldea Steakhouse ... **13**	Lions Dive **6**
Landhuis Daniel **14**	Papagayo Beach **9**
Mambo Beach **10**	Renaissance Curaçao Resort **3**
Scampi's **5**	Santa Barbara Beach & Golf Resort **10**
Shore **12**	Sunscape Curaçao **5**
Tempo Doeloe **6**	

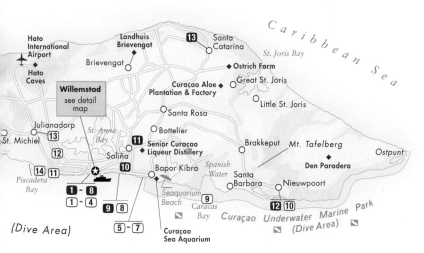

TOP REASONS TO VISIT CURAÇAO

1 Below the Belt: Because it sits below the hurricane belt, the weather in Curaçao is almost always alluring, even during the off-season.

2 Carnival: Curaçao's biggest party draws an increasingly large crowd.

3 Culture: The island's cultural diversity is reflected in the good food from many different cultures.

4 History You Can See: Striking architecture and fascinating historic sites give you something to see when you're not shopping or sunning on the charming beaches.

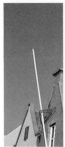

Updated by Vernon O'Reilly Ramesar

The sun smiles down on Curaçao, which sits on the outer fringe of the so-called hurricane belt. Gentle trade winds help keep temperatures generally in the 80s. Water sports—including outstanding reef diving—attract enthusiasts from all over the world. Curaçao claims 38 beaches—some long stretches of silky sand, most smaller coves suitable for picture postcards. In the countryside, the dollhouse look of plantation houses, or *landhuizen* (literally, "land houses"), makes a cheerful contrast to stark cacti and austere shrubbery.

The sprawling city of Willemstad is the island's capital. Its historic downtown and the natural harbor (*Schottegat*), around which it's built are included on UNESCO's World Heritage List, a coveted distinction reserved for the likes of the Palace of Versailles and the Taj Mahal. The "face" of Willemstad delights like a kaleidoscope—rows of sprightly painted town houses with gabled roofs sit perched alongside the steely blue Santa Anna Bay. Local lore has it that in the 1800s the governor claimed he suffered from migraines and blamed the glare from the sun's reflection off the then-white structures. To alleviate the problem, he ordered the facades painted in colors.

Curaçao was discovered by Alonzo de Ojeda (a lieutenant of Columbus) in 1499. The first Spanish settlers arrived in 1527. In 1634 the Dutch came via the Netherlands West Indies Company. Eight years later Peter Stuyvesant began his rule as governor (in 1647, Stuyvesant became governor of New Amsterdam, which later became New York). Twelve Jewish families arrived in Curaçao from Amsterdam in 1651, and by 1732 a synagogue had been built; the present structure is the oldest synagogue in continuous use in the Western Hemisphere. Over the years the city built fortresses to defend against French and British invasions—the standing ramparts now house restaurants and hotels. The Dutch claim to Curaçao was recognized in 1815 by the Treaty of

LOGISTICS

Getting to Curaçao: If you want to connect through Aruba, more likely than not you'll have to book your flight on a tiny island-hopper directly with the island-based airline InselAir. Hato International Airport (CUR) has car-rental facilities, duty-free shops, and restaurants.

Hassle Factor: Medium to high.

On the Ground: It takes about 20 minutes to get to the hotels in Willemstad by taxi. Taxis have meters, but drivers still use set fares when picking passengers up at the airport. Verify which method your driver will use before setting off; fixed rates apply for up to four passengers in a single vehicle. Fares from the airport to Willemstad and the nearby beach hotels run about $18 to $22, and those to hotels at the island's western end about $40 to $47.

Paris. From 1954 through 2006, Curaçao was the seat of government of the Netherlands Antilles, a group of islands under the umbrella of the Kingdom of the Netherlands. In 2010, after discussions with the Netherlands, Curaçao's island council granted the territory autonomy (the same status Aruba attained in 1986).

Tourism is on a fast track to surpassing harbor-related activities as the island's primary source of income, with a corresponding surge in hotel development in recent years. The government has committed funds to an expansion plan to accommodate future growth. The opening of a massive pier has boosted the number of cruise-ship passengers to record highs. In addition, the government and private sources have invested substantially in the restoration of the island's graceful colonial buildings.

Today Curaçao's population derives from nearly 60 nationalities—an exuberant mix of Latin, European, and African roots speaking a Babel of tongues—resulting in superb restaurants and a flourishing cultural scene. Although Dutch is the official language, Papiamento is the vernacular of all the Netherlands Antilles and the preferred choice for communication among the locals. English and Spanish are also widely spoken. The island, like its Dutch settlers, is known for its religious tolerance, and tourists are warmly welcomed.

9

PLANNING

WHEN TO GO

High season in Curaçao mirrors that in much of the Caribbean: basically from mid-December through mid-April. In the off-season, rates will be reduced at least 25% and often more. Hurricanes and severe tropical storms are rare—though still possible—in Curaçao, which means the island has good weather almost year-round.

GETTING HERE AND AROUND

AIR TRAVEL

Most travelers will make a connection in San Juan, Montego Bay, or Aruba. To connect through Aruba, you'll likely have to book your flight on a tiny island-hopper directly with the island-based airline.

Airline Contacts American Airlines ☎ *5999/869–5707.* **Avianca** ☎ *5999/820–2020* ⊕ *www.avianca.com.* **KLM** ☎ *5999/861–0195.*

Airport Hato International Airport. The airport has car-rental facilities, duty-free shops, and restaurants. ⊠ *CUR* ☎ *5999/839–1000.*

Nonstop Flights Atlanta (Delta, seasonal), Miami (American), and New York–Newark (United). American Airlines also offers service from San Juan.

CAR TRAVEL

Many of the larger hotels have free shuttles into Willemstad, or you can take a quick, cheap taxi ride; hotels in Willemstad usually provide a free beach shuttle, so it's possible to get by without a car. If you're planning to do country driving or rough it through Christoffel National Park, a four-wheel-drive vehicle is best. All you need is a valid driver's license. Driving in Curaçao is on the right-hand side of the road; right turns on red are prohibited. Seat belts are required, and motorcyclists must wear helmets. Children under age four must be in child safety seats.

Car Rental: You can rent a car from any of the major car agencies at the airport or have one delivered free to your hotel. Rates are about $40–$47 a day for a compact car to $55–$65 for a four-door sedan or four-wheel-drive vehicle; add 5% tax and optional daily insurance.

Contacts Avis ☎ *5999/461–1255, 800/331–1084* ⊕ *www.avis.com.* **Budget** ☎ *5999/868–3466, 800/472–3325* ⊕ *www.budget.com.* **Hertz** ☎ *5999/888–0088* ⊕ *www.hertz.com.* **National Car Rental** ☎ *5999/869–4433* ⊕ *www. nationalcuracao.com.* **Thrifty** ☎ *5999/461–3089* ⊕ *www.thrifty-curacao.com.*

TAXI TRAVEL

Fares from the airport to Willemstad and the nearby beach hotels run about $18 to $22, and those to hotels at the island's western end about $40 to $47 (be sure to agree on the rate before setting off). The government-approved rates, which do not include waiting time, can be found in a brochure called "Taxi Tariff Guide," available at the airport, hotels, cruise-ship terminals, and the tourist board. Rates are for up to four passengers. There's a 25% surcharge after 11 pm.

Central Dispatch. Taxis are readily available at hotels and at taxi stands at the airport, in Punda, and in Otrobanda; in other cases, call Central Dispatch. ☎ *5999/869–0752.*

ESSENTIALS

Addresses In street addresses that do not specify a house number, the *z/n* is a Dutch abbreviation for *zonder nummer* (no number).

Banks and Exchange Services U.S. dollars are accepted nearly everywhere. Currency in Curaçao is the florin (also called the guilder) and is indicated by *fl* or *NAf* on price tags. The official rate of exchange

at this writing was NAf 1.75 to US$1. The government is considering changing the currency to the Caribbean guilder, but at press time, plans for this change were not definitive.

Electricity 110–130 volts/50 cycles.

Emergency Services Ambulance ☎ *912.* **On-call doctors** ☎ *1111.* **Police and fire** ☎ *911.* **Tourist Emergencies** ☎ *917.*

Passport Requirements A valid passport is required. All visitors must be able to show an ongoing or return ticket as well as have proof of sufficient funds to support their stay on the island.

Phones To call Curaçao direct from the United States, dial 011–5999 plus the number in Curaçao. International roaming for most GSM mobile phones is available in Curaçao. Local companies are UTS (United Telecommunication Services) and Digicel. You can also rent a mobile phone or buy a prepaid SIM card for your own phone.

Taxes and Service Charges The departure tax is $32.50 (including flights to Aruba), and the departure tax to other former members of the Netherlands Antilles islands is $8. This must be paid in cash, in either florins or U.S. dollars. Hotels add a 12% service charge to the bill and collect a 7% government room tax; restaurants typically add 10% to 15%. Most goods and services purchased on the island will also have a 5% OB tax (a goods-and-services tax) added to the purchase price.

Tipping Service is usually included, but if you find the staff exemplary, you can add another 5% to 10% to the bill. Porters and bellhops, about $1 a bag; housekeeping, $2 to $3 per day; taxi, about 10%.

ACCOMMODATIONS

Resort development is concentrated around the capital, Willemstad, so most resorts are within easy reach of town, by shuttle or on foot. As the island becomes more developed, visitors have more options, and there are a few resorts farther removed as well, but it's the amenities that should drive your decision more than location. Choose the type of lodging that best appeals to your interests and style. Those spending a bit more time gravitate to villas and bungalows.

Resorts: Most of Curaçao's larger hotels are midsize resorts of 200 to 300 rooms, and many of them are within easy striking distance of town. The island offers a full range of resorts from the intimate and luxurious to historic properties—few other destinations offer a downtown hotel with a saltwater infinity pool complete with palm-lined beach.

Dive Resorts: Most of the resorts catering to divers are smaller operations of fewer than 100 rooms (often much smaller). Although some of these are in and around Willemstad, there are also a few on the secluded west end of the island, and that's where shore diving is best.

Villas and Bungalows: Though they are marketed primarily to European travelers who have more time to spend on the island, self-catering accommodations are an option for anyone who has at least a week to spend in Curaçao.

HOTEL AND RESTAURANT PRICES

Prices in the restaurant reviews are the average cost of a main course at dinner or, if dinner is not served, at lunch; taxes and service charges are generally included. Prices in the hotel reviews are the lowest cost of a standard double room in high season, excluding taxes, service charges, and meal plans (except at all-inclusives). Prices for rentals are the lowest per-night cost for a one-bedroom unit in high season.

For expanded lodging reviews and current deals, visit Fodors.com.

VISITOR INFORMATION

Contacts Curaçao Tourist Board ✉ *Pietermaai 19, Punda, Willemstad* ☎ *5999/434–8200* ⊕ *www.curacao.com.*

WEDDINGS

You and your partner must be living outside the Netherlands Antilles; you must report to the Office of the Registrar at least three days before your marriage. You'll need a birth certificate, passport, evidence that you are single, or evidence that you are divorced or a widow or widower.

EXPLORING

WILLEMSTAD

What does the capital of Curaçao have in common with New York City? Broadway, for one thing. Here it's called Breedestraat, but the origin is the same. Dutch settlers came here in the 1630s, about the same time they sailed through the Verazzano Narrows to Manhattan, bringing with them original red-tile roofs, first used on the trade ships as ballast and later incorporated into the architecture of Willemstad.

The city is cut in two by Santa Anna Bay. On one side is the Punda—crammed with shops, restaurants, monuments, and markets—and on the other is Otrobanda (literally, the "other side"), with lots of narrow, winding streets full of private homes notable for their picturesque gables and Dutch-influenced designs. In recent years the ongoing regeneration of Otrobanda has been apparent, marked by a surge in development of new hotels, restaurants, and shops; the rebirth, concentrated near the waterfront, was spearheaded by the creation of the elaborate Kura Hulanda complex.

There are three ways to cross the bay: by car over the Juliana Bridge; by foot over the Queen Emma pontoon bridge; or by free ferry, which runs when the pontoon bridge is swung open for passing ships. All the major hotels outside town offer free shuttle service to town once or twice daily. Shuttles coming from the Otrobanda side leave you at Riffort. From here it's a short walk north to the foot of the pontoon bridge. Shuttles coming from the Punda side leave you near the main entrance to Ft. Amsterdam.

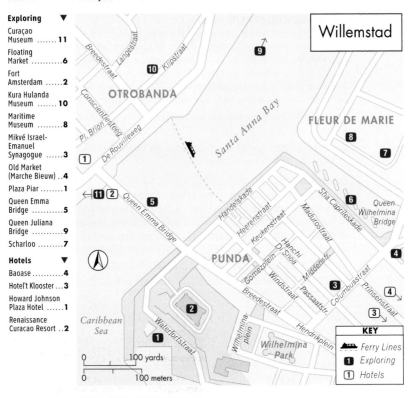

TOP ATTRACTIONS

Ft. Amsterdam. Step through the archway of this fort and enter another century. The entire structure dates from the 1700s, when it was the center of the city and the island's most important fortification. Now it houses the governor's residence, a church (which has a small museum), and government offices. Outside the entrance, a series of majestic gnarled *wayaka* trees are fancifully carved with human forms—the work of local artist Mac Alberto. ⊠ *Foot of Queen Emma Bridge, Punda, Willemstad* ☎ *5999/461–1139* ⊠ *Fort free, church museum $2* ⊙ *Weekdays 9:30–1, Sun. service at 10.*

Fodor'sChoice ★ **Kura Hulanda Museum.** This fascinating anthropological museum reveals the island's diverse roots. Housed in a restored 18th-century village—now largely off limits because the attached hotel has closed—the museum is built around a former mercantile square (Kura Hulanda means "Holland courtyard"), where the Dutch once sold slaves. An exhibit on the trans-atlantic slave trade includes a gut-wrenching replica of a slave-ship hold. Other sections feature relics from West African empires, examples of pre-Columbian gold, and Antillean art. The complex is the brainchild of Dutch philanthropist Jacob Gelt Dekker, and the museum grew from his personal collection of artifacts. ⊠ *Klipstraat 9, Otrobanda* ☎ *5999/434–7765* ⊕ *www.kurahulanda.com* ⊠ *$10* ⊙ *Thurs.–Sat. 10–5.*

Mikvé Israel-Emanuel Synagogue. The temple, the oldest in continuous use in the Western Hemisphere, is one of Curaçao's most important sights and draws thousands of visitors a year. The synagogue was dedicated in 1732 by the Jewish community, which had already grown from the original 12 families who came from Amsterdam in 1651. They were later joined by Jews from Portugal and Spain fleeing persecution from the Inquisition. White sand covers the synagogue floor for two symbolic reasons: a remembrance of the 40 years Jews spent wandering the desert, and a re-creation of the sand used by secret Jews, or *conversos*, to muffle sounds from their houses of worship during the Inquisition. English and Hebrew services are held Friday at 6:30 pm and Saturday at 10 am. Men who attend should wear a jacket and tie. Yarmulkes are provided to men for services and tours. ⊠ *Hanchi Snoa 29, Punda* ☎ *5999/461–1067* ⊕ *www.snoa.com* 🎫 *$10; donations also accepted* ⊙ *Weekdays 9–4:30.*

Jewish Cultural Museum. The Jewish Cultural Museum, in back of the synagogue, displays antiques—including a set of circumcision instruments—and artifacts from around the world. Many of the objects are used in the synagogue, making it a "living" museum. ☎ *5999/461–1633.*

WORTH NOTING

Curaçao Museum. Housed in an 1853 plantation house, this small museum is filled with artifacts, paintings, and antiques that trace the island's history. This is also a venue for visiting art exhibitions. ⊠ *V. Leeuwenhoekstraat z/n, Otrobanda* ☎ *5999/462–3873* 🎫 *Free* ⊙ *Weekdays 8:30–4:30, Sun. 10–4.*

Floating Market. Each morning dozens of Venezuelan schooners laden with tropical fruits and vegetables arrive at this bustling market on the Punda side of the city. Mangoes, papayas, and exotic vegetables vie for space with freshly caught fish and herbs and spices. The buying is best at 6:30 am—too early for many people on vacation—but there's plenty of action throughout the afternoon. Any produce bought here should be thoroughly washed or peeled before being eaten. ⊠ *Sha Caprileskade, Punda.*

NEED A BREAK?

Old Vienna Terrace Café. For a cooling break from your explorations, Old Vienna Terrace Café serves scrumptious homemade ice cream. Indulge your sweet tooth with such flavors as green apple, mango, and rum plum. There's also a full menu of light bites and outdoor seating along the harbor. ⊠ *Handelskade 6 C, Punda* ☎ *5999/736–1086.*

Maritime Museum. The museum—designed to resemble the interior of a ship—gives you a sense of Curaçao's maritime history, using model ships, historic maps, nautical charts, navigational equipment, and audiovisual displays. Topics explored in the exhibits include the development of Willemstad as a trading city, Curaçao's role as a contraband hub, the remains of *De Alphen* (a Dutch marine freighter that exploded and sank in St. Anna Bay in 1778 and was excavated in 1984), the slave trade, the development of steam navigation, and the role of the Dutch navy on the island. The museum also offers a two-hour guided tour (Wednesday and Saturday, 2 pm) on its "water bus" through Curaçao's harbor—a route familiar to traders, smugglers, and pirates. The museum is wheelchair accessible. ⊠ *Van der Brandhofstraat 7, Scharloo* ☎ *5999/465–2327* ⊕ *www.curacaomaritime.com* ⊠ *Museum $6.50, museum and harbor tour $15* ☉ *Tues.–Sat. 9–4.*

Old Market (*Marche Bieuw*). Local cooks prepare hearty Antillean lunches in coal pots at this covered market behind the post office. Enjoy such Curaçaoan specialties as *funchi* (polenta), goat stew, fried fish, or stewed okra. Prices range from $5 to $14. ⊠ *De Ruyterkade, Punda.*

Plaza Piar. This plaza is dedicated to Manuel Piar, a native Curaçaoan who fought for the independence of Venezuela under the liberator Simón Bolívar. On one side of the plaza is the Waterfort, built in the late 1820s to help defend the old city. The original cannons are still positioned in the battlements. The foundation, however, now forms the walls of the Howard Johnson Plaza Hotel Curaçao & Casino.

Queen Emma Bridge. Affectionately called the Swinging Old Lady by the locals, this bridge connects the two sides of Willemstad—Punda and Otrobanda—across the Santa Anna Bay. The bridge swings open at least 30 times a day to allow passage of ships to and from the sea. The original bridge, built in 1888, was the brainchild of the American consul Leonard Burlington Smith, who made a mint off the tolls he charged for using it: 2¢ per person for those wearing shoes, free to those crossing barefoot. Today it's free to everyone. The bridge was dismantled and completely repaired and restored in 2005.

Queen Juliana Bridge. This 1,625-foot-long bridge stands 200 feet above the water, and it's the highest bridge in the Caribbean. It's the crossing for motor traffic between Punda and Otrobanda and affords breathtaking views (and photo ops) of the city, day and night.

Scharloo. The Wilhelmina Drawbridge connects Punda with the once-flourishing district of Scharloo, where the early Jewish merchants built stately homes. The architecture along Scharlooweg (much of it from the 17th century) is magnificent, and, happily, many of the colonial mansions that had become dilapidated have been meticulously renovated. The area closest to Kleine Werf is a red-light district and fairly run-down, but the rest is well worth a visit.

ELSEWHERE ON CURAÇAO

The Weg Maar Santa Cruz through the village of Soto winds to the island's northwest tip through landscape that Georgia O'Keeffe might have painted: towering cacti, flamboyant dried shrubbery, and aluminum-roof houses. Throughout this *cunucu,* or countryside, you can see fishermen hauling nets, women pounding cornmeal, and an occasional donkey blocking traffic. Land houses—large plantation houses from centuries past—dot the countryside. To explore the island's eastern side from Willemstad, take the coastal road called Martin Luther King Boulevard about 2 miles (3 km) to Bapor Kibra. This is where you can find the Sea Aquarium and the Dolphin Academy. Farther east are a nature park at Caracas Bay and the upscale Spanish Water neighborhood and marina. To the far northeast is Groot St. Joris, home of Curaçao's aloe plantation and one of the largest ostrich-breeding farms outside Africa.

A daring, mast-eye view of the Handelskade in Punda

TOP ATTRACTIONS

Christoffel National Park. The 1,239-foot Mt. Christoffel, Curaçao's highest peak, is at the center of this 4,450-acre garden and wildlife preserve. The exhilarating climb up—a challenge to anyone who hasn't grown up scaling the Alps—takes about two hours for a reasonably fit person. On a clear day, the panoramic view from the peak stretches to the mountain ranges of Venezuela.

Throughout the park are eight hiking trails and a 20-mile (32-km) network of driving trails (use heavy-treaded tires if you wish to explore the unpaved stretches). All these routes traverse hilly fields full of prickly pear cacti, divi-divi trees, bushy-haired palms, and exotic flowers. Guided nature walks, horseback rides, and jeep tours can be arranged through the main park office. If you're going without a guide, first study the *Excursion Guide to Christoffel Park*, sold at the visitor center. It outlines the various routes and identifies the indigenous flora and fauna. Start out early, as by 10 am the park starts to feel like a sauna.

Watch for goats and small animals that might cross your path, and consider yourself lucky if you see any of the elusive white-tailed deer. Every day at 4 pm, guides lead 15-minute expeditions to track the protected herd. Birds are abundant, and experts lead the way twice daily. White-tailed hawks may be seen along the green hiking route, white orchids along the yellow hiking route. There are also ancient Indian drawings and caves where you might hear the rustling of bat wings or spot scuttling, nonpoisonous scorpions.

Most island sports outfitters offer some kind of activity in the park, such as kayaking, specialized hiking tours, and drive-through tours *(⇨ Sports and Activities, below).* ⊠ *Savonet* ☎ *5999/864–0363 for information and tour reservations, 5999/462–6262 for jeep tours* 🖃 *$12* ⊗ *Mon.– Sat. 8–4, Sun. 6–3; last admission 90 min before closing.*

Curaçao Aloe Plantation & Factory. Drop in for a tour that takes you through the various stages of production of aloe vera, renowned for its healing powers. You'll get a look at everything from the fields to the final products. At the gift shop, you can buy CurAloe products, including homemade goodies like soap, pure aloe gel, and pure aloe juice, as well as sunscreen and other skin-care products. The plantation is on the way to the Ostrich Farm and run by the same owner. Tours are offered throughout the day. ⊠ *Weg Naar Groot St. Joris z/n, Groot St. Joris* ☎ *5999/767–5577* ⊕ *www.aloecuracao.com* 🖃 *$7* ⊗ *Mon.–Sat. 9–4; last tour at 3.*

FAMILY **Curaçao Sea Aquarium.** You don't have to get your feet wet to see the island's underwater treasures. The aquarium has about 40 saltwater tanks filled with more than 400 varieties of marine life. A restaurant, a snack bar, two photo centers, and souvenir shops are on-site. ⊠ *Seaquarium Beach, Bapor Kibra z/n* ☎ *5999/461–6666* ⊕ *www. curacao-sea-aquarium.com* 🖃 *$20* ⊗ *Daily 8:30–5:30.*

Dolphin Academy. At the Dolphin Academy, you can watch a fanciful dolphin show (included with Sea Aquarium admission). For up-close interactions, you may choose from several special programs (extra charges apply and reservations are essential) to encounter the dolphins in shallow water, or to swim, snorkel, or dive with them. ⊠ *Seaquarium Beach, Bapor Kibra z/n* ☎ *5999/465–8900* ⊕ *www.dolphin-academy. com* 🖃 *$89–$159* ⊗ *Daily 8:30–4:30.*

Hato Caves. Stalactites and stalagmites form striking shapes in these 200,000-year-old caves. Hidden lighting adds to the dramatic effect. Indians who used the caves for shelter left petroglyphs about 1,500 years ago. More recently, slaves who escaped from nearby plantations used the caves as a hideaway. Hour-long guided tours wind down to the pools in various chambers. Keep in mind that there are 49 steps to climb up to the entrance and the occasional bat might not be to everyone's taste. To reach the caves, head northwest toward the airport, take a right onto Gosieweg, follow the loop right onto Schottegatweg, take another right onto Jan Norduynweg and a final right onto Rooseveltweg, and follow signs. ⊠ *Rooseveltweg z/n, Hato* ☎ *5999/868–0379* 🖃 *$8* ⊗ *Daily 10–4.*

FAMILY **Ostrich Farm.** If you (and the kids) are ready to stick your neck out for an adventure, visit one of the largest ostrich farms outside Africa. Every hour, guided tours show the creatures' complete development from egg to mature bird. Kids enjoy the chance to hold an egg, stroke a day-old chick, and sit atop an ostrich for an unusual photo op. At the **Restaurant Zambezi** you can sample local ostrich specialties and other African dishes (reservations are recommended; closed Monday; no dinner Tuesday). The gift shop sells handicrafts made in southern Africa, including leather goods and wood carvings, as well as products made by local artisans. ⊠ *Groot St. Joris* ☎ *5999/747–2777* ⊕ *www. ostrichfarm.net* 🖃 *$15* ⊗ *Tues.–Sun. 9–5.*

WORTH NOTING

Den Paradera. Dazzle your senses at this organic herb garden, where guides will explain the origins of traditional folk medicines used to treat everything from stomach ulcers to diabetes. Owner Dinah Veeris is a renowned expert and author in the field. The kitchen is a factory of sorts where three busy people turn homegrown plants like cactus, aloe vera, and calabash into homemade body- and skin-care products like shampoos, ointments, and oils—all for sale at the gift shop. Reservations are essential for guided tours. ⊠ *Seru Grandi 105A, Banda Riba* ☎ *5999/767–5608* ⊑ *$8 with guided tour* ⊘ *Mon.–Sat. 9–6.*

Landhuis Kenepa. With the island's largest slave population, this plantation was the site of a revolt in 1795 that spurred the abolition of slavery on the island. The renovated plantation house near the island's western tip is filled with period furnishings and clothing. ⊠ *Weg Naar Santa Cruz, Knip* ☎ *5999/864–0244* ⊑ *$3* ⊘ *Weekdays 9–4, weekends 10–4.*

Museo Curaçao (*Kas di Pal'i Maishi*). The thatch-roof cottage is filled with antique furniture, farm implements, and clothing typical of 19th-century colonial life. Out back is a small farm and vegetable garden. Look closely at the fence—it's made of living cacti. There's also a snack bar. A festival featuring live music and local crafts takes place here on the first Sunday of each month. ⊠ *Dokterstuin 27, on road to Westpunt from Willemstad, Westpunt* ☎ *5999/864–2742* ⊑ *$4* ⊘ *Tues.–Fri. 9–4, weekends 9–5.*

Senior Curaçao Liqueur Distillery. The famed Curaçao liqueur, made from the peels of the bitter Laraha orange, is produced at this mansion, which dates to the 1800s. Don't expect a massive factory—it's just a small showroom in an open-air foyer. There are no guides, but delightful old hand-painted posters explain the distillation process, and you can watch workers filling the bottles by hand. Assorted flavors are available to sample for free. If you're interested in buying—the orange-flavor chocolate liqueur is delicious over ice cream—you can choose from a complete selection in enticing packaging, including miniature Dutch ceramic houses. ⊠ *Landhuis Chobolobo, Saliña* ☎ *5999/461–3526* ⊑ *Free* ⊘ *Weekdays 8–noon and 1–5.*

Shete Boka. The name of this park means "Seven Inlets" in Papiamento. Indeed, the sea has carved out seven magnificent grottoes, the largest of which is Boka Tabla, where you can watch and listen to the waves crashing against the rocks beneath a limestone overhang. Boka Pistol is also spectacular, with thunderous waves smashing into the rocks and jetting up into towering plumes of spray, often leaving rainbows lingering in the mist. Several of the surrounding caverns serve as turtle nesting places; you might also spot flocks of parakeets emerge in formation, hawks soar and dip, and gulls dive-bomb for their lunch. ⊠ *Westpunt Hwy., just past village center, Soto* ⊑ *$5.50* ⊘ *Daily 9–5.*

9

Plantation house in Christoffel National Park with Mt. Christoffel in the distance

BEACHES

Beautiful beaches are not hard to find on Curaçao. The island boasts more than three dozen beaches, with many of the best ones on the western side. The more popular beaches offer a wide range of facilities and excellent restaurants.

Beaches in Curaçao range from small inlets shielded by craggy cliffs to longer expanses of sparkling sand. Beaches along the southeast coast tend to be rocky in the shallow water (wear reef shoes—some resorts lend them out for free); the west side has more stretches of smooth sand at the shoreline. Exploring the beaches away from the hotels is a perfect way to soak up the island's character. Whether you're seeking a lovers' hideaway, a special snorkeling adventure, or a great spot to wow the kids, you're not likely to be disappointed. There are snack bars and restrooms on many of the larger beaches, but it's at the smaller ones with no facilities where you might find utter tranquility, especially during the week. Most spots with entry fees offer lounge chairs for rent at an additional cost, typically $2 to $3 per chair.

EAST END

FAMILY **Seaquarium Beach.** This 1,600-foot stretch of sandy beach is divided into separate sections, each uniquely defined by a seaside resort or restaurant as its central draw. By day, no matter where you choose to enter the palm-shaded beach, you can find lounge chairs in the sand, thatched shelters, and restrooms. The sections at Mambo and Kontiki beaches also have showers. The island's largest water-sports center

(Ocean Encounters at Lions Dive) caters to nearby hotel guests and walk-ins. Mambo Beach is always a hot spot and quite a scene on weekends, especially during the much-touted Sunday-night fiesta that's become a fixture of the island's nightlife. The ubiquitous beach mattress is also the preferred method of seating for the Tuesday-night movies at Mambo Beach (check the *K-Pasa* guide for listings—typically B-films or old classics—and reserve your spot with a shirt or a towel). At Kontiki Beach, you can find a spa, a hair braider, and a restaurant that serves refreshing piña colada ice cream. Unless you're a guest of a resort on the beach, the entrance fee to any section is $3 until 5 pm, then free. After 11 pm, you must be 18 or older to access the beach. **Amenities:** food and drink; lifeguards; parking; showers; toilets. **Best for:** partiers; snorkeling; walking. ⊠ *About 1 mile (1½ km) east of downtown Willemstad, Bapor Kibra z/n.*

WEST END

FAMILY **Cas Abao.** This white-sand gem has the brightest blue water in Curaçao, a treat for swimmers, snorkelers, and sunbathers alike. You can take respite beneath the hut-shaded snack bar. The restrooms and showers are immaculate. The only drawback is the weekend crowds, especially Sunday, when local families descend in droves; come on a weekday for more privacy. You can rent beach chairs, paddleboats, and snorkeling and diving gear. The entry fee is $3, and the beach is open from 8 to 6. Turn off Westpunt Highway at the junction onto Weg Naar Santa Cruz; follow until the turnoff for Cas Abao, and then drive along the winding country road for about 10 minutes to the beach. **Amenities:** food and drink; lifeguards; parking; showers; toilets; water sports. **Best for:** partiers; snorkeling; swimming. ⊠ *West of St. Willibrordus, about 3 miles (5 km) off Weg Naar Santa Cruz.*

Playa Jeremi. No snack bar, no dive shop, no facilities, no fee—in fact, there's nothing but sheer natural beauty. Though the beach is sandy, there are rocky patches, so barefoot visitors should exercise care. The parking area is offset from the beach, and vehicle break-ins are common. Quite a bit of development is planned for this beach, so have a look before it's too late. **Amenities:** none. **Best for:** solitude; swimming. ⊠ *Off Weg Naar Santa Cruz, west of Lagun.*

Playa Kalki. Noted for its spectacular snorkeling, this beach is at the western tip of the island. Sunbathers may find the narrow and rocky beach less than ideal. The Ocean Encounters dive shop is here. **Amenities:** food and drink; parking; toilets; water sports. **Best for:** solitude; snorkeling; swimming. ⊠ *Near Jaanchi's, Westpunt.*

FAMILY **Playa Knip.** Two protected coves offer crystal clear turquoise waters. Big (Groot) Knip is an expanse of alluring white sand, perfect for swimming and snorkeling. You can rent beach chairs and hang out under the *palapas* (thatch-roof shelters) or cool off with ice cream at the snack bar. There are restrooms here but no showers. It's particularly crowded on Sunday and school holidays. Just up the road, also in a protected cove, Little (Kleine) Knip is a charmer, too, with picnic tables and palapas. Steer clear of the poisonous manchineel trees. There's no fee for these beaches. **Amenities:** food and drink; lifeguards; parking; toilets; water sports. **Best for:** snorkeling; sunrise; sunset; surfing; swimming. ✉ *Just east of Westpunt, Banda Abou.*

FAMILY **Playa Lagun.** This northwestern cove is caught between gray cliffs, which dramatically frame the Caribbean blue. Cognoscenti know this as one of the best places to snorkel—even for kids—because of the calm, shallow water. It's also a haven for fishing boats and canoes. There's a small dive shop on the beach, a snack bar (open weekends), and restrooms, but there's no fee. **Amenities:** food and drink; parking; showers; toilets. **Best for:** snorkeling; swimming; walking. ✉ *West of Santa Cruz, Banda Abou.*

FAMILY **Playa Porto Mari.** Calm, clear water and a long stretch of white sand are the hallmarks of this beach. Without the commercial bustle of Seaquarium Beach, it's one of the best for all-around fun, and it therefore draws throngs of local families and tourists on the weekends. A decent bar and restaurant, well-kept showers, changing facilities, and restrooms are all on-site; a nature trail is nearby. The double coral reef—explore one, swim past it, explore another—is a special feature that makes this spot popular with snorkelers and divers. The entrance fee (including one free beverage) is $2 on weekdays, $3 on Sunday and holidays. From Willemstad, drive west on Westpunt Highway for 4 miles (7 km); turn left onto Willibrordus Road at the Porto Mari billboard, and then drive 3 miles (5 km) until you see a large church; follow signs on the winding dirt road to the beach. **Amenities:** food and drink; lifeguards; parking; showers; toilets. **Best for:** partiers; snorkeling; swimming; walking. ✉ *Off Willibrordus Rd.*

WHERE TO EAT

Dine beneath the boughs of magnificent old trees, on the terraces of restored mansions and plantation houses, or on the ramparts of 18th-century forts. Curaçaoans partake of generally outstanding fare, with representation from a remarkable smattering of ethnicities. Outdoor or open-air sheltered dining is commonplace; note that most restaurants offer a smoking section or permit smoking throughout. Fine dining tends to be pricey, mostly because of the high cost of importing products to the island. For cheap eats with a local flair, drop by the Old Market for lunch, or stop at one of the snack bars or snack trucks found all over the island (have some guilders handy—many of them won't have change for dollars).

What to Wear. Dress in restaurants is almost always casual (though beachwear isn't acceptable). Some of the resort dining rooms and more elegant restaurants require that men wear jackets, especially in high season; ask when you make reservations.

$ CAFÉ 🍴 **Awa di Playa.** Formerly a fishermen's hangout, this ramshackle shed-like structure located on an ocean inlet gives way to an equally ramshackle interior and some of the best local lunches anywhere on the island. There's no menu—the waiter will tell you what's available, and you can watch it being cooked in the tiny kitchen. The presentation isn't fancy, and the occasional fly makes an appearance, but the food is honest and delicious. [$] *Average main: $8* ✉ *Behind Hook's Hut and Hilton, Piscadera Bay, Willemstad* ☎ *5999/462–6939* 💳 *No credit cards* ⏲ *No dinner.*

$$$ ✕ **Bistro Le Clochard.** Built into a 19th-century fort, this romantic gem
EUROPEAN anchors the entrance to the 21st-century Riffort Village complex, the
Fodor'sChoice waterside terrace offering an enchanting view of the floating bridge and
★ harbor. Switzerland and France are the key influences on the sublime
preparations. The signature dish is La Potence—a spike-covered metal
ball resembling a medieval weapon. It's brought to your table blazing
hot and covered with bits of sizzling tenderloin and sausage, served
with various dipping sauces. Though more gimmicky fun than fine
dining, it makes for a popular photo opportunity. The cheese fondue
definitely keeps diners coming back. Game lovers can have their fill
from the seasonal menu. No matter what, leave room for the sump-
tuous Toblerone chocolate mousse. $ *Average main: $52* ⊠ *Harbor-
side Terr., Riffort Village, Otrobanda, Willemstad* ☎ *5999/462–5666*
⊕ *www.bistroleclochard.com* ⌁ *Reservations essential.*

$$ ✕ **Blues.** Jutting out onto a pier over the ocean, this jazzy spot is an
EUROPEAN alluring place for dinner. The small menu is surprisingly comprehen-
sive, with a special emphasis on seafood. The fish, mussel, and shrimp
ceviche is a popular and refreshing appetizer. For meat lovers, the Spare
Ribs New Orleans Style holds a spot at the top of the charts. Live
music on Thursday and Saturday evenings includes seductive vocalists
and top-notch musicians. If you'd rather be removed from the scene,
you can arrange for a cozy dinner on the beach; whether it's a table
for two or for a larger group, you'll be nestled in the sand on colorful
oversize pillows. There's also a terrific prix-fixe tapas buffet on Friday.
$ *Average main: $23* ⊠ *Avila Hotel, Penstraat 130, Punda, Willemstad*
☎ *5999/461–4377* ⊕ *www.avilahotel.com* ☉ *Closed Mon. No lunch.*

$$$ ✕ **CRU Steak House & Wine Bar.** This elegant enclave on the grounds
STEAKHOUSE of the Renaissance has some of the best steaks while also catering to
those looking for nonsteak options. The dark-wood interior is made
a bit more whimsical by liberal displays of funky wallpaper. The CRU
trio appetizer featuring a crab cake, perfectly grilled jumbo shrimp and
buttery tuna each paired with a sauce is sure to please. Steak entrées
range in size from a manageable 6 ounce to an eye-popping 24 ounce
and are all priced reasonably by island standards. $ *Average main:
$25* ⊠ *Renaissance Mall, Otrobanda, Willemstad* ☎ *5999/435–5090*
⊕ *www.crusteakhousecuracao.com/.*

$$ ✕ **Dal Toro.** Built into the Waterfort Arches, this restaurant and its out-
ITALIAN door terrace are part of an adjoining strip of eateries in a coveted spot
perched over the Caribbean. Listen to the rippling waves crash against
the rocks as you sip wine and enjoy creative variations on homemade
pastas and pizza. The pretty Italian-themed dining room has huge
picture windows so the ocean is always visible. The menu changes
frequently, so there is usually something new to choose should you
make multiple visits. $ *Average main: $17* ⊠ *Waterfort Archesboog
12, Punda, Willemstad* ☎ *5999/461–3482.*

$$ ✕ **Fort Nassau Restaurant.** On a hill above Willemstad, this elegant restau-
EUROPEAN rant is built into an 18th-century fort with a 360-degree view. For the
Fodor'sChoice best perspective, sit beside the huge bay windows in the air-conditioned
★ interior; the terrace has a pleasant breeze and is generally more popular
with diners, but the view is not quite optimal. Among the highlights of

9

the diverse menu is the medley of Caribbean seafood with mahimahi, shrimp, and grilled octopus. Scrumptious desserts will leave you feeling sated. $ *Average main: $31* ⊠ *Schottegatweg 82, near Juliana Bridge, Otrobanda, Willemstad* ☎ *5999/461–3450, 5999/461–3086* ⚑ *Reservations essential* ☉ *No lunch weekends.*

$$ ✕ **Gouverneur de Rouville Restaurant & Café.** Dine on the verandah of a
ECLECTIC restored 19th-century Dutch mansion overlooking the Santa Anna
Fodor'sChoice Bay and the resplendent Punda skyline. Though often busy and pop-
★ ular with tourists, the ambience makes it worth a visit. Intriguing soup options include Cuban banana soup and Curaçao-style fish soup. *Keshi yena* (seasoned meat wrapped in cheese and then baked) and spareribs are among the savory entrées. After dinner, you can stick around for live music at the bar, which stays open until 1 am. The restaurant is also popular for lunch and attracts crowds when cruise ships dock. Reserve ahead if you would like a balcony table. $ *Average main: $22* ⊠ *De Rouvilleweg 9, Otrobanda, Willemstad* ☎ *5999/462–5999* ⊕ *www.de-gouverneur.com.*

$$ ✕ **Jaanchies Restaurant.** Over the years this has become something of a
CARIBBEAN road marker on Curaçao's beaten tourist path, with prices to match. You'll be greeted by the owner, Jaanchi himself, a self-described "walking, talking menu," who will recite your choices of dishes for lunch. Jaanchi's iguana soup, touted in folklore as an aphrodisiac, is famous on the island. It's quite a sight when so-called sugar-thief birds flock to feeders outside the restaurant when the owner periodically fills them with sugar. Although predominantly a lunch spot, the restaurant will accommodate groups of four or more for dinner by prior arrangement. $ *Average main: $23* ⊠ *Westpunt 15, Westpunt* ☎ *5999/864–0126.*

$$ ✕ **La Bahia Seafood & Steakhouse.** The sheltered terrace at La Bahia
SEAFOOD features a remarkable view of the harborfront and is so close to the
FAMILY passing ships you'll feel you can almost touch them. The menu runs the gamut from burgers and pastas to *keshi yena* (seasoned meat wrapped in cheese and then baked) and other local specialties. Even if the food doesn't appeal, this is a great spot to relax with a cup of coffee or a cocktail after a day of exploring. It is a short walk from the Queen Emma Bridge. $ *Average main: $22* ⊠ *Otrobanda Hotel & Casino, Breedestraat, Otrobanda, Willemstad* ☎ *5999/462–7400* ⊕ *www.otrobandahotel.com.*

$$$$ ✕ **L'aldea Steakhouse.** A long drive from downtown hotels along some-
STEAKHOUSE times bumpy roads leads to this Brazilian steak house with a decidedly Mayan theme. Clashing motifs are quickly forgotten as you enter the lush interior filled with stone carvings and greenery. The price of dinner includes the largest salad bar on the island and a nonstop procession of servers at your table, carving a delectable selection of grilled meats, until told to stop. Each table has three buttons—to hail the waiter, manager, and request the check. It isn't cheap, but the service and fare are top-notch. $ *Average main: $58* ⊠ *Sta. Catharina #66, Willemstad* ☎ *5999/767–6777* ⊕ *www.laldeacur.com/restaurant.html* ⚑ *Reservations essential* ☉ *Closed Mon. No lunch weekdays.*

$$ ✕ **Landhuis Daniel.** Many of the tasty meals served here have their roots
CARIBBEAN in the restaurant's garden. Fruits, vegetables, and herbs are organically grown at this landmark plantation house—dating from 1711—and used unsparingly in the menu, which changes according to seasonal crop yield. The chef draws on creole, French, and Mediterranean influences for his creations. One option is the prix-fixe "surprise menu"—just tell your waiter your preference for meat, fish, or vegetarian, and any dislikes. There's also a small inn here. $ *Average main: $21* ⊠ *Weg Naar, Westpunt* ☎ *5999/864–8400* ⊕ *www.landhuisdaniel.com.*

$$ ✕ **Mambo Beach.** Spread over the sand, this open-air bar and grill serves
EUROPEAN hearty sandwiches and burgers for lunch; steaks, fresh seafood, and pasta
FAMILY fill the dinner menu. There's a fish buffet on Friday and dinner with a movie on the beach on Tuesday. $ *Average main: $12* ⊠ *Seaquarium Beach, Bapor Kibra z/n* ☎ *5999/461–8999* ⊕ *www.mambocuracao.com.*

$$ ✕ **Scampi's.** Part of the Waterfort dining complex, this family-friendly
SEAFOOD eatery offers great basic food right next door to the decidedly more upscale eateries that share its waterfront location. The food is simple but well made, and better yet, very affordable. There is a good selection of fresh seafood and steaks at surprisingly reasonable prices, and kids can choose from their own menu. There's live music on Thursday. $ *Average main: $22* ⊠ *Waterfortstraat 41–42, Punda* ☎ *5999/465–0769.*

$$ ✕ **Shore.** Despite its setting in the upscale Santa Barbara Beach & Golf
AMERICAN Resort, this airy seafood grill overlooking the ocean is surprisingly relaxed. Appetizers range from a simple but exquisite gravlax salmon salad to a huge serving of bubbling crab dip served with bread that can easily feed two. The main grill courses require a bit of pleasing deliberation, as both meat and seafood offerings are fully customizable, with choices of seasoning, sauce, and side. Although the restaurant is quite a drive if you're not staying at the hotel, the ambience and excellent food are worth it. $ *Average main: $30* ⊠ *Santa Barbara Beach & Golf Resort, Santa Barbara Plantation, Nieuwpoort* ☎ *5999/840–1234.*

$$ ✕ **Tempo Doeloe.** The hillside location, Balinese decor, and authentic
INDONESIAN Indonesian cuisine draw both visitors and locals to this sprawling establishment. Although dishes may be ordered individually, the excess of either the full rijstaffel or more manageable—though without seafood—small rijstaffel is an experience not easily forgotten. Call ahead to request a table with a view. $ *Average main: $30* ⊠ *La Vista Resort, Piscaderaweg, Willemstad* ☎ *5999/461–2881* ⊕ *www.tempodoeloe.net* ⌔ *Reservations essential.*

WHERE TO STAY

You'll generally find that hotels at all price levels provide friendly, prompt, detail-oriented service; however, the finer points of service are in some cases still in nascent stages. Many of the large-scale resorts east and west of Willemstad proper have lovely beaches and provide a free shuttle to the city, 5 to 10 minutes away, but you'll find utmost seclusion at hotels on the island's southwestern end, a 30- to 45-minute drive from town. Most hotels in town provide beach shuttles.

9

VILLAS AND RENTALS

FAMILY Villa and bungalow rentals are especially popular with divers and European visitors and are generally good options for large groups or longer stays. The Curaçao Tourist Board (🌐 *www.curacao.com*) has a complete list of rental apartments, villas, and bungalows on its website.

Livingstone Jan Thiel Resort. The 128 villas at Livingstone Jan Thiel Resort surround a swimming pool in a low-rise complex that offers a minimarket on-site, free access to the beach across the street, Wi-Fi in the open-air lobby, and a playground and special programs for kids. Festive decor includes a large painted mural at the entrance and beaded shades on tabletop candleholders at the poolside restaurant. Reasonable rates even in high season make this an appealing choice for those looking for self-catering facilities. ✉ *Jan Thiel* ☎ *5999/747–0332* 🌐 *www.janthielresort.com* 🛏 *128 villas.*

FAMILY **Papagayo Beach Resort.** The bungalows at Papagayo Beach Resort give you a unique option: on a whim you can open up a full wall so that your wraparound wooden terrace becomes part of your living space. Suddenly you're as close as it gets to living outdoors. These well-designed and nicely furnished homes include two bedrooms, a full kitchen with dishwasher, and bathroom (showers only). The restaurant menu changes seasonally; the pool bar is a cozy place to meet your neighbors. There's no beachfront, but you get free access to the beach across the street. Special programs and entertainment for kids are offered during school vacation periods. ✉ *Jan Thiel* ☎ *5999/747–4333* 🌐 *www.papagayo-beach.com* 🛏 *75 bungalows.*

RECOMMENDED HOTELS AND RESORTS

$$ RESORT Fodor's Choice ★ 🏨 **Avila Hotel.** The right blend of old-world touches, modern amenities, alluring beachfront, and attentive staff makes this resort the place of choice for the visiting Dutch royalty (well, all guests actually). **Pros:** wide variety of room types and decor; old-world charm; excellent restaurants; choice of upscale shops on-site. **Cons:** bit of a walk to the city; because it caters to a largely European clientele, most rooms only have 220 outlets. [$] *Rooms from: $310* ✉ *Penstraat 130, Willemstad* ☎ *5999/461–4377, 800/747–8162* 🌐 *www.avilahotel.com* 🛏 *154 rooms, 11 suites* 🍴 *No meals.*

$$$$ RESORT Fodor's Choice ★ 🏨 **Baoase.** No other resort on Curaçao can match this Balinese-inspired gem for understated elegance and attention to detail. **Pros:** beautiful landscaping; complete privacy and quiet. **Cons:** lacks some of the distractions of a larger resort; a bit far from downtown shopping. [$] *Rooms from: $425* ✉ *Winterswijkstraat 2, Willemstad* ☎ *5999/461–1799* 🌐 *www.baoase.com* 🛏 *9 villas, 3 1-bedroom suites* 🍴 *No meals.*

$$ RENTAL 🏨 **Blue Bay Village.** This property is a 10-minute drive from Willemstad but offers a quiet setting, beautiful villas, thoughtfully decorated rooms, and the perfect location for golf lovers. **Pros:** spacious units; ideal location for golfers; far from the madding crowd; on-site restaurant is quite good for basic family meals. **Cons:** a bit isolated, so a car is absolutely necessary; no nightlife in the area. [$] *Rooms from: $160* ✉ *Landhuis*

Blauw z/n, Willemstad ☎ 5999/888–8800 🌐 www.bluebay-curacao.com 🛏 48 apartments, 36 3-bedroom villas 🍴 No meals.

$$$ RESORT FAMILY Fodor's Choice ★ 🏨 **Curaçao Marriott Beach Resort & Emerald Casino.** The cream of the crop of Curaçao's resorts beckons you to live it up from the moment you arrive. **Pros:** no need to leave the compound for anything but sightseeing; excellent beach location; first-class fitness center; five-star PADI dive shop. **Cons:** feels big and impersonal; pool area can get very busy. [$] *Rooms from: $266 ☎ 5999/736–8800 🌐 www.curacaomarriott.com 🛏 237 rooms, 10 suites 🍴 Multiple meal plans.*

$$ HOTEL 🏨 **Floris Suite Hotel.** Dutch interior designer Jan des Bouvrie has used warm mahogany shades offset by cool, sleek stainless-steel adornments in the suites of this modernist hotel, all of which have a balcony or porch and a full kitchen. **Pros:** great for a quiet escape; beautifully designed rooms and public spaces. **Cons:** decor lacks romantic feel; bit of a hike to decent shopping and restaurants. [$] *Rooms from: $195 ✉ Piscaderaweg, Piscadera Bay, Willemstad ☎ 5999/462–6111 🌐 www.florissuitehotel.com 🛏 72 suites 🍴 No meals.*

$$ RESORT FAMILY 🏨 **Hilton Curaçao.** Two beautiful beaches of pillowy white sand beyond the open-air lobby make this resort a jewel in its price range. **Pros:** gorgeous beachfront; close to great shopping and off-site restaurants; friendly staff. **Cons:** lacks the intimacy of smaller resorts. [$] *Rooms from: $229 ✉ Piscaderaweg, Willemstad ☎ 5999/462–5000 🌐 www.hiltoncuracaoresort.com 🛏 196 rooms, 12 suites 🍴 No meals.*

$$ 🏨 **Hotel 't Klooster.** Located in a former monastery ("klooster" means "cloister") in the Pietermaai district of the capital city this little hotel offers lots of historical charm. **Pros:** great base downtown; historical charm aplenty; reasonable price. **Cons:** nowhere near a beach; sounds from church service next door can bleed into rooms. [$] *Rooms from: $140 ✉ Veerstraat 12, Willemstad ☎ 5999/461-2650 🌐 www.hotelklooster.com/ 🛏 24 rooms 🍴 No meals.*

$$ HOTEL 🏨 **Howard Johnson Plaza Hotel & Casino.** Everything the city has to offer is at your doorstep at this colorful hotel on the main square of Otrobanda, an especially coveted location during the holidays and Carnival. **Pros:** in the heart of downtown with easy access to Punda; excellent price for a downtown location; some rooms have great views of Punda and Queen Emma Bridge. **Cons:** no beach; downtown noise can sometimes be a problem; pool isn't always maintained. [$] *Rooms from: $109 ✉ Brionplein, Otrobanda, Willemstad ☎ 5999/462–7800 🌐 www.hojo-curacao.com 🛏 70 rooms 🍴 No meals.*

$$ B&B/INN FAMILY 🏨 **Lagun Blou Dive & Beach Resort.** Travelers on a budget will love this family-owned and -run hotel that combines a great view with an intimate setting. **Pros:** relaxed atmosphere; family-run; intimate setting; bargain for families. **Cons:** far from shopping and restaurants; lacks the amenities of a big resort; rooms cleaned once each week; additional charges for cleaning and for electricity and water. [$] *Rooms from: $112 ✉ Playa Lagun L76, Bapor Kibra z/n ☎ 5999/864–0557 🌐 www.lagunblou.nl 🛏 13 rooms, 8 bungalows 🍴 No meals.*

$ RESORT FAMILY 🏨 **Lions Dive & Beach Resort.** Divers are lured by the first-rate program here, but this low-key resort has a lot to offer nondivers as well. **Pros:** ideal for diving; beautiful private beach and access to Seaquarium

Beach; family-friendly, Olympic-length pool. **Cons:** beach can get busy; kids everywhere. [$] *Rooms from: $199* ✉ *Seaquarium Beach, Bapor Kibra z/n* ☎ *5999/434–8888* 🌐 *www.lionsdive.com* 🛏 *102 rooms, 10 suites, 1 penthouse* 🍴 *No meals.*

$$ HOTEL 🏨 **Papagayo Beach & Design Hotel.** Designed by Costa Rican architect Ronald Zurcher, the clean lines and sharp angles of this brand new resort are eye-catching. **Pros:** quiet, uncrowded location; striking exterior and interior design. **Cons:** far from shopping; European esthetic may not be for those seeking plush comfort. [$] *Rooms from: $175* ✉ *Jan Thiel* ☎ *5999/766–1637* 🌐 *www.papagayo-designhotel.com* 🛏 *153 rooms* 🍴 *No meals.*

$$$ RESORT Fodor's Choice ★ 🏨 **Renaissance Curaçao Resort & Casino.** The four gabled buildings of this downtown resort are painted in colors that seem to mirror those of Punda across the harbor and fit in perfectly with the historic surroundings. **Pros:** coolest (and only) pool-beach in town; every amenity imaginable; walking distance to all the attractions of both Otrobanda and Punda; exceptionally helpful staff. **Cons:** Rif Fort area is a major tourist draw and can get busy; common-area color scheme is not exactly calming. [$] *Rooms from: $224* ✉ *Pater Euwensweg, Otrobanda, Willemstad* ☎ *5999/435–5000* 🌐 *www.renaissancecuracao.com* 🛏 *223 rooms, 14 suites* 🍴 *No meals.*

$$$ RESORT FAMILY 🏨 **Santa Barbara Beach & Golf Resort.** Miles away from any other property, this luxury resort was a Hyatt until the owners reclaimed the property and installed another management company. **Pros:** gorgeous location miles away from the hustle and bustle of downtown; elegant public areas. **Cons:** long drive or expensive taxi ride away from everything; feels a bit sterile even by large resort standards. [$] *Rooms from: $279* ✉ *Santa Barbara Plantation, Nieuwpoort* ☎ *5999/840–1234* 🌐 *www.santabarbararesortcuracao.com* 🛏 *335 rooms, 15 suites* 🍴 *No meals.*

$$ ALL-INCLUSIVE FAMILY 🏨 **Sunscape Curaçao Resort, Spa & Casino.** This family-friendly all-inclusive resort was formerly Beaches Curaçao and underwent extensive renovations to bring it up to its current standard. **Pros:** ample distractions for the whole family; renovated rooms are beautifully appointed and airy; nice laid-back atmosphere. **Cons:** Bit far from downtown; ongoing renovation could continue into 2014. [$] *Rooms from: $404* ✉ *Martin Luther King Blvd. 78, Willemstad* ☎ *5999/736–7888, 800/467–8737* 🌐 *www.sunscaperesorts.com/curacao* 🛏 *285 rooms, 56 suites* 🍴 *All-inclusive* ☞ *3-night minimum.*

NIGHTLIFE

Friday is a big night out, with rollicking happy hours and live music at many bars and hotels. And although it might sound surprising, Sunday-night revelry into the wee hours is an island tradition. Pick up a copy of the weekly free entertainment listings, *K-Pasa,* available at most restaurants and hotels.

Fodor's Choice ★ **Carnival.** Outrageous costumes, blowout parades, pulsating Tumba rhythms, mini processions known as jump-ups, and frenetic energy characterize Carnival. The season lasts longer here than on many other islands: the revelries begin at New Year's and continue until midnight the day before Ash Wednesday. One highlight is the Tumba Festival (dates vary), a four-day musical event featuring fierce competition between local musicians for the honor of having their piece selected as the official road march during parades. For the Grand Parade, space is rented along the route and people mark their territory by building wooden stands, some lavishly decorated and furnished.

BARS

De Gouverneur. Wednesday-night jam sessions are hot at De Gouverneur. ⊠ *De Rouvilleweg 9, Otrobanda, Willemstad* ☎ *5999/462–5999.*

Grand Café de Heeren. This is a great spot to grab a locally brewed Amstel Bright and meet a happy blend of tourists and transplanted Dutch locals. ⊠ *Zuikertuintjeweg, Bloempot* ☎ *5999/736–0491.*

Hook's Hut. By day Hook's Hut is a beach hangout for locals and tourists stationed at the nearby hotels. The daily happy hour from 5 to 6 kicks off a lively nighttime scene. The outdoor pool table is in terrible shape, but it's one of the few bar tables around. ⊠ *Next to Hilton Curaçao, Piscadera Bay* ☎ *5999/462–6575.*

Rif Fort Bar. Located within the stone walls of Rif Fort there's usually a lively crowd on weekends. A good place to sit outside and enjoy the evening breezes with one of their signature cocktails. ⊠ *Rif Fort, Otrobanda, Willemstad* ☎ *5999/518–8725.*

Waterfort Arches. The seaside outdoor deck at the Waterfort Arches comprises a connecting strip of several bars and restaurants that have live entertainment on various nights of the week. ⊠ *Waterfortstraat Boog 1, Punda, Willemstad* ☎ *5999/465–0769.*

Wet & Wild Beach Club. There's never a dull moment at Wet & Wild Beach Club, where the name speaks for itself every weekend. Friday happy hour features free barbecue; on Saturday a DJ or live band jams until it's too late to care about the time. On Sunday things get charged, starting with happy hour at 6; the fiesta goes on past midnight. ⊠ *Seaquarium Beach, Bapor Kibra z/n* ☎ *5999/561–2477.*

CASINOS

The following hotels have casinos that are open daily: Sunscape Curaçao, the Curaçao Marriott Beach Resort & Emerald Casino, the Hilton Curaçao, the Holiday Beach Hotel & Casino, Howard Johnson Plaza Hotel & Casino, and the Otrobanda Hotel & Casino. Even the biggest of these rooms offer only a few card games, and some are limited to slot machines. As for ambience, only the casino at the Marriott—which features pleasant live entertainment some nights—even approaches the class of a Bond-like establishment. A few Texas Hold 'Em tables are available here, but games start up only when enough players express interest. The Veneto Casino at the Holiday Beach Resort is the largest on the island, and the only one with sports betting—you can watch the live action on TV. Unfortunately, the casino is dreary. Around the island, slot machines open earlier than table games, between 10 am and 1 pm. Most of the rooms have penny and nickel slots in addition to the higher-priced machines. Tables generally open at 3 pm or 4 pm. Casinos close about 1 am or 2 am weekdays; some stay open until 4 am on weekend nights.

9

DANCE AND MUSIC CLUBS

Blues. Live jazz electrifies the pier at Blues on Thursday—*the* night to go—and Saturday. ⊠ *Avila Hotel, Penstraat 130, Punda, Willemstad* ☎ *5999/461–4377.*

Club Facade. Locals flock here on Thursday and Friday nights to dance the night away to local music on three floors. ⊠ *Lindberghweg 32–34, Willemstad* ☎ *5999/461–4640.*

Emerald Lounge. The dance floor at the Emerald Lounge comes alive on weekends, and is especially steamy on Friday salsa nights. ⊠ *Curaçao Marriott Beach Resort, Piscadera Bay* ☎ *5999/736–8800.*

Mambo Beach. This open-air bar and restaurant draws a hip, young crowd that dances the night away under the stars. On Sunday, come in time for happy hour and warm up for the nightlong party with some beach volleyball. ⊠ *Seaquarium Beach, Bapor Kibra z/n* ☎ *5999/461–8999.*

SHOPPING

From Dutch classics like embroidered linens, Delft earthenware, cheeses, and clogs to local artwork and handicrafts, shopping in Curaçao can turn up some fun finds. But don't expect major bargains on watches, jewelry, or electronics; Willemstad is not a duty-free port (the few establishments that claim to be "duty-free" are simply absorbing the cost of some or all of the tax rather than passing it on to consumers); however, if you come prepared with some comparison prices, you might still dig up some good deals.

SHOPPING AREAS

Willemstad's **Punda** is a treat for pedestrians, with most shops concentrated within a bustling area of about six blocks, giving you plenty of opportunity for people-watching to boot. Closed to traffic, Heerenstraat and Gomezplein are pedestrian malls covered with pink inlaid bricks. Other major shopping streets are Breedestraat and Madurostraat. Here you can find jewelry, cosmetics, perfumes, luggage, and linens—and no shortage of trinkets and souvenirs. Savvy shoppers don't skip town without a stop across the bay to Otrobanda, where the Riffort Village Shopping Mall houses a variety of retailers. It's worth noting that many of the bargain-price designer labels found in smaller clothing shops are just knockoffs from Latin America. The Renaissance Mall right next to Riffort has retailers such as Guess and Tiffany & Co. next to local shops offering a range of jewelry and fashion.

There are also some retail shops in the Kura Hulanda complex.

ART GALLERIES

Gallery Alma Blou. Works by top local artists are displayed at Gallery Alma Blou; you can find shimmering landscapes, dazzling photographs, ceramics, even African-inspired Carnival masks. ⊠ *Frater Radulphusweg 4, Otrobanda* ☎ *5999/462–8896.*

Hortence Brouwn Gallery. Sculpted human forms (sometimes abstract) in bronze, concrete, marble, and limestone are sold in the gardens of Landhuis Bloemhof. ⊠ *Landhuis Bloemhof, Willemstad* ☎ *No phone.*

Nena Sanchez Gallery. At the Nena Sanchez Gallery, you can find this local artist's cheerful paintings in characteristically bright yellows, reds, greens, pinks, and blues. Her work depicting marine life and island scenes is available in various forms, including posters, mouse pads, and picture frames. ⊠ *Bloempot Shopping Mall, Windstraat #15, Punda* ☎ *5999/461–2882.*

CIGARS

Cigar Emporium. A sweet aroma permeates Cigar Emporium, where you can find the largest selection of Cuban cigars on the island, including H. Upmann, Romeo y Julieta, and Montecristo. Visit the climate-controlled cedar cigar room. However, remember that Cuban cigars cannot be taken back to the United States legally. ⊠ *Gomezplein, Punda, Willemstad* ☎ *5999/465–3955.*

CLOTHING

Bamali. This shop sells funky, fabulous women's apparel, including Indonesian batik clothing; charming jewelry made of beads, shells, gemstones, and silver; handbags of leather and other fabrics; and lots of other unique accessories. Custom-made clothing is available here, too. ⊠ *Breedestraat, Punda, Willemstad* ☎ *5999/461–2258.*

Bikini Shop. Get suited up for the beach at the Bikini Shop, where you can find women's bathing suits (Vix, Becca, La Goufe) and accessories like cover-ups, flip-flops, and sunglasses. ⊠ *Seaquarium Beach, Bapor Kibra z/n* ☎ *5999/461–7343.*

Casa Janina. You can find a large selection of Calvin Klein apparel here along with an assortment of Levi's jeans. ⊠ *Madurostraat 13, Punda, Willemstad* ☎ *5999/461–1371.*

Tommy Hilfiger. This label's Curaçao outpost carries the full designer line for men, women, and children. ⊠ *Heerenstraat 3, Punda, Willemstad* ☎ *5999/461–2266.*

Wulfsen & Wulfsen. Come here for a large selection of smart men's and women's wear from European and American designers like Gant, Kenneth Cole, and Passport. ⊠ *Promenade Shopping Centre, Schottegatweg Noord, Willemstad* ☎ *5999/737–2922.*

FOOD

Centrum Supermarket. This is one of the better markets in terms of variety and quality. A bakery is on the premises, too. ⊠ *Weg Naar Bullenbaai z/n, Piscadera* ☎ *5999/869–6222.*

Plaza's Gourmet & Fresh Mart. Located in the upscale Zuikertuin Mall, Plaza's Gourmet & Fresh Mart is a relatively small market selling a variety of gourmet items in addition to the basics. ⊠ *Zuikertuintjeweg, Santa Rosa* ☎ *5999/737–0188.*

GIFTS

Boolchand's. Head here for electronics, jewelry, Swarovski crystal, Swiss watches, cameras, and more, sold behind a facade of red-and-white checkered tiles. ⊠ *Breedstraat 50, Punda, Willemstad* ☎ *5999/461–6233.*

Julius L. Penha & Sons. Near the Pontoon Bridge, Julius L. Penha & Sons sells French perfumes and cosmetics, clothing, and accessories in a baroque-style building dating from 1708. ⊠ *Heerenstraat 1, Punda, Willemstad* ☎ *5999/461–2266.*

Little Switzerland. You can find jewelry, watches, crystal, china, and leather goods at significant savings at Little Switzerland. ⊠ *Breedestraat 44, Punda, Willemstad* ☎ *5999/461–2111.*

HANDICRAFTS

Caribbean Handcraft Inc. It's worth visiting this shop just for the spectacular hilltop view; an elaborate assortment of locally handcrafted souvenirs is available here. ⊠ *Kaya Kakina 8, Jan Thiel* ☎ *5999/767–1171.*

Landhuis Groot Santa Martha. Artisans with disabilities make the ceramic vases, dolls, leather goods, and other products sold at Landhuis Groot Santa Martha. There's a $3 entrance fee, and it's closed weekends. ⊠ *Santa Martha Bay* ☎ *5999/864–1323, 5999/864–2969.*

JEWELRY

Clarisa. This shop specializes in cultured pearls and also carries European gold jewelry and watches. ⊠ *Gomezplein 10, Punda, Willemstad* ☎ *5999/461–2006.*

Different Design. Gorgeous custom-made pendants and rings of precious gems and gold are on display at Different Design. ⊠ *Gomezplein 7, Punda, Willemstad* ☎ *5999/465–2944.*

Freeport Jewelers. A fine selection of watches and jewelry (lines include Movado, David Yurman, and Maurice Lacroix) is available at Freeport Jewelers. ⊠ *Renaissance Mall #208, Otrobanda, Willemstad* ☎ *5999/461–2856.*

Pieters Jewelers. This jewelry store carries watches, including Seiko, Tissot, and Swatch, as well as gold jewelry, gemstones, and glassware. ⊠ *Promenade Shopping Center, Piscadera Bay, Willemstad* ☎ *5999/736–5833.*

LINENS

New Amsterdam. Hand-embroidered tablecloths, napkins, and pillowcases, as well as blue delft, are available at New Amsterdam. ⊠ *Gomezplein 14, Punda, Willemstad* ☎ *5999/461–2437* ⊠ *Breedestraat 29, Willemstad* ☎ *5999/461–3239.*

PERFUMES AND COSMETICS

Yellow House. This shop offers a vast selection of perfumes at low prices. ⊠ *Breedestraat 46, Punda, Willemstad* ☎ *5999/461–3222.*

SPORTS AND ACTIVITIES

FAMILY For the full gamut of activities in one spot, nature buffs (especially bird-watchers), families, and adventure seekers may want to visit **Caracas Bay Peninsula.** Things to do here include hiking, mountain biking, canoeing, kayaking, windsurfing, jet skiing, and snorkeling. There's a fully equipped dive shop, a restaurant, and a bar on the premises. Admission to the scenic area is $7; activities cost extra. ☎ *5999/747–0777.*

BIKING

Wanna Bike Curaçao. So you wanna bike Curaçao? This shop has the fix: kick into gear and head out for a guided mountain-bike tour through the Caracas Bay peninsula and the salt ponds at the Jan Thiel Lagoon. Although you should be fit to take on the challenge, mountain-bike experience is not required. Tour prices vary, depending on skill level and duration, and cover the bike, helmet, water, refreshments, park entrance fee, and guide—but don't forget to bring a camera. ⊠ *Jan Thiel Beach z/n, Jan Thiel, Willemstad* ☎ *5999/527–3720* ⊕ *www.wannabike.com.*

DIVING AND SNORKELING

The **Curaçao Underwater Marine Park** includes almost a third of the island's southern diving waters. Scuba divers and snorkelers can enjoy more than 12½ miles (20 km) of protected reefs and shores, with normal visibility from 60 to 150 feet. With water temperatures ranging from 75°F to 82°F (24°C to 28°C), wet suits are generally unnecessary. No coral collecting, spearfishing, or littering is allowed. An exciting wreck to explore is the SS *Oranje Nassau,* which ran aground in 1906. The other two main diving areas are Banda Abou, along the southwest coast between Westpunt and St. Marie, and along central Curaçao, which stretches between Bullen Bay to the Breezes Curaçao resort. The north coast—where conditions are dangerously rough—is not recommended for diving.

Introductory scuba resort courses run about $75 for one dive and $140 for two dives. Open-water certification courses run about $425 for the five-dive version. Virtually every operator charges $40 to $55 for a single-tank dive and $70 to $85 for a two-tank dive. One day of unlimited shore diving runs about $22 to $25. Snorkeling gear commonly rents for $10 to $16 per day.

Diversity Blue Bay. This outfitter offers a full range of dive services and equipment rental and is a fully certified PADI diving school. ⊠ *Blue Bay Golf & Dive Resort, Piscadera* ☎ *5999/888–6479* ⊕ *www. diveversity.com.*

9

FAMILY **Ocean Encounters.** This is the largest dive operator on the island. Its operations cover the popular east-coast dive sites, including the *Superior Producer* wreck, where barracudas hang out, and a tugboat wreck. West-end hot spots—including the renowned Mushroom Forest and Watamula dive sites—are accessible from the company's outlet at Westpunt. Ocean Encounters offers a vast menu of scheduled shore and boat dives and packages, as well as certified PADI instruction. In July, the dive center sponsors a kids' sea camp in conjunction with the Sea Aquarium. ⊠ *Lions Dive & Beach Resort, Seaquarium Beach, Bapor Kibra z/n* ☎ *5999/461–8131* ⊕ *www.oceanencounters.com.*

FISHING

Let's Fish. A 50-foot, fully rigged fishing boat, *Let's Fish* can accommodate groups of up to 11 people on half-day or full-day fishing trips to Klein Curaçao or Banda Abou in search of dolphinfish, marlin, wahoo, and more. ⊠ *Caracasbaaiweg 407N, Caracas Bay* ☎ *5999/747–4489.*

Miss Ann Boat Trips. The 43-foot *Second Chance* and an experienced crew will let you test your fishing skills. They boast the best catch ratio on the island. ⊠ *Jan Sofat 232, Van Engelen* ☎ *5999/767–1579* ⊕ *www.missannboattrips.com.*

GOLF

Blue Bay Curaçao Golf & Beach Resort. Set right on the Caribbean Sea, this course designed by Rocky Roquemore measures 6735 yards from the tips and beckons experts and novices alike. It's best feature is the spectacular views. You will be sure to enjoy the par-three 5th, which plays across and is guarded by the sea the entire left-hand side. Facilities include a golf shop, locker rooms, and a snack bar. You can rent carts, clubs, and shoes though don't expect too much with any of them or the facilities. If you'd like to drive your game to a new level, take a lesson from the house pro ($50 for a half hour). ⊠ *Landhuis Blauw, Blue Bay z/n* ☎ *5999/868–1755* ⊕ *www.golf.bluebay-curacao.com* ⅄ *18 holes, 6735 yards, par 72* ⬜ *$110 for 18 holes; $70 for 9 holes..*

Old Quarry Golf Course. This lush course designed by Pete Dye has incredible vistas on the sheltered bay known as Spanish Water. The course features a breathtaking mixture of ocean views and various forms of desert cactus along with Dye's dramatic bunkering. The 6920-yard layout is the best and toughest on the Island and includes an 8,000 square-foot clubhouse. There is a full range of facilities, and with the Santa Barbara Resort nearby, drinks and fine dining are mere steps away. Greens fees feature multiple play packages as well as resort discounts. You can rent carts, clubs, and shoes. ⊠ *Santa Barbara Plantation, Porta Blancu, Nieuwpoort z/n* ☎ *5999/840–6886* ⊕ *www.oldquarrygolf.com* ⅄ *18 holes, 6920 yards, par 72* ⬜ *From $55 to $175 in high season.*

GUIDED TOURS

Most tour operators have pickups at the major hotels, but if your hotel is outside the standard zone, there may be an additional charge of around $5. Tours are available in several languages, including English.

Atlantis Adventures. The so-called Trolley Train visits historic sites in Willemstad on a 1½-hour guided tour. This tour begins at Ft. Amsterdam, and there's no hotel pickup. ⊠ *Hilton Curaçao, J.F. Kennedy Blvd., Box 2133, Piscadera Bay* ☎ *5999/461–0011* ⊕ *www. atlantissubmarines.com/curacao.*

Blue Skies Helicopters. Those seeking a bird's eye view of things can take a 10-minute helicopter tour of Willemstad ($125) or a 30-minute island tour ($325). The photos alone might be worth it. ⊠ *Motetwerf Wharf, Willemstad* ☎ *5999/461–2088* ⊕ *www.blueskieshelicopters.com.*

Dutch Dream Adventures. This outfitter targets the action seeker with guided canoe and kayak safaris, mountain-bike excursions through Christoffel National Park for groups of 10 or more, or custom-designed tours to suit your group's interests. ☎ *5999/461–9393* ⊕ *www. dutchdreamcuracao.com.*

Peter Trips. Full-day island tours with Peter Trips depart from the hotels Tuesday, Wednesday, Friday, and Sunday at 9 am, with visits to many points of interest, including Ft. Amsterdam, Spanish Water, Scharloo, and Ft. Nassau. The cost is $50, and lunch is included. East-side half-day tours and a beach trip are offered Monday for $25 and $45, respectively. ☎ *5999/561–5368, 5999/465–2703* ⊕ *www.petertrips.com.*

Taber Tours. Among the favorites at Taber Tours is the Christoffel National Park–Cas Abou Beach combo: start the day with a guided hike up Mt. Christoffel followed by a tour of the park, and wind up at the beach to relax or snorkel. ⊠ *Kaya Schilling 170, Willemstad* ☎ *5999/868–7012.*

Yellow Tourism Solutions. This company offers a full range of half- and full-day tours, whether you want to check out town, beaches, or historical sites, or head out with a group for horseback riding, diving, or snorkeling. The company's Yellow Jeep Safari takes you to Christoffel National Park aboard a bright yellow Land Rover, driven by a guide who will take you off the beaten (and paved) path, deep into the park's natural terrain. ⊠ *Curaçao Marriott Beach Resort, Piscadera Bay* ☎ *5999/562–4895* ⊕ *www.tourism-curacao.com.*

WALKING TOURS

When making reservations for any tour, mention that you speak English.

Anko van der Woude. Walking tours of historic Otrobanda, focusing on the unique architecture of this old section of town, are led by architect Anko van der Woude upon request. ☎ *5999/461–3554.*

Eveline van Arkel. The Talk of the Town tour with Eveline van Arkel will take you through historical Punda to visit sites including Ft. Amsterdam, the restored Ft. Church, the Queen Emma pontoon bridge, and the Mikvé Israel-Emanuel Synagogue (call for reservations; English tours are on Tuesday at 9:30 am). ⊠ *Punda, Willemstad* ☎ *5999/747–4349.*

Gigi. Gigi leads expert tours of Punda focusing on Jewish heritage, including an insider's look at the synagogue. ✉ *Punda, Willemstad* ☎ *5999/697–0290.*

SEA EXCURSIONS

Many sailboats and motorboats offer sunset cruises and daylong snorkeling and picnic trips to Klein Curaçao, the uninhabited island between Curaçao and Bonaire, and other destinations. Prices are around $50 to $90 for a half-day trip (including food and drinks).

Insulinde. One option aboard the 120-foot Dutch sailing ketch *Insulinde* is a snorkeling-and-scenic-tour combo, capped off by a return cruise into the sunset. The cost is $50 (cash only). ☎ *5999/560–1340* ⊕ *www. insulinde.com.*

Jonalisa. The half-day lunch and snorkel trip on the *Jonalisa,* a 54-foot catamaran, features sailing, snorkeling, and swimming. It includes an open bar and barbecue lunch. ☎ *5999/767–9998* ⊕ *www. bountyadventures.com.*

Mermaid. This 66-foot motor yacht carries up to 60 people to Klein Curaçao three times a week. A buffet lunch, beer, and soft drinks are provided at the boat's exclusive beach house, which has picnic tables, shade huts, and facilities. ☎ *5999/560–1530* ⊕ *www.mermaidboattrips.com.*

Miss Ann. The 76-foot *Miss Justine* motorboat offers snorkeling or diving, moonlight, and party trips for up to 54 people. ☎ *5999/767–1579* ⊕ *www.missannboattrips.com.*

Seaworld Explorer. For a unique vantage point, soak up the local marine life on a 1½-hour-long tour of the coral reefs aboard the glass-bottom, semisubmersible *Seaworld Explorer.* ☎ *5999/461–0011* ⊕ *www. atlantissubmarines.com/curacao/explorer.*

WATER SPORTS

Caribbean Sea Sports. This quality company runs kayaking, windsurfing, banana boats, tube rides, diving, snorkeling, and more. ✉ *Curaçao Marriott Beach Resort, Piscadera Bay* ☎ *5999/462–2620* ⊕ *www. caribseasports.com.*

Let's Go Watersports. Captain "Goodlife" will help you plan kayaking and other boat outings for snorkeling in some special spots. He also grills up a tasty lunch at the dock. ✉ *Santa Cruz Beach 1, Santa Cruz* ☎ *5999/520–1147, 5999/864–0438.*

DOMINICA

WELCOME TO DOMINICA

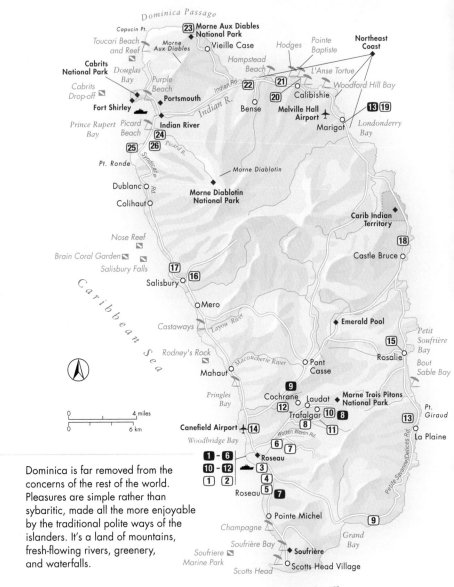

Dominica is far removed from the concerns of the rest of the world. Pleasures are simple rather than sybaritic, made all the more enjoyable by the traditional polite ways of the islanders. It's a land of mountains, fresh-flowing rivers, greenery, and waterfalls.

THE NATURE ISLAND

The island is 29 miles (47 km) long and 16 miles (26 km) wide, with approximately 73,000 citizens. Because it was a British colony (achieving independence in 1978), you may wonder about the prevalence of French names. Although the English first claimed Dominica in 1627, the French controlled it from 1632 until 1759, when it passed back into English hands.

KEY	
⌐	*Beaches*
🛳	*Cruise Ship Terminal*
◪	*Dive Sites*
1	*Restaurants*
①	*Hotels*

DOMINICA

10

TOP REASONS TO VISIT DOMINICA

1 **Fewer Crowds:** Dominica is a delightful respite from the more crowded, commercial islands.

2 **Unspoiled Nature:** The island's natural environment is the major draw.

3 **Great Dives:** Diving pristine reefs full of colorful sea life or in bubbly, volcanic water is amazing.

4 **Natural Spas:** Dominica has an abundance of natural sulfur pools, some of which have become makeshift spas.

THE ORIGINAL CARIBBEANS

Blame Christopher Columbus: his logs give accounts of the "gentle, laughing" Arawak and the "ferocious, cannibalistic" Carib, both stereotypes that pigeonholed the Caribbean's two indigenous peoples and persist to this day. Historians have had to wade through a lot of colonial romanticism to get at the truth.

Archaeologists have determined that the first Amerindian migration to the islands took place around 1000 BC from northern South America. "War and Peace" could describe the divergence between the agrarian Arawak and the more militant Carib. The Arawak—the umbrella term encompassed many smaller groups, most notably the Taíno people on the larger islands—were easily subjugated by Spanish explorers; the Carib, less so, but eventually they succumbed, too. Warfare and disease—the indigenous peoples had never encountered smallpox until the Europeans' arrival—caused populations of both groups to dwindle to a few thousand by the end of the 18th century.

Language. Carib warfare resulted in the capture of many Arawak women. As a result, early Spanish arrivals were puzzled by what appeared to be gender-specific languages, with men speaking the Carib Kalinago language, and women, one of several Arawakan tongues. Historians debate the notion of a persistent gender-communication divide between what the British would later call Island Carib and Island Arawak. The languages gave several of the islands their names: Bequia ("cloud"), Canouan ("turtle"),

Carriacou ("reef"), Saba ("rock"), and Tobago ("tobacco"). The English words barbecue, hurricane, and potato have their roots in indigenous Caribbean languages, too.

Religion. The Carib adopted many of the tenets of Arawak religion, essentially a system of animism and ancestor worship. Shamans held the keys to unlocking contact with the spirit world, thus occupying esteemed roles in their communities. Tobacco played a prominent role in worship ceremonies. Petroglyphs, rock carvings dedicated to objects of indigenous veneration, can be seen today in Puerto Rico, St. Kitts, St. John, and Grenada.

Innovations. With the construction of their *canoas*—source of the word canoe—indigenous Caribbean peoples were able to establish interisland transport. (The Arawak used their vessels for trade; the Carib, for warfare.) And the next time you laze in a hammock, acknowledge the Arawak. *Hamacas* were a regular fixture in their homes.

Women. Carib and Arawak women participated in surprisingly egalitarian societies. Women were eligible to be a community's *cacique* (chief) and frequently served on its ruling council. Society did, however, ascribe gender roles: men went off to war while women tended agriculture and took care of domestic chores.

Food. Fishing was a major source of nourishment for the Carib and Arawak. Perhaps no food is more identified with Caribbean indigenous peoples than the cassava or yuca, a starchy tuber and a major source of carbohydrates, with one major god even being the patron of this important crop.

Cannibalism? What of the charges of cannibalism among the Carib people? Columbus wrote that he saw the practice, but most historians side with today's Carib descendants who insist it never went on. They suggest that Spanish explorers had religious and economic motives for perpetuating the myth of cannibalism. Conversion to Christianity and even slavery would have to be better than such "barbarism" in their eyes.

—Jeffrey Van Fleet

10

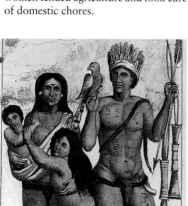

Updated
by Roberta
Sotonoff

Wedged between the two French islands of Guadeloupe and Martinique, Dominica (pronounced dom-in-ee-ka) is as close to the Garden of Eden as you're likely to get. Wild orchids, anthurium lilies, ferns, heliconia, and myriad fruit trees sprout profusely. Much of the interior is still covered by luxuriant rain forest and remains inaccessible by road.

With this bountiful natural abundance, there's also a lot of active watching—flying birds and butterflies, turtles hatching, plus jumping dolphins and breaching whales. Even when you're not looking, something is sure to capture your gaze. The sensory overload isn't just visual. Your soul may be soothed by the refreshing smell of clean river water and cleaner air, your taste buds will be tantalized by the freshest fruits and vegetables, and your skin will be caressed by the purest natural soaps.

A natural fortress, the island protected the Caribs (the region's original inhabitants) against European colonization. The rugged northeast is still reserved as home to the last survivors of the Caribs, along with their traditions and mythology.

Dominica—with a population of approximately 73,000—did eventually become a British colony. It attained independence in November 1978 and has a seat in the United Nations as the central Caribbean's only natural World Heritage Site. Its official language is English, although most locals communicate with each other in Creole; roads are driven on the left; family and place-names are a mélange of English, Carib, and French; and the economy is still heavily dependent on agriculture.

Dominica is an ideal place to be active—hike, bike, trek, kayak, dive, snorkel, or sail in marine reserves. Explore the rain forests, waterfalls, and geothermal springs, or search for whales and dolphins. Discover Dominica's vibrant Carib culture. To experience Dominica is really to know Earth as it was created.

LOGISTICS

Getting to Dominica: There are no nonstops from the United States, so you'll have to transfer in the British Virgin Islands, Antigua, Barbados, Martinique, San Juan, St. Maarten, or St. Vincent. There is also a ferry (90 minutes) from Guadeloupe or Martinique.

Hassle Factor: High.

On the Ground: Taxis and minibuses are available at the airports and in Roseau as well as at most hotels and guesthouses. Rates are fixed by the government (if you share a taxi with other passengers going in the same direction, you can negotiate a special price; a trip from Melville Hall Airport to Roseau can cost as little as $30 per person). Taxi drivers also offer tours anywhere on the island beginning at $30 an hour for up to four people; a four- to five-hour island tour costs approximately $150. It's best to get a recommendation from your hotel. You can recognize a taxi or minibus by the H, HA, and HB plates; simply flag them down or make your way to the nearest bus stop.

PLANNING

WHEN TO GO

Dominicans boast that they have the most spontaneous carnival in the region, Mas Domnik. It's fun to join a band, get all costumed and painted, and revel in the streets during Carnival Monday and Tuesday. Celebrations usually heat up the last 10 days or so before Ash Wednesday. Independence Day on November 3 celebrates not only Dominica's independence from Great Britain, but also the Creole culture. On the last weekend in October or first weekend of November, the awesome, three-day Annual World Creole Music Festival draws performers and Creole music enthusiasts from around the globe.

The high season is December to April, when many Americans and Europeans come. May 1 to November 1 is hurricane season.

GETTING HERE AND AROUND

AIR TRAVEL

There are no nonstops from the United States. Note that LIAT is not the most reliable airline; if you're flying them, it pays to double-check your reservation and to get to the airport with lots of time to spare.

Airport Contacts Canefield Airport (*DCF*). Canefield Airport is served by only a few small Caribbean-based airlines. ⚠ There is no longer an information office at this airport. ✉ *Canefield.* **Melville Hall Airport** (*DOM*). Melville Hall Airport, where most flights arrive, is 75 minutes from Roseau. ✉ *Marigot* ☎ *767/445–7101.*

Airline and Travel Agent Contacts BVI Airlines. BVI Airlines flies from Tortola, in the British Virgin Islands (about US$127.50), and from St. Maarten (about US$125) to Dominica (Melville Hall Airport). Flights can be booked online or through the Witchurch Travel Agency. ✉ *Terrance B. Lettsome International, Suite 234, British Virgin Islands* ⊕ *gobvi.com.* **Conviasa.** Conviasa flies from Venezuela to Dominica's Canfield Airport on Tuesday and Thursday. Tickets can be booked through the Whitchurch Travel Agency. ☎ 767/448–8227 ⊕ www.conviasa.aero. **LIAT.** LIAT flies from Melville Hall Airport. ☎ 767/440–2452 ⊕ www.liatairline.com. **Seaborne Airlines.** Seaborne Airlines flies direct to the island from San Juan, Puerto Rico as well as from St. Croix, BVI. Supersaver fares start at $159. ⊠ British Virgin Islands ☎ 866/359-8784 ⊕ www.seaborneairlines.com/. **Whitchurch Travel Agency.** This local travel agency can book you flights on local airlines, including Conviasa and BVI. ⊠ Old St., Roseau ☎ 767/448-2181 ⊕ www.whitchurch.com.

BOAT AND FERRY TRAVEL

There is a ferry (90 minutes) from Guadeloupe or Martinique.

Express des Isles. Express des Isles has regularly scheduled interisland jet catamaran ferry service connecting Dominica to Guadeloupe, Martinique, and St. Lucia. The ferry departs from Roseau and travels to Martinique or Guadeloupe on Monday, Wednesday, Friday, Saturday, and Sunday. (Schedules are subject to change.) From Guadeloupe, it continues south to St. Lucia. The Martinique or Guadaloupe round-trip crossing costs €129 and takes approximately 90 minutes. The voyage offers superb views of the other islands. Tickets can be booked through the Whitchurch Travel Agency. ⊠ H.V. Whitchurch & Co. Ltd., Old St., Roseau ⊕ www.express-des-iles.com/index.cfm?lng=en.

CAR TRAVEL

Unless you are staying in Roseau or doing extensive guided tours, a car may be a necessity. Cabs can be very expensive. Daily car-rental rates begin at about $35 to $70 per day (weekly and long-term rates can be negotiated). A refundable US$1,200 deposit or credit card confirmation is required at the time of pickup. You'll need to buy a visitor's driving permit for $12 at one of the airports or at the Traffic Division office on High Street in Roseau or at vehicle-rental offices. Gasoline stations are all over the island; at this writing, gas costs about $5.60 per gallon. Driving in Dominica is on the left side, though you can rent vehicles with a steering wheel on either the left or the right.

Contacts **Best Deal Rent-A-Car** ⊠ 15 Hanover St., Roseau ☎ 767/449–9204, 767/616–3325 ⊕ bestdealrentacar.dm. **Courtesy Car Rental.** There are two locations; one at Melville Hall Airport and one in the town of Roseau. ⊠ 10 Winston La., Goodwill ☎ 767/448–7763, 767/235–7763 ⊕ www.dominicacarrentals.com ⊠ Mellville Hall Airport, Mairgot ☎ 767/445–7677. **Road Runner Car Rental.** At all of its non-Portsmouth locations, the reasonably priced Road Runner Car Rental will deliver and pick up cars at no charge. ⊠ Canffield Hwy., Roseau ☎ 767/275–5337 ⊕ www.roadrunnercarrental.com.

TAXIS

Contacts **CombineTaxi.** There are fixed rates from Melville Hall Airport to different parts of the island. To Picard/Portsmouth, it's $26; a shared taxi from the airport runs $30–$35. ☎ 767/275–6005. **Dominica Taxi Association.** Dominica Taxi Association has fixed rates from the airport. From Melville Hall Airport to Canefield/Roseau/ Newtown/Portsmouth/Picard, rates are $26. A shared taxi from Melville Hall to Roseau is $30–$35. Other destinations run $15–$40. ☎ 767/275–8533, 767/449–8533.

ESSENTIALS

Banks and Exchange Services The official currency is the Eastern Caribbean dollar (EC$). The exchange rate hovers around EC$2.70 to the US$1. U.S. dollars and major credit cards are widely accepted. You can find ATMs in all the banks in Roseau and airports as well as some in larger villages such as Portsmouth. They dispense EC dollars only and accept international bank cards.

Emergencies Ambulance, police, and fire ☎ *999.*

Passport Requirements Valid passport plus a return or onward ticket.

Phones To call Dominica from the United States, dial the area code (767) and the local access code (44), followed by the five-digit local number. On the island, dial only the seven-digit number that follows the area code.

Taxes and Service Charges The departure-embarkation tax is EC$59, or about US$23, payable in cash only at the airport at the time of departure from the island. Hotels collect 10%, plus a 10% service charge. Restaurants collect a 15% government V.A.T. (value-added tax).

Tipping Most hotels and restaurants add a 10% service charge to your bill. A 5% tip for exceptionally good service on top of the service charge is always welcome; otherwise just tip accordingly.

ACCOMMODATIONS

There are a few upscale options in Dominica and no large resorts. Most accommodations are in small lodges and guesthouses.

HOTEL AND RESTAURANT PRICES

Prices in the restaurant reviews are the average cost of a main course at dinner or, if dinner is not served, at lunch; taxes and service charges are generally included. Prices in the hotel reviews are the lowest cost of a standard double room in high season, excluding taxes, service charges, and meal plans (except at all-inclusives). Prices for rentals are the lowest per-night cost for a one-bedroom unit in high season.

For expanded lodging reviews and current deals, visit Fodors.com.

VISITOR INFORMATION

Discover Dominica Authority (*Dominica Tourist Office*). The main tourism office is in the Financial Centre, but there's also a small branch at the airport. The Discover Dominica Authority's information offices at the Bayfront (Dame Charles Boulevard) can recommend hiking guides. ✉ *Financial Centre, Kennedy Ave., Roseau* ☎ *767/448–2045, 866/522–4057 in U.S.* ⊕ *www.discoverdominica.com* ✉ *Bayfront, Dame Charles Blvd., Roseau.*

WEDDINGS

Two days' minimum residency. A valid passport, original birth certificate, and divorce decree or death certificate for the former spouse (if applicable) is required. The parties must sign a statutory declaration on marital status, which must be obtained and sworn in Dominica in the presence of a local lawyer. At least two witnesses must be present at the ceremony.

10

EXPLORING

Despite the small size of this island, it can take a couple of hours to travel between the popular destinations. Many sights are isolated and difficult to find; you may be better off taking an organized excursion. If you do go it alone, drive carefully; roads can be narrow and winding. Plan at least eight hours to see the highlights. To fully experience the island, set aside about five days so you can enjoy the water and take some hikes.

ROSEAU

Although it's one of the smallest capitals in the Caribbean, Roseau has the highest concentration of inhabitants of any town in the eastern Caribbean. Caribbean vernacular architecture and a bustling marketplace transport visitors back in time. Although you can walk the entire town in about an hour, you'll get a much better feel for the place on a leisurely stroll.

For some years now, the Society for Historical Architectural Preservation and Enhancement (SHAPE) has organized programs and projects to preserve the city's architectural heritage. Several interesting buildings have already been restored. **Lilac House,** on Kennedy Avenue, has three types of gingerbread fretwork, latticed verandah railings, and heavy hurricane shutters. The **J.W. Edwards Building,** at the corner of Old and King George V streets, has a stone base and a wooden second-floor gallery. The **Old Market Plaza** is the center of Roseau's historic district, which was laid out by the French on a radial plan rather than a grid, so streets such as Hanover, King George V, and Old radiate from this area. South of the marketplace is the Fort Young Hotel, built as a British fort in the 18th century; the nearby statehouse, public library, and Anglican cathedral are also worth a visit. New developments at the bay front on Dame M.E. Charles Boulevard have brightened up the waterfront.

WORTH NOTING

FAMILY **Botanical Gardens.** The 40-acre Botanical Gardens, founded in 1891 as an annex of London's Kew Gardens, is a great place to relax, stroll, or watch a cricket match. In addition to the extensive collection of tropical plants and trees, there's also a parrot aviary. At the Forestry Division office, which is also on the garden grounds, you can find numerous publications on the island's flora, fauna, and national parks. The forestry officers are particularly knowledgeable on these subjects and can also recommend good hiking guides. ⊠ *Valley Rd., Roseau* ☎ *767/266–3807, 767/266–3812* ⊕ *www.da-academy.org/dagardens.html* 🎫 *Free* ☉ *Daily 8–4.*

SOUFRIÈRE

Tourism is quietly mingling with the laid-back lifestyle of the residents of this gently sunbaked village in the southwest, near one of the island's two marine reserves. Although it was first settled by French lumbermen in the 17th century, it's mainly fishermen you'll find here today. In the village sits one of the island's prettiest churches, a historic 18th-century Catholic church built of volcanic stone. The ruins of the L. Rose Lime

Oil factory; Sulphur Springs, with its hot mineral baths to the east; and some of the best diving and snorkeling on the island is within the **Soufrière/Scotts Head Marine Reserve.** To the west is Bois Cotlette (a historic plantation house) and to the south the Scotts Head Peninsula—at the island's southern tip—which separates the Caribbean from the Atlantic.

WORTH NOTING

The Waitukubuli National Trail. On an island that already brims with fabulous hiking tracks, this 114-mile trail is like the icing on the cake. In its 14 segments, paths wind from the southern part of the island at Scotts Head to Capuchin up north. Trekkers pass through woodlands, gorges, waterfalls, and lush rain forests as they make their way down rivers and up mountains. The trails weave through Fort Shirley and Carib villages, in some places following old runaway-slave trails. Paths and signage are sometimes hard to find, as the project is still a work in progress. Yellow and blue markings are on rocks, sticks, poles, and sometimes embedded into the ground. Pick and choose the segments that most interest you. Those ambitious enough to do the whole trail—which can take about a week—will come away with an intimate knowledge of the island's terrain and unique history. Via the Kalinago Home Stay, you can even stay overnight in a house or hut in Carib Territory. It is US$12 for a day pass or US$40 for a 15-day pass on any of the 14 segments. Passes are mandatory and available at the Forestry and Wildlife Division, the Waitukubuli Trail Headquarters in Pont Casse, and at vendors near the trail segments. ☎ *767/266–3593, 767/440–6125* ⊕ *www.waitukubulitrail.com.*

NORTHEAST COAST

Steep cliffs, dramatic reefs, and rivers that swirl down through forests of mangroves and fields of coconut define this section of Dominica. The road along the Atlantic, with its red cliffs, whipped-cream waves, and windswept trees, crosses the Hatton Garden River before entering the village of Marigot. In the northeastern region there are numerous estates—old family holdings planted with fruit trees. Beyond Marigot and the Melville Hall Airport is the beautiful Londonderry Estate. The beach here is inspiring, with driftwood strewn about its velvety black sands, which part halfway where the Londonderry River spills into the Atlantic (swimming isn't advised because of strong currents, but a river bath here is a memorable treat). Farther along the coast, beyond the village of Wesley (which has a gas station and a shop that sells wonderful bread) and past Eden Estate, there are still more beautiful beaches and coves. The swimming is excellent at Woodford Hill Bay, Hodges Beach, Hampstead Estate, Batibou Bay, and L'Anse Tortue (Turtle Bay), where you might glimpse a turtle plodding on the beach to lay her eggs. At the charming community of Calibishie you'll find beach bars and restaurants, as well as laid-back villas and guesthouses. At Bense, a village in the interior just past Calibishie, you can take a connector road to Chaudiere, a beautiful swimming spot in a valley; the only crowd you're likely to encounter is a group of young villagers frolicking in the 15-foot-deep pool and diving off the 25-foot-high rocks.

10

PORTSMOUTH

In 1782, Portsmouth was the site of the Battle of Les Saintes, a naval engagement between the French and the English. The English won the battle but lost the much tougher fight against malaria-carrying mosquitoes that bred in the nearby swamps. Once intended to be the capital, thanks to its superb harbor on Prince Rupert Bay, Portsmouth saw as many as 400 ships in port at one time in its heyday. But because of those swamps, Roseau, not Portsmouth, is the capital today. Maritime traditions are continued here by the yachting set, and a 2-mile (3-km) stretch of sandy beach fringed with coconut trees runs to the Picard Estate area.

ELSEWHERE ON DOMINICA

TOP ATTRACTIONS

FAMILY **Emerald Pool.** Quite possibly the most visited nature attraction on the island, this emerald-green pool fed by a 50-foot waterfall is an easy trip to make. To reach this spot in the vast Morne Trois Pitons National Park, you follow a trail that starts at the side of the road near the reception center (it's an easy 20-minute walk). Along the way, there are lookout points with views of the windward (Atlantic) coast and the forested interior. If you don't want a crowd, check whether there are cruise ships in port before going out, as this spot is popular with cruise-ship tour groups. ⊠ *Morne Trois Pitons National Park* ☎ *US$3 for pre-organized tours; US$5 for private and stay-over visitors; US$12 weekly site pass covers all parks.*

Morne Trois Pitons National Park. A UNESCO World Heritage Site, this 17,000-acre swath of lush, mountainous land in the south-central interior (covering 9% of Dominica) is the island's crown jewel. Named after one of the highest (4,600 feet) mountains on the island, it contains the island's famous "boiling lake," majestic waterfalls, and cool mountain lakes. There are four types of vegetation zones here. Ferns grow 30 feet tall, wild orchids sprout from trees, sunlight leaks through green canopies, and a gentle mist rises over the jungle floor. A system of trails has been developed in the park, and the Division of Forestry and Wildlife works hard to maintain them—with no help from the excessive rainfall and the profusion of vegetation that seems to grow right before your eyes. Access to the park is possible from most points, though the easiest approaches are via the small mountaintop villages of Laudat (pronounced lau-*dah*) and Cochrane.

About 5 miles (8 km) out of Roseau, the Wotten Waven Road branches off toward Sulphur Springs, where you can see the belching, sputtering, and gurgling releases of volcanic hot springs. At the base of Morne Micotrin you can find two crater lakes: the first, at 2,500 feet above sea level, is **Freshwater Lake.** According to a local legend, it's haunted by a vindictive mermaid and a monstrous serpent. Farther on is **Boeri Lake,** fringed with greenery and with purple hyacinths floating on its surface.

On your way to Boiling Lake you pass through the **Valley of Desolation,** a sight that definitely lives up to its name. Harsh sulfuric fumes have destroyed virtually all the vegetation in what must once have been a lush forested area. Small hot and cold streams with water of various colors—black, purple, red, orange—web the valley. Stay on the trail to avoid breaking through the crust that covers the hot lava. During this hike you'll pass rivers where you can refresh yourself with a dip (a particular treat is a soak in a hot-water stream on the way back). At the beginning of the Valley of Desolation trail is the **TiTou Gorge,** where you can swim in the pool or relax in the hot-water springs along one side. If you're a strong swimmer, you can head up the gorge to a cave (it's about a five-minute swim) that has a magnificent waterfall; a crack in the cave about 50 feet above permits a stream of sunlight to penetrate the cavern.

Also in the national park are some of the island's most spectacular waterfalls. The 45-minute hike to **Sari Sari Falls,** accessible through the east-coast village of La Plaine, can be hair-raising. But the sight of water cascading some 150 feet into a large pool is awesome. So large are these falls that you feel the spray from hundreds of yards away. Just beyond the village of Trafalgar and up a short hill is the reception facility, where you can purchase passes to the national park and find guides to take you on a rain-forest trek to the twin **Trafalgar Falls**; the 125-foot-high waterfall is called the Father, and the wider, 95-foot-high one, the Mother. If you like a little challenge, let your guide take you to the riverbed and the cool pools at the base of the falls (check whether there's a cruise ship in port before setting out; this sight is popular with the tour operators). You need a guide for the arduous 75-minute hike to **Middleham Falls.** It's best if you start at Laudat (the turnoff for the trailhead is just before the village); the trip is much longer from Cochrane Village. Guides for these hikes are available at the trailheads; still, it's best to arrange a tour before setting out. *US$3 for pre-organized tours; US$5 for private and stay-over visitors; US$12 weekly site pass covers all parks.*

Boiling Lake. The undisputed highlight of the park is the Boiling Lake. Reputedly one of the world's largest such lakes, it's a cauldron of gurgling gray-blue water—temperatures range 80°F to 197°F—70 yards wide and of unknown depth. Although generally believed to be a volcanic crater, the lake is actually a flooded fumarole—a crack through which gases escape from the molten lava below. As many visitors discovered in late 2004, the "lake" can sometimes dry up, though it fills again within a few months and, shortly after that, once more starts to boil. It has returned to its pre-2004 levels. The two- to four-hour (one way) hike up to the lake is challenging (on a very rainy day, be prepared to slip and slide the whole way up and back). You'll need clothes appropriate for a strenuous hike. Most guided trips start early (no later than 8:30 am) for this all-day, 7-mile (11-km) round-trip trek. Do not attempt this trek without a trained guide.

10

WORTH NOTING

FAMILY **Cabrits National Park.** Along with Brimstone Hill in St. Kitts, Shirley Heights in Antigua, and Ft. Charlotte in St. Vincent, the Cabrits National Park's Ft. Shirley ruins are among the most significant historic sites in the Caribbean. Just north of the town of Portsmouth, this

1,300-acre park includes a marine park and herbaceous swamps, which are home to several species of rare birds and plants. At the heart of the park is the Ft. Shirley military complex. Built by the British between 1770 and 1815, it once comprised 50 major structures, including storehouses that were also quarters for 700 men. With the help of the Royal Navy (which sends sailors ashore to work on the site each time a ship is in port) and local volunteers, historian Dr. Lennox Honychurch restored the fort and its surroundings, incorporating a small museum that highlights the natural and historic aspects of the park and an open canteen-style restaurant. ⊠ *Portsmouth* ⌨ *$5* ⊘ *Museum open daily 9–5.*

FAMILY **Carib Indian Territory.** In 1903, after centuries of conflict, the Caribbean's first settlers, the Kalinago (more popularly known as the Caribs), were granted approximately 3,700 acres of land on the island's northeast coast. Here a hardened lava formation, **L'Escalier Tête Chien** (Snake's Staircase), runs down into the Atlantic. The name is derived from a snake whose head resembles that of a dog. The ocean alongside Carib Territory is particularly fierce, and the shore is full of countless coves and inlets. According to Carib legend, every night the nearby Londonderry Islets transform into grand canoes to take the spirits of the dead out to sea.

The Kalinago people resemble native South Americans and are mostly farmers and fishermen. Others are entrepreneurs who have opened restaurants, guesthouses, and little shops that offer exquisite baskets and handcrafted items. Craftspeople have retained their knowledge of basket weaving, wood carving, and canoe building through generations. They fashion long, elegant canoes from the trunk of a single *gommier* tree. ⊕ *www.caribterritory.com.*

Kalinago Barana Autê. You might catch canoe builders at work at Kalinago Barana Autê, the Carib Territory's place to learn about Kalinago customs, history, and culture. A guided, 45-minute tour explores the village, stopping along the way to see some traditional dances and to learn about plants, dugout canoes, basket weaving, and cassava bread making. The path offers wonderful viewpoints of the Atlantic and a chance to glimpse Isukulati Falls. There's also a good souvenir shop. ⊠ *Crayfish River, Salybia* ☎ *767/445–7979* ⊕ *www. kalinagobaranaaute.com* ⌨ *Basic package is about $10* ⊘ *Daily 9–5.*

FAMILY **Indian River.** The mouth of the Indian River, which flows into the ocean at Portsmouth, was once a Carib Indian settlement. A rowboat ride down this river, which was featured in *Pirates of the Caribbean: Dead Man's Chest,* is both relaxing and educational. The river is lined with trees whose buttress roots spread up to 20 feet. Clear, brackish water is a playground for young barracudas and crayfish. Except for singing yellow warblers, flitting hummingbirds, or wing-flapping egrets, there is an eerie silence. To arrange such a trip, stop by the visitor center in Portsmouth and ask for one of the "Indian River boys," of the Portsmouth Indian River Tour Guides Association. Most boat trips take you up as far as Rahjah's Jungle Bar. You can usually do an optional guided walking tour of the swamplands and the remnants of one of Dominica's oldest plantations. Tours last one to three hours, for roughly $20–$25 per person, but the actual price depends on your guide.

Morne Aux Diables. This peak soars 2,826 feet above sea level and slopes down to Toucari and Douglas bays and long stretches of dark-sand beach on the north side of the island. To reach it, take the road along the Caribbean coast. It twists by coconut, cocoa, and banana groves, past fern-festooned embankments, over rivers, and into villages where brightly painted shanties are almost as colorful as all the flora and fauna.

FAMILY **Morne Diablotin National Park.** Here Dominica's highest mountain, Morne Diablotin, soars 4,747 feet. The peak takes its name from a bird known in English as the black-capped petrel. Now extinct on the island, it was prized by hunters in the 18th century. Dominica is still a major birding destination with many exotic—and endangered—species such as the green-and-purple Sisserou parrot (*Amazona imperialis*) and the Jaco, or red-neck, parrot (*Amazona arausiaca*). Before this national park was established, its Syndicate Nature Trail was aided by some 6,000 schoolchildren—each donated 25¢ to protect the area's habitat. The west-coast road (at the bend near Dublanc) runs through three types of forest and leads to the park. The trail offers a casual walk; just bring a sweater and binoculars. But the five- to eight-hour hike up Morne Diablotin is no walk in the park. You will need a guide, sturdy hiking shoes, warm clothing, and a backpack with refreshments and a change of clothes (including socks). All should be wrapped in plastic to keep them dry.

Bertrand Jno Baptiste. Local ornithology expert Bertrand Jno Baptiste is a good guide for Morne Diablotin. ☎ *767/245–4768.*

BEACHES

Most of Dominica's beaches are in the north and east; they are windswept, dramatic, and uncrowded, lending themselves more to relaxing than swimming. That is because many have undercurrents. Slightly farther north there are beautiful secluded beaches and coves. Although northeast-coast beaches offer excellent shallow swimming, their wind-tossed beauty can be dangerous; there are sometimes strong currents with the whipped-cream waves. From these beaches you can see the islands of Marie-Galante and Les Saintes and parts of Guadeloupe. On the southwest coast, beaches are fewer and made mostly of black sand and rounded volcanic rocks. In general, the west coast is more for scuba diving and snorkeling than for lounging on the beach.

FAMILY **Champagne.** On the west coast, just south of the village of Pointe Michel, this stony beach is hailed as one of the best spots for swimming, diving, and (especially) snorkeling. Forget the sunning, though, because the beach is strewn with rocks. Champagne gets its name from volcanic vents that constantly puff steam into the sea, which makes you feel as if you are swimming in warm champagne. A boardwalk leads to the beach from Soufrière/Scotts Head Marine Reserve. **Amenities:** none. **Best for:** snorkeling; swimming. ⊠ *1 mile (1½ km) south of Pointe Michel, Soufrière.*

10

Emerald Pool is one of Dominica's most popular natural attractions.

FAMILY **Hampstead Beach.** This isolated gold-with-speckled-black-sand shoreline on the northeast coast actually encompasses three bays. It is divided into two beaches. The Red River meets the sea at Hampstead Beach I. This is where Johnny Depp was chased by natives in *Pirates of the Caribbean: Dead Man's Chest*. The palm tree–lined Hampstead Beach II is on the sheltered and calm Batibou Bay. A 4x4 is the preferred mode of transportation to get here—or be prepared hike in from the road. Both beaches ooze with charm and are worth the effort. **Amenities:** none. **Best for:** solitude; swimming. ⊠ *Off Indian Rd., west of Calibishie, Calibishie.*

L'Anse Tortue. On the northeast coast, this isolated, golden-sand beach with dabs of black is also known as Turtle Bay. It is a favorite for egg-laying turtles and for those who want seclusion without having to drive all the way out to Hampstead Beach. Sitting on a cove just past Woodford Hill, it's an easy, although sometimes steep, walk down from the road. There is no sign marking the trail or the beach, but it starts just across the road from a brown-building snack shop with Fanta signs. This is another BYOBC (bring your own beach chair) beach with no amenities. Its charm is its solitude and beauty. **Amenities:** none. **Best for:** solitude. ⊠ *East of Calibishie, Calibishie.*

Mero Beach. The closest beach to Roseau, this silver-gray stretch of beach on the west coast, is just outside the village of Mero. Waters are warm and calm. The entire community comes here on Sunday. This is one of the few beaches with amenities. **Amenities:** food and drink; showers; toilets. **Best for:** partiers; swimming. ⊠ *Near Roseau, Mero.*

FAMILY **Pointe Baptiste.** Extravagantly shaped red-sandstone boulders surround this beautiful golden-sand beach. Access is a 15-minute walk, entering through private property (Pointe Baptiste Guest House or Red Rock Haven), so the beach is quiet and unpopulated. It is the place to relax, take a dip or climb the incredible rock formations. The Red Rock Haven luxury hotel is just behind it, so you can grab a snack at its Escape Beach Bar & Grill. **Amenities:** food and drink. **Best for:** solitude; swimming. ⊠ *Calibishie.*

Scotts Head. At the southernmost tip of the island, a small landmass is connected to the mainland by a narrow stretch of stony beach. It's a fantastic spot for snorkeling and diving. You can lunch at one of the village restaurants, where you'll always find fresh-caught red snapper and mahimahi. On the beach, there's also a small snack shop and a couple of venders. **Amenities:** food and drink. **Best for:** snorkeling; swimming. ⊠ *Near Soufriére, Scotts Head Village.*

WHERE TO EAT

You can expect an abundance of vegetables, fruits, and root crops to appear on menus around the island. Dominica's economy, after all, is based on agriculture. Sweet ripe plantains, *kushkush* (cornmeal), yams, breadfruit, dasheen (also called taro), fresh fish, and chicken prepared at least a dozen different ways are all staples. The local drink is a spiced rum steeped with herbs such as anisette (called nanny) and *pweve* (lemongrass). Dominican cuisine is also famous for its use of local game, such as the *manicou* (a small opossum) and the *agouti* (a large indigenous rodent), but you'll have to be an intrepid diner to go that route. The government had banned "mountain chicken" (a euphemism for a large frog called *crapaud*) because a fungal disease, over-hunting, and other problems have greatly reduced its numbers.

What to Wear: Most Dominicans dress nicely but practically when eating out—for dinner it's shirts and trousers for men and modest dresses for women. During the day, nice shorts are acceptable at most places; beach attire is frowned on unless you're eating on the beach.

10

$$ ╳ **The Banana Tree.** This former garage has become the only true grill
ECLECTIC on the island. It boasts "cool drinks, great food." The menu includes prime steaks, pasta, and seafood as well as creole food and jerk chicken. The bar stools here are anchored by old tires, and a selection of vittles like the 4x4 (ribs) and 6 Cylinders (spicy chicken wings) also recall the space's former incarnation. In early evening, it is a very happening space with the locals. Breakfast, lunch, and dinner is served. ⓢ *Average main: US$17* ⊠ *15 Hanover St. at Kennedy Ave., Roseau* ☎ *767/448–5433.*

$ ╳ **Cocorico.** It's hard to miss the umbrella-shaded chairs and tables at
ECLECTIC this Parisian-style café on a prominent bay-front corner in Roseau.
FAMILY Breakfast crepes, croissants, baguette sandwiches, and piping-hot café au lait are available beginning at 8:30 am. Throughout the day you can relax indoors or out and enjoy any of the extensive menu selections with the perfect glass of wine. You can also surf the Internet on

its computers. In the cellar downstairs, the Cocorico wine store has a reasonably priced selection from more than eight countries, plus a wide assortment of pâtés and cheeses, crepes, sausages, cigars, French bread, and chocolates. $ *Average main: US$10* ⊠ *Bay Front at Kennedy Ave., Roseau* ☎ *767/449–8686* ⊕ *www.natureisle.com/cocorico* ⊙ *No dinner. Closed Sun. unless ship is in port, then 10–4.*

$
AMERICAN

✕ **Cornerhouse Café.** This Internet café offers an eclectic menu to sustain you while surfing: bagels with an assortment of toppings, delicious soups, vegetarian dishes, Mexican, fish, sandwiches, salads, cakes, and coffee. Computers are rented by the half hour (US$3); relax on soft chairs and flip through books and magazines while you wait. $ *Average main: US$8* ⊠ *6 King George V St., Roseau* ☎ *767/449–9000* ▭ *No credit cards* ⊙ *Mon.–Sat. 8:30 am–10 pm.*

$$
CARIBBEAN

✕ **Guiyave.** This popular restaurant in a quaint Caribbean town house also has a shop downstairs serving a scrumptious selection of sweet and savory pastries, tarts, and cakes, which can also be ordered upstairs, along with breakfast and a Caribbean buffet for lunch. Choose to dine either in the airy dining room or on the sunny, narrow balcony perched above Roseau's colorful streets—the perfect spot to have one of the freshly squeezed tropical juices. $ *Average main: US$16* ⊠ *15 Cork St., Roseau* ☎ *767/448–2930* ⊙ *Closed Sun. No dinner.*

$$$
BISTRO
Fodor's Choice
★

✕ **Le Bistro.** At this intimate French bistro in downtown Roseau, the food gets raves and is as creative as the centerpieces on the tables—upside-down wineglasses with fresh flowers inside. Chef Vincent Binet's fare is constantly changing. You may find duck with a wine and ginger reduction, a marlin and mussels fricassee, or a rib-eye steak. The bistro also offers a simple lunch menu that includes steak frites, salads, and sandwiches. $ *Average main: US$25* ⊠ *19 Castle St., upstairs, Roseau* ☎ *767/440–8117* ⊙ *Closed weekends. No lunch.*

$
CARIBBEAN

✕ **Miranda's Corner.** Just past Springfield on the way to Pont Casse, you'll begin to see hills full of flowers. At a big bend, a sign on a tree reads "Miranda's Corner," referring to a bar, rum shop, and diner all in one. Here Miranda Alfred is at home, serving everyone from Italian tourists to banana farmers. Many of her ingredients are grown in her adjacent garden. The specialties are numerous, including tropical juices and *titiree,* fish balls made from a type of fish called titiree, which are served only in season. All the dishes are prepared with a potion of passion and a fistful of flavor. Miranda's is open for breakfast, lunch, and dinner and is a great pit stop if you are in the area; call ahead to make sure it's open. $ *Average main: US$11* ⊠ *Mount Joy, Springfield* ☎ *767/449–2509.*

$$$
ECLECTIC

✕ **Old Stone Bar and Grill.** Stone walls, lots of plants, and red accents make this restaurant near the waterfront a very cozy place. The menu offers tasty chicken, pork, seafood, and local dishes—the coconut battered fish is very good. The Old Stone's owner, Leonard Lewis, says they serve the biggest selection of specialty drinks on the island; many are made with fresh fruit. The very friendly waitstaff only enhances the experience. $ *Average main: US$32* ⊠ *15 Castle St., Roseau* ☎ *767/440–7549, 767/277–3652.*

$$ CARIBBEAN 🍴 **Pagua Bay Bar & Grill.** The small but comfortable Pagua Bay Bar & Grill has a lovely outdoor deck with a drop-dead bay view, a full-service bar, and free Wi-Fi. For breakfast, choose from homemade bagels or multigrain buns as well as egg and pancakes. From 11 am until closing, you can chow down out on sandwiches, salads, and the house specialty, the "Serious Taco." Crab ravioli and curried goat are both standouts on the dinner menu, which has mostly seafood and local dishes. The friendly eatery is also a good place for yummy shrimp fritters and other snacks. Breakfast and dinner are by reservation only. [$] *Average main: US$23* ✉ *Pagua Bay House, Pagua Bay, Marigot* ☎ *767/445–8888* 🌐 *www.paguabaybarandgrill.com* 🕑 *Breakfast and dinner by reservation only. Lunch noon–3.*

$ CARIBBEAN 🍴 **Pearl's Cuisine.** Located in downtown Roseau, chef Pearl, with her robust and infectious character, prepares some of the island's best local cuisine, such as callaloo soup, fresh fish, and rabbit. Her menu changes daily, but she offers such local delicacies as souse (pickled pigs' feet), blood pudding, and rotis. When sitting down, ask for a table on the open-air gallery that overlooks Roseau. Servings are large here, but make sure you leave space for dessert. If you're on the go, enjoy a quick meal from the daily, varied menu in the ground-floor snack bar. You're spoiled for choice when it comes to the fresh fruit juices. [$] *Average main: US$12* ✉ *Sutton Place Hotel, 25 Old St., Roseau* ☎ *767/448–8707* 🕑 *Closed Sun. No dinner.*

$$ CARIBBEAN 🍴 **Rainforest Restaurant at Papillote.** Dine at an altitude cool enough to demand a throw blanket and warm enough to inspire after-dinner conversation. First, try a strong rum punch while lounging in a hot mineral bath in the Papillote Wilderness Retreat gardens. The menu has expanded but still offers the bracing callaloo soup, dasheen puffs, fish "rain forest" (marinated with papaya and wrapped in banana leaves), or other creole-style delicacies. This handsome Caribbean restaurant has quite possibly one of the best views in the region. [$] *Average main: US$20* ✉ *Papillote Wilderness Retreat, Trafalgar Falls Rd., Trafalgar* ☎ *767/448–2287* 🌐 *www.papillote.dm* ✍ *Reservations essential* 🕑 *Closed Sept. and Oct.*

$$$$ CARIBBEAN 🍴 **Sea Surge Terrace Restaurant & Bar.** You can find classic local food with a very elegant twist at this restaurant in the Evergreen Hotel. Selections include starters like fresh soup or salad made with local produce, authentic creole and international main courses, and, when in season, tasty crab backs. Breakfast, lunch, and dinner is served daily. On Friday evenings there is entertainment as well as a special menu. [$] *Average main: US$32* ✉ *Evergreen Hotel, Castle Comfort* ☎ *767/448–3288* 🌐 *www.evergreenhoteldominica.com.*

$$ ECLECTIC 🍴 **TAO Lounge Bar & Grill.** Just across from the water sits a cottage that has been converted into a small bistro that's as lovely inside as it is on the patio. Dark woods decorate the interior; above the small bar is a portrait of Johnny Depp as Jack Sparrow in *Pirates of the Caribbean*. The menu features a mix of Peruvian, Japanese, Italian and international dishes as well as the more usual steaks, fish, and pork entrées. All are tastefully presented. Tao is the only place in Roseau that serves sushi—it's not quite traditional, but it is delicious. [$] *Average main: US$34* ✉ *7 Victoria St., south of Fort Young Hotel, Roseau* ☎ *767/316–6666* 🌐 *www.facebook.com/taodominica* 🕑 *No lunch Sat. Closed Sun.*

$$$ ECLECTIC FAMILY Fodor's Choice ★ 🍴 **Waterfront Restaurant.** At the southern end of Roseau's bay front, this elegant and romantic restaurant overlooks the Caribbean coastline. You can dine outdoors on the wraparound verandah while listening to the sounds of the sea or indoors in the air-conditioned formal dining room. The restaurant's menu incorporates spa-vegetarian choices alongside the traditional international and local dishes. The dishes range widely, including creole specialties like callaloo soup; beef, lamb, and duck dishes; and even skewered shrimp with a Thai sauce. Tropical desserts include cheesecake and guava tart. No matter what your choice, it will be served by a friendly and efficient waitstaff. Monday night manager's cocktail is served in the Bala's Bar, followed by a Caribbean fusion buffet in the Marquis Restaurant. The steel pan band adds a nice touch to the night's events. Waterfront Restaurant is closed in September and early October, but meals are served in the Marquis Restaurant, which has a regular Monday-night buffet. [$] *Average main: US$25* ✉ *Fort Young Hotel, Victoria St., Roseau* ☎ *767/448–5000* 🌐 *www.fortyounghotel.com* ✍ *Reservations essential.*

WHERE TO STAY

Many properties offer packages with dives, hikes, tours, and meal plans included, along with all the usual amenities. Some advertise winter rates with a discount for either summer or longer stays. You may also want to look into a stay among the Caribs, via Kalinago Territory Home Stay.

HOME STAYS

$ RENTAL 🏨 **Kalinago Home Stays.** Now you can experience life as the Kalinago (Carib) Indians live it by spending the night with a family and learning firsthand about their culture. ✉ *Carib Territory* 🌐 *kalinagoterritory.com/home-stays.*

RECOMMENDED HOTELS AND RESORTS

$ HOTEL FAMILY 🏨 **Anchorage Hotel.** Pioneers in Dominica's diving and whale-watching industry, the Anchorage Hotel attracts adventure seekers of every age, who come for these and other activities led by the in-house tour company. **Pros:** a fine range of water activities; wheelchair accessible; upstairs rooms have balconies; small meeting room. **Cons:** no-frills accommodations. [$] *Rooms from: US$95* ✉ *Castle Comfort* ☎ *767/448–2638, 888/790–5264 in U.S.* 🌐 *www.anchoragehotel.dm* 🛏 *32 rooms* 🍽 *No meals.*

$ HOTEL 🏨 **Atlantique View Resort & Spa.** Perched high on a hill overlooking the water, one of Dominica's newest properties has a lot to offer. **Pros:** free airport pickup; children under 12 stay free; breakfast, entertainment, including live music and movies; a nonsmoking hotel. **Cons:** though there is a small private beach, it's a five-minute walk down the hill. [$] *Rooms from: US$245* ✉ *Anse De Mai* ☎ *767/445–6719* 🌐 *atlantiqueview.com* 🛏 *42 rooms* 🍽 *Breakfast.*

$ B&B/INN 🏨 **Beau Rive.** Owner Mark Steele puts Zen-like elegance and creative soul into every detail of this secluded boutique hotel. **Pros:** lovely rooms; very good food; all rooms have fans and awesome ocean views; swimming pool. **Cons:** ocean is too rough for swimming; no TVs or room phones; no guests under 16 or a/c (though the latter is not needed). [$] *Rooms from: US$190* ☒ *Between Castle Bruce and Sineku* ☎ *767/445–8992* ⊕ *www.beaurive. com* ⇆ *10 rooms* ☾ *Closed Aug. and Sept. unless special arrangements made* ❮◯❯ *Multiple meal plans* ⇆ *2-night minimum.*

$ ⌗ **Calibishie Lodges.** Within walk-
HOTEL ing distance from one of Dominica's
FAMILY most picturesque seaside villages,
Fodor'sChoice these six self-contained one-bedroom
★ suites emerge from behind terraced lemongrass. **Pros:** plenty of charm; people-pleasing owners; meal plans available; 20 minutes from Melville airport. **Cons:** at least an hour's drive from Roseau; no a/c. [$] *Rooms from: US$110* ☒ *Calibishie Main Rd., Calibishie* ☎ *767/445–8537* ⊕ *www. calibishie-lodges.com* ⇆ *6 apartments* ❮◯❯ *Multiple meal plans.*

$ ⌗ **Castle Comfort Lodge.** The boats anchored just off the pier, the telltale
HOTEL dive log, and the guests with mask imprints on their foreheads give it all away—this is the best dive lodge in Dominica. **Pros:** a favorite retreat for divers; good location; free Wi-Fi. **Cons:** rooms are very basic. [$] *Rooms from: US$100* ☒ *Castle Comfort* ☎ *767/448–2188, 646/502–6800 U.S., 888/414–7626 U.S.* ⊕ *www.castlecomfortdivelodge.com* ⇆ *13 rooms* ☾ *Closed Sept.* ❮◯❯ *Some meals.*

$ ⌗ **Cocoa Cottage.** This eco-sensitive, hand-built wood-and-stone lodge
B&B/INN has a cozy tree-house feel, and, though very basic, it's still comfortable. **Pros:** immersive tropical mountain experience; artistic vibe; only 10 minutes from Roseau and the 10 minutes from Morne Piton Natinal Park. **Cons:** no-frill accommodations. [$] *Rooms from: US$125* ☒ *Trafalgar* ☎ *767/448–0412, 767/276–2920* ⊕ *www.cocoacottages.com* ⇆ *6 rooms* ❮◯❯ *Multiple meal plans.*

$ ⌗ **Comfort Cottages.** These one-bedroom cottages, which are surrounded
HOTEL by tropical gardens and have fully equipped kitchens, are perfect. **Pros:** a great deal; immersive tropical mountain experience; artistic vibe. **Cons:** a bit far removed, and somewhat difficult to find. [$] *Rooms from: US$149* ☒ *Terre Platte, Blenhiem* ☎ *767/445–3245* ⊕ *comfortcottages. com* ⇆ *4 rooms* ❮◯❯ *Breakfast.*

$ ⌗ **Crescent Moon Cabins.** In a hidden valley full of waterfalls and a river,
HOTEL this small, family-run, forest resort is so deep in the bush that you might
FAMILY almost believe you're camping—except you have the benefit of basic, eco-friendly facilities with balconies and hammocks. **Pros:** one-of-a-kind property; excellent food. **Cons:** facilities are about two steps above camping; road here is difficult to navigate but recently improvements have been made. [$] *Rooms from: US$154* ☒ *Sylvania* ☎ *767/449–3449* ⊕ *www.crescentmooncabins.com* ⇆ *4 cabins* ☾ *Closed Aug. and Sept.* ❮◯❯ *Multiple meal plans* ⇆ *2-night minimum.*

BEST BETS FOR LODGING

BEST FOR ROMANCE
Secret Bay, Beau Rive, Red Rock Haven

BEST BEACHFRONT
Red Rock Haven

BEST POOL
Fort Young

BEST SERVICE
Calibishie Lodges, Fort Young

BEST FOR KIDS
Calibishie Lodges, Fort Young

10

Fort Young Hotel

$

HOTEL

FAMILY

🏠 **Evergreen Hotel.** This family-run, modern, oceanfront inn is a non-diver's oasis in diver-friendly Castle Comfort. **Pros:** friendly staff; pleasant surroundings; breakfast included. **Cons:** though it's close to Roseau, it's a good idea to take a cab at night as the road is not well lit. *$ Rooms from: US$147 ✉ Castle Comfort ☎ 767/448–3288 ⊕ www.evergreenhoteldominica.com ➥ 16 rooms, 1 cottage ⎟○⎟ Breakfast.*

$

RESORT

FAMILY

Fodor'sChoice

★

🏠 **Fort Young Hotel.** This hotel's street-level entrance and lobby are in an old stone fort, cannons and all. **Pros:** cosmopolitan; friendly staff. **Cons:** gets crowded during the Friday-night happy hour. *$ Rooms from: US$102 ✉ Victoria St., Dutchman's Bay, Roseau ☎ 767/448–5000 ⊕ www.fortyounghotel.com ➥ 71 rooms ⎟○⎟ No meals.*

$

HOTEL

FAMILY

🏠 **Garraway Hotel.** Fronted by the bay, this city-style hotel on the western edge of Roseau offers lovely views from its higher floors—the rooms take in the town's quaint buildings, the ocean, and the imposing mountains. **Pros:** spacious rooms; well located in the heart of Roseau; free Wi-Fi. **Cons:** rooms are a bit sparse; lower-level rooms do not have good views. *$ Rooms from: US$105 ✉ Place Heritage, 1 Dame Eugenia Charles Blvd., Roseau ☎ 767/449–8800 ⊕ garrawayhotel.com ➥ 20 rooms, 10 suites ⎟○⎟ No meals.*

$

B&B/INN

🏠 **Hummingbird Inn.** The ocean vistas, lushly fragrant garden, and naturally sensuous atmosphere at this hillside retreat provide the perfect setting for honeymooners and, needless to say, hummingbirds. **Pros:** gorgeous view; if you are into lizards, this is a sanctuary for the rare local iguana. **Cons:** very basic rooms; a charge for in-room TV; road to the property has a very steep turn and is challenging after it rains; no a/c. *$ Rooms from: US$75 ✉ Rock-A-Way, Canefield ☎ 767/449–1042 ☎ 767/285–4285 ⊕ www.thehummingbirdinn.com ➥ 9 rooms, 1 suite ⎟○⎟ Breakfast.*

$ ⬚ **Itassi Cottages.** You forget how close these three cottages are to
RENTAL   Roseau as you swing on your hammock overlooking the ocean. **Pros:**
FAMILY   very friendly atmosphere; great bang for your buck; weekly and
monthly rates available. **Cons:** 20-minute drive to Mero, the closest beach. $ *Rooms from: US$60* ⊠ *Morne Bruce* ☎ *767/449–8700*
⊕ *www.avirtualdominica.com/itassi* ⤳ *3 cottages* ⟊ *No meals.*

$ ⬚ **Jungle Bay Resort & Spa.** Sweeping views of the untamed Atlantic
RESORT   surround this luxury eco-resort, which sits on 55 acres of the only
developed section of the island's southeast. **Pros:** perfect for active vacationers; lovely rooms; outdoor showers; tours of the island offered.
Cons: facility is remote; water is too rough for swimming; no a/c; long
trek to many of the rooms; not wheelchair accessible. $ *Rooms from:*
US$200 ⊠ *Point Mulatre* ☎ *767/446–1789* ⊕ *www.junglebaydominica.*
com ⤳ *35 cottages* ⊙ *Closed Sept.* ⟊ *Multiple meal plans.*

$ ⬚ **Pagua Bay House.** If you're after privacy and beautiful views, this is
B&B/INN   your place. **Pros:** nonmotorized sports equipment is complimentary,
as is airport drop-off. **Cons:** because of the strong currents, you can't
swim in the ocean; breakfast is not included. $ *Rooms from: US$140*
⊠ *Pagua Bay, Marigot* ☎ *767/445–8888* ⊕ *www.paguabayhouse.com*
⤳ *7 rooms* ⟊ *No meals.*

$ ⬚ **Papillote Wilderness Retreat.** Luxuriant vegetation abounds in this
B&B/INN   retreat's 4 acres of gardens. **Pros:** lovely grounds; adjacent to Morne
FAMILY   Trois Pitons National Park and close to Trafalgar Falls; only 10 minutes
by car from Roseau. **Cons:** though bus service to and from Roseau is
available, you'll probably want to rent a car. $ *Rooms from: US$115*
⊠ *Trafalgar Falls Rd., Trafalgar* ☎ *767/448–2287* ⊕ *www.papillote.dm*
⤳ *3 rooms, 4 suites* ⊙ *Closed Sept. and Oct.* ⟊ *Some meals.*

$$ ⬚ **Picard Beach Cottages.** Eighteen cottages, on the grounds of an old
B&B/INN   6-acre coconut plantation and its lovely landscaped gardens, are just
FAMILY   steps away from Dominica's longest grayish-sand beach. **Pros:** has
some spa facilities; nice beach; free Wi-Fi. **Cons:** property is not well
lighted and can be difficult to navigate at night without a flashlight;
this part of the island can get pretty buggy. $ *Rooms from: US$120*
⊠ *Prince Rupert Bay* ☎ *767/445–5131* ⊕ *picardbeachcottages.dm* ⤳ *18*
1-bedroom cottages ⟊ *No meals.*

$ ⬚ **Red Rock Haven.** Perched above the secluded Pointe Baptiste Beach and
HOTEL   surrounded by lush landscape, these posh accommodations are accented
FAMILY   with wood, stone, and bamboo, and also have laddered lofts for the
kids. **Pros:** modern and lovely. **Cons:** steep paths, so difficult for people
with mobility problems; you'll need a car. $ *Rooms from: US$125*
⊠ *Calibishie* ☎ *767/445–7997* ⤳ *3 1-bedroom suites, 1 2-bedroom*
villa ⟊ *Breakfast.*

$ ⬚ **Rejens Hotel.** Located between the airport and Roseau, this group
HOTEL   of Dominican-style suites is in quiet surroundings. **Pros:** very rea-
sonably priced; nice set of amenities. **Cons:** no handicap-accessible
rooms. $ *Rooms from: US$91* ⊠ *Portsmouth* ☎ *767/445–3529*
⊕ *www.rejens.com* ⤳ *6 standard suites, 3 deluxe suites, 4 social*
suites ⟊ *No meals.*

10

$ HOTEL Fodor's Choice ★ **Rosalie Bay Resort.** It's hard not to be charmed by this new boutique hotel, which is set on 22 acres along the Atlantic Ocean and overlooks the Rosalie River. **Pros:** tranquil; beautiful surroundings; discounts for stays of four nights or more. **Cons:** beach is small, and the currents make swimming dangerous. [$] *Rooms from: US$225* ✉ *Rosalie* ☎ *767/446–1010, 877/732–2864* 🌐 *www.rosaliebay.com* 🛏 *28 rooms* 🍴 *Breakfast.*

$ HOTEL FAMILY **Roseau Valley Hotel.** With tile floors and cheerful decor, this little hotel is quite inviting. **Pros:** reasonable and pleasant; kid-friendly; free parking, local calls, and Wi-Fi. **Cons:** a long walk to Roseau (but there is local bus service). [$] *Rooms from: US$60* ✉ *2 miles (3 km) east of Roseau, Roseau* ☎ *767/449–8176* 🌐 *www.roseauvalleyhotel.com* 🛏 *10 rooms* 🍴 *Breakfast.*

$$ B&B/INN Fodor's Choice ★ **Secret Bay.** Private and luxurious, the four villas and two bungalows here come with stunning panoramas and outdoor showers, plus lots of amenities—even a chef to cook two daily meals, which can be delivered to your accommodation (this costs $55 per day, plus food). **Pros:** perfect honeymoon hideaway; open verandah; free Wi-Fi; nonmotorized sports complimentary. **Cons:** tiny beach; no children under 12; pricey for Dominica; no restaurant. [$] *Rooms from: US$430* ✉ *Tibay Beach, northwest part of island, Portsmouth* ☎ *767/445–4444* 🌐 *www.secretbay.dm* 🛏 *6 rooms* 🍴 *Some meals.*

$ HOTEL FAMILY **Sunset Bay Club & Seaside Dive Resort.** Sunset is a simple but comfortable beachfront hotel on a stretch of Dominica's spectacular west coast. **Pros:** beautiful gardens and views; great food; kid-friendly. **Cons:** very basic rooms; in-room TVs are extra. [$] *Rooms from: US$132* ✉ *Batalie Beach, Coulibistrie* ☎ *767/446–6522* 🌐 *www.sunsetbayclub.com* 🛏 *12 rooms, 1 suite* 🍴 *Breakfast.*

$ B&B/INN FAMILY **Tamarind Tree Hotel & Restaurant.** The warmth and friendliness of owners Annette and Stefan Loerner-Peyer are this small inn's most valuable assets. **Pros:** extremely friendly owners; good food; one of the owners is a certified tour guide. **Cons:** no-frills rooms. [$] *Rooms from: US$94* ✉ *Salisbury* ☎ *767/449–7395, 767/449–7007* 🌐 *www.tamarindtreedominica.com* 🛏 *15 rooms* 🕒 *Closed Sept.* 🍴 *Breakfast.*

$ HOTEL **Tia's Bamboo Cottages.** Tia himself built these charming but rustic cabins, which sit on the side of a hill, amid a picturesque, natural setting. **Pros:** proximity to river and natural springs; extremely helpful staff. **Cons:** cottages are sparsely furnished. [$] *Rooms from: US$65* ✉ *Wotton Waven, in Roseau Valley* ☎ *767/225–4823, 767/448–1998* 🛏 *3 cottages* 💳 *No credit cards* 🕒 *Closed June* 🍴 *No meals.*

$ HOTEL **Zandoli Inn.** Overlooking a 111-foot cliff on the southeast Atlantic coast, this small inn has a stunning view—water and mountains. **Pros:** drop-dead vistas; full-service bar and restaurant. **Cons:** steep walk to the beach, which is not the best place to take a plunge. [$] *Rooms from: US$145* ✉ *Roche Cassée, Stowe* ☎ *767/446–3161* 🌐 *www.zandoli.com* 🛏 *5 rooms* 🍴 *No meals.*

NIGHTLIFE AND THE ARTS

The friendly, intimate atmosphere and colorful patrons at the numerous bars and hangouts will keep you entertained for hours. Jazz, calypso, reggae, steel band, soca (a variation of calypso), and cadence-zouk, or jing ping—a type of folk music featuring the accordion, the *quage* (a kind of washboard instrument), drums, and a "boom boom" (a percussion instrument)—are all heard on the island. Wednesday through Saturday nights are really lively, and during Carnival, Independence, and summer celebrations, things can be intense. Indeed, Dominica's Carnival, the pre-Lenten festival, is the most spontaneous in the Caribbean. Other big cultural events include Emancipation celebrations hosted by the National Cultural Council each August.

THE ARTS

Arawak House of Culture. Arawak House of Culture, managed by Harry Sealy at the Cultural Division, is Dominica's main performing-arts theater. A number of productions are staged here throughout the year, including plays, recitals, and dance performances. ✉ *Kennedy Ave., near Government Headquarters, Roseau.*

Old Mill Cultural Center. At this landmark, the island's first sugarcane processing mill and rum distillery, you can catch performances, art exhibits, cultural programs, and other events that take place throughout the year. ✉ *Canefield* ☎ *767/449–1804, 767/266–3421.*

Fodor's Choice ★ **World Creole Music Festival.** During the World Creole Music Festival, held for three days in late October or early November, fans come from all over the world to listen to the likes of Kassav, Aswad, and Tabou Combo. ⊕ *www.wcmfdominica.com.*

NIGHTLIFE

Balas Bar & Courtyard. Every Friday night from 6 to 8 Balas Bar has a very happening rum-punch happy hour, with a live band and drink specials. ✉ *Fort Young Hotel, Victoria St., Roseau* ☎ *767/448–5000* ⊕ *www.fortyounghotel.com/dining/balas-bar.*

Banana Leaf. Very popular with locals, this bar doesn't close until the last person leaves. ✉ *15 Hanover St., Roseau* ☎ *767/448–5433.*

Melvina's Champagne Bar & Restaurant. Melvina's Champagne Bar & Restaurant is a popular hangout for locals and tourists, especially on Friday and Saturday nights. ✉ *Pointe Michel Rd., Pointe Michel* ☎ *767/235–6072.*

Symes Zee's. At this crowd-pleasing bar, there's no cover, and the food, drinks, and cigars are reasonably priced. ✉ *34 King George V St., Roseau* ☎ *767/448–2494.*

10

SHOPPING

Dominicans produce distinctive handicrafts, with various communities specializing in their specific products. The crafts of the Carib Indians include traditional baskets made of dyed *larouma* reeds and water-proofed with tightly woven *balizier* leaves. These are sold in the Carib Indian Territory and Kalinago Barana Autê as well as in Roseau's shops. Vertivert straw rugs, screw-pine tableware, *fwije* (the trunk of the forest tree fern), and wood carvings are just some examples. Also notable are local herbs, spices, condiments, and herb teas. Café Dominique, the local equivalent of Jamaican Blue Mountain coffee, is an excellent buy, as are the Dominican rums Macoucherie and Soca. Proof that the old ways live on in Dominica can be found in the number of herbal remedies available. One stimulating memento of your visit is rum steeped with *bois bandé* (scientific name *Richeria grandis*), a tree whose bark is reputed to have aphrodisiacal properties. It's sold at shops, vendors' stalls, and supermarkets.

Dominican farmers island-wide bring their best crops to the Roseau Market, at the end of Dame Eugenia Boulevard and Lange Lane, every Friday and Saturday from 6 am to 1 pm.

One of the easiest places to pick up a souvenir is the Old Market Plaza, just behind the Dominica Museum, in Roseau. Slaves were once sold here, but today handcrafted jewelry, T-shirts, spices, souvenirs, batik, and trays, plus lacquered and woven bamboo boxes, are available from a group of vendors in open-air booths set up on the cobblestones.

ART

Indigo. The tree-house studio and café at Indigo sells works by in-house artists Clem and Marie Frederick and also serves fresh sugarcane juice or bush teas. ⊠ *Grandby Dr., Bournes* ☎ *767/445–3486* ⊕ *www.indigo.wetpaint.com.*

CLOTHING

There's such a wide selection when it comes to clothing stores in Roseau that it really is best to walk around and explore for yourself. However, for classic Caribbean and international designer clothing, there are several reliable boutiques to try. Kai-K, on the Dame Eugenia Charles Boulevard (Bayfront), is good for clothes made of linen. Desiderata, on King George V Street has a good selection of clothing.

GIFTS AND SOUVENIRS

Jeweller's International. Jeweller's International carries crystalware, liquor, and other gift items, such as gold and silver jewelry and baubles with emeralds, diamonds, and other gems. ⊠ *Fort Young Hotel, Victoria St., Roseau* ☎ *767/440–3319.*

Land. For high-quality leather goods and other personal accessories, try Land at the Duty-Free Emporium next to the Royal Bank. ⊠ *Bay Front, Roseau* ☎ *767/448–5709.*

Pirates. Pirates is the place for booze, Cuban cigars, cheese, watches, and souvenirs. ⊠ *6 Long La., Roseau* ☎ *767/449–3394* ⊘ *Weekdays 8:30–5, Sat. 8:30–2.*

Whitchurch Duty-Free. Whitchurch Duty-Free perfumes, leather goods, designer sunglasses, and many other items. ⊠ *Fort Young Hotel, Victoria St., Roseau* ☎ *767/448–2181* ⊕ *www.whitchurch.com.*

HANDICRAFTS

Kalinago Barana Autê. Kalinago Barana Autê sells carvings, pottery, and lovely handwoven baskets, which you can watch the women weave. ⊠ *Salybia, Carib Territory* ☎ *767/445–7979* ⊕ *www.kalinagobaranaaute.com* ⊘ *Daily 9–5.*

Papillote Wilderness Retreat. Papillote Wilderness Retreat has a small gift shop with local handcrafted goods and particularly outstanding wood carvings by Louis Desire. ⊠ *Trafalgar* ☎ *767/448–2287.*

SPORTS AND ACTIVITIES

ADVENTURE SPORTS

Extreme Dominica. Rappel alongside waterfalls, jump into clear pools, explore canyons in Dominica's lush rainforests or hike to Boiling Lake. Extreme Dominica will pick you up from Roseau, supply the necessary equipment and offer a short training session before setting out on your wet adventure. All levels of experience can be accommodated. Prices begin at $75 per person for Boiling Lake to $160 per person for canyoning tours. ⊠ *Cocoa Cottages, Trafalgar* ☎ *767/295–7272, 767/295–6828* ⊕ *www.extremedominica.com.*

FAMILY **Wacky Rollers.** Wacky Rollers will make you feel as if you are training for the marines as you swing on a Tarzan-style rope and grab onto a vertical rope ladder, rappel across zip lines, and traverse suspended log bridges, a net bridge, and four monkey bridges (rope loops). Including transportation, it costs $60 pp for the adult course and should take from 1½ to 3½ hours to conquer the 28 "games." There is also an abbreviated kids' course for $25 (kids 10 and under). Wacky Rollers also organizes adventure tours around the island plus kayak and tubing trips. Although the office is in Roseau, the park itself is in Hillsborough Estate, about 20 to 25 minutes north of Roseau. ⊠ *Office, Front St., Roseau* ☎ *767/440–4386* ⊕ *www.wackyrollers.com.*

10

BIKING

Nature Island Dive. Nature Island Dive has a fleet of bikes in good condition. You can rent a mountain bike for $25, which includes a helmet, but if your group prefers a knowledgeable guide to lead you through specific areas, the cost ranges from $65 for a half day to $96 for a full day, which includes lunch, snacks, and drinks. ⊠ *Soufrière* ☎ *767/449–8181.*

DIVING AND SNORKELING

Fodor'sChoice Not only is Dominica considered one of the top 10 dive destinations
★ in the world by *Skin Diver* and *Rodale's Scuba Diving* magazines,
but it has won many other awards for its underwater sites. They are
truly memorable. The west coast of the island has awesome sites, but
the best are those in the southwest—within and around **Soufrière/
Scotts Head Marine Reserve.** This bay is a submerged volcanic crater.
The Dominica Watersports Association has worked along with the
Fisheries Division for years to establish this reserve and has set stringent regulations to prevent the degradation of the ecosystem. Within
½ mile (¾ km) of the shore there are vertical drops from 800 feet
to more than 1,500 feet, with visibility frequently extending to 100
feet. Shoals of boga fish, Creole wrasse, and blue cromis are common, and you might even see a spotted moray eel or a honeycomb
cowfish. Crinoids (rare elsewhere) are also abundant here, as are
giant barrel sponges. There is a $2 fee per person to dive, snorkel,
or kayak in the reserve. Other noteworthy dive sites include **Salisbury
Falls, Nose Reef, Brain Coral Garden,** and—even farther north—**Cabrits
Drop-Off** and **Toucari Reef.** The conditions for underwater photography, particularly macrophotography, are unparalleled. Rates start at
about $55 for a single-tank dive and about $90 for a two-tank dive
or from about $75 for a resort course with one open-water dive. All
scuba-diving operators also offer snorkeling. Equipment rents for
$10 to $25 a day; trips with gear range from $15 to $35. A 10%
tax is not included.

Anchorage Dive & Whale Watch Center. The Anchorage Dive & Whale
Watch Center has two dive boats that can take you out day or night.
It also offers PADI instruction (all skill levels), snorkeling and whale-
watching trips, and shore diving. It has many of the same trips as Dive
Dominica. ⊠ *Anchorage Hotel, Castle Comfort* ☎ *767/448–2638,
888/790–5264 in U.S.* ⊕ *www.anchoragehotel.dm.*

Cabrits Dive Center. Cabrits Dive Center is the only PADI five-star dive
center in Dominica. Nitrox courses are also available for $250. Since
Cabrits is the sole operator on the northwest coast, its dive boats have
the pristine reefs almost to themselves, unlike other operations, whose
underwater territories may overlap. ⊠ *Picard Estate, Portsmouth*
☎ *767/445–3010* ⊕ *www.cabritsdive.com.*

Dive Dominica. Dive Dominica, one of the island's dive pioneers, conducts PADI courses as well as Nitrox certification courses. With four
boats, it offers diving, snorkeling, and whale-watching trips and packages, including accommodation at the Castle Comfort Lodge. Its trips
are similar to Anchorage's. ⊠ *Castle Comfort Lodge, Castle Comfort*
☎ *767/448–2188, 646/502–6800 in U.S.* ⊕ *www.divedominica.com.*

Fort Young Dive Centre. Fort Young Dive Centre conducts snorkeling, diving, and whale-watching trips that depart from the hotel's private dock.
⊠ *Fort Young Hotel, Victoria St., Roseau* ☎ *767/448–5000* ⊕ *www.
fortyounghotel.com/activities/diving.*

A diver pauses to admire a lavender stovepipe sponge (aplysina archeri).

Irie Safari. Irie Safari takes snorkelers to Champagne and the nearby tall grasses, where turtles like to hang out. ⊠ *Soufrière/Scotts Head Marine Reserve, Soufrière* ☎ *767/440–5085.*

Nature Island Dive. Nature Island Dive is run by an enthusiastic crew who offer diving, snorkeling, kayaking, and mountain biking as well as resort and full PADI courses. Some of the island's best dive sites are right outside its door. Dive prices are $84 for a two-tank dive and US$100 for a two-tank dive with BC vest and regulator. ⊠ *Soufrière* ☎ *767/449–8181* ⊕ *www.natureislanddive.com.*

FISHING

Anchorage Hotel. Contact the Anchorage Hotel for information about fishing excursions. Fees are $550 for a half-day trip and $1,050 for a full day. ⊠ *Castle Comfort* ☎ *767/448–2638, 888/790 in U.S., 0800/7297 in U.K.* ⊕ *www.anchoragehotel.com.*

GUIDED TOURS

Generally tours start off in the Roseau area, but most operators will arrange convenient pickups. Prices range between $35 and $75 per person, depending on the duration and the destination, amenities provided, and the number of people on the excursion.

Dominica Tours. Dominica Tours is one of the island's largest tour companies, offering a range of hikes and bird-watching trips. ☎ *767/448–2638* ⊕ *www.experience-dominica.com.*

Ken's Hinterland Adventure Tours & Taxi Service. Ken's Hinterland Adventure Tours & Taxi Service offers a range of island tours and guided hikes, including some specifically for families with children. ⊠ *Fort Young Hotel, Victoria St., Roseau* ☎ *767/448–4850, 767/448–1660, 866/880–0508 in U.S.* ⊕ *www.khattstours.com.*

HIKING

Dominica's majestic mountains, clear rivers, and lush vegetation conspire to create adventurous hiking trails. The island is crisscrossed by ancient footpaths of the Arawak and Carib Indians and of the Nègres Maroons, escaped slaves who established camps in the mountains. Existing trails range from easygoing to arduous. To make the most of your excursion, you'll need sturdy hiking boots, insect repellent, a change of clothes (kept dry), and a guide. Hikes and tours run $25 to $80 per person, depending on destinations and duration. A poncho or light raincoat is recommended. Some of the natural attractions within the island's national parks require visitors to purchase a site pass. These are sold for varying numbers of visits. A single-entry site pass costs $5, and a week pass $12. The Discover Dominica Authority's information offices at the Bayfront (Dame Charles Boulevard) can recommend guides.

Bertrand Jno Baptiste. Local bird and forestry expert Bertrand Jno Baptiste leads hikes up Morne Diablotin and along the Syndicate Nature Trail; if he's not available, ask him to recommend another guide. ☎ *767/245–4768.*

Forestry Division. The Forestry Division, which is responsible for the management of forests and wildlife, has numerous publications on Dominica as well as a wealth of information on reputable guides. ⊠ *Dominica Botanical Gardens, between Bath Rd. and Valley Rd., Roseau* ☎ *767/266–5856, 767/266–5853.*

WHALE-WATCHING

FAMILY
Fodor's Choice
★

Dominica records the highest species counts of resident cetaceans in the southern Caribbean region, so it's not surprising that tour companies claim 90% sighting success for their excursions. Humpback whales, false killer whales, minke, and orcas are all occasionally seen, as are several species of dolphin. But the resident sperm whales (they calve in Dominica's 3,000-foot-deep waters) are truly the stars of the show. During your 3½-hour expedition, which costs about $55 plus tax, you may be asked to assist in recording sightings, data that can be shared with local and international organizations. Although there are resident whale and dolphin populations, more species can be observed from November through February. Turtle-watching trips are also popular.

Anchorage Dive & Whale Watch Center. The Anchorage Dive & Whale Watch Center can arrange whale-watching trips. ⊠ *Anchorage Hotel, Castle Comfort* ☎ *767/448–2638* ⊕ *www.anchoragehotel.dm.*

Dive Dominica. Dive Dominica is a major whale-watching operator. ⊠ *Castle Comfort Lodge, Castle Comfort* ☎ *767/448–2188* ⊕ *www.divedominica.com.*

DOMINICAN REPUBLIC

WELCOME TO DOMINICAN REPUBLIC

Ocean World Adventure Park **7**
Cofresí Beach
Luperón Beach **12** **13**
Montecristi
Playa Dorada **6**
11
10 **5**
Playa Cabarete
Puerto Plata
Museo de Ambar **8** Sosúa Cabarete
Guayubin Dominicano
1 - **4**
8 - **9**
Cabo Francés Viejo
Laguna Grí-Grí
Mt. Isabel de Torres
Gregorie Luperón International Airport
Cabrera
Playa Grande
9 Santiago
Moca
Bahía Escocesa Las Terrenas **6** **5** **1**
Pico Duarte
La Vega Vieja
San Francisco de Macorís
Playa Cosón
Nagua **7**
Jarabacoa
Taino Park
Los Haitises National Park
Bahía de Samaná
← TO HAITI
H I S P A N I O L A
Sabana de la Mar
H A I T I
San Juan
Monte Plata
Lago Enriquillo
Neiba
Las Américas International Airport
Duvergé
Azua
San Cristóbal
Boca Chica Juan Dolio
Bahía de Ocoa
Bani
Santo Domingo see detail map
Barahona
Playa Bahoruco
Pto. Palenque
C a r i b b e a n   S e a
Oviedo
Cabo Beata

Like the merengue seen on all the dance floors in Santo Domingo, the Dominican Republic is charismatic yet sensuous, energetic yet elegant. The charm of the people adds special warmth: a gracious wave of greeting here, a hand-rolled cigar tapped with a flourish there. Dazzling smiles just about everywhere will quickly beguile you.

LA ISLA ESPAÑOLA

The Dominican Republic covers the eastern two-thirds of the island of Hispaniola (Haiti covers the other third). At 18,765 square miles (48,730 square km), it's the second-largest Caribbean country (only Cuba is larger), and with more than 8.8 million people, the second-most-populous country, too. It was explored by Columbus on his 1492 voyage to the New World.

Restaurants ▼

Baia Lounge	**1**
The Beach	**10**
The Beach Club	**5**
bliss	**4**
B.Y.O.W. Restaurant	**6**
Il Pasticcio	**9**
Lucía	**7**
Mares Restaurant	**8**
Miró's Tapas	**2**
Natura Restaurant at Natura Cabana	**3**
Peperoni	**12**
Porto	**11**

Hotels ▼

Balcones del Atlantico	**6**
The Bannister Hotel	**4**
Casa Colonial	**13**
Casa de Campo	**1**
Dreams La Romana	**2**
Gran Ventana Beach Resort	**12**
Hotel El Magnifico	**9**
Iberostar Costa Dorada	**11**
Natura Cabana	**8**
Peninsula House	**5**
Sea Horse Ranch	**10**
Sublime Samaná	**7**
Viva Wyndham Dominicus Palace	**3**

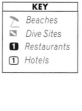

ATLANTIC OCEAN

10 **11**

Cabo Samaná

Samaná
4 Cayo Levantado

Miches

Hato Mayor
El Seibo

La Romana International Airport

Higüey

El Macao

Playa Bávaro

Río Chavón

Punta Cana
see detail map

Punta Cana International Airport

San Pedro de Macorís

12

1 La Romana

Punta Cana

Altos de Chavón

Minitas

Bayahibe

Bahía de Yuma

2 **3**

Isla Saona ♦ Isla Saona

Mona Passage

KEY

⌐	Beaches
◣	Dive Sites
1	Restaurants
1	Hotels

0 _____ 50 miles

0 _____ 75 km

TOP REASONS TO VISIT DOMINICAN REPUBLIC

1 Great Beaches. There are some 1,000 miles of excellent beaches, some of which are pearl-white.

2 Great Value. You'll find the best-value all-inclusive resorts in the Caribbean here.

3 Myriad Water Sports. Every imaginable activity—world-class golf, horseback riding, white-water rafting, surfing, diving, windsurfing, and more—is available here.

4 Friendly People. The genuine hospitality of the people and their love of norteamericanos.

5 Happening Nightlife. The Dominicans love to party, dance, drink, and have a good time at happening bars and clubs.

Updated by
Eileen Robin-
son Smith

Dominicans will extend a gracious welcome, saying, "This is your home!" and indeed are happy to share their beautiful island bathed by the Atlantic Ocean to the north and the Caribbean Sea to the south. Among its most precious assets are 1,000 miles (1,600 km) of gorgeous beaches studded with coconut palms and sands ranging from pearl-white to golden brown to volcanic black. The Caribbean sun kisses this exotic land, which averages 82°F year-round. It's a fertile country blessed with resources, particularly cocoa, coffee, rum, tobacco, and sugarcane.

A land of contrasts, the Dominican Republic has mountain landscapes, brown rivers with white-water rapids, rain forests full of wild orchids, and fences of multicolor bougainvillea. Indigenous species from crocodiles to the green cockatoo, symbol of the island, live in these habitats. Bird-watchers, take note: there are 29 endemic species flying around here.

The contrasts don't stop with nature. You can see signs of wealth, for the upper strata of society lives well indeed. In the capital, the movers and shakers ride in chauffeur-driven silver Mercedes. On the country roads you'll be amazed that four people with sacks of groceries and a stalk of bananas can fit on a smoky old *motoconcho* (motorbike–taxi). This is a land of mestizos who are a centuries-old mix of native Indians, Spanish colonists, and African slaves, plus every other nationality that has settled here, from Italian to Arabic.

Accommodations offer a remarkable range—surfers' camps, exclusive boutique hotels, and amazing megaresorts that have brought the all-inclusive hotel to the next level of luxury. Trendy restaurants, art galleries, boutique hotels, and late-night clubs help make Santo Domingo a superb urban vacation destination. Regrettably, most Dominican towns and cities are neither quaint nor particularly

LOGISTICS

Getting to the Dominican Republic: The D.R. has seven international airports. Plan your air travel carefully so you don't end up flying into Santo Domingo when you are staying in Punta Cana, a two-hour, $150 taxi ride away. Travel between the island's many developed tourism zones can be arduous and expensive, with few domestic flights available.

Hassle Factor: Low for popular destinations. High for off-the-beaten-path places.

Getting Around the Island: Most travelers to the Dominican Republic take guided tours or participate in organized excursions. Independent travel is easier if you rent a car, but car rentals are expensive and signage is bad (and some working knowledge of Spanish is strongly advisable). For longer distances, buses are the best alternative, but locally, taxis are widely available in all major resort areas.

On the Ground: Most travelers book packages that include airport transfers. Otherwise, you'll have to take a local taxi, which can be quite expensive.

pretty, and poverty still prevails. However, the standard of living has really come up along with the growth of North American tourism. Food prices are higher than they have been, which means prices at all-inclusive resorts are up; however, a vacation in the D.R. can still be a relative bargain. Even the new, small boutique hotels are still well priced for the Caribbean. Nevertheless, already high government taxes of 16% on hotels and restaurants increased to 18% in 2013 and must be considered when budgeting.

The vibrant lifestyle of this sun-drenched Latin-Caribbean country, where Spanish is the national language and where the people are hospitable and good-natured, makes the Dominican Republic a different cultural experience. If you pick up the rhythm of life here, as freewheeling as the island's trademark merengue, this can be a beguiling tourist destination.

PLANNING

WHEN TO GO

The D.R. is busy year-round. During the somewhat quieter summer season, Europeans keep rates high from mid-June through August. However, in late spring (after Easter until early June) and early fall (September to October—peak rainy season, with hurricanes a threat) you can get good deals.

Unlike on many islands, where rain showers are usually passing things, the rains in the D.R. can linger, especially from June through November.

GETTING HERE AND AROUND

AIR TRAVEL

You can fly nonstop to the Dominican Republic from Atlanta (Delta, AirTran), Baltimore (AirTran), Boston (JetBlue, US Airways), Charlotte (US Airways), Chicago–Midway (AirTran), Chicago–O'Hare (United), Cincinnati (Delta), Detroit (Delta), Fort Lauderdale (Spirit), Miami (American), Minneapolis (Delta), New York–Newark (United), New York–JFK (JetBlue, Delta), Orlando (JetBlue), Philadelphia (US Airways), and Washington Dulles (United). However, not all airlines fly to all the destinations in the D.R. and some flights connect in San Juan or various airports throughout the United States.

Many visitors fly nonstop on charter flights direct from the U.S. East Coast and Midwest, particularly into Punta Cana; these charters are part of a package and can be booked only through a travel agent.

Airport Transfers: If you book a package through a travel agent, your airport transfer fee will almost certainly be included. If you book independently, you will have to take a taxi, rent a car, or hire a private driver-guide. DominicanShuttles.com offers drivers and private transfers in addition to scheduling domestic airline flights and excursions.

Airline Contacts Air Antilles Express ☎ *809/621–8888 General Services, 809/560–0168* ⊕ *www.airantilles.com, www.flyairantillesexpress.com.* **Air Caraïbes** ☎ *809/621–8888 general services, 0590/82–47–00 in Guadeloupe* ⊕ *www.aircaraibes.com, www.aircaraibes-usa.com.* **Airtran Airways** ☎ *809/549–8151 in D.R., 800/247–8726 in U.S.* ⊕ *www.airtranairways.com, www.airtran. com.* **American Airlines** ☎ *809/959–2420 in Punta Cana, 800/433–7300 in U.S., 800/222–2377 web help, 809/200–5151, 809/542–5151 in Santo Domingo* ⊕ *www.aa.com.* **Delta** ☎ *809/549–8151 in D.R., 800/221–1212 in U.S.* ⊕ *www. delta.com.* **JetBlue** ☎ *809/273–2771 in D.R. (tickets), 809/200–9898 in D.R. (Las America's Airport, S.D.), 800/538–2583 in U.S.* ⊕ *www.jetblue.com.* **LIAT** ☎ *809/621–8888 general services, 888/844–5428 in D.R., 809/549–2036 in Santo Domingo* ⊕ *www.liatairline.com.* **Spirit Airlines** ☎ *801/401–2200 in U.S.* ⊕ *www.spirit.com.* **United** ☎ *809/262–1060 in D.R., 800/538–2929 in U.S., 800/864–8331* ⊕ *www.united.com.* **US Airways** ☎ *800/428–4322 in U.S., 800/622–1015 in D.R.* ⊕ *www.usairways.com.*

Airports Cibao International Airport (STI) in Santiago; **El Catey International Airport** (AZS) in Samaná; **Gregorio Luperon International Airport** (POP) in Puerto Plata; **La Isabella International Airport** (JBQ) in Higüero; **La Romana/ Casa de Campo International Airport** (LRM) in La Romana; **Las Américas International Airport** (SDQ) in Santo Domingo; and **Punta Cana International Airport** (PUJ) in Punta Cana.

Domestic and Charter Airlines Aerodomca ✉ *La Isabella International Dr. Joaquin Balaguer, Higuero* ☎ *809/931–4073 DomShuttle, 829/410–3326 DomShuttle, 809/696–2420* ⊕ *aerodomca.com.* **Air Century** ✉ *La Isabella International Dr. Joaquin Balaguer, Av. Presidente Antonio Guzmán Fernández, Higuero* ☎ *809/826–4222 for charters, 305/677–0641 in U.S., 809/931–4073 reses from Dominican-Shuttles* ⊕ *www.aircentury.com.* **DominicanShuttles.com** ✉ *Av. Romulo Betancourt 1856, Corner Calle Angel Maria Liz, Mirador Sul, Santo Domingo* ☎ *809/931–4073, 829/410–3326* ⊕ *www.dominicanshuttles.com.* **Helidosa Helicopters** ✉ *Punta Cana International Airport, Punta Cana* ☎ *809/552–6069* ⊕ *www.helidosa.com.*

BUS TRAVEL

Privately owned buses are the cheapest way to get around the country. For example, one-way bus fare from Santo Domingo to Puerto Plata is about RD$8, and the trip takes 3½ hours on Caribe Tours, less on Metro Buses, a more deluxe operation. Both bus lines go to Sosua, too, which takes another 15–20 minutes. There is no service to Cabarete, but taxis meet the bus and drivers are eager to take you, for about US$12. These bus companies make regular runs to Santiago, Puerto Plata, Punta Cana, and other destinations from Santo Domingo. Be forewarned that air conditioning can be frigid, and there might be a movie, possibly an American one, maybe not, as the equipment often is inoperable. There will be a restroom, but definitely B.Y.O. paper. ■TIP➜ **Motoconcho-men will try to lure you for significantly less but don't do it, especially if you have any kind of luggage and it's past sunset.**

Frequent service from Santo Domingo to the town of La Romana is provided by Express Bus, leaving every hour on the hour from 5 am to 9 pm. However, there's no office and no phone. They depart from Parque Enriquillo in the Zona Colonial. A ticket taker will take your US$ (actually the peso equivalent) just before departure, and will charge you double if you have large luggage. Travel time is about 1¾ hours and as these are usually small, second-class buses, without air conditioning, that make many stops, it is a rough ride—let it be your last choice. Once in La Romana, you can take a taxi from the bus stop to your resort. You will pay US$15–US$20 to Casa de Campo and US$30–US$35 to Bayahibe. Espreso Baváro buses depart from Plaza Los Girasoles at Avenida Máximo Gómez at Juan Sánchez Ruiz; the buses are said to be first-class, but . . . are not the best, yet cost only about US$6. They do make a stop in La Romano. If you're going to one of the Punta Cana resorts, you get off at the stop before the last and take a cab waiting at the taxi stand. Depending on which resort you are going to, that charge could be more than US$50.

Bus Contacts Caribe Tours ✉ *Esq. Leopoldo Navarro, Av 27 de Febrero, Ensanches Miraflores, Santo Domingo* ☎ *809/221–4422* ⊕ *www.caribetours. do.* **Espreso Santo Domingo Baváro** ✉ *Plaza Los Girasoles, Av. Máximo Gómez at Juan Sánchez Ruiz, Santo Domingo* ☎ *809/682–9670.* **Metro Buses** ✉ *Av. Winston Churchill and Calle Francisco Prats Ramirez Piantini, Santo Domingo* ☎ *809/582–9111 in Santiago, 809/227–0101 in Santo Domingo, 809/586–6062 in Puerto Plata* ⊕ *www.metroserviciosturisticos.com.*

CAR TRAVEL

Driving in the D.R. can be a harrowing and expensive experience; we don't recommend that the typical vacationer rent a car. It's best if you don't drive outside the major cities at night. If you must, use extreme caution, especially on narrow, unlighted mountain roads.

Local agencies exist, but it is highly advisable to rent only from internationally known companies. U.S. citizens should really consider only U.S.–based chains, so that if you have a major problem you have easier recourse. The major agencies can be found in most of the island's airports. At the capital's Las Americas International Airport, most agencies are open from 7 am to 11 pm.

Car-Rental Contacts Budget ☎ 800/472–3325 ⊕ www.budget.com ✉ Las Américas Airport, Santo Domingo ☎ 809/549–0351, 800/527–0700 in the U.S. ⊕ www.budget.com ✉ Gregorio Luperón International Airport, Puerto Plata ☎ 809/586–0413 ⊕ www.budget.com. **Europcar** ✉ Las Américas Airport, Santo Domingo ☎ 809/549–0942 in D.R. ⊕ www.europcar.com ✉ Gregorio Luperón International Airport, Puerto Plata ☎ 809/586–0215. ✉ Punta Cana International Airport, Bavaro, Punta Cana ☎ 809/959–0177, 809/480–8188. **National** ✉ Casa de Campo, La Romana ☎ 809/523–3333, 809/523–8191 ⊕ www.nationalcar.com.

TAXI TRAVEL

Wherever you are, hotel taxis are generally the best option. Carry small bills; drivers rarely have change. Recommendable radio-taxi companies in Santo Domingo are Tecni-Taxi (which also operates in Puerto Plata) and Apolo. You can use taxis to travel to out-of-town destinations at quoted rates. Check with your hotel or the dispatcher at the airport. From the Zona Colonial in Santo Domingo to Playa Dorada with Tecni-Taxi is $160. If you book through your hotel concierge, it can be more. Dominican Shuttles (⊕ *www.dominicanshuttles.com*) provides safe and reliable service.

Contacts Apolo Taxi ☎ 809/537–0000, 809/537–1245 for high-end cars or SUVs ⊕ www.apolotaxi.com. **Taxi-Cabarete** ☎ 809/571–0767 in Cabarete. **Taxi-Queen Santiago** ☎ 809/570–0000 in Santiago. **Taxi-Sosúa** ☎ 809/571–3097 in Sosúa. **Tecni-Taxi** ☎ 809/567–2010 in Santo Domingo, 809/320–7621 in Puerto Plata.

ESSENTIALS

Banks and Exchange Services Currency is the Dominican peso (written RD$). You will not need to change money unless you plan to travel independently around the D.R. Banco Popular has many locations throughout the country, with ATMs that accept international cards.

Electricity 110–120 volts/60 cycles, the same as in the United States.

Health Never drink tap water in the D.R. (look for a hotel or restaurant that has earned an *H* for food-service hygiene or that has a Crystal America certification). Don't buy food or even juice from the street vendors. Use mosquito repellent to protect yourself from mosquito-borne illnesses like Dengue fever; long sleeves and long pants also help.

Language Spanish is spoken in the D.R. Most staff at major tourist attractions and front-desk personnel in most major hotels speak English. Outside the popular tourist establishments, English is spoken less frequently.

Passport Requirements All U.S. citizens must carry a valid passport. Additionally, all visitors must have a valid tourist card, which costs US$10 (purchased on arrival in cash with U.S. currency only).

Phones To call the D.R. from the United States, dial 1–809, and the local number. From the D.R. you also need dial only 1–809, then the number. To make a local call, you must dial 809 plus the seven-digit number (dial 1–809 if you are calling a cell phone). Directory assistance is 1411.

Safety Violent crime is rare. Nevertheless, poverty is everywhere in the D.R., and petty theft, pickpocketing, and purse snatching are an increasing concern, particularly in Santo Domingo. Pay attention,

11

especially when leaving a bank or casino. Take hotel-recommended taxis at night.

Taxes The departure tax of $20 is almost always included in the price of your airline ticket. The government tax (IBIS) is a whopping 18% and is added to almost everything—bills at restaurants, hotels, sports activities, rental cars, and even many items at the supermarkets, definitely on anything imported.

Tipping A 10% service charge is included in all hotel and restaurant bills. In restaurants, the bill will say *propino incluido* or simply *servis*. Even then it's still expected that you will tip an extra 5% to 10% if the service was good. Hotel maids typically get $2 per day; taxi drivers, 10%; skycaps and hotel porters, $1 per bag.

ACCOMMODATIONS

All-inclusive resorts predominate in Punta Cana; some of these are quite luxurious. All-inclusives also make up the lion's share of resorts in Playa Dorada on the north coast, but Sosúa and Cabarete still have a few charming independent inns and small resorts. The Southeast Coast has nice beaches but some of the most mediocre resorts on the island, though the area around La Romana (Casa de Campo in particular) and nearby Bayahibe, has both wonderful beaches and some good resorts. Santo Domingo offers both large and small hotels with access to the capital's great restaurants, nightlife, and historical sights. Samaná is a bit more isolated, though becoming less so, and it offers a range of all-inclusive resorts as well as smaller properties both luxurious and simple.

HOTEL AND RESTAURANT PRICES

Prices in the restaurant reviews are the average cost of a main course at dinner or, if dinner is not served, at lunch; taxes and service charges are generally included. Prices in the hotel reviews are the lowest cost of a standard double room in high season, excluding taxes, service charges, and meal plans (except at all-inclusives). Prices for rentals are the lowest per-night cost for a one-bedroom unit in high season.

For expanded lodging reviews and current deals, visit Fodors.com.

VISITOR INFORMATION

Contacts Dominican Republic One. Dominican Republic One is a "trusted site" of the Secretariat de Turismo. It's written by bilingual staffers at the ministry and delivers the official word on the latest news, travel, and airline information. ⊕ *www.dr1.com.* **Dominican Republic Tourist Office** ☎ *212/588–1012 in New York City, 888/374–6361 in New York City, 888/358–9594 in Miami* ⊕ *www.godominicanrepublic.com.*

WEDDINGS

There are no residency requirements. Blood tests are not mandatory. Original birth certificates and passports are required. Divorce certificates and proof that the bride and groom are single must be stamped by the Dominican Consulate. Documents must be submitted two weeks before the wedding and translated into Spanish. Many couples are opting to marry in the United States, then hold a ceremony at the resort of their choice followed by a reception.

EXPLORING

SANTO DOMINGO

Parque Independencia separates the old city from modern Santo Domingo, a sprawling, noisy city with a population of close to 2 million. The 12 cobblestone blocks of Santo Domingo's Zona Colonial contain most of the major sights in town. It's one of the most appealing historic districts in the Caribbean and is best explored on foot. The Zone ends at the seafront, called the Malecón.

Spanish civilization in the New World began in Santo Domingo's 12-block **Zona Colonial.** As you stroll its narrow streets, it's easy to imagine this old city as it was when the likes of Columbus, Cortés, and Ponce de León walked the cobblestones, pirates sailed in and out, and colonists started settling. Tourist brochures claim that "history comes alive here"—a surprisingly truthful statement. Almost every Thursday to Sunday night at 8:30 a typical "folkloric show" is staged at Parque Colón and Plaza de España. During the Christmas holidays there is an artisans' fair and live-music concerts take place. A fun horse-and-carriage ride throughout the Zona costs $25 for an hour, with any commentary in Spanish. The steeds are no thoroughbreds, but they clip right along. You can also negotiate to use them as a taxi, say, to go down to the Malecón. The drivers usually hang out in front of the Hostal Nicolas de Ovando. You can get a free walking-tour map and brochures in English at the Secretaria de Estado de Turismo office at Parque Colón (Columbus Park), where you may be approached by freelance, English-speaking guides who will want to make it all come alive for you. They'll work enthusiastically for $25 an hour for four people. Simply put, the Zona is not as safe as it once was—particularly at night and during festivals. Don't carry a lot of cash or your passport (leave them in the hotel safe).

TOP ATTRACTIONS

Alcazar de Colón. The castle of Don Diego Colón, built in 1517, was the home to generations of the Christopher Columbus family. The Renaissance-style structure, with its balustrade and double row of arches, has strong Moorish, Gothic, and Isabelline influences. The 22 rooms are furnished in a style to which the viceroy of the island would have been accustomed—right down to the dishes and the vice regal shaving mug. The mansion's 40-inch-thick coral-limestone walls make air-conditioning impossible. Bilingual guides are on hand for tours peppered with fascinating anecdotes, like weddings once-upon-a time. ⊠ *Plaza de España, off Calle Emiliano Tejera, Zona Colonial* ☎ *809/ 682–4750* ⊠ *RD$100* ☉ *Mon.–Sat. 9–5, Sun. 9–4.*

Calle Las Damas. "Ladies Street" was named after the elegant ladies of the court: in the Spanish tradition, they promenaded in the evening. Here you can see a sundial dating from 1753 and the Casa de los Jesuitas, which houses a fine research library for colonial history as well as the **Institute for Hispanic Culture**; admission is free, and it's open weekdays from 8 to 4:30. The boutique Hostal Nicolas de Ovando is on this street, across from the French Embassy. If you follow the street going toward

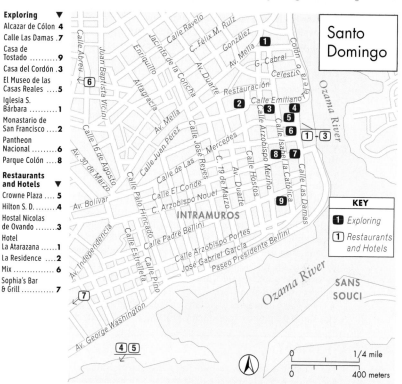

**Santo
Domingo**

11

INTRAMUROS

SANS
SOUCI

Ozama River

KEY

1 Exploring

1 Restaurants
and Hotels

0   1/4 mile

0   400 meters

the Malecón, you will pass a picturesque alley, fronted by a wrought-iron gate, where there are perfectly maintained colonial structures owned by the Catholic Church. ⊠ *Calle las Damas, Zona Colonial.*

WORTH NOTING

Iglesia Santa Bárbara. This combination church and fortress, the only one of its kind in Santo Domingo, was completed in 1562. ■TIP→ **For mass times, be sure to check the day before you want to attend.** ⊠ *Av. Mella, between Calle Isabel la Católica and Calle Arzobispo Meriño, Zona Colonial* ☎ *809/682–3307* ☎ *Free* ☉ *Mon.–Sat. 6 am–6:45 pm; Sun. masses begin at 8 am, last mass at 6 pm.*

Monasterio de San Francisco. Constructed between 1512 and 1544, the St. Francis Monastery contained the church, convent, and hospital of the Franciscan order. Sir Francis Drake's demolition squad significantly damaged the building in 1586, and in 1673 an earthquake nearly finished the job, but when it's floodlit at night, the eerie ruins are dramatic indeed. The Spanish government has donated money to turn this into a beautiful cultural center, but we are still waiting. In the meantime, there's music many nights at 7 pm (often live), and it becomes an old-fashioned block party. Zone residents mingle with expats and tourists, who snap pictures of the octogenarians dancing the merengue and the bachata. Others who come are content to just sit in white plastic chairs, swaying and clapping. It's nice. ⊠ *Calle Hostos at Calle Emiliano, Zona Colonial.*

Pantheon Nacional. The National Pantheon (circa 1714) was once a Jesuit monastery and later a theater. The real curiosity here is the military guard, who stays as still as the statues, despite the schoolchildren who try to make him flinch. ⊠ *Calle Las Damas, near Calle de Las Mercedes, Zona Colonial* ☎ *809/689–6010* 🖅 *Free* ☾ *Mon.–Sat. 8 am–9 pm.*

Parque Colón. The huge statue of Christopher Columbus in the park named after him dates from 1897, and is the work of sculptor Ernesto Gilbert. Like all the parks in the Zona Colonial, this one is quite a social gathering place. ⊠ *El Conde at Calle Arzobispo Meriño, Zona Colonial.*

Plaza de España. This wide esplanade, which goes past the Casas de Reales in front of Don Diego Columbus's former palace, El Alcazar de Colón, is the area in the Zona Colonial where national holidays are celebrated. The annual Coca-Cola–sponsored Christmas tree is here. It's bordered by what once were the ramparts of the original walled city. People enjoy the views of the Ozama River from here, and watch the cruise-ship activity below at the terminal. Lovers stroll by night, sharing a kiss under the gas lamps. When many people talk about the Plaza de España, they are often referring to the half-dozen restaurants in a row, which are on the upper level of these 16th- and 17th-century warehouses. The popular tables are on their outdoor decks. Cultural performances are held on a stage across from the Plaza on certain weekends. ■TIP→ **Make dinner reservations on those nights and you'll have a special Santo Domingo experience.** ⊠ *Calle La Atarazana, Zona Colonial.*

SOUTHEAST COAST

Las Américas Highway (built by the dictator Rafael Trujillo so his son could race his sports cars) runs east along the coast from Santo Domingo to La Romana—a two-hour drive. A new highway now connects La Romana and Bayahibe to Punta Cana and shortens the drive time to about 45 minutes. Midway are the well-established beach resorts such as Juan Dolio, and Sammy Sosa's hometown, San Pedro de Macorís. Much farther east are Punta Cana and Bávaro, glorious beaches on the sunrise side of the island. Along the way is Higüey, an undistinguished city notable only for its giant concrete cathedral and shrine, one of the country's most visited monuments.

LA ROMANA

78 km (48 miles) east of Juan Dolio.

Neither pretty nor quaint, La Romana has a central park, an interesting market, a couple of good restaurants, banks and small businesses, a public beach, and Jumbo, a major supermarket. ■TIP→ **If you are staying for a week or more you may want to buy a Dominican cell phone at Jumbo.** It's a mere $20 for a basic one, plus minutes. It can save you untold money if you'll be making local calls from your hotel/resort. It is, at least, a real slice of Dominican life. Casa de Campo is just outside La Romana, and other resorts are found in the vicinity of nearby Bayahibe. Although there are now more resorts in the area, this 7,000-acre luxury enclave put the town on the map. Casa de Campo Marina, with its Mediterranean design and impressive yacht club and villa complex, is as fine a marina facility as can be found anywhere; the shops and restaurants at the marina are a big draw for all tourists to the area.

The architecture in the town of Altos de Chavón re-creates a 16th-century Mediterranean village.

Fodor's Choice
★

Altos de Chavón. This re-creation of a 16th-century Mediterranean village sits on a bluff overlooking the Río Chavón, on the grounds of Casa de Campo but about 3 miles (5 km) east of the main facilities. There are cobblestone streets lined with lanterns, wrought-iron balconies, wooden shutters, courtyards swathed with bougainvillea, and **Iglesia St. Stanislaus,** the romantic setting for many a Casa de Campo wedding. More than a museum piece, this village is a place where artists live, work, and play. Dominican and international painters, sculptors, and artisans come here to teach sculpture, pottery, silk-screen printing, weaving, dance, and music at the school, which is affiliated with New York's Parsons School of Design. The artists work in their studios and crafts shops selling their finished wares. The village also has an amber museum, an archaeological museum, a handful of restaurants, and a number of unique shops. Strolling musicians enliven the rustic ambience of ceramic tiles and cobblestone terrace. ⊠ *Casa de Campo* ⊕ *www.casadecampo.com.do.*

Amphitheater at Altos de Chavon. A 5,000-seat, Grecian-style amphitheater features *Kandela,* a spectacular musical extravaganza showcasing the island's sensuous Afro-Caribbean dance moves, music, and culture (November–April only). Concerts and celebrity performances by such singers as Elton John, Julio Iglesias, his son Enrique, Sting, and the Pet Shop Boys share the amphitheater's schedule of events. Show dates vary to coincide with cruise-ship arrivals. Many people make dinner reservations at **La Piazzetta** (Altos de Chavón ☎ *809/523–3333*), the high-end Italian restaurant that is closest to the amphitheater. It's known for its antipasto selections, homemade pasta, and authentic regional dishes; outside guests are welcome. ⊠ *Casa de Campo* ☎ *809/523–2424 for Kandela tickets* ⊕ *www.kandela.com.do* 🎫 *$35 for Kandela; other concert prices vary.*

PUNTA CANA

The larger area known as Punta Cana encompasses Cabeza de Torres, Playa Bávaro, and continues all the way around the peninsula to Playa de Uvero Alto. Development continues in Galerias Punta-Cana Village, a shopping center that is a draw for visitors from around the area. A new Four Points by Sheraton just opened across from the area and is the only "airport" hotel in the region. Each hotel has its own strip of sand with rows of *chaise longues,* and most of these resorts will arrange in advance for day passes. The stretch between Club Med and the Puntacana Resort & Club is one of the most beautiful. Playa El Cortecito is more how life used to be, with fishermen bringing in their catch, and it is where the crazy restaurant Capitan Cook's is located. Farther north along the coast is a stretch of beach known as Arena Gorda, literally "fat sand." About 32 km (20 miles) from Punta Cana International Airport, it's an area brimming with coconut groves and the location of several resorts. Macao is a pastoral village, but its public beach is no longer a good option, having first been taken over by four-wheeler excursions and now dominated by the huge Hard Rock Hotel & Casino Punta Cana.

NORTH COAST

The farther east you go from Puerto Plata and Sosúa, the prettier and less spoiled the scenery becomes. The autopista runs past Cabarete, a town that's a popular windsurfing haunt, and Playa Grande, which has a miraculously unspoiled white-sand beach with amenities now being gentrified, a famous golf course, and a development project underway

PUERTO PLATA

Although it has been sleeping for decades, this was a dynamic city in its heyday, and it is coming back. You can get a feeling for this past in the magnificent Victorian gazebo in the central **Parque Independencia.** Recently painted a crisp white, the park looks postcard pretty, with gleaming new statuary. On Puerto Plata's own Malecón, which has had a multimillion-dollar refurbishment, the **Fortaleza de San Felipe** protected the city from many a pirate attack and was later used as a political prison. Nearby, a new amphitheater is in the planning stages. The nearby **lighthouse** has been restored.

Museo de Ambar Dominicano (*Dominican Amber Museum*). In an opulent, galleried mansion, restored to its former Victorian glamour, the museum displays and sells the Dominican Republic's national stone: semiprecious, translucent amber. Amber is essentially prehistoric hardened tree sap, and Dominican amber is considered the best in the world. Many pieces are fascinating for what they have trapped inside, and the second-floor museum contains a piece with a lizard reported to be 50 million years old, give or take a few millennia. The museum's English text is informative. Shops on the museum's first floor sell amber, souvenirs, and ceramics. ⊠ *Calle Duarte 61, Puerto Plata* ☎ *809/586-2848* ⊕ *www.ambermuseum.com* ⊡ *RD$50* ☉ *Mon.–Sat. 9–6.*

Ocean World Adventure Park. This multimillion-dollar aquatic park in Cofresí has marine and wildlife interactive programs, including dolphin and sea lion shows and encounters, a double-dolphin swim, a tropical reef aquarium, stingrays, shark tanks, an aviary, a rain forest, and the Tiger Grotto inhabited by Bengal tigers. You must make advance reservations if you want to

> **FLAT TIRE**
>
> Blowout? A *gomero* can make a flat tire round! There are many such fellows, because the rough roads are rubber-eaters. You will see their signs on the highways and if stranded in a town, just ask: *¿Donde esta un gomero?*

11

participate in one of the swims or encounters; children must be at least six and accompanied by an adult. The exhilarating (albeit expensive) double-dolphin swim will produce lifelong memories. If you are brave enough for the (nurse) shark encounter, you will feed them and touch them in the shark cove; the stingray encounter is also included. A photo lab and video service can capture the moment, but there is a charge. If you're staying at nearby Lifestyle resorts, or hotels in Puerto Plata, transfers are free. If in Sosua or Cabarete, transfers are $5 per person; hotels should have the tour schedules. ■ TIP➜ **There's a private beach, showers, and a locker room on-site.** ⊠ *Calle Principal 3, 3 miles (5 km) west of Puerto Plata, Cofresi, Puerto Plata* ☎ *809/291–1000* ⊕ *www. oceanworld.net* ⊠ *$69 entrance includes lunch; extra charge for some activities/encounters* ☉ *Tues.–Sun. 9–6.*

SOSÚA
24 km (15 miles) east of Puerto Plata.

Sosúa is called Puerto Plata's little sister, and consists of two communities—El Batey, the modern hotel development, and Los Charamicos, the old quarter—separated by a cove and one of the island's prettiest beaches. The sand is soft and nearly white, the water crystal clear and calm. The walkway above the beach is packed with tents filled with souvenirs, pizzas, and even clothing for sale. The town had developed a reputation for prostitution, but much is being done to eliminate that and to clean up the more garish elements. Conversely, there are many fine, cultured types here, both Dominican and expats, and the recent opening of a cultural center was a major coup for them. Upscale condos and hotels are springing up, and the up-and-coming Dominican families are returning to the big houses on the bay.

Casa de Arte de Sosua. The new cultural center of Sosúa was inaugurated with much celebration by Mayor Llana in November 2013. Classical concerts and choral performances by area residents characterized the long-awaited event. Open to the public and free of charge, the ground floor gallery has rotating exhibitions that primarily feature work by Sousa and area artists. Music lessons for local children are offered on the second floor, as are other culturally minded activities. ⊠ *Pedro Clisante, across from casino, Sosúa* ☉ *Weekdays 9–5.*

Museo Judio Sosúa. Sosúa is not a destination known for its sights. However, this museum stands as one of the exceptions, chronicling the immigration and settlement of the Jewish refugees in the 1940s. This is a fascinating place, and depending on the docent, you may hear that the Jewish settlers fleeing from Hitler, experienced a certain amount of prejudice here when they arrived. The adjacent small wooden synagogue is the wedding spot for many Jewish couples from abroad. At this writing there wasn't a working telephone and hours were irregular, but chances are good that someone will be at the museum to let you in. ■ TIP→ **You can try phoning Sosua Villas or the accommodating Hotel Casa Valeria nearby to confirm if the museum is open.** ⊠ *Calle Dr. Rosen at David Stern, Sosúa* ☏ *809/377–2038 Sosua Villas, 809/477–2038 Sosua Villas, 809/571–3565 Hotel Casa Valeria* ⊕ *www.sosua-villas.com/jewish-museum* ⊠ *RD$75* ☉ *Sun.–Fri. 10–1 (but hrs are irregular).*

CIBAO VALLEY

The heavily trafficked four-lane highway north from Santo Domingo, known as the Autopista Duarte, cuts through the banana plantations, rice and tobacco fields, and royal poinciana trees of the Cibao Valley. Along the road are stands where a few pesos buy pineapples, mangoes, avocados, *chicharrones* (fried pork rinds), and fresh-fruit drinks.

SANTIAGO

Although an industrial center, Santiago has a surprisingly charming, provincial feel; the women of Santiago are considered among the country's most beautiful. High on a plateau is an impressive monument honoring the restoration of the republic. Traditional yet progressive, Santiago is still relatively new to the tourist scene but already has several thriving restaurants and hotels. It's definitely worth setting aside some time to explore the city. Colonial-style buildings—with wrought-iron details and tiled porticoes—date from as far back as the 1500s. Others are from the Victorian era, with the requisite gingerbread latticework and fanciful colors, and recent construction is nouveau Victorian. Santiago is the DR's cigar-making center; the Fuente factory is here, though its cigars can be bought on the island only in special designated cigar stores and clubs. (If you see them for sale on the streets, they are counterfeit.)

Fodor'sChoice ★ **Centro León.** Without question, this is a world-class cultural center for Dominican arts and culture. A postmodern building with an interior space full of light from a crystal dome, the center includes several attractions, including a multimedia biodiversity show, a museum dedicated to the history of the Dominican Republic, a simulated local market, a dramatic showcase of Dominican art and sculpture, galleries for special exhibits, a sculpture garden, an aviary, classrooms, and a replica of La Aurora's first cigar factory, where cigar rollers turn out handmade cigars. Presently, an exhibition celebrates the Centennial of the León Jimenes family. There's even a first-rate cafeteria and a museum shop where you can buy high-quality, artsy souvenirs and jewelry. Check the website for activities and night events. It can be a fine way to meet sophisticated Santiagueros who have a high level of fluency in English. ■ TIP→ **It's best to give advance notice if you want a guided tour in English.** ⊠ *Av. 27 de Febrero 146, Villa Progreso, Santiago* ☏ *809/582–2315* ⊕ *www.centroleon.org.do* ⊠ *RD$150, guides in English RD$300* ☉ *Exhibitions Tues.–Sun. 10–7.*

Hand-rolling cigars in the Cibao Valley

SAMANÁ PENINSULA

Samaná (pronounced sah-mah-NAH) is a dramatically beautiful peninsula, like an island unto itself, of coconut trees stretching into the sea. It's something of a microcosm of the Dominican Republic: here you'll see poverty and fancy resorts, brand-new highways as well as bad roads, verdant mountainsides, tropical forests, tiny villages lined with streetside fruit vendors, secluded beaches, and the radiant warmth of the Dominican people. A visit here is really about two things: exploring the preserved natural wonders and relaxing at a small beachfront hotel. The latter is most readily accomplished in **Las Terrenas,** the only true tourist center, where you can find picturesque restaurants, accommodations of all types (including the new oceanfront Sublime Samaná and the luxury condo-hotel, Balcones del Atlantico), and great beaches. At Las Terrenas you can enjoy peaceful *playas,* take advantage of the vibrant nightlife, and make all your plans for expeditions on the peninsula. The other pleasures are solitary—quiet beaches, the massive national park Los Haitises, and water sports and hiking. A relatively new toll road connects Santo Domingo to the peninsula; it's about a 2- to 2½-hour drive. Small El Catey International Airport is near Las Terrenas and is now being served by twice-weekly JetBlue flights (Wednesday and Saturday).

SANTA BÁRBARA DE SAMANÁ
35 km (22 miles) southeast of Las Terrenas.

The official name of the city is Santa Bárbara de Samaná; but these days it's just called "Samaná." An authentic port town, it's getting its bearings as a tourist zone, and still is not a tourist magnet like Las Galeras and Las Terrenas. It has a typical *malecón* (seaside promenade) that's ideal for strolling and watching the boats in the harbor. Lookout "towers" have been built; ascend the stairs and see the whales in season or just look out to the horizon. Strong night lighting has been added, too, so you will see Dominicans and tourists alike taking walks after dinner. A small but bustling town, Samaná is filled with friendly residents, skilled local craftsmen selling their wares, and a handful of outdoor, sea-view, and courtyard restaurants.

A big all-inclusive resort, the Bahía Príncipe Cayacoa, is on one end of the bay road up on a hill. Day passes are available (and the resort has the only beaches in town). The hotel also operates a block of colorful gift shops and a small casino.

Fodor's Choice **Los Haitises National Park.** A highlight of a visit to the Samaná Peninsula
★ is a chance to explore Los Haitises National Park (pronounced Hightee-sis), which is across Samaná Bay. The park is famous for its karst limestone formations, caves, and grottoes filled with pictographs and petroglyphs left by the indigenous Taíno.

The park is accessible only by boat, and a professionally guided kayaking tour is highly recommended, plus a licensed guide from a tour company or the government is mandatory. You'll paddle around dozens of dramatic rock islands and spectacular cliff faces, while beautiful coastal birds—magnificent Frigatebirds, brown pelicans, brown booby, egrets and herons—swirl around overhead. A good tour will also include the caverns, where your flashlight will illuminate Taíno petroglyphs. It's a continual sensory experience, and you'll feel tiny, like a human speck surrounded by geological grandeur. DominicanShuttles.com can arrange a park tour and a stay at the adjacent, and rustic, Paraiso Caño Hondo Ecolodge, which has authentic creole cuisine and multiple waterfalls. ⊠ *Samaná Bay* ☎ *809/472–4204* ✑ *$4, not including manadatory use of licensed guide* ☼ *Daily dawn–dusk.*

BEACHES

SOUTHEAST COAST

BAYAHIBE

Playa Bayahibe. Playa Bayahibe, where several seafood restaurants are situated, is somewhat thin, with hard-packed taupe sand and no lounge chairs. However, as you move away from the village, a 10-minute walk along the shoreline, you'll reach the glorious, half-moon cove where you'll find the Dreams resort. Although you'll be able to get to the cove and the soft sand, bring a towel (the resort's security won't let you use the facilities). At night, when no one is on the playa and the silver moon illuminates the phosphorescence, it's the stuff that Caribbean dreams are made of. **Amenities:** food and drink; toilets. **Best for:** partiers; sunset; swimming; walking; windsurfing. ⊠ *Starts in center of town, Near Dreams resort, Bayahibe.*

PUNTA CANA

Playa Bávaro. Bávaro is the most developed stretch of the 35 miles of white-sand beach in the Punta Cana area, which is lined with massive all-inclusive resorts. Although it encompasses many smaller towns, the main area, which is past Cabeza de Toro, is thought to begin with the massive Barcelo Bávaro Beach Resort and extend to the funky, fun fishermen's beach, Playa El Cortecito, known for the landmark restaurant Capitan Cooks. The water is characteristically warm and fairly shallow, with seaweed kept in check by hotels. Each resort has its own designated area with its chaise longues lined up in neat rows. Although there are stretches that are idyllically quiet, for the most part it is nonstop action. Boats and watersports provide the entertainment, wandering beach vendors the aggravation. In several areas there are designated, makeshift markets. **Amenities:** food and drink; toilets; water sports. **Best for:** walking; swimming; windsurfing. ⊠ *Playa Bávaro, Bávaro.*

Playa Punta Cana. This long stretch of sandy coastline on the Caribbean side of the peninsula is where tourism first began in Punta Cana. This undulating beach with powdery white sand is shaded by lilting coconut palms. Much of it still looks like virgin beach since there is not the proliferation of all-inclusive hotels you find further north in Bávaro. The beach extends south to Playa Juanillo, which is similarly incredible and now the site of the Cap Cana development. The waters are generally calm, with more wave action in the winter and during hurricane season. Seaweed has become more of a problem in recent years, and resorts have crews that rake their stretch of sand. Coral rock can make areas difficult to walk in the water, which is often shallow close to shore; however, the reefs are super for snorkeling and one can walk or swim from shore. **Amenities:** food and drink; toilets; water sports. **Best for:** snorkeling; swimming; walking; windsurfing. ⊠ *Playa Punta Cana, Punta Cana.*

NORTH SHORE

Playa Cabarete. This is the main business district of Cabarete. If you follow the coastal road east from Playa Dorada, you can't miss it. The beach, which has strong waves after a calm entrance, and ideal, steady wind (from 15 to 20 knots), is an integral part of the international windsurfing circuit. Segments of this long beach are strips of sand punctuated only by palm trees. The regeneration of Cabarete Beach was a massive engineering project that made the beach some 115 feet wider, adding an infusion of white sand. In the most commercial area, restaurants and bars are back-to-back, spilling onto the sand. The informal scene is young and fun, with expats and tourists from everywhere. **Amenities:** food and drink; lifeguards; toilets; water sports. **Best for:** partiers; surfing; swimming; windsurfing; kitesurfing. ⊠ *Sosúa–Cabarete Rd., Cabarete.*

Playa Dorada. Playa Dorada is one of the island's most established resort areas. Each hotel has its own slice of the beach, which is covered with soft sand, nearly white now thanks to its participation in a $6 million beach rejuvenation. Reefs for snorkeling are right offshore. Gran Ventana Beach Resort, which is on a point, marks the easternmost end of the beach, followed by Casa Colonial and Blue Bay Villa Doradas. If you're not staying at one of the resorts in the Playa Dorada complex, then it's best to enter the beach before this point. Zealous hotel security guards try to keep you off "their" stretch of beach, but by law they cannot if you walk along the water's edge. They can keep you off the chaise longues and from coming into the resort's property. This is a good swimming beach with mild wave action. **Amenities:** none (though resorts on the beach offer full service). **Best for:** fishing; swimming; walking; waterskiing; windsurfing. ⊠ *Off Autopista Luperón, at entrance to Playa Dorada Complex, approximately 10-min drive east of town, Playa Dorada* ⊕ *www.playadorada.com.do.*

Fodor'sChoice **Playa Grande.** This dramatic, mile-long stretch is widely considered to be
★ one of the top beaches in the world. Many a photo shoot and postcard image were made at this picture-perfect beach with off-white sands and turquoise water. Just east of the famous golf course of the same name, Playa Grande's drama comes from craggy cliffs dropping into the crystalline sea. Shade can be found in the palm trees that thicken into Parque Nacional Cabo Frances Viejo, a jungle preserve south of the beach.

This simply gorgeous stretch of sand had food shacks and cheapie souvenir stands that marred its beauty, but the vendors now have brightly-painted, cutesy, Victorian-style huts that have been relocated to the end of the beach where a large parking area was constructed. The days of driving your car onto the beach are definitely over (a good thing since islanders with huge speaker systems in their cars would park right next to your table.)

Just behind the beach, screened by a palm-frond fence, are beach bungalows built by the development group of Playa Grande, available for rent—you know who you might spot sunbathing. **Amenities:** food and drink. **Best for:** surfing; walking. ⊠ *Carretera Río San Juan–Cabrera, Km 12, Río San Juan* ⊕ *www.playagrande.com* ⊠ *Free* ⚐ *Playa Grande Golf & Reserve.*

Playa Sosúa. This gorgeous beach on Sosúa Bay, renowned for its coral reefs and dive sites, is a 20-minute drive east of Puerto Plata. Here, calm waters gently lap at a shore of soft, golden sand. Swimming is delightful—except after a heavy rain, when litter floats in. But beware of sea urchins in the shallow water—beach shoes are definitely recommended—and bring your own mask and snorkel if possible. You can see mountains in the background, the cliffs that surround the bay, and seemingly miles of coastline. Snorkeling from the beach can be good, but the best spots are offshore, closer to the reefs. The beach is backed by a string of tents where hawkers push souvenirs, snacks, drinks, and water-sports equipment rentals. The weekend scene here is incredible—local families pack the beach, and the roar of Dominican fun fills the air. Alas, with the closing of the Sosua Bay Resort, the tourist presence has diminished. There is a small parking area on the beach's north end near the Big Blue Dive Center, at the south end of La Puntilla Street. **Amenities:** food and drink; parking (free). **Best for:** snorkeling; swimming; walking. ⊠ *Carretera Puerto Plata–Sosúa, El Batey, Sosúa.*

SAMANÁ PENINSULA

11

On the north coast of the Samaná Peninsula, tall palms list toward the sea, and the beaches are extensive and postcard perfect, with crystal-line waters and soft, golden sand. There's plenty of color—vivid blues, greens, and yellows—as well as colorful characters. To the west is Playa El Cosón, opposite Cayo Ballena, a great whale-watching spot (from January to April). Samaná has some of the country's best beaches and drop-dead scenery, the rough roads notwithstanding.

LAS TERRENAS

Fodor'sChoice **Playa Cosón.** This is a long, wonderful stretch of nearly white sand and
★   the best beach close to the town of Las Terrenas. Previously undevel-oped, it's now reachable by a new highway, Carretera Cosón, and there are a number of condo developments under construction (so the current sense of solitude probably won't last). One excellent restaurant, The Beach, serves the entire 15-mile shore, and there's the European-owned boutique hotel, Casa Cosón and its restaurant and bar. If beachgoers buy lunch and/or drinks at either, then they can use the restrooms. **Amenities:** food and drink; parking; toilets. **Best for:** swimming; sunset; walking; windsurfing. ⊠ *Las Terrenas.*

WHERE TO EAT

The island's culinary repertoire includes Spanish, Italian, Middle East-ern, Indian, Japanese, and *nueva cocina Dominicana* (contemporary Dominican cuisine). If seafood is on the menu, it's bound to be fresh. The dining scene in Santo Domingo is the best in the country and prob-ably offers as fine a selection of restaurants as you will find in most Caribbean destinations. Keep in mind that the touristy restaurants, such as those in the Zona Colonial, with mediocre fare and just-okay service, are becoming more and more costly, while the few fine-dining options here have lowered some of their prices. For example, La Residence now offers a daily prix-fixe chef's menu with three courses. Or you can order two generous appetizers for even less. You will have caring service and be sequestered in luxe surroundings away from the tourist hustle. Know that *capitaleños* (residents of Santo Domingo) dress for dinner and dine late. The crowds pick up after 9:30 pm.

What to Wear: In resort areas, shorts and bathing suits under beach wraps are usually (but not always) acceptable at breakfast and lunch. For dinner, long pants, skirts, and collared shirts are the norm. Restau-rants tend to be more formal in Santo Domingo, both at lunch and at dinner, with trousers required for men and dresses suggested for women. Ties aren't required anywhere, but jackets are (even at the midday meal) in some of the finer establishments.

SANTO DOMINGO

ZONA COLONIAL

$$$ FRENCH Fodor's Choice ★ 🍴 **La Residence.** This fine-dining enclave has the setting—Spanish-colonial architecture, with pillars and archways overlooking a courtyard—but with the classically grounded French chef, Dominique David, serving remarkably innovative cuisine, it has really grown into a destination restaurant. An amuse-bouche arrives before your meal, and there is an excellent bread service. Available for lunch and dinner, the three-course daily Menu de Chef is about $26, including tax. It could feature brochettes of spit-roasted duck, chicken au poivre, or vegetable risotto. Veer from this menu, and prices go higher, but they remain fair. A luscious foie gras parfait with a port wine velouté and house-made brioche will start you on your way; segue to grilled scallop skewers with a strong passion fruit jus and spinach tagliatelle. For a finale, we suggest the strawberry soup with basil and mint infusion. Musicians romantically serenade diners except on Jazzy Thursdays when they are close by, at the pool. [$] *Average main: $23* ✉ *Hostal Nicolas de Ovando, Calle Las Damas, Zona Colonial* ☎ *809/685–9955* 🌐 *www.accorhotels.com; mgallery.com* ✍ *Reservations essential.*

$$ INTERNATIONAL FAMILY 🍴 **Mix.** Mix, match, and *compartier* (share) is the thought behind this trendy restaurant that is in presently, with well-heeled capitalenos. Best enjoyed with a group, the round tables with banquette seating can easily accommodate six or more. Two-tops prevail out on the terrace, which is not as loud as the dining room. Neighboring tables talk back and forth. It's: "Pass the *Cocoloco* (ceviche with lime and green plantains) and "Where is the *Popeye* (a spinach dip au gratin with hot tortillas)?" "Did you finish the great balls of rice (risotto balls stuffed with pork and covered with a creamy Italian sauce)?" It's a fun atmosphere, though you might want your very own tamarind, grilled chicken salad. Italian-Dominican influences often prevail in the main courses. The cultivated wine list offers many fine Italian bottles and to finish, there are grappas. Family-friendly, with a convivial bar and late-night scene, this is a crowd-pleaser (translation: always packed). [$] *Average main: $17* ✉ *Gustavo Mejia Ricart #69, Torre Washington Local 102, Naco* ☎ *809/472–0100* 🕒 *Sun.–Thurs. noon–midnight, Fri. and Sat. noon–2 am.*

PIANTINI

$$$ ECLECTIC 🍴 **Peperoni.** One of Santo Domingo's long-standing destination restaurants, Peperoni continues to evolve, which keeps it on the list of "in" places for the well-heeled of all ages. The menu is contemporary and multinational, and only the highest-quality ingredients are used. You may not make it past the appetizers, like a warm goat-cheese salad, and, from the menu's "Asian Market," a sushi roll of sweet plantain, tuna, and avocado. But try to get to the main courses, giving the gnocchi, pastas, and risottos your first consideration. Many of the Italian offerings date back to the restaurant's beginning, but some of the latest specialties are lighter, like the polenta encrusted sea bass hit with cilantro oil. Service is laudable. Take the savvy wine steward's recommendations. Indoor dining rooms can be too cold and noisy; try for the terrace. ■ TIP→ **If you like this hot ticket, you will love its younger sister restaurant at the Casa de Campo Marina.** [$] *Average main: $24* ✉ *Sarasota 23, at Plaza Universitaria, Piantini* ☎ *809/508–1330, 809/508–2392* 🌐 *peperoni.com.do.*

SOUTHEAST COAST

LA ROMANA

$$$ ECLECTIC Fodor's Choice ★

🍴 **Peperoni.** Although the name may sound as Italian as *amore,* this restaurant's menu is much more eclectic than Italian. It has a classy, contemporary, white-dominated decor in a dreamy, waterfront setting. Strolling musicians perpetuate the mood. Astounding appetizers are found under the Asian section, like the sweet plantain roll or the Peperoni roll. Pasta dishes and risottos with rock shrimp or porcinis taste authentic, and the more inventive items such as house-made pear-and-goat-cheese ravioli with pine nuts and a key-lime emulsion are delectable. *Pulpo* (octopus) with fava beans stewed in limoncello vinaigrette is highly recommended. You can also opt for stylishly simple charcoal-grilled steaks (sauce or no), burgers, gourmet wood-oven pizzas, sandwiches, or even sushi and sashimi. Desserts are worthy here. [$] *Average main: $21* ✉ *Casa de Campo, Plaza Portafino 16, Casa de Campo Marina, La Romana* ☎ *809/523–2227, 809/523–3333.*

PUNTA CANA

$$$ SEAFOOD Fodor's Choice ★

🍴 **Blue Marlin.** You dine here beneath a palapa-shaded table on a pier that sits over the Caribbean's gentle waters—truly a paradisical island experience. The restaurant's own small fleet of fishing boats harvests the waters daily for fresh catch, which are among the most popular menu items, though other specialties come from around the world. The menu offers everything from ceviche to Asian calamari rolls with sweet-and-spicy chili sauce and cilantro to Caribbean lobster cakes. Healthful, vegetarian, or vegan offerings are flagged. Lunch offerings have such innovations as wasabi or spicy chipotle mayonnaise. Some may think the portions are small but on the all-inclusive plan you can order as much as you like. Service is caring and attentive. The blue Euro-tiles around the fireplace at the bar add an unexpected, decorative element. Nonhotel guests must have a reservation to pass through security. ■ **TIP→ Lobster and other high-ticket seafood items do come with a supplement if you have the Sanctuary Cap Cana AI plan.** [$] *Average main: $24* ✉ *Sanctuary Cap Cana, Cap Cana, Playa Juanillo* ☎ *809/562–9191* 🌐 *www.sanctuarycapcana.com* ✍ *Reservations essential.*

$$ SEAFOOD

🍴 **La Palapa by Eden Roc.** If you crave waterfront dining, this is a great option. Especially close to the blue-green is the new deck with its sushi menu. The main restaurant with its palapa (thatched) roof exudes Caribbean charisma, yet has an Italian accent. The aromas promise exceptional seafood specialties and guests are rarely disappointed. The fresh seafood, even hard finds like baby octopus, is enhanced by the deft preparations of the Italian executive chef. The quality of product is immediately apparent from the Parmigiano Reggiano to selections from the international wine list and wines by the glass. Details such as the contemporary Campari cocktails bespeak the high style of Eden Roc, the boutique hotel that has proud ownership. The manager and waiters are professionals, yet here it is as casual as the pareos on the beachgoers who come and the golf guys when they finish the nearby 18th hole of Punta Espada. [$] *Average main: $22* ✉ *Caleton Beach Club, Cap Cana, Juanillo* ☎ *809/469–7593, 809/695–5555* 🌐 *www.edenroccapcana.com.*

$$ ✕**Playa Blanca.** On a white-sand
SEAFOOD beach shaded by coco palms, this
Fodor's Choice understatedly cool seafood restau-
★ rant is efficient, friendly, and fun.
Start with a perfectly executed
cocktail—like a lime or mango
daiquiri. Food is savvy and sim-
ple—fresh fish is still a staple; opt
for fried or grilled with a sauce on
the side. Each winter season the
offerings have become more cre-
ative. The prices are an excellent
value for the amount of creativity
and skill involved in dish creations,
and there are paellas, pasta, risotto,
and ravioli dishes to fill out the rest
of the menu. You usually have to
pay for the sides, but a bit more
for some yucca mashed with blue
cheese—why not? The best dessert is the chocolate fondant filled with
molten *dulce de leche,* with vanilla ice cream. Live music weekly is just
one aspect of the beachfront entertainment; another is watching the
kitesurfers—poetry in motion. You could try it yourself. it is available
"next door." ⓢ *Average main: $20 ⊠ Puntacana Resort & Club, Playa
Blanca ☎ 809/959–2262 ⊕ www.puntacana.com.*

> **ON THE MENU**
>
> Among the best Dominican special-
> ties are *queso frito* (fried cheese),
> *sancocho* (a thick stew of meats,
> served with rice and avocado
> slices), *arroz con pollo* (rice with
> beans and chicken), *pescado
> al coco* (fish in coconut sauce),
> *platanos* (plantains), and *tostones*
> (fried green plantains). Presidente
> is the best local beer. Brugal rum
> is popular with the Dominicans,
> but Barceló *añejo* (aged) rum is
> as smooth as cognac, and Barceló
> Imperial is so special that it's sold
> only around Christmastime.

$$$ ✕**Simon Mansion & Supper Club.** This unique dining experience is found
CONTEMPORARY within the Hard Rock Hotel, nearly adjacent to its casino; it is the only
Fodor's Choice full-service restaurant that is open to outside guests. Celebrity Chef
★ Simon Kerry has contracted with Hard Rock to design the menu and
train the chefs at this signature restaurant featuring his brand of contemporary American cuisine. The setting is cleverly designed as a mythi-
cal rock star's mansion and the various dining rooms are decadent,
lavishly furnished like a living room, a library, even a bedroom and a
patio. Your dining experience will be a sensory rush from an innovative rum cocktail to a Pacific Rim appetizer, followed by a rack of lamb
that is perfection. All meats are natural, the produce organic, so feel
no guilt when you order a luscious dessert. Follow the wine and other
suggestions of the savvy German manager and prepare to be pampered.
ⓢ *Average main: $25 ⊠ Hard Rock Hotel & Casino Punta Cana, Blvd.
Turistico del Este 74, Km 28, Playa Macao ☎ 809/731–0094 restaurant,
809/687–0000 hotel* ⊘ *6 pm–midnight* ⊘ *No lunch.*

NORTH COAST

The Cabarete area in particular—where all-inclusive resorts don't yet
totally dominate the scene—has some fun, original restaurants, but
these are often small places, so it's important that you make reservations in advance. Expat residents complain that the prices in this town
have moved past the good-value-for-money mark. Also, more and more
restaurants are insisting on cash only, be it pesos, dollars, or euros. The
area has lovely fine-dining options, *listed below.*

11

PUERTO PLATA

$$$
CARIBBEAN
Fodor'sChoice
★

✕ **Lucía.** Lucia's menu is comprehensive and contemporary; billed as Caribbean Fusion cuisine, the new Italian chef might put his own accent on some items. The setting is as artistic as a gallery—befitting its location within Casa Colonial, a refined boutique hotel. Picture orchids galore, crisp white linens, and attentive waiters in white guayabera shirts. Guests love the one-of-a-kind appetizers, like the Tris-Viche, a ceviche of Chilean sea bass, tuna, and lobster. A main course might be a grilled breast, crispy leg confit, and foie gras served with rum-mango sauce and mashed pumpkin. Carnivores with more basic tastes can order an Angus filet. The molten chocolate volcano with vanilla ice cream is the dessert you want. When the digestif cart is rolled over, be daring with a Brunello grappa or the local Brugal Unico rum, and look through the glass wall to the orchids clinging to the trees and the tropical mangrove garden. It's the good life at Lucía. $ *Average main: $25 ⊠ Casa Colonial, Playa Dorada* ☎ *809/320–3232* ⊕ *www. casacolonialhotel.com* ⊘ *No lunch.*

$$
CONTEMPORARY
Fodor'sChoice
★

✕ **Mares Restaurant & Pool Lounge.** This residence-cum-restaurant is the home of the D.R.'s most acclaimed chef, Rafael Vasquez. Guests "knock on the door" with an oversized fork and spoon, which is indicative of this charismatic chef's mantra—he is a rule breaker. The indoor dining room is sophisticated with classy china, glassware and cutlery and lots of white, with contemporary art by Rafael's father, a recognized painter. The outdoor seating is arranged between the bar and the swimming pool and the twinkle lights of the former play on the latter. The candles make it as romantic as Valentine's Day. Vasquez' Dominican heritage always is represented in his global repertoire; his island version of sushi is a sweet plantain roll with tempura shrimp and mofonguitos have goat marinated with the local Brugal rum. The main courses go a bit more international, such as salmon or baby lobsters in a creamy pastis sauce that is so French. The staff is mature, discreet and professional. Ask if a dessert sampler is available . . . mmm. Mares can be like a house party or it can be your venue for a landmark celebration. $ *Average main: $18 ⊠ Francisco J. Peynado #6A, Puerto Plata* ☎ *809/261–3330, 809/224–1998* ⊕ *www. maresrestaurant.com* ⌕ *Reservations essential* ⊘ *No lunch, closed Mon.*

SOSÚA

$$$
CONTEMPORARY
Fodor'sChoice
★

✕ **Baia Lounge.** Perched above Sosua Bay, a new world-class culinary experience awaits with all the criteria for such a designation: innovative contemporary cuisine; a superlative setting; a classy but casual ambience; capable and caring servers; a young and fun spirit, and pricing that is fair. Baia Lounge is within the Ocean Club, an entity that is akin to a private club but is open to the public with reservation. Topside, past the infinity pool, is the alfresco dining area that includes a deck shaded by umbrellas. By day one can watch a fascinating parade of boats and at sunset vivid colors streak across a cerulean sky. Chef/partner Giancarlo Fiori works his magic by fusing four cuisines: Mediterranean; Asian; New World, and American Grill. Each forkful is a sensory rush and visually, his plates are eye candy. And if ever there was a "man-cave," the subterranean level is a wine cellar with hundreds of vintages, and a cigar lounge offering premium smokes. Sexy and edgy from the design space to the dessert wine, this is simply "the good life." An oasis in Sosua, it's more like a dream vision. [$] *Average main: $24* ✉ *The Ocean Club, Calle Bruno Phillip #5, El Batey, Sosúa* ☎ *849/816–2434* 🌐 *www.oceanclubdr.com* ✍ *Reservations essential.*

CABARETE

$$ INTERNATIONAL 🍴 **The Beach Club.** Overlooking a craggy shoreline, this restaurant has seen a number of evolutions but this reincarnation is the best ever. The couple in charge, the Avakians, is a well-known entity in the Cabarete expat community, with roots in Armenia, Ethiopia, and Italy. Consequently, the menu is international and runs the global gamut from Thai beef salad to Middle-Eastern baklava, lobster ravioli, and fragrant chicken Tikka Tandoori. Grilled tuna is served atop caramelized onions with a fresh herb sauce, and do ask what *zil zil* is. A lunch favorite is the salad of grilled mango, avocado, shrimp and cilantro, which you should pair with the signature yucca fries. The quality of the product is high, from the pancetta to the house-made gelato and excellent pizzas. The monthly music nights are sceney, and you may even see musicians from the annual jazz festival perform. As the music grooves, savor the panna cotta drizzled with caramel sauce. [$] *Average main: $18* ✉ *Sea Horse Ranch, Carretera Principal Sosua-Cabarete, Cabarete* ☎ *809/571–4995* 🕑 *Daily noon–10* 🕑 *Closed Mon. in low season.*

$$ MEDITERRANEAN 🍴 **bliss Restaurant–Lounge Bar Pool.** A white, stucco home where tables flank the night-lighted pool and soft, chill music plays—this is the kind of intimate place where wedding proposals are staged. Like its name, the mood is tranquillo and the restaurant is ideally suited to the concept of slow food, where diners savor each course. Charming and passionate, the young owners are Italian so anything from Italy is a wise choice. Start with antipastos, carpaccios, and tartares or the bliss salad of spinach, Gorgonzola, walnuts, bacon, and pear. For mains, try the gnocci in a Gorgonzola sauce, or ravioli stuffed with fresh smoked mozzarella, mascarpone, and parmigiano; pair it with a Tuscan red. Panna cotta is just like you hope to find, and marries well with a mild grappa or Sambuca. The chic set come to dinner and leave with an art piece under their arm—an adjacent room is an unexpected gallery. [$] *Average main: $19* ✉ *Callejon de la Loma 1, Cabarete* ✣ *This home is at entrance of a residential neighborhood off Sosua-Cabareta Hwy. #5. The side street is directly across from Ocean Dreams complex on other side of the hwy* ☎ *809/571–9721* 🌐 *www.activecabarete.com/bliss* 🕑 *Daily 6–10 pm* 🕑 *No lunch.*

$$ SEAFOOD 🍴 **Natura Restaurant at Natura Cabana.** If you're staying at this beachfront ecolodge, you'll likely take most of your meals here. If not, definitely go, not only for the freshest of seafood, but for the soothing ambience. Seafood is at the heart of the menu here, and appropriately so, because diners listen to the sounds of the waves crashing on coral rock as they fork the catch of the day. The menu changes with the seasons while holding tight to some perennial favorites. The vegetables and herbs are farmed at Natura's organic garden. An innovative ceviche has octopus and conch marinated with pineapple juice, honey, and tiger milk. That appetizer could be coupled with a filet mignon in a coconut-blue cheese sauce. For dessert, enjoy a classic such as tiramisu with a tropical twist—passion fruit. Know that rich, flavorful soups, many pastas and

vegetarian dishes round out the menu. The wines are French, Spanish, and Chilean (go for the *reservas*). Service is warm, caring, and efficient, the international music atmospheric. $ *Average main: $19* ✉ *Natura Cabana, Perla Marina, Cabarete* ☎ *809/571–1507, 809/858–5822* ⊕ *www.naturacabana.com* ⋐ *Reservations essential.*

SANTIAGO

$ ✕ **Il Pasticcio.** Everyone from college students to cigar kings, presidents
ITALIAN to politicos, photographers and movie stars pack this eccentrically-decorated culinary landmark. Tourists take photos of the bathrooms, with their ornate mirrors and Romanesque plaster sinks. Chef-owner Paolo's mouthwatering creations are authentic and fresh. Ask about the tasting menu, or try the great antipasto selections; commence with the Pasticcio salad, which might have smoked salmon, mozzarella, anchovies, capers, and baby arugula. Even the bread service comes with three sauces: one is like pesto, there's a pomodoro, and the best is a creamy anchovy sauce. Finish with a shot of limoncello and cheesecake or handmade gelato with strawberries marinated in wine. And if it's too dim to read the menu, just look up—it's also written on the ceiling. Who said Paolo is off the wall? ■ TIP→ **The value here is remarkable and it has won the hospitality award for Latin america and the Caribbean by the Italian Chamber of Commerce.** $ *Average main: $14* ✉ *Ave. El Lano corner, #3 Cerros de Guarbo* ☎ *809/582–6061* ⊕ *www.ilpasticciord.com* ۞ *Closed Mon.*

SAMANÁ PENINSULA

LAS TERRENAS

$$$ ✕ **The Beach.** Some of the best food in Samaná is served up for lunch (and
SEAFOOD lunch only) in a wooden, Victorian-style bungalow on Playa Cosón—
Fodor'sChoice decidedly not the usual beach shack. Hidden past a long stretch of lawn
★ and behind a grove of coconut trees it's on a 12-mile stretch of virgin beach. The Beach is an alfresco terrace restaurant decorated with the same exquisite taste as its big sister, the Peninsula House. The daily menu changes based on what fresh ingredients, fish, and lobster are available. Cooking is refined: a terrine of roasted beets and fresh goat cheese, or *langostinos* in passion fruit butter. Lunch here on fine china makes for a cherished travel memory. After you finish, you can dream about it while taking a siesta on the golden beach. $ *Average main: $22* ✉ *Playa Cosón, Antiqua carretera de Playa Coson (Old Beach Rd.), Las Terrenas* ☎ *809/962–7447* ⊟ *No credit cards* ۞ *Closed Mon. No dinner.*

$$ ✕ **Porto.** This jaw-dropping beachfront beauty is one of the newer play-
SEAFOOD ers in the ever-evolving, European-accented restaurant scene in Las Ter-
Fodor'sChoice renas. Sectioned off by ceiling-to-floor shell mobiles that divide the
★ space, the nautically themed dining room is one of the best efforts of the well-known Dominican designer Patricia Reid. Smart servers take pride in providing the kind of service that normally is found only in Santo Domingo's finest restaurants. Though beautiful, the setting is decidedly casual; in between courses, guests who come in their cover-ups can dive into the crystalline waters just past the sea grape trees. The Peruvian-influenced cuisine has roots in Italian cooking, with Asian undertones

and focuses primarily on fresh seafood, including delightful Peruvian-style ceviche. The wine cave is impressive as well. El Balconcito, the adjacent beach bar, is operated by Alex and Veronique of El Mosquito fame. ■TIP➔ In low season the hours are cut back some. $ *Average main: $18* ✉ *Across from Balcones del Atlántico, Playa Las Terrenas, Las Terrenas* ☎ *809/682–0954* ⊕ *www.balcones.com.do.*

WHERE TO STAY

The Dominican Republic has the largest hotel inventory (at this writing some 70,000 rooms, with even more under construction) in the Caribbean and draws large numbers of stateside visitors. Surfers can still find digs for $25 a night in Cabarete, and the new generation of luxurious all-inclusives in Punta Cana and Uvero Alto is simply incredible.

Santo Domingo properties generally base their tariffs on the European Plan (no meals)—though many include breakfast—and maintain the same room rates year-round. Beach resorts have high winter rates, with prices reduced for the shoulder seasons of late spring and early fall (summer has become another strong season). All-inclusives dominate in Punta Cana. Cabarete was a stronghold of the small inn, but it does have all-inclusives. Villa rentals are gaining in popularity all over the island, particularly in Cabarete and the Cabrera area.

During your stay your patience may be tested at times, particularly at all-inclusives. Even in the touristic zones, the D.R. still has vestiges of a third-world country. The nodding in and out of the electricity is one annoyance, and sometimes the *plantas* (generators) either don't kick in or wheeze and hiss from age. Service lapses and the language barrier can also be frustrating. But when an employee sincerely says, "How can I serve you, missus?" followed by, "It's a pleasure to help you. Have a happy day!" you're pleasantly reminded of the genuine hospitality of the locals. You gotta love it!

SANTO DOMINGO

The seaside capital of the country is in the middle of the island's south coast. In Santo Domingo, most of the better hotels are on or near the Malecón, with several small, desirable properties in the trendy Zona Colonial, allowing you to feel part of that magical environment. The capital is where you'll find some of the most sophisticated hotels and restaurants, not to mention nightlife. However, such an urban vacation is best coupled with a beach stay elsewhere on the island.

ZONA COLONIAL

$$ ▒ **Hostal Nicolas de Ovando–M Gallery Collection.** This historic, boutique
HOTEL hotel was sculpted from the residence of the first governor of the Ameri-
Fodor'sChoice cas, and it just might be the best thing to happen in the Zone since Diego
★ Columbus's palace was finished in 1517. **Pros:** lavish breakfast buffet;
beautifully restored historic section; its La Residence is one of the capi-
tal's best restaurants. **Cons:** breakfast, no longer included in rates, is $25;
pricey; rooms could be larger. $ *Rooms from: $185* ✉ *Calle Las Damas,
Zona Colonial* ☎ *809/685–9955, 800/763–4835* ⊕ *www.mgallery.com*
↪ *104 rooms* ⎮◎⎮ *No meals.*

$ B&B/INN **Hotel La Atarazana.** This artistically renovated town house near Plaza España offers comfortable accommodations in a central, safe location in the Zona Colonial. **Pros:** superior service and assistance; impressive rooftop terrace has views and both sunny and shaded sitting areas; $100 rate includes taxes, service, safe box and breakfast; super for solo travelers. **Cons:** no luxurious creature comforts beyond cable TV, Wi-Fi, and a/c; the multilingual owners aside, employees are not fluent in English; rooms are not large by American standards. [$] *Rooms from: $100* ✉ *Vicente Celestino Duarte 19, next door to police station, Zona Colonial* ☎ *809/688–3693* 🌐 *www.hotel-atarazana.com* 🛏 *6 rooms* 🍴 *Breakfast.*

BEST BETS FOR LODGING

BEST FOR ROMANCE
Eden Roc Resort, Peninsula House

BEST POOL
Casa Colonial Beach & Spa, Dreams Punta Cana Resort & Spa

BEST SERVICE
Hilton Santo Domingo, Tortuga Bay Villas

BEST FOR KIDS
Casa de Campo, Club Med Punta Cana

GAZCUE

$$ HOTEL **Hilton Santo Domingo.** This has become *the* address on the Malecón for businesspeople, convention attendees, and leisure travelers. **Pros:** Sunday brunch is one of the city's top tickets; 'luxe bedding; totally soundproof rooms; the executive-level lounge. **Cons:** little about the property is authentically Dominican; Vista Bar in lobby is closed on weekends and no longer has live entertainment. [$] *Rooms from: $129* ✉ *Av. George Washington 500, Gazcue* ☎ *809/685–0000* 🌐 *hiltoncaribbean.com/santodomingo* 🛏 *260 rooms* 🍴 *No meals.*

SOUTHEAST COAST

LA ROMANA

$$$$ ALL-INCLUSIVE FAMILY Fodor's Choice ★ **Casa de Campo.** The country's most illustrious resort, which set the benchmark for luxury travel in the Caribbean, recently had a dramatic renovation of its public spaces, rooms, and suites. **Pros:** excellent golf and tennis; La Cana by IL Circo and La Casita in the marina are on the meal plan. **Cons:** not the largest beach; food's expensive if not on an inclusive plan; a bit too sprawling although *gratis* golf carts minimize this. [$] *Rooms from: $832* ✉ *Casa de Campo Resort* ☎ *809/523–3333, 305/856–5405, 800/877–3643* 🌐 *www.casadecampo.com.do* 🛏 *173 rooms, 12 suites, 50 villas* 🍴 *All-inclusive.*

BAYAHIBE

$$$ ALL-INCLUSIVE FAMILY **Dreams La Romana.** This resort sits on an exceptional palm-fringed ribbon of white sand protected by a coral reef that offers great snorkeling from the beach, and a professional PADI dive school. **Pros:** with the new highway, the hotel is now a 50-minute drive from Las Americas Airport and 40 minutes from Punta Cana Airport; top-shelf liquors available at the lobby bar; free Wi-Fi in lobby and in-room at the club level; Cristal program for the food outlets. **Cons:** large

and busy property can feel overly full; lots of local groups book in August–October and can be noisy; caring and efficient staff is sometimes overwhelmed. [$] *Rooms from: $250* ✉ *Playa Bayahibe, Bayahibe* ☎ *809/221–8880* 🌐 *www.dreamsresorts.com/drelr* 🛏 *788 rooms* 🍴 *All-inclusive.*

$ ALL-INCLUSIVE FAMILY 🏨 **Viva Wyndham Dominicus Palace.** Older Americans may prefer this classier sister to the nearby Viva Wyndham Dominicus Beach resort, though the more fun-loving Beach has a reputation for strong animation programs and sports, and attracts young Americans and Canadians as well as Italians. **Pros:** lots of stylish European guests; big fun quotient; professional dive center. **Cons:** always heavily occupied and maintenance cannot keep up; no interior transportation; reservations needed for à la carte restaurants; Wi-Fi is free only in lobby. [$] *Rooms from: $230* ✉ *Playa Bayahibe, Bayahibe* ☎ *809/686–5658* 🌐 *www.vivaresorts.com* 🛏 *330 rooms* 🍴 *All-inclusive.*

PUNTA CANA

The easternmost coast of the island has 56 km (35 miles) of incredible beach punctuated by coco palms; add to that a host of all-inclusive resorts, an atmospheric thatch-roof airport, and many more direct flights than any other D.R. resort area, and it's easy to see why this region—despite having almost 50,000 hotel rooms (more than on most other Caribbean islands)—can regularly sell out. It has become the Cancún of the D.R. Most hotels in the region are clustered around Punta Cana and Bávaro beaches, where more than 90% of the existing properties are all-inclusive. But development continues to press outward—northward to the more remote locations of Macao and Uvero Alto, and southward to the nearby Juanillo—and several of the newer offerings are more luxurious and not all-inclusive.

The region commonly referred to as Punta Cana actually encompasses the beaches and villages of Juanillo, Punta Cana, Bávaro, Cabeza de Toro, El Cortecito, Arena Gorda, Macao, and Uvero Alto, which hug an unbroken stretch of the eastern coastline; however, Uvero Alto, the farthest developed resort area to the north, lies almost an hour from the Punta Cana airport.

PLAYA PUNTA CANA

$$$$ ALL-INCLUSIVE Fodor's Choice ★ 🏨 **Club Med Punta Cana.** Whimsy and camaraderie are characteristic of this family-friendly resort—Punta Cana's original all-inclusive—redesigned and situated on 75 tropical acres, with a coastline of incredible white-sandy shores. **Pros:** Tiara, the waterfront luxury section, is outstanding; animated, fun, interesting, global staff; themed weeks for music, dance, and sports. **Cons:** although buffets are praiseworthy, dining options are limited; Wi-Fi is expensive both in-room and in public spaces except the Internet cables (free) in Tiara suites; most guest complaints seem to occur during peak holiday times; standard rooms are aging although being renovated in stages. [$] *Rooms from: $575* ✉ *Playa Punta Cana* ☎ *809/686–5500, 800/258–2633* 🌐 *www.clubmed.com* 🛏 *553 rooms* 🍴 *All-inclusive.*

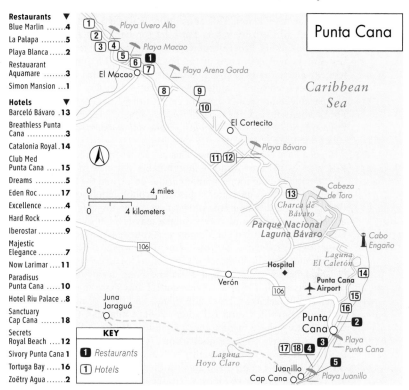

Restaurants ▼
Blue Marlin 4
La Palapa 5
Playa Blanca 2
Restauarant Aquamare 3
Simon Mansion ...1

Hotels ▼
Barceló Bávaro .13
Breathless Punta Cana 3
Catalonia Royal .14
Club Med Punta Cana 15
Dreams 5
Eden Roc 17
Excellence 4
Hard Rock 6
Iberostar 9
Majestic Elegance 7
Now Larimar 11
Paradisus Punta Cana 10
Hotel Riu Palace ..8
Sanctuary Cap Cana 18
Secrets Royal Beach 12
Sivory Punta Cana 1
Tortuga Bay 16
Zoëtry Agua 2

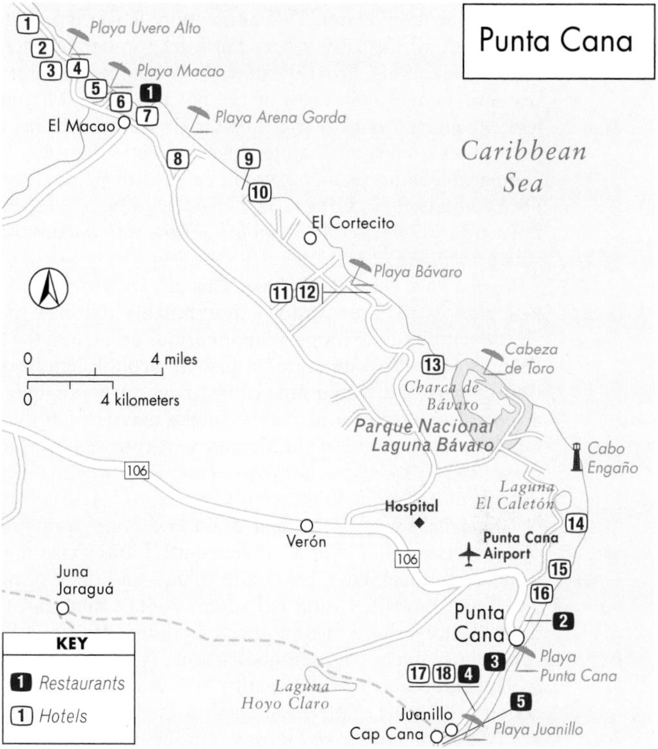

$$$$
RENTAL
Fodor's Choice ★

🏨 **Tortuga Bay.** Shuttered French windows that open to grand vistas of the sea and a cotton-white private beach are hallmarks of this luxury-villa enclave within the grounds of Puntacana Resort & Club. **Pros:** sprawling grounds with virgin beaches; VIP check-in at airport; breakfast poolside with fresh squeezed OJ. **Cons:** little nightlife; Bamboo restaurant is pricey; too isolating for singles unless you roll on over to Playa Blanca. [$] *Rooms from: $875* ✉ *Punta Cana Resort & Club, Playa Punta Cana* ☎ *809/959–8229, 888/442–2262* 🌐 *www.puntacana.com* 🛏 *30 suites* 🍴 *Breakfast.*

PLAYA BÁVARO

$$$
ALL-INCLUSIVE
FAMILY

🏨 **Barceló Bávaro Beach Resort.** Barceló deserves loud applause for the incredible face-lift that has totally transformed this property from an aging, middle-of-the-road has-been to a glamorous complex worthy of gushing praise. **Pros:** the whole place has been reinvented; enormous range of entertainment and activity options; no other kids' club is this contemporary; exceptionally comfortable beds. **Cons:** pool gets crowded and noisy; high-volume resort draws large conventions; tacky go-go girls have been moved from the disco to the casino. [$] *Rooms from: $387* ✉ *Carretera Bávaro, Km 1, Bávaro* ☎ *809/686–5797* 🌐 *www.barcelo.com* 🛏 *2887 rooms* 🍴 *All-inclusive.*

$$ ALL-INCLUSIVE Fodor's Choice ★ 🏨 **Catalonia Royal Resort.** This adults-only haven is a perfect example of how an all-inclusive resort can offer top-tier hospitality without the herd mentality. **Pros:** all rooms have hammocks on terraces; three restaurants at Royal, eight at the Bávaro, make 11 dining options; less expensive than other deluxe/luxurious AIs. **Cons:** even the bi-level suites need some maintenance and better lighting; busier than a comparable boutique hotel would be; the other Royal restaurants are not as wonderful as Cata Tapa. [$] *Rooms from: $225* ✉ *Playa Bávaro, Bávaro* ☎ *809/412–0011* 🌐 *www.hoteles-catalonia.com* 🛏 *255 rooms* 🍴 *All-inclusive.*

$$$ ALL-INCLUSIVE FAMILY 🏨 **Dreams Palm Beach Punta Cana.** This fine Dreams has a fabulous new look after its 2013 renovation—most notably in its new room category, 75 Premium Deluxe rooms with luxurious decor, and the new Dreams Pevonia Spa. **Pros:** unlimited top-shelf alcohol; handsome redecoration of bars and restaurants plus a new music lounge; close to the airport; free Wi-Fi for all. **Cons:** singles may feel left out with all the families; resort runs high occupancy year-round; a bit pricy. [$] *Rooms from: $420* ✉ *Cabeza de Toro, Bávaro* ☎ *809/552–6000* 🌐 *www.dreamsresorts.com/palmbeach* 🛏 *500 rooms* 🍴 *All-inclusive.*

$$ ALL-INCLUSIVE FAMILY 🏨 **Grand Palladium Resort Spa & Casino.** Four sprawling, contiguous resorts (with a shuttle service until 2 am) share these well-kept grounds and feel like a beachside village, and three of these—Grand Palladium Bávaro, Grand Palladium Punta Cana, and Grand Palladium Palace—share one another's facilities. **Pros:** excellent offshore snorkeling (extra charge); guest rooms are exceptionally spacious, and quiet, because of solid, quality construction and location far from activity centers; complete spa and health club. **Cons:** few rooms have sea views; the attractive lobby at Turquesa serves as the club lounge with the bar/café offering drinks but no contemporary hors d'oeuvres; the Royal section doesn't have a strong fun quotient but rather focuses on calm relaxation. [$] *Rooms from: $250* ✉ *Carretera El Cortecito, El Cortecito, Bávaro* ☎ *809/221–8149 Grand Palladiuim Bávaro, 809/221–0719 Grand Palladium Palace* 🌐 *www.fiestahotelgroup.com* 🛏 *1,823 rooms* 🍴 *All-inclusive.*

$$ ALL-INCLUSIVE FAMILY 🏨 **Iberostar Bávaro Resort.** Like its two sister resorts, this Spanish entry has panache—evidenced in its lobby, an artistic showpiece, and newly refurbished guest accommodations with contemporary style and bedding—making it competitive with Punta Cana's newer properties. **Pros:** fun entertainment—not too aggressive; a kids' water playground; good specialty restaurants; extra-special management keeps the staff in fine spirits. **Cons:** buffet not quite as good as it once was; the property is showing its age. [$] *Rooms from: $400* ✉ *Playa Bávaro, Bávaro* ☎ *809/221–6500, 888/923–2722* 📠 *809/688–6186* 🌐 *www.iberostar.com* 🛏 *596 rooms* 🍴 *All-inclusive.*

$$$$ ALL-INCLUSIVE Fodor's Choice ★ 🏨 **Iberostar Grand Hotel.** Iberostar's adults-only resort—an architectural gem—is a knockout from the moment you walk into the glamorous lobby and is one resort where the term "no expense was spared" is actually true. **Pros:** competent and caring management; impressive selection of designer restaurants with contemporary cuisine; idyllic beach weddings and honeymoons. **Cons:** although improving, there are still

service lapses from lack of English-language skills; chefs don't always let servers know when items are unavailable; the hotel is pricey for an all-inclusive in this area. $ *Rooms from: $850 ⊠ Playa Bávaro, Bávaro* ☎ *809/221–6500, 888/923–2722* ⊕ *iberostar.com* ⏎ *260 suites, 13 grand suites, 1 presidential* ¶⊙¶ *All-inclusive.*

$$$ ⊞ **Majestic Elegance.** The younger of Punta Cana's two Majestic resorts,
ALL-INCLUSIVE which is an all-suites property, is the more sophisticated sister—and a busy one. **Pros:** fun and welcoming staff; premium liquors at all bars and à la carte restaurants; at holidays decoration is full throttle as is the fun quotient. **Cons:** guests not in the VIP Club may feel second-class; consistent high occupancy makes it always feel crowded especially if not "in the Club"; rooms are not soundproof and there has been some bathroom plumbing issues. $ *Rooms from: $430 ⊠ Majestic St., Arena Gorda, Bávaro* ☎ *809/221–9898* ⊕ *www.majestic-resorts.com* ⏎ *596 rooms* ¶⊙¶ *All-inclusive.*

$$ ⊞ **Now Larimar Punta Cana.** This relatively new, moderately priced
ALL-INCLUSIVE branch of the AMResorts family—which welcomes children—has style
FAMILY as well as a gorgeous 700-yard beachfront. **Pros:** within walking distance of shops and off-site cafés; close to the airport; large housekeeping and entertainment team. **Cons:** some complaints about maintenance and repairs; guests say food is sometimes mediocre; in-room Wi-Fi is expensive (free at the Club level). $ *Rooms from: $430 ⊠ El Cortecito, Ave. Alemania s/n, Bávaro* ☎ *809/221–4646* ⊕ *www.nowresorts.com* ⏎ *822 rooms* ¶⊙¶ *All-inclusive.*

$$$$ ⊞ **Paradisus Palma Real Resort.** This luxury all-inclusive is a visual show-
ALL-INCLUSIVE stopper especially its central plaza by night, which sparkles under dra-
FAMILY matic lighting. **Pros:** enticing and professional spa with therapists winning
Fodor's Choice kudos for service and skill; adjacent Palma Real Shopping Center. **Cons:**
★ restaurants and nightlife are far from some rooms; most rooms at the Reserve do not have sea views and guests must take a shuttle to the private beach. $ *Rooms from: $520 ⊠ Bavaro Beach, Bávaro* ☎ *809/688–5000* ⊕ *www.paradisuspalmareal.com* ⏎ *554 rooms* ¶⊙¶ *All-inclusive.*

$$$ ⊞ **Paradisus Punta Cana.** Paradisus has so many new, innovative ameni-
ALL-INCLUSIVE ties, while also exuding a charismatic quality—like vintage wine—that
FAMILY produces the warm feeling that makes for loyal, repeat guests. **Pros:**
Fodor's Choice some impressive architecture and decor; professional and caring man-
★ agement has service down pat; the newly renovated YHI spa, which allows one to de-stress and revitalize. **Cons:** at the Reserve, kids can make the dining room noisy and the only water views are of the pool; no elevators; some rooms have yet to be renovated. $ *Rooms from: $430 ⊠ Bavaro Beach, Bávaro* ☎ *809/687–9923* ⊕ *www.paradisuspuntacana. solmelia.com* ⏎ *686 rooms* ¶⊙¶ *All-inclusive.*

$$$ ⊞ **Secrets Royal Beach.** The lobby at this sceney, adults-only all-suites
ALL-INCLUSIVE resort is like a modern art gallery, with suspended fish sculptures imme-
Fodor's Choice diately attracting the eye; however, the Caribbean-accented guest rooms
★ do not quite match. **Pros:** idyllic for weddings and honeymoons; nightly entertainment at the main plaza; good fun quotient with activities like cooking competitions on the beach; exceptional 17,000-square-foot Spa by Pevonia. **Cons:** beach vendors and excursion salespeople can be annoying; some clients think food is not as stellar as the environment;

tropical view rooms don't compare to more expensive accommodations; Wi-Fi is slow and costly. $ *Rooms from: $560* ✉ *El Cortecito, Avenida Alemania s/n, Bávaro* ☎ *809/221–4646* ⊕ *www.secretsresorts. com* ⤴ *372 rooms* ⦿⦿ *All-inclusive.*

PLAYA MACAO

$$$$ 🖵 **Hard Rock Hotel & Casino Punta Cana.** Hard Rock's first all-inclusive
ALL-INCLUSIVE property has its own unique identity, different from any other Dominican resort, and themed like its cafes. **Pros:** there is a large fun quotient here; mostly good service, particularly wait staff; variety and quality of the cuisine. **Cons:** complaints balloon when the resort is overly full particularly on long Dominican weekends and traditional holidays, like Christmas; some maintenance needed due to high occupancy; doesn't have a Caribbean feel except at the beach, which has a bad undertow; not for those who prefer a boutique property. $ *Rooms from: $508* ✉ *Blvd. Turístico del Este 74, Km 28, Playa Macao* ☎ *809/687–0000* ⊕ *www.hardrockhotels.com* ⤴ *1,787 rooms* ⦿⦿ *All-inclusive.*

$$ 🖵 **Hotel Riu Palace Macao.** After a major, much-needed renovation in
ALL-INCLUSIVE 2012, this adults-only resort has gone from dowdy to stellar, having
Fodor's Choice been brought up to a completely new level. **Pros:** the exterior, which
★ replicates a grand, white, Victorian edifice; good for a girls' getaway for the mannerly staff will ask you to dance to the live music in the lounge; fun and friendly staffers like the one dressed in a chauffer's uniform who opens the nightly buffet by reciting welcome in 25 languages. **Cons:** limited room views of the gorgeous beach; it is such a good value for the price, but don't expect luxury; its new popularity equals high occupancy. $ *Rooms from: $287* ✉ *Playa Arena Gorda, Bávaro* ☎ *809/221–7171* ⊕ *www.riu.com* ⤴ *328 rooms, 36 suites* ⦿⦿ *All-inclusive.*

PLAYA UVERO ALTO

$$ 🖵 **Breathless Punta Cana Resort & Spa.** Enter the lobby and the contempo-
ALL-INCLUSIVE rary decor with its explosion of vibrant colors—orchid, orange, flamingo pink—strong lighting, dangling sculptures, and retro-styled furniture may leave you breathless. **Pros:** everything new, clean and unique; premium liquors are served in the lobby bar Wink; Xhale level makes everything better; well suited for the wedding market and for conferences. **Cons:** some find the interior design overwhelming or slightly cheesy; standard rooms are basic and smallish, those near lobby noisy; no reservations needed for à la cartes is translating to long waits; new staff lacks sufficient English. $ *Rooms from: $510* ✉ *Playa Uvero Alto, Km 275, Uvero Alto* ☎ *809/551–0000* ⊕ *breathlessresorts.com* ⤴ *750 rooms* ⦿⦿ *All-inclusive.*

$$$ 🖵 **Dreams Punta Cana Resort & Spa.** This fun resort in a remote, pasto-
ALL-INCLUSIVE ral setting is super for families, young couples, wedding entourages,
FAMILY ladies getaways, and, yes, even singles. **Pros:** all-around camaraderie; nightly entertainment is a cut above; lovely guest rooms, most have been redecorated with new color schemes of magenta or aqua, and all were freshly painted. **Cons:** some rooms still need updating as do some of older public spaces; complaints are few, with some citing mediocre food, others insufficient outdoor furniture; expensive Wi-Fi (Club level it's free); resort runs at high occupancy. $ *Rooms from: $575* ✉ *Playa Uvero Alto, Km 269.5, Uvero Alto* ☎ *809/682–0404* ⊕ *www. dreamsresorts.com* ⤴ *620 rooms* ⦿⦿ *All-inclusive.*

Excellence Punta Cana

$$$$ ALL-INCLUSIVE **Excellence Punta Cana.** Originally, known to be a sumptuous lovers' lair, this adults-only all-inclusive is particularly appealing to couples (honeymooners, for sure) and wedding parties, and it now attracts a younger, fun clientele. **Pros:** no reservations are required at any of the eight individualistic restaurants; super-sized Excellence Club suites come with full bottles of top shelf liquor; the bi-level Excellence Club lounge has had its total redecoration. **Cons:** far from shopping, other restaurants, and nightlife; isolating for singles; service staff tries hard but doesn't always succeed. [$] *Rooms from: $528* ✉ *Playa Uvero Alto, Uvero Alto* ☎ *809/685–9880* 🌐 *www.excellence-resorts.com* 🛏 *456 rooms* 🍴 *All-inclusive.*

$$$$ RESORT **Sivory Punta Cana.** The best things really do come in small packages for this enchanting boutique hotel, which delivers on its promise of expressly personal service and utter tranquillity. **Pros:** caring and accommodating management and staff (mostly); free, strong Wi-Fi throughout; gay-friendly. **Cons:** can be too quiet as it's far from off-resort nightlife and shopping; guests from high-stress areas like NYC and D.C. appreciate the slowness here (others not always); food is frequently cited as disappointing; if accustomed to all-inclusive resorts, paying for each drink and every meal can be painful. [$] *Rooms from: $510* ✉ *Playa Uvero Alto, Uvero Alto* ☎ *809/333–0500* 🌐 *www.sivorypuntacana.com* 🛏 *55 rooms* 🍴 *No meals.*

$$$$ ALL-INCLUSIVE **Zoëtry Agua Punta Cana.** At this serene, oceanfront resort, rustic natural beauty and high architectural style blend seamlessly. **Pros:** the wellness spa has hydrotherapy, yoga, and Reiki classes; the petite gourmet room with its fusion menu and "wine cellar"; barista-style coffee shop/bakery. **Cons:** bathrooms can have too much nature and bugs can get into suites with thatched roofs, especially when it rains; limited nightlife

here or in the Uvero Alto area; guest reviews range from outstanding to dreadful, with an array of complaints ranging from service to food. $ *Rooms from: $835* ⊠ *Playa Uvero Alto, Uvero Alto* ☎ *809/468–0000* ⊕ *www.zoetryresorts.com* ⊅ *89 rooms, 5 villas* ⵏⵔ *All-inclusive.*

PLAYA JUANILLO

$$$$ | 🏨 **Eden Roc Cap Cana.** A new star in the luxury resort category, which
HOTEL | debuted in Cap Cana in 2012, has completed its wonderful components
Fodor'sChoice | like the Riva Bar and Mediterraneo restaurant, and the result is so stun-
★ | ning that it warrants our Fodor's Choice; it continues to garner other top awards. **Pros:** pampering, discreet service; a golf cart is included to zip around to reception; the charismatic, Riviera-style bar with its talented musicians. **Cons:** suites don't have sea views; only eight one-bedrooms, which are in demand; expensive, surely, but promotions appear on its website. $ *Rooms from: $944* ⊠ *Cap Cana, Juanillo* ☎ *809/469–7469* ⊕ *www.edenroccapcana.com* ⊅ *34 suites* ⵏⵔ *Breakfast.*

$$$$ | 🏨 **Sanctuary Cap Cana Golf & Spa Resort.** This stellar resort, the keystone
ALL-INCLUSIVE | of Cap Cana, welcomes families with the Fortress wing reserved for adults only; both all-inclusive and EP plans are offered. **Pros:** famous white-sand beach; professional management with many exceptional staffers; a wonderful spirit and fun-quotient especially in the Love Bar. **Cons:** the standard junior suites are long but narrow; areas of the resort are showing some wear; chef turnover has hurt food qual-ity; beach by main pool has coral, shallow and milky water but to the left of the Fortress is a phenomenal beach but BYO towel, and so on. $ *Rooms from: $450* ⊠ *Cap Cana, Blvd. Zona Hotelera, Playa Juanillo, Juanillo* ☎ *809/562–9191* ⊕ *www.sanctuarycapcana.com* ⊅ *142 rooms, 33 villas* ⵏⵔ *All-inclusive.*

NORTH COAST

The northern coast of the island, with mountains on one side, is also called the Amber Coast because of the large quantities of amber found in the area. The sands on its 121 km (75 miles) of beach are also golden. Major resort areas are Playa Dorada, Cabarete, and Sosúa. Plan to fly into Puerto Plata's Gregorio Luperon International Airport.

PUERTO PLATA

$$$ | 🏨 **Casa Colonial Beach & Spa.** Georgeously designed by architect Sara Gar-
HOTEL | cia, sophisticated Casa Colonial, a small property exuding refinement and
Fodor'sChoice | relaxation on the quietest end of the long beach, is a surprise among the
★ | chockablock all-inclusives of Playa Dorada. **Pros:** architectural gem offer-ing the full luxury, boutique experience; glorious spa; exceptional gourmet room (Lucia). **Cons:** can feel empty during the low season; large suites could use a splash of color; service is attentive but sometimes a bit off. $ *Rooms from: $395* ⊠ *Playa Dorada, Puerto Plata* ☎ *809/320–3232, 866/376–7831* ⊕ *www.casacolonialhotel.com* ⊅ *50 rooms* ⵏⵔ *No meals.*

$$ | 🏨 **Gran Ventana Beach Resort.** This all-inclusive is filled primarily with
ALL-INCLUSIVE | English-speaking clientele who like its sophisticated lobby, the color-
FAMILY | fully painted facades, and easy beach access. **Pros:** consistently good food and service for this price point; plenty of activities for the whole family; particularly efficient and caring front-desk staff. **Cons:** feels busy

year-round; some aspects of the rooms and restaurants are still dated. [$] *Rooms from: $295* ✉ *Playa Dorada* ☎ *809/320–2111, 809/320–3232* 🌐 *www.granventanahotel.com* ⇨ *506 rooms* 🍴 *All-inclusive.*

$$ ALL-INCLUSIVE **Presidential Suites–Puerto Plata Lifestyle.** This hilltop enclave consists mainly of apartment-style, two-bedroom suites decorated in a modern, masculine style with black leather chairs, cherry wood, and bedroom Jacuzzis. **Pros:** the sexy, *moderne* suites; pool with cascading waterfall and the lounging beds; variety and quality of lounges and restaurants; VIP beach club; caring employees and management try hard to please. **Cons:** a fast shuttle from the beach; popular, so can feel overly crowded; restaurants can jam up. [$] *Rooms from: $345* ✉ *1 Paradise Dr., Cofresí* ☎ *809/970–7777* 🌐 *www.lhvcresorts.com* ⇨ *60 rooms* 🍴 *All-inclusive.*

SOSÚA

$$$$ RENTAL **Sea Horse Ranch.** This enclave of private homes, each with large front and back yards and private pool, opened in 1993 as an elite bastion set within a vast country club–like setting. **Pros:** one of the most organized, well-managed groups of villas in the country; potent security makes your vacation worry-free; location close to Puerto Plata and the airport; all villas have free, unlimited Wi-Fi. **Cons:** guests usually feel the need to rent a car or hire a driver; small beaches; if your laptop has to be configured for the Wi-Fi, you will need to pay for a tech. [$] *Rooms from: $700* ✉ *Coastal Hwy., Cabarete* ☎ *809/571–3880, 800/635–0991* 🌐 *www.sea-horse-ranch.com* ⇨ *20 villas* 🍴 *No meals.*

CABARETE

$ HOTEL **Hotel El Magnifico.** You will find a healthy dose of unexpected pleasure `at this stellar, boutique condo-hotel. **Pros:** never feels crowded; the interior decor is très chic; the spaces are large and contemporary; children under 15 stay free. **Cons:** steep spiral staircases and no elevators; no restaurant or bar; no in-room phones and no way to communicate with reception unless you have a cell phone or rent one here. [$] *Rooms from: $92* ✉ *Calle del Cementario, Cabarete* ☎ *809/571–0868* 🌐 *www.hotelmagnifico.com* ⇨ *30 units* 🍴 *No meals.*

$$ RENTAL FAMILY Fodor's Choice ★ **Le Reef Beach Condos.** Le Reef is a small condominium complex with Euro-style and furnishings that reflect Cabarete's surfing craze (kite, wind, and otherwise). **Pros:** rooms are spacious and stylin'; beautiful beach; super food and service at the Front Loop Café. **Cons:** smaller property than some people may want; no elevator and three floors; some water views are hindered by the café's structure. [$] *Rooms from: $125* ✉ *Cabarete Beach, next to the Palms condos, Cabarete* ☎ *809/571–0848, 809/858–2589 cell* 🌐 *www.le-reef.com* ⇨ *6 condos* 🍴 *Breakfast.*

$ B&B/INN **Natura Cabana.** If your idea of perfection is thatched-roof cabanas and a quiet, private beach, then this is your oceanfront eco-lodge. **Pros:** natural, peaceful, beachfront stay; fresh seafood and innovative cuisine for dinner; caring owner, manager and long-term staff; spa with "Magic Mushroom" steam bath; free in-room Wi-Fi. **Cons:** no TVs, phones, or air-conditioning, but sea breezes; car is an asset but taxis to town are safer; boutique touches, yet not for those who crave luxurious creature comforts. [$] *Rooms from: $180* ✉ *Playa Perla Marina, Cabarete* ☎ *809/571–1507* 🌐 *www.naturacabana.com* ⇨ *10 rooms* 🍴 *Breakfast.*

$ HOTEL 🏨 **Velero Beach Resort.** You'll appreciate the location of this well-managed hotel and residential enclave with its own beachfront and gardens, just a few minutes' walk east of the noise of town yet also just minutes from the happening bars and restaurants. **Pros:** blenders, microwaves, and DVDs in the junior suites and above; draped Balinese sun beds at the pool are dreamy. **Cons:** no elevators—it's a climb up the spiral staircases; standard rooms are not spacious. [$] *Rooms from: $132* ✉ *Calle la Punta 1, Cabarete* ☎ *809/571–9727, 888/770–9886* 🌐 *www.velerobeach.com* 🛏 *29 units* 🍴 *No meals.*

CABRERA

$$ B&B/INN Fodor's Choice ★ 🏨 **Villa Castellamonte.** When not rented in its entirety, this elegant villa in Orchid Bay Estates operates as a high-end B&B. **Pros:** for all its grandeur, it's as laid-back as the garden hammock; sumptuous master suites have gas fireplaces; 24-hour security guards; three rooms have been updated with Italian-themed murals. **Cons:** beach is rocky and best visited with reef shoes; the staff of eight can be too much service. [$] *Rooms from: $195* ✉ *Orchid Bay Estates, Casa #10, Cabrera* ☎ *809/223–1072 cell, 888/589–8455 U.S./Canada toll-free, 702/900–3121 U.S. direct* 🌐 *www.villa-castellamonte.com* 🛏 *8 rooms* 🍴 *Breakfast.*

SAMANÁ

Samaná is the name of both the peninsula that curves around the eponymous bay and of the largest town. Conveniently, El Catey Airport (AZS) is served regularly by JetBlue from New York–JFK; otherwise, www.dominicanshuttles.com offers regular flights from several D.R. airports.

LAS TERRENAS

$$$$ RENTAL FAMILY 🏨 **Balcones del Atlantico.** A condo hotel on a large tract of virgin land; its spacious accommodations are beyond stellar, with exceptional interior design, dreamy bedding, and private Jacuzzis on terraces that are basically outdoor rooms. **Pros:** intelligent and caring concierge staff; everything is nearly new, clean, and fresh; ideal for longer stays. **Cons:** not smack on the beach, with marginal views; some planned amenities are still not in place; a second restaurant and minimart closer to accommodations is needed; hotel charges a resort fee; best with a rental car for trips to town and shopping. [$] *Rooms from: $400* ✉ *Carretera El Limon, across from Porto on Playa Las Terrenas, Las Terrenas* ☎ *809/240–5011* 🌐 *www.balconesdelatlantico.com.do* 🛏 *36 units* 🍴 *No meals.*

$$$$ B&B/INN Fodor's Choice ★ 🏨 **Peninsula House.** The gorgeous Victorian-style plantation house with wraparound verandahs overlooks acres of coconut palms down to the ocean and is one of the best bed-and-breakfasts in the Caribbean. **Pros:** quiet and remote; impeccable guest attention; ideal for honeymoons and babymoons. **Cons:** pricey; you may worry that you'll break something; unmarked entrance, just off a dirt road. [$] *Rooms from: $650* ✉ *Camino Cosón, Las Terrenas* ☎ *809/962–7447, 809/847–7540* 🌐 *www.thepeninsulahouse.com* 🛏 *6 rooms* 🍴 *Breakfast.*

Peninsula House, Las Terrenas

SANTA BÁBARA DE SAMANÁ

$$ 🛏 **The Bannister Hotel at Puerto Bahia Marina & Residences.** This stylish
HOTEL   marina complex smack on the Bay of Samaná has changed the face of
Fodor's Choice   tourism in this area and become the social center for the upscale residents,
★   a safe harbor for visiting yachtsmen, and a reasonable option for inter-
national visitors. **Pros:** wonderful ambience; natural beauty everywhere.
Cons: the bedrooms in the one-bedroom accommodations could be more
spacious; too far from town to walk. $ *Rooms from: $170* ⊠ *Puerto
Bahia, Carretera Sanchez Km 5, Santa Bárbara de Samaná* ☎ *809/503–
6363* ⊕ *www.thebannisterhotel.com* ✒ *30 rooms* ⊙ *No meals.*

LAS GALERAS

$$$ 🛏 **Sublime Samaná.** With dramatic, contemporary architecture that
HOTEL   allows each suite water views, this resort offers large two- and three-
Fodor's Choice   bedroom condo accommodations with designer kitchens and living
★   rooms, two LCD TVs and a balcony that looks down upon the labyrinth
of swimming pools. **Pros:** the beach bar offers a great lunch, tropical
cocktails, and fresh juices; chic interior furnishings are designed with
taste and Caribbean spirit; the pool complex is so inviting. **Cons:** relatively isolated (a taxi into town is $60 round-trip); restaurant options
are limited; not a lot of on-site activities. $ *Rooms from: $425* ⊠ *Bahia de Coson, Ramal Viva, Las Terrenas* ☎ *809/240–5050* ⊕ *www.
sublimesamana.com* ✒ *15 suites (in the rental pool)* ⊙ *Breakfast.*

$ 🛏 **Villa Serena.** Decidedly one of the better hotels in the eastern cor-
HOTEL   ner of the peninsula, Villa Serena makes for a wonderful, stress-free
Samaná vacation. **Pros:** private beachfront without vendors or loud
music; reliable Wi-Fi in lobby and all rooms; new Croatian manager

speaks English, as does front-desk staff. **Cons:** main section feels a bit dated; most rooms have a/c but no TVs. [$] *Rooms from: $140* ✉ *Las Galeras Beach, Las Galeras* ☎ *809/538–0000* 🌐 *www.villaserena.com* 🛏 *21 rooms* 🍴 *Breakfast.*

NIGHTLIFE

Santo Domingo's nightlife is vast and ever changing. Check with the concierges and hip capitaleños. At this writing, there is still a curfew for clubs and bars; they must close at midnight during the week, and 2 am on Friday and Saturday nights. There are some exceptions to the latter, primarily those clubs and casinos in hotels. Sadly, the curfew has put some clubs out of business, but it has cut down on the crime and late-night noise, particularly in the Zona Colonial. Some clubs are now pushing the envelope and staying open until 3, but they do get in trouble with the authorities when caught, and you probably don't want to be there then.

Dancing is as much a part of the culture here as eating and drinking. As in other Latin countries, after dinner it's not a question of *whether* people will go dancing but *where* they'll go. Move with the rhythm of the merengue and the pulsing beat of salsa (adopted from neighboring Puerto Rico). Among the young, the word is that there's no better place to party in the Caribbean than Santo Domingo. Almost every resort in Puerto Plata and Punta Cana has live entertainment, dancing, or both.

The action can heat up—and the island does have casinos—but gambling in the Dominican Republic is more a sideline than a raison d'être. Most casinos are in the larger hotels of Santo Domingo, with a couple on the North Coast, plus many more in Punta Cana. All offer slot machines, blackjack, craps, and roulette and are generally open daily from 3 pm to 4 am, the exception being those in Santo Domingo, which, for now, must close at midnight (2 am on Friday and Saturday). You must be 18 to enter.

PUNTA CANA

BARS AND CLUBS

Fodor's Choice ★ **Imagine.** Imagine you were dancing the night away in a natural cave, with earth-rocking acoustics. You can bounce back and forth between the various "cave" rooms with their stalactites and stalagmites, with equally hot dance floors, featuring house/club jams, merengue/salsa/world beats, current Top 40, and more. Come late and stay early: things start getting steamy well after midnight, when many club crawlers descend via shuttle (round-trip) from the local resorts. (The free bus is great, but know that it stops at every resort in the area, beginning around 11 pm. Service from Uvero Alto resorts is $10 extra. Taxis wait outside for those who can't hang.) Special rates (from $60) are offered for a weekly, multiple-entrance pass, with one night including an open bar. Although, most disco-goers are in awe, others say that it's a lot of hype. ✉ *Carretera Cocoloco–Riu, Coco Loco/Friusa, Bávaro* ☎ *809/466–1049, 809/466–1079* 🌐 *www.imaginepuntacana.com* 🎟 *$40 (includes cover, transportation, and 2 drinks)* 🕒 *11 pm–after 4 am.*

Continued on page 450

PIRATES
IN THE
CARIBBEAN

Susan MacCallum Whitcomb & Julie Collazo Schwietert

Peg legs, parrots, and an easy-to-imitate "ahoy matey" lexicon: these are requisite elements in any pirate tale, but so are avarice and episodes of unspeakable violence. The combination is clearly compelling. Our fascination with pirates knows no bounds.

The true history of piracy has largely been obscured by competing pop-culture images. On one hand, there is the archetypal opportunist—fearsome, filthy, and foul-mouthed. On the other is the lovable scallywag epitomized by Captain Jack Sparrow in Disney's *Pirates of the Caribbean* franchise. Actual pirates, however, usually fell somewhere between these two extremes.

They could be uneducated men with limited life choices or crewmen from legitimate commercial and exploratory vessels left unemployed in the wake of changing political agendas. In either case, the piratical career path offered tempting benefits. Making a fast doubloon was only the beginning. Piracy also promised adventure plus egalitarian camaraderie—a kind of social equality unlikely to be found elsewhere during that class-conscious period.

Life aboard ship was governed by majority, as opposed to autocratic, rule. Pirates moreover, adhered to the Pirate's Code (a sort of "honor among thieves" arrangement). On the ships, at least, the common good took precedence.

✗ MARKS THE SPOT

Movie *Pirates of the Caribbean.*

The Caribbean offered easy pickings for pirates because Spanish imperialists had already done the heavy lifting, extracting gems and precious metals from their South American colonies. Pirates from competing powers (namely England and France) could simply grab the spoils as Spanish ships island-hopped homeward.

Jamaica

Calico Jack Rackham, his lover Anne Bonny, and Mary Read were ultimately captured in **Bloody Bay** near Negril. Reportedly the male crew members were too busy drinking rum to mount a proper defense.

Dominican Republic

The centuries-old Spanish architecture in Santo Domingo's **Zona Colonial** is so well-preserved you can almost picture the area populated with tankard-toting buccaneers and corset-clad wenches.

Puerto Rico

Massive fortifications, like **Castillo San Felipe del Morro** in Old San Juan, show just how far the Spanish were prepared to go to protect their assets from seagoing attackers, whether authorized or otherwise.

British Virgin Islands

Sir Francis Drake Channel, Jost Van Dyke, and Great Thatch Island were named for pirates or privateers. Ditto for **Norman Island**, which reputedly inspired the setting for R.L. Stevenson's *Treasure Island.*

St. Thomas

A strategic location, protected anchorages, plus easy-to-hide-in inlets made the U.S. Virgin Islands an ideal habitat for plunderers. High points like **Drake's Seat** and Blackbeard's Castle were used to survey the terrain.

Anguilla

Underwater heritage preserves let divers explore vessels that sailed during piracy's Golden Age. **Stoney Ground Marine Park** contains a Spanish galleon wrecked in 1772, plus cannons, anchors, and other artifacts.

Santo Domingo, Dominican Republic

Stoney Ground Marine Park

Pirate ship arrives for Pirates Week, the Cayman Islands.

Peppered Pickled Pirate Party, Nevis.

Castillo de San Felipe del Morro, Puerto Rico.

Anguilla

St. Maarten
St. Martin

St. Barthélemy

Saba

St. Eustatius   St. Kitts

Nevis

Barbuda

Antigua

Montserrat

Guadeloupe

Marie
Galante

Dominica

Martinique

St. Lucia

St. Vincent

PIRATES OF THE CARIBBEAN

Dominica
Convoys of booty-filled Spanish ships often stopped at this lush island. Pirates followed—and so did Hollywood. Key scenes for the second and third *Pirates of the Caribbean* movies were shot here.

St. Vincent
Sequences for the first three *Pirates of the Caribbean* installments were filmed on location here. The meticulously detailed cluster of buildings built to represent Port Royal can be seen at **Wallilabou Bay.**

PIRATE PARTIES

Cayman Islands
In mid-November, islanders celebrate their piratical past with an 11-day festival featuring treasure hunts, mock trials, and other themed events. The highlight is an invasion of **George Town** staged by *faux* pirates.

Nevis
Taking a page from the Cayman Islands book, Nevis introduced the weeklong **Peppered Pickled Pirate Party.** Held twice during the last week of October and November, It celebrates William Kidd and Black Bart with an "invasion," regattas, cooking and cocktail competitions, treasure hunts, and more

St. Barthélemy
Logically enough, Frenchman Daniel Montbars used this French island as his home base. Legend has it some of his treasure remains hidden in the beachfront caves around **Anse du Gouverneur.**

St. Lucia
Now a peaceful national park, **Pigeon Island** (on St. Lucia's northern tip) was once the hideout of François Le Clerc. This peg-legged pirate orchestrated attacks from his hilly vantage point in the late 16th century.

TIMELINE

| | 1523 First Spanish treasure ships seized | 1577 Francis Drake begins circumnavigating the globe | 1604 James I revokes Letters of Marque |

1500   1550   1600

1492 onward exploitation of New World resources

1585–1604 Anglo-Spanish War

FAMOUS PIRATES

Years after they wreaked havoc on the high seas, history still remembers some of the most notorious pirates of the Caribbean.

SIR FRANCIS DRAKE

Drake was a busy fellow. The first Englishman to circumnavigate the globe, he popularized tobacco, led slave-trading expeditions, helped destroy the Spanish Armada, and still had time to terrorize treasure-laden ships with Queen Elizabeth's blessing. Drake led his country's fleet in epic encounters throughout the Caribbean.

HENRY MORGAN

Captain Morgan led a colorful life before lending his name to a ubiquitous brand of rum. Leaving Wales for the West Indies as a young man, he successfully segued from debauched buccaneer to semi-respectable privateer and, after dodging piracy charges in England, ended up

Captin Morgan

Edward "Blackbeard" Teach

as the Lieutenant Governor of Jamaica.

BLACKBEARD

Born Edward Teach, Blackbeard was notable for his business savvy (which included making profit-sharing deals with politicos) as well as his fiendish looks. His signature beard was braided and often laced with lit fuses to terrify enemies. Alas, in 1718 Blackbeard's head was severed in a dramatic showdown with Lt. Robert Maynard of the Royal Navy. It

was mounted on Maynard's ship as a warning to others.

WILLIAM KIDD

Life was a roller-coaster ride for the legendary Captain Kidd. Kidd was a retired privateer living in New York when he accepted a commission to hunt pirates and then became one himself with the encouragement of a mutinous crew. He was executed in London in 1701, but hopefuls still hunt for the treasure he supposedly left buried.

PIRATES, PRIVATEERS, AND BUCCANEERS

The "pirate" label is generally applied to sailors engaging in any type of maritime marauding. Yet there are variations on the theme.

Privateers such as Sir Francis Drake were licensed looters, their escapades were authorized by a royal Letter of Marque, which issued private commissions for strategic naval operations. Privateers were sanctioned to attack only specific enemy ships, with the goodies gained benefitting their government. Since this rogue diplomacy was intended to challenge Spain's dominance in the Americas, many privateers felt they were protecting national interests. Hence, they were pirates... but patriotic.

Buccaneers, conversely, were a motley crew. The word, originally reserved for pirates from Hispaniola (the island shared by Haiti and the Dominican Republic), eventually included anyone from

Sir Francis Drake

1618–1648
Thirty Years War

1689–1697
King William's War

1701–1714
War of Spanish Succession

William Kidd

Calico Jack Rackman

Anne Bonny

BLACK BART ROBERTS

Though not the most famous pirate, he is often considered the most successful. He racked up impressive credits, plundering some 400 ships between 1719 and 1722. A snappy dresser who was fashionably attired even in battle, he was also a strict disciplinarian. Roberts quashed onboard gambling and banned music on Sunday.

DANIEL MONTBARS

Montbars proved Brits didn't hold a monopoly on bad behavior. French lineage aside, he differed from his 17th-century peers in that he was affluent and educated. His manners needed polishing, though. Violent outbursts (disemboweling Spaniards was a favorite sport) earned Montbars the nickname "The Exterminator."

CALICO JACK RACKHAM

An Englishman who ascended from mate to captain, Rackham, secured his legend by adding women to his crew. Workwise, his favorite tactic was attacking small vessels close to shore. Such boldness led to an inglorious end. Rackham was hung then tarred, feathered, and displayed in a cage in Port Royal, Jamaica.

ANNE BONNY AND MARY READ

Thought to be unlucky, female pirates were rare. Yet the comely Bonny and cross-dressing Read were respected by their shipmates... and feared by their victims. Captured together in 1720, they were sentenced to death. Both, however, escaped the noose by claiming to be pregnant.

the "Boys Gone Wild" school. Coming from diverse ethnic backgrounds, many buccaneers were fugitive slaves, escaped criminals, or other social outcasts who became plunderers by choice or force. Operating solely in their own interests and typically lacking a strategy or social order, they were the bottom feeders.

Political shifts could turn privateers into pirates (James I's decision to revoke Letters of Marque was a case in point). Desperation or moral degeneration could just as easily turn pirates into buccaneers.

PIRATE FLAGS

Flashy flags were to pirates what coats of arms were to royal families: visible signs of group identity. Each crew flew its own, depending on what attributes the captain wanted to emphasize or the degree of menace he wanted to convey.

The most recognizable is the "Jolly Roger": an iconic white-on-black skull cradled by crossbones.

Pacha. A favorite among locals and still one of the best resort-based dance spots, Pacha plays more merengue and bachata than most of the other clubs, but still is geared to "young" contemporary music. The later it gets, typically the louder it gets. The place is not that large and is handsome in its decor, especially the bar. Drinks here are cheaper, too. For a beer, expect to pay about 80 pesos (about $2.50); the price can be double in some of the other clubs. Cover charges apply when live bands perform; otherwise it's free to enter, and nonresort guests are welcome. ■ TIP→ If you're staying at the Riu Macao complex, it's an easy, safe enough walk. ⊠ *Riu Naiboa Resort, Av. Estados Unidos, on Caribbean St., Bávaro* ☎ *809/221–7575.*

NORTH COAST

BARS AND CLUBS

LAX. LAX is a perennially popular open-air bar that really comes alive by night. You can sit in the sand in lounge chairs or jump into the action under the palapa, where a DJ will be spinning madly or a live band will be playing. There's good grazing chow, too, and special theme nights like Thai (it's not bad, either). Carefully made mojitos and other drinks (two-for-one specials from 5 to 7) mean you must be patient: getting one can take time when the bar backs up. It's next to a small hotel, so it must close early, around 1 am. ⊠ *Cabarete Beach, Cabarete* ☎ *829/745–8800.*

Onno's Bar. Onno's Bar, right next to LAX, remains a serious party place. It is usually wall-to-wall and back-to-back as the young and fit pack the dance floor and groove to techno sounds while other multinational youth sit at the tables in the sand. It's easier to get served at the beach bar than the main one, and as you chill, people will pass by, introduce themselves, chat, and then move on. It's fun and friendly, with theme nights—Wednesday is Mexican night and Thursday is Ladies night. Happy Hour is daily 6–9 pm and Killer Hour is 9–10 pm. A DJ cranks it up on Friday and Saturday nights, however, in high season, when it stays open until 3 am, the scene can get rowdy. (In fact, some local expats say that the crowd that it is now attracting is less than wonderful.) Cabarete's Onno's now has sister establishments in Bavaro, Altos de Chavon and Santo Domingo's Zona Colonial. ⊠ *Cabarete Beach, Calle Principal, Cabarete* ☎ *809/571–0461* ⊕ *www.onnosbar.com.*

SAMANÁ PENINSULA

BARS AND CLUBS

El Balconcito del Mosquito. A fun beach bar adjacent to Porto, the fabulous beachfront restaurant belonging to Balcones del Atlantico, El Balconcito is open all day, every day. It offers a special menu from Porto to help cushion the sting of the house specialty—*chupitos*. Served in tall pony glasses, these drinks consist of a lethal dose of white rum mixed with flavors such as passion fruit (*chinola*) or—the best—ginger. Run by the owners of the original Mosquito Art Bar which was destroyed by the devastating fire that tore through Pueblo Los Pescadores in 2012, they have regrouped and have opened a new Mosquito Art Bar, which is next to the Palapa Hotel in Punta Poppy. It's open from 6 pm until late, and it serves *chupitos,* of course, and light fare. ⊠ *Next to Porto, Carretera El Limon, Las Terrenas* ☎ *809/877–2844, 809/240–6715.*

SHOPS AND SPAS

Cigars continue to be the hottest commodity coming out of the D.R. Many exquisite hand-wrapped smokes come from the island's rich Cibao Valley, and Fuente Cigars—handmade in Santiago—are highly prized. Only reputable cigar shops sell the real thing, and many you will see sold on the street are fakes. You can also buy and enjoy Cuban cigars here, but they can't be brought back to the United States legally. Dominican rum and coffee are also good buys. Mamajuana, an herbal liqueur, is said to be the Dominican answer to Viagra. The D.R. is the homeland of designer Oscar de la Renta, and you may want to stop at the chic shops that carry his creations. La Vega is famous for its *diablos cajuelos* (devil masks), which are worn during Carnival. Look also for the delicate, faceless ceramic figurines that symbolize Dominican culture.

Though locally crafted products are often of a high caliber (and very affordable), expect to pay hundreds of dollars for designer jewelry made of amber and larimar. Larimar—a semiprecious stone the color of the Caribbean Sea—is found on the D.R.'s south coast in the hills above the city of Barahona. Prices vary according to the stone's hue and category, AAA being the highest. Amber has been mined extensively between Puerto Plata and Santiago. A fossilization of resin from a prehistoric pine tree, it often encases ancient animal and plant life, from leaves to spiders to tiny lizards. Beware of fakes, which are especially prevalent in street stalls. A reputable dealer can show you how to tell the difference between real larimar and amber and imitations.

Bargaining is both a game and a social activity in the D.R., especially with street vendors and at the stalls in El Mercado Modelo. Vendors are disappointed and perplexed if you don't haggle. They're also tenacious, so unless you really plan to buy, don't even stop to look.

SANTO DOMINGO

SHOPPING AREAS AND MALLS

Acropolis Mall, between Avenida Winston Churchill and Calle Rafael Augusto Sanchez, has become a favorite shopping arena for the young and/or hip capitaleños. Stores like Zara and Mango (both from Spain) have today's look without breaking your budget.

One of the main shopping streets in the Zona is **Calle El Conde,** a pedestrian thoroughfare. With the advent of so many restorations, the dull and dusty stores with dated merchandise are giving way to some hip, new shops. However, many of the offerings, including local designer shops, are still of a caliber and cost that the Dominicans can afford. Some of the best shops are on **Calle Duarte,** north of the Zona Colonial, between Calle Mella and Avenida de Las Américas. **El Mercado Modelo,** a covered market, borders Calle Mella in the Zona Colonial; vendors here sell a dizzying selection of Dominican crafts.

Piantini is a swanky residential neighborhood that has an increasing number of fashionable shops and clothing boutiques. Its borders run from Avenida Winston Churchill to Avenida Lope de Vega and from Calle Jose Amado Soler to Avenida 27 de Febrero.

RECOMMENDED STORES

Casa Virginia. One of the Dominican Republic's leading department stores, Casa Virginia was founded in 1945 by the mother of the present Virginia, who took it to the next level, adding a great day spa. The store is stocked mostly with high-end designer clothing (including a Jenny Polanco department) and fashion finds, but also has Italian jewelry and some moderately priced gift items. ⊠ *C/Av. Roberto Pastoriza 255, Naco* ☎ *809/566–4000, 809/566–1535 spa* ⊕ *casavirginia.com.*

Galería de Arte Nader. Top Dominican artists in various mediums are on display here. The gallery staff are well known in Miami and New York, and work with Sotheby's. ⊠ *Rafael Augusto Sanchez 22, Ensanche Piantini, Piantini* ☎ *809/544–0878.*

La Leyenda del Cigarro, S.R.L. This shop along El Conde in the Zona Colonial makes and sells its own branded premium cigars to clients worldwide and anyone who happens to walk into the cozy store. Enjoy the leather couch in the seating area, and let owner Julio Vilchez Rosso or a member of his personable staff regale you with the history of cigar making in the Dominican Republic and learn what makes a good cigar a good cigar. This store is perfect for experienced connoisseurs or those who'd like to become one. There's another branch in the Malecón Center. ⊠ *Calle El Conde, 4, Zona Colonial* ☎ *809/686–5489, 809/445–3728.*

L'Ile Au Tresor. L'Ile Au Tresor has a *Pirates of the Caribbean* theme, but that aside, it's fun. The owner, a talented tri-lingual Frenchman named Patrick, has some of the most attractive and creative designer pieces in native larimar and amber. If you have never bought any of these lovely stones because of cheesy settings or too high a price tag, then this is your chance. His innovative custom work, with sterling or gold, can be done in 48 hours. The shop crew does not speak English, but will call Patrick if he is not there. ⊠ *Arzobispo Meriño 258, Zona Colonial* ✛ *In front of Colonial Tour Agency* ☎ *829/688–8751, 809/688–8751.*

Lyle O. Reitzel Art Contemporaneo. Lyle O. Reitzel Art Contemporaneo has, since 1995, specialized in contemporary art. The gallery showcases mainly Latin artists from Mexico, South America, and Spain, and some of the most controversial Dominican visionaries. Their rotating collection can include the new, the strange, and the daring. ⊠ *Torre Piantini, Gustavo Mejia Ricart, Suites 1 and 2 A, Piantini* ☎ *809/227–8361, 809/519–9214 cell* ⊕ *www.lyleoreitzelgallery.com.*

Plaza Toledo Bettye's Galeria. A fascinating array of artwork, including Haitian voodoo banners and metal sculpture, and souvenirs, chandeliers, and estate jewelry, are sold at Plaza Toledo Bettye's Galeria. The gallery's second room is dedicated to Dominican fine art. The American expat owner, Bettye Marshall, has a great eye, and can also rent you a room in one of her bed-and-breakfasts; which are basic, but historic with some kind of art hanging on the walls and just $50 for two including breakfast. ⊠ *Isabel la Católica 163, Zona Colonial* ☎ *809/688–7649.*

SOUTHEAST COAST

SHOPPING AREAS AND MALLS

Altos de Chavón. Altos de Chavón is a re-creation of a 16th-century Mediterranean village on the grounds of the Casa de Campo resort, where you can find a church, art galleries, boutiques, restaurants and souvenir shops, and a 5,000-seat amphitheater for concerts grouped around a cobbled square. At the Altos de Chavón Art Studios you can find ceramics, weaving, and screen prints made by local artists. Extra special is Casa Montecristo, a chic cigar lounge, which also offers a tour with cigar history and trivia. The minimarket sells sundries and some food items. ✉ *Casa de Campo.*

The Casa de Campo Marina. Casa de Campo's top-ranked marina is home to shops and international boutiques, galleries, and jewelers scattered amid restaurants, an ice-cream parlor, bars, banks, beauty salons, and a yacht club. It's a great place to spend some time shopping, sightseeing, and staring at the extravagant yachts. The chic shopping scene at the marina includes Bleu Marine (cosmetics) and Everett Designs (high-end larimar and amber jewelry). Art Arena sells local artisan jewelry and gifts. Dominican designer Jenny Polanco sells clothes, purses, and jewelry. The Bibi Leon boutique, is known for its tropical-themed home accessories. There's also a marvelous Italian antiques shop, Nuovo Rinascimento, and the Club de Cigarro (Fumo). By the way, the supermercado Nacional at the marina has not only groceries but sundries, postcards, and snacks. ✉ *Casa de Campo Marina, Calle Barlovento.*

PUNTA CANA

SHOPPING AREAS AND MALLS

Fodor'sChoice **Galerias at Puntacana Village.** The Galerias at Puntacana Village lie
★ within a still-blossoming shopping, dining, and residential complex built on the road to the Punta Cana International Airport. Originally the village was built to house employees of the Puntacana Group, but now the shops, and restaurants are also a tourist draw. The village is comprised of churches, an international school, and this commercial area with its restaurants, shops, a supermarket, banks, a beauty salon, and doctors' offices. The Sheraton Four Points Puntacana Village opened across the street, a two-minute drive to the airport. ✉ *Blvd. Primero de Noviembre.*

Fodor'sChoice **Palma Real Shopping Village.** A standout among the region's shopping
★ centers, Palma Real Shopping Village is a swanky, partially enclosed mall (similar to something you would see in southern California), that is also overall the most expensive. Fountains and tropical plants infuse life into the bright and airy interiors beneath the blue-tile roof. Music pipes through the stone-floor plaza in the center, where seating is available and security is tight. Upscale retail shops, which sell beachwear, clothing, skin-care products, and jewelry, line the walls. Several restaurants give visitors welcome dining alternatives beyond the gates of their resorts. There's also a movie theater, the only one in

Punta Cana. There are two banks, ATMs, and a money exchange out-let. Stores are open 10–10, but the restaurants stay open later. It has the best pharmacy in the area. Shuttle buses run to and from many of the hotels, with pick-ups every two hours. ⊠ *Bávaro* ☎ *809/552–8725* ⊕ *www.palmarealshoppingvillage.com.*

RECOMMENDED STORES

Harrison's Fine Jewelry. It's hard to walk by the windows of Harrison's Fine Jewelry without stepping in to admire the collection of jewelry, including a large selection of larimar and amber pieces in striking settings, as well as diamonds and other classic gems. Outlets of this renowned chain are also in several resorts of Punta Cana. ⊠ *Palma Real Shopping Village, Bávaro* ☎ *809/552–8721* ⊕ *www.harrisons.com.*

SPAS

Fodor'sChoice **Six Senses Spa.** This spa offers the best treatments in the Dominican
★ Republic. Period. Here you will find master Thai therapists; you will melt in the hands of these gifted women and be transported to another zone. Whether you have a special manicure or facial with fresh product, a hot stone massage, or go on a magical Spa Sensory Journey, it will be exceptional. This exotic wellness center also has couples' accommodations which include luxurious baths. The spa belongs to the Puntacana Resort and is housed in its gorgeous golf club; gentlemen as well as ladies are made welcome, as are outside guests. ■TIP➔ **An added bonus for resort guests: you can book thera-pies in your guest rooms or villas.** ⊠ *Puntacana Resort and Club, ground fl. of Clubhouse* ⊕ *www.puntacana.com, sixsensesspa.com* ☉ *Daily 9 am–8 pm.*

SAMANÁ PENINSULA

Shopping isn't a big draw in Samaná, in general, but Las Terrenas has the most shops. They mainly sell souvenirs aimed at tourists.

SPAS

NI Spa & Salon. Walk up the steel, spiral staircase to a haven of peace, with New Age music, a professional staff dressed in white, and a chic, sparkling clean environment. Still moderately priced for the quality of the treatments, NI is one of the island's best spa values. Within its 3,500 square feet is a couples' treatment room and a boutique fitness center. When you're finished with your therapeutic and pleasurable treatments, head to the full-service beauty salon to get ready for that special night out. ⊠ *Bannister Hotel, Puerto Bahia Marina, Carretera Sanchez Km. 5, Santa Bárbara de Samaná* ☎ *809/503–6363.*

SPORTS AND ACTIVITIES

11

Although there's hardly a shortage of activities here, the resorts have virtually cornered the market on sports, including every conceivable water sport. In some cases, facilities may be available only to guests of the resorts.

BASEBALL

Baseball is a national passion, and Sammy Sosa is still a legend in his own time. But he is just one of many celebrated Dominican baseball heroes, including pitcher Odalis Revela. Triple-A Dominican and Puerto Rican players and some American major leaguers hone their skills in the D.R.'s professional Winter League, which plays from October through January. Some games are held in the Tetelo Vargas Stadium, in the town of San Pedro de Macorís, east of Boca Chica.

Estadio Francisco A. Michelli. Estadio Francisco A. Michelli is La Romana's baseball stadium. Know that *la temporada* (the season) is short; your window of opportunity is just October through December, with an occasional game in January. ⊠ *Av. Padre Abreu, near monument, La Romana* ☎ *809/556–6188.*

Liga de Béisbol Stadiums. Liga de Béisbol Stadiums can be a helpful information source if you're planning an independent trip to a baseball game. ⊠ *Santo Domingo* ☎ *809/567–6371.*

BIKING AND HIKING

Pedaling is easy on pancake-flat beaches, but there are also some steep hills in the D.R. Several resorts rent bikes to guests and nonguests alike.

NORTH COAST

Fodor's Choice
★

Iguana Mama. Iguana Mama's offerings include mountain bike tours that will take you along the coastal flats or test your mettle on steeper climbs in the National Parks. Downhill bike rides—which include a taxi up to 3,000 feet, breakfast and lunch—cost $99 for a full-day trip, $70 for a half-day trip without lunch. Advanced rides, on and off road, are $55 to $95.

Other half- and full-day trips—which range in price from $89 to $195—include hiking, swimming, climbing up and jumping off various waterfalls, rappelling, and natural waterslides. Guided day hikes cost $35 to $75; a three-day hike to the Caribbean's tallest peak, Pico Duarte in Jarabacoa, is $450. This well-established, safety-oriented company also offers horseback riding on the beach of Cabarete and in the countryside (from $45 for two hours), white-water rafting, ecotours, and lots of other adventure sports. ⊠ *Calle Principal 74(across from Scotia Bank), Cabarete, Dominican Republic* ☎ *809/571–0908, 809/571–0734, 809/654–2325* ⊕ *www.iguanamama.com.*

BOATING

Sailing conditions are ideal, with constant trade winds. Favorite excursions include day trips to Catalina and Saona islands—both in La Romana area—and sunset cruises on the Caribbean. Prices for crewed sailboats of 26 feet and longer, with a capacity of 4 to 12 people, are fixed according to size and duration, from a low of $200 a day to the norm of $700 a day. Examples of other prices, taken from the fleet at the upscale Cap Cana Marina, are as follows: sportfishermen from 47 to 51 feet accommodating up to eight people (crewed with all equipment, snacks, and beverages with sandwiches on all day trips), $1,800 for four hours, $2,500 for eight hours; a 62-foot custom, luxury power-sail catamaran, $1,650 for two hours (everything included for Cap Cana guests); a 56-foot Sea Ray Sedan Bridge motor yacht, $2,000 for two hours, $2,500 for four hours, $3,500 for eight hours (everything included); and a luxury 90-foot custom motor yacht, ideal for an incentive group, $3,500 for two hours, $5,000 for four hours, $8,500 for eight hours.

SOUTHEAST COAST

Casa de Campo Marina. Casa de Campo Marina has much going on, from sailing to motor yachting and socializing at the Casa de Campo Yacht Club. A first for the marina was hosting the Rolex FARR 40 World's Championship in April 2010. One of the world's most important annual sailing events, this was the first time it had come to the Caribbean. ⊠ *Casa de Campo, Calle Barlovento 3, La Romana* ☎ *809/523–3333, 809/523–3333* ⊕ *www.casadecampo.com.do.*

NORTH COAST

Carib Wind Cabarete. A renowned windsurfing center (known for decades as BIC Center) Carib Wind Cabarete has been operating since 1988. In the last decade it has transformed into a high performance Olympic training center for Laser sailors from around the world. Here you can rent Lasers, 17-foot catamarans, bodyboards, ocean kayaks, and paddle boards. ⊠ *Cabarete* ☎ *809/571–0640* ⊕ *www.caribwind.com.*

SAMANÁ PENINSULA

Puerto Bahia Marina. This stunning marina on the north end of pristine Samaná Bay is a relatively new entity and is a first-class, full-service facility with slips from 40 to 150 feet. This marina not only has the necessary amenities, including fuel, restrooms with showers, 24-hour security, garbage pick-up, Internet access, water taxis, car rentals, but all the services and facilities of the Bannister Hotel. ⊠ *Carretera Sanchez-Samaná, Km 5, Santa Bárbara de Samaná* ☎ *809/503–6363, 855/503–6363* ⊕ *www.puertobahiasamana.com.*

DIVING

Ancient sunken galleons, undersea gardens, and offshore reefs are among the lures here. Most divers head to the north shore. In the waters off Sosúa alone you can find a dozen dive sites (for all levels of ability) with such catchy names as Three Rocks (a deep, 163-foot dive), Airport Wall (98 feet), and Pyramids (50 feet). Some dive schools are represented on or near Sosúa Beach, in the town of Bayahibe and in Las Terrenas and Las Galeras on the Samaná Peninsula resorts have dive shops on-site or can arrange trips for you.

NORTH COAST

Northern Coast Aquasports. A five-star, Gold Palm PADI dive center, Northern Coast Aquasports is also the only National Geographic diver certification site in the Dominican Republic. They run diving courses from beginner to instructor level. Professionalism is apparent in the initial classroom and pool practice; classrooms have air-conditioning and DVDs. Successful completion of a three-day course earns you a PADI Open Water Certification card.

The selection of legendary dive sites around beautiful Sosúa Bay, includes reefs, walls, wrecks, and swim-throughs, from 25 to 130 feet. Sosua is close to Cabarete and there are trips to Paradise Island and Du Du Caverns (near Cabrera). Nondivers can snorkel. All activities are guided by (multilingual) PADI professionals. ⊠ *Calle Pedro Clisante #8, Sosúa* ☎ *809/571–1028* ⊕ *www.northerncoastdiving.com.*

SAMANÁ

In 1979 three atolls disappeared after a seaquake off Las Terrenas, providing an opportunity for truly memorable dives. Also just offshore from Las Terrenas are the Islas Las Ballenas (the Whale Islands), a cluster of four little islands with good snorkeling. A coral reef is off Playa Jackson, a beach accessible only by boat.

Las Galeras Divers. This is a professional, safety-conscious operation. Owner Serge is a PADI, OWSI and Nitrox instructor, and every level of PADI course is offered. Diving lessons and trips are offered in English, French, and Spanish, and diving equipment rentals are also available. Single tank dives are $45, two-tank dives $75, but equipment charge for either is an extra $10. Exciting night dives cost $70. Discounts are given to groups, families, and divers who want a package deal. ⊠ *Calle Principal, Las Galeras* ☎ *809/538–0220* ⊕ *www.las-galeras-divers.com.*

Las Terrenas Divers. This PADI and SSI dive center will teach novices as well as take experienced divers night-, canyon-, cave-, wreck-, and deepwater diving. A single dive is approximately $50; daily diving equipment rentals are $10. There are discounts for larger dive packages. Learn-to-dive programs begin at $100; an open-water dive course is $435. The German owner, Hanjo, is multilingual. ⊠ *Hotel Bahía Las Ballenas, Playa Punta Bonita, Las Terrenas* ☎ *809/889–2422* ⊕ *www.lt-divers.com.*

FISHING

Big-game fishing is big in Punta Cana, with blue and white marlin, wahoo, sailfish, and dorado among the most common catches in these waters. Several fishing tournaments are held every summer. The Punta-Cana Resort & Club hosted the ESPN Xtreme Billfishing Tournament for many years. Blue-marlin tournaments are held at La Mona Channel in Cabeza de Toro. Several tour operators offer organized deep-sea fishing excursions.

LA ROMANA

Casa de Campo Marina. Casa de Campo Marina is the best charter option in the La Romana area. Yachts (22 to 60 footers) are available for deep-sea fishing charters for half or full days. Prices go from $708 to $1,591. They can come equipped with rods, bait, dinghies, drinks, and experienced guides. Going out for the big billfish that swim the depths of the Caribbean is a major adrenaline rush. In 2014, (March 21–24) the marina hosted the annual Casa de Campo International Blue Marlin Classic Tournament, which was celebrated with a round of parties. ⊠ *Casa de Campo, Calle Barlovento 3, La Romana* ☎ *809/523–3333, 809/523–3333.*

PUNTA CANA

Puntacana Marina. At the Puntacana Marina, on the southern end of the resort, there are many, many nautical options available for rent, from banana boats and water skiing craft to sport fishing and diving charters. ⊠ *Puntacana Resort & Club, Punta Cana* ☎ *809/959–2262* ⊕ *www.puntacana.com.*

GOLF

Fodor's Choice ★ The D.R. has some of the best courses in the Caribbean, designed by top golf architects; among these leading designers are Pete Dye, P.B. Dye, Jack Nicklaus, Robert Trent Jones, Gary Player, Tom Fazio, Nick Faldo, Tom Watson, and Severiano Ballesteros. The Dominican Republic was voted Golf Destination of the Year by the International Association of Golf Tour Operators (IAGTO) during its IAGTO Awards 2009 celebrations in Spain. IAGTO operators control more than 80% of golf holiday packages sold worldwide. Criteria for choosing the winner included customer satisfaction, quality of courses and accommodations, value for money, support from suppliers and tourist boards, and professional conduct. Most courses charge higher rates during the winter high season; some, but not all, reduce their rates between April and October, so be sure to ask. Also, some have cheaper rates in the afternoon (mornings are cooler). And guests of certain hotels get better prices.

SOUTHEAST COAST

Fodor's Choice ★ **Casa de Campo Resort.** The Resort is considered by most to the premier multiple golf resort in the Caribbean. The famed 18-hole Teeth of the Dog course at Casa de Campo, with seven holes on the sea, is usually ranked as the number-one course in the Caribbean and is among the top courses in the world. Pete Dye regards Teeth of the Dog as one of his best designs and has long enjoyed living there part-time. The Teeth of the Dog requires a caddy for each round and an additional $25 (plus tip). Pete Dye has designed this and two other globally acclaimed courses here. Dye Fore, now with a total of 27 holes, is close to Altos de Chavón, hugging a cliff that features commanding vistas of the sea, a river, Dominican mountains, and the marina. The Links is a gamey 18-hole inland course. Resort guests must reserve tee times for all courses at least one day in advance; nonguests should make reservations earlier. Jim McLean operates a golf school at Casa de Campo; an instructor is on-site year-round. Half- and full-day lessons are available to individuals and groups; one-hour private lessons for adults cost $150. ✉ *Casa de Campo, La Romana* ☎ *809/523–3333 resort, 809/523–8115 golf director* ⊕ *www.casadecampo.com.do* 🏌 *Teeth of the Dog: 18 holes, 6989 yards, par 72; Dye Fore: 18 holes, 7740 yards, par 72; The Links: 18 holes, 6664 yards, par 71* 🏌 *Teeth of the Dog: for nonhotel guests, $325 per round per golfer; for guests, $185 per round per player. Dye Fore: $295 for nonguests, $218 for guests. The Links: $206.50 for nonguests; $182.90 for hotel guests.*

PUNTA CANA

Barceló Bávaro Golf. Integrated within the Barceló Bávaro Beach Golf & Casino Resort complex in the Punta Cana region, this course is open to both resort and nonresort guests. The course traverses a lush inland mangrove forest and features 22 inland lakes and 122 bunkers, and totals 6655 yards. It was actually the first course in the area and was designed by Juan Manuel Gordillo. Complete renovations, executed by designer P. B. Dye in 2010, breathed new life to the layout. The best rates are available for guests of the more upscale Barceló hotels, such as the Barceló Palace Deluxe. Walking is not permitted. ✉ *Barceló Bávaro Beach Golf & Casino Resort, Bávaro* ☎ *809/686–5797* ⊕ *www.barcelobavarogolf.net* 🏌 *18 holes, 6655 yards, par 72* 🏌 *Barceló guests, $65 for 18 holes; nonguests, $145.*

Catalonia Caribe Golf Club. Challenging and reasonably priced, Catalonia Caribe Golf Club is spread out on greens surrounded by five lakes and an abundance of shady palms. It's a relatively short course and features an island green. The architect, Alberto Sola, designed it to be challenging for both experienced and novice golfers. Rates include a cart. ✉ *Catalonia Bávaro Resort, Cabeza de Toro, Bávaro* ☎ *809/321–7059* ⊕ *www.cataloniabavaro.com* 🏌 *18 holes, 6950 yards, par 72* 🏌 *Catalonia Resort guests: $80 for 18 holes; nonresort guests: $130.*

Corales Golf Club. Corales Golf Club is "the Augusta National of the Caribbean" with expansive finely landscaped grounds. Designed by Tom Fazio it's a dramatic 18-hole course with six Caribbean seaside holes with a finishing hole that encourages players to cut off as much of the Caribbean as they dare off the tee. Laid out along the natural cliffs and coves of the sea and inland lakes and Coralina quarries, the 700 acres here are part of the extensive Puntacana Resort & Club. The club is open to its members and their guests, guests of Tortuga Bay, and Puntacana Resort guests who purchase the resort's Golf Experience packages. Caddies are mandatory at Corales. Inquiries and tee-time requests can be made by emailing golfcorales@puntacana.com. ✉ *Puntacana Resort & Club, Punta Cana* ☎ *809/959–4653* ⊕ *www. puntacana.com* 🏌 *18 holes, 7555 yards, par 72* 🏌 *Resort guests: from $275 in season and $195 during the off-season. Subject to availability, the Corales Golf Club accepts a limited number of external guests with a rate of $380 in season and $280 off-season.*

Fodor's Choice
★ **La Cana Golf Club.** You'll love the ocean views on 14 of La Cana Golf Club's 27 holes of championship golf designed by P. B. Dye. The three 9s: Tortuga, Hacienda, and Arrecife make for a very popular offering, particularly the oceanside finish on La Cana Nine. The latest nine, Hacienda, opened in January 2012, not as a full course but rather a set of nine individual holes; it is punctuated with many lakes amidst an unspoiled tropical landscape, a challenging addition to the existing, spectacular courses. All fees include a golf cart, taxes, and use of the expansive practice facility. Multiple round/twilight packages are available as well. Caddies are optional. Lessons and golf schools are offered by PGA professional staff. Rental clubs are available and reserve two weeks in advance from November through April. Golf packages may also include the nearby Corales Golf Course. ⊠ *Puntacana Resort & Club, Punta Cana* ☎ *809/959–2262* ⊕ *www.puntacana.com* ⅄ *27 holes: Tortuga Nine: 9 holes, 3483 yards, par 36; Arrecife Nine: 9 holes, 3676 yards, par 36; Hacienda Nine: 9 holes, 3768 yards, par 36* ⊠ *Resort guests: $135 for 18 holes in season, $105 off-season; nonguests: $175 in season, $140 off-season.*

Fodor's Choice
★ **Punta Espada Golf Course.** Jack Nicklaus casts his mark in the Caribbean with the magnificent Punta Espada Golf Course. You will discover a par-72 challenge with striking bluffs, lush foliage, and many gently tumbling fairways with spectacular water vistas. Incidentally, the water often does come into play. Having hosted the Champions Tour, the course is even better in person than it looks on TV, and you won't find smoother putting surfaces! Yes, there's a Caribbean view from all the holes, and eight of them play right along the sea. The course's length can be extended to nearly 7400 yards, but it's advisable to play a more forward tee. This exceptional golf club has concierge services, a restaurant, the Hole 19 bar, a pro shop, a members' trophy gallery, a library, lockers, an equipment repair shop, and a meeting room. Rates are discounted for guests in any of Cap Cana's accommodations and include golf cart, caddy, tees, water, and practice on the driving range. In high season, reservations are required and it's best to make them two weeks in advance for tee times. ⊠ *Cap Cana, Carretera Juanillo, Playa Juanillo* ☎ *809/221–1290 Ext. 2000* ⊕ *www.capcana.com* ⅄ *18 holes, 7396 yards, par 72* ⊠ *Resort guests:$225 ($160 after 2 pm); nonguests: $375 ($250 after 2 pm).*

NORTH COAST

Playa Dorada Golf Club. *Golf Digest* has named Playa Dorada Golf Club one of the top 100 courses outside the United States. It's open to guests of all the hotels in the area. Greens fees for 9 holes are $47, 18 holes $79; caddies are mandatory for foursomes and will cost about $15 for 18 holes, $8 for 9 (plus tip); carts are optional, at $24 and $18, for 18 or 9 holes, respectively. The attractive clubhouse has lockers, a pro shop, a bar, and a restaurant. Reservations during high season should be made as far in advance as possible. Guests at certain hotels in the Playa Dorada complex get discounts. ⊠ *Next door to Victoria Resort, Playa Dorada* ☎ *809/320–4262* ⊕ *www. playadoradagolf.com.*

Playa Grande Golf Course. Enjoy 10 holes that interface with the Atlantic at the Playa Grande Golf Course. Some describe the layout, located between Río San Juan and Cabrera on the North Coast, as "the Pebble Beach of the Caribbean" because it also features oceanside cliffs reaching 60-feet. The challenge has lots of muscle extending to more than 7000 yards and carries the signature of Robert Trent Jones Sr. (At this writing, only nine holes are available as the back is being renovated.) Fees include the cost of a mandatory cart. Caddies are also mandatory and cost an additional $20 for 18 holes, or $12 for 9, plus tip. Dress code dictates no tank tops, bikinis, or cutoffs. There's a pro shop as well as an open-air bar and restaurant offering a few dishes, including fish and burgers. ■TIP→ **Know that in the winter this course is heavily booked so call as far in advance as possible to find a time slot.** ✉ *Carretera Río San Juan–Cabrera, Km 9, Cabrera* ☎ *809/582–0860* ⊕ *www.playagrande.com* ⚑ *18 holes, 7090 yards, par 72* ✍ *$50 for 9 holes and $75 for 2 plays.*

GUIDED TOURS

Visitors to the Dominican Republic will have a plethora of excursions to choose from, but many options are not wonderful and are overpriced. Wait until you arrive before booking anything. As for group excursions, "interview" fellow guests to find out if their tour was worth the money and effort. Often the full-day excursions are too long and leave too early. Best are half-day trips—particularly boat excursions. Horseback riding can sound appealing, as the trails usually include some stretches of beach, but do not envision superior horseflesh, tack, instruction, or even guides who can speak English. And whatever, just enjoy! Clients traveling on a tour-company package tend to book excursions with the same company, or through the company affiliated with their resort.

SANTO DOMINGO

Private tours are a good option in Santo Domingo, but you will have to pay more than $125 a day for a guide—more if the tour guide works with a driver. Your hotel concierge can best arrange these for you, and he or she will know the best English-speaking guides. Be sure you hire a guide who is licensed by the government.

SOUTHEAST COAST

Tropical Tours. The primary tour operator on the Southeast Coast is Tropical Tours (with headquarters at Casa de Campo in La Romana), whose prices are even less than some nonpros and some cruise-ship excursions. Their vans are new or nearly new and well-maintained. Also, most of their staff speaks English as well as other languages. They can take you on a tour of Santo Domingo, and to fascinating caves.

Although most water-based excursions (outback safaris and zip lining too) now go through the concierges at Casa de Campo, they do have a new trip to the Marineaquarium and Reef Explorer where brave-hearts can swim with the sharks. The company also provides transfers to Las Americas and Punta Cana International Airports; $140 for 1–4 persons or a mere $28 per person for 5 or more. ✉ *Casa de Campo, La Romana* ☎ *809/523–2029, 809/523–2028* ⊕ *tropicaltoursromana.com.do.*

PUNTA CANA

Fodor'sChoice ★ **Amstar DMC–Apple Vacations.** Amstar is well-managed and reliable, and it is associated with Apple Vacations, a major player that packages all-inclusive vacations in the D.R., particularly in Punta Cana. ⊠ *Carretera Bávaro, Bávaro* ☎ *809/221–6626* ⊕ *www.amstardmc.com.*

Fodor'sChoice ★ **Go Golf Tours (GGT).** Go Golf has services tailored to clients seeking to make golf part of their getaway—whether it's the primary focus or just a one-time outing; the company will help arrange tee times, golf instruction, and transport to courses in Punta Cana or Casa de Campo by private driver at costs that are usually considerably less than those in a private taxi. ⊠ *Cocotal Golf & Country Club, Bávaro* ☎ *809/687–4653, 855/374–4653 toll-free in U.S., 809/200–9556 toll-free in D.R.* ⊕ *www.golfreservationcenter.com.*

NORTH COAST

Alf's Tours. In Sosúa, Alf's Tours has been a mainstay for years. Why? It only has multilingual, licensed tour guides, and it's open daily (9 am– 7 pm). Plus, it has excursions all over the island for moderate prices, and they offer complimentary pickup service at any hotel in Sosua, Puerto Plata, and Cabarete. Vehicles are closer to new than old, and guests are insured whether they are going to the famous waterfall, El Limon in Las Terrenas, or hopping aboard a Funny Buggy. They are now booking hotels, too. ⊠ *Eugenio Kunhardt 68, El Batey, Sosúa* ☎ *809/571–1461.*

Flora Tours. Considered one of the better tour operators in Las Terrenas, Flora Tours can arrange boating and guided hiking trips like to cacao plantations. A trip to the El Limón waterfall includes taxi pickup at your hotel, round-trip transportation, a horse, a meal and guides' tips. The company also arranges snorkeling trips to various beaches nearby. Their specialty is excursions to Los Haitises National Park, which leave on Wednesday and Saturday, but they also take clients whale-watching (January 1–March 15), on a safe catamaran with dual engines. In addition, this well-established, safety-oriented company offers daily ATV excursions into the mountains, where you rarely encounter any other tourists. They also go to Playa Moron by ATV. Flora will begin a new adventure, kayaking on a river coupled with a safari to a rice plantation and beyond. ⊠ *#278, Calle Principal Duarte, Las Terrenas* ☎ *809/240– 5482* ⊕ *www.flora-tours.net.*

HORSEBACK RIDING

SOUTHEAST COAST

Equestrian Center at Casa de Campo. The 250-acre Equestrian Center at Casa de Campo has something for both Western and English riders—a dude ranch, a rodeo arena (where Casa's trademark "Donkey Polo" is played), polo fields, guided trail rides, and jumping, riding and polo lessons. Guided rides run about $56 an hour, $88 for two hours; lessons cost $65 an hour, and jumping lessons are $88 an hour or $55 a half-hour. There are early morning and sunset trail rides, too. Handsome, old-fashioned carriages are available for hire as well. Unlimited horseback riding is included if you are a hotel guest staying on the all-inclusive plan. Great for families, trail rides are offered through the property's private cattle ranch, and upon request, can include a classy, catered lunch. ⊠ *Casa de Campo, La Romana* ☎ *809/523–3333* ⊕ *www.casadecampo.com.do.*

PUNTA CANA

Adventures Land. Long-established, the former Southfork Ranch (Rancho Pat), which has been the stable of choice for many visitors, is now a part of the Barceló resort complex (though the French owners are still the same). Trail rides are taken along Barceló's "private" beach and on open country roads. Prices begin at $55 per hour; for $15 more you get another hour. Morning rides start out at 9 am (and include a mojito break at a typical bar). Another includes an exploratory mission to Taíno caves and culminates in a lobster beach cookout ($130). Then there is the memorable sunset beach ride, which can end with a beach bonfire barbecue ($100). If you like speed and don't mind getting dusty, go for the outback adventures on the powerful quads or tamer buggies—or play it safer and discover the Dominican countryside in a Jeep. These multi-option activities are ideal for family groups. ⊠ *Barceló Resort Complex, Bávaro* ☎ *809/223–8896* ⊕ *adventures-puntacana.com.*

Rancho Punta Cana. Rancho Punta Cana is across from the main entrance of the resort. A one-hour trail ride winds along the beach, the golf course, and through tropical forests. The two-hour jungle trail ride has a stopover at a lagoon fed by a natural spring, so wear your swimsuit under your long pants. You can also do a three-hour full-moon excursion or take riding lessons. The stock is comprised of Paso Finos. ⊠ *Puntacana Resort & Club, Punta Cana* ☎ *809/959–9221* ⊕ *www.puntacana.com.*

NORTH COAST

Sea Horse Ranch Equestrian Center. This equestrian center is a professional, well-staffed operation. The competition ring is built to international regulations, and there is a large schooling ring. Lessons, including dressage instruction, start at $35 an hour, and endurance rides are $30 for 90 minutes, $50 for three hours, including drinks and snacks—but make reservations. The most popular ride includes stretches of beach and a bridle path across a neighboring farm's pasture that's full of wildflowers and butterflies. Feel free to tie your horse to a palm tree and jump into the waves. ⊠ *Sea Horse Ranch, Coastal Hwy., Cabarete* ☎ *809/571–3880, 809/571–4462* ⊕ *www.sea-horse-ranch.com.*

WHALE-WATCHING

SAMANÁ PENINSULA

Humpback whales come to Samaná Bay to mate and give birth each year for a relatively limited period, from approximately January 15 through March 30. Samaná Bay is considered one of the top 10 destinations in the world to watch humpbacks. If you're here during the brief season, this can be the experience of a lifetime. You can listen to the male humpback's solitary courting song and witness incredible displays as the whales flip their tails and breach (humpbacks are the most active species of whales in the Atlantic).

Fodor's Choice **Whale Samaná.** Whale Samaná is owned by Kim Beddall, a Canadian
★ who is incredibly knowledgeable about whales and Samaná in general,
having lived here for decades. Her operation is far and away the region's
best, most professional, and environmentally sensitive. On board Pura
Mia, a 55-foot motor vessel, a marine mammal specialist narrates and
answers questions in several languages. Kim herself conducts almost
all the English-speaking trips. The $59 price does not include the $3
Marine Mammal Sanctuary entrance fee (price is subject to change).
Normal departure times are 9 am for the morning trip and 1:30 pm
for the afternoon trip, but she is flexible whenever possible for cruise
ship passengers, yet does require advance reservations. ⊠ *Across street
from town dock, beside park, Calle Sra. Morellia Kelly, Santa Bárbara
de Samaná* ☎ *809/538–2042* ⊕ *www.whaleSamana.com.*

GRENADA

with Carriacou

WELCOME TO GRENADA

THE SPICE ISLAND

A small, mountainous island, Grenada is 21 miles (34 km) long and 12 miles (19 km) wide; much of the interior is covered by verdant rain forest. Grenada is a major producer of nutmeg, cinnamon, mace, cocoa, and other spices and flavorings. Carriacou—23 miles (37 km) north of Grenada—comprises just 13 square miles (34 square km). Tiny Petite Martinique is 2 miles (3 km) farther north.

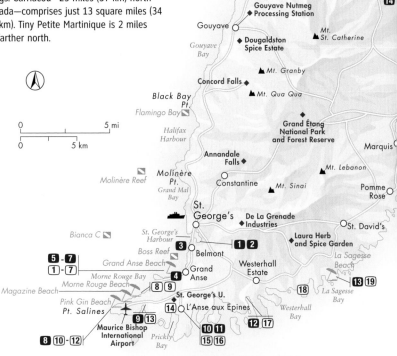

These days, local people on the Isle of Spice busy themselves cultivating nutmeg, cloves, and other spices. Renowned for its natural beauty, its fragrant air, and its friendly people, Grenada has lovely beaches and plenty of outdoor and cultural activities. Vestiges of its briefly turbulent past have all but disappeared.

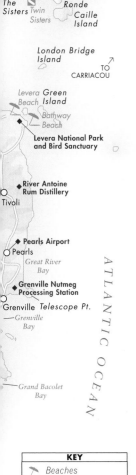

KEY

⌐ *Beaches*

⚓ *Cruise Ship Terminal*

◹ *Dive Sites*

❶ *Restaurants*

① *Hotels*

TOP REASONS TO VISIT GRENADA

1 Old and New: Grenada successfully blends an "original" Caribbean atmosphere with all of the comforts and amenities that you expect today.

2 The Aroma: The scent of spices fills the air, perfumes the soap, improves the drinks, and even flavors the ice cream.

3 Nature Abounds: Spot monkeys in the mountains, watch birds in the rain forest, join fish in the sea, and build sand castles on the beach.

4 Local Hospitality: Grenadians go out of their way to make you feel welcome.

5 A Great Getaway: With no megaresorts, you really can get away from it all.

Updated by
Jane E. Zarem

Independent since 1974, the lush, green isle of Grenada
has developed a healthy tourism sector and a modern infrastructure, including welcoming hotels and resorts, good
roads, up-to-date technology, and reliable utilities.

The nation of Grenada actually consists of three islands: Grenada, the largest, has a population of about 103,000; Carriacou (*car*-ree-a-coo), north of Grenada, has a population of just over 6,000; and Petite Martinique has a population of about 500. Carriacou and Petite Martinique are popular for day trips, fishing adventures, or diving and snorkeling excursions, but most of the tourist activity is on the island of Grenada itself. People interested in a really quiet, get-away-from-it-all vacation will, however, appreciate the simple pleasures of Carriacou during an extended stay.

The island of Grenada has 45 beaches and countless secluded coves. Crisscrossed by nature trails and laced with spice plantations, its mountainous interior is made up mostly of a nature preserve and rain forest. St. George's, the capital, is one of the most picturesque cities in the Caribbean; Grand Anse is one of the region's finest beaches.

Although Christopher Columbus never set foot on Grenada, he did sight it in 1498, naming it Concepción. Spanish sailors following in his wake renamed it Granada, after the city in the hills of their homeland. Adapted to Grenade by French colonists, the transformation of the name to Grenada was completed by the British in the 18th century.

Throughout the 17th century, Grenada was the scene of many bloody battles between the indigenous Carib Indians and the French. Rather than surrender to the Europeans after losing their last battle in 1651, the Caribs committed mass suicide by leaping off a cliff that's now called Carib's Leap or Leapers Hill. The French were later overwhelmed by the British in 1762, the beginning of a seesaw of power between the two nations. The Treaty of Versailles in 1783 ultimately granted Grenada to the British. Almost immediately, thousands of African slaves were brought in to work the sugar plantations (although slavery in Grenada actually began with the French colonization in 1650). Slavery on the island was finally abolished in 1834.

LOGISTICS

Getting to Grenada and Carriacou: Nonstop flights to Grenada are available several times per week from New York and Miami. Otherwise, connect through Barbados or another nearby island via a regional airline. Fairly frequent (20 minutes each way) air service on small planes and a daily ferry (105 minutes each way) connect Grenada and Carriacou.

Hassle Factor: Medium for Grenada, medium-high for Carriacou.

On the Ground: Maurice Bishop International Airport (GND), at Point Salines on the southwestern tip of

Grenada, is a modern facility suitable for the largest jets. Best of all, it's no more than a 10-minute drive from most hotels and resorts. On Carriacou, just west of Hillsborough, Lauriston Airport (CRU) has a lighted landing strip that accommodates small planes, with a small building for ticket sales and shelter. A $4 departure tax is payable in cash when leaving Carriacou by air.

On Grenada, taxis are always available for transportation between the airport and hotels.

At Carriacou's airport, taxis meet every plane.

12

Forts on which the French began construction, in order to protect St. George's Harbour during their colonization of Grenada, were later completed and used by the British during theirs. Today Ft. George and Ft. Frederick are two of the most visited sites in St. George's. Besides their historical interest, the two locations have magnificent views of the harbor, the capital city itself, and the distant mountains and countryside. Not a single shot was fired from either fort for more than two centuries. In 1983, however, Prime Minister Maurice Bishop and seven others were murdered at Ft. George during a coup d'état. That event triggered the request from Grenada's governor-general and the heads of state of neighboring islands for U.S. troops to intervene, which they did on October 25, 1983.

From that time forward, Grenada's popularity as a vacation destination has increased with each decade, as travelers continue to seek friendly, exotic islands to visit. Most hotels, resorts, and restaurants in Grenada are family-owned and -run (mostly by Grenadians); their guests often become good friends. All Grenadians, in fact, have a well-deserved reputation for their friendliness, hospitality, and entrepreneurial spirit.

PLANNING

WHEN TO GO

The high season stretches from December 15 to April 15. In the off-season, prices at Grenada resorts may be discounted by up to 40%. In September and early October, some hotels close for annual maintenance and renovations. There are fewer seasonal rate changes on Carriacou, where the small hotels and guesthouses are all relatively inexpensive anyway.

GETTING HERE AND AROUND

AIR TRAVEL

Nonstop flights to Grenada are available from New York and Miami. Regional flights between Grenada and Carriacou and between Grenada and neighboring islands operate several times each day.

Airline Contacts American Airlines. American flies nonstop to Grenada from Miami several times a week, with connecting service through Miami from other major cities. ☎ 473/444–2121, 800/744–0006 ⊕ www.aa.com. **Caribbean Airlines.** Caribbean provides service several times a week from New York, Ft. Lauderdale, Miami, and Orlando via Port-of-Spain, Trinidad. ☎ 800/744–2225 ⊕ www.caribbean-airlines.com. **Delta Air Lines.** From mid-December through August, Delta provides nonstop service from New York. ☎ 800/241–4141 ⊕ www.delta.com. **LIAT.** LIAT offers frequent scheduled service linking Grenada with more than a dozen neighboring islands. ☎ 473/444–4121, 888/844–5428 ⊕ www.liat.com. **SVG Air.** SVG Air flies between Grenada and Carriacou, as well as between Grenada and Union Island, Canouan, or Bequia in the Grenadines with connecting flights between Union Island and St. Vincent or Barbados. ☎ 473/444–3549, 800/744–7285, 473/443–8519 in Carriacou ⊕ www.svgair.com.

Airport Contacts Lauriston Airport (CRU). ✉ Carriacou ☎ 473/443–6306. **Maurice Bishop International Airport** (GND). ✉ Point Salines, St. George ☎ 473/444–4101.

Transfers On Grenada, taxis are always available for transportation between the airport and hotels. Fares to St. George's are $25; to the hotels of Grand Anse and L'Anse aux Épines, $15. Rides taken between 6 pm and 6 am incur a $4 surcharge. On Carriacou, taxis meet every plane; the fare to Hillsborough is $8; to Bogles, $13; to Tyrell Bay or Windward, $15.

CAR TRAVEL

On Grenada, having a car or jeep is a real convenience if you're staying at a resort in a location other than Grand Anse, which has frequent minibus service. If you don't have a car of your own, the round-trip taxi rides can get expensive if you plan to leave the resort frequently for shopping, meals, or visiting other beaches. Driving is also a reasonable option if you want to explore the island on your own. Most of Grenada's 650 miles (1,050 km) of paved roads are kept in fairly good condition—although they are steep, curving, and narrow beyond the Grand Anse area. Driving is on the left, British-style. Gas stations are in St. George's, Grand Anse, Grenville, Gouyave, and Sauteurs.

Renting a Car: To rent a car on Grenada, you need a valid driver's license and a temporary local permit (available at the Central Police Station on the Carenage in the capital city of St. George's and at most car-rental firms), which costs $12 (EC$30). You can rent a car on Carriacou, even for just a few hours, but it's easier to take taxis.

Some rental agencies impose a minimum age (18 or 21). Rental cars, including four-wheel-drive vehicles, cost $50 to $75 a day or $330 to $375 a week with unlimited mileage—rates are slightly lower in the low season. In high season there may be a three-day minimum rental. Rental agencies offer free pickup and drop-off at either the airport or your hotel.

12

Contacts on Grenada **Indigo Car Rentals** ☎ 473/439–3300
⊕ www.indigocarsgrenada.com. **McIntyre Bros. Ltd.** ☎ 473/444–3944
⊕ www.caribbeanhorizons.com. **ROC Rentals** ☎ 473/444–4786
⊕ www.rocrentalsgrenada.com. **Y & R Car Rentals** ☎ 473/444–4448
⊕ www.carrentalgrenada.com.

Contacts on Carriacou **Barba's Auto Rentals** ⊠ L'Esterre, Carriacou
☎ 473/407–5156. **Franklyn's Auto Rentals** ⊠ L'Esterre, Carriacou ☎ 473/407–
8496. **Wayne's Auto Rentals** ⊠ Hillsborough, Carriacou ☎ 473/443–6120.

FERRY TRAVEL

Osprey Express. The high-speed ferry Osprey Express makes one round-trip voyage daily from Grenada to Carriacou and on to Petite Martinique. The fare for the 105-minute trip from Grenada to Carriacou is $31 each way. For the 15-minute trip from Carriacou to Petite Martinique, the fare is $12 each way. The boat departs Grenada from the Carenage in St. George's Monday–Saturday at 9 am and Sunday at 8 am; the return trip leaves Carriacou at 3:30 pm. ⊠ The Carenage, St. George's, St. George ☎ 473/440–8126 ⊕ www.ospreylines.com.

TAXIS

On Grenada, taxis are plentiful, and rates are set. The trip between Grand Anse and St. George's is $20. A $4 surcharge is added for rides taken between 6 pm and 6 am. Taxis can be hired at an hourly rate of $30, as well.

In Carriacou the taxi fare from the jetty in Hillsborough to Belair is $10; to Prospect, Tyrell Bay, or Windward, $13. Carriacou minibus drivers will take up to four people on a 2½-hour island tour for $75.

ALTERNATIVE TRANSPORTATION

The best way to travel between Grenada and Carriacou is by air or high-speed ferry, but if you're looking for adventure and economy rather than comfort and speed—and aren't prone to motion sickness—then cargo boats from Grenada to Carriacou are another option. The cargo boat Amelia departs from the Carenage in St. George's every Wednesday and Saturday at 10 am for the four-hour voyage to Carriacou; the return trip to Grenada departs from Carriacou on Monday and Thursday at 10 am. The fare between Grenada and Carriacou on these boats is $15 each way.

Reservations aren't necessary, but get to the wharf before 10 am to be sure you don't miss the boat.

Water taxis are available along the Esplanade, near the port area. For about $8 (EC$20) a motorboat will transport you on a quick and picturesque cruise between St. George's and the jetty at Grand Anse Beach. Water taxis are privately owned, unregulated, and don't follow any particular schedule—so make arrangements for a pickup time if you expect a return trip.

ESSENTIALS

Banks and Exchange Services Grenada uses the Eastern Caribbean dollar (EC$). The official exchange rate is fixed at EC$2.67 to US$1; for convenience, taxis, shops, and hotels sometimes use a lower rate (EC$2.50). You can exchange money at banks and hotels, but major credit cards and U.S. paper currency (no coins) are widely accepted—although you'll get your change in local currency.

Electricity Current on Grenada is 220 volts/50 cycles. U.S. standard appliances (110 volts) require a transformer and adapter plug. For dual-voltage computers and other devices, you'll still need an adapter plug; most hotels will lend adapters.

Language English is the official language in Grenada.

Passport Requirements To enter Grenada, visitors must produce a valid passport and a return or onward ticket.

Phones The area code for Grenada and Carriacou is 473. Prepaid phone cards can be used for local or international calls from special card phones located throughout the Caribbean; the phone cards are sold in denominations of EC$20 ($7.50), EC$30 ($12), EC$50 ($20), and EC$75 ($28) at shops, attractions, transportation centers, and other convenient outlets. For international calls using a major credit card, dial 111; to place a collect call or use a calling card, dial 800/225–5872 from any telephone.

Taxes and Service Charges Grenada has a 10% V.A.T. (value-added tax) on hotel bills and a 15% V.A.T. on restaurant bills and retail sales. In addition, a 10% service charge is often added to hotel and restaurant bills.

Tipping If there is no service charge, then tip 10%; if a service charge has been included, additional tipping is optional: bellhops, $1 per bag; housekeeping, $1 or $2 per night; taxi drivers and tour guides, 10% of the fare or fee.

ACCOMMODATIONS

Grenada's tourist accommodations are located, for the most part, in the southwestern part of the island—primarily on or near Grand Anse Beach or overlooking small bays along the island's southern coast. Carriacou is a small island, and its hotels and guesthouses are primarily in or around Hillsborough.

Guesthouses: Small guesthouses predominate on Carriacou, where no property has more than 25 rooms.

Luxury Resorts: Grenada has a handful of luxurious inns and resorts. Spice Island Beach Resort on Grand Anse Beach is one of the finest boutique resorts in the Caribbean.

Modest Resorts and Apartment Complexes: Most resorts and hotels on Grenada are small, and many are modest; but that is part of their charm.

HOTEL AND RESTAURANT PRICES

Prices in the restaurant reviews are the average cost of a main course at dinner or, if dinner is not served, at lunch; taxes and service charges are generally included. Prices in the hotel reviews are the lowest cost of a standard double room in high season, excluding taxes, service charges, and meal plans (except at all-inclusives). Prices for rentals are the lowest per-night cost for a one-bedroom unit in high season.

For expanded lodging reviews and current deals, visit Fodors.com.

VISITOR INFORMATION

Contacts Grenada Hotel & Tourism Association ☎ 473/444–1353 ⊕ *www.gogrenada.gd.* **Grenada Tourism Authority** ☎ 800/927-9554 ⊕ *www.grenadagrenadines.com.* **Grenada Tourism Authority** ✉ *Burns Point, south end of Carenage, St. George's* ☎ 473/440-2001, 473/440-2279, 800/927-9554 ⊕ *www.grenadagrenadines.com* ✉ *Maurice Bishop International Airport, Point Salines, St. George* ☎ 473/444-4140 ✉ *Main St., Hillsborough, Carriacou* ☎ 473/443-7948.

WEDDINGS

Three days' residency is required to get a marriage license; no blood test is necessary. For scuba-loving couples, the Flamboyant Hotel will arrange an underwater ceremony, with a dive-certified pastor included, at the Underwater Sculpture Park.

EXPLORING

GRENADA

Grenada is divided into six parishes, including one named St. George that includes the communities of Grand Anse, Morne Rouge, True Blue, L'Anse aux Épines, and the capital city of St. George's. When exploring this beautiful island, please note that removing bark from trees, taking wildlife from the forest, and taking coral from the sea are all against the law.

ST. GEORGE'S

Grenada's capital is a bustling West Indian city, much of which remains unchanged from colonial days. Narrow streets lined with shops wind up, down, and across steep hills. Brick warehouses cling to the waterfront, and pastel-painted homes rise from the waterfront and disappear into steep green hills.

Horseshoe-shape **St. George's Harbour,** a submerged volcanic crater, is arguably the prettiest harbor in the Caribbean. Schooners, ferries, and tour boats tie up along the seawall or at the small dinghy dock. **The Carenage** (pronounced car-a-*nahzh*), which surrounds the harbor, is the capital's center. Warehouses, shops, and restaurants line the waterfront. The *Christ of the Deep* statue that sits on the pedestrian plaza at the center of the Carenage was presented to Grenada by Costa Cruise Line in remembrance of its ship, *Bianca C,* that burned and sank in the harbor in 1961; Bianca C is now a popular dive site.

An engineering feat for its time, the 340-foot-long **Sendall Tunnel** was built in 1895 and named for Walter Sendall, an early governor. The narrow tunnel, used by both pedestrians and vehicles, separates the harbor side of St. George's from the Esplanade on the bay side of town, where you will find the markets (produce, meat, and fish), the Cruise Ship Terminal, the Esplanade Mall, and the public bus station.

TOP ATTRACTIONS

Ft. Frederick. Overlooking the city of St. George's and the picturesque harbor, historic Ft. Frederick provides a panoramic view of about one-fourth of Grenada. The fort was started by the French and completed in 1791 by the British; it was also the headquarters of the People's Revolutionary Government before and during the 1983 coup. Today, it's simply a peaceful spot with a bird's-eye view of much of Grenada. ⊠ *Richmond Hill, St. George.*

FAMILY
Fodor's Choice
★

Ft. George. Ft. George is high on the hill at the entrance to St. George's Harbour. Grenada's oldest fort, it was built by the French in 1705 to protect the harbor. No shots were ever fired here until October 1983, when Prime Minister Maurice Bishop and several of his followers were assassinated in the courtyard. The fort now houses police headquarters but is open to the public daily. The 360-degree view of the capital city, St. George's Harbour, and the open sea is spectacular. ⊠ *Church St., St. George's* 🖼 *$2.*

FAMILY
Grenada National Museum. A block from the Carenage, the Grenada National Museum is built on the foundation of a French army barracks and prison that was originally built in 1704. The small museum has exhibitions of news items, photos, and proclamations relating to the 1983 intervention, along with the childhood bathtub of Empress Joséphine (who was born on Martinique), and other memorabilia. ⊠ *Young and Monckton Sts., St. George's, St. George* 🖀 *473/440–3725* 🖼 *$1* ☉ *Weekdays 9–4:30, Sat. 10–1:30.*

Fodor's Choice
★

Market Square. Definitely plan to visit St. George's Market Square, a block from the Cruise Ship Terminal and Esplanade Mall in downtown St. George's. This is the place to buy fresh spices, bottled sauces, and handcrafted gifts and souvenirs to take home. In addition to local spices and heaps of fresh produce, vendors sell baskets, brooms, clothing, knickknacks, coconut water, and more. The market is open every weekday morning but really comes alive on Saturday from 8 to noon. Historically, Market Square is where parades begin and political rallies take place. ⊠ *Granby St., St. George's, St. George.*

St. George's Methodist Church. Built in 1820, the oldest original church building in the city is still in use. It has no spire, unlike the more elaborate churches in St. George's. The building itself was severely damaged by Hurricane Ivan in 2004 but has been completely refurbished. ⊠ *Green St., near Herbert Blaize St., St. George's, St. George.*

St. George's Roman Catholic Church. The Gothic tower of St. George's Roman Catholic Church, the city's most visible landmark, dates from 1818. ⊠ *Church St., St. George's, St. George.*

ELSEWHERE ON GRENADA
TOP ATTRACTIONS

Fodor's Choice
★

Concord Falls. About 8 miles (13 km) north of St. George's, a turnoff from the West Coast Road leads to Concord Falls—actually three separate waterfalls. The first is at the end of the road; when the currents aren't too strong, you can take a dip under the 35-foot cascade. Reaching the two other waterfalls requires an hour's hike into the forest reserve. The third and most spectacular waterfall, at Fountainbleu, thunders 65 feet over huge boulders and creates a small pool. It's smart to hire a guide for that trek. The path is clear, but slippery boulders toward the end can be treacherous without assistance. ⊠ *Off West Coast Rd., Concord, St. John* 🚰 *Changing room $2* ⏱ *Daily 9–5.*

FAMILY
Fodor's Choice
★

Gouyave Nutmeg Processing Station. Touring the nutmeg-processing co-op, right in the center of the west-coast fishing village of Gouyave (pronounced *gwahv*), is a fragrant, fascinating way to spend a half-hour. You can learn all about nutmeg and its uses, see the nutmegs laid out in bins, and watch the workers sort them by hand and pack them into burlap bags for shipping worldwide. The three-story plant turned out 3 million pounds of Grenada's most famous export each year before Hurricane Ivan's devastating effect on the crop in 2004, when most of the nutmeg trees were destroyed. By 2013, production finally began to reach pre-hurricane levels. ⊠ *Palmiste La. (Main Rd.), Gouyave, St. John* 🕾 *473/444–8337* 🚰 *$1* ⏱ *Weekdays 10–1 and 2–4.*

FAMILY
Fodor's Choice
★

Grand Étang National Park & Forest Reserve. A rain forest and wildlife sanctuary deep in the mountainous interior of Grenada, Grand Étang has miles of hiking trails for all levels of ability. There are also lookouts to observe the lush flora and many species of birds and other fauna (including the Mona monkey) and a number of streams for fishing. **Grand Étang Lake** is a 36-acre expanse of cobalt-blue water—1,740 feet above sea level—that fills the crater of an extinct volcano. Although legend has it that the lake is bottomless, maximum soundings have been recorded at just 18 feet. The informative **Grand Étang Forest Center** has displays on the local wildlife and vegetation. A forest ranger is on hand to answer questions; a small snack bar and souvenir stands are nearby. ⊠ *Main interior road, between Grenville and St. George's, St. Andrew* 🕾 *473/440–6160* 🚰 *$1* ⏱ *Daily 8:30–4.*

FAMILY

Laura Herb & Spice Garden. The 6½ acres of gardens here are part of an old plantation at Laura Land, near the village of Perdmontemps in St. David Parish and about 6 miles (10 km) east of Grand Anse. On the 20-minute tour, you will learn all about spices and herbs grown in Grenada—including cocoa, clove, nutmeg, pimiento, cinnamon, turmeric, and tonka beans (sometimes used in vanilla substitutes)—and how they're used for flavoring and for medicinal purposes. ⊠ *Laura Land, St. David* 🕾 *473/443–2604* 🚰 *$2* ⏱ *Weekdays 8–4.*

FAMILY

Spice Basket. Half of the small but fascinating museum at this cultural center and performance venue covers Grenada's heritage—its Amerindian beginnings, its geology (including samples of sand representing all the different hues represented on local beaches), local birds and animals, early tools and implements, sugar and slavery, and the 1979–1983 Grenada Revolution. The other half of the museum is dedicated to cricket, making it "the world's first and only display offering an insight into Caribbean social history through cricket." The memorabilia, some dating to the 1800s, includes uniforms, bats, equipment, and more. It's all very fascinating and definitely worth a visit. A gift shop features locally made items. Spice Basket is in the countryside, not far from Annandale Falls. ⊠ *Beaulieu, St. George* 🕾 *473/437–9000, 473/232–9000* ⊕ *www. spicebasketgrenada.com* 🚰 *$10.*

WORTH NOTING

Annandale Falls. This is a lovely, cool spot for swimming and picnicking. A mountain stream cascades 40 feet into a natural pool surrounded by exotic vines. A paved path leads to the bottom of the falls, and a trail leads to the top. ✉ *Main interior road, 15 mins northeast of St. George's, Annandale, St. George* ☎ *473/440–2452* ✉ *$1* ⊘ *Daily 9–5.*

Carib's Leap. At Sauteurs (the French word for "leapers") on the island's northernmost tip, Carib's Leap (or Leaper's Hill) is the 100-foot vertical cliff from which the last of the indigenous Carib Indians flung themselves into the sea in 1651. After losing several bloody battles with European colonists, they chose suicide over surrender to the French. ✉ *Sauteurs, St. Patrick.*

De La Grenade Industries. In the suburb of St. Paul's, five minutes east of St. George's, De La Grenade produces syrups, jams, jellies, and a liqueur from nutmeg and other homegrown fruits and spices. You're welcome to watch the manufacturing process and stroll around the adjacent herb and spice gardens. ✉ *Morne Délice, St. Paul's, St. George* ☎ *473/440–3241* ⊕ *www.delagrenade.com* ✉ *$5* ⊘ *Weekdays 8–5, Sat. 9–12:30.*

FAMILY **Dougaldston Spice Estate.** Just south of Gouyave, this historic plantation still grows and processes spices the old-fashioned way. You can see cocoa, nutmeg, mace, cloves, and other spices laid out on giant racks to dry in the sun. A worker will be glad to explain the process (and will appreciate a small donation). You can buy spices for about $5 a bag. ✉ *Gouyave, St. John* ✉ *Free* ⊘ *Weekdays 9–4.*

FAMILY **Grand Anse.** A residential and commercial area about 5 miles (8 km) south of downtown St. George's, Grand Anse is named for the world-renowned beach it surrounds. Grenada's tourist facilities—resorts, restaurants, some shopping, and most nightlife—are concentrated in this general area. **Grand Anse Beach** is a 2-mile (3-km) crescent of sand, shaded by coconut palms and sea grape trees, with gentle turquoise surf. A public entrance is at Camerhogne Park, just a few steps from the main road. Water taxis carry passengers between the Esplanade in St. George's and a jetty on the beach. **St. George's University,** which for years held classes at its enviable beachfront location in Grand Anse, now has its sprawling main campus in True Blue, a nearby residential community. ✉ *Grand Anse, St. George.*

FAMILY **Grenville Nutmeg Processing Station.** Like its counterpart in Gouyave, this nutmeg-processing plant is open to the public for guided tours. You can see and learn about the entire process of receiving, drying, sorting, and packing nutmeg. ✉ *Grenville, St. Andrew* ☎ *473/442–7241* ✉ *$1* ⊘ *Weekdays 10–1 and 2–4.*

Levera National Park & Bird Sanctuary. This portion of Grenada's protected parkland encompasses 450 acres at the northeastern tip of the island, where the Caribbean Sea meets the Atlantic Ocean. A natural reef protects swimmers from the rough Atlantic surf at Bathway Beach. Thick mangroves provide food and protection for nesting seabirds and seldom-seen parrots. The southernmost islets of the Grenadines are visible from the beach. ✉ *Levera, St. Patrick* ✉ *Free* ⊘ *Daily dawn–dusk.*

Pearls Airport. Pearls, the island's original airport just north of Grenville on the Atlantic coast, was replaced in 1984 by Maurice Bishop International Airport in Point Salines. Here at Pearls, deteriorating Cuban and Soviet planes sit at the end of the old runway. The planes were abandoned after the 1983 intervention, during which Cuban "advisers" helping to construct the airport at Point Salines were summarily removed from the island. There's a good view north to the Grenadines and a small beach nearby. Interestingly, three decades later, Cuban workers helped build the new Argyll International Airport in neighboring St. Vincent (scheduled to open in 2014) with no similar international reaction. ⊠ *Pearls, St. Andrew.*

River Antoine Rum Distillery. At this rustic operation, kept open primarily as a museum, a limited quantity of Rivers rum is produced by the same methods used since the distillery opened in 1785. River Antoine (pronounced An-*twyne*) is the oldest functioning water-propelled distillery in the Caribbean. The process begins with the crushing of sugarcane from adjacent fields; the discarded canes are used as fuel to fire the boilers. The end result is a potent overproof rum, sold only in Grenada, that will knock your socks off. (A less strong version is also available.) ⊠ *River Antoine Estate, St. Patrick* ☎ 473/442–7109 ⚌ *$2* ☉ *Guided tours daily 9–4.*

Westerhall Estate. Back in the late 1800s, cocoa, sugarcane, coconuts (the oil was used for soap), and limes (used in perfume) were produced on the 951-acre Westerhall Estate, which was then called Bacaye. More recently, Westerhall has focused on rum. The Westerhall Estate tour includes an explanation of the ruins and sugar-processing machinery on the grounds, along with a small museum comprising the eclectic collection of the Grenadian journalist Dr. Alistair Hughes (1919–2005). Particularly interesting items on display in the museum include old rum bottles and labels, Carib artifacts, a number of vintage sewing machines, a World War I Maxim machine gun, and a 1915 Willys Overland automobile. ⊠ *Westerhall* ☎ 473/443–5477 ⊕ *www.westerhallrums.com* ⚌ *$4* ☉ *Mon., Wed., and Fri. 9–3.*

CARRIACOU

Carriacou, the land of many reefs, is a hilly island with neither lakes nor rivers, so its drinking water comes from rainwater caught in cisterns. It gets quite arid during the dry season (January through May). Nevertheless, pigeon peas, corn, and fruit are grown here, and the climate seems to suit the mahogany trees used for furniture making and the white cedar that's critical to the island's famed boatbuilding industry.

The lookout from Belair, with Hillsborough and Carriacou's western coast below

Hillsborough is Carriacou's main town. Just offshore, Sandy Island is one of the nicest beaches around (although recent storms and the gradually rising sea have taken their toll on this tiny spit of land). Almost anyone with a boat can give you a ride out to Sandy Island for a small fee (about $20 round-trip), and you can leave your cares on the dock. Rolling hills cut a wide swath through the middle of Carriacou, from Gun Point in the north to Tyrell Bay in the south.

Despite its tiny size, Carriacou has several distinct cultures. Hillsborough is decidedly English; the southern region, around L'Esterre, reflects French roots; and the northern town of Windward has Scottish ties. African culture, though, is the overarching influence.

WORTH NOTING

Belair. For a great bird's-eye view of Hillsborough and Carriacou's entire west coast, drive to Belair in the north-central part of the island. The vantage point for the magnificent view, 700 feet above sea level, is adjacent to Princess Royal Hospital. On the way to Belair, you'll pass by the photogenic ruins of an old sugar mill. ⊠ *Belair.*

Carriacou Museum. Housed in a building that once held a cotton gin, and just one block from the waterfront, Carriacou's little museum has exhibitions of Amerindian, European, and African artifacts, a collection of watercolors by native folk artist Canute Caliste, and a small gift shop with local items. ⊠ *Paterson St., Hillsborough* ☎ *473/443–8288* 🖃 *$2* ⊙ *Weekdays 10–4.*

High North Nature Reserve. At 955 feet, the highest peak on Carriacou is High North Nature Reserve, a designated national park site that allows breathtaking views as far as Grenada to the south and St. Vincent and all its Grenadines to the north. Visitors can hike the trails, either alone or with a guide, and are likely to encounter iguanas, land tortoises, soldier crabs, and various birds—perhaps even a few macaws—along the way. ⊠ *Windward.*

Tyrell Bay. Tyrell Bay, a waterfront village in Harvey Vale, is a large protected harbor in southwest Carriacou and the official port of entry for yachts. The bay is almost always full of sailboats, powerboats, and working boats—coming, going, or bobbing at their moorings. Restaurants, cafés, and grocery stores face the waterfront. If you take a short boat ride, you will find yourself in the middle of one of the few pristine ecosystems in the region, with oysters growing on the roots of the mangrove trees. ⊠ *Tyrell Bay, Harvey Vale.*

Windward. The small town of Windward is a boatbuilding community on the northeast coast of Carriacou. At certain times of year, primarily during school vacations, you may encounter a work in progress along the roadside. ⊠ *Windward.*

PETITE MARTINIQUE

Ten minutes north of Carriacou by boat or ferry lies the tiny residential island of Petite Martinique. There's a guesthouse or two but no tourist facilities or attractions—just peace and quiet. Meander along the beachfront and watch boatbuilders at work. If by chance there's a boat launching, sailboat race, traditional wedding, holiday, or festival taking place while you're there, you're in for a treat. The music is infectious, the food bountiful, and the spirit lively.

BEACHES

GRENADA

Grenada's best beaches are found along the island's southwestern coastline, which is also where you'll find most of the tourist facilities. Carriacou has lovely beaches that are an easy walk for day-trippers arriving by ferry, but the deserted islands just offshore are the most memorable.

Grenada has some 80 miles (130 km) of coastline, 65 bays, and 45 beaches—many in little coves. The best beaches are just south of St. George's, facing the Caribbean, where most resorts are also clustered. Nude or topless bathing that's done in view of others is against the law.

Bathway Beach. This broad strip of white sand on the northeastern tip of Grenada is part of Levera National Park. A natural coral reef protects swimmers and snorkelers from the rough Atlantic surf; swimming beyond the reef is dangerous. A magnet for local folks on national holidays, the beach is almost deserted at other times. Changing rooms are located at the park headquarters. A vendor or two sometimes sets up shop near the beach, but you're smart to bring your own refreshments. **Amenities:** parking (no fee); toilets. **Best for:** solitude; snorkeling; swimming; walking. ⊠ *Levera National Park, Levera, St. Patrick.*

Fodor's Choice ★ **Grand Anse Beach.** Grenada's loveliest and most popular beach is Grand Anse: a gleaming 2-mile (3-km) semicircle of white sand, lapped by gentle surf, and punctuated by sea grape trees and coconut palms that provide shady escapes from the sun. Brilliant rainbows frequently spill into the sea from the high green mountains that frame St. George's Harbour to the north. Several resorts face the beach, from Flamboyant and Mount Cinnamon at the southern end of the beach to Spice Island Beach Resort, Coyaba Beach Resort, Allamanda Beach Resort, and Radisson Grand Beach Resort as you head north. Several of these hotels have dive shops for arranging dive trips or renting snorkeling equipment. A water-taxi dock is at the midpoint of the beach, along with the Grand Anse Craft & Spice Market, where vendors also rent beach chairs and umbrellas. Restrooms and changing facilities are available at Camerhogne Park, which is the public entrance and parking lot. Hotel guests, cruise-ship passengers, and other island visitors love this beach, as do local people who come to swim and play on weekends. There's plenty of room for everyone. **Amenities:** food and drink; parking (no fee); toilets; water sports. **Best for:** sunset; swimming; walking. ⊠ *3 miles (5 km) south of St. George's, Grand Anse, St. George.*

La Sagesse Beach. Surrounding a sheltered bay along the southeastern coast at La Sagesse Nature Centre, this secluded crescent of the finest (gray) sand on the island is a 30-minute drive from Grand Anse. Surrounded by tropical vegetation, it provides a lovely, quiet refuge. The water is fairly shallow and always calm along the shoreline. Plan a full day of swimming, sunning, and nature walks, with lunch at La Sagesse Inn's restaurant, which is adjacent to the beach. **Amenities:** food and drink; parking (no fee); toilets. **Best for:** solitude; swimming; walking. ⊠ *La Sagesse Nature Center, La Sagesse, St. David.*

Magazine Beach. Not far from the international airport in Point Salines, Magazine Beach is a magnificent strip of pure white sand that stretches from Aquarium Restaurant and Maca Bana Villas at its southern end to the Grenadian by Rex Resort, farther north. Never crowded, it's excellent for swimming and sunbathing; the surf ranges from gentle to spectacular. Cool drinks, snacks, or a full lunch are available at the Aquarium's La Sirena Beach Bar—or stick around for happy hour. You can also rent snorkeling equipment and kayaks there. Access to the beach is next to the restaurant or next to the Rex. **Amenities:** food and drink; toilets; water sports. **Best for:** snorkeling; sunset; swimming; walking. ⊠ *Point Salines, St. George.*

FAMILY **Morne Rouge Beach.** One mile (1½ km) south of Grand Anse, a ½-mile-long (¾-km-long) crescent of pure white sand is tucked away on Morne Rouge Bay. The clear turquoise water is excellent for swimming, and the gentle surf makes this beach perfect for families with small children. Light meals and snacks are available at Gem Holiday Resort's beachfront bar and grill. **Amenities:** food and drink; parking (no fee); toilets. **Best for:** sunset; swimming. ⊠ *Morne Rouge, St. George.*

CARRIACOU

On Carriacou, you'll find beaches within walking distance of the ferry jetty in Hillsborough—miles of soft, white sand that slopes gently down to the warm (average 83°F), calm sea. Carriacou's best beach experience, though, is a day spent swimming, snorkeling, and picnicking on one of the otherwise uninhabited islands just offshore.

Anse La Roche. About a 15-minute hike north from the village of Prospect, on the northwestern tip of Carriacou, this often-deserted beach has white sand, sparkling clear water, and abundant marine life for snorkelers. The beach was named for a huge rock where pelicans gather, so birdwatchers will also be thrilled. And because of its relative inaccessibility, Anse La Roche is never crowded. **Amenities:** none. **Best for:** solitude; snorkeling; swimming; walking. ⊠ *Prospect, Carriacou.*

Hillsborough Beach. Day-trippers (and others) can take a dip at this strip of sand adjacent to the jetty where the ferry docks. The beach extends for quite a distance in each direction, so there's plenty of room to swim without interference from the boat traffic. The best part of the beach is at the northern end, along what's called the Esplanade. Ade's Dream House is across the street from the beach, and snack bars and restaurants are nearby. **Amenities:** food and drink. **Best for:** swimming. ⊠ *Hillsborough, Carriacou.*

Paradise Beach. This long, narrow stretch of beautiful sandy beach in L'Esterre, between Hillsborough and Tyrell Bay, has calm, clear, inviting water. Popular with local folks on weekends, it's very quiet—often deserted—at other times. The Hardwood Bar, at the southern end of the parking lot, serves local specialties for lunch. **Amenities:** food and drink; parking (no fee); showers; toilets. **Best for:** snorkeling; swimming; walking. ⊠ *L'Esterre, Carriacou.*

Fodor's Choice
★
Sandy Island. This is a truly deserted sandbar off Paradise Beach—just a few young palm trees on a spit of pure white, powdery soft sand—except for those who come by boat to snorkel and swim in the sparkling clear water. A 5-square-mile (3-square-km) Marine Protected Area surrounds the island. Arrange transportation to the island (about $20 round-trip) with a local boat owner at the jetty at Hillsborough or the restaurant at Paradise Beach; be sure to arrange the pick-up time! Wear your bathing suit and bring along snorkeling gear and everything else you'll need (sunscreen, towel, hat, shirt, food and water, etc.), making sure to leave only your footprints when you leave. **Amenities:** none. **Best for:** solitude; snorkeling; swimming. ⊠ *L'Esterre Bay, off Paradise Beach, Carriacou.*

White Island. On this deserted island off Carriacou's southeastern coast, your choice of beautiful white sandy beaches and calm Caribbean waters await you. The island is surrounded by reefs and has beaches on all sides except for the eastern (Atlantic Ocean) side, which has a high cliff. Arrange transportation from Tyrell Bay for about $25 to $30 (EC$70) round-trip, and be sure to bring everything you may need. **Amenities:** none. **Best for:** solitude; snorkeling; swimming; walking. ⊠ *Cassada Bay, off southeastern coast, Carriacou.*

WHERE TO EAT

Grenada's crops include all kinds of citrus, mangoes, papaya (called pawpaw here), callaloo (similar to spinach), dasheen (taro, a root vegetable), christophene (a squash, also known as chayote), yams (white, green, yellow, and orange), and breadfruit. All restaurants prepare dishes with local produce and season them with the many spices grown throughout the island. Be sure to try the local flavors of ice cream: soursop, guava, rum raisin, coconut (the best), or nutmeg.

Soups—especially pumpkin and callaloo—are divine and often start a meal. Pepper pot is a savory stew of pork, oxtail, vegetables, and spices. *Oildown,* the national dish, combines salted meat, breadfruit, onions, carrots, celery, dasheen, and dumplings all boiled in coconut milk until the liquid is absorbed and the savory mixture becomes "oily." A roti—curried chicken, beef, or vegetables wrapped in pastry and baked—is similar to a turnover and more popular in Grenada than a sandwich.

Fresh seafood of all kinds is plentiful, including lobster in season (September–April). Conch, known here as *lambi,* often appears curried or in a stew. Crab back, though, is not seafood—it's land crab. Most Grenadian restaurants serve seafood and at least some local dishes.

Rum punches are ubiquitous and always topped with grated nutmeg. Clarke's Court, Rivers, and Westerhall are local rums. Carib, the local beer, is refreshing, light, and quite good. If you prefer a nonalcoholic drink, opt for fruit punch—a delicious mixture of freshly blended tropical fruit.

What to Wear: Dining in Grenada is casual. At dinner, collared shirts and long pants are appropriate for men (even the fanciest restaurants don't require jacket and tie), and sundresses or dress pants are fine for women. Reserve beachwear and other revealing attire for the beach.

GRENADA

$$$
SEAFOOD
FAMILY
Fodor's Choice ★

🍴 **Aquarium Restaurant.** As the name suggests, fresh seafood is the specialty here. Spend the day at the adjacent Magazine Beach (you can rent kayaks or snorkeling gear) and then break for a cool drink or satisfying lunch—a salad, sandwich or burger, fresh fish, or pasta—served on the waterfront deck at the restaurant's La Sirena Beach Bar. Lush plants and palms surround the dining room, and a waterfall adds a touch of romance in the evening. The dinner menu always includes fresh fish, grilled lobster, and specialties such as callaloo cannelloni. On Sunday, there's a beach barbecue with live reggae music. [$] *Average main: $25* ✉ *Maurice Bishop Memorial Hwy., overlooking Magazine Beach, Point Salines, St. George* ☎ *473/444–1410* 🌐 *www.aquarium-grenada.com* 🕒 *Closed Mon.*

$$$
CARIBBEAN
FAMILY

🍴 **BB's Crabback Caribbean Restaurant.** Overlooking St. George's Harbour, on the north side of the Carenage, BB's Crabback features Grenadian and West Indian dishes prepared with special flair. Born in Grenada and trained in England, Chef BB (Brian Benjamin) turns out some of the best meals in town. Crab back (local land crab) is a house specialty, of course, but you'll want to try some of his seafood dishes, as well. Prawns in lobster sauce comes to mind. Or try the signature curried goat, the breast of chicken marinated in 12 herbs and spices, or the pan-fried barracuda in a crab and lobster sauce. Dining is alfresco here, and the views of the harbor and out to sea are nothing short of spectacular. It's definitely the place to go for lunch or dinner in downtown St. George's. [$] *Average main: $23* ✉ *Progress House, The Carenage, St. George's* ☎ *473/435–7058.*

$$$$ ECLECTIC 🍴 **The Beach House.** At this family-owned restaurant in an iconic Caribbean beach house, the gleaming white sand and sea views are the perfect backdrop for a casual salad or pasta lunch on the deck or a burger or ribs at the bar. At dinner, the casually elegant surroundings, the delectable entrées—rack of lamb, blackened fish, or prime rib—and superb wines give new meaning to the term beach party. There's a kid's menu available, and a quick snack menu is available anytime in high season. On Friday and Saturday night, there's a happy hour from 10 pm to midnight. Get to the restaurant via a short walk down the beach from Laluna resort, a longer walk up the beach from the Grenadian by Rex Resort, a water taxi ride from the Carenage in St. George's, or a drive from the airport road. [$] *Average main: $30* ✉ *Off Maurice Bishop Memorial Hwy., on Dr. Groom's Beach, Portici Bay, Point Salines, St. George* ☎ *473/444–4455* 🌐 *www.beachhousegrenada.com* ✍ *Reservations essential* 🕒 *Closed Sun. No lunch May–Nov.*

$$ CARIBBEAN FAMILY 🍴 **Belmont Estate.** If you're visiting the northern reaches of Grenada, plan to stop at Belmont Estate, a 400-year-old working nutmeg and cocoa plantation. Settle into the breezy open-air dining room, which overlooks enormous trays of nutmeg, cocoa, and mace drying in the sunshine. A waiter will offer some refreshing local juice and a choice of callaloo or pumpkin soup. Then head to the buffet and help yourself to salad, rice, stewed chicken, beef curry, stewed fish, local vegetables, and more. Dessert may be homemade ice cream, ginger cake, or another delicious confection. Afterward, feel free to take a tour of the museum, cocoa fermentary, sugarcane garden, and old cemetery. Farm animals (and a couple of monkeys) roam the property, and there's often folk music and dancing on the lawn. [$] *Average main: $17* ✉ *Belmont, St. Patrick* ☎ *473/442–9524* 🌐 *www.belmontestate.net* 🕒 *Closed Sat. No dinner.*

$$$ CARIBBEAN 🍴 **Coconut Beach Restaurant.** Take local seafood, add butter, wine, and Grenadian spices, and you have excellent French-creole cuisine. Throw in a beautiful location at the northern end of Grand Anse Beach, and this West Indian cottage becomes a perfect spot for either an alfresco lunch or a dinner by moonlight. Lobster is a specialty, whether it's lobster thermidor or perhaps wrapped in a crepe, dipped in garlic butter, or added to pasta. Homemade coconut pie is a winner for dessert. Dine "wet or fine," at a table on the beach or inside. At lunch, you can just walk down the beach to the restaurant; at night, either drive or opt for a taxi. And on Saturday, stick around for late-night drinks and DJ music. [$] *Average main: $25* ✉ *Grand Anse Main Rd., on beach, Grand Anse, St. George* ☎ *473/444–4644* 🕒 *Closed Tues.*

$$$$ ✕ **La Belle Creole.** The marriage of contemporary and West Indian cui-
CARIBBEAN   sines and a splendid view of the twinkling lights in distant St. George's
Fodor'sChoice   are the delights of this romantic hillside restaurant. The always-chang-
★   ing five-course prix fixe and à la carte menus are based on original
recipes from the owner's mother, a pioneer in incorporating local fruits,
vegetables, and spices into "foreign" dishes. Try, for instance, Grenadian caviar (roe of the white sea urchin), green-banana soup, callaloo
quiche, creole fish, baked chicken roulade, or ginger pork chops—with
homemade mango cheesecake for dessert. The inspired cuisine, romantic setting, and gracious service are impressive. $ *Average main: $35*
⊠ *Blue Horizons Garden Resort, Morne Rouge Rd., Grand Anse, St.*
George ☎ *473/444–4316* ⊕ *www.grenadabluehorizons.com* ⚹ *Reser-*
vations essential.

$$ ✕ **La Boulangerie.** This combination French bakery and Italian pizzeria,
CAFÉ   convenient to the hotels at Grand Anse, is perfect for an inexpensive
FAMILY   breakfast or light meal—to eat in, take out, or have delivered. You'll
find freshly baked croissants and Danish pastry, focaccia and baguette
sandwiches, homemade pizza and pasta, fresh-squeezed juice or house
wine, coffee and espresso, and homemade gelato. $ *Average main: $18*
⊠ *Le Marquis Complex, across from Spiceland Mall, Grand Anse, St.*
George ☎ *473/444–1131.*

$$$ ✕ **La Sagesse Restaurant.** The perfect spot to soothe a frazzled soul, this
SEAFOOD   open-air seafood restaurant is on a secluded cove in a nature preserve.
Combine your lunch or dinner with a nature walk or a day at the beach.
Linger over sandwiches, salads, or grilled lobster for lunch. Lambi
(conch), smoked marlin, tuna steak, chicken piccata, filet mignon, and
a daily vegetarian entrée may be joined on the dinner menu by Chef
Cecilia's specials, such as flying fish or an upscale version of Grenada's
national dish, oildown. All fish is locally caught; all vegetables, fruit,
and spices are grown on La Sagesse's own organic farm in the rain
forest. La Sagesse is a 25-minute drive from St. George's or Grand
Anse; public transportation is available. $ *Average main: $26* ⊠ *La*
Sagesse Nature Centre, La Sagesse, St. David ☎ *473/444–6458* ⊕ *www.*
lasagesse.com ⚹ *Reservations essential.*

$$$$ ✕ **Lighthouse Ship Restaurant.** Fine dining is served aboard *Västra Ban-*
ECLECTIC   *ken*, a historic lightship that was brought to Grenada in 2006 as the
centerpiece of Le Phare Bleu Marina Hotel. Guest chefs—a new one
each year—use local ingredients to create contemporary cuisine served
in a setting that's both nautical and intimate. You might enjoy seafood
ravioli or a callaloo and crab soufflé appetizer, followed by roasted
rack of lamb or seared swordfish. The warm home-baked breads are
wonderful, but the chocolate-plate dessert takes the cake. Before dinner, drinks are served on the top deck, under the stars. $ *Average main:*
$32 ⊠ *Le Phare Bleu Marina Hotel, Petite Calivigny Bay, Calvigny,*
St. George ☎ *473/444–2400* ⊕ *www.lepharebleu.com* ⚹ *Reservations*
essential ⊙ *No lunch. Closed Sun. Closed May–Nov.*

$$ ✕ **The New Nutmeg.** West Indian specialties, fresh seafood, hamburgers,
CARIBBEAN   and a waterfront view make the New Nutmeg a favorite with locals
FAMILY   and visitors alike. It's on the Carenage (above Sea Change bookstore),
with large, open windows from which you can view the harbor activity

and catch a cool breeze as you eat. Try the callaloo soup, curried lambi, fresh seafood, or a steak—or just stop by for a roti and a cold beer or rum punch, with grated nutmeg on top, of course. [$] *Average main: $18* ✉ *The Carenage, St. George's* ☎ *473/435–9525.*

$$$ CARIBBEAN 🍴 **Patrick's Local Homestyle Cooking.** The fixed tasting menu of 20 or so local dishes, served family-style, will astound you—it's Grenadian home-style cooking at its casual best. The restaurant, in a tiny cottage on the outskirts of St. George's, is named for the late and very charismatic chef Patrick Lavine. You'll sample successive helpings of superb callaloo or pumpkin soup, lobster salad, codfish fritters, breadfruit salad, ginger pork, fried jacks (fish), cou-cou (cornmeal cakes), lambi creole, curried goat, stir-fried rabbit, oildown, rice *pelau* (layered with meat and vegetables), starchy tannia (yautia) cakes with shrimp, green papaya in cheese sauce, carrot or banana cake, and more—all for $23 per person. Everything is cooked fresh, so you must call ahead for reservations. [$] *Average main: $23* ✉ *Lagoon Rd., opposite Grenada Yacht Services, St. George's* ☎ *473/440–0364* ✍ *Reservations essential.*

$$$ SEAFOOD 🍴 **The Red Crab.** West Indian basics such as curried lambi and garlic shrimp—and classics such as lobster Newburg, Coquilles St. Jacques, and veal Cordon Bleu—keep the regulars coming back to this family-run restaurant that's been serving locals and expats for decades. Seafood, particularly lobster, and steak (imported from the United States) are staples of the menu; hot garlic bread comes with every order. Dine inside or outside on the front patio. [$] *Average main: $24* ✉ *L'Anse aux Épines Rd., L'Anse aux Épines, St. George* ☎ *473/444–4424* ⏲ *Closed Sun.*

$$$$ INTERNATIONAL 🍴 **Rhodes' Restaurant.** Named after the acclaimed British chef Gary Rhodes, this open-air restaurant is surrounded by palms, flowering plants, and twinkling lights—a wonderful setting for a romantic dinner or special occasion. Local produce and spices have never appeared (or tasted) more elegant. Past menus have featured citrus-cured salmon with a lime, fennel, and pawpaw (papaya) salad as a starter, followed by grilled swordfish steak with Caribbean paella risotto or filet of beef on a roasted potato cake with whole-grain-mustard cream. The passion-fruit panna cotta, light as a soufflé, is nothing short of divine. [$] *Average main: $40* ✉ *Calabash Hotel, L'Anse aux Épines, St. George* ☎ *473/444–4334* 🌐 *www.calabashhotel.com* ✍ *Reservations essential* ⏲ *No lunch.*

$$ ECLECTIC FAMILY 🍴 **Umbrellas Beach Bar.** Whether you're spending the day on Grand Anse Beach or just looking for a quick bite, Umbrellas is the place to go. Right on the beach, next to Coyaba Beach Resort, this classic beach bar is open from breakfast until well into the evening. The burgers and sandwiches are great, the salads are freshly made, and there's barbecued fish or steak with wedge potatoes or sweet potato fries. Everything's reasonably priced—yet another reason it's so busy. Of course, you can also just sit on the top deck with a beer or rum punch and a plate of appetizers and stare at the waves—or watch the sunset. [$] *Average main: $15* ✉ *Next to Coyaba Beach Resort, Grand Anse, St. George* ☎ *473/439–9149* ⏲ *Closed Mon.*

CARRIACOU

$$$
CARIBBEAN
Fodor'sChoice
★
× **Bogles Round House.** Surrounded by gardens and a handful of cottages for rent, this small round structure was built with a concrete-filled tree trunk as its central support and a long bench that was once the jawbone of a whale. The food is less peculiar: Chef Roxanne Russell is celebrated for her elegant style of Caribbean cuisine. Her three-course menu, which changes according to market availability, may include starters such as fish cakes and cream of callaloo soup and entrées such as rack of lamb au jus and grilled lobster with garlic butter—there's always a vegetarian dish, too. Pasta and pizza are available for kids upon request. Desserts, including the ice cream, are all homemade. $ *Average main: $30* ✉ *Sparrow Bay, Bogles* ☎ *473/443–7841* ⊕ *www.boglesroundhouse.com* ⊲ *Reservations essential* ⊗ *Closed Wed.*

$$
CARIBBEAN
FAMILY
× **Laurena II.** As you approach this popular restaurant and bar, just a few giant steps from the ferry wharf, you're greeted by the unmistakable scent of authentic Jamaican jerk chicken and pork. That's the specialty (and personal favorite) of Chef Purgeon Reece, who hails from Negril, although his menu also includes other local and regional dishes such as curried goat, baked chicken, or grilled fish with rice and peas. Daily specials are posted on a street-side blackboard. This "jerk center" is definitely a casual spot, the best bet for a delicious lunch, and a good place to catch the local vibe. $ *Average main: $14* ✉ *Main St., Hillsborough* ☎ *473/443–8333* ⊗ *Closed Sun.*

$
DELI
× **Patty's Deli.** At this delicatessen, a short walk from the ferry jetty, you can get takeout sandwiches made to order with freshly sliced meats (ham, smoked turkey, herbed chicken, etc.) and cheeses. Baguettes, croissants, and pastries are fresh daily—and on Friday, there's usually cheesecake. Anyone provisioning a boat or a house will find a wide selection of coffee, tea, preserves, condiments, locally smoked fish, and a freezer full of USDA meats. $ *Average main: $12* ✉ *Main St., Hillsborough* ☎ *473/443–6258* ⊕ *www.pattysdeli.com.*

$$
ECLECTIC
× **Slipway Restaurant.** Slip right in for lunch or dinner—or Sunday brunch—overlooking the waterfront activity on Tyrell Bay. The menu depends on what's fresh that day, but you can depend on a juicy American-style hamburger, fresh salad, or creative pasta dish at lunch and fresh-caught seafood at night—lobster in season, pan-seared tuna, mahimahi, you name it. You can choose to dine inside or beachside. It's hard to decide what's most appealing—the outstanding food, the nautical ambience, the friendly service, or the very reasonable prices. Plus, the bar is open all day. $ *Average main: $20* ✉ *Tyrell Bay* ☎ *473/443–6500* ⊕ *www.slipwayrestaurant.com* ⊗ *Closed Mon. No dinner Sun.*

WHERE TO STAY

Hotels and resorts in Grenada tend to be small, with friendly management and attentive staff. All guest rooms are equipped with air-conditioning, an in-room TV, and telephone unless indicated otherwise. Most also offer Wi-Fi. During the off-season (April 15 to December 15), prices may be discounted up to 40%.

PRIVATE VILLAS AND CONDOS

Grenada was one of the last islands to have private villa communities, in which privately owned units are rented to nonowner vacationers through management companies. Only a few such properties are here now or in progress. Laluna Estate in Morne Rouge opened seven waterfront villas in 2012, and an extensive villa development is underway at Bacolet Bay in St. David (265 villas expected on completion) and is planned for Port Louis on The Lagoon in St. George's. Otherwise, apartments and houses are available for rent for a week or longer. The minimum staff includes a maid and laundress, but a cook, housekeeper, gardener, and others can be arranged.

In Grenada, many rental properties are located in and around L'Anse aux Épines, a beautiful residential peninsula that juts into the sea. In-season rates range from $1,000 a week for a small, two-bedroom house with no pool or air-conditioning to $8,000 a week for a five-bedroom house full of amenities, including a pool and beach access. In Carriacou, in-season rates range from $80 a day for a small cottage or in-town apartment suitable for two people to $350 a day for a two-bedroom villa with panoramic views and a swimming pool.

RENTAL CONTACTS

Altman Real Estate (Grenada) ⊠ *Le Marquis Shopping Complex, Grand Anse, St. George* ☎ *473/435–2081* ⊕ *www.altmangrenada.com.*

Down Island Villa Rentals ⊠ *Craigston, Carriacou* ☎ *473/443–8182* ⊕ *www.islandvillas.com.*

Spice Isle Villas ⊠ *Grand Anse, St. George* ☎ *473/439–2486* ⊕ *www.spiceislevillas.com.*

Villas of Grenada ⊠ *True Blue, St. George* ☎ *473/444–4462* ⊕ *www.villasofgrenada.com.*

GRENADA

$ 🏨 **Allamanda Beach Resort.** Well-situated facing Grand Anse Beach, this
HOTEL small hotel has some rooms with whirlpool baths; many rooms also have
FAMILY connecting doors, making Allamanda a good choice for families. **Pros:** location, location, location; great value; room rates include breakfast and free Wi-Fi. **Cons:** don't expect luxury at this price; rooms are attractive but somewhat dated; you have to walk down the beach for water sports. $ *Rooms from: $145* ⊠ *Grand Anse, St. George* ☎ *473/444–0095* ⊕ *www.allamandaresort.com* ⤳ *50 rooms* ⦿ *Breakfast.*

$ 🏨 **Blue Horizons Garden Resort.** Just 300 yards from Grand Anse Beach,
RESORT "Blue" is especially popular among divers, nature lovers, and family vaca-
FAMILY tioners looking for roomy self-catering accommodations. **Pros:** peaceful and quiet; walk to shopping and restaurants; lovely garden environment.

Cons: not directly on the beach; lots of steps up to the hilltop units—which also offer the best view. [$] *Rooms from: $210* ✉ *Morne Rouge Rd., Grand Anse, St. George* ☎ *473/444–4316, 473/444–4592* 🌐 *www.grenadabluehorizons.com* 🛏 *26 suites, 6 studios* 🍴 *Multiple meal plans.*

BEST BETS FOR LODGING

BEST FOR ROMANCE
Calabash, Laluna, Petite Anse Hotel, Spice Island Beach Resort

BEST BEACHFRONT
Coyaba Beach Resort, Radisson Grand Beach Resort, Grenadian by Rex, La Sagesse Nature Centre, Laluna, Spice Island Beach Resort

$$$$ HOTEL Fodor's Choice ★ **Calabash Hotel & Spa.** The posh suites here are in 10 two-story cottages distributed in a horseshoe around 8 acres of lawn and gardens that hug the beach on Prickly Bay (L'Anse aux Épines). **Pros:** excellent service; love those treats; breakfast served on your verandah. **Cons:** small beach, small pool, large lawn and gardens; Wi-Fi only in public areas; rental car suggested to get around the island. [$] *Rooms from: $735* ✉ *L'Anse aux Épines Rd., L'Anse aux Épines, St. George* ☎ *473/444–4334* 🌐 *www.calabashhotel.com* 🛏 *30 suites* ⏲ *Closed Aug. and Sept.* 🍴 *Multiple meal plans.*

$$ RESORT **Coyaba Beach Resort.** Rooms at Coyaba, one of a handful of hotels with direct access to beautiful Grand Anse Beach, are in pavilion-style buildings that surround a 5½-acre beachfront garden of palm trees, hibiscus, frangipani, and bougainvillea. **Pros:** excellent beachfront location; spacious grounds; pool with swim-up bar; on-site dive center. **Cons:** rooms are attractive but not extraordinary; "free" water sports have time limits, usually one hour per day. [$] *Rooms from: $360* ✉ *Grand Anse, St. George* ☎ *473/444–4129* 🌐 *www.coyaba.com* 🛏 *80 rooms* 🍴 *Multiple meal plans.*

$ RESORT FAMILY **Flamboyant Hotel & Villas.** Draped over the hillside at the southern end of Grand Anse Beach, Flamboyant offers roomy, reasonably priced accommodations—all with private verandahs that have stunning, panoramic views of the sea. **Pros:** reasonable prices; friendly staff; nightlife at the Owl bar; on-site dive center. **Cons:** rooms are pleasant but decidedly unflamboyant; hilly terrain. [$] *Rooms from: $250* ✉ *Morne Rouge Rd., Grand Anse, St. George* ☎ *473/444–4247* 🌐 *www.flamboyant.com* 🛏 *38 rooms, 27 suites, 2 cottages* 🍴 *Multiple meal plans.*

$ HOTEL FAMILY **Gem Holiday Beach Resort.** The one- and two-bedroom self-catering apartments are small and simply furnished at this no-frills hotel on pretty Morne Rouge Bay, but the beach it faces is one of Grenada's best. **Pros:** inexpensive; good restaurant and popular beach bar; nightclub on-site. **Cons:** air-conditioning only in bedrooms; no pool; nightclub attracts the public on Wednesday through Saturday nights. [$] *Rooms from: $126* ✉ *Morne Rouge Rd., Morne Rouge, St. George* ☎ *473/444–2288* 🌐 *www.gembeachresort.com* 🛏 *15 1-bedroom apartments, 5 2-bedroom apartments* 🍴 *No meals.*

$ ALL-INCLUSIVE FAMILY **Grenadian by Rex Resorts.** This massive, Palladian-style beachfront resort on a huge piece of property on Tamarind Bay is particularly popular with Europeans. **Pros:** large play area for kids; two excellent beaches—one quiet, the other for water sports; minutes from the airport. **Cons:** rooms are unremarkable; quite a hike from room to beach to lobby; rooms could use some TLC. $ *Rooms from: $254* ✉ *Tamarind Bay, Point Salines, St. George* ☎ *473/444–3333* ⊕ *www. rexresorts.com* ⤴ *152 rooms, 20 suites* ❍ *All-inclusive.*

$ ⬚ **Kalinago Beach Resort.** This contemporary beachfront hotel on Morne
HOTEL Rouge Bay, next to Gem Holiday Resort and with the same ownership,
FAMILY has stylish suites—all with a patio or deck and a view of the ocean. **Pros:** modern rooms; great beach; dive packages. **Cons:** walking to Grand Anse—or anywhere—requires negotiating a steep hill; a rental car is a good idea. $ *Rooms from: $210* ✉ *Morne Rouge Rd., Morne Rouge, St. George* ☎ *473/444–5255* ⊕ *www.kalinagobeachresort.com* ⤴ *29 rooms* ❍ *Multiple meal plans.*

$$$$ ⬚ **Laluna.** You may think you've landed on an island in the South
RESORT Pacific when you reach this upscale getaway, hidden away on a pris-
Fodor'sChoice tine beach near Grenada's Quarantine Point. **Pros:** nifty 650-square-
★ foot cottages; great restaurant; fabulous beach; free Wi-Fi. **Cons:** the long, bumpy, dirt access road; total seclusion could seem confining (if it weren't such a divine spot!). $ *Rooms from: $495* ✉ *Morne Rouge, St. George* ☎ *473/439–0001* ⊕ *www.laluna.com* ⤴ *16 cottages, 7 villas* ❍ *Multiple meal plans.*

$ ⬚ **La Sagesse.** Secluded on La Sagesse Bay, this country inn boasts its own
B&B/INN restaurant and beach bar, along with a salt-pond bird sanctuary, thick mangroves, nature trails, and ½ mile (¾ km) of palm-lined beach—one of the prettiest beaches in the entire Caribbean. **Pros:** perfect out-of-the-way escape; great place to commune with nature; excellent restaurant. **Cons:** far from everything; no TV, no phones, no Internet access, no noise; not the best choice for families with kids. $ *Rooms from: $185* ✉ *La Sagesse Nature Center, La Sagesse, St. David* ☎ *473/444–6458* ⊕ *www.lasagesse.com* ⤴ *9 rooms, 3 suites* ❍ *No meals.*

$ ⬚ **Le Phare Bleu Marina & Boutique Hotel.** The spacious, self-catering
RENTAL accommodations at the family-friendly Le Phare Bleu (The Blue Light-
FAMILY house) are perfectly situated for those who arrive by boat or who like to be around boats. **Pros:** boater's delight; on-site minimart has freshly baked bread daily; good restaurants. **Cons:** somewhat isolated; rental car advised; tiny beach. $ *Rooms from: $200* ✉ *Petite Calivigny Bay, Calvigny, St. George* ☎ *473/444–2400* ⊕ *www.lepharebleu.com* ⤴ *9 cottages, 4 apartments, 1 villa* ❍ *Breakfast.*

$$$$ ⬚ **Maca Bana.** Clustered on a 2-acre hillside overlooking mile-long
RENTAL Magazine Beach, each of Maca Bana's seven private villas ("banas")
Fodor'sChoice has a great view—of the white sand below, out to sea, up the coast-
★ line to pretty St. George's Harbour, and beyond toward cloud-capped mountains. **Pros:** roomy villas with huge kitchens; enormous decks with amazing views; fabulous beach. **Cons:** steep hill down to the restaurant and beach; expensive; tiny pool. $ *Rooms from: $515* ✉ *Magazine Beach, on hill above Aquarium restaurant, Point Salines, St. George* ☎ *473/439–5355* ⊕ *www.macabana.com* ⤴ *2 1-bedroom villas, 5 2-bedroom villas* ❍ *No meals.*

$$$$ ⬚ **Mount Cinnamon.** On a hillside overlooking Grand Anse Beach, Mount
RESORT Cinnamon's spacious one-, two-, or three-bedroom villas have full kitch-
FAMILY ens with a breakfast bar, Bose entertainment systems, cable TV, and

12

convenient extras that include washers and dryers. **Pros:** amazing views; great choice for families; pool, private beach club on Grand Anse Beach, on-site dive shop; grocery stocking service. **Cons:** villas are on a steep hill, but golf-cart transport to restaurant or beach is available. $ *Rooms from: $475 ⊠ Morne Rouge Rd., Grand Anse, St. George* ☎ *473/439–4400, 866/720–2616* ⊕ *www.mountcinnamongrenadahotel.com* ↘ *21 units* ❍ *Multiple meal plans.*

$ 🏠 **Petit Bacaye Villa Hotel.** Hidden along the coast in St. David, about
RENTAL   a half-hour drive east of Grand Anse and the hustle and bustle of St.
FAMILY   George's, Petit Bacaye is a tiny oasis of serenity. **Pros:** idyllically private, quiet spot; airport shuttle service; perfect for a quiet wedding or honeymoon. **Cons:** remote (you'll need a car); access driveway is steep and scary for drivers; no Internet access. $ *Rooms from: $205 ⊠ Westerhall, St. David* ☎ *473/443–2902* ⊕ *www.petitbacaye.com* ↘ *4 cottages* ☽ *Closed Aug. and Sept.* ❍ *No meals* ☞ *7-day minimum stay.*

$ 🏠 **Petite Anse Hotel.** Independent travelers love this delightful oceanfront
HOTEL   hotel at the northern tip of Grenada; it's surrounded by beautiful gardens on one side and an unobstructed view of the southern Grenadines on the other. **Pros:** romantic setting; secluded palm-studded beach; inviting and woodsy trails; free Wi-Fi. **Cons:** remote; rental car advised; it's a trek down to the beach. $ *Rooms from: $270 ⊠ Sauteurs, St. Patrick* ☎ *473/442–5252* ⊕ *www.petiteanse.com* ↘ *2 rooms, 9 cottages* ❍ *Multiple meal plans.*

$ 🏠 **Radisson Grand Beach Resort.** On 20 landscaped acres that stretch
RESORT   along 1,200 feet of Grand Anse Beach, this resort offers comfortable
FAMILY   rooms and extensive amenities. **Pros:** huge hotel full of amenities, including water sports and a dive shop; beautiful beachfront location; walking distance to Grand Anse shops and restaurants; excellent value; complimentary Wi-Fi throughout the resort. **Cons:** rooms are comfortable but not extraordinary; gets crowded when meetings are scheduled. $ *Rooms from: $147 ⊠ Grand Anse, St. George* ☎ *473/444–4371* ⊕ *www.grenadagrand.com* ↘ *238 rooms, 2 suites* ❍ *Breakfast.*

$$$$ 🏠 **Sandals LaSource Grenada Resort & Spa.** Sandals—a favorite retreat for
ALL-INCLUSIVE   young couples, honeymooners, and second honeymooners—entered the Grenadian market in 2013 by "Sandal-izing" what for years had been the LaSource property on pretty Pink Gin Beach. **Pros:** excellent beachfront location with lots to do; congenial atmosphere; brand new; Wi-Fi access. **Cons:** expensive for Grenada, though it's all-inclusive and a reliable brand; somewhat isolated; you'll need a taxi or rental car to venture beyond the property. $ *Rooms from: $717 ⊠ Pink Gin Beach, near airport, Point Salines, St. George* ☎ *473/444–2556, 888/726–3257* ⊕ *www.sandals.com* ↘ *150 rooms, 75 suites* ❍ *All-inclusive.*

$$$$ 🏠 **Spice Island Beach Resort.** Presenting the most luxurious resort experi-
RESORT   ence in Grenada: exquisite rooms fill gleaming white buildings that extend
FAMILY   along 1,600 feet of Grand Anse Beach, and the personalized service is
Fodor's Choice   impeccable. **Pros:** casually elegant and luxurious, yet family-friendly; per-
★   fect beachfront location; excellent service. **Cons:** luxury doesn't come cheap; the elegant nightly dinners may be limiting during long stays or for families with kids; all the pampering makes it very hard to go home. $ *Rooms from: $914 ⊠ Grand Anse, St. George* ☎ *473/444–4258* ⊕ *www.spiceislandbeachresort.com* ↘ *64 suites* ❍ *Multiple meal plans.*

12

$

RESORT

FAMILY

True Blue Bay Resort & Villas. Families with kids appreciate the lawns and gardens at this family-run resort, a former indigo plantation that overlooks True Blue Bay. **Pros:** pleasant environment at reasonable prices; convenient to St. George's University; complimentary shuttle to Grand Anse Beach; free Wi-Fi. **Cons:** no beach for swimming; rental car recommended. $ *Rooms from: $242* ⊠ *Old Mill Ave., True Blue Bay, True Blue, St. George* ☎ *473/443–8783, 866/325–8322* ⊕ *www.truebluebay.com* 🛏 *33 rooms, 5 villa suites* ❙⦿❙ *Multiple meal plans.*

$

B&B/INN

Twelve Degrees North. Named for the latitude here, this small, secluded, adults-only inn on 3 acres of hillside has one- and two-bedroom self-contained suites, all of which face the sea—and face west, providing beautiful sunset views from the balcony or patio. **Pros:** private getaway; personalized service; excellent snorkeling off the dock; free Wi-Fi. **Cons:** reef makes the beach unsuitable for swimming; rooms are comfortable but not stylish; no Internet. $ *Rooms from: $225* ⊠ *L'Anse aux Épines, St. George* ☎ *473/444–4580* ⊕ *www.twelvedegreesnorth.com* 🛏 *8 suites* ❙⦿❙ *No meals.*

CARRIACOU

$

HOTEL

Ade's Dream. By the jetty in Hillsborough, Ade's (pronounced add-ees) is a convenient—and popular—place to rest your weary head after a day snorkeling at Sandy Island or scuba diving at some of Carriacou's best dive spots. **Pros:** steps from the jetty; convenient for an overnight on Carriacou; very affordable; Internet café and Wi-Fi on premises. **Cons:** no frills here; noise may be an issue in street-facing rooms. $ *Rooms from: $45* ⊠ *Main St., Hillsborough* ☎ *473/443–7317* ⊕ *www.adesdream.com* 🛏 *23 rooms* ❙⦿❙ *No meals.*

$

RENTAL

FAMILY

Bayaleau Point Cottages. In a laid-back environment on a quiet hillside estate on the easternmost point of Windward Bay, four colorful gingerbread cottages are within earshot of one another but partially hidden by trees and other foliage. **Pros:** ideal for small groups or families (up to 16 people); swinging in your hammock is an "active" sport; beautiful Grenadines view; Wi-Fi access. **Cons:** very rustic; way off the beaten path; rental car advised. $ *Rooms from: $110* ⊠ *Bayaleau, Windward* ☎ *473/443–7984* ⊕ *www.carriacoucottages.com* 🛏 *4 cottages* ❙⦿❙ *No meals.*

$

B&B/INN

Bogles Round House. Three quaint cottages—called Lime, Mango, and Plum—are in a garden setting about 60 feet from Sparrow Bay, where guests enjoy swimming, snorkeling, and walks on the beach. **Pros:** the price; the restaurant; the ambience. **Cons:** one step up from camping out; no a/c; no telecommunications with the outside world (although that may appeal to some). $ *Rooms from: $97* ⊠ *Sparrow Bay, Bogles* ☎ *473/443–7841* ⊕ *www.boglesroundhouse.com* 🛏 *3 cottages* ⊗ *Closed May* ❙⦿❙ *Breakfast.*

$

HOTEL

Carriacou Grand View Hotel. Island visitors and local businesspeople alike relish the lovely view, particularly at sunset, from this perch high above Hillsborough Harbour. **Pros:** truly a grand view, even from the swimming pool; popular restaurant with late-night piano bar; free Wi-Fi. **Cons:** accommodations are basic; it's a hot walk uphill from town and the beach. $ *Rooms from: $65* ⊠ *Beausejour* ☎ *473/443–6348* ⊕ *www.carriacougrandview.com* 🛏 *7 rooms, 7 suites* ❙⦿❙ *No meals.*

$ ⚏ **Green Roof Inn.** You're guaranteed beautiful views of Hillsborough
B&B/INN   Bay and the offshore cays at this small inn, which is the perfect location
for a scuba-diving, snorkeling, or beachcombing vacation. **Pros:** pick a
room with a sea view; homey atmosphere; close to town; Wi-Fi access.
Cons: rooms are small and very basic; no a/c; showers only. $ *Rooms
from: $95* ⊠ *Hillsborough Bay, Hillsborough* ☎ *473/443–6399* ⊕ *www.
greenroofinn.com* ⇝ *5 rooms, 1 cottage* ⦿ *Breakfast.*

$ ⚏ **Hotel Laurena.** The family-owned, family-operated Hotel Laurena is
HOTEL   within walking distance of downtown Hillsborough, the ferry wharf,
FAMILY   shops, and some beaches. **Pros:** convenient to town; good dining at
the on-site restaurant and the nearby Laurena II Jerk Center; some
rooms are wheelchair accessible. **Cons:** not particularly attractive town
views; no pool; walk to beach. $ *Rooms from: $85* ⊠ *Hillsborough*
☎ *473/443–8759, 877/755–4386 in U.S.* ⊕ *www.hotellaurena.com*
⇝ *20 rooms, 6 apartments* ⦿ *Breakfast.*

NIGHTLIFE

Grenada's nightlife consists mainly of live music at resort hotels, a dinner theater in the countryside, a very popular street party, and a handful
of nightspots. During the winter season, some resorts present a steel
band or other local entertainment several nights a week.

BARS

Bananas. The students at nearby St. George's University like to "lime"
(hang out) at this casual restaurant and nightspot, especially on Friday
night when there's a DJ. Other nights, sports events on big-screen TVs
in the sports bar get much of the attention, as does the menu of wood-
fired pizza, burgers, wings, and cold beer. Every evening from 5 to 7 is
Happy Hour(s), with half-price drinks. ⊠ *True Blue Rd., True Blue, St.
George* ☎ *473/444–4662* ⊕ *www.bananas.gd.*

DANCE CLUBS

Fantazia 2001. On weekends, you can hear disco, soca, reggae, and
international pop music from 9:30 pm until the wee hours at this
spot. Wednesday night is "Oldie Goldies" night. There may be a cover
charge of EC$10 to EC$30, depending on the entertainment, although
admission is often free. Friday night is always ladies night—no charge.
⊠ *Morne Rouge Beach, adjacent to Gem Holiday Beach Resort, Morne
Rouge, St. George* ☎ *473/444–2288* ⊕ *www.fantazia2001niteclub.com.*

Karma. Inside this club's 10,000 square foot space are four bars, a
stage, dance floor, and a dozen plasma TV screens. The club features
karaoke on Wednesday night, "student night" on Thursday, video
DJ entertainment on Friday, and special parties and headliner concerts on certain Saturday nights. The nightclub entrance fee is EC$25;
admission for special events runs EC$50 and up. ⊠ *The Carenage, St.
George's* ☎ *473/409–2582* ⊕ *www.karmavip.com.*

The Owl. This club at the Flamboyant Hotel features crab racing on
Monday night, karaoke on Thursday night, calypso on Friday night,
and two happy hours (4–7 and 11–midnight) every night. It's open until
3 am nightly. ⊠ *Flamboyant Hotel, Morne Rouge Rd., Grand Anse, St.
George* ☎ *473/444–4247* ⊕ *www.owlgrenada.com.*

THEME NIGHTS

FAMILY

Fodor's Choice ★

Gouyave Fish Friday. Every Friday from 4 pm until 1 am, the town of Gouyave—the very proud hometown of the 2012 Olympic gold medalist Kirani James—celebrates its deep-sea fishing heritage. Street vendors sell freshly caught fish, lobster, and other seafood cooked on open fires, as well as your favorite beverages. Local music and cultural performances make it an entertaining family event—and the place to be on a Friday night. It's about 45 minutes north of St. George's. ⊠ *St. Francis and St. Dominic Sts., Gouyave, St. John* ☏ *473/444–8430, 473/444–9490* ⊕ *www.gogouyave.com.*

Rhum Runner. *Rhum Runner,* a 60-foot twin-deck catamaran and *Rhum Runner II,* a 72-foot sister ship, are floating party boats. The boats depart the Carenage on most weekends for day, sunset, and moonlight cruises—with plenty of rum and snacks—in and around St. George's and Grand Anse. Reservations are required. ⊠ *The Carenage, St. George's* ☏ *473/440–4386* ⊕ *www.rhumrunner.gd.*

FAMILY

Spice Basket Dinner Theatre. Combining music and theater, this colorful and family-friendly journey through history explores the sweep of Grenadian history. Performances are held every Tuesday night, beginning at 7:15 pm. The admission price for the buffet dinner, drinks, and the show is $50 per person, with an additional $10–$15 for transportation from your hotel, depending on its location. Reservations are recommended. ⊠ *Beaulieu, St. George* ☏ *473/437–9000, 473/232–9000* ⊕ *www.spicebasketgrenada.com.*

Spicy Fridays and Oldie Goldies at Spice Basket. At the Spice Basket cultural center, Spicy Fridays begin at 5 pm with a live band, drink specials, and a buffet with local foods; on Saturday, Oldie Goldies night begins at 8 pm. Admission is free except for special events or when the live entertainment is a major headliner. ⊠ *Beaulieu, St. George* ☏ *473/437–9000, 473/232–9000* ⊕ *www.spicebasketgrenada.com.*

SHOPPING

Some unique, locally made goods to look for in gift shops and supermarkets are locally made chocolate bars, nutmeg jam and syrup, spice-scented soaps and body oils, and (no kidding) Nut-Med Pain-Relieving Spray. Grenada's best souvenirs or gifts for friends back home, though, are spice baskets in a variety of shapes and sizes that are filled with cinnamon, nutmeg, mace, bay leaves, cloves, turmeric, and ginger. You can buy them for as little as $5 to $10 in practically every shop, at the open-air produce market at **Market Square** in St. George's, at vendor stalls along the Esplanade near the port, and at the Vendor's Craft & Spice Market on Grand Anse Beach. Vendors also sell handmade fabric dolls, coral jewelry, seashells, spice necklaces, and hats and baskets handwoven from green palm fronds.

Here's some local terminology you should know. If someone asks if you'd like a "sweetie," you're being offered a candy. When you buy spices, you may be offered "saffron" and "vanilla." The "saffron" is really turmeric, a ground yellow root rather than the (much more expensive) fragile pistils of crocus flowers; the "vanilla" is extracted from locally grown tonka beans rather than from actual (also much more expensive) vanilla beans. No one is trying to pull the wool over your eyes; these are common local terms. That said, the U.S. Food and Drug Administration warns that "vanilla" extracts made from tonka beans can have toxic effects and may pose a significant health risk for individuals taking certain medications.

SHOPPING AREAS AND MALLS

In St. George's, on the northern side of the harbor, **Young Street** is a main shopping thoroughfare; it rises steeply uphill from the Carenage and then descends just as steeply to **Market Square.** On Melville Street adjacent to the Cruise Ship Terminal, **Esplanade Mall** has shops that offer duty-free jewelry, electronics, liquor, and gift items, as well as local crafts. On Lagoon Road in Belmont, just south of St. George's Harbor, the **Grenada Craft Center** houses several shops with handmade art and craft items; some items are made in on-site workshops.

In Grand Anse, a short walk from the resorts, **Excel Plaza** has shops and services to interest locals and tourists alike, including a full-service health club and a three-screen movie theater. **Grand Anse Shopping Centre** has a supermarket and liquor store, a clothing store, a fast-food restaurant, a pharmacy, an art gallery, several small gift shops, and a doctor's office. **Le Marquis Complex** has restaurants, shops, and tourist services. **Spiceland Mall** has a modern supermarket with a liquor section, clothing and shoe boutiques for men and women, housewares stores, a wine shop, gift shops, an art gallery, a food court, a bank, and a video-game arcade.

SPECIALTY STORES

ART
Art and Soul Gallery. Owned by the noted Grenadian artist Susan Mains, Art and Soul is a full-service gallery with original works by local, regional, and international artists—including Mains herself. You can commission a portrait of yourself, your child, or even your pet. ⊠ *Spiceland Mall, Grand Anse, St. George* ☎ *473/439–3450* ⊕ *www. artandsoulgrenada.com.*

BOOKS
Sea Change. This handy bookstore is on the waterfront, below the New Nutmeg restaurant. ⊠ *The Carenage, St. George's* ☎ *473/440–3402.*

DUTY-FREE GOODS
Duty-free shops at the airport sell liquor at impressive discounts of up to 50%, as well as perfumes, crafts, and Grenadian syrups, jams, and hot sauces. You can shop duty-free at some shops in town, but you must show your passport and outbound ticket to get the duty-free prices.

Gittens. The three Gittens shops, spin-offs of a single pharmacy that opened in the 1940s, carry perfume and cosmetics. ⊠ *Halifax St., St. George's* ☎ *473/440–2165* ⊠ *Spiceland Mall, Grand Anse, St. George* ☎ *473/439–0860* ⊠ *Maurice Bishop International Airport, Point Salines, St. George* ☎ *473/444–2549.*

12

FOODS

FAMILY **Bonbon Chocolates.** The small Grenada Chocolate Company, founded in 1999, initially produced its now-famous chocolate bars in a small house-turned-factory in the village of Hermitage. Now the chocolate bars and a variety of chocolate bonbons are produced and sold at this outlet, located at the nearby Belmont Estate cocoa farm and fermentary. Employees use antique machinery powered by solar energy to roast cocoa beans supplied by a local cooperative of growers representing more than 150 acres of organic cocoa farms—the largest of which is Belmont Estate. They mix and temper small batches of rich, dark chocolate that are then molded and wrapped by hand into high-quality, organic chocolate bars (cocoa powder and cocoa butter are also available). The 82% chocolate bar was awarded the silver medal in 2011 by the London Academy of Chocolate. The candy bars also sell in supermarkets and gift shops for about $5 each. ⊠ *Belmont Estate, Belmont, St. Patrick* ☎ *473/442–0050* ⊕ *www.grenadachocolate.com.*

De La Grenade Industries. Nutmeg and guava jams and jellies, nutmeg syrup, nutmeg liqueur (from a 200-year-old family recipe), and a dozen other kinds of delicious jellies, marmalades, and condiments are all available from this famous local manufacturer. You can buy De La Grenade products at the processing plant, in food stores and gift shops throughout Grenada, and at duty-free shops in the airport departure lounge. ⊠ *Morne Délice, St. Paul's, St. George* ☎ *473/440–3241* ⊕ *www.delagrenade.com.*

Food Fair. The local supermarket chain is a great spot to buy spices, hot sauce, candy, snacks, and other edible gifts. Prices of locally produced goods are very reasonable; familiar brands imported from the United States may cost twice as much as back home. ⊠ *The Carenage, St. George's* ☎ *473/440–2488* ⊠ *Grand Anse Shopping Center, Grand Anse Main Rd., Grand Anse, St. George* ☎ *473/444–4573.*

Fodor's Choice ★ **Market Square.** This bustling produce market is open mornings. Saturday is busiest—and the best time and place to stock up on fresh fruit to enjoy during your stay and to buy packets of baskets of island-grown spices to take home. Vendors also sell crafts, leather goods, and decorative objects. ■**TIP**➜ **All in all, it's one of the best markets in the entire Caribbean.** ⊠ *Foot of Young St., on north side of town, St. George's.*

Marketing & National Importing Board. At this local market you'll find fresh fruits and vegetables, spices, hot sauces, and local syrups and jams at lower prices than in most gift shops. ⊠ *Young St., St. George's, St. George* ☎ *473/440–1791.*

Real Value IGA Supermarket. This large, modern supermarket carries a huge variety of familiar products, as well as local produce, meats and seafood, spices, sauces, snacks, sweets, and a broad selection of wines and spirits. ⊠ *Spiceland Mall, Grand Anse, St. George* ☎ *473/439–2121* ⊕ *www.realvalueiga.com.*

GIFTS

Arawak Islands. This workshop's spice-scented soaps, body oils, perfumes, insect repellents, balms, beeswax candles, and incense are all made by hand from 100% natural products, most of which are grown in Grenada. Visitors are welcome to watch the small group of workers sorting, blending, cutting, shaping, bottling, and labeling the products—and even cutting, sewing, hand-painting, and ironing the little cotton bags used for packaging. Arawak Islands products, including gift baskets, are sold in most gift shops. ✉ *Frequente Industrial Park, Airport Rd., Point Salines, St. George* ☎ *473/444–3577* ⊕ *www.arawak-islands.com.*

Imagine. The main draws at this gift shop are straw work, ceramics, island fashions, and batik fabrics. ✉ *Grand Anse Shopping Centre, Grand Anse Main Rd., Grand Anse, St. George* ☎ *473/444–4028.*

HANDICRAFTS

Art Fabrik. At Art Fabrik, you'll find batik fabric created by hand by as many as 45 home workers. It's sold by the yard or fashioned into pareos, dresses, shirts, shorts, hats, scarves, and bags. Part of the boutique is dedicated to demonstrating the batik process. ✉ *Young St., St. George's* ☎ *473/440–0568* ⊕ *www.artfabrikgrenada.com.*

Fidel Productions. Step inside this bright green shipping container planted in the Paradise Beach parking lot, and you'll be treated with a bevy of locally made gifts and souvenirs—hand-printed T-shirts, hand-painted calabashes, Arawak Island soaps and lotions, jewelry, caps, and more. ✉ *Paradise Beach, L'Esterre, Carriacou* ☎ *473/435–8866.*

Tikal. Regional artwork, carvings, jewelry, home goods, batik items, and a few fashions are the specialties at Tikal, established in 1959 as one of the first arts and crafts shops in Grenada. ✉ *Young St., St. George's* ☎ *473/440–2310.*

Vendor's Craft & Spice Market at Grand Anse. Managed by the Grenada Tourism Authority, this market has 82 booths for vendors who sell arts, crafts, spices, music tapes, clothing, produce, and refreshments. It's open daily from 7 to 7. ✉ *Grand Anse Beach, toward north end, Grand Anse, St. George* ☎ *473/444–3780.*

Veronica's Vision. Find colorful silk-screened lengths of fabric, along with handmade totes, bags, women's dresses, men's shirts and ties, T-shirts, scarves, belts, and cushions at this shop. The fabrics and other products are all designed and created by artist/designer Jessie-Ann Jessamy and hand-printed in her on-site workshop. The colors and themes celebrate the isle of spice—particularly the ubiquitous nutmeg. ✉ *Corner Lime Gap and Main Rd., opposite Excel Plaza, St. George* ☎ *473/437–8154* ⊕ *www.grenadaspicecloth.com.*

SPORTS AND ACTIVITIES

BOATING AND SAILING

12

As the "Gateway to the Grenadines," Grenada attracts boatloads of seasoned sailors to its waters. Large marinas are located at Port Louis along the Lagoon in St. George's, at Prickly Bay and True Blue on Grenada's southern coast, at Petite Calivigny Bay and St. David's in southeastern Grenada, and at Tyrell Bay in Carriacou. You can charter a yacht, with or without crew, for weeklong sailing vacations through the Grenadines. Scenic day sails along Grenada's coast cost about $145 per person (with a minimum of four passengers), including lunch or snacks and an open bar; a charter will cost $400 to $1,000 per day (with a five-day minimum), depending on the boat, for up to six people.

Carib Cats. Departing from Grand Anse Beach, Carib Cats' 60-foot sailing catamaran can be chartered for a full-day sail along the southwest coast, a half-day snorkel cruise to the Underwater Sculpture Park at Molinère Bay, or a two-hour sunset cruise along the west coast. ⊠ *Grand Anse Beach, St. George's* ☎ *473/444–3222.*

Footloose Yacht Charters. Operating from the Lagoon in St. George's, Footloose Yacht Charters has a catamaran spacious enough for three couples, as well as a 71-foot ocean ketch. Both are available for day trips around Grenada or longer charters to the Grenadines. ⊠ *Lagoon Rd., St. George's* ☎ *473/440–7949.*

Horizon Yacht Charters. Arrange either bareboat or crewed charters (there's a four-day minimum) on monohulls or catamarans through Horizon. ⊠ *True Blue Bay Marina, True Blue, St. George* ☎ *473/439–1000, 866/463–7245 in U.S.* ⊕ *www.horizonyachtcharters.com.*

Moorings. Based at Port Louis Marina in St. George's, Moorings offers bareboat or crewed charters on its custom-built 35-foot to 51-foot catamarans and monohulls. The diverse itinerary options include one-way charters to the company's bases in either Canouan or St. Lucia. ⊠ *Port Louis Marina, Lagoon Rd., St. George's* ☎ *800/535–7289* ⊕ *www.moorings.com.*

DIVING AND SNORKELING

You can see hundreds of varieties of fish and some 40 species of coral at more than a dozen sites off Grenada's southwestern coast—only 15 to 20 minutes away by boat—and another couple of dozen sites around Carriacou's reefs and neighboring islets. Depths vary from 20 to 120 feet, and visibility varies from 30 to 100 feet.

OFF GRENADA

For a spectacular dive, visit the ruins of *Bianca C,* a 600-foot cruise ship that caught fire in 1961, sank to 100 feet, and is now a coral-encrusted habitat for giant turtles, spotted eagle rays, barracuda, and jacks. **Boss Reef** extends 5 miles (8 km) from St. George's Harbour to Point Salines, with a depth ranging from 20 to 90 feet. **Flamingo Bay** has a wall that drops to 90 feet. It teems with fish, sponges, sea horses, sea fans, and coral. **Molinère Reef** slopes from about 20 feet below the surface to a wall that drops to 65 feet. Molinère is also the location of the Underwater Sculpture Park, a rather odd artificial reef consisting of more than 55 life-size figures that were sculpted by artist and scuba instructor Jason Taylor and placed on the sea bottom. An underwater bench gives divers a good view of the art gallery. Its most recent addition is a 2011 replica of Christ of the Deep, the statue that's on the promenade along the Carenage in St. George's. Molinère is a good dive for beginners; advanced divers can continue farther out to view the wreck of the *Buccaneer,* a 42-foot sloop.

OFF CARRIACOU

There's an active underwater volcano known as **Kick-em Jenny**, with plentiful coral and marine life in the vicinity and, usually, visibility up to 100 feet, though you can't dive down the 500 feet required to reach the actual volcano. **Sandy Island,** in Hillsborough Bay, is especially good for night diving and has fish that feed off its extensive reefs 70 feet below. For experienced divers, **Twin Sisters of Isle de Rhonde** is one of the most spectacular dives in the Grenadines, with walls and drop-offs of up to 185 feet and an underwater cave.

PADI-certified dive operators offer scuba and snorkeling trips to reefs and wrecks, including night dives and special excursions to the *Bianca C.* They also offer resort courses for beginning divers and certification instruction for more experienced divers. It costs about $60 for a one-tank dive, $105 for a two-tank dive, $65 for trips to the *Bianca C,* $145 to dive Isle de Rhonde, and $65 to $70 for night dives. Discounted 5- and 10-dive packages are usually offered. Resort courses cost about $100, and open-water certification runs from $265 to $460.

Most dive operators will take snorkelers along on dive trips or offer special snorkeling adventures. The best snorkeling in Grenada is at Molinère Point, north of St. George's; in Carriacou, magnificent Sandy Island is just a few hundred yards offshore. Snorkeling trips cost about $35 per person.

GRENADA DIVE OPERATORS

Aquanauts Grenada. Every morning Aquanauts Grenada heads out on two-tank dive trips, each accommodating no more than eight divers, to both the Caribbean and Atlantic sides of Grenada. Also available: guided snorkel trips; beach snorkeling; and special activities, courses, and equipment for children. ⊠ *Spice Island Beach Resort, Grand Anse Beach, Grand Anse, St. George* ☎ *473/444–1126, 850/3013–0330 in U.S.* ⊕ *www.aquanautsgrenada.com* ⊠ *True Blue Bay Resort, True Blue, St. George* ⊕ *www.aquanautsgrenada.com.*

Dive Grenada. Specializing in diving the *Bianca C* wreck and in family snorkeling trips, Dive Grenada heads out twice daily (at 10 am and 2 pm) to local dive sites. ⊠ *Flamboyant Hotel, Morne Rouge Rd., Morne Rouge, St. George* ☎ *473/444–1092* ⊕ *www.divegrenada.com.*

EcoDive. This full-service PADI dive shop offers two trips daily, both drift and wreck dives, as well as weekly trips to dive Isle de Rhonde and a full range of diving courses. EcoDive employs two full-time marine biologists who run Grenada's marine-conservation and education center and conduct coral-reef monitoring and restoration efforts. ⊠ *Coyaba Beach Resort, Grand Anse Beach, Grand Anse, St. George* ☎ *473/444–7777* ⊕ *www.ecodiveandtrek.com.*

ScubaTech Grenada. With three full-time diving instructors, ScubaTech Grenada offers the complete range of PADI programs—from "discover scuba," which allows novices to learn the basics and dive for the length of their vacation, to "dive master," the highest level a diver can achieve. Dive trips to local sites leave each morning. ⊠ *Calabash Hotel, Prickly Bay Beach, L'Anse aux Épines, St. George* ☎ *473/439–4346* ⊕ *www. scubatech-grenada.com.*

CARRIACOU DIVE OPERATORS

Arawak Divers. This company has its own jetty at Tyrell Bay; it takes small groups on daily dive trips and night dives, offers courses in German and English, and provides pickup service from yachts. ⊠ *Tyrell Bay, Harvey Vale, Carriacou* ☎ *473/443–6906* ⊕ *www.arawakdivers.com.*

Deefer Diving. Deefer Diving has two PADI dive masters and two PADI instructors that provide a full range of diving instruction on their catamaran, *Bobcat*, which accommodates up to 12 divers. The itinerary is flexible, so you can dive when and for as long as you like. There are two guided single-tank dives daily, as well as individually scheduled excursions. ⊠ *Main St., Hillsborough, Carriacou* ☎ *473/443–7882* ⊕ *www.deeferdiving.com.*

Lumbadive. The folks who operate Lumbadive share their enthusiasm for safe, exciting scuba-diving adventures with both new and experienced divers. Lumbadive offers open-water diving courses that range from "discover" to "dive master." ⊠ *On beachfront, Tyrell Bay, Harvey Vale, Carriacou* ☎ *473/443–8566* ⊕ *www.lumbadive.com.*

FISHING

Deep-sea fishing around Grenada is excellent. The list of likely catches includes marlin, sailfish, yellowfin tuna, and dorado (also known as mahimahi or dolphin). You can arrange sportfishing trips that accommodate up to five people starting at $475 for a half day and $700 for a full day.

True Blue Sportfishing. British-born Captain Gary Clifford, who has been fishing since the age of six, has run True Blue Sportfishing since 1998. He offers big-game charters for up to six passengers on the 31-foot *Yes Aye*. The boat has an enclosed cabin, a fighting chair, and professional tackle. Refreshments and transportation to the marina are included. ⊠ *True Blue Bay Marina, True Blue, St. George* ☎ *473/444–2048* ⊕ *www.yesaye.com.*

GOLF

Grenada Golf & Country Club. Determined golfers might want to try the 9-hole course at the Grenada Golf & Country Club. Separate tees allow for an 18-hole configuration. Located halfway between St. George's and Grand Anse, the layout features lateral hazards and challenging rough, and small, elevated sloping putting surfaces. Spread over the top of a hill, with strong winds fairly common, the course is more challenging than you might expect. Your hotel can make arrangements for you. Popular with local businesspeople, this course is convenient to most hotels and is the only public course on the island. The club has changing rooms as well as club rental, a bar and restaurant. ⊠ *Golf Course Hill, Belmont, St. George* ☎ *473/444–4128* ✝ *9 holes (played twice from different tees) 5165 yards, par 67* ⊴ *$16; $24 to play the course twice (from separate tees).*

GUIDED TOURS

Guided tours offer the historical sights of St. George's, Grand Étang National Park & Forest Reserve, spice plantations and nutmeg-processing stations, rain-forest hikes and treks to waterfalls, snorkeling trips to local islands, and day trips to Carriacou. A full-day sightseeing tour costs $70 to $90 per person, usually including lunch and admissions; a half-day tour, $45 to $60; a guided hike to Concord or Mt. Qua Qua, $55 to $60 per person. Grenada taxi drivers will conduct island sightseeing tours for $150 per day or $25 to $35 per hour for up to four people. Carriacou minibus drivers will take up to four people on a 2½-hour island tour for $60 and $20 per hour thereafter.

Adventure Jeep Tour. On Adventure Jeep Tour you ride in the back of a Land Rover, safari fashion, along scenic coastal roads, trek in the rain forest, have lunch at a plantation, take a swim, and skirt the capital. The company also combines a full-day jeep tour ($85 per person) with river tubing (add $45 per person) and offers guided bike tours ($15 an hour). ⊠ *St. George's, St. George* ☎ *473/444–5337* ⊕ *www. adventuregrenada.com.*

Caribbean Horizons. Personalized half- or full-day tours of historic and natural island sites, market and garden tours, and sailing excursions to Carriacou are all available from this company. ⊠ *True Blue, St. George* ☎ *473/444–1555* ⊕ *www.caribbeanhorizons.com.*

Edwin Frank's Tours. After 22 years as public relations officer for the Grenada Board of Tourism—and as a radio and TV personality in his own right—Edwin Frank brings to his daily island tours a wealth of information about Grenada's history, geography, politics, culture, flora, fauna, and cuisine, along with a range of contemporary perspectives about life in and on this lovely island. ⊠ *Calvigny, St. George* ☎ *473/407–5393.*

Henry's Safari Tours. Denis Henry knows Grenada like the back of his hand. He leads adventurous hikes and nature safaris in four-wheel-drive vehicles, or you can design your own half- or full-day "as you like it" tour for $25–$35 per hour, depending on the number of people. ⊠ *Woburn, St. George* ☎ *473/444–5313* ⊕ *www.henrysafari.com.*

Isle of Reefs Tours. A soft adventure tour operator, Isle of Reefs specializes in guided hiking treks, boat trips to the Tobago Cays, mountain bike rentals, offshore camping trips, dingy sailing lessons, and cookery classes. ⊠ *L'Esterre, Carriacou* ☎ *473/404–0415* ⊕ *www. isleofreefstours.com.*

Take an exciting safari-style tour of Grenada on an Adventure Jeep Tour.

Mandoo Tours. Whether for one or two people or for a busload, Mandoo (Simon Seales) offers half- or full-day standardized island tours that follow northern, southern, or eastern routes. An environmentalist at heart and determined advocate for the preservation of the island's heritage, he will gladly arrange customized tours, as well as hikes to waterfalls, the rain forest, and the mountains. ✉ *Mt. Moritz, St. George* ☎ *473/440–1428* ⊕ *www.grenadatours.com.*

Sunsation Tours. You can visit all the usual sites or go as far off the beaten track as you want to go on Sunsation Tours' customized island tours, market tours, home and garden tours, challenging hikes, and day sails. ✉ *Le Marquis Complex, Grand Anse, St. George* ☎ *473/444–1594* ⊕ *www.grenadasunsation.com.*

HIKING

EcoTrek. This company takes small groups on day trips to the heart of the rain forest, where you'll find hidden waterfalls and hot-spring pools. A half-day hike to Seven Sisters Waterfall ($55 per person) is suitable for the reasonably fit; full-day adventures to other destinations are more strenuous. ■TIP→ **Make arrangements at the main location at Coyaba Beach Resort in Grand Anse or at Port Louis Marina on Lagoon Rd. in St. George's.** ✉ *Coyaba Beach Resort, Grand Anse, St. George* ☎ *473/232–7777* ⊕ *www.ecodiveandtrek.com.*

Fodor's Choice
★ **Grand Étang National Park & Forest Reserve.** Mountain trails wind through Grand Étang National Park & Forest Reserve; if you're lucky, you may spot a Mona monkey or some exotic birds on your hike. There are trails

for all levels—from a self-guided nature trail around Grand Étang Lake to a demanding hike through the bush to the peak of Mt. Qua Qua (2,373 feet) or a major trek up Mt. St. Catherine (2,757 feet). Long pants and hiking shoes are recommended. Expect to pay $25 per person for a four-hour guided hike up Mt. Qua Qua, $20 each for two or more, or $15 each for three or more; the Mt. St. Catherine hike starts at $35 per person. ⊠ *Grand Étang, St. Andrew* ☎ *473/440–6160.*

Henry's Safari Tours. The personalized hiking excursions here include trips through rich agricultural land and rain forest to remote waterfalls, the summit of Mt. Qua Qua, and other fascinating spots. ⊠ *Woburn, St. George* ☎ *473/444–5313, 347/721–9271 in U.S.* ⊕ *www.henrysafari.com.*

Telfor Bedeau Hiking Tours. Over the years Telfor Bedeau has walked up, down, or across nearly every mountain, trail, and pathway on the island. He first began hiking at age 23. That was in 1962. By now, he has hiked more than 13,000 miles (21,000 km) over, around, and through Grenada. Even well into his 70s, his experience and knowledge of the trails and his inexhaustible energy and patience make him an excellent guide, whether it's an easy walk with novices or a strenuous hike with experts. ⊠ *Soubise, St. Andrew* ☎ *473/442–6200.*

GUADELOUPE

Visit Fodors.com for advice, updates, and bookings

WELCOME TO GUADELOUPE

Guadeloupe Passage

La Pointe d la Grande Vigie

Plage de la Chapelle à Anse Bertrand

Anse Bertrand `N8`

Campêche

`N6`

Port Louis `N8`

Les Mangles `N6`

Gros Cap

Beauport `N6`

Petit-Canal `D12`

G R A N D

Anse du Vieux Fort

Pte. Allègre

La Grande-Anse

`11`

Ilet à Fajou

Anse du Canal

Vieux-Bourg

Morne-à-l'Eau `N5`

`9` `12`

`12`

`13`

Ste-Rose

`N2`

Grand Cul-de-Sac Marin

Jabrun du Sud

Jabrun du Nord

`10`

Deshaies

`N2`

Abymes

Lamentin

✈ **Airport**

Pointe-Noire

Destrelan

`N1`

Pointe-à-Pitre

B A S S E

Fort Fleur d'Epée `1` `2`

`1` `2`

Anse Caraïbe

Cascade aux Ecrevisses

`N1`

Bas-du-Fort

Mahaut

La Traversée

`D23`

Petit-Bourg

Aquarium de Caravel la Guadeloupe

Plag

Ilet de Pigeon

Les Mamelles

Vernou

Pigeon Island 🔲

Malendure

Pigeon

Parc National de la Guadeloupe

Bouillante

`11`

Goyave

T E R R E

Marigot

La Soufrière

Ste-Marie

`N2`

`N1`

Vieux-Habitants

Le Musée Volcanologique

Capesterre-Belle-Eau

Plage de Rocroy

Matouba

St-Claude

Chutes du Carbet

Anse Chapelle

`D11`

Gourbeyre

St-Sauveur

`N1`

Bananier

`D6`

Trois-Rivières

Basse-Terre ✪

`D6`

`14`

Anse Turlet

Vieux Fort

`8` - `10`

`15` - `18`

Iles des Saintes (Les Saintes)

Pompierres

`19`

Terre-de-Haut

Terre-de-Bas

Anse Crawen

La Coche

Grand Ilet

Caribbean Sea

KEY	
⤓	Beaches
⚓	Cruise Ship Terminal
🔲	Dive Sites
▪	Restaurants
①	Hotels
⛴	Ferry

A heady blend of Afro-Caribbean customs, French style, and tropical delights, butterfly-shape Guadeloupe is actually two islands divided by a narrow channel: smaller, flatter, and drier Grande-Terre (Large Land) and wetter and more mountainous Basse-Terre (Low Land). Sheltered by palms, the beaches are beguiling, and the waterfront sidewalk cafés are a bit like the Riviera.

THE BUTTERFLY ISLAND

Guadeloupe, annexed by France in 1674, is not a single island but rather an archipelago. The largest parts of the chain are Basse-Terre and Grande-Terre, which together are shaped somewhat like a large butterfly. The "out" islands are the Iles des Saintes, La Désirade, and Marie-Galante.

13

GUADELOUPE

ATLANTIC OCEAN

Anse de la Savane Brûlée

Baie du Nord-Ouest
L'Autre Bord
Plage le Moule
N7
D101
Le Moule
D114
6
St. François Airport
Anse de la Gourde
Anse à la Baie
Pointe Tarare
TERRE
St-François
Ste-Anne
7 **5** **8**
Pointe des Châteaux
Anse Kahouanne
5
Plage du Helleux
4 **6**
3 **3** **4**
Iles de la Petite Terre

Porte d'Enfer
7 La Désirade
Le Soufleur Plage
Grande-Anse

0 ——— 10 miles
0 ——— 15 km

Anse de Vieux Fort
Grosse Pte.
Vieux Fort
21
Anse Carot
20
Baie de St. Louis
13
Saint Louis
Marie-Galante
Plage de Folle Anse
Châteaux Murat
Capesterre
22 **23** **15**
Grand-Bourg
D203
14
Petite-Anse
Pte. Des Basses
Aérodrome de Marie-Galante

Restaurants ▼		Hotels ▼	
Café Wango	4	Au Village de Menard	21
Chez Clara	12	Auberge de la Vieille Tour	1
Chez Henri	13	Bwa Chik Hotel	7
Couleurs du Monde	8	Caraib Bay Hotel	13
Iguane Café	5	Club Med La Caravelle	3
Restaurant La Savane	15	Habitation du Comté	9
La Toubana	3	Hotel Amundo	5
Le Rocher de Malendure	11	Hotel Les Petits Saints	15
La Porte	6	Langley Hotel	12
Le Touloulou	14	La Cocoteraie	6
Oualiri Breeze	7	La Créole Beach	2
Restaurant Les Petits Saints	9	La Rose de Bresil	22
Restaurant de la Vielle Tour	2	La Toubana Hôtel	4
Ti Kaz La	10	Le Jardin de Malanga	14
Zawag	1	Le Neem	8
		Le Soleil Levant	23
		Le Village de Canada	20
		Lô Bleu Hôtel	17
		Paradis Saintois	16
		Residence Anse Caraibe	18
		Residence Grand Baie	19
		Tainos Cottages	11
		Tendacayou Ecolodge	10

TOP REASONS TO VISIT GUADELOUPE

1 Creole Flavors: Guadeloupe's restaurants and hotel dining rooms highlight the island's fine creole cuisine.

2 Small Inns: Also called *relais* and *gites* (apartments) these intimate accommodations give you a genuine island experience.

3 Adventure Sports: Parc National has plenty of activities to keep the adrenaline pumping.

4 La Désirade: Remote and affordable, this friendly island provides an escape-from-it-all experience.

EATING AND DRINKING WELL IN THE FRENCH WEST INDIES

Creole cuisine, a sultry mélange of African, European, Arawak, even Asian traditions, reflects the islands' turbulent territorial tugs-of-war.

Deceptively simple yet robustly flavored, authentic "Kweyol" cuisine demands patience to make: continual macerating and marinating, then seasoning as the food simmers. Many dishes developed in response to economic necessities, recycling leftovers and incorporating ingredients such as starches (both hardy and impervious to spoilage). The indigenous Arawaks provided tubers such as tannia and yucca; lemongrass and capsicum for seasoning; arrowroot for thickening; and *roucou* (annatto, a yellowish-reddish seed) for coloring. The Africans imported plantains, pigeon peas, potatoes, and peppers. The French and British introduced tomatoes, onions, and less perishable salt cod. East Indian indentured servants brought cumin, cardamom, and coriander, notably used in *colombo*, a

meat (try *cabri*, goat), poultry, or seafood dish that detonates the palate. Wash it down with fresh local juices from pulpy papaya to puckering passion fruit or the fine rums. Bon appétit!

Blaff. This typical method of preparation is usually used for firm, flaky, white fish such as mahimahi or grouper. The fish is poached in a seasoned broth, often a classic court-bouillon (a quick stock perfumed with fresh herbs). The broth is then doctored with lime, onion, garlic, cilantro, chilies, and other ingredients to create the incendiary "condiment" *sauce chien* (whose etymology is obscure, but may indeed have been named "dog's sauce" because it would render even canines edible).

Cod. France contributed many basic ingredients over time to economize, notably dried salt cod, which required

13

no refrigeration and became a staple in creole cooking. *Accras de morue*, fluffy cod fritters, grace every menu. Other popular traditional dishes include *chiquetaille*, shredded cod usually served with a spicy vinaigrette, and *ferocé* (saltfish mixed with avocado and peppers, deep-fried in manioc flour). *Tinnain morue*, grilled cod and bananas believed to energize, still jump-starts many locals' days.

Crayfish. This spiky freshwater crustacean, both wild and, increasingly, farmed, is usually served whole with a variety of sauces. It goes by many names in the French West Indies, including the more Gallic *écrevisse*, patois *z'habitant* or *crebiche*, and *ouassou* (generally larger). A favorite preparation is stewed with *dombrés* (manioc dumplings served pancake-style); you may also see it *étouffée* (stewed with vegetables, served over rice), underscoring the similarity to Cajun cuisine (alongside such dishes as *boudin*, blood sausage).

Poulet Boucané. "Buccaneer's chicken" is smoked slowly over burnt sugarcane (a centuries-old warning signal that pirates were coming) in a closed, chimney-topped barbecue. *Boucanage* is also a French preservation technique, "drying" seasoned meats and poultry on a wood fire (in this case using sugarcane husks). Roughly similar to Jamaica's jerk, it mingles smokiness, sweetness,

and spiciness; the marinade typically is a variant of the combustible sauce chien, though milder versions might combine vinegar, lime, garlic, and clove.

'Ti Punch. The primary ingredient in this aperitif is 100-proof rum, occasionally fruit-infused, muddled with lime and simple cane syrup. Novices can request the lighter (weight) *ti-bete*. Another concoction worth sampling is the classic *planteur* (rum with fruit juices and spices); finish dinner with a *rhum vieux* (aged, cognac-quality rum) like Reimonenq's Ste. Rose, or *shrubb*, an orange-and-spice-tinged rum-based liqueur.

Tripe. Another old-fashioned method of economizing was the use of internal organs, offal, which eventually became appropriated by haute cuisine. Tripe (small intestines) is particularly popular. The classic dish is *bébélé*, a stew of tripe, green bananas, tubers (usually breaded as croquettes or *domblés*), and gourds such as *giraumon* (similar to pumpkin).

—Jordan Simon

(Top left) Lobster Barbecue (Bottom right) 'Ti Punch
(Top right) Accras—Salt Cod Fritters

Updated by
Eileen Robin-
son Smith

Sail the waters around the Isles of Guadeloupe and you'll observe nuances in the ocean's color palette as you glide through the gin-clear sea. Things look better from the bow of a sailboat, from the storybook islands of Les Saintes to towns not as postcard pretty. This Caribbean coastline is dramatic with white and golden beaches, rocky promontories, and rugged cliffs that span the horizon.

Although Guadeloupe is thought of as one island, it is several, each with its own personality. "The mainland" consists of the two largest islands in the Guadeloupe archipelago: Basse-Terre and Grande-Terre, which look something like a butterfly. The outer islands—Les Saintes, Marie-Galante, and La Désirade—are finally being acknowledged as wonderfully unique, unspoiled travel destinations. Tourism officials are now wisely marketing their country as a plural, Les Iles de Guadeloupe. See which one is your place in the sun. *Vive les vacances!*

It's no wonder that in 1493 Christopher Columbus welcomed the sight of this emerald paradise, where fresh, sweet water flows in cascades. And it's understandable why France annexed it in 1674 and why the British schemed to wrench it from them. In 1749 Guadeloupe mirrored what was happening in the motherland. It, too, was an island divided between royalists and revolutionaries.

The resident British sided with the royalists, so Victor Hugues was sent to banish the Brits. While here, he sent to the guillotine more than 300 planters loyal-to-the-royals and freed the slaves, thus all but destroying the plantocracy. An old saying of the French Caribbean refers to *les grands seigneurs de la Martinique et les bonnes gens de la Guadeloupe* (the lords of Martinique and the bourgeoisie of Guadeloupe), and that still rings true. You'll find more aristocratic descendants of the original French planters on Martinique (known as *békés*) and also more "expensive" people both living and vacationing there. That mass beheading is one of the prime reasons. Napoléon—who ultimately ousted the royals—also ousted Hugues and reestablished slavery. It wasn't until 1848 that an Alsatian, Victor Schoelcher, abolished it for good.

LOGISTICS

Getting to Guadeloupe: You can now connect in Miami with American Airlines direct flight on Saturday or go through San Juan or another Caribbean island. Some travelers prefer the regularly scheduled ferry service from Dominica, St. Lucia, and Martinique, but the extra travel time certainly increases the hassle factor. The smaller islands—though charming and rewarding—are harder to reach; even with regular ferries and air service, you will almost always need to spend some time on Guadeloupe both coming and going. Aéroport International Pôle Caraïbes, 3 miles (5 km) from Pointe-à-Pitre (PTP), is a fairly modern airport by Caribbean standards.

Hassle Factor: Medium for Guadeloupe to high for the smaller islands.

On the Ground: Cabs meet flights at the airport if you decide not to rent a car. The metered fare is about €25 to Pointe-à-Pitre, €30 to Gosier, and €70 or more to St-François. Fares go up 40% on Sunday and holidays and from 7 pm to 7 am. You can take a public bus from the airport to downtown Pointe-à-Pitre, but that's not a good option if you have a lot of luggage. And there are no recommendable hotels in the city.

13

Guadeloupe became one of France's *départements d'outremer* in 1946, meaning that it's a dependent of France. It was designated a region in 1983, making it a part of France, albeit a distant part. This brought many benefits to the islanders, from their fine highway systems to the French social services and educational system, as well as a high standard of living. Certain tensions still exist, though the anticolonial resentment harbored by the older generations is dying out. Guadeloupe's young people realize the importance of tourism to the island's future, and you'll find them welcoming, smiling, and practicing the English and tourism skills they learn in school. Some *français* is indispensable, though you may receive a bewildering response in Creole.

Guadeloupe has a little bit of France, but the culture of this tropical paradise is more Afro-influenced. Savor the earthier pleasures here, exemplified by the wonderful potpourri of whole spices whose heady aromas flood the outdoor markets.

PLANNING

WHEN TO GO
The tourism industry thrives during the high season, which lasts from mid-November through May, and then the island is quiet the rest of the year. Prices decline 25% to 40% in the off-season.

GETTING HERE AND AROUND
AIR TRAVEL
The nonstop service now available is from Miami on American Airlines and on Seaborne Airlines, flying out of San Juan direct, four times weekly. It has interline agreements (codeshares) with both American

Airlines and JetBlue. Air Canada flies weekly nonstops between Montreal (YUL) and Pointe-à-Pitre. Air Antilles Express has service to Martinique; St. Martin; Cayenne, French Guiana; St. Lucia; and Santo Domingo, Dominican Republic.

Air Caraïbes connects the island to St. Maarten; Martinique; Haiti; St. Barth; French Guiana, St. Lucia; Santo Domingo, Dominican Republic; Havana, Cuba; and Paris.

Air France's weekly flights between Miami and Guadeloupe stop in Haiti before landing in Pointe-a-Pitre. Air France is a Parisian connection, of course, and from the islands you can sometimes get good prices to France.

LIAT mainly services the English-speaking Caribbean islands, including Antigua, Barbados, and St. Lucia. St. Lucia has direct service from New York, Miami, Atlanta, and Toronto. These flights are one way for U.S. and Canadian travelers to get to Guadeloupe with fewer stopovers. LIAT code-shares with Air Caraïbes.

A carrier new to the French Islands, Seaborne Airlines now flies to Guadeloupe four times a week out of San Juan on Monday, Tuesday, Thursday, and Saturday. Flights are timed for connections to and from the United States and Canada. A new code-share program between American Airlines and Seaborne Airlines allows you to book your American Airlines and Seaborne Airlines combined itinerary on *www.aa.com* while earning AAdvantage program miles. They have just entered into a similar agreement with JetBlue.

Airline Contacts Air Antilles Express. ☏ *0890/64–86–48* ⊕ *www.airantilles. com.* **Air Canada.** ☏ *888/247–2262, 0590/21–12–77* ⊕ *www.aircanada.com.* **Air Caraïbes.** ☏ *0820/83–58–35* ⊕ *www.aircaraibes.com.* **Air France.** ☏ *0590/21–13–03, 0820/82–08–20, 800/237–2747* ⊕ *www.airfance.com.* **American Airlines.** ⊕ *www.aa.com.* **LIAT.** ☏ *0590/21–13–93, 888/844–5428* ⊕ *www.liatairline.com.* **Seaborne Airlines.** ☏ *866/359–8784* ⊕ *www.seaborneairlines.com.*

AIRPORTS AND TRANSFERS

Aéroport International Pôle Caraïbes (PTP). Aéroport International Pôle Caraïbes (PTP), usually called the Pointe-à-Pitre Airport, is one of the largest and most modern in the Caribbean. Excellent signage makes it very manageable. It has shops, restaurants, and car-rental agencies. There is a tourism information booth in the terminal with bilingual staffers, an ATM, and a currency exchange. Ask your resort if airport transfers can be arranged, as they are almost always cheaper than taking a taxi. ✉ *Morne Mamiel, Abymes* ☏ *0590/21–71–71, 0590/21–14–00* ⊕ *www.guadeloupe.aeroport.fr.*

Taxi fare to Pointe-à-Pitre is about €25, to Gosier resorts about €30, to Ste-Anne €60, and to St-François more than €70. Cabs meet flights at the airport if you decide not to rent a car.

CAR TRAVEL

Renting a Car: If you're based in Gosier or at a large resort, you'll probably need a car only for a day or two of sightseeing. That may be enough, since roundabouts, mountain roads, and fast, aggressive drivers are stressful. Your valid driver's license will suffice for up to 20 days. You can get a rental car from the airport or your hotel. Count on spending between €48 and €70 a day for a small car with standard shift; automatics are considerably more expensive and must be reserved in advance. Note that some companies, including Europcar, charge a €20 drop-off fee for the airport, even if you pick the car up there. Allow at least 30 to 60 minutes to drop off your car at the end of your stay. The chances of your getting lost on the way to the airport and to where you need to leave the car are such that you should probably allow a full hour. Conscientiously follow every sign that has a picture of a plane. You must return the car to the old (former) airport and wait for a shuttle to bring you back to the current airport. An alternative is to return it in Gosier and put that €20 toward a stress-free taxi ride. Return your vehicle with the same amount of gas or you'll be charged an exorbitant rate.

DRIVING TIPS

Guadeloupeans are fast and often impatient drivers, and they tailgate. Driving around Grande-Terre is relatively easy for there is a well-maintained system of highways. Basse-Terre requires more skill to navigate the hairpin bends in the mountains and around the eastern shore; at night the roads are unlighted and treacherous. Roundabouts (*rond-pointes*) are everywhere. Use your turn signal and proceed cautiously. If you're lost, don't ask people standing on the side of the road; they are waiting for a lift and may jump in. Try to find a gas station. *"Je suis perdue!"* (I am lost!) is a good phrase to know.

Car Rental Contacts **Avis** ☎ 0590/85–69–00, 0590/21–13–54, 800/331–1212 ⊕ www.avis.fr. **Budget** ☎ 0590/21–13–49 ⊕ www.budgetantilles.com. **Europcar** ☎ 0590/21–13–52 ⊕ www.europcar-guadelooupe.com. **Hertz** ☎ 0590/21–13–46 ⊕ www.hertzantilles.com. **Jumbo Car** ☎ 0820/22–02–30 ⊕ www.jumbocar.com. **Sixt** ☎ 0590/21–13–44 ⊕ www.sixt.com.

FERRY TRAVEL

Ferry schedules and fares often change, so phone ahead to confirm. You normally travel to the outlying islands in the archipelago in the morning, returning in the afternoon. Both Comatrile and Express des Isles operate ferries between Terre-de-Haut and Marie-Galante.

One of the newer ferries, Jeans for freedom, is owned by L'Express des Isles. Its ferries go between Pointe-à-Pitre, Guadeloupe, and St-Pierre, Martinique; they also make a brief stop in Dominica. The price is approximately €79. Jeans also connects Fort-de-France to St. Lucia (€70). In Guadeloupe, service is also available between Pointe-à-Pitre and Marie-Galante or Les Saintes for €19. Round trip tickets are discounted, as are children's.

BABOU One. This ferry runs between St-François and La Désirade and on certain days, Marie Galante and/or Les Saintes. ☎ 0690/50–05–10, 0590/22–26–31. **Comatrile.** Comatrile travels from St-François on Grande Terre to Désirade, to St. Louis on Marie-Galante and Terre de Haut on Les Saintes. January through March the boat leaves Saint Francois at 7:05 am and returns from Marie Galante at 3:45 pm. From April onward the schedule will be 7:15 am from Saint Francois and 3 pm from Marie-Galante. The cost is €56 RT if you are staying more than one night. If you are doing a day trip (coming back the same day) then the promotion is €38. Bwa Chik, the ecohotel in St. Francois, is offering a special package with the newly refreshed Cap Reva property in Marie Galante. Year-round the schedule to Les Saintes is Monday–Sunday 7:15 am, Sant Francois departure; at 3 pm it returns from Terre de Haut. Fare: €58 RT. If doing a same-day round-trip, there is a promotion for €39. To and from Desirade, the schedule is Monday–Sunday the ferry leaves St Francois at 4:45 pm and departs from Desirade at 5:06 am. Cost is €28 RT. ✉ *Marina de St-François, St-François* ☎ *0690/50–05–09 port, 0590/22–26–31.* **C.T.M. DEHER.** C.T.M. DEHER goes between Trois-Rivieres and Terre-de-Haut, Les Saintes, departing at 9 am and returning to Guadeloupe at 4 pm daily. ☎ *0590/99–50–68* ⊕ *www.ctmdeher.com.* **Jeans for freedom.** This company is owned by L'Express des Isles and operates two ferries to Martinique and Les Saintes, also. ✉ *St-Pierre, Martinique* ☎ *0825/01–01–25* ⊕ *www.jeansforfreedom.com.* **L'Express des Isles.** L'Express des Isles runs ferries to Marie-Galante and to Les Saintes (about €19), from Pointe-à-Pitre. Longer trips to other islands like Dominica, Martinique, and St. Lucia cost about €79 one-way (€109 round-trip) and take between three and four hours. ■ TIP➔ **Be prepared for bad weather and choppy seas, which are especially likely on longer runs, when the boats are in open water.** That said, the company uses larger ferries when heading to and from Dominica and Martinique, and that makes for a smoother ride. French films (sometimes R-rated) on flat-screen TVs help pass the time. There are extra departures on weekends and holidays and for special events, when the ferries can be crowded. Note that the company enforces its overweight baggage rules and uses the same limits as the airlines. A snack bar on board sells beverages, including snacks and oftentimes simple sandwiches, which they sometimes run out of. Be prepared and B.Y.O. food. ☎ *0825/35–90–00* ⊕ *www.express-des-iles.com.*

TAXI TRAVEL

Taxis are metered and fairly pricey. Fares jump by 40% between 7 pm and 7 am and on Sunday and holidays.

CDL Taxi. If your French is in order, you can call this company, which has "radio cabs" (or ask your hotel receptionist to call them for you). ☎ *0590/20–74–74.* **Jean Luc of St-François.** Accommodating and punctual, this pleasant driver has multiple vehicles and speaks English well. ☎ *0690/57–59–40.*

ESSENTIALS

Banks and Exchange Services Few places accept U.S. dollars, so plan on exchanging them for euros. You must exchange cash at a bank, your hotel or a *bureau de change*, which has a better exchange rate. One favorite company is Change Caraïbe, with branches near the tourist office and market in Pointe-à-Pitre. It's easier to use your ATM card to get euros. There are a number of banks that have outdoor ATMs in downtown Pointe-à-Pitre. To use them, make sure you have a four-digit PIN, and be aware that they will charge a fee of about 2 euros for withdrawals and your own bank as much as $5. ATMs, particularly those in smaller towns, don't always accept foreign bank cards. Visa and MasterCard are most often accepted, followed by American Express.

There are just two ATMs on the main island of Iles des Saintes, one at the ferry dock and the other at the post office, which has erratic hours. Come with extra cash reserve, because it's not unusual for ATMs to run out of euros or to malfunction during electrical blackouts.

Electricity 220 volts/50 cycles. North American electronics and laptops (sometimes) require an adapter and a plug converter.

Emergency Services **Ambulance** ☎ *15*. **Fire** ☎ *18*. **Police emergencies** ☎ *17*. **SAMU**. SAMU is a medical service when you need to see a doctor fast. ☎ *0590/89–11–00*.

13

Etiquette Guadeloupeans are deeply religious and traditional, particularly the older generations. Revealing shorts or swimwear away from the beach may be considered indecorous by some, and you should ask before taking a picture of any islander. The children, however, will probably flash you one of their happy smiles. Observe the courtesy of saying *bonjour* or *bonsoir* when you enter or leave a place or before asking someone a question or directions.

Language The official language is French, though most of the islanders also speak Creole, a lyrical patois that you won't be able to understand. Often, their French has a heavy Creole accent. Most of the staff in hotels knows some English as do some taxi drivers, but communicating is decidedly more difficult in the countryside. Arm yourself with a phrase book, a dictionary, patience, and a sense of humor.

Passport Requirements You must have a valid passport as well as a return or ongoing ticket to enter Guadeloupe.

Phones To make on-island calls, dial 0590 (0690 if it is a cellular phone) and then the six-digit phone number. To call Guadeloupe from the United States, dial 00–590–590, then the local number. For cell phone numbers, dial 00–590–690, then the local number. If you're on one of the other islands in the French West Indies, dial 0590 and then the local number.

Taxes and Service Charges The *taxe de séjour* (room tax), which varies by hotel, is usually €1 but never exceeds €1.80 per person per day. Most hotel prices include a 10% to 15% service charge in their rates; if not, it'll be added to your bill. A 15% service charge is included in all restaurant prices, as are taxes.

Tipping Restaurants are required to include that 15% service charge in the menu price. No additional gratuity is necessary (although it's appreciated if service is particularly good). Tip skycaps and porters about €2 a bag, cabdrivers 10% of the fare (if they work for a cab company rather than having their own taxi), and housekeeping €2 per night.

ACCOMMODATIONS

Guadeloupe is actually an archipelago of large and small islands. Grande-Terre has the big package hotels that are concentrated primarily in four or five communities on the south coast, whereas wilder Basse-Terre has more locally owned hotels. More distant and much quieter are the Iles des Saintes, Marie-Galante, and La Désirade, in that order. On each of these smaller islands tourism is only a part of the economy and development is light, and any of them will give you a sense of what the Caribbean used to be.

Relais and Gites: These small inns offer a more personal—and authentic—kind of Caribbean experience.

Resorts: You can certainly opt for a big, splashy resort with all the amenities. Many of the island's large chain hotels cater to French package groups and are relatively bare-bones, though an increasing number of them are being renovated to the degree that they will appeal more to Americans as well.

Villas: Private villas are another option—particularly for families—but the language barrier is often a deterrent to Americans. Best to go through one of the rental agencies recommended here.

HOTEL AND RESTAURANT PRICES

Prices in the restaurant reviews are the average cost of a main course at dinner or, if dinner is not served, at lunch; taxes and service charges are generally included. Prices in the hotel reviews are the lowest cost of a standard, double room in high season, which generally include taxes and service charges but not any optional meal plans. Prices for rentals are the lowest per-night cost for a one-bedroom unit in high season.

For expanded lodging reviews and current deals, visit Fodors.com.

VISITOR INFORMATION

Contacts Comité du Tourisme des Iles de Guadeloupe ⊠ *5 sq. de la Banque, Pointe-à-Pitre* 📠 *0590/82–09–30* ⊕ *www.lesilesdeguadeloupe.com.* **Office de Tourisme de Désirade** ⊠ *La Capitainerie-Beausejour, waterfront at ferry dock, La Désirade* 📠 *0590/85–00–86.* **Office du Tourisme de Marie-Galante.** Located right in town, this office has staff who speak English and who are quite helpful. ⊠ *Rue du Fort, BP 15, Grand-Bourg, Marie-Galante* 📠 *0590/97–56–51* ⊕ *www.ot-mariegalante.com* ⊘ *Mid-July–mid-Aug. and Dec.–May, weekdays 9–4, weekends 9–noon; mid-Aug.–Nov. and June–mid-July, weekdays 9–1.* **Office du Tourisme de St-François** ⊠ *Av. de l'Europe, St-François, Grande-Terre* 📠 *0590/68–66–81* ⊘ *Weekdays 8–noon and 2–5, weekends 9–noon and 3–5).* **Office du Tourisme de Terre de Haut** ⊠ *Ferry Dock, Jean Calot St., PB 10, Terre-de-Haut, Iles des Saintes* 📠 *0590/94–30–61* ⊕ *www.lessaintes.fr.*

WEDDINGS

A long residency requirement makes weddings prohibitive.

EXPLORING

To see each "wing" of the butterfly, you'll need to budget at least one day. They are connected by a bridge, and Grande-Terre has pretty villages along its south coast and the spectacular Pointe des Châteaux. You can see the main sights in Pointe-à-Pitre in a half day. Touring the rugged, mountainous Basse-Terre is a challenge. If time is a problem, head straight to the west coast; you could easily spend a day traveling its length, stopping for sightseeing, lunch, and a swim. You can make day trips to the islands, but an overnight or more works best. Leave your heavy luggage in the baggage room of your "mainland" hotel.

GRANDE-TERRE

POINTE-À-PITRE

Although not the capital, this is the island's largest city, a commercial and industrial hub in the southwest of Grande-Terre. The Isles of Guadeloupe have 450,000 inhabitants, 99.6% of whom live in the cities. Pointe-à-Pitre is bustling, noisy, and hot—a place of honking horns and traffic jams and cars on sidewalks for want of a parking place. By day its pulse is fast, but at night, when its streets are almost deserted, you don't want to be there.

The heart of the old city is Place de la Victoire; surrounded by wooden buildings with balconies and shutters (including the tourism office) and by sidewalk cafés, it was named in honor of Victor Hugues's 1794 victory over the British. During the French Revolution Hugues ordered the guillotine set up here so that the public could witness the bloody end of 300 recalcitrant royalists.

Even more colorful is the bustling marketplace, between rues St-John Perse, Frébault, Schoelcher, and Peynier. It's a cacophonous place, where housewives bargain for spices, herbs (and herbal remedies), and a bright assortment of papayas, breadfruits, christophenes, and tomatoes.

WORTH NOTING

Musée St-John Perse. Those with a strong interest in French literature and culture will want to see the Musée St-John Perse, which is dedicated to the poet Alexis Léger, Guadeloupe's most famous son. Better known as Saint-John Perse, he was the winner of the Nobel Prize for literature in 1960. Some of his finest poems are inspired by the history and landscape—particularly the sea—of his beloved Guadeloupe. The museum, in a restored colonial house, contains a collection of his poetry and some of his personal belongings. Before you go, look for his birthplace at 54 rue Achille René-Boisneuf. ⊠ *9 rue Nozières, Pointe-à-Pitre* ☎ *0590/90–01–92* 🖾 *€2.50* ⊙ *Weekdays 9–5, Sat. 8:30–12:30.*

ELSEWHERE ON GRANDE-TERRE

WORTH NOTING

FAMILY **Aquarium de la Guadeloupe.** Unique in the Antilles, this aquarium in the marina near Pointe-à-Pitre is a good place to spend an hour. Its motto is: "Visit the sea." The well-planned facility has an assortment of tropical fish, crabs, lobsters, moray eels, coffer fish, and some live coral. It's also a turtle rescue center, and the shark tank is spectacular. A restaurant serves kid-friendly fare, snacks, salads, and pastas. A small shop stocks marine toys and souvenirs. The aquarium also offers a half-day ecotour, in which small boats travel through the mangroves, reefs, and a lagoon, with a biologist guide and a diving instructor on board. Leaving daily at 8:30 am and 1 pm, the tours are €59. Snorkeling gear is included, and kids are more than welcome. A full-day ecotour includes lunch and a visit to the aquarium (€95). ⊠ *Marina Pl. Créole, off Rte. N4, Gosier* ☎ *0590/90–92–38* ⊕ *www.aquariumdelaguadeloupe.com* 🖾 *€11* ⊙ *Daily 9–6.*

13

Ft. Fleur d'Épée. The main attraction in Bas-du-Fort is this fortress, built between 1759 and 1763. It hunkers down on a hillside behind a deep moat. The fort was the scene of hard-fought battles between the French and the English in 1794. You can explore its well-preserved dungeons and battlements and take in a sweeping view of Iles des Saintes and Marie-Galante. The free guided tour here explores the fort's history and architecture and helps explain the living conditions of the soldiers who lived here. Included on the tour is an exploration of its underground galleries, now decorated with graffiti. If a bilingual person is on duty, she will explain it all in English. Call ahead, and to make certain of that day's hours. Registered as an historic monument since 1979, the fort also provides superb views for walkers. ⊠ *Bas-du-Fort* ☎ *0590/90–94–61* 🖃 *Free* ⊗ *Mon.–Sun. 9–5.*

Gosier. Gosier was still a tiny village in the 1950s, a simple stopping place between Pointe-à-Pitre and Ste-Anne. However, it grew rapidly in the 1960s, when the beauty of the southern coastline began to bring tourists in ever-increasing numbers. Today Gosier is one of Guadeloupe's premier tourist areas while at the same time serving as a chic suburb of Pointe-à-Pitre. People sit at sidewalk cafés reading *Le Monde* as others flip-flop their way to the beach. This resort town has several hotels, nightclubs, shops, a casino, rental car agencies, and a long stretch of sand.

Musée Camélia Costumes et Traditions. This museum is a labor of love by its creators, and seeing the dress of black, white, and *métisseé* (mixed-race, or brown) societies is a fascinating way to visualize the island's tumultuous history. Items that you will remember: madras headdresses; baptism outfits; embroidered maternity dresses; colonial pith helmets and other various chapeaux as well as the doll collection. Make sure to go out back and visit the replica of a Guadeloupean case circa 1920. The small museum is privately owned; the founder, Camelia Bausivoir, is a retired English teacher, and she can act as your guide. This represents a collection accrued over decades, and Bausivoir sewed many of the costumes. Call before you go for directions and to make sure that a school group is not there. ⊠ *1 Perinette, Gosier* ☎ *0590/83–21–70, 0690/41–51–90* 🖃 *€9* ⊗ *Tues.–Sun. 9–1 and 3–5.*

Pointe des Châteaux. The island's easternmost point offers a breathtaking view of the Atlantic crashing against huge rocks, carving them into shapes resembling pyramids. There are spectacular views of Guadeloupe's southern and eastern coasts and the island of La Désirade. The beach has few facilities now that vendors have been relocated to Petit Anse Kahouanne, about a mile up the road, so bring your own food and drink. In high season and taxis run every hour to shuttle beach-people back and forth to town. On weekends locals come in numbers to walk their dogs, surf, or look for romance. ⊠ *St-François.*

NEED A BREAK?

If you don't want to take time for a two-hour French lunch, watch for gas stations such as Shell Boutique, Total Boutique, and Esso Tigermart, which sell food. The VITO station on the left going into St-François has good pizza for €8, roast chicken, and panini, as well as tables and chairs. A Total "fillin' station" might have barbecue ribs, chicken, and turkey.

DID YOU KNOW?

There are numerous hiking trails that climb La Soufrière volcano, and some of them can be pretty treacherous. Go with a guide and you can safely take in breathtaking sights, such as the views from Piton Dolomieu.

Ste-Anne. In the 18th century this town, 8 miles (13 km) east of Gosier, was a sugar-exporting center. Sand has replaced sugar as the town's most valuable asset. La Caravelle and the other beaches are among the best in Guadeloupe. On its main drag, which parallels the waterfront, is a lively group of inexpensive eateries, shops, and artisan stalls. On a more spiritual note, Ste-Anne has a lovely cemetery with stark-white tombs.

St-François. This was once a simple little village, primarily involved with fishing and harvesting tomatoes. The fish and tomatoes are still here, as are the old creole houses and the lively market with recommendable food stalls in the centre villa, but increasingly, the St-François marina district is overtaking Gosier as Guadeloupe's most fashionable tourist resort area. Its avenue de l'Europe runs between the marina and the fairways and water obstacles of the municipal golf course, which was designed by Robert Trent Jones. On the marina side is a string of shops (including a huge supermarket), hotels, bars, and restaurants. The Bwa Chik Hotel & Golf, an eco-chic study in recyclable materials, is here; it's a favorite with golfers. Other attractions include an array of beaches and the St. François casino. ⊠ *St-François.*

NEED A BREAK? There's no wagering at **Hyper Casino**, a *supermarché* on l'avenue de l'Europe at the St-François Marina, but there are esoteric cheeses and baked goods such as pie-size tropical-fruit tarts. Other supermarkets with good deli or bakery departments are those in the Leader Price and Carrefour chains.

BASSE-TERRE

Basse-Terre (which translates as "low land") is by far the highest and wildest of the two wings of the Guadeloupe butterfly, with the peak of the Soufrière volcano topping off at nearly 4,811 feet. Basse-Terre, where you can find the island's national park, is also an ecotourist's treasure, with lush, equatorial plant life and adventurous opportunities for hikers and mountain bikers on the old *traces,* routes that porters once took across the mountains. You can still find numerous fishing villages and banana plantations stretching as far as the eye can see. The northwest coast, between Bouillante and Grande-Anse, is magnificent; the road twists and turns up steep hills smothered in vegetation and then drops down and skirts deep-blue bays and colorful seaside towns. Constantly changing light, towering clouds, and frequent rainbows only add to the beauty. In fact, Basse-Terre is gaining in popularity each year, and is especially appreciated by young sporty couples.

BASSE-TERRE

Because Pointe-à-Pitre is so much bigger, few people suspect that this little town of 15,000 is the capital and administrative center of Guadeloupe. But if you have any doubts, walk up the hill to the state-of-the-art Théâtre Nationale, where some of France's finest theater and opera companies perform.

FAMILY **Jardin Botanique.** This exquisite 10-acre park is filled with parrots and flamingos. A circuitous walking trail takes you by ponds with floating lily pads, cactus gardens, and every kind of tropical flower and plant, including orchids galore. Amid the exotic ferns and gnarled, ancient trees are little wooden bridges and a gazebo. A panoramic restaurant with a surprisingly sophisticated lunch menu plus a snack bar are housed in terraced gingerbread buildings, one overlooking the park's waterfall, the other the mountains. The garden has a children's park and nature-oriented playthings in the shop. A local juice and a snack is included with admission. ⊠ *Deshaies* ☎ *0590/28–43–02* ⊕ *www.jardinbotanique.com* 🎫 *€15.50* ⊗ *Daily 9–5:30; last tickets sold at 4:30.*

13

VIEUX-HABITANTS

This was the island's first colony, established in 1635. Beaches, a restored coffee plantation, and the oldest church on the island (1666) make this village worth a stop.

Musée du Café/Café Chaulet. From the riverfront Musée du Café/Café Chaulet, dedicated to the art of coffee making, the tantalizing aroma of freshly ground beans reaches the highway. Plaques and photos tell of the island's coffee history. The shop sells excellent Arabic coffee, rum punches, Schrubb, (an orange liqueur), hot sauces, achets of spices, bay-rum lotion, marmalades, and jewelry made from natural materials. The "resident" chocolate-maker, a young French woman, also crafts bonbons and festive holiday candies. You will even see the coffee cars—emblazoned Volkswagen Beetles. ⊠ *Vieux-Habitants* ☎ *0590/98–54–96* ⊕ *www.cafechaulet.com* 🎫 *€6* ⊗ *Daily 9–5.*

POINTE-NOIRE

Pointe-Noire is a good jumping-off point from which to explore Basse-Terre's little-visited northwest coast. A road skirts magnificent cliffs and tiny coves, dances in and out of thick stands of mahogany and gommier trees, and weaves through unspoiled fishing villages with boats and ramshackle houses as brightly colored as a child's finger painting. This town has two small museums devoted to local products.

STE-ROSE

In addition to a sulfur bath, there are two good beaches (Amandiers and Clugny) and several interesting small museums in Ste-Rose.

Domaine de Séverin. At this historic rum distillery, a small train crosses the plantation at 9:30, 10:45, and 11:30 am and again at 2:30 and 3:45 pm from Sunday to Friday. (Hours are abbreviated in the low season, as is the train schedule.) The train passes by crayfish ponds (they farm the jumbo ouassous), golden fields of sugarcane, the distillery's working waterwheel, and the Big House, the former mansion of the Marsolle family, which has owned the habitation since 1928. The impressive great house, white-pillared with verandahs on two stories, has two apartments and two guest rooms for overnight or longer stays. They aren't beautifully furnished but are atmospheric indeed. A combination tasting room and gift shop sells rum, rum punches (liqueurs) spices, and hot sauces. The simple, open-air dining room here has a good menu and sometimes offers the jumbo crayfish. ⊠ *Ste-Rose* ☎ *0590/28–91–86* ⊕ *www.severinrhum.com* 🎫 *Free; train tour €11, children €6* ⊗ *Nov.–Mar., daily 8:30–5:30; Apr.–Oct. 8:30–1:00 and sometimes 2:30–5:30.*

ELSEWHERE ON BASSE-TERRE
TOP ATTRACTIONS

Chutes du Carbet. You can reach three of the Carbet Falls (one drops from 65 feet, the second from 360 feet, the third from 410 feet) via a long, steep path from the village of Habituée. On the way up you pass the Grand Étang (Great Pond), a volcanic lake surrounded by interesting plant life. For horror fans there's also the curiously named Étang Zombi, a pond believed to house evil spirits. If there have been heavy rains, though, don't even think about going here. ⊠ *St-Claude.*

Fodor's Choice **La Bonifierie/Ti café.** When it comes to the island's coffee and choco-
★ late experiences, this place takes the cake. Within the attractive complex comprised of fieldstone and wooden colonial houses (circa 1760), there's a display case for the truffles, chocolate candies, and confections. They are created from 100% local products, including cacao and tropical fruits. The French chocolatier produces excellent chocolate. The sophisticated courtyard café has a contemporary menu. The beef, like the coffee, is grown on the plantation. If you can get a group together, call and they will give you a price for a participatory demonstration as to how to make candy bars followed by a Franco-Caribbean buffet with tastings of island rum. There are no more guided tours, so visitors can just tour on their own. Again, if a group of 10 or more, they can reserve a guided tour. The café does not serve dinner, however if there is a group reservation they will open for it. What anyone fit can do is the zip line in the new adventure park. ⊠ *Section Morin Rte. de Morin, St-Claude* ☎ *0590/80–06–05* ☒ *Free to tour* ☺ *Tues.–Sun. noon–2:30.*

Parc National de la Guadeloupe. This 74,100-acre park has been recognized by UNESCO as a Biosphere Reserve. Before going, pick up a *Guide to the National Park* from the tourist office; it rates the hiking trails according to difficulty, and most are quite difficult indeed. Most mountain trails are in the southern half. The park is bisected by the route de la Traversée, a 16-mile (26-km) paved road lined with masses of tree ferns, shrubs, flowers, tall trees, and green plantains. It's the ideal point of entry. Wear rubber-soled shoes and take along a swimsuit, a sweater, water, and perhaps food for a picnic. Try to get an early start to stay ahead of the hordes of cruise-ship passengers making a day of it. Check on the weather; if Basse-Terre has had a lot of rain, give it up. In the past, after intense rainfall, rockslides have closed the road for months. ⊠ *Habitation Beausoleil-Montéran, BP-93, St-Claude* ☎ *0590/80–86–00* ⊕ *www. guadeloupe-parcnational.com* ☒ *Free* ☺ *Weekdays 8–5:30.*

WORTH NOTING

Bouillante. The name means "boiling," and so it's no surprise that hot springs were discovered here. However, the biggest attraction is scuba diving on nearby Pigeon Island, which is accessed by boat from Plage de Malendure. There's a small information kiosk on the beach at Plage de Malendure that can help you with diving and snorkeling arrangements. ⊠ *Bouillante.*

Les Mamelles. Two mountains—Mamelle de Petit-Bourg, at 2,350 feet, and Mamelle de Pigeon, at 2,500 feet—rise in the Parc National de la Guadeloupe. *Mamelle* means "breast," and when you see the mountains, you'll understand why they got their name. Trails ranging from easy to arduous lace up into the surrounding mountains. There's a glorious view from the lookout point 1,969 feet up Mamelle de Pigeon. If you're a climber, plan to spend several hours exploring this area. If there have been heavy rainfalls, cancel your plans. ⊠ *St-Claude* ⊕ *www. guadeloupe-parcnational.com.*

ILES DES SAINTES

The eight-island archipelago of Iles des Saintes, often referred to as Les Saintes, dots the waters off the southern coast of Guadeloupe. The islands are Terre-de-Haut, Terre-de-Bas, Ilet à Cabrit, Grand Ilet, La Redonde, La Coche, Le Pâté, and Les Augustins. Columbus discovered them on November 4, 1493, and christened them Los Santos (Les Saintes in French) for All Saints' Day.

Only Terre-de-Haut and Terre-de-Bas are inhabited, with a combined population of little more than 3,000. Many of the Saintois are fair-haired, blue-eyed descendants of Breton and Norman sailors. Unless they are in the tourism industry, they tend to be taciturn and standoff-ish. Fishing still is their main source of income, and they take pride in their work. The shores are lined with their boats and *filets bleus* (blue nets dotted with orange buoys).

DID YOU KNOW?

For generations, the Saintois fishermen wore hats called *salakos*, which look like large, inverted saucers, patterned after a hat said to have been brought here by a seafarer from China. You're now more likely to see the younger fishermen in visors and French sunglasses piloting boats with powerful motors rather than the traditional small sailboats of their predecessors. A fun, three-day event in late May celebrates the fishing industry and its hardy fishermen (⊕ *www.omtlessaintes.fr*).

TERRE-DE-HAUT

With 5 square miles (13 square km) and a population of about 1,500, Terre-de-Haut is the largest and most developed of Les Saintes. Its "big city" is Bourg, with one main street lined with bistros, cafés, and shops. Clutching the hillside are trim white houses with bright red or blue doors, balconies, and gingerbread frills.

Terre-de-Haut's ragged coastline is scalloped with lovely coves and beaches, including the semi-nude beach at Anse Crawen. The beautiful bay, complete with a "sugarloaf" mountain, has been called a mini Rio. There are precious few vehicles or taxis on island, so you'll often find yourself walking, despite the hilly terrain. Or you can add to the din and rent a motorbike. Take your time on these rutted roads, as around any bend there might be a herd of goats chomping on a fallen palm frond. Two traffic lights have brought a small amount of order to the motorbike hordes. When aggressively soliciting you, the scooter agencies will not tell you that it is prohibited to scoot in town from 9 to noon and from 2 to 4.

This island makes a great day trip, but you can really get a feel for Les Saintes if you stay overnight. It's not unlike St. Barth, but for a fraction of the price. Note: most shops and restaurants close for two hours in the afternoon.

13

■TIP➔ A wonderful introduction to the island as well as a travel keep-sake, is the coffee-table book Carnet de Route-Les Saintes on sale in shops for €20.

Fort Napoléon. Also known as Louis Castle, this fort was built in 1777 by order of King Louis XVI, and was first known as a military tower. Renamed Napoléon Castle in 1805, it was strengthened by Vauban, a famous architect. However, it was never used for military purposes, although it did serve as a penitentiary in wartime. The museum here is notable for its exhaustive exhibit of the greatest sea battles ever fought. You can also visit the well-preserved barracks and prison cells, or admire the botanical gardens, which specialize in cacti. ■TIP➔ This is a hill climb, and if you decide to walk, allow 30 minutes from the vil-lage, wear comfortable footwear, and bring water. You will be rewarded with outstanding views of the bay and neighboring islands. ⊠ *Grand Bourg* ☎ *0690/50–73–43* 🖃 *€4* ⊗ *Daily 9–12:30.*

MARIE-GALANTE

Columbus sighted this 60-square-mile (155-square-km) island on November 3, 1493, named it after his flagship, the *Maria Galanda,* and sailed on. It's dotted with ruined 19th-century sugar mills, and sugar is still its major product. Honey and 59% rum are its other favored harvests. You should make it a point to see one of the distill-eries. With its rolling hills of green cane still worked by oxen and men with broad-brim straw hats, it's like traveling back in time to when all of Guadeloupe was still a giant farm.

Although it's only an hour by high-speed ferry from Pointe-à-Pitre, the country folk here are still sweet and shy, and crime is a rarity. You can see swarms of yellow butterflies, and maybe a marriage car-riage festooned with flowers, pulled by two white oxen. A daughter of the sea, Marie-Galante has some of the archipelago's most gorgeous, uncrowded beaches. Take time to explore the dramatic coast. You can find soaring cliffs—such as the Gueule Grand Gouffre (Mouth of the Giant Chasm) and Les Galeries (where the sea has sculpted a natural arcade)—and enormous sun-dappled grottos, such as Le Trou à Diable, whose underground river can be explored with a guide. Port Louis, the island's "second city," is the new hip spot. The ferry dock is in Port Louis, and it's also on the charts for yachts and regattas. After sunset, the no-see-ums and mosquitoes can be a real irritation, so always be armed with repellent.

TOP ATTRACTIONS

Fodor's Choice
★
Domaine de Bellevue. If time allows just one distillery, choose the mod-ern Domaine de Bellevue. Its rum has taken home the gold during official French competitions. Free tastings are just one inviting ele-ment here. There are award-winning, pure rums (50%–59%); excel-lent tropical liqueurs (punches); coffee-table books; and local organic products. Down from the windmill (circa 1821), is a boutique with everything made from natural materials, such as calabash gourds. ⊠ *Section Bellevue, Capesterre, Marie-Galante* ☎ *0590/97–26–50* 🖃 *Free* ⊗ *Daily 9:30–1.*

Kreol West Indies. This fascinating museum, in a renovated bungalow, houses information and graphics on Guadeloupe's early Indians, as well as some pirate artifacts. Rooms are furnished with antiques and collectibles that depict island life during various eras, up through the 1950s. Devoted to Creole culture, the museum also doubles as an art gallery, with attractive contemporary paintings by island artists. This labor of love, displays works owned by a professional French hotelier, Vincent Nicaudie. The gift shop carries quality, Marie Galante logoized T-shirts and caps, beach wear, and island food products. Also, this is a friendly, Wi-Fi hot spot. ⊠ *Grand-Bourg, Marie-Galante* ☎ *0590/97–21–56* ⊕ *www.kreolwestindies.com* ✉ *Free* ⊘ *Daily 9:30–6:30.*

> **COMPETITIONS DES BOEUFS TIRANTS**
>
> The annual ox-pulling competitions on Marie-Galante go on for two weeks in November. Oxen were used for the sugar mills and still power the agriculture. Where else will you see this in your lifetime?

13

WORTH NOTING

Distillerie Poisson "Rhum du Père Labat." The Poisson Distillery produces rum (nearly 200,000 liters a year) that is considered some of the finest in the Caribbean, and its atelier turns out lovely pottery. Tastings are available, but watch out—those samples are quite strong, especially considering that it is only open in the morning! ⊠ *Section Poisson, Grand-Bourg, Marie-Galante* ✉ *Free* ⊘ *Mon.–Sat. 7–noon.*

LA DÉSIRADE

Desirable is the operative word here. This small, safe, somewhat remote island is an absolute find for those who prefer a road less traveled, who want their beaches long and white, and who don't mind that accommodations are simple if the price is right. The Désirade populace (all 1,700 of them) welcome tourism, and these dear hearts have a warm, old-fashioned sense of community.

According to legend, the "desired land" was so named by the crew of Christopher Columbus, whose tongues were dry for want of fresh water when they spied the island; alas, it was the season for drought. The 8-square-mile (21-square-km) island, 5 miles (8 km) east of St-François, is a chalky plateau, with an arid climate, perennial sunshine, cacti, and iguanas. You may even see two male iguanas locked in a prehistoric-looking battle. Rent a four-wheel drive to climb the zigzag road that leads to the Grande Montagne. Make a photo stop at the diminutive white chapel, which offers a panorama of the sea below. Afraid that you might zig instead of zag down the precipice? Then take a fun, informative van tour that you join near the tourist office at the harbor. The ruins of the original settlement—a leper colony— are on the tour.

Only one road runs around the perimeter of the island, and if you're interested in visiting one of the many gorgeous beaches shaded by coco palms and sea grape trees, you can do that on a scooter. Driving is safer here than most anywhere.

BEACHES

Guadeloupe is an archipelago of five paradises surrounded by both the Caribbean and the Atlantic. Its beaches run the spectrum from white to black. There are idyllic beaches, long stretches of unspoiled beach shaded by coconut palms, with soft, warm sand. Hotel beaches are generally narrow, although well maintained. Some hotels allow nonguests who patronize their restaurants to use their beach facilities. The popular public beaches tend to be cluttered with campers-turned-cafés and cars parked in impromptu lots on the sand. Sunday is the big day, but these same (free) beaches are often quiet during the week.

On the southern coast of Grande-Terre, from Ste-Anne to Pointe des Châteaux, you can find stretches of soft white sand and some sparsely visited areas. The Atlantic waters on the northeast coast are too rough for swimming. Along the western shore of Basse-Terre signposts indicate small beaches. The sand starts turning gray in Malendure; it becomes volcanic black farther south. There's only one official nude beach, Pointe Tarare, but topless bathing is common.

GRANDE-TERRE

L'Autre Bord. The waves on this Atlantic beach give the long expanse of sand a wild look. The beach is protected by an extensive coral reef, which makes it safe for children. Further out, the waves draw surfers and windsurfers. From its location right in the town of Moule, you can stroll along a seaside promenade fringed by flamboyant trees (also known as flame trees). Many shade trees offer protection; the swaying coconut palms are more for photo composition. Sidewalk cafes provide sustenance. **Amenities:** food and drink; parking (no fee); toilets. **Best for:** surfing; swimming; walking; windsurfing. ⊠ *Moule, Grande-Terre.*

Plage Caravelle. Just southwest of Ste-Anne is one of Grande-Terre's longest and prettiest stretches of sand, the occasional dilapidated shack notwithstanding. Protected by reefs, it's also a fine snorkeling spot. Club Med occupies one end of this beach, and nonguests can enjoy its beach and water sports, as well as lunch and drinks, by buying a day pass. You can also have lunch on the terrace of La Toubana Hotel & Spa, then descend the stairs to the beach or enjoy lunch at its beach restaurant, wildly popular on Sunday. **Amenities:** food and drink; parking (no fee); toilets; water sports. **Best for:** partiers; snorkeling; sunset; swimming; walking; windsurfing. ⊠ *Rte. N4, southwest of Ste-Anne, Grande-Terre.*

Plage de la Chapelle à Anse-Bertrand. If you want a delightful day trip to the northern tip of Grande-Terre, aim for this spot, one of the loveliest white-sand beaches, whose gentle midafternoon waves are popular with families. It's shaded by coco palms, there are the ruins of a chapel to explore, and the sea kayaking's excellent. When the tide rolls in, it's equally popular with surfers. Several little terrace restaurants are at the far end of the beach, but you might want to bring your own mat or beach towel, because no one rents chaise longues. The town has

Looking out over Marie-Galante

remained relatively undeveloped. **Amenities:** food and drink; showers; toilets. **Best for:** solitude; sunrise; sunset; surfing; swimming; walking; windsurfing. ⊠ *4 miles (6½ km) south of La Pointe de la Grand Vigie, Grande-Terre.*

Plage du Helleux. Except on Sunday, this long stretch of wild beach— framed by dramatic cliffs—is often completely deserted in the morning or early afternoon. By 4 pm, though, you might find 70 or so young surfers. Many locals take their young children here, but use caution with your own, because the current can be strong. The beach has no facilities of its own, but you can get lunch and drinks at the Hotel Eden Palm. To get here, follow the signs to Hotel Eden Palm and pass the hotel; the beach is down the dirt road to the right. **Amenities:** none. **Best for:** solitude; partiers; surfing; swimming; walking. ⊠ *Rte. N4, Lieu-dit le Helleux, Ste-Anne, Grande-Terre.*

Pointe Tarare. This secluded strip just before the tip of Pointe des Châteaux is the island's only nude beach. (Technically, this is not allowed by French law.) Small bar–cafés are in the parking area, but it's still best to bring some water, snacks, and beach chairs, because there's no place to rent them. What you do have is one of the coast's most dramatic landscapes; looming above are rugged cliffs topped by a huge crucifix. When approaching St-François Marina, go in the direction of Pointe des Châteaux at the roundabout and drive for about 10 minutes. **Amenities:** food and drink; parking (no fee); toilets. **Best for:** solitude; partiers; sunset; swimming; walking. ⊠ *Rte. N4, southeast of St-François, Grande-Terre.*

BASSE-TERRE

Plage de la Grande-Anse. One of Guadeloupe's widest beaches has soft beige sand sheltered by palms. To the west it's a round verdant mountain. It has a large parking area and some food stands, but no other facilities. The beach can be overrun on Sunday, not to mention littered, due to the food carts. Right after the parking lot, you can see signage for the creole restaurant Le Karacoli; if you have lunch there (it's not cheap), you can *sieste* on the chaise longues. At the far end of the beach, which is more virgin territory, is Tainos Cottages, which has a restaurant. **Amenities:** food and drink; parking (no fee). **Best for:** partiers; solitude; swimming; walking. ⊠ *Rte. N6, north of Deshaies, Deshaies, Basse-Terre.*

Plage de Malendure. Across from Pigeon Island and the Jacques Cousteau Underwater Park, this long, gray, volcanic beach on the Caribbean's calm waters has restrooms, a few beach shacks offering cold drinks and snacks, and a huge parking lot. There might be some litter, but the beach is cleaned regularly. Don't come here for solitude, as the beach is a launch point for many dive boats. The snorkeling's good. Le Rocher de Malendure, a fine seafood restaurant, is perched on a cliff over the bay. Food carts work the parking lot. **Amenities:** food and drink; parking (no few); toilets. **Best for:** partiers; snorkeling; swimming. ⊠ *Rte. N6, Bouillante, Basse-Terre.*

ILES DES SAINTES

FAMILY **Pompierres.** This beach is particularly popular with families with small children, as there's a gradual slope, no drop-off, and a long stretch of shallow water. The calm water also makes for good snorkeling. To get here, go to the seamen's church near the main plaza, and then head in the direction of Marigot. Continue until you see Le Salako Snack Bar and some scurrying chickens, maybe some goats and—*voilà!*—you'll spy a palm-fringed, half-moon bay with tawny sand. Saintois women may be at the entrance selling snacks and drinks. The curve of the beach is called the Bridge of Stone and you can walk it—carefully—taking a dip in the crater that fills with water from the Atlantic. Morning sun is best; then, return to Salako for some grilled fresh fish and a cold one. **Amenities:** food and drink. **Best for:** snorkeling; sunrise; swimming; walking. ⊠ *Terre-de-Haut, Iles des Saintes.*

LA DÉSIRADE

Le Soufleur Plage. To reach one of La Désirade's longest and best beaches from the ferry dock, face town and follow the main road to the right. It's about 15 minutes by car or motor scooter (about €20 a day). White sand, calm waters, and snacks and cold drinks from the beach restaurant await, but there are no chaises, so BYO beach towel or mat. **Amenities:** food and drink; toilets. **Best for:** solitude; snorkeling; sunset; swimming; walking. ⊠ *Dpmt. Rd. 207, La Désirade.*

MARIE-GALANTE

Anse de Vieux Fort. This gorgeous Marie-Galante beach stretches alongside crystal-clear waters that border a large body of freshwater that is ideal for canoeing. It's a surprising contrast from the nearby mangrove swamp you can discover on the hiking trails. The beaches in this area are wide because of the erosion of the sand dunes. It's known as a beach for lovers because of the solitude. Bring your own everything. You can pair a visit to Château Murat with your beach day. **Amenities:** none. **Best for:** solitude; snorkeling; sunset; swimming; walking. ☒ *Rte. D205, Marie-Galante.*

13

Plage de Petite-Anse. This long, golden beach on Marie-Galante is punctuated with sea grape trees. It's idyllic during the week, but on weekends the crowds of locals and urban refugees from the main island arrive. Le Touloulou's great creole seafood restaurant provides the only facilities. The golden sands are ideal for shelling. **Amenities:** food and drink; parking (no fee); toilets. **Best for:** partiers; snorkeling; sunset; swimming; walking. ☒ *6½ miles (10 km) north of Grand-Bourg via rte. D203, Petite-Anse.*

WHERE TO EAT

Creole cooking is the result of a fusion of influences: African, European, Indian, and Caribbean. It's colorful, spicy, and made up primarily of local seafood and vegetables (including squashlike christophenes), root vegetables, and plantains, always with a healthy dose of pepper sauce. Favorite appetizers include *accras* (salted codfish fritters), *boudin* (highly seasoned blood sausage), and *crabes farcis* (stuffed land crabs). *Langouste* (lobster), *lambi* (conch), *chatrou* (octopus), and *ouassous* (crayfish) are considered delicacies. *Souchy* (Tahitian-style ceviche), raw fish that is "cooked" when marinated in lime juice or similar marinades, is best at seafront restaurants. *Moules et frites* (mussels in broth served with fries) can be found at cafés in Gosier and both the Marina in St. Francois and Bas du Fort Marina. Also in the marina is Rôtisseur des Isles, with aromatic roasted meats, a salad bar, and classic French desserts. Many of the most contemporary, gastronomic restaurants are in Jarry, a commercial area near Pointe-à-Pitre. All restaurants and bars are smoke-free, as decreed by French law.

Diverse culinary options range from pizza and crepes to Indian cuisine. For a quick and inexpensive meal, visit a *boulangerie*, where you can buy luscious French pastries and simple baguette sandwiches. Look for the recommendable chain Baguettoo. Good news: menu prices seem high but include tax and service (which is split among the entire staff). If service is to your liking, be generous and leave some extra euros, and they will think of Americans as "the good guys." In most restaurants in Guadeloupe (as throughout the Caribbean), lobster is the most expensive item on the menu. It can easily top €40 and often comes as part of a prix-fixe menu; *price ranges for the restaurants listed in this chapter do not include lobster for this reason.*

What to Wear: Dining is casual at lunch, but beach attire is a no-no except at the more laid-back marina and beach eateries. Dinner is slightly more formal. Long pants, collared shirts, and skirts or dresses are appreciated, although not required. Guadeloupean ladies like to "dress," particularly on weekends, so don't arrive in flip-flops—they'll be in heels.

GRANDE-TERRE

$$ ✕ **Café Wango.** At this alfresco hotspot, Asian wok dishes, sushi, skew-
ECLECTIC ers, fish carpaccios, and tartares dominate the menu, and there are no fewer than nine better-than-average salads. There are also pricey pastas, daily specials like a classic sirloin in a Roquefort-poivre sauce, and two prix-fixes ($$$–$$$$). Kids are crazy for the ice cream. Facing the marina's boat slips, the modern furnishings here are often filled with a fun, discerning crowd of mainly French expats; parked nearby there may be a couple diners' Harleys, flying tiny American flags. $ *Average main:* €18 ⊠ *St-François Marina, Marines 1, St-François* ☎ *0590/83–50–41* ⊕ *www.cafewango.com* ⊗ *Closed June 17–July 6.*

$$$ ✕ **Iguane Café.** Iguanas are indeed the theme here, and you can still spy
ECLECTIC them in unexpected places—but their numbers have diminished and the
Fodor'sChoice room now has a clean, contemporary appeal, just like the china and
★ glassware. The salon seating for cocktails has a homey feel, with basket-weave rattan furniture and hot-pink accent pillows. Unquestionably original cuisine with Asian, Indian, Creole, and African influences is chef Sylvain Serouart's trademark. Two amuse-bouches will arrive, and there is usually a wonderful foie-gras appetizer. Another good beginning is the duo of marlin, a tartare and a mousse. The menu is always evolving. Desserts are little contemporary marvels. This is a pricey place, but recently it's become a bit more egalitarian, now allowing guests to compose their own three-course prix-fixe. (The prix fixe is 45.50 euros.) $ *Average main:* €30 ⊠ *Rte. de La Pointe des Châteaux, ½ mile (¾ km) from airport, St-François* ☎ *0590/88–61–37* ⊕ *www.iguane-cafe.com* ⊗ *Closed Tues. No lunch Mon.–Sat.*

$$$ ✕ **La Porte des Indes.** Dining here is truly a departure: the open-air per-
INDIAN gola, the blue gates, the pungent aromas, and the bust of Ganesha. Within the paisley-covered menu you can find authentic Indian dishes alongside such adaptations as boneless curried chicken with crème fraîche, cashews, and raisins. Vegetarian are catered to here, and an eggplant puree is one of the better options. Children may fill up on the addictive Indian cheese naan bread and be too stuffed for *kulfi*, Indian ice cream that's topped here with ginger confit. The welcome here is always warm, and the service dignified. The Indian chef-owner, Karious Arthur, has a culinary degree from Paris and worked for years in France. Consistently good, La Porte's perennial popularity means that on weekends you really should make reservations. $ *Average main:* €30 ⊠ *Desvarieux, St-François* ☎ *0590/21–30–87* ⊗ *Closed mid-Sept.–mid-Oct. and Mon. No lunch Tues.–Sat. No dinner Sun.*

$$$$ ✕ **La Toubana Restaurant** (*Le Gran Bleu*). Fresh lobsters, which swim in
FRENCH the canals that beautify the deck, draw many diners. The chef prepares an impressive foie gras duo—a sauté and a torchon—paired with onion and fig compotes. The French food here often gets a delicious Caribbean

STILL WATERS

Guadeloupe has some of the best-tasting mountain water in the Caribbean isles, but you'll rarely see anyone drinking it out of the tap (*robinet*). Some say that is because the city pipes are rusty, others that they can taste the chlorine. At restaurants, the server will usually ask if you want a bottle of water, and if so, what kind: *plat?* (pronounced plah, meaning "still"). Say "*Oui, Capes*" to request the main island brand. You'll pay €3 to €4 for a big bottle (1½ liter), half the price of Evian. In your hotel minibar, a small bottle may cost that much. Stop at a gas station, minimart, or supermarche and buy the big ones for anywhere from €0.70 to €1.50. Or join the new movement to help save the environment by not using plastic bottles, and at restaurants ask for *une carafe d'eau du robinet*—tap water. Is it safe? Guadeloupe sells water to all the big ships.

infusion, as in the fillet of *daurade* (sea bream) with a vanilla sauce, or the passion-fruit tart with a meringue. The inside dining room, although open-air, has deep leather chairs, and, on occasion, a piano player and live music by pop-rock vocalists; local music is the norm on Thursday night. You can listen whether you just "take a pop" (drink) or have dinner. Lunch patrons dine on the terrace near the infinity pool. With your feet dangling in the water and an exotic cocktail in hand, you can watch the sea churn below. [$] *Average main: €35* ✉ *La Toubana Hotel & Spa, B. P. 63-Fonds Thezan, Ste-Anne* ☎ *0590/88–25–57.*

$$$ FRENCH 🍴 **Restaurant de la Vieille Tour.** A historic sugar mill is the backdrop for the artistic creations here, which take refined French cuisine and incorporate culinary trends and local produce. As the hotel's only restaurant, it has to be all things to all guests. The lunch menu is a mix of classic restaurant food and lighter dishes. A *formule* (prix fixe) of a main course, a starter or dessert, a glass of wine, and coffee is available for €42. A Creole menu is available on Thursday and Sunday nights; other evenings feature a more classically French menu. Roasted veal rib with chanterelles and seared sea scallops topped with passion-fruit butter are elegantly delicious. Desserts are dazzling, with lots of towers, sauces, and glacés. On Friday and Saturday nights, a piano man plays. [$] *Average main: €26* ✉ *Auberge de la Vieille Tour, Rte. 1, Montauban 97, Gosier* ☎ *0590/84–23–23* 🌐 *www.mgallery.com* ✍ *Reservations essential.*

$$ SEAFOOD 🍴 **Zawag.** At this secret hideaway you'll see the churning sea below and hear the waves crashing against the coral rock on which it sits. The interior architecture is all hardwood with matching furniture and white linen napkins. Primarily a grill, the simplicity is reflected in the food offerings. Kids are particularly fascinated when the lobster net is dipped into the tank and the thrashing begins. The fish of the night is fresh from the waters below, often accompanied by creole or tropical-fruit sauces. Creole dishes and sides that were gently contemporized by a French chef, are offered as nightly specials. Zawat—why that's a tropical fish that swims in the water that guests see through the open shutters. [$] *Average main: €18* ✉ *La Créole Beach Hotel & Spa, Pointe de la Verdure, Gosier* ☎ *0590/90–46–66* ✍ *Reservations essential* ⏲ *Late spring–early fall, closed Sun.*

BASSE-TERRE

$$
CARIBBEAN
✕ **Chez Clara.** As a jazz dancer, Clara worked her way through Europe's capitals and was briefly a "Claudette," backup dancer for Claude François, a French music idol in the 1970s. She's always been a colorful character, and her landmark restaurant is equally vivid; even the napkins offer a splash of color. She, however, is draped in her signature white garb. The food here is haute Creole, the curries intoxicating. Clara buys some spices from an Indian shop in Manhattan, and they're used here along with more local ones. The chef has a remarkable way of preparing *lambi* (conch), octopus, and local fish. A dessert surprise is sweet potato pie, a recipe from a Carolina girl who was her roomie in Paris. $ *Average main: €21* ⊠ *Bord de Mer, St. Rose* ☎ *0590/28–72–99* ☯ *No dinner Wed. and Sun.*

$$$
FRENCH
✕ **Le Rocher de Malendure.** Guests first climb the worn yellow stairs because of the panoramic sea views, but they return again and again for the food. If you arrive before noon, when the divers pull in, you might snag one of the primo tables in a gazebo that literally hangs over the Caribbean. Begin with a perfectly executed mojito. With fish just off the boat, don't hesitate to try the sushi *antillaise* or grilled crayfish and lobster from the pool. $ *Average main: €25* ⊠ *Bord de Mer, Malendure de Pigeon, Bouillante* ☎ *0590/98–70–84* ☯ *Closed Tues. and Sept.–early Oct.*

$$$
FRENCH
✕ **Restaurant La Savane.** Even if there's a downpour, a terrace table right on the crystalline Deshaies Bay is a dream fulfilled. Besides, La Savane's roof overhang (with gingerbread fretwork) will keep you dry, and the music and food does a lot to keep spirits high here. Part of the fascination with this gastronomique outpost is that the owning family has a most unusual, vastly international background that influences the operation. The mother is Portuguese, yet she lived in Angola (Africa) for 15 years, thus the African decor and name. The father is French and was a candy maker in Switzerland where they lived when their three children were born. Daughter Tatiana is the welcoming English-speaking server. Her dad's desserts are not to be missed, like the tarte tatin with a Calvados-infused butter. On the latest menu and among the "mains," the giant crayfish in red curry/coconut milk has proved successful, as has the guinea hen in a honey peanut sauce. As a starter, a standout is the shrimp in remoulade with green papaya. Some diners feel that it is expensive, but quality ingredients coupled with creativity make for happy forks. $ *Average main: €22* ⊠ *Blvd. des Poissonniers, Deshaie* ☎ *0690/75–70–57* ⊕ *www.restaurant-la-savane-deshaies.com* ⌂ *Reservations essential* ☯ *Closed Wed. No lunch in low season. No lunch Mon.–Thurs. in high season.*

ILES DES SAINTES

$$$
CAFÉ
✕ **Couleurs du Monde.** Vivid Caribbean colors of pink, yellow, and green all pop at this fun waterfront café, where the books and newspapers, teas and coffees, wine, and icy rum cocktails all encourage lounging. Sushi, smoked-fish plates, and smoked duck salad often appear on the appetizer-fille menu. The catch of the day with an exotic sauce is usually a choice. After sunset there are aperitifs, and although reservations are requested for dinner, the friendly, accommodating staff also takes

walk-ins. Finish off with the house-made punch *du monde*. To get here from the main dock, take a left to the main street and walk two blocks. It's across from the kayak-rental company. [$] *Average main: €25* ✉ *Le Mouillage, Terre-de-Haut* ☎ *0590/92–70–98* ⏲ *Closed Thurs.*

$$$ ECLECTIC 🍴 **Restaurant Les Petits Saints.** Chef Xavier Simon is remarkably inventive with the fresh local produce and seafood, as in his Asian-style *lambi* (conch) Asian-style. Duck breast with a hibiscus/honey sauce is a fine choice, as is grilled lobster. However, guests could benefit from more selections on the menu. Contemporary dinnerware brought from France complements the menu and presentation. A lot of effort has gone into the wine menu, and the selection of a full range of aged rums from Guadeloupe. For the finale, there are some dazzling desserts. Service is on the verandah, where the night sounds of the tropics vie with jazz and French music. [$] *Average main: €24* ✉ *Hotel Restaurant les Petits Saints, La Savane, Terre-de-Haut* ☎ *0590/99–50–99* 🌐 *www.petitssaints.com* ✍ *Reservations essential* ⏲ *Closed Mon. and Sept. No lunch.*

$$$ FRENCH 🍴 **Ti Kaz La.** This small, convivial waterfront restaurant has a lot to recommend it—it's artsy, with contemporary originals, hanging plants, hip music, and a talented chef-owner, Philippe Dade. Brochettes are the popular items, due to their dramatic presentation. Metal skewers of beef, lamb, shrimp, or the jumbo crayfish *ouassous* are hooked to what looks like a hangmen's scaffold, and are accompanied by chien and passion-fruit sauces—plus authentic *pomme frites. Le choucroute de la mer* has fish, scallops, and mussels in a bath of white wine. For dessert, one pouffed marvel—a mango soufflé with raspberry coulis—must be ordered in advance. [$] *Average main: €22* ✉ *10 rue Benoit Cassin, Terre-de-Haut* ☎ *0590/92–40–00, 0590/99–57–63* ⏲ *Closed on Wed. from Jan. to May and in Aug. Closed on Tues. and Wed. from June through July and Sept. through Dec.*

MARIE-GALANTE

$$ CARIBBEAN 🍴 **Chez Henri.** This hip place on the water, flanked by the town pier, is named for its passionate chef–owner, Henri Vergerolle. An island character, he spent much of his life in France and returned to create this combination restaurant and cultural center. Begin with a rum and fresh-squeezed juice. Smoked fish can be a component of a salad or an appetizer; the creole omelet is an app, too. It's quite an original, with breadfruit and sweet potatoes. Another innovation is the fish of the day with a Caribe sauce. Kick back and listen to African blues and view the latest art or sculpture exhibits. You might have the good luck to be here when there's a live music concert. [$] *Average main: €17* ✉ *8 rue des Caraibes, St. Louis, Marie Galante* ☎ *0590/97–04–57* 🌐 *www.chezhenri.net* ⏲ *Closed Mon. No lunch Tues.–Thurs. from Sept.–early Oct.*

$$ SEAFOOD 🍴 **Le Touloulou.** On the curve of Plage de Petite-Anse, this casual eatery has tables in the sand. Stylish Euro furnishings are here, as are marine-blue hammocks—perfect for chilling between courses. Chef José Viator serves the freshest seafood; his standout dish just might be fricassee of conch or octopus with breadfruit. Set menus start at €20-something, and a simple, fresh lobster prix-fixe is €35. For lunch, the best value is the *formule rapid*. Both the chicken and the *ouassous* (jumbo crayfish)

13

in coconut sauce are exceptional. And on weekends, the Creole Brunch (from 11 to 4) is particularly celebratory. Pergola's, the circular bar, has the best in rum cocktails for sipping as a sundowner. On weekend nights the anteroom is a dance club, with salsa lessons on Friday and a disco beat on Saturday. $ *Average main: €18* ⊠ *Plage de Petite-Anse, Capesterre* ☎ *0590/97–32–63* ⊕ *www.letouloulou.com* ☉ *Closed mid-Sept.–mid-Oct. No dinner Sun.*

LA DÉSIRADE

$$

CARIBBEAN

FAMILY

✕ **Oualiri Breeze Restaurant.** On tables in the sand, on the covered terrace, and under a conical tent, this beachfront eatery lays out a bountiful creole buffet on Friday nights and for Sunday brunch. Both are accompanied by live entertainment. You can always grab a continental breakfast, lunch, or dinner, and customize your own €15.50 prix fixe. Seafood is the obvious specialty, particularly creole fricassees of lambi (conch) and chatrou. Sidle up to the fieldstone bar for a perfect planter's punch, and between courses, jump into the sea. Children have their own menus and love that this is also a *glacier* (ice-cream shop) with a litany of flavors; drizzle your scoops with cajou (cashew) syrup. P.S. You can check your email here. Also, the affable, English-speaking owner, Theodore Compper, will pick you up at the dock or airport. $ *Average main: €15* ⊠ *Plage Beausejour, Beau Sejour, Le Désirade* ☎ *0590/20–20–08, 0690/71–24–76* ⊕ *www.im-caraibes.com/oualiri.*

WHERE TO STAY

Most of the island's resort hotels are on Grande-Terre: Gosier, St-François, and Bas-du-Fort are generally considered major resort areas, as is Ste-Anne. With each passing year, the hotels here improve. The Swedish-owned Langley Resort Fort Royal has breathed new life into the north of Basse-Terre, the closest area of that island to Pointe-à-Pitre and Grande-Terre. In general, more tourists are discovering this area, loving the small hotels and unspoiled nature.

Often, hotel rates include a generous buffet breakfast; ask whether this is included in your rate quote. (It usually is.) Many smaller properties do not accept American Express. As dictated by French law, all public spaces in hotels are no-smoking, but hotel rooms are considered private, and properties can choose to offer smoking rooms.

For expanded reviews, facilities, and current deals, visit Fodors.com.

PRIVATE VILLAS AND RENTALS

French Caribbean International. French Caribbean International handles hotel arrangements and private villa rentals, from charming cottages in Basse-Terre ($130 to $350 a night) to deluxe sea-view villas in Grande-Terre ($2,600 to $7,000 per week), all with pools. With three decades of experience in the French Caribbean, including Les Saintes and Marie-Galante, the company has a global reputation for honesty, exceptional service, and professionalism. They can also dispense information on just about everything you need to know about the French islands. ☎ *805/967–9850 in U.S.* ⊕ *www.frenchcaribbean.com.*

Nouvelles Antilles. The first online travel agency dedicated to the French West Indies acts as an agent for some 30 villas around the islands, most of them luxurious. The company can also book your villa or hotel accommodations, flight, rental car, and sports activities, and create a well-priced package. It deals with all the Guadeloupe isles, Martinique, St. Barth, and St. Martin, too, and can customize a multidestination package for groups up to 15. ✉ *St-François, Grande-Terre* ☎ *0590/85–00–00* 🌐 *www.nouvellesantilles.com.*

prestigevillarental.com. An online agency that provides luxury villa rental services to the French Caribbean, their site is contemporary and comprehensive with an excellent English version, photos of every room and detailed descriptions. Rental properties range from deluxe to over-the-top, such as the most high-end rental in Terre de Haut, Villa Les Saintes. It's a real blend of luxury and the island's unique charm. Prestige has villas that are handpicked for celebratory occasions, everything from Honeymoon hideaways to contemporary mansions for family reunions. They have handled corporate retreats and anniversaries. Their concierge service can provision villas or arrange private chefs and housekeepers, orchestrate tours and shopping excursions, and in-house spa services. Villas can have everything from Wi-Fi to pool guys. The agency's young bilingual owner, who grew up on Guadeloupe, writes an impressive blog giving tips on "doing" the French islands. He honed his rental skills in St. Bart's, where he became a villa specialist. ✉ *Grande-Terre* ☎ *917/720–3120, 336/851–853–01* 🌐 *www.prestigevillarental.com.*

RECOMMENDED HOTELS AND RESORTS

GRANDE-TERRE

$$$ HOTEL 🏨 **Auberge de la Vieille Tour.** At this island classic built around an historic sugar mill, everyone loves the initial welcome: a cool drink and citrus-scented towels dispensed by ladies in white eyelet lace. **Pros:** most rooms have great views; breakfast is a highlight; restaurant is one of the island's best. **Cons:** expensive; exteriors of some sections are unattractive 1960s-style; it's a hill climb back from the beach and pool, which is slated to be redone, but not soon enough. [$] *Rooms from: €365* ✉ *Rte. de Montauban, Gosier, Grande-Terre* ☎ *0590/84–23–23* 🌐 *www.mgallery.com* 🛏 *70 rooms, 32 deluxe rooms, 1 suite* 🍴 *Breakfast.*

$ HOTEL 🏨 **Bwa Chik Hotel & Golf.** This ecochic, boutique hotel at the marina is the buzz in St. Francois for its unique decor; recycled wood and driftwood are juxtaposed with ultracontemporary Euro furnishings and gauzy, salmon-hued drapes. **Pros:** ideal location; car unnecessary; welcoming staff; live jazz nights in season. **Cons:** small pool; not all the staff speaks English; no elevators or bellmen. [$] *Rooms from: €146* ✉ *Av. de l'Europe, St-François, Grande-Terre* ☎ *0590/88–60–60* 🌐 *www.bwachik.com* 🛏 *43 rooms, 11 duplexes* 🍴 *Breakfast.*

$$$ ALL-INCLUSIVE FAMILY Fodor's Choice ★ 🏨 **Club Med La Caravelle.** Facing the island's best white-sand beaches, La Caravelle is one of the original clubs in the Caribbean, yet all the facilities—including the seafront restaurant and its deck—have a smashing, contemporary look. **Pros:** a large fun quotient; exceptional boutique; good service. **Cons:** Club Med experience and kid-friendly atmosphere

is not for everyone; older standard rooms are small; Wi-Fi is extra. $ *Rooms from: €392* ✉ *Quartier Caravelle, Ste-Anne, Grande-Terre* ☎ *0590/85–49–50, 800/258–2633* ⊕ *www.clubmed.us* ⌁ *297 rooms, 37 suites* ☾ *Closed Sept.– early Nov.* ⏀ *All-inclusive.*

$
B&B/INN
⊞ **Hotel Amaudo.** This *hôtel de charme* (boutique hotel) is a small *madam-et-monsieur* operation, the mom 'n' pop being the sophisticated French managers. **Pros:** a moderate price tag for unobstructed sea views; safe (mechanized security gate). **Cons:** you need a car, as it is not in the tourist zone of St-François; no bar, restaurant or activities; could be too quiet and peaceful. $ *Rooms from: €145* ✉ *Anse à la Barque, St-François, Grande-Terre* ☎ *0590/88–87–00* ⊕ *www.amaudo.fr* ⌁ *10 rooms* ⏀ *Multiple meal plans.*

$$
HOTEL
⊞ **La Cocoteraie.** This boutique hotel's lobby, overlooking a glorious pool and with basket-weave rattan furnishings and decorative masks, is a study in refinement. **Pros:** by a calm lagoon; sophisticated clientele; international crowd and light fare at the Indigo Bar; new general manager who is busy revitalizing the resort. **Cons:** generic, white-plastic furniture on terraces; some ongoing maintenance issues; not as fun as it used to be. $ *Rooms from: €298* ✉ *Av. de l'Europe, St-François, Grande-Terre* ☎ *0590/88–79–81* ⊕ *www.lacocoteraie.com* ⌁ *52 suites* ⏀ *Breakfast.*

$
RESORT
Fodor'sChoice
★
⊞ **La Créole Beach Hotel & Spa.** This 10-acre complex has a contemporary, colorful lobby, cosmopolitan bar, and dual pools that are surrounded by mauve market umbrellas and silver patio furniture. **Pros:** excellent management and long-term staff; lovely tropical gardens; exceptionally good buffets and the entire restaurant is to be renovated. **Cons:** some rooms quite a hike from lobby; beach is nice but small; Wi-Fi costs extra. $ *Rooms from: €230* ✉ *Pointe de la Verdure, Gosier, Grande-Terre* ☎ *0590/90–46–46* ⊕ *www.deshotelsetdesiles.com* ⌁ *276 rooms, 16 junior suites, 6 suites, 13 apartments* ⏀ *No meals.*

$$
RESORT
Fodor'sChoice
★
⊞ **La Toubana Hôtel & Spa.** Few hotels on Guadeloupe command such a panoramic view of the sea—spanning four islands, no less. **Pros:** a special boutique experience with sophisticated style; glass-enclosed cocktail lounge–library has remarkable views; praise-worthy restaurant continues to evolve. **Cons:** the little beach is down the hill, via a very steep paved path; bedrooms and TVs are small by American standards; some bungalows need renovation. $ *Rooms from: €304* ✉ *Ste-Anne, Grande-Terre* ☎ *0590/88–25–57* ⊕ *www.toubana.com* ⌁ *32 bungalows, 1 studio suite, 5 1-bedroom suites, 9 2-bedroom suites* ⏀ *Breakfast.*

BASSE-TERRE

$
B&B/INN
FAMILY
⊞ **Caraïb'Bay Hotel.** This complex of colorful duplex bungalows may not impress you at first, but its service and customer satisfaction have earned it many kudos. **Pros:** homey feel with multilingual library; moderate prices, especially with weekly offers; innovative bar and flavorful, creole specialties by night. **Cons:** good, long beach, but it's down and across the road; not luxe; statesiders sometimes consider duplexes' furnishings dated. $ *Rooms from: €148* ✉ *Allée du Coeur, Ziotte, Deshaies* ☎ *0590/28–41–71* ⌁ *12 duplex bungalows (for 2–5 persons), 4 villas (3–8 persons)* ⏀ *Multiple meal plans.*

La Toubana Hotel & Spa

$ B&B/INN **Habitation Du Comté.** A decidedly special place, this was the great house for the owner of a sugarcane plantation, but the stalwart, hurricane-proof mansion wasn't built eons ago, only in 1948. **Pros:** shutters for sleeping that block out any light; blissfully quiet; in-room Wi-Fi is strong and free. **Cons:** not much goes on; need a car; no resort-style amenities. [$] *Rooms from: €160* ✉ *Comté de Lohéac, St. Rose* ☎ *0590/21–78–81* 🌐 *www.hotelducomte.com* 🛏 *7 rooms, 1 2-bedroom suite, 1 2-bedroom bungalow* 🍴 *Breakfast.*

$ ALL-INCLUSIVE FAMILY **Langley Hotel Fort Royal.** This well-priced, friendly, and fun hotel was formed by a major renovation of a 1970s seafront mid-rise with the addition of conical bungalows (14 beachfront). **Pros:** nonguests can sample the fun by paying €49 for a day pass; free Internet; food and service surprisingly good. **Cons:** not all hotel rooms have a sea view; bungalows are small and some are subject to noise from the restaurant and bar; the single restaurant, which mainly serves buffets, gets crowded. [$] *Rooms from: €250* ✉ *Petit Bas Vent, Deshaies* ☎ *0590/68–76–70* 🌐 *www.fortroyal.eu* 🛏 *126 rooms, 7 suites, 82 bungalows* 🕐 *Closed Sept. and Oct.* 🍴 *All-inclusive.*

$ B&B/INN Fodor's Choice ★ **Le Jardin de Malanga.** At this former coffee plantation, trees laden with fruit are like the temptations of the Garden of Eden. **Pros:** a romantic hideaway with history and character; lovely food (half-board is a good option). **Cons:** not easy to find and best navigated by day; no TV or Internet in the bungalows; the nearest beach is 20 minutes away by car. [$] *Rooms from: €233* ✉ *#60 Rte. de l'Hermitage, Hermitage, Trois-Rivières* ☎ *0590/92–67–57* 🌐 *www.deshotelsetdesiles.com* 🛏 *9 rooms, 1 suite* 🍴 *Breakfast.*

$ ⚼ **Le Neem Bungalows.** These three attractive gites, or suites, have spicy
RENTAL names—Vanille, Safron, and Canela (cinnamon), and that is the order
of preference. **Pros:** fine beach just across the street; good prices; young
owning couple are caring, and Joel's wife, Ancette, speaks English.
Cons: no space between suites; no views; no hotel amenities. **$** *Rooms
from: €100* ✉ *Rte. de la Pointe des Chateaux, St-François, Grande-
Terre* ⊕ *www.leneem.fr* ⌨ *3 suites.*

$$ ⚼ **Tainos Cottages.** Now *this* is a story: a globe-trotting Frenchman
B&B/INN designed seven teakwood cottages resembling Guadeloupean *cases* from
the 1920s, had them constructed in Indonesia, and imported the cottages
to a site overlooking a long unspoiled beach, Plage de Grande-Anse.
Pros: from the smallest to the largest, the cottages are large; a discount
is available by booking online; a hip, multigenerational family owns the
place. **Cons:** the mosquito netting's there for a reason; no glass on the
windows; the dark wood and some other features need maintenance.
$ *Rooms from: €300* ✉ *Plage de Grande-Anse, Deshaies* ☎ *0590/28–
44–42* ⊕ *www.tainoscottages.com* ⌨ *7 bungalows* ⊙ *Closed mid-Aug.–
mid-Oct.* ⅠⓄⅠ *Breakfast.*

$$ ⚼ **Tendacayou Ecolodge & Spa.** This complex is the result of a remarkable
B&B/INN 10-year saga, as an expat French family learned to live off a parcel of
rain forest, building tree houses for their large brood, then construct-
ing additional ones for paying guests, as well as a seafood restaurant,
Le Poisson Rouge. **Pros:** boardwalks rather than scary ladders to the
tree houses; fun, funky, quirky and inventive; ample breakfast with lots
house-made; a boutique jammed with wonderfully exotic clothes and
treasures from Thailand and elsewhere. **Cons:** open-air sleeping (particularly in the older tree houses) might be too one-with-nature for you;
no beach (but sea views and a pool); no phones, TVs, or in-room Wi-Fi.
$ *Rooms from: €257* ✉ *Matouba La Hauf, Deshaies* ☎ *0590/28–42–
72* ⊕ *www.tendacayou.com* ⌨ *7 1-bedroom bungalows, 2 3-bedroom
bungalows* ⅠⓄⅠ *Breakfast.*

ILES DES SAINTES

$ ⚼ **Hotel Restaurant Les Petits Saints.** This charismatic landmark inn, which
B&B/INN draws mainly couples and families, was bought by a French couple
who discovered the property while on vacation from their home in
California. **Pros:** reminiscent of the island guesthouses of the 1970s;
village just down the hill; free Wi-Fi, including in some rooms. **Cons:**
do not expect luxury, though improvements continue; not the house
party it once was. **$** *Rooms from: €150* ✉ *La Savane, Terre-de-Haut*
☎ *0590/99–50–99* ⊕ *www.petitssaints.com* ⌨ *3 bungalows, 3 suites,
2 studios, 2 rooms* ⊙ *Closed Sept.* ⅠⓄⅠ *Breakfast.*

$ ⚼ **Lô Bleu Hôtel.** This cheerful hotel is painted sunset orange with marine-
HOTEL blue trim; dramatic nightlights illuminate the beach area, which is furnished with chaises. **Pros:** right on the bay; large front rooms with sea
view and balconies; family-friendly, with baby monitors and some bunk
beds. **Cons:** no grounds or resort amenities; no restaurant; the "front
desk" does not always speak English. **$** *Rooms from: €140* ✉ *Fond
de Curé, Terre-de-Haut* ☎ *0590/92–40–00, 0690/63–80–36* ⊕ *www.
lobleuhotel.com* ⌨ *10 rooms.*

Le Jardin de Malanga

$ RENTAL **Paradis Saintois.** You'll feel like the king of the hill as you rock yourself to sleep in your hammock while gazing down on the Caribbean below. **Pros:** lots of fun; super managers; radio/CD/mp3 players in all units; TVs in apartments and some studios. **Cons:** no phones or TVs in some rooms; a hike up the hill from town. [$] *Rooms from: €70* ✉ *211 Rte. des Pres Cassin, B. P. I., Terre-de-Haut* ☎ *0590/99–56–16* 🌐 *www.paradissaintois.com* 🛏 *5 apartments, 3 studios, 1 room* 🍴 *No meals* ☞ *3-night minimum.*

$ RENTAL **Residence Anse Caraibe.** This residence, which in French means a rental complex, is perched on a hill right in the village, a five-minute walk from the ferry dock. **Pros:** English-speaking, accommodating French manager, who can even arrange transportation on the mainland; four apartments (F2 is the best) open onto spacious, private terraces that look to the bay; Wi-Fi is now in all units. **Cons:** no phones or cable channels for little TVs; steep hill; no cushy creature comforts; three-night minimum in high season, two in low season. [$] *Rooms from: €57* ✉ *Emmanuel Laurent St., Terre-de-Haut, Iles des Saintes* ☎ *0690/57–68–13, 0683/05–63–67* 🌐 *www.grandbaie.com* 🛏 *4 studio apartments, 1 2-bedroom apartment, 1 3-bedroom apartment* 🍴 *No meals.*

$$ RENTAL **Résidence Grand Baie.** A luxe, hilltop complex that houses several different accommodations, it offers privacy and a seafront existence, 15 minutes from the village. [$] *Rooms from: €68* ✉ *Rte. du Figuier, Terre-de-Haut, Iles des Saintes* ☎ *0690/57–68–13, 0683/05–63–67* 🌐 *www.grandbaie.com* 🛏 *5 units* 🍴 *No meals.*

MARIE-GALANTE

Accommodations here run the gamut from inexpensive, locally owned beachfront bungalows to complexes with international owners. For an overnight or longer, a special promotion put together by Bwa Chik Hotel in St. Francois involves the ferry BABOU that runs from that town. There is one to Marie Galante and one to a new hotel option, Cap Reva.

$ **Au Village de Menard.** Village de Menard consists of 15 crisp and B&B/INN colorful bungalows surrounding a pool, in a pastoral setting. **Pros:** it has been in business for decades; moderate price, especially for weekly rentals. **Cons:** accommodations are not very stylish; you're not on the beach. $ *Rooms from: €75* ⊠ *Section Vieux Fort, St. Louis* ☎ *0590/97–09–45* ⊕ *www.villagedemenard.com* ➴ *15 rooms* ⏐⊖⏐ *No meals.*

$ **La Rose de Bresil.** Indeed, this should be called the Rose of Marie-B&B/INN Galante, for if there is any "address" here that would appeal to a stateside clientele, this be the place. **Pros:** flat-screen, satellite TV; free Wi-Fi even in-room; quality mattresses are replaced every three years. **Cons:** no sea views; no resort amenities; older rooms not as lovely. $ *Rooms from: €120* ⊠ *Rte. du litoral, Capesterre* ☎ *0590/97–47–39* ⊕ *www.larosedubresil.com* ➴ *7 rooms, 2 2-bedroom suites; 1 3-bedroom suite.*

$ **Le Soleil Levant.** Several features keep this simple, family-owned comHOTEL plex filled, the first being its low price, followed by its hilltop views and dual pools. **Pros:** family-friendly; good air-conditioning; Wi-Fi is free and consistent in hotel rooms. **Cons:** need a car; hotel rooms are not large; staff not accustomed to American guests. $ *Rooms from: €55* ⊠ *Section Marie-Louise, 42 rue de la Marine, Les Hauteurs de Capesterre, Capesterre* ☎ *0590/97–31–55* ⊕ *www.hotel-soleil-levant.fr* ➴ *8 rooms, 5 apartments, 10 bungalows* ⏐⊖⏐ *No meals.*

$ **Le Touloulou.** Le Touloulou has four simple stucco one-bedroom bunRENTAL galows, two of which have kitchenettes, as well as a two-bedroom bungalow, also with a kitchenette. **Pros:** beachfront location at a budget price; adjacent restaurant and fun bar; genial, bilingual chef-owner. **Cons:** simple, no-frills place; lacks the usual resort amenities. $ *Rooms from: €60* ⊠ *Plage de Petite-Anse* ☎ *0590/97–32–63* ⊕ *www. letouloulou.com* ➴ *5 bungalows* ⏐⊖⏐ *Multiple meal plans.*

$ **Le Village de Canada.** Le Village de Canada has studios, bungalows RENTAL (villas), and apartments, some with sea views; there's a pool but no beach, though one is close by. **Pros:** friendly; private terraces; moderate prices, especially on a weekly basis; good central location, being equidistant between Grand Bourg and St. Louis. **Cons:** not on the beach; needs updating; no breakfast or restaurant. $ *Rooms from: €70* ⊠ *Section Canada, Grand-Bourg* ☎ *0590/97–86–11* ⊕ *www.villagedecanada. com* ➴ *5 studios, 3 villas, 7 apartments* ⏐⊖⏐ *No meals.*

NIGHTLIFE

Guadeloupeans maintain that the beguine began here, and for sure, the beguine and mazurkas were heavily influenced by the European quadrille and orchestrated melodies. Their merging is the origin of West Indian music, and it gave birth to zouk (music with an African-influenced Caribbean rhythm) at the beginning of the 1980s. Still the rage here, it has spread not only to France but to other European countries. Many resorts have dinner dancing or offer regularly scheduled entertainment by steel bands and folkloric groups.

BARS AND NIGHTCLUBS

Club Med By Night. Club Med sells night passes (6 pm–2 am) for €93 that include all cocktails, dinner with wine, and a show in the theater, followed by admission to the disco. Go on Friday for the gala dinner and the most creative show, or on a Tuesday, another special night. A night pass is a good option for single women, who will feel comfortable and safe at the disco, where there are plenty of fun staffers (G.O.s) willing to be dance partners. ⊠ *Quartier Caravelle, Ste-Anne, Grande-Terre* ☎ *0590/85–49–50* ⊘ *Closed Sept.– early Nov.*

Eden Palm Theater Spectacles. The jazzed-up Eden Palm Theater usually presents Cuban-influenced Caribbean musical reviews on Saturday nights (though phone ahead to make sure, as it is tending to happen more on major holidays). The fast-moving, grand *spectacle*—like nothing else on the island—has plumage, imaginative costumes, a super sound system, special effects, a bevy of dancers, and even trapeze artists. The cost varies along with what one receives for it. The program (and the price) escalates during the Christmas holidays and on New Year's Eve; both are celebratory happenings here. Always there is the dinner—multicourse and Franco-Caribbean, and some alcoholic beverage. Example: one can expect to pay €120 at Christmas with a glass of wine and €350 per couple for New Year's Eve, with a champagne accompanying dessert. ⊠ *Hotel Eden Palm, Ste-Anne, Grande-Terre* ☎ *0590/88–48–48* ⊕ *www.edenpalm.com.*

La Créole Beach Hotel & Spa Bar and Lounge. Something is always happening at this hotel. The entertainment is often bands playing beguine and zouk, or a piano man accompanied by a bass guitar, all of which are very danceable and add to the hotel's conviviality. The tom-tom drummers accompanied by a bevy of native dancers are exciting. A steel band also plays, usually on Monday and Wednesday. The busy bar specializes in quality rums from various Caribbean islands, and serves some tasty, light dishes. ⊠ *La Créole Beach Hotel & Spa, Pointe de la Verdure, Gosier, Grande-Terre* ☎ *0590/90–46–46.*

Le Bar at Auberge de la Vieille Tour. Entertainment at Auberge de la Vieille Tour ranges from the talented piano man to jazz combos. The atmospheric piano bar with its planter's chairs and whirring fan blades is as memorable as Rick's Café in *Casablanca*. Accras (salt-fish fritters) and other munchies usually arrive with your cocktail. A selection of tapas is available, as is an extensive number of rums, some of which are available by the flight. In high season, there's live music often nightly, and in low season it's on Friday and Saturday evenings only. ⊠ *Rte. de Montauban, Gosier, Grande-Terre* ☎ *0590/84–23–23.*

13

Zoo Rock Café. Open nightly, this bar, *rhumerie* (rum distillery), restaurant, and café often has live music. Theme nights are a house party, be it Havana night, Halloween, or their takeoff on New Orleans' Mardi Gras. The crowd is young and mostly European French. Food is secondary to the fun and good humor—on a busy night, the crowd spills out of this alfresco cafe as they rock to the wild DJ sounds. If you are hungry, go earlier—doors open at 6—before the party begins and have one of their signature brochettes off the grill. ☒ *La Marina Gosier, Gosier* ☎ *0590/90–77–77* ⊕ *www.zoorockcafe.com.*

CASINOS

Both of the island's casinos are on Grande-Terre and have American-style roulette, blackjack, and stud poker. The legal age for gambling is 21, and French law dictates that everyone show a passport, or for locals, a driver's license. Jacket and tie aren't required, but "proper attire" means no shorts, T-shirts, jeans, flip-flops, or sneakers.

DISCOS

Night owls should note that carousing here isn't cheap. On the weekend and when there's live music, most discos charge a cover of at least €10, which might go up to as much as €20. Your cover usually includes a drink, and other drinks cost about €12 each.

SHOPPING

The island has a lot of desirable French products, from designer fashions for women and men and sensual lingerie to French china and liqueurs. As for local handicrafts, you can find attractive wood carvings, madras table linens, island dolls dressed in madras, woven straw baskets and hats, and *salakos*—fishermen's hats made of split bamboo, some covered in madras—which make great wall decorations. Of course, the favorite Guadeloupean souvenir is rum. Look for *rhum vieux*, the top of the line. Be aware that the only liquor bottles allowed on planes have to be bought in the duty-free shops at the airport. Usually the shops have to deliver purchases to the aircraft. For foodies, the market ladies sell aromatic fresh spices, crisscrossed with cinnamon sticks, in little baskets lined with madras.

AREAS AND MALLS

Bas-du-Fort. Bas-du-Fort's two shopping areas are the Cora Shopping Center and the marina, where there are 20 or so shops and some restaurants, many right on the water. ☒ *Pointe-à-Pitre, Grande-Terre.*

Destreland. Grande-Terre's largest, most modern shopping mall, Destreland, has more than 180 boutiques, restaurants and stores. This commercial center is a few minutes from the airport, which is a shopping destination in its own right. ☒ *Abymes, Grande-Terre* ⊕ *www.destreland.com.*

Pointe-à-Pitre. In Pointe-à-Pitre you can browse in the street stalls around the harbor quay and at the two markets (the best is the Marché de Frébault). The town's main shopping streets are rue Schoelcher, rue de

Basse-Terre Market

Nozières, and the busy rue Frébault. At the St-John Perse Cruise Terminal, there's an attractive mall with about two dozen shops. ⊠ *Pointe-à-Pitre, Grande-Terre.*

St-François. In St-François there are more than a dozen shops surrounding the marina, some selling French lingerie, swimsuits, and fashions. The supermarket has particularly good prices on French wines and cheeses, and if you pick up a fresh baguette, you'll have a picnic. (Then you can go get lost at a secluded beach.) ⊠ *St-François, Grande-Terre.*

SPECIALTY STORES

ART

Pascal Foy. Artist Pascal Foy produces stunning homages to traditional Creole architecture: paintings of houses that incorporate collage make marvelous wall hangings. As his fame has grown, his media attention has expanded, so prices have risen. You are more likely to find a family member manning the shop nowadays. ⊠ *Rte. à Pompierres, Terre-de-Haut, Iles des Saintes* ☎ *0690/43–13–09.*

CLOTHING

Côté Plage. In addition to T-shirts and other ideal island necessities, Côté Plage sells bikinis, sundresses, and straw beach totes. There's also a line of simple jewelry—turtles, geckos, and sea horses—made of sand and resin. It's directly across from the produce market. ⊠ *Pl. du Marché, Pointe-à-Pitre, Grande-Terre.*

Dody. Across from the market, Dody is the place to go if you want white eyelet lace (blouses, skirts, dresses, even bustiers). A single item can cost from €100 to €300. There's lots of madras, too, which is especially cute in children's clothing. Hark! Now those who love designer ensembles based in Guadeloupean tradition, can shop online. Online models include Miss Guadeloupe and bebes creole. Many styles have reduced prices and there are special-occasion "costumes"—wedding, communion, and confirmation dresses all in white eyelet. ⊠ *31 rue Frébault, Pointe-à-Pitre, Grande-Terre* 🕿 *0590/82–18–73* ⊕ *www.dodyshop.com.*

Le Gall. Le Gall handles a line of fashionable resort wear for women and children, designed by French painter Jean Claude Le Gall, that has hand-painted figures like turtles and dolphins on high-quality cotton knits. There are several other branches of this French favorite across the island, at the Bas-du-Fort Marina and even on Les Saintes. A gift from this store is considered prestigious back in mainland France. ⊠ *La Marina–La Coursive, St-François, Grande-Terre.*

COSMETICS AND PERFUME

L'Atelier du Savon. L'Atelier du Savon makes all of its soaps from vegetable products, with scents including marine spice and mandarin orange. Beautifully packaged gift baskets include bath salts and aromatic oils. You never know when the sign: "Closed today, we are making soap," will go up. ⊠ *Impasse du Mouillage, near pharmacy on rue Jean Calot, Terre-de-Haut, Iles des Saintes* 🕿 *0590/99–56–24.*

HANDICRAFTS

Centre Artisanat. The Centre Artisanat offers a wide selection of local crafts, including art composed of shells, wood, and stone. One of the outlets sells authentic Panama hats. It is located under a tent across from the waterfront as you first drive into the village. ⊠ *Ste-Anne, Grande-Terre.*

Madras Bijoux. Bijoux is the French word for jewelry and Madras Bijoux specializes in replicas of authentic Creole jewelry, like the multistrand gold bead necklaces. The shop also creates custom designs and does repairs. ⊠ *115 rue Nozières, Pointe-à-Pitre, Grande-Terre* 🕿 *0590/ 82–88–03.*

Maogany Boutique. At this shop, which resembles a yacht, the best of the offerings are batiks and clothing in luminescent seashell- and blue shades. Ladies love *pareos* (wraparound fabric for skirts) in the colors of the sea, from pale green to deep turquoise, as well as the jewelry. For men and ladies, there are authentic Panama hats—tropical fedoras in classic white *and* tropical colors. There are also several lines of women's clothing by French designers, tunics, crocheted tops, and tiered long skirts. Now if you can't get to the island you can shop online with their new site. ⊠ *26 rue Jean Calot, Terre-de-Haut, Iles des Saintes* 🕿 *0590/99–55–69, 0690/50–48–44* ⊕ *www.maogany.com* ⊗ *Closed Mon. in low season.*

LIQUOR AND TOBACCO

The airport duty-free stores have a good selection of rum and tobacco.

SPORTS AND ACTIVITIES

BIKING

The French are mad about *le cyclisme*. If you rent a bicycle, expect to be asked to leave a deposit, but the amount seems to vary; normally you can use a credit card to secure your rental. On Terre-de-Haut, there are a number of shops to the immediate left and right of the ferry dock; the farther from the dock they are, the lower the rates. At least one shop has bikes with small motors on them to help climb the hills. And you can usually negotiate the price down—a little.

BOATING AND SAILING

Generally speaking, most of the towns and cities of Guadeloupe are not beautiful; however, the craggy coastline and the waters of variegated blues and greens are gorgeous. If you plan to sail these waters, you should be aware that the winds and currents tend to be strong. There are excellent, well-equipped marinas in Pointe-à-Pitre, Bas-du-Fort, Deshaies, St-François, and Gourbeyre. You can rent a yacht (bareboat or crewed) from several companies. To make a bareboat charter, companies will evaluate your navigational and seamanship skills. If you do not pass, you must hire a skipper or be left on dry land.

Antilles Sail. Antilles Sail is a charter operation specializing in catamarans from 40 to 62 feet, which can accommodate eight guests. A new, exciting addition to their fleet is a 45' Neel trimaran. For those who don't qualify to captain their own ship, or for those who want to just relax and be pampered, a skipper and crew can be hired. Provisioning and meal service can be arranged and VIP, dive, and other packages are available. The fleet also contains monohulls from 35 to 55 feet, which are used mainly for bareboating. Antilles Sail can also arrange flights, land stays, and other arrangements. ⊠ *Bas-du-Fort Marina, Quai No. 9, Boutique des Moulins, Bas-du-Fort, Grande-Terre* ☎ *0590/90–16–81* ⊕ *www.antilles-sail.com.*

DIVING

The main diving area at the **Cousteau Underwater Park,** just off Basse-Terre near Pigeon Island, offers routine dives to 60 feet. The numerous glass-bottom boats and other craft make the site feel like a marine parking lot; however, the underwater sights are spectacular. Guides and instructors are certified under the French CMAS (some also have PADI, but none have NAUI). Most operators offer two-hour dives three times per day for about €45 to €50 per dive; three-dive packages are €120 to €145. Hotels and dive operators usually rent snorkeling gear.

FAMILY **Les Heures Saines.** Les Heures Saines is the premier operator for dives in the Cousteau Underwater Park. Trips to Les Saintes offer one or two dives for average and advanced divers, with plenty of time for lunch and sightseeing. Wreck, night, and Nitrox diving are also available. The instructors, many of them English speakers, are excellent with children. The company also offers winter whale- and dolphin-watching trips with marine biologists as guides. These tours, aboard a 60-foot catamaran, cost €55 (less for children). Inquire also about going canyoning and/or hiking with Les Heures Saines. ⊠ *Le Rocher de Malendure, Plage de Malendure, Bouillante, Basse-Terre* ☎ *0590/98–86–63* ⊕ *www.heures-saines.gp.*

FAMILY **Pisquettes Club de Plongée Des Saintes.** With more than 10 years of experience, dive master Cedric Phalipon of Pisquettes Club de Plongée Des Saintes knows all the best sites. He gives excellent lessons, and in English, too. Equipment is replaced frequently and is of a high caliber. Small tanks are available for kids, who are taken buddy diving. PADI divers are welcomed. Sec Pate is a famous underwater mountain, off the island's coast, in open seas. Les Saintes is known for its underwater hills, caves, canyons, and wall dives. Divers can see sponges of varied colors and gorgeous underwater trees that sway. Sec Pate is a famous underwater mountain, off the island's coast, in open seas. ⊠ *Le Mouillage, Terre-de-Haut, Iles des Saintes* ☎ *0590/99–88–80* ⊕ *www.pisquettes.com.*

Plaisir Plongee Karokera (PPK). Plaisir Plongee Karokera (PPK) has a good reputation and is well established among those who dive off Pigeon Island. One dive boat departs three times daily and charges €30 a dive. A second dive boat goes to Les Saintes, with two dives, one at a wreck, the other at a reef. The €85 price includes lunch. English-speaking dive masters are PADI certified. Show your Fodor's guide and ask for a discount. ⊠ *Plage de Malendure, Bouillante, Basse-Terre* ☎ *0590/98–82–43.*

FISHING

Not far offshore from Pigeon-Bouillante, in Basse-Terre, is a bounty of big-game fish such as bonito, dolphinfish, captain fish, barracuda, kingfish, and tuna. You can also thrill to the challenge of the big billfish such as marlin and swordfish. Anglers have been known to come back with as many as three blue marlins in a single day. For Ernest Hemingway wannabes, this is it. To reap this harvest, you'll need to charter one of the high-tech sportfishing machines with flying bridges, competent skippers, and mates. The price is $430 to $600 a day, with lunch and drinks included. The boats can accommodate up to six passengers.

Captain Tony. Like father, like son: Tony Burel has officially taken over the sportfishing boat that he and his dad, Michel, worked for years. It's outfitted to go into combat with the big game fish and he has hauled many a billfish aboard. It's outfitted to go into combat with big game fish and he has hauled many a billfish aboard. It has the latest generation of electronics and is considered the most commodious sportfisherman on the island. This Burel has 10 fishing years to his credit, five as a guide. Not only does he know where to find blue marlin but yellow-fin tuna, wahoo—"what you like." Rates are €160 for each fisherman, and €90 if someone is just coming along for the ride. This reliable big-fishing charter outfit can usually pick anglers up at their hotel for an extra 30 euros. The skipper will be happy to take your picture with your catch of the day. And if you are not into jigging or chumming check the website for snorkeling adventures and other excursions. ⊠ *Les Galbas, Ste-Anne, Basse-Terre* ☎ *0690/55–21–35* ⊕ *captaintonyb.com.*

EN ROUTE

If you're driving from Ste-Anne to the St-François Marina area, follow signs first to St-François, then look for signs to the marina and Pointe des Châteaux, not St-François centre ville. That is the old town, and although it's a nice detour to see the market, it's also a circuitous route to the marina.

GOLF

Golf Municipal St-François. Golf Municipal St-François is a par-72 course that was designed by Robert Trent Jones in 1978, with later alterations that made it more challenging, though many feel that the putting surfaces could use improvement. The course has an English-speaking pro and electric carts for rent. It's best to reserve tee times a day or two in advance. There are no caddies. Clubs can be rented for about €2. Guests at Bwa Chik Hotel & Golf get a 20% discount. Le Birdy restaurant serves lunch daily and dinner Wednesday and Friday through Sunday and tapas are offered at the bar. Sunday buffets in season or during competitions are €35. ✉ *97118 Saint Francois, St-François, Grande-Terre* ☎ *0590/88–41–87* ☉ *Daily 7 am–6:30 pm.* ⚑ *18 holes, 6755 yards, par 71* ⛳ *€28 for 9 holes, €45 for 18 holes.*

HIKING

Fodor's Choice
★

With hundreds of trails and countless rivers and waterfalls, the **Parc National de la Guadeloupe** on Basse-Terre is the main draw for hikers. Some of the trails should be attempted only with an experienced guide. All tend to be muddy, so wear a good pair of boots. Know that even the young and fit can find these outings arduous; the unfit may find them painful. Start off slowly, with a shorter hike, and then go for the gusto. All water sports—even canoeing and kayaking—are forbidden in the center of the park. Scientists are studying the impact of these activities on the park's ecosystem.

Vert Intense. Vert Intense organizes hikes in the national park and to the volcano. You move from steaming hot springs to an icy waterfall in the same hike. Guides are patient and safety-conscious, and can bring you to heights that you never thought you could reach, including the top of Le Soufrière. The volcano hike costs €30 and must be booked four days in advance. Note that when you are under the fumaroles you can smell the sulfur (like rotten eggs) and you, your hair and clothes will smell like sulfur until you take a shower. A mixed-adventure package spanning three days costs €225. The two-day bivouac and other adventures can be extreme, so before you decide to play Indiana Jones, know what is expected. The French-speaking guides, who also know some English and Spanish, can take you to other tropical forests and rivers for canyoning (climbing and scrambling on outcrops, usually along and above the water). If you are just one or two people, the company can team you up with a group. Vert Intense now has a guesthouse where you can combine a stay with trekking and other activities. ✉ *Rte. de la Soufrière, Mourne Houel, Basse-Terre* ☎ *0590/99–34–73, 0690/55–40–47* ⊕ *www.vert-intense.com.*

HORSEBACK RIDING

Le Haras de Saint-François. A 50-horse stable, Le Haras de Saint-François has English lessons and Western trail rides for two hours (€50) or three hours (€60). The latter will take you to the beach, where you can go bareback into the sea. ⊠ *Chemin de la Princesse, St-François, Grande-Terre* ☎ *0690/39–90–00.*

JET SKIING

Atmosphere. The young and sporty French are wild for their *scooters de mer,* but you can't rent a Jet Ski in Guadeloupe unless you have a special license. Instead, Atmospheres organizes group excursions for two to five hours that cost €270 (one person on one Jet Ski) to €135 per person on one Jet Ski. It's a pricey but exhilarating way to enjoy the sea, and you can experience a number of different sites speedily; the full day includes lunch at a remote islet. If you have knee or back problems or are afraid of speed, stay on your chaise longue: even twentysomethings are sore afterward. ⊠ *La Créole Beach Hotel & Spa, Pointe de la Verdure, Gosier, Grande-Terre* ☎ *0590/88–08–62, 0690/49–47–28* ⊕ *atmosphere-antilles.com.*

KAYAKING AND OTHER WATER SPORTS

Centre Nautique. On the beach, Centre Nautique rents sea kayaks for €10 an hour and Hobie Cats for €40 an hour, and can arrange fishing, catamaran, kayaking, diving, and motorboat excursions. It also runs water taxis to the Islet du Gosier (€10). There are PADI instructors for the dive segment of the operation, and certifications are possible. Jet Ski rentals include a guide, and range from a half hour for €70 to €270 for one Jet Ski for five hours including lunch. Nonguests are welcome but must call in advance. ⊠ *La Créole Beach Hotel & Spa, Pointe de la Verdure, Gosier, Grande-Terre* ☎ *0590/90–46–59.*

Centre Éconautique. Centre Éconautique aka Clear Blue Caraibes has mastered the art of underwater exploration without ever getting your hair wet. Rent a transparent kayak, which allows you to see the myriad colors of one of the world's most beautiful bays here. Paddleboards and clear-bottom, dinghy-like inflatables also enable you to play in the water. The tours, which last either two-hours or a half-day, will let you be privy to the marine beauty of the coral reefs and sea life. The cost is €20 per person, with special family and group rates available. Also, trips to the nearby Isle de Cabrito for a picnic and snorkeling are now offered. To find Centre Éconautique, take a left from the main dock, go two blocks and look for its colorful signage on the right. It is across from Couleurs du Monde. ⊠ *Ruelle Lasserre, Mouillage, Terre-de-Haut, Iles des Saintes* ☎ *0690/65–79–81* ⊕ *www.clearbluecaraibes.fr.*

SEA EXCURSIONS

FAMILY **Evasion Tropicale.** Evasion Tropicale operates daylong whale-watching cruises. With the help of the onboard hydrophone and the skipper's 20 years of experience humpback whales are easy to find from December through March, sperm whales and many species of small cetaceans all year round. Food and drinks are served and when you arrive back in port, you follow the leader to the small whale museum "Balen ka Souflé."

Trips on the 51-foot motor sailor cost €65 per person (10 passengers maximum), but every passenger must also buy an annual membership in the Association for Study and Census of Turtles, Marine and Mammals of the Caribbean for €25. Contributing to the conservation of marine life is a good way to discover and learn about the underwater world, especially for children. Evasion Tropicale received the biodiversity Conservation Award Special Mention in 2013. ✉ *Rue des paletuviers, Pigeon-Bouillante, Basse-Terre* ☎ *0590/92–74–24, 0690/57–19–44* ⊕ *www.evasiontropicale.org.*

Paradoxe Croisieres. A top-of-the-line catamaran, *Paradoxe* sails to Marie-Galante (anchoring at the idyllic beach, Anse Canot) for €90 in high season, usually on Thursday, but most days it departs from St. Francois for Petite-Terre, an uninhabited island that's a nature preserve. This isn't your typical booze cruise. Bottles of rum aboard? Sure, but passengers are more likely to be in it for the sailing experience and to see an out-island. In the morning when it anchors off Petite-Terre, the passengers take guided walking tours, always on the lookout for iguanas. Then it's back to the beach to eat lunch. Normally lunch is grilled fish with side dishes, which is served on the beach and prepared by the boat's crew. In the afternoon guests can snorkel in the lagoon. The lunch is tasty, and the music on board's soothing. The trip to Marie-Galante usually includes a bus tour around the island and a visit to a distillery. Marina ticket booth is open from 8–noon and 5–7. ✉ *St-François Marina, St-François, Grande-Terre* ☎ *0590/88–41–73* ⊕ *paradoxe-croisieres.com.*

WIND- AND KITESURFING

Most beachfront hotels can help you arrange lessons and rentals.

LookaSurf. This retail surf shop also rents surf and stand-up paddleboards (SUP). The action takes place on the remarkable Caravelle Beach. ✉ *Ste-Anne Lagoon, 17 Lot Marguerite-Valette, Ste-Anne, Grande-Terre* ☎ *0590/88–15–17* ⊕ *www.lookasurf.com.*

UCPA Hotel Club. Windsurfing buffs congregate at the UCPA Hotel Club, where for moderate weekly rates (beginning at €805 or €115 a day) they sleep in hostel-style quarters, eat three meals a day, and do a lot of windsurfing. Lessons and boards (also available to nonguests) are included in the package, as are bikes to pedal to the lagoon. UCPA has a water-sports center in the middle of town, though the hotel itself is out on isolated Baie de Marigot. There is a lot of action at *le centre* UCPA, where island visitors can rent windsurfing equipment for €25, take a lesson for €30, or take a kitesurfing lesson for €70 (€20 if part of a group). Kayaks, Hobie Cats, and dive tanks are available, too, and you can explore the beautiful seabeds and remote beaches of the archipelago. ✉ *Terre-de-Haut, Iles des Saintes* ☎ *0590/99–56–34 in-town sport center, 0590/99–54–94 hotel reservations* ⊕ *www.ucpa.com.*

JAMAICA

WELCOME TO JAMAICA

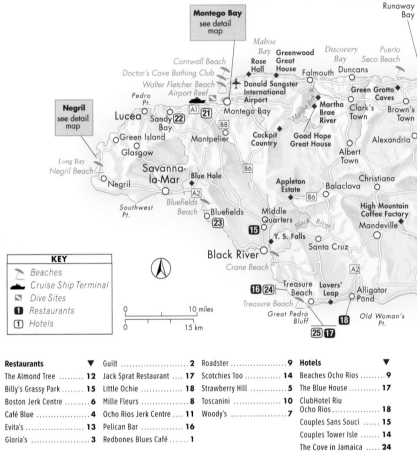

Montego Bay
see detail map

Negril
see detail map

Runaway Bay

KEY

- Beaches
- Cruise Ship Terminal
- Dive Sites
- **1** Restaurants
- **1** Hotels

0   10 miles
0   15 km

Restaurants ▼		
The Almond Tree **12**	Guilt **2**	Roadster **9**
Billy's Grassy Park **15**	Jack Sprat Restaurant **17**	Scotchies Too **14**
Boston Jerk Centre **6**	Little Ochie **18**	Strawberry Hill **5**
Café Blue **4**	Mille Fleurs **8**	Toscanini **10**
Evita's **13**	Ocho Rios Jerk Centre **11**	Woody's **7**
Gloria's **3**	Pelican Bar **16**	

Hotels ▼
Beaches Ocho Rios **9**
The Blue House **17**
ClubHotel Riu Ocho Rios **18**
Couples Sans Souci **15**
Couples Tower Isle **14**
The Cove in Jamaica **24**

Chances are you will never fully understand Jamaica in all its delightful complexity, but you will probably have a good time trying. You can party in Montego Bay, enjoy the sunset in Negril, or simply relax at one of the island's many all-inclusive resorts. One thing's for sure, along the way you'll discover a rich culture and delicious island cuisine that you'll not soon forget.

The third-largest island in the Caribbean (after Cuba and Hispaniola), Jamaica is 146 miles (242 km) long and is slightly smaller than the state of Connecticut. It has a population of 2.7 million. With about 800,000 people, the capital, Kingston, is the largest English-speaking city south of Miami (in the Western Hemisphere, at least). The highest point is Blue Mountain Peak at 7,402 feet.

14

JAMAICA

TOP REASONS TO VISIT JAMAICA

1 All-Inclusive Resorts: Come to where they were invented.

2 Great Golf: Golfers will be delighted by the many wonderful courses.

3 Fun for the Kids: Every conceivable activity, great beaches, and many child-friendly resorts appeal to families.

4 Negril Beach: It's simply one of the Caribbean's best.

5 Unique Culture: Jamaica has rich cultural traditions—particularly local music, art, and cuisine.

EATING WELL IN JAMAICA

The multicultural values embodied in Jamaica's national motto, "Out of Many, One People," serve equally well to describe its melting-pot cuisine: a savvy, savory fusion of African, Asian, Arawak-Taíno, and European influences, ingredients, techniques, and traditions.

Even the humble patty blends African peppers, Chinese soy sauce, and Cornish pasties. Sizzling Scotch bonnet peppers are indigenous, as are pimento—from which allspice is produced (Jamaica produces 80% of the world's supply), and the liberally used native ginger is stronger in Jamaica than elsewhere. Aspiring Anthony Bourdains should try beachfront or roadside vans, kiosks, and shacks dishing out darkly bubbling grub from cow foot to curried goat. They offer authentic fare such as succulent slow-cooked jerk with heaping helpings of rice 'n' peas (beans) and provisions (tubers such as yam and cassava).

JERK

Arguably Jamaica's most famous export after reggae and Olympic-caliber runners, jerk (usually chicken or pork) but now including everything from goat, fish, and even conch, is marinated for hours in a fiery blend of peppers, pimento, scallion, and thyme, then cooked over an outdoor pit lined with pimento wood. Low, slow heating retains the natural juices while infusing the meat with the flavor of the wood and spices and ensures that the meat lasts in the tropical heat.

The Culinary Jerk Trail spans the island from Negril through Mo'Bay and Ocho Rios to Kingston and Port Antonio. The attraction features 10 of the hottest jerk spots where diners can interact with chefs and learn the origins behind jerk cooking. For more information, go to ⊕ *www.visitjamaica.com/jerk*.

ACKEE AND SALTFISH

The British brought salt cod with them as a cheap, long-lasting foodstuff for sailors and slaves alike. Ackee, a red tree fruit introduced to Jamaica from western Africa via Britain, is actually poisonous in its natural state. Once the pear-shape fruit's tough, toxic, ruddy membrane is removed, however, the boiled, yellowish, pulpy arils surprisingly resemble scrambled eggs in taste and texture.

EXOTICA (TO SOME)

Goat figures in incendiary curries, as well as in "mannish water," a lusty soup, believed to be an aphrodisiac, that's traditionally served on wedding nights, wakes and other festive occasions. The soup includes the head, brains, and various other organs slow-cooked with various seasonings and tubers. Oxtail is a culinary constant from Italy to Indonesia. Jamaicans serve it stewed, braised, or in soup; inventive chefs might toss it with pasta in rum-cream sauce or use it to stuff quesadillas.

SEAFOOD ESCOVEITCH

Freshly caught fish—including snapper, tuna, wahoo, grouper, and marlin—is often served as *escoveitch* aka *escoveech* (fried to a golden crisp then topped

with pickled hot peppers, onions, chayote, carrots and pimento). Despite the linguistic and gastronomic similarity to ceviche and *escabeche*, escoveitch is rarely served cold, though it is usually marinated in vinegar and lime juice before it is cooked.

PROVISIONS

Farmers traditionally cultivated carbrich crops that could furnish energy for islanders' hardscrabble heavy labor without requiring refrigeration. Pumpkins, coconuts, plantains, breadfruit, sweet potatoes, cassava, yams, and other "provisions" (root and gourd vegetables as well as some fruits) became staples, sometimes replacing expensive imported ingredients (chayote was used in mock-apple crumble). Most homeowners still have kitchen gardens; the Olympic sprinter Usain Bolt credits yams from his native Trelawny Parish for his speed. Today lots of sophisticated chefs here are returning to the "grow what you eat" locavore ethos.

(Top left) Lobster at Evita's Italian Restaurant (Bottom right) A bounty of native Jamaican fruits (Top right) Fresh seafood, a part of many memorable Jamaican meals

Updated by Jonique Gaynor and Richard Sitler

Jamaicans define enthusiasm. Whether the topic is track and field, or politics, the spirit of this island comes out in every interaction. Although the country is well known for its tropical beauty, reggae music, and cuisine, you may find that your interactions with local residents are what you truly remember.

The island is rich in beauty, but a quick look around reveals widespread poverty and a land where the disparity between the lives of the resort guests and the resort employees is often staggering. Where vacationers opt to make their Jamaican home away from home depends on factors ranging from the length of their vacation to personal interests. With its direct air connections to many cities in the United States, Montego Bay (or Mo'Bay) is favored by Americans taking short trips; many properties are just minutes from the airport. Other parts of the island can be reached from Montego Bay in 60 to 90 minutes; more Eastern areas may be more accessible through the island's other major airport in the capital, Kingston.

Some of the island's earliest residents were the Arawak Indians, who arrived from South America around AD 650 and named the island Xaymaca, or "land of wood and water." Centuries later, the Arawaks welcomed Christopher Columbus on his second voyage to the New World. Later, when the Spanish arrived, the peaceful inhabitants were executed or taken as slaves.

The Spanish maintained control of the island until 1655, when the English arrived. Soon, slavery increased as sugar became a booming industry. In 1834 slavery was abolished, but the sugar as well as banana industries continued. Jamaica's plantation owners looked for another source of labor. From 1838 to 1917, more than 30,000 Indians immigrated here, followed by about 5,000 Asians as well as immigrants from the Middle East, primarily from what is now Lebanon.

In the early 1900s the boats that took the banana crop off the island began returning with travelers. By 1960 the tourism industry had become Jamaica's most important form of income. In 1962, Jamaica became an independent nation.

LOGISTICS

Getting to Jamaica: Donald Sangster International Airport (MBJ), in Montego Bay, is the most efficient point of entry for travelers destined for Mo'Bay, Ocho Rios, Runaway Bay, the South Coast, and Negril. Norman Manley International Airport (KIN), in Kingston, is the best arrival point for travelers headed to the capital or to Port Antonio.

Hassle Factor: Low–high, depending on your distance from the resort areas of Montego Bay, Ocho Rios, and Negril.

On the Ground: Most all-inclusive resorts include transfers. If transfers are not included for your trip, you can get shared-van service or charter a taxi from the airport in Montego Bay to your final destination. You can rent a car at either airport.

Getting Around the Island: Most travelers to Jamaica take guided tours on trips outside their resorts. The average traveler will not want to rent a car, which can be expensive. In most places, a taxi may suffice for occasional trips around town, but your resort may have a free shuttle, so ask.

14

Although 95% of the population traces its bloodlines to Africa, Jamaica is a stockpot of cultures, including those of other Caribbean islands, Great Britain, the Middle East, India, China, Germany, Portugal, and South America. The third-largest island in the Caribbean (after Cuba and Hispaniola), Jamaica enjoys a considerable self-sufficiency based on tourism, agriculture, and mining.

PLANNING

WHEN TO GO

High season in Jamaica runs roughly from mid-December through mid-April. From May through mid-December, you can save from 20% to as much as 40% on rates, more if you use value-oriented travel packagers. There are several annual events in Jamaica that draw huge numbers of visitors.

GETTING HERE AND AROUND

AIR TRAVEL

You can fly to Jamaica from Atlanta (AirTran, Delta), Boston (Jet-Blue, US Airways), Charlotte (US Airways), Chicago (American), Dallas (American), Detroit (US Airways), Fort Lauderdale (Caribbean Airlines, Spirit), Houston (Continental), Las Vegas (American), Los Angeles (American), Miami (American), New York–JFK (Caribbean Airlines, American, JetBlue), New York–Newark (Continental), Orlando (Jet-Blue), Philadelphia (, US Airways), Phoenix (US Airways), San Diego (American), or Tampa (American). Most flights come into Montego Bay, but some nonstops go to Kingston.

All international flights arrive in Montego Bay or Kingston.

Domestic Airline Contacts Captain John's Island Hoppers ☎ *876/974–1285* ⊕ *www.jamaicahelicopterservices.com.* **Tim Air.** Tim Air offers charter service between Montego Bay's Sangster International Airport and airports in Port Antonio, Ocho Rios, Kingston, Negril and Treasure Beach. ☎ *876/952–2516, 876/979–1114* ⊕ *www.timair.com.*

Domestic Airports Ian Fleming International Airport (*OCJ*). ⊠ *8 miles [14 km] east of Ocho Rios, Oracabessa* ☎ *876/975–3101* ⊕ *www.ifia.aero.* **Negril Aerodrome** ⊠ *Norman Manley Blvd., Negril* ☎ *876/957–5016.* **Port Antonio Ken Jones Aerodrome** ⊠ *North Coast Hwy., Port Antonio* ☎ *876/913–3926, 876/913–3173.*

International Airline Contacts Caribbean Airlines ⊕ *www.caribbean-airlines.com.* **Air Tran** ☎ *800/247–8726* ⊕ *www.airtran.com.* **American Airlines** ☎ *800/744–0006* ⊕ *www.aa.com.* **Cayman Airways** ☎ *876/926–1762* ⊕ *www. caymanairways.com.* **Delta Airlines** ☎ *800/221–1212* ⊕ *www.delta.com.* **JetBlue** ☎ *800/963–3014* ⊕ *www.jetblue.com.* **United Airlines** ☎ *800/538–2929* ⊕ *www.united.com.* **US Airways** ☎ *800/455–0123* ⊕ *www.usairways.com.*

International Airports Donald Sangster International Airport (*MBJ*). ⊠ *Montego Bay* ☎ *876/952–3124* ⊕ *www.mbjairport.com.* **Norman Manley International Airport** (*KIN*). ⊠ *Kingston* ☎ *876/924–8452* ⊕ *www.nmia.aero.*

CAR TRAVEL

Driving in Jamaica can be an extremely frustrating chore. You must constantly be on guard—for enormous potholes, people and animals darting out into the street, and aggressive drivers. Local drivers are quick to pass other cars—and sometimes two cars will pass simultaneously. Gas stations are open daily, and some now accept credit cards, though you shouldn't count on it. Driving in Jamaica is on the left, British-style.

Car Rentals To rent a car, you must be at least 23 years old, have a valid driver's license (from any country), and have a valid credit or debit card. You may be required to post a security deposit of several hundred dollars before taking possession of your car; ask about it when you make the reservation. Rates average $70 to $120 a day after the addition of the compulsory insurance, which you must usually purchase even if your credit card offers it.

Car-Rental Contacts Avis Rent a Car ⊠ *Donald Sangster International Airport* ☎ *876/952–0762, 876/979–1060* ⊕ *www.avis.com.jm.* **Budget** ⊠ *Donald Sangster International Airport* ☎ *876/952–3838* ⊕ *www.budgetjamaica.com.* **Fiesta Car Rentals** ☎ *876/926–0133* ⊕ *www.fiestacarrentals.com.* **Hertz** ☎ *876/979–0438* ⊕ *www.hertzjamaica.com.* **Island Car Rentals** ☎ *876/924–8075 in Kingston, 876/952–7225 in Montego Bay* ⊕ *www.islandcarrentals.com.*

TAXI TRAVEL

Some but not all of Jamaica's taxis are metered. If you accept a driver's offer of his services as a tour guide, be sure to agree on a price before the vehicle is put into gear. (Note that a one-day tour should run about $150 to $200, in U.S. dollars, depending on distance traveled.) All licensed taxis display red Public Passenger Vehicle (PPV) plates. Your hotel concierge can call a taxi for you, or you can flag one down on the street. Rates are per car, not per passenger, and 25% is added to the rate between midnight and 5 am. Licensed minivans are also available and bear the red PPV plates. JUTA is the largest taxi franchise, with offices in most resort areas.

Taxi Contacts JCAL Tours ☎ 876/952–7574, 876/952–8277 ⊕ www.jcaltours. com. **JUTA Montego Bay** ☎ 876/952–0813 ⊕ www.jutatoursltd.com. **Pat's Taxi Service & Car Rental Co.** ⊠ 5 Lewis St., Savannah-la-Mar ☎ 876/918–0431, 876/955–3335 ⊕ www.patscarrentaljamaica.com.

ESSENTIALS

Banks and Exchange Services The official currency is the Jamaican dollar, but few Americans bother to exchange money, since U.S. dollars are widely accepted. At this writing, an American dollar is worth roughly 105 Jamaican dollars. Most ATMs in Jamaica accept American ATM cards and will dispense either U.S. or Jamaican dollars. Major credit cards are widely accepted, although cash is often required at gas stations, in markets, and in many small stores.

Electricity As in North America, the current in Jamaica is 110 volts but only 50 cycles, with outlets that take two flat prongs. Some hotels provide 220-volt plugs as well as special shaver outlets.

Emergency Services Police, Ambulance, and Fire Emergencies ☎ 110, 911. **Police Emergencies & Air Rescue** ☎ 119. **Scuba-Diving Emergencies** ⊠ St. Ann's Bay Hospital, Edge Hill Rd., St. Ann's Bay ☎ 876/972–2272.

Passport Requirements All visitors must have a valid passport.

Phones Cellular service is available throughout Jamaica. GSM cell phones equipped with tri-band or world-roaming service will find coverage throughout much of the coastal region. Cellular service averages about J$1.50 to J$2 per minute on the island. Rates for local calls start at about 10¢ per minute, and incoming calls are free. Outgoing international calls to the United States start at about 19¢ per minute. Prepaid SIM cards cost about J$500. Providers Digicel and Lime also offer prepaid international calling to the United States and Canada. Cellular-phone rentals are also available starting at about $20 per week.

Most hotels offer direct-dial telephone services with a substantial service charge; local businesses provide fax services for a fee. Pay phones are now hard to find across the island. To dial Jamaica from the United States, just dial 1 + area code 876. Some U.S. phone companies provide only limited credit-card calls from Jamaica because they've been victims of fraud. The best option is to buy Jamaican phone cards, sold in most stores across the island.

Safety Crime in Jamaica is, unfortunately, a persistent problem, so don't let the beauty of the island cause you to abandon the caution you would practice in any unfamiliar place. Many of the headlines are grabbed by murders in Kingston, often gang-related; violent crimes are, for the most part, largely a problem for residents who live in certain areas of the city. Visitors should be extremely cautious about visiting many of the neighborhoods in Kingston that are outside the business district of New Kingston.

Property crime is an island-wide problem. Use your in-room safe and be sure to lock all doors—including balconies—when you leave your room or villa. Never leave your car unlocked, and never leave valuables inside it, even when it is locked. Ignore efforts, however persistent, to sell you drugs, including ganja (marijuana), which is illegal across the island.

Taxes Almost all airline ticket prices include the departure tax, which varies in amount depending which country you are flying to and from; otherwise, it must be paid in cash. A General Consumption Tax (G.C.T.) of 17.5% is included in the cost of most goods and services; there is also a $1 per room hotel tax introduced in 2012.

Tipping Most hotels and restaurants add a 10% service charge to your bill. When a service charge isn't included, a 10% to 20% tip is expected. Tips of 10% to 20% are customary for tour guides and drivers as well. However, many all-inclusives have a strict no-tipping policy.

ACCOMMODATIONS

Montego Bay has the largest concentration of resorts on the island; Negril, known as the "Capital of Casual," is a more relaxed haven on the west coast. Both offer a mix of large and small resorts, plus good nightlife. Runaway Bay and Ocho Rios are more than an hour east of Mo'Bay. Port Antonio, a sleepy, laid-back haven, has a few resorts and a quiet atmosphere and is usually accessed by a short flight or long drive from Kingston. The South Coast has a few small resorts, uncrowded beaches, and only one large resort. Few vacationers choose to stay in **Kingston,** the capital, but it can be a good weekend-break destination, and the surrounding area also includes the Blue Mountains, home of the luxe Strawberry Hill resort. Jamaica was the birthplace of the Caribbean all-inclusive resort, which is still the most popular vacation option here. Several of these are open only to couples. The island also has some high-end villas for rent, many near Runaway Bay.

HOTEL AND RESTAURANT PRICES

Prices in the restaurant reviews are the average cost of a main course at dinner or, if dinner is not served, at lunch; taxes and service charges are generally included. Prices in the hotel reviews are the lowest cost of a standard double room in high season, excluding taxes, service charges, and meal plans (except at all-inclusives). Prices for rentals are the lowest per-night cost for a one-bedroom unit in high season.

For expanded lodging lodging reviews and current deals, visit Fodors.com.

VISITOR INFORMATION

Contacts Jamaica Tourist Board ☎ *305/665–0557 in Miami, 876/929–9200 in Kingston, 876/952–4425 in Montego Bay* ⊕ *www.visitjamaica.com.*

WEDDINGS

A 24-hour waiting period is required; many resorts offer free weddings.

EXPLORING

Touring Jamaica can be both thrilling and frustrating. Rugged (albeit beautiful) terrain and winding (often potholed) roads make for slow going. *Always* check conditions before you set off to explore the island by car, but especially in the rainy season from June through October, when roads can easily be washed out. Primary roads that loop around and across the island are two-lane routes but are not particularly well marked. Numbered addresses are seldom used outside major townships, locals drive aggressively, and people and animals seem to have a knack for appearing on the street out of nowhere. That said, Jamaica's scenery shouldn't be missed. To be safe and avoid frustration, stick to guided tours and licensed taxis.

If you're staying in Kingston or Port Antonio, set aside at least one day for the capital's highlights and another for a guided excursion to the Blue Mountains. You can find at least three days' worth of activity right along Mo'Bay's boundaries; you should also consider a day trip to Negril or Ocho Rios. If you're based in Ocho Rios, be sure to visit Dunn's River Falls; you may also want to stop by Bob Marley's birthplace, Nine Mile, or Firefly, the restored home of Noël Coward. If Negril is your hub, take in the South Coast, including Y.S. Falls and the Black River.

MONTEGO BAY

As home of the north-shore airport, Montego Bay is the first taste most visitors have of the island. It's the second-largest city in Jamaica and has a busy cruise pier west of town. Travelers from around the world come and go in this bustling community year-round. Home to a number of all-inclusive resorts and some of the island's best beaches, Montego Bay is often top-of-the-mind when vacationers think of Jamaica. It's relative proximity to nearby resort towns like Ocho Rios and Negril also make this town a popular choice. Throughout the surrounding areas, adventures and one-of-a-kind experiences await, not to mention some interesting colonial sights.

TOP ATTRACTIONS

Greenwood Great House. Unlike Rose Hall, Greenwood has no spooky legend to titillate, but it's much better than Rose Hall at evoking life on a sugar plantation. The Barrett family, from whom the English poet Elizabeth Barrett Browning descended, once owned all the land from Rose Hall to Falmouth; on their vast holdings they built this and several other great houses. (The poet's father, Edward Moulton Barrett, "the Tyrant of Wimpole Street," was born at nearby Cinnamon Hill, later the estate of country singer Johnny Cash.) Highlights of Greenwood include oil paintings of the Barretts, china made for the family by Wedgwood, a library filled with rare books from as early as 1697, fine antique furniture, and a collection of exotic musical instruments. There's a pub on-site as well. It's 15 miles (24 km) east of Montego Bay. ⊠ *Greenwood* ☎ *876/953–1077* ⊕ *www.greenwoodgreathouse. com* 🎟 *$20* ⊙ *Daily 9–6; last tour at 5.*

Fodor's Choice **Rose Hall.** In the 1700s it may well have been one of the greatest great
★ houses in the West Indies. Today it's popular less for its architecture
than for the legend surrounding its second mistress, Annie Palmer. As
the story goes, Annie was born in 1802 in England to an English mother
and Irish father. When she was 10, her family moved to Haiti, and
soon her parents died of yellow fever. Annie was adopted by a Haitian
voodoo priestess and soon became skilled in the practice of witchcraft.
Annie moved to Jamaica, married, and became mistress of Rose Hall,
an enormous plantation spanning 6,600 acres with more than 2,000
slaves. You can take a spooky nighttime tour of the property and then
have a drink at the White Witch pub, located in the great house's cellar.
■TIP→ **If you're up for a scare, opt for the night tour!** ⊠ *North Coast
Hwy., St. James* ✛ *15 miles (24 km) east of Montego Bay* ☎ *876/953–
2323* ⊕ *www.rosehall.com* ⊠ *$20* ⊙ *Daily 9:15–5:15. Night tours,
daily 6:30–9:15 pm.*

WORTH NOTING

Martha Brae River. This gentle waterway about 25 miles (40 km) southeast of Montego Bay takes its name from an Arawak woman who
killed herself because she refused to reveal the whereabouts of a local
gold mine. According to legend, she agreed to take her Spanish inquisi-
tors there and, on reaching the river, used magic to change its course,
drowning herself and the greedy Spaniards with her. Her *duppy* (ghost)
is said to guard the mine's entrance. Rafting on this river is a very
popular activity—many operators are on hand to take you for a glide
downstream. ⊠ *Montego Bay.*

Rocklands Bird Sanctuary. A great place to spot birds is this sanctuary,
which is south of Montego Bay. The station was the home of the late
Lisa Salmon, one of Jamaica's first amateur ornithologists. Here you
can sit quietly and feed a variety of birds—including the doctor bird
(also known as the streamer-tail hummingbird), recognizable by its long
tail—from your hand. ⊠ *Rock Pleasant District, Anchovy, Montego
Bay* ☎ *876/952–2009* ⊠ *$15* ⊙ *Daily 10–5.*

FALMOUTH

Fodor's Choice **Good Hope Estate.** A visit to Good Hope Estate, about a 20-minute drive
★ inland from Falmouth, will give you a real sense of Jamaica's rich history as a sugar-estate island and also provides loads of fun! Newly
expanded, the estate sits on more than 2,000 acres and boasts incredible views of the Martha Brae River. This fun-filled adventure park now
offers zip lining, river tubing, a great house tour, access to the new colonial village, a challenge course for adults, aviary, swimming pool, and
a kids play area with its own challenge course. Guests may get a taste
of Jamaica at the Appleton Estate Jamaica Rum Tavern and Jablum
Cafe or enjoy spicy goodness from the Walkerswood Jerk Hut. Adventure Park Passes entitle visitors to all adventures offered on the Estate.
⊠ *Falmouth* ☎ *876/356–8502, 876/276–2082* ⊕ *chukkacaribbean.com*
⊠ *US$55.*

OCHO RIOS

Although Ocho Rios isn't near eight rivers as its name would seem to indicate, it does have a seemingly endless series of cascades that sparkle from limestone rocks along the coast. (The name Ocho Rios came about because the English misunderstood the Spanish *las chorreras*—"the waterfalls.") The town itself isn't very attractive and can be traffic-clogged, but the area has several worthwhile attractions, including the very popular Dunn's River Falls. A few steps from the main road in Ocho Rios are some of the most charming inns and oceanfront restaurants in the Caribbean. Lying on the sand of what seems to be your very own cove or swinging gently in a hammock while sipping a tropical drink, you'll soon forget the traffic that's just a stroll away. The original "defenders" stationed at the Old Fort, built in 1777, spent much of their time sacking and plundering as far afield as St. Augustine, Florida, and sharing their booty with the local plantation owners who financed their missions. Discovery Bay, 15 miles (24 km) west, is where Columbus landed and where there's a small museum with such artifacts as ships' bells and cannons and iron pots used for boiling sugarcane. Don't miss a drive through Fern Gully, a natural canopy of vegetation filtered by sunlight. (Jamaica has the world's largest number of fern species, more than 570.) To reach the stretch of road called Fern Gully, take the A3 highway south of Ocho Rios.

14

TOP ATTRACTIONS

Bob Marley Centre and Mausoleum. Travelers with an interest in Bob Marley won't want to miss Nine Mile, the community in the parish of Ste-Ann where the reggae legend was born and is buried. Today his former home is a shrine to his music and values. Tucked behind a tall fence, the site is marked with green and gold flags. Tours are led by Rastafarians, who take visitors through the house and point out the single bed that Marley wrote about in "Is This Love." Visitors also step inside the mausoleum where the singer is interred with his guitar. The site includes a restaurant and gift shop. It is best to take a guided excursion from one of the resorts. If you're driving here yourself, be ready for some bad roads. And note that the hustlers that meet you outside the Bob Marley Centre are some of the most aggressive in Jamaica. ⊠ *Nine Mile, Calderwood Post Office, Ste-Ann* ☎ *876/843–0498* ⊕ *www.bobmarleymovement.com* ✉ *$19* ⊙ *Daily 9–5.*

Coyaba Gardens and Mahoe Waterfalls. Jamaica's national motto is "Out of Many, One People," and here you can see exhibits on the many cultural influences that have contributed to the creation of the one. The museum covers the island's history from the time of the Arawak Indians up to the present day. A guided 45-minute tour through the lush 3-acre garden, which is 1½ miles (2½ km) south of Ocho Rios, introduces you to the flora and fauna of the island. The complex includes a crafts and gift shop and a snack bar. ⊠ *Shaw Park Estate, Shaw Park Ridge Rd., Ocho Rios* ☎ *876/974–6235* ⊕ *www.coyabagardens.com* ✉ *$10* ⊙ *Daily 8–5.*

Fodor's Choice **Dunn's River Falls.** One of Jamaica's most popular attractions is an eye-
★ catching sight: 600 feet of cold, clear mountain water splashing over
a series of stone steps to the warm Caribbean. The best way to enjoy
the falls is to climb the slippery steps: don a swimsuit, take the hand of
the person ahead of you, and trust that the chain of hands and bodies
leads to an experienced guide. The leaders of the climbs are personable fellows who reel off bits of local lore while telling you where to
step; you can hire a guide's service for a tip of a few dollars. After the
climb, you exit through a crowded market, another reminder that this
is one of Jamaica's top tourist attractions. If you can, try to schedule a
visit on a day when no cruise ships are in port. ■TIP→ **Always climb
with a licensed guide at Dunn's River Falls. Freelance guides might be
a little cheaper, but the experienced guides can tell you just where to
plant each footstep—helping you prevent a fall.** ⊠ *Off Rte. A1, between
St. Ann's Bay and Ocho Rios, Ocho Rios* ☎ *876/974-4767* ⊕ *www.
dunnsriverfallsja.com* ⊠ *$20* ☉ *Daily 8:30–5; last entry at 4.*

Fern Gully. Don't miss a drive through Fern Gully, a natural canopy of
vegetation that sunlight barely penetrates. (Jamaica has the world's
largest number of fern species, with more than 570 types.) The 3-mile
(5-km) stretch of fern-shaded forest includes many walking paths as
well as numerous crafts vendors. Most tours through the area include
a drive through Fern Gully, but to experience the damp, shady forest,
stop and take a walk. The winding road through Fern Gully has recently
been resurfaced making for a smoother drive through this natural wonder. ⊠ *Rte. A3, south of Ocho Rios.*

Mystic Mountain. This attraction covers 100 acres of mountainside
rain forest near Dunn's River Falls. Visitors board the Rainforest Sky
Explorer, a chairlift that soars through and over the pristine rain forest
to the apex of Mystic Mountain. On top, there is a restaurant with spectacular views of Ocho Rios, arts-and-crafts shops, and the attraction's
signature tours, the Rainforest Bobsled Jamaica ride and the Rainforest
Zipline Canopy ride. Custom-designed bobsleds, inspired by Jamaica's
Olympic bobsled team, run downhill on steel rails with speed controlled
by the driver, using simple push-pull levers. Couples can run their bobsleds in tandem. The zip-line tours streak through lush rain forest under
the care of an expert guide who points out items of interest. The entire
facility was built using environmentally friendly techniques and materials in order to leave the native rain forest undisturbed. ⊠ *North Coast
Hwy., Ocho Rios* ☎ *876/974-3990* ⊕ *www.rainforestbobsledjamaica.
com* ⊠ *$47–$137* ☉ *Daily 9–5; activities 9–3:30.*

WORTH NOTING

Firefly. About 20 miles (32 km) east of Ocho Rios near Port Maria,
Firefly was once Noël Coward's vacation home and is now a national
monument managed by Chris Blackwell's Island company. Although the
setting is Eden-like, the house is surprisingly spartan. Coward decamped
from his original setting at Blue Harbour up the hill to this remote
setting to escape the numerous jet-setters who came to Blue Harbour
to visit. He wrote *High Spirits, Quadrille* and other plays here, and
his simple grave is on the grounds next to a small stage where his
works are occasionally performed. Recordings of Coward singing about

Climbing Dunn's River Falls, Ocho Rios

"mad dogs and Englishmen" echo over the lawns. Tours include a walk through the house and grounds where Coward is buried. The view from the house's hilltop perch, which was a lookout for Captain Morgan, is one of the best on the north coast, making Firefly well worth the price of admission. ⌧ *Port Maria* ☎ *876/420–5544* ⊕ *www.firefly-jamaica. com* ⌧ *$10* ☉ *Daily 9–4.*

Prospect Plantation. To learn about Jamaica's agricultural heritage, a trip to this working plantation, just east of town, is a must. It's not just a place for history lovers, however. Everyone enjoys the views over the White River Gorge and the tour in a tractor-pulled cart. The grounds are full of exotic flowers and tropical trees, some planted over the years by such celebrities as Winston Churchill and Charlie Chaplin. The estate includes a small aviary with free-flying butterflies. You can also saddle up for horseback rides and camel safaris on the plantation's 900 acres, but the actual tour times are usually geared toward the cruise-ship schedule, so call ahead. There's also a Segway tour. You can even take a lesson in cooking Jamaican style. Prices vary depending on the tour. ⌧ *Rte. A1, 4 miles (3.2 km) east of Ocho Rios, Ocho Rios* ☎ *876/994–1058* ⊕ *www.prospectplantationtours.com.*

Shaw Park Gardens and Waterfalls. Originally used for growing sugarcane and later oranges, this estate became the original site of the exclusive Shaw Park Hotel (today relocated to the beach). The owner's daughter, appropriately named Flora, worked to create the lush gardens, which now fill the 25-acre site with flame flowers, birds of paradise, and orchids. ⌧ *Shaw Park Rd., Ocho Rios* ☎ *876/974–2723, 876/893–5899* ⊕ *www.shawparkgardens.com* ⌧ *$10* ☉ *Daily 8–5.*

PORT ANTONIO

Port Antonio is one of Jamaica's quietest getaways, primarily preferred by long-staying Europeans. Even with the recent improvement of the North Coast Highway from Ocho Rios to Port Antonio, tourism remains slow here. However, in 2013, Trident Castle reopened as part of the Geejam chain, a development that's expected to give a boost to the area's tourism.

Port Antonio has also long been a center for some of the Caribbean's finest deep-sea fishing. Dolphin (the delectable fish, not the lovable mammal) is the likely catch here, along with tuna, kingfish, and wahoo. In October the weeklong Blue Marlin Tournament attracts anglers from around the world. By the time they've all had their fill of beer, it's the fish stories—rather than the fish—that carry the day.

TOP ATTRACTIONS

Blue Lagoon. One of Port Antonio's best-known attractions is the Blue Lagoon, whose azure waters have to be seen to be believed. The colors of the spring-fed lagoon are a real contrast to the warmer waters of the ocean. Catch some rays on the floating docks, or relax on the small beach. Just how deep is the Blue Lagoon? You might hear it's bottomless, but the lagoon has been measured at a depth of 180 feet. Guests of nearby hotels may have access to the lagoon, while those staying farther away can hire an operator for rafting trips. ✉ *9 miles (13 km) east of Port Antonio, 1 mile (1½ km) east of San San Beach, Port Antonio.*

Boston Beach. A short drive east of Port Antonio is Boston Beach, a not-to-be-missed destination for lovers of jerk pork. The recipe's origins may go back to the Arawak, the island's original inhabitants, but modern jerk was perfected by the Maroons. Eating almost nothing but wild hog preserved over smoking coals enabled these former slaves to survive years of fierce guerrilla warfare with the English. Jerk resurfaced in the 1930s, and the spicy barbecue drew diners from around the island. Today a handful of small jerk stands, collectively known as the Boston Jerk Centre, offers fiery flavors cooled by some *festival* bread (similar to a southern hush puppy) and a cold Red Stripe beer. ✉ *Rte. A4, east of Port Antonio, Port Antonio.*

▌QUICK BITES **Coronation Bakery.** Grab some hard-dough bread (originally brought to Jamaica by the Chinese), an unleavened bun called *bulla,* or spicy patties. The bakery's been open for more than seven decades. ✉ *18 West St., Port Antonio* ☎ *876/993–2710.*

WORTH NOTING

Folly. A favorite photo stop in Port Antonio, Folly is little more than ruins these days. This structure, spanning 60 rooms in its heyday and built in 1905, was the home of a Tiffany heiress. The house didn't last long because seawater, rather than freshwater, was used in the cement. The ruins have been featured in music videos. In July, the grounds serve as the setting for the annual Portland Jerk Festival. ✉ *Folly Point, Port Antonio.*

Folly Lighthouse. Since 1888, this red-and-white-stripe masonry lighthouse has stood watch at the tip of Folly Point. Administered by the Jamaica National Heritage Trust, the lighthouse is an often-photographed site near Port Antonio's East Harbour. ⊠ *Folly Point, Port Antonio* ⊕ *www. jnht.com/site_folly_point_lighthouse.*

Rio Grande. Jamaica's river-rafting operations began here, on an 8-mile-long (13-km-long), swift, green waterway from Berrydale to Rafter's Rest. (Beyond that, the Rio Grande flows into the Caribbean Sea at St. Margaret's Bay.) The trip of about three hours is made on bamboo rafts pushed along by a guide who is likely to be quite a character. You can pack a picnic lunch to enjoy on the raft or on the riverbank; wherever you lunch, a Red Stripe vendor is likely to appear. A restaurant, a bar, and several souvenir shops can be found at Rafter's Rest. ⊠ *Rte. A4, 5 miles (8 km) west of Port Antonio, Port Antonio.*

Somerset Falls. On the Daniels River, these falls are in a veritable botanical garden. A concrete walk to the falls takes you past the ruins of a Spanish aqueduct and Genesis Falls before reaching Hidden Falls. At Hidden Falls, you board a boat and travel beneath the tumbling water; more daring travelers can swim in a whirlpool or jump off the falls into a pool of water. The bar and restaurant specializing in local seafood here is a great place to catch your breath. ⊠ *Rte. A4, 13 miles (21 km) west of Port Antonio, Port Antonio* ☎ *876/913–0046* ⊕ *www. somersetfallsjamaica.com* ☎ *$12* ☉ *Daily 9–5.*

KINGSTON

Few travelers—particularly Americans—take the time to visit Kingston, although organized day trips make the city accessible from Ocho Rios and Montego Bay. That's understandable, as Kingston can be a tough city to love. It's big and has a bad reputation, with gang-controlled neighborhoods that are known to erupt into violence. However, New Kingston is a vibrant and exciting business district with many places for visitors to enjoy. If you've seen other parts of the island and yearn to know more about the heart and soul of Jamaica, Kingston is worth a visit. This government and business center is also a cultural capital, home to numerous dance troupes, theaters, and museums. It's also home to the University of the West Indies, one of the Caribbean's largest universities. In many ways, Kingston reflects the true Jamaica—a wonderful cultural mix—more than the sunny havens of the North Coast. As one Jamaican put it, "You don't really know Jamaica until you know Kingston."

Serving as a magnificent backdrop for the city are the Blue Mountains, with fabulous homes in the foothills. The views become increasingly grand as the roads wind up into one of the island's least developed yet most beautiful regions.

TOP ATTRACTIONS

Bob Marley Museum. At the height of his career, Bob Marley purchased a house on Kingston's Hope Road and added a recording studio—painted Rastafarian red, yellow, and green. It now houses this museum, the capital's best-known tourist site. The guided tour takes you through rooms wallpapered with magazine and newspaper articles that chronicle his rise to stardom. There's a 20-minute biographical film on Marley's career. You can also see the bulletholes in the walls from a politically motivated assassination attempt in 1976. ⊠ *56 Hope Rd., Kingston* 🕾 *876/927–9152* ⊕ *www.bobmarley-foundation.com* 🖾 *$20* ☾ *Mon.– Sat. 9:30–5; last tour begins at 4.*

Devon House. Built in 1881 as the mansion of the island's first black millionaire, who made his fortune from gold mining in South America, Devon House was bought and restored by the Jamaican government in the 1960s. You can only visit the two-story mansion, furnished with Venetian-crystal chandeliers and period reproductions, on a guided tour. On the grounds there are two restaurants, crafts shops, a bakery, a wine bar, and one of the few mahogany trees that have survived Kingston's ambitious but not always careful development. ⊠ *26 Hope Rd., Kingston* 🕾 *876/929–6602* ⊕ *www.devonhousejamaica.com* 🖾 *$10.*

Hope Royal Botanic Gardens. The largest botanical garden in the Caribbean, originally called the Hope Estate, was founded in the 1600s by an English army officer. Today it's often referred to as Hope Gardens and features areas devoted to orchids, cacti, and palm trees. The gardens are also home to the Hope Zoo Kingston. ⊠ *Old Hope Rd., Kingston* 🕾 *876/927–1257, 876/970–3505* 🖾 *Gardens free* ☾ *Daily 6–6.*

FAMILY **Hope Zoo Kingston.** Lucas, a regal male lion, is Hope Zoo's most popular sight, but there are many other interesting animals to see in the recently refurbished zoo. The colorful array of parrots and other tropical birds are worth the admission. Current exhibits also include zebras, crocodiles, monkeys, deer, and more. At this writing there is a five-year development plan that includes increasing programs and attractions. ⊠ *Hope Gardens, Kingston 6, Kingston* 🕾 *876/927–1085* ⊕ *https://twitter.com/ ZooKingston* 🖾 *J$1,500.*

WORTH NOTING

Bank of Jamaica Money Museum. You don't have to be a numismatist to enjoy the exhibits at this museum, which offers a fascinating look at Jamaica's history through its monetary system. It includes everything from glass beads used as currency by the Taíno Indians to Spanish gold pieces to currency of the present day. Ultraviolet lights enable the viewing of detailed features of historic bank notes. There's also a parallel exhibit on the general history of currency through world history. ⊠ *Duke St., at Nethersole Pl., Kingston* 🕾 *876/922–0750* ⊕ *www.boj. org.jm* 🖾 *Free* ☾ *Weekdays 10–4.*

Emancipation Park. The 7 acres of Emancipation Park's lush greenery is a popular place for respite from the New Kingston concrete jungle. Locals come here to jog, play table tennis, see concerts, take wedding photos, and relax. There are also clowns to entertain the children and photographers to take romantic pictures of couples by the fountain. The south entrance is graced by Redemption Song, a pair of monumental statues of slaves that serve as a reminder of the island's colonial past. ⊠ *Knutsford Blvd., at Oxford Rd., Kingston* 🕾 *876/926–6312* ⊕ *www. emancipationpark.org.jm* 🖾 *Free* ☾ *Closes at 6 pm on public holidays.*

National Gallery of Jamaica. The artists represented at the National Gallery may not be household names, but their paintings are sensitive and moving. You can find works by such Jamaican masters as painter John Dunkley and sculptor Edna Manley. The gallery's exhibition program introduces visitors to the work of contemporary Jamaican artists through events such as the National Biennial and the National Visual Arts Competition and Exhibition, which are staged annually each July and August, respectively. Guided tours are offered for J$3,000 for groups of up to 25 people and must be booked in advance of your visit. ⊠ *12 Ocean Blvd., near waterfront, Kingston* ☎ *876/922–1561* ⊕ *www.natgalja.org.jm/ioj_wp* ☑ *J$400; free last Sun. of month* ☉ *Tues.–Thurs. 10–4:30, Fri. 10–4, Sat. 10–3, last Sun. of every month 10–3.*

14

BLUE MOUNTAINS

Fodor's Choice ★ Best known as the source of Blue Mountain coffee, these mountains rising out of the lush jungle north of Kingston are a favorite destination with adventure travelers, as well as hikers, birders, and anyone looking to see what lies beyond the beach. You can find guided tours to the mountains from the Ocho Rios and Port Antonio areas, as well as from Kingston. ■TIP➜ **Unless you're traveling with a local, don't try to go on your own; the roads wind and dip without warning, and hand-lettered signs blow away, leaving you without a clue as to which way to go. It's best to hire a taxi (look for red PPV license plates to identify a licensed cab) or book a guided tour.**

WORTH NOTING

Holywell. In this recreation area, a part of the Blue and John Crow Mountains National Park, nature trails winding through the rugged terrain offer you the chance to spot some of the island's most reclusive creatures. Be on the lookout for the national bird, the streamer-tail hummingbird (known locally as the doctor bird) and the rare swallowtail butterfly. Rustic camping facilities are available, including showers and shelters. It's about 15 miles (25 km) north of Kingston on a very slow and winding road. ⊠ *Rte. B1, northwest of Newcastle, Kingston* ☎ *876/960–2849, 876/960–2848* ⊕ *www.blueandjohncrowmountains.org, www.jcdt.org.jm* ☑ *US$5* ☉ *Tues.–Sun. 9–5.*

Mavis Bank Coffee Factory. An hour-long guided tour of Mavis Bank Coffee Factory takes you through the processing of coffee, from planting to distribution and includes a sample cup of the drink. Inquire about tours when you arrive at the main office. Mavis Bank is high up in the Blue Mountains above Kingston. ⊠ *Gordon Town Rd., Mavis Bank* ☎ *876/977–8005, 876/977–8527* ⊕ *www.jablumcoffee.com* ☑ *US$8* ☉ *Weekdays 9–3 (with break for lunch noon–1).*

SOUTH COAST

TOP ATTRACTIONS

Appleton Estate. Before the rise of tourism as Jamaica's main industry, the island was highly prized for its sugarcane production. Vast fortunes were made here during colonial times, and many of the island's historic greathouses remain as reminders of that time. Much of the sugarcane was processed into molasses, the main ingredient in the production of rum. Appleton Estate, still one of the Caribbean's premier rum distillers, offers guided tours illustrating the history of rum making in the region. After a lively discussion of the days when sugarcane was crushed by donkey power, the tours move on to a behind-the-scenes look at the modern facility. After the tour, samples flow freely, and every visitor receives a complimentary bottle of rum. ⊠ *Hwy. B6, Siloah* ☎ *876/963–9215* ⊕ *uk.appletonestate.com/the-place/rum-tour* ☞ *$25, lunch costs an additional $15. Reservations required for lunch* ☉ *Mon.–Sat. 9–3:30.*

Lovers' Leap. As legend has it, two slaves who were in love chose to jump off this 1,700-foot cliff rather than be captured by their master. Today it's a favorite stop with travelers, who enjoy a drink at the bar along with one of the most stunning sea views in Jamaica. ⊠ *Yardley Chase, St. Elizabeth* ☎ *876/365–6577* ☞ *J$300* ☉ *Daily 9–7.*

WORTH NOTING

FAMILY **Y.S. Falls.** A quiet alternative to Dunn's River Falls in Ocho Rios, these falls are part of a cattle and horse farm and are reached via a tractor and trailer. Newly revamped, this attraction now offers an exhilarating zip line that takes adventurers over the cascading falls. If you aren't staying on the South Coast, companies in Negril offer excursions. The last tour of the day begins at 3:30. ⊠ *North of A2, just past town of Middle Quarters* ☎ *876/997–6360* ⊕ *www.ysfalls.com* ☞ *$17, zip line $42* ☉ *Tues.–Sun. 9:30–4:30; last admission 3:30* ☉ *Closed Mon.*

NEGRIL

Negril stretches along the coast south from horseshoe-shape Bloody Bay (named when it was a whale-processing center) along the calm waters of Long Bay to the lighthouse. Nearby, divers spiral downward off 50-foot-high cliffs into the deep green depths as the sun turns into a ball of fire and sets the clouds ablaze with color. Sunset is also the time when Norman Manley Boulevard and West End Road, which intersect, come to life with busy waterside restaurants and reggae stage shows.

TOP ATTRACTIONS

Blue Hole Mineral Spring. Located about 20 minutes from Negril near the community of Little Bay, the Blue Hole is a mineral spring and swimming pool. You can jump 22 feet off the cliff into the hole or climb down a ladder to swim and bathe in the icy water. Mud around the water's edge is said to be good for your skin, and the water itself is reputed to have therapeutic properties. For those who cannot jump or climb down into the hole, water has been pumped up into a swimming pool on the surface. A bar, a grill, cabanas, and a volleyball court add to the attractions. Take a chartered taxi from Negril, or call to organize a pickup. ⌂ *Brighton, Negril* ⊕ *www. blueholejamaica.ning.com.*

FAMILY **Kool Runnings Adventure Park.** Billing itself as the place where "Jamaica Comes to Play," this park has 10 waterslides and a ¼-mile lazy-river float ride, as well as a go-cart track and kayaking. The park's adventure zone features outdoor laser combat games and "Jamboo" rafting, which allows the family to take to the water on floating bamboo. There is also bungee jumping, a "kool kanoe" adventure, a wave pool, and paintball. Admission prices vary according to age and area, but with the "All For One Plan," you can have access to both the waterpark and funzone for one rate. The park opens for the year only after Jamaica's Labor Day, in May. ⌂ *Norman Manley Blvd., Negril* ☎ *876/957–5400* ⊕ *www. koolrunnings.com* ⌂ *$33, general admission. $75 for the All For One Plan* ☼ *Labor Day (May)–early Sept., daily 11–5:30.*

14

BEACHES

Although hotel beaches are generally private above the high-water mark and restricted to guests of the property, other beaches are public and are open to all kinds of vendors, who can sometimes get aggressive. At resort areas, even if the beach area is considered private, the area below the high-water mark is always public, so vendors will roam longer beaches looking for business. In most cases, a simple "no thanks" will do.

MONTEGO BAY

FAMILY **Doctor's Cave Bathing Club.** Montego Bay's tourist scene has its roots right on the "Hip Strip," the bustling entertainment district along Gloucester Avenue. Here, a sea cave whose waters were said to have healing powers drew travelers from around the world. Although the cave was destroyed by a hurricane long ago, the beach is always busy and has a perpetual spring-break feel. The clubhouse has changing rooms, showers, a gift shop, and restaurant. You can rent beach chairs, pool floats and umbrellas. Its location within the Montego Bay Marine Park—with protected coral reefs and plenty of marine life—makes it a good spot for snorkeling. Glass-bottom boat rides are offered at the beach. **Amenities:** food and drink; lifeguards; parking (fee); showers; toilets; water sports. **Best for:** partiers; snorkeling; swimming; sunsets. ⌂ *Gloucester Ave., Montego Bay* ☎ *876/952–2566* ⊕ *www.doctorscavebathingclub. com* ⌂ *US$6* ☼ *8:30–5.*

FAMILY **Walter Fletcher Beach.** Although it's not as pretty as Doctor's Cave Beach, Walter Fletcher Beach is home to Aquasol Theme Park, which offers a large beach (with lifeguards and security personnel) and for an additional cost, glass-bottom boats, snorkeling, go-kart racing, a skating rink at night, and a bar and restaurant. Near the center of town, the beach has unusually fine swimming; the calm waters make it a good bet for children. **Amenities:** food and drink; lifeguards; parking; showers; toilets; water sports; **Best for:** partiers; snorkeling; sunset; swimming. ⌂ *Gloucester Ave., Montego Bay* ☎ *876/979–9447* ⌂ *J$400 adults* ☼ *Daily 9–6.*

RUNAWAY BAY

FAMILY   **Puerto Seco Beach.** This public beach looks out on Discovery Bay, the location where, according to tradition, Christopher Columbus first came ashore on this island. The explorer sailed in search of freshwater but found none, naming the stretch of sand Puerto Seco, or "dry port." Today the beach is anything but dry; concession stands sell Red Stripe beer and local food, including jerk and patties, to a primarily local beach crowd. **Amenities:** food and drink; lifeguards; parking; showers; toilets. **Best for:** snorkeling; swimming. ⊠ *Discovery Bay, 5 miles (8 km) west of Runaway Bay, Runaway Bay.*

OCHO RIOS

Dunn's River Falls Beach. You'll find a crowd (especially if there's a cruise ship in town) at the small beach at the foot of the falls. Although tiny—especially considering the crowds that pack the falls—it's got a great view. Dunn's River Falls is one of the most recognized and visited landmarks in Jamaica. Look up from the sands for a spectacular vista of the cascading water, the roar from which drowns out the sea as you approach. All-day access to the beach is included in the entrance fee to Dunn's River Falls. **Amenities:** lifeguards; parking; toilets. **Best for:** swimming. ⊠ *Rte. A1, between St. Ann's Bay and Ocho Rios, Ocho Rios* ☎ *876/974–4767* ⊕ *www.dunnsriverfallsja.com* 🖅 *$20* ☉ *Daily 8:30–5; last entry at 4.*

PORT ANTONIO

Boston Bay Beach. Considered the birthplace of Jamaica's famous jerk-style cooking, Boston Bay is the beach that some locals visit just to buy dinner. You can get peppery jerk pork at any of the shacks spewing scented smoke along the beach. While you're there, you'll also find a small beach perfect for an after-lunch dip, although these waters are occasionally rough and much more popular for surfing. **Amenities:** food and drink; parking; toilets; showers. **Best for:** snorkeling; sunrise; surfing; windsurfing. ⊠ *11 miles (18 km) east of Port Antonio, Port Antonio.*

FAMILY   **Frenchman's Cove.** This beautiful, somewhat secluded beach is petite perfection. Protected by two outcroppings that form the cove, the inlet's calm waters are a favorite with families. A small stream trickles into the cove. You'll find a bar and restaurant serving fried chicken right on the beach. If this stretch of sand looks a little familiar, it just might be because you've seen it in the movies; it has starred in *Club Paradise, Treasure Island* (the 1990 TV-movie version), and *The Mighty Quinn.* **Amenities:** food and drink; lifeguards; parking; showers; toilets. **Best for:** partiers; sunrise; swimming. ⊠ *Rte. A4, 5 miles (8 km) east of Port Antonio, Port Antonio* ☎ *876/993–7270* 🖅 *$8 for those not staying at Frenchman's Cove Resort.*

SOUTH COAST

If you're looking for something off the main tourist routes, head for Jamaica's largely undeveloped South Coast. Because the population in this region is sparse, these isolated beaches are some of the island's safest, with hasslers practically nonexistent. You should, however, use common sense; never leave valuables unattended on the beach.

Bluefields Beach Park. On the south coast road to Negril, you'll find this relatively narrow stretch of sand and rock near the small community of Bluefields. A free beach, it's typically crowded only on weekends and local holidays. The swimming here is good, although the sea is sometimes rough. **Amenities:** food and drink; lifeguards; parking (fee); showers (fee); toilets (fee). **Best for:** sunset; swimming. ⊠ *Bluefields.*

FAMILY **Treasure Beach.** The most atmospheric beach in the southwest is in the community of Treasure Beach, which has several long stretches of sand as well as many small coves. Though it isn't as pretty as those to the west or north—it has more rocks and darker sand—the idea that you might be discovering a bit of the "real" Jamaica more than makes up for the small negatives. Both locals and visitors use the beaches here, though you're just as likely to find it completely deserted, beyond a friendly beach dog. Treasure Beach attracts a bohemian crowd, and you won't find as many of the "hustlers" as in north coast resort towns. **Amenities:** food and drink; parking. **Best for:** solitude; sunset; walking. ⊠ *Treasure Beach township.*

NEGRIL

Fodor's Choice ★ **Negril Beach.** Stretching for 7 miles (11 km), the long, white-sand beach in Negril is probably Jamaica's finest. It starts with the white sands of Bloody Bay north of town and continues along Long Bay all the way to the cliffs on the southern edge of town. Some stretches remain undeveloped, but these are increasingly few. Along the main stretch of beach, the sand is public to the high-water mark, so a nonstop line of visitors and vendors parade from end to end. The walk is sprinkled with many good beach bars and open-air restaurants, some of which charge a small fee to use their beach facilities. Bloody Bay is lined with large all-inclusive resorts, and these sections are mostly private. Jamaica's best-known nude beach, at Hedonism II, is always among the busiest; only resort guests or day-pass holders may sun here. **Amenities:** food and drink; lifeguards; parking; toilets; showers; water sports. **Best for:** partiers; sunset; swimming; walking. ⊠ *Norman Manley Blvd., Negril.*

14

WHERE TO EAT

Probably the most famous Jamaican dish is jerk pork—the ultimate island barbecue. The pork (purists cook a whole pig) is covered with a paste of Scotch bonnet peppers, pimento berries (also known as allspice), and other herbs, and cooked slowly over a coal fire. Many aficionados believe the best jerk comes from Boston Beach, near Port Antonio. Jerk chicken and fish are also seen on many menus. The ever-so-traditional rice and peas is similar to the *moros y cristianos* of Spanish-speaking islands: white rice cooked with red kidney beans, coconut milk, scallions, and seasonings.

There are fine restaurants in all the resort areas, many in Kingston and in the resorts themselves. Many restaurants outside the hotels in Mo'Bay and Ocho Rios will provide complimentary transportation.

What to Wear: Dinner dress is usually casual chic (or just plain casual at many local hangouts, especially in Negril). There are a few exceptions in Kingston and at the top resorts; some require semiformal wear (no shorts; collared shirts for men) in the evening during high season. People tend to dress up for dinner; men might be more comfortable in nice slacks, women in a sundress.

MONTEGO BAY

$$ BARBECUE 🍴 **Biggs BBQ Restaurant & Bar.** New to the "Hip Strip," this authentic BBQ joint is the real deal. Featuring down-home favorites like pulled pork, corn bread, mac and cheese, baked beans, and of course some good ole Memphis-style ribs, Biggs is the perfect place for a little taste of Americana in paradise. Diners have the option of sitting outside to enjoy amazing views of the Montego Bay coastline or inside around wooden tables draped in checkered fabric. Drinks like the must-try Bluegrass Lemonade, a heady mix of house-made lemonade and "bluebeery" vodka, are served in traditional jars and meals are served in both half-pound and one-pound portions. [$] *Average main: $15* ✉ *Gloucester Ave., Montego Bay* ☎ *876/952–9488.*

$$$$ SEAFOOD 🍴 **Marguerites Seafood By the Sea.** At this romantic seaside restaurant, lobster, shrimp, and fish are the specialties, as is the Caesar salad. Dine on the patio-style terrace or at the water's edge. Walk-in guests can often be accommodated, but it's best to make a reservation. [$] *Average main: $40* ✉ *Gloucester Ave., Montego Bay* ☎ *876/952–4777* 🌐 *www.margaritavillecaribbean.com* ✍ *Reservations essential* ⏲ *No lunch.*

$$$ SEAFOOD 🍴 **Pier 1.** After tropical drinks at the deck bar, you'll be ready to dig into the international variations on fresh seafood; the best are the grilled lobster and any preparation of island snapper. Occasional party cruises leave from the marina here, and on Friday night the restaurant is mobbed by locals who come to dance at the weekly party dubbed "Pier Pressure." [$] *Average main: $22* ✉ *Off Howard Cooke Blvd., Montego Bay* ☎ *876/952–2452* 🌐 *www.pieronejamaica.com.*

$ JAMAICAN Fodor's Choice ★ 🍴 **Pork Pit.** A favorite with many Mo'Bay locals, this no-frills eatery serves Jamaican specialties including some fiery jerk—note that it's spiced to local tastes, not watered down for tourists. Many people get their food to go, but you can also eat at picnic tables. [$] *Average* *main:* $12 ✉ *27 Gloucester Ave., Montego Bay* ☎ *876/940–3008* ⌘ *Reservations not accepted.*

$ × **Scotchies.** Many call this open-air
JAMAICAN jerk eatery the best in Jamaica, but the Scotchies Too branch in Ocho Rios certainly makes it a tough call. Both serve genuine jerk—chicken, pork, fish, sausage, and more— with fiery sauce and delectable side dishes including festival (bread that's similar to a hush puppy) and rice and peas. This restaurant is a favorite with Montego Bay residents; on a typical day, you're likely to see a slap-the-table game of dominoes. Ⓢ *Average main: J$350* ✉ *North Coast Hwy., across from Holiday Inn SunSpree, 10 miles (16 km) east of Montego Bay, Montego Bay* ☎ *876/953–3301.*

$$$$ × **Seagrape Terrace.** Named for the trees that line the beach at the Half
INTERNATIONAL Moon resorts, this beachside restaurant is open to the public throughout the day and evening. At lunchtime, a superb buffet as well as an à la carte menu is available. Standout buffet options include roast meats and freshly baked breads. At dinner there's a good selection of seafood, steaks, and ribs including the herb-roasted Angus beef tenderloin, redwine braised short ribs, and grilled yellow fin tuna. Ⓢ *Average main:* $38 ✉ *Half Moon, North Coast Hwy., 7 miles (11 km) east of Montego Bay, Montego Bay* ☎ *876/953–2211* ⊕ *www.halfmoon.com.*

$$$$ × **Sugar Mill.** Caribbean dishes with an Asian twist are served with flair
ECLECTIC at this terrace restaurant on the Half Moon golf course. The menu includes the likes of coconut- and saffron-poached snapper fillet, pork tenderloin in a rum and plum sauce and a tea-smoked duck breast. A well-stocked wine cellar rounds out the experience. The dress code is "casual elegant." Ⓢ *Average main:* $38 ✉ *Half Moon, North Coast Rd., 7 miles (11 km) east of Montego Bay, Montego Bay* ☎ *876/953–2211* ⊕ *www.halfmoon.com* ⌘ *Reservations essential* ⊗ *No lunch.*

OCHO RIOS

$$$ × **The Almond Tree.** This restaurant is named for the massive tree growing
ECLECTIC through the roof. For many diners, the evening starts with a drink at the terrace bar overlooking the sea. Dinner, which can be enjoyed on the terrace or in the dining room, begins with pumpkin or pepper pot soup before moving on to seafood, pasta, and dishes with a Jamaican flavor, such as jerk lamb. Ⓢ *Average main:* $21 ✉ *Hibiscus Lodge Hotel, 83–85 Main St., Ocho Rios* ☎ *876/974–2813* ⊕ *www.hibiscusjamaica.com.*

$$$ × **Evita's Italian Restaurant.** Set in an 1860's gingerbread house Evita's has
ECLECTIC a commanding a view above Ocho Rios. For 25 years, this chic and
Fodor's Choice charming restaurant has been the self-proclaimed "Best Little Pasta
★ House in Jamaica," and there's no doubt it's an island institution. Their

---

BEST BETS FOR DINING

Fodor's Choice ★

Evita's Italian Restaurant, Ivan's Restaurant & Bar, Kuyaba on the Beach, Pelican Bar, Redbones Blues Café, Rockhouse Restaurant, Toscanini

BEST LOCAL FOOD

Boston Jerk Centre, Just Natural, Pork Pit, Scotchies, Scotchies Too

BEST FOR A SPECIAL OCCASION

Rockhouse Restaurant, Strawberry Hill

14

pasta is offered up with a spicy zing as they serve a mash-up of the best of Italian and Jamaican cuisine. The friendly staff, and sometimes the proprietor herself, the effervescent Eva Myers, will guide you through the many inventive choices, which include lasagna Rastafari, jerk spaghetti, and One-Love Penne. Make time for desert and enjoy the view from the verandah. [$] *Average main: $23* ✉ *Eden Bower Rd., Ocho Rios* ☎ *876/974–2333* 🌐 *www.evitasjamaica.com.*

$ JAMAICAN 🍴 **Ocho Rios Jerk Centre.** This canopied, open-air eatery is a great place for fiery jerk pork, chicken, or seafood such as fish and conch. Frosty Red Stripe beers or cocktails such as their special Jerk Center Cooler—a colorful mix featuring rum and vodka—are perfect complements to their island fare. Milder barbecued meats, also sold by weight (typically, a quarter- or half-pound makes a good serving), turn up on the daily chalkboard menu posted on the wall. It's busy at lunch, especially when passengers from cruise ships swamp the place. [$] *Average main: $8* ✉ *Da Costa Dr., Ocho Rios* ☎ *876/974–2549.*

$ JAMAICAN 🍴 **Roadster.** A simple, rustic eatery across the road from Jamaica Inn, Roadster is a great place for good Jamaican food at unbeatable prices. You can eat under a tree or inside the basic restaurant, which is run by longtime German resident Marion Rose and her Jamaican husband. The menu has local favorites such as fried chicken and oxtail. Go early or call ahead with your order, because there's a limited amount of food prepared each day. [$] *Average main: $400* ✉ *Hibiscus Dr., Ocho Rios* ☎ *876/974–2910, 876/402–1602* 💳 *No credit cards.*

$ JAMAICAN Fodor's Choice ★ 🍴 **Scotchies Too.** The Ocho Rios branch of the longtime Montego Bay favorite has been lauded by international chefs for its excellent jerk. The plates of jerk chicken, sausage, fish, pork, and ribs at this open-air restaurant are all accompanied by festival, bammy, and some fire-breathing hot sauce. Be sure to step over to the kitchen to watch the preparation of the jerk over the pits. [$] *Average main: J$500* ✉ *Drax Hall, North Coast Hwy., Ocho Rios* ☎ *876/794–9457.*

$$$ INTERNATIONAL Fodor's Choice ★ 🍴 **Toscanini.** At Harmony Hall, this longtime favorite offers seating in the dining room and on the garden verandah. The menu features classic Italian dishes and Jamaican fusion cuisine, all made with fresh, local produce. Look out for marinated marlin, caught in local waters, and the tuna, which customers will come specially from Kingston to enjoy. Huge juicy south coast prawns also draw in customers. Desserts such as tiramisu, chocolate profiteroles, and a wicked affogato round off the meal beautifully. If you are staying in Ocho Rios, call for the complimentary shuttle. [$] *Average main: $25* ✉ *Harmony Hall, North Coast Hwy., Ocho Rios* ☎ *876/975–4785* 🌐 *www.harmonyhall.com.*

PORT ANTONIO

$ JAMAICAN Fodor's Choice ★ 🍴 **Boston Jerk Centre.** Actually a collection of about half a dozen open-air stands, this is a culinary landmark thanks to its popular jerk pits. Stroll up to the open pits, fired by pimento logs and topped with a piece of corrugated roofing metal, locally known as zinc, and order meat by the quarter, half, or full pound; chicken, pork, goat, and fish are top

Fresh shrimp offered at a colorful roadside stand

options. Side dishes are few but generally include festival and rice and peas. $ *Average main: J$800* ✉ *Boston Beach, Rte. A4, east of Port Antonio, Port Antonio* ▭ *No credit cards.*

$$$
CARIBBEAN

✕ **Mille Fleurs.** Sit on a terrace surrounded by tropical vegetation and enjoy European, Jamaican, and Caribbean cuisine while you watch the sunset. The menu changes daily but always includes dishes prepared with local ingredients, such as ackee-fruit soufflé or plantain fritters with black-bean dip. Lobster medallions in a creamy passion sauce is a favorite. Innovative vegetarian options, such as ratatouille with feta and herb crumble, are always on the menu, and "Meatless Mondays" are a weekly feature. $ *Average main: $29* ✉ *Hotel Mockingbird Hill, Port Antonio* ☎ *876/993–7267* ⊕ *www.hotelmockingbirdhill.com.*

$
JAMAICAN

✕ **Woody's Low Bridge Place Fast Food Restaurant & Bar.** Positive vibes and burgers are featured at this roadside eatery. Charles "Woody" Cousins and his wife Cherry serve up simple fare from a white-washed shack that has walls decorated with Cherry's handwritten affirmations. Besides quintessential American fare from fries to hot dogs you can order veggie or plantain burgers. They will cook a traditional Jamaican dinner made to order. A full range of drinks including homemade ginger beer and blended drinks are available. $ *Average main: $8* ✉ *Drapers Main Rd., Port Antonio* ☎ *876/993–7888* ▭ *No credit cards.*

KINGSTON

$$ ╳ **Gloria's.** The unassuming setting belies the excellent food served at
JAMAICAN Gloria's. Frequented by Kingston residents who are more than happy
to take the long drive to Port Royal to enjoy quality seafood. Fresh
fish is served up steamed, fried, escoveitched or in brown stew. Garlic
or curry lobster and shrimp are some of the other delicious offerings.
Sit on the upper deck to catch the cooling sea breeze. Ⓢ *Average main:
J$1600* ⊠ *15 Foreshore Rd., Port Royal* ☎ *876/967–8220.*

$$$ ╳ **Guilt Restaurant.** For bold creations by an imaginative chef go to the
JAMAICAN terrace of the venerable Devon House and savor dishes that transform
traditional Jamaican cuisine into novel, sumptuous meals that will
please the most discerning palate. Exclusive private dining is available
in the vault. Do not pass up desert as chef/owner Colin Hylton made
his name and reputation originally as a pastry chef. Ⓢ *Average main:
J$1600* ⊠ *Devon House, 26 Hope Rd., Kingston* ☎ *876/968–5488*
◷ *Closed Mon.*

$$$$ ╳ **Redbones Blues Café.** At this hip restaurant and bar, there's a lively
INTERNATIONAL music and arts scene, and the family owners take their social and
Fodor'sChoice environmental responsibilities seriously. Not only is the food some of
★ the best in Kingston, but much of the produce is grown on the owners' farm in the hills above the city. The pork is raised at a children's
home in Mandeville that has its own farm. The waiters at Redbones
also attended a children's home in Kingston, going on to train and
make a career at the restaurant. Choose from delicious dishes such
as lamb chops or jerked chicken kebabs, served with a Caribbean
fruit salsa. Redbones comes alive at night, with movies nights, literary evenings, music, and other events. There is also a gallery with
revolving exhibitions. Ⓢ *Average main: J$2450* ⊠ *1 Argyle Rd., Kings-
ton* ☎ *876/978–8262, 876/978–6091* ⊕ *www.redbonesbluescafe.com*
◷ *Closed Sun. No lunch Sat.*

BLUE MOUNTAINS

$ ╳ **Cafe Blue.** Perched on the hillside in Irish Town more than 3,000 feet
CAFÉ up, Cafe Blue could be one of the most stunning places in the world to
enjoy a cup of coffee in the region where it's produced. It's a hip hideaway spot for Kingstonians and is popular with Strawberry Hill guests.
On offer are many different styles of Blue Mountain, from espresso to
latte, as well as a selection of freshly baked cakes. Other café branches
are in the Shoppes at Rosehall in Montego Bay and the Sovereign Centre in Kingston. Ⓢ *Average main: J$375* ⊠ *Irishtown* ☎ *876/944–8918*
⊕ *www.jamaicacafeblue.com.*

$$$$ ╳ **Strawberry Hill.** A favorite with Kingstonians for its elegant Sunday
JAMAICAN brunch, Strawberry Hill is a stunning location to have lunch or din-
Fodor'sChoice ner and is well worth the drive from the city. The open-air terrace has
★ spectacular views of Kingston and the countryside. The restaurant
serves a prix-fixe menu with constantly changing dishes for lunch and
dinner. Entrées include curried shrimp, coconut-crusted snapper, and
Jamaican favorites such as curried goat and jerk chicken. The greens,
the milk, and much of the other ingredients comes from the Island

Outpost farm in the parish of Trelawny and from local farmers. The bar area, a good place for cocktails or after-dinner drinks, features a piano and a fireplace that's usually ablaze in the cool evenings of the Blue Mountains. $ *Average main: $38* ⊠ *Strawberry Hill, New Castle Rd., Irishtown* ☎ *876/944–8400* ⊕ *www.islandoutpost.com* ⏶ *Reservations essential.*

SOUTH COAST

$
JAMAICAN

✕ **Billy's Grassy Park.** A true side-of-the-road stop in the famous Middle Quarters strip along the South Coast Highway, Billy's Grassy Park serves fiery Jamaican food, including scorching peppered shrimp caught just behind the kitchen. Billy cooks favorites such as fried fish, curry goat, and chicken over a wood fire. Also on the menu is peanut porridge, a hearty Jamaican breakfast, which remains a favorite among locals and visitors alike. $ *Average main: $5* ⊠ *A2, about 30 mins east of Whitehouse, Middlequarters* ☎ *876/366–4182* ▭ *No credit cards.*

$$
ECLECTIC
Fodor'sChoice
★

✕ **Jack Sprat Seafood and Pizza Restaurant.** It's no surprise that this restaurant shares its home resort's bohemian style (it's the beachside dining spot at Jakes). From the casual outdoor tables to the late-night dance-hall rhythm, it's a place to come and chill out. Jerk crab, conch, fish and lobster join favorites like pizzas and jerk chicken on the menu, all followed by Devon House ice cream. Tables are either shaded by trees or in the open-sided dining porch. $ *Average main: $15* ⊠ *Jakes, Calabash Bay, Treasure Beach* ☎ *876/965–3000* ⊕ *www.jakeshotel.com.*

$$
JAMAICAN

✕ **Little Ochie.** This casual beachside eatery, a favorite with locals and travelers, is known for its genuine Jamaican dishes like "fish tea" (a spicy bouillon), escoveitch fish, peppered shrimp, jerk chicken, seapuss (octopus), and lobster. Most of the seafood is brought in by fishermen just yards away. For those staying in Treasure Beach, a popular way to reach Little Ochie is by boat. Each year in the second week of July, Little Ochie comes alive with the Little Ochie Seafood Fest, a veritable paradise for seafood lovers featuring several stalls serving fresh seafood with all the trimmings, music, and all-day entertainment. $ *Average main: $17* ⊠ *About 7 miles (11 km) south of A2, Alligator Pond* ☎ *876/852–6430, 876/508–3578* ⊕ *www.littleochie.com.*

$
SEAFOOD
Fodor'sChoice
★

✕ **Pelican Bar.** One of the funkiest places in Jamaica to down a cold Red Stripe, this whimsical structure sits on stilts ½ mile (1 km) offshore between Treasure Beach and Black River, atop a small sandbar, and reachable only by boat. It has become a local legend and a mandatory stop for many visitors to the South Coast. The place serves platters of lobster and other fresh seafood for lunch and dinner. Floyde Forbes (who runs the bar) or one of the hotels of Treasure Beach and Black River can arrange boat transportation, although these short rides can be pricey. $ *Average main: $10* ⊠ *St. Elizabeth* ☎ *876/354–4218* ▭ *No credit cards.*

14

NEGRIL

$$ INTERNATIONAL 🍴 **Annie's Restaurant.** For a special occasion or a night of romantic indulgence, book the private dining cave overlooking the sea at this casual but upscale small restaurant at Moon Dance Cliffs. You'll be set up with an intimate table in the small cavern underneath the main dining area, where waiting staff will pamper you with flowers, candles, champagne, and your own music system. The restaurant's main menu is also first-class, with appetizers such as creamy pumpkin soup, cracked conch, and grilled tomatoes topped with goat cheese. The beef filet mignon is melt-in-your-mouth tender, and the shrimp is also a great option. There's a good mix of seafood, international, local, and vegetarian dishes. [$] *Average main: $20* ✉ *Moon Dance Cliffs, West End Rd., Negril* ☎ *876/957–0872* 🌐 *www.moondanceresorts.com/cliffs.*

$$$ INTERNATIONAL 🍴 **Bongos Restaurant.** A grand piano and a well-stocked premium bar add to the upscale feeling at this restaurant, with stylish indoor seating and patio tables. The cuisine is a fusion of the foods from the many cultures that have settled in the Caribbean over the centuries from Africa, Spain, the Netherlands, France, Portugal, Denmark, Great Britain and, later, India and China. The resulting melting pot of flavors makes for mouthwatering contemporary cuisine. The seafood paella for two is a good bet, as is the Lime 'n' Thyme grilled chicken breast with ackee, callaloo, and a mango broad-bean sauce. Alternatively, opt for the vegetarian choice such as the ackee, vegetable and mixed-bean Stew with a cilantro-tomato sauce. [$] *Average main: $25* ✉ *Sandy Haven Hotel, Norman Manley Blvd., Negril* ☎ *876/957–3200* 🌐 *www.sandyhavenresort.com* ⏲ *No lunch.*

$$$$ JAMAICAN 🍴 **The Caves Restaurant.** This gorgeous Island Outpost boutique resort on Negril's West End has opened up its restaurant to nonguests if they make a reservation. The price of US$100 per person covers a three-course dinner, a welcome drink, and a bottle of wine. The cuisine is authentic Jamaican with a twist. For US$300 per couple, you can book private, romantic candlelit five-course dinner in one of the sea-front caves. The hotel's bar, the Sands, is open Wednesday and Saturday 4–7, during which you can join in cliff-jumping, a popular West End pastime, and enjoy exotic cocktails and fare from the smoky jerk grill. The Blackwell Rum Bar located in a private cave is open Wednesday to Saturday, 5 pm to 10 pm. You can also dine under the stars on Thursday evenings at the Sands for US$100 per person, when a mento band plays. Much of the produce served here comes from the hotel's organic farm in the parish of Trelawny. [$] *Average main: $100* ✉ *The Caves, West End, Negril* ☎ *876/957–0270, 876/618–1081* 🌐 *www.islandoutpost.com* ✍ *Reservations essential* ⏲ *No lunch.*

$$ SEAFOOD 🍴 **Cosmo's Seafood Restaurant and Bar.** Owner Cosmo Brown has made this seaside, open-air bistro a pleasant place to spend the afternoon—and maybe stay on for dinner. Fish is the main attraction, and the conch soup—a house specialty—is a meal in itself. You can also find lobster (grilled, thermidore, or curried), fish-and-chips, and the catch of the morning. After lunch, customers often drop cover-ups to take a dip before coffee and dessert and return to lounge in chairs scattered under almond and seagrape trees (there's an entrance fee of

J$400 for the beach if you want to use the facilities, and JS$150 to rent a lounge chair). This is where many Jamaicans chill out when they come to Negril. [$] *Average main: $16* ✉ *Norman Manley Blvd., Negril* ☎ *876/957–4330, 876/957–4784.*

$$ ECLECTIC 🍴 **The Hungry Lion.** A small but intimate restaurant with stylish decor, the Hungry Lion has long been a favorite restaurant on Negril's West End. You'll find an eclectic crowd gathered here to enjoy the excellent vegetarian fare and seafood, although there are also Jamaican jerk-chicken kebabs available. Try the Thai tofu, which has chunks of tofu in a coconut-curry-and lemongrass sauce—you may be tempted to lick the plate. Other favorites include "shepherd's pie"—a spicy lentil stew topped with mashed potatoes—or Killer Shrimp, which are marinated and grilled in herbs and coconut milk. There is also a good selection of fresh juices. The good-health accent is set to the tune of world music, jazz and blues, and roots reggae. [$] *Average main: $13* ✉ *West End Rd., Negril* ☎ *876/957–4486* ⏲ *No lunch.*

14

$$$ CARIBBEAN Fodor's Choice ★ 🍴 **Ivan's Restaurant & Bar.** A combination of upscale Caribbean cuisine, stunning cliffside dining, and romance make this one of the best places to eat on Negril's West End. Arrive just before dusk and watch the spectacular sunset while enjoying a cocktail by the simple thatched bar and eatery, which is decorated with lots of funky art pieces. Dinner opens with a delicious complimentary conch soup. Beautifully presented appetizers include options like the Calypso Trio—three of Ivan's most requested dishes all in one—chicken, sweet pepper, tomato, and pineapple skewer; jerk shrimp; and a Caribbean crab cake with Ivan dip. Don't miss entrées like grilled lobster with garlic butter and mashed potatoes or the seafood linguine, which has a mixture of shrimp, lobster, and snapper in a creamy white-wine sauce. Try the flambéed banana or pineapple for dessert—the waitress will set overproof rum on fire for you to blow out after two minutes and pour over ice cream. Frozen cheesecakes in flavors such as chocolate mocha, key-lime pie, and peanut butter swirl are also available. You can dress up or dine in casual wear. [$] *Average main: $25* ✉ *Catcha Falling Star, West End Rd., Negril* ☎ *876/957–0390, 876/967–0045* 🌐 *www.catchajamaica.com* ⏲ *No lunch.*

$ VEGETARIAN 🍴 **Just Natural.** This low-key eatery serves vegetarian and seafood dishes as well as fresh fruit and vegetable juices, but it's the surroundings—an enchanting garden on Negril's West End—that really make it stand out. The tables and chairs are all mismatched, some of them furnished from recycled materials, and they're all scattered in the garden, surrounded by orange trees, pretty flowers, and lush vegetation, so that each dining area is private. All food is made to order and well priced. A small soup and dessert are both included with dinner. At this laid-back spot, the motto is "come and relax." [$] *Average main: $7* ✉ *Hylton Ave., ½ mile (0.8 km) after lighthouse, Negril* ☎ *876/957–0235, 876/354–4287* 💳 *No credit cards.*

$$ JAMAICAN Fodor's Choice ★ 🍴 **Kuyaba on the Beach.** This charming thatch-roofed restaurant is open all day and right on the beach: it's one of the top spots for dinner on Negril's 7-mile (11.3-km) strip of sand. The menu specializes in Jamaican cuisine with an international twist, with meals split into the categories of sea, breeze, land and earth. There are a few good vegetarian

options like the veggie stewed peas or the rasta pasta. All food is cooked to order, so come prepared for a long languorous meal. During the day you can lounge on the beach chairs. The restaurant will bring you here for free if you're staying in Negril. $ *Average main: $20* ✉ *Norman Manley Blvd., Negril* ☎ *876/957–4318* ⊕ *www.kuyaba.com.*

$$ ✕**LTU Pub.** This thatched bar and eatery is one of the prettiest on the
INTERNATIONAL   West End. Located right on the cliffs and practically next door to Rick's Cafe, the views are dazzling during the day and at sunset, with steps down to the water to swim. At night, you can dine under the stars. Expats and long-term visitors hang out here to enjoy the laid-back vibe that put Negril on the map. Appetizer highlights include chicken-and-cheese quesadillas and coconut shrimp. Entrees feature beef tenderloin in red-wine sauce, chicken Lola, and snapper stuffed with callaloo. There are lots of pasta choices too. All dinner orders come with a delicious complimentary pumpkin soup. $ *Average main: $15* ✉ *West End Rd., Negril* ☎ *876/957–0382.*

$$ ✕**The Rockhouse Restaurant.** One of the top dining spots in Negril, Rock-
CARIBBEAN   house Restaurant is must for a dinner at least once while you're here.
Fodor'sChoice   The open-air dining area has huge comfy bamboo sofas where you
★   can relax for an aperitif or an after-dinner drink, while the tables are arranged near the cliff for sensational seaside dining. For special occasions there is a cabana, an intimate terrace, and a lower deck where a private table can be set up for a group. The menu features both traditional Jamaican cooking and Rockhouse's interpretation of "New Jamaican cuisine," which is inspired by the many cultures, which have come to the island over the centuries. The staff are friendly and attentive. $ *Average main: $17* ✉ *Rockhouse, West End Rd., Negril* ☎ *876/957–4373* ⊕ *www.rockhousehotel.com.*

$ ✕**Shark's Restaurant.** This nicely decorated, thatched roadside restaurant
JAMAICAN   with just three tables is opposite Tensing Pen. It's one of the best places in Negril to sample local cooking in a friendly and laid-back atmosphere. Juliet, who owns and runs the tiny place, also cooks. All the food is delicious, including chicken fricassee, curried goat, and grilled lobster with lashings of garlic butter. The panfried snapper is also a crowd pleaser. $ *Average main: $6* ✉ *West End Rd., Negril* ☎ *876/428–8411* ▬ *No credit cards.*

WHERE TO STAY

Jamaica is the birthplace of the Caribbean all-inclusive resort, a concept that started in Ocho Rios and later spread throughout the island, so that now most hotel rates are all-inclusive. Package prices usually include airport transfers, accommodations, three meals a day, snacks, all bar drinks (often including premium liquors) and soft drinks, a full menu of sports options (including scuba diving and golf at high-end establishments), nightly entertainment, and all gratuities and taxes. At most all-inclusive resorts, the only surcharges are for such luxuries as spa and beauty treatments, telephone calls, tours, vow-renewal ceremonies, and weddings (though even weddings are often included at high-end establishments).

The all-inclusive market is especially strong with couples and honeymooners. To maintain a romantic atmosphere (no Marco Polo games by the pool), some resorts have minimum age requirements ranging from 12 to 18. Other properties court families with supervised kids' programs, family-friendly entertainment, and in-room amenities especially for young travelers.

PRIVATE VILLA RENTALS

Ocho Rios is filled with private villas, especially in the Discovery Bay area. In Jamaica, most luxury villas come with a full staff, including a housekeeper, a cook, a butler, a gardener, and often a security guard. Many can arrange for a driver, either for airport transfers, for daily touring, or for a prearranged number of days for sightseeing.

BEST BETS FOR LODGING

Fodor's Choice ★

The Blue House, Catcha Falling Star, The Caves, Geejam, Hermosa Cove, Hotel Mocking Bird Hill, Jakes, Jamaica Inn, Rockhouse, Round Hill, Sandals Royal Plantation Ocho Rios, Spanish Court Hotel, Strawberry Hill, Tensing Pen

BEST FAMILY RESORTS

Beaches Ocho Rios, Hilton Rose Hall, Spa Holiday Inn SunSpree, Sunset Beach Resort

BEST FOR ROMANCE

Catcha Falling Star, The Caves, Strawberry Hill, Tensing Pen

14

Recent years have seen an increased demand for larger, more luxurious properties. Numerous villas have five or more bedrooms spread around different parts of the building—or in different buildings altogether—for extra privacy.

Most villas come fully stocked with linens. You can often arrange for the kitchen to be stocked with groceries upon your arrival. Air-conditioning, even in the most luxurious villas, is typically limited to the bedrooms.

A four-night minimum stay is average for many villas although this can vary by season and property. Gratuities, usually split among the staff, typically range from 10% to 15%. Several private companies specialize in villa rentals, finding vacationers places with the right size and price.

Jamaica Association of Villas and Apartments. Since 1967, the Jamaica Association of Villas and Apartments has handled villas, cottages, apartments, and condos across the island. ☎ *800/845–5276, 773/463–6688* ⊕ *www.villasinjamaica.com.* **Jamaica Villas by Linda Smith.** More than 90 fully staffed villas are available from this company. ✉ *8029 Riverside Dr., Maryland, USA* ☎ *301/229–4300* ⊕ *www.jamaicavillas.com.*

Montego Bay

MONTEGO BAY

Mo'Bay has miles of hotels, villas, apartments, and duty-free shops. Although without much in the way of must-see culture, at least for the average visitor, it presents a comfortable island backdrop for the many conventions it hosts. And it has the added advantage of being the closest resort area to the Donald Sangster International Airport.

$$ RESORT **Coyaba Beach Resort and Club.** Privately owned and operated, this intimate property is relaxing, welcoming, and just 10 minutes east of Montego Bay airport. **Pros:** quiet atmosphere of an inn; excellent restaurants; good-size private beach. **Cons:** directly on North Coast Highway; fairly small pool: climb to third-floor rooms can be difficult without elevator. [$] *Rooms from: $365* ✉ *Little River, Montego Bay* ☎ *876/953–9150* 🌐 *www.coyabaresortjamaica.com* 🛏 *50 rooms* 🍴 *Multiple meal plans.*

$$$$ HOTEL FAMILY **Half Moon, A Rockresort.** With its many room categories, massive villas (with three to seven bedrooms), shopping village, hospital, school, dolphin attraction, golf course, and equestrian center, Half Moon seems more like a town than a mere resort. **Pros:** huge beach; many room categories, including villas; numerous on-site activities. **Cons:** some accommodations are a long walk from public areas, and some haven't been renovated that recently; not all activities are within walking distance. [$] *Rooms from: $615* ✉ *Rose Hall Montego Bay, Montego Bay* ☎ *876/953–2211* 🌐 *www.halfmoon.com* 🛏 *45 rooms, 152 suites, 33 villas* 🍴 *Multiple meal plans.*

$$$ ALL-INCLUSIVE FAMILY **Hilton Rose Hall Resort and Spa.** Popular with romance-minded couples, conference groups, and families, this self-contained resort 4 miles (6 km) east of the airport is on the grounds of the 400-acre Rose Hall Plantation. **Pros:** family-friendly dining and pool area; easy access to golf. **Cons:** beach is not as good as others in the area; kid-filled pool can be noisy; some activities are across the highway. [$] *Rooms from: $410* ✉ *Rose Hall Main Rd., St. James* ✣ *15 miles (24 km) east of Montego Bay* ☎ *876/953–2650* 🌐 *www.rosehallresort.com* 🛏 *488 rooms, 14 suites* 🍴 *All-inclusive.*

$$ ALL-INCLUSIVE FAMILY **Holiday Inn SunSpree Resort Montego Bay.** Family fun is tops here, although many couples and singles are also drawn to the not-crazy prices and good location, 6 miles (10 km) east of the airport. **Pros:** good family atmosphere; easy access to shopping area; free self-serve laundry. **Cons:** numerous children mean some areas can be noisy; only nonmotorized water sports included in rates; hotel is directly beside North Coast Highway. [$] *Rooms from: $264* ✉ *North Coast Hwy., 10 miles (16 km) east of Montego Bay, Montego Bay* ☎ *876/953–2485* 🌐 *www.caribbeanhi.com/jamaica* 🛏 *524 rooms, 27 suites* 🍴 *All-inclusive.*

$$ ALL-INCLUSIVE FAMILY **Iberostar Rose Hall Beach.** Twenty minutes east of the Montego Bay airport, this all-inclusive resort was the first (and least expensive) of three adjacent Ibersotar properties. **Pros:** numerous on-site activities; easy access to airport and into Montego Bay; complimentary minibar. **Cons:** high-rise setup can mean elevator wait; more limited all-inclusive program than some others. [$] *Rooms from: J$394* ✉ *North Coast Hwy., 8 miles (13 km) east of Montego Bay city center, Montego Bay* ☎ *876/680–0000* 🌐 *www.iberostar.com* 🛏 *366 rooms* 🍴 *All-inclusive.*

14

$$$ ALL-INCLUSIVE

🏨 **Riu Palace Montego Bay.** This newly opened adult-only resort, with its well-appointed 238 rooms, is trendy and sophisticated. **Pros:** right on the beach and near activities; free Wi-Fi, double-glass; noise-canceling doors in all rooms; hydro-massage tubs in every room. **Cons:** parking lot right at the entrance of the resort takes away from the aesthetics; the contemporary design overpowers the expected island flavor; small gym. [$] *Rooms from: $272* ✉ *Blue Mahoe Bay, Ironshore, Montego Bay* ☎ *800/810–9822* 🌐 *www.riu.com* 🛏 *238 rooms* 🍴 *All-inclusive.*

$$$$ HOTEL Fodor's Choice ★

🏨 **Round Hill Hotel and Villas.** A favorite of celebrities and other wealthy people thanks to its private and elegant villas, this peaceful resort 8 miles (13 km) west of Mo'Bay also offers 36 stylish hotel rooms in the Pineapple House. **Pros:** personal service; spa, stylish rooms; quiet; bathrooms have deep tubs and large walk-in showers. **Cons:** somewhat remote; expensive; some villas do not have pools. [$] *Rooms from: $639* ✉ *North Coast Hwy., 8 miles (13 km) west of Montego Bay, Montego Bay* ☎ *876/956–7050* 🌐 *www.roundhill.com* 🛏 *36 rooms, 27 villas* 🍴 *No meals.*

$$$$ ALL-INCLUSIVE

🏨 **Sandals Royal Caribbean Resort and Private Island.** Four miles (6 km) east of the airport, this elegant resort consists of Jamaican-style buildings arranged in a semicircle around attractive gardens. **Pros:** lots of room categories; offshore dining; complimentary airport shuttle and shuttle to other Sandals resorts in Montego Bay. **Cons:** too quiet for some; smaller beach than Sandals Montego Bay. [$] *Rooms from: $450* ✉ *North Coast Hwy., 6 miles (9 km) east of Montego Bay city center, Montego Bay* ☎ *876/953–2231* 🌐 *www.sandals.com* 🛏 *197 rooms and suites* 🍴 *All-inclusive.*

$$$$ ALL-INCLUSIVE FAMILY

🏨 **Sunset Beach Resort.** Often packed with charter groups, this expansive resort can be a good value if you don't mind mass tourism. **Pros:** excellent beaches; good restaurants; numerous on-site activities. **Cons:** can be crowded; high-rise setup means lines for the elevator; too far to walk to other attractions in Montego Bay. [$] *Rooms from: $440* ✉ *Freeport, Montego Bay* ☎ *876/979–8800* 🌐 *www.sunsetbeachresortjamaica.com* 🛏 *430 rooms, 16 suites* 🍴 *All-inclusive.*

$$$$ RESORT

🏨 **Tryall Club.** The sumptuous villas—each with a private pool—and pampering staff, lend a home-away-from-home atmosphere to this golfers' haven west of Mo'Bay. **Pros:** excellent golf; villa experience with the conveniences of a resort; complimentary kids' club plus a nanny service. **Cons:** nonmembers have to pay an extra US$20 a day to become temporary members of Tryall Club; shared public facilities; somewhat formal atmosphere. [$] *Rooms from: J$550* ✉ *North Coast Hwy., 15 miles (24 km) west of Montego Bay, Sandy Bay* ☎ *876/956–5660, 800/238–5290 in U.S.* 🌐 *www.tryallclub.com* 🛏 *77 villas* 🍴 *No meals.*

Sandals Royal Caribbean Resort & Private Island, Montego Bay

RUNAWAY BAY

The smallest of the resort areas, Runaway Bay, 50 miles (80 km) east of Montego Bay and about 12 miles (19 km) west of Ocho Rios, has a handful of modern hotels, a few all-inclusive resorts, and an 18-hole golf course.

$$$$ **ALL-INCLUSIVE** **Jewel Paradise Cove Beach Resort & Spa.** A new full-service spa is the center piece of this resort that has been taken over by the Jewel chain and totally refurbished to focus on fitness, health, and well-being. **Pros:** free Wi-Fi; complimentary greens fees at the Runaway Bay Golf Club; excellent fitness facilities. **Cons:** spa treatments are at additional cost; beach is not the best. [$] *Rooms from: $650* ✉ *Paradise Cove Dr., Runaway Bay* ☎ *876/972–7400* 🌐 *www.jewelresorts.com* 🛏 *225 rooms* 🍴 *All-inclusive.*

$$$$ **RESORT** **Jewel Runaway Bay Beach & Golf Resort.** This is a luxury all-inclusive geared to active adults and families complete with a championship golf course. **Pros:** extensive sports and water sports options; complimentary airport shuttle; complimentary green fees. **Cons:** small property; low-rise room blocks easy beach access. [$] *Rooms from: $540* ✉ *North Coast Hwy., Runaway Bay* ☎ *876/973–6099* 🌐 *www.jewelresortsrunawaybay.com* 🛏 *266 rooms, 20 suites* 🍴 *Multiple meal plans.*

OCHO RIOS

Ocho Rios lies on the North Coast, halfway between Port Antonio and Mo'Bay. Rivers, waterfalls, fern-shaded roads, and tropical lushness fill this fertile region. It's a favorite with honeymooners as well as Jamaicans who like to escape crowded Kingston for the weekend. The area's resorts, hotels, and villas are all a short drive from the frenetic, traffic-clogged downtown, which has a crafts market, boutiques, duty-free shops, restaurants, and several scenic attractions. The community lies 67 miles (111 km) east of Montego Bay, a drive that takes just under two hours thanks to an improved highway.

$$$$ ALL-INCLUSIVE FAMILY **Beaches Ocho Rios Resort and Golf Club.** The company that specializes in the all-inclusive resort brings its brand of luxury, attention to detail, and an attentive staff to a property that is designed for the entire family. **Pros:** excellent children's program; numerous dining options; great spa, compact enclosed property. **Cons:** no room service unless you get the butler service, each restaurant has different hours and are not always open; Wi-Fi isn't free. [$] *Rooms from: $970* ✉ *North Coast Hwy., St. Ann's Bay* ☎ *876/975–7777* 🌐 *www.beaches.com* 🛏 *223 rooms, 90 suites* 🍴 *All-inclusive* ☞ *2 night minimum.*

$ B&B/INN Fodor's Choice ★ **The Blue House.** This stylish boutique bed-and-breakfast is a nice alternative to the all-inclusive hotels on the north coast. **Pros:** homey; great for single travelers; pool on the property. **Cons:** not many rooms, so you need to book early during busy season; not on the beach; far from amenities. [$] *Rooms from: $240* ✉ *Marcliff, White River Estate, Ocho Rios* ☎ *876/994–1367* 🌐 *www.thebluehousejamaica.com* 🛏 *5 rooms* 🍴 *Multiple meal plans.*

$ ALL-INCLUSIVE **ClubHotel Riu Ocho Rios.** This sprawling resort, built in two U-shape wings each overlooking a pool, is one of the largest in Jamaica. **Pros:** lots of places to eat; large rooms; expansive beach. **Cons:** long walk to beach; some public areas feel cramped; all-inclusive package is limited. [$] *Rooms from: $178* ✉ *North Coast Hwy., Mammee Bay* ☎ *876/972–2200* 🌐 *www.riu.com* 🛏 *478 rooms, 386 junior suites* 🍴 *All-inclusive.*

$$$$ ALL-INCLUSIVE **Couples Sans Souci Resort and Spa.** This classy all-inclusive encourages its guests to check their cares at the entrance and indulge in some soul-nurturing pampering. **Pros:** excellent spa; free weddings and expansive all-inclusive package; complimentary round-trip airport shuttle from Montego Bay airport; trips to Dunn's River Falls and shopping in Ocho Rios are included. **Cons:** some rooms are very isolated and a long walk from public areas; beaches are not as good as others in area. [$] *Rooms from: $950* ✉ *North Coast Hwy., 2 miles (3 km) east of Ocho Rios, Ocho Rios* ☎ *876/994–1206* 🌐 *www.couples.com* 🛏 *150 suites* 🍴 *All-inclusive.*

$$$$ ALL-INCLUSIVE **Couples Tower Isle.** This all-inclusive resort has beautiful contemporary decor. **Pros:** some free weddings; excellent beach facilities; reciprocal arrangement with Couples Sans Souci on Monday, Wednesday, and Friday. **Cons:** long distance from Montego Bay airport. [$] *Rooms from: $950* ✉ *Tower Isle, Rte. A1, 5 miles (8 km) east of Ocho Rios, St. Mary* ☎ *876/975–4271* 🌐 *www.couples.com* 🛏 *280 rooms, 14 suites* 🍴 *All-inclusive.*

$ RENTAL **Glory be.** When owner Karen Schleifer's aunt Marion Simmons first set eyes on this property, she exclaimed, "Glory be," and that's what the house, frequented by the fashionable art and literary crowd of the 1950s and 1960s, became known as. **Pros:** private; pool; great location on the cliffs; close to Reggae Beach. **Cons:** no natural-sand beach on property; 4 miles from Ocho Rios town center. [$] *Rooms from: $150* ✉ *Tower Isle, Ocho Rios* ☎ *876/975–4213* 🛏 *3 cottages* 🍴 *No meals.*

$$$$ RENTAL Fodor's Choice ★ **Goldeneye.** Whether you're a James Bond buff or just a fan of luxury getaways, this exclusive address 20 minutes east of Ocho Rios holds special appeal. **Pros:** unique and spacious place to stay; plenty of privacy. **Cons:** remote location; limited dining options; may be too quiet for some. [$] *Rooms from: $840* ✉ *North Coast Hwy., Oracabessa* ☎ *876/622–9007* 🌐 *www.goldeneye.com* 🛏 *1 5-bedroom villa, 21 villas/cottages* 🍴 *No meals.*

$$$ RESORT Fodor's Choice ★ **Hermosa Cove Villa Resort & Suites.** Secluded in a walled-in complex, Hermosa Cove's contemporary one- and two-story villas are artfully decorated and set in verdant lush grounds. **Pros:** quiet, stylish, and comfortable suites and villas; safe and secure. **Cons:** small beach; limited menu at restaurant; isolated; walled-in. [$] *Rooms from: $301* ✉ *Hermosa Cove, Hermosa St., Ocho Rios* ☎ *876/974–3699* 🌐 *www.hermosacove.com* 🛏 *9 cottages* 🍴 *Breakfast.*

$$$$ HOTEL Fodor's Choice ★ **Jamaica Inn.** The Jamaica inn is a link to the heyday of tourism in Jamaica that exemplified elegance, luxury, and exquisite service, attracting such luminaries as Marilyn Monroe, who honeymooned here with playwright Arthur Miller. **Pros:** elegant accommodations; exceptional service; good spa. **Cons:** no in-room TV. [$] *Rooms from: $513* ✉ *North Coast Hwy., 2 miles (3 km) east of Ocho Rios, Ocho Rios* ☎ *876/974–2514* 🌐 *www.jamaicainn.com* 🛏 *48 suites, 4 2-bedroom cottages* 🍴 *Some meals.*

$$$$ ALL-INCLUSIVE **The Jewel Dunn's River Beach Resort & Spa.** From the waterfall in the main pool inspired by the famous nearby attraction, to the bag of jewels placed on your pillow by the attentive staff, this upscale resort for adults lives up to its name. **Pros:** more intimate than most all-inclusives; 9-hole golf course; high-quality service and amenities **Cons:** crowded beach [$] *Rooms from: $600* ✉ *Mammee Bay, Ocho Rios* ☎ *876/972–7400* 🌐 *www.jewelresorts.com* 🛏 *234 rooms, 16 suites* 🍴 *All-inclusive.*

$$$$ ALL-INCLUSIVE **Sandals Grande Riviera Beach & Villa Golf Resort.** This sprawling resort began years ago as two separate properties, and today it continues to have a split personality. **Pros:** airport shuttle; lots of privacy; numerous swimming options; romantic dining options. **Cons:** villas a long way from the beach; some rooms removed from public areas; long wait for the shuttle. [$] *Rooms from: $1000* ✉ *Main St., Ocho Rios* ☎ *876/974–5691* 🌐 *www.sandals.com* 🛏 *260 rooms, 268 villas* 🍴 *All-inclusive.*

$$$$ ALL-INCLUSIVE Fodor's Choice ★ **Sandals Royal Plantation Ocho Rios.** During its heyday, guests at what was then called Plantation Inn included members of the British royal family, Sir Winston Churchill, and the authors Noël Coward and Ian Fleming. **Pros:** accommodations are expansive and stylish; good dining; room service available. **Cons:** guest rooms and beach are on different levels; small pool and beach. [$] *Rooms from: $1470* ✉ *Main St., Ocho Rios* ☎ *876/974–5601* 🌐 *www.sandals.com* 🛏 *74 suites, 1 villa* 🍴 *All-inclusive.*

PORT ANTONIO

There's a genuine alternative to the hectic tourist scene in Jamaica's bustling resorts Montego Bay and Ocho Rios: Port Antonio. This quiet community is on Jamaica's east end, 133 miles (220 km) east of Montego Bay, and is favored by those looking to get away from it all. Don't look for mixology classes or limbo dances here; this end of Jamaica is quiet and relaxed. The fun is usually found outdoors, followed by a fine evening meal. The area's must-do activities include rafting Jamaica's own Rio Grande, taking an eco-hike, and having lunch or a drink at the Jamaica Palace.

$ **Demontevin Lodge Hotel.** On Titchfield Hill, Demontevin Lodge is a
HOTEL   fine example of elegant 19th-century Victorian architecture, with period decor and furnishings as well. **Pros:** offers the opportunity to sample "old Jamaica;" central location **Cons:** limited amenities beyond a modest restaurant; some rooms have shared bathrooms. $ *Rooms from: $40* ✉ *21 Fort George St., Port Antonio* ☎ *876/993–2604* 🖷 *876/715–5987* ⤶ *13 rooms* ⏣ *No meals.*

$$$$ **Geejam.** Located 10 minutes east of Port Antonio, this stylish rockers'
HOTEL   getaway (Gwen Stefani recorded an album here, and it's a favorite of
Fodor'sChoice   Grace Jones) was once a music producer's hideaway. **Pros:** A five-night
★   stay includes ground transfer from Kingston airport; complimentary transportation to nearby beaches; personalized service; Apple TV in all rooms. **Cons:** remote location; limited on-site amenities; may be too quiet for some guests. $ *Rooms from: $495* ✉ *North Coast Hwy., San San, Port Antonio* ☎ *876/993–7000* ⊕ *www.geejam.com* ⤶ *1 3-bed villa, 1 suite, 3 cabins* ⏣ *Breakfast.*

$$ **Goblin Hill Villas at San San.** Hummingbirds flit about this property,
RESORT   which consists entirely of one- and two-story villas but has the conve-
FAMILY   niences of a hotel. **Pros:** full maid service; roomy, family friendly. **Cons:** no restaurant; not directly on the beach. $ *Rooms from: $225* ✉ *Rte. A4, 3 miles (5 km) east of Port Antonio, San San* ☎ *876/925–8108* ⊕ *www.goblinhill.com* ⤶ *28 villas* ⏣ *No meals.*

$$ **Hotel Mocking Bird Hill.** This ecofriendly boutique hotel is a delight
HOTEL   for those who are environmentally conscience and socially aware, and
Fodor'sChoice   has luxury that is bound to please anyone. **Pros:** numerous ecotourism
★   options; environmentally conscious; carbon offsetting; excellent (but limited) dining. **Cons:** somewhat remote, not directly on the beach. $ *Rooms from: $695* ✉ *North Coast Hwy., Point Ann, Port Antonio* ☎ *876/993–7267* ⊕ *www.hotelmockingbirdhill.com* ⤶ *10 rooms* ⏣ *Some meals.*

$$$$ **Trident Hotel.** What was once a stiff formal and traditional hotel has
HOTEL   been remade into a contemporary stylish resort and is now part of the Geejam collection. **Pros:** stylish; movie-screening room; full service spa; nanny service; private beach **Cons:** only 13 rooms, so it can be difficult to book during busy times. $ *Rooms from: $563* ✉ *North Coast Hwy., Point Ann, Port Antonio* ☎ *876/993–2602* ⊕ *www.geejam.com, www.tridentportantonio.com* ⤶ *13 suites* ✎ *Minimum 5-nights stay required Dec. 20–26 and Easter, minimum 7-nights stay Dec. 26–Jan. 3.*

KINGSTON

Visited by few vacationers but a frequent destination for business travelers and visitors with a deep interest in Jamaica heritage and culture, the sprawling city of Kingston is home to some of the island's finest business hotels. Skirting the city are the Blue Mountains, a completely different world from the urban frenzy of the capital city.

$$
HOTEL

The Courtleigh Hotel & Suites. Aimed at business people, this hotel is in the city's financial district, in the heart of New Kingston and less than a half-hour from Norman Manley International Airport). **Pros:** large rooms; lively nightlife; good business facilities. **Cons:** limited dining options; noisy location; most rooms lack balconies. $ *Rooms from: $205* ⊠ *85 Knutsford Blvd., Kingston* ☎ *876/929–9000* ⊕ *www. courtleigh.com* ⪻ *127 rooms, 38 suites* ‖○‖ *Breakfast.*

$
B&B/INN

Neita's Nest. For travelers who want to get away from the corporate hotels of New Kingston and the hustle and bustle of the city, there's this bed-and-breakfast. **Pros:** inexpensive; an intimate experience; quiet location; the chance to stay in a Jamaican family's house. **Cons:** far from restaurants and attractions; no amenities within walking distance. $ *Rooms from: $80* ⊠ *Bridgemount, Stony Hill, Kingston* ☎ *876/469–3005* ⊕ *www.neitasnest.com* ⪻ *3 rooms* ▬ *No credit cards* ‖○‖ *Breakfast.*

$$$
HOTEL
Fodor's Choice
★

Spanish Court Hotel. Quickly becoming the go-to hotel in Kingston, providing service to business travelers, wedding parties, and tourists, Spanish Court is a calm oaisis in New Kingston. **Pros:** great location in the city center; business center is open 24 hours; reasonable prices; energy-conserving features. **Cons:** limited dining options. $ *Rooms from: $245* ⊠ *1 St. Lucia Ave., Kingston* ☎ *876/926–0000* ⊕ *www. spanishcourthotel.com* ⪻ *111 rooms, 10 suites* ‖○‖ *Breakfast.*

$
HOTEL

Terra Nova All Suite Hotel. This graceful hotel, which was a former colonial mansion, features elegant touches that are sure to please the most discerning traveler. **Pros:** elegant; great open-air dining; near shops and restaurants. **Cons:** fills up quickly on weekends. $ *Rooms from: $220* ⊠ *17 Waterloo Rd., Kingston* ☎ *876/926–2211* ⊕ *www. terranovajamaica.com* ⪻ *49 suites* ‖○‖ *Breakfast.*

BLUE MOUNTAINS

$$
HOTEL
Fodor's Choice
★

Strawberry Hill. A 45-minute drive from Kingston—but worlds apart in terms of atmosphere—this exclusive resort was developed by Chris Blackwell, former head of Island Records (the label of Bob Marley, among many others). **Pros:** stylish accommodations with breathtaking mountain views; cool retreat from the heat, great for hiking or exploring nearby coffee plantations. **Cons:** remote location a distance from the beaches; limited on-site dining options. $ *Rooms from: $355* ⊠ *New Castle Rd., Irishtown, Kingston* ☎ *876/944–8400* ⊕ *www. islandoutpost.com* ⪻ *12 cottages* ‖○‖ *Multiple meal plans.*

14

SOUTH COAST

In the 1970s Negril was Jamaica's most relaxed place to hang out. Today that distinction is held by the South Coast, a long stretch of coastline ranging from Whitehouse to Treasure Beach. Here local residents wave to cars, and travelers spend their days exploring local communities and their nights in local restaurants. The best way to reach the South Coast is from Montego Bay, driving overland, or via Savannah-la-Mar from Negril. Both methods take around 90 minutes to two hours, depending on your final destination.

$ **The Cove in Jamaica.** A newcomer to the South Coast, this boutique
HOTEL hotel on the outskirts of Treasure Beach is an excellent choice if you want complete relaxation. **Pros:** great sea views; romantic and intimate atmosphere. **Cons:** far from the main drag of Treasure Beach; may be too quiet for some. $ *Rooms from: $150* ✉ *Fort Charles, Treasure Beach* ☎ *876/815–9029* ⊕ *www.thecovejamaica.com* ⤳ *12 rooms* ⦿| *No meals.*

$ **Jakes Hotel Villas & Spa.** Jakes takes seaside charm and combines it
HOTEL with art and individuality to create a chic place that oozes personality.
Fodor's Choice **Pros:** unique accommodations; infused with South Coast friendliness;
★ personalized service. **Cons:** some rooms can be cramped when housebound during the occasional rainy periods; a long drive from the airports at Montego Bay or Kingston. $ *Rooms from: $115* ✉ *Calabash Bay, Treasure Beach* ☎ *876/965–3000* ⊕ *www.jakeshotel.com* ⤳ *50 rooms, including villas* ⦿| *No meals.*

$$$$ **Sandals Whitehouse European Village and Spa.** The first major resort
ALL-INCLUSIVE on the South Coast, this property is one of the most upscale properties in the Sandals chain. **Pros:** great private beach; lots of restaurants and an extensive all-inclusive package that includes airport shuttle; stylish rooms at all levels. **Cons:** some travelers won't like Disney-ish re-creation of Euro styles; far from independent restaurants and attractions. $ *Rooms from: $468* ✉ *Whitehouse, Westmoreland* ☎ *876/640–3000* ⊕ *www.sandals.com* ⤳ *360 rooms and suites* ⦿| *All-inclusive.*

NEGRIL

Some 50 miles (80 km) west of Mo'Bay, the so-called "Capital of Casual" was once a hippie hangout, favored for its inexpensive mom-and-pop hotels and laid-back atmosphere. Today there's still a little bohemian flair, but the town is one of the biggest tourist draws on the island, with several large all-inclusives along Bloody Bay, northeast of town. The main strip of Negril Beach and the cliffs are still favored by vacationers who like to get out and explore.

$$$$ **Breezes Grand Resort and Spa Negril.** Fancy touches at this resort are
ALL-INCLUSIVE balanced by an expansive clothing-optional beach (including its own hot tub, bar, and grill), giving you one of Jamaica's best all-inclusive resorts, where it's fun to dress for dinner but equally good to strip down for a day of fun in the sun. **Pros:** excellent beaches; super-inclusive package, including 24-hour room service for all rooms; elegant. **Cons:** some rooms need updating; central public area lacks view; clothing-optional pool is small. $ *Rooms from: $320* ✉ *Norman Manley Blvd., Negril* ☎ *876/957–5010* ⊕ *www.breezes.com* ⤳ *210 suites* ⦿| *All-inclusive.*

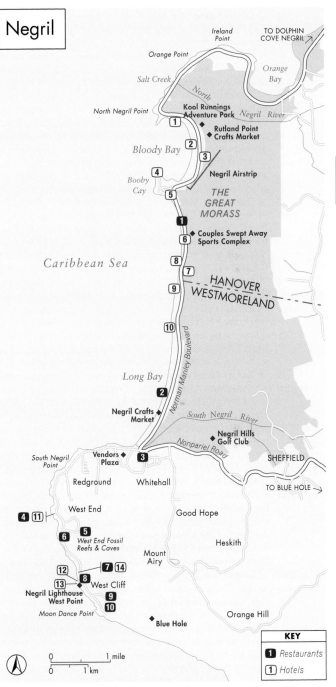

Negril

14

Ireland
Point

TO DOLPHIN
COVE NEGRIL

Orange Point

Orange
Bay

Salt Creek

North

North Negril Point

Kool Runnings
Adventure Park

Negril River

Rutland Point
Crafts Market

Bloody Bay

Negril Airstrip

Booby
Cay

THE
GREAT
MORASS

Caribbean Sea

Couples Swept Away
Sports Complex

HANOVER
WESTMORELAND

Norman Manley Boulevard

Long Bay

Negril Crafts
Market

South Negril River

Negril Hills
Golf Club

Nonpariel Road

SHEFFIELD

South Negril
Point

Vendors
Plaza

Redground

Whitehall

TO BLUE HOLE

West End

Good Hope

West End Fossil
Reefs & Caves

Heskith

Mount
Airy

Negril Lighthouse
West Point

West Cliff

Moon Dance Point

Orange Hill

Blue Hole

0   1 mile
0   1 km

KEY

1 *Restaurants*

1 *Hotels*

$$
HOTEL
Fodor's Choice
★

Catcha Falling Star. Surely one of the prettiest properties on the West End cliffs, Catcha Falling Star is, as it proclaims, a place "to rekindle the romance." **Pros:** rooms for different budgets; romantic; every room is individual. **Cons:** no beach; the cheapest gatehouse cottage may get noise from the street. $ *Rooms from: $135* ✉ *West End Rd., Negril* 📞 *876/957–0390* ⊕ *www.catchajamaica.com* ⌘ *6 suites, 11 cottages* ◯ *No meals.*

$$$$
RESORT
Fodor's Choice
★

The Caves. At this boutique resort, the thatched-roof cottages are individually designed and furnished, most with balconies overlooking the deep water off Negril's West End honeycombed cliffs. **Pros:** intimate spa on clifftop; quiet and friendly; unobtrusive but excellent service. **Cons:** limited on-site dining options; a couple of rooms have no sea views, no beach (hotel is on the cliffs); really expensive. $ *Rooms from: $650* ✉ *One Love Dr., Negril* 📞 *876/957–0270, 876/618–1081* ⊕ *www.islandoutpost.com/the_caves* ⌘ *13 villas and cottages* ◯ *Breakfast.*

$
HOTEL

Charela Inn. This quiet, family-run hotel is on one of the nicest parts of Negril beach and recently benefitted from a renovation project. **Pros:** friendly owners and staff; great dining; good beach location; good value for families. **Cons:** some guest rooms are small; facilities are not luxurious. $ *Rooms from: $190* ✉ *Norman Manley Blvd., Negril* 📞 *876/957–4648, 876/957–4277* ⊕ *www.charela.com* ⌘ *50 rooms* ◯ *Multiple meal plans.*

$
ALL-INCLUSIVE
FAMILY

ClubHotel Riu Negril. At the far north end of Negril on Bloody Bay, this massive resort has a decent, sandy beachfront. **Pros:** economical all-inclusive; family travelers find plenty of children on-site; good on-site dining. **Cons:** pools and public areas can be overcrowded with families; many rooms are a long walk from public areas; long walk from attractions of Negril Beach. $ *Rooms from: $314* ✉ *Norman Manley Blvd., Negril* 📞 *876/957–5700, 876/940–8020* ⊕ *www.riu.com* ⌘ *400 rooms* ◯ *All-inclusive.*

$
B&B/INN

Country Country Beach Cottages. Owned by Kevin and Joanne Robertson, who also own Montego Bay's Coyaba, this small hotel carries the same home-away-from-home feel of its north-coast cousin but with a distinct Negril charm. **Pros:** charming guest rooms; oversized accommodations; good location on Negril Beach. **Cons:** may be too small for some travelers; some rooms can be noisy at night because of nearby Margaritaville; limited on-site dining options. $ *Rooms from: $198* ✉ *Norman Manley Blvd., Negril* 📞 *876/957–4273* ⌘ *17 cottages, 2 apartments* ◯ *Breakfast.*

$$$$
ALL-INCLUSIVE

Couples Negril. This couples-only resort emphasizes romance and relaxation and is a more laid-back alternative to the nearby Sandals Negril. **Pros:** free weddings for guests staying six nights or more; complimentary airport shuttle; good stretch of beach. **Cons:** it's a long walk along the beach to the heart of the action if you want to sample life outside the all-inclusive. $ *Rooms from: $975* ✉ *Norman Manley Blvd., Negril* 📞 *876/957–5960* ⊕ *www.couples.com* ⌘ *234 rooms, 18 suites* ◯ *All-inclusive.*

$$$$
ALL-INCLUSIVE

Couples Swept Away Negril. Sports-minded couples are welcomed to this all-suites resort known for its expansive menu of sports offerings, top-notch facilities (the best in Jamaica and among the best in the Caribbean), and emphasis on healthy cuisine. **Pros:** excellent fitness and sports facilities; complimentary round-trip airport shuttle; great spa. **Cons:** the healthy angle's not for everyone; some facilities are across the road from resort; fairly expensive. $ *Rooms from: $1000* ✉ *Norman Manley Blvd., Negril* 📞 *876/957–4061* ⊕ *www.couples.com* ⌘ *312 suites* ◯ *All-inclusive* ⌚ *3-night minimum.*

$ ALL-INCLUSIVE **Grand Pineapple Beach Resort Negril.** This low-rise resort, dubbed "the cutest little resort in Negril" epitomizes the relaxed and funky style that Negril is still known for. **Pros:** a nice pool on the garden side with snacks available; good value; lovely beach; helpful staff; nice spa **Cons:** some rooms don't have balconies; nearby bars can be noisy; limit of three to a room. [$] *Rooms from: $230* ✉ *Norman Manley Blvd., Negril* ☎ *876/957–4408* 🌐 *www.grandpineapple.com* 🛏 *65 rooms* 🍴 *All-inclusive.*

$$$ ALL-INCLUSIVE **Hedonism II.** Promising a perpetual spring break for adults who are drawn to the legendary party atmosphere, this resort gets a lot of repeat business. **Pros:** good beaches; more economical than some adult all-inclusives; numerous activities. **Cons:** spring-break atmosphere not for everyone; nude beach and pool frequently overcrowded; rooms are basic. [$] *Rooms from: $436* ✉ *Norman Manley Blvd., Rutland Point, Negril* ☎ *876/957–5200* 🌐 *www.hedonism.com* 🛏 *268 rooms, 12 suites* 🍴 *All-inclusive.*

14

$ HOTEL Fodor's Choice ★ **Rockhouse Hotel.** Attracting discerning travelers, honeymooners, and celebrities, this boutique hotel has its cottages and villas placed along a cliff. **Pros:** unique accommodations; beautiful setting; natural, tropical style throughout; great dining options. **Cons:** no beach; may be too quiet for vacationers looking for a party scene. [$] *Rooms from: $180* ✉ *West End Rd., Negril* ☎ *876/957–4373* 🌐 *www.rockhousehotel.com* 🛏 *9 rooms, 20 villas, 5 studios* 🍴 *No meals.*

$$ HOTEL **Sandy Haven.** This small boutique hotel, which opened in 2012, is a good value, particularly since it's on a lovely stretch of Negril's famed beach. **Pros:** good value for money; lovely beach location on beach; good restaurant. **Cons:** beach is not private; limited options on-side for lunch. [$] *Rooms from: $300* ✉ *Norman Manley Blvd., Negril* ☎ *876/957–3200, 800/583–8365 toll-free from U.S.* 🌐 *www.sandyhavenresort.com* 🛏 *17 rooms, 18 suites* 🍴 *Multiple meal plans.*

$$$ HOTEL **The Spa Retreat.** This boutique resort on the cliffs features seven seaside cottages and five rooftop cottages with sea views as well as five similar garden cottages. **Pros:** large groups and wedding parties can rent the whole property; shuttle to beach; restaurant on-site; lovely yoga deck. **Cons:** no natural beach; sea's sometimes too rough for swimming; no relaxation area in the spa section. [$] *Rooms from: $250* ✉ *West End Rd., Negril* ☎ *876/957–4329, 855/843–7725* 🌐 *www.thespajamaica.com* 🛏 *17 cottages, 1 suite* 🍴 *No meals.*

$$$$ ALL-INCLUSIVE **Sunset at the Palms Resort.** A sister property of the Sunset Resorts in Montego Bay and Ocho Rios—but far different in scale and atmosphere—this relaxed all-inclusive is a favorite with ecotourists thanks to its emphasis on environmentally sustainable tourism. **Pros:** environmentally conscious hotel; beautiful grounds; unique accommodations. **Cons:** beach is across street; ecotheme not for everyone; expensive; not within walking distance of many Negril Beach attractions and restaurants. [$] *Rooms from: $540* ✉ *Norman Manley Blvd., Negril* ☎ *876/957–5350* 🌐 *www.sunsetatthepalms.com* 🛏 *85 rooms* 🍴 *All-inclusive.*

$ B&B/INN Fodor's Choice ★ **Tensing Pen.** At this rustic but elegant resort, the cottages are made of stone and wood, with thatch roofs—some of the cottages are on stilts, and they all have big beds. **Pros:** unique accommodations; great snorkeling; spa; spacious rooms. **Cons:** not on beach; barking dogs and other noise sometimes interrupts the quiet. [$] *Rooms from: $250* ✉ *West End Rd., Negril* ☎ *876/957–0387* 🌐 *www.tensingpen.com* 🛏 *21 rooms* 🍴 *Breakfast.*

NIGHTLIFE

For the most part, the liveliest late-night happenings throughout Jamaica that tourists take part in are in the major resort hotels, and on the beach in Negril. Some of the all-inclusives offer a dinner-and-entertainment pass from about $50 to $100; call ahead to check availability and be sure to bring a photo ID with you. Consult *Daily Gleaner,* the *Jamaica Observer,* or the *Star* (available online and at newsstands throughout the island) for listings of who's playing when and where. In Negril, cars with loudspeakers travel through the streets in the afternoon announcing the hot spot for the evening.

MONTEGO BAY

ANNUAL EVENTS

Fodor'sChoice **Jamaica Jazz & Blues.** Held the last Thursday, Friday, and Saturday of
★ January, Jamaica Jazz & Blues festival is one of the biggest music events of the year. It attracts followers from around the world, with previous headlines acts including Mary J. Blige, Michael Bolton, Celine Dion, Kenny Rogers, and Alicia Keys. Tickets usually go on sale online in late November or early December. The event is held at Greenfield Stadium, a 25-minute drive east of Montego Bay. ⊠ *Greenfield Stadium, Trelawny* ⊕ *www.jamaicajazzandblues.com.*

Fodor'sChoice **Reggae Sumfest.** Those who know and love reggae should visit Montego
★ Bay between mid-July and August for this weeklong concert, which attracts big names. Tickets are sold for each night's performances or by multi-event passes. ⊠ *Catherine Hall, Montego Bay* ☎ *876/953–8360* ⊕ *www.reggaesumfest.com.*

BARS AND CLUBS

Blue Beat. This lounge moves to a jazz groove on Friday nights and features techno and house music other nights. It closes around 10:30 most nights, but goes until the wee hours on Friday and Saturday. ⊠ *Gloucester Ave., Montego Bay* ☎ *876/952–4777.*

Club Ville. After 10, the Margaritaville restaurant turns into a hip and happening nightspot. DJs play reggae, house, and R&B along with occasional live performances. Thursday night is Ladies Night and is especially popular among locals. ⊠ *Margaritaville, Gloucester Ave., Montego Bay* ☎ *876/952–4777* ⊕ *www.margaritavillecaribbean.com.*

CASINOS

Acropolis Gaming Lounge. Formerly called Coral Cliff, the completely renovated gaming lounge is a hot spot on Montego Bay's "Hip Strip." Guests can try their luck at the slot machines and roulette tables. ⊠ *165 Gloucester Ave., Montego Bay* ⊕ *www.supremeventures.com.*

Mosino Gaming Lounge. The newest gaming lounge to open in Montego Bay, Mosino is fast becoming a favorite for gamers and non-gamers alike. It houses a full restaurant and sports bar serving tasty apps and entrees. Visitors may try their luck at any of the 214 machines available here, including an assortment of virtual tables and slot machines. ⊠ *Catherine Hall, Montego Bay* ☎ *876/620-9202.*

Treasure Hunt Gaming Lounge. One of the newer additions to Montego Bay's gaming scene, this lounge is located in Ironshore's Whitter Village Shopping Complex. Guests can try their luck at slot machines or roulette tables or have a drink from the well-stocked bar. ⊠ *Whitter Village, Ironshore, Montego Bay.*

OCHO RIOS

ANNUAL EVENTS

Jamaica Ocho Rios International Jazz Festival. Held each June and the biggest event in Ocho Rios, this jazz festival has been running since 1991, when it was just a one-day event. Now it spans nine days and draws many top names. ⊠ *Ocho Rios* ☎ *876/927–3544* ⊕ *www. ochoriosjazz.com.*

Fodor's Choice ★ **Rebel Salute.** Over the years, Rebel Salute has grown to be one of the biggest annual reggae festivals in Jamaica: in 2013 it moved from St. Elizabeth to the Richmond Estate and is now a two-day celebration. As thus is a family-oriented, roots-reggae event, no meat or alcohol is served within the showground. The festival is held in January. ⊠ *Richmond Estate, St Ann* ⊕ *www.rebelsaluteprod.com.*

BARS AND CLUBS

Club Ville. After 10, Margaritaville transforms into Club Ville, where there's a mix of the hottest tunes of the moment, along with occasional live performances from local entertainers. ⊠ *Island Village, Ocho Rios* ☎ *876/675–8800* ⊕ *www.margaritavillecaribbean.com.*

Five Star Watersports. Carnival only occurs once a year, but thanks to Five Star Watersports, you can experience a party atmosphere during the weekly "Jiggy Thursdays," which take place aboard a special evening cruise. They also have these offerings: snorkle/Dunn's River Falls cruise, sunset cruise, private group charters and onboard weddings. ⊠ *121 Main St., Ocho Rios* ☎ *876/974–2446, 876/974–4593* ⊕ *www. fivestarwatersports.com* 🖃 *$79.*

KINGSTON

As the cultural hub of Jamaica, Kingston has the island's largest selection of nightlife. Unlike the more tourist-oriented resort communities, nightlife here is aimed at locals, and varies from live music to DJs. Because of Kingston's high crime rate, check with your concierge or a local who knows the scene before heading out for the night's activities.

BARS AND CLUBS

Friday nights in Kingston bring on the Friday Night Jam, an impromptu street party that begins when office doors close and entrepreneurial chefs roll out oil drums transformed into jerk pits. Street corners sizzle with spicy fare, music blares, and the city launches into weekend mode.

The *Daily Gleaner,* the *Jamaica Observer,* and the *Star* have listings of who's playing when and where. Also look out for roadside posters.

Redbones Blues Cafe. For sophisticated entertainment, you can't beat the jazz, world music, and other low-key performances on Thursdays at this café and performance space. On Friday, it's rock, reggae, or alternative fusion, and once a month house music is the attraction—Redbones is one of the few venues for electronic music in Kingston. The Redbones Gallery rotates art shows once or twice a month, showcasing paintings, photography, sculptures, and sometimes even furniture. Films are screened once a week in the movie garden, usually on Tuesday or Saturday. And the last Wednesday of every month brings a literary evening with poetry and fiction. There's a cover for some events. ⊠ *1 Argyle Rd., Kingston* ☎ *876/978–8262, 876/978–6091* ⊕ *www. redbonesbluescafe.com.*

Usain Bolt's Tracks and Records. For fans of sprinting superstar Usain Bolt, no trip to Kingston would be complete without a visit to his club, a combination casual restaurant and sports bar that's designed to look like a stadium. There are (of course) large-screen TVs for the big game. Upstairs, on the mezzanine, you can see the running shoes Bolt wore on many of his record-breaking sprints as well as signed outfits from medal-winning events. A gift shop sells all the Bolt gear you could wish for. When not breaking Olympic records or outrunning competitors at other meets around the world, the Big Man himself regularly shows up at the bar. ⊠ *The Marketplace, Constant Spring Rd., Kingston* ☎ *876/906–3903* ⊕ *www.tracksandrecords.com.*

NEGRIL

BARS AND CLUBS

Alfred's Ocean Palace. You can find some of Negril's best live music at this bar, which stages reggae band performances right on the beach on Sunday, Tuesday, and Friday nights. ⊠ *Norman Manley Blvd., Negril* ☎ *876/957–4669* ⊕ *www.alfreds.com* ☜ *J$500.*

Bourbon Beach. This beach bar is popular for its live reggae music on Monday, Thursday, and Saturday nights. ⊠ *Norman Manley Blvd., Negril* ☎ *876/957–4432, 876/374–4982* ⊕ *www.bbnegril.com.*

Hedonism II. The sexy, always-packed disco at Hedonism II is a wild night out. For nonguests, passes are $100 for a couple, $50 for a single lady and $100 for a single man, and include meals, drinks, and use of the facilities from 6 pm to 2 am; bring a photo ID to obtain a pass, and call ahead for a reservation. ⊠ *Norman Manley Blvd., Negril* ☎ *876/957–5200* ⊕ *www.hedonism.com.*

The Jungle. The Jungle nightclub is one of the hottest nightspot in Negril, with two raised bars and a circular dance floor. ⊠ *Norman Manley Blvd., Negril* ☎ *876/957–4005.*

Rick's Café. Sunset brings the crowds to Rick's Café to watch live reggae band performances. ⊠ *West End Rd., Negril* ☎ *876/957–0380.*

Continued on page 602

REGGAE

Julie Schwietert Collazo
& Eric Wechter

There's an undeniable, universal appeal to reggae music. Its feel-good beat and impassioned lyrics resonate with listeners across the globe, but experiencing reggae in the country of its birth is the best way to enjoy the music.

Widely considered to be Jamaica's seminal music form, reggae was born out of other genres, including ska and rocksteady, and is relatively young compared to other Jamaican musical styles. In fact, the history of Jamaican music is as long as the history of the island itself. Reggae's origins are firmly rooted in traditions of African music, and its lyrics are inspired by Jamaicans' fervid resistance to colonialism and imperialism. Reggae can be distinguished from earlier music forms by its comparatively faster beat, its experimental tendencies, and a more prominent role for the guitar. Reggae is also more "ragged"—both in sound and in concept. That is it's both more earthy and down to earth, or folkloric. Lyrically, reggae is rife with social themes, primarily those that explore the plight of the working classes.

BUILDING A BEAT

Sly Dunbar, touring with Peter Tosh, 1979

Robbie Shakespeare, on tour with Peter Tosh, 1978

Pioneering reggae musicians, such as drummer **Sly Dunbar** and bassist **Robbie Shakespeare**, shaped the genre by distilling what they viewed as the best elements of ska and rocksteady. Reggae is not complex in terms of chord structure or rhythmic variation. There may be only one to three chords in a typical reggae song, and the danceable feel is propelled most commonly by a rhythm—or "riddim"—called the "drop beat" or "one drop." The bass drum emphasizes the third beat in a four-beat cycle, creating an anchor, or a pull, that the guitar and bass play on top of. For a more propulsive feel, the drummer may equally emphasize all four beats in each measure. Layered on top of this repetitive, solid foundation are socially conscious lyrics, which often preach resistance to the establishment or beseech listeners to love one another.

REGGAE AND RASTA

Reggae is a musical genre of, by, and for the people, and the influence of Rastafarianism has expanded its folk appeal. Rasta became pervasive in Jamaica in the 1950s, when resistance to colonialism peaked. Rasta, combining spiritual, political, and social concerns, had its origins in the crowning of **Haile Selassie I** as the emperor of Ethiopia in 1930. Selassie, the only black man to head an independent African nation at the time, became a vital figure and symbol of freedom for Africans in the diaspora. Greatly inspired by Selassie, Jamaicans integrated his empowering messages into many aspects of their culture. Musically, the Rasta influence is felt in reggae in two ways. The lyrics often advocate the idea of returning to Africa, and minor chords and a simple "riddim" structure characterize the songs. In the words of music historian Lloyd Bradley, Rastas were the "underclass of the underclass," and by 1959 more than one in every 25 Jamaicans identified with Rastafarianism. One of them was Bob Marley.

Haile Selassie I of Ethiopia

BOB MARLEY

Bob Marley is reggae's oracle, a visionary who introduced the world to the music of Jamaica and the struggles of its people. A stirring performer with a preternatural talent for connecting with audiences, Marley revealed the oppression of his countrymen and their indomitable spirit through his songs of hope, freedom, and redemption. His legacy extends far beyond reggae, influencing generations of artists across multiple genres.

Born in February 1945, Robert Nesta Marley left his home in rural St. Ann's Parish, Jamaica, at 14 to pursue a music career in Kingston. In 1963 Marley joined with singers Peter Tosh and Bunny Livingston to form the group the Wailers, and they began recording singles with a renowned local producer. After a series of stops and starts and a strengthened devotion to the teachings of the Rastafari faith, Bob Marley and the Wailers released *Catch a Fire* in 1973. It was their first release outside of Jamaica, and nearly instantly it became an international success. Mar-

ley's global popularity and acclaim grew with albums like *Burnin'* and *Natty Dread.* As Marley's stardom increased abroad, his influence at home became transcendent. Regarded by many of his countrymen as a prophet, Marley, whose songs of freedom and revolution reverberated throughout Jamaica, was perceived as threat in some corridors. In December 1976, he was wounded in an assassination attempt. Marley left Jamaica for more than a year and in 1977 released his biggest record thus far, *Exodus,* which included the hits "Jammin" and "One Love/People Get Ready." By 1980, Marley was poised to reach even greater heights with an extensive U.S. tour, but while jogging in New York he suddenly collapsed. Cancer had silently invaded his brain and lungs. He died in May, 1981, at age 36. Marley's spirit and music endure in the hearts and minds of fans worldwide. His greatest hits collection, *Legend,* is the top-selling reggae album of all time.

Bob Marley at Reggae Sunsplash

COMMUNING WITH THE SPIRIT

Bob Marley Museum, Kingston

Whether you're a serious enthusiast or have just a passing curiosity, Jamaica offers visitors plenty of opportunities to experience the music and culture of reggae.

Zion Bus Line Tour to Nine Mile. Marley fans won't want to miss this bus pilgrimage to the reggae icon's birthplace and final resting place. With the sounds of familiar reggae tunes thumping through the bus speakers, the guided tour takes you through the mountains to the small town of Nine Mile. The half-day tour includes a visit to Marley's house, a stop at Mount Zion (a rock where Marley meditated) and the opportunity to view Marley's mausoleum. The tour leaves from Ocho Rios. On the return trip from Nine Mile, the group stops at the Jerk Center for an authentic Jamaican lunch.

Reggae Sumfest in Montego Bay. This week-long reggae festival is held each July. In addition to featuring musical line-ups of the most popular reggae, dance hall, R&B, and hip hop acts, the Sumfest offers traditional Jamaican food and local crafts. Recent festivals have featured local favorite Tarrus Riley, as well as international performers, like LL Cool J and Mary J. Blige.

DID YOU KNOW?

The first appearance of the word *reggae* is widely attributed to the 1968 single by the Maytals called "Do the Reggay."

Burning Spear   Jimmy Cliff   The Congos

Bob Marley Museum in Kingston (☎ *876/ 927–9152*). If the Zion Bus Tour only whets your appetite for Marley, visit the Bob Marley Museum for a glimpse at another chapter of his life. Housed inside the former headquarters of Marley's label, Tuff Gong Records, it is also the site of the failed attempt on Marley's life that inspired his song, "Ambush."

And, of course, your Jamaican reggae experience would not be complete with-

out catching some live bands. Local acts play at **Bourbon Beach** (☎ *876/957–4432*) in Negril on Monday, Thursday, and Saturday nights. Also in Negril is **Rick's Cafe** (☎ *876/957–0380*), which features an in-house reggae band nightly, and **Alfred's Ocean Palace** (☎ *876/957–4669*) where you can dance on the beach to live reggae.

REGGAE LINGO

Dancehall. A modern style that introduces elements of electronic dance music and improvised singing or rapping by DJs to raw reggae tracks.

Dub. A form of reggae characterized by the use of re-mixes of previously recorded material.

One-drop rhythm. The definitive beat of reggae characterized by a steady "drop" of the bass drum on the strong beat in each measure.

Ragamuffin (ragga). Similar to dancehall, ragga

combines electronic dance music, hip-hop, and R&B with reggae for a more contemporary, club feel.

Riddim. The rhythmic foundation for nearly all reggae styles, characterized by a repetitive, driving drum and bass feel.

Rocksteady. A style of reggae that followed ska, rocksteady is marked by a slower tempo.

Ska. Precursor to reggae that combines traditional Caribbean rhythms, jazz, and calypso

RECOMMENDED LISTENING

Bob Marley
Uprising, Legend, Exodus, Burnin', Catch a Fire

Peter Tosh
Legalize It

Toots and the Maytals
Funky Kingston

Jimmy Cliff
The Harder They Come

Burning Spear
Marcus Garvey

Alton Ellis
Alton Ellis Sings Rock and Soul

The Congos
The Heart of the Congos

SHOPPING

Shopping is not really one of Jamaica's high points, though you will certainly be able to find things to buy. Good choices include Jamaican crafts, which range from artwork to batik fabrics to baskets. Wood carvings are one of the top purchases; the finest carvings are made from the Jamaican national tree, lignum vitae, or tree of life, a dense, blond wood that requires a talented carver to transform it into dolphins, heads, or fish. Bargaining is expected with crafts vendors. Naturally, Jamaican rum is another top souvenir—there's no shortage of opportunities to buy it or Tia Maria, the Jamaican-made coffee liqueur, at gift shops and liquor stores. Coffee (both Blue Mountain and the less expensive High Mountain) is sold at nearly every gift shop on the island as well. The cheapest prices are often found at the local grocery stores, where you can buy coffee beans or ground coffee.

Unless you have an extremely early flight, you'll find plenty of shopping at the Sangster International Airport, which has a large shopping mall. Fine handmade cigars are available there, or at one of the island's many cigar stores. You can also buy Cuban cigars almost everywhere, though they can't be taken back legally into the United States.

As a rule, only rum distilleries, such as Appleton's and Sangster's, have better deals than the airport stores. Best of all, if you buy your rum at the airport stores, you don't have to tote all those heavy, breakable bottles to your hotel and then to the airport. (Note that if you purchase rum—or other liquids, such as duty-free perfumes—outside the airport, you'll need to place them in your checked luggage when returning home. If you purchase liquids inside the secured area of the airport, you may board with them, but, after clearing U.S. Customs on landing, you will need to place them in your checked bag if continuing on another flight.)

MONTEGO BAY

AREAS AND MALLS

Half Moon Shopping Village. Half Moon Shopping Village, at Half Moon hotel, has bright yellow buildings filled with some of the finest and most expensive wares money can buy, as well as more affordable boutiques. There is also a post office, bank, and restaurants. ⊠ *Half Moon, North Coast Hwy., 7 miles (11 km) east of Montego Bay, Montego Bay* ☎ *876/953–2211* ⊕ *www.halfmoon.com.*

Holiday Shopping Centre. Directly across the street from the Holiday Inn Sunspree Resort, this casual shopping area has jewelry, clothing, and crafts stores. ⊠ *Holiday Inn SunSpree Resort, North Coast Hwy., 10 miles (16 km) east of Montego Bay, Montego Bay.*

The Shoppes at Rose Hall. This upscale, open-air shopping center was designed to resemble an old-fashioned main street. The center, five minutes from the Hilton Rose Hall Resort & Spa, includes jewelry, cosmetics, and designer-clothing shops. Some hotels offer free shuttle service here. ⊠ *Rose Hall, North Coast Hwy., 7 miles (11 km) east of Montego Bay, St. James.*

HANDICRAFTS

In Montego Bay, the largest crafts market can be found on Fort Street and on **Market Street.** Both streets have a bunch of stalls, each selling pretty much the same thing. Come prepared to haggle over prices and to be given the hard sell; if you're in the right mood, though, the whole experience can be a lot of fun and a peek into Jamaican commerce away from the resorts.

Things Jamaican. Find some of the best Jamaican crafts—from carved wooden bowls and trays to reproductions of silver and brass period pieces—at Things Jamaican. ⊠ *Sangster International Airport, Montego Bay* ☎ *876/971–0775* ⊕ *www.thingsjamaicanstores.com* ⊠ *Devon House, 26 Hope Rd., Kingston* ☎ *876/926–1961.*

OCHO RIOS

14

AREAS AND MALLS

Ocho Rios has several malls that draw day-trippers from the cruise ships. The best are **Soni's Plaza** and the **Taj Mahal,** two malls on the main street with stores selling jewelry, cigars, and clothing. Another popular mall on the main street is **Ocean Village.** On the North Coast Highway slightly east of Ochos Rios are **Pineapple Place** and **Coconut Grove.**

Ocho Rios Crafts Market. The largest craft market is the Ocho Rios Crafts Market, with stalls selling everything from straw hats to wooden figurines to T-shirts. Vendors can be aggressive, and haggling is expected for all purchases. Your best chance of getting a good price is to come on a day when there's no cruise ship in port. ⊠ *Main St., Ocho Rios.*

Pineapple Craft Market. The Pineapple Craft Market is a small, casual market on the outskirts of Ocho Rios. Look for everything from carved figurines to coffee-bean necklaces. ⊠ *North Coast Hwy., Ocho Rios.*

HANDICRAFTS

Harmony Hall. An eight-minute drive east of the main part of town, is a restored 19th-century house of a minister, now known for the original works of art sold inside. Owner Annabella Proudlock sells her unique wooden boxes (their covers are decorated with reproductions of Jamaican paintings). Also on sale—and magnificently displayed—are larger reproductions of paintings, lithographs, and signed prints of Jamaican scenes and hand-carved wooden combs. In addition, Harmony Hall is well known for its shows by local artists. ⊠ *Rte. A3, Ocho Rios* ☎ *876/974–2870* ⊕ *www.harmonyhall.com* ☉ *Tues.–Sun. 10–5:30.*

Wassi Art Handcrafted Caribbean Home Accessories. Wassi Art sells pottery and ceramics and other local arts and crafts, all of which are made in Jamaica. ⊠ *Bonham Spring, Ocho Rios* ☎ *876/974–5044* ⊕ *www. wassiart.com.*

NEGRIL

SHOPPING CENTERS

The Boardwalk Village. Set right on the beach in Negril, this is a nice place to spend half a day perusing souvenir stores and clothing boutiques, and perhaps also having lunch at the restaurant. ⊠ *The Boardwalk Village, Norman Manley Blvd., Negril* ⊕ *www.theboardwalkvillagenegril.com.*

Time Square. The mall is known for its luxury goods and souvenirs, including cigars and jewelry. ⊠ *Norman Manley Blvd., Negril* ☎ *876/ 957–9263* ⊕ *timesquareplaza.com.*

MARKETS

Craft Market by Beach Park. This craft market on the beach side of the bridge at Negril's town center roundabout sells arts and crafts aplenty. ⊠ *Norman Manley Blvd., Negril.*

Rutland Point. With its laid-back atmosphere, it's no surprise that most Negril shopping involves straw hats, woven baskets, and T-shirts, all plentiful at Rutland Point, a crafts market on the northern edge of town. The atmosphere is less aggressive here than at similar establishments in Montego Bay and Ocho Rios. ⊠ *Norman Manley Blvd., Negril.*

PORT ANTONIO

Shopping is not a major attraction in Port Antonio, compared with the duty-free shopping of Ocho Rios and Montego Bay. The marina and cruise-ship port offers limited shopping opportunities and takes a backseat to other activities.

MARKETS

Musgrave Market. This traditional market, unlike those in Ocho Rios and Montego Bay, is primarily aimed at locals. Although you can find some crafts here, look for luscious fruits and vegetables, household goods, and clothing in these stalls. ⊠ *West St., Port Antonio.*

HANDICRAFTS

Carriacou Gallery. The work of Hotel Mocking Bird Hill owner Barbara Walker and other local artists is showcased at Carriacou Gallery. It also offers art classes. ⊠ *Hotel Mocking Bird Hill, off Rte. A4, 6 miles (9½ km) east of Port Antonio, Port Antonio* ☎ *876/993–7267.*

Things Jamaican. As its name suggests, Things Jamaican sells local items: books, music, crafts, spices, sauces, beachwear, and more. ⊠ *Errol Flynn Marina, Ken Wright Dr., Port Antonio* ☎ *876/715–5247* ⊕ *www. thingsjamaican.com.*

KINGSTON

Unlike the island's North Coast towns, Kingston isn't known for its duty-free stores. Shopping here is mostly limited to shops for residents. The city's Constant Spring Road and King Street are home to a growing roster of shopping malls offering fashions, housewares, and more.

SHOPPING CENTERS

Shops at Devon House. This cluster of mostly upscale shops sells clothing, crafts, and other items. The location, at the historic Devon House, makes it a pleasant spot to spend a morning or afternoon. Don't miss the famous Devon House ice cream. ⊠ *26 Hope Rd., Kingston* ☎ *876/929–6602.*

SPECIALTY ITEMS

Starfish Oils. Find aromatherapy products, such as fragrant oils, scented candles, and soaps here. Lemongrass, which grows locally, goes in one of the most popular oils, and Blue Mountain coffee is a favorite ingredient in both soap and candles. Another Starfish Oils shop is in Manor Park Plaza, and its products are sold in shops throughout the island. ⊠ *Devon House, Kingston* ☎ *876/901–7113* ⊕ *www.starfishoils.com* ⊠ *Manor Park Plaza, Kingston.*

Tuff Gong Recording Studio. This studio is part of the Bob Marley group of companies, with international clients including Maxi Priest, Steele Pulse, and Sinéad O'Connor, and is itself a tourist attraction for reggae-music buffs. It also houses the Tuff Gong music shop and the Rita Marley Foundation. ⊠ *220 Marcus Garvey Dr., Kingston* ☎ *876/923–9380* ⊕ *www.tuffgong.com.*

SPORTS AND ACTIVITIES

The tourist board licenses all recreational activity operators and outfitters, which should assure you of fair business practices as long as you deal with companies that display its decals.

BIRD-WATCHING

Jamaica is a major bird-watching destination, thanks to its various natural habitats. The island is home to more than 200 species, some seen only seasonally or in particular parts of the island. Many bird-watchers flock here for the chance to see the vervain hummingbird (the world's second-smallest bird, larger only than Cuba's bee hummingbird) or the Jamaican tody (which nests underground).

PORT ANTONIO

Jamaica Explorations. Jamaica is a bird watcher's paradise. There are more than 265 species of birds with more than 20 native to Jamaica. There are more species native to Jamaica than any other Caribbean Island. Among the several guided tours for birders is a special hummingbird tour. Hotel Mockingbird Hill, listed in "Birds of West Indies" as one of the best places for bird watching, is where these tours originate. Tours are given in two areas—either in the Reach Falls area or Blue Mountains. Rates include transportation. ⊠ *Hotel Mockingbird Hill, Port Antonio* ☎ *876/993–7267* ⊕ *www.jamaicaexplorations.com* ⊠ *$330 Blue Mountains tour; $130 Reach Falls tour.*

14

KINGSTON AND THE BLUE MOUNTAINS

Arrowhead Birding Tours. This company runs birding tours across the island, including customized trips and annual eight-day trips in November, February, and March. Customized tours available. ⊠ *Kingston* ☎ *876/260–9006* ⊕ *www.arrowheadbirding.com* ✉ *$130.*

Birdlife Jamaica. The nonprofit Birdlife Jamaica organizes bird-watching trips into the Blue Mountains and nearby John Crow Mountains, as well as other parts of the island. ⊠ *University of the West Indies Mona, Dept. of Life Sciences, Mona Rd., Kingston* ☎ *876/260–9006.*

Sun Venture Tours. Billed as tours for nature lovers Sun Venture Tours offers 25 different special-interest tours across the island, including bird-watching. ⊠ *30 Balmoral Ave., Kingston* ☎ *876/960–6685, 876/408–6973 after office hrs and weekends* ⊕ *www.sunventuretours.com.*

DIVING AND SNORKELING

Jamaica isn't a major dive destination, but you can find a few rich underwater regions, especially off the North Coast. Mo'Bay, known for its wall dives, has **Airport Reef** at its southwestern edge. The site is known for its coral caves, tunnels, and canyons. The first marine park in Jamaica, the **Montego Bay Marine Park,** was established to protect the natural resources of the bay; a quick look at the area and it's easy to see the treasures that lie beneath the surface. The North Coast is on the edge of the Cayman Trench, so it boasts a wide array of marine life.

Thanks to a marine area protected since 1966, the Ocho Rios region is also a popular diving destination. Through the years, the protected area grew into the **Ocho Rios Marine Park,** stretching from Mammee Bay and Drax Hall to the west to Frankfort Point on the east. Top dive sites in the area include **Jack's Hall,** a 40-foot dive dotted with all types of coral; **Top of the Mountain,** a 60-foot dive near Dunn's River Falls with many coral heads and gorgonians; and the **Wreck of the** *Katryn,* a 50-foot dive to a deliberately sunk 140-foot former minesweeper.

With its murkier waters, the southern side of the island isn't as popular for diving. However, **Port Royal,** which is near Kingston's airport, is filled with sunken ships that are home to many different varieties of tropical fish, although a special permit is required to dive some sites here. Prices range from $45 to $80 for a one-tank dive. Most of the large resorts have dive shops, and the all-inclusive places sometimes include scuba diving in their rates. To dive, you need to show a certification card, though it's possible to get a small taste of scuba diving and do a shallow dive—usually from shore—after taking a one-day resort diving course, which almost every resort with a dive shop offers. A couple of places stand out.

MONTEGO BAY

Jamaica Scuba Divers. Here are serious scuba facilities for dedicated divers as well as beginners. This PADI and NAUI operation also offers nitrox diving and instruction as well as instruction in underwater photography, night diving, and open-water diving. Operations are based at Travellers Beach Resort in Negril and Franklyn D. Resort in Runaway Bay. Pick-up can be arranged from most hotels and other locations along the North Coast. ☏ *876/381–1113* ⊕ *www.scuba-jamaica.com* ✉ *Travellers Beach Resort, Negril.*

OCHO RIOS

Five Star Watersports. The company's "Cool Runnings" catamaran cruises to Dunn's River Falls. The trips leave from Mahogany Beach at 12:30 pm and cost US$85. ✉ *121 Main St., Ocho Rios* ☏ *876/974–2446, 876/974–4593* ⊕ *www.fivestarwatersports.com* ☾ *Closed Sun.*

PORT ANTONIO

Lady G'Diver. The only dive operator in Port Antonio runs trips to interesting sites almost every days. Two-tank dive trips depart at around 11 am. Call two or three days in advance to set up the trip. ✉ *Errol Flynn Marina, Ken Wright Dr., Port Antonio* ☏ *876/995–0246* ⊕ *www.ladygdiver.com.*

14

FISHING

Port Antonio makes deep-sea-fishing headlines with its annual Blue Marlin Tournament in October, and Mo'Bay and Ocho Rios have devotees who exchange tales (tall and otherwise) about sailfish, yellowfin tuna, wahoo, dolphinfish, and bonito. Licenses aren't required, and you can arrange to charter a boat at your hotel. A chartered boat (with captain, crew, and equipment) costs about $500 to $900 for a half day or $900 to $1,500 for a full-day excursion, depending on the size of the boat.

MONTEGO BAY

No Problem Sport Fishing. Charter fishing excursions are available aboard the *E-Zee*. Half- and full-day excursions take anglers in search of big catch. Plan on spending US$600 for a half-day charter and US$1,200 for a full day on the seas. A discount is available if paying by cash. Fees include drinks and equipment. ✉ *The Yacht Club, Montego Bay* ☏ *876/381–3229* ⊕ *www.montego-bay-jamaica.com/ajal/noproblem.*

FALMOUTH

Glistening Waters Marina. This marina offers deep-sea fishing and other charter trips from Glistening Waters, which is 20 minutes east of Montego Bay. The marina also has night tours for a look at the lagoon, which is iridescent due to microscopic dinoflagellates that glow when they move. ✉ *North Coast Hwy., Falmouth* ☏ *876/954–3229* ⊕ *www.glisteningwaters.com.*

GOLF

Caddies are almost always mandatory throughout the island, and rates are $15 to $45 per round of golf. Cart rentals are available at most courses; costs are $20 to $40. Some of the best courses in the country are found near Mo'Bay. Many resorts have their own courses (including several of the Sandals resorts) and allow both guests and nonguests to play.

MONTEGO BAY

Cinnamon Hill Gold Course. Situated on 400 lush acres, Cinnamon Hill will take you to the water's edge and then up into the hilly jungles for a most entertaining golf experience. The course was designed by Robert von Hagge and Rick Baril and is on the Rose Hall estate. Rates include greens fees, cart, caddy, and tax. The replay rate is $49. Nike golf clubs are available for rental. ⊠ *Rose Hall, North Coast Hwy., St. James* ☎ *876/953–2984* ⊕ *www.cinnamonhilljamaica.com* ⅃ *18 holes, 6828 yards, par 72* ⌦ *$169 per person in winter.*

Half Moon Golf Course. Swaying palms, abundant bunkering, and large greens greet you on this flat Robert Trent Jones Sr.–designed course, home of the Jamaica Open. The course was renovated in 2005 by Jones protégé Roger Rulewich to better position the hazards for today's longer hitting golfers. The course is also the home of the Half Moon Golf Academy, which offers one-day sessions, multiday retreats, and hour-long private sessions. ⊠ *Half Moon, North Coast Hwy., 7 miles (11 km) east of Montego Bay, Montego Bay* ☎ *876/953–2211* ⊕ *www. halfmoongolf.com* ⅃ *18 holes, 7141 yards, par 72* ⌦ *Nonguest cost is US$181 for 18 holes, US$118 for 9 holes.*

Ritz-Carlton Golf and Spa Resort, Rose Hall. One of the nicest courses in Montego Bay, if not Jamaica, is the White Witch course, named for Annee Palmer, the wicked 19th-century plantation mistress who reportedly did away with three unsuspecting husbands. It occupies mountainous terrain high above the sea and features bold, attractive bunkering and panoramic views. Legend has it that Annee still haunts the area, but not your golf game. Rental clubs are available for $60. Pre-booking is recommended. ⊠ *1 Ritz Carlton Dr., Rose Hall, St. James* ⊕ *www. whitewitchgolf.com* ⅃ *18 holes, 6758 yards, par 71* ⌦ *$159.*

Fodor's Choice ★ **Tryall Club Golf Course.** Want to experience first-class golf where traces of storied history still abound? One of the best-known courses in Jamaica and the Caribbean is at this exclusive country club resort 15 miles (24 km) west of Montego Bay. The 18-hole championship course on the site of a 19th-century sugar plantation exudes a peaceful ambience where no one is hurried and playing with a caddy is the norm. The layout visits the Caribbean coast before heading up into the hills featuring some more expansive vistas. Golfers will enjoy the 4th hole whose green hugs the sea. The course, designed by Ralph Plummer, has hosted events such as the Johnnie Walker World Championship. ⊠ *Tryall Club, North Coast Hwy., Sandy Bay* ☎ *876/956–5601* ⊕ *www.tryallclub.com* ⅃ *18 holes, 6836 yards, par 71* ⌦ *For Tryall guests: $105 for 18 holes and $75 for 9 holes; nonguests: $150 and $115.*

NEGRIL

Negril Hills Golf Club. Lush tropical foliage, picturesque water hazards, elevated tees, and gently rolling fairways greet you at Negril Hills Golf Club. Beyond that you will enjoy tropical mountain vistas and hard-sloping greens. Located an hour and a half drive west of Montego Bay on Jamaica's north shore, it sits inland from the longest stretch of private beach in Jamaica. This 6333-yard course is walkable, but plays longer due to its elevated putting surfaces. ⊠ *Sheffield, Negril* ☎ *876/957–4638* ⊕ *www.negrilhillsgolfclub.com* ⅃ *18 holes, 6333 yards, par 72* ⌦ *$60.*

GUIDED TOURS

Because most vacationers avoid renting cars for safety and cost reasons, guided tours are a popular option if you want to take a break from the beach and explore. Check with your hotel concierge or go online for information on half- and full-day tours that offer pickup at your resort. Jamaica's size and slow interior roads mean that you can't expect to see the entire island on any one trip; even a full-day tour will concentrate on just one part of the island. Most of the tours are similar in both content and price. If you're in Montego Bay, tours often include one of the plantation houses in the area. Several Negril-based companies offer tours to Y.S. Falls on the South Coast. Tours from Ocho Rios might include any of the area's top attractions, including Dunn's River Falls or Kingston. In almost all cases, you'll arrange your tour through the tour desk of your resort. However, a few tours stand out, including the following.

MONTEGO BAY

Most of the large Montego Bay resorts have tour desks where you can book a number of excursions and activities. Guided plantation and countryside visits are also popular. Almost all tour operators will pick you up if you are staying in one of the large resorts.

Croydon Plantation Tour. Take a tour of the birthplace of the Jamaican hero Sam Sharpe, who led the rebellion that helped put an end to slavery on the island. The tour, run on Tuesday, Thursday, and Friday, visits Croydon Plantation, an hour and a half from Montego Bay, where pineapples, sugarcane, and citrus fruits are grown in the foothills of the Catadupa mountains. Pick-up is available from hotels in and around Montego Bay and the Grand Palladium Resort in Hanover. ☎ *876/979–8267* ⊕ *www.croydonplantation.com* ✉ *US$70 adults, $50 children. Infants are free.*

Glamour Destination Management. One of the island's large tour operators, this company offers a wide selection of guided visits to Rose Hall and Greenwood Great House. ✉ *1225 Providence Dr., Montego Bay* ☎ *876/953–3810* ⊕ *www.glamourtoursdmc.com.*

Island Routes Caribbean Adventures. Run by Sandals, Island Routes provides luxury tours of Jamaica to both guests and nonguests of Sandals resorts. The company offers group and private guided tours with certified partners to a host of attractions. Guests have a choice of booking via the website or on-island at one of the Island Routes tour desks at participating resorts. ✉ *Montego Bay* ☎ *888/768–8370 U.S. and Canada, 888/429–5478 Jamaica* ⊕ *www.islandroutes.com.*

JUTA. The island's largest tour operator offers a great house tour and a rafting tour, as well as tours to other parts of the island like Black River, Negril, and Ocho Rios. ☎ *876/952–0813* ⊕ *www.jutatoursltd.com.*

OCHO RIOS

Chukka Caribbean Zion Bus Tour. This tour will appeal to anyone visiting the Ocho Rios area who wants to visit Bob Marley's boyhood home. Travelers ride a country-style bus painted in bright colors to the island's interior and the village of Nine Mile. The tour includes a look at the simple house where Marley was born and is now buried. The tour (US$100, including lunch at a local jerk stand) lasts for five hours and is limited to guests age 18 and older. ⊠ *Ocho Rios* ☎ *876/619–1441 Digicel in Jamaica, 876/656–8026 Lime in Jamaica, 877/424–8552 U.S.* ⊕ *www.chukkacaribbean.com.*

Jamaica Tours Limited. This operator offers several Ocho Rios tours with stops that include gardens and Dunn's River Falls. ☎ *876/974–6447* ⊕ *www.jamaicatoursltd.com.*

PORT ANTONIO

Tours in Port Antonia. Joanna Hart leads an in-depth cultural and historical tour of the Port Antonio area, incorporating the history of the Maroons. ⊠ *Port Antonio* ☎ *876/859–3758* ⊕ *www.toursinportantonio.com.*

KINGSTON

Numerous operators offer tours of the Kingston area, as well as excursions into the Blue Mountains. Professional tour operators provide a valuable service, as neither destination is particularly suited to exploration without a guide. In Kingston, certain areas can be dangerous; an organized tour provides a measure of security compared with going it alone. Think twice before roaming too freely in the Blue Mountains, as roads are narrow or in poor condition, and signs are few and far between.

Typical city tours include a city overview with stops at Devon House, the Bob Marley Museum, and Port Royal. Other tour options cover the Blue Mountains. Niche operators such as Olde Jamaica Heritage Tours provide theme tours, including a tour of churches and museums and one that visits the athletic grounds where Usain Bolt and other world sprinting champions have trained.

Jessa Tours, Ltd. Tours run by this company visit the Bob Marley Museum, the National Gallery, the craft market, and other heritage sites. ⊠ *19 Herb McKenley Dr., Kingston* ☎ *876/978–2259* ⊕ *www. jessatours.com.*

Olde Jamaica Tours. This company runs heritage, cultural, and sporting attraction tours. Island-wide trips are offered but the focus is on the Kingston area. As well as churches, great houses, and the like, Olde Jamaica Tours can also take visitors to the cricket field and to the athletics training ground where Usain Bolt and others have developed their sporting prowess. ⊠ *5 Cowper Dr., Kingston* ☎ *876/371–3613, 876/328–1385* ⊕ *www.oldejamaicatours.com.*

Sun Island Executive Tours & Services Ltd. This company offers tours to places of interest around Jamaica and can work with you to design your own itinerary. ⊠ *8 Bower Bank Ave., Kingston* ☎ *876/931–8826.*

SOUTH COAST

Countrystyle Community Experiences Tours. This company designs community experience tours combining your choice of accommodation—whether a homestay or in a hotel—with your special interests. The tours and other parts of the package showcase community lifestyles, helping you enjoy Jamaican culture, heritage, cuisine and music with a personal touch. The Community Experience tours—Jamaica Roots Experience, Jamaica Taste Experience, and Jamaica Nature

Experience—are offered in Kingston and Montego Bay, where you're matched up with residents based on your interests. ✉ *62 Ward Ave., Mandeville* ☎ *876/507–6326, 876/488–7207* ⊕ *www.jamaica-no-problem.com/community-tours.html, www.villagesasbusinesses.com.*

Jakes Biking Tour. Jakes can arrange for various tours throughout the area, whether biking or hiking. In this tour, a guide will take you around to places like the gorgeous stretch of sand at Fort Charles or Great Bay. Treasure Beach is quite flat, so almost all fitness levels can enjoy the tour. The three-hour tour is $60 per person. ✉ *Treasure Beach* ☎ *876/965–3000* ⊕ *www.jakeshotel.com.*

NEGRIL

Tropical Tours. This company offers Negril visitors a highlights tour with a look at the Lighthouse and a stop for shopping, as well as Rick's Cafe. The tours leave at 2 from Club Riu for shopping and the Lighthouse, and at 4 for Rick's Cafe. ✉ *Norman Manley Blvd., Negril* ☎ *876/957–4110 in Negril* ⊕ *www.tropicaltours-ja.com.*

HELICOPTER TOURS

MONTEGO BAY

Captain John's Island Hoppers. Departing from the domestic terminal of Montego Bay's Sangster International Airport, Captain John's Island Hoppers offers three helicopter tours of the Montego Bay area. The longest is the Western Showcase (US$1,280 for up to four persons), which flies as far away as Negril and the South Coast The Memories of Jamaica tour (US$640 for up to four persons) travels west over the cruise pier and over Round Hill. On Montego Bay Ecstasy Tour (US$440 for up to four persons) you fly east over Rose Hall. Tours also take place in Ocho Rios leaving from Reynold's Pier and, by request, from Rodney Street in Falmouth. ✉ *Sangster International Airport, Montego Bay* ☎ *876/952–1059* ⊕ *www.jamaicahelicopterservices.com.*

OCHO RIOS

Captain John's Island Hoppers (Ocho Rios). Just west of the small fort in Ocho Rios, Island Hoppers offers three helicopter tours of the region. The longest tour is the Jamaican Showcase (US$1,280 for up to four persons), circling over Spanish Town, Kingston, and the Blue Mountains. The Memories of Jamaica tour (US$640 for up to four persons) travels east to Port Maria for an aerial view of Noël Coward's and Ian Fleming's former homes. For diehard 007 fans, James Bond's Jamaica Tour (US$440 for up to four persons) provides a look at the sites made famous by the movies and novels. ✉ *Reynolds Pier, Ocho Rios* ☎ *876/974–1285* ⊕ *www.jamaicahelicopterservices.com.*

HIKING

PORT ANTONIO

Jamaica Explorations. The guided tours from this company include a Reich Falls excursion and a Blue Mountain hike. ✉ *Hotel Mocking Bird Hill, Port Antonio* ☎ *876/993–7267* ⊕ *www.jamaicaexplorations.com.*

14

HORSEBACK RIDING

MONTEGO BAY

Braco Stables. These stables are in the Braco area near Duncans in Trelawny, between Montego Bay and Ocho Rios. Two estate rides are offered a day for US$70, and riders are matched to horses based on riding ability. The trip also includes complimentary refreshments served poolside at the Braco great house. Experienced riders can also opt for a mountain ride ($100) for a more-rugged two-hour tour. ✉ *Braco, Duncans* ☎ *876/954–0185* ⊕ *www.bracostables.com and www.bracotours.com.*

OCHO RIOS

Annandale Plantation. The 600-acre plantation is high above Ocho Rios and today serves as a working farm; in its glory days it hosted dignitaries such as the Queen Mother. The great house is open for the tours. Horseback rides start at Drax Hall and include trails to the beach and, upon request, to the great house. ✉ *4 miles (6 km) southwest of Ocho Rios, near town of Epworth* ☎ *876/974–2323* ⊕ *tourwise.org.*

Fodor'sChoice **Chukka Caribbean Adventures.** Ocho Rios has excellent horseback riding,
★ and a great option is Chukka Caribbean's two-hour ride-and-swim tour, which takes you along Papillion Cove (where the 1973 movie *Papillion* was filmed), as well as locations used in *Return to Treasure Island* (1985) and *Passion and Paradise* (1988). The trail continues along the coastline to Chukka beach and a bareback ride in the sea. The tour costs US$74 for adults, US$52 for children. Note that Chukka also has another location west of Montego Bay at Sandy Bay, and that the outfitter handles many other activities and tours beyond just horseback riding. ✉ *Ocho Rios* ☎ *876/619–1441 Digicel in Jamaica, 876/656–8026 Lime in Jamaica, 877/424–8552 from U.S.* ⊕ *www. chukkacaribbean.com.*

Hooves. This stable offers several guided tours, including a popular 2½-hour beach ride ($85 from Ocho Rios, $89 from Runaway Bay) suitable for adults and children taller than three feet. The trip begins with a visit to the Seville Great House estate before making its way to the beach for a ride. Hooves is home to many rescue horses that have been rehabilitated. ✉ *Windsor Rd., St. Ann's Bay* ☎ *876/972–0905* ⊕ *www.hooves-jamaica.com.*

Prospect Plantation. The plantation offers a horseback rides for ages eight and older. The price (US$64) includes use of helmets; advance reservations are required. For the adventurous, Prospect Plantation also offers guided camel rides. ✉ *Rte. A1, about 3 miles (5 km) east of Ocho Rios* ☎ *876/974–5335* ⊕ *www.prospectplantationtours.com.*

SOUTH COAST

Paradise Park. This working farm has been owned and operated by the same family for more than 100 years. Visitors can take horseback rides to explore the farm's fields and pastures and the beaches on the property. Afterward you can take a dip in Sweet River, and have a picnic if you bring your own food. Rides are US$50 per person, and reservations must be made at least 24 hours in advance. ✉ *Rte. A2, 1 miles (2 km) west of Ferris Cross, Savannah-la-Mar* ☎ *876/955–2675.*

Rafting on the Rio Grande, near Port Antonio

NEGRIL

Rhodes Hall Eco Tours. Just 15 minutes from Negril, Rhodes Hall is a former sugar plantation that now offers eco tours and adventures in a nature reserve. A recent overhaul has seen the introduction of horseback riding, a nature walk trail, bird-watching, a crocodile lake, and an animal reserve featuring a bird sanctuary and peacock haven. Visitors may also snorkel, scuba dive, take a trip around the Samuel's Bay National Marine Park in a glass bottom boat or bathe in Rhodes Hall's Magic Blue Mud Mineral Spring Bath.

Also new to this facility is the addition of 27 ocean front rooms. Guests staying here receive a 20% discount off all Rhodes Hall Eco Tours. Day passes to Rhodes Hall are $10 and they assist with arranging transportation from Negril area hotels. ⊠ *Green Island, Hanover* ☎ *876/957–6422* ⊕ *www.rhodesresort.com.*

RIVER BOATING AND RAFTING

Jamaica's many rivers mean a multitude of freshwater experiences, from mild to wild. Jamaica's first tourist activity off the beaches was relaxing rafting trips aboard bamboo rafts poled by local boatmen. Soft-adventure enthusiasts can also opt for white-water action with guided tours through several operators.

Fodor'sChoice ★ Bamboo rafting in Jamaica originated on the **Río Grande,** a river in the Port Antonio area. Jamaicans had long used the bamboo rafts to transport bananas downriver; decades ago actor and Port Antonio resident Errol Flynn saw the rafts and thought they'd make a good tourist attraction, and local entrepreneurs quickly rose to the occasion. Today the slow rides are a favorite with romantic travelers and anyone looking to get off the beach for a few hours. The popularity of the Río Grande's trips spawned similar trips down the **Martha Brae River,** about 25 miles (40 km) from Mo'Bay. Near Ocho Rios, the **Great River** has lazy river rafting as well as energetic kayaking.

MONTEGO BAY

Jamaica Tours Limited. This big tour company conducts raft trips down at Martha Brae, approximately 12 miles (19 km) east of Mo'Bay; the excursion can include lunch if requested. Bookings can be made through hotel tour desks. Price depends on the number of people on the trip and your pickup location. They also offer several other tours as well as airport transfers. ⊠ *Providence Dr., Montego Bay* ☎ *876/953–3700* ⊕ *www.jamaicatoursltd.com.*

River Raft Ltd. This company leads trips down the Martha Brae River, about 25 miles (40 km) from most hotels in Mo'Bay. The cost is $60 per person for the 1½-hour river run. ⊠ *Martha Brae* ☎ *876/940–6398* ⊕ *www.jamaicarafting.com.*

SOUTH COAST

FAMILY **South Coast Safaris Ltd.** This company takes visitors on slow boat cruises (US$20) up the river. Keep an eye peeled for crocodiles basking on the banks and swimming in the water—the boat captain has pet names for some of them. The cruise also passes through a thick mangrove area where you can see egrets and other birds. Back at the landing stage there is a crocodile nursery where visitors are shown the young crocs being raised for release into the wild. ⊠ *1 Crane St., Black River* ☎ *876/965–2513* ⊕ *www.jamaica-southcoast.com.*

SAILING

MONTEGO BAY

Dreamer Catamaran Cruises. Dreamer Catamaran Cruises offers sails on four catamarans ranging from 53 to 65 feet. The cruise (US$83) includes a snorkel stop and a visit to Margaritaville before the final leg of the cruise. There are foot massages for women, followed by dance instruction for all. Children are allowed on only the morning and sunset cruises. ⊠ *Cornwall Beach, Gloucester Ave., Montego Bay* ☎ *876/979–0102* ⊕ *www.dreamercatamarans.com.*

PORT ANTONIO

Errol Flynn Marina. This official national port of entry has 24-hour customs and immigration services. The 32-berth marina, reached via a deepwater channel, includes 24-hour security, an Internet center, a swimming pool, a laundry, and a 100-ton boat lift, and the only facility in the area which can handle vessels up to 600 feet. There are also scuba diving and other water sports attractions onsite. ⊠ *Ken Wright Dr., Port Antonio* ☎ *876/715–6044* ⊕ *www.errolflynnmarina.com.*

MARTINIQUE

WELCOME TO MARTINIQUE

PARIS IN THE TROPICS

The largest of the Windward Islands, Martinique is 425 square miles (1,101 square km). The southern part of the island is all rolling hills and sugarcane fields; it's also where you'll find the best beaches and most development. In the north are craggy cliffs, lush vegetation, and one of the Caribbean's largest volcanoes, Mont Pelée.

Restaurants ▼	Hotels ▼
Chez Les Pecheurs 4	Cap Est Lagoon 8
Fleur de Sel 9	Club Med Buccaneer's Creek 9
La Cave à Vins 1	Engoulevent 2
La Table de Mamy Nounou 6	Hotel Bakoua 10
Le Bélem 8	Hotel L'Impératrice 1
Le Colibri 5	Hotel La Caravelle 6
Le Foyall 2	Hotel Plein Soleil 7
Le Petibonum 3	Hotel Villa St. Pierre 3
Le Plein Soleil 7	La Suite Villa 11
Le Zandoli 10	Le Domaine St. Aubin ... 5
Restaurant Le Golf 11	Le Hameau du Morne des Cadets 4

0 ___ 5 mi
0 ___ 5 km

KEY
➤ Beaches
❶ Restaurants
① Hotels

Joie de vivre is the credo in this French enclave, which is often characterized as a Caribbean suburb of Paris. Exotic fruit grows on the volcanoes' forested flanks amid a profusion of wild orchids and hibiscus. The sheer lushness of it all inspired the tropical paintings of onetime resident Paul Gauguin.

Basse-Pointe

ATLANTIC OCEAN

D21
N3
N1
Le Lorrain
Marigot

Morne Jakob

5 Ste-Marie **5**

Havre de la Trinité

Anse Tartane

Caravelle Peninsula

Presqu'île du Caravelle

Dubuc Castle

Tartane

6 6

Pointe Caracoli

La Trinité

D1
D2
N4

Baie du Galion

Pitons du Carbet

N3

St-Joseph

Balata

Gros-Morne

Le Robert

Havre du Robert

N1

Pte. Larose

Le Plein Soleil

7 7

8 8

2
N4
Schoelcher
Fort-de-France

1 2 1

N1

Lamentin

Le François

Baie des Flamands

Lamentin International Airport

Mt. Vauclin

Baie de Fort-de-France
Anse-à-l'Ane

Pointe du Bout
N5

Anse-Mitan

Ducos

N6

Le Vauclin

Pointe Bout

11 Les Trois-Îlets

9 – 11

Rivière Salée

10

D7
D7
N5

Forêt de Montravail

Mt. Bigot

Anse-d'Arlets

Le Diamant

D37
D7

Diamant Beach

D17
D18

Rivière-Pilote

D18A
N5

Ste-Luce

N6

Le Marin

Anse Corps de Garde
Pte. Figuier

Pointe du Marin

Cap Chevalier

9 D9

Ste-Anne

Baie des Anglais

Diamond Rock

Cul-de-Sac du Marin

La Savane (Petrified Forest)

Les Salines

Anse-Trabaud

Grande Anse

Pte. d'Enfer

Pte. des Salines

15

MARTINIQUE

TOP REASONS TO VISIT MARTINIQUE

1 **The Romance:** A magical sensuality infuses everything; it will awaken dormant desires and fuel existing fires.

2 **Beautiful Beaches:** A full roster of beautiful beaches will let you enjoy sun and sand.

3 **The French Connection:** Excellent French food, not to mention French music and fashion, makes the island a paradise for those in search of the finer things.

4 **Range of Accommodations:** Hospitable, stylish small hotels abound; big resorts, too. Or play expat in a private, luxe villa.

5 **Inviting Waters:** The sea, Caribbean; the ocean, Atlantic—experience the water in a kayak or on a sailboat. Even a ferry works.

Updated by
Eileen Robin-
son Smith

Numerous scattered ruins and other historical monuments reflect the richness of Martinique's sugarcane plantation past, *rhum,* and the legacy of slavery. Called the Rum Capital of the World, it is widely considered the best gourmet island in the Caribbean. It stirs the passions with its distinctive brand of culinary offerings. If you believe in magic, Martinique has it, along with a sensuality that fosters romance. It has become known as the island of *revenants,* those who always return. *Et pourquoi non?*

Martinique is simply one of the most enchanting destinations in the Western Hemisphere. Francophiles adore this island for its food, rum, *musique,* and élan, and the availability of the finest French products, from Chanel fashions to Limoges china. It is endowed with lots of tropical beauty, including white-sand beaches and rain forests. The volcano Mont Pelée looms over the harbor town of St-Pierre, known as the Pompeii of the Caribbean. Its largest city, Fort-de-France, comes with lots of charm as well as some great restaurants and clubs. Martinicans will be glad you came, and you will be greeted with warm smiles and politesse.

Christopher Columbus first sighted this gorgeous island in 1502, when it was inhabited by the fierce Caraïbes, who had terrorized the peaceloving Arawaks. The Arawaks called their home Madinina (the Isle of Flowers), and for good reason. Exotic wild orchids, frangipani, anthurium, jade vines, flamingo flowers, and hundreds of vivid varieties of hibiscus still thrive here.

The island reflects its rich cultural history. In colonial days Martinique was the administrative, social, and cultural center of the French Antilles; this rich, aristocratic island was famous for its beautiful women. The island even gave birth to an empress, Napoléon's Joséphine. It saw the full flowering of a society ruled by planters, with servants and soirees, wine cellars, and lots of snobbery.

Martinique's economy still depends on *les bananes* (bananas), *l'ananas* (pineapples), cane sugar, rum, and fishing. It's also the largest remaining stronghold of the *békés*—the descendants of the original French planters—and they are still the privileged class on any of the French-Caribbean islands. Numbering around 4,000, many control Martinique's most profitable businesses, from banana plantations and rum distilleries to car dealerships. The elite dress in designer outfits straight off the Paris runways. In general, the islanders have style. In the airport waiting room you can almost always tell the Martiniquaises by their fashionable clothes.

Of the island's 400,000 inhabitants, 100,000 live in Fort-de-France and its environs. It has 34 separate municipalities. Though the actual number of French residents from the Metropole (France) does not exceed 15% of the total population, Martinique is a part of France, an overseas *département* to be exact, and French is the official language, though the vast majority of the residents also speak Creole.

Thousands are employed in government jobs offering more paid holidays than most Americans can imagine. Martinicans work hard and enjoy their time off, celebrating everything from *le fin de la semaine* (the weekend) to Indian feast days, sailboat races, and Carnival. Their joie de vivre is infectious. Once you experience it, you'll be back.

PLANNING

WHEN TO GO

High season runs from mid-December through mid-April, and the island can be quiet the rest of the year, with some hotels closing down for months, particularly in September and October. Those places that remain open offer discounts. Check ⊕ *www.martinique.org* for the latest deals.

GETTING HERE AND AROUND

AIR TRAVEL

There are now nonstop flights from the United States on American Airlines, flying out of Miami twice a week. New service by Seaborne Airlines has flights leaving four times a week from San Juan. Most travelers are able to connect in San Juan or in Miami and to Air France, as well, which departs Miami three times a week with a stop in a neighboring island.

Air Antilles Express flies to Martinique from Guadeloupe, St. Maarten, St. Barth, Cayenne, French Guiana, St. Lucia, and Santo Domingo. ☎ *0890/64–86–48, 0596/42–16–71, 0596/42–16–72* ⊕ *www.airantilles.com.* **Air Canada** flies every Saturday from Montreal to Martinique, and on Tuesday from early January to early April. The return flight is just on Sunday. If you live near the Canadian border this may be your best option. ☎ *1-888/247–2262* ⊕ *www.aircanada.com.* **Air Caraïbes** flies to Martinique, Guadeloupe, St. Martin, St. Barth, Guyane, Haiti and St. Lucia and the Dominican Republic (Santo Domingo). (This airline offers substantial discounts for seniors on some routes.) ☎ *0820/*

15

83–58–35, 0590/82–47–47 Guad. reservation ⊕ *www.aircaraibes.com.*
Air France has service to and from Miami, with stops in neighboring
islands, three times a week in the winter season. ☎ *0820/82–08–20,*
0892/68–29–72, 0596/55–34–72, 800/237–27–47 in U.S., 0596/82–
61–61 ⊕ *www.airfrance.com.* **American Airlines** uses a Boeing 737 aircraft for its new, twice weekly service from Miami; it flies nonstop on
Saturday and Wednesday. ☎ *800/433–7300* ⊕ *www.aa.com.* **LIAT** connects Martinique with the English-speaking "down islands," like St.
Lucia, Barbados, and Antigua. It also flies into San Juan, the Dominican
Republic, the U.S. and British Virgin Islands, and more. LIAT code-
shares with Air Caraïbes. ■**TIP**➜ **Daily flights from Saint-Lucia (UVF)—**
which has direct service from New York, Miami, Atlanta and Toronto—is
one way for U.S. and Canadian visitors to get to Martinique with fewer
stopovers. ☎ *0596/42–16–11* ⊕ *www.liatairline.com.* **Seaborne Airlines**
now flies to Martinique four times a week out of San Juan. The airline
uses a SAAB 340B aircraft, offering the comfort of 34 economy class
seats, with in-flight service. Flights are timed for connections to and
from the United States and Canada. A new code-share program between
American Airlines and Seaborne Airlines now allows you to book your
American Airlines and Seaborne Airlines combined itinerary on the AA
website, while earning AAdvantage program miles. ☎ *866/359–8784*
⊕ *www.seaborneairlines.com.*

AIRPORT

Martinique Aimé Césaire Airport. Martinique Aimé Césaire Airport, in the
commercial area of Lamentin, is relatively small and easy to maneuver; some staff members speak English. The airport is 15 minutes from
Fort-de-France via taxi; it's 40 minutes from Les Trois-Ilets Peninsula.
✉ *FDF, Lamentin* ☎ *0596/42–16–00.*

CAR TRAVEL

The main highways, about 175 miles (280 km) of well-paved and well-
marked roads, are excellent, but only in a few areas are they lighted at
night. Many hotels are on roads that are barely passable, so get wherever you're going by nightfall or you could lose your way. Then tell
a stranger, *"Je suis perdu!"* ("I am lost!"). It elicits sympathy. If they
say, *"Suivez-moi!"*—that's "Follow me!"—stay glued to their bumper.
Finally, drive defensively; although Martinicans are polite and lovely
people, they drive with aggressive abandon.

Martinique, especially Fort-de-France and environs, is plagued with
heavy traffic; if you must drive into Fort-de-France, do it on a weekend. Absolutely avoid the Lamentin Airport area and Fort-de-France
during weekday rush hours, roughly 7 to 10 am and 4 to 7:30 pm,
and on Sunday night going in the direction of Fort-de-France. That's
when everyone comes off the beaches and heads back to the city. Even
smaller towns such as La Trinité have rush hours. Watch, too, for *dos*
d'ânes (literally, donkey backs), speed bumps that are hard to spot—
particularly at night. Gas is costly, some $US6.50 per gallon. Diesel is
somewhat cheaper, around $5.20, but if you rent an economy car for
a full week, you should budget at least $100 for fuel.

LOGISTICS

Getting to Martinique: There are now nonstop flights from the United States aboard American Airlines, departing from Miami twice weekly. There are also year-round, nonstop, direct flights from Montreal, with connections from most major cities. A new carrier, Seaborne Airlines, now flies to Martinique four times a week out of San Juan; it code-shares with American Airlines which allows you to book your American Airlines and Seaborne Airlines combined itinerary on the AA website while earning AAdvantage program miles.

Many travelers can connect in San Juan or Miami. Air Canada flies to Martinique every Sunday. A second flight on Tuesday is available January 8–April 9. Air Antilles Express flies from Guadeloupe, St. Maarten, and St. Barth. Air Caraïbes flies from Guadeloupe, St. Maarten, St. Barth, and Santo Domingo. (This airline offers substantial discounts for seniors on its shorter flights.) Air France is another connection option; during the peak tourist season (winter), it has service from Miami three times a week, with stops in neighboring islands. LIAT connects Martinique with the English-speaking "down islands" such as St. Lucia. Other airlines, including Air Antilles Express, also offer service to Martinique from nearby islands (some of which are also connected to Martinique by ferries).

Hassle Factor: Medium to high.

On the Ground: Taxis in Martinique are expensive, so factor airport-transfer costs into your vacation budget. From the airport to Fort-de-France, you'll pay at least €30 (€40 at night or on Sunday); from the airport to Pointe du Bout, it's about €50 (€60 at night or on Sunday); fares to François or Tartane are approximately €60 (€70 at night or on Sunday). If you arrive at night or on Sunday, depending on where your hotel is, it may be cheaper (although not safer) to rent a car from the airport and keep it for 24 hours than to take a taxi to your hotel. ■ TIP➔ **Better yet, stay closer to the airport or in Fort de France, pick up your rent-a-car after a good night's sleep, and then navigate to your resort.**

Be aware that the French gendarmes set up roadblocks, often on Sunday, to stop speeders and drunk drivers, and just to check papers. Now they even have video cameras on the highways. Visitors are not absolved from speeding tickets, because you can be tracked down through the rental car's license plate.

Renting a Car: It's worth the hassle to rent a car—if only for a day or two—so that you can explore more of this beautiful island. Just be prepared for a manual shift, steep mountainous roads, and heavy traffic. Prices are expensive, about €70 per day or €400 per week (unlimited mileage) for a manual shift, perhaps more for an automatic, which must be ordered in advance (and not all agencies have them). You may save money by waiting to book your car rental on the island for a reduced weekly rate from a local agency. Some of the latter, though, make up their own rules, and they will not be in your favor. There's an extra charge (about $20) if you drop the car off at the airport after having rented it somewhere else on the island. A valid U.S. driver's license or International Driver's Permit is needed to rent a car for up to 20 days. ■TIP→ Often, the airline you fly in with will have a discount coupon for a rental car, right on the ticket, or in their in-flight magazine. Also, local publications have ads with discounts that can be as much as 40% off (in low season). You can find these at the Tourism Information counter in the airport.

Contacts **Avis.** This is one of the agencies that will have an automatic; reserve it as far in advance as possible. ☎ *0596/42–11–00* ⊕ *www. avis-antilles.fr.* **Budget.** A presence on island for 20 years, Budget has three locations, the airport location is the one that is open the most hours. ✉ *Martinique Aimé Césaire Airport, Lamentin* ☎ *0596/42–04– 04* ⊕ *www.budget-martinique.com.* **Europcar.** Europcar will sometimes deliver the car to you and pick it up later, and its rates are usually among the lowest. The downside is that employees don't usually speak English. That said, at its location near the airport, which is behind a gas station on the national road, there are several English-speaking employees who are particularly helpful. If you go first to the Europcar counter at the airport a shuttle will transport you to the site. With advance notice, you can get an automatic. ☎ *0596/42–42–42* ⊕ *www. europcar-martinque.com.* **Hertz.** Hertz has the advantage of three locations, more multilingual staffers and the assurance that you are dealing with a U.S. franchise. Like in the states, it's more expensive than most, but they have some automatics including BMWs, as well as French cars, both economy and higher-end models. ✉ *Martinique Aime Cesare Airport, Lamentin* ☎ *0596/51–01–01, 0810/32–31–13* ⊕ *www.hertzantilles.com or www.hertzantilles.com/location_voiture_ martinique.* **JumboCar.** Of the many agencies, JumboCar is the most likely to cut a deal (but few of its staffers speak English). The airport location is open until 10 pm. They have a large selection of cars, more standard and economy models, but they do have some convertibles; automatics may be possible with advance reservations. ✉ *Martinique Aimé Césaire Aéroport, Lamentin* ☎ *0596/42–16–99, 0820/22–02–30* ⊕ *www.jumbocar.com.* **Sixt.** This well-oiled operation is the agency most likely to have automatics and higher-end cars, notably BMWs, as well as more affordable options. ✉ *Martinique Aimé Césaire Airport, Lamentin* ☎ *0596/42–17–01* ⊕ *www.sixt.fr.*

FERRY TRAVEL

Weather permitting, *vedettes* (ferries) operate daily between Quai d'Esnambuc in Fort-de-France and the marinas in Pointe du Bout, Anse-Mitan, and Anse-à-l'Ane and are the best way to go into the capital. Any of these trips takes about 20 minutes. Ferries depart every 30 minutes on weekdays; less often in the low season. Round-trip tickets cost €6.50.

Contacts **Compagnie Maritime West Indies.** Compagnie Maritime West Indies provides rapid sea shuttle service from neighboring St. Lucia. Boats (capacity 15 persons) usually depart daily at 11 am and 4 pm from Castries, St. Lucia. Fares are approximately €89 for adults and €69 for children. The departures from Le Marin are at 8 am and 1:30 pm. A number of airlines fly into St. Lucia, so making arrangements to land there and take Compagnie can be a good way to get to Martinique (especially if you are staying at Club Med or another resort in the south). ☎ *0696/21–77–76, 0758/452–8757 in St. Lucia, 0758/45–81–61 in St. Lucia, 0696/45–12–00* ⊕ *www.sail-stlucia.com*. **Jeans for Freedom.** This branch of the L'Express des Îles company goes between Pointe-à-Pitre, Guadeloupe, and St-Pierre, Martinique; it also makes a brief stop in Dominica; the price is now up to €79. In Guadeloupe, service is also available between Pointe-à-Pitre and Marie-Galante or Les Saintes for €19. Jeans also runs specials like a day-trip out of Fort-de-France to St. Lucia for €89 round-trip. ⊠ *Pl. du Marche, rue Victor Hugo, St-Pierre* ☎ *0825/01–01–25, 0596/78–11–50* ⊕ *www.jeansforfreedom.com*. **L'Express des Îles.** *L'Express des Îles* connects Martinique with Dominica, St. Lucia, Guadeloupe—it also services Guadeloupe's "out-islands." Each one-way trip is €75. The crossings generally take between three and four hours; if it is raining and the waters are choppy, it can be a rough passage. However, the newest ferry is much larger and stabilized and gives a smooth ride. French films (sometimes R-rated) on flat screens help pass the time. Most of these services are daily, with extra departures on weekends and holidays or for special events—the ferries can often get crowded then. Boats depart from the Terminal Inter Îles–Quai Ouest in Fort-de-France; head there for to-go options that are better than what the boats' snack bars carry; boat doesn't always get its food delivery, so it pays to bring some snacks aboard. There are discounted fares for babies, youths, seniors, and families. Note that the ferry charges for luggage that exceeds its weight limits. If traveling from Martinique to Dominica, Guadeloupe, or St. Lucia, a passenger is allowed three pieces of luggage that weigh no more than 25 kg (55 pounds) each; if traveling from Guadeloupe to its out-islands, Les Saintes and Marie-Galante you're allowed one less bag. In either direction, you're also allowed to carry on one piece of baggage that weighs 10 kg (22 pounds) or less. Be aware that this ferry company also follows airline rules for what you're allowed to pack inside checked and carry-on baggage; check the website for more information. ⊠ *Terminal Inter Isles Quai Ouest, Fort-de-France* ☎ *0825/35–90–00, 0596/63–12–11* ⊕ *www.express-des-iles.com*.

TAXI TRAVEL

Taxis, which are metered, are expensive, though you can try bargaining by offering to pay a flat rate to your destination or offering them an hourly rate—try for €40, but you may have to compromise at €50.

Contacts J. Peloponese Taxis. J. Peloponese Taxis provides luxury service in new Mercedes-Benz cars. The taxis have meters but you can also arrange an hourly rate for touring. English speaking, politeness, and patience are characteristics. ☎ *0696/25–61–02*. **M. Martial Mercedes Taxis.** Drivers of M. Martial Mercedes Taxis speak English, Spanish, and German as well as French. ☎ *0596/64–20–24, 0696/45–69–07 mobile*. **Taxi de Place.** At this government-designated stand, you will find some English-speaking drivers, lots of courtesy, and new SUVs. ⊠ *Rue Victoire sévre, Fort-de-France* ☎ *0596/60–59–12*.

ESSENTIALS

Banks and Exchange Services The euro is the official currency in Martinique. U.S. dollars are accepted in some hotels, but generally at an unfavorable rate. You can usually get the best rate by withdrawing euros from ATMs, which you'll find at the airport and at branches of the Crédit Agricole and other major banks. Be aware that your bank will probably charge $5 for each foreign withdrawal; the ATM will advise you of its fee before they release the cash. Consequently, it may make sense to take the maximum amount allowed out at one time, but be diligent about stashing the cash in your hotel safe. Most hotels and restaurants accept major credit cards, but this is somewhat less common once you get away from Fort-de-France and Pointe du Bout. Many establishments don't accept American Express in any case. There is a change office at the beginning of Ernest Deproge Street next to the Banque Francaise. Change Caraïbes is at 14 rue Victor Hugo and Le Bord de Mer.

Electricity 220-volt outlets. North American appliances require a converter and an adapter.

Emergency Services Ambulance ☎ *15, 0596/71–15–75.* **Fire** ☎ *18.* **Police** ☎ *17.*

Passport Requirements All visitors must have a valid passport and a return or ongoing ticket.

Phones To call Martinique from the United States, dial 011–596–596 plus the local six-digit number (yes, you must dial *596 twice*). To call the United States from Martinique, dial 001, then the area code, then the local number.

Taxes and Service Charges A resort tax varies from city to city. Each has its own tax, with most between €0.76 and €1.25 per person per day; the maximum is €2.25. Rates quoted by hotels usually include a 10% service charge.

Tipping All restaurants include a 15% service charge in their menu prices. You can always add to this if you feel that service was particularly good. Although you may have some initial sticker shock at the prices, remember that they include the tax and tip.

ACCOMMODATIONS

At Martinique, you can stay in tiny inns called *relais créoles,* boutique hotels, and private villas as well as splashy tourist resorts and restored plantation houses. Several hotels are clustered in Point du Bout on Les Trois-Ilets Peninsula, which is connected to Fort-de-France by ferry. Other clusters are in Ste-Luce, and Le François has become known for its boutique properties. Hotels and relais can be found all over the island. Because Martinique is the largest of the Windward Islands, this can mean a substantial drive to your hotel after a long flight or ferry trip. You may want to stay closer to the airport on your first night—for instance, at the Hotel Galleria, a no-nonsense hotel within a shopping mall just 10 minutes from the airport, or at a hotel in Fort-de-France. If you need to make a last-minute hotel reservation, head for the Tourism Information counter in the airport arrival hall (☎ *0596/42–18–05*); it is open between 8 am and 9 pm every day except Sunday, when it's open from 2 pm to 9 pm.

MARTINIQUE TRANSPORTATION TIPS

Taxi: Taxis in Martinique are expensive, and you will pay more after dark. From the airport to Fort-de-France you'll pay at least €30 during the day, €40 at night; from the airport to Pointe du Bout, it's about €50 (€60 at night); to François or Tartane, the fare is approximately €60 (€70 at night). A 40% surcharge is levied between 7 pm and 6 am and on Sunday. If you arrive at night, depending on where your hotel is, it may be cheaper (although not safer) to rent a car from the airport and keep it for 24 hours than to take a taxi to your hotel.

Car Rental: Be prepared for a manual shift, steep mountainous roads, and heavy traffic. Prices are about €70 per day or €400 per week (unlimited mileage), substantially more for an automatic, which is rare. Usually, you won't find them unless you book in advance.

Alternative Transportation: Locals take *collectifs* (white vans holding up to 10 passengers) that cost just a few euros and depart from Pointe Simon, on the waterfront in Fort-de-France, to all parts of the island. Don't be shy; the difference can be €3 versus, say, €60 for a taxi to reach the same destination. Drivers don't usually speak English, and there's no a/c.

Bus Mozaik. The air-conditioned buses of this private company stop within the city; they service Lamentin, Fort-de-France suburbs such as Schoelcher, and as far into the interior of the island as St. Joseph. Buses leave from Pointe Simon, on the waterfront, where the public buses and shared-taxis (white vans) congregate. Fares start at €1.20. For schedules, visit *www.aquelleheure. fr/bus.htm.* ⊕ *www.aquelleheure.fr/ bus.htm.*

The tourist offices can help with maps and information.

15

Large Resorts: There are only a few deluxe properties on the island. Those that lack megastar ratings offer an equally appealing mixture of charisma, hospitality, and French style. Larger hotels often have the busy, slightly frenetic feel that the French seem to like.

Relais Créoles: Small, individually owned inns are still available on Martinique, though they may be far removed from the resorts.

Villas: Groups and large families can save money by renting a villa, but the language barrier can be problematic, and often you will need a car.

HOTEL AND RESTAURANT PRICES

Prices in the restaurant reviews are the average cost of a main course at dinner or, if dinner is not served, at lunch; taxes and service charges are generally included. Prices in the hotel reviews are the lowest cost of a standard double room in high season, excluding taxes, service charges, and meal plans (except at all-inclusives). Prices for rentals are the lowest per-night cost for a one-bedroom unit in high season.

For expanded lodging reviews and current deals, visit Fodors.com.

VISITOR INFORMATION
Contacts **Comité Martiniquais du Tourisme** ✉ *Immeuble Beaupre, Pointe de Jaham, Schoelcher, Fort-de-France* ☎ *0596/61–61–77* ⊕ *www.martiniquetourisme.com.* **Martinique Promotion Bureau** ✉ *825 3rd Ave., 29th fl., New York, New York, USA* ☎ *212/838–6887 in New York* ⊕ *www.martinique.org.* **Office du Tourisme de Fort-de-France** ✉ *76 rue Lazare Carnot, Fort-de-France* ☎ *0596/60–27–73* ⊕ *www.tourismefdf.com.*

WEDDINGS
Martinique has a long residency requirement, so it's not really feasible to plan a wedding on the island. It is, however, a very romantic place for honeymoons.

EXPLORING

The northern part of the island will appeal to nature lovers, hikers, and mountain climbers. The drive from Fort-de-France to St-Pierre is particularly impressive, as is the one across the island, via Morne Rouge, from the Caribbean to the Atlantic. This is Martinique's wild side—a place of waterfalls, rain forest, and mountains. The highlight is Mont Pelée. The south is the more developed half of the island, where the resorts and restaurants are located, as well as the beaches.

FORT-DE-FRANCE

With its historic fort and superb location beneath the towering Pitons du Carbet on the Baie des Flamands, Martinique's capital—home to about one-quarter of the island's 400,000 inhabitants—should be a grand place. It hasn't been for decades, but it's now coming up fast. An ambitious redevelopment project, still under way, hopes to make it one of the most attractive cities in the Caribbean. Already done is the renovation of the park La Savane and the construction of a spectacular waterfront promenade. Also on the radar is the Pointe Simon Business and Tourist Center, which will include a 100-room hotel and luxury apartment building. The apartments are now being heavily advertised for sale, but the hotel will take some time to open. The striking 215,000-square-foot Cour Perrinon Mall, bordered by rue Perrinon, houses a Carrefour supermarket, a bookstore, perfume shops, designer boutiques, a French bakery, and a café–brasserie. Near the mall is the Hôtel de Ville (mayor's office), in a gorgeous and ornate building.

There is a small Office of Tourism de Fort-de-France at 76 rue Lazare Carnot. It has some brochures in English and helpful, English-speaking staffers. They can organize English-language tours with advance notice. Walking tours are scheduled for Wednesday and Friday at 9 am. They take in a number of historic sites in about an hour and 45 minutes and cost €12. Another Point d'Information Touristique is near the cathedral, at the junction of rues Antoine Siger and Victor Schoelcher.

The new Stewards Urbains, easily recognized by their red caps and uniforms, are able to answer most visitor questions about the city and

Anglers sit on a dock in Fort-de-France harbor.

give directions. These young gals and *garçons* are multilingual and knowledgeable. When a large cruise ship is in port, they are out in force, positioned in heavily trafficked tourist zones and at the front entrance of Lafayette's department store.

The most pleasant districts of Fort-de-France—Didier, Bellevue, and Schoelcher—are up on the hillside, and you need a car (or a taxi) to reach them. But if you try to drive here, you may find yourself trapped in gridlock in the narrow streets downtown. Parking is difficult, and it's best to try for one of the garages or—as a second choice—outdoor public parking areas. Come armed with some euro coins for this purpose. A taxi or ferry from Pointe du Bout may be a better alternative. Even if your hotel isn't there, you can drive to the marina and park nearby.

There are some fine shops with Parisian wares (at Parisian prices), including French lingerie, St. Laurent clothes, Cacharel perfume, and sexy stiletto heels. Near the harbor is a lively indoor marketplace (*grand marché*), where produce and spices are sold.

A playground on the Malecon, which now has a half-mile wooden boardwalk, has swings, trampolines, benches, and grounds for playing *pétanque*. The urban beach between the Malecon and the fort, La Française, is covered with white sand that was brought in.

TOP ATTRACTIONS

La Savane. The heart of Fort-de-France, La Savane is a 12½-acre park filled with trees, fountains, and benches. A massive revitalization, completed in 2010, made it the focal point of the city again, with entertainment, shopping, and a pedestrian mall. Attractive wooden stands have been constructed along the edge of the park that house a tourism information office, public restrooms, arts-and-crafts vendors, a crepe stand, an ice-cream stand, and numerous other eateries. There are some homeless types around, but everyone considers them harmless.

The Hotel L'Imperatrice, directly across from the park, has become a real gathering place—particularly for its café, which opens to the sidewalk. The hotel also has one of the best kiosks in the area for lunch and snacks.

Diagonally across from La Savane, you can catch the ferries for the 20-minute run across the bay to Pointe du Bout and the beaches at Anse-Mitan and Anse-à-l'Ane. It's relatively cheap as well as stress-free—much safer, more pleasant, and faster than by car.

The most imposing historic site in Fort-de-France is **Ft. St-Louis**, which runs along the east side of La Savane. Now a military installation, it's closed to the public.

WORTH NOTING

Bibliothèque Schoelcher. This wildly elaborate Romanesque public library was named after Victor Schoelcher, who led the fight to free the slaves in the French West Indies in the 19th century. The eye-popping, historic structure was built for the 1889 Paris Exposition, after which it was dismantled, shipped to Martinique, and reassembled piece by piece. ⊠ *At rue de la Liberté, which runs along west side of La Savane* ☎ *0596/55–68–30* 🎫 *Free* ☯ *Mon. 1–5, Tues.–Thurs. 8:30–5:30, Fri. 8:30–5, Sat. 8:30–noon.*

Le Musée Régional d'Histoire et d'Ethnographie. This museum is best undertaken at the beginning of your vacation, so you can better understand the history, background, and people of the island. Housed in an elaborate former residence (circa 1888) with balconies and fretwork, the museum displays some of the garish gold jewelry that prostitutes wore after emancipation as well as the sorts of rooms that a proper, middle-class Martinican would have lived in. Oil paintings, engravings, and old historical documents also help sketch out the island's culture. ⊠ *10 bd. Général de Gaulle* ☎ *0596/72–81–87* 🎫 *€3* ☯ *Mon. and Wed.–Fri. 8:30–5, Tues. 2–5, Sat. 8:30–12:30.*

Rue Victor Schoelcher. Stores sell Paris fashions and French perfume, china, crystal, and liqueurs, as well as local handicrafts along this street running through the center of the capital's primary shopping district, a six-block area bounded by rue de la République, rue de la Liberté, rue Victor Severe, and rue Victor Hugo.

St-Louis Cathedral. This Romanesque cathedral with lovely stained-glass windows was built in 1878, the sixth church on this site (the others were destroyed by fires, hurricanes, and earthquakes). ⊠ *Rue Victor Schoelcher* ☯ *Dawn—dusk.*

SOUTH OF FORT-DE-FRANCE

LE FRANÇOIS

With some 16,000 inhabitants, this is the main city on the Atlantic coast. Many of the old wooden buildings remain and are juxtaposed with concrete structures. The classic West Indian cemetery, with its black-and-white tiles, is still here, and a marina is at the end of town. Two of Martinique's best hotels are in this area, as well as some of the most upscale residences. Le François is also noted for its snorkeling. Offshore are the privately owned Ilets de l'Impératrice. The islands received that name because, according to legend, this is where Empress Joséphine came to bathe in the shallow basins known as *les fonds blanc* because of their white-sand bottoms. Group boat tours leave from the harbor and include lunch and drinks. Prices vary (⇨ *Sports and Activities*). You can also haggle with a fisherman to take you out for a while on his boat. There's a fine bay 6 miles (10 km) farther along the coast where you can swim and go kayaking. The town itself is rather lackluster but authentic, and you'll find a number of different shops and supermarkets, owned by truly lovely, helpful residents.

15

TOP ATTRACTIONS

Fodor's Choice ★ **Habitation Clément.** Get a glimpse into Martinique's colonial past. Visitors are given a multilingual audio headset, which explains tour highlights Signage further describes the rum-making process and other aspects of plantation life. The Palm Grove, with an avenue of palms and park benches, is delightful. It was all built with the wealth generated by its rum distillery, and its 18th-century splendor has been lovingly preserved. The plantation's creole house illustrates the adaption to life in the tropics up through the 20th century. An early French typewriter, a crank-up telephone, and decades-old photos of the Clements and Hayots (béké families), are juxtaposed with modern Afro-Caribbean art. Enjoy the free tastings at the bar of the retail shop. Consider the Canne Bleu, Grappe Blanche, or one of the aged rums, some bottled as early as 1952. ■ TIP→ Children get a discount, but so do parents with children! Also, allow 1½–2 hours to see everything. The ticket office closes at 5. ⊠ *Domaine de l'Acajou, Le François* ☎ *0596/54–62–07* ⊕ *www.habitation-clement.fr* ☜ €12 ☉ *Daily 9–5.*

LES TROIS-ILETS

Named after the three rocky islands nearby, this lovely little village (population 3,000) has unusual brick-and-wood buildings roofed with antique tiles. It's known for its pottery, straw, and woodwork, but above all as the birthplace of Napoléon's empress, Joséphine. In the square, where there's also a market and a fine *mairie* (town hall), you can visit the simple church where she was baptized Marie-Joseph Tascher de la Pagerie. The Martinicans have always been enormously proud of Joséphine, even though her husband reintroduced slavery on the island and most historians consider her to have been rather shallow.

WORTH NOTING

La Savane des Esclaves (*The Savannah of the Slaves*). Down a dirt road, in the countryside outside the tourist zone, stands La Savane des Esclaves, a re-created slave village (circa 1800). This labor of love was created by Gilbert Larose, who has a fascination with his ancestors who were "Nèg'Marrons," slaves who fled the plantations to live free, off the land.

The Antan Lontan Village, the name Larose gave his settlement, reveals much about this major element in Martinique's history and culture, with food tastings and artisan demonstrations. Shows utilizing the various groups of Martinican folklorico dancers are held several times a year, both in the day and by night. On Saturdays from 9 am to noon, there are often more elaborate tastings, demonstrations, and traditional dance lessons. Allow an hour and 15 minutes for the guided tour in French. ✉ *Quartier La Ferme* ☎ *0596/68–33–91* ⊕ *www.lasavanedesesclaves. fr* ☞ *€6* ⊗ *Daily 9–noon and 2–5:30.*

Musée de la Pagerie. A stone building that held the kitchen of the estate where Joséphine grew up houses the Musée de la Pagerie. It contains an assortment of memorabilia pertaining to her life and rather unfortunate loves, including a marriage certificate and a love letter written straight from the heart by Napoléon in 1796. The main house blew down in the hurricane of 1766, when she was 3, and the family lived for years above the sugarcane factory—a hot, smelly, and fly-ridden existence. At 16 she was wed (an arranged marriage because her father was a gambling man in need of money) to Alexandre de Beauharnais. After he was assassinated during the Revolution, she married Napoléon. ■ TIP➔ **Museum hours sometimes change, so be sure to call in advance.** ☎ *0596/68–33–06* ☞ *€5* ⊗ *Tues.–Fri. 9–4:30, weekends 9:30–1.*

OTHER ATTRACTIONS SOUTH OF FORTE-DE-FRANCE

TOP ATTRACTIONS

Diamond Rock. This volcanic mound, 1 mile (1.5 km) offshore from the small, friendly village of Le Diamant, is one of the island's best diving spots. In 1804, during the squabbles over possession of the island between the French and the English, the latter commandeered the rock, armed it with cannons, and proceeded to use it as a strategic battery. The British held the rock for nearly a year and a half, attacking any French ships that came along. The French got wind that the British were getting cabin fever on their isolated island and arranged for barrels of rum to float up on the rock. The French easily overpowered the inebriated sailors, ending one of the most curious engagements in naval history. ✉ *Le Diamant.*

Le Marin. The yachting capital of Martinique, Le Marin is also known for its colorful August carnival and its Jesuit church, circa 1766. From Le Marin a narrow road leads to picturesque Cap Chevalier, about 1 mile (1.5 km) from town. Most of the buildings are white and very European. The marina, a hub for charter boats, is often busy. There are waterfront restaurants and clubs that are a magnet for the younger crowd as well as for sailors and tourists at large.

Diamond Rock

Pointe du Bout. This tourist area has a marina and several resort hotels, among them the deluxe Hotel Bakoua. The ferry to Fort-de-France leaves from here. The Village Creole complex with its cluster of boutiques, ice-cream parlors, and rental-car agencies, forms the hub from which various restaurants and hotels radiate. It's a pretty quiet place in the low season. The beach at Anse-Mitan, which is a little west of Pointe du Bout proper, is one of the best on the island. There are also several small restaurants, and inexpensive guesthouses here. ⊠ *Les Trois-Ilets*.

WORTH NOTING

Forêt de Montravail. A few miles north of Ste-Luce, this tropical rain forest is ideal for a short hike. Look for the interesting group of Carib rock drawings. ⊠ *Le Diamant*.

NEED A BREAK? **Le Grand Trianon Boulangerie.** If you need a fast French lunch break in Le François, try this bakery, which is in town, near the Carrefour Supermarket. Crisp baguettes and luscious pastries and ice cream are sold, as are prix-fixe lunches with sandwiches or salads. French ladies love to "do lunch" here. ⊠ *Centre Cial Ancienne Usine* ☏ *0596/77–46–01*.

Le Vauclin. The return of the fishermen at noon is the big event in this important fishing port on the Atlantic. There's also the 18th-century Chapel of the Holy Virgin. Nearby is the highest point in the south, Mont Vauclin (1,654 feet). A hike to the top rewards you with one of the best views on the island. The Hotel Cap Macabou has added activity and tourism to this quiet town.

Ste-Anne. A long, nearly white-sand beach and a Catholic church are the highlights of this town on the island's southern tip. A bevy of small, inexpensive cafés offer seafood and creole dishes, pizza parlors, produce markets, and barbecue joints—it's a fun and lively place. To the south of Ste-Anne is Pointe des Salines, the southernmost tip of the island and site of one of Martinique's best beaches.

Ste-Luce. This quaint fishing village has a sleepy main street with tourist shops and markets, and you can see some cool types taking a Pernod. Many young, single people live in this town. From the sidewalk cafés there are panoramic sea views of St. Lucia. Nearby are excellent beaches, nearly white, and several resorts, including three from the Karibea Hotel chain. To the east is Pointe Figuier, an excellent spot for scuba diving. On the way, the Trois-Rivieres Distillery is just off the highway, and Club Med is nearby, on its own peninsula.

NORTH OF FORT-DE-FRANCE

ST-PIERRE

The rise and fall of St-Pierre is one of the most remarkable stories in the Caribbean. Martinique's modern history began here in 1635. By the turn of the 20th century St-Pierre was a flourishing city of 30,000, known as the Paris of the West Indies. As many as 30 ships at a time stood at anchor. By 1902 it was the most modern town in the Caribbean, with electricity, phones, and a tram. On May 8, 1902, two thunderous explosions rent the air. As the nearby volcano erupted, Mont Pelée split in half, belching forth a cloud of burning ash, poisonous gas, and lava that raced down the mountain at 250 mph. At 3,600°F, it instantly vaporized everything in its path; 30,000 people were killed in two minutes.

The **Cyparis Express,** a small tourist train, will take you around to the main sights with running narrative (in French) for a half hour on Saturday, an hour on weekdays, for €10 (€5 for children).

An Office du Tourisme is on the *moderne* seafront promenade. Stroll the main streets and check the blackboards at the sidewalk cafés before deciding where to lunch. At night some places have live music. Like stage sets for a dramatic opera, there are the ruins of the island's first church (built in 1640), the imposing theater, and the toppled statues. This city, situated on its naturally beautiful harbor and with its narrow, winding streets, has the feel of a European seaside hill town. With every footstep you touch a page of history. Although many of the historic buildings need work, stark modernism has not invaded this burg. There is now a recommendable small hotel on the bay as well as new ferry service between the town and Guadeloupe. As much potential as it has, this is one place in Martinique where real estate is cheap—for obvious reasons.

TOP ATTRACTIONS

Fodor's Choice ★ **Depaz Distillery.** An excursion to Depaz Distillery is one of the best things to do on the island. Established in 1651, it sits at the foot of the volcano. After a devastating eruption in 1902, the fields of blue cane were replanted, and in time, the rum-making began all over again. A self-guided tour includes the workers' gingerbread cottages. The tasting room sells its rums, including golden and aged rum, and liqueurs made from orange, ginger, and basil, among other flavors, that can enhance your cooking. Unfortunately, the plantation's great house, or château, is closed to the public. The restaurant **Le Moulin a Canne** (☎ *0596/69–80–44*), open only for lunch—even on Sunday when the distillery is closed. It has both Creole specialties and some French classics on the menu, plus—you guessed it—Depaz rum to wash it down. ■ TIP→ Shutters are drawn at the tasting room and the staff leaves at exactly 5 pm (or 4 on Saturday), so plan to be there at least an hour before. ⊠ *Mont Pelée Plantation* ☎ *0596/78–13–14* ⊕ *www. depazrhum.com* ☑ *Distillery free* ⊙ *Weekdays 10–5, Sat. 9–4.*

FAMILY **Musée Vulcanologique Frank Perret.** For those interested in Mont Pelée's eruption of 1902, the Musée Vulcanologique Frank Perret is a must. It was established in 1933 by Frank Perret, a noted American volcanologist. The museum houses photographs of the old town, documents, and a number of relics—some gruesome—excavated from the ruins, including molten glass, melted iron, and contorted clocks stopped at 8 am. An English-speaking guide is often available. ⊠ *Rue Victor Hugo (D10), corner of rue du Theatre* ☎ *0596/78–15–16* ☑ *€3* ⊙ *Daily 9–5.*

WORTH NOTING

Le Centre de Découverte des Sciences de la Terre. If you want to know more about volcanoes, earthquakes, and hurricanes, check out Le Centre de Découverte des Sciences de la Terre. Housed in a sleek building that looks like a dramatic white box, this earth-science museum has high-tech exhibits and interesting films. Watch the documentary on the volcanoes in the Antilles, highlighting the eruption of the nearby Mont Pelée. Le Centre has fascinating summer programs on Wednesday on dance, food, and ecotourism. ■ TIP→ The Depaz Distillery is nearby, and it's easy to visit both on the same day. ⊠ *Habitation Perinelle, Quartier la Galere* ☎ *0596/52–82–42* ⊕ *cdst.e-monsite.com* ☑ *€5* ⊙ *Sept.–June, Tues.–Sun. 9–4; July and Aug., Tues.–Sun. 10–5.*

MACOUBA

Named after the Carib word for "fish," this village was a prosperous tobacco town in the 17th century. Today its cliff-top location affords magnificent views of the sea, the mountains, and—on clear days—the neighboring island of Dominica. (Do not confuse it with Cap Macabou, which is near Le Vauclin.)

Route to Grand' Rivière. Macouba is the starting point for a spectacular drive, the 6-mile (10-km) Route to Grand' Rivière on the northernmost point. This is Martinique at its greenest: groves of giant bamboo, cliffs hung with curtains of vines, and human-size tree ferns that seem to grow as you watch them. Literally at the end of the road is Grand' Rivière, a colorful, sprawling fishing village at the foot of high cliffs. The Syndicat d'Initiative Riverain, the local tourism office in Macouba, can arrange hiking and boating excursions. ☎ *0596/55–72–74.*

STE-MARIE

The winding, hilly route to this town of some 20,000 offers breathtaking views of the rugged Atlantic coastline. Ste-Marie is the commercial capital of the island's north. Look for a picturesque mid-19th-century church here. Most come to the area to visit the St. James Distillery and its Musée du Rhum, but the north is also filled with immense natural beauty.

St. James Distillery & Rum Museum. The Musée du Rhum, operated by the St. James Rum Distillery, is housed in a graceful, galleried Creole house. Interestingly, the distillery was founded in 1765 in Ste. Pierre by a priest who was also an alchemist. It was relocated to Ste. Marie after the 1902 eruption of Mt. Pelee. Guided tours can take in the plantation and the displays of the tools of the trade, the art gallery, and include a visit and tasting at the distillery. You can opt to take a little red train tour for €5 that traverses the cane fields while a guide narrates. This runs on Tuesday and Thursday mornings and Saturday afternoons—maybe.

The museum is known for its "happenings," including beauty contests as well as the huge Fête du Rhum, in December. The party can get somewhat wild when a dozen or more tour buses pull in. ■TIP→ **The museum and distillery are closed during the cane harvest, and weekend hours sometimes change; tours may not happen during December. It's a good idea to call ahead.** ⊠ *Plan d l'union, St. James Distillery* ☎ *0596/69–30–02* ✆ *Free* ⊙ *Daily 9–5.*

OTHER ATTRACTIONS NORTH OF FORTE-DE-FRANCE
TOP ATTRACTIONS

FAMILY **Aqualand.** This U.S.-style water park is a great place for families to have a wet, happy day. The large wave pool is well tended; little ones love it, as they do the pirate's galleon in their own watery playground. Older kids may prefer to get their thrill from the slides, including the hairpin turns of the Giant Slalom, the Colorado slide, and the Black Hole, which winds around in total darkness before it drops you into a tidal pool. In the best French tradition, the fast-food options are top-notch, including crepes, salads, and beer. ⊠ *Rte. des Pitons, Carbet* ☎ *0596/78–40–00* ⊕ *www.aqualand-martinique.fr* ✆ *€21.50; €17.5 for children under 12* ⊙ *June 16–Sept. 2, daily 10–5.*

Le Morne Rouge. This town sits on the southern slopes of the volcano that destroyed it in 1902. Today it's a popular resort spot and offers hikers some fantastic mountain scenery. From Le Morne Rouge you can start the climb up the 4,600-foot **Mont Pelée.** But don't try scaling this volcano without a guide unless you want to get buried alive under pumice stones. Instead, drive up to L'Auberge de la Montagne Pelée. (Ask for a room with a view.) From the parking lot it's 1 mile (1.5 km) up a well-marked trail to the summit. Bring a hooded sweatshirt, because there's often a mist that makes the air damp and chilly. From the summit follow the route de la Trace (Route N3), which winds south of Le Morne Rouge to St-Pierre. It's steep and winding, but that didn't stop the *porteuses* (female porters) of old: balancing a tray, these women would carry up to 100 pounds of provisions on their heads for the 15-hour trek to the Atlantic coast.

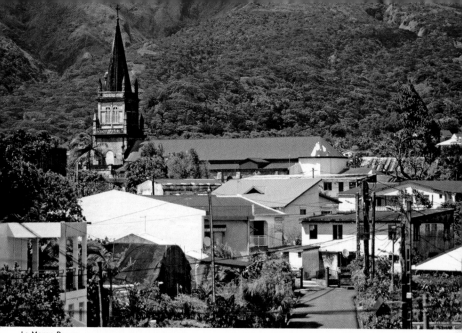

Le Morne Rouge

WORTH NOTING

Ajoupa-Bouillon. Near pineapple fields and filled with flowers, this 17th-century village is the jumping-off point for several sights. The Saut Babin, a 40-foot waterfall, is a half-hour walk from Ajoupa-Bouillon. The Gorges de la Falaise is a river gorge where you can swim. ⊠ *Ajoupa-Bouillon.*

Basse-Pointe. On the route to this village on the Atlantic coast at the island's northern end you pass many banana and pineapple plantations. Just south of Basse-Pointe is a **Hindu temple**, which was built by descendants of the East Indians who settled in this area in the 19th century. The view of Mont Pelée from the temple is memorable.

Bellefontaine. This colorful fishing village has pastel houses on the hillsides and beautifully painted *gommiers* (fishing boats) bobbing in the water. Look for the restaurant built in the shape of a boat.

Dubuc Castle. At the eastern tip of the Presqu'île du Caravelle are the ruins of this castle, once the home of the Dubuc de Rivery family, who owned the peninsula in the 18th century. According to legend, young Aimée Dubuc de Rivery was captured by Barbary pirates, sold to the Ottoman Empire, became a favorite of the sultan, and gave birth to a son.

You can park your car right after the turnoff for Résidence Oceane and walk the dirt road to the ruins. The castle still has a skeleton of stone walls, but it is mostly rubble. Hikers go for the dramatic ocean views, raw nature, and birdlife, but for others, it might not be worth the price of admission. ⊠ *Tartane, La Trinité* 🖾 *€4.*

Making Nice in Martinique

Martinique is a polite society. Doors will open to you and you will win the favor of the Martinicans if you demonstrate proper French manners. Preface questions, particularly if asking directions, with *Bonjour* or *Bonsoir*, followed by *Excusez-moi*. When finished, say, *"Merci beaucoup. Bonne journée"* ("Thank you very much. Have a good day") or *"Bonne nuit"* ("Good night"). Bone up on your French, and bring your phrase book with you, please (*s' il vous plait*, or when written, *s.v.p.*).

INTRODUCTIONS

If you're a woman over 30 or so, the honorific when you're introduced will likely be Madame rather than *mademoiselle*, even if you are single. When introduced say, *"Enchanté"* ("Enchanted").

Do not call someone by their first name, especially someone who is older, until they tell you to. When they call you by your Christian name, you have carte blanche. It pays to remember to say, *"Merci, madame"* (not *ma'am*) and *"No merci, monsieur."* If you're speaking French, remember to use the formal *vous* for you, not the familiar *tu*, unless you are sure of yourself.

The French islanders will kiss each other on both cheeks if they know the other person and often if they do not. If they realize that you are not French, they will most likely extend their hand for a handshake. And yes, the older gentlemen still kiss a lady's hand, although it will likely be a mock kiss, not touching skin.

Le Prêcheur. This quaint village, the last on the northern Caribbean coast, is surrounded by volcanic hot springs. It was the childhood home of Françoise d'Aubigné, who later became the Marquise de Maintenon and the second wife of Louis XIV. At her request, the Sun King donated the handsome bronze bell that still hangs outside the church. The Tomb of the Carib Indians commemorates a sadder event. It's a formation of limestone cliffs, from which the last of the Caraïbes are said to have flung themselves to avoid capture by the marquise's forebears.

Neisson Distillery. The producers of one of the best rums on the island, Neisson is a small, family-run operation. Its rum is distilled from pure sugarcane juice rather than molasses. It's open for tours and tastings, and the shop sells *rhum extra-vieux* (vintage rum) that truly rivals cognac. Neisson is one of the distilleries that consistently brings home the gold (and the silver) from rum competitions in France. A passion for history and tradition characterizes the distillery, as does the design of its bottles. Proud of its independence, at a time when most distilleries are absorbed by large groups, the distillery is now run by the daughter and grandson of Hildevert Pamphille Neisson, who founded the distillery in 1931. ⊠ *Domaine Thieubeurt-Bourg, Carbet* ☎ *0596/78–03–70* ⊕ *www.neisson.com* ✉ *Free* ☺ *Weekdays 8:30–5, Sat. 8–noon*.

Presqu'île du Caravelle. Much of the Caravelle Peninsula, which juts 8 miles (13 km) into the Atlantic Ocean, is under the protection of the Regional Nature Reserve and offers places for trekking, swimming, and sailing. This is also the site of Anse-Spoutourne, an open-air sports and leisure center operated by the reserve. The town of Tartane has a popular surfing beach with brisk Atlantic breezes. ⊠ *Tartane.*

BEACHES

Take to the beach in Martinique and experience the white sandbars known as Joséphine's Baths, where Napoléon's Joséphine would bathe. All of Martinique's beaches are open to the public, but hotels charge a fee for nonguests to use changing rooms and other facilities. There are no official nudist beaches, but topless bathing is prevalent, as is the case on most French islands. Unless you're an expert swimmer, steer clear of the Atlantic waters, except in the area of Cap Chevalier (Cape Knight) and the Presqu'île du Caravelle (Caravelle Peninsula). The white-sand beaches are south of Fort-de-France; to the north, the sand turns darker, and there are even beaches with silvery-black volcanic sand. Some of the most pleasant strips of sand are around Ste-Anne, Ste-Luce, and Havre du Robert. Some 15 minutes from Le François harbor, the white sandbars that form Joséphine's Baths stand in the middle of the sea.

SOUTH OF FORTE DE-FRANCE

Anse Corps de Garde. On the southern Caribbean coast, this is one of the island's best long stretches of white sand. The public beach has picnic tables, restrooms, sea grape trees (which offer some shade), and crowds on weekends, when you'll also usually find plenty of wandering food vendors and the litter that follows them. During the week, the beach is much less busy, usually just with a few tourists and some local kids after school. The water is calm, with just enough wave action to remind you that it's the sea. There are no beach-chair rentals. From Fort-de-France, exit to the right before you get to the town of Ste-Luce. You first see signs for the Karibea Hotels and then one for Corps de Garde, which is on the right. At the stop sign take a left. **Amenities:** food and drink; toilets. **Best for:** swimming; walking, partiers. ⊠ *Ste-Luce.*

Anse-Mitan. There are often yachts moored offshore in these calm waters. This long stretch of beach can be particularly fun on Sunday. Small, family-owned seaside restaurants are half-hidden among palm trees and are footsteps from the lapping waves. Nearly all offer grilled lobster and some form of music on weekends, perhaps a zouk band. Inexpensive waterfront hotels line the clean, golden beach, which has excellent snorkeling just offshore. Chaise longues are available for rent from hotels for about €7, and there are also usually vendors on weekends. When you get to Pointe du Bout, take a left at the yellow office of Budget Rent-A-Car, then the next left up a hill, and park near the little white church. **Amenities:** food and drink. **Best for:** partiers; snorkeling; swimming; walking. ⊠ *Pointe du Bout, Les Trois-Ilets.*

15

The town of St-Pierre is beneath the 4,600-foot Mont Pelée.

Diamant Beach. The island's longest beach has a splendid view of Diamond Rock, but the Atlantic waters are rough, with lots of wave action—it's not known as a surfers' beach, though. Diamant is often deserted, especially midweek, which is more reason to be careful if you do go swimming. The sand is black here, and it is an experience to snorkel above it. Happily, it's a great place for picnicking and beachcombing; there are shade trees aplenty, and parking is abundant and free. The hospitable, family-run Diamant les Bains hotel is a good lunch spot; if you eat lunch there, the management may let you wash off in the pool overlooking the beach. From Les Trois-Ilets, go in the direction of Rivière Salée, taking the secondary road to the east, toward Le Diamant. A coastal route, it leads to the beach. **Amenities:** food and drink; parking. **Best for:** solitude; snorkeling; walking. ⊠ *Le Diamant.*

FAMILY **Les Salines.** A short drive south of Ste-Anne brings you to a mile-long (1.5-km-long) cove lined with soft white sand and coconut palms. The beach is awash with families and children during holidays and on weekends, but quiet during the week. The far end—away from the makeshift souvenir shops—is most appealing. The calm waters are safe for swimming, even for the kids. You can snorkel, but it's not that memorable. Food vendors roam the sand, and there are also pizza stands and simple seafood restaurants. From Le Marin, take the coastal road toward Ste-Anne. You will see signs for Les Salines. If you see the sign for Pointe du Marin, you have gone too far. **Amenities:** food and drink; parking; showers; toilets. **Best for:** partiers; swimming; walking. ⊠ *Ste-Anne.*

FAMILY **Pointe du Bout.** The beaches here are small, man-made, and lined with resorts. Each little strip is associated with its resident hotel, and security guards and closed gates make access difficult. However, if you take a left across from the main pedestrian entrance to the marina—after the taxi stand—then go left again, you will reach the beach for Hotel Bakoua, which has especially nice facilities and several options for lunch and drinks. If things are quiet—particularly during the week—one of the beach boys may rent you a chaise; otherwise, just plop your beach towel down, face forward, and enjoy the delightful view of the Fort-de-France skyline. The water is dead calm and quite shallow, but it eventually drops off if you swim out a bit. **Amenities:** food and drink; showers. **Best for:** snorkeling; sunset; swimming. ⊠ *Pointe du Bout, Les Trois-Ilets.*

Pointe du Marin. Stretching north from Ste-Anne, this is a good windsurfing and waterskiing spot. It's also a popular family beach, with restaurants, campsites, and clean facilities available for a small fee. Club Med is on the northern edge, and you can purchase a day pass. From Le Marin, take the coastal road to Ste-Anne. Make a right before town, toward Domaine de Belfond. You can see signs for Pointe du Marin. **Amenities:** food and drink; toilets. **Best for:** swimming; walking; windsurfing. ⊠ *Ste-Anne.*

NORTH OF FORTE DE-FRANCE

Anse Tartane. This patch of sand is on the wild side of the Presqu'île du Caravelle. Ungroomed and in a fairly natural state, it's what the French call a *sauvage* beach. The only people you are likely to see are brave surfers who ride the high waves or some local families. Bliss, the surf school here, has taught many kids. Résidence Oceane looks down on all of this action; it doesn't have a restaurant, but you can get a drink. **Amenities:** parking; toilets (at surf school); water sports. **Best for:** partiers; surfing; walking. ⊠ *Tartane, La Trinité ✛ Turn right before you get to La Trinité, and follow rte. de Château past Caravelle hotel. Instead of following signs to Résidence Oceane, veer left and go downhill when you see ocean. The road runs right beside beach. There are several bays and pointes here, but if you keep heading to right, you can reach surf school.*

WHERE TO EAT

Martinique cuisine, a fusion of African and French, is certainly more international and sophisticated than that of its immediate island neighbors. The influx of young chefs, who favor a contemporary and lighter approach, has brought exciting innovations to the table. This haute-nouvelle creole cuisine emphasizes local products, predominantly starchy tubers such as plantains, white yams, yucca, and island sweet potatoes, as well as vegetables such as breadfruit, christophene (also known as chayote), and taro leaves. Many creole dishes have been Frenchified, transformed into mousselines, terrines, and gratins topped with creamy sauces. And then there's the bountiful harvest of the sea—*lambi* (conch), *langouste* (clawless local lobsters), and dozens of species of fish predominate, but you can also find *crevisses* (freshwater crayfish, which are as luscious as jumbo prawns).

Some local creole specialties are *accras* (cod or vegetable fritters), which are the signature appetizer of Martinique, *crabes farcis* (stuffed land crab), and *feroce* (avocado stuffed with saltfish and farina). You can perk up fish and any other dish with a hit of hot *chien* (dog) sauce. Not to worry—it's made from onions, shallots, hot peppers, oil, and vinegar. To cool your jets, have a 'ti punch—four parts white rum and one part sugarcane syrup.

Supermarkets often have snack bars that serve sandwiches, as do the bakeries and larger gas stations such as Esso and Total. Supermarkets, such as Carrefour, have good deli sections and sell French wines for significantly less than at home. Another French chain, Le Baguet Shop, has locations in most tourist areas. Travelers on a budget will find creperies and pizzerias, even an African pizza place in Le François. And there may be times when you just want to drive in to Mickey Ds—however, brace yourself for the price hike.

In Fort-de-France's city market, ladies serve up well-priced creole prix-fixe meals that can include accras, fricassee of octopus and conch, chicken in coconut milk, or grilled whole fish.

As for euro sticker shock, the consolation is that although menu prices may seem steep, they include tax and service. Prix-fixe menus, sometimes with wine, can help keep costs in line.

What to Wear. For dinner, casual resort wear is appropriate. Generally, men wear collared shirts. Women typically wear light cotton sundresses, short or long. At dinnertime, beach attire is too casual for most restaurants. Both the French ladies and the Martiniquais often "dress." They have an admirable French style, and almost always wear high heels.

Nice shorts are okay for lunch, depending on the venue, but jeans and shorts aren't acceptable at dinner. Keep in mind that in Martinique lunch is often a wonderful three-course, two-hour affair.

SOUTH OF FORT-DE-FRANCE

$$$ FRENCH FUSION

🍴 **Fleur de Sel.** Everything comes together in this 19th-century *maison bourgeoise*—the cuisine, the music, the location, the service. The talented chef-owner, Damien Pelé, is from France and has worked in some top spots in Martinique, as well as five-star hotels and prestigious restaurants all over Europe and the Caribbean. The ambience is relaxed, the service personalized, and the cuisine sophisticated. The interesting clientele is a mix of locals and tourists (even some kids—children's plates are €10.) Sailors tie up their dinghies close by. They all applaud Damien's innovations like his cheeseburger in paradise—a conch burger with a "pancake" made with pumpkin, curry, mozzarella, and a wasabi/soy cream. The menu changes every three months; if you chance on the rhubarb and mascarpone cream with a ginger coulis and chocolate crumbles, it will be a blissful ending. [$] *Average main: €24* ✉ *27 ave. de l'Impératrice Josephine, Les Trois-Ilets* ☎ *0596/68–42–11* 🕒 *No lunch (except for brunch in Jan. and Feb.) Closed Sun. in low season.*

$$$ FRENCH 🍴 **Le Bélem.** To really experience Le Bélem, start with a cocktail in the super-chic bar lined with old black-and-white photographs of the island; a simple 'ti punch gets an elaborate presentation. At this special-occasion restaurant for the well-heeled, the innovative cuisine is served in a contemporary setting, with a bevy of servers who try hard to please. A cylindrical wine "cave" is the dramatic focal point. It's all definitely expensive, but the complimentary amuse-bouche may save you an appetizer. The menu changes seasonally: the latest favorite is red snapper with lime crust, socca pancake, and eggplant cavier. Grand cru chocolate souffle with tonka beans, tangerine and cumbava sorbet, is an unexpected dessert. **TIP→ Although less glamorous, lunch at Campeche, the beach restaurant, is still a treat, and provides a more affordable alternative.** It opens for dinner in high season. Hotel guests take breakfast at Le Bélem, and during the season, it's open seven nights a week. [$] *Average main: €29* ✉ *Cap Est Lagoon Resort & Spa, Quartier Cap Est, Le François* ☎ *0596/54–80–80* ✍ *Reservations essential* ⏲ *No lunch. Closed some nights in low season.*

$$$ FRENCH FUSION Fodor's Choice ★ 🍴 **Le Plein Soleil Restaurant.** Perennially popular with the chic set, Le Plein Soleil has a smashing contemporary, Creole look. But it's the inventive, beautifully executed menu that cements its well-deserved reputation. It continues to draw applause for the use of the latest techniques from France coupled with remarkable twists on local products. Take a long and leisurely lunch (€35) on the terrace, which has a hilltop sea view; by night the mood is romantic, the service fine, the music heady. Soups are like a mixed-media collage. A velouté can be the canvas for a ravioli made of foie gras or pineapple. For the evening's three-course prix-fixe dinner (€45), a thick tuna steak roasted with lemon confit and stacked on mushroom risotto might be the main. At dinner, guests can choose from five main courses, two of which are fresh lobster and a steak. A memorable finale is a basil custard topped with a red berry coulis. On Sunday nights a tapas menu is available. [$] *Average main: €45* ✉ *Hôtel Le Plein Soleil, Pointe Thalèmont, Le François* ☎ *0596/38–07–77* ✍ *Reservations essential* ⏲ *No lunch Mon., Tues., and Thurs.*

$$$ FRENCH FUSION Fodor's Choice ★ 🍴 **Le Zandoli.** Although "le zandoli" is the Creole term for the lowly gecko, there's nothing humble about the culinary presentation or the wildly colorful dining room here, which are as slick as anything you might encounter in Paris. The executive chef has worked in Michelin three-star restaurants in France, and the owning couple has artistic taste that is off the charts. At the start of the meal, two amuse-bouches arrive, one in a tall shooter glass, another on a white, contemporary spoon. The three-course, prix-fixe menu is continually evolving and influenced by five continents—one favorite main is the filet of beef with girolles (chanterelle mushrooms). **TIP→ One can opt for just two courses for €33.** You may want to arrive for your dinner reservation early, so that you can sit at the bar, which looks like an avant-garde movie set, and have a fanciful, fresh juice cocktail with tiny accoutrements. [$] *Average main: €42* ✉ *La Suite Villa, Rte. du Fort d'Alet, Anse Mitan, Les Trois-Ilets* ☎ *0596/59–88–00* 🌐 *www.la-suite-villa.com* ✍ *Reservations essential* ⏲ *No lunch.*

$$ MODERN FRENCH 🍴 **Restaurant Le Golf.** A golf course isn't the usual place for a great restaurant, but once you're at this terraced, alfresco location, you might find yourself wowed. It opens to acres of rolling greens, followed by the turquoise blue of the Caribbean. The interior is bright with colorful place settings, but the real eye candy is on the plates the French chef sends out—he can elevate a red snapper filet to art with a puree of sweet potato here and a colorful (and spicy) rouille sauce there. Golfers sit down to torchon de foie gras with spiced fruit condiments, or cold avocado soup with apples and citronelle. And the food's usually light enough to allow for a rich and satisfying dessert like caramel "Lutti." [$] *Average main: €18* ✉ *Golf de Trois-Ilets, Quartier la Pagerie, Trois-Ilets* ☎ *0596/48–20–84* 🕒 *No dinner Sun. and Mon.*

FORT-DE-FRANCE AND POINTS NORTH

$$ SEAFOOD 🍴 **Chez Les Pecheurs.** At the sign of the billfish, you'll find the kind of beach restaurant you search for but seldom find. It's your basic "feet-in-the-sand" spot, but it's authentic and it opened when owner M. Palmont still made his living by fishing. Now Palmont's pink-and-blue boat is the best one bobbin'. People come for the fisherman's platter, *literally* the catch of the day (which could be *loup de mer* [branzino], flying fish, or marlin) with a flavorful red sauce, ripe tomatoes, perfect red beans and rice, and lentil salad. Grilled crayfish can usually be had Thursday through Saturday. In fact, the best offerings are on the weekend; these might include the fricassee of octopus or conch, which are among the more expensive dishes. Bottles of Neisson rum are plunked in front of a table of the convivial groups of diners here. On Friday night, local bands usually play; they get everyone up and dancing in the sand. [$] *Average main: €16* ✉ *Le Bord de Mer, Carbet* ☎ *0596/76–98–39, 0696/23–95–59* 🕒 *No dinner Sun.*

$$$ FRENCH 🍴 **La Cave à Vins.** The front door of this landmark restaurant opens on a small shop selling French food items and wine. What follows are two dining rooms, the first modern and whimsical, the second with murals of the French countryside and an impressive, domed skylight that compensates somewhat for the lack of windows. Meals begin with an amuse bouche, such as coriander sorbet. One signature dish is duck breast Rossini finished with a sauce of morels. Contemporary desserts complement such richness. The menu is the same for lunch and dinner, with not much in the way of light fare. [$] *Average main: €23* ✉ *124 rue Victor-Hugo, Fort-de-France* ☎ *0596/70–33–02* 🕒 *No dinner Sun. and Mon. Closed Aug.*

$$$ FRENCH 🍴 **La Table de Mamy Nounou.** Although the name may sound like a local eatery, it's actually quite a civilized setting with cuisine rafinee. Sip an aperitif while listening to the mesmerizing music and admiring the view from the lounge decorated with African art. Chef Jean-Paul Mahler has been the recipient of a number of culinary awards. He is continually outdoing himself, as the à la carte menu becomes more inventive, with additions like foie gras served with vanilla bourbon, red pepper jam, and prunes in an orange sauce. An amuse-bouche arrives before the outstanding appetizers. Finish with a trio of desserts, which might feature gingerbread ice cream. Lunch is served outdoors on the terrace and has a simpler, less pricey menu, and includes some salads, even

CLOSE UP

Dining in Martinique

Dining in Martinique is a delightful culinary experience, but as with driving here, it is best to get some directions before you head out. First of all, as in France, *entrées* are appetizers; the main courses will usually be labeled as follows: *poissons* (fish); *viandes* (meat); or *principal plats* (main dishes). The appetizers are almost as expensive as the mains—and if the appetizer is foie gras, you'll pay just as much as for a main course, but it is oh so worth it.

Entrecôte is a sirloin steak, usually cut too thin. A filet mignon is a rarity, but you will see *filet mignon du porc*, which is pork tenderloin. *Ecrivesses* (known also as *ouassous* or *z'habitants*) are incredible freshwater crayfish, usually served with their heads on. Similarly, if a fish dish does not specify fillet, it will be served whole.

Every respectable restaurant has an admirable wine *carte*, and the offerings will be almost completely French, with few half bottles. Wines by the glass are often swill and best avoided.

Finally, don't ever embarrass yourself by asking for a doggie bag, unless you're willing to risk being considered gauche.

one with smoked chicken. [$] *Average main: €22* ✉ *Anse L'Etang, Tartane, La Trinité* ☎ *0596/58–07–32* 🌐 *hotel-la-caravelle-martinique.com* ⏲ *Closed Tues. and June and Sept.*

$$ CARIBBEAN 🍴 **Le Colibri.** Gregarious Joel Paladino is lovingly continuing a family culinary tradition with this little local spot in the island's northeastern reaches. You'll be impressed by the ocean views as well as the cuisine that his twin sisters prepare. Begin with deep-green callaloo soup with crab or delicious conch pie, then move on to grilled lobster with a christophine gratin (assuming you don't mind the splurge) or the rabbit baked with prunes (if you do). Some of the traditional creole dishes, such as stuffed pigeon with coconut sauce, conch fricassee, and *cochon au lait* (suckling pig), are favorites for Sunday lunch. **TIP→ The restaurant is in the house and you have to walk through the yard, but the food is authentic, and the warm hospitality genuine.** [$] *Average main: €23* ✉ *4 rue des Colibris, Morne-des-Esses, Ste-Marie* ☎ *0596/69–91–95* ⏲ *Closed Mon.*

$$ BISTRO 🍴 **Le Foyall.** At this versatile place on the main drag, you can choose your experience. Downstairs is like a brasserie or a gastropub, while upstairs, at Le Cesaire, things are more refined, elegant, and expensive. There is seating on a covered terrace with a view of the sea, but the traffic, noise, and dust make it a bad choice. For a light lunch there are many possibilities, including a crepe with shrimp in coconut sauce and a small salad, smoked marlin, fried Camembert with jam and nuts, and a perfect burger. If you want to go with something more substantial, and creative, there's local octopus with green papaya and passion-fruit sauce or duck in a citrusy sauce. Some waiters speak English, and most are fun and helpful. **TIP→ Foyall serves all day and into the late night, even on Sundays.** Try sitting at the bar; it's fun and for a lot of French expats, this is their "Cheers." [$] *Average main: €20* ✉ *Bord de Mer, 38 rue de Ernest Proges, Fort-de-France* ☎ *0596/63–00–38.*

$$$ ✕ **Le Petibonum.** Billed as an artisan restaurant, Le Petibonum is a mar-
SEAFOOD   riage of French island funkiness and Miami's South Beach. It's a one-
of-a-kind in Martinique. So is charismatic owner Guy Ferdinand, a
tall Martinican with curly, blond-streaked hair who has made this a
destination restaurant in the north coast's tiny town of Carbet. Smack
on the beach, it's an ideal stopover if you're visiting nearby St-Pierre.
Remember to wear your swimsuit. Kick off your shoes and order a
perfect mojito. You can lounge on coral rubber chaises, shaded by
umbrellas, and be sprayed intermittently with a gentle, cool mist. The
appetizers—blue marlin tartare or fried flying fish right from the Carbet
shore—are appropriate for a feet-in-the-sand restaurant. For mains, the
signature dish is jumbo crayfish in a vanilla cream sauce flambeed with
rhum vieux and it is decadently rich. There's lobster on Friday night,
when local bands play. It's a scene. $ *Average main: €25* ✉ *Le Coin, Le
Bord de Mer, Carbet* ☎ *0596/78–04–34* ⊕ *www.babaorum.net.*

WHERE TO STAY

Larger hotels usually include a big buffet breakfast of eggs, fresh fruit,
cheese, yogurt, croissants, baguettes, jam, and café au lait. Smaller relais
(inns) often have open-air, terrace kitchenettes. There are only a few
hotels that still have rooms in which smoking is allowed. Most hotels
do not have elevators and many are built on hillsides, so if you have
issues with stairs or with climbing paths, be sure to ask about that.

For expanded reviews, facilities, and current deals, visit Fodors.com.

PRIVATE VILLAS AND CONDOS

If you're staying a week or longer, you can often save money by rent-
ing a villa or apartment with a kitchen for preparing your own meals.
The more upscale rentals come with French-speaking maids and cooks.
Don't forget to add the cost of a car rental to your vacation budget.

RENTAL CONTACTS

French Caribbean International. French Caribbean International, a highly
professional English-speaking reservation service operated for decades
by Gerard Hill, can help you with both villa rentals and hotel rooms in
Martinique; it covers all of the French West Indies. ✉ *Santa Barbara,
California, USA* ☎ *800/322–2223, 805/967–9850 U.S. office* ⊕ *www.
frenchcaribbean.com.*

Nouvelles Antilles. Nouvelles Antilles, based in St-François, Guadeloupe,
acts as an agent for some 30 villas around the islands, most of them
luxurious. In addition, the first online travel agency dedicated to the
French West Indies can book your flight, rental car, and sports activi-
ties, and create a well-priced package. It deals with all the Guadeloupe
isles, St. Barth, and St. Maarten, in addition to Martinique, and can cus-
tomize a multidestination package for groups up to 15. ✉ *St-François,
Guadeloupe* ☎ *0590/85–00–00* ⊕ *www.nouvellesantilles.com.*

FRENCH PLUMBING

If you aren't familiar with handheld showers and intricate levers, you can easily flood the bathroom and scald yourself. The French are not big on shower curtains either. So when the bellman gives you the walk-through, ask him to explain the plumbing. For example, toilets have two depressors; one is for a quick flush, the other a strong and serious flush and you'd better step aside. You can try for too long to figure out how to get the stopper in a bathtub to hold the water. Step into the tub and stomp down on that silver stopper. That should do it. It's as difficult to drain it. Leave it for the maid and tip heavily? Bidets are common. In self-catering villas, if there is a washing machine or a dishwasher, make sure you have a lesson before touching those dials or you'll be sorry.

In some *toilettes* (public restrooms) there are new sanitary sinks where you depress a lever on the left, or a foot pedal. If you are looking to get some water and don't see any handles near the faucet, look down.

15

SOUTH OF FORT-DE-FRANCE

$$$$
RESORT
Fodor's Choice
★
🛎 **Cap Est Lagoon Resort & Spa.** At Martinique's most exclusive resort, the caring staff strives to make sure that guests leave satisfied. **Pros:** large central infinity pool; really special lounge/bar, with a Martinican feel. **Cons:** somewhat isolated; beach is not that big; some suite renovations are needed; pricey. $ *Rooms from: €406* ⊠ *Quartier Cap Est, Le François* ☎ *0596/54–80–80, 800/735–2478* ⊕ *www.capest.com* ⮌ *50 suites* ⦿ *Breakfast.*

$$$
ALL-INCLUSIVE
🛎 **Club Med Buccaneer's Creek.** At what's one of the French chain's most upscale resorts, the suites have contemporary everything, and the huge, seaside pool has sensual Indonesian beds. **Pros:** on one of the island's best beaches; Club Med energy is contagious; even waterskiing is included. **Cons:** annual membership is $60 for each adult; some first-timers just don't like the Club Med style. $ *Rooms from: €457* ⊠ *Pointe Marin, Ste-Anne* ☎ *0596/76–72–72* ⊕ *www.clubmed.us* ⮌ *250 rooms, 44 suites* ⦿ *All-inclusive.*

$$
RESORT
🛎 **Hotel Bakoua.** Wrought-iron gates open to what's one of Martinique's best resorts, what French guests call a "human hotel," where you can cocoon. **Pros:** the Bakoua exudes vintage Caribbean charisma; it's a classy classic; you don't necessarily need a car. **Cons:** constructed in stages, so some rooms show age and others are fresh; facades are not all pretty. $ *Rooms from: €300* ⊠ *Pointe du Bout, Les Trois-Ilets* ☎ *0596/66–02–02* ⊕ *www.mgallery.com* ⮌ *132 rooms, 6 suites* ⦿ *Breakfast.*

$
HOTEL
Fodor's Choice
★
🛎 **Hotel Plein Soleil.** Long one of our favorites, this heavenly hideaway is now a Martinique landmark. **Pros:** stimulating client mix; owner Jean Christophe is on-site and accessible; sophisticated and artistic ambience is unique in Martinique; deluxe breakfast. **Cons:** rough road (particularly in rainy season) to somewhat remote hilltop location; smallest rooms have small bathrooms; Wi-Fi seldom works in accommodations. $ *Rooms from: €164* ⊠ *Pointe Thalèmont, Le François* ☎ *0596/38–07–77* ⊕ *www.hotelpleinsoleil.fr* ⮌ *12 rooms, 4 suites* ☽ *Sept.–mid-Oct.* ⦿ *No meals.*

$ 🏠 **La Suite Villa.** This hilltop *hôtel de charme* (boutique hotel) gives Les
HOTEL   Trois-Ilets some art-infused glamour. **Pros:** inimitable, whimsical style
Fodor'sChoice   with a profusion of Caribbean colors; entertaining and artistic owners;
★   the upbeat social scene. **Cons:** greathouse has three floors and no elevator; no beach (nearest one is 2,000 feet away.) **$** *Rooms from: €255*
☒ *Rte. du Fort d'Alet, Anse Mitan, Les Trois-Ilets* 🕾 *0596/59–88–00*
⊕ *www.la-suite-villa.com* ⌇ *6 suites, 9 villas (6 2-bedrooms, 3 3-bed-
rooms)* ⊺⊙⊺ *Breakfast.*

FORT-DE-FRANCE AND POINTS NORTH

$ 🏠 **Engoulevent.** This small B&B in a suburban house (about 10 minutes
B&B/INN   from Fort-de-France) has deluxe suites with contemporary decor, as well
as Wi-Fi and other attractive amenities and high-end touches. **Pros:** rooms
are attractive, particularly Nos. 2 and 5; unique on the island. **Cons:** not
all the benefits of a hotel; best with a car; no restaurant here, but many are
nearby. **$** *Rooms from: €165* ☒ *22 rte. de l'Union Didier, Fort-de-France*
🕾 *0596/64–96–00* ⌇ *5 suites* ⊙ *Closed Aug.* ⊺⊙⊺ *Breakfast.*

$ 🏠 **Hotel La Caravelle.** The energetic Mahler family transformed this
HOTEL   simple hotel with a renovation and their artwork from Africa, where
patriarch Jean-Paul worked for several decades as a manager of five-
star hotels. **Pros:** caring service; interesting international family; very
good food. **Cons:** no pool; still a simple French hotel; you'll need a
car. **$** *Rooms from: €84* ☒ *Anse L'Etang, Tartane, La Trinité* 🕾 *0596/
58–07–32* ⊕ *www.hotel-la-caravelle-martinique.com* ⌇ *14 studios, 1
apartment* ⊺⊙⊺ *No meals.*

$ 🏠 **Hôtel L'Impératrice.** Right across from La Savane stands this hotel; like
HOTEL   the park, it's another landmark that's been revived in recent years. **Pros:**
personalized service; shades of a small Parisian hotel; some English is
spoken. **Cons:** the small standard rooms in back are not desirable albeit
quiet; narrow hallways; window a/c units break often. **$** *Rooms from:*
€125 ☒ *15 rue de la Libert, Fort-de-France* 🕾 *0596/63–06–82* ⊕ *www.
limperatricehotel.fr* ⌇ *22 rooms* ⊺⊙⊺ *No meals.*

$ 🏠 **Hotel Villa St. Pierre.** A simple, modern decor typifies this modest bay-
HOTEL   front property that is somewhere between a *hôtel de charme* (boutique
hotel) and a French business hotel. **Pros:** caring managers Maryse and
Andre; downtown location. **Cons:** little English spoken; not luxurious; price is somewhat high for the accommodations. **$** *Rooms from:*
€145 ☒ *108 rue Bouillé, St-Pierre* 🕾 *0596/78–68–45* ⊕ *www.hotel-
villastpierre.fr* ⌇ *9 rooms* ⊙ *Closed Sept.* ⊺⊙⊺ *Breakfast.*

$ 🏠 **Le Domaine Saint Aubin.** This former estate perched on a verdant hilltop,
HOTEL   has breathtaking views overlooking the Atlantic. **Pros:** daydream yourself
into a more gracious era; hip owners make scintillating company; wheel-
chair-accessible rooms (and the pool has a chair-lift). **Cons:** somewhat
remote location requires a car; original rooms are not stylish; breakfast is an
additional €14. **$** *Rooms from: €119* ☒ *Petite Rivière Salée, off Rte. 1, La
Trinité* 🕾 *0596/69–34–77, 0696/41–88–23* ⊕ *www.ledomainesaintaubin.
com* ⌇ *30 rooms, 6 2-bedroom apartments* ⊺⊙⊺ *No meals.*

$ 🏠 **Le Hameau du Morne des Cadets.** A prosperous farmer known to all as
B&B/INN   Tonton (uncle in Creole) Léon constructed these Creole-style bungalows so as to share his verdant north-side estate with ecotourists. **Pros:**

inexpensive; outstanding views of Mt. Pelée and terraced farmland; great place for hikers. **Cons:** need a car; Creole meals are tasty but not that creative; just some English spoken. [$] *Rooms from: €90* ⊠ *Morne des Cadets, Fonds-Ste. Denis* ☎ *0596/55–83–30* ⊕ *www. tonton-leon.com* ⤳ *3 1-bedroom bungalows; 1 lodge that sleeps 6* ⊟ *No credit cards.*

NIGHTLIFE AND THE ARTS

To enter a casino, French law requires everyone to show a passport or license; the legal gambling age is 18.

There are lively discos and nightclubs in Martinique, but a good deal of the fun is to be had by befriending Martinicans and French residents and other expats and hoping they will invite you clubbing or to their private parties. For art openings and other cultural events, check with the Fondation Clément (⊕ *www.fondation-clement.org*), which runs the Habitation Clément, to see what's coming up. In addition to its art exhibits, the foundation throws some of the best parties on the island, which are a chance to toast and clink rum glasses with some of Martinique's leading citizens and culture mavens.

CASINOS

Casino Batelière Plaza. On the outskirts of Fort-de-France, the classy Casino Batelière Plaza is built in a striking nouveau-plantation-house style, all yellow and white. It has slot machines, video poker, and table games like Texas hold 'em, blackjack, stud poker, and American roulette. Slots open at 10 am, but table games don't start until after 8 pm. There's always a bar open, and you can often catch live entertainment on weekends from 8–midnight. Closing time is 4 am on Friday and Saturday, 3 am the rest of the week. It's open Sunday night, when most places are shut tight. Restaurant Le Club Seven, which serves Franco-Creole food, is open from noon until 2:30 then from 7:30 to midnight and the food is quite good. ■ TIP→ You may see billboards that say: CASINO or even GEANTE CASINO, with directionals. Do not follow them if you are looking for a gambling casino. CASINO is the name of a supermarket chain. GEANTE means a megasupermarket. ⊠ *Rue de Alizes, Schoelcher* ☎ *0596/61–73–23.*

Casino Trois-Ilets. The interior of this casino was designed in a French Quarter style. It houses 70 slot machines, blackjack, U.S. roulette, stud poker, and craps (Friday and Saturday). The casino is open daily 10 am to 3 am, but the gaming tables don't start cranking until 9 pm. On weekends in high season a DJ spins Caribbean, Creole, and international beats, and there's a dance floor. There are three restaurants: a buffet that serves breakfast and dinner; a Creole restaurant; and one that serves more international fare. None of the food is noteworthy, and the tables are right in the middle of the floor, which is not conducive to fine dining. Although it's popular with islanders, this casino isn't as fun as the competition. ■ TIP→ **The gaming age is now 21. Bring your passport, and be prepared for a possible entrance fee of about US$7.** ⊠ *Rte. de Pointe du Bout, near rte. de Trois-Ilets, Trois-Ilets* ☎ *596/66–00–30.*

DANCE CLUBS

Your hotel or the tourist office can put you in touch with the current popular places. It's also wise to check on opening and closing times and cover charges. Several free tourist publications that can be found at hotels tell of the latest happenings at the clubs. For the most part, the discos draw a mixed crowd of Martinicans and tourists, and although a younger crowd is the norm, people of all ages go dancing here.

Coconuts Club. A long-standing nocturnal institution, the Coconuts Club houses a restaurant, bar–lounge, and disco. It attempts to appeal to all tastes, and quite successfully, as long as you like reggaetton, R&B, crunk, hip-hop, salsa, bacchata, or merengue. The motto here is "Life is a party!" Nothing wrong with that. ⊠ *Quartier Laugier, Riviére-Salée* ☎ *0596/68–20–49* ⊛ *www.coconutsclub.fr* ☉ *Closed Sun.–Wed.*

Crazy Nights. This club remains popular because it's all about having one crazy time. With upward of 1,000 partying people, your chances of enjoying yourself are good. Live concerts are frequent, but dancing and hip-swinging are the priorities. Islanders are drawn to this club, and some young 'n' fun tourists follow suit. Like most clubs here, Crazy Nights has a hefty entrance fee, especially if there's a popular group in concert. ⊠ *ZAC Les Côteaux, Ste-Luce* ☎ *0596/68–56–68.*

Le Negresko. This is a prime example of a French Antilles urban disco. It's hot, it rocks, there are lots of glam outfits, and on busy nights when people are feelin' their dances and waving their arms in the air, well, you just have to be there. The weekend is when it really cranks up. On most nights you can expect a cover charge, especially when there's live entertainment. Negresco generally opens at 9 pm, although that can change due to after-work parties or if they've decided to close. Not only is security tight, but there's a free parking lot just across the street. ⊠ *Pointe Simon, 109 rue Ernest Deproge, Fort-de-France* ☎ *0596/70–07–03.*

FOLKLORIC PERFORMANCES

Most leading hotels offer nightly entertainment in season, including the marvelous **Grands Ballets de Martinique,** one of the finest folkloric dance troupes in the Caribbean. Consisting of a bevy of musicians and dancers dressed in traditional costume, the ballet revives the Martinique of yesteryear through dance rhythms such as the beguine and the mazurka. They usually appear on Tuesday at the Hotel Carayou & Spa in Les Trois-Ilets in a dinner performance coupled with an authentic creole buffet. Call first to be sure of the time, and to make reservations (or have your hotel make them). You can sometimes catch a performance elsewhere.

Traditional madras costumes in Martinique

ISLAND CULTURE

Theatre Aimé Cesaire. This ornate, historical building—built around 1901—is the main theater downtown. Now named after Martinique's literary great, Aimé Cesaire, it has an Italian Proscenium stage with excellent acoustics. Cesaire's former office has been arranged as an exhibition space, open for visits. The schedule of events includes national and international music and/or dance companies, and more. ⊠ *Rue Victor Sévère, Fort-de-France* ☎ *0596/59–43–29.*

MUSIC CLUBS AND LOUNGES

Jazz musicians, like their music, tend to be informal and independent. They rarely hold regular gigs. Zouk mixes Caribbean rhythm with Creole lyrics. Jacob Devarieux is the leading exponent of this style, and he occasionally performs on the island. Otherwise, you're likely to hear one of his followers.

Hotel Cap Macabou, in Vauclin, has "dancing dinners" and theme nights, most often on Friday and Saturday. On Sunday, there's usually a midday buffet with dancing to a band—you can even bring your bathing suit. Check the site for holiday parties.

Calebasse Café. A diverse, mostly older, crowd gravitates to Calebasse Café. Jazz is the norm, but there may be soul or R&B, and there's often a talented local singer. Concerts may be combined with art exhibitions, like the recent "percussion and painting." Funky and hip, the interior is a bit rough but convivial, albeit artsy. If you don't make a reservation on Saturday night, you won't have a seat. The food here isn't wonderful, but if you have the conch tart and the grilled lobster, you'll leave satisfied and avoid the cover charge. Friday and Saturday nights are banging, but call before you go on other nights. Doors open at 6 pm, but the music doesn't start till later in the evening. ■TIP→ **If an event is destined to be a big draw, a white tent is erected outside.** ✉ *19 bd. Allègre, Le Marin* 🕾 *596/74–91–93* ☾ *Closed Mon. Low season: closed Tues., Thurs., and Sun.*

Club Med Buccaneer's Creek. At Club Med Buccaneer's Creek, you can buy a night pass that, at €93, might seem expensive; it is, but it includes an extensive buffet dinner with wine, a show in the theater, and dancing. Tuesdays and Fridays cost more, at €113. Friday's entertainment, called the gala, is the best night to come, with elaborate food and the most impressive show, which might be a Brazilian spectacle. Entertainment changes based on a two-week cycle; for example, Sunday there might be Celtic dancers. Following the show, it's on to dancing at the disco until 2 if you can hang. Single women feel comfortable here, and they find willing and very able dance partners. The pass system allows you to decide whether it is your next vacation. Or plan on spending one overnight here; for a couple, the price difference is not that great. ✉ *Pointe du Marin, Ste-Anne* 🕾 *0596/76–83–36.*

Hotel Cap Macabou. Hotel Cap Macabou in Vauclin has "dancing dinners" and theme nights, most often on Friday and Saturday. On Sunday, there's usually a midday buffet with dancing to a band—you can even bring your bathing suit. There are often salsa soirees with Latin music, as well as holiday parties in season, which are quite celebratory. ✉ *Petit Macabou, Le Vauclin* 🕾 *0596/74–24–24* ⊕ *www. capmacabou.com.*

La Villa Créole. This restaurant's Martinican owner, Guy Bruere-Dawson, has been singing and strumming the guitar since the 1980s—in five languages, everything from François Cabrel to Elton John, some Italian and Creole ballads, even original ditties. Other singers perform, too, on Friday and Saturday nights, when there might also be a limbo show, a Brazilian group, Caribbean musicians, and perhaps an art expo. To see the show, you must order dinner; grilled lobster from the tank is often the best option. That said, the present chef has a fine repertoire of contemporary French-Creole cuisine. There's also a small dance floor, and a few tables are outside the open-air restaurant. If patrons aren't using them for dinner, you can just drink and more or less hear the music. The crowd tends to be mature. ✉ *Anse Mitan* 🕾 *0596/66–05–53* ⊕ *www.la-villa-creole.fr.*

Le Kano Bar-Lounge Restaurant. At this trendy, beachfront lounge and bar, Creole-influenced tapas and creative Caribbean cocktails with lyrical creole names are happily consumed while listening to weekend music events—a full menu is available, too. In season, a DJ cranks until 2:30 on Saturday night and on Sundays the music is live. Kano is handy to the Casino des Trois-Ilets, and the ample parking here makes it easy to visit both. ✉ *Facing the casino, rue des Bougainvilliers, Les Trois-Ilets* 🕾 *0596/78–40–33.*

Lili's Beach Bar. Partying on this strip of white sand, you'd never know that right above was a business hotel and a casino, or that Fort-de-France's fashionable suburb of Schoelcher lies just beyond. At this thatched-roof beach bar, London-trained bartenders put their spin on tropical cocktails while they do their flamboyant bottle-juggling. On any given night DJs spin local and international sounds, helping make the place a great alternative to clubbing downtown, and there are special theme nights and happenings. Lili's attracts a mainly young crowd, although those who come to eat at the restaurant often linger due to the happy vibe and edgy French scene. The creative cuisine is a definite cut above the usual beach fare. With free parking and tight security because of the casino, it is a safe, happy, haven for tourists and one sexy party place. ✉ *The Beach at l'Hotel Bateliere, Schoelcher* ☎ *0596/42–89–02.*

SHOPPING

15

French fragrances; designer clothes, scarves, and sunglasses; fine china and crystal; leather goods; wine (inexpensive at supermarkets); and liquor are all good buys in duty-free Fort-de-France. Purchases are further sweetened by the 20% discount on luxury items when paid for with certain credit cards. Among the items produced on the island, look for *bijoux creole* (local jewelry, such as hoop earrings and heavy bead necklaces); white, dark, and aged rum; and handcrafted straw goods, pottery, and tapestries.

AREAS AND MALLS

The area around the cathedral in Fort-de-France has a number of small shops that carry luxury goods. Of particular note are the shops on rue Victor Hugo, rue Moreau de Jones, rue Antoine Siger, and rue Lamartine. The **Galleries Lafayette** department store on rue Schoelcher in downtown Fort-de-France sells everything from perfume to pâté. On the outskirts of Fort-de-France, the **Centre Commercial de Cluny, Centre Commercial de Dillon, Centre Commercial de Bellevue,** and **Centre Commercial la Rond Point** are among the major shopping malls.

You can find more than 100 thriving businesses—from shops and department stores to restaurants, pizzerias, fast-food outlets, a superb supermarket, and the simple Galleria Hotel (the closest hotel to the airport)—at **La Galleria** in Lamentin. In Pointe du Bout there are a number of appealing tourist shops and boutiques, both in and around **Village Créole,** which alone has 26, plus seven restaurants–bars, an ice-cream shop, free Wi-Fi, and the Residence Hotelière, with small and family-size furnished apartments. Village Creole often has live entertainment at night.

SPECIALTY STORES

CLOTHING

Coté Plage Sarl. Stop in here for French sailor jerseys in creative colors, youthful straw purses in bold hues, fun teenage jewelry, and ladies' bathing suits. ⊠ *Village Créole, Pointe du Bout, Les Trois-Ilets* ☎ *0596/66–13–00.*

La Chamade. So you wanna look French? *Femmes*, this urban boutique is a good start, although the chic doesn't come cheap here. You will recognize some well-known brands like Saint-Hillaire, Escada, and Blue Label, and the sexy French shoes are nearly irresistible. The shop does have some good *soldes* (sales), though—and make sure you check the second level. ⊠ *25 rue Schoelcher, Fort-de-France* ☎ *0596/73–28–78.*

La Petite Boutique. La Petite Boutique offers a unique children's collection, including jewelry, madras dollies, and teeny underwear. There are also contemporary ministyles from Hip Up and Funky Family. ⊠ *Village Créole, Pointe du Bout, Les Trois-Ilets* ☎ *0596/38–00–65.*

Lynx Optique. Lynx Optique has the latest designer sunglasses from Chanel, Gucci, Dior, Cartier, and Versace. (French designer brands are less expensive here.) And if you need a pair of prescription lenses, they can take care of that, too. ⊠ *20 rue Lamartine, Fort-de-France* ☎ *0596/71–38–48.*

Mounia. Owned by a former Yves St. Laurent model, Mounia carries the top French designers for women and men. It will have you opening your wallet wide. Hope for a *solde* (sale). ⊠ *Rue Perrinon, near old House of Justice, Fort-de-France* ☎ *0596/73–77–27.*

HANDICRAFTS

Antan Lontan. The work of Antan Lontan has to be seen. Sculptures, busts, statuettes, and artistic lamps portray Creole women and the story of the Martiniquaise culture. ⊠ *Centre Commercial, La Veranda, rue du Professeur Raymond Garcin, Fort-de-France* ☎ *0696/92–15–50.*

Art et Nature. Art et Nature carries unique wood paintings, daubed with 20 to 30 shades of earth and sand. They depict simple Martinican scenes. ■TIP➔ **The small-size artwork makes good take-home gifts.** ⊠ *Distillerie Trois Rivieres, Quartier Rivieres, Ste-Luce* ☎ *0596/62–59–19* ⊕ *www.artetnaturemartinique.com.*

Artisanat & Poterie des Trois-Ilets. This complex lets you watch the creation of Arawak- and Carib-style pots, vases, and jars. On the site of an old Jesuit compound, this group of shops is now a major tourist attraction it the area. There are shops with interesting gifts, jewelry, and clothing, especially pareus (wraparound skirts). Several appealing restaurants also make it a good stopover for lunch. ⊠ *Rte. des Trois-Ilets, Les Trois-Ilets* ☎ *0596/68–03–44.*

Atelier Céramique. On display at Atelier Céramique are the ceramics, paintings, and miscellaneous souvenirs of the owners, David and Jeannine England, who are members of the island's small British expat community and talented artists in their own right. ⊠ *Le Diamant* ☎ *0596/76–42–65.*

Bois Nature. This place is all about mood and mystique and eco-sensitivity. Gift items at Bois Nature begin with scented soap, massage oil, aromatherapy sprays, and perfumes. Then there are wind chimes, mosquito netting, shell mobiles, and sun hats made of coconut fiber. The interior decor accessories are unique and worth carrying home on the plane, but they can also ship things home for you. The big stuff includes natural wood-frame mirrors and furniture à la Louis XV. ⊠ *Parking Centre, commercial place d'armes, Lamentin* ☎ *0596/65–77–65* ⊕ *www.boisnature.fr.*

Domaine Château Gaillard. A large two-story shopping complex designed like a plantation house, Domaine Château Gaillard sells handicrafts and tropical floral compositions at its nursery. You can also find pottery, jewelry, toys, paintings, and food, including coffee and chocolate—there's a small museum chronicling both island products. Antique creole hats and madras items are on display, too. The restaurant is a good spot for lunch. A boutique with Wi-Fi helps keep you connected. There's even a medical clinic and a heliport; **Héli Blue** (☎ *0596/66–10–80* ⊕ *www.heliblue.com*) gives great 'copter tours of the island or to others, for a mere €1,300 an hour (four passengers possible). ⊠ *SARL SH11, rte. des Trois-Ilets, Les Trois-Ilets* ☎ *0596/68–15–68.*

Galerie de Sophen. Across from the Village Créole, this gallery combines Sophie and Henry, both in name and content. On sale are the originals and limited prints of a French couple who live aboard their sailboat and paint the beauty of the sea and the island, from exotic birds to banana trucks. ⊠ *Pointe du Bout, Les Trois-Ilets* ☎ *0596/66–13–64.*

Galerie Jecy. At Galerie Jecy, owner Stephanie designs fanciful, colorful metalwork; her island themes include starfish, octopus, geckos, and impressive billfish. She also sells more portable souvenirs such as colorful wooden napkin rings, fruit plates, and trivets. Have a look while you wait for the ferry. ⊠ *Pointe du Bout Marina, Pointe du Bout, Les Trois-Ilets* ☎ *0596/66–04–98.*

JEWELRY

Thomas de Rogatis. Authentic Creole jewelry, popularized after the abolition of slavery and seen in many museums, is for sale here, at what's the number-one jewelry store in Martinique. ⊠ *22 rue Antoine Siger, Fort-de-France* ☎ *0596/70–29–11.*

PERFUME

NOCIBE Roger Albert. This classy store stocks popular scents by Dior, Chanel, Guerlain, and the like. It has a total of three locations, but the one at Centre Commerical is the most accessible. It's worth going. Walk into the shop, have a whiff, and think *Amour*! Also available is delicate designer crystal. ⊠ *Centre Commercial at Rond-Point, Lamentin* ☎ *0596/61–22–00.*

SALON

Hair du Temps. If you want to look French, you can put on the right designer resort wear, but the secret is a cool, sexy French haircut. Both ladies and men vie for appointments at Hair du Temps. Note that haircut prices are reasonable but do not include a blow-dry—that's extra, as are hairspray and mousse—€6 extra for whichever you choose. ⊠ *Arcade La Pagerie, Point du Bout, Les Trois-Ilets* ☎ *0596/66–02–51.*

15

SPORTS AND ACTIVITIES

BOATING AND SAILING

You can rent Hobie Cats, Sunfish, and Sailfish by the hour from most hotel beach shacks. As for larger craft, bareboat charters (that is, ones with no crew) can be had for $1,900 to $7,000 a week, depending on the season and the size of the craft. The Windward Islands are a joy for experienced sailors, but the channels between islands are often windy and have high waves. You must have a sailing license or be able to prove your nautical prowess, though you can always hire a skipper and crew. Before setting out, you can get itinerary suggestions; the safe ports in Martinique are many. If you charter for a week, you can go south to St. Lucia or Grenada or north to Dominica, Guadeloupe, and Les Saintes. One-way sailing to St. Martin or Antigua is a popular choice.

⚠ Don't even consider striking out on the rough Atlantic side of the island unless you're an experienced sailor. The Caribbean side is much calmer—more like a vast lagoon.

Punch Croisières. A local, French-owned charter company, Punch Croisières has a fleet of 17 sailboats, 14 of which are catamarans from 40 to 47 feet; they go out bareboat or crewed, and you can take a boat to a neighboring island. Rentals from one week to 11 months are available. ⊠ *Marina, bd. Allègre, Le Marin* ☎ *0596/74–89–18* ⊕ *www.punch-croisieres.com.*

Windward Island Cruising Company. Windward Island Cruising Company has sailboats from 30 to 70 feet, catamarans and motor yachts, for bareboat or crewed charters. Luxury is what characterizes their fleet. If crewed, there is a choice of full- or half-board. This is a worldwide operation, with 40 locations around the globe. ⊠ *Le Marin* ☎ *0596/74–31–14* ⊕ *www.windward-islands.net.*

■ TIP→ Located on the west coast, Anse-d'Arlets is a delightful fishing village with a historic church and wooden gingerbread houses. It is yacht-friendly and has several sheltered coves; charter boats usually anchor on Grand Anse or Petite Anse. Ti Sable is a waterfront restaurant that has a fun scene. Sunday brunch is a big event, with a good and moderately priced buffet. They now have art exhibits and other happenings as well.

CANOPY TOURS

Even younger kids can join in the fun on some of these zip-line courses, which are also known as tree-topping tours. However, if your body parts—particularly knees and elbows—are not as supple as they once were, or if you're afraid of heights, stay back at the hotel pool. The "tour" consists of a series of wooden ladders and bridges suspended from the trees, connected with zip lines. Participants are secured in harnesses and ropes that are hitched to them like dog leashes. You connect to a cable and then fly and bellow like Tarzan until you get to the other side. Advance reservations are recommended.

Mangofil. This professionally-run zip-line park is overseen by Frenchmen who came from a similar park in France. All of the platforms, ladders,

Kayaking is a popular activity on Martinique.

and stations were installed by members of a special union in France that specializes in such work. Safety is key here, but there's also a lot of fun; there are upgraded food offerings and a picnic area. The cost is €25 per person for adults, €15–€20 for children, depending on height. It's open Wednesday–Sunday 9–5 and every day during French school holidays. For kids age 18 months and up, there's also a huge safety net for them to frolic and "dance" among the trees, with toys galore to bounce around with. Here Happy Hour on the weekends refers to discounted prices for their minigolf. ■ TIP→ **If a Big Mango (adult) comes with a little Parc-about (kid), it is €25 plus €5. They also rent quads (4x4s) Wednesday and weekends.** ⊠ *Forêt Rateau, rte. de Trois-Ilets, near Le Potterie, Les Trois-Ilets* ☏ *0596/68–08–08* ⊕ *www.mangofil.eu.*

CANYONING

Bureau de la Randonnée et du Canyoning. Since 1995, the professionals at this company have been leading hikes that take in the island's gorge, canyons, and volcanic landscape. The tours also include some canyoning, which involves climbing up, down, in, and around rocky areas, which are usually near falls or along a stream. For this adrenaline rush, you must be fit and able to hike in the forest for hours. If you are not sure about that, book just the half-day trip, not the full day. These tropical adventures can take you to the Presqu'île du Caravelle, through canals, to Mont Pelée, even to the borders of the craters. Price depends on the destination and the duration. For example, a hike to Mont Pelée takes six to seven hours and is €35—should you want to test fate, that is. ⊠ *Joliment, Morne Vert* ☏ *0596/55–04–79, 0696/24–32–25* ⊕ *www.bureau-rando-martinique.com.*

DAY SAILS

Kata Mambo. The catamaran *Kata Mambo* offers two full-day excursions now. For €74, you can sail north to historic St-Pierre and snorkel in clear, Atlantic waters. For €79, you can have a sail coupled with a 4x4 adventure through sugarcane and banana plantations in the south of the island. The full-day trips include rum drinks and a good, multicourse, creole lunch. The boat pulls into its slip at the marina at 5 pm. This is a fun day, and although there's no guarantee, chances are you'll meet some dolphins. The fact that it's been in the biz since the early 1990s attests to its professionalism. ⊠ *Pointe du Bout Marina, Les Trois-Ilets* ☎ *0696/25–23–16, 0596/66–11–83* ⊕ *www.kata-mambo.com.*

La Belle Kréole. La Belle Kréole runs one of the most popular excursion boats to les fonds blanc, also known as Empress Joséphine's baths. (These are natural, shallow pools with white-sand bottoms.) You can experience the unique Martinican custom of "baptism by rum" (tilt your head back while standing in waist-deep water, and one of the crew pours rum into your mouth). The cost of the day trip depends it part on what you choose to have for lunch, which is taken on the remote Isle de Thierry. There's planter's punch and dancing to Martinican CDs. Yes, it is touristy— you're basically on a booze cruise that lasts from 9 am to 5 pm, with lots of loud music. The price, which starts at around €50, varies depending on what you chose for lunch. A two-hour excursion directly to the baths is also available. ⊠ *Baie du Simon, slip 36, Le François* ☎ *0596/54–95–57, 0696/29–93–13* ⊕ *www.baignoiredejosephine.com.*

Fodor's Choice ★ ***Les Ballades du Delphis.*** This civilized full-day tour (€79) uses one of three commodious catamarans, with two departure points: François Bay and Anse Spoutourne (Tartane). The sail from François takes in the famous fond blancs and then the Baie du Robert and l'Ilet Chancel to see sea iguanas and ruins. The Tartane route heads to Treasure Bay, one of the most appealing nature preserves on the island. You'll be served planter's punch, accras (fritters), and a creole-style lunch with fish or chicken. This can be an idyllic travel memory, especially when you are sailing from islet to islet, between coral reefs and swimming in shallow pools with white-sand bottoms. The boats are available for private party charters, or a romantic couple sail. ⊠ *La Marina du François, Baie du Simon, Le François* ☎ *0696/90–90–36* ⊕ *www.catamaran-martinique.com.*

DIVING AND SNORKELING

Martinique's underwater world is decorated with multicolor coral, crustaceans, turtles, and sea horses. Expect to pay €40 to €45 for a single dive; a package of three dives is around €110.

Okeanos Club. This landmark dive operation has a morning trip close to shore; in the afternoon the boats go farther into open water. Lessons (including those for kids eight to 12) with a PADI-certified instructor can be conducted in English. It's always a fun experience. The dive shop looks out to Diamant Rock, which has wonderful underwater caves and is one of the preferred dives on the island. Okeanos Club goes to 12 different sites, many with catchy names like Little Turtle, and the Gardens of St. Luce, an underwater spot chock-full of colorful sponges. Trips are geared to the level of the clients, from rank beginners to certified divers. A single, one-tank dive costs €45, and there are a variety of packages. Guests from all hotels are welcome, and Okeanos provides pickup from some of them. ⊠ *Pierre & Vacances, Pavilion-Pointe Philippeau rte. de Gros Raisin, Ste-Luce* ☎ *0596/62–52–36* ⊕ *www.okeanos-club.com.*

Planète Bleue. Planète Bleue has a big up-to-date dive boat, hand-painted with tropical fish and waves, so it's impossible to miss. The English-speaking international crew is proud to have been in business since the early 1990s. The company hits 20 sites, including the Citadel and Salomon's Pool, and you'll also see the quaint town of Anses d'Arlet. A boat goes out mornings and afternoons. Thursday is a full day on the north coast, with breakfast, lunch, and all drinks included. A one-tak dive is €50; a half-day dives includes gear and a 'ti punch. Sunday is a day of rest, except for the first one in the month, when it's off to Diamant Rock. ⊠ *Pointe du Bout Marina, Pointe du Bout, Les Trois-Ilets* ☎ *0596/58–61–43* ⊕ *planetebleue-plongee.com.*

GOLF

Golf de l'Impératrice Josephine (*Martinique Golf and Country Club*). Although it's named in honor of Empress Joséphine Napoléon, this Robert Trent Jones Sr. course is completely American in design, with an English-speaking pro, a pro shop, a bar, and an especially good restaurant. The best hole on the course may just be the par-five 15th. Sandwiched between two good par-threes, the 15th plays to an island fairway and then to a green situated by the shore. (You can finish your visit here with foie gras or a full meal, being mesmerized by the turquoise waters all the while.)

The club offers special greens fees to cruise-ship passengers. For those who don't mind walking while admiring the Caribbean view between the palm trees, club trolleys (called "chariots") are €6 for 18 holes, €4 for 9. There are no caddies. ⊠ *Quartier la Pagerie, Les Trois-Ilets* ☎ *0596/61–05–24* 🖃 *€30 for 9 holes, €45 for 18; €25 for a cart, 9 holes; €40 for cart, 18 holes.* ⯮ *18 holes, 6640 yards, par 71.*

GUIDED TOURS

Your hotel front desk can help arrange a personalized island tour with an English-speaking driver. It's also possible to hire a taxi for the day or half day; there are set rates for certain itineraries, and if you share the ride with others, the per-person price will be whittled down.

The Office du Tourisme de Fort-de-France also arranges tours, from walking tours of the city to bus excursions, and can find you English-speaking guides, too.

HD Madinina Rental-SARL. A guided tour of Martinique's sinuous mountain roads makes sense on a Harley-Davidson motorcycle, especially since weather's good for cruising year-round. This company's include some for those new to motorcycles, as well daily and weekly rentals, luggage transport, and maps and advice. ⊠ *Residence Les Capetiens, Le François* ☎ *0696//02–67–52* ⊕ *www.hdmadininarental.com.*

15

HIKING

Parc Naturel Régional de la Martinique. Two-thirds of Martinique is designated as protected land. Trails, all 31 of them, are well marked and maintained. At the beginning of each, a notice is posted advising on the level of difficulty, the duration of a hike, and any interesting facts. The Parc Naturel Régional de la Martinique organizes inexpensive guided excursions year-round. If there have been heavy rains, though, give it up. The tangle of ferns, bamboo trees, and vines is dramatic, but during rainy season, the wet, muddy trails will temper your enthusiasm. ⊠ *9 bd. Général de Gaulle, Fort-de-France* ☏ *0596/64–42–59 secretary, 0596/0596 communication department.*

HORSEBACK RIDING

FAMILY   Horseback-riding excursions can traverse scenic beaches, palm-shaded forests, sugarcane fields, and a variety of other tropical landscapes. Trained guides often include running commentaries on the history, flora, and fauna of the island.

Ranch Jack. Ranch Jack has a large stable of some 30 horses. Its trail rides (English-style) cross some beautiful country for country for €38 for an hour and a half (to two); half-day excursions for €55 (inquire about transfers from nearby hotels) go through the fields and forests to the beach. Short rides can range from €16 to €25. They also have a wonderful program to introduce kids ages 3–7 to horses. ⊠ *Morne habitué, Trois-Ilets* ☏ *0596/68–37–69, 0696/92–26–58* ✍ *ranch. jack@wanadoo.fr.*

KAYAKING

Les Kayaks du Robert. You'll receive one of the island's warmest welcomes at Les Kayaks du Robert. After a memorable paddle through shallow lagoons and mangrove swamps chasing colorful fish, you can enjoy a complimentary glass of juice or planter's punch, all for €15 per kayak for a half-day; a full day is €21. A guide is available with advance reservation. If you're going without a guide, ask how to get to various small islets, especially Iguana Island. Masks and fins are available and it's a joy to snorkel in the *fonds blancs.* ⊠ *Pointe Savane, Le Robert* ☏ *0596/64–33–93.*

MONTSERRAT

WELCOME TO MONTSERRAT

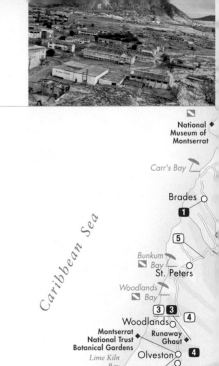

Although the Soufrière Hills volcano continues to rumble, the island is otherwise as peaceful as the Caribbean gets—almost a throwback to another time, with the occasional modern convenience (and convenience store) thrown in. Montserrat draws ecotourists, divers, and those who simply want to experience the Caribbean as it once was.

Restaurants ▼	Hotels ▼
Gourmet Gardens **2**	Erindell Villa **4**
Olveston House **3**	Gingerbread Hill **2**
Tina's **1**	Grand View
Ziggy's **4**	Bed & Breakfast **5**
	Olveston House **3**
	Tropical Mansion **1**

National ◆
Museum of
Montserrat

Carr's Bay

Brades ○ **1**

Caribbean Sea

5

*Bunkum
Bay* ○
St. Peters

*Woodlands
Bay*

3 **3** **4**
Woodlands ○

Montserrat ◆   Runaway
National Trust   Ghaut ◆
Botanical Gardens
Lime Kiln   Olveston ○ **4**
Bay   ○
2   Salem

Old Towne ○

*Old Road
Bay*

Garibaldi
Hill ◆
Iles Bay   Cork Hill ○

Foxes Bay

Bransby
Pt.

Richmond ◆
Hill
Plymouth ○

KEY	
↗	*Beaches*
◥	*Dive Sites*
1	*Restaurants*
①	*Hotels*

TOP REASONS TO VISIT MONTSERRAT

1 Geology: Volcano lovers will experience a landscape that's been pretty much left alone for more than a decade.

2 Diving: The diving is one of the Caribbean's unsung secrets, as the underwater terrain has also remained largely undisturbed.

3 Peace and Quiet: You'll find tranquillity in abundance; if you want to lie back and relax, this is the place for you.

4 Peace of Mind: There's virtually no crime, and you won't find a friendlier place in the Caribbean.

North West Bluff

Little Redonda

Hell's Gate

Silver Hill

Pinnacle Rock

Rendezvous Bay

Yellow Bay

Little Bay

Gerald's Airport

[1]

St. John's

Cudjoehead

[2]

EXCLUSION ZONE BOUNDARY

Jack Boy Viewing Facility

ATLANTIC OCEAN

The Cot

Katy Hill

CENTER HILLS

Montserrat Volcano Observatory

Farm Bay

Spanish Point

Harris

St. George's Hill

DAYTIME ENTRY ZONE

EXCLUSION ZONE

Roche Bluff

Soufrière Hills Volcano

Sugar Bay

Guadeloupe Passage

Shoe Rock

Landing Bay

0 —————— 2 miles
0 —————— 3 km

THE EMERALD ISLE OF THE CARIBBEAN

Montserrat is a small island about 25 miles (40 km) southwest of Antigua. Named by Columbus after a Catholic abbey near Barcelona—Santa Maria de Montserrate—the island was settled predominantly by Irish Catholics who had once been indentured servants in the West Indies. The numbers of Irish waned, but their influence remained. The island rumbled into the media in 1995, when the Soufriére Hills volcano suddenly erupted and covered the capital, Plymouth, in ash.

16

MONTSERRAT

Updated by
Jordan Simon

Aficionados have always regarded Montserrat as an idyllic, fairy-tale island. But in 1995, Grimm turned grim when the Soufrière Hills volcano erupted, literally throwing the island into the fire. The frilly Victorian gingerbreads of the capital, Plymouth, were buried, much of the tourism infrastructure was wiped out, and more than half the original 11,000 residents departed and have not been able to return.

Though the volcano still belches (plumes of ash are visible from as far as Antigua), plucky locals joke that new beachfront is being created. The volcano itself is an ecotourism spot, drawing travelers curious to see the awesome devastation. Ironically, other fringe benefits exist. Volcanic deposits enriched the already fertile soil; locals claim their fruit and vegetable crops have increased and improved. The slightly warmer waters have attracted even more varied marine life for divers and snorkelers to appreciate, along with new underwater rock formations.

Although an "Exclusion Zone" covers half the island, the rest is safe; in fact, the zone was slightly retracted after the volcano's lava dome partially collapsed during a pyroclastic flow in 2003. Seismologists and volcanologists conduct regular risk analyses and simulation studies; as a result, the Daytime Exclusion Zone shrank after a 2006 collapse, and then expanded again after activity in early 2008 and 2009. Borders retracted slightly in 2010 and 2011, opening parts of Old Towne and Isles Bay to as far as Richmond Hill. Visitors expecting mass devastation are in for a surprise; Montserrat ranks among the region's most pristine, serene destinations, its luxuriant vegetation and jagged green hills justifying the moniker Emerald Isle.

Though Christopher Columbus named the island in 1493 (after the hillside Santa Maria de Montserrate monastery outside Barcelona), most locals are descended from 17th-century Irish Catholic settlers escaping English persecution and indentured servitude. They routed the resident Caribs (who themselves had "evicted" the indigenous

LOGISTICS

Getting to Montserrat: There are no nonstop flights to Montserrat from North America. You can transfer on Antigua for a FlyMontserrat flight or the ABM/SVG Air service. You can also take a ferry from Antigua.

Hassle Factor: Medium to high.

Getting Around the Island: The fixed taxi fare from the airport ranges from $10 (for Tropical Mansion) to $26 (to the Olveston/Salem area villas). Though you can take taxis, you'll best appreciate Montserrat's quiet beauty if you rent a car and do some exploring on your own. Rates start at around $35 a day, but gas is expensive, so be sure to budget for that.

One main road runs from the north, down each side of the island, with little unnamed side roads streaming inland. Most addresses don't have street names or house numbers. Driving is on the left; the well-paved main road zigs, zags, climbs, and plummets precipitously, and many equally winding side roads are pocked with potholes. There are no traffic lights, but there are a few zebra pedestrian crossings; beware wandering pigs and goats.

16

Saladoids and Arawaks) and eventually imported slaves to work the plantations. The Gaelic influence lingers in place and family names, folklore, jigs, and even a wispy brogue.

The island's captivating beauty, low profile, and difficult access made it a hip destination in the 1970s and '80s. Sir George Martin (The Beatles' producer) founded Air Studios in 1979, luring icons such as Eric Clapton, Sir Paul McCartney, and Stevie Wonder to record. Destroyed by Hurricane Hugo in 1989, it was never rebuilt. But locals and expats alike still like a good band. The combined Carnival and Christmas festivities go on for nearly a month, when the island is awash with color, from calypso competitions to parades and pageants.

Other than the volcano, the steamiest activities are the fiercely contested domino games outside rum shops. That may soon change. The government speaks optimistically of building a new golf course, developing spa facilities to offer volcanic mud baths, even running tours—pending safety assessments—of Plymouth as a haunting Caribbean answer to Pompeii. An airport was constructed, partly in the hope of recapturing the villa crowd that once frequented the island. But these developments—as well as debates over the new capital and threatened lawsuits against the British government for restricting access and utility service to homesites—will simmer for quite some time. One thing won't change: the people, whether native-born or expat, are among the warmest anywhere. Chat them up, and don't be surprised if you're invited to a family dinner or beach picnic.

PLANNING

WHEN TO GO

The year's big event is **St. Patrick's Day**, which ushers in more than a week of festivities, highlighted by musical concerts and masquerades à la Carnival. July's annual weeklong Calabash Festival is becoming quite popular. **Tourism Week**, usually late September or early October, encourages village competitions in music, dance, crafts, and food.

Late October's **Police, Fire, Search, and Rescue Services Community Week** also explodes with sound and color, as jump-ups, concerts, and barbecues lure hundreds of revelers. Early December welcomes the literary celebration, Alliouagana Festival of the Word. Mid-December into the New Year sees **Christmas festival celebrations,** from calypso competitions to pageants and parades.

GETTING HERE AND AROUND

AIR TRAVEL

There are nonstop flights to Antigua, where you can transfer to a Fly-Montserrat flight (most departures are scheduled to coincide with the international flight schedule) into the John A. Osborne Airport (MNI) in Geralds. ABM Air, a sister carrier of well-known SVG Air, also offers flights from Antigua.

Airline Contacts ABM/SVG Air. A service and subsidiary of SVG Air, ABM flies twice daily between Antigua and Montserrat. ☏ 268 ⊕ www.abm-air.com. **FlyMontserrat.** FlyMontserrat offers several daily flights from Antigua on nine-seat Britten Norman Islanders, and charter service to and from other destinations. ☏ 664/491-3434 ⊕ www.flymontserrat.com.

CAR TRAVEL

A temporary driver's license is required if you wish to drive on the island; you can get one for $20 at the police headquarters in Brades, which is open 24 hours on weekdays. You can rent jeeps and cars for roughly $35–$50 per day. Even if you rent a car, you're best off hiring a local guide, who will know where the best views are—and which parts of the island are off-limits because of volcanic activity. Respect the signs and closed gates that indicate the Exclusion Zone boundaries; though the Daytime Entry Zone is usually open 24/7, you should avoid it at night.

Car-Rental Contacts Montserrat Enterprises ✉ Old Towne ☏ 664/491-2431. **Yvette Lee's Agency** ✉ Olveston ☏ 664/491-5270, 664/493-1947.

FERRY TRAVEL

There's year-round ferry service between Little Bay and Antigua's Bryson's Pier at Heritage Quay in St. John's, though the schedule changes constantly and has halted abruptly in the past. The one-hour-long trip takes place Wednesday–Sunday on the new 195-passenger *Caribe Sun*. The fare is EC$150 each way. Call Ferry Agent Roosevelt Jemmotte (☏ 664/496-9912) on Montserrat or Jennifer Burke (☏ 268/788-9786) on Antigua for more info. Also check the Montserrat Tourist Board's website for updates and schedule.

Ferry Contact Carib World Travel ✉ Antigua ☏ 268/480-2999 ⊕ www.caribworldtravel.com.

TAXI TRAVEL

Taxis don't have meters. Rates are fixed, and drivers can often serve as useful guides. Many have set rates for this service.

ESSENTIALS

Banks and Exchange Services Local currency is the Eastern Caribbean dollar (EC$). US$1 is worth approximately EC$2.70. American dollars are readily accepted, although you usually receive change in EC$. If you decide to change money, you will get a slightly better exchange rate if you change your money in a bank than at your hotel (the exchange is sometimes rounded down to EC$2.50 in simpler transactions). Major credit cards are widely accepted. ATMs (dispensing EC$) are available at the Royal Bank of Canada and the Bank of Montserrat.

Electricity 220 volts, 50 to 60 cycles, but most lodgings also use 110 volts, permitting use of small North American appliances such as electric shavers. Outlets may be either two- or three-pronged, so bring an adapter.

Emergency Services Ambulance ☎ 411, 664/491–2802. **Fire** ☎ 911. **Glendon Hospital** ✉ St. John's ☎ 664/491–2552, 664/491–7404. **Police** ☎ 999.

Passport Requirements All visitors need a valid passport. All visitors must present a return or ongoing ticket.

Phones To place a local call, simply dial the local seven-digit number. To call Montserrat from the United States, dial 1 + 664 + the local seven-digit number. To call the United States and Canada from Montserrat, dial 1 + the area code + the seven-digit number. LIME phone cards are available at most hotels and post offices if you want to make an international call. LIME provides the island's cell-phone service.

Taxes and Service Charges The departure–airport-security tax is US$21—cash only. Most flights come through Antigua, as it is the main hub; be sure to bring copies of your onward travel documents for check-in on both flight legs (you may also be asked to fill out a form upon check-in) to avoid the US$37.50 Antiguan airport tax, normally assessed each way. Day-trippers from Antigua spending less than 24 hours on Montserrat or people with onward connections to and from Montserrat within 24 hours pay only an EC$10 "security charge" and no departure tax on Antigua. Hotels collect a 10% government room tax, guesthouses and villas 7%. Hotels and restaurants also usually add a 10% service charge to your bill.

Tipping In restaurants, it's customary to leave 5% beyond the regular service charge added to your bill if you're pleased with the service. Taxi drivers expect a 10% tip; porters and bellmen, about $1 per bag; maids are not often tipped, but if you do, leave $2 to $3 per night.

ACCOMMODATIONS

With a few small guesthouses, villas, and one small hotel, Montserrat has no large-scale development. The island's best hotel, Vue Point, is permanently closed because of continued volcanic activity.

HOTEL AND RESTAURANT PRICES

Prices in the restaurant reviews are the average cost of a main course at dinner or, if dinner is not served, at lunch; taxes and service charges are generally included. Prices in the hotel reviews are the lowest cost of a standard double room in high season, excluding taxes, service charges, and meal plans (except at all-inclusives). Prices for rentals are the lowest per-night cost for a one-bedroom unit in high season.

For expanded lodging reviews and current deals, visit Fodors.com.

VISITOR INFORMATION

Contact **Montserrat Tourist Board.** The Montserrat Tourist Board keeps track of accommodations, restaurants, activities, car-rental agencies, and tours available on the island and will prove to be an invaluable resource for those traveling to Montserrat. ⊠ *Main Rd., upstairs from Public Market, Little Bay* ☎ *664/491–2230* ⊕ *www.visitmontserrat.com* ✉ *Montserrat Government Office, 180-186 King's Cross Rd., London, England* ☎ *0207/031–0317, 0207/520–2622.*

WEDDINGS

Getting married on Montserrat is relatively easy. No blood test is required. For adults 18 years and over, the minimum residency is three days. Apply for a special or Governor's marriage license through the Department of Administration Human Resource Unit via email or by calling between 8 am and 4 pm weekdays. They will ask you to bring valid passports as proof of citizenship and, in the case of previous marriages, the original divorce or annulment decree; widows or widowers will need the original marriage and death certificates. Given the lack of on-island wedding planners and difficulty in transportation, most visitors choose to get married on Antigua and then take a honeymoon trip to Montserrat, which would certainly allow you to spend some quiet time together.

Contact **Department of Administration.** You can reach the Department of Administration Human Resource Unit via email or by calling between 8 am and 4 pm weekdays. ☎ *664/491–2365* ✉ *hrmu@gov.ms.*

EXPLORING

Though the more fertile—and historic—southern half of Montserrat was destroyed by the volcano, emerald hills still reward explorers. Hiking and biking are the best ways to experience this island's unspoiled rain forest, glistening black-sand beaches, and lookouts over the devastation.

TOP ATTRACTIONS

Jack Boy Viewing Facility. This vantage point—replete with telescope, barbecue grill and tables for picnickers, landscaped grounds, and washrooms—provides bird's-eye views of the old W.H. Bramble airport and eastern villages damaged by pyroclastic flows. ⊠ *Jack Boy Hill.*

Montserrat National Trust Botanical Gardens. The MNT's main headquarters and collections relocated to Little Bay's new Montserrat National Museum in late 2012. But the lovingly tended botanical gardens and nature trails at the original site make for a pleasant, self-guided stroll. Among the plants are herbs used in folkloric medicine, former economic staples like Sea Island cotton and limes, and uniquely indigenous flora. You'll also find charming local keepsakes in the gift shop on the premises. ⊠ *Main Rd., Olveston* ☎ *664/491–3086* ⊕ *www.montserratnationaltrust.ms, www.visitmontserrat.com/national_trust* 🖃 *$2* ⊙ *Weekdays 10–4.*

Montserrat Volcano Observatory. The island's must-see sight occupies capacious, strikingly postmodern quarters with stunning vistas of the Soufrière Hills volcano—a lunarscape encircled by brilliant green—and Plymouth in the distance. Unfortunately, the MVO staff no longer offers tours that explain monitoring techniques on sophisticated computerized equipment in riveting detail. But you can see graphic photos, artifacts like rock and ash, and diagrams that describe the various pyroclastic surge deposits. The Interpretation Center screens a high-impact film with IMAX footage. ⊠ *Flemings* ☎ *664/491–5647* ⊕ *www.mvo.ms* 🖃 *Observatory free, screening EC$10* ⊙ *Mon.–Thurs. 10:15–3.*

St. George's Hill/Garibaldi Hill. The only access to this incredible vantage point over the devastation is across the Belham Valley, through a once-beautiful golf course now totally covered by volcanic mudflow, resembling a lunarscape. The area is sometimes reinstated in the Daytime Entry Zone when decreased volcanic activity permits. If it's accessible on your visit, be aware that routes aren't signposted on the rough road, which is often impassable after heavy rains, so it's best to hire an experienced guide. You'll drive through Cork Hill and Weekes, villages for the most part spookily intact (there's no way to provide utilities, though geothermal drilling as an alternate energy source is underway). Close to the summit, the equally eerie, abandoned, stark-white windgenerator project and the giant satellite dishes of the Gem and Antilles radio stations resemble abstract-art installations awaiting completion by Christo. At the top, Ft. St. George contains sparse ruins, including a few cannons, but the overwhelming sight is the panorama of destruction, an unrelenting swath of gray offset by vivid emerald fields and the turquoise Caribbean. If access is restricted to St. George's, you may be able to drive partway to Garibaldi Hill, which also affords sweeping vistas of the devastation. ⊠ *St. George's Hill* ⊙ *Daylight hrs when open.*

WORTH NOTING

The Cot. A fairly strenuous Centre Hills trail leads to one of Montserrat's few remaining historic sites—the ruins of the once-influential Sturges family's summer cottage—as well as a banana plantation. Its Duck Pond Hill perch, farther up the trail, dramatically overlooks the coastline, Garibaldi Hill, Old Towne, abandoned villages, and Plymouth.

NEED A BREAK?

D&D Bar and Grocery. This unprepossessing shack is just downhill off the first right turn from the MVO. Owner Dawn Davis mastered mixology while working at Nisbet Plantation on Nevis, and she proudly offers more than 30 libations at her Lilliputian bar (and accepts challenges). She also bakes sublime bread and serves delectable, cheap, local fare—souse, fishwater (fish soup), macaroni pie, baked chicken—on weekdays, and just heavenly fried chicken for Saturday lunch. ⊠ *Flemings* ☎ *664/491–9730, 664/496–9781.*

16

National Museum of Montserrat. The National Trust, which aims to conserve and enhance the island's natural beauty and cultural heritage, moved its headquarters and collection to this handsome new building in March 2012. The museum features permanent and rotating exhibits on Arawak canoe building, colonial sugar and lime production (the term limey was first applied here to English sailors trying to avoid scurvy), indigenous marine life, West Indian cricket, the annual Calabash Festival, island folklore like mocko jumbies (spirits), and the history of Sir George Martin's Air Studios, which once lured top musicians from Dire Straits to Stevie Wonder and Paul McCartney. The back room houses a charming small-scale recreation of pre-eruption Plymouth via blown-up photos, cutouts, and dioramas. Eventually one archival exhibit will screen videos of Montserrat's oral history related by its oldest inhabitants. ⊠ *Little Bay* 📞 *664/491–3086* ⊕ *www.montserratnationaltrust. ms, www.visitmontserrat.com/national_trust* 🎟 *$2, children 12 and under free* ⊙ *Weekdays 10–2.*

Plymouth. Montserrat's former capital has been off-limits to general tourists because of volcanic activity since the May 2006 dome collapse. Before that, the adventuresome could stroll its streets, albeit at their own risk; check with the police department to see if the situation has changed again. Once one of the Caribbean's loveliest towns, facing the vividly hued sea, it now resembles a dust-covered lunarscape, with elegant Georgian buildings buried beneath several feet of ash, mud, and rubble (though rain is slowly washing layers away). Entry is officially possible only with a police escort (lest you fall through a rickety roof), and can be arranged with the police headquarters in Salem if you are able to obtain clearance from the Volcano Observatory (generally, permission is restricted to scientists and historians). A hazard allowance of EC$150 is charged per individual or group. ⊠ *Plymouth* 📞 *664/491–2230 for Montserrat Tourist Board.*

Richmond Hill. This once affluent suburb of Plymouth, which is back in the Daytime Entry Zone, is just north of the former capital and also offers a riveting panorama. You can see the 18th-century sugar mill that once housed the Montserrat Museum and poke around the abandoned Montserrat Springs Hotel, where a few items remain just as they were left on the front desk during the mass exodus in 1997. You might encounter a goat or cow nibbling mushrooms growing through the cracks in the pool and tennis court. The hotel's hot springs are down the hill by the beach, which has grown substantially and become a favorite liming spot of locals and expats. ⊠ *Richmond Hill* ⊙ *Daylight hrs when open.*

Runaway Ghaut. Montserrat's *ghauts* (pronounced guts) are deep ravines that carry rainwater down from the mountains to the sea. This natural spring, a short, well-marked walk into the hilly bush outside Woodlands, was the site of bloody colonial skirmishes between the British and French. The legend is more interesting than the trail: "Those that drink its water clear they spellbound are, and the Montserrat call they must obey." If you don't want to hike or picnic, a drink from the roadside faucet should ensure that you return to Montserrat in your lifetime. ⊠ *Main Rd., just south of Woodlands.*

BEACHES

Montserrat's beaches are public and, with one exception, composed of soft, light- to dark-gray volcanic sand.

Little Bay. Boats chug in and out of the port at the northern end of this otherwise comely crescent with calm waters. Several beach bars—Pont's (fine cheap local lunch Tuesday–Sunday), Soca Cabana, Seaside and Sylvia's—provide cool shade and cooler drinks. Carlton's Fish Net Bar specializes in barbecued stuffed trunkfish (a shellfish delicacy). A number of bars and restaurants are being built in the adjacent section dubbed "Marine Village," including Monty's Bar and Dive Centre, which opened January 2014. You may see locals casting lines for their own dinner. **Amenities:** food and drink. **Best for:** partiers; snorkeling; swimming. ⊠ *Approximately 1½ miles (2½ km) north of Brades off main road; look for turnoffs to Little Bay.*

Rendezvous Bay. The island's sole white-sand beach is a perfect cove tucked under a forested cliff whose calm, unspoiled waters are ideal for swimming and offer remarkable snorkeling. It's accessible only via the sea or a steep trail that runs over the bluff to adjacent Little Bay (you can also negotiate boat rides from the fishermen who congregate there). There are no regular facilities or shade, but its very remoteness and pristine reef teeming with marine life lend it exceptional charm. Quan Jo Boat Tours and Camping offers Sunday beach activities including boat rides and snorkeling, as well as food, music and tents for shade. **Amenities:** none. **Best for:** snorkeling; solitude; swimming. ⊠ *Rendezvous Bay.*

Woodlands. The only drawback to this secluded strand is the occasionally rough surf (children should be closely monitored). The breezy but covered picnic area on the cliff is one of the best vantage points to watch migratory humpback whales in spring and nesting green and hawksbill turtles in early fall. From here, you can hike north, then down across a wooden bridge to even less trammeled Bunkum Bay, which has a friendly guesthouse and beach bar. **Amenities:** none. **Best for:** solitude; surfing. ⊠ *At turnoff just outside Woodlands Village.*

16

WHERE TO EAT

Restaurants are casual affairs indeed, ranging from glorified rum shops to hotel dining rooms. Most serve classic Caribbean fare, including such specialties as goat water (a thick stew of goat meat, tubers, and vegetables that seems to have been bubbling for days), salt fish cake (codfish fritters), home-brewed ginger beer, and freshly made juices from soursop, mango, blackberry (different from the North American species), guava, tamarind, papaya, and gooseberry.

What to Wear: Dress is informal even at dinner, though skimpy attire is frowned upon by the comparatively conservative islanders. Long pants are preferred, albeit not required, for men in the evening.

$$ ✕**Gourmet Gardens.** This tranquil, secluded spot—a classic gingerbread
ECLECTIC chattel-house replica echoing the adjacent historic buildings of the for-
mer Olveston estate—fulfills more than half the name's promise. There
are few more delightful experiences than relaxing on Mariet's verandah
amid a virtual botanical garden or beneath the huge, shady tamarind
tree. Lunches are excellent value, but Sunday brunch is the winner
(scrumptious eggs Benedict). "Gourmet" is a slight exaggeration, but
the all-homemade global menu more than satisfies most palates and
wallets. Specialties include stroganoff, chicken cordon bleu, Wiener
schnitzel, shrimp stir-fry, and any dessert (try the chocolate mousse
or cheesecake). $ *Average main: US$16* ✉ *Olveston* ☎ *664/491–7859*
⌂ *Reservations essential* ▭ *No credit cards.*

$$ ✕**Olveston House.** Five different rums power the knockout Olveston
ECLECTIC Rum Punch, but the animated chatter of locals, expats, and interna-
tional guests also generates its own potent buzz. Picture windows overlook the handsome verandah and gardens at this popular eatery. Chef
Margaret Wilson creatively uses whatever ingredients are available.
You might luck into fresh wahoo in orange-ginger sauce, scrumptious
garlic shrimp, pork tenderloin glazed with homemade preserves, or
flaky savory pies that elevate traditional English pub grub to an art
form. The sublime sticky toffee pudding, mango-ginger crumble, and
pear tart justify Margaret's declaration, "I'd rather make desserts than
clean the house," though daughter Sarah's luscious cheesecakes (mango,
chocolate hazelnut) are also winners. Sailing etchings, period cabinets
with mismatched china, and serenading tree frogs create the ambience
of dining at someone's country estate, Caribbean-style. Wednesday bar-
beque, Friday Pub Night, and Sunday classic English brunch are casual
and cheap, with no reservations required. $ *Average main: US$18*
✉ *Olveston* ☎ *664/491–5210, 664/495–5210* ⊕ *www.olvestonhouse.
com* ⌂ *Reservations essential* ⊘ *Closed Jan., Mon., and dinner Sun.*

$$ ✕**Tina's.** This pretty, coral-and-white wooden building is garlanded year-
CARIBBEAN round with Christmas lights, a harbinger of the good vibes within. It's
the best place to eavesdrop on island gossip, as government function-
aries file in for lunch (at least when day-trippers don't take over). Dine
either in a trim room or on a breezy verandah (admittedly sans view).
Occasionally you'll find old-time dishes like souse, but the menu is gen-
erally more upscale: specialties include velvety pumpkin soup, proper
escargots, and tender lobster in sultry creole sauce or (even better)
tangy garlic sauce. Entrées are served with heaping helpings of salads
and sides. Fine desserts (moist carrot cake, cheesecake, and wonderfully
textured coconut pie) end the meal and, surprisingly, good take-out
pizza is available. $ *Average main: US$18* ✉ *Brades* ☎ *664/491–3538*
▭ *No credit cards* ⊘ *Closed Sun.*

$$$ ✕**Ziggy's.** Vivacious owners John and Marcia Punter literally hacked
ECLECTIC Montserrat's most elegant eatery from the rain forest. They poured
a concrete floor and dressed it with a billowing, white, rectangular
tent, pergolas, palm fronds, potted plants, hardwood chairs, jade hurricane shutters, bronze sculpted candlesticks, and colorful Moroccan-
inspired table settings: the ultimate in shack chic. The menu (posted on
a blackboard) changes daily, but always offers one red meat, one white

meat, and one seafood entrée. Generally well-executed dishes lean more toward bistro fare (emphasizing beef entrecote or goat cheese soufflé over such island staples as fish, though specials like oxtail ravioli happily marry both culinary traditions); the signature butterfly shrimp usually precedes entrées. A decent wine list enhances the meal; save room for the Chocolate Sludge. Despite an erratic schedule (reconfirm reservations), hard-to-find location, and overly relaxed service, the ambience is appealingly serene and upscale. $ *Average main: US$28* ⊠ *Mahogany La., Woodlands* ☎ *664/491–8282* ⊕ *www.ziggysrestaurant.com* ⌁ *Reservations essential* ☺ *No lunch.*

WHERE TO STAY

Currently, the island primarily offers villas (housekeepers and cooks can be arranged) or guesthouses, the latter often incorporating meals in the rate by request (ask if the 7% tax and 10% service charge are included), and there is one small hotel. Note that inns rarely have air-conditioning, relying instead on hillside breezes.

PRIVATE VILLA RENTALS

Fodor's Choice ★

In the pre-volcano (and pre–Hurricane Hugo) days, when an international roster of celebrity musicians (Elton to Eric, the Rolling Stones to Sting) recorded at Sir George Martin's Air Studios, Montserrat was a favored spot for many rich and famous Britons (and the occasional American) to vacation. Today you can luxuriate in one of the handsome villas they called home when visiting and do so for comparatively affordable rates.

Montserrat Enterprises. In business since 1962, Montserrat Enterprises has a generally smaller inventory but most of its properties offer splendid views and amenities. ☎ *664/491–2431* ⊕ *www.montserratenterprises.com.*

Tradewinds Real Estate. The leading villa rental company in Montserrat is Tradewinds Real Estate. Many of its 20-plus deluxe properties, ranging from one to four bedrooms, have plunge pools, amazing water vistas, and ultramodern conveniences from DVD players and Internet access to gourmet kitchens. Recommended properties with beach access and/or strategic hillside locations include Mango Falls, Vest View, Cythera, and Mango Pointe (owned by the former drummer of the Turtles). Caring owner Susan Edgecombe really tries to match guest to villa, remaining available throughout your stay to make any additional arrangements and offer touring and activity suggestions; she'll keep you updated back home with her informative newsletter. Rates run from $800 to $3,000 per week in high season. ⊠ *Main Rd., Olveston* ☎ *664/491–2004* ⊕ *www.tradewindsmontserrat.com.*

RECOMMENDED HOTELS AND INNS

$

B&B/INN

Erindell Villa Guesthouse. This tranquil rain-forest retreat is a photo album in the making, overflowing with character and characters. **Pros:** engaging owners; beautiful landscaping; fun makeshift entertainment; abundant freebies. **Cons:** hike to beach; occasionally raucous fun makeshift entertainment; occasional ash dustings. $ *Rooms from: US$75* ⊠ *Gros Michel Dr., Woodlands* ☎ *664/491–3655* ⊕ *www.erindellvilla. com* ⇄ *2 rooms* ▭ *No credit cards* ⎢⦿⎢ *Breakfast.*

16

$ **Gingerbread Hill.** This secluded mountainside retreat offers remarkable
HOTEL   value, splendid views, utter tranquillity, and exquisite grounds. **Pros:** environmentally conscious; fascinating owners; delightful menagerie, including birds; free Wi-Fi and airport transfers; access to washer/dryer. **Cons:** car necessary; no beachfront; perhaps too "granola" for some. $ *Rooms from: US$125 ⊠ Virgin Island Rd., St. Peter's* ☎ *664/491–5812, 813/774–5270* ⊕ *www.volcano-island.com* ↪ *2 rooms, 2 villas, 1 cottage* |○| *No meals.*

$ **Grand View Bed & Breakfast.** This aptly named inn is run by energetic
B&B/INN   dynamo Theresa Silcott, who prides herself on being Montserrat's top hostess. **Pros:** splendid views; delightful gardens; congenial hostess; excellent local food (ask about medicinal folklore); free Wi-Fi. **Cons:** no beachfront; very basic if clean rooms. $ *Rooms from: US$55 ⊠ Baker Hill* ☎ *664/491–2284* ⊕ *www.mnigrandview.com* ↪ *2 suites, 5 rooms* ▭ *No credit cards* |○| *Breakfast.*

$ **Olveston House.** This 1950s villa, rented to island hotelier Carol
HOTEL   Osborne by Beatles producer Sir George Martin, brims with history
Fodor's Choice   (including the owner's fabled AIR Studios where Sting, Elton John,
★   Eric Clapton, and Paul McCartney recorded). **Pros:** incredible value; gorgeous pool; glorious views of the glowing Soufrière; invigorating blend of locals, expats, and guests at the bar and dining room. **Cons:** no beach; occasional dusting of ash; Wi-Fi spotty. $ *Rooms from: US$119 ⊠ Olveston* ☎ *664/491–5210, 664/495–5210* ⊕ *www.olvestonhouse. com* ↪ *6 rooms* ⊘ *Closed Jan.* |○| *Breakfast.*

$$ **Tropical Mansion Suites.** Despite the grandiose name, this is little more
HOTEL   than a motel with neocolonial architectural pretensions and clean, spacious rooms. **Pros:** currently the island's only full-service lodging; centrally located. **Cons:** far from beaches; extra charge for air-conditioning; mediocre and comparatively pricey food. $ *Rooms from: US$129 ⊠ Main Rd., Sweeney's* ☎ *664/491–8767* ⊕ *www.tropicalmansion.com* ↪ *17 rooms, 1 suite* |○| *Breakfast.*

NIGHTLIFE AND THE ARTS

Although Montserrat is better known for another kind of wildlife, Friday-night revelers lime in roadside rum shops scattered around the island, often spilling out on the street as part of the informal evening culture. There's no closing time, and many bars serve yummy, authentic local food. Salem is party central (the roadside sign says, "Welcome to fun and revelry"). Little Bay is being developed as the island capital (the government will remain in Brades); in season the Hot Spot is a collection of a dozen watering holes between the "town" and Cultural Center; Festival Village is a gathering of pop-up bars during festivals.

NIGHTLIFE

Garry Moore's Wide Awake Bar. This perennial favorite doesn't close as long as customers are thirsty. The name was a teasing reference to Garry's penchant for napping at the bar (when he wasn't complaining—mostly humorously—about a plumber's hard life and long hours). Sadly, Garry passed in 2012, but his son vows to carry on the tradition. ⊠ *Salem* ☎ *664/491–7156.*

Howe's Rum Shop. This is the best spot on the island for shooting pool and the breeze; get here early for luscious fried and barbecued chicken, liberally daubed with mouth- and eye-watering homemade sauces and seasonings, accompanied by frosty beers and local firewater liqueurs. ⊠ *St. John's* ☎ *664/491–3008.*

Let's Go Limin'. In season, artist Harriet Peakes runs a rollicking "Rumshop Tour" of three to four truly local watering holes where you can lime, drink, sample local fare, and play spirited dominoes. ☎ *664/491–7156.*

Soca Cabana. This hot spot offers live Caribbean beats, as the name implies. But expat owner Tom Walker is passionate about the island's musical heritage, including the halcyon days of Air Studios. He salvaged the "Bar of the Stars" from Sir George Martin's celebrated recording space, where weekly Montserrat Idol competitions take place. It's a delightful liming spot, with the bamboo bar and whitewashed patio accented in mint and turquoise overlooking the beach. Seemingly half the island descends on the hotspot Sunday for meals, music, and merriment. Karaoke Saturdays also reel partiers in. ⊠ *Little Bay* ☎ *664/492–1677* ⊕ *www.socacabana.com* ✉ *Admission varies* ☉ *Open for lunch daily; dinner by request and live music Wed., Fri., and Sat. nights; dinner Sun.*

Treasure Spot Cafe. Lydia, the owner of the Treasure Spot, often books the island's up-and-coming musicians (usually One Man Band but also Pops Morris, Hero, and Basil—reggae and soca artists beginning to develop a reputation outside Montserrat) to play weekends. Locals also savor breakfast, lunch and weekend BBQs. ⊠ *Cudjoe Head* ☎ *664/493–2003.*

THE ARTS

Montserrat Cultural Centre. Eight years in development, the impressive, colonnaded Montserrat Cultural Centre and its 500-seat, state-of-the-art Sir George Martin Auditorium present craft demonstrations, folkloric and fashion shows, pageants, movies (with popcorn and hot dogs), and the occasional dance and theatrical performance. During intermission, check out the Wall of Fame (bronzed handprints of musicians who recorded or performed on Montserrat, such as Sir Paul McCartney, Sir Elton John, and Mark Knopfler). Check with the tourist board or local newspaper listings for the current schedule. ⊠ *Little Bay* ☎ *664/491–4242, 664/491–4700* ⊕ *www.themontserratculturalcentre.com.*

SHOPPING

Montserrat offers a variety of local crafts and does a brisk trade in vulcanology mementos (many shops sell not only postcards and striking photographs but also small bottles of gray ash capped by colorful, homemade cloth).

David Lea. David Lea has chronicled Montserrat's volcanic movements in a fascinating eight-part video–DVD series, *The Price of Paradise,* each entry a compelling glimpse into the geological and social devastation—and regeneration. These, as well as rollicking local-music CDs by his son (named Sun) and other musicians, are available at his studio. ⊠ *Gingerbread Hill, St. Peter's* ☎ *664/491–5812* ⊕ *www.volcano-island.com.*

16

Luv's Cotton Store. This is the island's best source for sportswear made from Sea Island cotton, celebrated for its softness and high quality. ✉ *Salem* ☎ *664/491–3906.*

Montserrat Philatelic Bureau. Occupying the Government Headquarters Building, the Montserrat Philatelic Bureau sells a wealth of highly prized unusual stamps, including handsome first-day covers, that highlight local treasures from the Montserrat Oriole to the late great musician, the Mighty Arrow. ✉ *Government Headquarters Bldg., Brades* ☎ *664/491–2042, 664/491–2996.*

Oriole Gift Shop. Oriole Gift Shop in the National Museum, run by the Montserrat National Trust, is an excellent source for books on Montserrat (look for the *Montserrat Cookbook* and works by the island's former acting governor, Sir Howard Fergus), as well as trail maps, handicrafts (wonderful dolls, hand-painted boxes, and calabash purses) and locally made food products. ✉ *Little Bay* ☎ *664/491–3086.*

Woolcock's Craft & Photo Gallery. This gallery promotes the work of local artists such as Donaldson Romeo and sells spectacular photos of the volcano as well as of indigenous birds and other wildlife. ✉ *BBC Bldg., Little Bay Public Market, Little Bay* ☎ *664/491–2025.*

SPORTS AND ACTIVITIES

BIKING

Mountain biking is making a comeback, with a wide network of trails through the lush Centre Hills. Bikes are also a wonderful way to explore the island and enjoy the lovely coastal vistas along the main road.

DIVING

More than 30 practically pristine dive sites surround Montserrat. The even more bountiful marine life has had time to recover from the predations of human activities, and the pyroclastic flows formed boulders, pinnacles, ledges, and walls that anchor new coral reefs. **Carr's Bay** is a favorite for shore dives, with arrow crabs, basket stars, turtles, and shimmering blue tang darting about hulking boulders and a small, colorful cave; night dives are particularly memorable, as millions of bioluminescent microorganisms glow when disturbed. The shallow reefs surrounding **Woodlands Bay** feature varied underwater topography, including a small, colorful cave and thousands of banded coral shrimp, copper sweepers, sergeant majors, four-eyed butterfly fish, jackknife, attenuated trumpetfish, and turtles. **Rendezvous Bay** may be the finest spot for both snorkeling and diving, thanks to a sheltered reef and lack of ash or silt. You come face-to-face with spotted morays, porcupine fish, snake eels, octopuses, and more. You can even hang out with thousands of (harmless) fruit bats in partly submerged caves. Other top dive sites include **Lime Kiln Bay** and **Bunkum Bay,** as well as the spectacular submarine rock formations around **Little Redonda** and the **Pinnacles** off the rougher, more challenging northeastern shores.

FAMILY **Scuba Montserrat.** Andrew Myers and Emmy Aston of Scuba Montserrat provide experienced PADI certification; lengthy shore, boat, and kayak dives; snorkeling excursions (including a stop at a very cool bat cave); specialty courses from drift diving to digital underwater photography; and down the road the possibility of helping regenerate volcano-damaged sites. They're particularly family focused, stocking underwater Frisbees, torpedoes, and specialized children's gear. They also rent inflatable two-person Hanauma kayaks. ⊠ *Little Bay* ☏ *664/496–7807* ⊕ *www.scubamontserrat.com.*

FISHING

Danny Sweeney. Deep-sea fishing (wahoo, bonito, shark, marlin, and yellowfin tuna) is superb, since the waters aren't disturbed by leviathan cruise ships. Affable Danny Sweeney (ask him why Dire Straits' "Walk of Life" allegedly memorializes him) has won several regional tournaments, including Montserrat's Open Fishing Competition. Half-day charters (up to four people) are $300. Though schools of game fish amazingly cavort just 2 to 3 miles (3 to 5 km) offshore, Danny's depth sounder picks up action in deeper waters. An extra bonus on the open sea is the gripping views of the volcanic devastation. He also runs Plymouth/island circumnavigation boat tours for $50 per person. ⊠ *Olveston* ☏ *664/491–5645.*

GUIDED TOURS

Avalon Tours. Joe "Fergus" Phillip, who operates Avalon Tours, often emails updates on Montserrat to visitors. ⊠ *Manjack* ☏ *664/491–3432, 664/492–1565* ✎ *joephillip@live.com.*

Furlonge Taxi & Tours. Reuben Furlonge of Furlonge Taxi & Tours is another hardy helpful local (and a "goat water specialist"; you may be stopped along the way by locals inquiring if he's made a batch). All the staff here are friendly, knowledgeable, and reliable taxi and tour drivers. ⊠ *Gerald's* ☏ *664/491–4376, 664/492–2790.*

HIKING

Montserrat's lush, untrammeled rain forest teeming with exotic flora, fauna, and birdlife is best experienced on foot. The tourist office provides lists of hiking trails, from easy to arduous. The most dramatic routes are gradually being upgraded as part of the Montserrat Tourism Development Project; in addition to improving their definition, the government will also be building viewing platforms and providing interpretative information at strategic points. Still, if you're not experienced or fit, go with a guide; always wear sturdy shoes and bring water. Most marked trails run through the biologically diverse, scenic Centre Hills region, offering stirring lookouts over the volcano's barren flanks, surrounding greenery, and ash-covered villages in the Exclusion Zone. The rain forest is home to many regionally endemic wildlife species (tree frogs, dwarf geckos, anoles, mountain chicken—actually a type of frog—and the half-snake-half-lizard galliwasp), as well as most of the

34 resident birds, from red-billed tropic birds to the rare national bird, the Montserrat oriole, with its distinctive orange-and-black plumage. The Silver Hills in the north are vastly different, with dry and deciduous forests and open plains blanketing a defunct, heavily faulted and eroded volcano; views here might provide a glimpse of how southern Montserrat will look millions of years from now.

Scriber's Adventure Tours. These excellent tours are run by James "Scriber" Daley ("a describer since I was little"), an employee of the Agricultural Department legendary for his uncanny birdcalls. He leads nature hikes through the rain forest for $20 to $50; he'll hire additional guides if there are more than 10 people per group, ensuring personal attention. Scriber also explains indigenous flora, from 42 fern species (kids love when he "tattoos" them with silver fern leaves) to others prized for medicinal properties (you might collect the makings of bush tea for back pain or menstrual cramps). He also conducts a memorable, if brief, evening mountain-chicken tour, distributing flashlights to find the foot-long frogs. ☎ 664/491–2546, 664/491–3412, 664/492–2943.

PUERTO RICO

WELCOME TO PUERTO RICO

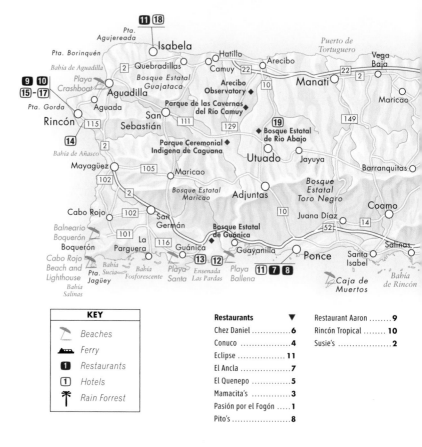

KEY	
⚖	Beaches
⛴	Ferry
❶	Restaurants
①	Hotels
🌴	Rain Forrest

Restaurants ▼

Chez Daniel **6**
Conuco **4**
Eclipse **11**
El Ancla **7**
El Quenepo **5**
Mamacita's **3**
Pasión por el Fogón **1**
Pito's **8**

Restaurant Aaron **9**
Rincón Tropical **10**
Susie's **2**

Mother Spain is always a presence here—on a sun-dappled cobblestone street, in the shade of a colonial cathedral or fort. Yet multifaceted Puerto Rico pulses with New World energy. The rhythms of the streets are of Afro-Latin salsa and bomba. And the U.S. flag flaps in the salty breezes wherever you go.

SPANISH AMERICAN

Puerto Rico is 110 miles (177 km) long and 35 miles (56 km) wide. With a population of almost 4 million, it's among the biggest Caribbean islands. The first Spanish governor was Juan Ponce de León in 1508; he founded Old San Juan in 1521. The United States won the island in the Spanish-American war in 1898 and made it a commonwealth in 1952.

17

PUERTO RICO

Hotels ▼	Hacienda Tamarindo **6**	Mary Lee's by the Sea . **12**
Casa Grande **19**	Hix Island House **9**	Río Mar Beach
Club Seaborne **5**	Horned Dorset	Resort & Spa **1**
Copamarina	Primavera **15**	St. Regis Bahia **3**
Beach Resort **13**	Hotel Meliá **11**	Tres Sirenas **16**
Dorado Beach, A Ritz	Inn on the	Villa Montaña **18**
Carloton Resort **20**	Blue Horizon **7**	W Retreat & Spa **10**
El Conquistador **4**	Lazy Parrot **17**	
Gran Meliá	Lemontree **14**	
Puerto Rico **2**	Malecón House **8**	

TOP REASONS TO VISIT PUERTO RICO

1 The Nightlife: Happening clubs and discos make San Juan one of the Caribbean's nightlife capitals, rivaling even Miami.

2 The Food: Great restaurants run the gamut from elegant places in San Juan to simple spots serving delicious comida criolla.

3 The Beaches: Both developed and wild, beaches here suit the needs of surfers, sunbathers, and families.

4 The Nature: Nature abounds, from the underground Río Camuy to El Yunque, the only Caribbean national forest.

5 The Unexpected: Puerto Mosquito— kayak after dark on the astounding bioluminescent bay on Vieques.

EATING AND DRINKING WELL IN PUERTO RICO

More chefs and restaurateurs are developing menus in the line of a Nuevo Latino cuisine. However, even the most modern chefs here include traditional ingredients as they update old favorites.

Standard meats like chicken, pork, and lamb are given an added zest by sauces made from such tropical fruits as tamarind, mango, or guava. Puerto Rican cooking uses a lot of local vegetables: plantains are cooked a hundred different ways, and yams and other root vegetables are served baked, fried, stuffed, boiled, and mashed. Rice and beans are accompaniments to almost every dish. *Sofrito*—a garlic, onion, sweet pepper, cilantro, oregano, and tomato puree—is used as a base for practically everything. *Arroz con pollo* (chicken with rice), pernil (roasted pork shoulder), *sancocho* (beef, chicken, or pork feet and tuber soup), and *bistec encebollado* (steak and onions) are all typical plates. Also look for fritters served along highways and beaches. You may find *empanadillas* (stuffed fried turnovers), *sorullitos* (cheese-stuffed corn sticks), and *bacalaítos* (codfish fritters).

Cocina Criolla: *Cocina criolla*—literally, creole cooking—is an aggregate of Caribbean cuisines, sharing basic ingredients common to Cuban, Dominican, and even Brazilian culinary traditions. Conventional wisdom says that the secret of the cocina criolla depends on the use of sofrito, achiote (the inedible fruit of a small Caribbean shrub whose seeds are sometimes ground as a spice or simmered in oil to release their color), lard, and the *caldero* (cooking pot).

Coffee. Cultivated at high altitudes in cool, moist air and mineral-rich soil, the island's coffee beans (called cherries)

are black and aromatic. Look for local brands: Yauco Selecto, Rioja, Yaucono, Café Rico, Crema, Adjuntas, Coqui, and Alto Grande Super Premium.

Fruits and Vegetables: Tropical fruits often wind up at the table in the form of delicious juices. A local favorite is pineapple juice from crops grown in the north of the island. Coconut, mango, papaya, lime, and tamarind are other local favorites. Puerto Rico is home to terrific lesser-known fruits; these include the *caimito* (also called a star apple), *quenepa* (a Spanish lime with a yellow sweet-tart pulp surrounded by a tight, thin skin), and *zapote* (a plum-size fruit that tastes like peach, avocado, and vanilla). The Plaza del Mercado in Santurce is a good place to look for the unusual.

Local Seafood: The freshest seafood is to be found on the northern and western coasts, where seaside shacks and kiosks serve up red snapper, conch, crab, and spiny lobster in traditional recipes. Fried fish is also popular, served with *mojo isleño*, a sauce made with olives, onions, pimientos, capers, tomatoes, and vinegar.

Plantains and Mofongo: *Plátanos,* or plantains, are related to bananas but are larger and starchier. They are served mostly as side dishes and may be eaten green or ripe. They can be fried, baked, boiled, or roasted and served either

whole or in slices. Of all the delicious plantain preparations, one of the tastiest is also the simplest—*mofongo*. Green plantains are mashed with a wooden *pilón*, mixed with garlic, pork fat, and other flavorings and fried in a pan. Served plain, it's often a side dish. But when it's stuffed with chicken, beef, or some other meat, *mofongo* becomes one of Puerto Rico's signature entrées.

Rice: Rice is omnipresent, and most often it's served with *habichuelas* (beans). Rice stuck to the pot, known as *pegao,* is the most highly prized, full of all the ingredients that have sunk to the bottom.

Rum: Although rum was first exported in 1897, it took a bit longer for it to become the massive industry it is today. The Bacardí family set up shop near San Juan in 1959, after fleeing Cuba. The company's product, lighter-bodied than those produced by most other distilleries, gained favor around the world. Today Puerto Rico produces more than 35 million gallons of rum a year. You might say it's the national drink.

17

Updated by Paulina Salach and Julie Schwietert

Sunrise and sunset are both worth waiting for when you're in Puerto Rico. The pinks and yellows that hang in the early-morning sky are just as compelling as the sinewy reds and purples that blend into the twilight. It's easy to compare them, as Puerto Rico is small enough to have breakfast in Fajardo, looking eastward over the boats headed to Vieques and Culebra, and lobster dinner in Rincón as the sun is sinking into the inky-blue water.

Known as the Island of Enchantment, Puerto Rico conjures a powerful spell. Here traffic actually leads you to a "Road to Paradise," whether you're looking for a pleasurable, sunny escape from the confines of urbanity or a rich supply of stimulation to quench your cultural and entertainment thirst. On the island you have the best of both worlds, natural and urban thrills alike, and although city life is frenetic enough to make you forget you're surrounded by azure waters and warm sand, traveling a few miles inland or down the coast can easily make you forget you're surrounded by development.

Puerto Rico was populated primarily by Taíno Indians when Columbus landed in 1493. In 1508 Ponce de León established a settlement and became the first governor; in 1521 he founded what is known as Old San Juan. For centuries, while Africans worked on the coastal sugarcane fields, the French, Dutch, and English tried unsuccessfully to wrest the island from Spain. In 1898, as a result of the Spanish-American War, Spain ceded the island to the United States. In 1917 Puerto Ricans became U.S. citizens, and in 1952 Puerto Rico became a semiautonomous commonwealth.

Since the 1950s, Puerto Rico has developed exponentially, as witnessed in the urban sprawl, burgeoning traffic, and growing population (estimated at nearly 4 million); yet *en la isla* (on the island) a strong Latin sense of community and family prevails. Puertorriqueños are fiercely proud of their unique blend of heritages.

Music is another source of Puerto Rican pride. Like wildflowers, *velloneras* (jukeboxes) pop up almost everywhere, and when one is playing, somebody will be either singing or dancing along—or both. Cars often vibrate with *reggaetón,* an aggressive beat with lyrics that express social malaise. Salsa, a fusion of West African percussion, jazz, and other Latin beats, is the trademark dance. Although it may look difficult to master, it's all achieved by just loosening your hips. You may choose to let your inhibitions go by doing some clubbing *a la vida loca* made famous by pop star Ricky Martin. Nightlife options are on par with any cosmopolitan city—and then some.

By day you can drink in the culture of the old world; one of the richest visual experiences in Puerto Rico is Old San Juan. Originally built as a fortress by the Spaniards in the early 1500s, the Old City has myriad attractions that include restored 16th-century buildings and 200-year-old houses with balustraded balconies of filigreed wrought iron that overlook narrow cobblestone streets. Spanish traditions are also apparent in the countryside festivals celebrated in honor of small-town patron saints. For quiet relaxation or experiences off the beaten track, visit coffee plantations, colonial towns, or outlying islets where nightlife is virtually nonexistent.

And you don't come to a Caribbean island without taking in some of the glorious sunshine and natural wonders. In the coastal areas the sun mildly toasts your body, and you're immediately healed by soft waves and cool breezes. In the misty mountains, you can wonder at the flickering night flies and the star-studded sky while the *coquís* (tiny local frogs) chirp their legendary sweet lullaby. On a moonless night, watch the warm ocean turn into luminescent aqua-blue speckles on your skin. Then there are the island's many acres of golf courses, numerous tennis courts, rain forests, and dozens of beaches that offer every imaginable water sport.

17

PLANNING

WHEN TO GO

San Juan in particular is very expensive—many would say overpriced—during the busy tourist season from mid-December through mid-April; during the off-season, you can get good deals all over the island, with discounts of up to 40% off high-season rates.

GETTING HERE AND AROUND

AIR TRAVEL

San Juan's busy Aeropuerto Internacional Luis Muñoz Marín (SJU) receives flights from all major American carriers, and there are dozens of daily flights to Puerto Rico from the United States. Nonstop options include AirTran from Atlanta, Baltimore, Fort Lauderdale, Orlando, and Tampa; American Airlines from Atlanta, Chicago, Dallas, Miami, New York–JFK, and San Diego; Delta from Atlanta and New York–JFK; JetBlue from Boston, Fort Lauderdale, Hartford, Jacksonville, Newark, New York–JFK, Orlando, and Tampa; Spirit Air from Fort Lauderdale; United from Chicago, Houston, Newark, Philadelphia, and Washington, D.C.–Dulles; and US Airways from Charlotte, Chicago, Philadelphia, and Washington, D.C.–Dulles.

San Juan is a major regional hub; many travelers make connections here to other islands in the Caribbean. Air Flamenco and Vieques Air Link offer daily flights from SJU and Isla Grande Airport (SIG) in San Juan to Vieques and Culebra. Seaborne Airlines and Cape Air both fly between SJU and Vieques.

Airline Contacts American Airlines ☎ *800/433-7300* ⊕ *www.aa.com.* **Delta Airlines** ☎ *800/221-1212 for U.S. reservations, 800/241-4141 for international reservations* ⊕ *www.delta.com.* **JetBlue** ☎ *800/538-2583* ⊕ *www.jetblue.com.* **Spirit Airlines** ☎ *800/772-7117* ⊕ *www.spirit.com.* **United Airlines** ☎ *800/864-8331* ⊕ *www.united.com.* **US Airways** ☎ *800/428-4322 for U.S. and Canada reservations, 800/622-1015 for international reservations* ⊕ *www.usairways.com.*

Regional Airlines Air Flamenco ☎ *787/724-1818, 877/535-2636* ⊕ *www.airflamenco.net.* **Cape Air** ☎ *866/227-3247* ⊕ *www.capeair.com.* **Seaborne Airlines** ☎ *866/359-8784* ⊕ *www.seaborneairlines.com.* **Vieques Air Link** ☎ *787/741-8331, 888/901-9247* ⊕ *www.viequesairlink.com.*

Airports From either airport you can catch flights to Culebra, Vieques, and other destinations on Puerto Rico and throughout the Caribbean. **Aeropuerto Internacional Luis Muñoz Marín** (*SJU*). Puerto Rico's main airport serves as the gateway to the Caribbean, with flights from AirTran, American Airlines, Delta, JetBlue, Southwest, Spirit Air, United, and US Airways. ✉ *Carolina, San Juan* ☎ *787/289-7240* ⊕ *www.aeropuertosju.com.* **Aeropuerto Fernando L. Ribas Dominicci** (*SIG*). Sometimes known as Isla Grande, the Aeropuerto Fernando L. Ribas Dominicci is in Miramar, near the Convention Center. It handles most short hops to Vieques and other nearby islands. ✉ *Calle Lindbergh, San Juan* ☎ *787/729-8751* ⊕ *prpa.pr.gov/aeropuertos.*

BOAT AND FERRY TRAVEL

Ferry service is from the ferry terminal in Fajardo, about a 90-minute drive from San Juan. There are a limited number of seats on the ferries, so get to the terminal in plenty of time.

Contact Autoridad de Transporte Marítimo. Part of the Department of Transportation, the Maritime Transport Authority runs passenger and cargo ferries from Fajardo to Culebra and Vieques. ✉ *Carr De Maternillo, Fajardo* ☎ *787/494-0934* ⊕ *www.dtop.gov.pr.*

CAR TRAVEL

In San Juan it's often more trouble than it's worth to rent a car. Elsewhere a car is probably a necessity. A valid driver's license from your country of origin can be used in Puerto Rico for three months. Rates start as low as $25 a day. Several well-marked multilane highways link population centers. Driving distances are posted in kilometers, but speed limits are posted in miles per hour. Road signs are in Spanish.

International Agencies Avis ✉ *San Juan International Airport, Terminal Building, Carolina* ☎ *787/253-5926* ⊕ *www.avis.com.* **Hertz** ☎ *800/654-3030* ⊕ *www.hertz.com.* **National** ☎ *888/222-9058* ⊕ *www.nationalcar.com.* **Thrifty** ☎ *800/847-4389* ⊕ *www.thrifty.com.*

Local Agencies Charlie Car Rental ☎ *787/728-2418* ⊕ *www.charliecars.com.* **Vias** ☎ *787/791-4120* ⊕ *www.viascarrental.com.*

LOGISTICS

Getting to Puerto Rico: There are dozens of daily flights to Puerto Rico from the United States. San Juan's international airport is a major regional hub, so many travelers headed elsewhere in the Caribbean make connections here. Fares to San Juan are among the most reasonably priced in the region. The island also has airports in Aguadilla (BQN), Fajardo (FAJ), Ponce (PSE), and Mayagüez (MAZ), and on the islands of Vieques (VQS) and Culebra (CPX). Culebra and Vieques can also be reached by ferry.

Hassle Factor: Low.

On the Ground: Before arriving, check with your hotel about transfers: some hotels and resorts provide transport from the airport—free or for a fee—to their guests; some larger resorts run regular shuttles. Otherwise, your best bets are *taxis turísticos* (tourist taxis). Uniformed officials at the airport can help you make arrangements. They will give you a slip with your exact fare to hand to the driver. Rates are based on your destination. There's a $1 charge for each bag handled by the driver.

TAXI TRAVEL

The Puerto Rico Tourism Company has instituted a well-organized taxi program. White taxis with the "taxi turistico" logo run from the airport or the cruise-ship piers to Isla Verde, Condado/Ocean Park, and Old San Juan, with fixed "zone" rates ranging from $10 to $24. If you take a cab going somewhere outside the fixed zones, insist on setting the meter. City tours start at $36 per hour. In other towns you can flag down cabs on the street, but it's easier to have your hotel call one for you. ■TIP→ **Make sure the driver is clear on whether he or she will charge a flat rate or use a meter to determine the fare. In most places, the cabs are metered.**

Contacts Major Cab Company ☎ *787/723–2460.* **Metro Taxi** ☎ *787/725–2870* ⊕ *www.metrotaxipr.com.*

ESSENTIALS

Banks and Money The U.S. dollar is the official currency. Major credit cards are widely accepted, ATMs are readily available and reliable in the cities and less frequently in rural areas. Look to local banks such as Banco Popular and First Bank.

Electricity 110 volts/60 cycles.

Emergencies Dial 911. For nonemergencies, the Tourist Zone Police are particularly helpful to visitors. **Tourist Zone Police** ☎ *787/725–7015 for Condado, 787/726–2981 for Isla Verde.*

Language Puerto Rico is officially bilingual, but Spanish dominates, particularly outside the tourist areas of San Juan. Although English is widely spoken, you'll probably want to take a Spanish phrase book along on your travels about the island.

Passport Requirements U.S. citizens don't need passports. You will not pass through immigration, but there is an agriculture inspection before you check in for your flight home.

Phones Most U.S. mobile phone users will not pay roaming charges in Puerto Rico; confirm with your company. Area codes are 787 and 939. Toll-free numbers (prefix 800, 888, or 877) are widely used, and many can be accessed from North America (and vice versa). To make a local call in Puerto Rico you must dial 1, the area code, and the seven-digit number. For international calls, dial 011, the country code, the city code, and the number. Dial 00 for an international long-distance operator. Phone cards are widely available (most drugstores carry them).

Taxes Accommodations incur a tax: for hotels with casinos it's 11%, for other hotels it's 9%, and for government-approved paradores it's 7%. Ask your hotel before booking. The tax, in addition to the standard 5% to 12% service charge or resort fee applied by most hotels, can add a hefty 20% or more to your bill. There's a 5.5% sales tax in Puerto Rico, and some municipalities charge an additional 1.5%.

Tipping Tips are expected, and appreciated, by restaurant waitstaff (15% to 20% if a service charge isn't included), hotel porters ($1 per bag), maids ($1 to $2 a day), and taxi drivers (15% to 18%).

ACCOMMODATIONS

If you want easy access to shopping, dining, and nightlife, then you should stay in San Juan, which also has decent—though by no means the island's best—beaches. Most of the other large, deluxe resorts are along the northeast coast. There are also a few resorts along the southern coast. Rincón, in the west, has a concentration of resorts and great surfing. Other small inns and hotels are around the island in the interior, including a few around El Yunque. Look to Vieques and Culebra if you want to find excellent beaches and little development. Many larger resorts in Puerto Rico charge resort fees, which are uncommon elsewhere in the Caribbean.

Big Hotels: San Juan's beaches are lined with large-scale hotels that include happening restaurants and splashy casinos. Most are spread out along Condado and Isla Verde beaches.

Paradores: Small inns (many offering home-style comida criolla cooking) are spread out around the island, though they are rarely on the beach.

Upscale Beach Resorts: All over the island—but particularly along the north coast—large tourist resorts offer all the amenities along with a hefty dose of isolation. Just be prepared for expensive food and few off-resort restaurants nearby.

HOTEL AND RESTAURANT PRICES

Prices in the restaurant reviews are the average cost of a main course at dinner or, if dinner is not served, at lunch; taxes and service charges are generally included. Prices in the hotel reviews are the lowest cost of a standard double room in high season, excluding taxes, service charges, and meal plans (except at all-inclusives). Prices for rentals are the lowest per-night cost for a one-bedroom unit in high season.

For expanded lodging reviews and current deals, visit Fodors.com.

VISITOR INFORMATION

Contact **Puerto Rico Tourism Company** ⊠ *Ochoa Bldg., Calle Tanca and Calle Comercio, across from Pier 1, Old San Juan, San Juan* ☎ *787/721–2400* ⊕ *www. seepuertorico.com* ⊠ *Luis Muñoz Marín International Airport, Carolina, San Juan* ☎ *787/791–1014.*

WEDDINGS

There are no special residency requirements, but U.S. citizens must produce a birth certificate, as well as a driver's license or other state-issued photo identification. Both you and your intended must appear together at the office to purchase a marriage license. A judge or any member of the clergy may then perform your ceremony. The fee is usually between $150 and $350. Most large hotels on the island have marriage coordinators who can explain the necessary paperwork and help you complete it on time for your marriage ceremony.

EXPLORING

OLD SAN JUAN

Old San Juan, the original city founded in 1521, contains carefully preserved examples of 16th- and 17th-century Spanish colonial architecture. More than 400 buildings have been beautifully restored. Graceful wrought-iron balconies with lush hanging plants extend over narrow streets paved with *adoquines* (blue-gray stones originally used as ballast on Spanish ships). The Old City is partially enclosed by walls that date from 1633 and once completely surrounded it. Designated a U.S. National Historic Zone in 1950, Old San Juan is chockablock with shops, open-air cafés, homes, tree-shaded squares, monuments, and people. You can get an overview on a morning's stroll (bear in mind that this "stroll" includes some steep climbs). However, if you plan to immerse yourself in history or to shop, you'll need a couple of days.

17

TOP ATTRACTIONS

FAMILY
Fodor's Choice
★
Castillo San Cristóbal. This huge stone fortress, built between 1634 and 1790, guarded the city from land attacks from the east. The largest Spanish fortification in the New World, San Cristóbal was known in the 17th and 18th centuries as the Gibraltar of the West Indies. Five freestanding structures divided by dry moats are connected by tunnels. You're free to explore the gun turrets (with cannon in situ), officers' quarters, re-created 18th-century barracks, and gloomy passageways. Along with El Morro, San Cristóbal is a National Historic Site administered by the U.S. Park Service; it's a World Heritage Site as well. Rangers conduct tours in Spanish and English. ⊠ *Calle Norzagaray at Av. Muñoz Rivera, Old San Juan* ☎ *787/729–6777* ⊕ *www.nps.gov/saju* ☜ *$3; $5 includes admission to El Morro* ⊙ *Daily 9–6.*

FAMILY
Fodor's Choice
★
Castillo San Felipe del Morro (*El Morro*). At the northwestern tip of the Old City is El Morro ("the promontory"), a fortress built by the Spaniards between 1539 and 1786. Rising 140 feet above the sea, the massive six-level fortress was built to protect the harbor entrance. It is a

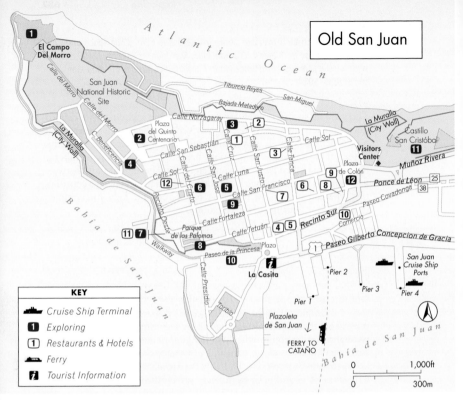

Old San Juan

KEY

🚢 Cruise Ship Terminal
1️⃣ Exploring
1️⃣ Restaurants & Hotels
⛴ Ferry
ℹ️ Tourist Information

labyrinth of cannon batteries, ramps, barracks, turrets, towers, and tunnels. Built to protect the port, El Morro has a commanding view of the harbor. You're free to wander throughout. The cannon emplacement walls and the dank secret passageways are a wonder of engineering. The fort's small but enlightening museum displays ancient Spanish guns and other armaments, military uniforms, and blueprints for Spanish forts in the Americas, although Castillo San Cristóbal has more extensive and impressive exhibits. There's also a gift shop. The fort is a National Historic Site administered by the U.S. Park Service; it's a World Heritage Site as well. Various tours and a video are available in English. ⊠ *Calle del Morro, Old San Juan* ☎ *787/729–6960* ⊕ *www.nps.gov/saju* ☜ *$3; $5 includes admission to Castillo San Cristóbal* ⊙ *Daily 9–6.*

La Fortaleza. Sitting atop the fortified city walls overlooking the harbor, La Fortaleza was built between 1533 and 1540 as a fortress, but it proved to be insufficient, mainly because it was built inside the bay. It was attacked numerous times and was occupied twice, by the British in 1598 and the Dutch in 1625. When El Morro and the city's other fortifications were finished, the Fortaleza became the governor's palace. Numerous changes have been made to the original primitive structure over the past four centuries, resulting in the current eclectic yet eye-pleasing collection of marble and mahogany, medieval towers, and stained-glass galleries. It is still the official residence of the island's governor, and is the Western Hemisphere's oldest executive mansion in continual use. Guided tours of the gardens and the building's exterior are conducted several times a day in English and Spanish. Call ahead, as the schedule changes daily. Proper attire is required: no sleeveless shirts or very short shorts. The tours begin near the main gate in a yellow building called the Real Audiencia, housing the Oficina Estatal de Preservación Histórica. ⊠ *Western end of Calle Fortaleza, Old San Juan* ☎ *787/721–7000* ⊕ *www.fortaleza.gobierno.pr* ☜ *Free* ⊙ *Weekdays 9–4:30.*

Paseo de la Princesa. Built in the mid-19th century to honor the Spanish princess of Asturias, this street has a broad pedestrian walkway and is spruced up with flowers, trees, benches, and street lamps. Unfurling westward from Plaza del Inmigrante along the base of the fortified city walls, it leads to the Fuente Raíces, a striking fountain depicting the various ethnic groups of Puerto Rico. Take a seat and watch the boats zip across the water. Beyond the fountain is the beginning of Paseo del Morro, a well-paved shoreline path that hugs Old San Juan's walls and leads past the city gate at Calle San Juan and continues to the tip of the headland, beneath El Morro. ⊠ *Paseo de la Princesa, Old San Juan.*

WORTH NOTING

Alcaldía. San Juan's city hall was built between 1602 and 1789. In 1841, extensive alterations were made so that it would resemble the city hall in Madrid, with arcades, towers, balconies, and an inner courtyard. Renovations have refreshed the facade of the building and some interior rooms, but the architecture remains true to its colonial style. Only the patios are open to public viewings. A municipal tourist information center and an art gallery with rotating exhibits are in the lobby. ⊠ *153 Calle San Francisco, Plaza de Armas, Old San Juan* ☎ *787/480–2548* ☜ *Free* ⊙ *Weekdays 8–4.*

17

Museo de las Américas. On the second floor of the imposing former military barracks, Cuartel de Ballajá, this museum houses four permanent exhibits: Popular Arts, African Heritage, the Indian in America, and Conquest and Colonization. You'll also find a number of temporary exhibitions of works by regional artists. A wide range of handicrafts is available in the gift shop. ⊠ *Calle Norzagaray and Calle del Morro, Old San Juan* ☎ *787/724–5052* ⊕ *www.museolasamericas.org* 🖾 *$3* ☺ *Tues.–Sat. 9–noon, 1–4, Sun. noon–5.*

Plaza de Armas. The Old City's original main square was once used as military drilling grounds. Bordered by Calles San Francisco, Rafael Cordero, San José, and Cruz, it has a fountain with 19th-century statues representing the four seasons as well as a bandstand, a small café and kiosk that sells local snacks and fruit frappés. The Alcaldía commands the north side. This is one of the most popular meeting places in Old San Juan, so you're likely to encounter lots of bustle: artists sketching caricatures, pedestrians waiting in line at food carts, and hundreds of pigeons waiting for handouts. ⊠ *Calle San José, Old San Juan.*

Plaza de Colón. The tallest statue of Christopher Columbus in the Americas stands atop a soaring column and fountain in this bustling Old San Juan square, kitty-corner to Castillo San Cristóbal. What was once called St. James Square was renamed in 1893 to honor the 400th anniversary of Columbus's arrival in Puerto Rico. Bronze plaques on the statue's base relate various episodes in the life of the explorer. Local artisans often line the plaza, so it's a good place to stop for souvenirs. Cool off with a fresh fruit frappé or smoothie at the newly opened kiosk. ⊠ *Old San Juan.*

GREATER SAN JUAN

Taxis, buses, *públicos* (shared vans), or a rental car are needed to reach the points of interest in "new" San Juan. Avenida Muñoz Rivera, Avenida Ponce de León, and Avenida Fernández Juncos are the main thoroughfares that cross Puerta de Tierra, east of Old San Juan, to the business and tourist districts of Santurce, Condado, Ocean Park, and Isla Verde. Dos Hermanos Bridge connects Puerta de Tierra with Miramar, Condado, and Isla Grande. Isla Grande Airport, from which you can take short hops, is on the bay side of the bridge. On the other side, the Condado Lagoon is bordered by Avenida Ashford, which goes past the high-rise Condado hotels, and Avenida Baldoriorty de Castro Expreso, which barrels east to the airport and beyond. Due south of the lagoon is Miramar, a residential area with fashionable turn-of-the-20th-century homes and a few hotels and restaurants. Isla Verde, with its glittering beachfront hotels, casinos, discos, and public beach, is to the east, near the airport.

TOP ATTRACTIONS

Museo de Arte Contemporáneo de Puerto Rico. This Georgian-style structure, once a public school, displays a dynamic range of works by both established and up-and-coming Latin American artists. Many of the works on display have strong political messages, including pointed

Hear your footsteps echo throughout Castillo San Felipe's vast network of tunnels, designed to amplify the sounds of approaching enemies.

commentaries on Puerto Rico's status as a commonwealth. Only a small part of the more than 900 works in the permanent collection is on display at any time, but it might be anything from an exhibit of ceramics to a screening of videos. ⊠ *1220 Av. Ponce de León, at Av. R.H. Todd, Santurce* ☎ *787/977–4030* ✉ *$5* ☉ *Tues.–Fri. 10–4, Sat. 11–5, Sun. 1–5.*

Fodor'sChoice ★ **Museo de Arte de Puerto Rico.** One of the biggest museums in the Caribbean, this beautiful neoclassical building was once the San Juan Municipal Hospital. The collection of Puerto Rican art starts with works from the colonial era, most of them commissioned for churches. Here you'll find works by José Campeche, the island's first great painter. His *Immaculate Conception*, finished in 1794, is a masterpiece. Also well represented is Francisco Oller y Cestero, who was the first to move beyond religious subjects to paint local scenes. Another gallery room is filled with works by artists inspired by Oller. The original building, built in the 1920s, proved to be too small to house the museum's collection: the newer east wing is dominated by a five-story-tall stained-glass window, the work of local artist Eric Tabales. Entrance is free on Wednesday 2–8. There's much more to the museum, including a beautiful garden filled with a variety of native flora and a 400-seat theater that's worth seeing for its remarkable hand-crocheted lace curtain. ⊠ *299 Av. José de Diego, Santurce* ☎ *787/977–6277* ⊕ *www.mapr.org* ✉ *$6* ☉ *Tues. and Thurs.–Sat. 10–5, Wed. 10–8, Sun. 11–6.*

Continued on page 696

WALKING OLD SAN JUAN

Old San Juan is Puerto Rico's quintessential colonial neighborhood. Narrow streets and plazas are still enclosed by thick fortress walls, and bougainvillea bowers spill over exquisite facades. A walk along streets paved with slate-blue cobblestones leads past colonial mansions, ancient churches, and intriguing museums and galleries. Vivacious restaurants and bars that teem with life young and old are always nearby, making it easy to refuel and reinvigorate anytime during your stroll. *by Christopher P. Baker*

left, strolling down Calle del Cristo; top right, a view from El Morro; bottom right, dancers in front of Castillo San Cristóbal

A STROLL THROUGH OLD SAN JUAN

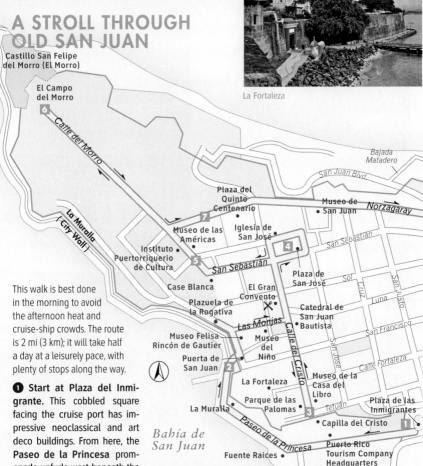

Castillo San Felipe del Morro (El Morro)

El Campo del Morro

Calle del Morro

La Muralla (City Wall)

La Fortaleza

Bajada Matadero

San Juan Blvd.

Plaza del Quinto Centenario

Museo de San Juan

Norzagaray

Museo de las Américas

Iglesia de San José

San Sebastián

Instituto Puertorriqueño de Cultura

San Sebastián

Sol

Cruz

San Justo

Case Blanca

El Gran Convento

Plaza de San José

Luna

Plazuela de la Rogativa

Catedral de San Juan Bautista

Las Monjas

San Francisco

Museo Felisa Rincón de Gautier

Museo del Niño

Calle del Cristo

San José

Calle Fortaleza

Puerta de San Juan

La Fortaleza

Museo de la Casa del Libro

Plaza de las Inmigrantes

Parque de las Palomas

Tetuán

La Muralla

Paseo de la Princesa

Capilla del Cristo

Bahía de San Juan

Fuente Raíces

Puerto Rico Tourism Company Headquarters

This walk is best done in the morning to avoid the afternoon heat and cruise-ship crowds. The route is 2 mi (3 km); it will take half a day at a leisurely pace, with plenty of stops along the way.

❶ Start at Plaza del Inmigrante. This cobbled square facing the cruise port has impressive neoclassical and art deco buildings. From here, the **Paseo de la Princesa** promenade unfurls west beneath the ancient city wall, **La Muralla**. Artisans set up stalls under the palms on weekends. Midway along the brick-paved walkway, stop to admire the **Fuente Ra-**

ices monument and fountain: dolphins cavort at the feet of figures representing Puerto Rico's indigenous, Spanish, and African peoples.

❷ Pass through the Puerta de San Juan. This fortified entrance in La Muralla was built in 1520 and still retains its massive wooden gates, creaky on their ancient hinges. Immediately beyond, turn left and ascend to **Plazuela de la Rogativa**, a tiny plaza where a contemporary statue recalls

the torch-lit procession that thwarted an English invasion in 1797. The harbor views are fantastic. Then, walk east one block to reach the **Catedral de San Juan Bautista**, the neoclassical 19th-century cathedral containing the mausoleum of Ponce de León.

❸ Head south on Calle del Cristo. Sloping gradually, this lovely cobbled street is lined with beautifully restored colonial mansions housing cafés, galleries, and boutiques. Pass-

Puerta de San Juan

Castillo San Cristóbal   Calle del Cristo   Catedral de San Juan Bautista

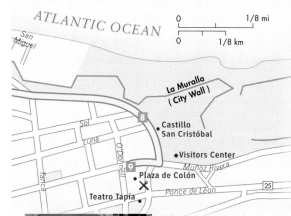

ATLANTIC OCEAN

0   1/8 mi
0   1/8 km

La Muralla (City Wall)

Castillo San Cristóbal

◆Visitors Center

Plaza de Colón

Teatro Tapía

Castillo San Felipe del Morro

ing Calle Fortaleza, note **La Fortaleza**, the official residence of the Puerto Rican Governor at the end of the street. Calle del Cristo ends at **Capilla del Cristo**, a chapel adorned within by silver *milagros* (token requests).

❹ Return via Calle del Cristo and continue to Plaza de San José. Catercorner to the cathedral you'll find **El Gran Convento**, a former convent turned hotel, with an excellent restaurant, tapas bar, and café. At **Plaza de San José** visit the

Iglesia de San José, a simple church dating from 1532.

❺ Walk west on Calle San Sebastián. This narrow street with colonial mansions painted in vibrant pastels ends at the gleaming white **Casa Blanca**. The oldest continually occupied residence in the Americas was originally the home of Ponce de León. Today it's a delightful museum furnished with period pieces. The garden is a tranquil spot for contemplation.

❻ Follow Calle del Morro north. One block from Casa Blanca you'll emerge upon a broad grassy headland—the Campo del Morro—popular with kite-flying families. It's skewered by an arrow-straight gravel path that aims at the imposing **Castillo San Felipe del Morro (El Morro)**, guarding the harbor entrance. Allow one-hour to roam the small museum, tur-

rets, labyrinthine tunnels, and six levels of ramparts soaring 140 feet above the ocean.

❼ Retrace your steps and turn left on Calle Norzagaray. This street runs atop the Atlantic shoreline, offering sweeping ocean vistas. On your right you'll pass the **Plaza del Quinto Centenario**, pinned by an impressive statue: the *Tótem Telúrico*. Beyond, stroll past the Convento de los Dominicos to reach the **Museo de San Juan**. Housed in a former market, it traces the city's history and displays works by Puerto Rico's master painters.

❽ Continue east to Castillo San Cristóbal. Spanning 27 acres, this multitiered fortress was completed in 1771 with mighty bulwarks that protected the city from eastern attack by land. It features superb historical exhibits and reenactments by soldiers in period costumes.

❾ Exit the castle, turn south and walk one block to Plaza de Colón, This leafy square is lined with excellent cafés and restaurants where you can rest your feet and enjoy a great meal.

WORTH NOTING

El Capitolio. The white-marble Capitol, a fine example of Italian Renaissance style, dates from 1929. The grand rotunda, which can be seen from all over San Juan, was completed in the late 1990s. Fronted by eight Corinthian columns, it's a very dignified home for the commonwealth's constitution. Although the Senate and the House of Representatives have offices in the more modern buildings on either side, the Capitol is where the legislators meet. Guided tours, which last about an hour and include visits to the rotunda and other parts of the building, are by appointment only. ⊠ *Av. Constitución, Puerta de Tierra* ☎ *787/724–2030* ☜ *Free* ⊙ *Weekdays 9:15–3:45.*

Museo de Historia, Antropología y Arte. The Universidad de Puerto Rico's small Museum of History, Anthropology and Art offers rotating exhibitions in three areas. Its archaeological and historical collection covers the Native American influence on the island and the Caribbean, the colonial era, and the history of slavery. There's also a small collection of Egyptian antiquities. Art holdings include a range of Puerto Rican popular, graphic, folk, and fine art; the museum's prize exhibit is the painting *El Velorio* (*The Wake*), by the 19th-century artist Francisco Oller. If you're looking to see something in particular, call before you go, as only a small portion of the collection is on display at a time. Guided tours in English are available; call ahead to make a reservation. ⊠ *Universidad de Puerto Rico, Av. Ponce de León, Río Piedras* ☎ *787/763–3939* ☜ *Free* ⊙ *Mon., Tues., Thurs., and Fri. 9–4:30, Wed. 9–8:30, Sun. 11:30–4:30.*

SAN JUAN ENVIRONS

WORTH NOTING

Casa Bacardí Visitor Center. Exiled from Cuba, the Bacardí family built a small rum distillery here in the 1950s. Today it's the world's largest, with the capacity to produce 100,000 gallons of spirits a day and 21 million cases a year. You can hop on a little tram to take an approximately 45-minute tour of the visitor center, though you don't visit the distillery itself. Yes, you'll be offered two free samples. If you don't want to drive, you can reach the factory by taking the ferry from Pier 2 for 50¢ each way and then a *público* (public van service) from the ferry pier to the factory for about $2 or $3 per person. ⊠ *Bay View Industrial Park, Rte. 165, Km 2.6, at Rte. 888, Cataño* ☎ *787/788–1500* ⊕ *www.casabacardi.org* ☜ *Free* ⊙ *Mon.–Sat. 9–6, last tour at 4:15; Sun. 10–5, last tour at 3:45.*

EASTERN PUERTO RICO

EL YUNQUE

FAMILY

Fodor'sChoice

★

El Yunque is the only tropical rain forest in the U.S. National Forest System, spanning 28,000 acres, reaching an elevation of more than 3,500 feet and receiving an estimated average of 200–240 inches of rain each year. The forest's 13 hiking trails are extremely well maintained; many of them are easy to navigate and less than 1 mile (1½ km) long. It's about 73°F year-round, so weather isn't much of a factor for seasonal planning. For easy parking and fewer crowds, be sure to arrive early in the day, although the park rarely gets crowded by U.S. National Park standards. Expect rain nearly every day, but keep eyes peeled post-showers for the best bird-watching.

Carve out some time to stop at the cathedral-like **El Portal Visitor Center** (⊠ *Rte. 191, Km 4.3, off Rte. 3* ☎ *787/888–1880* ⊕ *www.fs.usda.gov/elyunque* ☞ *$4* ⊘ *Daily 9–4:30*). Enter via an elevated walkway that transports visitors across the forest canopy, 60 feet above the ground. Signs identify and explain the birds, animals, and other treasures seen among the treetops. Below the walkway, there's a ground-level nature trail with stunning views of the lower forest and coastal plain. Inside the center, interactive exhibits explain the El Yunque National Forest's history, topography, flora, and fauna. The facility also has a well-stocked bookstore and gift shop.

The trails on the north side of El Yunque, the park's main tourist hub, tend toward folks with minimal or no hiking experience. There are several short trails (about ½ mile [.8 km]) that are completely paved. On the south side, expect fewer people and moderate to challenging hikes. These trails are not as well maintained as the marked trails found lower in the forest. Regardless of where you go, you'll be immersed in the sounds, smells, and scenic landscape of the park. For avid outdoor adventurers, it's possible to hike between the north and south sides of El Yunque. If you prefer to see the sights from a car, as many people do, simply follow Route 191 as it winds into the mountains and stop at several observation points along the way.

FAJARDO

Founded in 1772, Fajardo was once known as a port where pirates stocked up on supplies. It later developed into a fishing community and an area where sugarcane flourished. (There are still cane fields on the city's fringes.) Today it's a hub for the yachts that use its marinas; the divers who head to its good offshore sites; and the day-trippers who travel by catamaran, ferry, or plane to the out-islands of Culebra and Vieques. With the most-significant docking facilities on the island's eastern side, Fajardo is often congested and difficult to navigate.

Reserva Natural Las Cabezas de San Juan. The 316-acre reserve on a headland north of Fajardo is owned by the nonprofit Conservation Trust of Puerto Rico. You ride in open-air trolleys and wander down boardwalks through seven ecosystems, including lagoons, mangrove swamps, and dry-forest areas. Green iguanas skitter across paths, and guides identify other endangered species. A half-hour hike down a wooden walkway brings you to the mangrove-lined **Laguna Grande,** where bioluminescent microorganisms glow at night. The restored **Fajardo Lighthouse** is the final stop on the tour; its Spanish-colonial tower has been in operation since 1882, making it Puerto Rico's second-oldest lighthouse. The first floor houses ecological displays; a winding staircase leads to an observation deck. The only way to see the reserve is on one of the many guided tours; reservations are required through the Conservation's comprehensive website. ⊠ *Rte. 987, Km 6* ☎ *787/722–5882 weekdays, 787/860–2562 weekends* ⊕ *www.paralanaturaleza.org* ☞ *$10.*

VIEQUES AND CULEBRA

CULEBRA

Culebra is known around the world for its curvaceous coastline. Playa Flamenco, the tiny island's most famous stretch of sand, is considered one of the two or three best beaches in the world. If Playa Flamenco gets too crowded, as it often does around Easter and Christmas, there are many other beaches that will be nearly deserted. There's archaeological evidence that Taíno and Carib peoples lived on Culebra long before the arrival of the Spanish in the late 15th century. The Spanish didn't bother laying claim to it until 1886; its dearth of freshwater made it an unattractive location for a settlement. Although the island now has modern conveniences, its pace seems little changed from a century ago. There's only one town, Dewey, named after U.S. Admiral George Dewey. When the sun goes down, Culebra winds down as well. But during the day it's a delightful place to stake out a spot on Playa Flamenco or Playa Soni and read, swim, or search for shells. So what causes stress on the island? Nada.

VIEQUES

This island off Puerto Rico's east coast is famed for its Playa Sun Bay, a gorgeous stretch of sand with picnic facilities and shade trees. In 2003 the U.S. Navy withdrew from its military operations and turned over two-thirds of Vieques to the local government, which is transforming it into the Vieques National Wildlife Refuge. Vieques has two communities—Isabel Segunda, where the ferries dock, and the smaller Esperanza. Both have restaurants and hotels that will surprise you with their sophistication.

Fodor's Choice   **Puerto Mosquito Bioluminescent Bay.** East of Esperanza, Puerto Mosquito
★   Bioluminescent Bay is one of the world's best spots to have a glow-in-the-dark experience with undersea dinoflagellates. Local tour operators offer kayak trips or excursions on nonpolluting boats to see the bay's microorganisms, which light up when the water around them is agitated. Look behind your boat, and you'll see a twinkling wake. Even the fish that swim through and jump from the water will bear an eerie glow. The high concentration of dinoflagellates sets the bay apart from the other spots around the world (including others in Puerto Rico) that are home to these microorganisms. The bay is at its best when there's little or no moonlight; rainy nights are beautiful, too, because the raindrops splashing in the water produce ricochet sparkles that shimmer like diamonds. ⊠ *Reach via unpaved roads off Rte. 997, Vieques.*

SOUTHERN PUERTO RICO

Bosque Estatal de Guánica (*Guánica State Forest*). The 9,900-acre Bosque Estatal de Guánica, a United Nations Biosphere Reserve, is a great place for hiking expeditions. It's an outstanding example of a tropical dry coastal forest, with some 700 species of plants, ranging from the prickly-pear cactus to the gumbo limbo tree. It's also one of the best places on the island for bird-watching, since you can spot more than 100 species, including the pearly-eyed thrasher, the lizard cuckoo, and the nightjar.

One of the most popular hikes is the **Ballena Trail,** which begins at the ranger station on Route 334. This easy 1¼-mile (2-km) walk follows a partially paved road and takes you past a mahogany plantation to a dry plain covered with stunted cactus. A sign reading "Guayacán centenario" leads you to an extraordinary guayacán tree with a trunk that measures six-feet across. The moderately difficult **Fuerte Trail** takes you on a 3½-mile (5½-km) hike to an old fort built by the Spanish Armada. It was destroyed during the Spanish-American War in 1898, but you can still see the ruins of the old observatory tower.

In addition to going in the main entrance on Route 334, you can enter on Route 333, which skirts the forest's southwestern quadrant. You can also try the less explored western section, off Route 325. ⌧ *Rte. 334, Guánica* ☎ *787/821–5706* ⌧ *Free* ☽ *Daily 9–5.*

PONCE

The island's second-largest urban area, Ponce shines in 19th-century style with pink-marble-bordered sidewalks, painted trolleys, and horse-drawn carriages. Stroll around the main square, the Plaza de las Delicias, with its perfectly pruned India-laurel fig trees, graceful fountains, gardens, and park benches. View the Catedral de Nuestra Señora de la Guadalupe (Our Lady of Guadalupe Cathedral), perhaps even attend the 6 am Mass, and walk down Calles Isabel and Cristina to see turn-of-the-20th-century wooden houses with wrought-iron balconies.

TOP ATTRACTIONS

FAMILY

Fodor'sChoice

★

Hacienda Buena Vista. Built by Salvador de Vives in 1838, Buena Vista was one of the area's largest coffee plantations. It's a technological marvel—water from the nearby Río Canas was funneled into narrow brick channels that could be diverted to perform any number of tasks, including turning the waterwheel. (Seeing the two-story wheel slowly begin to turn is fascinating, especially for kids.) Nearby is the two-story manor house, filled with furniture that gives a sense of what it was like to live on a coffee plantation nearly 150 years ago. Make sure to take a look in the kitchen, dominated by a massive hearth. In 1987 the plantation was restored by the Puerto Rican Conservation Trust, which leads four tours a day (at least one in English). The tours are by reservation only, so make sure to call several days ahead. After seeing the plantation, you can buy coffee beans and other souvenirs at the gift shop. Allow yourself an hour to travel the winding road from Ponce. ⌧ *Rte. 123, Km 16.8, Sector Corral Viejo* ☎ *787/722–5882 weekdays, 787/284–7020 weekends* ⊕ *www.paralanaturaleza.org* ⌧ *$10* ☽ *Wed.–Sun., tours at 8:30, 10:30, 1:30 and 3:30.*

Fodor'sChoice

★

Museo de Arte de Ponce. Designed by Edward Durrell Stone, who also designed the original Museum of Modern Art in New York City and the Kennedy Center in Washington, D.C., Ponce's Art Museum is easily identified by the hexagonal galleries on the second story. The museum has one of the best art collections in Latin America, which is why residents of San Juan frequently make the trip down to Ponce. The 4,500-piece collection includes works by famous Puerto Rican artists such as Francisco Oller, represented by a lovely landscape called *Hacienda Aurora*. There are plenty of European works on display as well, including paintings by Peter Paul Rubens and Thomas Gainsborough. The highlight of the European collection is the pre-Raphaelite paintings, particularly the

17

mesmerizing *Flaming June,* by Frederick Leighton, which has become the museum's unofficial symbol. You can take a break in the museum's three sculpture gardens, or relax in Restaurant Al Sur. Watch for special exhibits, such as a recent one examining the work of video artists. ✉ *2325 Blvd. Luis A. Ferre Aguayo, Sector Santa María* ☎ *787/840–1510* ⊕ *www.museoarteponce.org* 🎟 *$6* ⊗ *Wed.–Mon. 10–6.*

FAMILY
Fodor'sChoice
★

Parque de Bombas. After El Morro in Old San Juan, this distinctive red-and-black-striped building may be the second-most-photographed structure in Puerto Rico. Built in 1882 as a pavilion for an agricultural and industrial fair, it was converted the following year into a firehouse. Today it's a museum tracing the history—and glorious feats—of Ponce's fire brigade. Kids love the antique fire truck on the lower level. Short tours in English and Spanish are given on the half hour, and you can sign up for free trolley tours of the historic downtown here. Helpful tourism officials staff a small information desk inside the door. ✉ *Plaza de las Delicias, Ponce Centro* ☎ *787/284–3338* ⊕ *www.visitponce.com* 🎟 *Free* ⊗ *Daily 9–5.*

WORTH NOTING

Museo de la Historia de Ponce. Housed in two adjoining neoclassical mansions, this museum includes 10 rooms with exhibits covering the city's residents, from Taíno Indians to Spanish settlers to the mix of the present. Hour-long guided tours in English and Spanish give an overview of the city's history. The descriptions are mostly in Spanish, but displays of clothing from different eras are interesting to see. ✉ *53 Calle Isabel, at Calle Mayor* ☎ *787/844–7071* 🎟 *Free* ⊗ *Tues.–Sun. 8–4.*

SAN GERMÁN

Around San Germán's (population 39,000) two main squares—Plazuela Santo Domingo and Plaza Francisco Mariano Quiñones (named for an abolitionist)—are buildings done in every conceivable style of architecture found on the island, including Mission, Victorian, Creole, and Spanish colonial. The city's tourist office offers a free, guided trolley tour. Students and professors from the Inter-American University often fill the center's bars and cafés.

CENTRAL PUERTO RICO

Fodor'sChoice
★

Arecibo Observatory. Hidden among pine-covered hills, the Arecibo Observatory is home to the world's largest radar-radio telescope. Operated by the National Astronomy and Ionosphere Center of Cornell University, the 20-acre dish lies in a 563-foot-deep sinkhole in the karst landscape. If the 600-ton platform hovering eerily over the dish looks familiar, it may be because it was featured in the movie *Contact.* You can walk around the viewing platform and explore two levels of interactive exhibits on planetary systems, meteors and weather phenomena in the visitor center. There's also a gift shop. Note that the trail leading up to the observatory is extremely steep. For those who have difficulty walking or have a medical condition, ask a staff member at the gate about a van that provides courtesy shuttle service to the observatory entrance. ✉ *Rte. 625, Km 3.0, Arecibo* ☎ *787/878–2612* ⊕ *www.naic. edu* 🎟 *$10* ⊗ *June, July, and mid-Dec.–mid-Jan., daily 9–4; Aug.–mid-Dec. and mid-Jan.–May, Wed.–Sun. 9–4.*

Today it's a museum, but for more than 100 years Parque de Bombas served as Ponce's main firehouse.

Parque de las Cavernas del Río Camuy. The 268-acre Parque de las Cavernas del Río Camuy contains one of the world's largest cave networks.
After watching an introductory film, a tram takes you down a trail
shaded by bamboo and banana trees to Cueva Clara, where the stalactites and stalagmites turn the entrance into a toothy grin. Hour-long
guided tours in English and Spanish lead you on foot through the
180-foot-high cave, which is teeming with wildlife. You're likely to
see the blue-eyed river crabs and long-legged tarantulas. More elusive
are the bats that make their home here. They don't come out until
dark, but you can feel the heat they generate at the cave's entrance.
The visit ends with a tram ride to the Tres Pueblos sinkhole, where
you can see the third-longest underground river in the world passing from one cave to another. Tours are first-come, first-served; plan
to arrive early on weekends, when locals join the crowds. There's a
picnic area, cafeteria, and gift shop. ⊠ *Rte. 129, Km 18.9, Camuy*
☎ *787/898–3100* ⊕ *www.parquesnacionalespr.com* ☎ *$15* ⊙ *Wed.–*
Sun. 8:30–5; last tour at 3:30.

WESTERN PUERTO RICO

MAYAGÜEZ

With a population of slightly more than 100,000, this is the largest
city on Puerto Rico's west coast. Although bypassed by the mania for
restoration that has spruced up Ponce and Old San Juan, Mayagüez is
graced by some lovely turn-of-the-20th-century architecture, such as the
landmark art deco Teatro Yagüez and the Plaza de Colón.

FAMILY **Zoológico de Puerto Rico.** Puerto Rico's only zoo, the 45-acre Zoológico de Puerto Rico, is just north of downtown. Its 45-foot-tall aviary allows you to walk through a rain-forest environment as tropical birds fly freely above your head. There's also a butterfly park where you can let brilliant blue morphos land on your hand, and an arthropodarium where you can get up close and personal with spiders and their kin. Video monitors are built into the floor to show off the bugs that normally get trampled underfoot. The older section of the park has undergone an extensive renovation, so most of the cages have been replaced by fairly natural-looking environments. One of the most popular residents is Mundi, a female elephant who arrived as a baby more than two decades ago. There are also plenty of lions, tigers—and even bears. ⊠ *Rte. 108, north of Rte. 65, Miradero* 🕾 *787/834–8110* ⊕ *www. parquesnacionalespr.com* 🖃 *$13; parking $3* ⊙ *Wed.–Sun. 8:30–4.*

RINCÓN

Jutting out into the ocean along the rugged western coast, Rincón, meaning "corner" in Spanish, may have gotten its name because it's tucked into a bend of the coastline. Some, however, trace the town's name to Gonzalo Rincón, a 16th-century landowner who let poor families live on his land. Whatever the history, the name suits the town, which is like a little world unto itself.

The most famous hotel in the region is the Horned Dorset Primavera—the only Relais & Chateaux property in Puerto Rico. It's one of the most luxurious resorts on the island, not to mention in the Caribbean. A couple of larger hotels, including the Rincón of the Seas and Rincón Beach Resort, have been built, but Rincón remains a laid-back place. The town is still a mecca for wave-seekers, particularly surfers from the East Coast of the United States, who often prefer the relatively quick flight to Aguadilla airport direct from New York–area airports instead of the long haul to the Pacific. One of Rincón's greatest attractions is the diving and snorkeling at nearby Desecheo Island, but the town continues to cater to all sorts of travelers, from budget-conscious surfers to families to honeymooners seeking romance.

BEACHES

In Puerto Rico the Foundation for Environmental Education, a non-profit agency, designates Blue Flag beaches. They have to meet 27 criteria, focusing on water quality, the presence of a trained staff, and the availability of facilities such as water fountains and restrooms.

Playa Flamenco, on the island of Culebra, made the cut. After all, it's rated one of the world's best beaches. More surprisingly, two of the beaches are in San Juan: Balneario Escambrón, in Puerta de Tierra, and Balneario Carolina, in Isla Verde. The fourth is Luquillo's Balneario Monserrate (Playa Luquillo). This means that three of Puerto Rico's finest beaches are within an hour's drive of the capital. In total the government maintains 13 *balnearios* (public beaches). They're gated and equipped with dressing rooms, lifeguards, parking, and, in some cases, picnic tables, playgrounds, and camping facilities.

SAN JUAN

The city's beaches can get crowded, especially on weekends. There's free access to all of them, but parking can be an issue in the peak sun hours—arriving early or in the late afternoon is a safer bet.

FAMILY **Balneario de Carolina.** When people discuss a "beautiful Isla Verde beach," this is the one they're talking about. East of Isla Verde, this Blue Flag beach is so close to the airport that the leaves rustle when planes take off. Thanks to an offshore reef, the surf is not as strong as other nearby beaches, so it's especially good for children and families. There's plenty of room to spread out underneath the palm and almond trees. For meals there are picnic tables and barbecue grills. Although there's a charge for parking, there's not always someone there to take the money. **Amenities:** lifeguards; showers; toilets. **Best for:** swimming; walking. ⊠ *Ave. Los Gobernadores, Carolina* ☎ *787/791–2410* 🖅 *$3 parking* ⊙ *Tues.–Sun. 8–5.*

FAMILY **Balneario El Escambrón.** In Puerta de Tierra, this government-run beach has a patch of honey-colored sand shaded by coconut palms. An offshore reef means that the surf is generally gentle, so it's favored by families. Nearby restaurants make picnicking a breeze. **Amenities:** food and drink; lifeguards, showers; toilets. **Best for:** swimming; walking. ⊠ *Ave. Muñoz Rivera, Puerta de Tierra* 🖅 *Parking $5* ⊙ *Daily 8–5:30.*

EASTERN PUERTO RICO

FAMILY
Fodor's Choice
★
Balneario La Monserrate. Just off Route 3, gentle Balneario La Monserrate is a magnet for families. Also known as Playa Luquillo, it's one of Puerto Rico's distinguished Blue Flag beaches. Lined with colorful lifeguard stations and shaded by soaring palm trees, it's well equipped with food stands, picnic areas, and even cocktail kiosks. Lounge chairs and umbrellas are available to rent, as are kayaks and Jet Skis. Its most distinctive facility is the Mar Sin Barreras (Sea Without Barriers), a low-sloped ramp leading into the water that allows wheelchair users to take a dip. **Amenities:** food and drink; lifeguards, parking (fee); showers; toilets. **Best for:** partiers; swimming; walking. ⊠ *Off Rte. 3, Luquillo* ☎ *787/889–5871* ⊕ *www.parquesnacionalespr.com* 🖅 *$4 per car* ⊙ *Wed.–Sun. 8:30–5.*

FAMILY **Balneario Seven Seas.** One of Puerto Rico's prized Blue Flag beaches, Balneario Seven Seas may turn out to be the best surprise of your trip. This long stretch of powdery sand near the Reserva Natural Las Cabezas de San Juan has calm, clear waters that are perfect for swimming. There are plenty of picnic tables, as well as restaurants just outside the gates. **Amenities:** food and drink; parking (fee); showers; toilets. **Best for:** swimming. ⊠ *Rte. 195, Km 4.8, Las Croabas* ☎ *787/863–8180* ⊕ *www.parquesnacionalespr.com* 🖅 *$4 parking* ⊙ *Wed.–Sun. 8:30–5.*

VIEQUES AND CULEBRA

Balneario Sun Bay. Just east of Esperanza, this mile-long stretch of sand skirts a perfect crescent-shaped bay. Dotted with picnic tables, this beach gets packed on holidays and weekends. On weekdays, when the crowds are thin, you might see wild horses grazing among the palm trees. Parking is $3, but often there is no one at the gate to take your money. **Amenities:** food and drink; parking (fee); showers; toilets. **Best for:** snorkeling; swimming; walking. ⊠ *Rte. 997, Esperanza, Vieques* ☎ *787/741–8198* ⊕ *www.parquesnacionalespr.com* 🖅 *$3 parking* ⊙ *Wed.–Sun. 8:30–5.*

17

Playa Caracas (*Red Beach*). Also known as Red Beach, Playa Caracas is one of the first stretches of sand you reach when you head east of Esperanza on Route 997. This beach is well-maintained and boasts covered cabañas for lounging away from the sun. Less rustic than some of the nearby beaches, this spot is sheltered from waves. **Amenities:** toilets. **Best for:** snorkeling; swimming; walking. ⊠ *Off Rte. 997, Vieques.*

FAMILY
Fodor'sChoice
★

Playa Flamenco. Consistently ranked one of the most beautiful beaches in the world, Playa Flamenco has snow-white sands, turquoise waters, and lush hills that rise on all sides. During the week, it's pleasantly uncrowded; on weekends it fills up fast with day-trippers from the mainland. With kiosks selling simple dishes and vendors for lounge-chair and umbrella rentals, it's easy to make a day of it. Don't miss the tanks on the northern end of the beach—a reminder that this area was once a military base. **Amenities:** food and drink; parking (free); showers; toilets. **Best For:** swimming; walking. ⊠ *Rte. 251, west of airport, Culebra* 🖀 *787/742–0700* ☉ *Daily dawn–dusk.*

SOUTHERN PUERTO RICO

Isla Caja de Muertos (*Coffin Island*). Named "Coffin Island" due to its shape, Isla Caja de Muertos is 5 miles off the coast and has the best beaches in the Ponce area. Stretching for 2 miles, it's one of the best snorkeling spots in southern Puerto Rico, second only to La Parguera. Due to the hawksbill turtles that nest between May and December, the island is protected by the Reserva Natural Caja de Muertos but you can still swim, snorkel, and dive here. A 30-minute hike across the island will take you to a small lighthouse that dates back to 1887. Scheduled boats leave La Guancha Friday through Sunday at 8:30 am and daily in high season. You'll need to pack in what you need (drinks and food) and pack out your garbage. **Amenities:** toilets. **Best for:** snorkeling; swimming; walking. ⊠ *Boats leave from La Guancha, at end of Rte. 14, Ponce.*

WESTERN PUERTO RICO

Balneario de Rincón. Swimmers enjoy the tranquil waters at this beach. There's a playground for the kids and shelters where families can enjoy seaside picnics. The beach is within walking distance of the center of town. **Amenities:** parking (free); showers; toilets. **Best for:** sunset; swimming. ⊠ *Calle Caubija, Rincón.*

Playa Crashboat. Here you'll find the colorful fishing boats that are portrayed on postcards all over the island. Named after the rescue boats used when the nearby Ramey Air Force Base was in operation, the beach has soft and sugary sand, and the water's as smooth as glass. A food stand run by locals serves the catch of the day with cold beer. Right before you cross the bridge leading down to the beach, a lookout point on your left is a perfect place for a photo op. **Amenities:** food and drink; parking (free); showers; toilets. **Best for:** partiers; snorkeling; swimming. ⊠ *End of Rte. 458, off Rte. 107, Aguadilla.*

WHERE TO EAT

In cosmopolitan San Juan, European, Asian, Middle Eastern, and chic fusion eateries vie for your attention with family-owned restaurants specializing in seafood or *comida criolla* (creole cooking, or local Puerto Rican food). Many of the most innovative chefs here have restaurants in the city's large hotels, but don't be shy about venturing into stand-alone establishments—many concentrated in Condado and Old San Juan. The historic center is also home to a number of notable new restaurants and cafés, offering more artisanal-style cuisine—crop-to-cup coffee, rustic homemade pizzas, and creative vegetarian food—at affordable prices. Throughout the island, there's a radiant pride in what the local land can provide, and enthusiastic restaurateurs are redefining what Puerto Rican food is, bite by tasty bite.

What to Wear: Dress codes vary greatly, though a restaurant's prices are a fairly good indicator of its formality. For less expensive places, anything but beachwear is fine. Ritzier eateries will expect collared shirts for men (jacket and tie requirements are rare) and chic attire for women. When in doubt, do as the Puerto Ricans often do and dress up.

OLD SAN JUAN

$$$ ✕ **Aguaviva.** The name means "jellyfish," which explains why this
SEAFOOD ultramodern place has dim blue lighting like a tranquil ocean, and lamps shaped like jellyfish floating overhead. Eating here is like submerging oneself into the sea. The extensive, ever-changing menu by Chef Hector Crespo features inventive ceviches, including the truffle tuna tartare with cucumber and green apple. For something more filling, try the lobster yucca gnocchi or the orzo paella, which is generously covered with an assortment of seafood. Chicken and chorizo with saffron beurre blanc are added to the dish making it oh so tasty and enough for two. You could also splurge on one of the *torres del mar,* or "towers of the sea." This gravity-defying dish comes hot or cold and includes oysters, mussels, shrimp—you name it. Don't pass up the Oysters Rockefeller, those alone are worth the trip. $ *Average main: $31* ⊠ *364 Calle Fortaleza, Old San Juan* ☎ *787/722–0665* ⊕ *www.oofrestaurants.com* ⊘ *No lunch.*

$ ✕ **Bistro Burger.** After exploring El Morro, head to Bistro Burger on
BURGER Calle San Sebastian for what locals consider the best burgers in town. Choose from the house burgers, all named after local artists or build your own burger with homemade ingredients. The Daphne Elvira is a great choice made with chorizo and pork, manchego cheese, red onion, and *acerola* (Caribbean cherry) ketchup on fresh foccacia bread. Don't leave without trying the *ropa vieja* egg rolls made with tender, stewed beef. The kitchen is open late on weekends, making Bistro Burger the perfect place to grab a bite after bar hopping on Calle San Sebastian. $ *Average main: $9* ⊠ *157 Calle San Sebastian, Old San Juan* ☎ *787/245–9062* ⊘ *Closed Mon. and Tues. No dinner Sun.*

17

$ CAFÉ Fodor's Choice ★ 🍴 **Café Cuatro Sombras.** If you want to try locally grown, single-origin, shade-grown coffee, this micro-roastery and café is the place to do it. Owners Pablo Muñoz and Mariana Suárez grow their beans in the mountains of Yauco on a hacienda that has been in Muñoz family since 1846. The wood planks that line the banquette are from repurposed coffee storage pallets, and the red accents that catch your eye throughout the room recall perfectly ripe coffee beans. The name Cuatro Sombras, or "four shades," refers to the four types of trees traditionally used in Puerto Rico to provide shade for coffee plants. And although it's the delicious, medium-bodied brew that steals the show, there's also a small but tasty menu of pastries and sandwiches. [$] *Average main: $7* ✉ *259 Calle Recinto Sur, Old San Juan* ☎ *787/724–9955* 🌐 *www.cuatrosombras.com* 🕒 *No dinner.*

$ CONTEMPORARY 🍴 **Casa Cortés ChocoBar.** The Cortés family has been making bean-to-bar chocolate for more than 85 years and in 2013, they opened up Puerto Rico's first Choco Bar to share their passion with the world. The walls in this vivid, modern space are decorated with vintage ads from the '50s, original chocolate bar molds, a timeline of chocolate, and two flat screens that depict the family's chocolate-making process. From pastries to tapas, breakfast dishes to panini sandwiches, the chef successfully integrates chocolate into every bite without overpowering the dish. Try the ripe plantain *mofonguitos* filled with chocolate and bacon bits. The panfried jumbo shrimp with a chocolate lemon sauce are delicious! Locals from all over the San Juan Metro area flock to ChocoBar for weekend brunch—arrive early to avoid a long wait. On Thursday, Saturday, and Sunday head upstairs to the gallery for a glimpse of the family's private art collection. [$] *Average main: $10* ✉ *210 Calle San Francisco, Old San Juan* ☎ *787/722–0499* 🌐 *www.casacortespr.com* 🕒 *Closed Mon. No dinner.*

$$$ LATIN AMERICAN 🍴 **Dragonfly.** Dark and sexy, this popular Latin-Asian restaurant, all done up in Chinese red, feels more like a fashionable after-hours lounge than a restaurant. The romantic ambience, created partly through tightly packed tables and low lighting, is a big draw. The small plates, meant to be shared, come in generous portions. Don't miss the Peking duck nachos and the pork and sweet plantain dumplings. Tuna sushi is turned on its head and served atop a deep-fried rice cake dressed with spicy mayo and seaweed salad. Make sure to try the inventive cocktails that nicely complement the food. Reservations aren't accepted, but we'll let you in on a secret to save yourself a frustrating wait: you can call ahead and get yourself put on the waiting list. [$] *Average main: $21* ✉ *364 Calle Fortaleza, Old San Juan* ☎ *787/977–3886* 🌐 *www.oofrestaurants.com* ✍ *Reservations not accepted* 🕒 *No lunch.*

$$ PUERTO RICAN 🍴 **La Fonda del Jibarito.** The menus are handwritten and the tables wobble, but *sanjuaneros* have favored this casual, no-frills, family-run restaurant—tucked away on a quiet cobbled street—for years. The *bistec encebollado,* goat fricassee, and shredded beef stew are among the specialties on the menu of typical Puerto Rican *comida criolla* dishes. The tiny back porch is filled with plants, and the dining room is filled with fanciful depictions of life on the street outside.

Troubadours serenade patrons, which include plenty of cruise-ship passengers when ships are in dock. $ *Average main: $14* ✉ *280 Calle Sol, Old San Juan* ☎ *787/725–8375.*

$$$ ✕ **Marmalade.** Prepare to be impressed when you enter Old San Juan's
ECLECTIC hippest—and finest—restaurant. Its U.S.-born owner-chef, Peter
Fodor's Choice Schintler, apprenticed with Raymond Blanc and Gordon Ramsay; here
★ he's created a class act that's famous for its ultra-chic lounge bar. The restaurant's sensual and minimalist orange-and-white decor features high-back chairs and cushioned banquettes beneath recessed halogen lights. The menu uses many sustainable and nonmodified ingredients prepared California-French fashion, resulting in complex flavors and strong aromas. The yellowtail is served with lemongrass and compressed watermelon while the pork cheeks are served with a peach-poblano marmalade. For dessert, indulge in the Millionnaire's ice cream, topped with honeycomb and shaved truffles. You can build your own four- to six-course tasting menu, with or without pairings from the *Wine Spectator* Award of Excellence wine list, or order à la carte. In addition, the restaurant is accommodating to vegetarians, vegans, and those with food allergies and/or dietary restrictions. $ *Average main: $32* ✉ *317 Calle Fortaleza, Old San Juan* ☎ *787/724–3969* ⊕ *www.marmaladepr. com* ⌕ *Reservations essential* ⊙ *No lunch.*

$$ ✕ **Verde Mesa.** With punched-tin ceilings, mason-jar lighting fixtures,
VEGETARIAN and eclectic decor inspired by Versailles' Petit Trianon, the focus
Fodor's Choice at this vegetarian restaurant is on pleasing the senses. Much of the
★ organic produce used in the regularly changing menu comes from the owners' farm and other local sources. The flavor combinations are anything but accidental. Start with a garlicky "hummus" of local pigeon peas. The signature Verde Mesa rice is a mixture of in-season vegetables and chickpeas that the owners say has turned many a skeptic into further exploring the culinary potential of vegetables. You'll also find quite a few expertly prepared tuna, salmon and scallop dishes, if you don't want to go all veggie. Your salmon might be cured with lavender and ginger and your scallop dish migh be served on a bed of parsnip mash, dressed with fig foam. Reservations are not accepted so arrive early; restaurant opens at 6 pm. $ *Average main: $22* ✉ *107 Calle Tetuán, at Calle San José, Old San Juan* ☎ *787/390–4662* ⊕ *www.verdemesa.com* ⌕ *Reservations not accepted* ⊙ *Closed Sun. and Mon. No lunch.*

$ ✕ **Waffle-era Tea Room.** The only tearoom in Puerto Rico is hugely popu-
CAFÉ lar, and it recently relocated to a larger space where they now take reservations, making locals very happy. You can choose from nearly 30 loose teas, including white and fruity blends as well as black. The carefully crafted cocktail menu is a nice addition to the new space. But you'll probably be even more curious about the coffee setup, which looks like a mad-science experiment. It's a siphon fire-brewing system, a painstaking process popular in Japan. The menu consists of house-made sweet or savory waffles—or smaller "wafflitos," and a revamped tapas menu that includes the signature ham hugged dates. These savory delicacies are stuffed with gorgonzola and cherry tomatoes, wrapped in fire-torched, brandy infused prosciutto. You might also choose a

17

"waffe-izza" with fresh tomato sauce and blowtorch-melted mozza-rella. We're still thinking of the decadent crème brûlée wafflito. At the time of this writing, the plan is to keep open the original location at 103 Calle Tetuan. $ *Average main: $9* ⌧ *252 Calle San José, Old San Juan* ☎ *787/721–9512* ⊕ *www.waffle-era.com* ⊙ *Closed Tues. and Wed. No dinner.*

GREATER SAN JUAN

$$$$
ECLECTIC
Fodor'sChoice
★

✕ **1919.** Michelin-starred Chef José Cuevas successfully operates this fine-dining restaurant in San Juan's most striking hotel, once home to the Vanderbilt family. The main dining room is set on the Atlantic Ocean, elegant and sophisticated, large yet intimate where tables are spread out to allow for privacy and comfort. Brazilian tiger wood tables, dark wooden floors, and three striking chandeliers with drooping pearl shells are reminiscent of the Gatsby era. The Puerto-Rican born chef presents international cuisine with a strong focus on local ingredients. Choose from the prix-fixe menu or order à la carte. Standout dishes include eggplant confit in tomato water with local cucumber, clams esca-beche, calabaza ravioli with sage brown butter, and the chicharrones gremolata. For pairings, choose from a 200-plus wine selection or take advantage of the champage table service. $ *Average main: $36* ⌧ *The Vanderbilt Hotel, 1055 Av. Ashford, Condado* ☎ *787/724–1919* ⊕ *www.1919restaurant.com* ⊙ *Closed Sun and Mon. No lunch Sat.*

$$$
PUERTO RICAN
Fodor'sChoice
★

✕ **Jose Enrique.** Since 2007, Chef Jose Enrique's eponymous restaurant in La Placita de Santurce has been the preferred dining choice for locals. In 2013, the world started catching on when José was nominated for *Food & Wine* magazine's Best New Chefs. He is also the first Puerto Rican chef to receive the prestigious James Beard award nomination, for a second consecutive year. At Jose Enrique, elevated Puerto Rican cuisine is served in a very casual setting that fits right in with the surround-ings. The menu, brought to your table on an eraser board, changes all the time. The crab fitters are a staple as is the whole fried yellowtail snapper served over a root mash with avocado and papaya salsa. The restaurant's no reservation policy means that you will have to wait for your table. Put your name on the list and wander around La Placita, where you can sip on cheap drinks and mingle with the locals. $ *Average main: $30* ⌧ *176 Calle Duffaut, La Placita de Santurce, San-turce* ☎ *787/725–3518* ⊕ *www.joseenriquepr.com* ⌲ *Reservations not accepted* ⊙ *Closed Sun. and Mon. No lunch Sat.*

$$
CAFÉ

✕ **Kasalta.** Those who think coffee can never be too strong should make a beeline to Kasalta, which has an amazing pitch-black brew that will knock your socks off. Make your selection from the display cases full of luscious pastries, particularly the famous *quesito* (cream cheese–filled puff pastry) and other tempting treats. Walk up to the counter and order a sandwich, such as the Medianoche, made famous after President Obama ordered one during his campaign on the island. For dinner, dive into a fish dish, paella, or do like the locals and make a meal out of the savory Spanish tapas. Occasionally the quality can be uneven, and some staff members are curt with tourists. $ *Average main: $16* ⌧ *1966 Calle McLeary, Ocean Park* ☎ *787/727–7340* ⊕ *www.kasalta.com.*

$$$ ✗**Pamela's.** If you've always dreamed of fine dining for two right on
CARIBBEAN   the beach, only steps from where crashing waves meet the shore, head
to this local favorite in Ocean Park. If you prefer air-conditioning, an
elegant glassed-in solarium awaits, complete with black cobblestone
floors and slow-turning ceiling fans. The menu is a contemporary, cre-
ative mix of Caribbean spices and other tropical ingredients. To start,
try the corn fritters with a spicy cilantro aioli. The restaurant prides
itself on its fresh seafood, so move on to the rainbow trout, stuffed with
crab and coconut and steamed in a banana leaf, or choose the seared
salmon served with an *acerola* (Caribbean cherry) chimichurri. $ *Aver-
age main: $30* ✉ *Numero Uno Guest House, 1 Calle Santa Ana, Ocean
Park* ☎ *787/726–5010* ⊕ *www.numero1guesthouse.com.*

$$$$ ✗**Pikayo.** Celebrity chef and Puerto Rico native Wilo Benet's flagship
ECLECTIC   restaurant makes the most of its elegant surroundings at the Conrad
Fodor'sChoice   San Juan Condado Plaza hotel. Works from local artists line the walls,
★   and the atmosphere is formal but never hushed. The menu offers a
twist on traditional Puerto Rican classics as well as more international
flavors. Choose from the thoughtfully crafted tasting menu or order à
la carte. There is a large selection of starters; particularly good are the
pork belly sliders, the spicy tuna on crispy rice (known here as *pegao*),
and the foie gras with ripe plantains and black truffle honey. For main
courses, options include succulent petit duck magret with crimini mush-
rooms and a raspberry vinegar gastrique and North Atlantic swordfish
in a pigeon pea escabeche with a ripe plantain emulsion. Don't be
surprised if Benet himself stops by your table to make sure everything
is just to your liking. $ *Average main: $37* ✉ *Conrad Condado Plaza,
999 Ashford Ave., Condado* ☎ *787/721–6194* ⊕ *www.wilobenet.com/
pikayo* ☽ *No lunch.*

EASTERN PUERTO RICO

$$$$ ✗**Chez Daniel.** When the stars are out, it would be hard to find a more
FRENCH   romantic setting than this waterfront eatery in the Anchor's Village
Fodor'sChoice   Marina. Dozens of gleaming white boats are anchored so close that
★   you could practically hit them with a baguette. The dining room has a
chummy atmosphere, probably because many patrons seem to know
each other. If you'd prefer alone time, ask for a table on one of the pri-
vate terraces. Chef Daniel Vasse's French-country-style dishes are some
of the best on the island. The exceptional Marseille-style bouillabaisse is
full of fresh fish and bursts with the flavor of a white garlic sauce. Some-
thing less French, you say? Choose steak or fish simply prepared on the
grill, and pair it with a bottle from the extensive wine cellar. Sunday
brunch, with its seemingly endless seafood bar, draws people from all
over the island, and runs $45 per person with drinks. $ *Average main:
$33* ✉ *Palmas del Mar, Anchor's Village Marina, Rte. 906, Km 86.4,
Humacao* ☎ *787/850–3838* ⚭ *Reservations essential* ☽ *Closed Tues.*

$$$ ✗**Pasión por el Fogón.** At one of Fajardo's most beloved restaurants, Chef
CARIBBEAN   Myrta Pérez Toledo possesses a talent for taking traditional dishes and
making them into something special. Succulent cuts of meat and fish
are presented in unexpected ways—witness a perfectly cooked flank
steak rolled into a cylinder standing on one end. But what makes this

17

dish remarkable is the slightly sweet tamarind sauce that brings out the meat's earthy flavors. If you're a seafood lover, start with the lime-infused red-snapper ceviche, and then move on to the lobster medallions broiled in butter. For dessert, order the "Caribbean Sun," a version of an ice cream sundae that blends caramel, cinnamon, and chocolate toppings. $ *Average main: $28* ⊠ *Rte. 987, Km 2.3, Barrio Sardinera, Fajardo* ☎ *787/863–3502* ⊕ *www.pasionporelfogon.net* ⌂ *Reservations essential* ⊘ *No lunch weekdays.*

VIEQUES AND CULEBRA

CULEBRA

$$ ✕ **Mamacita's.** Pull your dinghy up to the dock and watch the resident
CARIBBEAN iguanas plod past at this simple open-air, tin-roofed restaurant on a rough-plank deck beside the Dewey canal. Tarpon cruise past in the jade waters below, and the to and fro of boaters also keeps patrons amused. Doubling as Culebra's favorite local watering hole and gringo hangout, palm tree trunks litter the space, which is painted in a rainbow of pink, purple, and green. With a nightly changing menu, Mamacita's down-home dishes play a part in the appeal. The menu is heavy on burgers and sandwiches, but seafood dishes include an excellent mahimahi. $ *Average main: $12* ⊠ *66 Calle Castelar, Dewey, Culebra* ☎ *787/742–0322* ⊕ *www.mamacitasguesthouse.com.*

$$$ ✕ **Susie's.** Susie's is truly the island's only upscale restaurant, yet it's
ECLECTIC casual and unpretentious. Sanjuanera owner-chef Susie Hebert learned her culinary skills at San Juan's swank Caribe Hilton and Ritz-Carlton hotels before settling on Culebra and opening her fine-dining restaurant, a soothing Zen space filled with banquettes, pillows, and couches. A lively bar opens onto patio dining off the canal. The Caesar salad here excels; follow with sautéed jumbo shrimp in ginger-lime and coconut vinaigrette, Szechuan-style sesame-crusted tuna, or mahimahi with beurre blanc and scallion-ginger sauce. Feeling carnivorous? The filet mignon with a simple truffle au jus is divine. $ *Average main: $21* ⊠ *Rte. 250, Dewey, Culebra* ☎ *787/340–7058* ⊕ *www.susiesculebra. com* ⌂ *Reservations essential* ⊘ *Closed Thurs.*

VIEQUES

$$ ✕ **Conuco.** A mix of locals and gringos frequent Conuco, soft-spoken
PUERTO RICAN Puerto Rico native Rebecca Betancourt's homage to local food with
Fodor'sChoice an upscale twist. Barnlike open windows look out onto one of Isabel
★ Segunda's main streets, and within, the airy room is simple but cozy, enhanced by bright yellow walls, seafoam chairs, white table tops, and ceiling fans. A back patio offers alfresco dining. Start with sangria rum punch, then move onto *any* of the menu's many selections; they're all that wonderful. Piping-hot arepas are piled high with pepper and octopus salad, while small *tostones rellenos* (fried plantains) are shaped into cups filled with a citrusy ceviche. *Sorullitos* (cheesy corn fritters) and *bacalaítos* (cod fritters) are reimagined with modern flair. The only thing trumping the flavors of a juicy *churrasco* (skirt steak) and overflowing seafood *mofongo* is the wow-factor of Betancourt's presentations. Elevating cooking to art form, this local spot is one that will

have you dreaming about Vieques long after you've left the island. [$] *Average main: $15* ✉ *110 Luis Muñoz Rivera, Isabel Segunda, Vieques* ☎ *787/741–2500* 🌐 *www.restauranteconuco.com* ⏲ *Closed Sun. and Mon. No lunch.*

> **DID YOU KNOW?**
>
> The seafood shacks of Joyuda are so well known for fresh fish that locals flock there from as far away as Ponce and San Juan. In Boquerón people line up at pushcarts where vendors sell oysters on the half shell.

$$$ ECLECTIC Fodor's Choice ★ 🍴 **El Quenepo.** Elegant yet unpretentious, El Quenepo brings fine dining and a touch of class to the Esperanza waterfront. Six stable doors on an inviting powder blue building open to expose ocean views. The menu, which changes yearly, features local herbs and fruits such as *quenepas* and breadfruit in the artfully prepared dishes that owners Scott and Kate Cole call "fun, funky island food." Scott is the chef, known for his seafood specials highlighting the daily catch; Kate is the consummate hostess. Start with the popular grilled Caesar salad followed by sensational *mofongo* stuffed with shrimp and lobster in sweet-and-spicy *criollo* sauce. Oenophiles will appreciate the large wine list, and the sangria is delicious. Lucky walk-ins can grab a seat at the more casual high bar tables, but for the true experience of this gem, make a reservation. [$] *Average main: $25* ✉ *148 Calle Flamboyan, Esperanza, Vieques* ☎ *787/741–1215* ✍ *Reservations essential* ⏲ *No lunch. Closed Mon.*

17

SOUTHERN PUERTO RICO

PONCE

$$ SEAFOOD 🍴 **El Ancla.** Families favor this laid-back restaurant, whose dining room sits at the edge of the sea. The kitchen serves generous and affordable plates of fish, crab, and other fresh seafood with *tostones* (fried plantains), french fries, and garlic bread. Try the shrimp in garlic sauce, salmon fillet with capers, or the delectable mofongo stuffed with seafood. Finish your meal with one of the fantastic flans. The piña coladas—with or without rum—are exceptional. [$] *Average main: $20* ✉ *805 Av. Hostos Final, Ponce Playa, Ponce* ☎ *787/840–2450* 🌐 *www.restauranteelancla.com.*

$$$ SEAFOOD 🍴 **Pito's Seafood.** Choose from the waterfront terrace or one of the enclosed dining rooms at this longtime favorite east of Ponce in Las Cucharas. No matter where you sit, you'll have a view of the ocean. The main attraction is the freshly caught seafood, ranging from lobster and crab to salmon and red snapper. For total indulgence, try the fresh oysters or shrimp wrapped in bacon—both specialties of the house. There's also a wide range of chicken and beef dishes. The plantain cups stuffed with chicken or seafood make an excellent starter. From the expansive wine cellar you can select more than 25 different wines by the glass. Listen to live music on Friday and Sunday night. [$] *Average main: $20* ✉ *Rte. 2, Km 218.5, Sector Las Cucharas, Ponce* ☎ *787/841–4977* 🌐 *www.pitosseafoodpr.com.*

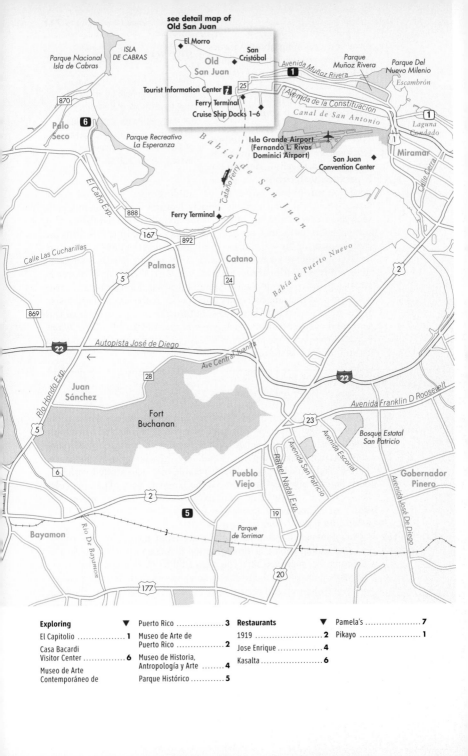

**see detail map of
Old San Juan**

El Morro

San
Cristóbal

Old
San Juan

Tourist Information Center

Ferry Terminal
Cruise Ship Docks 1–6

25

ISLA
DE CABRAS

Parque Nacional
Isla de Cabras

870

Palo
Seco

6

Parque Recreativo
La Esperanza

Avenida Muñoz Rivera

Parque
Muñoz Rivera

Parque Del
Nuevo Milenio

Escambrón

Avenida de la Constitución

Canal de San Antonio

1

Laguna
Condado

Isla Grande Airport
(Fernando L. Rivas
Dominici Airport)

San Juan
Convention Center

Miramar

Calle Cerra

Bahía de San Juan

El Caño Exp.

888

Ferry Terminal

Cataño Ferry

167   892

Calle Las Cucharillas

Palmas

5

869

Cataño

24

Bahía de Puerto Nuevo

2

22   Autopista José de Diego

Ave Central Iuanita

Río Hondo Exp.

28

Juan
Sánchez

5

6

Fort
Buchanan

22

Avenida Franklin D Roosevelt

23

Avenida Escorial

Avenida San Patricio

Bosque Estatal
San Patricio

Gobernador
Piñero

Avenida José De Diego

Pueblo
Viejo

2

Rafael Nadal Exp.

5

19

Río De Bayamón

Bayamón

Parque
de Torrimar

177

20

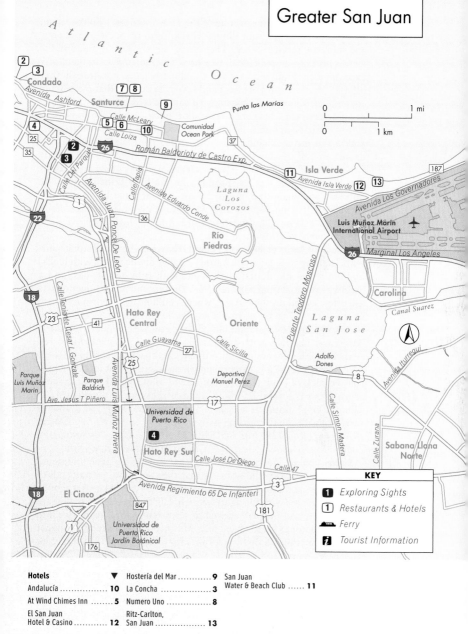

Greater San Juan

Atlantic Ocean

Condado
Avenida Ashford
Santurce
Calle McLeary
Calle Loiza
Comunidad
Ocean Park
Punta las Marías

Román Baldorioty de Castro Exp.

Isla Verde
Avenida Isla Verde

Avenida Los Governadores

Laguna
Los
Corozos

Luis Muñoz Marín
International Airport

Río
Piedras

Marginal Los Angeles

Calle Tapia
Avenida Eduardo Conde

Avenida Juan Ponce de León

Carolina

Canal Suarez

Hato Rey
Central

Oriente

Laguna
San Jose

Calle Guayama
Calle Sicilia

Adolfo
Dones

Parque
Luis Muñoz
Marín

Parque
Baldrich

Ave. Jesus T Piñero

Deportivo
Manuel Perez

Avenida Luis Muñoz Rivera

Universidad de
Puerto Rico

Sabana Llana
Norte

Hato Rey Sur
Calle José De Diego

Calle 47

El Cinco

Avenida Regimiento 65 De Infanteri

Universidad de
Puerto Rico
Jardín Botánical

0   1 mi
0   1 km

KEY

1 Exploring Sights
1 Restaurants & Hotels
Ferry
i Tourist Information

Hotels

Andalucía **10**

At Wind Chimes Inn **5**

El San Juan
Hotel & Casino **12**

Hostería del Mar **9**

La Concha **3**

Numero Uno **8**

Ritz-Carlton,
San Juan **13**

San Juan
Water & Beach Club **11**

WESTERN PUERTO RICO

$$$ ECLECTIC Fodor's Choice ★ 🍴 **The Eclipse.** The Eclipse is one of the best restaurants on the island with beautiful beachfront dining: check, farm-to- table ingredients, and fantastic service: check. The setting is rustic yet elegant and the view is nothing short of ideal. Executive Chef Jeremie Cruz flawlessly executes dishes full of local flavors and ingredients. For brunch, they offer a wonderful mix of sweet and savory selections that range from coconut brioche French toasts with caramelized bananas and nuts, to an assortment of pizza frittatas. For lunch, they make some delicious classic Neapolitan pizzas crafted from the freshest ingredients and baked in their handmade brick oven. Try their perfectly marinated catch of the day (from Isabela) ceviche. On top of the already varied dinner menu, Chef Jeremie creates a three-course menu daily that highlights the freshest products he can find. Wine pairings are optional and suggested, given the spectacular wine list. Enjoy live Caribbean Jazz on Sunday and Wednesday night. [$] *Average main: $28* ✉ *Villa Montaña, Carretera 4466, Km 1.9, Isabela* ☎ *787/872–9554* 🌐 *www.VillaMontana.com.*

$$$$ CARIBBEAN 🍴 **Restaurant Aaron at the Horned Dorset Primavera.** A pair of stone stairways leads up to Restaurant Aaron's elegant dining room, with black-and-white marble floors, chandeliers with ruby-red shades, and a Steinway piano dating back to 1901. Dessert and after-dinner drinks are often served on the terrace, where you'll hear the constant crash of the waves. The seven-course tasting menu, an extravagant meal with a $125 price tag, might include foie gras with maple berry glaze, pan-seared scallops with asparagus risotto, or poached *chillo* (red snapper) with apricot gnocchi. Adding Caribbean accents to classical French cuisine, the à la carte menu changes weekly but might include roasted rack of lamb and wahoo (a kind of mackerel) in a pistachio crust. Dress is formal by island standards, except in the downstairs "Blue Room" dining area, where a similar menu is served. Lunch is served outside, on the terrace. [$] *Average main: $36* ✉ *Horned Dorset Primavera, Rte. 429, Km 3* ☎ *787/823–4030* 🌐 *www.horneddorset.com* ✍ *Reservations essential* ⏲ *Closed Mon.–Wed. Apr.–Nov.*

$$ PUERTO RICAN 🍴 **Rincón Tropical.** Don't be scared off by the cheap plastic tables and chairs. What you should notice is that they are almost always full of locals enjoying the area's freshest seafood. The kitchen keeps it simple, preparing dishes with the lightest touch. Highlights include mahimahi with onions and peppers as well as fried red snapper with rice and bean and octopus salad. Fried plantains make a nice accompaniment to almost anything. Stop by weekdays for the affordable lunch special. [$] *Average main: $15* ✉ *Rte. 115, Km 12* ☎ *787/823–2017* 🌐 *www.rinconpr.com/rincontropical.*

WHERE TO STAY

In San Juan, the best beaches are in Isla Verde, though Condado is more centrally located. Old San Juan offers easy access to dining and nightlife. Outside San Juan, particularly on the east coast, you can find self-contained luxury resorts that cover hundreds of acres. Around the island, government-sponsored *paradores* are rural inns, others offer no-frills apartments, and some are large hotels close to either an attraction or beach.

PRIVATE VILLAS AND CONDOS

In the west, southwest, and south—as well as on the islands of Vieques and Culebra—smaller inns and condominiums for short-term rentals are the norm. Villa rentals are increasingly popular.

RENTAL CONTACTS

Island West Properties. This office can help you rent villas in Rincón by the day, week, or month. The company has been around for years, so it corners the market. ✉ *Rte. 413, Km 0.7* ☎ *787/823–2323* 🌐 *www.islandwestrentals.com.*

Rainbow Realty. A list of rental properties is available from this gay-friendly company. ✉ *278 Calle Flamboyán, Esperanza, Vieques* ☎ *787/741–4312* 🌐 *www.viequesrainbowrealty.com.*

San Juan Vacations. Many properties in Condado and Isla Verde can be rented from this real estate company. ✉ *Marbella del Caribe Oeste, Av. Isla Verde, S-5, Isla Verde, San Juan* ☎ *787/727–1591* ✍ *sanjuvac@gmail.com.*

17

OLD SAN JUAN

$$ B&B/INN 🏨 **The Gallery Inn.** No two rooms in this 200-year-old mansion are alike, but all have four-poster beds, hand-woven tapestries, and quirky antiques in every nook and cranny. **Pros:** one-of-a-kind lodging; ocean views; wonderful classical music concerts. **Cons:** several narrow, winding staircases; an uphill walk from rest of Old San Juan; sometimes raucous pet macaws and cockatoos. [$] *Rooms from: $160* ✉ *204–206 Calle Norzagaray, Old San Juan* ☎ *787/722–1808* 🌐 *www.thegalleryinn.com* 🛏 *20 rooms, 5 suites* 🍴 *Breakfast.*

$$$ HOTEL Fodor's Choice ★ 🏨 **Hotel El Convento.** There's no longer anything austere about this 350-year-old former convent. **Pros:** lovely building; atmosphere to spare; plenty of nearby dining options. **Cons:** near some noisy bars; small pool and small bathrooms. [$] *Rooms from: $285* ✉ *100 Calle Cristo, Old San Juan* ☎ *787/723–9020* 🌐 *www.elconvento.com* 🛏 *52 rooms, 6 suites* 🍴 *No meals.*

GREATER SAN JUAN

$ B&B/INN 🏨 **Andalucía.** In a Spanish-style house, this friendly little inn evokes its namesake region with such details as hand-painted tiles and ceramic pots filled with greenery. **Pros:** terrific value; helpful hosts; gorgeous courtyard. **Cons:** not right on the beach; some rooms are smaller than others. [$] *Rooms from: $99* ✉ *2011 Calle McLeary, Ocean Park* ☎ *787/309–3373* 🌐 *www.andalucia-puertorico.com* 🛏 *11 rooms* 🍴 *No meals.*

$
B&B/INN
At Wind Chimes Inn. Hidden behind a whitewashed wall covered with bougainvillea, this Spanish-style villa gives the impression of an exclusive retreat. **Pros:** charming architecture; on the edge of Condado; bar on site (opens at 5 pm); includes use facilities at Acacia Seaside Inn. **Cons:** on a busy street; old-fashioned rooms; only a few rooms have closets. $ *Rooms from: $109* ⊠ *1750 Av. McLeary, Condado* ☎ *787/727–4153, 800/946–3244* ⊕ *www.atwindchimesinn.com* ⮧ *17 rooms, 5 suites, 1 apartment* ¶○¶ *No meals.*

$$$
RESORT
FAMILY
Fodor'sChoice
★
El San Juan Resort & Casino. Much of the classical appeal remains at this don't-miss destination in Isla Verde: the intricately hand-carved mahogany walls and ceiling in the lobby date back to 1955. **Pros:** beautiful pool; great dining options in and near hotel; on a fantastic beach. **Cons:** noise in the lobby from bars and casino; self-parking lot is a long walk from the hotel entrance; small bathrooms. $ *Rooms from: $450* ⊠ *6063 Av. Isla Verde, Isla Verde* ☎ *787/791–1000* ⊕ *www.elsanjuanhotel.com* ⮧ *386 rooms, 22 suites* ¶○¶ *No meals.*

$
B&B/INN
Hostería del Mar. Decorated in bright blues and whites, the stylish rooms at this beachfront inn have an Asian feel, with influences from Bali, Malaysia, and India. **Pros:** plasma-screen televisions; right on the beach; good on-site dining. **Cons:** long walk to other restaurants; no pool; Wi-Fi in lobby only. $ *Rooms from: $139* ⊠ *1 Calle Tapia, Ocean Park* ☎ *787/727–3302* ⊕ *www.hosteriadelmarpr.com* ⮧ *23 rooms, 2 suites* ¶○¶ *No meals.*

$$$
RESORT
Fodor'sChoice
★
La Concha—A Renaissance Resort. Every detail at La Concha feels tropical and sexy, from the undulating ceiling in the sprawling lobby to Perla, the signature shell-shape restaurant and an architectural marvel. **Pros:** stunning architecture; numerous on-site social activities; beautiful guestrooms. **Cons:** noisy bar/lobby, particularly when there's live music; beach can be narrow during high tide. $ *Rooms from: $299* ⊠ *1077 Av. Ashford, Condado* ☎ *787/721–7500* ⊕ *www.laconcharesort.com* ⮧ *257 rooms, 226 suites* ¶○¶ *No meals.*

$$
HOTEL
Fodor'sChoice
★
Numero Uno Guest House. It seems that first-time visitors to Numero Uno are destined to become repeat customers because it's quite common to hear guests trading stories about how often they've returned to this relaxing retreat. **Pros:** friendly atmosphere; great restaurant; right on the beach. **Cons:** a long walk to other restaurants; small pool. $ *Rooms from: $150* ⊠ *1 Calle Santa Ana, Ocean Park* ☎ *787/726–5010, 866/726–5010* ⊕ *www.numero1guesthouse.com* ⮧ *11 rooms* ¶○¶ *Breakfast.*

$$$$
RESORT
FAMILY
Fodor'sChoice
★
The Ritz-Carlton, San Juan. Elegant marble floors and fountains don't undermine the feeling that this is a true beach getaway. **Pros:** top-notch service; excellent restaurant options; spruce guest rooms and modern spa and fitness center. **Cons:** not much is within walking distance; expensive for San Juan lodging. $ *Rooms from: $629* ⊠ *6961 Av. de los Gobernadores, Isla Verde* ☎ *787/253–1700, 800/241–3333* ⊕ *www.ritzcarlton.com/sanjuan* ⮧ *416 rooms, 11 suites* ¶○¶ *No meals.*

$$
HOTEL
San Juan Water & Beach Club. Water is everywhere at this boutique hotel, from the droplets that decorate the reception area to the deluge that runs down the glass walls of the elevators. **Pros:** fun atmosphere; interesting design; great nightlife option; on the beach. **Cons:** dark hallways; small pool. $ *Rooms from: $219* ⊠ *2 Calle Tartak, Isla Verde* ☎ *787/728–3666, 888/265–6699* ⊕ *www.waterbeachclubhotel.com* ⮧ *76 rooms, 4 suites* ¶○¶ *No meals.*

Hotel El Convento

BEYOND SAN JUAN

$$$$ RESORT Fodor's Choice ★

Dorado Beach, A Ritz-Carlton Reserve. Following a recent $342 million renovation, this Ritz-Carlton Reserve ups the ante with a roster of posh offerings, including a restaurant from Fodor's Tastemaker Chef Jose Andres, and an incredible setting along 3 miles of Puerto Rican coastline. **Pros:** all rooms are beachfront; top-notch facilities; golf, tennis and water activities; award-winning spa; gourmet dining. **Cons:** daily added $95 resort fee; a 45-minute drive from San Juan. [$] *Rooms from: $1399* ✉ *100 Dorado Beach Dr., Dorado* ☎ *787/626–1100* 🌐 *www.ritzcarlton.com/en/Properties/DoradoBeach* 🛏 *100 rooms, 14 suites, 1 villa* 🍴 *No meals.*

EASTERN PUERTO RICO

$$$$ RESORT

El Conquistador Resort. Perched on a bluff overlooking the ocean, El Conquistador (The Conqueror) is a sprawling complex that has claimed the northern tip of the island and is one of Puerto Rico's most popular destination resorts. **Pros:** bright, spacious rooms; unbeatable views of nearby islands; good dining options; various meal plans available. **Cons:** must take a boat to reach the beach; long waits at the funicular taking guests between levels; self-parking is far from the hotel entrance; hidden fees like parking ($16/day) and kids club ($70/day). [$] *Rooms from: $400* ✉ *1000 Av. El Conquistador* ☎ *787/863–1000, 888/543–1282* 🌐 *www.elconresort.com* 🛏 *750 rooms, 15 suites, 234 villas* 🍴 *Multiple meal plans.*

$$$ ▢ **Gran Meliá Puerto Rico.** This massive resort, on an enviable stretch of
RESORT pristine coastline, has an open-air lobby with elegant floral displays
that resemble a Japanese garden, and the swimming pool's columns call
to mind ancient Greece. **Pros:** beautiful setting; lovely pool area; short
walk to the beach. **Cons:** parking spots are scarce; facade is blank and
uninviting. $ *Rooms from: $305* ⊠ *200 Coco Beach Blvd., Coco Beach*
☎ *787/809–1770, 877/476–3542* ⊕ *www.gran-melia-puerto-rico.com*
⌨ *544 suites, 6 villas* ⦿ *Multiple meal plans.*

$$$$ ▢ **Rio Mar Beach Resort & Spa, a Wyndham Grand Resort.** Guests come
RESORT to this sprawling 500-acre resort to enjoy a host of outdoor activities,
FAMILY including championship golf and tennis, as well as hiking excursions
in the nearby rain forest. **Pros:** expansive beachfront; good restau-
rants in hotel; plenty of outdoor activities. **Cons:** dark and depressing
parking garage; sometimes there are long lines at the check-in desk.
$ *Rooms from: $305* ⊠ *6000 Río Mar Blvd.* ☎ *787/888–6000* ⊕ *www.
wyndhamriomar.com* ⌨ *600 rooms, 72 suites* ⦿ *No meals.*

$$$$ ▢ **St. Regis Bahia Beach Resort.** Between El Yunque National Forest and
RESORT the Río Espíritu Santo, this luxurious, environmentally aware property
Fodor's Choice has raised the bar for lodgings in Puerto Rico. **Pros:** privacy; impeccable
★ service; luxurious amenities. **Cons:** isolated location; slim off-property
restaurant selection; very, very expensive. $ *Rooms from: $800* ⊠ *Rte.
187, Km 4.2* ☎ *787/809–8000* ⊕ *www.stregisbahiabeach.com* ⌨ *104
rooms, 35 suites* ⦿ *No meals.*

VIEQUES AND CULEBRA

$$ ▢ **Club Seaborne.** The most sophisticated place to set down roots in
HOTEL Culebra, this cluster of slate-blue plantation-style cottages paints a
Fodor's Choice pretty picture on a hilltop overlooking Fulladoza Bay. **Pros:** lovely cot-
★ tages; lush gardens; rates include airport or ferry transfers. **Cons:** some
steps to negotiate; no elevator; spotty Internet and cell phone reception. $ *Rooms from: $249* ⊠ *Rte. 252, northwest of town, Culebra*
☎ *787/742–3169* ⊕ *www.clubseabourne.com* ⌨ *3 rooms, 8 villas, 1
cottage* ⦿ *Breakfast.*

$$ ▢ **Hacienda Tamarindo.** The 250-year-old tamarind tree rising more
HOTEL than three stories through the center of the main building gives this
plantation-style house and former dance hall its name. **Pros:** beautiful
views; nicely designed rooms; excellent breakfasts. **Cons:** you have to
drive to beaches; small parking lot; no full-service restaurant; no eleva-
tor. $ *Rooms from: $155* ⊠ *Rte. 997, Km 4.5, Esperanza, Vieques*
☎ *787/741–8525* ⊕ *www.haciendatamarindo.com* ⌨ *16 rooms, 1 pent-
house suite* ⦿ *Breakfast.*

$$ ▢ **Hix Island House.** Constructed entirely of concrete and set in the mid-
HOTEL dle of Vieques's tropical forest surroundings, Hix House echoes the
gray granite boulders strewn around Vieques, and the four buildings
do manage to blend seamlessly with the environment. **Pros:** acclaimed
architecture; secluded setting; friendly staff. **Cons:** the lack of windows
means bugs (especially pesky mosquitos) get in; damp linens and clothing after tropical showers; no elevator. $ *Rooms from: $175* ⊠ *Rte.
995, Km 1.5, Vieques* ☎ *787/741–2302* ⊕ *www.hixislandhouse.com*
⌨ *19 rooms* ⦿ *Breakfast.*

El San Juan Hotel & Casino

$$ B&B/INN **Malecón House.** Posh boutique spots like this seaside escape in Esperanza are raising the bar on lodging in Vieques. **Pros:** affordable rates for a waterfront property; tasty breakfasts; welcoming hosts. **Cons:** in-town location isn't for those seeking seclusion. [$] *Rooms from: $175* ✉ *105 Calle Flamboyan, Esperanza, Vieques* ☎ *787/741–0663* 🌐 *www.maleconhouse.com* *13 rooms* 🍴 *Breakfast.*

$$$$ RESORT Fodor's Choice ★ **W Retreat & Spa.** Hovering over two gorgeous beaches, the über-hip W Retreat & Spa is the island's hot spot for urbane fashionistas, yet remarkably, it manages to simultaneously be family-friendly. **Pros:** sensational decor; full-service spa; free transfers to/from airport. **Cons:** high prices even in low season; $60 daily resort fee. [$] *Rooms from: $919* ✉ *Rte. 200, Km 3.2, Isabel Segunda, Vieques* ☎ *787/741–4100* 🌐 *www.wvieques.com* *156 rooms, 20 suites* 🍴 *No meals.*

SOUTHERN PUERTO RICO

$$ RESORT FAMILY Fodor's Choice ★ **Copamarina Beach Resort & Spa.** Without a doubt the most beautiful resort on the southern coast, Copamarina is set on 16 palm-shaded acres facing the Caribbean Sea. **Pros:** tropical decor; plenty of activities; great dining options. **Cons:** somewhat distant from other attractions; noise from all the kids. [$] *Rooms from: $190* ✉ *Rte. 333, Km 6.5* ☎ *787/821–0505, 800/468–4553* 🌐 *www.copamarina.com* *104 rooms, 2 villas* 🍴 *Multiple meal plans.*

$ HOTEL **Hotel Meliá.** In the heart of the city, this family-owned hotel has been a local landmark for over a century. **Pros:** great location on the main square; walking distance to downtown sites; good dining options near hotel. **Cons:** decor is somewhat outdated; front rooms can be noisy.

[$] *Rooms from: $120* ✉ *75 Calle Cristina, Ponce Centro, Ponce* ☎ *787/842–0260, 800/448–8355* 🌐 *www.hotelmeliapr.com* ⇆ *68 rooms, 6 suites* 🍴 *Breakfast.*

$ RENTAL Fodor's Choice ★ **Mary Lee's by the Sea.** This meandering cluster of apartments sits on quiet grounds full of brightly colored flowers. **Pros:** feels like a home away from home; warm and friendly owner; near pristine beaches and forests. **Cons:** weekly maid service unless requested daily; no nightlife and no pool. [$] *Rooms from: $110* ✉ *Rte. 333, Km 6.7* ☎ *787/821–3600* 🌐 *www.maryleesbythesea.com* ⇆ *10 apartments* 🍴 *No meals.*

WESTERN AND CENTRAL PUERTO RICO

$ HOTEL Fodor's Choice ★ **Casa Grande Mountain Retreat.** Here you'll come as close as you can to sleeping in a tree house. **Pros:** unspoiled setting with spectacular views; accessible for people with disabilities; outdoor activities. **Cons:** no air-conditioning; long drive to other sights/restaurants. [$] *Rooms from: $126* ✉ *Rte. 612, Km 0.3, Utuado* ☎ *787/894–3939* 🌐 *www.hotelcasagrande.com* ⇆ *20 rooms* 🍴 *No meals.*

$$$$ RESORT Fodor's Choice ★ **Horned Dorset Primavera.** This is, without a doubt, the most luxurious hotel in Puerto Rico. **Pros:** unabashed luxury; unmatched meals; lovely setting; pet-friendly; beautiful decor; yoga "treehouse." **Cons:** on a very narrow beach; long staircase to some villas. [$] *Rooms from: $770* ✉ *Rte. 429, Km 3* ☎ *787/823–4030, 800/633–1857* 🌐 *www.horneddorset.com* ⇆ *17 villas* 🍴 *Multiple meal plans.*

$ HOTEL **The Lazy Parrot.** Painted in eye-popping tropical hues, this mountainside hotel doesn't take itself too seriously. **Pros:** economy rooms available; tropical setting; microwaves in rooms. **Cons:** not on the beach; stairs to climb; some may consider the whimsical style tacky. [$] *Rooms from: $135* ✉ *Rte. 413, Km 4.1* ☎ *787/823–5654, 800/294–1752* 🌐 *www.lazyparrot.com* ⇆ *21 rooms* 🍴 *Breakfast.*

$$ HOTEL **Lemontree Oceanfront Cottages.** Sitting right on the beach, this pair of lemon-yellow buildings holds six apartments named after such fruits as Mango, Cocoa, Banana, and Piña. **Pros:** far from the crowds; on-call massage therapist; spacious balconies. **Cons:** beach is very narrow; you have to drive to reach shops and restaurants; no elevator. [$] *Rooms from: $155* ✉ *Rte. 429, Km 4.1* ☎ *787/823–6452* 🌐 *www.lemontreepr.com* ⇆ *6 apartments* 🍴 *No meals.*

$$ B&B/INN Fodor's Choice ★ **Tres Sirenas.** Waves gently lap against the shores at this boutique inn named "Three Mermaids" in honor of the owners' daughters. **Pros:** in-room massages; spotless and tastefully decorated, discounted rates May through October. **Cons:** usually booked; set breakfast hour; Wi-Fi signal occasionally drops. [$] *Rooms from: $230* ✉ *26 Seabeach Dr.* ☎ *787/823–0558* 🌐 *www.tressirenas.com* ⇆ *2 rooms, 1 studio, 2 apartments* 🍴 *Breakfast.*

$$$ RESORT Fodor's Choice ★ **Villa Montaña.** This secluded cluster of villas, situated on a deserted stretch of beach between Isabela and Aguadilla, feels like a little town. **Pros:** bikes and playground for children; on a secluded beach; great food. **Cons:** a bit pricey; far from any off-site restaurants; airplane noise. [$] *Rooms from: $255* ✉ *Rte. 4466, Km 1.9, Isabela* ☎ *787/872–9554* 🌐 *www.villamontana.com* ⇆ *74 rooms, 52 villas* 🍴 *No meals.*

Tres Sirenas

NIGHTLIFE AND THE ARTS

Qué Pasa, the official visitor's guide, has listings of events in San Juan and out on the island. For daily listings, pick up a copy of the English-language edition of the *San Juan Star.* The Thursday edition's weekend section is especially useful. For the gay scene, check out the monthly *Puerto Rico Breeze*; the free newspaper is found in many businesses, especially in the Condado area.

NIGHTLIFE

Wherever you go, dress to impress. Puerto Ricans have flair, and both men and women love getting dressed up to go out. Bars are usually casual, but if you have on jeans, sneakers, and a T-shirt, you may be refused entry at swankier nightclubs and discos.

In Old San Juan, Calle San Sebastián is lined with bars and restaurants. Salsa music blaring from jukeboxes in cut-rate pool halls competes with mellow Latin jazz in top-flight nightspots. Evenings begin with dinner and stretch into the late hours (often until 3 or 4 in the morning) at the bars of the more upscale, so-called SoFo (south of Fortaleza) end of Old San Juan. An eclectic crowd heads to the Plaza del Mercado in Santurce after work to hang out in the plaza or enjoy drinks and food in one of the small establishments skirting the farmers' market. Condado and Ocean Park have their share of nightlife, too. Most are restaurant-and-bar environments.

Just east of San Juan along Route 187, funky Piñones has a collection of open-air seaside eateries that are popular with locals. On weekend evenings many places have merengue combos, Brazilian jazz trios, or reggae bands. In the southern city of Ponce, people embrace the Spanish tradition of the *paseo*, an evening stroll around the Plaza de las Delicias. The boardwalk at La Guancha in Ponce is also a lively scene. Live bands often play on weekends. Elsewhere *en la isla*, nighttime activities center on the hotels and resorts.

OLD SAN JUAN AND GREATER SAN JUAN

BARS AND MUSIC CLUBS

Mist. On the roof of the San Juan Water & Beach Club Hotel, this sexy spot offers some of the best ocean views anywhere in Isla Verde. On the weekends there's a DJ, and locals pack in to relax at the bar or on the leather beds reserved for bottle service. If you get hungry, order from the eclectic Socializers menu. Try the serrano ham flatbread with fig marmalade and goat cheese or the pork belly *banh mi*. ⊠ *San Juan Water & Beach Club, 2 Calle Tartak, Isla Verde, San Juan* ☎ *787/725–4664* ⊕ *www.waterbeachclubhotel.com.*

Nuyorican Café. There's something interesting happening at this hipper-than-hip, no-frills, wood-paneled performance space nearly every night, be it an early evening play, poetry reading, or talent show or, later on, a band playing Latin jazz, Cuban *son*, Puerto Rican salsa, or rock. On Wednesday nights, watch the owner play the conga drums with the house salsa band, Comborican. During breaks between performances the youthful, creative crowd chats in an alley outside the front door. There is usually a $5 cover charge. ⊠ *312 Calle San Fransico, entrance on Callejón de la Capilla, Old San Juan* ☎ *787/977–1276* ⊕ *www.nuyoricancafepr.com* ۞ *Closed Mon. and Tues.*

CASINOS

By law, all casinos must be in hotels, and most of them are in San Juan. The government keeps a close eye on them. Dress for the larger casinos is on the formal side, and the atmosphere is refined, particularly in the Isla Verde resorts. Casinos set their own hours but are generally open from noon to 4 am. In addition to slot machines, typical games include blackjack, roulette, craps, Caribbean stud (a five-card poker game), and *pai gow* poker (a combination of American poker and the Chinese game pai gow). Hotels with casinos have live entertainment most weekends, as well as restaurants and bars. The minimum age to gamble (and to drink) is 18.

DANCE CLUBS

Atlantic Beach. The oceanfront deck bar of this hotel is famed in the gay community for its weekday happy hours from 5 to 10 pm. But the pulsating tropical music, exotic drinks, and ever-pleasant ocean breeze would make it a hit in any case. ⊠ *Atlantic Beach Hotel, 1 Calle Vendig, Condado, San Juan* ☎ *787/721–6900* ⊕ *www.atlanticbeachhotel.com.*

Brava. A long line of young people can be spotted at the door of this chic club at the El San Juan Hotel. The two-level club, each with its own DJ and dance floor, is one of the best places for dancing. Dress to impress at this 21-plus club. ⊠ *El San Juan Hotel & Casino, 6063 Av. Isla Verde, Isla Verde, San Juan* ☎ *787/791-2781* ⊕ *www.bravapr.com* ⊙ *Thurs.–Sat. 10 pm–5 am.*

THE ARTS

Orquesta Sinfónica de Puerto Rico (*Puerto Rico Symphony Orchestra*). Under the direction of conductor Maximiano Valdés, the 80 members of this prominent orchestra perform a full 52-week season that includes classical-music concerts, operas, ballets, and popular-music performances. The orchestra plays most shows at Centro de Bellas Artes Luis A. Ferré, but it also gives outdoor concerts at museums and university campuses around the island, and it has an educational outreach program in island schools. Pablo Casals, the impetus for this group, helped create it in 1956. ⊠ *San Juan* ☎ *787/918–1108* ⊕ *www. sinfonicapr.gobierno.pr.*

Teatro Tapia. Named for Puerto Rican playwright Alejandro Tapia y Rivera, Teatro Tapia is the oldest theater in Puerto Rico and hosts traveling and locally produced theatrical and musical productions. Matinee performances with family entertainment are also held here, especially around the holidays. Stop by the box office to find out what's showing. ⊠ *Plaza Colón, Calle Fortaleza, Old San Juan, San Juan* ☎ *787/480–5004* ⊕ *www.teatropr.com.*

17

SHOPPING

San Juan has the island's best range of stores, but it isn't a free port, so you won't find bargains on electronics and perfumes. You can, however, find excellent prices on china, crystal, clothing, and jewelry. Shopping for local crafts can also be gratifying: you'll run across a lot that's tacky, but you can also find treasures, and in many cases you can watch the artisans at work. Popular items include *santos* (small carved figures of saints or religious scenes), hand-rolled cigars, handmade *mundillo* lace from Moca, *vejigantes* (colorful masks used during Carnival and local festivals) from Loíza and Ponce, and fancy men's shirts called guayaberas.

In Old San Juan—especially on Calles Fortaleza and Cristo—you can find T-shirt emporiums, selective crafts stores, bookshops, art galleries, jewelry boutiques, and even shops that specialize in made-to-order Panama hats. Calle Cristo has a number of factory outlets, including stores for Coach and Ralph Lauren.

With many stores selling luxury items and designer fashions, the shopping spirit in the San Juan neighborhood of Condado is reminiscent of that in Miami. Avenida Ashford is considered the heart of San Juan's fashion district, and you'll find plenty of high-end clothing stores here.

OLD SAN JUAN AND GREATER SAN JUAN

CLOTHES

Cappalli. Noted local designer Lisa Cappalli sells her feminine, sensuous designs in this elegant boutique, which specializes in ready-to-wear and custom fashions including a small collection of whimsical, lacy wedding gowns. ⊠ *206 Calle O'Donnell, Old San Juan, San Juan* ☏ *787/289–6565* ⊕ *www.lisacappalli.net.*

David Antonio. Prolific designer David Antonio runs a shop that's small but full of surprises. His joyful creations range from updated versions of the men's classic guayabera to fluid chiffon and silk tunics and dresses for women. ⊠ *69 Ave. Condado, Condado, San Juan* ☏ *787/725–0600* ⊕ *www.davidantoniopr.com.*

Nativa. The window displays at Nativa are almost as daring as the clothes it sells. The shop caters to trendy, young ladies looking for party dresses, jumpers, accessories, shoes, and more. ⊠ *55 Calle Cervantes, Condado, San Juan* ☏ *787/724–1396* ⊕ *www.nativaboutique. net* ⊗ *Closed Sun.*

Nono Maldonado. Nono Maldonado is well known for his high-end, elegant clothes for men and women, particularly those done in linen. He should know a thing or two about style—he worked for many years as the fashion editor of *Esquire* and presents a periodic couture collection. This second-floor store also serves as the designer's studio. ⊠ *1112 Av. Ashford, 2nd fl., Condado, San Juan* ☏ *787/721–0456* ⊕ *www. nonomaldonado.com* ⊗ *Closed Sun.*

Otto. In his shop, Otto Bauzá stocks international lines of casual and formal wear for younger men. ⊠ *69 Av. Condado, Condado, San Juan* ☏ *787/722–4609* ⊗ *Closed Sun. and Mon.*

GIFTS

Eclectika. At this boutique, you'll find a variety of items, mostly from Indonesia. From bed spreads to beaded and wooden jewelry, furnishings to hand fans, you could easily lose track of time as you browse through the shop for unique gift ideas. Everything is reasonably priced and you might just end up keeping everything you bought for yourself! ⊠ *204 Calle O'Donnell, Plaza Colón, Old San Juan, San Juan* ☏ *787/721–7236.*

Spicy Caribbee. Kitchen items, cookbooks, jams, spices, and sauces from around the Caribbean are on offer at Spicy Caribbee. ⊠ *154 Calle Cristo, Old San Juan, San Juan* ☏ *888/725–7259* ⊕ *www. spicycaribbee.com.*

JEWELRY

Bared & Sons. If you're in the market for a Rolex, Cartier, Bvlgari, or Brietling watch, visit Bared. The store also carries a large selection of fine jewelry. Look for the massive clock face on the corner. ⊠ *206 San Justo, Old San Juan, San Juan* ☏ *787/724–4811.*

Catalá Joyeros. A family-run business since the 1930s, Catalá Joyeros is known for its large selection of pearls, precious stones, and jewelry design. ⊠ *Plaza de Armas, 152 Rafael Cordero, Old San Juan, San Juan* ☏ *787/722–3231* ⊕ *www.catalajoyeros.com* ⊗ *Closed Sun.*

SOUVENIRS

Mi Pequeño San Juan. You might manage to find the hotel where you're staying reproduced in plaster at this shop, which specializes in tiny ceramic versions of San Juan doorways. The works, all created by hand right in the shop, make a wonderful souvenir. You can also pick up fine art prints. ✉ *152 Calle Fortaleza, Old San Juan, San Juan* ☎ *787/721–5040* ⊕ *www.mipequenosanjuan.com.*

SPECIALTY STORES

Galería Botello. The very influential Galería Botello displays the works of the late Angel Botello, who was hailed as the "Caribbean Gauguin" as far back as 1943. His work, which often uses the bright colors of the tropics, usually depicts island scenes. His paintings hang in the Museo de Arte de Puerto Rico. There are works on display here by other prominent local artists as well. ✉ *208 Calle Cristo, Old San Juan, San Juan* ☎ *787/723–9987* ⊕ *www.botello.com* ⊘ *Closed Sun.*

SPORTS AND ACTIVITIES

BOATING AND SAILING

East Island Excursions. At East Island Excursions catamarans ranging in size from 45 feet to 65 feet take you offshore for snorkeling. Two of the catamarans are powered, and this cuts down tremendously on travel time to outlying islands. Trips include stops at isolated beaches and a lunch buffet. East Island Excursions can accommodate those who wish to see the bioluminescent bay on Vieques and return to the mainland on the same evening. Transportation to Vieques is included, as is dinner at a local restaurant. All craft are outfitted with swimming decks, freshwater showers, and full-service bars. These vessels are some of the plushest for day sails in the area. ✉ *Marina Puerto del Rey, Rte. 3, Km 51.4, Fajardo* ☎ *787/860–3434, 877/937–4386* ⊕ *www.eastwindcats.com.*

17

DIVING AND SNORKELING

The diving is excellent off Puerto Rico's south, east, and west coasts, as well as its nearby islands. Particularly striking are dramatic walls created by a continental shelf off the south coast near La Parguera and Guánica. There's also some fantastic diving near Fajardo and around Vieques and Culebra, two small islands off the east coast. It's best to choose specific locations with the help of a guide or outfitter. Escorted half-day dives range from $65 to $120 for one or two tanks, including all equipment; in general, double those prices for night dives. Packages that include lunch and other extras are more. Snorkeling excursions, which include transportation, equipment rental, and sometimes lunch, start at $50. Equipment rents for about $5 to $10.

Aquatic Adventures. Captain Taz Hamrick takes guests out on snorkeling and PADI-certified scuba trips, as well as charters to the surrounding keys. You can also book a sunset cruise on their 26-foot boat, the *Raz-Ma-Taz*. ✉ *372 Sector Fulladoza, Dewey, Culebra* ☎ *787/209–3494, 515/290–2310* ⊕ *www.diveculebra.com.*

Culebra Divers. Run by Monika and Walter Rieder, Culebra Divers is the island's premiere dive shop, catering to those new to scuba as well as those adept at underwater navigation. Travel to more than 50 local sites on one of the company's 25-foot cabin cruisers and hope to spot wildlife like spotted eagle rays, octopus, moray eels, and turtles. Spring for an underwater scooter, which propels you through the sea like James Bond. You can also rent a mask and snorkel to explore on your own. ✉ *4 Calle Pedro Marquez, Dewey, Culebra* ☎ *787/742–0803* ⊕ *www.culebradivers.com.*

Sea Ventures Dive Center. At Sea Ventures Pro Dive Center you can get your diving certification, arrange dive trips to 20 offshore sites, and organize boating and sailing excursions. ✉ *Marina Puerto del Rey, Rte. 3, Km 51.4, Fajardo* ☎ *787/863–3483, 800/739–3483* ⊕ *www. divepuertorico.com.*

FISHING

Puerto Rico's waters are home to large game fish such as marlin, wahoo, dorado, tuna, and barracuda; as many as 30 world records for catches have been set off the island's shores.

Karolette Sport Fishing. At Karolette Sport Fishing, you're in the capable hands of Captain Bill Burleson, who has fished these waters since 1966. He'll take you out for excursions in his bright yellow 46-foot Bertram powerboat. A half day of fishing along the continental shelf costs $750, while a full day (usually more than nine hours) of deep-water fishing costs $1,450. If nobody makes a catch, he'll cut the fee in half. ✉ *Palmas del Mar, Anchor's Village Marina, Humacao* ☎ *787/637–7992* ⊕ *www. puertoricodeepseafishing.com.*

GOLF

Aficionados may know that Puerto Rico is the birthplace of golf legend Chi Chi Rodríguez—and that he had to hone his craft somewhere. Currently, you can find nearly 20 courses on the island, including many championship links. Be sure to call ahead for tee times; hours vary, and several hotel courses give preference to guests. Greens fees start at about $20 and go up as high as $165.

The **Puerto Rican Golf Association** (✉ *264 Av. Matadero, Suite 11, San Juan* ☎ *787/793–3444* ⊕ *www.prga.org*) is a good source for information on courses and tournaments.

Arthur Hills Golf Course at El Conquistador Resort & Waldorf Astoria Spa. Named for its designer, the 18-hole course at El Conquistador Resort is famous for its mountainous terrain that features elevation changes of more than 200 feet—rare in the Caribbean. From the highest spot, on the 15th hole, you have great views of the surrounding mountains and rain forest. The trade winds make every shot challenging—if the gorgeous views, strategic bunkering, and many water hazards haven't already distracted you. You are also likely to spot the harmless and generally timid iguana that populate the area. ⊠ *1000 Av. El Conquistador, Fajardo* ☎ *787/863–6784* ⊕ *www.elconresort.com* ✉ *Up to $185* ⚑ *18 holes, 6746 yards, par 72.*

Dorado Beach Resort Golf. If you want Caribbean luxury and great golf with four flavors, go no further than the Dorado Beach Resort, an iconic name for golf with a storied tradition in Puerto Rico with four 18-hole regulation courses. The famous East and the West Courses (closed for renovations at this writing) were designed by Robert Trent Jones Sr. and are located in a secluded seaside sanctuary along two miles of northeasterly shore within the former Rockefeller estate. Two "Plantation Courses" the Sugarcane (more challenging) and the Pineapple (easier) complete the 72-hole offering. ⊠ *5000 Plantation Dr., Dorado* ☎ *787/262–1010* ⊕ *www.doradobeach clubs.com* ✉ *East/ West Courses, $255; Plantation Courses, $154.* ⚑ *East Course: 18 holes, 7000 yards, par 72; West Course: 18 holes, 6975 yards, par 72; Sugarcane: 18 holes, 7119 yards, par 72; Pineapple: 18 holes 7030 yards, par 72.*

Fodor'sChoice
★
The Golf Links at Royal Isabela. Picture one of the most dramatic golf courses to be built in recent years, add in an ecologically sensitive, but luxurious service and surroundings and you have the Golf Links at Royal Isabela. Featuring an incomparable setting along the dramatic bluffs at the northwest edge of Puerto Rico, this magnificent 18-hole golf course, which opened in 2011, is already being described as among the best in the Caribbean if not beyond. Designed and developed by Stanley and Charles Pasarell with assistance from Course Architect David Pfaff, it can play to as much as 7,667 yards and a par of 72 or 73 depending on how you play the "Fork in the Road" 6th. This course is not built on one signature moment, but many: from the 6th to the island green at 9, to the carry over the sea at 12 just to name a few. Carts are available though walking is encouraged and caddies are mandatory. ⊠ *396 Ave. Noel, Estrada, Isabela* ☎ *787/609–5888* ⊕ *www.royalisabela.com.* ✉ *$250 for outside guests and $125 for in-house guests, plus a $90 caddie fee for 2 players* ⚑ *18 holes, 7667 yards, par 73.*

17

HORSEBACK RIDING

Horseback riding is a well-established family pastime in Puerto Rico, with *cabalgatas* (group day rides) frequently organized on weekends through mountain towns.

Carabalí Rainforest Park. A family-run operation, this hacienda is a good place to jump in the saddle and ride one of Puerto Rico's Paso Fino horses. Hour-long rides take you around the 600-acre ranch, while two-hour treks take you to a river where you and your horse can take a dip. If you prefer something more high-tech, rent a four-wheeler for an excursion through the foothills of El Yunque. ⊠ *Rd. 3, Km 31.6, Luquillo* ☎ *787/889–5820* ⊕ *www.carabalirainforestpark.com.*

SURFING

The very best surfing beaches are along the northwestern coast from Isabela south to Rincón, which gained notoriety by hosting the World Surfing Championship in 1968. Today the town draws surfers from around the globe, especially in winter, when the waves are at their best.

Desecheo Surf & Dive Shop. Desecheo Surf & Dive Shop rents snorkeling equipment, Boogie boards, and a variety of short and long surfboards. The company also has a small shop with swimwear, sandals, sunglasses, and surf gear. ⊠ *Rte. 413, Km 2.5* ☎ *787/823–0390* ⊕ *www. desecheosurfshop.com.*

Mar Azul. Mar Azul has Rincon's best selection of performance surfboards and stand-up paddleboards to buy or rent. Paddleboard lessons are also available. This is one of the best surf shops on the entire island. ⊠ *Rte. 413, Km 4.4* ☎ *787/823–5692* ⊕ *www.puertoricosurfinginfo.com.*

SABA

WELCOME TO SABA

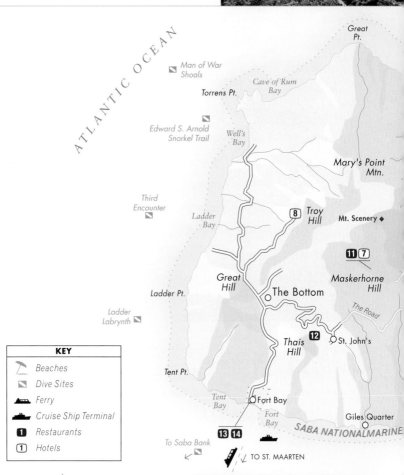

KEY

⤳	Beaches
◪	Dive Sites
⛴	Ferry
🚢	Cruise Ship Terminal
1	Restaurants
①	Hotels

Great Pt.

Man of War Shoals

Cave of Rum Bay

Torrens Pt.

ATLANTIC OCEAN

Edward S. Arnold Snorkel Trail

Well's Bay

Mary's Point Mtn.

Third Encounter

Ladder Bay

8 *Troy Hill*

Mt. Scenery ◆

11 **7**

Maskerhorne Hill

Great Hill

The Bottom

Ladder Pt.

Ladder Labrynth

The Road

12 *St. John's*

Thais Hill

Tent Pt.

Tent Bay

Fort Bay

Fort Bay

Giles Quarter

13 **14**

SABA NATIONAL MARINE

To Saba Bank

TO ST. MAARTEN

Mountainous Saba's precipitous terrain allows visitors to choose between the heights and the depths. The Bottom, the island's capital, was once thought to be the crater of a dormant volcano. From here a trail of 400 rough-hewn steps drops to the sea. Divers can take a different plunge to view the pristine reef.

THE UNSPOILED QUEEN

Tiny Saba—an extinct volcano that juts out of the ocean to a height of 2,855 feet—is just 5 square miles (13 square km) in size and has a population of about 1,500. Part of the Dutch Caribbean, it's 28 miles (45 km) south of St. Maarten and surrounded by some of the richest dive sites in the Caribbean.

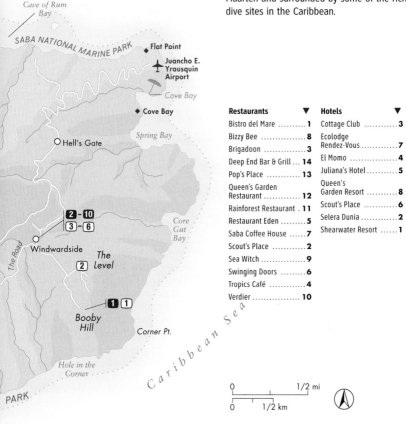

Restaurants	▼
Bistro del Mare	1
Bizzy Bee	8
Brigadoon	3
Deep End Bar & Grill	14
Pop's Place	13
Queen's Garden Restaurant	12
Rainforest Restaurant	11
Restaurant Eden	5
Saba Coffee House	7
Scout's Place	2
Sea Witch	9
Swinging Doors	6
Tropics Café	4
Verdier	10

Hotels	▼
Cottage Club	3
Ecolodge Rendez-Vous	7
El Momo	4
Juliana's Hotel	5
Queen's Garden Resort	8
Scout's Place	6
Selera Dunia	2
Shearwater Resort	1

18

SABA

TOP REASONS TO VISIT SABA

1 Diving: Divers flock to Saba because of the clear water and spectacular ocean life.

2 Hiking: Hikers can climb the island's pinnacle, Mt. Scenery, but the less intense trails offer many sweeping vistas as well.

3 Authenticity: Saba reminds you of what nearly all of the Caribbean used to be: the locals are genuine, and tourist traps are just about nonexistent.

4 Ecotourism: Several hotels cater to ecotourists, with resident nature pros who can tell you everything about local flora and fauna.

5 Quirkiness: On this unusual island, the airport landing and "the Road" are thrill rides, Wells Bay beach disappears at the end of every summer, and the Bottom is not on the bottom.

Updated
by Roberta
Sotonoff

Though Saba (pronounced *say*-ba) is just south of St. Maarten (if you've seen the original *King Kong*, you may recognize its majestic silhouette from the beginning of the film), the islands couldn't be more different. St. Maarten is all beaches, gambling, and duty-free shopping; Saba is ecotourism, diving, and hiking.

Nearly half of Saba's 5 square miles (13 square km) is covered in verdant tropical rain forest; the other half is sprinkled with hamlets composed of white, green-shuttered houses trimmed in gingerbread, roofed in red, and built on grades so steep, they seem to defy physics. Flower-draped walls and neat picket fences border narrow paths among the bromeliads, palms, hibiscus, orchids, and Norfolk Island pines. The land dips and climbs à la San Francisco and eventually drops off into sheer cliffs that fall right into the ocean, the fodder for some of the world's most striking dive sites and the primary reason for Saba's cultlike following. Divers seem to relish the fact that they're in on Saba's secret.

But word about this Dutch Caribbean island has gotten out. Every year, more tourists are turned on to Saba's charms and make the 11-minute, white-knuckle flight from St. Maarten into the tiny airport with a runway not much larger than an aircraft carrier's. Indeed, traffic jams along the winding, narrow road (yes, there's really just one) are rare, unless the driver in front of you stops to chat. The past few years have seen the opening of more restaurants and most recently, a minimall (big advances, considering around-the-clock electricity was established only in 1970). But don't come expecting a booming metropolis; even as it changes, Saba retains an old-world charm.

A major point of local pride is that many Saban families can be traced all the way back to the island's settlement in 1640 (the surnames Hassell, Johnson, and Peterson fill the tiny phone book). And Sabans hold their traditions dear. Saba lace—a genteel art that dates back to the 1870s—is still hand-stitched by local ladies who, on the side, also distill potent, 151-proof Saba Spice, which is for sale in most of the island's mom-and-pop shops. And islanders like to keep their ancestors close in a very literal sense: in keeping with a generations-old tradition, the dead are buried in local families' neatly tended gardens.

Like the residents of most small towns, the Sabans are a tight-knit group; nothing happens without everyone hearing about it, making crime pretty much a nonissue. That said, they are eager to welcome newcomers and tend to make travelers feel less like tourists and more like old friends. After all, they're proud to show off their home, which they lovingly call "the unspoiled queen."

LOGISTICS

Getting to Saba: There are no nonstops from the United States. You have to transfer in St. Maarten for the short flight.

Hassle Factor: Medium to high.

On the Ground: Taxis can take you around, or you can rent a car. There's just one road, so it's not as if you could get lost. Some people even hitchhike.

PLANNING

WHEN TO GO

High season runs from mid-December through April. The Saba Day long weekend is usually at the end of the first week of December, and Carnival is in the summer (July or August).

GETTING HERE AND AROUND

AIR TRAVEL

All flights arrive in St. Maarten, where you have to transfer for a short flight.

Airlines Winair. The only airline to fly to Saba (SAB) is Winair; all the flights originate in St. Maarten. Round-trip fees are $141 and up. ☎ 599/416–2255 ⊕ www.fly-winair.com.

Airport The approach to Saba's tiny airstrip is as thrilling as a roller-coaster ride; luckily, the de Havilland Twin Otter aircraft are built for it. In fact, the pilot needs only half the length of the runway to land properly. (If you're nervous, don't sit on the right. The wing seems almost to scrape against the cliff side on the approach.) **Juancho E. Yrausquin Airport** (*SAB*). Once you've touched down on the airstrip, the pilot taxis an inch or two, turns, and deposits you just outside the airport. ☎ 599/416–2222 *control tower, 599/416–2860 airport manager.*

BOAT AND FERRY TRAVEL

Dawn II. A 65-foot aluminum vessel that holds 50 people, the *Dawn II* runs on Tuesday, Thursday, and Saturday between Philipsburg and Fort Bay. It leaves Saba at 7 am, arriving at St. Maarten at 9 am, and departs St. Maarten at 5 pm, arriving at Fort Bay at 7 pm. The one-way fare from St. Maarten to Saba is $48 plus a $7 harbor fee; the opposite direction is $45 plus a $5 harbor fee. A same-day return (round-trip) ticket is $68 plus an additional $12 harbor fee. Call ahead to check current schedules. ⊠ *Fort Bay Ferry Terminal* ☎ 599/416–2299 ⊕ *www. sabactransport.com.*

18

The Edge. This high-speed ferry leaves St. Maarten's Pelican Marina in Simpson Bay for Fort Bay on Saba every Wednesday through Sunday at 9 am (check in for the trip an hour before). It departs for the return trip about 3:30 pm. The trip, which can be rough, takes just over an hour each way. Round-trip fare is $80 per person for a Saba day trip, plus a $12 port fee, and 5% extra if you pay by credit card. One-way tickets are $55 plus $7 port fee. Passports are necessary for travel. ⊠ *Fort Bay Ferry Terminal* ☎ *721/544–2631* ⊕ *www.stmaarten-activities.com.*

CAR TRAVEL

You won't need long to tour the island by car—you can cover the entire circuitous length of the Road in the space of a morning. If you want to shop, have lunch, and do some sightseeing, plan on a full day.

Gasoline Station. The island has only one gasoline station, which is located in Fort Bay. If you are renting a car, make sure you do not let your tank run too low. The station has abbreviated hours. At this writing, gasoline costs $5.90 per gallon. ⊠ *Fort Bay* ⊙ *Weekdays 8–3:30, Sat. 8–noon. Closed Sun.*

Morgan's Car Rental. Rentals average about US$55–US$65 a day depending on the size of the car. Weekly rates are available. ⊠ *Windwardside* ☎ *599/416–2881 ICS (Island Communication Services).*

TAXI TRAVEL

Taxis charge a set rate for up to four people per taxi, with an additional cost for each person more than four. The fare from the airport to Hell's Gate is $10, to Windwardside it's $12.50, and to the Bottom it's $20. The fare from the Fort Bay ferry docks to Windwardside is $15. A taxi from Windwardside to the Bottom is $10.

ESSENTIALS

Banks and Exchange Services U.S. dollars are accepted everywhere, but Saba's official currency is the Netherlands Antilles florin (NAf; also called the guilder). The exchange rate is fixed at NAf 1.79 to US$1. Both First Caribbean International Bank and the Royal Bank of Trinidad and Tobago are in Windwardside and provide foreign-exchange services. The Windward Island Bank in the Bottom offers full banking services, weekdays 8:30–3:30.

Electricity 110 volts/60 cycles; visitors from North America should have no trouble using their electronics or travel appliances.

Emergency Services Ambulance ☎ *599/416–2210, 599/416–3710.* **Fire** ☎ *599/416–3710, 599/416–2210.* **Police** ⊠ *The Bottom* ☎ *599/416–3737.*

Passport Requirements Visitors must carry a valid passport and have an ongoing or return ticket.

Phones Phones take prepaid phone cards, which can be bought at stores throughout the island, or local coins. To call Saba from the United States, dial 011 + 599 + 416, followed by the four-digit number.

Taxes and Service Charges You must pay a $5 departure tax when leaving Saba by plane. There is also a $5 departure tax by boat, which is sometimes covered in the cost of the ticket. Several of the larger hotels will tack on a 10%–15% service charge; others include it in rates.

Hotels add a 5% government tax plus a 3% turnover tax to the cost of a room. A $1 per person, per night nature fee is automatically added to your hotel bill.

ACCOMMODATIONS

There are no big resorts on Saba, just some small hotels and guesthouses, as well as a few rental apartments and villas.

HOTEL AND RESTAURANT PRICES

Prices in the restaurant reviews are the average cost of a main course at dinner or, if dinner is not served, at lunch; taxes and service charges are generally included. Prices in the hotel reviews are the lowest cost of a standard double room in high season, excluding taxes, service charges, and meal plans (except at all-inclusives). Prices for rentals are the lowest per-night cost for a one-bedroom unit in high season.

For expanded lodging reviews and current deals, visit Fodors.com.

VISITOR INFORMATION

Saba Tourist Office ⊠ *Windwardside* ☎ *599/416–2231, 599/416–2322* ⊕ *www.sabatourism.com.*

WEDDINGS

Lt. Governor of Saba. If you want to be married in Saba at somewhere other than the Government Building's courtroom, you must submit a written request to the Lt. Governor of Saba. Same-sex marriages are now the norm. ☎ *599/416–3313, 599/416–3311, 599/416–3312.*

EXPLORING

18

Getting around the island means negotiating the narrow, twisting roadway that clings to the mountainside and rises from sea level to almost 2,000 feet. Although driving isn't difficult, be sure to go slowly and cautiously. If in doubt, leave the driving to a cabbie so you can enjoy the scenery.

TOP ATTRACTIONS

FAMILY **Harry L. Johnson Museum.** Small signs mark the way to the Harry L. Johnson Museum. This 160-year-old former sea captain's home is surrounded by lemongrass, clover, and a playground for small children. It has recently been renovated but period pieces like the handsome mahogany four-poster bed, an antique organ, and the kitchen's rock oven still remain. You can also look at old documents, such as a letter a Saban wrote after the hurricane of 1772, in which he sadly says, "We have lost our little all." Don't miss the delightful stroll to the museum down the stone-walled Park Lane, one of the prettiest walks in the Caribbean. ⊠ *Windwardside* ☎ *$2* ⊙ *Weekdays 11–4.*

Fodor's Choice **Mt. Scenery.** Stone and concrete steps—1,064 of them—rise to the top of
★ Mt. Scenery. En route to the mahogany grove at the summit, the steps pass giant elephant ears, ferns, begonias, mangoes, palms, and orchids; there are six identifiable ecosystems in all. The staff at the Trail Shop in Windwardside can provide a field guide. Have your hotel pack a picnic lunch, wear sturdy shoes, and take along a jacket and a canteen of water. The round-trip excursion, which takes about three hours, is best begun in the early morning.

WORTH NOTING

The Bottom. Sitting in a bowl-shape valley 820 feet above the sea, this town is the seat of government and the home of the lieutenant governor. The governor's mansion, next to Wilhelmina Park, has fancy fretwork, a steeply pitched roof and wraparound double galleries.

On the other side of town is the Wesleyan Holiness Church, a small stone building with white fretwork. Though it's been renovated and virtually reconstructed over the years, its original four walls date from 1919; go inside and look around. Stroll by the church, beyond a place called the Gap, to a lookout point where you can see the 400 rough-hewn steps leading down to Ladder Bay. This and Fort Bay were the two landing sites from which Saba's first settlers had to haul themselves and their possessions up to the heights. Sabans sometimes walk down to Ladder Bay to picnic. Think long and hard before you do: climbing back requires navigating the same 400 steps.

Cove Bay. Near the airport on the island's northeastern side, this 20-foot-long strip of rocks and pebbles laced with gray sand is really the only place for sunning. There's also a small tide pool here for swimming. Sand has been added to make it more beachy. ⊠ *Cove Bay.*

Flat Point. This is the only place on the island where planes can land. The runway here is one of the world's shortest, with a length of approximately 1,300 feet. Only STOL (short takeoff and landing) prop planes dare land here, as each end of the runway drops off more than 100 feet into the crashing surf below. ⊠ *Flat Point.*

Fort Bay. The end of the Road is also the jumping-off place for all of Saba's dive operations and the location of the St. Maarten ferry dock. The island's only gas station is here, as is a 277-foot pier that accommodates the tenders from ships. On the quay is a decompression chamber, which at this writing is not in use, and three dive shops. Deep End Bar and Grill and Pop's Place are two good places to catch your breath while enjoying some refreshments and the view of the water. ⊠ *Fort Bay.*

Hell's Gate. The Road makes 14 hairpin turns up nearly 2,000 vertical feet to Hell's Gate. Holy Rosary Church, on Zion's Hill, is a stone structure that looks medieval but was built in 1962. In the community center behind the church, village ladies sell their intricate lace. The same ladies make the potent rum-based Saba Spice, each according to her old family recipe. The intrepid can venture to Lower Hell's Gate, where the Old Sulphur Mine Walk leads to bat caves (with a sulfuric stench) that can—with caution—be explored. ⊠ *Holy Rosary Church.*

Saba National Marine Park. Established in 1987 to preserve and manage the island's marine resources, the Saba National Marine Park encircles the entire island, dipping down to 200 feet. It's zoned for diving, swimming, fishing, boating, and anchorage. A unique aspect of Saba's diving is the submerged pinnacles at about the 70-foot depth mark. Here all forms of sea creatures rendezvous. The information center offers talks and slide shows for divers and snorkelers and provides literature on marine life. (Divers are charged $3 a dive to help maintain the park facilities.) Before you visit, call first to see if anyone is

Looking down from Mt. Scenery

around. ✉ *Saba Conservation Foundation/Marine Park Visitors Center, Fort Bay* ☎ *599/416-3295, 599/416-3435* ⊕ *www.sabapark.org* ⊙ *Weekdays 8–5.*

Windwardside. The island's second-largest village, perched at 1,968 feet, commands magnificent views of the Caribbean. Here amid the oleander bushes are rambling lanes and narrow alleyways winding through the hills, and clusters of tiny, neat houses and shops as well as the Saba Tourist Office. At the village's northern end is the Church of St. Paul's Conversion, a colonial building with a red-and-white steeple. ✉ *Windwardside.*

WHERE TO EAT

The island might be tiny, but there's no shortage of mouthwatering fare, including French dishes, fresh seafood, and Caribbean specialties. Reservations are necessary, as most of the restaurants are quite small. In addition, some places provide transportation.

What to Wear: Restaurants are informal. Shorts are fine during the day, but for dinner you may want to put on pants or a casual sundress. Just remember that nights in Windwardside can be cool because of the elevation.

$$$
SEAFOOD
✕ **Bistro del Mare.** While dining alongside the pool at the Shearwater Resort, savor the sounds of the sea, soft jazz, and a panorama from 2,000 feet above sea level. On the frequently changing menu, fresh seafood is a given; specialties include a mushroom-and-cheese risotto and braised lamb. Unfortunately, the staff could stand to be a little friendlier

here. The road to and from this resort is particularly steep, something to keep in mind if you visit the bar, the largest in Saba. $ Average main: $27 ⊠ Shearwater Resort, Booby Hill, Windwardside ☏ 599/416–2498 ⊕ www.shearwater-resort.com ⌂ Reservations essential ⊘ No dinner Sun. and Mon.

$ ✕ **Bizzy Bee Bakery.** Chat with the locals while you buy sandwiches
BAKERY   or something sweet to have with your tea or coffee. They also create
FAMILY   good turkey panini and a variety of tasty breads including cornbread, multigrain, sunflower seed, pumpkin seed, and milk bread. $ Average main: $7 ⊠ Breadline Plaza, Windwardside ☏ 599/416–2900 ═ No credit cards ⊘ No dinner. Closed Sun.

$$$ ✕ **Brigadoon.** The exceptional fare draws just as many people to this
ECLECTIC   local favorite as the entertaining atmosphere, which stars eccentric co-owner Tricia Chammaa. She livens things up with jokes and brassy banter while her husband, Michael, toils over dinner in the back. The result is a great experience. Brigadoon's glass-top tables are accented with Caribbean-style runners and string lights. Specialties include Chowder Michael and Shrimp Michael, a pasta dish that also includes mushrooms and olives. Thursday and Saturday are prime rib and sushi nights. As for desserts, the cheesecake, which comes in a variety of flavors, and the peanut-butter pie are standouts. Also worth a try: Madagascar vanilla bean–ginger rum, made in-house (as are all the ice creams). $ Average main: $23 ⊠ Windwardside ☏ 599/416–2380 ⌂ Reservations essential ⊘ No lunch. Closed Tues. Closed Aug. or Sept. (call ahead).

$$ ✕ **Deep End Restaurant and Bar.** Now owned by Queen's Garden Resort,
AMERICAN   its interior and menu have been recently renovated. The $10 "1-2-3" breakfast special allows you to choose your egg style, bread, and enhancer (Gouda cheese, bacon, sausage, ham, or cream cheese). Lunch features a variety of customized pastas sandwiches, salads, and wok dishes. $ Average main: $15 ⊠ Fort Bay ☏ 599/416–3438 ⊘ Closed Mon. No dinner.

$ ✕ **Pop's Place.** You'll find this itty-bitty come-as-you-are, Caribbean-flavor
AMERICAN   shack directly on the water, overlooking the pier in Fort Bay. It's cozy, it's fun, and its bar resembles a ship. Fast food and sandwiches are on offer. Note that Pop's sometimes closes on slow days. $ Average main: $8 ⊠ Fort Bay ☏ 599/416–3640 ═ No credit cards ⊘ Closed Mon.

$$$ ✕ **Queen's Garden Restaurant.** Set in a lovely garden and showcasing
ECLECTIC   sweeping views of the Bottom, this dimly lit venue is the perfect place
Fodor's Choice   for a romantic meal. For true honeymooners, there's the "Bird's Nest,"
★   a tree house for private dining. Regardless of where you sit, you can expect excellent service to go with superb Saban lobster or some other tasty menu offering, or the chef will create something to your liking. The smoked-duck-breast salad starter is mouthwatering. Come early for cocktails at the outdoor bar, which overlooks the pool—and, below that, the ocean—then stay late and be awed by the stars above you. Poolside parties, musical events, and theme nights with international flavors spice things up. A jacket is required for dinner only. $ Average main: $30 ⊠ 1 Troy Hill Dr., Troy Hill ☏ 599/416–3494 ⊕ www. queensaba.com/theresort ⌂ Reservations essential ⊘ No dinner Mon.

$$ **CARIBBEAN** ✕ **Rainforest Restaurant.** You might need a flashlight for the five-minute hike down the Crispeen Track, by way of the Mt. Scenery Trail, to find this restaurant in the middle of the rain forest. Once you arrive, you'll feel truly away from it all. There's a different menu every week. At night, you are surrounded by music—the lilting sound of the tree frogs. Ⓢ *Average main: $15* ⊠ *Ecolodge Rendez-Vous, Crispeen Track, Windwardside* ☎ *599/416–7012, 599/416–7032* ⊕ *www.ecolodge-saba.com* ✆ *Closed Mon.*

$$$$ **EUROPEAN** **Fodor's**Choice ★ ✕ **Restaurant Eden.** On a rooftop amid a lovely garden setting, Chef Norbert Schippers concocts an eclectic, European-French menu that might include anything, risotto, seafood, and steaks. Sample the Frutti del Mare, pasta with seafood and garden vegetables, which is topped with a lobster cream sauce. The restaurant prides itself on the freshness of its ingredients. Ⓢ *Average main: $31* ⊠ *Lambee's Pl., above Sea Saba Dive Center, Windwardside* ☎ *599/416–2539* ⊕ *www.edensaba.com* ⌕ *Reservations essential* ✆ *Closed Tues. No lunch.*

$ **CAFÉ** ✕ **Saba Coffee House.** Saba's answer to Starbucks, this local hangout roasts its own coffee. And there are a lot to choose from—15 to be exact—as well as mochas, cappuccinos, lattes, and frozen drinks like chais and smoothies. You can also get salads, soup, sandwiches, and beer and wine. The Wi-Fi's free, too. The café is open by 7 am on weekdays and at 11 am on weekends. Ⓢ *Average main: $3* ⊠ *The Bottom* ☎ *599/416–3636* ▤ *No credit cards* ✆ *No dinner.*

$$ **CARIBBEAN** ✕ **Scout's Place.** At this spacious, fun-loving restaurant and bar, you'll find dishes like goat stew and spit-roasted chicken. Theme nights include Friday fish-and-chips or gyros ($18) and Saturday barbecue ($19). In addition to the good food, a great reason to come here is the atmosphere. Locals flock to Scout's Place on Friday for karaoke, but there's bound to be a group looking for fun every other night of the week. Sit on the outdoor verandah, which has stunning views of the water, the tiny houses, and the lush forest that make Saba so picturesque. Ⓢ *Average main: $19* ⊠ *Windwardside* ☎ *599/416–2740, 599/416–2205* ⊕ *www.scoutsplace.com* ✆ *No dinner Sun.*

$$ **ECLECTIC** ✕ **Sea Witch Bar & Grill.** Find both indoor and outdoor dining at this newly opened eatery (formerly Saba's Treasure). Start off your meal with a cocktail or imported beer. Then enjoy pizza, pasta, steak or seafood. Desserts are homemade. Ⓢ *Average main: $19* ⊠ *Windwardside* ☎ *599/416–2013.*

$$ **BARBECUE** ✕ **Swinging Doors.** A cross between an English pub and an Old West saloon (yes, there are swinging doors), this busy watering hole serves not-to-be-missed barbecue on Tuesday and Friday nights. Pick from ribs, chicken, or ribs and chicken ($12), and don't forget to ask for peanut sauce—you'll be glad you did. Steak night is Sunday ($16–$18); if you'd like to cook your own steak, you're quite welcome to do it. The rest of the week it's just drinks. Expect plenty of conversation, including some local gossip. Ⓢ *Average main: $15* ⊠ *Windwardside* ☎ *599/416–2506* ▤ *No credit cards* ✆ *No lunch. No dinner Mon., Weds., Thurs., or Sat.*

18

$$ ECLECTIC 🍴 **Tropics Café.** Breakfast and lunch are served at the cabana-style, open-air dining room at the pool or in a small room dominated by a bar. Sandwiches, salads, and fresh fish dominate the menu, and tapas is the Sunday-night treat here. Every Friday starting at 4, there is a T.G.I.F party with snack platters and music by local DJs. [$] *Average main: $20* ✉ *Juliana's Hotel, Windwardside* ☎ *599/416–2469, 888/289–5708* 🌐 *www.sabatropics.com* 🕒 *No lunch Mon.*

$ SPANISH 🍴 **Verdier.** Dine outdoors in the Plaza and enjoy lunch or dinner at the new mini-mall. A delightful eatery and pub, it mostly specializes in Spanish fare but also offers burgers and chicken nuggets. The restaurant is open daily for lunch and dinner, but depending on the dinner business, they may close earlier or later. [$] *Average main: $10* ✉ *Breadline Plaza, Windwardside* ☎ *599/416–2001* 💳 *No credit cards.*

WHERE TO STAY

Saba's few hotel rooms are primarily in a handful of friendly, tidy inns or guesthouses perched on ledges or tucked into tropical gardens. Because the island is so small, it doesn't much matter where you stay. Among the choices are a couple of delightful small inns and ecoresorts. There are also more than a dozen apartments, cottages, and villas for rent. Cable TV is common, but air-conditioning is rare.

$ HOTEL FAMILY 🏨 **Cottage Club.** Form follows function at these gingerbread bungalows, where the price is right and the proximity to downtown is ideal. **Pros:** walking distance to Windwardside; lushly landscaped pool with a gorgeous view; majestic lobby–reception room. **Cons:** stark suites; no on-site dining; some of the walks to the rooms are steep; no a/c. [$] *Rooms from: $130* ✉ *Windwardside* ☎ *599/416–2486* 🌐 *www.cottage-club.com* 🛏 *6 cottages* 🍽 *No meals* ☞ *4 additional cottages are long-term rentals.*

$ HOTEL 🏨 **Ecolodge Rendez-Vous Saba.** If you like hiking and getting back to nature, then this lodge, a five-minute walk deep in the rain forest, is for you. **Pros:** quiet; candlelit restaurant; nature-theme cottages. **Cons:** it's a hike to get here; only three cottages have ocean views; no electricity or Internet; steep climb to rooms. [$] *Rooms from: $60* ✉ *Crispeen Track, Windwardside* ☎ *599/416–7012, 599/416–7032* 🌐 *www.ecolodge-saba.com* 🛏 *12 cottages* 🍽 *No meals.*

$ HOTEL 🏨 **El Momo.** If you want to feel as if you're doing your ecological part without giving up every modern convenience, consider these tiny cottages. **Pros:** snack bar–lounge with hammock; cottages buried in the woods; smoke-free property; free Wi-Fi; gift shop. **Cons:** tiny accommodations; strenuous hike to get here; no a/c. [$] *Rooms from: $50* ✉ *Booby Hill* ☎ *599/416–2265* 🌐 *www.elmomocottages.com* 🛏 *7 cottages* 🍽 *No meals.*

$ HOTEL FAMILY 🏨 **Juliana's Hotel.** Reasonable prices, in town, great views, and accommodations from good to luxurious—it's all here. **Pros:** across the street from Tropics Café; outdoor, in-rock shower in Orchid Cottage; two on-site computers with free Internet; full breakfast. **Cons:** close quarters; a hike to get off the property; not all rooms have a/c. [$] *Rooms from: $130* ✉ *Windwardside* ☎ *599/416–2269, 888/783–3319* 🌐 *www.julianas-hotel.com* 🛏 *9 rooms, 1 apartment, 4 cottages* 🍽 *Breakfast.*

$ 🏠 **Queen's Gardens Resort.** Everything about this romantic miniresort
HOTEL reflects the island of Saba, from the quaint stone stairway that winds up
Fodor'sChoice past the largest pool on the island to the patio in front of the main build-
★ ing, which houses the lovely Queen's Garden restaurant, serving fresh
island fare. **Pros:** local flavor; large pool with bar; private Jacuzzis with
sweeping views. **Cons:** occasional noisy parties; not wheelchair accessible; not kid-friendly. **$** *Rooms from: $230* ⊠ *1 Troy Hill Dr., Troy
Hill* 🕾 *599/416–3494* ⊕ *www.queenssaba.com* ⤳ *12 1- or 2-bedroom
suites, 1 house* ⦿ *No meals.*

$ 🏠 **Scout's Place.** Owned by the dive instructors Wolfgang and Barbara
HOTEL Tooten, this all-in-one dive resort is especially good for the diver on a
tight budget. **Pros:** on-site dive shop; multilingual owners; "Sabaoke"
on Friday; free Nitrox diving with packages. **Cons:** smallish rooms;
some don't get much sunlight. **$** *Rooms from: $114* ⊠ *Windwardside* 🕾 *599/416–2740, 599/416–2205, 866/656–7222 for reservations*
⊕ *www.scoutsplace.com* ⤳ *10 rooms, 1 2-bedroom cottage* ⦿ *Breakfast.*

$ 🏠 **Selera Dunia.** The managing director, Hemmie van Xanten, has traveled
B&B/INN the world amassing a vast collection of objects from Africa, Morocco,
Fodor'sChoice Asia, and Colombia. **Pros:** accommodations are very well appointed;
★ tranquillity and privacy. **Cons:** if you want to explore the island, you'll
need car or taxi. **$** *Rooms from: $135* ⊠ *The Level, Windwardside*
🕾 *599/416–5443* ⊕ *www.seleradunia.com* ⤳ *2 rooms* ⦿ *No meals.*

$ 🏠 **Shearwater Resort.** It's worth the trip here just for the view—the
RESORT sea from 2,000 feet above. **Pros:** location, location, location! **Cons:**
it's a schlep to get here because the road is so steep; standoffish staff.
$ *Rooms from: $175* ⊠ *Booby Hill, Windwardside* 🕾 *599/416–2498*
⊕ *shearwater-resort.com* ⤳ *8 rooms* ⦿ *Breakfast.*

NIGHTLIFE

Guido's. There's often dancing and local DJs on weekends here. ⊠ *Windwardside* 🕾 *599/416–2230.*

Scout's Place. When night rolls around, the convivial bar here can get
crowded, and sometimes there's dancing. Go on Friday for "Sabaoke
Night" (the Sabaen version of karaoke), when people swarm the spacious dining area. ⊠ *Windwardside* 🕾 *599/416–2740.*

SHOPPING

The history of Saba lace, one of the island's most popular goods, goes
back to the late 19th century. Gertrude Johnson learned lace making at
a Caracas convent school. She returned to Saba in the 1870s and taught
the art that has endured ever since. Saban ladies display and sell their
creations at the community center in Hell's Gate and from their houses;
just follow the signs. Collars, tea towels, napkins, and other small articles are relatively inexpensive; larger ones, such as tablecloths, can be
pricey. The fabric requires some care—it's not drip-dry. Saba Spice is
another island buy. Although it *sounds* as delicate as lace, and the
aroma is as sweet as can be, the base for this liqueur is 151-proof rum.

Breadline Plaza. Saba's one and only mini shopping mall opened in Windwardside in 2013. It contains a variety of shops including Bluemint Boutique, Bizzy Bee Bakery, Eye Care Optical, Island Communication Service (a business and Internet café), and Verdier Bar & Restaurant. ⊠ *Windwardside.*

El Momo Folk Art. The shelves here overflow with regional crafts, local postcards, handmade jewelry, knickknacks, and anything else El Momo can find a spot for. It's next door to the Peanut Gallery and has the same owners. ⊠ *Windwardside* ☎ *599/416–2518* ⊕ *emfa-saba.com* ⊘ *Mon.– Sat. 9–6, Sun noon–3.*

JoBean Glass. Artist-owner Jo Bean's handmade glass-bead jewelry and sterling silver and gold pieces are delicate and unique. Workshops in beadwork are available. A branch is also in the main part of Windwardside. ⊠ *Windwardside* ☎ *599/416–2490* ⊕ *www.jobeanglassart.com.*

Little Green Shop. Marie Petit crafts jewelry from polished sea glass, stones, seeds, and porcelain. The store also sells locally made items, including lace and Saba Spice. ⊠ *Across from Sea Saba, Windwardside* ☎ *599/416–2792* ⊘ *Wed.–Sun. 10–5.*

Peanut Gallery. From watercolors of local houses to ocean-inspired sculpture, the Peanut Gallery offers the island's best selection of local and Caribbean art. Take time to browse through the offerings, and you might just walk away with something better than a refrigerator magnet to remember your trip with. ⊠ *Windwardside* ☎ *599/416–2792* ⊕ *thepeanutgallery.vpweb.co.uk.*

Saba Artisan Foundation. Here you can buy hand-screened fabrics by the yard or already made into resort clothing. The foundation also serves as a central location for buying the famous Saba lace as well as T-shirts and spices. ⊠ *The Bottom* ☎ *599/416–3260* ⊘ *Mon.–Thurs. 8:30–4, Fri. 8:30–3:30.*

SPORTS AND ACTIVITIES

DIVING AND SNORKELING

Fodor's Choice
★

Saba is one of the world's premier scuba-diving destinations. Visibility is extraordinary, and dive sites are alive with corals and other sea creatures. Within ½ mile (¾ km) of shore, seawalls drop to depths of more than 1,000 feet. The Saba National Marine Park, which includes shoals, reefs, and seawalls rich with corals and fish, is dedicated to preserving its marine life.

Divers have a pick of 28 sites, including **Third Encounter,** a top-rated pinnacle dive (usually to about 110 feet) for advanced divers, with plentiful fish and spectacular coral; **Man of War Shoals,** another popular pinnacle dive (70 feet), with myriad fish and coral; and **Ladder Labyrinth,** a formation of ridges and alleys (down to 80 feet), where likely sightings include grouper, sea turtles, and sharks.

Snorkelers shouldn't feel left out: the marine park has several marked spots where reefs or rocks sit in shallow water. Among these sites is

Divers will find spectacular marine life and coral in Saba's 28 dive sites.

Torrens Point on the northwest side of the island. Waterproof maps are available from the marine park, the Saba Conservation Foundation, or dive shops.

Expect to pay about $60 for a one-tank dive, around $110 for a two-tank dive. There is also a mandatory $3 dive fee imposed by the Saba Marine Park and a $1 charge per dive for the hyperbaric chamber.

Saba Deep. If you're looking for a very personal, one-on-one dive experience, try Saba Deep, which tends to take out smaller groups. The company provides PADI certifications from beginner to dive master. They also offer Nitrox diving and equipment if needed. One tank dive is $60; two tank, $110. ⊠ *Fort Bay* ☎ *599/416–3347, 599/416–6301* ⊕ *www.sabadeep.com.*

Saba Divers. Saba Divers offers multilingual instruction, making it a great option for anyone interested in meeting international divers or in practicing their language skills. It's the only outfit on the island that allows its customers to dive with Nitrox for free. ⊠ *Windwardside* ☎ *599/416–2740* ⊕ *www.sabadivers.com.*

Sea Saba. All of Sea Saba's excursions are accompanied by at least two dive instructors and can include up to 10 divers on one of two 40-foot boats. The staff is both knowledgeable and jovial, making a day on the boat illuminating and enjoyable for any diver. ⊠ *Windwardside* ☎ *599/416–2246, 800/883–7222 in U.S.* ⊕ *www.seasaba.com.*

FAMILY **Sea and Learn.** Every October, local dive operator Lynn Costenaro, of Sea Saba, orchestrates an event that has become an international attraction. Sea and Learn is when pharmacologists, biologists, and other nature experts from all over the world descend on Saba to give presentations, lead field trips, and show off research projects, all of which are designed to increase environmental awareness. Past events have included monitoring undersea octopus checkpoints and studying the medicinal value of indigenous plants. There are even special events for kids. And best of all, it's free. You can sign up online. ☎ *599/416–2246* ⊕ *www.seaandlearn.org.*

GUIDED TOURS

The taxi drivers who meet the planes at the airport or the boats at Fort Bay conduct tours of the island. Tours can also be arranged by dive shops or hotels. A full-day trek costs $50 for one to four passengers and $12.50 per person for groups larger than four. If you're in from St. Maarten for a day trip, you can do a full morning of sightseeing, stop off for lunch (have your driver make reservations before starting), complete the tour afterward, and return to the airport in time to make the last flight back to St. Maarten. Guides are available for hiking; arrangements may be made through the tourist office or the Trail Shop in Windwardside. Or check out the island in a guided boat tour available for groups of up to 10 on Tuesday and Wednesday. In an hour and a half you can circle the island while learning about its history, its local seabirds, and its coral reefs.

HIKING

On Saba you can't avoid hiking, even if you just go to mail a postcard. The big deal, of course, is Mt. Scenery, with 1,064 steps leading to its top.

Saba Conservation Foundation. For information about Saba's 18 recommended botanical hikes, check with the Saba Conservation Foundation, which maintains trails, at its office in Fort Bay or at its shop in Windwardside. The charges for trail use are a $1 per day or $3 per stay. This nature fee is automatically added to your hotel bill. Botanical tours are available on request. Crocodile James (James Johnson) will explain the local flora and fauna. A guided, strenuous, full-day hike through the undeveloped side of Mt. Scenery costs about $50. ✉ *Fort Bay* ☎ *599/416–2630 trail shop, 599/416–3295* ✉ *$3 donation requested* ✉ *Trail Shop, Windwardside* ☎ *599/416–2630* ⊕ *www.sabapark.org.*

ST. BARTHÉLEMY

WELCOME TO ST. BARTHÉLEMY

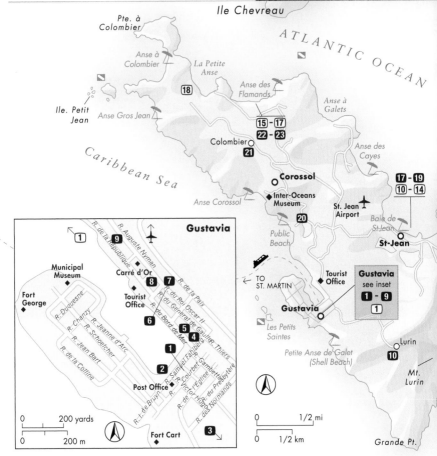

Ile Chevreau

ATLANTIC OCEAN

Pte. à Colombier

Anse à Colombier

La Petite Anse

Anse des Flamands

Anse à Galets

18

Ile. Petit Jean

Anse Gros Jean

15 - 17
22 - 23

Colombier

Anse des Cayes

Caribbean Sea

21

Anse Corossol

Corossol

Inter-Oceans Museum

St. Jean Airport

17 - 19
10 - 14

20

Gustavia

Municipal Museum

Carré d'Or

Public Beach

St-Jean

Fort George

Tourist Office

8 7

6

5
4

1

2

Post Office

R. de la République
R. Auguste Nyman
R. de la Paix
R. du Roi Oscar II
R. du Général de Gaulle
R. Thiers
R. Victor Hugo
R. de l'Église
R. du Presbytère
R. des Normands
R. Samuel Fahlberg
R. Courbet
R. Gambetta
R.-t. de Bruyn
R. de la Colline
R. Jean Bart
R. Schoelcher
R. Jeanne d'Arc
R. Charzy
R. Duquesne
R. du Bord de Mer

TO ST. MARTIN

Tourist Office

Gustavia
see inset

1 - 9
1

Gustavia

Les Petits Saintes

Lurin

10

Petite Anse de Galet (Shell Beach)

Mt. Lurin

0   200 yards
0   200 m

Fort Cart

3

0   1/2 mi
0   1/2 km

Grande Pt.

Chic travelers put aside their cell phones long enough to enjoy the lovely beaches— long, surf-pounded strands; idyllic crescents crowned by cliffs or forests; glass-smooth lagoons perfect for windsurfing. Nothing on St. Barth comes cheap. But on a hotel's awning-shaded terrace St. Barth's civilized ways seem worth every penny.

LA RIVIERA DES CARAÏBES

Just 8 square miles (21 square km), St. Barth is a hilly island with many sheltered bays. Development is tightly controlled, so you will find no high-rise resorts to spoil your views. The French, who had controlled the island since the late 17th century, gave it to Sweden in 1784 but finally reclaimed it in 1877.

ST.BARTHÉLEMY

19

TOP REASONS TO VISIT ST. BARTHÉLEMY

1 The Scene: The island is active, sexy, hedonistic, and hip, and the human scenery is as beautiful as the sparkling-blue sea vistas.

2 Super Style: St. Barth continues to change and evolve, becoming ever more chic.

3 Great Dining: New restaurants continue to tempt gourmets and gourmands.

4 Shopping Galore: If you're a shopper, you'll find bliss stalking the latest in clothes and accessories in dozens of the Caribbean's best boutiques.

5 Getting Out on the Water: Windsurfing, kitesurfing, and other water sports make going to the beach more than just a lounging experience.

Updated by
Elise Meyer

St. Barthélemy blends the respective essences of the Caribbean, France, and *Architectural Digest* in perfect proportions. A sophisticated but unstudied approach to relaxation and respite prevails: you can spend the day on a beach, try on the latest French fashions, and watch the sunset while nibbling tapas over Gustavia Harbor, then choose from nearly 100 excellent restaurants for an elegant or easy evening meal. You can putter around the island, scuba dive, windsurf on a quiet cove, or just admire the lovely views.

A mere 8 square miles (21 square km), St. Barth is a hilly island, with many sheltered inlets providing visitors with many opportunities to try out picturesque, quiet beaches. The town of Gustavia wraps itself around a modern harbor lined with everything from size-matters megayachts to rustic fishing boats to sailboats of all descriptions. Red-roof villas dot the hillsides, and glass-front shops line the streets. Beach surf runs the gamut from kiddie-pool calm to serious-surfer dangerous, beaches from deserted to packed. The cuisine is tops in the Caribbean, and almost everything is tidy, stylish, and up-to-date. French *savoir vivre* prevails throughout the island.

Christopher Columbus discovered the island—called "Ouanalao" by its native Caribs—in 1493; he named it for his brother Bartolomé. The first group of French colonists arrived in 1648, drawn by the ideal location on the West Indian Trade Route, but they were wiped out by the Caribs, who dominated the area. Another small group from Normandy and Brittany arrived in 1694. This time the settlers prospered—with the help of French buccaneers, who took advantage of the island's strategic location and protected harbor. In 1784 the French traded the island to King Gustav III of Sweden in exchange for port rights in Göteborg. The king dubbed the capital Gustavia, laid out and paved streets, built three forts, and turned the community into a prosperous free port. The island thrived as a shipping and commercial center until the 19th century, when earthquakes, fires, and hurricanes brought financial ruin. Many residents fled for newer lands of opportunity, and Oscar II of Sweden decided to return the island to France. After briefly considering selling it to America, the French took possession of St. Barthélemy again on August 10, 1877.

Today the island is a free port, and in 2007 it became a Collectivity, a French-administered overseas territory outside of continental France. Arid, hilly, and rocky, St. Barth was unsuited to sugar production and thus never developed an extensive slave base. Some of today's 3,000 current residents are descendants of the tough Norman and Breton settlers of three centuries ago, but you are more likely to encounter attractive French twenty- and thirtysomethings from Normandy and Provence who are friendly, English speaking, and here for the sunny lifestyle.

PLANNING

WHEN TO GO

High season in St. Barth is typical for the Caribbean, from mid-December through mid-April (or until after Easter). During busy holiday periods prices can shoot up to the highest levels, but in the summer (particularly June and July), there are some remarkable bargains on the island, though some restaurants still close over the summer months, and hotels tend to do their annual maintenance during this time as well.

GETTING HERE AND AROUND

AIR TRAVEL

There are no direct flights to St. Barth. Most North Americans fly first into St. Maarten's Queen Juliana International Airport (⇨ *Chapter 23, St. Maarten/St. Martin for more information)*, from which the island is 10 minutes by air. Winair, which celebrated its 50th anniversary of service to St. Barth in 2013, has regularly scheduled flights from St. Maarten. Tradewind Aviation has regularly scheduled service from San Juan and also does V.I.P charters. Anguilla Air Services and St. Barth Commuter have scheduled flights and also do charters. You must reconfirm your return interisland flight, even during off-peak seasons, or you may very well lose your reservations. Be certain to leave ample time between your scheduled flight and your connection in St. Maarten—three hours is the minimum recommended (and be aware that luggage frequently doesn't make the trip; your hotel or villa-rental company may be able to send someone to retrieve it). It's a good idea to pack a change of clothes, required medicines, and a bathing suit in your carry-on—or better yet, pack very light and don't check baggage at all.

Airports Gustaf III Airport (SBH) ⊠ *St. Jean Rd., St-Jean* 🕾 *0590/27-75-81.*

Local Airline Contacts Anguilla Air Services 🕾 *264/498-5922* ⊕ *www.anguillaairservices.com.* **St. Barth Commuter** 🕾 *0590/27-54-54* ⊕ *www.stbarthcommuter.com.* **Tradewind Aviation** 🕾 *800/376-7922, 203/267-3305 in Connecticut* ⊕ *www.tradewindaviation.com.* **Winair** 🕾 *0590/27-61-01, 866/466-0410* ⊕ *www.fly-winair.com.*

19

BOAT AND FERRY TRAVEL

St Barth can be reached by sea via ferry service or charter boat. There are three companies that provide passenger ferry service between St. Maartin/St. Martin and St. Barth, so check each provider's timetable to determine the most convenient departure. All service is to and from Quai de la République in Gustavia. Voyager offers round-trips for about $100 per person from either Marigot or Oyster Pond. Great Bay Express has several round-trips a day from Bobby's Marina in St. Maarten for €55 if reserved in advance, or €60 for same-day departures. Private boat charters are also available, but they are very expensive; Master Ski Pilou is one of the companies that offer the service.

Boat and Ferry Contacts Great Bay Express Ferry. This express service provides quick ferry transportation between Phillipsburg and Gustavia two or three times daily. Online reservations are available on their website. Round-trip fares are €90 for adults and €45 for children, less if booked in advance. A same-day round-trip is €56 for adults, €40 for kids. ✉ *Quai Gustavia, Gustavia* ☎ *690/71-83-01, 917/652-7346* ⊕ *www.sbhferry.com.* **Master Ski Pilou.** Private boat transfers from St. Maarten to St. Barth are available with Master Ski Pilou. ☎ *0590/27-91-79* ⊕ *www.masterski-pilou.com.* **Voyager.** This service offers several daily departures to Gustavia from Marigot or Oyster Pond in St. Martin. You can book online. ☎ *0590/87-10-68* ⊕ *www.voy12.com.*

CAR TRAVEL

Roads are sometimes unmarked, so get a map and look for signs pointing to a destination. These will be nailed to posts at all crossroads. Roads are narrow and sometimes very steep, but recent work has improved roads all over the island; even so, check the brakes and gears of your rental car before you drive away. ■ TIP➔ **Take a careful inventory of existing dents and scrapes on your rental vehicle with pictures on your smartphone or digital camera.** Maximum speed on the island is 30 mph (50 kph). Driving is on the right, as in the United States and Europe. Parking is an additional challenge. There are two gas stations on the island, one near the airport and one in Lorient. They aren't open after 5 pm, or on Sunday, but the station near the airport has pumps that accept automated payment by chip-and-pin credit card (such as those used throughout Europe), although at this writing most U.S. credit cards don't have the chip required for credit payments. Considering the short distances, a full tank of gas should last you most of a week.

Car Rentals: You must have a valid driver's license and be 25 or older to rent, and in high season there may be a three-day minimum. During peak periods, such as Christmas week and February, be sure to arrange for your car rental ahead of time. When you make your hotel reservations, ask if the hotel has its own cars available to rent; some hotels provide 24-hour emergency road service—something most rental companies don't offer. A tiny but powerful Smart car is a blast to buzz around in, and also a lot easier to park than larger cars. Expect to pay at least $55 per day. A Mini-Cooper convertible makes the most of sunny drives.

LOGISTICS

Getting to St. Barth: There are no direct flights to St. Barth (SBH). You must fly to another island and then catch a smaller plane for the hop over, or you can take a ferry. Most Americans fly first to St. Maarten, and then take the 10-minute flight to St. Barth, but you can connect through St. Thomas or San Juan as well.

Hassle Factor: Medium–high.

On the Ground: Many hotels offer free airport transfers; before you arrive, they will contact you for your arrival information. Otherwise, there's a taxi stand at the airport; unmetered taxis cost about €10 to €25 to reach most hotels. If you are renting a car, you may pick it up from the airport; if you have a reservation (strongly recommended in high season), rental agents will meet you at the ferry if you arrive by boat.

Getting Around the Island: Most people coming to St. Barth rent a car. Taxis are expensive, but some visitors are happy to let an experienced driver negotiate the roads at night. Any restaurant will be happy to call a cab back to your hotel after dinner. Otherwise, there is no other transportation option on the island. It's also possible to rent a motorbike, but steep roads can make driving a stressful experience if you aren't experienced.

Car-Rental Contacts Avis ✉ *Gustaf III Airport (SBH), St Jean Rd., St-Jean* ☎ *0590/27–71–43, 0590/27–71–52* ⊕ *www.avis-stbarth.com.* **Budget** ✉ *Gustaf III Airport, St. Jean Rd., St-Jean* ☎ *0590/29–62–40* ⊕ *www.st-barths.com/budget/en/home.html.* **Cool Rental** ✉ *Maison I, Flamands* ☎ *590/27–52–58* ⊕ *www.cool-rental.com.* **Europcar** ✉ *Gustaf III Airport, St. Jean Rd., St-Jean* ☎ *0590/27–74–34* ⊕ *www.st-barths.com/europcar/index.html.* **Gumbs** ✉ *Gustaf III Airport, St. Jean Rd., St-Jean* ☎ *0590/27–75–32* ⊕ *www.gumbs-car-rental.com.* **Hertz** ✉ *Gustaf III Airport, St-Jean* ☎ *0590/27–71–14* ⊕ *www.hertzstbarth.com.* **Turbé** ✉ *Gustaf III Airport, St-Jean* ☎ *0590/27–71–42* ⊕ *www.turbe-car-rental.com.*

19

MOPED, SCOOTER, AND BIKE TRAVEL

Several companies rent motorbikes, scooters, mopeds, and mountain bikes. Motorbikes go for about $30 per day and require a $100 deposit. Helmets are required. Scooter and motorbike rental places are mostly along rue de France in Gustavia and around the airport in St-Jean.

Contacts Barthloc Rental ✉ *Rue de France, Gustavia* ☎ *0590/27–52–81* ⊕ *www.barthloc.com.* **Chez Béranger** ✉ *21 rue du général de Gaulle, Gustavia* ☎ *0590/27–89–00* ⊕ *www.beranger-rental.com.*

TAXI TRAVEL

Taxis are expensive and not particularly easy to arrange, especially in the evening. There's a taxi station at the airport and another in Gustavia; from elsewhere you must contact a dispatcher in Gustavia or St-Jean. Fares are regulated by the Collectivity, and drivers accept both dollars and euros. If you go out to dinner by taxi, let the restaurant know if you will need a taxi at the end of the meal, and they will call one for you. Limo-style private car-and-driver service is also available through Taxi Prestige 24/7.

DID YOU KNOW?

The largest hotel on St. Barth has just over 70 rooms, which means you get a great deal of personal service and attention wherever you stay.

Contacts Gustavia taxi dispatcher
☎ *0590/27–66–31* ⊕ *www.stbarth-taxis.com.* **St-Jean taxi dispatcher**
✉ *Gustaf III Airport, St-Jean*
☎ *0590/27–75–81.***Taxi Prestige**
☎ *0590/27–70–57* ⊕ *www.stbarts-limousine.com.*

ESSENTIALS

Banks and Exchange Services Legal tender is the euro, but U.S. dollars are widely accepted. ATMs are common and dispense only euros.

Electricity Voltage is 220 AC/60 cycles, as in Europe. You'll need a converter and perhaps a transformer for electronic devices. Most hotels have converters available for guests' use.

BACK-UP FERRY

Even if you are flying to St. Barth, it's a good idea to keep the numbers and schedules for the three ferry companies handy in case your flight is delayed. If you are planning to spend time in St. Maarten before traveling on to St. Barth, the ferry is half the cost and somewhat more reliable than the puddle-jumper, and you can leave from Marigot, Oyster Pond, or Philipsburg. Check at the brand-new St. Barth Tourist Information counter at Princess Juliana Airport for specifics.

Emergency Services Ambulance and Fire ☎ *18, 590/27–66–13.*
Hospital Emergency ☎ *590/27–60–35.* **Police** ☎ *11, 0590/27–11–70.*

Language French, but English is widely spoken.

Passport Requirements All visitors must carry a valid passport and have a return or ongoing ticket. A visa is not necessary for stays of up to a month. Passports must be valid for at least three months from the date of entry to the territory of St. Barthélemy.

Phones Many hotels will provide or rent you a cell phone to use during your stay. Some U.S. cell companies work in St. Barth, but ask your provider before you leave; you may need to have your phone authorized for international use. The country code for St. Barth is 590. Thus, to call St. Barth from the United States, dial 011 + 590 + 590 and the local six-digit number. Some cell phones use the prefix 690. For calls on St. Barth, you must dial 0590 plus the six-digit local number.

Taxes and Service Charges The island charges a $5 departure tax when your next stop is another French island, $10 to anywhere else payable in cash only (dollars or euros). Some hotels add a 10% service charge. Sometimes it is included in the room rate, so check. There is a 5% room tax on hotels and villa rentals.

Tipping Restaurants include a 15% service charge in their published prices, but it's common French practice to leave 5% to 10% more in cash, even if you have paid by credit card. Most taxi drivers don't expect a tip.

ACCOMMODATIONS

Most hotels on St. Barth are small (the largest has fewer than 70 rooms) and stratospherically expensive, but there are some reasonable options. About half of the accommodations on St. Barth are in private villas. Prices drop dramatically after March, and summer is a great time for a visit. Check hotel websites for updates of discounts and special offers that seem to be becoming more common with the current economy.

19

HOTEL AND RESTAURANT PRICES

Prices in the restaurant reviews are the average cost of a main course at dinner or, if dinner is not served, at lunch; taxes and service charges are generally included. Prices in the hotel reviews are the lowest cost of a standard double room in high season, excluding taxes, service charges, and meal plans (except at all-inclusives). Prices for rentals are the lowest per-night cost for a one-bedroom unit in high season.

For expanded lodging reviews and current deals, visit Fodors.com.

VISITOR INFORMATION

Contact Office du Tourisme ⊠ *Quai Général-de-Gaulle, Gustavia* ☎ *0590/27–87–27* ⊕ *www.saintbarth-tourisme.com.*

WEDDINGS

Because of the long legal residency requirement, it's not really feasible to get married on St. Barth unless you're a French citizen.

EXPLORING

With a little practice, negotiating St. Barth's narrow, steep roads soon becomes fun. Recent infrastructure upgrades and the prevalence of small, responsive cars have improved things a lot. Free maps are everywhere, roads are smooth and well-marked, and signs will point the way. The tourist office has annotated maps with walking tours that highlight sights of interest. Parking in Gustavia is still a challenge, especially during busy vacation times.

GUSTAVIA

You can easily explore all of Gustavia during a two-hour stroll. Some shops close from noon to 3 or 4, so plan lunch accordingly, but stores stay open past 7 in the evening.

FAMILY **Le Musée Territorial de Saint Barthélemy.** On the far side of the harbor known as La Pointe is the charming Municipal Museum, where you can find watercolors, portraits, photographs, and historic documents detailing the island's history, as well as displays of the island's flowers, plants, and marine life. ⊠ *La Pointe, Gustavia* ☎ *590/29–71–55* ⊠€2 ☉ *Mon. and Tues. 8:30–1 and 2:30–5:30, Wed. 9–1, Thurs. and Fri. 8:30–1 and 2:30–5, Sat. 9–1* ☉ *Call for summer closing hrs.*

Tourist Office. A good spot to park your car is rue de la République, alongside the catamarans, yachts, and sailboats. The tourist office on the pier can provide maps and a wealth of information. During busier holiday periods, the office may be open all day. ⊠ *Rue de la République, Gustavia* ☎ *0590/27–87–27* ⊕ *www.saintbarth-tourisme.com* ☉ *Mon. 8:30–12:30, Tues.–Fri. 8–noon and 2–5, Sat. 9–noon.*

COROSSOL

FAMILY Traces of the island's French provincial origins are evident in this two-street fishing village with a little rocky beach.

LORIENT

Site of the first French settlement, Lorient is one of the island's two parishes; a restored church, a school, and a post office mark the spot. Note the gaily decorated graves in the cemetery.

ELSEWHERE ON THE ISLAND

St-Jean. There is a monument at the crest of the hill that divides St-Jean from Gustavia. Called *The Arawak,* it symbolizes the soul of St. Barth. A warrior, one of the earliest inhabitants of the area (AD 800–1,800), holds a lance in his right hand and stands on a rock shaped like the island; in his left hand he holds a conch shell, which sounds the cry of nature; perched beside him are a pelican (which symbolizes the air and survival by fishing) and an iguana (which represents the earth). The half-mile-long crescent of sand at St-Jean is the island's most popular beach. A popular activity is watching and photographing the hair-raising airplane landings (though you should note that it is extremely dangerous to stand in the area at the beach end of the runway). You'll also find some of the best shopping on the island here, as well as several restaurants. ⊠ *St-Jean.*

Toiny Coast. Over the hills beyond Grand Cul de Sac is this much-photographed coastline. Stone fences crisscross the steep slopes of Morne Vitet, one of many small mountains on St. Barth, along a rocky shore that resembles the rugged coast of Normandy. Nicknamed the "washing machine" because of its turbulent surf, it is not recommended even to expert swimmers because of the strong undertow. ■ TIP➔ **There is an tough but scenic hike around the point. Take the road past Le Toiny hotel to the top to find the start of the trail.**

BEACHES

19

There is a beach in St. Barth to suit every taste. Whether you are looking for wild surf, a dreamy white-sand strand, or a spot at a chic beach club close to shopping and restaurants, you will find it within a 20-minute drive.

There are many *anses* (coves) and nearly 20 *plages* (beaches) scattered around the island, each with a distinctive personality; all are open to the public, even if the beach fronts the toniest resorts. Because of the variety and number of beaches, even in high season you can find a nearly empty beach, despite St. Barth's tiny size. That's not to say that all the island's beaches are equally good or even equally suitable for swimming, but each beach has something unique to offer. Unless you are having lunch at a beachfront restaurant that has lounging areas set aside for its patrons, you should bring your own umbrella, beach mat, and water (all of which are easily obtainable all over the island if you haven't brought yours with you on vacation). Topless sunbathing is common, but nudism is supposedly forbidden—although both Grande Saline and Gouverneur are de facto nude beaches, albeit less today than in the past. Shade is scarce.

Anse à Colombier. The beach here is the least accessible, thus the most private, on the island; to reach it you must take either a rocky footpath from Petite Anse or brave the 30-minute climb down (and back up) a steep, cactus-bordered trail from the top of the mountain behind the beach. Appropriate footgear is a must, and you should know that once you get to the beach, the only shade is a rock cave. But this is a good place to snorkel. Boaters favor this beach and cove for its calm anchorage. **Amenities:** none. **Best for:** snorkeling; swimming. ⊠ *Anse à Colombier, Colombier.*

PICKING THE RIGHT BEACH

For long stretches of talcum-soft pale sand choose La Saline, Gouverneur, or Flamands. For seclusion in nature, pick the tawny grains of Corossol. But the most remarkable beach on the island, Shell Beach, is right in Gustavia and hardly has sand at all! Millions of tiny pink shells wash ashore in drifts, thanks to an unusual confluence of ocean currents, sea-life beds, and hurricane action.

Anse de Grand Cul de Sac. The shallow, reef-protected beach is nice for small children, fly-fishermen, kayakers, and windsurfers—and for the amusing pelicanlike frigate birds that dive-bomb the water fishing for their lunch. There is a good dive shop. You needn't do your own fishing; you can have a wonderful lunch at one of the excellent restaurants, and use their lounge chairs for the afternoon. **Amenities:** food and drink; parking (no fee); toilets; water sports. **Best for:** swimming; walking. ⊠ *Grand Cul de Sac.*

FAMILY

Fodor's Choice

★

Anse de Grande Saline. With its peaceful seclusion and sandy ocean bottom, this is just about everyone's favorite beach and is great for swimming, too. Without any major development (although there is some talk of developing a resort here), it's an ideal Caribbean strand, though there can be a bit of wind at times. In spite of the prohibition, young and old alike go nude. The beach is a 10-minute walk up a rocky dune trail, so be sure to wear sneakers or water shoes, and bring a blanket, umbrella, and beach towels. Although there are several good restaurants for lunch near the parking area, once you get here, the beach is just sand, sea, and sky. The big salt ponds here are no longer in use, and the place looks a little desolate when you approach, but don't despair. **Amenities:** parking (no fee). **Best for:** nudists; swimming; walking. ⊠ *Grande Saline.*

FAMILY

Anse de Lorient. This beach is popular with St. Barth's families and surfers, who like its rolling waves and central location. Be aware of the level of the tide, which can come in very quickly. Hikers and avid surfers like the walk over the hill to Point Milou in the late afternoon sun when the waves roll in. **Amenities:** parking (no fee). **Best for:** snorkeling; surfing; swimming. ⊠ *Lorient.*

Anse des Flamands. This is the most beautiful of the hotel beaches—a roomy strip of silken sand. Come here for lunch and then spend the afternoon sunning, enjoying long beach walks, and swimming in the turquoise water. From the beach, you can take a brisk hike along a paved sidewalk to the top of the now-extinct volcano believed to have given birth to St. Barth. **Amenities:** food and drink; toilets. **Best for:** snorkeling; swimming; walking. ⊠ *Anse des Flamands, Flamands.*

FAMILY **Anse du Gouverneur.** Because it's so secluded, this beach is a popular place for nude sunbathing. It is truly beautiful, with blissful swimming and views of St. Kitts, Saba, and St. Eustatius. Venture here at the end of the day and watch the sun set behind the hills. The road here from Gustavia also offers spectacular vistas. Legend has it that pirates' treasure is buried in the vicinity. There are no restaurants, toilets, or other services here, so plan accordingly. **Amenities:** parking (no fee). **Best for:** nudists; sunset; swimming; walking. ⊠ *Anse du Gouverneur, Gouverneur.*

FAMILY **Baie de St-Jean.** Like a mini–Côte d'Azur—beachside bistros, terrific shopping, bungalow hotels, bronzed bodies, windsurfing, and day-trippers who tend to arrive on BIG yachts—the reef-protected strip is divided by Eden Rock promontory. Except when the hotels are filled to capacity you can rent chaises and umbrellas at La Plage restaurant or at Eden Rock, where you can lounge for hours over lunch. **Amenities:** food and drink; toilets. **Best for:** partiers, walking. ⊠ *Baie de St-Jean, St-Jean.*

WHERE TO EAT

Dining on St. Barth compares favorably to almost anywhere in the world. Varied and exquisite cuisine, a French flair in the decor, sensational wine, and attentive service make for a wonderful epicurean experience in almost any of the more than 80 restaurants. On most menus, freshly caught local seafood mingles on the plate with top-quality provisions that arrive regularly from Paris. Interesting selections on the Cartes de Vins are no surprise, but don't miss the sophisticated cocktails whipped up by island bartenders. They are worlds away from cliché Caribbean rum punches with paper umbrellas. The signature drink of St. Barth is called "'ti punch," a rum concoction similar to a Brazilian Caipirinha. It's also fun to sit at a bar and ask the attractive bartender for their own signature cocktail.

Most restaurants offer a chalkboard full of daily specials that are usually a good bet. But even the pickiest eaters will find something on every menu. Some level of compliance can be paid to dietary restrictions within reason, and especially if explained in French; just be aware that French people generally let the chef work his or her magic. Expect your meal to be costly; however, you can dine superbly and somewhat economically if you limit pricey cocktails, watch wine selections, share appetizers or desserts, and pick up snacks and picnic meals from one of the well-stocked markets. Or you could follow the locals to small *crêperies,* cafés, sandwich shops, and pizzerias in the main shopping areas. Lunch is usually less costly than dinner. *Ti Creux* means "snack" or "small bite."

Lavish publications feature restaurant menus and contacts. Ask at your hotel or look on the racks at the airport for current issues. Reservations are strongly recommended and, in high season, essential. Lots of restaurants now accept reservations through their website or by email. Check social media. Except during the Christmas–New Year's season it's not usually necessary to book far in advance. A day's—or even a few hours'—notice is usually sufficient. At the end of the meal, as in France, you must request the bill. Until you do, you can feel free to linger at the table and enjoy the complimentary vanilla rum that's likely to appear.

19

Check restaurant bills carefully. A *service compris* (service charge) is always added by law, but you should leave the server 5% to 10% extra in cash. You'll usually come out ahead if you charge restaurant meals on a credit card in euros instead of paying with American currency, as your credit card might offer a better exchange rate than the restaurant (though since some credit cards nowadays have conversion surcharges around 3%, the benefit of using plastic is rapidly disappearing). Many restaurants serve locally caught *langouste* (lobster); priced by weight, it's usually the most expensive item on a menu and, depending on its size and the restaurant, will range in price from $40 to $60. *In menu prices below, it has been left out of the range.*

What to Wear: A bathing suit and *gauzy top or shift* is acceptable at beachside lunch spots, but not really in Gustavia. Jackets are never required and are rarely worn by men, but most people do dress fashionably for dinner. Casual chic is the idea; women wear whatever is hip, current, and sexy. You can't go wrong in a tank dress or anything clingy and ruffly with white jeans and high sandals. The sky is the limit for high fashion at nightclubs and lounges in high season, when you might (correctly) think everyone in sight is a model. Leave some space in your suitcase; you can buy the perfect outfit here on the island. Nice shorts (not beachy ones) at the dinner table may label a man *américain,* but many locals have adopted the habit, and nobody cares much. Wear them with a pastel shirt to really fit in (never tucked in). Pack a light sweater or shawl for the occasional breezy night.

ANSE DE TOINY

$$$ BISTRO

🍴 **La Table de Jules.** Reinvented for 2013, the former K'fe Massai is now a charming and attractive "Bistrot Gourmand." The restaurant's decor and music pays hommage to French jazz singers like Edith Piaf, Charles Aznavour, and Jacques Brel, and the cuisine is the perfect match. French bistro classics like soup de poisson, house-made foie gras, and herb-wrapped beef tenderloin join tasty fish and grilled dishes, and the Tarte Tatin is the best on the island. [$] *Average main: €23* ✉ *Lorient* ☎ *590/29–76–78.*

$$$$ MODERN FRENCH Fodor's Choice ★

🍴 **Le Gaïac.** Hôtel Le Toiny's dramatic, tasteful, cliff-side dining porch showcases gastronomic art. Less stuffy than you might remember from seasons past, the food is notable for its innovation and extraordinary presentation, and the warm but consummately professional service sets a high standard. The menu changes frequently but rare ingredients and unique preparations always delight: beet ravioli filled with raspberries; tender roasted Iberian pork grilled and confit; lamb medallions accompanied by tender zucchini toasts. A greenhouse on-site produces organic produce for the restaurant. Tuesday is Fish Market Night when you choose your own fish to be grilled; there's a €43 buffet brunch on Sunday from 11 to 2. [$] *Average main: €36* ✉ *Hôtel Le Toiny, Anse à Toiny* ☎ *590/29–77–47* 🌐 *www.letoiny.com* ✍ *Reservations essential* 🕒 *Closed Sept.–mid-Oct.*

Le Gaïac, Anse de Toiny

FLAMANDS

$$$ FRENCH FUSION

🍴 **La Langouste.** This tiny but friendly beachside restaurant in the pool courtyard of Hôtel Baie des Anges lives up to its name by serving fresh-grilled local lobster, and lobster thermidor, at prices that are somewhat gentler than at most other island venues. Try starters like creole stuffed crab, scallop carpaccio, a warm goat cheese salad, or one of the five soups including classic Caribbean fish soup and lobster bisque. The well-prepared fish or pasta dishes are great main options, and there are choices for meat fans as well. Classic French desserts like Floating Island with vanilla sauce, crepes suzette, and mango tart are worth the calories. [$] *Average main: €27* ✉ *Hôtel Baie des Anges, Anse des Flamands* ☎ *0590/27–63–61* 🌐 *www.hotelbaiedesanges.fr* ✍ *Reservations essential* 🕒 *Closed May–Oct.*

$$$$ MODERN FRENCH Fodor's Choice ★

🍴 **Le Case a L'Isle.** You can't top the view or the fine service at this waterfront restaurant at the renowned Hotel Isle de France. Light and tasty fare with a hint of Asia is served at lunch and dinner; at lunch you can have your toes in the sand and a perfect Club Sandwich. There is something for everyone on the dinner menu, from sparkling fresh local tuna tartare with guacamole sauce to lobster risotto scented with coconut and lime, and the rack of lamb is beyond compare. A fashion show featuring the lovely beachwear from the on-site boutique occurs daily during lunch and during Tuesday dinner. ■ TIP→ **At night, there is no more romantic spot on St. Barth.** [$] *Average main: €27* ✉ *Hotel Isle de France, Flamands Beach, Flamands* ☎ *0529/27–61–81* 🌐 *www.isle-de-france.com* ✍ *Reservations essential.*

GRAND CUL DE SAC

$$$$ ITALIAN FAMILY 🍴 **Bar'tô.** Locavores will like the pretty restaurant in the gardens of the Guanahani hotel, which showcases the refined cuisine of executive chef Philippe Masseglia. Influenced by Provence and Italy, dishes are presented beautifully, and use some organic and local products. Try the Burrata with lightly smoked tomato, which is garnished with anchovy, olives, and basil seeds. Or, splurge on the black truffle risotto. There are €90 and €120 tasting menus if the whole table is adventurous and likes to eat on the early side. Don't miss the caramelized pear cloaked in almond brittle and chocolate. There is a €20 children's menu, too, and veggie and gluten-free items are marked on the menu. ■ TIP→ **Long pants are required at dinner.** [$] *Average main: €42* ✉ *Hotel Guanahani, Grand Cul de Sac* ☎ *590/27–66–60* ✍ *Reservations essential* ⊙ *Closed Mon. and Tues.*

> **WORD OF MOUTH**
>
> "If you've been to France and like the culture then I'm sure you will enjoy St. Barth. It's France in the tropics."
>
> —Sharona

GRANDE SALINE

$$$$ MODERN FRENCH FAMILY Fodor's Choice ★ 🍴 **L'Esprit.** Jean-Claude Dufour, a renowned chef on the island (formerly of Eden Rock) brings tasty and innovative dishes to a romantic terrace close to Saline Beach. The menu has lots of variety, from light French dishes with a Provencale twist to interesting salads (like house-smoked mahimahi on fennel slaw), pastas, burgers, and steak. Tasty vegetarian options keep nonmeat eaters happy, too. Don't miss the chocolate tart for dessert, but the memory of the sweet service will last longer. [$] *Average main: €36* ✉ *Anse de Grande Saline, Grande Saline* ☎ *590/52–46–10* ⊙ *No lunch Wed. and Sun.*

$$$ STEAKHOUSE 🍴 **Meat and Potatoes.** If you think that St. Barth is sometimes too "girly," you will love this restaurant at the end of the road to Saline Beach. The white interior is lined with banquettes heaped with red, black, and gray pillows; there are almost a dozen different cuts of steak, from tenderloins to T-bones, at least a dozen starchy sides, and some vegetables for good measure (all à la carte). There is also fresh fish for the red-meat averse, and a vegetarian menu. Don't miss the Provençal *pommes ratte,* wedges of potatoes cooked in duck fat, fresh rosemary, and sea salt. The wine list is full of complementary bottles, heavy on Bordeaux's best. [$] *Average main: €30* ✉ *Grande Saline* ☎ *590/51–15–98.*

$$$ FRENCH FAMILY 🍴 **Santa Fé.** Perched at the top of the Lurin hills on the way to Gouverneur Beach, this relaxed and scenic restaurant serves panoramic views with both lunch and dinner to visitors and locals alike. The chef comes from Provence, and trained at some of the region's best restaurants before moving to the Caribbean. Salads and light lunch offerings are perfect on the way to the beach, but come back for dinner—especially if you are a fan of authentic French cuisine—for delicious veal osso bucco, coq au vin, and crisp tomato tarts with pesto. [$] *Average main: €34* ✉ *Rte. de Lurin, Lurin* ☎ *590/27–61–04* ⊙ *No dinner Wed. Closed Sept.–mid-Oct.*

GUSTAVIA

$$$$ ✕**Bagatelle St Barth.** New in 2012, the sophisticated St. Tropez–inspired
BISTRO interior, right on the harbor, is a scene-y place to watch big boats and
enjoy a menu of classic French bistro favorites such as truffled roast
chicken, pastis-flamed shrimp, and steak tartare. There are platters of
charcuterie and fromage for sharing, and a great wine list. Fans of
the popular sister establishments in New York's Meatpacking District
and Los Angeles will recognize the friendly service and lively atmosphere, and the great music provided by resident DJs–come late, the
party really gets going after 11. Book a table on the terrace. $ *Average
main: €34 ⌧ Rue Samuel Fahlberg, Gustavia* ☎ *590/27–51–51* ⊕ *www.
bistrotbagatelle.com* ⌕ *Reservations essential.*

$$$$ ✕**Bonito.** Decorated like a chic beach house, Bonito features big, white,
LATIN AMERICAN canvas couches for lounging in the center, tables around the sides, an
Fodor's Choice open kitchen, and three bar areas—all located on a hill above Gustavia
★ Harbor. The young Venezuelan owners go to great lengths to see that
guests are having as much fun as they are. The specialty is ceviche
with eight different varieties, in combos that are prettily arrayed on
poured-glass platters for culinary experimentation. Try octopus and
shrimp, or wahoo garnished with sweet potatoes and popcorn. Tradi-
tionalists might like the fricassee of escargots, or foie gras served with
mango, soy, and preserved lemon. Carnivores will love the rack of lamb.
French pastry classics are on the dessert menu. ■TIP→ **A sister location,
with the same terrific food, but a quieter ambience is open in the chic
beachside Le Sereno resort.** $ *Average main: €35 ⌧ Rue Lubin Brin,
Gustavia* ☎ *590/27–96–96* ⊕ *www.ilovebonito.com* ⌕ *Reservations
essential* ⊘ *Closed Mon. in low season. No lunch.*

$$$$ ✕**Dõ Brazil.** Right on Gustavia's Shell Beach, this restaurant is open
ECLECTIC every day for lunch and dinner and offers live music for sundown
cocktail hour on Thursday, Friday, and Saturday evenings, as well as
top DJs spinning the latest club mixes for evening events, which are
listed in the local papers. You'll find tasty light fare like chilled soups,
fruit-garnished salads with tuna, shrimp, and chicken, plus sandwiches,
burgers, pastas, and grilled fresh fish for lunch. Everyone loves the Dõ
Brazil hot pot: Mahimahi, shrimp, and sea scallops in a sauce of lemongrass and coconut milk. The extensive cocktail menu tempts, but at
€12 each, your bar bill can quickly exceed the price of dinner. There is
a €10 children's menu. $ *Average main: €26 ⌧ Shell Beach, Gustavia*
☎ *0590/29–06–66* ⊕ *www.dobrazil.com.*

$$$ ✕**Eddy's.** By local standards, dinner in the pretty, open-air, tropical gar-
ASIAN den here is reasonably priced. The cooking is French-creole-Asian. Fish
specialties, especially the sushi tuna sampler, are fresh and delicious,
and there are always plenty of notable daily specials. Just remember
some mosquito repellent for your ankles. $ *Average main: €24 ⌧ 12
rue Samuel Fahlberg, Gustavia* ☎ *0590/27–54–17* ⌕ *Reservations not
accepted* ⊘ *Closed Sun. and Sept.–Oct. No lunch.*

$$$ ✕**Le Carré d'Or.** Franck Mathevet, the esteemed Burgundy-born chef for-
ECLECTIC merly of Wall House, opened this attractive and lively outdoor restaurant
in 2012, right in the center of Le Carré d'Or, Gustavia's glam shopping
enclave. Team terrific cocktails with tasty and modern small plates, fresh

19

seafood from the Raw Bar, or sandwiches like lobster rolls and pastrami-cured salmon on bagels. Sliders, both beef and mahimahi, are a favorite on the lunch menu, while fun sharable appetizers and simple grills make a perfect combo at night. The restaurant is open for breakfast, lunch, snacks, dinner, and Sunday brunch—and it's a great spot for a special event, too. [$] *Average main: €21* ✉ *Rue Auguste Nyman, Le carré d'or, Gustavia* ☎ *0590/52–46–11* 🌐 *www.lecarresbh.com.*

$$$ CARIBBEAN 🍴 **Le Palace.** Tucked into a tropical garden, this popular in-town restaurant, also known as Pipiri Palace, is famous for its barbecued ribs, beef fillet, and rack of lamb; it is consistently one of our absolute favorites. Fish-market specialties like red snapper cooked in a banana leaf or grilled tuna are good here, as are grilled duck with mushroom sauce and a skewered surf-and-turf with a green curry sauce. The blackboard lists daily specials that are usually a great choice, like St. Marcellin cheese roasted in a crock of honey. [$] *Average main: €31* ✉ *Rue Général-de-Gaulle, Gustavia* ☎ *0590/27–53–20* ✍ *Reservations essential* ⏲ *Closed Sun. and mid-June–July.*

$$ BRASSERIE FAMILY 🍴 **Le Repaire.** This friendly classic French brasserie overlooks Gustavia's harbor, and is a popular spot from its early morning opening to its late-night closing. The flexible hours are great if you arrive on the island midafternoon and need a substantial snack before dinner. Grab a cappuccino, pull a captain's chair up to the street-side rail, and watch the pretty people go by. The menu ranges from cheeseburgers, which are served only at lunch along with the island's best fries, to simply grilled fish and meat, pastas, and risottos. The mixed salads always please. Wonderful ice cream sundaes round out the menu. [$] *Average main: €19* ✉ *Rue de la République, Gustavia* ☎ *0590/27–72–48* ⏲ *Closed Sun. in June.*

$$$ FRENCH 🍴 **Les Bananiers.** Ask the locals where to eat, and they will surely recommend this casual spot in Colombier adjacent to a wonderful bakery. The food is classic French, the service is warm, the prices are gentle, and you can eat in or take out. Choose from dishes like grilled duck breast, classic escargots in garlic butter, pizza, or fresh fish. The classic fish soup is a favorite. [$] *Average main: €23* ✉ *Rte. de Columbier, Colombier* ☎ *590/27–93–48.*

$$$ ITALIAN Fodor's Choice ★ 🍴 **L'Isola.** St. Barth's chic sister to the Santa Monica (California) favorite, Via Veneto, packs in happy guests for classic Italian dishes, dozens of house-made pasta dishes, prime meats, and the huge, well-chosen wine list. Restaurateur Fabrizio Bianconi wants it all to feel like a big Italian party, and with all the celebrating you can hear at dinner in this pretty and romantic room, it sure sounds like he succeeded. Favorite dishes include a hearty veal chop in a sage-butter sauce, and heavenly risotto with either wild mushrooms or wild boar. [$] *Average main: €27* ✉ *33 Rue du roi Oscar II, Gustavia* ☎ *590/51–00–05* 🌐 *www.lisolastbarth.com* ✍ *Reservations essential* ⏲ *Closed Sept. and Oct.*

$$ PIZZA 🍴 **L'Isoletta.** New in 2012, this casual Roman-style pizzeria run by the popular L'Isola restaurant is a chic lounge-style gastropub serving delicious thin-crust pizzas by the slice or by the meter. Lasagnas and sandwiches are also available to eat in or take out. Stop in anytime as they are open from lunch straight through until 11 pm. Don't miss the dessert pizzas. [$] *Average main: €10* ✉ *Rue du Roi Oscar II, Gustavia* ☎ *590/52–02–02* 🌐 *www.lisolettastbarth.com* ✍ *Reservations not accepted.*

$$$$ ✕ **Maya's.** New Englander Randy Gurley and his wife Maya (the French-
FRENCH   born chef) provide returning guests with a warm welcome and a very
pleasant, albeit expensive, dinner on their cheerful dock decorated with
big, round tables and crayon-colored canvas chairs, all overlooking
Gustavia Harbor. A market inspired menu of good, simply prepared and
garnished dishes—like roasted quail and Indian-spiced fish—changes
daily, assuring the ongoing popularity of a restaurant that seems to be
on everyone's list of favorites. Ⓢ *Average main: €39* ✉ *Public, Gustavia*
☎ *0590/27–75–73* ⊕ *www.mayas-stbarth.com* ⚓ *Reservations essential*
◷ *Closed Sun.*

$$$ ✕ **Ocean.** New in 2013, this romantic and delicious seafood restau-
SEAFOOD rant is family-run and features fresh-caught local fish and attentive,
friendly service. Plates are distinctive, creative, refined, and beauti-
fully presented—think a whole sea bass baked in a salt-pastry shell.
There are also beautiful steaks on offer for nonfish lovers, and spec-
tacular, classic French desserts to round out your meal. The daily
prix-fixe lunch menu, which includes a main course and dessert,
ranges from €11 to €19; the choices are listed on their Facebook page.
▰ TIP➔ **Long-time visitors will fondly remember this as the charming
old–St. Barth–style space that once housed Le Sapotillier.** Ⓢ *Average
main: €26* ✉ *13 Rue Samuel Falberg, Gustavia* ☎ *590/52–45–31*
⚓ *Reservations essential.*

$$$$ ✕ **Wall House.** There's a new chef at the helm of this steak house–
ECLECTIC style restaurant on the far side of Gustavia Harbor. Favorite dishes,
such as the light-as-air gnocci with pesto and the roasted duck mari-
nated in honey, remain while others have been revised or replaced.
Steaks are Prime Angus Beef from the USA, and are offered in sizes
from "queen" to "emperor"; there are vegetarian options too. Local
businesspeople crowd the restaurant for the bargain €11 prix-fixe
lunch menu (posted daily on their Facebook page), with classic dishes
like duck-leg confit, but there are big salads too. For €18 the menu
includes the main dish or salad of the day, coffee and petits fours, and
a glass of wine or beer. An old-fashioned dessert trolley showcases
yummy classic sweets. Ⓢ *Average main: €33* ✉ *La Pointe, Gustavia*
☎ *590/27–71–83* ⊕ *www.wallhouserestaurant.com* ⚓ *Reservations
essential* ◷ *No lunch Sun.*

19

POINTE MILOU

$$$$ ✕ **Le Ti St. Barth Caribbean Tavern.** Chef-owner Carole Gruson captures
ECLECTIC the funky, sexy spirit of the island in her wildly popular hilltop hot spot.
Fodor's Choice We always come here to dance to great music with the attractive crowd
★ lingering at the bar, lounge at one of the pillow-strewn banquettes, or
chat on the torch-lighted terrace. By the time your appetizers arrive,
you'll be best friends with the next table. Top quality fish and meats
are cooked on the traditional charcoal barbecue; big spenders will love
the Angus beef filet Rossini with truffles, but there are lighter options
like wok shrimp with Chinese noodles, and seared tuna with caviar.
Provocatively named desserts, such as Nymph Thighs (airy lemon
cake with vanilla custard), Daddy's Balls (passion-fruit sorbet and ice
cream), and Sweet Thai Massage (kiwi, pineapple, mango, and lychee

salad) end the meal on a fun note. Around this time someone is sure to be dancing on top of the tables. There's an extensive wine list. The famously raucous full-moon parties, cabarets, and Monday "Plastic Boots" Ladies' Nights are all legendary. $ *Average main: €53* ⊠ *Pointe Milou* ☎ *0590/27–97–71* ⊕ *www.letistbarth.com* ⌂ *Reservations essential* ☼ *Closed Sun. and Mon.*

ST-JEAN

$$$$ ✕ **La Plage.** Beachfront dining in quintessential St. Barth style is spot-
FRENCH   on at this eatery in the Tom Beach Hotel. Passion-fruit martinis are a must, as is the fresh-caught grilled spiny lobsters and roasted beet "carpaccio." There are beach lounges for daytime, and music all day long. It's a prime spot for people-watching and all the action on St. Jean Beach. Check local papers for special events like Full Moon White Parties or Saturday Bikini Brunch. $ *Average main: €36* ⊠ *Tom Beach Hotel, Plage de St. Jean, St-Jean* ☎ *590/27–53–13* ⊕ *www. tombeach.com.*

$$$$ ✕ **The Sand Bar.** At this Eden Rock Hotel eatery, lunch on the terrace with
ECLECTIC   the beautiful blue water sparkling beyond is incomparable. Star chef
Fodor'sChoice   Jean Georges Vongerichten's cuisine is tailored to the setting and the
★   ambience—you'll find all the things you would expect to be tempted to eat at the beach. Delicious light salads, soups, and carpaccio are menu highlights, but there are also heartier salads with fish and chicken, and simple grilled fish and meat entrées. The wood-oven pizzas are delicious—try the fontina and truffle option. Beautiful and delicious desserts include the chocolate and lemon tart dessert. And, there's brunch on Sunday. You can be sure of world-class people-watching opportunities at the Eden Rock—you never know who'll be checking out a menu next to you. $ *Average main: €32* ⊠ *Eden Rock Hotel, Baie de St. Jean, St-Jean* ☎ *590/29–79–99* ⊕ *www.edenrockhotel.com* ⌂ *Reservations essential.*

WHERE TO STAY

There's no denying that hotel rooms and villas on St. Barth carry high prices. You're paying primarily for the privilege of staying on the island, and even at $800 a night the bedrooms tend to be small. Still, if you're flexible—in terms of timing and in your choice of lodgings—you can enjoy a holiday in St. Barth and still afford to send the kids to college.

The most expensive season falls during the holidays (mid-December to early January), when hotels are booked far in advance, may require a 10- or 14-day stay, and can be double the high-season rates. A 5% government tourism tax on room prices (excluding breakfast) is in effect; be sure to ask if it is included in your room rate or added on.

When it comes to booking a hotel on St. Barth, the reservation manager can be your best ally. Rooms within a property can vary greatly. It's well worth the price of a phone call or the time investment of an email correspondence to make a personal connection, which can mean a lot when it comes to arranging a room that meets your needs or

CLOSE UP

St. Barth's Spas

Visitors to St. Barth can enjoy more than the comforts of home by taking advantage of any of the myriad spa and beauty treatments that are available on the island. The major hotels, the Isle de France, the Guanahani, and Le Christopher, have beautiful, comprehensive, on-site spas. Others, including the Hôtel le Village St-Jean, Le Sereno, and Le Toiny, have added spa cottages, where treatments and services can be arranged on-site.

Depending on availability, all visitors to the island can book services at all of these. In addition, scores of independent therapists will come to your hotel room or villa and provide any therapeutic discipline you can think of, including yoga, Thai massage, shiatsu, reflexology, and even manicures, pedicures, and hairdressing. You can get up-to-date recommendations at the tourist office in Gustavia.

---

preferences. Details of accessibility, views, recent redecorating, meal options, and special package rates are topics open for discussion. Quoted hotel rates are per room, not per person, and include service charges and, often, airport transfers. Bargain rates found on Internet booking sites can sometimes yield unpleasant surprises in terms of the actual room you get. Consider contacting the hotel about a reservation and mentioning the rate you found. Often they will match it, and you'll end up with a better room.

VILLAS AND CONDOMINIUMS

On St. Barth the term *villa* is used to describe anything from a small cottage to a luxurious, modern estate. Today almost half of St. Barth's accommodations are in villas, and we recommend considering this option, especially if you're traveling with friends or family. Ever more advantageous to Americans, villa rates are usually quoted in dollars, thus bypassing unfavorable euro fluctuations. Most villas have a small private swimming pool and maid service daily except Sunday. They are well furnished with linens, kitchen utensils, and such electronic playthings as CD and DVD players, satellite TV, and broadband Internet. Weekly in-season rates range from $1,400 to "oh-my-gosh." Most villa-rental companies are based in the United States and have extensive websites that allow you to see pictures or panoramic videos of the place you're renting; their local offices oversee maintenance and housekeeping and provide concierge services to clients. Just be aware that there are few beachfront villas, so if you have your heart set on "toes in the sand" and a cute waiter delivering your Kir Royale, stick with the hotels or villas operated by hotel properties.

VILLA RENTAL CONTACTS

Marla. This local St. Barth villa-rental company represents more than 100 villas, many of which are not listed with other companies. ✉ *Rue du Roi Oscar II, Gustavia* ☎ *0590/27–62–02* ⊕ *www.marlavillas.com.*

19

St. Barth Properties, Inc. Owned by American Peg Walsh—a regular on St. Barth since 1986, St. Barth Properties represents more than 120 properties and can guide you to the perfect place to stay. Weekly peak-season rates range from $1,400 to OMG! depending on the property's size, location, and amenities. The excellent website offers virtual tours of most of the villas and even details of availability. An office in Gustavia can take care of any problems you may have and offers some concierge-type services. ✉ *Gustavia* ☎ *508/528–7727, 800/421–3396* 🌐 *www.stbarth.com.*

Wimco. Based in Rhode Island, Wimco oversees bookings for more than 230 properties on St. Barth. Rents range from $2,000 to $10,000 for two- and three-bedroom villas; larger villas rent for $7,000 per week and up. Properties can be previewed and reserved on Wimco's website (which occasionally lists last-minute specials). There are even interactive floor plans, so you can see exactly what you will be getting, or you can obtain a catalog by mail. The company will arrange for babysitters, massages, chefs, and other in-villa services for clients, as well as private air charters. ☎ *800/932–3222* 🌐 *www.wimco.com.*

ANSE DE TOINY

$$$$ HOTEL Fodor's Choice ★ 🏨 **Hôtel Le Toiny.** The privacy, serenity, and personalized service pleases the international mogul set; it's remote, but you never have to leave if you don't want to. **Pros:** extremely private; luxurious rooms; flawless service; environmental awareness. **Cons:** not on the beach; isolated (at least half an hour's drive from town). [$] *Rooms from: €1350* ✉ *Anse de Toiny* ☎ *590/27–88–88* 🌐 *www.letoiny.com* 🛏 *14 1-bedroom villas, 1 3-bedroom villa* 🕒 *Closed Sept.–late Oct.* 🍴 *Breakfast.*

COLOMBIER

$$ B&B/INN 🏨 **Le P'tit Morne.** Each of the modestly furnished but clean and freshly decorated, painted mountainside studios has a private balcony with panoramic views of the coastline. **Pros:** reasonable rates; great area for hiking. **Cons:** rooms are basic; remote location. [$] *Rooms from: €204* ✉ *Colombier* ☎ *0590/52–95–50* 🌐 *www.timorne.com/fr* 🛏 *14 rooms* 🍴 *Breakfast.*

FLAMANDS

$$$ HOTEL FAMILY 🏨 **Hôtel Baie des Anges.** Everyone is treated like family at this casual retreat with 10 clean, spacious units, two of which are brand-new, two-bedroom oceanfront suites. **Pros:** on St. Barth's longest beach; family-friendly; excellent value. **Cons:** the area is a bit remote from the town areas, necessitating a car. [$] *Rooms from: €385* ✉ *Anse des Flamands* ☎ *0590/27–63–61* 🌐 *hotel-baie-des-anges.com* 🛏 *10 rooms* 🕒 *Closed Sept.* 🍴 *No meals.*

$$$$ RESORT Fodor's Choice ★ 🏨 **Hotel St-Barth Isle de France.** An obsessively attentive management team ensures that this intimate, casual, refined resort remains among the very best accommodations in St. Barth—if not the entire Caribbean. **Pros:** prime beach location; terrific management; great spa; excellent restaurant. **Cons:** you will definitely want a car to get around; unfortunately, the day will come when you will have to leave this paradise. [$] *Rooms from: €725* ✉ *B.P. 612 Baie des Flamands, Flamands* ☎ *590/27–61–81* 🌐 *www.isle-de-france.com* 🛏 *32 rooms, 2 villas* 🕒 *Closed Sept.–mid-Oct.* 🍴 *Breakfast.*

Hotel Guanahani and Spa, Grand Cul de Sac

$$$$
RESORT
FAMILY
Fodor's Choice
★

🏨 **Hotel Taïwana.** This classic island retreat reopened in 2012 under new management to the delight of the young, international guests who appreciate the spiffy updates to the spacious rooms and suites clustered around a charming atrium garden. **Pros:** newly renovated; busy social scene; great beach access. **Cons:** maybe too scene-y for some; every room is different so choose carefully. $ *Rooms from: €538* ⊠ *Baie De Flamands, Anse des Flamands* ☎ *0590/29–80–08* ⊕ *www.hoteltaiwana. com* 🛏 *7 rooms, 15 suites* ❍| *Breakfast.*

GRAND CUL DE SAC

$$$$
RESORT
FAMILY
Fodor's Choice
★

🏨 **Hotel Guanahani and Spa.** The largest full-service resort on the island has lovely rooms and suites (14 of which have private pools) and impeccable personalized service, not to mention one of the island's only children's programs (though it's more of a nursery). **Pros:** fantastic spa; beach-side sports; family-friendly; great service. **Cons:** lots of walking all around the property; steep walk to beach. $ *Rooms from: €646* ⊠ *Grand Cul de Sac* ☎ *0590/27–66–60* ⊕ *www.leguanahani.com* 🛏 *35 suites, 32 rooms* ⊗ *Closed Sept.* ❍| *Breakfast.*

$$
RENTAL
FAMILY

🏨 **Hotel Les Ondines Sur La Plage.** Right on the beach of Grand Cul de Sac, this reasonably priced, intimate gem comprises modern, comfortable apartments with room to really spread out. **Pros:** spacious beachfront apartments; close to restaurants and water sports; pool; airport transfers. **Cons:** not a resort; beach is narrow in front of the property; will need a car to get around. $ *Rooms from: €425* ⊠ *Grand Cul de Sac* ☎ *590/27–69–64* ⊕ *www.stbarth-lesondineshotel.com* 🛏 *6 rooms* ❍| *Breakfast.*

$$$$ RESORT Fodor'sChoice ★ **Le Sereno.** Those seeking a restorative, sensous escape will discover true nirvana at the quietly elegant, aptly named Le Sereno, set on a beachy cove of turquoise sea, between the island's highest mountain and the foamy waves. **Pros:** romantic rooms; beach location; superchic comfort; friendly atmosphere. **Cons:** no a/c in bathrooms; some construction planned for this part of the island over the next few years. [$] *Rooms from: €730* ✉ *B.P. 19 Grand-Cul-de-Sac, Grand Cul de Sac* ☎ *590/29–83–00* 🌐 *www.lesereno.com* 🛏 *37 suites and villas* 🍴 *Multiple meal plans.*

GRANDE SALINE

$ RENTAL **Salines Garden Cottages.** Budget-conscious beach lovers who don't require a lot of coddling need look no further than these petite garden cottages, a short stroll from what is arguably St. Barth's best beach. **Pros:** only property walkable to Salines Beach; quiet; reasonable rates. **Cons:** far from town; not very private; strict cancellation policy. [$] *Rooms from: €160* ✉ *Grand Saline* ☎ *0590/51–04–44* 🌐 *www.salinesgarden.com* 🛏 *5 cottages* 🕒 *Closed mid-Aug.–mid-Oct.* 🍴 *Breakfast.*

GUSTAVIA

$ HOTEL **Sunset Hotel.** Ten simple, utilitarian rooms (one can accommodate three people) right in Gustavia sit across from the harbor and offer an economical and handy, if not luxurious option for those who want to stay in town. **Pros:** reasonable rates; in town. **Cons:** no elevator; not resortlike in any way. [$] *Rooms from: €110* ✉ *Rue de la République, Gustavia* ☎ *590/27–77–21* 🌐 *www.saint-barths.com/sunset-hotel* 🛏 *10 rooms* 🍴 *No meals.*

LORIENT

$ RENTAL FAMILY **Les Mouettes.** This guesthouse offers clean, simply furnished, and economical bungalows that open directly onto the beach. **Pros:** right on the beach; family-friendly. **Cons:** rooms are basic; right near the road; strict pre-payment and cancellation policies; no pool; no TV. [$] *Rooms from: €150* ✉ *Lorient Beach* ☎ *0590/27–77–91* 🌐 *www.lesmouetteshotel.com* 🛏 *7 bungalows* 💳 *No credit cards* 🍴 *No meals.*

$ B&B/INN **Normandie Hotel.** The immaculate rooms here are small but stylish, and there's nothing on the island at this price range that compares. **Pros:** friendly management; pleasant atmosphere; good value. **Cons:** tiny rooms; small bathrooms. [$] *Rooms from: €135* ✉ *Lorient* ☎ *0590/27–61–66* 🌐 *www.normandiehotelstbarts.com* 🛏 *8 rooms (7 double, 1 single)* 🍴 *Breakfast.*

POINTE MILOU

$$$ RESORT FAMILY **Christopher.** This longtime favorite of European families delivers a high standard of courteous professionalism and personalized service. **Pros:** comfortable elegance; family-friendly; reasonable price. **Cons:** resort is directly on the water but not on a beach; three-night minimum stay. [$] *Rooms from: €480* ✉ *Pointe Milou* ☎ *590/27–63–63* 🌐 *www.hotelchristopher.com* 🛏 *42 rooms* 🕒 *Closed Sept.–mid-Oct.* 🍴 *Breakfast.*

Eden Rock, St-Jean

ST-JEAN

$$$$ RESORT FAMILY Fodor's Choice ★ 🏨 **Eden Rock.** Even on an island known for gourmet cuisine and luxury hotels, this iconic property stands out—thanks to its two Jean-Georges Vongerichten eateries, spacious rooms, stunning bay views, and cosseting service. **Pros:** two Vongerichten-overseen restaurants; chic clientele; beach setting; stylish facilities; walk to shopping and restaurants. **Cons:** some suites are noisy because of proximity to street. [$] *Rooms from: €715* ✉ *Baie de St-Jean, St-Jean* ☎ *0590/29–79–99, 877/563–7015 in U.S.* 🌐 *www.edenrockhotel.com* 🛏 *32 rooms, 2 villas* 🕓 *Closed Aug. 29–Oct. 17* 🍴 *Breakfast.*

$$$ HOTEL FAMILY Fodor's Choice ★ 🏨 **Emeraude Plage.** Right on the beach of Baie de St-Jean, this petite resort consists of small but immaculate bungalows and villas with modern, fully equipped outdoor kitchens on small private patios. **Pros:** beachfront and in-town location; good value; cool kitchens on each porch. **Cons:** smallish rooms. [$] *Rooms from: €405* ✉ *Baie de St-Jean, St-Jean* ☎ *0590/27–64–78* 🌐 *www.emeraudeplage.com* 🛏 *28 bungalows* 🕓 *Closed Sept.–mid-Oct.* 🍴 *No meals.*

$ HOTEL FAMILY Fodor's Choice ★ 🏨 **Hôtel le Village St. Barth.** You get the advantages of a villa and the services of a hotel at Hôtel Le Village, where for two generations the Charneau family has offered friendly service and reasonable rates, making guests feel like a part of the family. **Pros:** great value; convenient location; wonderful management, friendly clientele. **Cons:** a walk up a steep hill to the hotel; can be noisy, depending on how close your room is to the street below. [$] *Rooms from: €280* ✉ *Colline de St-Jean, St-Jean* ☎ *0590/27–61–39, 800/651–8366* 🌐 *www.villagestjeanhotel.com* 🛏 *5 rooms, 20 cottages, 1 3-bedroom villa, 2 2-bedroom villas* 🍴 *Breakfast.*

$$$ HOTEL **Le Tom Beach Hôtel.** This chic but casual boutique hotel right on busy St-Jean beach is fun for social types, and the nonstop house party often spills out onto the terraces and lasts into the wee hours. **Pros:** party central at beach, restaurant, and pool; in-town location. **Cons:** trendy social scene is not for everybody, especially light sleepers. [$] *Rooms from: €320* ✉ *Plage de St-Jean, St-Jean* ☎ *0590/52–81–20* 🌐 *www.tombeach.com* 🛏 *12 rooms* 🍴 *Breakfast.*

WORD OF MOUTH

"We've seen up and down nightlife in Gustavia and St-Jean in March and April, better experiences in June, late September/October, and November. Depends who and what fancy boats are in dock and whether the jet set are partying publicly or privately. Some nights the bars can be a snooze, other times packed and Bohemian."

—Mathieu

$$$ RENTAL FAMILY **Les Îlets de la Plage.** On the far side of the airport, tucked away at the far corner of Baie de St-Jean, these well-priced, comfortably furnished island-style one-, two-, and three-bedroom bungalows (four right on the beach, seven up a small hill) have small kitchens, pleasant open-air sitting areas, and comfortable bathrooms. **Pros:** beach location; apartment conveniences; front porches. **Cons:** TVs by request only and offer limited French programming; a/c only in bedrooms; right next to the airport. [$] *Rooms from: €460* ✉ *Plage de St-Jean, St-Jean* ☎ *0590/27–88–57* 🌐 *www.lesilets.com* 🛏 *11 bungalows* 🕒 *Closed Sept.–Nov. 1* 🍴 *No meals.*

NIGHTLIFE

Most of the nightlife in St. Barth is centered on Gustavia, though there are a few places to go outside of town. "In" clubs change from season to season, so you might ask around for the hot spot of the moment, but none really get going until about midnight. Theme parties are the current trend. Check the daily *St. Barth News* or *Le Journal de Saint-Barth* for details. A late (10 pm or later) reservation at one of the club–restaurants will eventually become a front-row seat at a party. *Saint-Barth Collector Guest Book* contains current information about sports, spas, nightlife, and the arts.

GUSTAVIA

Bar de l'Oubli. This is where young locals gather for drinks. Bring cash, they don't accept plastic. ✉ *Rue du Roi Oscar II, Gustavia* ☎ *0590/27–70–06.*

Le Repaire. This restaurant lures a crowd for cocktail hour and its pool table. ✉ *Rue de la République, Gustavia* ☎ *0590/27–72–48.*

Le Sélect. This is St. Barth's original hangout, commemorated by Jimmy Buffett's song, "Cheeseburger in Paradise." The boisterous garden is where the barefoot boating set gathers for a cold Carib beer, at prices somewhat lower than usual. ✉ *Rue du Centenaire, Gustavia* ☎ *0590/27–86–87.*

Le Yacht Club. Although ads call it a private club, dress right and you can probably get in to this hot spot anyway. Nothing much happens 'til midnight, when the terrific DJs get things going. Check the local papers for details of special parties. Above the Yacht Club you'll find one of the island's newest hotspots, the First Floor, where there are tapas, drinks, and music. Check the club's Facebook page or in local papers for details of current events. ⊠ *Rue Jeanne d'Arc, Gustavia* ☎ *0690/49–23–33* ⊕ *www.caroleplaces.com.*

ST-JEAN

Le Nikki Beach. This place rocks on weekends during lunch—especially Sunday afternoons—when the scantily clad young and beautiful lounge on the white canvas banquettes. ⊠ *St-Jean* ☎ *0590/27–64–64* ⊕ *www. nikkibeach.com.*

SHOPPING

Fodor's Choice
★

St. Barth is a duty-free port, and with its sophisticated crowd of visitors, shopping in the island's 200-plus boutiques is a definite delight, especially for beachwear, accessories, jewelry, and casual wear. It would be no overstatement to say that shopping for fashionable clothing, jewels, and designer accessories is better in St. Barth than anywhere else in the Caribbean. New shops open all the time, so there's always something to discover. Some stores close for lunch from noon to 3, but they are open until 7 in the evening. A popular afternoon pastime is strolling about the two major shopping areas in Gustavia and St-Jean.

In Gustavia, boutiques line the three major shopping streets. Quai de la République, which is right on the harbor, rivals New York's Madison Avenue or Paris's avenue Montaigne for high-end designer retail, including shops for **Louis Vuitton, Bulgari, Cartier, Chopard,** Eres, and **Hermès.** These shops often carry items that are not available in the United States. The elegant Carré d'Or plaza is great fun to explore. Shops are also clustered in **La Savane Commercial Center** (across from the airport), **La Villa Créole** (in St-Jean), and **Espace Neptune** (on the road to Lorient). It's worth working your way from one end to the other at these shopping complexes—just to see or, perhaps, be seen. Boutiques in all three areas carry the latest in French and Italian sportswear and some haute couture. Bargains may be tough to come by, but you might be able to snag that *Birkin* that has a long waiting list stateside, and in any case, you'll have a lot of fun hunting around.

If you are looking for locally made art and handicrafts, call the tourist office, which can provide information, and arrange visits to the studios of some of the island artists, including Christian Bretoneiche, Robert Danet, Nathalie Daniel, Patricia Guyot, Rose Lemen, Aline de Lurin, and Marion Vinot. A few good gallery/craft boutiques are also scattered around Gustavia, Villa Créole, and the larger hotels.

19

ANSE DE TOINY

CLOTHING

La Chemise Tropezienne. Beautiful tailored cotton shirts in fun prints and stripes for men and women, and colorful Bermuda shorts to coordinate, are popular in St. Tropez and St. Barth. ⊠ *Carré d'Or, Gustavia* ☎ *590/27–54–33* ⊕ *www.be-shorts.com.*

HANDICRAFTS

French Indies Design. This beautiful shop on the far side of Gustavia Harbor is the brainchild of Karine Bruneel, a St. Barth-based architect and interior designer. There are lovely items to accent your home (or yacht) including furniture, textiles, glassware, and unusual decorative baskets, candles, and pottery. ⊠ *Maison Suédoise, Gustavia* ☎ *590/29–66–38* ⊕ *www.frenchindiesdesign.fr.*

GUSTAVIA

ART GALLERIES

Le P'tit Collectionneur. Encouraged by his family and friends, André Berry opened his private museum, "le P'tit Collectionneur," in early 2007 to showcase his lifelong passion for collecting fascinating objects such as 18th-century English pipes and the first phonograph to come to the island. He will happily show you his treasures. ⊠ *La Pointe, Gustavia* ⬚ *€2* ☾ *Mon.–Sat. 10–noon and 4–6.*

BOOKS

La Case Aux Livres. This is a full-service bookstore and newsstand with hundreds of English titles for adults and kids. Booklovers can follow their blog to learn about author appearances. ⊠ *Quai de la République, 9 Rue de la République, Gustavia* ☎ *0590/27–15–88* ⊕ *lacaseauxlivres. over-blog.com.*

CLOTHING

Bamboo St. Barth. Beach fashions like cotton tunics, cocktails-on-the-yacht dresses, and sexy Australian swimsuits by Nicole Olivier and Seafolly, can be paired with sassy sandals and costume jewelry. ⊠ *Pélican Beach, St-Jean* ☎ *590/52–08–82.*

Black Swan. This shop has an unparalleled selection of bathing suits for men, women, and children. The wide range of styles and sizes is appreciated. They also have souvenir-appropriate island logo-wear and whatever beach equipment you might require. ⊠ *Le Carré d'Or, Gustavia* ☎ *590/52–48–30.*

Boutique Lacoste. This store has a huge selection of the once-again-chic alligator-logo wear, as well as a shop next door with a complete selection of the Petit Bateau line of T-shirts popular with teens. ⊠ *Rue Du Bord de Mer, Gustavia* ☎ *0590/27–66–90.*

Calypso. This well-known retailer carries sophisticated, sexy resort wear and accessories by Balenciaga, Chloe, and D Squared, among others. ⊠ *Le Carré d'Or, Gustavia* ☎ *0590/27–69–74* ⊕ *www.saint-barths. com/calypso/.*

Hermès. The Hermès store in St. Barth is an independently owned franchise, and prices are slightly below those in the States. ⊠ *Rue de la République, Gustavia* ☎ *0590/27–66–15.*

Human Steps. Two boutiques, one for women and one for men, have a well-edited selection of chic shoes and leather accessories from names like YSL, Prada, Balenciaga, Miu Miu, and Jimmy Choo. ⊠ *39 rue de la République, Gustavia* ☎ *590/27–93–79* ⊕ *www.human-steps.fr.*

Kokon. This boutique offers a nicely edited mix of designs for on-island or off, including the bo'em, Lotty B. Mustique, and Day Birger lines, and cute shoes to go with them by Heidi Klum for Birkenstock. ⊠ *Rue Samuel Fahlberg, Gustavia* ☎ *0590/29–74–48.*

Linde Gallery. Linde sells vintage sunglasses, accessories, vintage ready-to-wear from the 1970s and '80s, as well as books, CDs, and DVDs. ⊠ *Les Hauts de Carré d'Or, Gustavia* ☎ *590/29–73–86* ⊕ *www. lindegallery.com.*

Linen. This shop offers tailored linen shirts for men in a rainbow of soft colors, and their soft slip-on driving mocs in classic styles are a St. Barth must. ⊠ *Rue Lafayette, Gustavia* ☎ *0590/27–54–26.*

Lolita Jaca. Don't miss this store for trendy, tailored sportswear. ⊠ *Le Carré d'Or, Gustavia* ☎ *0590/27–59–98* ⊕ *www.lolitajaca.com.*

Longchamp. Fans of the popular travel bags, handbags, and leather goods will find a good selection at about 20% off stateside prices. ⊠ *Rue Général de Gaulle, Gustavia* ☎ *0590/51–96–50.*

Mademoiselle Hortense. Shop for cute tops and dresses for the young and young at heart in pretty Liberty prints, which are made right on the island. You'll also find great crafty bracelets and necklaces to accent your new styles. ⊠ *Rue de la République, Gustavia* ☎ *590/27–13–29.*

Marina St. Barth. A great spot for the typical sexy resort-wear worn by the young and the beautiful on the island. If you forgot your floaty beachwear, you can stop here. Lines include Ondade, Façonnable, and Caffé. ⊠ *Rue du Roi Oscar II, Gustavia* ☎ *0590/29–37–30* ⊕ *www. marina-stbarth.com.*

Pati de Saint Barth. This is the largest of the three shops that stock the chic, locally made T-shirts, totes, and beach wraps that have practically become the logo of St. Barth. The newest styles have hand-done graffiti-style lettering. The shop also has some handicrafts and other giftable items. ⊠ *Rue Du Bord de Mer, Gustavia* ☎ *0590/29–78–04* ⊕ *www. madeinstbarth.com.*

Poupette St. Barth. All the brilliant color-crinkle silk, chiffon batik, and embroidered peasant skirts and tops are designed by the owner. There also are great belts and beaded bracelets. A new outpost is at Hotel Taïwana. ⊠ *Rue de la République, Gustavia* ☎ *0590/27–55–78* ⊕ *www. poupettestbarth.com.*

Saint-Barth Stock Exchange. On the far side of Gustavia Harbor is the island's consignment and discount shop. It's a blast to explore. ⊠ *La Pointe-Gustavia, Gustavia* ☎ *0590/27–68–12.*

19

Shops on rue de la France, Gustavia

Stéphane & Bernard. This store stocks a large, well-edited selection of superstar French fashion designers, including Rykiel, Missoni, Valentino, Versaci, Ungaro, Christian Lacroix, and Eres beachwear. ⊠ *Rue de la République, Gustavia* ☎ *0590/27–65–69* ⊕ *www.stephaneandbernard.com.*

Vanita Rosa. This store showcases beautiful lace and linen sundresses and peasant tops, with accessories galore, as well as some very cool designer vintage. ⊠ *Rue du Roi Oscar II, Gustavia* ☎ *0590/52–43–25* ⊕ *www.vanitarosa.com.*

Victoire. Classic, well-made sportswear in luxurious fabrics and great colors, with a French twist on preppy, will please shoppers eager for finds that will play as well in Nantucket or Greenwich as they do on St. Barth. There is even a small sidewalk café with Wi-Fi if you need a pick-me-up or a simple lunch. ⊠ *Rue du Général de Gaulle, Gustavia* ☎ *590/29–84–60* ⊕ *www.victoire-paris.com.*

FOODSTUFFS

A.M.C. This supermarket is a bit older than Marché U in St-Jean but able to supply nearly anything you might need for housekeeping in a villa or for a picnic. ⊠ *Quai de la République, Gustavia.*

La Rotisserie. For exotic groceries, dinner at your villa, or picnic fixings, stop by St. Barth's gourmet *traiteur* (takeout shop) for salads, prepared meats, groceries from Fauchon, and Iranian caviar. ⊠ *Rue du Roi Oscar II, Gustavia* ☎ *0590/27–63–13.*

HANDICRAFTS

Fabienne Miot. Look for unusual and artistic jewelry featuring rare stones and natural pearls at this shop. ✉ *Rue de la République, Gustavia* ☎ *0590/27–73–13* ⊕ *www.saint-barths.com/fabiennemiot.*

Kalinas Perles. Beautiful freshwater pearls are knotted onto the classic St. Barth–style leather thongs by artist Jeremy Albaledejo, who also showcases other artisans' works in a gallery-like setting. ✉ *23 Rue du General de Gaulle, Gustavia* ☎ *690/65–93–00.*

JEWELRY

Bijoux de la Mer. This store carries beautiful and artistic jewelry made of South Sea pearls in wonderful hues strung in clusters on leather to wrap around the neck or arms. ✉ *Rue de la République, Gustavia* ☎ *590/52–37–68* ⊕ *www.bijouxdelamerstbarth.com.*

Carat. Carat has Chaumet and a large selection of Breitling watches, plus rarities by Richard Mille and Breguet. ✉ *Rue de la République, Gustavia* ☎ *590/27–67–22* ⊕ *www.caratsaintbarth.com.*

Donna del Sol. Designer Donna del Sol carries beautiful handmade gold chains, Tahitian pearl pieces, and baubles in multicolor diamonds of her own designs. Have something special in mind? She'll work with clients to design and produce custom items. ✉ *Quai de la République, Gustavia* ☎ *590/27–90–53* ⊕ *www.donnadelsol.com.*

Sindbad. This tiny shop, an island favorite since 1977, curates funky, unique couture fashion jewelry by Gaz Bijou of St-Tropez, crystal collars for your pampered pooch, and other reasonably priced, up-to-the-minute styles. Current favorites are the south-sea pearls strung on leather thongs or colorful silky cords. ✉ *Carré d'Or, Gustavia* ☎ *0590/27–52–29* ⊕ *www.sindbad-st-barth.com.*

LIQUOR AND TOBACCO

M'Bolo. Be sure to sample the varieties of infused rums, including lemongrass, ginger, and the island favorite, vanilla. Bring some home some in beautiful hand-blown bottles. Chefs will like the selection of Laguiole knives, and the local spices, too. ✉ *Rue Général-de-Gaulle, Gustavia* ☎ *0590/27–90–54.*

19

LORIENT

COSMETICS

St. Barth Spa. Don't miss the superb skin-care products made on-site from local tropical plants by this St. Barth company. Call in advance to request personal visits from the beauticians or therapists at your villa or yacht. ✉ *Rte. de Saline, Lorient* ☎ *0590/27–82–63* ⊕ *www.lignestbarth.com.*

FOODSTUFFS

JoJo Supermarché. JoJo is the well-stocked counterpart to Gustavia's large supermarket and gets daily deliveries of bread and fresh produce. JoJoBurger, next door is the local surfers' favorite spot for a (very good) quick burger. ✉ *Lorient.*

ST-JEAN

CLOTHING

Black Swan. Black Swan has an unparalleled selection of bathing suits. The wide range of styles and sizes is appreciated. ⊠ *La Villa Créole, St-Jean* ⊕ *www.blackswanstbarth.com.*

Iléna. This boutique has incredible beachwear and lingerie by Chantal Thomas, Sarda, and others, including Swarovski crystal–encrusted bikinis for the young and gorgeous. ⊠ *Villa Creole, St-Jean* ☎ *0590/29–84–05.*

Lili Belle. Check out Lili Belle for a nice selection of wearable and current styles. ⊠ *Pelican Plage, St-Jean* ☎ *0590/87–46–14.*

Morgan. This shop has a line of popular casual wear in the trendy vein. ⊠ *La Villa Créole, St-Jean* ☎ *0590/27–71–00.*

St. Tropez KIWI. Look to this popular boutique with two branches (one in Gustavia and one in St-Jean) for resort wear. ⊠ *3 Villa Créole, St-Jean* ☎ *0590/27–57–08.*

SUD SUD.ETC.Plage. This store stocks everything for the beach: inflatables, mats, bags, and beachy shell jewelry, as well as bikinis and gauzy cover-ups. ⊠ *Galerie du Commerce, St-Jean* ☎ *0590/27–90–56.*

FOODSTUFFS

La Rotisserie. For exotic groceries or picnic fixings, stop by St. Barth's gourmet *traiteur* (takeout) for salads, sandwiches, prepared meats, groceries from Fauchon, and Iranian caviar. ⊠ *Centre Vaval, St-Jean* ☎ *0590/29–75–69.*

Marche U. This modern, fully stocked supermarket across from the airport has a wide selection of French cheeses, pâtés, cured meats, produce, fresh bread, wine, and liquor. There is also a good selection of prepared foods and organic grocery items. ⊠ *Face à l'aéroport, St-Jean* ☎ *0590/27–68–16.*

Maya's to Go. This is the place to go for prepared picnics, meals, salads, rotisserie chickens, and more from the kitchen of the popular restaurant in Gustavia. ⊠ *Galleries du Commerce, St-Jean* ☎ *0590/29–83–70* ⊕ *www.mayastogo.com* ⊗ *Closed Mon.*

SPORTS AND ACTIVITIES

BOATING AND SAILING

St. Barth is a popular yachting and sailing center, thanks to its location midway between Antigua and St. Thomas. Gustavia's harbor, 13 to 16 feet deep, has mooring and docking facilities for 40 yachts. There are also good anchorages available at Public, Corossol, and Colombier. You can charter sailing and motorboats in Gustavia Harbor for as little as a half day, staffed or bare-boat. Stop at the tourist office in Gustavia, or ask at your hotel for an up-to-the minute list of recommended charter companies.

Carib Waterplay. On St. Jean beach for 30 years, Carib Waterplay lets you try windsurfing, kayaking, and stand-up paddling. They also have new waterbikes for rent and there are kids' windsurf lessons, too. ⊠ *St-Jean* ☎ *0590/61–80–81* ⊕ *www.caribwaterplay.net.*

Jicky Marine Service. This company offers full-day outings, either on a variety of motorboats, Zodiacs, or 42- or 46-foot catamarans, to the uninhabited Île Fourchue for swimming, snorkeling, cocktails, and lunch. The cost starts at about $100 per person; an unskippered motor rental runs about $260 a day. ⊠ *26 rue Jeanne D'Arc, Gustavia* ☎ *0590/27–70–34* ⊕ *www.jickymarine.com.*

FAMILY **Yellow Submarine.** Go "six feet under" (the surface of the sea) for a one-hour, close-up view of St. Barth's coral reefs through large glass portholes. It costs €40 for adults, €25 for children under 11. Trips depart daily, from the Ferry Dock in Gustavia with departures at 11 am and 2 pm, with Night Excursions Wednesday and Friday at 5:45 pm but more often depending on demand, so call first. ⊠ *Ferry Dock, Gustavia* ☎ *0590/52–40–51* ⊕ *www.yellow-submarine.fr.*

DIVING AND SNORKELING

Several dive shops arrange scuba excursions to local sites. Depending on weather conditions, you may dive at **Pain de Sucre, Coco Island,** or toward nearby **Saba.** There's also an underwater shipwreck to explore, plus sharks, rays, sea tortoises, coral, and the usual varieties of colorful fish. The waters on the island's leeward side are the calmest. For the uncertified who still want to see what the island's waters hold, there's an accessible shallow reef right off the beach at Anse de Cayes that you can explore if you have your own mask and fins, and a hike down the hill to the beach at Corossol brings you to a very popular snorkeling spot for locals.

FAMILY **Plongée Caraïbe.** This company is recommended for its up-to-the-minute equipment and dive boat. Their Scuba discovery program is very well regarded. They also run two-hour group snorkeling trips on the *Blue Cat Catamaran*; a half-day is €40. ☎ *0590/27–55–94* ⊕ *www.plongee-caraibes.com.*

Réserve Marine de St-Barth. Most of the waters surrounding St. Barth are protected in the island's Réserve Marine de St-Barth, which also provides information at its office in Gustavia. The diving here isn't nearly as rich as in the more dive-centered destinations like Saba and St. Eustatius, but the options aren't bad either, and none of the smaller islands offer the ambience of St. Barth. ⊠ *Gustavia* ☎ *590/27–88–18* ⊕ *reservenaturellestbarth.com.*

Splash. In Gustavia, Splash offers PADI and CMAS (Confederation Mondiale des Activites Subaquatiques—World Underwater Federation) courses in diver training at all levels. All the instructors speak French, Russian, and English. Although their boat normally leaves daily at 9 am, 11:30 am, 2 pm, and in the evening for a night dive, they will adjust their times to suit your preferences. They feature "seabob" scuba scooters. ⊠ *Gustavia* ☎ *590/56–90–24* ⊕ *www.divestbarth.com.*

19

FISHING

Most fishing is done in the waters north of Lorient, Flamands, and Corossol. Popular catches are tuna, marlin, wahoo, and barracuda. There's an annual St. Barth Open Fishing Tournament, organized by Océan Must, in mid-July.

Jicky Marine Service. This private marina in the heart of Gustavia organizes catamaran day charters, champagne sunset sails, luxury motorboat day cruise, interisland transfer, bareboat sailboat rentals, diving, jet-skiing and more. ⊠ *Gustavia* ☎ *0590/27–70–34* ⊕ *www. jickymarine.com.*

Océan Must Marina. This outfitter arranges deep-sea fishing expeditions as well as bare boat and staffed boat charters. ⊠ *La Pointe, Gustavia* ☎ *0590/27–62–25* ⊕ *www.oceanmust.com.*

GUIDED TOURS

You can arrange island tours by minibus or car at hotel desks or through any of the island's taxi operators in Gustavia or at the airport. The tourist office runs a variety of tours with varying itineraries that run about €46 for a half day for up to eight people. You can also download up-to-the-minute walking and driving tour itineraries from the Tourist Board's website.

JC Taxi. Since 1986, native-born Jean-Claude has been providing safe and comfortable transportation for island visitors and residents alike in a 10 passenger minivan. Island tours and night driving are available. ⊠ *Gustavia* ☎ *0690/49–02–97.*

Mat Nautic. This company can arrange for you to tour the island by water on a Jet Ski or WaveRunner. ⊠ *Quai du Yacht Club, Rue Jeanne d'Arc, Gustavia* ☎ *0690/49–54–72.*

ST. EUSTATIUS

20

WELCOME TO ST. EUSTATIUS

FRIENDLY TRANQUILITY

A tiny part of the Dutch Caribbean, St. Eustatius (often just called "Statia") is just under 12 square miles (30 square km), which is still twice as large as Saba. The island, which is 38 miles (63 km) south of St. Maarten, has a population of less than 4,000. And although there are some beaches, they are better for strolling than swimming.

Boven Bay

Cocoluch Bay

Jenkins Bay

Boven

Little Mountain

Tumble Down Dick Bay

Signal Hill

Interlopers Pt. ◆ *Ft. Royal*

Stenara ◥
Reef

Smoke Alley Beach
(Oranje Beach)

Hotels ▼
Country Inn **1**
Statia Lodge **2**

Gallows Bay

Crooks ◥
Castle

◥
Double
Wreck

KEY	
⟋	*Beaches*
◥	*Dive Sites*
🌴	*Rain Forest*
①	*Hotels*

Barracuda
Reef ◥

Like Saba, tiny Statia is a quiet Caribbean haven for scuba divers and hikers. When the island was called the Emporium of the Western World, warehouses stretched for miles along the quays, and 200 merchant ships could anchor at its docks. These days it's the day-trippers from St. Maarten who walk the quays.

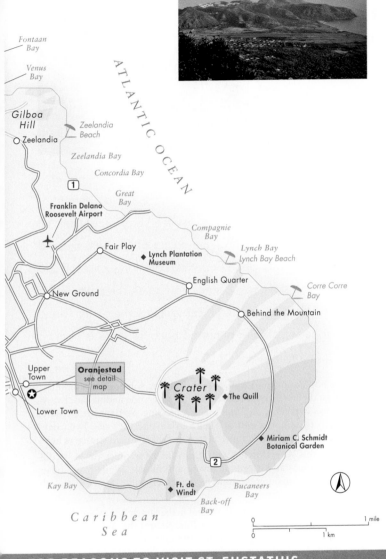

TOP REASONS TO VISIT ST. EUSTATIUS

1 Diving: Visiting the many varied wrecks in Statia's protected waters is a highlight.

2 Hiking: Hiking the Quill, an extinct volcano that holds a primeval rain forest, is the top activity for landlubbers.

3 Welcoming: The genuine friendliness of the people here is overwhelming.

4 History: For anyone interested in 18th-century history, even a day trip from St. Maarten is a satisfying experience.

Updated
by Roberta
Sotonoff

The stars are ablaze, but it's dark on the road between the Blue Bead Bar & Restaurant and the Old Gin House hotel. A chicken running across the road constitutes all the traffic, and except for the sound of crickets, there is silence. The island of St. Eustatius, commonly called Statia (pronounced *stay*-sha), is safe. How safe? The scuttlebutt is that a St. Maarten police officer sent to serve on the island thought he was being punished because there is nothing for him to do.

With a population of 3,800, it's difficult for someone to commit a crime—or do most anything else—without everyone finding out. Everyone knows everyone, and that's also a blessing. Statians are friendly; they beep their horns and say hello to anyone they see. Even day-trippers are warmly welcomed as friends. There are no strangers here.

Think of this tiny Dutch Caribbean island for quiet times, strolls through history, and awesome diving and hiking. While many of its neighbors are pursuing the tourist business big-time, Statia just plods along. That's its charm.

During the late 18th century, the island in the Dutch Windward Triangle was a hub for commerce between Europe and the Americas. When ships carrying slaves, sugar, cotton, ammunition, and other commodities crowded its harbor, it was known as the Emporium of the Western World and the Golden Rock.

With an 11-gun salute to the American Stars and Stripes on the brig-of-war the *Andrew Doria* on November 16, 1776, Statia's golden age ended. Statia's noteworthy role as the first country to recognize U.S. independence from Great Britain was not a gesture appreciated by the British. In 1781, British Admiral George Rodney looted and economically destroyed the island. It has never really recovered.

Indeed, chaos ensued between 1781 and 1816 as the Dutch, English, and French vied for control of the island. It changed hands 22 times. The Netherlands finally won out, and Statia has been a Dutch possession since 1816. Today, it's part of the Dutch Caribbean and a special municipality of the Netherlands.

Remnants of those bygone days are evident around the island. Hanging off the cliff at the only village, Oranjestad, is the nearly 370-year-old Fort Oranje, the site

LOGISTICS

Getting to St. Eustatius: There are no nonstop flights here from the United States, and the only way to get here is a Winair flight from St. Maarten.

Hassle Factor: Medium to high.

On the Ground: This is a small place. You can rent a car or scooter for trips out of town, or you can take a taxi.

from where the famous shots were fired. The original Dutch Reformed Church, built in 1755, sits in its courtyard. Oranjestad itself, on a ridge above the sea, is lush with greenery and bursting with bougainvillea, oleander, and hibiscus. The rest of the island is rather pristine. The eastern side, bordered by the rough waters of the Atlantic, has an untamed quality to it, and extinct volcanoes and dry plains anchor the north end. Statia's crown is the Quill, a 1,968-foot extinct volcano, its verdant crater covered with a primeval rain forest. Hiking to the peak is a popular pastime.

Beaches on the island come and go as the waters see fit, but first-class dive sites lure most visitors to the island. Wrecks and old cannons are plentiful at archaeological dive sites, and modern ships, such as the cable-laying *Charles L. Brown*, have been sunk into underwater craters. Stingrays, eels, turtles, and barracudas live in the undersea Caribbean neighborhood where giant pillar coral, huge yellow sea fans, and reef fingers abound. The sea has reclaimed the walls of Dutch warehouses that have sunk into the Caribbean over the past several hundred years, but these underwater ruins serve as a day-care center for abundant schools of juvenile fish.

20

On land, beachcombers hunt for blue beads. The 17th-century baubles, found only on Statia, were used to barter for rum, slaves, tobacco, and cotton. The chance of finding one is slim, though you can see them at the island's museum. Pre-Columbian artifacts, dating back to 500 BC, are also on display there.

Statia is mostly a short-flight day-trip destination from nearby St. Maarten. That might be just enough for some visitors. But those who linger can appreciate the unspoiled island, its history, and its peacefulness. Most of all, it's the locals who make a visit to the island special.

PLANNING

GETTING HERE AND AROUND

AIR TRAVEL

Flights to Statia from St. Maarten are timed to coincide with the arrival of international flights. There is no regularly scheduled ferry service. Reconfirm your flight, because schedules can change abruptly. The departure fee from the island is $10. If flying out of St. Maarten, check to see if the international departure fee has already been added into your airline ticket.

Airline Contact Winair. The only way to get to Statia is on one of the regularly scheduled Winair flights from St. Maarten. You'll have to book this flight directly with Winair, either by phone or online. Winair has five daily flights from St. Maarten to St. Eustatius. Prices range from roughly $150 to $200. ☎ 599/545–4237, 866/466–0410 ⊕ www.fly-winair.com.

Airport Contact Franklin Delano Roosevelt Airport (*EUX*). The flight from St. Maarten to Statia's Franklin Delano Roosevelt Airport takes 16 minutes. ✉ Oranjestad ☎ 599/318–2887.

CAR TRAVEL

Driving in Statia is not difficult, mostly because there are not that many places to go. Street signs are not plentiful, but anyone you ask for directions will be more than happy to help you. The roads are generally in good condition. Daily rates for a car rental begin at $35.

Car-Rental Contacts ARC Car Rental ✉ Oranjestad ☎ 599/318–2595. **Brown's** ✉ White Wall Rd. 8, Oranjestad ☎ 599/318–2266. **Rainbow Car Rental** ✉ Statia Mall, Oranjestad ☎ 599/318–1480, 599/318–2444.

SCOOTER TRAVEL

Zipping around by scooter is another option. Scooter rentals start at $25 per day, including insurance.

Contacts I.F. Rivers ✉ Oranjestad ☎ 599/318–2309. **LNP Scooter and Bike Rental** ☎ 599/318–1476.

TAXI TRAVEL

You could literally walk from the airport runway into town; one or two taxis are usually waiting for arriving passengers at the airport, and you'll be whisked into Oranjestad for about $8.

ESSENTIALS

Banks and Currency Exchange The U.S. dollar has been the legal tender here since 2011. **CIBC First Caribbean Bank.** The Upper Town branch of this bank provides exchange services. ☎ 599/318–2392 ⊕ www.cibcfcib.com ⊗ Weekdays 8:30–3:30. **Windward Islands Bank.** The bank has an ATM at the airport and at Mazinga Square, as well as exchange services in town. ☎ 599/318–2846, 599/318–2847 ⊕ www.wib-bank.net ⊗ Weekdays 8–3:30.

Emergency Services Ambulance ☎ 912, 599/318–2211. **Fire** ☎ 913, 599/318–2360. **Police** ☎ 911, 599/318–2333.

Mail The post office is on Ruby Hassell Road, Upper Town. Airmail letters to North America and Europe are $1.59, postcards 92¢. When sending letters to the island, be sure to include "Dutch Caribbean" in the address.

Passport Requirements All visitors must present a valid passport and a return or ongoing ticket for entry to Statia.

Phones To call Statia from North America, dial 011 + 599 + 318, followed by the four-digit number. To call the United States using an AT&T card, the access number is 001–800–872–2881. To call within the island, dial only the five-digit number that starts with an 8.

Taxes and Service Charges The departure tax—$10 for flights to Dutch Caribbean islands and foreign destinations—is payable in cash only. Note: When flying home through St. Maarten, list yourself as "in transit" to avoid paying the tax levied in St. Maarten if you will be there for less than 24 hours. Hotels collect a 7% government tax and 3% turnover tax. Restaurants charge a 3% government tax and a 10% service charge.

Tipping Taxi drivers, 10%; housekeeping, a dollar or two per day; waitstaff, an extra 5%–10%.

Visitor Information Tourist Office. There is also a tourist information booth at the airport, open daily. ⊠ *Fort Oranjestraat, Oranjestad* ☎ *599/318–2433, 599/318–2433 Airport Tourism Booth* ⊕ *www.statiatourism.com* ⊗ *Mon.–Thurs. 8–noon and 1–5, Fri. 8–noon and 1–4:30.*

ACCOMMODATIONS

Statia has only five hotels with 20 rooms or fewer—and except for Statia Lodge, all are within Oranjestad. There are also a handful of bed-and-breakfasts. Nothing on the island could be described as luxurious.

HOTEL AND RESTAURANT PRICES

Prices in the restaurant reviews are the average cost of a main course at dinner or, if dinner is not served, at lunch; taxes and service charges are generally included. Prices in the hotel reviews are the lowest cost of a standard double room in high season, excluding taxes, service charges, and meal plans (except at all-inclusives). Prices for rentals are the lowest per-night cost for a one-bedroom unit in high season.

For expanded lodging reviews and current deals, visit Fodors.com.

WEDDINGS

Foreign couples must be at least 21 and Dutch nationals at least 18. Documents should be received 14 days before the wedding date. The application requires notarized original documents, including birth certificates, passports (for non-Dutch people), divorce decrees, and death certificates of deceased spouses. The ceremony can be performed in English, Dutch, Spanish, or Papiamento. For more information, visit ⊕ *www.statiatourism.com.*

20

EXPLORING

Statia is an arid island with a valley between two mountain peaks. Most sights lie in the valley, making touring the island easy. From the airport you can rent a car or take a taxi and be in Oranjestad in minutes; to hike the Quill, Statia's highest peak, you can drive to the trailhead in less than 15 minutes from just about anywhere. Other trails with their breathtaking views include Boven, 450 feet elevation, Gilboa, 400 feet, and Venus Bay.

TOP ATTRACTIONS

Fodor'sChoice ★ **Oranjestad.** Statia's only town, Oranjestad sits on the west coast facing the Caribbean. Both Upper Town—with cobblestone streets that designate its historic section—and Lower Town are easy to explore on foot.

Fort Oranje. Three bastions have clung to these cliffs since 1636. In 1976, Statia participated in the U.S. bicentennial celebration by restoring the fort, and now the black cannons extend beyond the ramparts. In the parade grounds a plaque, presented in 1939 by Franklin D. Roosevelt, reads "Here the sovereignty of the United States of America was first formally acknowledged to a national vessel by a foreign official."

Built in 1775, the partially restored **Dutch Reformed Church,** on Kerkweg (Church Way), has lovely stone arches that face the sea. Ancient tales can be read on the gravestones in the adjacent 18th-century cemetery, where people were often buried atop one another. On Synagogepad (Synagogue Path) off Kerkweg is **Honen Dalim** ("She Who Is Charitable to the Poor"), one of the Caribbean's oldest synagogues. Dating from 1738, its exterior is partially restored.

Lower Town sits below Fort Oranjestraat (Fort Orange Street) and some steep cliffs. It is accessible from Upper Town on foot via the zigzagging, cobblestone Fort Road or by car via Van Tonningenweg. Warehouses and shops that were piled high with European imports in the 18th century are either abandoned or simply used to store local fishermen's equipment. One of them has been restored and now holds the **Mazinga-on-the-Bay** gift shop.

Along the waterfront is a lovely park with palms, flowering shrubs, and benches—the work of the historical foundation. Peeking out from the shallow waters are the crumbling ruins of 18th-century buildings, reminders of Statia's days as the merchant hub of the Caribbean. The sea has slowly advanced since then, and it now surrounds many of the stone-and-brick ruins, making for fascinating snorkeling. ⊠ *Oranjestad.*

Fodor'sChoice ★ **The Quill.** This extinct, perfectly formed, 1,968-foot volcano has a primeval rain forest in its crater. Hike and be surrounded with giant elephant ears, ferns, flowers, wild orchids, and fruit trees, and maybe if you're lucky, glimpse the elusive and endangered *iguana delicatissima* (a large—sometimes several feet long—greenish-gray lizard with spines down its back). The volcanic cone rises 3 miles (5 km) south of Oranjestad on the main road. Local boys go up to the Quill by torchlight to catch delectable land crabs. The tourist board or Statia Marine Park will help you make hiking arrangements, and you must purchase a $6 permit before beginning the hike. Figure on two to four hours to hike the volcano.

St. Eustatius Historical Foundation Museum

St. Eustatius National Parks. There are three national parks in Statia: National Marine Park, Quill/Boven National Park, and Miriam C. Schmidt Botanical Garden. To hike the Quill or Boven or dive in the marine park you must purchase a $6 permit at the St. Eustatius National Parks, the information booth at the airport or at your hotel. ⊠ *STENAPA Parks Office, Gallows Bay* ☎ *599/318–2884* ⊕ *www.statiapark.org.*

WORTH NOTING

Lynch Plantation Museum. Also known as the Berkel Family Plantation, or the Berkel's Domestic Museum, these two one-room buildings show what life was like almost 100 years ago. A remarkable collection preserves this family's history—pictures, eyeglasses, original furnishings, and farming and fishing implements—and gives a detailed perspective of life on Statia. Call ahead to arrange a private tour. Since it's on the northeast side of the island, you need either a taxi or a car to get there. ⊠ *Lynch Bay* ☎ *599/318–2338* ✉ *Free* ⊙ *By appointment only.*

FAMILY **Miriam C. Schmidt Botanical Garden.** Relaxation and quiet abound on these 52 acres, where there's a greenhouse, a palm garden, a kitchen garden, and an observation bird trail. Its location, on the Atlantic side of the Quill on a plot called Upper Company, reveals a superb view of St. Kitts. For a picnic, there's no better place, but the only way to get there is by car or taxi, and some of the road is not well paved. ☎ *599/318–2884 STENAPA* ⊕ *www.statiapark.org* ✉ *Suggested donation $5* ⊙ *Daily sunrise–sunset.*

St. Eustatius Historical Foundation Museum. In the center of Upper Town is the former headquarters of Lord George Rodney, a British admiral during the American Revolution. While here, Rodney confiscated everything from gunpowder to wine in retaliation for Statia's gallant

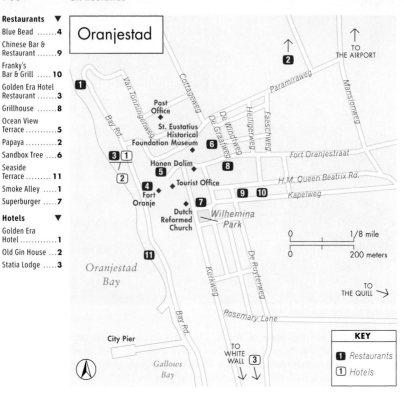

support of the fledgling country. The completely restored house is Statia's most important intact 18th-century dwelling. Exhibits trace the island's history from the pre-Columbian 6th century to the present. At the museum you can also buy a booklet with a self-guided walking tour of the sights. The tour begins in Lower Town at the marina and ends at the museum. ⊠ *Doncker House, 3 Wilhelminaweg, Upper Town, Oranjestad* ☎ *599/318–2288* ⊕ *www.steustatiushistory.org* ⊟ *$3* ⊗ *Mon.–Sat. 9–5.*

BEACHES

If you desire a white sandy beach, calm waters, and a place to cool yourself off with a quick dip, you're looking at the wrong island. Statia's beaches are mostly deserted, rocky stretches of pristine shoreline. Many of the beaches on the Caribbean side are here today and reclaimed by the sea tomorrow. The Atlantic side is an untamed mass of wild swells and vicious undertow. Walking, shelling, and searching for the elusive blue beads are popular pastimes for beachgoers. It's more likely, however, that the only place you will find real blue beads is at the St. Eustatius Historical Foundation Museum.

Lynch Bay Beach. Just two bends north of Corre Corre Bay on the island's Atlantic side, light-brown sand and rock cover this small beach, which is really an extension of Zeelandia Beach. Opt for walking instead of swimming here. There are turbulent swells, and there's a strong undertow. **Amenities:** none. **Best for:** walking. ✉ *Lynch Bay.*

Smoke Alley Beach (*Oranje Beach*). The color of the sand varies from light beige to black at this beach on the Caribbean side near Gallows Bay. Sometimes, much of the beach is claimed by ebb and flow. The waters are sometimes calm, so snorkeling is possible, but it's usually a better place for a swim or sunning. **Amenities:** none. **Best for:** swimming. ✉ *North end of Bay Rd., Oranjestad.*

Zeelandia Beach. Walking, shelling, and sunbathing are popular pastimes on this 2-mile (3-km) stretch of black-and-tan sand. Its Atlantic-side location makes it dangerous for swimming. **Amenities:** none. **Best for:** walking. ✉ *Oranjestad.*

WHERE TO EAT

As with most everything on the island, low-key and casual is the name of the game when it comes to Statia's restaurants.

$$ ECLECTIC Fodor's Choice ★

🍴 **Blue Bead Bar & Restaurant.** This delightful little blue-and-yellow restaurant, a favorite with locals, is the perfect place to watch the sunset. It is one of those places where everyone talks to everyone. There are always daily specials; the menu includes pizza, seafood, Italian and French food. [$] *Average main: $18* ✉ *Bay Rd., Gallows Bay, Lower Town, Oranjestad* ☎ *599/318–2873* ⏲ *Closed Mon.*

$ ECLECTIC

🍴 **Franky's Bar & Restaurant.** There isn't much more to this nondescript place than a bar, some tables, and a patio. But its goat dishes have made it well known. Every Saturday there is a barbecue and a steel band. The barbecue is a great deal—ribs, chicken, potatoes, satay rice, vegetables and salad—all for $12. [$] *Average main: $12* ✉ *Black Harry La., Oranjestad* ☎ *599/318–0166* 💳 *No credit cards* ⏲ *Closed Tues.*

$$ CARIBBEAN

🍴 **Golden Era Hotel Restaurant.** The surroundings may be bland, but the tasty seafood and fine creole dishes are anything but. It has another thing going for it: it's alongside the water, so the sound of the Caribbean is always playing in the background. Wednesday is chicken night; Friday, they serve pasta. [$] *Average main: $15* ✉ *Golden Era Hotel, Bay Rd., Lower Town, Oranjestad* ☎ *599/318–2445, 599/318–2345, 599/318–2355* 🌐 *www.goldenerahotel.com.*

$ CHINESE

🍴 **Grillhouse/San Yen Chinese Bar & Restaurant.** Short on decor—a few tables and a bar on the verandah—but long on taste, this Chinese restaurant has a special—a dish combining chicken, scallops, shrimp, beef, and sausage with vegetables—that's delicious, filling, and well worth the trip. [$] *Average main: $11* ✉ *White Wall Rd., White Wall* ☎ *599/318–2915* 💳 *No credit cards.*

$ CHINESE

🍴 **Kem WENG Chinese Bar & Restaurant.** Unless you're into Formica, don't expect to be wowed by the atmosphere at this simple spot. What you will find are large portions of dishes such as *bami goreng* (Indonesian-style noodles with bits of beef, pork, or shrimp as well as tomatoes, carrots, bean sprouts, cabbage, soy sauce, and spices); or pork chops with a spicy sauce. It's do-it-yourself table hauling if you want to eat outside. [$] *Average main: $12* ✉ *Queen Beatrix Rd., Upper Town, Oranjestad* ☎ *599/318–2389* ▭ *No credit cards.*

$ CARIBBEAN 🍴 **Ocean View Terrace.** This spot in the courtyard overlooking Fort Oranje is a favorite for those who like to watch the sunset. It hasn't changed over the years. Owner Lauris Redan serves sandwiches and burgers for lunch and local dishes—baked snapper with shrimp sauce, spicy chicken, and tenderloin steak—at dinner. Every now and then there's a succulent barbecue. [$] *Average main: $11* ✉ *Fort Oranjestraat, Upper Town, Oranjestad* ☎ *599/318–2934* ▭ *No credit cards* ⏲ *No lunch Sun.*

$ BAKERY 🍴 **Sandbox Tree Bakery.** This is the perfect spot for a quick sandwich; to satisfy your sweet tooth; or to order a wedding, birthday, or other special-occasion cake. [$] *Average main: $4* ✉ *Kerkweg, opposite Dutch Reformed Church, Upper Town, Oranjestad* ☎ *599/318–2469* ▭ *No credit cards* ⏲ *Closed Sun. Closed at noon on Sat.*

$$ ECLECTIC 🍴 **Seaside Terrace.** This extension of the Old Gin House faces the water. The simple menu includes great scrambled eggs for breakfast and sandwiches and tasty salads for lunch. Caribbean BBQ Night is every Wednesday. **TIP→ Service is slow, but on this island there is no reason to rush.** [$] *Average main: $13* ✉ *Across street from the Old Gin House, Bay Rd., Lower Town, Oranjestad* ☎ *599/318–2319.*

$$ ECLECTIC 🍴 **Smoke Alley Bar & Grill.** Owner Michelle Balelo cooks Tex-Mex, Italian, Caribbean, and American food to order at this beachfront hangout. The open-air eatery is the only place on the island where you can get draft beer. There's a barbecue every Friday night. [$] *Average main: $14* ✉ *Gallows Bay, Lower Town, Oranjestad* ☎ *599/318–2002* ▭ *No credit cards* ⏲ *Closed Sun.*

$ BURGER FAMILY 🍴 **Superburger.** Statia's version of fast food comes from this little hangout, which serves burgers, shakes, and ice cream as well as local West Indian dishes. It's a local favorite for lunch. [$] *Average main: $6* ✉ *De Graaffweg, Upper Town, Oranjestad* ☎ *599/318–2412* ▭ *No credit cards* ⏲ *Closed Sun.*

WHERE TO STAY

Statia has several basic rental apartments available as alternatives to hotel rooms, and a few are available for $60 or less per night. Don't expect much beyond cable TV, a bathroom, and a kitchenette. Check with the tourist office for options.

$ B&B/INN 🏨 **Country Inn.** Facing Zeelandia Bay and close to the airport, this folksy little inn is surrounded by a lush tropical garden. **Pros:** very homey; tropical garden is lovely. **Cons:** not on the water; a 15-minute walk to town; a vehicle is recommended. [$] *Rooms from: $70* ✉ *3 Passionfruit Rd., Concordia* ☎ *599/318–2484* 🛏 *6 rooms* ▭ *No credit cards* 🍽 *Multiple meal plans.*

$ HOTEL 🏨 **Golden Era Hotel.** On the waterfront across the street from the Old Gin House, this property has a funky, retro-1960s feel. **Pros:** friendly staff; right on the waterfront; breakfast included. **Cons:** rooms are

DID YOU KNOW?

The Quill's highest peak is known as Manzinga. The last eruption of the now-dormant volcano was in AD 400.

basic and dark. $ *Rooms from: $110* ✉ *Bay Rd., Lower Town, Oran-jestad* ☎ *599/318–2555, 599/318–2345, 599/318–2545* ⊕ *www. goldenerahotel.com* 🔅 *20 rooms, 1 suite* ⏸ *Breakfast.*

$$ 🔅 **King's Well Resort.** Win and Laura Piechutzki, along with their
B&B/INN macaws, iguanas, fishponds, cats, and Great Danes, warmly welcome visitors to their little inn, which is on the wooded cliffs between Upper and Lower Town. **Pros:** the cliff-side patio, which overlooks Oranje, is a pleasant place to watch the sunset and has a good view of the bay; breakfast included; observatory with telescope. **Cons:** not for those who don't love animals, particularly iguanas; not on the water or in town. $ *Rooms from: $150* ✉ *On curve of Van Tonningenweg, Smoke Alley, Oranjestad* ☎ *599/318–2538* ⊕ *www.kingswellstatia.com* 🔅 *5 rooms, 2 apartments* ⏸ *Breakfast.*

$$ 🔅 **The Old Gin House.** Built from 17th- and 18th-century cobblestones,
HOTEL this old cotton warehouse is now a hotel and restaurant with a recently renovated lobby. **Pros:** conveniently located; American breakfast at the Seaside Terrace is included. **Cons:** rooms are dark; rooms could use some sprucing up; pricey for what you get. $ *Rooms from: $225* ✉ *Bay Rd., Lower Town, Oranjestad* ☎ *599/318–2319* ⊕ *www. oldginhouse.com* 🔅 *20 rooms that include 2 ocean suites and 2 ocean view rooms* ⏸ *Breakfast.*

$$ 🔅 **Statia Lodge.** Look out from your cottage patio of the island's best digs
RENTAL and enjoy drop-dead-gorgeous views of St. Kitts and Nevis. **Pros:** the
FAMILY best views and most modern accommodations on the island; landscaping is lovely; French, English, and German spoken. **Cons:** no a/c; not near the water or town (which is why you need the car or scooter); not accessible for people with disabilities. $ *Rooms from: $165* ✉ *White Wall* ☎ *599/318–1900* ⊕ *www.statialodge.com* 🔅 *8 1-bedroom bunga-lows, 2 2-bedroom bungalows* ⊙ *Closed Aug. and Sept.* ⏸ *No meals.*

NIGHTLIFE

Kool Korner Bar & Restaurant. The island's oldest bar, the tiny Kool Korner is a lively after-work and weekend hangout. It's across from the St. Eustatius Historical Foundation Museum. ✉ *Wilhelminaweg, Oran-jestad* ☎ *599/318–3386.*

SHOPPING

The limited shopping here is all duty-free. But other than the predictable souvenirs, there's not much to buy. Several shops carry Dutch cheeses and chocolates.

Mazinga-on-the-Bay Gift Shop. Beads and other souvenirs are for sale at this store in a refurbished warehouse. It's on the seaside across from the Gin House. ✉ *Gallows Bay, Oranjestad* ☎ *599/318–2245* ⊙ *Wed.–Sat. 2–6.*

Paper Corner. Magazines, a few books, computer accessories, and stationery supplies are for sale here. ✉ *Van Tonningenweg, Upper Town, Oranjestad* ☎ *599/318–2208* ⊙ *Weekdays 9–noon and 2–5.*

SPORTS AND ACTIVITIES

DIVING AND SNORKELING

Fodor's Choice ★ Forget about glitz and nightlife. Statia is the quintessential low-key island. Finding an elusive *iguana delicatissima* on the Quill is probably the most exciting thing you can do on land. Statia's real thrills are underwater.

Long ago the ocean reclaimed the original seawall built by the Dutch in the 1700s. The sunken walls, remnants of old buildings, cannons, and anchors are now part of an extensive reef system populated by reef fingers, juvenile fish, and other sea creatures.

Statia has more than 30 dive sites protected by the Statia Marine Park. The park office is on Bay Road in Lower Town. Barracuda swim around colorful coral walls at **Barracuda Reef,** off the island's southwest coast. At **Double Wreck,** just offshore from Lower Town, you can find two tall-masted ships that date from the 1700s. The coral has taken on the shape of these two disintegrated vessels, and the site attracts spiny lobsters, stingrays, moray eels, and large schools of fish. About 100 yards west of Double Wreck is the Japanese ship *Cheng Tong,* which was sunk in 2004. Off the south end of the island, the sinking of the *Charles L. Brown,* a 1957 cable-laying vessel that was once owned by AT&T, created another artificial reef when it was sunk in a 135-foot underwater crater. Off the island's western shore, **Stenapa Reef** is an artificial reef created from the wrecks of barges, a harbor boat, and other ship parts. Large grouper and turtles are among the marine life you can spot here. For snorkelers, **Crooks Castle** has several stands of pillar coral, giant yellow sea fans, and sea whips just southwest of Lower Town.

There are dive shops along Bay Road in Lower Town that rent all types of gear (including snorkeling gear for about $14 a day), offer certification courses, and organize dive trips. One-tank dives start at $49; two-tank dives are about $98.

Dive Statia/Scubaqua. This fully equipped dive shop in a remodeled warehouse features PADI and CMS certification plus Nitrox diving and underwater photography courses. DVPs (diver propulsion vehicles) are available for diving or snorkeling. Dive courses are offered in several different various languages. ⊠ *Bay Rd., Lower Town, Oranjestad* ☎ *599/318–5450, 599/587–5481* ⊕ *www.scubaqua.com.*

Golden Rock Dive Center. Operated by Glenn and Michele Faires, Golden Rock Dive Center has PADI's Gold Palm designation. In addition to certification courses, the shop offers a National Geographic program that emphasizes conservation. ⊠ *Gallows Bay, Lower Town, Oranjestad* ☎ *599/318–2964* ⊕ *www.goldenrockdive.com.*

Statia National Parks. Both the Saba Marine Park and Quill/Boven National Park (STENAPA) are under the supervision of Statia National Parks. The marine tag fee, which all divers must buy, is used to help offset the costs of preserving the coral and other sea life here; the cost is $4 per day or $30 annually. There are two decompression chambers on the island. ⊠ *Headquarters, Gallows Bay, Lower Town, Oranjestad* ☎ *599/318–2884* ⊕ *www.statiapark.org.*

20

GUIDED TOURS

Statia's three taxis and two large buses are available for island tours. A 2½-hour outing costs $20 per person per vehicle for five people (extra people are $5 each), usually including airport transfer. (If you'd rather head out on your own, there's a self-guided walking tour booklet available from the St. Eustatius Historical Foundation Museum.)

HIKING

Trails range from the easy to the "Watch out!" The big thrill here is the Quill, the 1,968-foot extinct volcano with its crater cradling a rain forest. Give yourself two to four hours to complete the hike. The tourist office has a list of 12 marked trails and can put you in touch with a guide. Quill National Park includes a trail into the crater, which is a long, winding but safe walk. Maps and the necessary $6 permit, which is good for a year, are available at the Statia Marine Park headquarters on Bay Road. Wear layers: it can be cool on the summit and steamy in the interior.

ST. KITTS
AND NEVIS

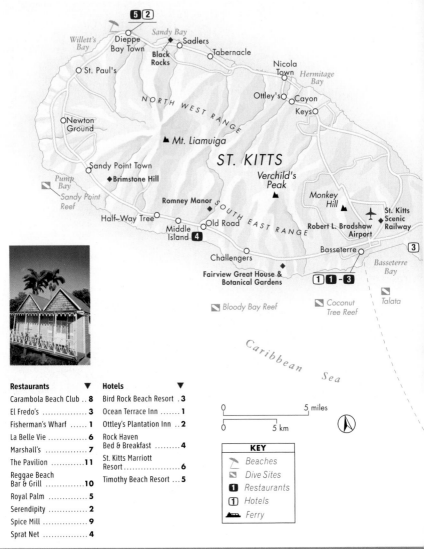

Restaurants ▼

Carambola Beach Club .. **8**
El Fredo's **3**
Fisherman's Wharf **1**
La Belle Vie **6**
Marshall's **7**
The Pavilion **11**
Reggae Beach
Bar & Grill **10**
Royal Palm **5**
Serendipity **2**
Spice Mill **9**
Sprat Net **4**

Hotels ▼

Bird Rock Beach Resort . **3**
Ocean Terrace Inn **1**
Ottley's Plantation Inn .. **2**
Rock Haven
Bed & Breakfast **4**
St. Kitts Marriott
Resort **6**
Timothy Beach Resort ... **5**

KEY

🏖 *Beaches*
◪ *Dive Sites*
❶ *Restaurants*
① *Hotels*
🚢 *Ferry*

TOP REASONS TO VISIT ST. KITTS AND NEVIS

1 History: Both St. Kitts and Nevis are steeped in history; Brimstone Hill Fortress is a man-made UNESCO World Heritage Site.

2 Luxury: Luxurious, restored plantation inns can be found on both islands.

3 Landscape: Both islands have extinct volcanoes and luxuriant rain forests ideal for hikes, as well as fine diving and snorkeling sites.

4 Unspoiled: You'll find less development—particularly on Nevis—and more cordial and courteous islanders than on more touristy islands.

5 Water Activities: Both islands feature aquatic activities aplenty, with fine sailing, deep-sea fishing, diving (especially off St. Kitts), and windsurfing (especially around Nevis).

WELCOME TO
ST. KITTS AND NEVIS

THE MOTHER COLONY
AND HER SISTER

St. Kitts, a 65-square-mile (168-square-km) island, is 2 miles (3 km) from smaller Nevis, about 40 square miles (121 square km). The two former British colonies are joined in a sometimes strained independence. St. Kitts is often called "The Mother Colony," because it was the first permanent English settlement in the Caribbean.

A yucca watches over North Friar's Bay on St. Kitts's narrow peninsula where Nevis, its diminutive companion, looms on the horizon. On both islands, green fields of sugarcane run to the sea, once-magnificent plantation houses are now luxurious inns, and lovely stretches of uncrowded beach stretch before you.

Updated by
Jordan Simon

These idyllic sister islands, 2 miles (3 km) apart at their closest point, offer visitors a relatively authentic island experience. Both have luxuriant mountain rain forests; uncrowded beaches; historic ruins; towering, long-dormant volcanoes; charming if slightly dilapidated Georgian capitals in Basseterre (St. Kitts) and Charlestown (Nevis); intact cultural heritage; friendly if shy people; and restored 18th-century sugar plantation inns run by elegant, if sometimes eccentric, expatriate owners.

The islands' history follows the usual Caribbean route: Amerindian settlements, Columbus's voyages, fierce colonial battles between the British and French, a boom in sugar production second only to that of Barbados. St. Kitts became known as the mother colony of the West Indies: English settlers sailed from there to Antigua, Barbuda, Tortola, and Montserrat, and the French dispatched colonists to Martinique, Guadeloupe, St. Martin, and St. Barth.

St. Kitts and Nevis, in addition to Anguilla, achieved self-government as an associated state of Great Britain in 1967. Anguillians soon made their displeasure known, separating immediately, whereas St. Kitts and Nevis waited until 1983 to become an independent nation. The two islands, despite their superficial similarities, have taken increasingly different routes regarding tourism. Nevis received an economic boost from the Four Seasons, which helped establish it as an upscale destination. St. Kitts, however, has yet to define its identity at a time when most islands have found their tourism niche. A fierce sibling rivalry has ensued.

Though its comparative lack of development is a lure, the Kittitian government is casting its economic net in several directions. Golf, ecotourism, and scuba diving are being aggressively promoted. And the government hopes the number of available rooms will increase roughly 30% by 2016 to more than 2,000, according to the "build it and they will come" philosophy. But is St. Kitts ready to absorb all this? The island offers a surprisingly diverse vacation experience while retaining its essential Caribbean flavor. Divers have yet to discover all its underwater attractions, and nature lovers will be pleasantly surprised by the hiking. There's now every kind of accommodation, as well as gourmet dining, golf, and gaming.

Meanwhile, Nevis seems determined to stay even more unspoiled (there are still no traffic lights). Its natural attractions and activities certainly rival those of St. Kitts, from mountain biking and ecohiking to windsurfing and deep-sea fishing, though lying in a hammock and dining on romantic candlelit patios remain cherished pursuits. Pinney's Beach, despite occasional hurricane erosion, remains a classic Caribbean strand. Its historic heritage, from the Caribbean's first hotel to Alexander Hamilton's childhood home, is just as pronounced, including equally sybaritic plantation inns that seem torn from the pages of a romance novel.

Perhaps it's a warning sign that many guests call the catamaran trip to Nevis the high point of their stay on St. Kitts—and many Kittitians build retirement and second homes on Nevis. The sister islands' relationship remains outwardly cordial if slightly contentious. Nevis papers sometimes run blistering editorials advocating independence, though one plebiscite has already failed. St. Kitts and Nevis may separate someday, but for now their battles are confined to ad campaigns and political debates. Fortunately, well-heeled and barefoot travelers alike can still happily enjoy the many energetic and easygoing enticements of both blissful retreats.

PLANNING

WHEN TO GO
The high season is relatively short, starting in mid-December and stretching into early or mid-April. The shoulder season (roughly April to mid-June and November to mid-December) offers lower rates. Rates are lower still from mid-June through November, but some establishments close for a month or longer.

GETTING HERE AND AROUND
AIR TRAVEL
Many travelers connect in Antigua, San Juan, St. Maarten, or St. Thomas. To Nevis, it's almost always cheaper to fly into St. Kitts and then take a regularly scheduled ferry, but check the schedules or book a transfer from your resort (if available) in advance.

There are nonstop flights to St. Kitts from Atlanta (Delta), Charlotte (US Airways), Miami (American), and New York–JFK (American). There are no nonstops from the United States to Nevis.

Airline Contacts American. American has daily flights from Miami into St. Kitts (twice daily Thursday–Sunday) and twice-weekly flights from New York's JFK. ☎ *869/465–2273, 869/469–8995.* **LIAT.** Other major domestic airlines (US Airways once weekly nonstop from Charlotte and Delta once weekly from Atlanta) fly from their eastern hubs either into Antigua, St. Maarten, San Juan, or St. Thomas, where connections to St.

Kitts (and, less frequently, to Nevis) can be made on LIAT. ☎ *869/465–1330, 869/469–5238 on Nevis* ⊕ *www.liatairline.com.* **Robert L. Bradshaw International Airport** (*SKB*). St. Kitts' airport is Robert L. Bradshaw International Airport. ✉ *Golden Rock* ☎ *465–8013.* **Vance W. Amory International Airport** (*NEV*). The Nevis airport is Vance W. Amory International Airport. ✉ *Newcastle, Nevis* ☎ *869/469–9343.* **Winair.** Nevis connections can also be made from St. Maarten on Winair. ☎ *869/469–5302* ⊕ *www.fly-winair.com.*

BOAT AND FERRY TRAVEL

There are several ferry services between St. Kitts and Nevis, all with schedules that are subject to abrupt change. Most companies make two or three daily trips. All the ferries take about 30 to 45 minutes and cost $8–$10.

Contacts Ferry Schedule ⊕ *www.thestkittsnevisobserver.com/ferry-schedules.html.*

There's an additional EC$1 tax for port security, paid separately on departure.

CAR TRAVEL

Driving Tips: One well-kept main road circumnavigates St. Kitts and is usually clearly marked, making it difficult to get lost, though the northeast can get a bit bumpy and the access roads to the plantation inns are notoriously rough.

The roads on Nevis are generally smooth, at least on the most traveled north, west, and south sides of the island. The east coast has some potholes, and pigs, goats, and sheep still insist on the right-of-way all around the island. Drivers on both islands tend to travel at a fast clip and pass on curves, so drive defensively. Driving is on the left, British-style, though you will probably be given an American-style car.

Renting a Car: You can get by without a car if you are staying in the Frigate Bay–Basseterre area, but elsewhere you'll need to rent a car. On Nevis it's often easier to just take taxis and guided tours. On St. Kitts, present your valid driver's license and $24 at the police station traffic department on Cayon Street in Basseterre or Fire Station in Frigate Bay to get a temporary driving permit (on Nevis the car-rental agency will help you obtain the $24 local license at the police station). The license is valid for three months on both islands. On either island, car rentals start at about $45 per day for a compact; expect to pay a few extra bucks for air-conditioning. Most agencies offer substantial multiday discounts.

Contacts Avis. Avis has the best selection of Hyundai and Daihatsu four-wheel-drive vehicles on St. Kitts, as well as rental exchange on Nevis and complimentary pickup. ✉ *South Independence Sq., Basseterre* ☎ *869/465–6507* ⊕ *www.avisstkitts.com.* **Delisle Walwyn.** Delisle Walwyn provides an excellent selection and the option of a replacement car for one day on Nevis if you rent for three days or more on St. Kitts. ✉ *Liverpool Row, Basseterre* ☎ *869/465–8449.* **Funky Monkey Tours & Rentals.** Funky Monkey Tours & Rentals lets you ride on the wild side in Polaris Ranger and Razor 4x4s; prices start at $115 per half day. You can also rent Vespas for $75 per day, as well as Sea-Doo wave runners.

LOGISTICS

Getting to St. Kitts and Nevis: Many travelers connect in Antigua, San Juan, St. Maarten, or St. Thomas. When going to Nevis, it's almost always cheaper to fly into St. Kitts and then take a regularly scheduled ferry to Nevis, but check the schedules. Robert L. Bradshaw International Airport on St. Kitts (SKB) and the smaller, simpler Vance W. Armory International Airport on Nevis (NEV) are still fairly sleepy.

Hassle Factor: Low to medium for St. Kitts, medium for Nevis.

On the Ground: Taxis meet every ferry and flight to St. Kitts or Nevis.

The taxis are unmetered, but fixed rates, in EC dollars, are posted at the airport and at the jetty. Note that rates are the same for one to four passengers. On St. Kitts the fares from the airport range from EC$32 to Frigate Bay to EC$72 for the farthest point. From the airport on Nevis it's EC$27 to Nisbet Plantation, EC$54 to the Four Seasons, and EC$67 to Montpelier. There is a 50% surcharge between 10 pm and 6 am. Before setting off in a cab, be sure to clarify whether the rate quoted is in EC or U.S. dollars.

Or follow in their tire tracks, off-roading through the island on a three-hour Funky Monkey tours. ⊠ *Nelson Springs, Nevis* ☎ *869/665–6045, 869/665–6245* ⊕ *www.funkymonkeytours.com.* **Nevis Car Rentals.** Nevis Car Rentals has quality vehicles and service. ⊠ *Newcastle, Nevis* ☎ *869/469–9837.* **Striker's Car Rental.** Striker's Car Rental has a good selection of vehicles. ⊠ *Hermitage Rd., Gingerland, Nevis* ☎ *869/469–2654* ⊕ *www.strikerscarrentals.com.* **TDC/Thrifty Rentals.** TDC/Thrifty Rentals has a wide selection of vehicles and outstanding service; it offers a three-day rental that includes a car on both islands. ⊠ *West Independence Sq., Central St., Basseterre* ☎ *869/465–2991* ⊕ *www.tdclimited. com/dept_content.asp?did=8* ⊠ *Bay Rd., Charlestown, Nevis* ☎ *869/469–5430* ⊕ *www.tdclimited.com/dept_content.asp?did=8.*

TAXI TRAVEL

Taxi rates are government regulated and posted at the airport, the dock, and in the free tourist guide. Be sure to clarify whether the fare is in EC or U.S. dollars. There are fixed rates to and from all the hotels and to and from major points of interest.

Airport Transfers: On St. Kitts the fares from the airport range from EC$32 to Frigate Bay to EC$72 for the farthest point. From the airport on Nevis it's EC$27 to Nisbet Plantation, EC$54 to the Four Seasons, and EC$67 to Montpelier. There is a 50% surcharge between 10 pm and 6 am.

Contacts St. Kitts Taxi Association ☎ *869/465–8487, 869/465–4253, 869/465–7818 after hrs.* **Nevis Taxi Service.** Nevis Taxi Service provides taxi information for Nevis, but does not operate a fleet of taxis. ☎ *869/469–5631, 869/469–9790 for the airport, 869/469–5515 after dark.*

ESSENTIALS

Banks and Exchange Services Legal tender is the Eastern Caribbean (EC) dollar. The rate of exchange at this writing is EC$2.70 to US$1. U.S. dollars are accepted everywhere, but change is usually EC currency. Most large hotels, restaurants, and shops accept major credit cards, but small inns and shops often do not. All banks, including the Royal Bank of St. Kitts and Scotia Bank, have ATMs. There are ATMs on Nevis at the airport, Bank of Nova Scotia, First Caribbean International Bank, Royal Bank of Trinidad & Tobago, and St. Kitts–Nevis National Bank.

Electricity 110 volts, 60 cycles.

Emergency Services **Ambulance and Emergencies** ☎ 911. **Fire emergencies on St. Kitts** ☎ 869/465-2515, 333. **Fire emergencies on Nevis** ☎ 869/469-3444. **Police** ☎ 869/465-2241 on St. Kitts, 869/469-5391 on Nevis, 911 on St. Kitts.

Passport Requirements All travelers must have a valid passport and a return or ongoing ticket. Canadian citizens (not connecting through U.S. territory) need either a valid passport or a birth certificate (with a raised seal) accompanied by a government-issue photo ID.

Phones Phone cards, which you can buy in denominations of EC$5, $10, and $20, are handy for making local phone calls, calling other islands, and accessing U.S. direct lines. To call St. Kitts and Nevis from the United States, dial area code 869, then access code 465, 466, 468, or 469 and the local four-digit number.

Taxes The departure tax of US$22 is included in your plane ticket; if it isn't, the gate agent will request payment, in cash only. There's no sales tax on either St. Kitts or Nevis. Hotels collect a 9% government tax.

Tipping Hotels add a 10%–12% service charge to your bill. Restaurants occasionally do the same; ask if it isn't printed on the menu; a 15% tip is appropriate when it isn't included. Taxi drivers typically receive a 10% tip, porters and bellhops $1 per bag; housekeeping staff, $2 to $3 per night.

ACCOMMODATIONS

St. Kitts has a wide variety of places to stay—beautifully restored plantation inns, full-service affordable hotels, simple beachfront cottages, and all-inclusive resorts. One large resort—the Marriott—is more mid-range than upscale and attracts large groups and package tourists. Choose St. Kitts if you want a wider choice of activities and accommodations (you can always do Nevis as a day trip). Nevis is a small island with no large resorts, and most accommodations are upscale—primarily plantation inns and the luxurious Four Seasons. It's much quieter than St. Kitts, so choose it if you want to get away from the hectic island scene and simply relax in low-key comfort and surprisingly high style.

Four Seasons Resort Nevis: Really in a class by itself, the Four Seasons is the only sizable, lavish, high-end property on either island until the Park Hyatt opens on Banana Bay (the first phase is tentatively scheduled to debut by 2016). If you can afford it, the resort is certainly one of the Caribbean's finest; recent post-hurricane renovations improved on near-perfection.

21

Plantation Inns: St. Kitts and Nevis feature renovated, historic plantation houses that have been turned into upscale inns. On Nevis, the inns are the most distinctive form of lodging. They are usually managed by hands-on owner-operators and offer fine cuisine and convivial hospitality; though not usually on a beach, most of these inns have beach clubs with free private shuttle service.

HOTEL AND RESTAURANT PRICES

Prices in the restaurant reviews are the average cost of a main course at dinner or, if dinner is not served, at lunch; taxes and service charges are generally included. Prices in the hotel reviews are the lowest cost of a standard double room in high season, excluding taxes, service charges, and meal plans (except at all-inclusives). Prices for rentals are the lowest per-night cost for a one-bedroom unit in high season.

For expanded lodging reviews and current deals, visit Fodors.com.

VISITOR INFORMATION

Contacts Nevis Tourism Authority ✉ *Elm House, Park La., Lower Froyle, Alton, Hampshire, England* ☎ *01420/520810* ⊕ *www.nevisisland.com.* **St. Kitts Tourism Authority** ☎ *212/535–1234 in New York City, 800/582–6208, 866/556–3847 for Nevis alone* ⊕ *www.stkittstourism.kn.* **St. Kitts–Nevis Hotel and Tourism Association** ✉ *Sands Complex, Box 438, Unit C9, Basseterre* ☎ *869/465–5304* ⊕ *www.stkittsnevishta.org.*

WEDDINGS

Two-business day residency requirement. License and application are EC$200. Valid passport or birth certificate required; if divorced, a divorce decree; if widowed, a death certificate of the deceased spouse.

ST. KITTS

EXPLORING

You can explore Basseterre, the capital city, in a half hour or so, and should allow four hours for an island tour. Main Road traces the northwestern perimeter of the island through seas of sugarcane and past breadfruit trees and stone walls. Villages with tiny pastel-color houses of stone and weathered wood are scattered across the island, and the drive back to Basseterre around the island's other side passes through several of them. The most spectacular stretch of scenery is on Dr. Kennedy Simmonds Highway, which goes to the tip of the Southeast Peninsula. This modern road twists and turns through the undeveloped grassy hills that rise between the calm Caribbean and the windswept Atlantic, passing the shimmering pink Great Salt Pond, a volcanic crater, and seductive beaches. Major developments are under way, including the Beaumont Park Racetrack near Dieppe Bay. The 6-furlong racetrack and state-of-the-art stables opened in 2009. Cards include some stakes races with horses from as far afield as France and Ireland competing; admission and parking are free; up to 9,000 spectators converge on the site, enhancing the exciting equine environment. At this writing a planned entertainment complex, with an upscale restaurant as well as polo grounds, go-karts, a retail complex, and bird and butterfly parks, is on hold.

BASSETERRE

On the south coast, St. Kitts's walkable capital is graced with tall palms and flagstone sidewalks; although many of the buildings appear run-down, there are interesting shops, excellent art galleries, and some beautifully maintained houses. Duty-free shops and boutiques line the streets and courtyards radiating from the octagonal **Circus,** built in the style of London's famous Piccadilly Circus.

WORTH NOTING

Independence Square. There are lovely gardens and a fountain on the site of a former slave market at Independence Square. The square is surrounded on three sides by 18th-century Georgian buildings. ⊠ *Off Bank St.*

National Museum. In the restored former Treasury Building, the National Museum presents an eclectic collection of artifacts reflecting the history and culture of the island. ⊠ *Bay Rd.* ☎ *869/465–5584* ▣ *US$3* ◔ *Weekdays 9:15–5, Sat. 9:15–1.*

Port Zante. Port Zante is an ambitious, ever-growing 27-acre cruise-ship pier and marina in an area that has been reclaimed from the sea. The domed welcome center is an imposing neoclassical hodgepodge, with columns and stone arches, shops, walkways, fountains, and West Indian–style buildings housing luxury shops, galleries, restaurants, and a small casino. A second pier, 1,434 feet long, has a draft that accommodates even leviathan cruise ships. The selection of shops and restaurants (Twist serves global fusion cuisine and rocks with DJs several nights of the week) is expanding as well. ⊠ *Waterfront, behind Circus* ⊕ *www.portzante.com.*

St. George's Anglican Church. This handsome stone building has a crenellated tower originally built by the French in 1670 that is called Nôtre-Dame. The British burned it down in 1706 and rebuilt it four years later, naming it after the patron saint of England. Since then it has suffered a fire, an earthquake, and hurricanes and was once again rebuilt in 1869. ⊠ *Cayon St.*

NEED A BREAK?

Ballahoo. The tropically themed second-floor terrace eatery Ballahoo draws a crowd for breakfast, lunch, and dinner. Specialties include chili shrimp, Madras beef curry, and a toasted rum-and-banana sandwich topped with ice cream. At lunchtime, you can watch the bustle of the Circus and enjoy special prices on such dishes as roti bursting with curried chicken or vegetables. Grab fresh local juices (tamarind, guava) if you can. Though the service is lackadaisical bordering on rude, the food is at least plentiful, the daiquiris are killer, the Wi-Fi free, and the people-watching delightful. ⊠ *Fort St.* ☎ *869/465–4197* ⊕ *www.ballahoo.com.*

ELSEWHERE ON ST. KITTS

TOP ATTRACTIONS

Brimstone Hill. This 38-acre fortress, a UNESCO World Heritage Site, is part of a national park dedicated by Queen Elizabeth in 1985. After routing the French in 1690, the English erected a battery here; by 1736 the fortress held 49 guns, earning it the moniker Gibraltar

Cannons at Brimstone Hill, a UNESCO World Heritage Site on St. Kitts

of the West Indies. In 1782, 8,000 French troops laid siege to the stronghold, which was defended by 350 militia and 600 regular troops of the Royal Scots and East Yorkshires. When the English finally surrendered, they were allowed to march from the fort in full formation out of respect for their bravery (the English afforded the French the same honor when they surrendered the fort a mere year later). A hurricane severely damaged the fortress in 1834, and in 1852 it was evacuated and dismantled. The beautiful stones were carted away to build houses.

The citadel has been partially reconstructed and its guns remounted. It's a steep walk up the hill from the parking lot. A seven-minute orientation film recounts the fort's history and restoration. You can see remains of the officers' quarters, redoubts, barracks, ordnance store, and cemetery. Its museum collections were depleted by hurricanes, but some pre-Columbian artifacts, objects pertaining to the African heritage of the island's slaves (such as masks and ceremonial tools), weaponry, uniforms, photographs, and old newspapers remain. The spectacular view includes Montserrat and Nevis to the southeast; Saba and St. Eustatius to the northwest; and St. Barth and St. Maarten to the north. Nature trails snake through the tangle of surrounding hardwood forest and savanna (a fine spot to catch the green vervet monkeys—inexplicably brought by the French and now outnumbering the residents—skittering about). ⊠ *Main Rd., Brimstone Hill* ☎ *869/465–2609* ⊕ *www.brimstonehillfortress.org* ✑ *$10* ⊙ *Daily 9:30–5:30.*

St. Kitts Scenic Railway. The old narrow-gauge train that had transported sugarcane to the central sugar factory since 1912 is all that remains of the island's once-thriving sugar industry. Two-story cars bedecked in bright Kittitian colors circle the island in just under four hours (a new Rail and Sail option takes guests going or on the return via catamaran). Each passenger gets a comfortable, downstairs air-conditioned seat fronting vaulted picture windows and an upstairs open-air observation spot. The conductor's running discourse embraces not only the history of sugar cultivation but also the railway's construction, local folklore, island geography, even other agricultural mainstays from papayas to pigs. You can drink in complimentary tropical beverages (including luscious guava daiquiris) along with the sweeping rain-forest and ocean vistas, accompanied by an a cappella choir's renditions of hymns, spirituals, and predictable standards like "I've Been Workin' on the Railroad." ⊠ *Needsmust* ☎ *869/465–7263* ⊕ *www.stkittsscenicrailway.com* ✉ *$89, children 4–12 $44.50* ⊗ *Departures vary according to cruise-ship schedules (call ahead, but at least once daily Dec.–Apr., usually 8:30 am).*

WORTH NOTING

Black Rocks. This series of lava deposits was spat into the sea ages ago when the island's volcano erupted. It has since been molded into fanciful shapes by centuries of pounding surf. ⊠ *Atlantic coast, outside town of Sadlers, Sandy Bay, Sand Bank Bay.*

Fairview Great House & Botanical Gardens. Parts of this French colonial greathouse set on more than 2 lush tropical acres date back to 1701, including original ipe beams. The interior has been impeccably restored in period fashion, with each room painted in different colors from pomegranate to lemon. Furnishings include a 16-seat mahogany dinner table set with china and silver; docents relate fascinating factoids (chaises were broadened to accommodate petticoats—or "can-can skirts," in local parlance). Cross the cobblestone courtyard to the original kitchen, replete with volcanic stone and brick oven, and bathing room (heated rocks warmed spring water in the tub). The fieldstone cellar now contains the gift shop, offering local pottery, art, and honey harvested on-site at the apiary. You can wander meticulously maintained gardens with interpretive signage, filled with chattering birds and monkeys. The Nirvana restaurant offers worthy local food (lunch buffets, Caribbean tapas, creative Mediterranean-tinged fare for dinner) as well as Island Flavours cooking classes; dips in the pool are a bonus. ⊠ *Artist's Level Hill, Boyd's* ☎ *869/465–3141* ⊕ *www.nirvanafairview. com* ✉ *$10* ⊗ *Daily 9–5; last entrance 4:30.*

Old Road. This site marks the first permanent English settlement in the West Indies, founded in 1624 by Thomas Warner. Take the side road toward the interior to find some Carib petroglyphs, testimony of even earlier habitation. The largest depicts a female figure on black volcanic rock, presumably a fertility goddess. Less than a mile east of Old Road along Main Road is **Bloody Point,** where French and British soldiers joined forces in 1629 to repel a mass Carib attack; reputedly so many Caribs were massacred that the stream ran red for three days. ✛ *Main Rd. west of Challengers.*

Romney Manor. The ruins of this somewhat restored house (reputedly once the property of Thomas Jefferson) and surrounding replicas of chattel-house cottages are set in 6 acres of glorious gardens, with exotic flowers, an old bell tower, and an enormous, gnarled 350-year-old saman tree (sometimes called a rain tree). Inside, at **Caribelle Batik,** you can watch artisans hand-printing fabrics by the 2,500-year-old Indonesian wax-and-dye process known as batik. You can also stroll to the17th-century ruins of Wingfield Manor, site of the first land grant in the British West Indies, and home to a ziplining outfit. Look for signs indicating a turnoff for Romney Manor near Old Road. ⊠ *Old Rd.* ☎ *869/465–6253* ⊕ *www.caribellebatikstkitts.com* 🖾 *Free* ☾ *Daily 9–5.*

BEACHES

Beaches on St. Kitts are free and open to the public (even those occupied by hotels). The best beaches, with powdery white sand, are in the Frigate Bay area or on the lower peninsula. The Atlantic waters are rougher, and many black-sand beaches northwest of Frigate Bay double as garbage dumps.

Banana/Cockleshell Bays. These twin connected eyebrows of glittering champagne-color sand—stretching nearly 2 miles (3 km) total at the southeastern tip of the island—feature majestic views of Nevis and are backed by lush vegetation and coconut palms. The first-rate restaurant–bar Spice Mill (next to Rasta-hue Lion Rock Beach Bar—order the knock-out Lion Punch) and Reggae Beach Bar & Grill bracket either end of Cockleshell. At this writing, plans for a 125-room mixed-use Park Hyatt (with additional residential condos and villas) are back on schedule for development by late 2015. The water is generally placid, ideal for swimming. The downside is irregular maintenance, with seaweed (particularly after rough weather) and occasional litter, especially on Banana Bay. Follow Simmonds Highway to the end and bear right, ignoring the turnoff for Turtle Beach. **Amenities:** food and drink; parking. **Best for:** partiers; snorkeling; swimming; walking. ⊠ *Banana Bay.*

Friar's Bay. Locals consider Friar's Bay, on the Caribbean (southern) side, the island's finest beach. It's a long, tawny scimitar where the water always seems warmer and clearer. The upscale Carambola Beach Club has co-opted roughly one third of the strand. Still, several happening bars, including Jam Rock (great grouper and jerk), ShipWreck and Sunset, serve terrific, inexpensive local food and cheap, frosty drinks. Chair rentals cost around $3, though if you order lunch, you can negotiate a freebie. Friar's is the first major beach along Southeast Peninsula Drive (aka Simmonds Highway), approximately a mile (1½ km) southeast of Frigate Bay. **Amenities:** food and drink. **Best for:** snorkeling; swimming; walking. ⊠ *Friar's Bay.*

Frigate Bay. The Caribbean side offers talcum-powder-fine beige sand framed by coconut palms and sea grapes, and the Atlantic side (a 15-minute stroll)—sometimes called North Frigate Bay—is a favorite with horseback riders. South Frigate Bay is bookended by the Timothy Beach Club's Sunset Café and the popular, pulsating Buddies Beach Hut. In between are several other lively beach spots, including Cathy's (fabulous jerk ribs), Chinchilla's, Vibes, Elvis Love Shack, and Mr. X

Shiggidy Shack. Most charge $3 to $5 to rent a chair, though they'll often waive the fee if you ask politely and buy lunch. Locals barhop late into Friday and Saturday nights. Waters are generally calm for swimming; the rockier eastern end offers fine snorkeling. The incomparably scenic Atlantic side is—regrettably—dominated by the Marriott (plentiful dining options), attracting occasional pesky vendors. The surf is choppier and the undertow stronger here. On cruise-ship days, groups stampede both sides. **Amenities:** food and drink; water sports. **Best for:** partying; snorkeling; swimming; walking. ⊠ *Frigate Bay* ✛ *Less than 3 miles (5 km) from downtown Basseterre.*

Sand Bank Bay. A dirt road, nearly impassable after heavy rains, leads to a long mocha crescent on the Atlantic. The shallow coves are protected here, making it ideal for families, and it's usually deserted. Brisk breezes lure the occasional windsurfer, but avoid the rocky far left area because of fierce sudden swells and currents. This exceptionally pretty beach lacks shade; Christophe Harbour has constructed several villas and a beach club (whose upscale Pavilion restaurant is open to the public only for dinner). As you drive southeast along Simmonds Highway, approximately 10 miles (16 km) from Basseterre, look for an unmarked dirt turnoff to the left of the Great Salt Pond. **Amenities:** none. **Best for:** solitude; swimming; windsurfing. ⊠ *Sand Bank Bay.*

White House Bay. The beach is rocky, but the snorkeling, taking in several reefs surrounding a sunken tugboat, as well as a recently discovered 18th-century British troop ship, is superb. It's usually deserted, though the calm water (and stunning scenery) makes it a favorite anchorage of yachties. There are no facilities and little shade, but there's also little seaweed. A dirt road skirts a hill to the right off Simmonds Highway approximately 2 miles (3 km) after Friar's. **Amenities:** none. **Best for:** snorkeling; solitude. ⊠ *White House Bay.*

WHERE TO EAT

St. Kitts restaurants range from funky beachfront bistros to elegant plantation dining rooms (most with prix-fixe menus); most fare is tinged with the flavors of the Caribbean. Many restaurants offer West Indian specialties such as curried mutton, pepper pot (a stew of vegetables, tubers, and meats), and Arawak chicken (seasoned and served with rice and almonds on breadfruit leaf).

What to Wear. Throughout the island, dress is casual at lunch (but no bathing suits). Dinner, although not necessarily formal, definitely calls for long pants and sundresses.

$$$$ ✕ **Carambola Beach Club.** This ultrastylish restaurant unfurls sensu-
ECLECTIC   ously down South Friar's Bay, like something out of St. Tropez. More
Fodor'sChoice   casual lunches take full advantage of the beachfront setting, with
★   white tents and hedonistic beach beds. But nighttime is truly spectacular, as outdoor fiber-optic fountains enhance the visual flair of
the vast, sleek-but-not-slick interior replete with eat-in wine cellar,
exhibition kitchen, and tile-and-layered-wood sushi bar. You might
start with intensely flavored butternut squash ravioli or one of the
original maki, such as the fiery Kittitian roll (lobster, avocado, chili

Royal Palm

paste, and honey-mustard sauce). Seafood such as breaded grouper in orange beuure blanc is masterfully executed; nothing at Carambola is overcooked. The Chef's Table prix fixe is often a steal. The sole letdown is the wine list. Although it's the island's largest, it lacks imagination; however, the by-the-glass selections are at least reasonably priced, as are such prizes as the 2007 Antinori Cervaro della Sala. [$] *Average main: US$32* ✉ *Friar's Bay* ☎ *869/465–9090* 🌐 *www.carambolabeachclub.com* ⚠ *Reservations essential.*

$ CARIBBEAN 🍴 **El Fredo's.** This humble wood shack across from the waterfront dishes out some of the finest local fare on St. Kitts. No surprise you'll find politicians and expats grabbing a quick lunch (it's a terrific place to eavesdrop on local gossip) alongside local workers shyly flirting with the waitresses. With just a few genre paintings for atmosphere, the decor is humble. The draw is the traditional stewed oxtail, curry goat, or swordfish Creole served with heaping helpings of fungi (cornmeal), rice and peas, and dumplings. Join the locals for bounteous dishes that they swear will cure—or at least absorb—any hangover. [$] *Average main: US$10* ✉ *Corner of Newtown Bay Rd. and Sanddown Rd., Basseterre* ☎ *869/764–9228* 💳 *No credit cards* 🕑 *No dinner. Closed Sun.*

$$$ SEAFOOD 🍴 **Fisherman's Wharf.** Part of the Ocean Terrace Inn, this extremely casual waterfront eatery, completely reinvented in late 2013, is decorated in contemporary nautical style, with sails, walls splashed with aqua waves, colorful painted fish, a mauve plexiglass marine display case, and a stylish open kitchen. Try the excellent conch chowder, followed by fresh grilled lobster or other shipshape seafood, and finish off your meal with a slice of the memorable banana cheesecake. The place is generally hopping, especially on weekend nights between karaoke and

live bands jamming atop the split-level, breeze-swept bar. [$] *Average main: US$24* ✉ *Ocean Terrace Inn, Wigley Ave., Fortlands, Basseterre* ☎ *869/465–2754* 🌐 *www.oceanterraceinn.com* ⏲ *No lunch.*

$$$ FRENCH 🍴 **La Belle Vie.** This très sympa nod to St. Kitts' French heritage is aptly titled "the good life." The cozy antiques-strewn lobby–bar leads to the semi-enclosed garden dining patio. Everything brims with brio from the brioches baked on-site to Brel and Aznavour on the soundtrack (accompanied by tree frogs). Nantes-born Fabien Richard deftly executes bistro fare at fair prices. You could feast on appetizers alone: salad *chabichoux* (warm goat cheese, *lardons*, mesclun) or velvety tomato *bavarois* with prosciutto. But opt for the bargain $41 three-course prix fixe; main courses might include salmon with aniseed emulsion, duck "steaklet" with green- and black-peppercorn sauce, or rack of lamb in thyme jus. Even the old-fashioned veggies delight, including smashing potatoes *dauphinoise*. Save room for an unimpeachable peach sable (tart) with crème anglaise. A few minor complaints include: mosquitoes on still nights, limited wine selection, and the occasional overcooked if tasty entrée. [$] *Average main: US$34* ✉ *19 Golf View, Frigate Bay* ☎ *869/465–5216, 869/764–6035* 🌐 *www.labelleviestkitts.com* ✍ *Reservations essential* ⏲ *No lunch. Closed Sun.*

$$$ ECLECTIC 🍴 **Marshall's.** The pool area of Horizons Villa Resort is transformed into a stylish eatery thanks to smashing ocean views, potted plants, serenading tree frogs, and elegant candlelit tables. Jamaican chef Verral Marshall fuses ultrafresh local ingredients with global influences. Recommended offerings include grilled swordfish with passionfruit beurre blanc, pan-roasted duck breast with raspberry-balsamic sauce, or homemade sorbets. Most dishes are regrettably orthodox (rack of lamb in port reduction) if artfully plated, and the execution is uneven. [$] *Average main: US$30* ✉ *Horizons Villa Resort, Frigate Bay* ☎ *869/466–8245* 🌐 *www.marshalls-stkitts.com* ✍ *Reservations essential* ⏲ *No lunch.*

$$$$ ECLECTIC Fodor's Choice ★ 🍴 **The Pavilion.** Imagine a semi-alfresco cathedral constructed of raw limestone coral overlooking a palm-fringed sandy crescent: that's the Pavilion, the ritzy Christophe Harbour beach club open to nonmembers for dinner only. The soaring interior blends colonial and contemporary with aplomb: a curved exhibition kitchen, streamlined bar stools, and abstract pendant lamps contrast with "found" sculptural sea fans and driftwood, antique settees, and 19th-century black-and-white photos of Kittitian scenes. Executive Chef Damien Heaney similarly blends tradition and innovation, taking the confusion out of fusion cuisine. Even such "traditional" fare as conch fritters is goosed with pickled ginger and passion fruit coulis and artfully presented with swirls of jerk mayo. Stunners such as beef tenderloin rubbed with five peppercorn, accompanied by fresh figs, local greens, and sorrel glaze or Creole-spiced swordfish with clams, pale-ale sofrito, and sweet pea risotto provide textbook examples of how to juxtapose textures, flavors, even colors. Wednesday night's $39 Chef's Appreciation prix fixe is an amazing buy. The wine list features some surprising bargains, especially among whites, and you can finish your meal in style with one of a dozen aged rums. [$] *Average main: US$35* ✉ *Christophe Harbour, Sandy Bank Bay* ☎ *869/465–8304* 🌐 *www.christopheharbour.com* ⏲ *No lunch unless member. Closed Sun. and Mon. dinner.*

$$ ITALIAN 🍴 **PJ's Bar and Restaurant.** "Garbage pizza"—topped with everything but the kitchen sink—is a favorite, or you can create your own pie at this longtime hangout owned by three expats (two Canadians and a Texan: Pat, Jude, and Janet). Sandwiches, calzones, simple but lustily flavored pastas (try the goat cheese ravioli in sun-dried tomato sauce or spaghetti with humongous garlicky meatballs), and mamma-mia classics (eggplant Parmesan to chicken piccata) are also served. Finish your meal with delicious, moist rum cake. This casual spot, bordering the golf course and open to cooling breezes, is always boisterous (especially during the 9–10 pm happy hour, overseen with good spirits by bartending fixture Ashton), despite—or perhaps because of—its ironic location beside the Frigate Bay police station. [$] *Average main: US$18* ✉ *Frigate Bay* ☎ *869/465–8373* 🌐 *www.pjsrestaurantstkitts.com* 🕒 *Closed Mon. and Sept. No lunch.*

$$ ECLECTIC 🍴 **Reggae Beach Bar & Grill.** Treats at this popular daytime watering hole include honey-mustard ribs, coconut shrimp, grilled lobster, decadent banana bread pudding with rum sauce, and an array of tempting tropical libations. Business cards and pennants from around the world plaster the bar, and the open-air space is decorated with nautical accoutrements, from fishnets and turtle shells to painted wooden crustaceans. You can snorkel here, spot hawksbill turtles and the occasional monkey, visit the enormous house pig Wilbur (who once "ate" beer cans whole, then moved to "lite" beers—but feeding is no longer encouraged), laze in a palm-shaded hammock, or rent a kayak, Hobie Cat or snorkeling gear. Beach chairs and Wi-Fi are free. Locals come Friday nights for bonfire dinners and Sunday afternoons for dancing to live bands. [$] *Average main: US$21* ✉ *S.E. Peninsula Rd., Cockleshell Beach* ☎ *869/762–5050* 🌐 *www.reggaebeachbar.com* 🕒 *No dinner.*

$$$$ ECLECTIC Fodor's Choice ★ 🍴 **Royal Palm.** A 65-foot, spring-fed pool bisects this elegant restaurant at Ottley's Plantation Inn into a semi-enclosed lounge with sea views and a breezy alfresco stone patio. Three-course extravaganzas (dishes are also available à la carte) blend indigenous ingredients with Asian, Mediterranean, and Latin touches: sweet potato, chile, and lime soup; portobello-caramelized onion ravioli with creamy spinach pesto; crab salpicon on Caribbean crab cake with mango vinaigrette and ginger remoulade. Finish with simple yet sinful indulgences such as coconut-cream cheesecake or mango mousse with raspberry coulis. The combination of superb food, artful presentation, romantic setting, and warm bonhomie is unbeatable. [$] *Average main: US$39* ✉ *Ottley's Plantation Inn, Ottley's Village, Basseterre* ☎ *869/465–7234* 🌐 *www.ottleys.com* ✍ *Reservations essential* ☞ *Prix-fixe: $66.*

$$$ ECLECTIC 🍴 **Serendipity.** This stylish restaurant occupies an old Creole home whose charming enclosed patio offers lovely views of Basseterre and the bay. The interior lounge is even more conducive to romantic dining, with cushy sofas, patterned hardwood floors, porcelain lamps, and African carvings. The menu reflects co-owner–chef Alexander James's peripatetic postings: you might start with wonderfully crispy fried Brie with sweet-and-sour blackberry sauce or beautifully presented spring rolls with plum-soy dipping sauce. Mahimahi crusted with cheddar, Parmesan, basil, and garlic floating on pools of creole and saffron cream

sauces; or prosciutto-wrapped beef tenderloin topped with pâté, prosciutto, and Madeira sauce paired with tiger shrimp in garlic sauce typify the ambitious main courses. The wine list is well considered; vegetarians will be delighted by the many creative options; and very affordable lunches feature gargantuan tapas-style selections. $ *Average main: US$35* ⊠ *3 Wigley Ave., Fortlands, Basseterre* ☎ *869/465–9999* ⊕ *www.serendipitystkitts.com* ⚑ *Reservations essential* ⊙ *Closed Mon. No lunch weekends.*

$$$$
ECLECTIC
Fodor's Choice
★

✕ **Spice Mill.** This beachfront beauty references the Caribbean's multiethnic cuisine, a melting pot of African, French, English, Iberian, Asian, and Dutch influences. But the kitchen also stays home in proper locavore fashion, as does the bar, sourcing as much local produce as possible from Kittitian farmers and fishermen (who might troop through the restaurant with 30 just-caught snapper for "De Bossman"). Spice Mill merrily marries those gastronomic traditions, juxtaposing colors, tastes, and textures right from the dips served with scrumptious homemade breads. Panko-crusted crab cake might be served with mango-lemon aioli and green papaya ceviche. Lobster risotto contrasts sweet pumpkin with savory truffle oil. The culinary globe-trotting approach also dictates the decor—a mix of regional (coconut-wood-top bar, Carib canoe, and crayfish baskets from Dominica) and cosmopolitan (white beach beds, cushioned couches) elements, making even the bar (open daily and serving light snacks) a barefoot-chic hangout. Lunch is considerably cheaper and more island-flavored. $ *Average main: US$35* ⊠ *Cockleshell Beach* ☎ *869/465–6455* ⊕ *www.spicemillrestaurant.com* ⚑ *Reservations essential* ⊙ *Closed Sun. No dinner Mon.*

$$
SEAFOOD

✕ **Sprat Net.** This simple cluster of picnic tables—sheltered by a brilliant-turquoise corrugated-tin roof and decorated with driftwood, life preservers, photos of coastal scenes, and fishnets—sits on a sliver of sand. Nonetheless, it's an island hot spot. There's nothing fancy on the menu: just grilled fish, lobster, ribs, and chicken served with mountains of coleslaw and peas and rice. But the fish is amazingly fresh: the fishermen–owners heap their catches on a center table from which you choose your own dinner, then watch it grilled to your specification before dining family-style on paper plates. An adjacent hut serves up the final food group: pizza, Wednesday–Sunday. Sprat Net offers old-style Caribbean flavor, with the cheapest drinks and best bands on weekends. No wonder cars line up along the road, creating an impromptu jump-up. $ *Average main: US$15* ⊠ *Main Rd., Old Road Town* ☎ *869/466–7535* ▭ *No credit cards* ⊙ *Closed Sept. No lunch.*

WHERE TO STAY

St. Kitts has an appealing variety of places to stay—beautifully restored plantation inns (where a meal plan including afternoon tea in addition to breakfast and dinner is the norm), full-service, affordable hotels, simple beachfront cottages, and all-inclusive resorts. There are also several guesthouses and self-serve condos. Increasing development has been touted (or threatened) for years. At this writing, the ritzy Park Hyatt plans to debut its first Caribbean property on Banana Bay, in partnership with the grand Christophe Harbour development that will sprawl across the Southeast Peninsula replete with spectacular villas, beach clubs, celebrity restaurants, megayacht marina, Tom Fazio–designed golf course, and other boutique hotels. Several upscale villa compounds are being developed, such as the culture-oriented, ecocentric Kittitian Hills (architect Bill Bensley designed some of Thailand's most remarkable resorts), which will include an "edible" golf course (greens will intersect with farmland), spa, cosmopolitan retail village, farm-to-table restaurants, and a variety of sustainable lodgings in vernacular style, most with fabulous views. The first phase of spectacular hillside cottages opened in 2013; the resort is scheduled for completion in 2015. Another deluxe condo complex, the sparkling 185-unit Ocean's Edge on the Atlantic side of Frigate Bay, opened its first two beachfront blocks in late 2012; hillside villas, a stunning tiered pool, additional water features, and a high-end restaurant are planned by 2015.

$ **Bird Rock Beach Resort.** This basic scuba-set resort crowns a bluff
RESORT above Basseterre, delivering amazing views of the town, sea, and mountains from every vantage point. **Pros:** exuberant clientele; great diving; excellent value; superb views; complimentary Frigate Bay shuttle. **Cons:** small man-made beach; insufficient parking; difficult for physically challenged to maneuver; several rooms leased longterm to students; poor lighting; dilapidated decor. $ *Rooms from: US$100* ✉ *2 miles (3 km) east of Basseterre, Basseterre Bay* ☎ *869/465–8914, 877/244–6285* ⊕ *www.birdrockbeach.com* ⌁ *30 rooms, 18 studios* ¶⊙¶ *Multiple meal plans.*

$ **Ocean Terrace Inn.** "OTI," as locals call it, is a rarity: a smart, inti-
HOTEL mate business hotel that also appeals to vacationers. **Pros:** excellent service; fine facilities for a small hotel; good restaurants; walking distance to Basseterre attractions and restaurants; suites represent excellent value for families. **Cons:** must drive to beaches; sprawling layout; difficult for physically challenged to navigate. $ *Rooms from: US$219* ✉ *Wigley Ave., Fortlands* ☎ *869/465–2754, 800/524–0512* ⊕ *www.oceanterraceinn.com* ⌁ *65 rooms* ¶⊙¶ *Multiple meal plans.*

$$ **Ottley's Plantation Inn.** You're treated like a beloved relative rather
HOTEL than a commercial guest at this quintessential Caribbean hotel, for-
Fodor'sChoice merly a sugar plantation, at the foot of Mt. Liamuiga. **Pros:** posh
★ yet unpretentious luxury; wonderfully helpful staff and owners; gorgeous gardens; excellent dining. **Cons:** no beach; bumpy access road; long walk from farthest cottages to office. $ *Rooms from: US$268* ✉ *Southwest of Nicola Town, Ottley's Village, Basseterre* ☎ *869/465–7234, 800/772–3039* ⊕ *www.ottleys.com* ⌁ *24 rooms* ¶⊙¶ *Some meals.*

$ **Rock Haven Bed & Breakfast.** This restful, cozy bed-and-breakfast,
B&B/INN a two-minute drive from Frigate Bay beaches (airport transfers are included), provides true local warmth, courtesy of Judith and Keith Blake. **Pros:** genuine island hospitality; immaculately maintained; delicious breakfasts. **Cons:** long walk to beach; car recommended to get around. $ *Rooms from: US$179* ✉ *Frigate Bay* ☎ *869/465–5503* ⊕ *www.rock-haven.com* ⌁ *2 rooms* ¶⊙¶ *Breakfast.*

Ottley's Plantation Inn

$$ **St. Kitts Marriott Resort.** This big, bustling beachfront resort offers
RESORT something for everyone from families to conventioneers, golfers to
gamblers. **Pros:** great range of activities; good bars; recently refur-
bished rooms; plentiful on-site duty-free shopping; enormous main
pool. **Cons:** impersonal service; occasional time-share pitches; surprise
extra charges; mostly mediocre food; not enough units feature ocean
views. $ *Rooms from: US$259* ⊠ *858 Frigate Bay Rd., Frigate Bay*
☎ *869/466–1200, 800/223–6388* ⊕ *www.stkittsmarriott.com* ⥮ *320
rooms, 73 suites* ❙❖❙ *No meals.*

$ **Timothy Beach Resort.** The only St. Kitts resort sitting directly on a
RENTAL Caribbean beach is incomparably located and restful, a great budget
find thanks to smiling service and simple but sizable apartments. **Pros:**
complimentary Wi-Fi; close to the beach action; pleasant on-site res-
taurant and bar; plentiful deals. **Cons:** occasionally worn decor; can
hear boisterous beach bar music weekend nights; no view from most
bedrooms. $ *Rooms from: US$150* ⊠ *1 S. Frigate Bay Beach, Frig-
ate Bay* ☎ *869/465–8597, 845/201–0047, 888/229–2747* ⊕ *www.
timothybeach.com* ⥮ *60 apartments* ❙❖❙ *No meals.*

NIGHTLIFE

Most nightlife revolves around the hotels, which host folkloric shows
and calypso and steel bands of the usual limbo-rum-and-reggae variety.
The growing Frigate Bay "strip" of beach bars, including Rainbow, Mr.
X Shiggidy Shack, Monkey Bar, Inon's, Buddies Beach Hut, Chinchilla,
and Vibes, is the place to party hearty on weekend nights.

Bob & Elvis The Party Bus. A wild, wacky evening is promised by Bob & Elvis The Party Bus ("What Happens on the Bus.. Stays on the Bus," reads the slogan) as they escort an increasingly raucous crowd via their psychedelically hued bus Wednesday and Friday to four of the island's top liming spots. ■ TIP→ **The bus will pick you up at your hotel.** ⊠ *Frigate Bay* ☎ *869/466–8110* ⊕ *www.caribbeanjourneymasters.com/BobElvis.cfm.*

Look for such hard-driving local exponents of soca music as Nu-Vybes, Grand Masters, Small Axe, and Royalton 5; and "heavy dance-hall" reggae group House of Judah. The Marriott's large, glitzy casino has table games and slots.

BARS AND CLUBS

Circus Grill. A favorite happy-hour watering hole is the Circus Grill, a second-floor eatery whose verandah offers views of the harbor and the activity on the Circus. ⊠ *Bay Rd., Basseterre* ☎ *869/465–0143.*

Keys Cigar Bar. This low-key, classy hangout has jazz-salsa duos, cushy sofas, high-back straw chairs, chess-set tables, and a superlative selection of aged rums and *Cubanos* (as well as top Dominican and Nicaraguan brands). If it's packed, try the hotel's Lobby Bar for tapas on tap or 'tinis with 'tude. ⊠ *St. Kitts Marriott Resort, Frigate Bay* ☎ *869/466–1200.*

Mr. X Shiggidy Shack. Mr. X Shiggidy Shack is known for its sizzling Thursday-night bonfire parties replete with fire-eaters, and raucous karaoke Saturdays. For locals it's a must-stop on the Friday-night liming circuit of Frigate Bay bars. ⊠ *Frigate Bay* ☎ *869/762–3983, 869/465–0673* ⊕ *www.mrxshiggidyshack.com.*

SHOPPING

St. Kitts has limited shopping, but several duty-free shops offer good deals on jewelry, perfume, china, and crystal. Numerous galleries sell excellent paintings and sculptures. The batik fabrics, scarves, caftans, and wall hangings of Caribelle Batik are well known. British expat Kate Spencer is an artist who has lived on the island for years, reproducing its vibrant colors on everything from silk pareus (beach wraps) and scarves to note cards. Other good island buys include crafts, jams, and herbal teas. Don't forget to pick up some CSR (Cane Spirit Rothschild), which is distilled from fresh wild sugarcane right on St. Kitts. The Brinley Gold Company has made a splash among spirits connoisseurs with its coffee, mango, coconut, lime, and vanilla rums (there is a tasting room at Port Zante).

AREAS AND MALLS

Most shopping plazas are in downtown Basseterre, on the streets radiating from the Circus.

All Kind of Tings. All Kind of Tings, a peppermint-pink edifice on Liverpool Row at College Street Ghaut, functions as a de facto vendors' market, where several booths sell local crafts and cheap T-shirts. Its courtyard frequently hosts folkloric dances, fashion shows, poetry readings, and steel-pan concerts. ⊠ *Liverpool Row, Basseterre.*

Pelican Mall. This shopping arcade, designed to look like a traditional Caribbean street, has 26 stores (purveying mostly resort wear, souvenirs, and liquor), a restaurant, tourism offices, and a bandstand near the cruise-ship pier. ⊠ *Bay Rd., Basseterre.*

Port Zante. Directly behind Pelican Mall, on the waterfront, is Port Zante, the deepwater cruise-ship pier where a much-delayed upscale shopping–dining complex is becoming a 30-shop area (including the usual ubiquitous large jewelry concerns like Abbott's, Diamonds International, and Kay Jewelers); the Amina Market here is a fine source for cheap local crafts. If you're looking for inexpensive, island-y T-shirts and souvenirs, check out the series of vendors' huts behind Pelican Mall to the right of Port Zante as you face the sea. ⊠ *Cruise Ship Pier, Basseterre* ⊕ *www.portzante.com.*

Shoreline Plaza. Shoreline Plaza is next to the Treasury Building, right on Basseterre's waterfront. The shops mainly sell locally made souvenirs and handicrafts, as well as T-shirts. ⊠ *Basseterre.*

TDC Mall. TDC Mall is just off the Circus in downtown, with a few boutiques and Chef's Garden restaurant, which serves great local food in a courtyard adorned with gingerbread and sports photos. ⊠ *Bank St., Basseterre.*

ART

Spencer Cameron Art Gallery. Spencer Cameron Art Gallery has historical reproductions of Caribbean island charts and prints, in addition to owner Rosey Cameron's popular Carnevale clown prints and a wide selection of exceptional artwork by Caribbean artists. It also showcases the work of Glass Island (exquisite Italianate art glass from frames to plates in sinuous shapes and seductive colors) and various local craftspeople. The gallery will mail anywhere. Rosey and Kate Spencer also run an offshoot in the Marriott called the Art Cooperative, where you can often watch Rosey at work. ⊠ *10 N. Independence Sq., Basseterre* ☎ *869/465–1617, 869/664–4157.*

HANDICRAFTS

Caribelle Batik. Caribelle Batik sells gloriously colored batik wraps, kimonos, caftans, T-shirts, dresses, wall hangings, and the like; you can watch the process in back. ⊠ *Romney Manor, Old Road Town* ☎ *869/465–6253.*

Crafthouse. The Crafthouse is one of the best sources for local dolls, wood carvings, and straw work. ⊠ *Southwell Industrial Site, Bay Rd., Basseterre* ☎ *869/465–7754.*

Fodor'sChoice
★
Kate Design. This boutique showcases the highly individual style of Kate Spencer, whose brilliantly colored original paintings, serigraphs, note cards, and other pieces including lovely art scarves are available from her studio outside Rawlins Plantation. ⊠ *Mount Pleasant House, St. Paul's* ☎ *869/465–7740* ⊕ *www.katedesign.com.*

Palms Court Gardens. Talk about multitasking: this little oasis offers a restaurant, an infinity pool and hot tub with bay views, miniature botanical gardens, and the Shell Works atelier and gift shop, where artisans fashion graceful napkin holders, candlesticks, stemware, wall hangings, and jewelry from coral, sea fans, mother-of-pearl, and other marine materials. ⊠ *Corner of Wilkin and Wigley Sts., Basseterre* ☎ *869/465–6060* ⊕ *www.palmscourtgardens.com.*

Potter's House. The atelier of Carla Astaphan celebrates Afro-Caribbean heritage with beautifully glazed ceramics and masks, and also carries marvelous Haitian pieces. Her work is also found at various craft markets around the island. ⊠ *New St., Camps Village* ☎ *869/465–5947, 869/662–5545.*

SPORTS AND ACTIVITIES

BOATING AND FISHING

Most operators are on the Caribbean side of Frigate Bay, known for its gentle currents. Turtle Bay offers stronger winds and stunning views of Nevis. Though not noted for big-game fishing, several steep offshore drop-offs do lure wahoo, barracuda, shark, tuna, yellowtail snapper, and mackerel. Rates are occasionally negotiable; figure approximately $350 for a four-hour excursion with refreshments.

Leeward Island Charters. The knowledgeable Todd Leypoldt of Leeward Island Charters takes you out on his charter boats, *Spirit of St. Kitts, Caona* and *Eagle*. He's also available for snorkeling charters, beach picnics, and sunset-moonlight cruises. ⊠ *Basseterre* ☎ *869/465–7474* ⊕ *www.leewardislandscharters.com.*

Mr. X Watersports. Found within Mr. X Shiggidy Shack *(⇨ see Nightlife above)*, this shop rents small craft, including motorboats (waterskiing and jet skiing are available). Paddleboats are $15 per hour, sailboats $25 per hour. Deep-sea fishing charters, snorkeling tours, water taxis, sunset cruises, and private charters with captain and crew are available. Mr. X and his cohorts are usually hanging out at the adjacent open-air Monkey Bar. ⊠ *Frigate Bay* ☎ *869/465–0673* ⊕ *www.mrxshiggidyshack.com.*

Reggae Beach Bar & Grill. This establishment rents kayaks and snorkeling equipment from the restaurant, offers sailing lessons, and can also arrange fishing trips, as well as water taxis to Nevis. ⊠ *S.E. Peninsula Rd., Cockleshell Beach* ☎ *869/762–5050* ⊕ *www.reggaebeachbar.com.*

DIVING AND SNORKELING

Though unheralded as a dive destination, St. Kitts has more than a dozen excellent sites, protected by several new marine parks. The surrounding waters feature shoals, hot vents, shallows, canyons, steep walls, and caverns at depths from 40 to nearly 200 feet. The St. Kitts Maritime Archaeological Project, which surveys, records, researches, and preserves the island's underwater treasures, has charted several hundred wrecks of galleons, frigates, and freighters dating back to the 17th century. **Bloody Bay Reef** is noted for its network of underwater grottoes daubed with purple anemones, sienna bristle worms, and canary-yellow sea fans that seem to wave you in. **Coconut Tree Reef,** one of the largest in the area, includes sea fans, sponges, and anemones, as well as the Rocks, three enormous boulders with impressive multilevel diving. The only drift-dive site, **Nags Head,** has strong currents, but experienced divers might spot gliding rays, lobsters, turtles, and reef sharks. Since it sank in 50 feet of water in the early 1980s, the *River Taw* makes a splendid site for less experienced divers. **Sandy Point Reef** has been designated a National Marine Park and includes Paradise Reef, with swim-through 90-foot sloping canyons, and Anchors Away, where anchors have been encrusted with coral formations. The 1985 wreck of the *Talata* lies in 70 feet of water; barracudas, rays, groupers, and grunts dart through its hull.

Dive St. Kitts. This PADI–NAUI facility, offers competitive prices, computers to maximize time below, wide range of courses from refresher to technical, and friendly, laid-back dive masters. The Bird Rock location features superb shore diving (unlimited when you book packages): common sightings 20 to 30 feet out include octopuses, nurse sharks, manta and spotted eagle rays, sea horses, even barracudas George and Georgianna. It also offers kayak and snorkeling tours. ⊠ *2 miles (3 km) east of Basseterre, Frigate Bay* ☎ *869/465–1189, 869/465–8914* ⊕ *www. divestkitts.com.*

Kenneth's Dive Center. Kenneth Samuel, the owner of this a PADI company, takes small groups of divers with C cards to nearby reefs on his two custom-built catamarans. Rates average $70 for single-tank dives, $105 for double-tank dives; add $10 for equipment. Night dives, including lights, are $80–$100, and snorkeling trips (four-person minimum) are $40, drinks included. After 25 years' experience, former fisherman Samuel is considered an old pro (Jean-Michel Cousteau requested his guidance upon his first visit in the 1990s) and strives to keep groups small and prices reasonable. ⊠ *Bay Rd., Newtown* ☎ *869/465–2670* ⊕ *www.kennethdivecenter.com.*

Pro-Divers. Owned by Auston Macleod, a PADI-certified dive master–instructor, this outfitter offers resort and certification courses running $125–$600, including specialty options from deep diving to digital underwater photography. Dive computers are included gratis. He offers introductory scuba courses Sunday through Thursday at 10 am and Friday and Saturday at 2:30 pm at the Marriott for guests only (the $20 fee is refunded if you purchase dives), plus a $30 Bubblemaker PADI course for kids eight and younger. He also takes groups to snorkeling sites accessible only by boat via his custom-built 38-foot catamaran, *Kuriala.* ⊠ *Ocean Terrace Inn, Basseterre* ☎ *869/660–3483* ⊕ *www. prodiversstkitts.com.*

GOLF

St. Kitts hopes to market itself as a golf destination with the remodeling of the Royal St. Kitts Golf Course and two upcoming resort and villa developments that include 18-hole courses, one designed by Tom Fazio (which promises to be one of the Caribbean's most spectacular, with huge elevation drops, ruins, extraordinary sweeping vistas, and carries over ravines: "Scottsdale meets Pebble Beach").

Royal St. Kitts Golf Club. This 18-hole links-style championship course underwent a complete redesign by Thomas McBroom to maximize Caribbean and Atlantic views and increase the challenge (there are 12 lakes and 83 bunkers). Holes 15 through 17 (the latter patterned after Pebble Beach No. 18) skirt the Atlantic in their entirety, lending new meaning to the term *sand trap*. The sudden gusts, wide but twisting fairways, and extremely hilly terrain demand pinpoint accuracy and finesse, yet holes such as 18 require pure power. The development includes practice bunkers, a putting green, a short-game chipping area, and the fairly high-tech Royal Golf Academy. Twilight and super-twilight discounts are offered. ⊠ *St. Kitts Marriott Resort, 858 Zenway Blvd., Frigate Bay* ☎ *869/466–2700, 866/785–4653* ⊕ *www. royalstkittsgolfclub.com* ⌦ *$150 for Marriott guests in high season, $165 for nonguests* ⚑ *18 holes, 6900 yards, par 71.*

GUIDED TOURS

The taxi driver who picks you up will probably offer to act as your guide to the island. Each driver is knowledgeable and does a three-hour tour of Nevis for $75 or a four-hour tour of St. Kitts for $80. He can also make a lunch reservation at one of the plantation restaurants, and you can incorporate this into your tour.

Kantours. On St. Kitts, Kantours offers comprehensive general island tours, as well as a variety of specialty excursions, including ATV expeditions. ⊠ *Liverpool Row, Basseterre* ☎ *869/465–2098, 869/465–3054 in St. Kitts, 869/469–0136 in Nevis* ⊕ *www.kantours.com.*

Tropical Tours. The friendly guides at Tropical Tours can run you around St. Kitts (from $27 per person), arrange kayaking and snorkeling, deep-sea fishing (from $135 per person), and take you to the volcano or rain forest for $52 per person and up. ☎ *869/465–4167* ⊕ *www. tropicalstkitts-nevis.com.*

HIKING

Trails in the central mountains vary from easy to don't-try-it-by-yourself. Monkey Hill and Verchild's Peak aren't difficult, although the Verchild's climb will take the better part of a day. Don't attempt Mt. Liamuiga without a guide. You'll start at Belmont Estate—at the west end of the island—on horseback, and then proceed on foot to the lip of the crater, at 2,600 feet. You can go down into the crater—1,000 feet deep and 1 mile (1½ km) wide, with a small freshwater lake—clinging to vines and roots and scaling rocks, even trees. Expect to get muddy. There are several fine operators (each hotel recommends its favorite); tour rates generally range from $50 for a rain-forest walk to $95 for a volcano expedition and usually include round-trip transportation from your hotel and picnic lunch.

Duke of Earl's Adventures. Owner Earl "The Duke of Earl" Vanlow is as entertaining as his nickname suggests—and his prices are slightly cheaper ($50 for a rain-forest tour includes refreshments, $75 volcano expeditions add lunch; hotel pickup and drop-off is complimentary). He genuinely loves his island and conveys that enthusiasm, encouraging hikers to swing on vines or sample unusual-looking fruits during his rain-forest trip. He also conducts a thorough volcano tour to the crater's rim and a drive-through ecosafari tour ($55 with lunch). ☎ *869/465–1899, 869/663–0994.*

Greg's Safaris. Greg Pereira of Greg's Safaris, whose family has lived on St. Kitts since the early 19th century, takes groups on half-day trips into the rain forest and on full-day hikes up the volcano and through the grounds of a private 18th-century greathouse. The rain-forest trips include visits to sacred Carib sites, abandoned sugar mills, and an excursion down a 100-foot coastal canyon containing a wealth of Amerindian petroglyphs. The Off the Beaten Track 4x4 Plantation Tour provides a thorough explanation of the role sugar and rum played in the Caribbean economy and colonial wars. He and his staff relate fascinating historical, folkloric, and botanical information. ☎ *869/465–4121* ⊕ *www.gregsafaris.com.*

HORSEBACK RIDING

Wild North Frigate Bay and desolate Conaree Beach are great for riding, as is the rain forest.

Trinity Stables. Guides from Trinity Stables offer beach rides ($50) and trips into the rain forest ($60), both including hotel pickup. The latter is intriguing, as guides discuss plants' medicinal properties along the way (such as sugarcane to stanch bleeding) and pick oranges right off a tree to squeeze fresh juice. Otherwise, the staffers are cordial but shy; this isn't a place for beginners' instruction. ✉ *Palmetto Point* ☎ *869/465–3226* ⊕ *www.trinityinnapartments.com/Stables.asp.*

SEA EXCURSIONS

In addition to the usual snorkeling, sunset, and party cruises (ranging in price from $40 to $95), most companies offer whale-watching excursions during the winter migrating season, January through April. And on land, turtle watches during nesting season are becoming popular.

Blue Water Safaris. Blue Water Safaris offers half-day snorkeling trips or beach barbecues on deserted cays, as well as sunset and moonlight cruises on its 65-foot catamarans *Irie Lime* and *Swaliga,* and the smaller *Falcon.* It also runs kayaking tours. Boats depart from Port Zante. ✉ *Princess St., Basseterre* ☎ *869/466–4933* ⊕ *www.bluewatersafaris.com.*

Leeward Island Charters. This reliable charter offers day and overnight charters on two catamarans—the 67-foot *Eagle* and 78-foot *Spirit of St. Kitts.* Day sails are from 9:30 to 4:30 and include a barbecue, an open bar, and use of snorkeling equipment. The Nevis trip stops at Pinney's Beach for a barbecue and at Shooting Bay, a tiny cove in the bullying shadow of a sheer cliff, where petrels and frigate birds inspect your snorkeling skills. The crews are mellow, affable, and knowledgeable about island life. ✉ *586 Fort St., Basseterre* ☎ *869/465–7474* ⊕ *www.leewardislandscharters.com.*

ZIP-LINING

FAMILY **Sky Safari Tours.** On these popular tours, would-be Tarzans and Janes whisk through the "Valley of the Giants" (so dubbed for the towering trees) at speeds up to 50 mph (80 kph along five cable lines); the longest (nicknamed "The Boss") stretches 1,350 feet through towering turpentine and mahogany trees draped thickly with bromeliads, suspended 250 feet above the ground. Following the Canadian-based company's mantra of "faster, higher, safer," it uses a specially designed trolley with secure harnesses attached. Many of the routes afford unobstructed views of Brimstone Hill and the sea beyond. The outfit emphasizes environmental and historic aspects. Guides provide nature interpretation and commentary, and the office incorporates Wingfield Estate's old sugar plantation, distillery, and church ruins, which visitors can explore. Admission is usually $65–$75, depending on the tour chosen. It's open daily 9–6, with the first and last tours departing at 10 and 3. ⊠ *Wingfield Estate, Wingfield Estate* ☎ *869/466–4259, 869/465–4347* ⊕ *www.skysafaristkitts.com.*

NEVIS

Nevis's charm is its rusticity: there are no traffic lights, goats still amble through the streets of Charlestown, and local grocers announce whatever's in stock on a blackboard (anything from pig snouts to beer).

EXPLORING

Nevis's Main Road makes a 21-mile (32-km) circuit through the five parishes; various offshoots of the road wind into the mountains. You can tour Charlestown, the capital, in a half hour or so, but you'll need three to four hours to explore the entire island.

CHARLESTOWN

About 1,200 of Nevis's 10,000 inhabitants live in the capital. If you arrive by ferry, as most people do, you'll walk smack onto Main Street from the pier. It's easy to imagine how tiny Charlestown, founded in 1660, must have looked in its heyday. The weathered buildings still have fanciful galleries, elaborate gingerbread fretwork, wooden shutters, and hanging plants. The stone building with the clock tower (1825, but mostly rebuilt after a devastating 1873 fire) houses the courthouse and second-floor library (a cool respite on sultry days). The little park next to the library is Memorial Square, dedicated to the fallen of World Wars I and II. Down the street from the square, archaeologists have discovered the remains of a Jewish cemetery and synagogue (Nevis reputedly had the Caribbean's second-oldest congregation), but there's little to see.

Alexander Hamilton Birthplace. The Alexander Hamilton Birthplace, which contains the Hamilton Museum, sits on the waterfront. This bougainvillea-draped Georgian-style house is a reconstruction of what is believed to have been the American patriot's original home, built in 1680 and likely destroyed during a mid-19th earthquake. Born here in 1755, Hamilton moved to St. Croix when he was about 12. He moved to the American colonies to continue his education at 17; he became George Washington's Secretary of the Treasury and died in a duel with political rival Aaron Burr in 1804. The Nevis House of Assembly occupies the second floor; the museum downstairs contains Hamilton memorabilia, documents pertaining to the island's history, and displays on island geology, politics, architecture, culture, and cuisine. The gift shop is a wonderful source for historic maps, crafts, and books on Nevis. ⊠ *Low St., Charlestown* ☎ *869/469–5786* ⊕ *www. nevis-nhcs.org* 💰 *$5, with admission to Museum of Nevisian History $7* ☉ *Weekdays 9–4, Sat. 9–noon.*

ELSEWHERE ON NEVIS

TOP ATTRACTIONS

Botanical Gardens of Nevis. In addition to terraced gardens and arbors, this remarkable 7.8-acre site in the glowering shadow of Mt. Nevis has natural lagoons, streams, and waterfalls, superlative bronze mermaids, Buddhas, egrets and herons, and extravagant fountains. You can find a proper rose garden, sections devoted to orchids and bromeliads, cacti, and flowering trees and shrubs—even a bamboo garden. The entrance to the Rain Forest Conservatory—which attempts to include every conceivable Caribbean ecosystem and then some—duplicates an imposing Mayan temple. A splendid re-creation of a plantation-style greathouse contains the appealing Oasis in the Gardens Thai restaurant with sweeping sea views, and the upscale World Art & Antiques Gallery selling artworks, textiles, jewelry, and Indonesian teak furnishings sourced during the owners' world travels. ⊠ *Montpelier Estate* ☎ *869/469–3509* ⊕ *www.botanicalgardennevis.com* ☞ *$13; $8 children 6–12* ⊘ *Mon.–Sat. 9–4.*

Museum of Nevis History. Purportedly this is the Western Hemisphere's largest collection of Lord Horatio Nelson memorabilia, including letters, documents, paintings, and even furniture from his flagship. Nelson was based in Antigua but came on military patrol to Nevis, where he met and eventually married Frances Nisbet, who lived on a 64-acre plantation here. Half the space is devoted to often-provocative displays on island life, from leading families to vernacular architecture to the adaptation of traditional African customs, from cuisine to Carnival. The shop is an excellent source for gifts, from homemade soaps to historical guides. ⊠ *Bath Rd., Charlestown* ☎ *869/469–0408* ⊕ *www.nevis-nhcs. org* ☞ *$5, with Hamilton Museum $7* ⊘ *Weekdays 8:30–4, Sat. 10–1.*

WORTH NOTING

Bath Springs. The Caribbean's first hotel, the Bath Hotel, built by businessman John Huggins in 1778, was so popular in the 19th century that visitors, including such dignitaries as Samuel Taylor Coleridge and Prince William Henry, traveled two months by ship to "take the waters" in the property's hot thermal springs. It suffered extensive hurricane and earthquake damage over the years and long languished in disrepair. Local volunteers have cleaned up the spring and built a stone pool and steps to enter the waters; now residents and visitors enjoy the springs, which range from 104°F to 108°F, though signs still caution that you bathe at your own risk, especially if you have heart problems. The development houses the Nevis Island Administration offices; there's still talk of adding massage huts, changing rooms, a restaurant, and a cultural/history center on the original hotel property. ⊠ *Charlestown* ⊹ *Follow Main St. south from Charlestown.*

Eden Brown Estate. This government-owned mansion, built around 1740, is known as Nevis's haunted house, or haunted ruins. In 1822 a Miss Julia Huggins was to marry a fellow named Maynard. However, come wedding day, the groom and his best man killed each other in a duel. The bride-to-be became a recluse, and the mansion was closed down. Local residents claim they can feel the presence of "someone" whenever they go near the eerie old house with its shroud of weeds and

Mt. Nevis rising behind the Botanical Gardens of Nevis

wildflowers. Though memorable more for the story than the hike or ruins, it's always open, and it's free. ⊠ *East Coast Rd., between Lime Kiln and Mannings, Eden Brown Bay.*

Ft. Ashby. Overgrown with tropical vegetation, this site overlooks the place where the settlement of Jamestown fell into the sea after a tidal wave hit the coast in 1680. Needless to say, this is a favorite scuba-diving site. ⊠ *Main Rd., 1½ miles southwest of Hurricane Hill, Fort Ashby Beach.*

Fothergills Nevisian Heritage Village. On the grounds of a former sugar plantation–cotton ginnery, this ambitious, ever-expanding project traces the evolution of Nevisian social history, from the Caribs to the present, through vernacular dwellings that re-create living conditions over the centuries. The Carib chief's thatched hut includes actual relics such as weapons, calabash bowls, clay pots, and cassava squeezers. Wattle-and-daub structures reproduce slave quarters; implements on display include coal pots and sea fans (used as sieves). A postemancipation gingerbread chattel house holds patchwork quilts and flour-bag dresses. There's a typical sharecropper's garden explaining herbal medicinal folklore and blacksmith's shop. Docents are quite earnest and go on at great (mostly fascinating) length. ⊠ *Gingerland* ☎ *869/469–5521, 869/469–2033* ✉ *$3* ⏱ *Mon.–Sat. 9–4; sometimes close early, call ahead.*

Mansa's Farm. Anyone who wants a real sense of island daily life and subsistence should call Mervin "Mansa" Tyson. He'll take you past his fruit trees and herb gardens through rows of tomatoes, cucumbers, string beans, eggplant, zucchini, sweet pepper, melons, and more. Discussing the needs for at least partial organic growing practices, he passionately explains how he adapted traditional folk pesticides and describes the medicinal properties of various plants, cultivated and wild. He'll prepare a lunch using his produce, including delectable refreshing fruit drinks at his Mansa's Last Stand grocery across from the beach. Weekend barbecues are a highlight. All in all, this agritourism foray redefines food for thought. ⊠ *Cades Bay* ☏ *869/469–8520* 🍴 *Varies* ⊙ *Call for appointment.*

St. John's Figtree Church. Among the records of this church built in 1680 is a tattered, prominently displayed marriage certificate that reads "Horatio Nelson, Esquire, to Frances Nisbet, Widow, on March 11, 1787." ⊠ *Church Ground* ✛ *Located about 10 min south of Charlestown on main road.*

St. Thomas Anglican Church. The island's oldest church was built in 1643 and has been altered many times over the years. The gravestones in the old churchyard have stories to tell, and the church itself contains memorials to Nevis's early settlers. ⊠ *Main Rd. just south of Cotton Ground, Jessups.*

BEACHES

All beaches on Nevis are free to the public (the plantation inns cordon off "private" areas on Pinney's Beach for guests), but there are no changing facilities, so wear a swimsuit under your clothes.

Newcastle Beach. This broad swath of soft ecru sand shaded by coconut palms is near Nisbet Plantation, on the channel between St. Kitts and Nevis. It's popular with snorkelers, but beware stony sections and occasional strong currents that kick up seaweed and roil the sandy bottom. **Amenities:** food and drink. **Best for:** snorkeling. ⊠ *Newcastle, St. Kitts.*

Oualie Beach. South of Mosquito Bay and north of Cades and Jones Bays, this beige-sand beach lined with palms and sea grapes is where the folks at Oualie Beach Hotel can mix you a drink and fix you up with water-sports equipment. There's excellent snorkeling amid calm water and fantastic sunset views with St. Kitts silhouetted in the background. Several beach chairs and hammocks (free with lunch, $3 rental without) line the sand and the grassy "lawn" behind it. Oualie is at the island's northwest tip, approximately 3 miles (5 km) west of the airport. **Amenities:** food and drink; water sports. **Best for:** snorkeling; sunset. ⊠ *Oualie Beach, St. Kitts.*

Pinney's Beach. The island's showpiece has soft, golden sand on the calm Caribbean, lined with a magnificent grove of palm trees. The Four Seasons Resort is here, as are the plantation inns' beach clubs and casual beach bars such as Sunshine's, Chevy's, and the Lime. Beach chairs are gratis when you purchase a drink or lunch. Regrettably, the waters can be murky and filled with kelp if the weather has been inclement anywhere within a hundred miles, depending on the currents. **Amenities:** food and drink; water sports. **Best for:** swimming; walking. ⊠ *Pinney's Beach, St. Kitts.*

WHERE TO EAT

Dinner options range from intimate meals at plantation guesthouses (where the menu is often prix fixe) to casual eateries. Seafood is ubiquitous, and many places specialize in West Indian fare. The island is trying to raise its profile as a fine-dining destination by holding NICHE (Nevis International Culinary Heritage Exposition), a gastronomic festival with guest chefs and winemakers offering cooking seminars and tastings during the second half of October.

What to Wear. Dress is casual at lunch, although beach attire is unacceptable. Dress pants and sundresses are appropriate for dinner.

$$$ ECLECTIC 🍴 **Bananas.** Peripatetic English owner Gillian Smith has held jobs with Disney and Relais & Châteaux, and everything about Bananas (read lovably nuts) borrows from her wildly diverse experiences. Even the setting is delightfully deceptive: the classic stone, brick, and wood plantation greathouse nestled amid extravagant gardens was painstakingly built by Gillian herself in 2006. Her fun, shabby-chic sensibility informs every aspect of the restaurant and adjacent art gallery in a faux chattel house. The colonial look (pith helmets, steamer trunks, beamed ceiling, chandeliers dangling from a corrugated tin roof) contrasts with Turkish kilims and Moroccan lamps. The food is equally eclectic and globe-trotting, running from bourbon-glazed guava ribs to baked gnocchi in roast pumpkin-Gorgonzola or portobello sauce. Despite the improvisational ambience, there's no monkeying around with quality at Bananas. [$] *Average main: US$27* ✉ *Upper Hamilton Estate* ☎ *869/469–1891* 🌐 *www.bananasrestaurantnevis.com* ✍ *Reservations essential* ⏲ *No lunch. Closed Sun.*

$$$$ ECLECTIC 🍴 **Coconut Grove.** This thatched-palm roof, rough-timber structure sports a sensuous South Seas look, best appreciated on the deck as the sun fireballs across the Caribbean. Inside, handsome teak furnishings are animated by Buddhas, parrot-hue throw pillows, batik hangings, and gauzy curtains. The service is warm, the champagne is properly chilled, and the splendid Pacific Rim–Mediterranean fusion fare seems designed to complement the admirable, 8,000-bottle wine cellar rather than the other way around. Stephen "Chef Steve" Smith, a CIA grad and registered dietitian, introduced heart-healthier options such as curry-scented pumpkin soup with fat-free soy cream and a miraculously fiber-licious 100-calorie whole-wheat-flour–and–black-bean brownie. Nonetheless, the menu also includes such indulgences as homemade foie gras steeped in aged rum and candied cherries served with a balsamic reduction or baby Camembert baked in Calvados with cranberry confiture. Happy hour, 11 pm–midnight, often ushers in impromptu dancing, continuing the "Bali high" theme. The downstairs "Coco Beach" has an infinity pool for use, sensational St. Kitts views, affordable, creative, lighter daytime fare when open for lunch (call ahead), and live music many evenings. [$] *Average main: US$37* ✉ *Nelson's Spring, Pinney's Beach* ☎ *869/469–1020* 🌐 *www.coconutgroverestaurantnevis.com* ✍ *Reservations essential* ⏲ *Closed Aug.–Oct.*

$$$$ STEAKHOUSE Fodor's Choice ★ 🍴 **Coral Grill.** Coral Grill is Four Seasons' successful "de-formalized" conversion of its former haute Dining Room into a stunning steak house. It eschews the venue's typical men's-club decor, lightening and brightening the original's imposing space. The graceful patio, beamed cathedral ceilings, flagstone hearth, and parquet floors remain; yet an open contemporary lounge that wouldn't be out of place in Santa Monica bisects the vast interior. The grilled items shine here, from Wagyu steak that dissolves in your mouth to intensely flavored yet meltingly tender Berkridge Kurobata pork chops to gossamer lobster tails. Corn-fed USDA prime cuts are Black Angus- or Black Diamond–labeled, sourced from select Midwest farms. Meats are served with a choice of Shiraz reduction, béarnaise, or chimichurri; seafood with rum-citrus glaze, lemongrass emulsion, or hollandaise. The comprehensive wine list features some surprisingly fair prices. The hotel can arrange a unique interactive dive-and-dine experience, plunging you into the deep to pluck lobster and other marine creatures that the chefs will cook for you later. [$] *Average main: US$36* ✉ *Four Seasons Nevis, Pinney's Beach* ☎ *869/469–1111, 869/469–6238* 🌐 *www.fourseasons.com/nevis* ✍ *Reservations essential* ⏲ *No lunch.*

$$ SEAFOOD 🍴 **Double Deuce.** Mark Roberts, the former chef at Montpelier, decided to chuck the "five-star lifestyle" and now co-owns this jammed, jamming bar just off Pinney's, which lures locals with fine, fairly priced fare and creative cocktails. The overgrown shack is plastered with sailing and fishing pictures, as well as Balinese masks, fish nets, license plates, and wind chimes. Behind the cool mauve bar is a gleaming modern kitchen where Mark (and fun-loving firebrand partner Lyndeta) prepare sublime seafood he often catches himself, as well as organic beef burgers, velvety pumpkin soup, inventive pastas, and lip-smacking ribs. The "DD" is as cool and mellow as it gets. Stop by for free Wi-Fi and proper espresso, a game of pool, riotous karaoke Thursdays, Sunday bingo, or just to hang out with a Double Deuce Stinger (Lyndy's answer to Sunshine's Killer Bee punch). Kids have their own trampoline. Dinner can be arranged for parties of 6 to 10. [$] *Average main: US$20* ✉ *Pinney's Beach* ☎ *869/469–2222* 🌐 *www.doubledeucenevis.com* ✍ *Reservations essential* 💳 *No credit cards* ⏲ *Closed Mon.*

$$ SEAFOOD 🍴 **Gallipot.** Gallipot attracts locals with ultrafresh seafood at reasonable prices, marvelous views of St. Kitts across the road, and sensational sunsets. Large Sunday lunches with ample portions (musts are lobster eggs Benedict and classic roast beef and Yorkshire pudding) are a big draw. The Fosberys originally built the octagonal bar as an addition to their small beach house down the road, and their daughter and son-in-law, Tracy and Julian Rigby, provide the catch (fishnets and photos from their sportfishing championships grace the bar). Julian built a smoker (Tracy dubs it "the eyesore"), where he cures melt-in-your-mouth wahoo, kingfish, and sailfish carpaccio. Those seeking land specialties can happily tuck into the smoked duck, steak-and-kidney pie, or chicken korma curry, seasoned with herbs from Tracy's garden. [$] *Average main: US$22* ✉ *Jones Bay* ☎ *869/469–8230* ⏲ *Closed Mon.–Wed. No dinner Sun.*

$$$
ECLECTIC

⤫ **Hermitage Plantation Inn.** After cocktails in the inn's antiques-filled parlor (the knockout rum punches are legendary), dinner is served on the verandah. Many ingredients are harvested from the inn's herb garden, fruit trees, piggery, and livestock collection; the scrumptious cured meats, baked goods, preserves, and ice creams are homemade. Sumptuous dishes lovingly prepared by the incomparable (and delightfully named) chef Lovey Boddie and team might include breadfruit-cheddar soufflé, seafood quenelles in gossamer curry cream, lemongrass-lime fish cakes with ginger aioli, lobster with tomato-basil butter and conch stuffing, herb-crusted lamb with rosemary and guava, and passion fruit–ginger cheesecake. A traditional wood-burning oven yields savory items as well. Wednesday night pig roasts are an island must. The ever-growing wine list is exceptionally priced. Bon mots and bonhomie serve as prelude, intermezzo, and coda for a lively evening. $ *Average main: US$32* ⊠ *Gingerland* ☎ *869/469–3477* ⊕ *www.hermitagenevis. com* ⚏ *Reservations essential.*

$$$
CARIBBEAN

⤫ **Mango.** This sophisticated beach bar at the Four Seasons is a perennial hot spot, thanks to a gorgeous outdoor deck overlooking the illuminated water, sizzling music, fab drinks (as well as an extensive rum list), hip decor, and a farm-and-sea-to-table menu showcasing local ingredients, many grown by the staff. You can savor artfully presented, robustly flavored Caribbean classics with inventive accents such as crab-cassava-and-ginger cake with tomato chutney or and mouth- and eye-watering mango-Myers rum barbecued baby back ribs with cooling coconut coleslaw. The kitchen also delights with updated twists, such as ethereal coconut foam floating in silken, roasted-butternut-squash soup infused with ginger and cinnamon. Half the menu is gluten-free. $ *Average main: US$29* ⊠ *Four Seasons Resort, Pinney's Beach* ☎ *869/469–1111, 869/469–6238* ⊙ *No lunch.*

$$$$
ECLECTIC
Fodor's Choice
★

⤫ **Montpelier Plantation & Beach.** The Hoffman family presides over a scintillating evening, starting with canapés and cocktails in the civilized plantation great room. Dinner is served on the breezy west verandah, dubbed Restaurant 750, overlooking the lights of Charlestown and St. Kitts. Executive chef Benjamin Voisin uses the inn's organic herb gardens and fruit trees to full advantage. The changing three-course menu might present vanilla-scented parsnip soup with morel powder; signature pan-seared sea scallops with green asparagus cream, serrano ham crisp, and apple chutney; and dark chocolate tart with caramelized banana, vanilla milk shake, and almond crumble. The exemplary wine list is perfectly matched to the cuisine. The Mill Privée opens with sufficient reservations, offering a different set multicourse menu accompanied by champagne and sorbets. Torches illuminate cobblestone steps up to this theatrical sugar mill with crystal sconces, floating candles, and an antique mahogany gear wheel suspended from the ceiling. Tapas, salads, and grilled items are available at the poolside Indigo. Finish with one of the infused rums. Benjamin offers cooking classes as well as tasty souvenirs under the M logo. $ *Average main: US$60* ⊠ *Montpelier Estate* ☎ *869/469–3462* ⊕ *www.montpeliernevis.com* ⚏ *Reservations essential* ⊙ *Closed late Aug.–early Oct.*

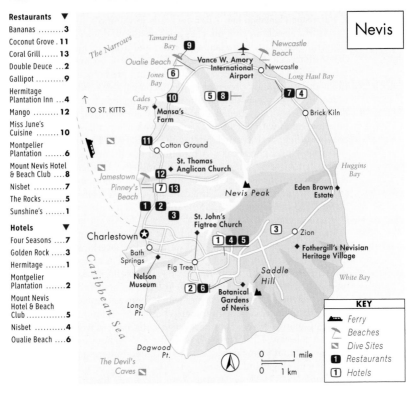

Restaurants ▼

Bananas 3
Coconut Grove . 11
Coral Grill...... 13
Double Deuce ...2
Gallipot 9
Hermitage Plantation Inn ...4
Mango 12
Miss June's Cuisine 10
Montpelier Plantation 6
Mount Nevis Hotel & Beach Club 8
Nisbet 7
The Rocks 5
Sunshine's 1

Hotels ▼

Four Seasons 7
Golden Rock 3
Hermitage 1
Montpelier Plantation 2
Mount Nevis Hotel & Beach Club..............5
Nisbet 4
Oualie Beach 6

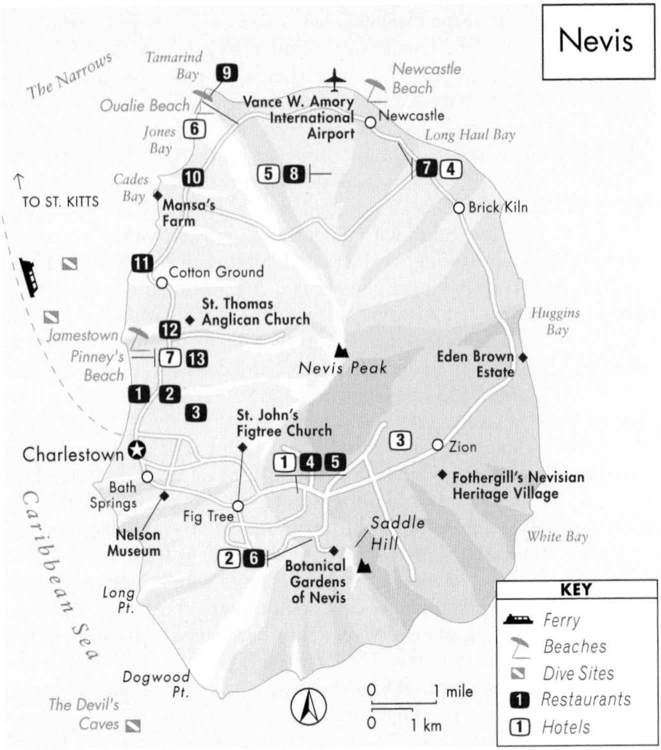

$$$ ECLECTIC 🍴 **Mount Nevis Hotel & Beach Club.** Mount Nevis's sublime open-air dining room by the pool offers a splendid view of St. Kitts. Before dinner, savor cocktails in the distinctive lounge, accented by sisal rugs, mosaic tiles, towering bamboo stalks, and flowers floating in crystal bowls. Acapulco-born chef Vicente Zaragoza and cohort Rajul Kinja deftly blend local ingredients, many grown in the organic garden, with a cornucopia of Caribbean-Continental cuisines. Sterling starters on the ever-changing menu might be crisp Brie with mango chutney or homemade conch ravioli in tomato-basil sauce. Worthy main courses include roast Cornish hen in caper-lime beurre blanc with polenta and grilled local tomatoes, or cured salmon crusted with sunflower seeds, vegetable couscous and sauce Vierge. Finish with tropical variations on classics such as ginger crème brûlée or passion fruit cheesecake. Vicente also runs the more affordable alfresco grill whose convection oven turns out marvelous baked goods in minutes. [$] *Average main: US$28* ✉ *Shaws Rd., Mt. Nevis Estates* ☎ *869/469–9373* 🌐 *www.mountnevishotel.com* ✍ *Reservations essential.*

$$$$ ECLECTIC 🍴 **Nisbet Plantation Beach Club.** The blissfully air-conditioned greathouse is an oasis of polished hardwood floors, mahogany and cherrywood furnishings, equestrian bronzes, antique hurricane lamps, wicker furnishings, and works by famed Nevisian artist Eva Wilkin. Tables on the verandah look down the palm-tree-lined fairway to the sea. The

four-course menu combines Continental, Pacific Rim, and Caribbean cuisines with local ingredients. The more mature clientele dictates less complex options from house-cured gravlax to filet mignon with chipotle butter in Zinfandel reduction. But Executive chef Antonio Piani might sneak in conch-breadfruit-and-dumpling soup, lobster stuffed with king crab–leg ragout in coconut Creole glaze, and lemon-and-vanilla mascarpone mousse with hazelnut praline. Enjoy an impressively cosmopolitan selection of cocktails or coffee with soft live music in the front bar. Witty, dapper maître d' Patterson Fleming (his cravat collection, more than 1,000 augmented by guests over the years, is enviable!) ensures a smooth, swank experience. $ *Average main: US$65* ⊠ *Newcastle* ☎ *869/469–9325* ⊕ *www.nisbetplantation.com* ⊛ *Reservations essential.*

$$$ ✕ **The Rocks at Golden Rock.** This glam eatery's tiered setting may be a
ECLECTIC genuine artistic and engineering masterpiece. Glass panels and ceilings display the night sky while reflecting patio lights. A series of cascading waterfalls, chutes, limpid pools, lily ponds, and fountains filigree the surrounding landscaped jungle with liquid silver. Strategically placed boulders resemble hulking Henry Moore sculpture; even the cut stone was painstakingly joined without mortar. Decor playfully contrasts classic and modern. A stone gazebo recalls an upside-down plantation-era copper boiler (the patio's barrel-vaulting also slyly mimics sugar equipment). Contemporary and colonial artworks from Mali and Afghanistan grace the interior. Sadly the kitchen doesn't quite match the setting's splendor or creativity. But the atmosphere more than compensates, and solid choices include jerk pork with pineapple relish or pan-roasted snapper with crispy risotto cake and red-pepper coulis. $ *Average main: US$28* ⊠ *Gingerland* ☎ *869/469–3346* ⊕ *www.goldenrocknevis.com* ⊛ *Reservations essential* ⊘ *No lunch.*

$$ ✕ **Sunshine's.** Everything about this shack overlooking (and spilling
CARIBBEAN onto) the beach is larger than life, including the Rasta man Llewelyn "Sunshine" Caines himself. Flags and license plates from around the world complement the international patrons (including an occasional movie or sports star wandering down from the Four Seasons). Picnic tables are splashed with bright sunrise-to-sunset colors; even the palm trees are painted, though "it gone upscaled," as locals say, with VIP cabanas. Fishermen cruise up with their catch—you might savor lobster rolls or snapper creole. Don't miss the lethal house specialty, Killer Bee rum punch. As Sunshine boasts, "One and you're stung, two, you're stunned, three, it's a knockout." $ *Average main: US$18* ⊠ *Pinney's Beach* ☎ *869/469–5817* ⊕ *www.sunshinesnevis.com.*

WHERE TO STAY

Many lodgings are in restored manor or plantation houses scattered throughout the island's five parishes (counties). The owners often live at these inns, and it's easy to feel as if you've been personally invited down for a visit. Before dinner you may find yourself in the drawing room having a cocktail and conversing with the family, other guests, or visitors who have come for a meal. Meal plans for most inns include breakfast and dinner (plus afternoon tea) and offer a free

Four Seasons Resort Nevis

shuttle service to their "private" stretch of beach. If you require TVs and air-conditioning, you're better off staying at hotels and simply dining with the engaging inn owners. Two major (by Nevisian standards) condo developments, with at least Phase 1 completed by late 2014, will nearly double the island's room inventory. Hamilton Beach Villas & Spa opened its first fully equipped condos on Cotton Ground Beach in 2013; the 10-building project will comprise a total of 79 self-catering units, as well as a spa, gym, pool, and tennis courts upon expected completion in 2014. The even more ambitious Tamarind Cove broke ground in 2012; plans call for six buildings housing 91 units, plus a pool, clubhouse with restaurant and shopping arcade, seafront boardwalk with more retail and dining, and a 120-berth marina. Other small upscale compounds are in various stages of development, including the overhauled Cliffdwellers at Tamarind Bay and the Zenith Beach houses, connected with the delightful Chrishi Beach Club on Cades Bay.

$$$$ Four Seasons Resort Nevis. This beachfront beauty impeccably com-
RESORT   bines world-class elegance with West Indian hospitality while scru-
FAMILY   pulously maintaining and upgrading facilities. **Pros:** luxury without
Fodor'sChoice   attitude; superlative service; marvelous food; dazzling golf and spa;
★   **Cons:** pricey; sometimes overrun by conventions and incentive groups
(off-season mainly), berms added as secondary defense against storm
surges impede some beachfront room views. $ *Rooms from: US$745*
✉ *Pinney's Beach* 📠 *869/469–1111, 869/469–6238, 800/332–3442 in*
U.S., 800/268–6282 in Canada ⊕ *www.fourseasons.com/nevis* 🛏 *179*
rooms, 17 suites, 61 villas ⊙ *No meals.*

$$ HOTEL **Golden Rock Plantation Inn.** Acclaimed artists Brice Marden and wife Helen Harrington have imparted a chic, modernist sensibility to this 18th-century estate property while respecting its storied past. **Pros:** ecofriendly; arty crowd; glorious grounds; free Wi-Fi. **Cons:** no actual beach though there are two beach clubs; lack of air-conditioning can be a problem on still days. [$] *Rooms from: US$298* ✉ *Gingerland* ☎ *869/469–3346* 🌐 *www.goldenrocknevis.com, www.golden-rock.com* 🛏 *16 rooms, 1 suite* ⏲ *Closed mid-Aug.–mid-Oct.* 🍴 *Breakfast.*

$$ HOTEL Fodor's Choice ★ **Hermitage Plantation Inn.** A snug 1670 greathouse—reputedly the Caribbean's oldest surviving wooden building—forms the heart of this breeze-swept hillside hideaway. **Pros:** wonderful sense of history; delightful owners and clientele; delicious food. **Cons:** long drive to beach; hillside setting difficult for physically challenged to negotiate. [$] *Rooms from: US$255* ✉ *Hermitage Rd., Gingerland* ☎ *869/469–3477, 800/682–4025* 🌐 *www.hermitagenevis.com* 🛏 *8 rooms, 8 cottages, 1 house* 🍴 *Multiple meal plans.*

$$$$ RESORT Fodor's Choice ★ **Montpelier Plantation & Beach.** This Nevisian beauty epitomizes understated elegance and graciously updated plantation living. **Pros:** impeccable service and attention to detail; lovely cuisine; exquisite gardens; trendily minimalist decor; complimentary Wi-Fi. **Cons:** some may find it a little stuffy; no beach on-site. [$] *Rooms from: US$405* ✉ *Montpelier Estate* ☎ *869/469–3462, 800/735–2478* 🌐 *www.montpeliernevis.com* 🛏 *17 rooms, 2 1-bedroom villas, 1 2-bedroom villa* ⏲ *Closed mid-Aug.–mid-Oct.* 🍴 *Multiple meal plans.*

$$$ HOTEL **Mount Nevis Hotel & Beach Club.** The personable, attentive Meguid family blends the intimacy of the plantation inns, contemporary amenities of the Four Seasons, and typical Nevisian warmth in this hilltop aerie. **Pros:** friendly staff; fantastic views; free Wi-Fi; complimentary cell phone (pay for card). **Cons:** lacks beach; long drive to many island activities; occasional plane noise. [$] *Rooms from: US$350* ✉ *Shaws Rd., Mt. Nevis* ☎ *869/469–9373, 800/756–3847* 🌐 *www.mountnevishotel.com* 🛏 *8 rooms, 8 junior suites, 16 suites, 10 villas* 🍴 *Breakfast.*

$$$$ RESORT Fodor's Choice ★ **Nisbet Plantation Beach Club.** At this beachfront plantation inn, pale yellow cottages face a regal, palm-lined grass avenue that sweeps to a lovely champagne-hue beach. **Pros:** glorious setting; the definition of casual elegance; environmentally conscious practices; plentiful recreational options such as mountain bikes, kayaks, even Vespa scooters; extras such as free use of digital video recorders and handheld GPS locators. **Cons:** long drive to most activities on island; airplanes occasionally whoosh by; food is variable; occasionally dodgy Wi-Fi signal. [$] *Rooms from: US$712* ✉ *Newcastle* ☎ *869/469–9325, 800/742–6008* 🌐 *www.nisbetplantation.com* 🛏 *36 rooms* 🍴 *Some meals.*

$$ RESORT **Oualie Beach Hotel.** These creole-style gingerbread cottages daubed in cotton-candy colors sit just steps a beach overlooking St. Kitts and are carefully staggered to ensure sea views from every room. **Pros:** fantastic water-sports operations; affordable (especially with recreational packages); appealing beach; Green Globe–certified. **Cons:** showing some wear; not ideal for less active types. [$] *Rooms from: US$250* ✉ *Oualie Beach* ☎ *869/469–9735* 🌐 *www.oualiebeach.com* 🛏 *32 rooms* 🍴 *Multiple meal plans.*

NIGHTLIFE

In season it's usually easy to find a local calypso singer or a steel or string band performing at one of the hotels, notably the Four Seasons and Oualie Beach (which also features string musicians on homemade instruments Tuesday evening), as well as at the Pinney's bars. Scan the posters plastered on doorways announcing informal jump-ups. Though Nevis lacks high-tech discos, many restaurants and bars have live bands or DJs on weekends.

FAMILY **Chrishi Beach Club.** Though more a daytime hangout (especially Sunday when Nevisians descend on the lovely beach with their families), Chrishi Beach Club remains happening through sunset thanks to vivacious Norwegian expats Hedda and Christian "Chrishi" Wienpahl. You can sprawl on comfy chaises and thatched, white, beach waterbeds (exemplifying the couple's wit and whimsy). Enjoy the righteous lounge mix (and mixology) and the glorious St. Kitts views, and what Hedda calls "European café-style" food (salads, pizzas, sandwiches like Brie with sun-dried tomatoes and cranberries). Kids have their own club with fresh-fruit smoothies, DJs spin on Sexy Saturday Nights, and Hedda's fun funky HWD jewelry line (incorporating leather, coins, found objects) is on sale. Their new Zenith Resort, an adjacent villa development, has some spectacular units. ⊠ *Next to Sea Bridge and Mansa's, Cades Bay* ☎ *869/662–3958, 869/662–3959* ⊕ *www.chrishibeachclub.com.*

Water Department Barbecue. The Water Department Barbecue is the informal name for a lively Friday-night jump-up that's run by two fellows from the local water department. Friday afternoons the tents go up and the grills are fired. Cars line the streets and the guys dish up fabulous barbecue ribs and chicken—as certain customers lobby to get their water pressure adjusted. It's a classic Caribbean scene. ⊠ *Pump Rd., Charlestown.*

SHOPPING

CLOTHING

Most hotels have their own boutiques.

Island Fever. The island's classiest shop carries an excellent selection of everything from bathing suits and dresses to straw bags and jewelry. ⊠ *Main St., Charlestown* ☎ *869/469–0867.*

HANDICRAFTS

CraftHouse. This marvelous source for local specialties, from vetiver mats to leather moccasins, also has a smaller branch in the Cotton Ginnery. ⊠ *Pinney's Rd., Charlestown* ☎ *869/469–5505.*

Nevis Handicraft Co-op Society. This shop across from the tourist office offers works by local artisans (clothing, ceramic ware, woven goods) and locally produced honey, hot sauces, and jellies (try the guava and soursop). ⊠ *Main St., Charlestown* ☎ *869/469–1746.*

Newcastle Pottery. This cooperative has continued the age-old tradition of hand-built red-clay pottery fired over burning coconut husks. It's possible to watch the potters and purchase wares at their small Newcastle factory. ⊠ *Main Rd., Newcastle* ☎ *869/469–9746.*

Philatelic Bureau. St. Kitts and Nevis are famous for their decorative, and sometimes valuable, stamps. Collectors will find real beauties here including the butterfly, hummingbird, and marine-life series. ⊠ *Cotton Ginnery, opposite tourist office, Charlestown* ☎ *869/469–0617.*

SPORTS AND ACTIVITIES

BIKING

Windsurfing Nevis/Wheel World. This shop offers mountain-bike rentals, apparel, and specially tailored tours on Gary Fisher, Trek, Hybrid, and MTB bikes. The tours ($55–$75), led by Winston Crooke, a master windsurfer and competitive bike racer, encompass lush rain forest, majestic ruins, and spectacular views. Costs vary according to itinerary and ability level but are aimed generally at experienced riders. Winston and his team delight in sharing local knowledge, from history to culture. For those just renting (rates from $25 daily, $150 weekly), Winston determines your performance level and suggest appropriate routes. ⊠ *Oualie Beach* ☎ *869/469–9682* ⊕ *www.bikenevis.com.*

DIVING AND SNORKELING

The **Devil's Caves** make up a series of grottoes where divers can navigate tunnels, canyons, and underwater hot springs while viewing lobsters, sea fans, sponges, squirrelfish, and more. The village of **Jamestown**, which washed into the sea around Ft. Ashby, just south of Cades Bay, makes for superior snorkeling and diving. Reef-protected Pinney's Beach offers especially good snorkeling. Single-tank dives are usually $80, two-tank dives $100; packages provide deep discounts.

FAMILY **Scuba Safaris.** This PADI five-star facility and NASDS Examining Station is staffed by experienced dive masters who offer everything from a resort course to full certification to Nitrox. Their equipment is always state-of-the-art, including underwater scooters. It also provides a snorkeling learning experience that enables you not only to see but to listen to sea life, including whales and dolphins, as well as an exhilarating underwater scooter safari, night dives, and kids' bubblemakers. ⊠ *Oualie Beach* ☎ *869/469–9518* ⊕ *www.scubanevis.com.*

FISHING

Fishing here focuses on kingfish, wahoo, grouper, tuna, and yellowtail snapper, with marlin occasionally spotted. The best areas are Monkey Shoals and around Redonda. Charters cost approximately $450–$500 per half day, $850–$1,000 per full day, and usually include an open bar.

Deep Venture. Run by fisherman–chef Matt Lloyd, Deep Venture does day-fishing charters (he keeps the catch), providing a real insight into both commercial fishing and the Caribbean kitchen. ⊠ *Oualie Beach* ☎ *869/469–5110.*

Nevis Water Sports. Nevis Water Sports offers sportfishing aboard the Bertram 31-foot *Sea Brat* under the supervision of tournament-winning captain Ian Gonzaley. The company helps organize the annual Nevis Yacht Club Sports Fishing Tournament, which reels in competitors from all over the Caribbean. ⊠ *Oualie Beach* ☎ *869/469–9060* ⊕ *www. fishnevis.com.*

GOLF

Fodor's Choice
★

Four Seasons Golf Course. The Robert Trent Jones Jr.–designed Four Seasons Golf Course is beautiful and impeccably maintained. The front 9 holes are fairly flat until Hole 8, which climbs uphill after your tee shot. Most of the truly stunning views are along the back 9. The signature hole is the 15th, a 660-yard monster that encompasses a deep ravine; other holes include bridges, steep drops, rolling pitches, extremely tight and unforgiving fairways, sugar-mill ruins, and fierce doglegs. Attentive attendants canvas the course with beverage buggies, handing out chilled, peppermint-scented towels and preordered Cubanos that help test the wind. There are huge kids', twilight, and off-season discounts. ⊠ *Four Seasons Resort Nevis, Pinney's Beach* ☏ *869/469–1111* ⊕ *www.fourseasons.com/nevis* ⅃ *18 holes, 6766 yards, par 72* ⊠ *$225 for hotel guests, $235 for nonguests.*

GUIDED TOURS

Fitzroy "Teach" Williams. Guide Fitzroy "Teach" Williams is the former president of the taxi association—even older cabbies call him "the Dean." He's an excellent tour guide. ☏ *869/469–1140.*

TC's Island Tours. TC, a Yorkshire lass who used to drive a double-decker bus in England and has been married to a Nevisian for more than a decade, offers entertaining explorations via TC's Island Tours. ☏ *869/469–2911.*

HIKING

The center of the island is Nevis Peak—also known as Mt. Nevis—which soars 3,232 feet and is flanked by Hurricane Hill on the north and Saddle Hill on the south. If you plan to scale Nevis Peak, a day-long affair, it's highly recommended that you go with a guide. Your hotel can arrange it (and a picnic lunch) for you. The 9-mile (15-km) **Upper Round Road Trail** was constructed in the late 1600s and cleared and restored by the Nevis Historical and Conservation Society. It connects the Golden Rock Plantation Inn, on the east side of the island, with Nisbet Plantation Beach Club, on the northern tip. The trail encompasses numerous vegetation zones, including pristine rain forest, and impressive plantation ruins. The original cobblestones, walls, and ruins are still evident in many places.

Peak Heaven at Herbert Heights. This tour company is run by the Herbert family, who lead four-hour nature hikes up through the rain forest to panoramic Herbert Heights, where you drink in fresh local juices and views of Montserrat; the powerful telescope, donated by Greenpeace, makes you feel as if you're staring right into that island's simmering volcano (or staring down migratory whales). The trail formed part of an escape route for runaway slaves, and you can also inspect recent archaeological excavations providing insight into the indigenous peoples. Shorter bush tea walks and monkey excursions are available. The Herberts painstakingly reconstructed thatched cottages that offer a glimpse of village life a century ago, dubbed Peak Heaven, at Nelson's Lookout. These include a small, poignant, history museum; local crafts shop; gallery; and massage room. The solar-powered Coal Pot restaurant offers heaping helpings of affordable island fare (try

CLOSE UP

Nevis's Day at the Races

21

One of the Caribbean's most festive, endearingly idiosyncratic events is the Nevis Turf and Jockey Club's Day at the Races, held 9 to 12 times a year on the wild and windswept Indian Castle course. I first experienced the event in the mid-1990s, when I met club president Richard "Lupi" Lupinacci, owner of the Hermitage Plantation Inn. Before even introducing himself, Richard sized me up in the driveway: "You look about the right size for a jockey. How's your seat?" His equally effervescent wife, Maureen, then interceded, "Darling, if you loathe horses, don't worry. In fact, Lupi and I have an agreement about the Jerk and Turkey Club. I get major jewels for every animal he buys."

Since my riding skills were rusty, it was decided that I should be a judge (despite questionable vision, even with glasses). "If it's really by a nose, someone will disagree with you either way," I was reassured. The next day presented a quintessential Caribbean scene. Although a serious cadre of aficionados (including the German consul) talked turf, the rest of the island seemed more interested in liming and enjoying lively music. Local ladies dished out heavenly barbecued chicken and devilish gossip. Sheep and cattle unconcernedly ambled across the course. But when real horses thundered around the oval, the wooden stands groaned under the weight of cheering crowds, and bookies hand-calculated the payouts.

The irregularly scheduled races continue, albeit now on a properly sodded track, as does the equine hospitality.

Hermitage Stables. Here you can opt for everything from horseback riding to jaunts in hand-carved mahogany carriages. ⌧ *Hermitage Plantation Inn, Hermitage Rd., Gingerland* ☎ *869/469–3477* ⊕ *www.hermitagenevis.com.*

Nevis Equestrian Centre. The Nevis Equestrian Centre offers leisurely beach rides as well as more demanding canters through the lush hills, starting at $55. ⌧ *Clifton Estate, Cotton Ground, Pinney's Beach* ☎ *869/662-9118* ⊕ *www.nevishorseback.com.*

—Jordan Simon

any soup, the thyme-seared snapper, and scrumptious homemade ice creams) alongside the splendid vistas. There's even a small playground at the entrance. Hike prices start at $25. ☎ 869/469–2856, 869/665–6926 ⊕ *www.peakheavennevis.com.*

Sunrise Tours. Run by Lynell and Earla Liburd, Sunrise Tours offers a range of hiking trips, but their most popular is Devil's Copper, a rock configuration full of ghostly legends. Local people gave it its name because at one time the water was hot—a volcanic thermal stream. The area features pristine waterfalls and splendid bird-watching. They also do a Nevis village walk, a Hamilton Estate Walk, a Charlestown tour, an Amerindian walk along the wild southeast Atlantic coast, and trips to the rain forest and Nevis Peak. They love highlighting Nevisian heritage, explaining time-honored cooking techniques, the many uses of dried grasses, and medicinal plants. Hikes range from $25 to $40 per person, and you receive a certificate of achievement. ☎ 869/469–2758 ⊕ *www.nevisnaturetours.com.*

WINDSURFING

Windsurfing Nevis. Waters are generally calm and northeasterly winds steady yet gentle, making Nevis an excellent spot for beginners and intermediates. Windsurfing Nevis offers top-notch instructors (Winston Crooke is one of the best in the islands) and equipment for $30 per hour. Beginners get equipment and two-hour instruction for $60. Groups are kept small (eight maximum), and the equipment is state-of-the-art from Mistral, North, and Tushingham. It also offers kayak rentals and tours along the coast, stopping at otherwise inaccessible beaches. ⊠ *Oualie Beach* ☎ 869/469–9682.

ST. LUCIA

WELCOME TO ST. LUCIA

THE CARIBBEAN'S TWIN PEAKS

St. Lucia, 27 miles (43.5 km) by 14 miles (22.5 km), is a volcanic island covered to a large extent by lush rain forest, much of which is protected as a national park. The most notable geological features are the Pitons, some 2,600-foot-high twin peaks designated a UNESCO World Heritage Site in 2004.

KEY	
⟋	Beaches
◨	Dive Sites
⛴	Ferry
⛴	Cruise Ship Terminal
1	Restaurants
1	Hotels
🌴	Rain Forest

Explorers, pirates, soldiers, sugar planters, and coal miners have made their mark on this lovely landfall, and the lush tropical peaks known as the Pitons (Gros and Petit) have witnessed them all. Today's visitors come to snorkel and scuba dive in St. Lucia's calm cobalt-blue waters, sun themselves on its multihued beaches, and experience nature at its finest.

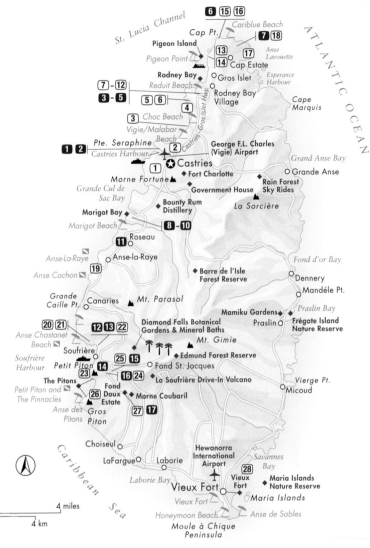

TOP REASONS TO VISIT ST. LUCIA

1 The Beauty: Magnificent, lush scenery makes St. Lucia one of the most beautiful Caribbean islands.

2 The Romance: A popular honeymoon spot, St. Lucia has abundant romantic retreats.

3 Indulgent Accommodations: Sybaritic lodging options include an all-inclusive spa resort, a posh sanctuary sandwiched between

a mountain and the beach, and two resorts with prime locations between the Pitons.

4 St. Lucia Jazz: Performers and fans come from all over the world for this annual music festival.

5 The Welcome: The friendly St. Lucians love sharing their island and their cultural heritage with visitors.

Updated by
Jane E. Zarem

A verdant, mountainous island halfway between Martinique and St. Vincent, St. Lucia has evolved into one of the Caribbean's most popular vacation destinations—particularly for honeymooners and other romantics enticed by the island's striking natural beauty, its many splendid resorts and appealing inns, and its welcoming atmosphere.

The capital city of Castries and nearby villages in the northwest are home to 40% of the 160,000 St. Lucians. This area, along with Rodney Bay Village farther north, Marigot Bay just south of the capital, and Soufrière on the southwestern coast are the destinations of most vacationers. In the central and southwestern parts of the island dense rain forest, jungle-covered mountains, and vast banana plantations dominate the landscape. A tortuous road follows most of the coastline, bisecting small villages, cutting through mountains, and passing by fertile valleys. Petit Piton and Gros Piton, the island's unusual twin peaks that anchor the southwestern coast and rise out of the sea to more than 2,600 feet, are familiar landmarks for sailors and aviators alike. Divers are attracted to the reefs in the National Marine Reserve between the Pitons and extending north past Soufrière, which was the capital during French colonial times. Most of the natural tourist attractions are in this area, along with several fine resorts and inns.

The pirate François Le Clerc, nicknamed Jambe de Bois (Wooden Leg) for obvious reasons, was the first European "settler" in St. Lucia. In the late 16th century Le Clerc holed up on Pigeon Island, just off the island's northernmost point, and used it as a staging ground for attacking passing ships. Now, Pigeon Island is a national park, connected by a causeway to the mainland; and Sandals Grande St. Lucian Spa & Beach Resort, one of the largest resorts in St. Lucia, and The Landings, a luxury villa community, sprawl along that causeway.

Like most of its Caribbean neighbors, St. Lucia was first inhabited by Arawaks and then the Carib people. British settlers attempted to colonize the island twice in the early 1600s, but it wasn't until 1651, after the French West India Company suppressed the local Caribs,

LOGISTICS

Getting to St. Lucia: St. Lucia's primary gateway is Hewanorra International Airport (UVF) in Vieux Fort, on the island's southern tip. Regional airlines fly into George F.L. Charles Airport (SLU) in Castries, commonly called Vigie Airport, which is more convenient to resorts in the north. The 40-mile (64 km) drive between Hewanorra and resorts in the north takes about 90 minutes; the trip between Hewanorra and Soufrière takes about 45 minutes.

Hassle Factor: Medium to high due to the long drive from Hewanorra International Airport.

On the Ground: Taxis are available at both airports, although transfers may be included in your travel package. It's an expensive ride to the north from Hewanorra—$80–$90 for up to four passengers—and $75–$80 to Soufrière. A helicopter shuttle cuts the transfer time to about 10 minutes, but the cost doubles.

Getting Around the Island: A car is more important if you are staying at a small inn or hotel away from the beach. If you're staying at an all-inclusive beach resort and you don't plan to leave for meals, taxis may be the better bet.

that Europeans gained a foothold. For 150 years, battles between the French and the British over possession of the island were frequent, with a dizzying 14 changes in power before the British finally took possession in 1814. The Europeans established sugar plantations, using slaves from West Africa to work the fields. By 1838, when the slaves were emancipated, more than 90% of the population was of African descent—roughly the same proportion as today's 170,000 St. Lucians.

On February 22, 1979, St. Lucia became an independent state within the British Commonwealth of Nations, with a resident governor-general appointed by the queen. Still, the island appears to have retained more relics of French influence—notably the island's patois, cuisine, village names, and surnames—than of the British. Most likely, that's because the British contribution primarily involved the English language, the educational and legal systems, and the political structure, whereas the French culture historically had more influence on the arts—culinary, dance, and music.

PLANNING

WHEN TO GO
The high season runs from mid-December through mid-April and during the annual St. Lucia Jazz and Carnival events; at other times of the year, hotel rates may be significantly cheaper. December and January are the coolest months, and June through August are the hottest. Substantial rain (more than just a tropical spritz) is more likely from June through November.

GETTING HERE AND AROUND

AIR TRAVEL

American Airlines flies nonstop from Miami, with connecting service from New York and other major cities. Delta flies nonstop from Atlanta. JetBlue flies nonstop from New York (JFK). US Airways flies nonstop from Philadelphia and Charlotte. Air Caraïbes flies from Guadeloupe and Martinique; LIAT flies from several neighboring islands.

Airline Contacts Air Caraïbes ☎ *758/453–0357* ⊕ *www.aircaraibes-usa.com.* **American Airlines** ☎ *800/744–0006, 758/459–6500* ⊕ *www.aa.com.* **Delta** ☎ *758/454–5594* ⊕ *www.delta.com.* **JetBlue** ☎ *758/454–6355* ⊕ *www.jetblue. com.* **LIAT** ☎ *888/844–5428, 758/452–2348* ⊕ *www.liatairline.com.* **US Airways** ☎ *800/622–1015* ⊕ *www.usairways.com.*

Airports George F.L. Charles Airport (*SLU*). ⊠ *Vigie, Castries* ☎ *758/452–1156.* **Hewanorra International Airport** (*UVF*). ⊠ *Vieux Fort* ☎ *758/454–6355.*

Air Transfers St. Lucia Helicopters ☎ *758/453–6950* ⊕ *www.stluciahelicopters.com.*

BOAT AND FERRY TRAVEL

When cruise ships are in port in Castries, a water taxi shuttles back and forth between Pointe Seraphine (on the north side of the harbor) and La Place Carenage (on the south side) for $2 per person each way. L'Express des Iles travels between St. Lucia and Martinique, Dominica, and Guadeloupe.

Contacts L'Express des Iles ☎ *758/456–5000* ⊕ *www.express-des-iles.com.*

BUS TRAVEL

Privately owned and operated minivans constitute St. Lucia's bus system, an inexpensive and efficient means of transportation used primarily by local people. Buses have green number plates beginning with the letter "M." They are a good way to travel between Castries and the Rodney Bay area; the fare is EC$2 (ideally payable in local currency). You can also travel from Castries to Soufrière (two-plus hours, EC$10), but that is definitely an arduous ride. Wait at a marked stop and hail the passing minivan. Let the conductor or driver know where you need to go, and he'll stop at the appropriate place.

CAR TRAVEL

Roads in St. Lucia are winding and mountainous, except north of Castries, making driving a challenge for timid or apprehensive drivers and exhausting for everyone else. You drive on the left, British-style. Seat belts are required, and speed limits are enforced, especially in Castries.

Car Rentals To rent a car you must be at least 25 years old and provide a valid driver's license and a credit card. If you don't have an international driver's license, you must buy a temporary St. Lucia driving permit for $20 (EC$54), which is valid for three months, or a daily permit for $12 (EC$32) at the car-rental office or the immigration office at either airport. Car-rental rates are usually quoted in U.S. dollars and range from $45 to $80 per day or $300 to $450 per week.

Car-Rental Contacts **Avis** ⊠ *Vide Bouteille, Castries* ☎ *758/452–2700* ⊕ *www. avisstlucia.com* ⊠ *Hewanorra International Airport, Vieux Fort* ☎ *758/454–6325* ⊠ *George F. L. Charles Airport, Vigie* ☎ *758/452–2046.* **Cool Breeze Jeep/Car Rental** ⊠ *Soufrière* ☎ *758/459–7729* ⊕ *www.coolbreezecarrental.com.* **Cost-Less Rent-a-Car & Internet Café** ⊠ *Harmony Suites, Rodney Bay Village, Gros Islet* ☎ *758/450–3416* ⊕ *www.costless-rentacar.com.* **Courtesy Car Rental** ⊠ *Bois d'Orange, Gros Islet* ☎ *758/452–8140* ⊕ *www.courtesycarrentals.com.*

22

TAXI TRAVEL

Fully licensed taxis have number plates beginning with "TX." They are unmetered, although fares are fairly standard. Sample fares for up to four passengers are: Castries to Rodney Bay, $25; Rodney Bay to Cap Estate, $12; Castries to Cap Estate, $25; Castries to Marigot Bay, $30; Castries to Anse La Raye, $40; Castries to Soufrière, $80–$100; Castries to Vieux Forte, $80; and Soufrière to Vieux Forte, $75–$80. Always ask the driver to quote the price *before* you get in, and be sure that you both understand whether it's quoted in EC or U.S. dollars. Drivers are generally careful, knowledgeable, and courteous.

ESSENTIALS

Banks and Exchange Services The official currency is the Eastern Caribbean dollar (EC$), but U.S. dollars (not coins) are accepted nearly everywhere—although you may get your change in local currency. Major credit cards and traveler's checks are also widely accepted. ATMs dispense only local currency. Major banks on the island include Bank of St. Lucia, Bank of Nova Scotia (Scotiabank), FirstCaribbean International Bank, and Royal Bank of Canada.

Electricity The electric current on St. Lucia is 220 volts, 50 cycles, with a square, three-pin plug (U.K. standard). You'll need a transformer to convert voltage and a plug adapter to use most North American appliances; dual-voltage computer and phone chargers or other appliances will still need a plug adapter, which you can often borrow from the hotel. More and more hotels and resorts have added 110-volt outlets for general use but sometimes only for electric razors. Many hotels and resorts also provide iPod docking stations.

Emergency Services Ambulance and Fire ☎ *911.* **Police** ☎ *999.*

Passport Requirements U.S. and Canadian citizens must have a valid passport to enter St. Lucia and a return or ongoing ticket.

Phones The area code for St. Lucia is 758. You can make direct-dial overseas and interisland calls from St. Lucia, and the connections are excellent. You can charge an overseas call to a major credit card with no surcharge; from public phones and many hotels, dial 811 to charge the call to your credit card. Some hotels charge a small fee (usually about EC$1) for local calls. Many retail outlets sell phone cards to use for either local or international calls from any touch-tone telephone (including pay phones) in St. Lucia. Cell phones may be rented from LIME or Digicel offices in Castries, Gablewoods Mall, Bay Walk Mall in Rodney Bay Village, and Vieux Fort, or you can purchase a prepaid SIM card to use in your own (unlocked) cell phone in those same locations. The prepaid cards may be topped up at hundreds of business locations around the island.

Safety Although crime isn't a significant problem, take the same precautions that you would at home—lock your door, secure your valuables, and don't carry too much money or flaunt expensive jewelry on the street or at the beach.

Taxes A government V.A.T. (value-added tax) of 9.5% is added to all hotel and restaurant bills. Most restaurants and some hotels also add a service charge of 10% in lieu of tipping.

ACCOMMODATIONS

Nearly all St. Lucia's resorts and small inns face unspoiled beaches or are hidden away on secluded coves or tucked into forested hillsides in three locations along the calm Caribbean (western) coast. They're in the greater Castries area between Marigot Bay, a few miles south of the city, and Labrelotte Bay in the north; in and around Rodney Bay Village and north to Cap Estate; and in and around Soufrière on the southwest coast near the Pitons. There's only one resort in Vieux Fort, near Hewanorra. The advantage of being in the north is that you have access to a wider range of restaurants and nightlife; in the south, you may be limited to your hotel's offerings and a few other restaurants—albeit some of the best—in and around Soufrière.

HOTEL AND RESTAURANT PRICES

Prices in the restaurant reviews are the average cost of a main course at dinner or, if dinner is not served, at lunch; taxes and service charges are generally included. Prices in the hotel reviews are the lowest cost of a standard double room in high season, excluding taxes, service charges, and meal plans (except at all-inclusives). Prices for rentals are the lowest per-night cost for a one-bedroom unit in high season.

For expanded lodging reviews and current deals, visit Fodors.com.

VISITOR INFORMATION

Contacts St. Lucia Tourist Board ☎ 212/867–2950 in New York, 800/456–3984 ⊕ www.saintlucianow.com.

WEDDINGS

Wedding licenses cost $125 with a required three-day waiting period or $200 with no waiting period, plus $60 for the associated registrar and certificate fees. Some resorts offer free weddings when combined with a honeymoon stay.

EXPLORING

Except for a small area in the extreme northeast, one main highway circles all of St. Lucia. The road snakes along the coast, cuts across mountains, makes hairpin turns and sheer drops, and reaches dizzying heights. It takes at least four hours to drive the whole loop. Even at a leisurely pace with frequent sightseeing stops, and whether you're driving or being driven, the curvy roads make it a tiring drive in a single outing.

The West Coast Road between Castries and Soufrière (a 1½-hour journey) has steep hills and sharp turns, but it's well marked and incredibly scenic. South of Castries, the road tunnels through Morne Fortune, skirts the island's largest banana plantation (more than 127 varieties

CLOSE UP

Embracing Kwéyòl

English is St. Lucia's official language, but most St. Lucians speak Kwéyòl—a French-based Creole language—and often use it for informal conversations among themselves. Primarily a spoken language, Kwéyòl in its written version doesn't look at all like French; pronounce the words phonetically, though—*entenasyonnal* (international), for example, or the word *Kwéyòl* (Creole) itself—and you indeed sound as if you're speaking French.

Pretty much the same version of the Creole language, or patois, is spoken in the nearby island of Dominica. Otherwise, the St. Lucian Kwéyòl is quite different from that spoken in other Caribbean islands that have a French and African heritage, such as Haiti, Guadeloupe, and Martinique—or elsewhere, such as Mauritius,

Madagascar, and the state of Louisiana. The Kwéyòl spoken in St. Lucia and Dominica is mostly unintelligible to people from those other locations—and vice versa.

St. Lucia embraces its Creole heritage by devoting the month of October each year to celebrations that preserve and promote Creole culture, language, and traditions. Events and performances highlight Creole music, food, dance, theater, native costumes, church services, traditional games, folklore, native medicine—a little bit of everything, or *tout bagay*, as you say in Kwéyòl.

Creole Heritage Month culminates at the end of October with all-day events and activities on Jounen Kwéyòl Entenasyonnal, or International Creole Day, which is recognized by all countries that speak a version of Creole.

of bananas, called "figs" in this part of the Caribbean, grow on the island), and passes through tiny fishing villages. Just north of Soufrière the road negotiates the island's fruit basket, where most of the mangoes, breadfruit, tomatoes, limes, and oranges are grown. In the mountainous region that forms a backdrop for Soufrière, you will notice 3,118-foot Mt. Gimie (pronounced Jimmy), St. Lucia's highest peak. Approaching Soufrière, you'll have spectacular views of the Pitons; the spume of smoke wafting out of the thickly forested mountainside just east of Soufrière emanates from the so-called "drive-in" volcano.

The landscape changes dramatically between the Pitons and Vieux Fort on the island's southeastern tip. Along the South Coast Road traveling southeasterly from Soufrière, the terrain starts as steep mountainside with dense vegetation, progresses to undulating hills, and finally becomes rather flat and comparatively arid. Anyone arriving at Hewanorra International Airport, which is in Vieux Fort, and staying at a resort near Soufrière will travel along this route, a journey of about 45 minutes each way.

From Vieux Fort north to Castries, a 1½-hour drive, the East Coast Road twists through Micoud, Dennery, and other coastal villages. It then winds up, down, and around mountains, crosses Barre de l'Isle Ridge, and slices through the rain forest. Much of the scenery is breathtaking. The Atlantic Ocean pounds against rocky cliffs, and acres and acres of bananas and coconut palms blanket the hillsides. If you arrive at Hewanorra and stay at a resort near Castries or Rodney Bay, you'll travel along the East Coast Road.

CASTRIES AND THE NORTH

Castries, the capital city, and the area north and just south of it are the island's most developed areas. The roads are mostly flat, straight, and easy to navigate. The beaches are some of the island's best. Rodney Bay Marina and most of the resorts, restaurants, and nightspots are north of Castries. Pigeon Island, one of the important historical sites, is at the island's northwestern tip. About 15 minutes south of Castries lies lovely Marigot Bay, which is both a yacht haven and a lovely destination for landlubbers.

TOP ATTRACTIONS

Castries. The capital, a busy commercial city of about 65,000 people, wraps around a sheltered bay. Morne Fortune rises sharply to the south of town, creating a dramatic green backdrop. The charm of Castries lies in its liveliness rather than its architecture, since four fires that occurred between 1796 and 1948 destroyed most of the colonial buildings. Freighters (exporting bananas, coconut, cocoa, mace, nutmeg, and citrus fruits) and cruise ships come and go frequently, making Castries Harbour one of the Caribbean's busiest ports. **Pointe Seraphine** is a duty-free shopping complex on the north side of the harbor, about a 20-minute walk or 2-minute cab ride from the city center; a launch ferries passengers across the harbor when cruise ships are in port. Pointe Seraphine's attractive Spanish-style architecture houses more than 20 duty-free shops, a tourist information kiosk, a taxi stand, and car-rental agencies. **La Place Carenage,** on the south side of the harbor near the pier and markets, is another duty-free shopping complex with a dozen or more shops and a café. **Derek Walcott Square,** a green oasis bordered by Brazil, Laborie, Micoud, and Bourbon streets, honors the hometown poet who won the 1992 Nobel Prize in Literature—one of two Nobel laureates from St. Lucia (the late Sir W. Arthur Lewis won the 1979 Nobel in economic science). Some of the few 19th-century buildings that survived fire, wind, and rain can be seen on Brazil Street, the square's southern border. On the Laborie Street side, there's a huge, 400-year-old samaan (monkeypod) tree with leafy branches that shade a good portion of the square. Directly across Laborie Street from Derek Walcott Square is the Roman Catholic **Cathedral of the Immaculate Conception,** which was built in 1897. Though it's rather somber on the outside, its interior walls are decorated with colorful murals by St. Lucian artist Dunstan St. Omer that were reworked just before Pope John Paul II visited in 1985. This church has an active parish and is open daily for both public viewing and religious services. ⊠ *Castries.*

Castries Market. Under a brilliant orange roof, the bustling **Castries Market** is at its liveliest on Saturday morning, when farmers bring their produce and spices to town—as they have for more than a century. Next door to the produce market is the **Craft Market,** where you can buy pottery, wood carvings, and handwoven straw articles. At the **Vendors' Arcade,** across Peynier Street from the Craft Market, you'll find still more handicrafts and souvenirs. ⊠ *Jeremie and Peynier Sts., Castries* ⊙ *Closed Sun.*

DID YOU KNOW?

Dunstan St. Omer, whose frescoes can be found in Castries's Cathedral of the Immaculate Conception, also designed the nation's flag.

Fodor'sChoice **Marigot Bay.** This is one of the prettiest natural harbors in the Caribbean.
★ In 1778, British admiral Samuel Barrington sailed into this secluded bay-within-a-bay and, the story goes, covered his ships with palm fronds to hide them from the French. Today this small community is a favorite anchorage for boaters and a peaceful destination for landlubbers, with a luxury resort, several small inns and restaurants, and a marina village with a snack shop, grocery store, bakery, and boutiques. A 24-hour ferry ($2 round-trip) connects the bay's two shores—a voyage that takes a minute or two each way. ⊠ *Marigot Bay.*

FAMILY **Our Planet Centre.** The only such attraction of its kind in the world,
Fodor'sChoice at least to date, Our Planet Centre is devoted to the many facets of
★ the Earth's environment. It's a fascinating, educational stop for the entire family and an especially good option on a rainy day. The exhibits include an Immersion Tunnel, where you can see how the planet was created and grew into its current state; Hurricane Island, where touch screens allow you to manipulate weather patterns to create a hurricane; Mirrorsphere, which gives a kaleidoscopic view of Earth's plants and animals; Science on a Sphere, installed by NOAA/NASA, which views the Earth from space complete with real-time weather patterns that might include storms, earthquakes, volcanoes, and tsunamis; and—the best part—a laser show in the Special Effects Theatre, where the lighting, shaking seats, wind, and mist mimic extreme weather events. The personalized guided tour takes about 90 minutes, but you'll probably want to linger longer at some of the exhibits and interactive games—which is fine. A gift shop features locally made recycled, reused, and natural products. ⊠ *La Place Carenage, Jeremie St., Castries* ☎ *758/453-0107* ⊕ *www.ourplanetcentre.org* ⊠ *$38* ☉ *Mon.–Sat. 9–4:30; last booking at 3:30; Sun. by reservation or when cruise ship is in port.*

FAMILY **Rain Forest Sky Rides.** Ever wish you could get a bird's-eye view of the rain forest? Or at least experience it without hiking up and down miles of mountain trails? Here's your chance. Depending on your athleticism and spirit of adventure, choose a two-hour aerial tram ride, a zip-line experience, or both. Either guarantees a magnificent view as you peacefully ride above or actively zip through the canopy of the 3,442-acre Castries Waterworks Rain Forest in Babonneau, 30 minutes east of Rodney Bay. On the tram ride, eight-passenger gondolas glide slowly among the giant trees, twisting vines, and dense thickets of vegetation accented by colorful flowers as a tour guide explains and shares anecdotes about the various trees, plants, birds, and other wonders of nature found in the area. The zip line, on the other hand, is a thrilling experience in which you're rigged with a harness, helmet, and clamps that attach to cables strategically strung through the forest. Short trails connect 10 lines, so riders come down to earth briefly and hike to the next station before speeding through the forest canopy to the next stop. ■ TIP→ Bring binoculars and a camera; there's a special nighttime zip-line tour. ⊠ *Chassin, Babonneau* ☎ *758/458-5151, 866/759-8726 in U.S.* ⊕ *www.rainforestadventure.com* ⊠ *Tram $72, zip line $69, combo $85, night zip, $79* ☉ *Tues.–Thurs. and Sun. 9–4.*

Rodney Bay. Hotels, popular restaurants, a huge mall, and the island's only casino surround a natural bay and an 80-acre man-made lagoon named for Admiral George Rodney, who sailed the British Navy out of Gros Islet Bay in 1780 to attack and ultimately destroy the French fleet. With 232 slips, Rodney Bay Marina is one of the Caribbean's premier yachting centers: each December, it's the destination of the Atlantic Rally for Cruisers (a transatlantic yacht crossing). Yacht charters and sightseeing day trips can be arranged at the marina. Rodney Bay is about 15 minutes north of Castries; a ferry makes hourly crossings between the marina and the mall, as well as daily excursions to Pigeon Island. ⊠ *Rodney Bay Village, Gros Islet.*

WORTH NOTING

Bounty Rum Distillery. St. Lucia Distillers, which produces the island's own Bounty and Chairman's Reserve rums, offers 90-minute Rhythm of Rum tours that cover the history of sugar, the background of rum, a detailed description of the distillation process, colorful displays of local architecture, a glimpse at a typical rum shop, Caribbean music, and a chance to sample the company's rums and liqueurs. The distillery is at the Roseau Sugar Factory in the Roseau Valley, on the island's largest banana plantation, a few miles south of Castries and not far from Marigot. Reservations for the tour are essential. ⊠ *Roseau Sugar Factory, West Coast Rd., near Marigot, Roseau* ☎ *758/451–4528* ⊕ *www.saintluciarums.com* 🖼 *$10* ⊙ *Weekdays 9–3.*

Ft. Charlotte. Begun in 1764 by the French as the Citadelle du Morne Fortune, Ft. Charlotte was completed after 20 years of battling and changing hands. Its old barracks and batteries are now government buildings and local educational facilities, but you can drive around and look at the remains of redoubts, a guardroom, stables, and cells. You can also walk up to the Inniskilling Monument, a tribute to the 1796 battle in which the 27th Foot Royal Inniskilling Fusiliers wrested the Morne from the French. At the military cemetery, first used in 1782, faint inscriptions on the tombstones tell the tales of French and English soldiers who died in St. Lucia. Six former governors of the island are also buried here. From this point atop Morne Fortune, you have a beautiful view of Castries Harbour, Martinique farther north, and the Pitons to the south. ⊠ *Morne Fortune, Castries.*

Government House. The official residence of the governor-general of St. Lucia—one of the island's few remaining examples of Victorian architecture—is perched high above Castries, halfway up Morne Fortune—the "Hill of Good Fortune"—which forms a backdrop for the capital city. Morne Fortune has also overlooked more than its share of *bad* luck over the years, including devastating hurricanes and four fires that leveled Castries. Within Government House itself is **Le Pavillon Royal Museum,** which houses important historical photographs and documents, artifacts, crockery, silverware, medals, and awards; original architectural drawings of Government House are displayed on the walls. Note that you must make an appointment to visit. ⊠ *Morne Fortune, Castries* ☎ *758/452–2481* 🖼 *Free* ⊙ *Tues. and Thurs. 10–noon and 2–4, by appointment only.*

FAMILY **Pigeon Island National Landmark.** Jutting out from the northwest coast, Pigeon Island is connected to the mainland via a causeway. Tales are told of the pirate Jambe de Bois (Wooden Leg), who once hid out on this 44-acre hilltop islet—a strategic point during the French and British struggles for control of St. Lucia. Now Pigeon Island is a national park and a venue for concerts, festivals, and family gatherings. There are two small beaches with calm waters for swimming and snorkeling, a restaurant, and picnic areas. Scattered around the grounds are ruins of barracks, batteries, and garrisons that date from 18th-century French and English battles. In the Museum and Interpretative Centre, housed in the restored British officers' mess, a multimedia display explains the island's ecological and historical significance. Pigeon Island National Landmark is administered by the St. Lucia National Trust. ☒ *Pigeon Island, Gros Islet* ☎ *758/452–5005* ⊕ *www.slunatrust.org* ☜ *$5* ⊘ *Daily 9–5.*

SOUFRIÈRE

The oldest town in St. Lucia and the island's former French colonial capital, Soufrière was founded by the French in 1746 and named for its proximity to the volcano of the same name. The wharf is the center of activity in this sleepy town (population, 9,000), particularly when a cruise ship anchors in pretty Soufrière Bay. French colonial influences are evident in the second-story verandahs, gingerbread trim, and other appointments of the wooden buildings that surround the market square. The market building itself is decorated with colorful murals.

Soufrière, the site of much of St. Lucia's renowned natural beauty, is the destination of most sightseeing trips. This is where you can get up close to the iconic Pitons and visit colonial capital of St. Lucia, with its "drive-in" volcano, botanical gardens, working plantations, waterfalls, and countless other examples of the natural beauty for which St. Lucia is deservedly famous.

VISITOR INFORMATION

Soufrière Tourist Information Centre. Head here for information about area attractions. Note that souvenir vendors station themselves outside some of the popular attractions in and around Soufrière, and they can be persistent. Be polite but firm if you're not interested. ☒ *Maurice Mason St.* ☎ *758/459–7200.*

TOP ATTRACTIONS

Fodor'sChoice **Diamond Falls Botanical Gardens and Mineral Baths.** These splendid gardens ★ are part of Soufrière Estate, a 2,000-acre land grant presented by King Louis XIV in 1713 to three Devaux brothers from Normandy in recognition of their services to France. The estate is still owned by their descendants; Joan DuBouley Devaux maintains the gardens. Bushes and shrubs bursting with brilliant flowers grow beneath towering trees and line pathways that lead to a natural gorge. Water bubbling to the surface from underground sulfur springs streams downhill in rivulets to become Diamond Waterfall, deep within the botanical gardens. Through the centuries, the rocks over which the cascade spills have become encrusted with minerals tinted yellow, green, and purple. Near the falls, mineral baths are fed by the underground springs. King Louis XVI of France

DID YOU KNOW?

The Devaux family has owned Diamond Botanical Gardens since 1713; the sulfurous water has stained the surrounding rocks different colors.

provided funds in 1784 for the construction of a building with a dozen large stone baths to fortify his troops against the St. Lucian climate. It's claimed that the future Joséphine Bonaparte bathed here as a young girl while visiting her father's plantation nearby. During the Brigand's War, just after the French Revolution, the bathhouse was destroyed. In 1930 André DuBoulay had the site excavated, and two of the original stone baths were restored for his use. Outside baths were added later. For a small fee, you can slip into your swimsuit and soak for 30 minutes in one of the outside pools; a private bath costs slightly more. ⊠ *Soufrière Estate, Diamond Rd.* ☎ *758/459–7155* 🖵 *$8, public bath $5, private bath $8* ⊙ *Mon.–Sat. 10–5, Sun. 10–3.*

Fodor'sChoice **The Pitons.** Rising precipitously from the cobalt-blue Caribbean Sea just
★ south of Soufrière Bay, these two unusual mountains are a UNESCO World Heritage Site and also the iconic symbol of St. Lucia. Covered with thick tropical vegetation, the massive outcroppings were formed by lava from a volcanic eruption 30 to 40 million years ago. They are not identical twins, since 2,619-foot Petit Piton is taller than 2,461-foot Gros Piton and Gros Piton is broader. It's possible to climb the Pitons, but it's a strenuous trek. Gros Piton is the easier climb and will take about two hours to reach the top. Either climb requires the permission of the Forest & Lands Department and the use of a knowledgeable guide. ☎ *758/450–2231, 758/450–2078 for St. Lucia Forest & Lands Department* 🖵 *Guide services $45* ⊙ *Daily by appointment only.*

WORTH NOTING

Edmund Forest Reserve. Dense tropical rain forest that stretches from one side of St. Lucia to the other, sprawling over 19,000 acres of mountains and valleys, is home to a multitude of exotic flowers and plants and rare birds—including the brightly feathered Jacquot parrot. The Edmund Forest Reserve, on the island's western side, is most easily accessible from the road to Fond St. Jacques, which is just east of Soufrière. A trek through the verdant landscape, with spectacular views of mountains, valleys, and the sea beyond, can take three or more hours. The ranger station at the entrance to the reserve is a 30-minute drive from Soufrière and 90 minutes or more from the northern end of St. Lucia. You'll need a four-wheel-drive vehicle to drive inland to the trailhead, which can take another hour. The trek itself is a strenuous hike, so you need plenty of stamina and sturdy hiking shoes. Your hotel can help you obtain the permission from the Forest & Lands Department to access reserve trails and to arrange for a naturalist or forest officer guide—necessary because the vegetation is so dense. ☎ *758/450–2231, 758/468–5649 for Forest & Lands Department* 🖵 *Guide for nature trails $10; hiking trails $25; bird-watching $30; guided tours including hotel transfers $65–$95* ⊙ *Daily by appointment only.*

FAMILY **Fond Doux Estate.** One of the earliest French estates established by land grants (1745 and 1763), this plantation still produces cocoa, citrus, bananas, coconut, and vegetables on 135 hilly acres. The restored 1864 plantation house is still in use, as well. A 30-minute walking tour begins at the cocoa fermentary, where you can see the drying process under way. You then follow a trail through the cultivated area, where a guide points out various fruit- or spice-bearing trees and tropical flowers. Additional trails lead to old military ruins, a religious shrine, and a vantage point for viewing the spectacular Pitons. Cool drinks and a Creole buffet lunch are served at the Cocoa Pod restaurant. Souvenirs, including just-made chocolate sticks, are sold at the boutique. ⊠ *Chateaubelair* ☎ *758/459–7545* ⊕ *www.fonddouxestate.com* ⊠ *$30, includes lunch* ⊗ *Daily 11–2.*

FAMILY **La Soufrière Drive-In Volcano.** As you approach, your nose will pick up the strong scent of the sulfur springs—more than 20 belching pools of murky water, crusty sulfur deposits, and other multicolor minerals baking and steaming on the surface. Despite the name, you don't actually drive all the way in. Instead, you drive within a few hundred feet of the gurgling, steaming mass and then walk behind your guide—whose service is included in the admission price—around a fault in the substratum rock. It's a fascinating, educational half hour, though it can also be pretty stinky on a hot day. ☎ *758/459–5500* ⊠ *$2* ⊗ *Daily 9–5.*

FAMILY **Morne Coubaril.** On the site of an 18th-century estate, a 250-acre land grant by Louis XIV of France in 1713, the original plantation house has been rebuilt and a farm workers' village has been re-created. It does a good job of showing what life was like for both the owners (a single family owned the land until 1960) and those who did all the hard labor over the centuries producing cotton, coffee, sugarcane, and cocoa. Cocoa, coconuts, and manioc are still grown on the estate using traditional agricultural methods. Guides show how coconuts are opened and roasted for use as oil and animal feed and how cocoa is fermented, dried, crushed by dancing on the beans, and finally formed into chocolate sticks. Manioc roots (also called cassava) are grated, squeezed of excess water, dried, and turned into flour used for baking. The grounds are lovely for walking or hiking, and the views of mountains and Soufrière Harbour are spellbinding. More adventurous visitors can learn how to climb a palm tree or enjoy Soufrière Hotwire Rides, an hour-long zip-line excursion with eight stations, taking you by Petit Piton and through the adjacent rain forest. The large, open-air restaurant serves a creole buffet luncheon by reservation only. ⊠ *2 miles (3 km) south of town* ☎ *758/459–7340, 758/712–5808 for reservations* ⊕ *www.mornecoubarilestate.com, www.stluciaziplining.com* ⊠ *$7, with lunch $210; zip line $69; tree-climbing $5* ⊗ *Daily 8–5.*

VIEUX FORT AND THE EAST COAST

Vieux Fort, on the southeastern tip of St. Lucia, is the island's second-largest town (Castries is the only "official" city). Vieux Fort is the location of Hewanorra International Airport, which serves all commercial jets arriving and departing the island. Although less developed for tourism than the island's north and west, the area around Vieux Fort and points north along the eastern coast are home to some of St. Lucia's unique ecosystems and interesting natural attractions.

WORTH NOTING

Barre de l'Isle Forest Reserve. St. Lucia is divided into eastern and western halves by Barre de l'Isle ridge. A mile-long (1½-km-long) trail cuts through the reserve, and four lookout points provide panoramic views. Visible in the distance are Mt. Gimie, immense green valleys, both the Caribbean Sea and the Atlantic Ocean, and coastal communities. The trailhead is about a half-hour drive from Castries. It takes about an hour to walk the trail—an easy hike—and another hour to climb Mt. LaCombe Ridge. Permission from the St. Lucia Forest & Lands Department is required to access the trail in Barre de l'Isle; a naturalist or forest officer guide will accompany you. ⊠ *Micoud Hwy., midway between Castries and Dennery, Ravine Poisson* ☎ *758/450–2231, 758/450–2078* ⌨ *Guide services $10* ⊙ *Daily, by appointment only.*

Frégate Island Nature Reserve. A mile-long (1½-km) trail encircles the nature reserve, which you reach from the East Coast Road near the fishing village of Praslin. In this area, boat builders still fashion traditional fishing canoes, called *gommiers* after the trees from which the hulls are made. The Amerindian people, who originally populated the Caribbean, used the ancient design. A natural promontory at Praslin provides a lookout from which you can view the two small islets, Frégate Major and Frégate Minor, and—with luck—the frigate birds that nest here from May to July. The only way to visit is on a guided tour, which includes a ride in a gommier to Frégate Minor for a picnic lunch and a swim; all trips are by reservation only and require a minimum of two people. Arrange visits through your hotel, a tour operator, or the St. Lucia National Trust; many tours include round-trip transportation from your hotel. ⊠ *Micoud Hwy., Praslin* ☎ *758/452–5005, 758/453–7656, 758/454–5014 for tour reservations* ⊕ *www.slunatrust. org* ⌨ *$18* ⊙ *Daily by appointment only.*

Mamiku Gardens. One of St. Lucia's largest and loveliest botanical gardens surrounds the hilltop ruins of the Micoud Estate. Baron Micoud, an 18th-century colonel in the French Army and governor general of St. Lucia, deeded the land to his wife, Madame de Micoud, to avoid confiscation by the British during one of the many times when St. Lucia changed hands. Locals abbreviated her name to "Ma Micoud," which, over time, became "Mamiku." (The estate did become a British military outpost in 1796, but shortly thereafter was burned to the ground by slaves during the Brigand's War.) The estate is now primarily a banana plantation, but the gardens themselves—including several secluded or "secret" gardens—are filled with tropical flowers and plants, delicate orchids, and fragrant herbs. ⊠ *Micoud Hwy., just north of Micoud, Praslin* ☎ *758/455–3729* ⌨ *$6; guided tour, $8* ⊙ *Daily 9–5.*

Vieux Fort. St. Lucia's second-largest town is where you'll find Hewanorra International Airport. From the Moule à Chique Peninsula, the island's southernmost tip, you can see much of St. Lucia to the north and the island of St. Vincent 21 miles (34 km) to the south. This is where the waters of the clear Caribbean Sea blend with those of the deeper blue Atlantic Ocean. ⊠ *Vieux Fort.*

BEACHES

The sand on St. Lucia's beaches ranges from golden to black, and the island has some of the best off-the-beach snorkeling in the Caribbean—especially along the western coast north of Soufrière.

St. Lucia's longest, broadest, and most popular beaches are in the north, which is also the flattest part of this mountainous island and the location of most resorts, restaurants, and nightlife. Many of the island's biggest resorts front the beaches from Choc Bay to Rodney Bay and north to Cap Estate. Elsewhere, tiny coves with inviting crescents of sand offer great swimming and snorkeling opportunities. Beaches are all public, but hotels flank many along the northwestern coast. A few secluded stretches of beach on the southwestern coast, south of Marigot Bay and accessible primarily by boat, are popular swimming and snorkeling stops on catamaran day sails or powerboat sightseeing trips. Don't swim along the windward (eastern) coast, as the Atlantic Ocean is too rough—but the views are spectacular. At Coconut Bay Resort, which has a beautiful beach facing the Atlantic at the southernmost tip of the island, the water is rough—but an artificial reef makes it safe for swimming and water sports, especially kitesurfing.

Anse Chastanet. In front of the resort of the same name and Jade Mountain, this palm-studded, dark-sand beach just north of Soufrière has a backdrop of green mountains, brightly painted fishing skiffs bobbing at anchor, calm waters for swimming, and some of the island's best reefs for snorkeling and diving right from shore. Anse Chastanet Resort's gazebos are among the palms; its dive shop, restaurant, and bar are on the beach and open to the public. The mile-long dirt road from Soufrière, though, is a challenge given its usual (and colossal) state of disrepair. **Amenities:** food and drink; parking (no fee); toilets; water sports. **Best for:** snorkeling; sunset; swimming. ⊠ *Anse Chastanet Rd., 1 mile (1½ km) north of town, Soufrière.*

Anse Cochon. This dark-sand beach in front of Ti Kaye Village is accessible by boat or via Ti Kaye's mile-long, tire-crunching access road. The calm water and adjacent reefs, part of the National Marine Reserve, are superb for swimming, diving, and snorkeling. Moorings are free, and boaters and swimmers can enjoy refreshments at Ti Kaye's beach bar. Snorkeling equipment is available at the dive shop on the beach. **Amenities:** food and drink; toilets; water sports. **Best for:** snorkeling; swimming. ⊠ *Off West Coast Rd., 3 miles (5 km) south of Anse la Raye, Anse la Raye.*

Anse des Pitons (*Sugar Beach, Forbidden Beach*). The white sand on this crescent beach, snuggled between the Pitons, was imported and spread over the natural black sand. Accessible through the Sugar Beach resort or by boat, Anse des Pitons offers crystal-clear water for swimming, excellent snorkeling and diving, and breathtaking scenery—you're swimming right between the Pitons, after all. The underwater area here is protected as part of the National Marine Reserve. **Amenities:** food and drink; toilets; water sports. **Best for:** snorkeling; sunset; swimming. ⊠ *Val des Pitons, 3 miles (5 km) south of Soufrière, Soufrière.*

22

Marigot Beach (*Labas Beach*). Calm waters rippled only by passing yachts lap a sliver of sand on the north side of Marigot Bay and adjacent to the Marigot Beach Club and Dive Resort. Studded with palm trees, the tiny but extremely picturesque beach is accessible by a ferry ($2 round-trip) that operates continually from one side of the bay to the other, with pickup at the Marina Village; you can find refreshments at adjacent restaurants. **Amenities:** food and drink; toilets; water sports. **Best for:** swimming. ⊠ *Marigot Bay.*

FAMILY **Pigeon Point.** At this small beach within the Pigeon Island National Historic Landmark site, on the northwestern tip of St. Lucia, you'll find golden sand, a calm sea, and a view that extends from Rodney Bay to Martinique. It's a perfect spot for picnicking, and you can take a break from the sun by visiting the nearby Museum and Interpretive Centre. **Amenities:** food and drink; toilets. **Best for:** solitude; snorkeling; swimming. ⊠ *Pigeon Island National Landmark, Pigeon Island, Gros Islet* ☜ *$5 park admission.*

FAMILY **Reduit Beach.** Many feel that Reduit (pronounced red-wee) is the island's
Fodor's Choice finest beach. The long stretch of golden sand that frames Rodney Bay
★ is within walking distance of many hotels and restaurants in Rodney Bay Village. Bay Gardens Beach Resort, Royal by Rex Resorts, and St. Lucian by Rex Resorts all face the beachfront; blu St. Lucia, Harmony Suites, and Ginger Lily hotels are across the road. The Royal has a water-sports center, where you can rent sports equipment and beach chairs and take windsurfing or waterskiing lessons. **Amenities:** food and drink; toilets; water sports. **Best for:** snorkeling; sunset; swimming; walking; windsurfing. ⊠ *Rodney Bay Village, Gros Islet.*

Vigie/Malabar Beach. This 2-mile (3-km) stretch of lovely white sand runs parallel to the George F.L. Charles Airport runway in Castries and continues on past the Rendezvous resort, where it becomes Malabar Beach. In the area opposite the airport departure lounge, a few vendors sell refreshments. **Amenities:** food and drink. **Best for:** swimming. ⊠ *Adjacent to George F.L. Charles Airport runway, Castries.*

WHERE TO EAT

Bananas, mangoes, passion fruit, plantains, breadfruit, okra, avocados, limes, pumpkins, cucumbers, papaya, yams, christophenes (also called chayote), and coconuts are among the fresh fruits and vegetables that grace St. Lucian menus. The French influence is strong, and most chefs cook with a creole flair. Resort buffets and restaurant fare include standards like steaks, chops, pasta, and pizza—and every menu lists fresh fish along with the ever-popular lobster which is available in season—August through March.

Soups and stews are traditionally prepared in a coal pot—unique to St. Lucia—a rustic clay casserole on a matching clay stand that holds the hot coals. Chicken and pork dishes and barbecues are also popular here. As they do throughout the Caribbean, local vendors set up barbecues along the roadside, at street fairs, and at Friday-night "jump-ups" and do a bang-up business selling grilled fish or chicken legs, bakes (fried biscuits), and beer—you can get a full meal for less than $10.

Guests at St. Lucia's many popular all-inclusive resorts take most meals at hotel restaurants—which are generally quite good and in some cases exceptional—but it's fun when vacationing to try some of the local restaurants as well—for lunch when sightseeing or for a special night out.

What to Wear: Dress on St. Lucia is casual but conservative. Shorts are usually fine during the day, but bathing suits and immodest clothing are frowned upon anywhere but at the beach. Nude or topless sunbathing is prohibited. In the evening, the mood is casually elegant, but even the fanciest places generally expect only a collared shirt and long pants for men and a sundress or slacks for women.

THE NORTH: RODNEY BAY TO CAP ESTATE

$$$
SEAFOOD
✕ **Buzz.** Opposite the Royal by Rex Resorts hotel and Reduit Beach, Buzz is part of Rodney Bay's "restaurant central." Starting with cool drinks (maybe a Buzz cooler) and warm appetizers (perhaps lobster and crab cakes, crispy calamari, or tempura shrimp) at the bar, diners make their way to the dining room or garden for some serious seafood or a good steak, baby back ribs, West Indian pepper-pot stew, spicy lamb shanks, or simple chicken and chips. The seared yellowfin tuna, potato-crusted red snapper, and seafood creole are big hits, too. There's also a vegetarian menu. Fresh lobster is available in season (September–April). ⓢ *Average main: US$26* ✉ *Reduit Beach Ave., Rodney Bay Village, Gros Islet* ☎ *758/458–0450* ⊕ *www.buzzstlucia.com* ⚖ *Reservations essential* ⊗ *No lunch. Closed Mon.*

$$$$
ECLECTIC
✕ **The Cliff at Cap.** High on top of a cliff at the northern tip of St. Lucia, the open-air dining room at Cap Maison welcomes diners to what Executive Chef Craig Jones calls "nouveau" French West Indian cuisine. True, he incorporates local vegetables, fruits, herbs, and spices with the best meats and fresh-caught seafood you'll find on the island, but the technique and presentation—and the service—leans more toward the French. In addition to the mouthwatering à la carte menu, guests may choose the five-course, prix-fixe Tasting Menu ($86, or $134 with course-matching wines). Lucky Cap Maison guests who choose a meal plan get to dine here daily, but nonguests make up about 40% of the dinner clientele. Day or night, this is one of the loveliest dining venues on St. Lucia. At lunch, the view on a clear day stretches to Martinique; in the evening, twinkling stars and waves crashing far below lend an air of romance. ⓢ *Average main: US$38* ✉ *Cap Maison, Smugglers Cove Dr., Cap Estate* ☎ *758/457–8681* ⊕ *www.capmaison.com* ⚖ *Reservations essential.*

$$$$
ECLECTIC
Fodor's Choice
★
✕ **The Edge.** Innovative Swedish chef Bobo Bergstrom has brought "Eurobbean" cuisine to his own restaurant, which overlooks the harbor at Harmony Suites hotel. St. Lucian locals and visitors alike rave about chef Bobo's culinary feats, the excellent wine list, and the sushi bar. The contemporary fusion style combines the chef's European heritage, Caribbean traditions and ingredients, and a touch of Asian influence. Follow one of a dozen starters with pan-seared red snapper and lobster medallions au gratin, jerk-marinated-and-grilled beef tenderloin, or pecan- and cardamom-rubbed rack of lamb. Or you might want to consider the five-course tasting menu. There's sure to be a dish on the extensive menu (or

at the sushi bar) that suits everyone in your party, including vegetarians. **TIP→ Leave room for a fabulous dessert.** [$] *Average main: US$39* ✉ *Harmony Suites, Reduit Beach Ave., Rodney Bay* ☎ *758/450–3343* 🌐 *www.edge-restaurant.com* ✍ *Reservations essential.*

$$$$ FRENCH 🍴 **Jacques Waterfront Dining.** Chef–owner Jacky Rioux creates magical dishes in his waterfront restaurant overlooking Rodney Bay. The cooking is decidedly French, as is Rioux, but fresh produce and local spices create a fusion cuisine that's memorable at either lunch or dinner. You might start with a bowl of creamy tomato-basil or pumpkin soup, a grilled portobello mushroom, or octopus and conch in curried coconut sauce. Choose among main dishes such as fresh seafood, perhaps oven-baked kingfish with a white wine–and–sweet pepper sauce, or breast of chicken stuffed with smoked salmon in a citrus-butter sauce. The wine list is impressive. Coming by boat? You can tie up at the dinghy dock. [$] *Average main: US$32* ✉ *Reduit Beach Ave., at end of road, Rodney Bay Village, Gros Islet* ☎ *758/458–1900* 🌐 *www.jacquesrestaurant.com* ✍ *Reservations essential* 🕒 *Closed Sun.*

$$$ CARIBBEAN 🍴 **KoKo Cabana.** Poolside at the Coco Palm hotel in Rodney Bay, KoKo Cabana is an open-air bistro and bar. Breakfast attracts mostly hotel guests, but the attractive restaurant attracts a wider range of clientele for lunch and dinner. Lunch is a good bet if you're poking around Rodney Bay, need a break from Reduit Beach, or are just looking for a good meal in an attractive spot. In the evening, the breezy dining room is where the magic really comes through. The dinner menu focuses on Caribbean favorites such as jerk baby back ribs with guava barbecue sauce; perfectly grilled fish or steak with local vegetables; tamarind-glazed chicken breast; and always a pasta dish or two. Leave room for dessert—perhaps the dark chocolate truffle cake or vanilla profiteroles with chocolate sauce. A live band entertains most evenings and always at the Friday night barbecue buffet. [$] *Average main: US$27* ✉ *Coco Palm, Rodney Bay Village, Gros Islet* ☎ *758/456–2866* 🌐 *www.coco-resorts.com* ✍ *Reservations essential.*

$$$$ ASIAN Fodor's Choice ★ 🍴 **Tao.** For exquisite dining, head for this Cap Estate restaurant. As you dine on a second-floor balcony at the edge of Cariblue Beach, you're guaranteed a pleasant breeze and a starry sky while you enjoy fusion cuisine—Asian tastes with a Caribbean touch. Choose from appetizers such as seafood dumplings, sashimi salad, or miso-eggplant timbale, followed by tender slices of pork loin teriyaki, twice-cooked duck, wok-seared calves' liver, or tandoori chicken—the results are mouthwatering. Fine wines accompany the meal, desserts are extravagant, and service is superb. Seating is limited; hotel guests have priority, so reserve early. [$] *Average main: US$35* ✉ *The Body Holiday, Cap Estate* ☎ *758/457–7800* 🌐 *www.thebodyholiday.com* ✍ *Reservations essential* 🕒 *No lunch.*

CASTRIES

$$$$ FRENCH Fodor's Choice ★ 🍴 **Coal Pot.** Popular since the early 1960s, this tiny waterfront restaurant overlooking pretty Vigie Cove is managed by local artist Michelle Elliott. For a light lunch, opt for a bowl of creamy pumpkin soup, Greek or shrimp salad, or broiled fresh fish. Dinner might start with a divine lobster bisque, followed by fresh seafood accompanied by

one (or more) of the chef's fabulous sauces—ginger, coconut-curry, lemon-garlic butter, or wild mushroom. Heartier eaters may prefer duck, lamb, beef, or chicken laced with peppercorns, red wine, onion, or Roquefort sauce. [$] *Average main: US$32* ✉ *Vigie Cove* ☎ *758/452–5566* 🌐 *www.coalpotrestaurant.com* ✍ *Reservations essential* 🕒 *Closed Sun. No lunch Sat.*

MARIGOT BAY

$$ ECLECTIC FAMILY

🍴 **Chateau Mygo.** Walk down a garden path to Chateau Mygo (a corruption of the word Marigot), pick out a table on the deck, pull up a chair, and soak up the waterfront atmosphere of what is probably the prettiest bay in the Caribbean. The tableau is mesmerizing—and that's at lunch, when you can order a sandwich, burger, fish- or chicken-and-chips, salads, or grilled fish or savory coconut chicken with peas and rice and vegetables. At dinner, chef–owner Doreen Rambally—whose family has owned and operated this popular dockside restaurant since the mid-1970s—draws on three generations of East Indian and creole family recipes. Beautifully grilled fresh tuna, red snapper, kingfish, mahimahi, and local lobster are embellished with flavors such as ginger, mango, papaya, or passion fruit, and then dished up with regional vegetables—perhaps callaloo, okra, dasheen, breadfruit, christophene, or yams. You can also have roast pork, beef, a chicken dish, or pizza. This is a very casual restaurant where locals, yachties, and frequent visitors know they'll get a delicious, reasonably priced meal right on the waterfront. And oh, that view! [$] *Average main: US$20* ✉ *Marigot Bay* ☎ *758/451–4772.*

$$ SEAFOOD FAMILY

🍴 **Doolittle's.** Named for the protagonist in the original (1967) *Dr. Dolittle* movie, part of which was filmed right here in Marigot Bay, Doolittle's is the inside–outside waterfront restaurant at the Marigot Beach Club & Dive Center on the north side of the bay. You'll have a beautiful view of the bay—watch yachts quietly slip by as you enjoy your meal. The menu includes light meals such as sandwiches, burgers, grilled chicken, and salads at lunchtime and, in the evening, seafood, steak, chicken, and Caribbean specials such as curries and stews. Take the little ferry across the bay to reach Doolittle's. During the day, bring your bathing suit. The beach is just outside the restaurant's door. ■ TIP→ **In the evening, it's a great spot for drinks and entertainment.** [$] *Average main: US$20* ✉ *Marigot Beach Club, Marigot Bay* ☎ *758/451–4974* 🌐 *www.marigotbeachclub.com.*

$$$$ INTERNATIONAL Fodor's Choice ★

🍴 **Rainforest Hideaway.** Exotic Caribbean tastes and flavors are paired with classical French techniques and recipes at this romantic and upscale hideaway on the north shore of pretty Marigot Bay. It's definitely worth the 20-minute-or-so drive from Castries. A little ferry whisks you to the alfresco restaurant, perched on a dock, where you're greeted with complimentary champagne. Fresh local fish—including the ubiquitous (and foreign) lionfish that is the scourge of local waters but tastes delicious—and prime meats are enhanced by fresh herbs grown in the backyard garden, which is also the source of exotic local vegetables and fruits featured in various dishes. You'll be duly impressed by entrées such as pan-fried mahimahi with creole buerre blanc; marinated loin of lamb with cucumber relish; or grilled beef tenderloin with papaya confit.

All are accompanied by excellent wines—not to mention the blanket of stars in the sky overhead and the live jazz Wednesday and Saturday nights. $ *Average main: US$48* ⊠ *Marigot Bay* ☎ *758/286–0511* ⊕ *www.rainforesthideawaystlucia.com* ⌕ *Reservations essential* ⊙ *No lunch. Closed Sun.–Tues. in summer.*

$ ✕ **Rowley's Café/Baguet Shop.** Join the yachties and nearby hotel guests
CAFÉ   for breakfast, lunch, afternoon tea, an evening snack, or just dessert
FAMILY   at this French bakery and café in the Marina Village on Marigot Bay. Open every day from 7 am to 7 pm, it offers freshly baked French bread, crusty croissants, and delicious French pastries. Sandwiches are prepared on a baguette, croissant, or focaccia—your choice. Pair your favorite with a cup of cappuccino, mocha, or latte, or save the coffee to go with something sweet, perhaps a fruit tart, *pain au chocolat*, or a coconut flan. Eat in (well, outside on the dock) or take it out. Even if you eat in, you'll probably also want a baguette—or a bagful—to take out. $ *Average main: US$10* ⊠ *Marina Village, Marigot Bay* ☎ *758/451–4275* ⌕ *Reservations not accepted.*

SOUFRIÈRE

$$$ ✕ **Boucan.** Ahh, chocolate! Here at Boucan on the Rabot Estate, a working
CARIBBEAN   cocoa plantation, you'll find that heavenly flavor infused into just about every dish: cacao gazpacho or citrus salad with white chocolate dressing for starters. The main course might be red snapper roasted in cacao butter, rib-eye steak "matured and infused" with cacao nibs, cacao- and herb-encrusted pork medallions, or handmade cocoa ravioli with a tomato and fresh herb sauce. You get the picture. Dessert, of course, is the grand chocolate finale: cacao crème brûlée, meringue floating in a sea of chocolate crème anglaise, dark chocolate mousse .. even cacao sorbet. Yum. $ *Average main: US$29* ⊠ *Boucan Hotel, Rabot Estate, West Coast Rd., 3 miles (5 km) south of Soufrière* ☎ *758/457–1624* ⌕ *Reservations essential.*

$$$ ✕ **Dasheene Restaurant and Bar.** The terrace restaurant at Ladera resort
CARIBBEAN   has breathtakingly close-up views of the Pitons and the sea between
Fodor's Choice   them, especially beautiful at sunset. The ambience is casual by day
★   and magical at night. Appetizers may include grilled crab claws with a choice of dips or silky pumpkin soup with ginger. Typical entrées are "fisherman's catch" with a choice of flavored butters or sauces, shrimp Dasheene (panfried with local herbs), grilled rack of lamb with coconut risotto and curry sauce, or pan-seared fillet of beef marinated in a lime-and-pepper seasoning. Light dishes, pasta dishes, and fresh salads are also served at lunch—along with that million-dollar view. $ *Average main: US$30* ⊠ *Ladera, 2 miles (3 km) south of Soufrière* ☎ *758/459–7323* ⊕ *www.ladera.com.*

$$ ✕ **Jardin Cacao at Fond Doux Estate.** The small, rustic restaurant at Fond
CARIBBEAN   Doux Estate—a working plantation—is one of the most popular spots
FAMILY   to enjoy a creole lunch when touring the natural sights in and around Soufrière. Help yourself at the buffet, where you'll find stewed chicken, grilled fish, rice and beans, macaroni and cheese, caramelized plantains, figs (green bananas), breadfruit balls, purple yams, salad, and more. Nearly all ingredients are locally sourced. Wash it all down with a rum punch or local fruit juice, and finish with something sweet such

Amazing views at Dasheene Restaurant in the Ladera Resort

as coconut or banana cake. Dinner, by candlelight, is à la carte; you'll find a choice of seafood, chicken, beef, and pasta dishes with a local twist—pepperpot, for example. Most people who come for lunch also take a short tour and learn the process of turning the cacao growing on the plantation into delicious chocolate. ■TIP→ **You can buy chocolate in the gift shop to take home!** $ *Average main: US$25* ⊠ *Fond Doux Holiday Plantation, Chateaubelair* ☎ *758/459–7545* ⊕ *www. fonddouxestate.com* ✍ *Reservations essential.*

$$
CARIBBEAN

✕ **Lifeline Restaurant at the Hummingbird.** The cheerful restaurant-bar in the Hummingbird Beach Resort specializes in creole cuisine, starting with fresh seafood or chicken seasoned with local herbs and accompanied by vegetables just picked from the Hummingbird's garden. Sandwiches (on homemade bread) and salads are also available. If you stop for lunch, sit outside by the pool for a magnificent view of the Pitons (you're welcome to take a dip), and be sure to visit the batik studio and art gallery of proprietor Joan Alexander, which is next to the dining room. ■TIP→ **Wednesday night is Creole night with live entertainment, dancing, and special dishes on the menu.** $ *Average main: US$18* ⊠ *Hummingbird Beach Resort, Anse Chastanet Rd.* ☎ *758/459–7985* ⊕ *www.hummingbirdbeachresort.com.*

$$$
CARIBBEAN
Fodor'sChoice
★

✕ **Orlando's.** Chef Orlando Satchell, British-born of Jamaican/Barbadian heritage and certainly a man on a mission, spent a dozen years as executive chef at Ladera's famed Dasheene Restaurant. Now he has spread his wings even further and opened his own restaurant and bar in downtown Soufrière. Orlando's self-described style of cooking is, and always has been, "Share The Love," or STL, with a focus on Caribbean cuisine. He supports local farmers and fishers by using only locally grown meats and organic produce and freshly caught fish in his delicious—and definitely world-class—dishes. Although he is known to be somewhat flexible, dinner offers a choice of two set five-course menus—starting with soup (pumpkin is *the* best!) and salad, then a fish dish followed by beef or chicken, and ultimately dessert. It's clear that Orlando loves St. Lucia, especially Soufrière. $ *Average main: US$30* ⊠ *Cemetery Rd.* ☎ *758/572–6613* ⌕ *Reservations essential* ⊘ *Closed Mon. and Tues.*

$$
CARIBBEAN

✕ **The Still.** When you're visiting Diamond Waterfall and other attractions in Soufrière, this is a convenient lunch spot. Located on a picturesque plantation just outside of town, the two dining rooms here seat up to 400 people, so it's also a popular stop for tour groups and cruise passengers. The emphasis is on local cuisine, using vegetables such as christophene, breadfruit, yam, and callaloo along with grilled fish or chicken; there are also pork and beef dishes. All fruits and vegetables used in the restaurant are organically grown on the estate. Lunch is a buffet. $ *Average main: US$20* ⊠ *The Still Plantation, Sir Arthur Lewis St.* ☎ *758/459–7261* ⊕ *www.thestillplantation.com* ⊘ *No dinner.*

WHERE TO STAY

Most people—particularly honeymooners—choose to stay in one of St. Lucia's many grand beach resorts, most of which are upscale and pricey. Several are all-inclusive, including the three Sandals resorts, two resorts owned or managed by Sunswept (the Body Holiday and Rendezvous), Morgan Bay Beach Resort, East Winds Inn, and Smugglers Cove Resort & Spa.

If you're looking for lodgings that are smaller and less expensive, St. Lucia has dozens of small inns and hotels that are primarily locally owned and frequently quite charming. They may or may not be directly on the beach. Luxury villa communities and independent private villas are another alternative in St. Lucia.

PRIVATE VILLAS AND CONDOS

Luxury villa and condo communities are an important part of the accommodations mix on St. Lucia, as they can be an economical option for families and other groups, or couples vacationing together. The villa units themselves are privately owned, but nonowners can rent individual units directly from the property managers for a vacation or short-term stay, much like reserving hotel accommodations.

All rental villas are staffed with a housekeeper and cook who specializes in local cooking; in some cases, a caretaker lives on the property and a gardener and night watchman are on staff. All properties have telephones, and some have Internet access. Telephones may be barred against outgoing overseas calls; plan to use a phone card, calling card, or your own cell phone. Most villas have TVs, DVDs, and CD players. All private villas have a swimming pool; condos share a community pool. Vehicles are generally not included in the rates, but rental cars can be arranged for and delivered to the villa upon request. Linens and basic supplies (such as bath soap, toilet tissue, and dish-washing detergent) are included. Pre-arrival grocery stocking can be arranged.

Units with one to nine bedrooms and the same number of baths run $200 to $2,000 per night, depending on the size of the villa, the amenities, the number of guests, and the season. Rates include utilities and government taxes. Your only additional cost will be for groceries and staff gratuities. A security deposit is required upon booking and refunded after departure less any damages or unpaid miscellaneous charges.

Rental Contacts Discover Villas of St. Lucia ☎ 758/484–3066 ⊕ www.a1stluciavillas.com. **Island Villas St. Lucia** ☎ 758/458–4903, 866/978–8499 in the U.S. ⊕ www.island-villas.com/st-lucia. **Tropical Villas** ✉ Cap Estate ☎ 758/450–8240 ⊕ www.tropicalvillas.net.

THE NORTH: RODNEY BAY TO CAP ESTATE

$$
RESORT
FAMILY
Fodor's Choice
★
⌂ Bay Gardens Beach Resort & Spa. One of three Bay Gardens properties in Rodney Bay Village, this family-friendly beach resort has a prime location directly on beautiful Reduit Beach. **Pros:** perfect spot on St. Lucia's best beach; self-catering suites work well for families; excellent value. **Cons:** very popular, so book ahead in season. $ *Rooms from: US$290* ✉ *Reduit Beach Ave., Rodney Bay Village, Gros Islet* ☎ *758/457–8006, 877/620–3200 in the U.S.* ⊕ *www.baygardensbeachresort.com* ⊅ *36 rooms, 36 suites* ⦿ *Multiple meal plans.*

$
HOTEL
⌂ Bay Gardens Hotel. Independent travelers and regional businesspeople swear by this cheerful, well-run boutique hotel at Rodney Bay Village. **Pros:** great value; Croton suites are a best bet; free Wi-Fi. **Cons:** not beachfront, although there's a beach shuttle; heavy focus on business travelers. $ *Rooms from: US$102* ✉ *Castries-Gros Islet Hwy., Gros Islet* ☎ *758/457–8010, 877/620–3200* ⊕ *www.baygardenshotel.com* ⊅ *59 rooms, 28 suites* ⦿ *No meals.*

$$
ALL-INCLUSIVE
⌂ blu St. Lucia. Singles, couples, families, and business travelers alike find blu St. Lucia to be a good base—and a reasonably priced one—in Rodney Bay Village and just across the road from Reduit Beach. **Pros:** excellent location; a peaceful refuge close to the Rodney Bay restaurants and action; complimentary Wi-Fi. **Cons:** not beachfront, although pretty close; rooms have showers only. $ *Rooms from: US$280* ✉ *Reduit Beach Ave., Rodney Bay Village, Gros Islet* ☎ *758/458–3300, 855/212–1972 in the U.S.* ⊕ *www.harlequinblu.com* ⊅ *72 rooms* ⦿ *All-inclusive.*

$$$$
ALL-INCLUSIVE
Fodor's Choice
★
⌂ The Body Holiday. At this adults-only spa resort on picturesque Cariblue Beach—where daily treatments are included in the rates— you can customize your own "body holiday" online even before you leave home. **Pros:** daily spa treatment included; excellent dining; interesting activities such as archery (including free instruction). **Cons:** expensive; unremarkable rooms; small bathrooms; lots of steps to the spa, although they'll give you a ride if you'd like. $ *Rooms from: US$1132* ✉ *Cariblue Beach, Cap Estate* ☎ *686/457–7800* ⊕ *www. thebodyholiday.com* ⊅ *152 rooms, 3 suites* ⦿ *All-inclusive.*

$$$
RESORT
Fodor's Choice
★
⌂ Calabash Cove Resort & Spa. The luxurious suites and Balinese-inspired cottages at this inviting resort spill gently down a tropical hillside to a secluded beach on Bonaire Bay, just south of Rodney Bay. **Pros:** stylish, sophisticated, and friendly; great food; wedding

Sandals Grande St. Lucian Spa & Beach Resort

parties can reserve the entire resort. **Cons:** the long, bone-crunching dirt road at the entrance; the many steps may be difficult for those with physical challenges. *§ Rooms from: US$475 ☒ Bonaire Estate, off Castries-Gros Islet Hwy., south of Rodney Bay, Marisule, Gros Islet ☎ 758/456-3500 ⊕ www.calabashcove.com ⇌ 17 suites, 9 cottages ⫶◯⫶ Multiple meal plans.*

\$\$\$ ⚏ **Cap Maison.** Prepare to be spoiled by the doting staffers at this inti-
RESORT mate villa resort—the luxurious service includes unpacking (if you
Fodor's Choice wish), an honor bar, and a personal butler for any little needs that arise.
★ **Pros:** private and elegant; outstanding service; rooftop plunge pools; cocktails with a view at the Cliff Bar or surfside at Rock Maison; free Wi-Fi. **Cons:** a/c in bedrooms only; all those steps can make it tough to reach the beach. *§ Rooms from: US$376 ☒ Smugglers Cove Dr., Cap Estate ☎ 758/457-8670, 888/765-4985 in the U.S. ⊕ www.capmaison. com ⇌ 10 rooms, 39 suites in 22 villas ⫶◯⫶ Breakfast.*

\$ ⚏ **Coco Palm.** This boutique hotel in Rodney Bay Village overlooks an
HOTEL inviting pool and a cozy guesthouse, Coco Kreole, at the edge of the
FAMILY property. **Pros:** excellent value; fabulous swim-up rooms; family suites. **Cons:** not directly on the beach; nightly entertainment can get noisy. *§ Rooms from: US$195 ☒ Rodney Bay Village, Gros Islet ☎ 758/456-2800, 877/655-2626 in the U.S. ⊕ www.coco-resorts.com ⇌ 91 rooms, 12 suites ⫶◯⫶ Multiple meal plans.*

\$\$ ⚏ **Cotton Bay Village.** Wedged between a quiet ocean beach and the
RESORT St. Lucia Golf Resort & Country Club, these luxurious, individually
FAMILY designed and decorated colonial-style town houses and château-style villas surround a village center and a free-form lagoon pool. **Pros:** beautiful remote beach; very private surroundings; family-friendly. **Cons:** a/c

in bedrooms only; bathrooms have showers only; you'll probably need a rental car if you plan to leave the place. [$] *Rooms from: US$276* ✉ *Cap Estate* ☎ *758/456–5700, 866/460–5755* 🌐 *www.cottonbayvillage.com* 🛏 *206 suites in 74 villas* 🍴 *No meals.*

$$$$ ALL-INCLUSIVE **East Winds Inn.** Guests keep returning to East Winds Inn, a small all-inclusive resort on a secluded beach halfway between Castries and Rodney Bay, where 7 acres of botanical gardens surround 13 duplex gingerbread-style cottages, three ocean-view rooms, and a suite. **Pros:** long-established clientele is the best recommendation; lovely beach; excellent dining; peaceful and quiet. **Cons:** not the best choice for families (though children are welcome); very expensive; minimum six-night stay. [$] *Rooms from: US$890* ✉ *Labrelotte Bay, Castries* ☎ *758/452–8212* 🌐 *www.eastwinds.com* 🛏 *30 rooms* 🍴 *All-inclusive.*

$$$$ RESORT FAMILY **The Landings.** On 19 acres along the Pigeon Point Causeway at the northern edge of Rodney Bay, this villa resort surrounds a private, 80-slip harbor where residents can dock their own yachts, literally, at their doorstep. **Pros:** spacious, beautifully appointed units; perfect place for yachties to come ashore; personal chef service. **Cons:** very expensive; condo atmosphere; a little hike to the beach from some rooms. [$] *Rooms from: US$849* ✉ *Pigeon Island Causeway, Gros Islet* ☎ *758/458–7300* 🌐 *www.thelandingsstlucia.com* 🛏 *122 units* 🍴 *Multiple meal plans.*

$$$ RESORT FAMILY **Royal by Rex Resorts.** This luxurious all-suites resort on St. Lucia's best beach caters to every whim—for the whole family. **Pros:** great beachfront; roomy rooms; family-friendly; convenient to restaurants, clubs, and shops. **Cons:** don't expect "all day" dining—get some snacks at the nearby supermarket. [$] *Rooms from: US$379* ✉ *Reduit Beach Ave., Rodney Bay Village, Gros Islet* ☎ *758/452–8351, 305/471–6170* 🌐 *www.rexcaribbean.com* 🛏 *96 suites* 🍴 *Multiple meal plans.*

$$$$ ALL-INCLUSIVE Fodor's Choice ★ **Sandals Grande St. Lucian Spa & Beach Resort.** Couples love this place—particularly young honeymooners and those getting married here at the biggest and splashiest of the three Sandals resorts on St. Lucia; it's grand, and busy, busy, busy. **Pros:** excellent beach; lots of activities; free scuba for certified divers; service with a smile; airport shuttle. **Cons:** the really long ride to and from Hewanorra; buffet meals are uninspired. [$] *Rooms from: US$770* ✉ *Pigeon Island Causeway, Gros Islet* ☎ *725/455–2000* 🌐 *www.sandals.com* 🛏 *272 rooms, 29 suites* 🍴 *All-inclusive.*

$$$$ ALL-INCLUSIVE **Sandals Halcyon Beach St. Lucia.** This is the most intimate and low-key of the three Sandals resorts on St. Lucia; like the others, it's beachfront, all-inclusive, for couples only, and loaded with amenities and activities. **Pros:** all the Sandals amenities in a more intimate setting; lots of dining and activity choices; exchange privileges (including golf) at two other Sandals properties. **Cons:** it's Sandals, so it's a theme property that's not for everyone; and it's small, so book well in advance. [$] *Rooms from: US$525* ✉ *Choc Bay, Castries* ☎ *758/453–0222, 888/726–3257* 🌐 *www.sandals.com* 🛏 *169 rooms* 🍴 *All-inclusive.*

$$$$ ALL-INCLUSIVE **Sandals La Toc Golf Resort & Spa.** One of three Sandals resorts on St. Lucia, this is the second-largest and distinguishes itself with its own 9-hole golf course (for guests only). **Pros:** lots to do; picturesque

Sandals Halcyon Beach, the Pier Restaurant

location; on-site golf; airport shuttle. **Cons:** somewhat isolated; expert golfers will prefer the St. Lucia Golf Resort & Country Club at Cap Estate. $ *Rooms from: US$596* ✉ *La Toc Rd., La Toc, Castries* ☎ *758/452–3081* ⊕ *www.sandals.com* ⇋ *212 rooms, 116 suites* ⊙| *All-inclusive.*

$$$$
ALL-INCLUSIVE
FAMILY

⊞ **Smugglers Cove Resort & Spa.** This huge, all-inclusive, resort on 60 acres overlooking pretty Smugglers Cove has more food, fun, and features than you and your family will have time to enjoy in a week. **Pros:** family rooms sleep five; excellent children's program; superlative tennis facilities; family-friendly nightly entertainment. **Cons:** busy, busy, busy; not the place for a quiet getaway; guest rooms are spread far and wide on the hillside. $ *Rooms from: US$729* ✉ *Smugglers Cove Rd., Cap Estate* ☎ *758/457–4140, 866/297–1685 in the U.S.* ⊕ *www. smugglersresort.com* ⇋ *257 rooms, 100 suites* ⊙| *All-inclusive.*

$$$$
ALL-INCLUSIVE
FAMILY

⊞ **St. James's Club Morgan Bay.** This all-inclusive resort offers singles, couples, and families tons of sports and activities—as well as quiet seclusion on 22 acres surrounding a stretch of white-sand beach. **Pros:** lots to do; children's club with organized activities; waterskiing, sailing, and tennis lessons are free; great dining atmosphere evenings at Morgan's Pier. **Cons:** resort is huge and can be very busy, especially when all rooms are filled; beach is relatively small given the resort's size; Wi-Fi only in public areas and in some rooms for a fee. $ *Rooms from: US$725* ✉ *Choc Bay, Castries* ☎ *758/450–2511* ⊕ *www. morganbayresort.com* ⇋ *225 rooms, 100 suites* ⊙| *All-inclusive.*

$
RESORT
FAMILY

⊞ **Windjammer Landing Villa Beach Resort.** As perfect for families as for a romantic getaway, Windjammer Landing offers lots to do yet still provides plenty of privacy. **Pros:** lovely, spacious units; beautiful sunset views; family-friendly, in-unit dining. **Cons:** some units have living rooms with no a/c; you'll want to rent a car if you plan to leave the property often, as it's far from the main road. $ *Rooms from: US$269* ⊠ *Trouya Point Rd., Labrelotte Bay, Castries* ☎ *758/456–9000, 877/522–0722 in the U.S.* ⊕ *www.windjammer-landing.com* ⟿ *41 suites, 72 villas* ⦾ *Multiple meal plans.*

22

GREATER CASTRIES

$$$$ ⬜ **Rendezvous.** Romance is alive and well at this easygoing, all-
ALL-INCLUSIVE inclusive, couples resort that stretches along the dreamy white sand of Malabar Beach opposite the George F.L. Charles Airport runway. **Pros:** convenient to Castries and Vigie Airport; great beach; romance in the air; popular wedding venue. **Cons:** no room TVs; occasional flyover noise. $ *Rooms from: US$732* ⊠ *Malabar Beach, Vigie, Castries* ☎ *758/457–7900* ⊕ *www.theromanticholiday.com* ⟿ *57 rooms, 35 suites, 8 cottages* ⦾ *All-inclusive.*

MARIGOT BAY TO ANSE LA RAYE

$$$ ⬜ **Ti Kaye Village.** Rustic elegance is not an oxymoron, at least at this
RESORT upscale cottage community on the hillside above Anse Cochon beach.
Fodor'sChoice **Pros:** perfect for a wedding, honeymoon, or private getaway; love those
★ garden showers; good restaurant; excellent beach for snorkeling; dive shop on-site. **Cons:** far from anywhere; long and very bumpy dirt access road; all those steps to the beach; not a good choice for anyone with physical challenges; no kids under age 12. $ *Rooms from: US$390* ⊠ *Off West Coast Rd., halfway between Anse La Raye and Canaries, Anse Cochon* ☎ *758/456–8101* ⊕ *www.tikaye.com* ⟿ *33 rooms* ⦾ *Multiple meal plans.*

SOUFRIÈRE

$$$$ ⬜ **Anse Chastanet Resort.** This resort is magical: spectacular rooms—
RESORT some with fourth walls completely open to the stunning Piton views— peek out of the thick rain forest that cascades down a steep hillside to the sea. **Pros:** great for divers; Room 14B has a huge tree growing through the bathroom; the open-wall Piton views. **Cons:** no pool; entrance road is annoying even in a 4WD vehicle; steep hillside certainly not conducive to strolling; no in-room TVs, phones, or a/c. $ *Rooms from: US$540* ⊠ *Anse Chastanet Rd.* ☎ *758/459–7000, 800/223–1108 in U.S.* ⊕ *www.ansechastanet.com* ⟿ *49 rooms* ⦾ *Multiple meal plans.*

$$$ ⬜ **Boucan by Hotel Chocolat.** Anyone who loves chocolate will love this
HOTEL themed boutique hotel just south of Soufrière and within shouting dis-
Fodor'sChoice tance of the Pitons. **Pros:** small and sophisticated; chocolate lover's
★ dream hotel; free Wi-Fi. **Cons:** no a/c; no TV; no children under 12; rental car advised; not for anyone allergic to or less than thrilled by the idea of all that chocolate. $ *Rooms from: US$395* ⊠ *Rabot Estate, West Coast Rd., 2 miles (3 km) south of town* ☎ *758/572–9600* ⊕ *www. thehotelchocolat.com* ⟿ *14 rooms* ⦾ *Multiple meal plans.*

Jade Mountain

$ 🏨 **Fond Doux Holiday Plantation.** Here at one of Soufrière's most active agricultural plantations, a dozen historic homes salvaged from all around the island have been rebuilt on the 135-acre estate and refurbished as guest accommodations. **Pros:** an exotic, ecofriendly experience; striking location on an 18th-century plantation. **Cons:** no a/c; no TV; a rental car is advised, as beach and local sights are a few miles away; not all cottages have a kitchen. [$] *Rooms from: US$275* ✉ *Fond Doux Estate, 4 miles south of Soufrière* ☎ *758/459–7545* 🌐 *www.fonddouxestate.com* 🛏 *12 cottages* 🍴 *Multiple meal plans.*
RESORT

$ 🏨 **Hummingbird Beach Resort.** Unpretentious and welcoming, this delightful little inn on Soufrière Harbour has simply furnished rooms—a traditional motif emphasized by four-poster beds and African wood sculptures—in small seaside cabins. **Pros:** local island hospitality; small and quiet; small beach; good food. **Cons:** few resort amenities—but that's part of the charm. [$] *Rooms from: US$100* ✉ *Anse Chastanet Rd.* ☎ *758/459–7985* 🌐 *www.hummingbirdbeachresort.com* 🛏 *9 rooms, 2 with shared bath, 1 suite, 1 cottage* 🍴 *Some meals.*
B&B/INN

$$$$ 🏨 **Jade Mountain.** This premium-class, premium-priced, adults-only hotel is an architectural wonder perched on a picturesque mountainside overlooking Anse Chastanet Bay. **Pros:** amazing accommodations; huge in-room pools; incredible Piton views. **Cons:** sky-high rates; no a/c; not a good choice for anyone with disabilities. [$] *Rooms from: US$1350* ✉ *Anse Chastanet, Anse Chastanet Rd.* ☎ *758/459–4000* 🌐 *www.jademountainstlucia.com* 🛏 *28 rooms* 🍴 *Multiple meal plans.*
RESORT
Fodor's Choice ★

$$$$ B&B/INN Fodor's Choice ★ 🏨 **Ladera.** The elegantly rustic Ladera, perched 1,100 feet above the sea directly between the two Pitons, is one of the most sophisticated small inns in the Caribbean but, at the same time, takes a local, ecofriendly approach to furnishings, food, and service. **Pros:** local flavor and style; breathtaking Pitons vista; in-room pools; excellent cuisine; complimentary Wi-Fi. **Cons:** expensive; the communal infinity pool is small; open fourth walls and steep drops make this the wrong place for kids or anyone with disabilities; no a/c (but no real need due to the breezy setting); rental car suggested. [$] *Rooms from: US$805* ✉ *West Coast Rd., 3 miles (5 km) south of town, Val de Pitons* ☎ *758/459–6600* 🌐 *www.ladera.com* 🛏 *32 suites, 5 villas* 🍴 *Multiple meal plans.*

$$$ RESORT 🏨 **Stonefield Estate Villa Resort & Spa.** The 18th-century plantation house and several gingerbread-style cottages that dot this 26-acre family-owned estate, a former lime and cocoa plantation that spills down a tropical hillside, have eye-popping views of Petit Piton. **Pros:** very private; beautiful pool; great sunset views from villa decks; lovely wedding venue; complimentary Wi-Fi. **Cons:** a rental car is recommended; you have to drive to off-site restaurants. [$] *Rooms from: US$402* ✉ *West Coast Rd., 1 mile (1½ km) south of Soufrière* ☎ *758/459–7037* 🌐 *www.stonefieldvillas.com* 🛏 *17 villas* 🍴 *Multiple meal plans.*

$$$$ ALL-INCLUSIVE FAMILY Fodor's Choice ★ 🏨 **Sugar Beach, A Viceroy Resort.** Located in Val des Pitons, the steep valley (once a sugar plantation) between the Pitons and the most dramatic 192 acres in St. Lucia, the resort's magnificent private villas are tucked into the dense tropical foliage that covers the hillside and reaches down to the sea. **Pros:** amazing accommodations; incomparable scenery, service, and amenities; perfect for a honeymoon; huge infinity-edge pool; complimentary Wi-Fi, with an iPad to use during your stay. **Cons:** very expensive; fairly isolated, so a meal plan makes sense; rental car advised. [$] *Rooms from: US$790* ✉ *Val des Pitons, 2 miles (3 km) south of town* ☎ *800/235–4300, 758/456–8000* 🌐 *www.viceroyhotelsandresorts.com/sugarbeach* 🛏 *11 rooms, 59 villas, 8 beachfront bungalows* 🍴 *All-inclusive.*

VIEUX FORT

$$$$ ALL-INCLUSIVE FAMILY 🏨 **Coconut Bay Beach Resort & Spa.** The only resort in Vieux Fort, Coconut Bay is a sprawling (85 acres), family-friendly, seaside retreat minutes from St. Lucia's Hewanorra International Airport. **Pros:** great for families; perfect for kitesurfing; friendly and sociable atmosphere. **Cons:** bathrooms have showers only; rough surf. [$] *Rooms from: US$689* ☎ *758/459–6000, 877/352–8898 in the U.S.* 🌐 *www.cbayresort.com* 🛏 *223 rooms, 27 suites* 🍴 *All-inclusive.*

NIGHTLIFE AND THE ARTS

THE ARTS

St. Lucia Jazz. A weeklong festival held in early May, St. Lucia Jazz is one of the premier events of its kind in the Caribbean. International jazz greats perform at outdoor venues on Pigeon Island and at various hotels, restaurants, and nightspots throughout the island; free concerts are also held at Derek Walcott Square in downtown Castries. ⊠ *Pigeon Island* ⊕ *www.stluciajazz.org.*

NIGHTLIFE

Most resort hotels have entertainment—island music, calypso singers, or steel bands, as well as disco, karaoke, or staff/guest talent shows—every night in high season and a couple of nights per week in the off-season. Otherwise, Rodney Bay Village is the best bet for nightlife. The many restaurants and bars there attract a crowd nearly every night.

BARS

Jambe de Bois. Enjoy live jazz on Sunday evenings at this cozy Old English–style pub within the Pigeon Island National Landmark. ⊠ *Pigeon Island, Gros Islet* ☎ *758/450–8166.*

CASINOS

Treasure Bay Casino. At St. Lucia's first (and only, so far) casino, you'll find more than 250 slot machines, along with 22 gaming tables (poker, blackjack, roulette, and craps) and a sports bar with 31 television screens. ⊠ *Bay Walk Shopping Mall, Reduit Beach Ave., just off Castries-Gros Islet Hwy., Rodney Bay Village, Gros Islet* ☎ *758/459–2901* ⊕ *www.treasurebaystlucia.com* ⊗ *Sun.–Thurs. 10 am–3 am, Fri. and Sat., 10 am–4 am.*

DANCE CLUBS

Rodney Bay Village has the most bars and clubs. Most dance clubs with live bands have a cover charge of $10 to $20 (EC$25 to EC$50), and the music usually starts at 11 pm.

Delirius. At Delirius, visitors and St. Lucians alike "lime" over cocktails at the horseshoe-shaped bar and at tables in the garden. The atmosphere is casual, the decor is contemporary, and the music (live bands or DJs on Wednesday, Friday, and Saturday nights) is often from the 1960s, '70s, and '80s. ⊠ *Reduit Beach Ave., Rodney Bay Village, Gros Islet* ☎ *758/451–3354* ⊗ *Closed Sun.*

Doolittle's. The music at Doolittle's, on the north side of the prettiest bay in St. Lucia, changes nightly. Expect live bands and a mix of calypso, soul, salsa, steel band, reggae, limbo, and other music for dancing. ⊠ *Marigot Beach Club, Marigot Bay* ☎ *758/451–4974.*

STREET PARTIES

Anse La Raye "Seafood Friday." For a taste of St. Lucian village life, head for this street festival, which is held every Friday night. Beginning at 6:30 pm, the main street in this tiny fishing village—about halfway between Castries and Soufrière—is closed to vehicles, and the residents prepare what they know best: fish cakes, grilled or stewed fish, hot bakes (biscuits), roasted corn, boiled crayfish, and lobster (grilled before your eyes). Prices range from a few cents for a fish cake or bake to $10 or $15 for a whole lobster, depending on its size. Walk around, eat, chat with the local people, and listen to live music until the wee hours of the morning. ⊠ *Main St., off West Coast Hwy., Anse la Raye.*

Fodor's Choice ★ **Gros Islet Jump-Up.** The island's largest street party is a Friday-night ritual for locals and visitors alike. Huge speakers set up on the street in this little fishing village blast Caribbean music all night long. Sometimes there are live bands. When you take a break from dancing, you can buy barbecued fish or chicken, rotis, beer, and soda from villagers who set up grills right along the roadside. It's the ultimate "lime" experience. ⊠ *Dauphin St., off Castries-Gros Islet Hwy., Gros Islet.*

SHOPPING

The island's best-known products are artwork and wood carvings, straw mats, clay pottery, and clothing and household articles made from batik and silk-screened fabrics that are designed and produced in island workshops. You can also take home straw hats and baskets and locally grown cocoa, coffee, spices, sauces, and flavorings.

AREAS AND MALLS

Bay Walk Mall, at Rodney Bay Village, is a 60-store complex of boutiques, restaurants, banks, a beauty salon, jewelry and souvenir stores, and the island's first (and only, so far) casino.

Along the harbor in Castries, rambling structures with bright-orange roofs house several markets that are open from 6 am to 5 pm Monday through Saturday. Saturday morning is the busiest and most colorful time to shop. For more than a century, farmers' wives have gathered at the **Castries Market** to sell produce—which, alas, you can't import to the United States. But you can bring back spices (such as cocoa sticks or balls, turmeric, cloves, bay leaves, ginger, peppercorns, cinnamon sticks, nutmeg, and mace), as well as locally bottled hot-pepper sauces—all of which cost a fraction of what you'd pay back home. The **Craft Market,** adjacent to the produce market, has aisles and aisles of baskets and other handmade straw work, rustic brooms made from palm fronds, wood carvings, leather work, clay pottery, and souvenirs—all at affordable prices. The **Vendors' Arcade,** across the street from the Craft Market, is a maze of stalls and booths where you can find handicrafts among the T-shirts and costume jewelry.

Gablewoods Mall, on the Gros Islet Highway in Choc Bay, a couple of miles north of downtown Castries, has about 35 shops that sell groceries, wines and spirits, jewelry, clothing, crafts, books and overseas newspapers, music, souvenirs, household goods, and snacks.

Along with 54 boutiques, restaurants, and other businesses that sell services and supplies, a large supermarket is the focal point of each **J.Q.'s Shopping Mall**; one is at Rodney Bay Village, and another is at Vieux Fort.

Marigot Marina Village in Marigot Bay has shops and services for boaters and landlubbers alike, including a bank, grocery store, business center, art gallery, assortment of boutiques, and French bakery and café.

Duty-free shopping areas are at **Pointe Seraphine,** an attractive Spanish-motif complex on Castries Harbour with a dozen shops, and **La Place Carenage,** an inviting three-story complex on the opposite side of the harbor. You can also find duty-free items at Bay Walk Mall, in a few small shops at the arcade at the Royal by Rex Resorts hotel in Rodney Bay Village, and, of course, in the departure lounge at Hewanorra International Airport. You must present your passport and airline ticket to purchase items at the duty-free price.

Vieux Fort Plaza, near Hewanorra International Airport in Vieux Fort, is the main shopping center in the southern part of St. Lucia. You'll find a bank, supermarket, bookstore, toy shop, and several clothing stores there.

ART

Caribbean Art & Antiques. On offer here are original artwork by local artists, along with antique maps and prints and hand-painted silk. ⊠ *Golf Park Rd., Mount du Cap, Cap Estate* ☎ *758/450–9740.*

Llewellyn Xavier. World-renowned St. Lucian artist Llewellyn Xavier creates modern art, ranging from vigorous oil abstracts that take up half a wall to small objects made from beaten silver and gold. Much of his work has an environmental theme and is created from recycled materials. Xavier's work is owned by major museums in New York and Washington, D.C. Others are sold in gift shops throughout the island. ■TIP➔ **Call to arrange a visit to his studio.** ⊠ *Mount du Cap, Cap Estate* ☎ *758/450–9155* ⊕ *www.llewellynxavier.com.*

CLOTHES AND TEXTILES

The Bagshaws of St. Lucia. Using Sydney Bagshaw's original designs, this shop sells clothing and table linens in colorful tropical patterns. The fabrics are silk-screened by hand in the adjacent workroom. You can also find Bagshaw boutiques at Pointe Seraphine and La Place Carenage, as well as a selection of items in gift shops at Hewanorra Airport. Visit the workshop to see how the designs are turned into colorful silk-screened fabrics, which are then fashioned into clothing and household articles. It's open weekdays from 8:30 to 5, Saturday 8:30 to 4, and Sunday 10 to 1. Weekend hours may be extended if a cruise ship is in port. ⊠ *La Toc Rd., La Toc, Castries* ☎ *758/451–9249.*

The Batik Studio. The superb batik sarongs, scarves, and wall panels sold here are designed and created on-site by the store's proprietor, Joan Alexander. ⊠ *Hummingbird Beach Resort, Anse Chastanet Rd., Soufrière* ☎ *758/459–7985* ⊕ *www.hummingbirdbeachresort.com.*

Caribelle Batik. At Caribelle Batik, craftspeople demonstrate the art of batik and silk-screen printing. Meanwhile, seamstresses use the batik fabric to make clothing and wall hangings, which you can buy in the shop. The studio is in an old Victorian mansion, high atop Morne Fortune and a 10-minute drive south of Castries. There's a terrace where you can have a cool drink and a garden full of tropical orchids and lilies. Caribelle Batik creations are also available in many gift shops throughout St. Lucia. ⊠ *Howelton House, Old Victoria Rd., Morne Fortune, Castries* ☎ *758/452–3785* ⊕ *www.caribellebatikstlucia.com.*

Sea Island Cotton Shop. High-quality T-shirts, Caribelle Batik clothing and other resort wear, and colorful souvenirs are all for sale here. ⊠ *Bay Walk Shopping Mall, Reduit Beach Ave., just off Castries-Gros Islet Hwy., Rodney Bay Village, Gros Islet* ☎ *758/458–4220* ⊕ *www.seaislandstlucia.com.*

GIFTS AND SOUVENIRS

Caribbean Perfumes. Using exotic flowers, fruits, tropical woods, and spices, Caribbean Perfumes blends eight lovely scents for women and two aftershaves for men. The reasonably priced fragrances, all made in St. Lucia, are available at most gift shops. ⊠ *Vigie Marina, Castries* ☎ *758/453–7249* ⊕ *www.caribbeanperfumes.com.*

HANDICRAFTS

Choiseul Arts & Crafts Centre. You can find handmade furniture, clay pots, wood carvings, and straw items at the Choiseul Arts & Crafts Centre, a project of the Ministry of Education to encourage skill development and local crafts. It's on the southwest coast, halfway between Soufrière and Vieux Fort; many of St. Lucia's artisans come from this area. ⊠ *South Coast Hwy., 5 miles south of Choiseul Village, La Fargue* ☎ *758/454–3226* ⊗ *Closed Sun.*

Eudovic's Art Studio. Head to this workshop, studio, and art gallery for wall plaques, masks, and abstract figures hand-carved by sculptor Vincent Joseph Eudovic from local mahogany, red cedar, and eucalyptus wood. ⊠ *West Coast Hwy., just below Morne Fortune, Goodlands, Castries* ☎ *758/452–2747* ⊕ *www.eudovicart.com.*

Zaka. At Zaka, you may get a chance to talk with artist and craftsman Simon Gajhadhar, who fashions totems and masks from driftwood, branches, and other environmentally friendly sources of wood—taking advantage of all the natural nibs and knots that distinguish each piece. Once the "face" is carved, it is painted in vivid colors to highlight the exaggerated features and provide expression. Each piece is unique. ⊠ *on road to Sugar Beach resort, off West Coast Hwy., Malgretoute, Soufrière* ☎ *758/457–1504* ⊕ *www.zaka-art.com.*

SPORTS AND ACTIVITIES

BIKING

22

Bike St. Lucia. This company takes small groups of bikers on Jungle Biking tours along 8 miles of trails that meander through the remnants of the 18th-century plantation, part of the 600-acre Anse Chastanet estate in Soufrière. Stops are made to explore the French colonial ruins, study the beautiful tropical plants and fruit trees, have a picnic lunch, and take a dip in a river swimming hole or a swim at the beach. There's a training area for learning or brushing up on off-road riding skills. If you're staying in the north, you can arrange a tour that includes transportation to the Soufrière area. ⊠ *Anse Mamin Plantation, adjacent to Anse Chastanet, Soufrière* ☎ *758/459–2453* ⊕ *www.bikestlucia.com.*

Palm Services Bike Tours. Tour participants first take a jeep or bus across the central mountains to Dennery, on the east coast. After cycling 3 miles (5 km) through the countryside, bikes are exchanged for shoe leather. The short hike into the rain forest ends with a cool drink and a refreshing swim next to a sparkling waterfall—then the return leg to Dennery. All gear is included, and the four-hour tours are suitable for all fitness levels. ⊠ *Rodney Bay, Gros Islet* ☎ *758/458–0908* ⊕ *www.adventuretoursstlucia.com.*

BOATING AND SAILING

Rodney Bay and Marigot Bay are both centers for bareboat and crewed yacht charters. Charter prices range from $1,700 to $8,000 per week, depending on the season and the type and size of vessel, plus $130 extra per day if you want a skipper and $100 per day for a cook. Some boat charter companies do not operate in August and September—the height of hurricane season.

Bateau Mygo. Choose a monohull or catamaran for your customized private sailing charter for either a couple of days or a week. ⊠ *Chateau Mygo Villas, Marigot Bay* ☎ *758/458–3957* ⊕ *www.sailstlucia.com.*

Destination St. Lucia (DSL) Ltd. For its bareboat yacht charters, DSL's vessels include two 42-foot catamarans and several monohulls ranging in length from 32 to 50 feet. ⊠ *Rodney Bay Marina, Rodney Bay, Gros Islet* ☎ *758/452–8531* ⊕ *www.dsl-yachting.com.*

Moorings Yacht Charters. Bareboat and crewed catamarans and monohulls ranging from Beneteau 39s to Morgan 60s are available for charter from this company. You can also pick up or drop off the boat at the company's facilities in nearby Canouan (in the Grenadines) or Grenada. ⊠ *Rodney Bay Marina, Rodney Bay* ☎ *758/451–4357, 800/952–8420* ⊕ *www.moorings.com* ☉ *Closed Aug. and Sept.*

DIVING AND SNORKELING

Fodor'sChoice ★ You'll find on-site dive shops at several resorts, including the Body Holiday, Sandals Grande. Royal by Rex, and Rendezvous in the north; Ti Kaye farther south; and Anse Chastanet and Sugar Beach, a Viceroy Resort, in Soufrière. Nearly all dive operators, regardless of their own location, provide transportation from Rodney Bay, Castries, Marigot Bay, or Soufrière. Depending on the season and the particular trip, prices range from about $35 for a one-tank shore dive or $65 for a one-tank boat dive to $175 to $250 for a six-dive package over three days and $350 to $400 for a 10-dive package over five days—plus a Marine Reserve permit fee of $6 per day. Dive shops provide instruction for all levels (beginner, intermediate, and advanced). For beginners, a resort course (pool training), followed by one open-water dive, runs about $100 to $130, depending on the number of days and dives included. Snorkelers can rent equipment for $5 to $10; they are also generally welcome on dive trips and usually pay $50 to $70. All prices generally include taxi/boat transfers, lunch, and equipment.

Anse Chastanet, near the Pitons on the southwestern coast, is the best beach-entry dive site. The underwater reef drops from 20 feet to nearly 140 feet in a stunning coral wall.

A 165-foot freighter, *Lesleen M,* was deliberately sunk in 60 feet of water near **Anse Cochon** to create an artificial reef; divers can explore the ship in its entirety and view huge gorgonians, black coral trees, gigantic barrel sponges, lace corals, schooling fish, angelfish, sea horses, spotted eels, stingrays, nurse sharks, and sea turtles.

Anse La Raye, midway up the west coast, is one of St. Lucia's finest wall and drift dives and a great place for snorkeling.

At the **Pinnacles,** four coral-encrusted stone piers rise to within 10 feet of the surface.

Superman's Flight is a dramatic drift dive along the steep walls beneath the Pitons. At the base of **Petit Piton,** a spectacular wall drops to 200 feet, where you can view an impressive collection of huge barrel sponges and black coral trees; strong currents ensure good visibility.

DIVE OPERATORS

Dive Fair Helen. In operation since 1992 and owned by a St. Lucian environmentalist, this PADI center offers half- and full-day excursions on two custom-built dive boats to wreck, wall, and marine reserve areas, as well as night dives and instruction. ⊠ *Marina Village, Marigot Bay* ☎ *758/451–7716, 888/855–2206 in U.S. and Canada* ⊕ *www.divefairhelen.com.*

Island Divers. Found at the edge of the Soufriere Marine Park at Anse Cochon, with two reefs and an offshore wreck accessible from shore, Island Divers has a convenient location for boat dives, PADI certification, and specialty courses. A day package includes hotel transfers, lunch at Ti Kaye's beachside bar and grill, a two-tank dive, and the use of snorkel gear for the day. ⊠ *Ti Kaye Village, off West Coast Hwy., between Anse La Raye and Canaries, Anse Cochon* ☎ *758/456–8110* ⊕ *www.islanddiversstlucia.com.*

Scuba St. Lucia. Daily beach and boat dives and resort and certification courses are available from this PADI Five Star facility on Anse Chastanet Beach, and so is underwater photography and snorkeling equipment. Day trips from the north of the island include round-trip speedboat transportation. ⊠ *Anse Chastanet Resort, Anse Chastanet Rd., Soufrière* ☎ *758/459–7755, 888/465–8242 in the U.S.* ⊕ *www.scubastlucia.com.*

FISHING

Among the deep-sea creatures you can find in St. Lucia's waters are dolphin (the fish, also called dorado or mahimahi), barracuda, mackerel, wahoo, kingfish, sailfish, and white and blue marlin. Sportfishing is generally done on a catch-and-release basis, but the captain may permit you to take a fish back to your hotel to be prepared for your dinner. Neither spearfishing nor collecting live fish in coastal waters is permitted. Half- and full-day deep-sea fishing excursions can be arranged at Vigie Marina. A half day of fishing on a scheduled trip runs about $85 to $90 per person to join a scheduled party; a private charter will cost $500 to $1,200 for up to six or eight people, depending on the size of the boat and the length of time. Beginners are welcome.

Captain Mike's. Named for Captain Mike Hackshaw and run by his family, Bruce and Andrew, this operation's fleet of Bertram powerboats (31 to 46 feet) accommodate as many as eight passengers for half-day or full-day sport-fishing charters; tackle and cold drinks are supplied. Customized sightseeing or whale-watching trips ($50 per person) can also be arranged for small groups (four to six people). ⊠ *Vigie Marina, Ganthers Bay, Castries* ☎ *758/452–7044* ⊕ *www.captmikes.com.*

Hackshaw's Boat Charters. In business since 1953, Hackshaw's Boat Charters runs charters on boats that include the 31-foot *Blue Boy* and the 38-foot *Sea Hunter* (both Bertrams) and the 50-foot, custom-built *Lady Hack* (a Newton Special, also used for whale watching). ⊠ *Vigie Marina, Ganthers Bay, Castries* ☎ *758/453–0553, 758/452–3909* ⊕ *www.hackshaws.com.*

GOLF

St. Lucia has only one 18-hole championship course: **St. Lucia Golf Resort & Country Club,** which is in Cap Estate. **Sandals La Toc Golf Resort and Spa** has a 9-hole course for its guests.

St. Lucia Golf Resort & Country Club. The island's only public course is at its northern tip, featuring wide views of both the Atlantic and the Caribbean and many spots adorned with orchids and bromeliads. Wind and the demanding layout present challenges. The Cap Grill serves breakfast and lunch until 7 pm; the Sports Bar is a convivial meeting place all day long. You can rent clubs and shoes and arrange lessons at the pro shop and perfect your swing at the 350-yard driving range. Fees include carts, which are required; club and shoe rentals are available. Reservations are essential. Complimentary transportation from your hotel (north of Castries) or cruise ship is provided for parties of three or more people. ⊠ *Cap Estate* ☎ *758/452–8523* ⊕ *www.stluciagolf.com* ⛳ *18 holes, 6685 yards, par 71* 🏷 *$100 for 9 holes, $140 for 18 holes.*

GUIDED TOURS

Taxi drivers are well informed and can give you a full tour and often an excellent one, thanks to government-sponsored training programs. Full-day island tours cost about $140 for up to four people, depending on the route and whether entrance fees and lunch are included; half-day tours, $100. If you plan your own day, expect to pay the driver $40 per hour plus tip.

Island Routes. Island Routes offers a variety of adventure tours, including a guided, drive-it-yourself dune buggy safari (two hours) departing either from Rodney Bay Marina for a tour of Pigeon Island and the north or from Soufriere in the south for a tour of the natural sites and attractions in that area. Other tours are via ATV, jeep, horseback, or boat. ☎ *877/768–8370 in the U.S.* ⊕ *www.islandroutes.com.*

Jungle Tours. This company specializes in rainforest hiking tours for all levels of ability. You're required only to bring hiking shoes or sneakers and have a willingness to get wet and have fun. The cost is $95 per person and includes lunch, fees, and transportation via an open Land Rover truck. ⊠ *Cas en Bas, Gros Islet* ☎ *758/715–3438* ⊕ *www. jungletoursstlucia.com.*

St. Lucia Helicopters. How about a bird's-eye view of the island? A 10-minute North Island tour ($95 per person) leaves from Pointe Seraphine, in Castries, continues up the west coast to Pigeon Island, then flies along the rugged Atlantic coastline before returning inland over Castries. The 20-minute South Island tour ($160 per person) starts at Pointe Seraphine and follows the western coastline, circling beautiful Marigot Bay, Soufrière, and the majestic Pitons before returning inland over the volcanic hot springs and tropical rain forest. A complete island tour combines the two and lasts 30 minutes ($200 per person). ⊠ *George F. L. Charles Airport, at hangar, Vigie, Castries* ☎ *758/453–6950* ⊕ *www.stluciahelicopters.com.*

St. Lucia Heritage Tours. The Heritage Tourism Association of St. Lucia (HERITAS), a volunteer group that represents local sites and institutions, puts together "authentic St. Lucia experiences" that focus on local culture and traditions. Groups are kept small, and the tours can be tailored to your interests. Some of the sites visited include a 19th-century plantation house surrounded by nature trails, a 20-foot waterfall hidden away on private property, and a living museum presenting Creole practices and traditions as well as turtle watching, horseback riding, garden walks, and rainforest treks. ⊠ *Pointe Seraphine, Castries* ☎ *758/451–6058* ⊕ *www.heritagetoursstlucia.org.*

Sunlink Tours. This huge tour operator offers dozens of land, sea, and combination sightseeing tours, as well as shopping tours, plantation, and rain-forest adventures via jeep safari, deep-sea fishing excursions, and day trips to other islands. Prices range from $30 for a half-day shopping tour in Castries to $135 for a full-day land-and-sea jeep safari to Soufrière. ⊠ *Place Creole Bldg., Reduit Beach Ave., Rodney Bay Village, Gros Islet* ☎ *758/456–9100* ⊕ *www.sunlinktours.com.*

HIKING

St. Lucia Forestry Department. Trails under this department's jurisdiction include the Barre de L'Isle Trail (just off the highway, halfway between Castries and Dennery), the Forestiere Trail (20 minutes east of Castries), the Des Cartiers Rain Forest Trail (west of Micoud), the Edmund Rain Forest Trail and Enbas Saut Waterfalls (east of Soufrière), the Millet Bird Sanctuary Trail (east of Marigot Bay), and the Union Nature Trail (north of Castries). Most are two-hour hikes on 2-mile loop trails; the bird-watching tour lasts four hours. The Forestry Department provides

22

guides ($2–$30, depending on the hike), who explain the plants and trees that you'll encounter and keep you on the right track. Seasoned hikers climb the Pitons, the two volcanic cones rising 2,461 feet and 2,619 feet from the ocean floor just south of Soufrière. Hiking is recommended only on Gros Piton, which offers a steep but safe trail to the top. The first half of the hike is moderately difficult; reaching the summit is challenging and should be attempted only by those who are physically fit. The view from the top is spectacular. Tourists are also permitted to hike Petit Piton, but the second half of the hike requires a good deal of rock climbing, and you'll need to provide your own safety equipment. Hiking either Piton requires permission from the St. Lucia Forestry Department and a guide. ⊠ *Stanislaus James Bldg., Waterfront, Castries* ☎ *758/468–4104, 758/450–2231 for Piton permission* ⊕ *malff.com.*

St. Lucia National Trust. The St. Lucia National Trust provides fascinating educational programs and tours. Its Eco-South Tours include a hike through a mangrove forest, a boat trip and trek to Maria Islands Nature Reserve, a native fishing tour on a traditional pirogue, handicraft production, horseback riding, and sea moss harvesting. ⊠ *Castries* ☎ *758/452–5005* ⊕ *www.slunatrust.org.*

HORSEBACK RIDING

Creole horses, a breed native to South America and popular on St. Lucia, are fairly small, fast, sturdy, and even-tempered animals suitable for beginners. Established stables can accommodate all skill levels. They offer countryside trail rides, beach rides with picnic lunches, plantation tours, carriage rides, and lengthy treks. Prices run about $40 for a one-hour guided ride, $60 for two hours, and $70–$90 for a three- or four-hour beach rides with swimming (with the horses) and lunch. Transportation is usually provided between the stables and nearby hotels. Local people sometimes appear on beaches with their steeds and offer 30-minute rides for $10 to $15; ride at your own risk.

Atlantic Shores Riding Stables. The two-hour trail rides from Atlantic Shores can take place on the beach and through the countryside. Beginners are welcome. ⊠ *Savannes Bay, Vieux Fort* ☎ *758/285–1090.*

Trim's National Riding Stable. At the island's oldest riding stable there are four sessions per day, plus beach tours, trail rides, and carriage tours to Pigeon Island. ⊠ *Cas en Bas, Gros Islet* ☎ *758/450–8273* ⊕ *horserideslu.50megs.com.*

SEA EXCURSIONS

Fodor'sChoice
★ A day sail or sea cruise from Rodney Bay or Vigie Cove to Soufrière and the Pitons is a wonderful way to see St. Lucia and a great way to get to the island's distinctive natural sites. Prices for a full-day sailing excursion to Soufrière run about $100 per person and include a land tour to the Diamond Botanical Gardens, lunch, a stop for swimming and snorkeling, and a visit to pretty Marigot Bay. You can even add zip-lining, if you wish! Half-day cruises to the Pitons, three-hour whale-watching tours, and two-hour sunset cruises along the northwest coast will cost $45 to $60 per person.

Captain Mike's Whale-Watching Tours. With 20 species of whales and dolphins that live in the Caribbean waters, your chances of sighting some are very good on Captain Mike's three-hour dolphin- and whale-watching trips ($50 per person) aboard *Free Willie*, a 60-foot Defender. ⊠ *Vigie Marina, Ganthers Bay, Castries* ☎ *758/452–7044* ⊕ *www.captmikes.com.*

Endless Summer. On *Endless Summer*, a 56-foot "party" catamaran, you can take a day trip along the coast to Soufrière—hotel transfers, tour, entrance fees, lunch, and drinks included—for $105 per person. A half-day swimming and snorkeling trip is also available. For romantics, there's a weekly sunset cruise, with dinner and entertainment. ⊠ *Reduit Beach Ave., Rodney Bay Village, Gros Islet* ☎ *758/450–8651* ⊕ *www.stluciaboattours.com.*

Mystic Man Tours. This company operates glassbottom boat, sailing, catamaran, deep-sea fishing, snorkeling, and whale- and dolphin-watching tours—all great family excursions—and sunset cruises in the evening. Most trips depart from Soufrière. ⊠ *Maurice Mason St., Soufrière* ☎ *758/459–7783, 800/401–9804* ⊕ *www.mysticmantours.com.*

Sea Spray Cruises. Sail down the West Coast on *Mango Tango*, a 52-foot catamaran, or on *Tango Too*, an 80-foot cat', from Rodney Bay to Soufrière. The all-day Tout Bagay (a little bit of everything) tour includes a visit to the sulfur springs, drive-in volcano, Morne Coubaril Estate, and more. The view of the Pitons from the water is majestic. You'll have lunch and drinks on board, plenty of music, and an opportunity to swim at a remote beach. Tout Bagay operates Monday, Wednesday, and Saturday. Sea Spray operates several other boat tours, including a sunset cruise, on other days of the week. ⊠ *Rodney Bay Marina, Rodney Bay, Gros Islet* ☎ *758/458–0123, 321/220–9423 in the U.S.*

WINDSURFING AND KITEBOARDING

Reef Kite and Surf Centre. You can rent windsurfing or kitesurfing equipment and take lessons from certified instructors at this water-sports center. Windsurfing equipment rental is $50 for a half day; $70 for a full day. Kitesurfing equipment rental is $60 for a half day; $80 for a full day. A three-hour beginning windsurfing course costs $10, including equipment. For kitesurfing, the three-hour starter course costs $200, including equipment and safety gear. Kitesurfing is particularly strenuous, so participants must be excellent swimmers and in good physical health. ⊠ *The Reef Beach Café, Anse de Sables, Vieux Fort* ☎ *758/454–3418.*

ST. MAARTEN/
ST. MARTIN

WELCOME TO ST. MAARTEN/ ST. MARTIN

TO ANGUILLA

Bell F

Baie d
Grand Cas

Anse Heureuse
des Pères

11 - 14 32 - 43

31 Grand
Case

Baie de
Friar

Aeroport de
l'Espérance

30

Pt. Arago

Colombier

ST.
MARTIN

Pte. du Bluff

Baie de la
Potence

Pt. du Plum

Baie
Rouge

Pte. des
Pierres
à Chaux

Le Fort Louis

Terres
Basses

Baie Nettlé

Baie de
Marigot

23 ★Marigot

Sandy Ground

24 - 28

10

Baie Longue

9

Cupecoy Beach

17 - 19

20

21

22

Musée de
Saint-Martin

Simpson Bay
Lagoon

Sentry
Hill

Dutch
Cul-de-Sac

Mullet
Bay

8

Princess Juliana
International
Airport

12 13

ST.
MAARTEN

16

15

7 6 14

11
The Carousel

Maho
Bay

Simpson
Bay

8

7

Koolbaai

Annie

5

9 10

4

Pelican
Key

Cole
Bay

Great Bay

Little Bay
Beach

3

KEY

📐 Beaches
⚓ Cruise Ship Terminal
◺ Dive Sites
⚓ Ferry
1 Restaurants
1 Hotels

Little
Bay

Grea
Bay

Caribbean Sea

TWO NATIONS, ONE ISLAND

St. Maarten/St. Martin is home to approximately 77,000 people from some 70 different countries, but governance of the 37-square-mile (96-square-km) island is split between France and the Netherlands. It's the smallest island in the world divided between two ruling powers. The Dutch capital is Philipsburg; the French capital is Marigot.

TOP REASONS TO VISIT ST. MAARTEN/ST. MARTIN

1 Great Food: The island has so many good places to dine that you could eat out for a month and never repeat a restaurant visit.

2 Lots of Shops: Philipsburg is one of the top shopping spots in the Caribbean, and Marigot brings a touch of France.

3 Beaches Large and Small: Thirty-seven picture-perfect beaches are spread out all over the island.

4 Water Sports Galore: The wide range of water sports will satisfy almost any need and give you the perfect excuse to finally try stand-up paddleboarding or kitesurfing.

5 Nightlife Every Night: There is a wide variety of nightlife: shows, discos, beach bars, and casinos.

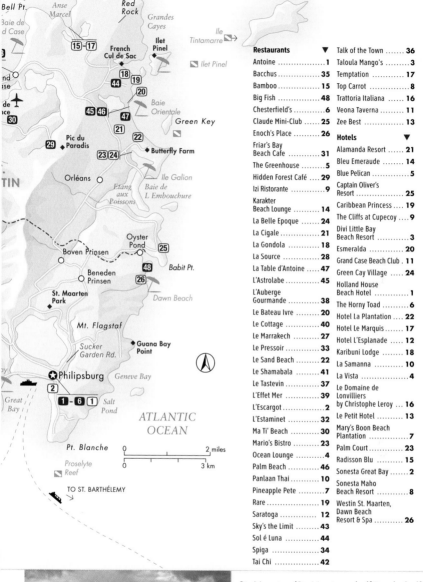

Creole Rock
Anse Marcel
Red Rock
Grandes Cayes
Bell Pt.
Baie de d Case
Pt. des Froussards
Île Tintamarre →
Îlet Pinel
French Cul de Sac
15 – 17
18
19
44
20
45 46
47
21
22
23 24
29 Pic du Paradis
Orléans
Butterfly Farm
Île Galion
Baie de L'Embouchure
Étang aux Poissons
Baie Orientale
Green Key
30
Oyster Pond
25
Boven Prinsen
48
Babit Pt.
Beneden Prinsen
26
St. Maarten Park
Mt. Flagstaf
Sucker Garden Rd.
Guana Bay Point
Dawn Beach
Philipsburg
Geneve Bay
2
1 – 6 1
Salt Pond
Great Bay
ATLANTIC OCEAN
Pt. Blanche
0 ___ 2 miles
0 ___ 3 km
Proselyte Reef
TO ST. BARTHÉLEMY →
Îlet Pinel
TIN

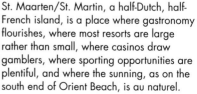

St. Maarten/St. Martin, a half-Dutch, half-French island, is a place where gastronomy flourishes, where most resorts are large rather than small, where casinos draw gamblers, where sporting opportunities are plentiful, and where the sunning, as on the south end of Orient Beach, is au naturel.

Updated by
Elise Meyer

St. Maarten/St. Martin is virtually unique among Caribbean destinations. The 37-square-mile (96-square-km) island is a seamless place (there are no border gates), but it is governed by two nations—the Netherlands and France—and has residents from 70-some different countries. A call from the Dutch side to the French is an international call, currencies are different, and even the vibe is different. Only the island of Hispaniola, which encompasses two distinct countries, Haiti and the Dominican Republic, is in even a similar position in the Caribbean.

Happily for Americans, who make up the majority of visitors to St. Maarten/St. Martin, English works in both nations. Dutch St. Maarten might feel particularly comfortable for Americans: the prices are lower (not to mention in U.S. dollars), the big hotels have casinos, and there is more nightlife. Huge cruise ships disgorge masses of shoppers into the Philipsburg shopping area at midmorning, when roads can quickly become overly congested. But once you pass the meandering, unmarked border into the French side, you will find a bit of the ambience of the south of France: quiet countryside, fine cuisine, and in Marigot, a walkable harbor area with outdoor cafés, outdoor markets, and plenty of shopping and cultural activities.

Almost 4,000 years ago, it was salt and not tourism that drove the little island's economy. Arawak Indians, the island's first known inhabitants, prospered until the warring Caribs invaded, adding the peaceful Arawaks to their list of conquests. Columbus spotted the isle on November 11, 1493, and named it after St. Martin (whose feast day is November 11), but it wasn't populated by Europeans until the 17th century, when it was claimed by the Dutch, French, and Spanish. The Dutch and French finally joined forces to claim the island in 1644, and the Treaty of Concordia partitioned the territory in 1648. According to legend the border was drawn along the line where a French man and a Dutch man, running from opposite coasts, met.

Both sides of the island offer a touch of European culture along with a lot of laid-back Caribbean ambience. Water sports abound—diving, snorkeling, sailing, windsurfing, and in early March, the Heineken Regatta. With soft trade winds cooling the subtropical climate, it's easy to while away the day relaxing on one of the 37 beaches, strolling Philipsburg's boardwalk, and perusing the shops on Philipsburg's Front Street or the *rues* (streets) of the very French town of Marigot. Although luck is an important commodity at St. Maarten's 13 casinos, chance plays no part in finding a good meal at the excellent eateries or after-dark fun in the subtle to sizzling nightlife. Heavy development—especially on the Dutch side—has stressed the island's infrastructure, but slowly some of the more dilapidated roads are showing signs of improvement. A series of large roundabouts, with the beginnings of some decent signage, and attractive monumental sculptures has improved traffic flow (remember, the cars already in the roundabout have right-of-way). At long last, the eyesore of hurricane-wrecked buildings that line the golf course at Mullet Bay have been demolished, and most welcome is the new swing bridge that crosses Simpson Bay Lagoon, connecting the airport and Cole Bay.

When cruise ships are in port (and there can be as many as seven at once), shopping areas are crowded and traffic moves at a snail's pace. We suggest spending the days on the beach or the water, and planning shopping excursions for the early morning or at cocktail hour, after "rush hour" traffic calms down. Still, these are minor inconveniences compared with the feel of the sand between your toes or the breeze through your hair, gourmet food sating your appetite, and having the ability to crisscross between two nations on one island.

PLANNING

WHEN TO GO
The high season begins in December and runs through the middle of April. During the off-season, hotel rooms can be had for as little as half the high-season rates.

GETTING HERE AND AROUND
AIR TRAVEL
There are nonstop flights from Atlanta (Delta, seasonal), Boston (Jet-Blue), Charlotte (US Airways), Miami (American), New York–JFK (American, Delta, JetBlue), New York–Newark (United), and Philadelphia (US Airways).There are also some nonstop charter flights (including GWV/Apple Vacations from Boston). You can also connect in San Juan on JetBlue, LIAT, or Air Sunshine. Many smaller Caribbean-based airlines, including Air Caraïbes, Anguilla Air Services, Caribbean Airlines, Copa, Dutch Antilles Express, Insel, LIAT, and Winair (Windward Islands Airways), offer service from other islands in the Caribbean.

Airline Contacts Air Caraïbes ☎ *590/590–52–05–10* ⊕ *www.aircaraibes-usa. com.* **American Airlines** ☎ *721/545–2040, 800/433–7300* ⊕ *www.aa.com.* **Caribbean Airlines** ☎ *721/546–7660* ⊕ *www.caribbean-airlines.com.* **Delta Airlines** ☎ *721/546–7615* ⊕ *www.delta.com.* **Insel Air** ☎ *599/546– 7621* ⊕ *www.fly-inselair.com.* **JetBlue** ☎ *721/546–7797, 877/306–4939* ⊕ *www.jetblue.com.* **LIAT** ☎ *888/844–5428* ⊕ *www.liatairline.com.* **St. Barths Commuter** ☎ *590/87–80–73* ⊕ *www.stbarthcommuter.com.* **United Airlines** ☎ *721/546–7663* ⊕ *www.united.com.* **US Airways** ☎ *721/546–7680* ⊕ *www. usairways.com.* **Winair** ☎ *721/545–2568* ⊕ *www.fly-winair.com.*

Airports Aéroport de L'Espérance. This airport, on the French side, is small and handles only island-hoppers. ✉ *SFG rte. l'Espérance, Grand Case, St. Martin* ☎ *590/27–11–00* ⊕ *www.aeroport-saintmartin.com.* **Princess Juliana International Airport.** This airport on the Dutch side handles all the large jets. ☎ *721/546–7542* ⊕ *www.sxmairport.com.*

BOAT AND FERRY TRAVEL

You can take ferries to St. Barth (45–80 minutes, €67–€93 from the Dutch or French side, though you can pay in dollars); to Anguilla (20 minutes, $25 from the French side); and to Saba (one to two hours, $90–$100 from the Dutch side). *Babou One,* a stabilized, air-conditioned boat run by West Indies Ferry Express, offers service between Marigot and Gustavia in only 70 minutes, timed to connect with international flights to and from St. Maarten's Princess Juliana Airport.

Contacts *Dawn II.* Ferry service to Saba. ✉ *Philipsburg, St. Maarten* ☎ *599/416–2299* ⊕ *www.sabactransport.com.* **Edge I and *Edge II.*** Day trips to Saba, St. Barth, and Anguilla. ✉ *Pelican Marina, Simpson Bay, St. Maarten* ☎ *721/544–2640, 721/544–2631* ⊕ *www.stmaarten-activities.com.* **Great Bay Express.** Service to St. Barth several times a day on a high-speed ferry. ✉ *Bobby's Marina Village, Phillipsburg, St. Maarten* ☎ *721/542–0032* ⊕ *www. greatbayferry.com.* **Link Ferries.** Ferry service to Anguilla from both Marigot and Princess Juliana Airport. ✉ *Marigot, St. Martin* ☎ *264/497–2231 in Anguilla, 264/497–3290 in Anguilla* ⊕ *www.link.ai.* **Shauna.** Service to Anguilla. ✉ *Simpson Bay, St. Maarten* ☎ *599/553–1820 in Anguilla.* **Voyager II.** Service to St. Barth from both Marigot and Oyster Pond. ✉ *Marigot, St. Martin* ☎ *590/87–10–68* ⊕ *www.voy12.com.*

CAR TRAVEL

It's easy to get around the island by car. Most roads are paved and in generally good condition. However, they can be crowded, especially when the cruise ships are in port; you might experience traffic jams, particularly around Marigot and Philipsburg. Be alert for potholes and speed bumps, as well as the island tradition of stopping in the middle of the road to chat with a friend or yield to someone entering traffic. Few roads are identified by name or number, but most have signs indicating the destination. Driving is on the right. There are gas stations in Simpson Bay near the airport as well as in Cole Bay, and on the French side, in Sandy Ground and Marigot.

Car Rentals: You can book a car at Juliana International Airport, where all major rental companies have booths, but it is often much cheaper to reserve a car in advance from home. A shuttle to the rental-car lot

LOGISTICS

Getting to St. Maarten/St. Martin: There are nonstop flights to St. Maarten from the United States, as well as connecting service through San Juan. Further, St. Maarten is a hub for smaller, regional airlines. The island's main airport is Princess Juliana International Airport (SXM), on the Dutch side. Aeroport de L'Espérance (SFG), on the French side, is small and handles only small planes.

Hassle Factor: Low to medium.

On the Ground: Most visitors rent a car upon arrival, but taxi service is available at the airport with fixed fares to all hotels on the island, and you'll be able to pay the fare in U.S. dollars. Although the island is small, it's still a long drive to many hotels on the French side, and the fares will add up.

Getting Around the Island: Most visitors rent a car because rates are fairly cheap and the island is easy to navigate. It's possible to get by with taxis if you are staying in a major hub such as Philipsburg or Baie Orientale, but you may spend more money than if you rented a car.

is provided. Rates are among the best in the Caribbean, as little as $20–$35 per day. You can rent a car on the French side, but this rarely makes sense for Americans because of the unfavorable exchange rates.

Car-Rental Contacts Avis ⌧ *Simpson Bay, St. Maarten* ☎ *721/545–2847* ⊕ *www.avis.com.* **Dollar/Thrifty Car Rental** ☎ *721/545–2393* ⊕ *www.dollar. com.* **Empress Rent-a-Car** ☎ *721/545–2062* ⊕ *www.empressrentacar.com.* **Golfe Car Rental** ☎ *0590/51–94–81 on French side* ⊕ *www.golfecarrental.com.* **Hertz** ☎ *721/545–4541* ⊕ *www.hertz.com.* **Unity** ⌧ *Simpson Bay, St. Maarten* ☎ *721/520–5767* ⊕ *www.unitycarrental.com.*

SCOOTER TRAVEL

Though traffic can be heavy, speeds are generally slow, so a moped can be a good way to get around. Scooters rent for as low as €25 per day and motorbikes for €37 a day at Eugene Moto, on the French side. The Harley-Davidson dealer, on the Dutch side, rents hogs for $150 a day or $900 per week.

Contacts Eugene Moto ⌧ *Sandy Ground Rd., Sandy Ground, St. Martin* ☎ *590/87–13–97.* **Harley-Davidson** ⌧ *71 Union Rd., Cole Bay, St. Maarten* ☎ *721/544–2704* ⊕ *www.h-dstmartin.com.*

TAXI TRAVEL

There is a government-sponsored taxi dispatcher at the airport and at the harbor. Posted fares are for one or two people. Add $5 for each additional person, $1 to $2 per bag. It costs about $18 from the airport to Philipsburg or Marigot, and about $30 to Dawn Beach. After 10 pm fares go up 25%, and after midnight 50%. Licensed drivers can be identified by the "taxi" license plate on the Dutch side and the window sticker on the French. You can hail cabs on the street or call the taxi dispatch to have one sent for you. Fixed fares apply from Juliana International Airport and the Marigot ferry to the various hotels around the island.

ESSENTIALS

Banks and Exchange Services Legal tender on the Dutch side is the Netherlands Antilles florin, but almost everyone accepts dollars. On the French side, the currency is the euro, but most establishments accept dollars. At this writing, quite a few restaurants continue to offer one euro for one dollar exchanges in cash. ATMs dispense dollars or euros, depending on where you are.

Electricity Generally, 110 volts AC (60-cycle) on the Dutch side, just as in the United States. The French side operates on 220 volts AC (60-cycle), with round-prong plugs; there, you'll need an adapter (many hotels can supply these for you).

Language Dutch is the official language of St. Maarten, and French is the official language of St. Martin, but almost everyone speaks English.

Passport Requirements A valid passport is required for all visitors.

Phones Calling from one side of the island to another is an international call. To phone from the Dutch side to the French, you first must dial 00–590–590 for local numbers, or 00–590–690 for cell phones, then the six digit number. To call from the French side to the Dutch, dial 00–721, then the local number. To call a local number on the French side, dial 0590 plus the six-digit number. On the Dutch side, just dial the seven-digit number with no prefix. Any of the local carriers—and most hotel concierges—can arrange for a prepaid rental phone for your use while you are on the island for about $5 a weekday plus a per-minute charge.

Taxes and Service Charges Departure tax from Juliana Airport is $10 to destinations within the Netherlands Antilles and $30 to all other destinations. It is usually included in your air ticket. It will cost you €3 (usually included in the ticket price) to depart by plane from Aéroport de L'Espérance and $5 (the rate can change) by ferry to Anguilla from Marigot's pier. Hotels on the Dutch side add a 15% service charge to the bill as well as a 5% government tax. Hotels on the French side add 10%–15% and generally 5% tax.

Tipping Service charges may be added to hotel and restaurant bills on the Dutch side (otherwise tip 15%–18%). Check bills carefully so you don't inadvertently tip twice. On the French side, a service charge is customary; on top of the included service it is customary to leave an extra 5%–10% *in cash* for the server. Taxi drivers, porters, and maids depend on tips. Give 10% to 15% to cabbies, $1 per bag for porters, and $2 to $5 per night per guest for chambermaids.

ACCOMMODATIONS

The island, though small, is well developed—some say overdeveloped—and offers a wide range of lodging. The larger resorts and time-shares are mostly on the Dutch side; the French side has more intimate properties. Just keep in mind that the popular restaurants around Grand Case, on the French side, are a long drive from most Dutch-side hotels. French-side hotels often charge in euros. Be wary of some of the very lowest-price alternatives, as some of these can be very run-down time-shares, or properties that function as short-term housing for temporary workers or tourists with very low-end tour companies. Additionally, make note of locations of properties very close to the airport, to avoid unpleasant surprises related to noise. In general, the newer a property, the better off you will be.

HOTEL AND RESTAURANT PRICES

Prices in the restaurant reviews are the average cost of a main course at dinner or, if dinner is not served, at lunch; taxes and service charges are generally included. Prices in the hotel reviews are the lowest cost of a standard double room in high season, excluding taxes, service charges, and meal plans (except at all-inclusives). Prices for rentals are the lowest per-night cost for a one-bedroom unit in high season.

For expanded lodging reviews and current deals, visit Fodors.com.

VISITOR INFORMATION

Contacts Dutch-side Tourist Information Bureau ✉ *Vineyard Park Bldg., 33 W. G. Buncamper Rd., Philipsburg, St. Maarten* ☎ *721/542–2337* ⊕ *www. vacationstmaarten.com.* **French-side Office de Tourisme** ✉ *Rte. de Sandy Ground, facing Marina de la Port-Royale, Marigot, St. Martin* ☎ *590/87–57–21* ⊕ *www.iledesaintmartin.org.*

WEDDINGS

There's a three-day waiting period on the Dutch side. Getting married on the French side is not a viable option because of long wait times.

EXPLORING

The best way to explore St. Maarten/St. Martin is by car. Though often congested, especially around Philipsburg and Marigot, the roads are fairly good, though narrow and winding, with some speed bumps, potholes, roundabouts, and an occasional wandering goat herd. Few roads are marked with their names, but destination signs are common. Besides, the island is so small that it's hard to get really lost—at least that is what locals tell you.

If you're spending a few days, get to know the area with a scenic "loop" around the island. Be sure to pack a towel and some water shoes, a hat, sunglasses, and sunblock. Head up the east shoreline from Philipsburg, and follow the signs to Dawn Beach and Oyster Pond. The road winds past soaring hills, turquoise waters, quaint West Indian houses, and wonderful views of St. Barth. As you cross over to the French side, turn into Le Galion for a stop at the calm sheltered beach, the stables, the butterflies, or the windsurfing school, then keep following the road toward Orient Bay, the St-Tropez of the Caribbean. Continue to Anse Marcel, Grand Case, Marigot, and Sandy Ground. From Marigot, the flat island of Anguilla is visible. Completing the loop brings you past Cupecoy Beach, through Maho and Simpson Bay, where Saba looms in the horizon, and back over the mountain road into Philipsburg.

DUTCH SIDE

PHILIPSBURG

The capital of Dutch St. Maarten stretches about a mile (1½ km) along an isthmus between Great Bay and the Salt Pond and has five parallel streets. Most of the village's dozens of shops and restaurants are on Front Street, narrow and cobblestone, closest to Great Bay. It's generally congested when cruise ships are in port, because of its many duty-free shops and several casinos. Little lanes called *steegjes* connect Front Street with Back Street, which has fewer shops and considerably less congestion. Along the beach is a ½-mile-long (1-km-long) boardwalk with restaurants and several Wi-Fi hot spots.

St Maarten Museum. The Sint Maarten Museum hosts rotating cultural exhibits addressing the history, industry, geology, and archaeology of the island. Artifacts range from Arawak pottery shards to objects salvaged from the wreck of the HMS *Proselyte*. An interesting exhibit about hurricanes focuses on Hurricane Luis, which devastated the island in 1995. There is a good reference and video library as well. ⊠ 7 *Front St., Philipsburg* 🕾 *721/542–4917* ⊕ *www.museumsintmaarten. org* 🖃 *$1* ⊘ *Weekdays 10–4.*

Wathey Square (pronounced *watty*) is in the heart of the village. Directly across from the square are the town hall and the courthouse, in the striking white building with the cupola. The structure was built in 1793 and has served as the commander's home, a fire station, a jail, and a post office. The streets surrounding the square are lined with hotels, duty-free shops, restaurants, and cafés. The **Captain Hodge Pier,** just off the square, is a good spot to view Great Bay and the beach that stretches alongside.

ELSEWHERE IN ST. MAARTEN

FAMILY **The Carousel.** Ride a beautiful restored Italian carousel and enjoy dozens of flavors of homemade Italian gelato and French pastries. Adults will love the espresso bar with great coffee drinks, and there is even a small cocktail bar. It's a perfect attraction for kids of all ages. ⊠ *60 Welfare Rd., Cole Bay* 🕾 *721/544–3112* 🖃 *$2* ⊘ *Tues.–Sun. 2–10.*

Yoda Guy Movie Exhibit. This odd-sounding exhibit is actually a nonprofit museum run by Nick Maley, a movie industry artist who was involved in the creation of Yoda and other movie icons. Learn how the artist worked while you enjoy the models and memorabilia on display. While it's certainly a must-see for any *Star Wars* fan, Maley's work should interest every movie buff out there. There are also souvenirs for sale that Maley is happy to autograph. ⊠ *19a Front St., Philipsburg* 🕾 *721/542–4009* ⊕ *www.netdwellers.com/mz/planetp/home.html.*

FRENCH SIDE

MARIGOT

It is great fun to spend a few hours exploring the bustling harbor, shopping stalls, open-air cafés, and boutiques of St. Martin's biggest town, especially on Wednesday and Saturday, when the daily open-air crafts markets expand to include fresh fruits and vegetables, spices, and all manner of seafood. The market might remind you of Provence, especially when

CLOSE UP

Concordia

The smallest island in the world to be shared between two different countries, St. Maarten/St. Martin has existed peacefully in its subdivided state for more than 360 years. The Treaty of Concordia, which subdivided the island, was signed in 1648 and was really inspired by the two resident colonies of French and Dutch settlers (not to mention their respective governments) joining forces to repel a common enemy, the Spanish, in 1644. Although the French were promised the side of the island facing Anguilla and the Dutch the south side of the island, the boundary itself wasn't firmly established until 1817 and only then after several disputes (16 of them, to be exact).

Visitors to the island will likely not be able to tell that they have passed from the Dutch to the French side unless they notice that the roads on the French side feel a little smoother. In 2003 the population of St. Martin (and St. Barthélemy) voted to secede from Guadeloupe, the administrative capital of the French West Indies. That detachment became official in 2007, and St. Martin is now officially known as the Collectivité de Saint-Martin.

aromas of delicious cooking waft by. Be sure to climb up to the fort for the panoramic view, stopping at the museum for an overview of the island. **Marina Port La Royale** is the shopping–lunch-spot central to the port, but rue de la République and rue de la Liberté, which border the bay, have duty-free shops, boutiques, and bistros. The West Indies Mall offers a deluxe (and air-conditioned) shopping experience, with such shops as Lacoste. There's less bustle here than in Philipsburg, but the open-air cafés are still tempting places to sit and people-watch. From the harborfront you can catch ferries for Anguilla and St. Barth. Parking can be a real challenge during the business day, and even at night during the high season.

Fort Louis. Though not much remains of the structure itself, Fort Louis, which was completed by the French in 1789, is great fun if you want to climb the 92 steps to the top for the wonderful views of the island and neighboring Anguilla. On Wednesday and Saturday there is a market in the square at the bottom. ⊠ *Marigot.*

FAMILY **Saint Martin Museum.** At the southern end of Marigot, next to the Marina Port La Royale, is a museum dedicated to preserving St. Martin's history and culture. A new building houses a variety of pre-Columbian treasures unearthed by the Hope Estate Archaeological Society. ⊠ *Terre Basse Rd., Marigot* ☎ *0690/29–48–36* ⊕ *museesaintmartin.e-monsite. com* ☛ *$5* ☉ *Weekdays 9–1 and 3–5.*

FRENCH CUL DE SAC

North of Orient Bay Beach, the French colonial mansion of St. Martin's mayor is nestled in the hills. Little red-roof houses look like open umbrellas tumbling down the green hillside. The area is peaceful and good for hiking. From the beach here, shuttle boats make the five-minute trip to **Ilet Pinel,** an uninhabited island that's fine for picnicking, sunning, and swimming. There are full-service beach clubs there, so just pack the sunscreen and head over.

GRAND CASE

The Caribbean's own Restaurant Row is the heart of this French-side town, a 10-minute drive from either Orient Bay or Marigot, stretching along a narrow beach overlooking Anguilla. You'll find a first-rate restaurant for every palate, mood, and wallet. At lunchtime, or with kids, head to the casual *lolos* (open-air barbecue stands) and feet-in-the-sand beach bars. Twilight drinks and tapas are fun. At night, stroll the strip and preview the sophisticated offerings on the menus posted outside before you settle in for a long and sumptuous meal. If you still have the energy, there are lounges with music (usually a DJ) that get going after 11 pm.

ORLÉANS

North of Oyster Pond and the Étang aux Poissons (Fish Lake) is the island's oldest settlement, also known as the French Quarter. You can still find a few classic, vibrantly painted West Indian–style homes with the original gingerbread fretwork. There are also large areas of the nature and marine preserve that is working to save the fragile ecosystem of the island.

Fodor'sChoice **PIC DU PARADIS**
★   Between Marigot and Grand Case, "Paradise Peak," at 1,492 feet, is the island's highest point. There are two observation areas. From them, the tropical forest unfolds below, and the vistas are breathtaking. The road is quite isolated and steep, best suited to a four-wheel-drive vehicle, so don't head up here unless you are prepared for the climb. There have also been some problems with crime in this area, so it might be best to go with an experienced local guide.

Fodor'sChoice **Loterie Farm.** Halfway up the road to Pic du Paradis is Loterie Farm, a
★   peaceful 150-acre private nature preserve opened to the public in 1999 by American expat B. J. Welch. There are hiking trails and maps, so you can go on your own (€5) or arrange a guide for a group (€25 for six people). Along the marked trails you will see native forest with tamarind, gum, mango, and mahogany trees, and wildlife including greenback monkeys if you are lucky. In 2011 Loterie opened a lovely spring-fed pool and Jacuzzi area with lounge chairs, great music, and chic tented cabanas called L'Eau Lounge; if you're with a group, consider the VIP package there. Don't miss a treetop lunch or dinner at **Hidden Forest Café** (⇨ *Where to Eat, below*), Loterie Farm's restaurant, where Julie Perkis cooks delicious, healthy meals and snacks. If you are brave—and over 4 feet 5 inches tall—try soaring over trees on one of the longest zip lines in the Western Hemisphere. ⊠ *Rte. de Pic du Paradis 103, Rambaud* ☎ *590/87–86–16, 590/57–28–55* ⊕ *www.loteriefarm.com* ⊡ *€35–€55* ⊙ *Tues.–Sun. 9–4.*

ELSEWHERE IN ST. MARTIN

FAMILY **Butterfly Farm.** If you arrive early in the morning when the butterflies
Fodor'sChoice first break out of their chrysalis, you'll be able to marvel at the absolute
★   wonder of dozens of butterflies and moths from around the world and the particular host plants with which each evolved. At any given time, some 40 species of butterflies—numbering as many as 600 individual insects—flutter inside the lush screened garden and hatch on the plants housed there. Butterfly art and knickknacks are for sale in the gift shop. In case you want to come back, your ticket, which includes a guided tour, is good for your entire stay. ⊠ *Le Galion Beach Rd., Quartier d'Orléans* ☎ *590/87–31–21* ⊕ *www.thebutterflyfarm.com* ⊡ *$12* ⊙ *Daily 9–3:30.*

Plantation Mont Vernon. Wander past indigenous flora, a renovated 1786 cotton plantation, and an old-fashioned rum distillery at a unique outdoor history and ecomuseum. Along the rambling paths of this former wooded estate, with beautiful views of Orient Bay, bilingual signs give detailed explanations of the island's agricultural history when its economy was dependent on salt, rum, coffee, sugar, and indigo. There's a complimentary coffee bar along the way and a delightful gift shop at the entrance. ⊠ *Rte. d'Orient-Baie* ☎ *590/29–50–62* ⊕ *www. plantationmontvernon.com* ✉ *€12* ⊘ *Daily 9–5.*

23

BEACHES

For such a small island, St. Maarten/St. Martin has a wide array of beaches, from the long expanse of Baie Orientale on the French side to powdery-soft Mullet Bay on the Dutch side.

Warm surf and a gentle breeze can be found at the island's 37 beaches, and every one of them is open to the public. What could be better? Each is unique: some bustling and some bare, some refined and some rocky, some good for snorkeling and some for sunning. Whatever you fancy in the beach landscape department, it's here, including a clothing-optional one at the south end of Baie Orientale, one of the Caribbean's most beautiful beaches. The key to enjoying beach life on St. Maarten and St. Martin is to try out several beaches; one quickly discovers that several of the island's gems don't have big hotels lining their shores. ⚠ **Petty theft from cars in beach parking lots is an unfortunate fact of life in St. Maarten and St. Martin. Leave nothing in your parked car, not even in the glove compartment or the trunk.**

DUTCH SIDE

Several of the best Dutch-side beaches are developed and have large-scale resorts. But others, including Simpson Bay and Cupecoy, have little development. You'll sometimes find vendors or beach bars to rent chairs and umbrellas (but not always).

Cupecoy Beach. Near the Dutch-French border, this picturesque area of sandstone cliffs, white sand, and shoreline caves is a necklace of small beaches that come and go according to the whims of the sea. Even though the western part is more developed, the surf can be rough. It's popular with gay locals and visitors. Break-ins have been reported in cars, so don't leave anything at all in your vehicle. **Amenities:** food and drink. **Best for:** sunset; solitude. ⊠ *Between Baie Longue and Mullet Bay, Cupecoy, St. Maarten.*

Dawn Beach. True to its name, Dawn Beach is the place to be at sunrise. On the Atlantic side of Oyster Pond, just south of the French border, this is a first-class beach for sunning and snorkeling, but the winds and rough water mean only strong swimmers should attempt to take a dip. It's not usually crowded, and there are several good restaurants nearby. To find it, follow the signs to the Westin or Mr. Busby's restaurant. **Amenities:** food and drink. **Best for:** snorkeling; sunrise. ⊠ *South of Oyster Pond, Dawn Beach, St. Maarten.*

The view from Fort Louis, high above Marigot

Great Bay. A bustling, white-sand beach, Great Bay is just behind Front Street and curves around Phillipsburg, making it very easy to find. Here you'll find boutiques, eateries, a pleasant boardwalk, and even Segway tours. Busy with cruise-ship passengers, the beach is best west of Captain Hodge Pier or around Antoine Restaurant. **Amenities:** food and drink. **Best for:** swimming; walking ⊠ *Philipsburg, St. Maarten.*

Guana Bay. If you're looking for seclusion, you'll find it here. There are no umbrellas and no lounge chairs; even the beach shack has no regular service. What this bay does have is a long expanse of soft sand. The surf is strong, making this beach a popular surfer hangout, but it's definitely not recommended for kids because of the rough surf. It's five minutes northeast of Philipsburg. Turn on Guana Bay Road, which is behind Great Bay Salt Pond. **Amenities:** none. **Best for:** surfing; solitude; walking. ⊠ *Upper Prince's Quarter, St. Maarten.*

Little Bay. Despite its popularity with snorkelers and divers as well as kayakers and boating enthusiasts, Little Bay isn't usually crowded, perhaps due to its gravelly sand. But, it does boast panoramic views of St. Eustatius, Philipsburg, the cruise-ship terminal, Saba, and St. Kitts. The beach is west of Fort Amsterdam and accessible via the Divi Little Bay Beach Resort. **Amenities:** food and drink; parking; toilets. **Best for:** snorkeling; swimming; walking. ⊠ *Little Bay Rd., Little Bay, St. Maarten.*

Mullet Beach. Many believe that this mile-long, powdery white-sand beach behind the Mullet Bay Golf Course is the island's best. Swimmers like it because the water is usually calm, but when the swell is up, the surfers take over the beach. It's also the place to listen for the "whispering pebbles" as the waves wash up. **Amenities:** none. **Best for:** surfing; swimming. ⊠ *South of Cupecoy, Mullet Bay, St. Maarten.*

Simpson Bay Beach. This secluded, half-moon stretch of white-sand beach on the island's Caribbean side is a hidden gem. It's mostly surrounded by private residences, with no big resorts, no Jet Skiers, and no crowds. It's just you, the sand, and the water (along with one funky beach bar to provide some nourishment). Southeast of the airport, follow the signs to Mary's Boon and the Horny Toad guesthouses. **Amenities:** food and drink; toilets; showers. **Best for:** solitude; swimming; walking. ⊠ *Simpson Bay, St. Maarten.*

FRENCH SIDE

Almost all the French-side beaches, whether busy Baie Orientale or less busy Baie des Pères (Friar's Bay), have beach clubs and restaurants. For about $25 a couple you get two chaises (*transats*) and an umbrella (*parasol*) for the day, not mention chair-side service for drinks and food. Only some beaches have bathrooms and showers, so if that is your preference, inquire.

Anse Heureuse (*Happy Bay*). Not many people know about this romantic, hidden gem. Happy Bay has powdery sand, gorgeous luxury villas, and stunning views of Anguilla. The snorkeling is also good. To get here, turn left on the rather rutted dead-end road to Baie des Péres (Friars Bay). The beach itself is a 10- to 15-minute walk from the last beach bar. **Amenities:** food and drink; toilets. **Best for:** solitude; walking; swimming; snorkeling. ⊠ *Happy Bay, St. Martin.*

Baie de Grand Case. Along this skinny stripe of a beach bordering the culinary capital of Grand Case, the old-style gingerbread architecture sometimes peeps out between the bustling restaurants. The sea is calm, and there are tons of fun lunch options from bistros to beachside barbecue stands (called *lolos*). Several of the restaurants rent chairs and umbrellas; some include their use for lunch patrons. In between there is a bit of shopping—for beach necessities but also for the same kinds of handicrafts found in the Marigot market. **Amenities:** food and drink; toilets. **Best for:** swimming; walking. ⊠ *Grand Case, St. Martin.*

FAMILY **Baie des Pères** (*Friars Bay*). This quiet cove close to Marigot has beach grills and bars, with chaises and umbrellas, calm waters, and a lovely view of Anguilla. Kali's Beach Bar, open daily for lunch and (weather permitting) dinner, has a Rasta vibe and color scheme—it's the best place to be on the full moon, with music, dancing, and a huge bonfire, but you can get lunch, beach chairs, and umbrellas any time. Friar's Bay Beach Café is a French Bistro on the sand, open from breakfast to sunset. To get to the beach, take National Road 7 from Marigot, go toward Grand Case to the Morne Valois hill, and turn left on the dead-end road at the sign. **Amenities:** food and drink; toilets. **Best for:** partiers; swimming; walking. ⊠ *Friar's Bay, St. Martin.*

Baie Longue (*Long Bay*). Though it extends over the French Lowlands, from the cliff at La Samanna to La Pointe des Canniers, the island's longest beach has no facilities or vendors. It's the perfect place for a romantic walk, but be warned that car break-ins are a particular problem here. To get here, take National Road 7 south of Marigot. Baie Longue Road is the first entrance to the beach. It's worth it to splurge for lunch or a sunset cocktail at the elegant La Samanna. **Amenities:** none. **Best for:** solitude; walking. ⊠ *Baie Longue, St. Martin.*

Baie Orientale (*Orient Bay*). Many consider this the island's most beautiful beach, but its 2 miles (3 km) of satiny white sand, underwater marine reserve, variety of water sports, beach clubs, and hotels also make it one of the most crowded. Lots of "naturists" take advantage of the clothing-optional policy, so don't be shocked. Early-morning nude beach walking is de rigueur for the guests at Club Orient, at the southeastern end of the beach. Plan to spend the day at one of the clubs; each bar has different color umbrellas, and all boast terrific restaurants and lively bars. You can have an open-air massage, try any sea toy you fancy, and stay until dark. To get to Baie Orientale from Marigot, take National Road 7 past Grand Case, past the Aéroport de L'Espérance, and watch for the left turn. **Amenities:** food and drink; parking; toilets; water sports. **Best for:** partiers; nudists; swimming; walking; windsurfing. ⊠ *Baie Orientale, St. Martin.*

Baie Rouge (*Red Bay*). Here you can bask with the millionaires renting the big-ticket villas in the "neighborhood," joining them on the gorgeous Baie Rouge. The beach and its salt ponds make up a nature preserve, the location of the oldest habitations in the Caribbean. This area is widely thought to have the best snorkeling beaches on the island. You can swim the crystal waters along the point and explore a swim-through cave. The beach is fairly popular with gay men in the mornings and early afternoons. There are two restaurants here; only Chez Raymond is open every day, and cocktail hour starts when the conch shell blows, so keep your ears open. There is a sign and a right turn after you leave Baie Nettlé. **Amenities:** food and drink; toilets. **Best for:** snorkeling; swimming; walking. ⊠ *Baie Rouge, St. Martin.*

Ilet Pinel. A protected nature reserve, this kid-friendly island is a five-minute ferry ride from French Cul de Sac ($7 per person round-trip). The ferry runs every half hour from midmorning until dusk. The water is clear and shallow, and the shore is sheltered. If you like snorkeling, don your gear and paddle along both coasts of this pencil-shape speck in the ocean. You can rent equipment on the island or in the parking lot before you board the ferry for about $10. Plan for lunch any day of the week at a palm-shaded beach hut, Karibuni (except in September, when it's closed) for the freshest fish, great salads, tapas, and drinks—try the frozen mojito for a treat. **Amenities:** food and drink; parking. **Best for:** swimming, snorkeling. ⊠ *Ilet Pinel, St. Martin.*

FAMILY **Le Galion.** A coral reef borders this quiet beach, part of the island's nature preserve, which is paradise if you are traveling with children. The water is calm, clear, and quite shallow, so it's a perfect place for families with young kids. It's a full-service place, with chair rentals, restaurants, and water-sports operators. Kite-boarders and windsurfers like the trade winds at the far end of the beach. On Sunday there are always groups picnicking and partying. To get to Le Galion, follow the signs to the unmissable Butterfly Farm and continue toward the water. **Amenities:** food and drink; parking; toilets; water sports. **Best for:** partiers; swimming; windsurfing. ⊠ *Quartier d'Orléans, St. Martin.*

WHERE TO EAT

Although most people come to St. Maarten/St. Martin for sun and fun, they leave praising the cuisine. On an island that covers only 37 square miles (96 square km), there are more than 400 restaurants from which to choose. You can sample the best dishes from France, Thailand, Italy, Vietnam, India, Japan, and, of course, the Caribbean.

Many of the best restaurants are in Grand Case (on the French side), but you should not limit your culinary adventures to that village. Great dining thrives throughout the island, from the bistros of Marigot to the hopping restaurants of Cupecoy to the low-key eateries of Simpson Bay. Whether you enjoy dining on fine china in one of the upscale restaurants or off a paper plate at the island's many lolos (roadside barbecue stands), St. Maarten/St. Martin's culinary options are sure to appeal to every palate. Loyalists on both "sides" will cheerfully try to steer you to their own favorites, and it's common to cite high euro prices to deter exploration, but quite a few restaurants still offer a one-to-one exchange rate between dollars and euros if you use cash, and main-course portions are often large enough to be shared.

During high season, it's essential to make reservations, and making them a month in advance is advisable for some of the best places. Dutch-side restaurants sometimes include a 15% service charge, so check your bill before tipping. On the French side, service is always included, but it is customary to leave 5% to 10% extra in cash for the server. Don't count on leaving tips on your credit card—it's customary to tip in cash. A taxi is probably the easiest solution to the parking problems in Grand Case, Marigot, and Philipsburg. Grand Case has two lots—each costs $4—at each end of the main boulevard, but they're often packed by 8 pm.

What to Wear: Although appropriate dining attire ranges from swimsuits to sport jackets, casual dress is usually appropriate throughout restaurants on the island. For men, a jacket and khakis or jeans will take you anywhere; for women, dressy pants, a skirt, or even fancy shorts are usually acceptable. Jeans are fine in the less formal eateries.

DUTCH SIDE

CUPECOY

$$$
ITALIAN

✕ **La Gondola.** Under new management, but still in the hands of chef Matteo Puccini, the kitchen rolls out the dough for the dozens of pasta dishes on the encyclopedic Italian menu, which also includes favorites like veal parmigiana, chicken piccata in marsala sauce, and osso buco Milanese. Save room for desserts like the *fantasia di dessert del Carnevale di Venezia* (a warm chocolate tart and frozen nougat served with raspberry sauce) or tiramisu. The service is professional and high-tech—the waiters take orders with earpieces and handheld computers. $ *Average main: $29* ⊠ *Atlantis World Casino, Rhine Rd. 106, Cupecoy* ☎ *721/544–3938* ⊕ *www.lagondola-sxm.com* ☽ *No lunch.*

BEST BETS FOR DINING

Fodor's Choice ★
L'Astrolabe, Bacchus, Bamboo, La Cigale, L'Effet Mer, Mario's Bistro, Le Pressoir, Sky's The Limit, Le Tastevin, Temptation, Top Carrot

MOST ROMANTIC
Le Domaine de Lonvilliers, Le Marrakech, Le Pressoir, La Samanna, Sol é Luna, Temptation

BEST VIEW
La Cigale, La Samanna, Sol é Luna, Taloula Mango's

BEST LOCAL FOOD
Chesterfield's

BEST FOR FAMILIES
Taloula Mango's, Top Carrot

BEST FOR A SPECIAL OCCASION
Le Pressoir, La Samanna (especially the wine dinner in the cellar)

HIP AND YOUNG
Bamboo, Calmos Café, Karakter, Palm Beach, Temptation, Treelounge/Hidden Forest Café

$$$$ STEAKHOUSE 🍴 **Rare.** Within an intimate, clubby setting, a guitarist provides background music while carnivores delight in chef Dino Jagtiani's creative menu. The focus is steak: certified Angus prime cuts topped with chimichurri, béarnaise, horseradish, peppercorn, or mushroom sauce. Not into red meat? You can also choose from seafood, pork, lamb, or veal. Sample some delicious sides like truffled mashed potatoes or cultivated mushroom sauté (a tasty fungi variety). Luscious desserts will make you forget that you will want to look good in your bathing suit tomorrow morning. Check the restaurant's website for specials. [$] *Average main: $54* ✉ *Atlantis World Casino, Rhine Rd. 106, Cupecoy* ☎ *721/545–5714* 🌐 *www.rareandtemptation.com* ✍ *Reservations essential* 🕓 *Closed Sept. and Mon. June–Oct. No lunch.*

$$$$ ECLECTIC 🍴 **Temptation.** Supercreative chef Dino Jagtiani, who trained at the Culinary Institute of America, is the mastermind behind dishes like seared foie gras PB and J (melted foie gras accented with peanut butter and homemade port-wine fig jam) and lump crab-stuffed jumbo shrimp wrapped in salmon bacon with pasta pearls primavera. The chef, who compares dessert to lovemaking ("both intimate, and not to be indulged in lightly"), offers a crème brûlée tasting, as well as tempura apple pie with cinnamon ice cream and caramel sauce. The wine list is extensive, and features a number of reasonably priced selections. The dining room is pretty and intimate, in spite of its location behind the casino. There's outdoor seating as well. [$] *Average main: $36* ✉ *Atlantis Casino Courtyard, Rhine Rd. 106, Cupecoy* ☎ *721/545–2254* 🌐 *www.rareandtemptation.com* ✍ *Reservations essential* 🕓 *Closed Sun. June–Oct. No lunch.*

MAHO

$$ ASIAN Fodor's Choice ★ 🍴 **Bamboo.** This dramatic and hip addition to the top level of the Maho central shopping area features red lacquer walls, lounging tables, Indonesian art, a first-rate bar, and electro-house tunes. You can get terrific sushi and sashimi, both the classic Japanese varieties and the Americanized ones (California roll, for example). All are good, as are the

Asian hot appetizers and exotic cocktails like the Tranquillity (citrus vodka and smoky oolong tea). If you're not into Asian fare, try the salmon, ribs, or beef. The young crowd keeps this place hopping way past midnight. If you're solo, you will have a great time hanging and even dining at the bar. There is a sake and sushi happy hour from 5 to 7 nightly. $ *Average main: $20* ⊠ *Sonesta Maho Beach Resort & Casino, 1 Rhine Rd., Maho* 📞 *721/545–3622* ⊕ *www.bamboo-sxm. com* ⊘ *No lunch Sat. or Sun.*

$$$ ✗ **Big Fish.** A chic, white interior, fresh-caught fish, and friendly, if some-
SEAFOOD times relaxed, service, are the draw at this Oyster Pond restaurant. The
FAMILY location is convenient whether you are staying in Oyster Pond or Dawn Beach. Stick with whatever was most recently in the sea, and you will be happy with your food. If offered, grouper in curry-coconut is a yummy option, and the hurricane shrimp is a local favorite. Light eaters will love the huge fresh salads. The owners also run a fishing-charter outfit, and they will happily cook up your daily catch here, too. $ *Average main: $28* ⊠ *14 Emerald Merrit Rd., Oyster Pond* 📞 *721/586–1961.*

$$$ ✗ **Le Bateau Ivre.** Located in the middle of an anonymous-looking
MEDITERRANEAN plaza in the new-ish Porto Cupecoy Marina complex, the big salads,
FAMILY American-style sandwiches, and varied crepes make this place a good choice for an easy lunch around the marina. At night there are all the French bistro classics, plus seafood specials; all are frequently accompanied by a singer performing Edith Piaf. You can sit outdoors and admire the yachts, or indoors for a more lounge-y feel. $ *Average main: $26* ⊠ *Marina Porto Cupecoy, Maho* 📞 *721/526–2157.*

$$$ ✗ **Trattoria Italiana.** Tucked behind Casino Royale, this plain Italian eat-
ITALIAN ery is extremely popular with locals. The menu includes favorites like
FAMILY penne Bolognese and eggplant Parmesan, but the real winners are the thin-crust pizzas. The freshly brewed iced tea is great on a hot day. With its laid-back atmosphere and friendly staff, this is a cozy spot for families with small children or a place where you just run in and grab a quick bite. $ *Average main: $22* ⊠ *Maho Shopping Plaza, Maho* 📞 *721/545–4034* ⊘ *No lunch Sun.*

PHILIPSBURG

$$ ✗ **Chesterfield's.** Both locals and tourists seem to love this restaurant
CARIBBEAN at Great Bay Marina. Seafood is the main focus, but steaks, burgers,
FAMILY pasta, and poultry are all on the dinner menu, and you can also get breakfast and lunch. If you love sophisticated cuisine, look elsewhere, but the portions are big and the prices reasonable. Happy hour is every night from 5 to 7. Delivery is available if you're staying in a condo or timeshare in the area. $ *Average main: $19* ⊠ *Great Bay Marina, Philipsburg* 📞 *721/542–3484.*

$$$ ✗ **The Greenhouse.** The famous happy hour with two-for-one drinks
ECLECTIC is just one of the reasons people flock to the Greenhouse. This water-
FAMILY front restaurant balances a relaxed atmosphere, reasonable prices, and popular favorites like burgers, prime rib, and steaks. If you're seeking something spicy, try the creole shrimp. The daily specials, like the Friday-night Lobster Mania, are widely popular. $ *Average main: $21* ⊠ *Bobby's Marina, Philipsburg* 📞 *721/542–2941* ⊕ *www. thegreenhouserestaurant.com.*

$$$ ECLECTIC FAMILY 🍴 **Ocean Lounge.** An airy modern veranda perched on the Philipsburg boardwalk gives Ocean Lounge its distinct South Beach vibe. You'll want to linger over fresh fish and steaks as you watch the scene with tourists passing by on romantic strolls by night or determined cruise-ship passengers surveying the surrounding shops by day. The $45 daily three-course tasting menu is a great deal. There is also a fun menu of bar snacks and martinis. It's a bit hard to park here so consider taking a taxi at night. [$] *Average main: $29* ✉ *Holland House Beach Hotel, 43 Front St., Philipsburg* ☎ *721/542–2572* 🌐 *www.hhbh.com.*

$$ ECLECTIC FAMILY 🍴 **Taloula Mango's.** Ribs are the specialty at this casual beachfront restaurant, but the jerk chicken and thin-crust pizza, not to mention a few vegetarian options like the tasty falafel, are not to be ignored. On weekdays lunch is accompanied by (warning: loud) live music; every Friday during happy hour a DJ spins tunes. In case you're wondering, the restaurant got its name from the owner's golden retriever. [$] *Average main: $17* ✉ *Sint Rose Shopping Mall, off Front St. on beach boardwalk, Philipsburg* ☎ *721/542–1645* 🌐 *www.taloulamango.com.*

SIMPSON BAY

$$$ ITALIAN FAMILY 🍴 **Izi Ristorante Italiano.** The former chef of La Gondola serves up huge, shareable portions of more than 400 different dishes in this cheerful, centrally located space. For something fun and different, diners are invited to create their own menu: pick a pasta and a sauce, then add in your choice of meat, fish, and veggies. [$] *Average main: $23* ✉ *Paradise Mall, 67 Welfare Rd., Simpson Bay* ☎ *721/544–3079* 🌐 *www.iziristoranteitaliano.com* ✍ *Reservations essential* ⏲ *Closed Tues. May–Nov.*

$$ ECLECTIC FAMILY Fodor's Choice ★ 🍴 **Karakter Beach Lounge.** Karakter, a funky and charming modern beach bar, is right behind the airport, serving up fun, great music, relaxation, and a lot of style. The vibe is more like St. Tropez than St. Maarten. Open from 9 am till 10 pm, the restaurant serves up healthy and tasty choices for any appetite: fresh fruit smoothies, tropical cocktails, fresh fruit salads, healthy sandwiches, and tapas. A sign near the shower/bathhouse invites guest to "come hang out here and shower before you go to the airport." So this is a place to keep in mind in case your flight is delayed or if you have a layover between flights, or even if you just want to spend every last second of your vacation on the sand. [$] *Average main: $14* ✉ *121 Simpson Bay Rd., Simpson Bay* ☎ *721/523–9983* 🌐 *www.karakterbeach.com.*

$$$ THAI FAMILY 🍴 **Panlaan Thai on the Bay.** This new Thai restaurant serves up big portions of fresh-tasting and nicely presented classic Thai dishes like curries and satays in a pretty, centrally located waterfront deck on Simpson Bay. There's delivery and take-out if you don't have time for a sit-down meal. Happy hour in high season (November–June) features $4 martinis served with $5 appetizers, and there is live music on Sunday nights. **TIP→ It can be breezy at night, so bring a light sweater.** [$] *Average main: $22* ✉ *Welfare Rd., Simpson Bay* ☎ *721/559–2811* 🌐 *www.panlaansxm.com.*

$$ SEAFOOD FAMILY 🍴 **Pineapple Pete.** This popular, casual, and fun (if slightly touristy) place is well located, with a game room that includes seven pool tables, four dart boards, an arcade, and flat-screen TVs tuned to sports. A friendly, efficient staff will serve you burgers, seafood, and ribs, but for a real

treat try one of the specialties like the tasty crab-stuffed shrimp appetizer. Follow it up with succulent, herb-crusted rack of lamb. There's free Wi-Fi and live entertainment Tuesday through Sunday. It's an easy choice for a bite near the airport, and is open from 11 am through closing. Note the 15% service charge included in the check. There's also a little shop for with T-shirts and local crafts for sale. $ *Average main: $20* ✉ *56 Welfare Rd., Simpson Bay* ☎ *721/544–6030* ⊕ *www. pineapplepete.com* ⚓ *Reservations essential.*

$ ✕ **Top Carrot.** Open from 7:30 am to 6 pm, this friendly café and juice bar is a popular breakfast and lunch stop. It features fresh and tasty vegetarian entrées, sandwiches, salads, homemade pastries, and fresh fish. Favorites include a pastry stuffed with pesto, avocado, red pepper, and feta cheese, or a cauliflower, spinach, and tomato quiche. The house-made granola and yogurt are local favorites, but folks also drop in just for espresso and the large selection of teas. Many also come for the free Wi-Fi. Adjacent to the restaurant is a gift shop with Asian-inspired items, spiritual books, and half-price cotton beach cover-ups. $ *Average main: $8* ✉ *Airport Rd., near Simpson Bay Yacht Club, Simpson Bay* ☎ *721/544–3381* ⊘ *Closed Sun. No dinner.*

VEGETARIAN
FAMILY
Fodor's Choice
★

$ ✕ **Vesna Taverna and Bagel House.** Centrally located near the Simpson Bay Bridge, this casual eatery is open all day long, with tasty but healthy options like smoothies, bagel sandwiches, omelets, crepes, pancakes, and salads (burgers are available for dinner). The patio makes for great outdoor eating, plus there's free Wi-Fi. $ *Average main: $10* ✉ *15 Airport Rd., Unit 1, Simpson Bay* ☎ *721/524–5283.*

DELI
FAMILY

$ ✕ **Zee Best.** This friendly bistro serves one of the best breakfasts on the island. There's a huge selection of fresh-baked pastries—try the almond croissants—plus sweet and savory crepes, omelets, quiches, and other treats from the oven. When you sit down a basket of assorted pastries arrives, and you are charged for the ones you select. Specialties include the St. Martin omelet, filled with ham, cheese, mushrooms, onions, green peppers, and tomatoes. Best of all, breakfast is served from 7:30 am until 2 pm. Lunch includes sandwiches, salads, and the chef's famous spaghetti Bolognese. ■ TIP→ **There are also locations near the Airport, and at Port de Plaisance.** $ *Average main: $8* ✉ *Plaza del Lago, Simpson Bay* ☎ *721/544–2477* ▭ *No credit cards.*

CAFÉ

FRENCH SIDE

BAIE NETTLÉ

$$$$ ✕ **La Cigale.** On the edge of Baie Nettlé, La Cigale has wonderful views of the lagoon from its dining room and its open-air patio, but the charm of the restaurant comes from the devoted attention of adorable owner Olivier, helped by his mother and brother, and various cousins, too. Stephane Istel's delicious food is edible sculpture: ravioli of lobster with wild mushrooms and foie gras is poached in an intense lobster bisque, and house-smoked swordfish and salmon is garnished with goat cheese and seaweed salad drizzled with dill-lime vinaigrette. For dessert, the raspberry macaroon is a favorite. $ *Average main: €43* ✉ *101 Laguna Beach, Baie Nettlé* ☎ *599/87–90–23* ⊕ *www.restaurant-lacigale.com* ⚓ *Reservations essential* ⊘ *Closed Sun. No lunch.*

FRENCH
Fodor's Choice
★

23

$$$$ FRENCH FAMILY 🍴 **Le Sand Beach.** A stylish St. Barth vibe and a beachfront location make Le Sand Beach a great choice for any meal. Relax on the terrace and enjoy cocktails and snacks, or park yourself on a lounge chair on the beach with an umbrella (no charge if you're dining), and enjoy the music and ambience. The refined food is fresh and nicely presented; the snapper and fish tartares are stand-outs, but real credit is due to the management and staff who are friendly and attentive. [$] *Average main: $35* ✉ *Sandy Bay, Baie Nettlé* ☎ *690/73–14–38* 🌐 *www.whereisstmartin.com.*

$$$ FRENCH FAMILY 🍴 **Ma Ti' Beach.** Here's a great choice for a casual beach bar with better-than-average food, right across from the Mercure Resort on the road to Marigot. Open for lunch and dinner, it offers great views across the turquoise water to Anguilla. You can always get fresh lobster from the tank, and don't forget the excellent traditional French onion soup with a cheesy crust. If the *moules frites* (fresh mussels) are a special, snap them up. [$] *Average main: €23* ✉ *Anse Margot, across the road from Mercure Resort, Baie Nettlé* ☎ *590/87–01–30* 🕒 *Closed Tues.*

BAIE ORIENTALE

$$$ FRENCH 🍴 **L'Astrolabe.** Chef Maxime Orea gets raves for his modern interpretations of classic French cuisine served around the pool at this cozy, relaxed restaurant in the Esmeralda Resort. Corn soup; foie gras terrine with apricot and quince jam; an amazing roast duck with pineapple-ginger sauce; and deliciously fresh fish dishes are just some of the offerings. There are lots of choices for vegetarians, a three-course prix fixe, a children's menu, and a lobster party with live music every Friday night. [$] *Average main: $26* ✉ *Esmeralda Resort, Baie Orientale* ☎ *0590/87–11–20* 🌐 *www.esmeralda-resort.com* ✍ *Reservations essential* 🕒 *No lunch. No dinner Wed.*

$$$$ FRENCH FAMILY 🍴 **La Table d'Antoine.** Settle in here for an evening of attentive, friendly service and hearty French-country food with a side dish of lively people-watching. The varied menu features slightly unfamiliar dishes that are worth a try, like the *Tartiflette* (a kind of cheese and potato gratin), beef baked in a salt crust, and duck magret with foie gras. Desserts are delicious, as is the selection of house-made infused rums. [$] *Average main: €35* ✉ *Pl. de la Baie Orientale, Baie Orientale* ☎ *590/62–82–28.*

$$$ FRENCH FUSION 🍴 **Palm Beach.** Just as stylish as its Florida namesake, this Baie Orientale beach club sets the stage with Balinese art and furniture, big comfy chaises on the beach, and an active bar. There are three big tree-house-like lounges for lunch or if you are looking for a place to spend the afternoon, plus a spa for beachside massages. The menu of salads, tartares, and Thai-influenced salads and noodle specialties is served in a pavilion shaded by sail-like awnings. The Sunday night beach party is the place to be for locals and guests alike. [$] *Average main: €21* ✉ *Baie Orientale* ☎ *690/35–99–06* 🌐 *www.palmbeachsxm.net* 🕒 *No dinner.*

FRIAR'S BAY

$$ BISTRO 🍴 **Friar's Bay Beach Café.** There is a sophisticated vibe at this quiet, rather elegant beach club that may make patrons feel as if they are on a private beach. The decor is not as funky as some of the other beach-club restaurants, but look out for the red and black signs on the road between Grand Case and Marigot so you'll know where to

turn. Drive slow because the road is rough. You can rent lounge chairs and umbrellas and spend the whole day relaxing, drinking, and dining. The restaurant is open from breakfast through the spectacular sunset, offering a menu reminiscent of a French bistro. Be sure to look at the specials on the blackboard, but carpaccios of meat and fish are sparklingly fresh, and the salads are terrific. Plus, you'll also find French standbys such as tomato and goat cheese tartlets, as well as "international" ones like burgers and sandwiches. On Sunday evening there is live music until 9 pm. $ *Average main: $18* ✉ *Friar's Bay Rd., Friar's Bay* 📞 *590/49–16–87* 🚫 *No credit cards.*

FRENCH CUL DE SAC

$$$
MODERN FRENCH

✕ **Anse Marcel Beach.** Beachside calm with a side order of chic is on the menu at this lovely and private cove, where the restaurant/beach club is a perfect choice for couples or families looking for a beach day, a sunset cocktail, or a great swimming spot. You can dine and lounge all day long, either in the tented pavilion or right on the beach. The food changes according to market availabilities but there are always salads, tasty mussels, fresh grilled fish and lobster, steaks, and sandwiches; try the smoked salmon and bagel combo if it's offered. The desserts are amazing, especially the crepes. There is safe, private parking for your car and moorings available for boats. $ *Average main: €24* ✉ *Anse Marcel Beach, Anse Marcel* 📞 *690/26–38–50.*

$$$
FRENCH

✕ **Le Ti Bouchon.** This tiny restaurant, close to Anse Marsel hotels, captures the spirit of Lyon, the capitol of French gastronomy, where casual small restaurants serve hearty traditional cuisine, wine comes by the pitcher, and the patron is very much part of the party. The eight tables are set on the porch of a traditional cottage and the menu (written on a chalkboard) changes frequently, assuring that each visit will be unique. Chances are you will become fast friends with the owner Momo, join in conversations with the next table, and linger over your chocolate mousse. Dietary restrictions are handled with grace and accuracy. $ *Average main: €30* ✉ *110 rte. de Cul de Sac, French Cul de Sac* 📞 *690/64–84–64* ⊕ *www.tibouchonrestaurant.com* ⬥ *Reservations essential.*

$$$
CARIBBEAN

✕ **Sol é Luna.** Charming and romantic, with modern decor, this restaurant puts its best tables on the balcony, from which you can best appreciate the great views. Begin your meal with an appetizer like curry tuna carpaccio, monkfish spring rolls, or roasted vegetables with goat cheese; then move on to an entree such as fresh pasta with mixed seafood or beef tenderloin flamed with Cognac. Try the chocolate soufflé for dessert. Don't be surprised if you see a proposal or two during your meal, as this is one of the most romantic restaurants on the island. ■TIP➔ Before ordering one of the "specials" ask about the prices; sometimes they can be surprisingly high compared to regular menu items. $ *Average main: €28* ✉ *61 rte. de Mont Vernon, French Cul de Sac* 📞 *590/29–08–56* ⊕ *www.solelunarestaurant.com* ⬥ *Reservations essential* ⊘ *Closed mid-June–early July and Sept.–early Oct.*

GRAND CASE

> **WORD OF MOUTH**
>
> "You should not visit St. Martin without enjoying at least one dinner at Le Pressoir (we chose to eat there twice on our last visit). Each course was outstanding, and the wine list is superb. Though the menu is a bit pricey, the food, service, and charm of the place make it worth every penny."
>
> —AddieLangdon

$$ FRENCH Fodor's Choice ★ 🍴 **Bacchus.** If you want to lunch with the savviest locals, you have to scrape yourself from the beach and head into the industrial park outside Grand Case, where Benjamin Laurent, the best wine importer in the Caribbean, has built this lively, deliciously air-conditioned, reconstruction of a wine cellar. He serves up first-rate starters, salads, and main courses made from top ingredients brought in from France, lovingly prepared by top chefs. Shop here for gourmet groceries for your villa, or order from the extensive take-out menu. Smokers love to hang in the new cigar–rum lounge. The wines are sublime, and you will get an amazing education along with a great lunch. You won't mind eating indoors here—just think of it as the perfect sunblock. Enter at the "Hope Estate" sign in the roundabout across from the road that leads to the Grand Case Airport. [$] *Average main: $20* ✉ *18–19 Hope Estate, Grand Case Rd., Grand Case* ☎ *0590/87–15–70* 🌐 *www.bacchussxm.com* 🕒 *No dinner. Closed Sun.*

$$$ FRENCH 🍴 **L'Auberge Gourmande.** A fixture of Boulevard Grand Case, L'Auberge Gourmande is in one of the oldest Creole houses in St. Maarten/St. Martin. The formal dining room is framed by elegant arches. The light Provençal cuisine includes menu choices like roasted rack of lamb with an herb crust over olive mashed potatoes, Dover sole in lemon butter, and pork filet mignon stuffed with apricots and walnuts. There are vegetarian options, a kids' menu, and a good selection of wines. Ask for an outside table. [$] *Average main: $21* ✉ *89 bd. de Grand Case, Grand Case* ☎ *590/87–73–37* 🌐 *www.laubergegourmande.com* 🕒 *Closed Sept. No lunch.*

$$$ FRENCH 🍴 **Le Cottage.** The inventive French cuisine is prepared with a light touch and presented with flair, and perhaps a bit of humor here. On the "fooding-tasting" menus, you can create your own selection from a tempting list of beautifully-plated mini-servings. Or try a prix-fixe meal. Huge portions of hearty French food are served by a genial staff to a lively community gathered on the street-front porch. Don't miss the caramel dessert tasting, which features a perfect soufflé, or the house-made salted caramel meringues. [$] *Average main: $27* ✉ *97 bd. de Grand Case, Grand Case* ☎ *590/29–03–30* 🌐 *www.lecottagesxm.com* ✍ *Reservations essential.*

$$$$ MODERN FRENCH Fodor's Choice ★ 🍴 **L'Effet Mer.** Longtime visitors to St. Martin are sure to remember the award-winning cuisine prepared by chef Stephane Decluseau at L'Astrolabe. Now, along with his partner Damien Pointeau, he's opened this Grand Case waterfront restaurant. You can hang out on beach chairs outside if you'd like, but the real action is inside, where creative and first-rate cooking is served with charm, precision, and panache. A tasting-plate of foie gras, or the incomparable foamy "lobster

cappuccino" soup are fine starters, mains are lively and unique, and the desserts are gorgeous edible art (try the crème brûlée tasting, with three variations on the theme). The €29 prix-fixe is a good deal. [$] *Average main: €34* ✉ *48 bd. de Grand Case, Grand Case* ☎ *590/87–05–65* 🌐 *www.effetmer.net* ✍ *Reservations essential* 🕒 *Closed Sun.*

$$$ FRENCH Fodor's Choice ★ 🍴 **L'Estaminet.** The name of this restaurant is an old-fashioned word for "tavern" in French, but the food is anything but archaic. The creative, upscale cuisine served in this modern, clean space is fun and surprising, utilizing plenty of molecular gastronomy. This means that intense liquid garnishes might be inserted into your goat cheese appetizer or perhaps given to you in a tiny toothpaste tube, or even a plastic syringe. The bright flavors, artistic plating, and novelty make for a lively meal that will be remembered fondly. Under no circumstances should you pass up the chocolate tasting for dessert. [$] *Average main: €23* ✉ *139 bd. de Grand Case, Grand Case* ☎ *590/29–00–25* 🌐 *www.estaminet-sxm.com* 🕒 *Closed Mon. in June–Nov.*

$$$ FRENCH Fodor's Choice ★ 🍴 **Le Pressoir.** In a carefully restored West Indian house painted in brilliant reds and blues, Le Pressoir has charm to spare. The name comes from the historic salt press that sits opposite the restaurant, but the thrill comes from the culinary creations of chef Franc Mear and the hospitality of his beautiful wife Melanie. If you are indecisive, or just plain smart, try any (or all) of the degustations (tastings) of four soups, four foie gras preparations, or four fruit desserts, each showcasing sophisticated preparations with adorable presentations. Foie gras is served in a dollhouse-size terrine, with a teensy glass of Sauternes. [$] *Average main: $30* ✉ *30 bd. de Grand Case, Grand Case* ☎ *590/87–76–62* 🌐 *www.lepressoir-sxm.com* ✍ *Reservations essential* 🕒 *Closed mid-Sept.–mid-Oct. and Sun. in May–Dec. No lunch.*

$$$$ FRENCH FUSION 🍴 **Le Shambala.** Romantic and beachy-chic, this waterfront restaurant has a lavish south-of-France vibe, with prices to match. Come for the sunset and start out with an interesting cocktail, before moving on to grilled rib-eye steaks, veal T-bone, or simply prepared fish garnished with fresh veggies. All the sophisticated desserts are made in-house; try pairing yours with a glass of champagne (there are more than a dozen types to choose from). [$] *Average main: €31* ✉ *28 bd. de Grand Case, Grand Case* ☎ *590/29–17–09* 🌐 *www.leshambala.com* ✍ *Reservations essential.*

$$$ FRENCH 🍴 **Le Tastevin.** In the heart of Grand Case, Le Tastevin is on everyone's list of favorites. The attractive wood-beamed room is the "real" St. Martin style, and the tasty food is enhanced by Joseph, the amiable owner, who serves up lunch and dinner every day on a breezy porch over a glittering blue sea. Salads and simple grills rule for lunch; at dinner, try one of the two tasting menus, either a "brasserie" style menu or a more expensive "gourmet" menu that includes excellent wines. [$] *Average main: $29* ✉ *86 bd. de Grand Case, Grand Case* ☎ *590/87–55–45* 🌐 *www.letastevin-restaurant.com* ✍ *Reservations essential* 🕒 *Closed mid-Aug.–Sept.*

$ CARIBBEAN Fodor's Choice ★ 🍴 **Sky's the Limit.** Although St. Martin is known for its upscale dining, each town has its roadside barbecue stands, called lolos, including the island's culinary capital of Grand Case. They are open from lunchtime until evening, but earlier in the day you'll find fresher offerings. Locals flock to the square of a half-dozen stands in the middle of Grand

Case, on the water side. Not to say that these stands offer haute or fine cuisine, but they are fun, relatively cheap, and offer an iconic St. Martin meal. With plastic utensils and paper plates, Sky's the Limit couldn't be more informal. The menu includes everything from succulent grilled ribs to stewed conch, fresh snapper, and grilled lobster at the most reasonable price on the island. Don't miss the johnnycakes and side dishes like plantains, curried rice, beans, and coleslaw that come with your choice. The service is friendly, if a bit slow, but sit back with a $1.50 beer and enjoy the experience. On weekends there is often live music. At this writing the lolos are still offering a one-to-one exchange between euros and dollars. [$] *Average main: €10* ✉ *Bd. de Grand Case, Grand Case* ☎ *590/35–67–84* ✍ *Reservations not accepted* 💳 *No credit cards.*

$$$ ITALIAN 🍴 **Spiga.** In a beautifully restored Creole house, Spiga's tasty cuisine fuses Italian and Caribbean ingredients and cooking techniques. Appetizers are tasty and ample. Follow with one of the excellent pasta dishes or a main course featuring fresh fish or meat such as the delicious pesto-crusted rack of lamb. Save room for the lemon-ricotta cake and try the selection of grappas. [$] *Average main: $28* ✉ *4 rte. de L'Esperance, Grand Case* ☎ *590/52–47–83* 🌐 *www.spiga-sxm.com* ✍ *Reservations essential* 🕒 *Closed mid-Sept.–late Oct. and Tues. in June–mid-Sept. No lunch Sun.*

$$$ ASIAN 🍴 **Tai Chi.** Sushi and Thai-fusion dishes are served with flashy cocktails at the end of the Orient Bay Plaza on the way from the beach. There are innovative sushi rolls, lots of choices for vegetarians and vegans, and congenial happy-hours. [$] *Average main: $23* ✉ *Pl. du Parc de la Baie Orientale, Grand Case* ☎ *590/87–73–98.*

MARIGOT

$$ CARIBBEAN 🍴 **Enoch's Place.** The blue-and-white-striped awning on a corner of the Marigot Market makes this place hard to miss. But Enoch's lolo-style cooking is what draws the crowds. Specialties include garlic shrimp, fresh lobster, and rice and beans like your St. Martin mother used to make. Try the saltfish and fried johnnycake—a great breakfast option. The food more than makes up for the lack of decor, and chances are you'll be counting the days until you can return. [$] *Average main: €13* ✉ *Marigot Market, Front de Mer, Marigot* ☎ *590/29–29–88* ✍ *Reservations not accepted* 💳 *No credit cards* 🕒 *Closed Sun. No dinner.*

$$ ECLECTIC FAMILY 🍴 **La Belle Epoque.** A favorite among locals, this brasserie is a good choice at the Marigot marina. Whether you stop for a drink or a meal, you'll soon discover that it's a great spot for boat- and people-watching. The menu has a bit of everything: big salads, thin-crust pizza, and seafood are always good bets. There's also a good wine list. And it's open nonstop seven days a week for breakfast through late dinner. [$] *Average main: €20* ✉ *Marina de la Port Royale, Marigot* ☎ *590/87–87–70* 🌐 *www.belle-epoque-sxm.com.*

$$ CONTEMPORARY 🍴 **La Source.** Somewhat hidden behind the boutiques in Marina La Royale (look near Vilbrequin), this tiny "healthy" restaurant features a French seasonal menu as well as sandwiches, salads, soups, fair-trade coffee and teas, and organic pastries. A bargain lunch special includes the special of the day and a drink, and the organic pasta dishes are

CLOSE UP

St. Maarten vs. St. Martin

If this is your first trip to St. Maarten/St. Martin, you're probably wondering which side will better suit your needs. That's hard to say, because in some ways the difference between the two can seem as subtle as the hazy boundary line dividing them. But there are some major distinctions.

St. Maarten, the Dutch side, has the casinos, more nightlife, smaller price tags, and bigger hotels. St. Martin, the French side, has no casinos, less nightlife, and hotels that are smaller and more intimate. Many have kitchenettes, and most include breakfast. There are many good restaurants on the Dutch side, but if fine dining makes your vacation, the French side rules.

The biggest difference might be currency—the Netherlands Antilles guilder (also called the florin) on the Dutch side, the euro on the French side. And the relative strength of the euro can translate to some expensive surprises. Many establishments on both sides (even the French) accept U.S. dollars.

delicious and inventive. The light choices, which include crab tartare with seaweed and organic-chicken salad, are terrific. Even the pastries are organic. [$] *Average main: $14* ✉ *Port La Royale Marina, Marigot* ☎ *590/27–17–27.*

$$$ MOROCCAN 🍴 **Le Marrakech.** Some 20 years ago, the charming owners renovated this beautifully historic St. Martin *case*. After several other restaurant ventures, they have returned to the original cottage to serve up delicious, authentic Moroccan cuisine in a beautiful and romantic space with an open garden that feels just like Morocco. The food is fragrant and delicious, with portions so huge you will have enough lunch for the next day. The couscous and tagines are authentically spiced and served with professional friendliness by an affable staff in Moroccan serving pieces. The mixed appetizers (*meze*) are delectable, and the royal couscous is justly popular. Kebabs and tajines are a great change of pace from the usual Caribbean and French fare. Lounge in the tented courtyard after dinner—and don't be surprised to be entertained by a talented belly-dancer. The restaurant is on Marigot's main road across from the stadium. [$] *Average main: $24* ✉ *169 rue de Hollande, Marigot* ☎ *590/27–54–48* ✍ *Reservations essential* ⏲ *Closed Sun.*

$$$ FRENCH 🍴 **Tropicana.** This bustling bistro at the Marina Port La Royale is busy all day long, thanks to a varied menu, (relatively) reasonable prices, and friendly staff. Salads are a must for lunch, especially the salad Niçoise with medallions of crusted goat cheese. Dinner includes some exceptional steak and seafood dishes. The wine list is quite extensive. Desserts are tasty, and you'll never be disappointed with old standbys like the crème brûlée. You can dine outside or inside along the yacht-filled waterfront, which is busy with shoppers during the day. [$] *Average main: $21* ✉ *Marina de la Port Royale, Marigot* ☎ *590/87–79–07.*

PIC DU PARADIS

$$ CARIBBEAN FAMILY Fodor's Choice ★

🍴 **Hidden Forest Café.** Schedule your trip to Loterie Farm to take advantage of the lovely tree-house pavilions where lunch or dinner has a safari vibe the hip clientele can appreciate and the yummy, locally sourced food is inventive and fresh. You can also enjoy the L'Eau Lounge, a giant spring-fed pool with Jacuzzis, lounge-cabanas, and a St. Barth-meets–Wet 'n' Wild atmosphere. Curried-spinach chicken with banana fritters is a popular pick, but there are great choices for vegetarians, too, including cumin lentil balls; those with stouter appetites dig into the massive black Angus tenderloin. Loterie Farm's other eatery, Treelounge, features great cocktails and tapas, is open Monday through Saturday, and stays open late with frequent live music. [$] *Average main: $20* ✉ *Loterie Farm, Pic Paradis 103, Rambaud* ☎ *590/87–86–16* 🌐 *www.loteriefarm.com* ⏲ *Closed Mon.*

SANDY GROUND

$$$$ FRENCH FUSION Fodor's Choice ★

🍴 **Mario's Bistro.** Don't miss dinner at this romantic eatery, a perennial favorite for its ravishing cuisine, romantic ambience, and most of all the marvelously friendly owners. Didier Gonnon and Martyne Tardif are out front, while chef Mario Tardif is in the kitchen creating ravishing dishes such as bouillabaisse with green Thai curry, a duet of grilled lamb chops and braised lamb shank shepherd pie, and sautéed jumbo scallops with crab mashed potatoes and leek tempura. Leave room for the heavenly upside-down banana coconut tart with caramel sauce and coconut ice cream. The restaurant is rather strict about reservations for large groups, so be sure to call and get the details. They don't take American Express. [$] *Average main: $31* ✉ *48 Rue Morne Rd., at Sandy Ground Bridge, Sandy Ground* ☎ *590/87–06–36* 🌐 *www.mariosbistro.com* ✍ *Reservations essential* ⏲ *Closed Sun., Aug., and Sept. No lunch.*

WHERE TO STAY

St. Maarten/St. Martin accommodations range from modern megaresorts such as the Radisson and the Westin St. Maarten to condos and small inns. On the Dutch side many hotels cater to groups, and although that's also true to some extent on the French side, you can find a larger collection of intimate accommodations there. ■ TIP→ **Off-season rates (April through the beginning of December) can be as little as half the high-season rates.**

TIME-SHARE RENTALS

Time-share properties are scattered around the island, mostly on the Dutch side. There's no reason to buy a share, as these condos are rented out whenever the owners are not in residence. If you stay in one, be prepared for a sales pitch. Most rent by the night, but there's often substantial savings if you secure a weekly rate. Not all offer daily maid service, so make sure to ask before you book. As some properties are undergoing renovations at this writing, be sure to ask about construction conditions, and in any case, ask for a recently renovated unit.

The Westin Dawn Beach Resort & Spa, St. Maarten

PRIVATE VILLAS

Villas are a great lodging option, especially for families who don't need to keep the kids occupied, or groups of friends who just like hanging out together. Since these are for the most part freestanding houses, their greatest advantage is privacy. These properties are scattered throughout the island, often in gated communities or on secluded roads. Some have bare-bones furnishings, whereas others are over-the-top luxurious, with gyms, theaters, game rooms, and several different pools. There are private chefs, gardeners, maids, and other staffers to care for both the villa and its occupants.

Villas are secured through rental companies. They offer properties with weekly prices that range from reasonable to more than many people make in a year. Check around, as prices for the same property vary from agent to agent. Because of the economy, many villas are now offered by the night rather than by the week, so it's often possible to book for less than a full week's stay. Rental companies usually provide airport transfers and concierge service, and for an extra fee will even stock your refrigerator.

RENTAL CONTACTS

French Caribbean International. This company offers rental properties on the French side of the island. ☎ *800/322–2223 in the U.S.* ⊕ *www. frenchcaribbean.com.*

Island Hideaways. The island's oldest rental company rents villas on both sides. ☎ *800/832–2302 in the U.S., 703/378–7840* ⊕ *www. islandhideaways.com.*

BEST BETS FOR LODGING

Fodor's Choice★
Blue Pelican, L'Esplanade, the Horny Toad, Palm Court, Le Petit Hotel, Radisson Blu St. Martin, La Samanna, Westin St. Maarten Dawn Beach Resort & Spa

BEST FOR ROMANCE
Le Domaine, Hotel le Marquis, Palm Court, La Samanna

BEST BEACHFRONT
Le Domaine, Esmeralda, the Horny Toad, Le Petit Hotel, Radisson Blu St. Martin, La Samanna

BEST POOL
Radisson Blu St. Martin, Westin St. Maarten Dawn Beach Resort & Spa

BEST SERVICE
Radisson Blu St. Martin, La Samanna

BEST FOR KIDS
Alamanda Resort, Divi Little Bay Beach Resort, Hotel Mercure, Radisson Blu St. Martin

Island Properties. This company's properties are scattered around the island. ✉ *62 Welfare Rd., Simpson Bay, St. Maarten* ☎ *599/544–4580, 866/978–5852 in the U.S.* 🌐 *www.remaxislandproperties.com.*

Jennifer's Vacation Villas. You can rents villas on both sides of the island from this company. ✉ *Plaza Del Lago, Simpson Bay Yacht Club, Simpson Bay, St. Maarten* ☎ *631/546–7345 in New York, 721/544–3107 in St. Maarten* 🌐 *www.jennifersvacationvillas.com.*

Pierres Caraïbes. Owned by American Leslie Reed, Pierres Caraïbes has been renting and selling upscale St. Martin villas to satisfied clients for more than a decade. The company's well-designed website makes it easy to get a sense of the first-rate properties available in all sizes and prices. The company is associated with Christies Great Estates. ✉ *Plaza Caraibes, rue Kennedy, Bldg. A, Marigot, St. Martin* ☎ *590/51–02–85 in St. Martin* 🌐 *www.pierrescaraibes.com.*

Villas of Distinction. This company is one of the oldest villa-rental companies on both the French and Dutch sides of the island. Check their website for special deals. ☎ *800/289–0900 in the U.S.* 🌐 *www.villasofdistinction.com.*

WIMCO. Go here for more hotel, villa, apartment, and condo listings in the Caribbean than just about any other company. ☎ *401/849–8012 in Rhode Island, 800/449–1553 in the U.S.* 🌐 *www.wimco.com.*

DUTCH SIDE

CUPECOY

$$$ RENTAL **The Cliff at Cupecoy Beach.** These luxurious, high-rise condos are rented out when the owners are not in residence and depending on the owner's personal style, they can be downright fabulous. **Pros:** great views; good for families; close to Maho casinos and restaurants; tight security. **Cons:** it's apartment living, so if you're looking for resort-y or beachy, this is not your place; there is a concierge, but no other hotel services. [$] *Rooms from: $425* ✉ *Rhine Rd., Cupecoy* ☎ *866/978–5839, 721/546–6633* 🌐 *www.cliffsxm.com* 🛏 *72 apartments* 🍴 *No meals.*

Le Domaine de Lonvilliers

LITTLE BAY

$$ RESORT FAMILY

🏨 **Divi Little Bay Beach Resort.** Bordering the lovely but sparsely populated Little Bay, this semi-renovated property is well located and is awash with water sports. **Pros:** good location; lovely beach, kids stay and eat free. **Cons:** ongoing renovations; pool areas not great. [$] *Rooms from: $299* ✉ *Little Bay Rd., Little Bay* ☎ *721/542–2333, 800/367–3484 in the U.S.* 🌐 *www.divilittlebay.com* 🛏 *218 rooms* 🍴 *No meals.*

OYSTER POND

$$ RESORT FAMILY Fodor's Choice ★

🏨 **Westin St. Maarten Dawn Beach Resort & Spa.** Straddling the border between the Dutch and French sides, the modern Westin sits on one of the island's best beaches. **Pros:** on Dawn Beach; plenty of activities; no smoking allowed. **Cons:** very big; a bit off the beaten track; time-share salespeople can be bothersome. [$] *Rooms from: $345* ✉ *144 Oyster Pond Rd., Oyster Pond* ☎ *599/543–6700, 800/228–3000 in the U.S.* 🌐 *www.westinstmaarten.com* 🛏 *317 rooms, 15 suites, 99 1-, 2-, and 3-bedroom condo units* 🍴 *No meals.*

PELICAN KEY

$$ RENTAL Fodor's Choice ★

🏨 **Blue Pelican.** The 13 modern and chic apartment units hidden in this private enclave in Pelican Key were built by the owners of Hotel L'Esplanade and Le Petit Hotel on the French side and share the French management's vision, graciousness, obsessive attention to detail, and concern for the comfort and safety of their guests. **Pros:** nicest place to stay in the area; great pool; excellent management and security. **Cons:** residence, not a resort; not on the beach; definitely need a car to get around because there is no restaurant. [$] *Rooms from: $290* ✉ *Billy Folly Rd., Pelican Key* ☎ *590–690/50–60–20* 🌐 *www.bluepelicansxm.com* 🛏 *13 apartments* 🍴 *No meals.*

PHILIPSBURG

$ HOTEL **Holland House Beach Hotel.** An ideal location for shoppers and sun worshippers, this historic hotel faces the Front Street pedestrian mall; to the rear are the boardwalk and a long stretch of Great Bay Beach. **Pros:** easy access to beach and shops; free Wi-Fi; young, engaging management. **Cons:** in a busy, downtown location; no pool; not very resort-y. [$] *Rooms from: $215 ✉ 43 Front St., Philipsburg ☎ 721/542–2572 🌐 www.hhbh.com 🛏 48 rooms, 6 suites 🍴 Multiple meal plans.*

$ RESORT FAMILY **Sonesta Great Bay Beach Resort and Casino.** St. Maarten's only all-inclusive is well positioned even if it doesn't offer the height of luxury: away from the docks that are usually crawling with cruise ships, but only a 10-minute walk from downtown Philipsburg. **Pros:** all-inclusive unlimited food and bar; nice beach and pool; enough activities to keep you busy. **Cons:** hallways are white and bare, giving them a hospital-like feel; expensive Wi-Fi; although the beach is beautiful, pollution can be a problem; staff can be indifferent. [$] *Rooms from: $260 ✉ 19 Little Bay Rd., Philipsburg ☎ 721/542–2446, 800/223–0757 in the U.S. 🌐 www.sonesta.com/greatbay 🛏 257 rooms 🍴 Some meals.*

SIMPSON BAY

$ B&B/INN Fodor's Choice ★ **The Horny Toad.** Because of its stupendous view of Simpson Bay and the simple but comfortable rooms with creative decor, this lovely guesthouse is widely considered the best on this side of the island. **Pros:** tidy rooms; friendly vibe thanks to the fantastic owner; beautiful beach is usually deserted. **Cons:** rooms are very basic; need a car to get around; no kids under seven allowed; no pool. [$] *Rooms from: $218 ✉ 2 Vlaun Dr., Simpson Bay ☎ 721/545–4323, 800/417–9361 in the U.S. 🌐 www.thtgh.com 🛏 8 rooms 🍴 No meals.*

$ RENTAL **La Vista.** Hibiscus and bougainvillea line brick walkways that connect the 32 wood-frame bungalows and beachfront suites of this intimate and friendly, family-owned time-share resort perched at the foot of Pelican Key. **Pros:** close to restaurants and bars. **Cons:** no-frills furnishings; need a car to get to more swimmable beaches. [$] *Rooms from: $210 ✉ 53 Billy Folly Rd., Simpson Bay ☎ 721/544–3005, 888/790–5264 in the U.S. 🌐 www.lavistaresort.com 🛏 50 suites, penthouses, and cottages 🍴 No meals.*

FRENCH SIDE

ANSE MARCEL

$$ HOTEL **Hotel Le Marquis.** If you crave spectacular vistas and intimate surroundings and don't mind heights or steep walks, this is a fun property, with a funky St. Barth vibe. **Pros:** romantic honeymoon destination; doting staff; amazing views. **Cons:** not on the beach; on a steep hill. [$] *Rooms from: $280 ✉ Pigeon Pea Hill, Anse Marcel ☎ 590/29–42–30 🌐 www.hotel-marquis.com 🛏 17 rooms 🍴 Breakfast.*

$$$ RESORT FAMILY **Le Domaine Beach Resort and Spa by Christophe Leroy.** This classic property on 148 acres of lush gardens borders the exceptionally beautiful and secluded beach in Anse Marcel. **Pros:** all-inclusive option; lovely gardens; beachfront setting. **Cons:** some rooms have round bathtubs right in the middle of the room; you will need a car to get around; beach

La Samanna

is shared with the busy Radisson Blu. $ *Rooms from: $420* ✉ *Anse Marcel* ☎ *590/52–35–35* ⊕ *www.hotel-le-domaine.com* ⇆ *124 rooms, 5 suites* ⊘ *Closed Sept. and Oct.* ▯◯▯ *Multiple meal plans.*

$$$
RESORT
FAMILY
Fodor's Choice
★

▭ **Radisson Blu St. Martin Resort, Marina and Spa.** A $10-million renovation in 2011 has brought a new level of service, design, and comfort to this family-friendly resort with 18 prime acres on one of the island's prettiest beachy coves. **Pros:** attentive service; activities galore; great beach; excellent breakfast buffet. **Cons:** no oceanfront rooms, they either face the garden or the marina; need a car to get around; lots of families at school-vacation times; beach can be busy. $ *Rooms from: $395* ✉ *BP 581, Anse Marcel* ☎ *590/87–67–09, 800/333–3333 in the U.S.* ⊕ *www.radissonblu.com/resort-stmartin* ⇆ *189 rooms, 63 suites* ▯◯▯ *Breakfast.*

BAIE LONGUE

$$$$
RESORT
FAMILY
Fodor's Choice
★

▭ **La Samanna.** A long stretch of pretty, white-sand beach borders this classic resort where service is warm and professional. **Pros:** chic new decor; great beach; convenient location; romantic; excellent spa. **Cons:** rather pricey for standard rooms; small pools. $ *Rooms from: $845* ✉ *Baie Longue* ☎ *590/87–64–00, 800/854–2252 in the U.S.* ⊕ *www.lasamanna.com* ⇆ *27 rooms, 54 suites* ⊘ *Closed Sept. and Oct.* ▯◯▯ *Breakfast.*

BAIE NETTLÉ

$
RESORT
FAMILY

▭ **Hotel Mercure St. Martin and Marina.** Families and couples who want to stay in a centrally located part of the island should try this modern option by a quiet beach bay. **Pros:** good location; pet and family-friendly; great spa; lots of activities, including for kids. **Cons:** beach isn't great for swimming; ground-floor rooms are noisy and have no view; no elevators. $ *Rooms from: $232* ⊠ *Baie Nettlé, Baie Nettlé* ☎ *590/87–54–54* ⊕ *www.mercure.com/gb/hotel-1100-hotel-mercure-saint-martin-marina/index.shtml* ⬎ *170 rooms* ⦿ *Breakfast.*

BAIE ORIENTALE

$$ 🖫 **Alamanda Resort.** One of the few resorts directly on the white-sand beach of Orient Bay, this hotel has a funky feel and spacious, colonial-style suites with terraces that overlook the pool, beach, or ocean. **Pros:** pleasant property; friendly staff; right on Orient Beach. **Cons:** some rooms are noisy; could still use some updating despite renovations. $ *Rooms from: $375* ⊠ *Baie Orientale* ☎ *590/52–87–40, 800/622–7836* ⊕ *www.alamanda-resort.com* ⬎ *42 rooms* ⦿ *Breakfast.*

RESORT
FAMILY

$$$ 🖫 **Caribbean Princess.** These 12 large, well-equipped, and updated two- and three-bedroom condos have big kitchens and living rooms, lovely balconies over Orient Beach (a few steps away), and share a pretty pool. **Pros:** the comforts of home; nice interior design; direct beach access. **Cons:** not a full-service resort. $ *Rooms from: $400* ⊠ *C5 Parc de la Baie Orientale, Baie Orientale* ☎ *0590/52–94–94* ⊕ *www.caribbeanprincesscondos.com* ⬎ *12 condos* ☉ *Closed Sept.* ⦿ *Breakfast.*

RENTAL
FAMILY
Fodor'sChoice
★

$$ 🖫 **Esmeralda Resort.** Almost all of these traditional Caribbean-style, kitchen-equipped villas, which can be configured to meet the needs of different groups, have their own private pool, and the fun of Orient Beach, where the hotel has its own private beach club, is a two-minute walk away. **Pros:** beachfront location; private pools; plenty of activities; frequent online promotions. **Cons:** need a car to get around; iffy Wi-Fi service. $ *Rooms from: $375* ⊠ *Baie Orientale* ☎ *590/87–36–36, 800/622–7836* ⊕ *www.esmeralda-resort.com* ⬎ *65 rooms* ☉ *Closed Sept. and Oct.* ⦿ *Breakfast.*

RESORT
FAMILY

$$$$ 🖫 **Green Cay Village.** Surrounded by five acres of lush greenery high above Baie Orientale, these villas are perfect for families or groups of friends who are looking for privacy and the comforts of home. **Pros:** beautiful setting near Baie Orientale; perfect for families with teens or older kids. **Cons:** need a car to get around; beach is a five-minute walk; need to be vigilant about locking doors, as there have been reports of crime in the area. $ *Rooms from: $660* ⊠ *Parc de la Baie Orientale, Baie Orientale* ☎ *590/87–38–63* ⊕ *www.greencay.com* ⬎ *9 villas* ⦿ *Breakfast.*

RENTAL
FAMILY

$ 🖫 **Hotel La Plantation.** Perched high above Orient Bay, this colonial-style hotel is a charmer. **Pros:** relaxing atmosphere; eye-popping views; lots of restaurants in the area. **Cons:** small pool; beach is a 10-minute walk away. $ *Rooms from: $240* ⊠ *C5 Parc de La Baie Orientale, Baie Orientale* ☎ *590/29–58–00* ⊕ *www.la-plantation.com* ⬎ *51 rooms* ☉ *Closed Sept.–mid-Oct.* ⦿ *Breakfast.*

HOTEL
FAMILY

$ 🖫 **Palm Court.** The romantic beachfront units of this *hotel de charme* are steps from the fu w; nice garden. **Cons:** across from, but not on the beach. $ *Rooms from: $252* ⊠ *Parc de la Baie Orientale, Baie Orientale* ☎ *590/87–41–94* ⊕ *www.sxm-palm-court.com* ⬎ *24 rooms* ☉ *Closed Sept.* ⦿ *Breakfast.*

HOTEL
Fodor'sChoice
★

Palm Court Hotel

FRENCH CUL DE SAC

$$ B&B/INN Fodor's Choice ★ 🏨 **Karibuni Lodge.** Lovely in every way, this superchic yet reasonably priced enclave of spacious suites surrounded by gorgeous tropical gardens offer stunning views of tiny Pinel Island. **Pros:** stylish; ecofriendly; lushly comfortable; amazing views. **Cons:** removed from the action; definitely need a car; not a resort, and not on the beach. [$] *Rooms from: $340* ✉ *29 Terrasses de Cul de Sac, French Cul de Sac* ☎ *690/64–38–58* 🌐 *www.lekaribuni.com* 🛏 *6 suites* 🍴 *Breakfast.*

GRAND CASE

$$ RENTAL FAMILY 🏨 **Bleu Emeraude.** The 11 spacious apartments in this tidy complex sit right on a sliver of Grand Case Beach. **Pros:** brand-new; walk to restaurants; attractive decor. **Cons:** it's not resort-y at all. [$] *Rooms from: $360* ✉ *240 bd. de Grand Case, Grand Case* ☎ *0590/87–27–71* 🌐 *www.bleuemeraude.com* 🛏 *4 studios, 6 1-bedroom apartments, 1 2-bedroom apartment* 🍴 *Breakfast.*

$$ RESORT FAMILY 🏨 **Grand Case Beach Club.** This beachfront property on a cove at the east end of Grand Case has a friendly staff and spectacular sunset views. **Pros:** reasonably priced; comfortable rooms; walking distance to restaurants. **Cons:** small beach; dated decor and buildings; need a car to explore island. [$] *Rooms from: $345* ✉ *21 rue de Petit Plage, at north end of Bd. de Grand Case, Grand Case* ☎ *590/87–51–87, 800/344–3016 in the U.S.* 🌐 *www.grandcasebeachclub.com* 🛏 *72 apartments* 🍴 *Breakfast.*

$$ HOTEL FAMILY Fodor's Choice ★ **Hôtel L'Esplanade.** Enthusiasts return again and again to the classy, loft-style suites in this immaculate boutique hotel. **Pros:** attentive management; very clean; updated room decor; family-friendly feel. **Cons:** lots of stairs to climb; not on the beach. [$] *Rooms from: $295* ✉ *Grand Case* ☎ *590/87–06–55, 866/596–8365 in the U.S.* 🌐 *www.lesplanade.com* 🛏 *24 units* 🍴 *No meals.*

$$ HOTEL FAMILY Fodor's Choice ★ **Le Petit Hotel.** Surrounded by some of the best restaurants in the Caribbean, this beachfront boutique hotel, sister hotel to Hotel L'Esplanade, oozes charm and has the same caring, attentive management. **Pros:** walking distance to everything in Grand Case; friendly staff; clean, updated rooms. **Cons:** many stairs to climb; no pool. [$] *Rooms from: $315* ✉ *248 bd. de Grand Case, Grand Case* ☎ *590/29–09–65* 🌐 *www.lepetithotel.com* 🛏 *9 rooms, 1 suite* 🍴 *Breakfast.*

OYSTER POND

$ HOTEL **Captain Oliver's Resort.** This cluster of pink bungalows is perched high on a hill above a lagoon with lots of lush landscaping and a fine view of the Caribbean and St. Barth. **Pros:** restaurant is reasonably priced; ferry trips leave from the hotel. **Cons:** not on the beach; not fancy or modern; must have a car to get around. [$] *Rooms from: $241* ✉ *Oyster Pond* ☎ *590/87–40–26* 🌐 *www.captainolivers.com* 🛏 *50 suites* ⏲ *Closed Sept. and Oct.* 🍴 *Breakfast.*

NIGHTLIFE

St. Maarten has lots of evening and late-night action. To find out what's doing on the island, pick up *St. Maarten Nights* or *St. Maarten Events,* both of which are distributed free in the tourist office and hotels. The glossy *Discover St. Martin/St. Maarten* magazine, also free, has articles on island history and on the newest shops, discos, and restaurants. Or buy a copy of Thursday's *Daily Herald* newspaper, which lists all the week's entertainment.

The island's casinos—all 13 of them—are found only on the Dutch side. All have craps, blackjack, roulette, and slot machines. You must be 18 years or older to gamble. Dress is casual (but excludes bathing suits or skimpy beachwear). Most casinos are found in hotels, but there are also some independents.

DUTCH SIDE

CUPECOY

CASINOS

Atlantis World Casino. With some of the best restaurants on the island, Atlantis World is a popular destination even for those who don't gamble. It has more than 400 slot machines and gaming tables offering roulette, baccarat, three-card poker, Texas Hold'em poker, and Omaha high poker, not to mention some of the best restaurants on the Dutch side of the island. ✉ *106 Rhine Rd., Cupecoy* ☎ *721/545–4601* 🌐 *www.atlantisworld.com.*

Gambling is the most popular indoor activity in St. Maarten.

MAHO
BARS AND CLUBS

Bliss. The open-air nightclub and lounge, which is good for dancing, rocks till late. Connect with them on social media for invitations to events. ⊠ *Caravanserai Resort, Maho* ☎ *721/544–3410* ⊕ *www.bliss-sxm.com.*

Cheri's Café. Across from Maho Beach Resort and Casino, Cheri's (you can't miss it—look for pink) is an open air club featuring Sweet Chocolate, a lively band that will get your toes tapping and your tush twisting. Snacks and hearty meals are available all day long on a cheerful verandah decorated with hundreds of inflatable beach toys. ⊠ *45 Rhine Rd., Maho* ☎ *721/545–3361* ⊕ *www.cheriscafe.com* ⊗ *Closed Tues.*

Fodor'sChoice ★ **Sky Beach.** The Sky Beach Rooftop Beach and Lounge is perfect for visitors who don't want to leave the beach vibe after the sun goes down (there's also a tent in case of rain). The elegant rooftop pulses with techno and house music while guests lounge on beds in cabanas. There is sand volleyball for fun and great cocktails at the happening bar. Great views and stargazing come with the territory. In-the-know clubbers come here before Tantra starts to wake up after midnight. It's open every day from 4 pm until 1 am. ⊠ *Sonesta Maho Resort & Casino, 1 Rhine Rd., Maho* ☎ *721/520–1757* ⊕ *www.theskybeach.com.*

Soprano's. Starting each night at 8, the pianist at Soprano's takes requests for oldies, romantic favorites, or smooth jazz. Come for happy hour from 8 to 9 pm with a full menu that includes pizza. The bar is open until 3 am nightly. ⊠ *Sonesta Maho Beach Resort & Casino, 1 Rhine Rd., Maho* ☎ *721/545–2485* ⊕ *www.sopranospianobar.com.*

Sunset Bar and Grill. This popular spot offers a relaxed, anything-goes atmosphere. Enjoy live music Wednesday through Sunday as you watch planes from the airport next door fly directly over your head. Bring your camera for stunning photos, but expect a high noise level. ⊠ *Maho Beach, Beacon Hill # 2, Maho* ☎ *721/545-2084* ⊕ *www.sunsetsxm.com.*

Tantra Nightclub & Sanctuary. This is definitely the hottest nightclub at the Sonesta Maho. Come late—things don't really get going until after 1 am. On Wednesday nights ladies drink champagne for free, and drinks are $2 for everyone on Friday. Celebrity DJs spin on Saturday. Feel free to dress up. There is bottle and table service by reservation. ⊠ *Sonesta Maho Beach Resort & Casino, 1 Rhine Rd., Maho Bay* ☎ *721/545-2861* ⊕ *www.tantrasxm.com.*

CASINOS

Casino Royale. This is the largest casino on the island, with some 1,300 square meters of gaming and a full theater with 750 seats for events and shows. There are 30 tables for gaming, including roulette (American and French), craps, blackjack, and poker (three-card and Caribbean). The 400 slot machines include a variety of classics and modern video slots. ⊠ *Maho Beach Resort & Casino, 1 Rhide Rd., Maho* ☎ *721/545-2590* ⊕ *www.playmaho.com.*

OYSTER POND

CASINOS

Westin Casino. This is somewhat more sedate than other island casinos. If you ever get tired of the slot machines and gaming tables, beautiful Dawn Beach is just outside the door. ⊠ *Westin Dawn Beach Resort and Spa, 144 Oyster Pond Rd., Oyster Pond* ☎ *721/543-6700* ⊕ *www.westinstmaarten.com.*

PHILIPSBURG

BARS AND CLUBS

Ocean Lounge. The quintessential people-watching venue, sip a guava-berry colada here and point your chair toward the boardwalk. ⊠ *Holland House Hotel, 43 Front St., Philipsburg* ☎ *721/542-2572.*

CASINOS

Beach Plaza Casino. In the heart of the shopping area, Beach Plaza Casino has more than 180 slots and multigame machines with the latest in touch-screen technology. Because of its location, it is popular with cruise-ship passengers. ⊠ *Front St., Philipsburg* ☎ *721/543-2031* ⊕ *www.atlantisworld.com.*

SIMPSON BAY

BARS AND CLUBS

Buccaneer Beach Bar. Located on Kim Sha Beach, this is the place to enjoy a BBC (Bailey's banana colada), a slice of pizza, a sunset, and a nightly fireball show. It's family-friendly and conveniently located. ⊠ *Behind Atrium Beach Resort, 10 Billy Folly Rd., Simpson Bay* ☎ *721/522-9700* ⊕ *www.buccaneerbeachbar.com.*

Le Shore. This nighttime hot spot located in the middle of Simpson Bay will remind you of Miami or Vegas, with its special events and parties almost every night. It's billed as a private club, but if you call for a reservation or just dress nicely, you shouldn't have a problem getting in. ⊠ *111 Welfare Rd, Simpson Bay* ☎ *721/586–4499* ⊕ *www.shoreclubsxm.com.*

Pineapple Pete. At Pete's you can groove to live music or visit the game room for a couple of rounds of pool. ⊠ *Airport Rd., Simpson Bay* ☎ *721/544–6030* ⊕ *www.pineapplepete.com.*

Red Piano. This bar has a great pool room, terrific live music, and tasty cocktails every night till 3 am. On Monday, check out the oldies hits of the '60s, '70s, and '80s. ⊠ *Hollywood Casino, 35 Billy Folly Rd., Simpson Bay* ☎ *721/544–6008* ⊕ *www.theredpianosxm.com.*

CASINOS

Paradise Plaza Casino. Betting on sporting events is the big thing here, which explains the 20 televisions tuned to whatever game happens to be on at the time. There are also 250 slots and multigame machines. ⊠ *69 Welfare Rd., Simpson Bay* ☎ *721/543–4721* ⊕ *www.paradisecasinosxm.com.*

FRENCH SIDE

BAIE DES PÈRES

BARS AND CLUBS

Kali's Beach Bar. This happening spot has featured live music late into the night since the late 1980s. On the night of the full moon and on every Friday night, the beach bonfire and late-night party here is the place to be, but it's a great place to hang out all day long on chaises you can rent for the day. Be sure to ask Kali for some tastes of his homemade fruit-infused rum. ⊠ *Baie des Pères* ☎ *690/49–06–81.*

GRAND CASE

BARS AND CLUBS

Calmos Café. Join the young local crowd at Caimos by just walking through the boutique and around the back to the sea, then pull up a beach chair or park yourself at a picnic table. It's open all day, but the fun really begins at the cocktail hour, when everyone enjoys tapas. The little covered deck at the end is perfect for romance. On Thursday and Sunday there is often live reggae on the beach. ⊠ *40 bd. de Grand Case, Grand Case* ☎ *590/29–01–85* ⊕ *www.lecalmoscafe.com.*

SHOPPING

It's true that the island sparkles with its myriad outdoor activities—diving, snorkeling, sailing, swimming, and sunning—but shopaholics are drawn to the sparkle in the jewelry stores. The huge array of stores is almost unrivaled in the Caribbean. In addition, duty-free shops can offer substantial savings—about 15% to 30% below U.S. and Canadian prices—on cameras, watches, liquor, cigars, and designer clothing, but not always, so make sure you know the U.S. price of anything you intend to buy to know if you're actually getting a deal. Stick with the big vendors that advertise in the tourist press, and you will be more likely to avoid today's ubiquitous fakes and replicas. On both sides of the island, be alert for idlers. They can snatch unwatched purses.

23

Prices are in dollars on the Dutch side, in euros on the French side. As for bargains, there are more to be had on the Dutch side; prices on the French side may sometimes be higher than those you'll find back home, and the fact that prices are in euros doesn't help affordability. Merchandise may not be from the newest collections, especially with regard to clothing, but there are items available on the French side that are not available on the Dutch side.

DUTCH SIDE

MAHO

You'll find a moderately good selection of stores in Maho Plaza, near the Sonesta resort in Maho. Many Americans prefer to shop here because they can pay in U.S. dollars and get better deals than on the French side. Blue Mall, a glitzy new shopping mall, opened in December 2013, but at this writing, the full list of shops is still in formation.

PHILIPSBURG

Philipsburg's **Front Street** has reinvented itself. Now it's mall-like, with a redbrick walk and streets, palm trees lining the sleek boutiques, jewelry stores, souvenir shops, outdoor restaurants, and the old reliables, such as McDonald's and Burger King. Here and there a school or a church appears to remind visitors there's more to the island than shopping. Back Street is where you'll find the **Philipsburg Market Place,** a daily open-air market where you can haggle for bargains on items such as handicrafts, souvenirs, and beachwear. **Old Street,** near the end of Front Street, has stores, boutiques, and open-air cafés offering French crepes, rich chocolates, and island mementos.

HANDICRAFTS

Guavaberry Emporium. Visitors to the Dutch side of the island come for free samples at the small factory where the Sint Maarten Guavaberry Company makes its famous liqueur. You'll find a multitude of versions, including one made with jalapeño peppers. Check out the hand-painted bottles. The store also sells the Gourmet BBQ & Hot Sauce Collection and souvenir hats ✉ *8–10 Front St., Philipsburg* ☎ *721/542–2965* ⊕ *www.guavaberry.com.*

Shipwreck Shop. This company has outlets all over the island that stock a little of everything: colorful hammocks, handmade jewelry, and lots of the local Guavaberry liqueur, but the main store on Front Street in Philipsburg has the largest selection of wares. ✉ *42 Front St., Philipsburg* ☎ *721/542–2962, 721/542–6710* ⊕ *www.shipwreckshops.com.*

JEWELRY AND GIFTS

Jewelry is big business on both the French and Dutch sides of the island, and many stores have outlets in both places. The so-called duty-free prices, however, may not give you much savings (if anything) over what you might pay at home, and sometimes prices are even higher. Compare prices in a variety of stores before you buy, and if you know you want to search for an expensive piece of jewelry or high-end watch, make sure you price your pieces at home and bargain hard to ensure you get a good deal.

Little Europe. Come here to buy fine jewelry, crystal, and china in the store's two branches in Philipsburg. ⊠ *80 Front St., Philipsburg* ☎ *721/542–4371* ⊠ *2 Front St., Philipsburg* ☎ *721/542–4371* ⊕ *www.littleeurope.com.*

Little Switzerland. The large Caribbean duty-free chain sells watches, fine crystal, china, perfume, and jewelry. ⊠ *52 Front St., Philipsburg* ☎ *721/542– 2523* ⊕ *www.littleswitzerland.com.* ⊠ *Westin Dawn Beach Resort & Spa, Dawn Beach* ☎ *721/543–6451* ⊕ *www.littleswitzerland.com.*

Oro Diamante. This store carries loose diamonds, jewelry, watches, perfume, and cosmetics. They specialize in natural colored diamonds, and also sell the popular stackable rings by Gabriel & Co. ⊠ *62-B Front St., Philipsburg* ☎ *599/543–0342, 800/635–7950 in the U.S.* ⊕ *www. oro-diamante.com.*

23

FRENCH SIDE

GRAND CASE

ART GALLERIES

Tropismes Gallery. Contemporary Caribbean artists, including Paul Elliot Thuleau, who is a master of capturing the unique sunshine of the islands, and Nathalie Lepine, whose portraits show the influence of Modigliani, are showcased at Tropismes. This is a serious gallery with some very good artists. It's open 10 am until 1 pm, and then from 5 pm until 9 pm daily, so you can browse before dinner. ⊠ *107 bd. de Grand Case, Grand Case* ☎ *690/54–62–69* ⊕ *www.tropismesgallery.com.*

MARIGOT

On the French side, wrought-iron balconies, colorful awnings, and gingerbread trim decorate Marigot's smart shops, tiny boutiques, and bistros in the **Marina Port La Royale** complex and on the main streets, **rue de la Liberté** and **rue de la République.** Also in Marigot are the pricey **West Indies Mall** and the **Plaza Caraïbes,** which house designer shops, although some shops are closing in the economic downturn.

ART GALLERIES

Galerie Camaïeu. This gallery sells both originals and copies of works by Caribbean artists. ⊠ *8 rue de Kennedy, Marigot* ☎ *590/87–25–78* ⊕ *www.camaieu-artgallery.com* ☾ *Closed Sun. Closed Sat. May–Nov.*

CLOTHING

On the French side, the best luxury-brand shops are found either in the modern, air-conditioned West Indies Mall or the Plaza Caraïbes center across from Marina Port La Royale in Marigot. There is also a small center in Grand Case, called La Petite Favorite, with four shops and a café.

JEWELRY AND GIFTS

Art of Time. This reputable shop carries Mikimoto, Pandora, and David Yurman, among many others, as well as high-end designer watches, including Chanel, Baum & Mercier, Technomarine, Bidat, and Chopard. ⊠ *3 rue Du General de Gaulle, Marigot* ☎ *590/52–24–80* ⊕ *www.artoftimejewelers.com.*

Manek's. Here you'll find two floors selling electronics, luggage, perfume, jewelry, Cuban cigars, duty-free liquors, and tobacco products. ⊠ *Rue de la République, Marigot* ☎ *590/87–54–91.*

SPORTS AND ACTIVITIES

BOATING AND SAILING

The island is surrounded by water, so why not get out and enjoy it? The water and winds are perfect for skimming the surf. It'll cost you around $1,200 to $1,500 per day to rent a 28- to 40-foot powerboat, considerably less for smaller boats or small sailboats. Drinks and sometimes lunch are usually included on crewed day charters.

DUTCH SIDE

Random Wind. This company offers full-day sailing and snorkeling trips on a traditional 54-foot clipper. Charter prices depend on the size of the group and whether lunch is served. The regularly scheduled Paradise Daysail costs $95 per person ($50 for kids) and includes food and drink. Departures are on the Dutch side, from Skipjack's at Simpson Bay, promptly at 8:30 am Tuesday through Friday. ■ TIP→ **You can get the best rates by booking directly from the website, rather than through your hotel or cruise.** ⊠ *Ric's Pl., Simpson Bay* ☎ *721/587–5742* ⊕ *www.randomwind.com.*

St. Maarten 12-Metre Challenge. Sailing experience is not necessary for the St. Maarten 12-Metre Challenge, one of the island's most popular activities. Participants compete on 68-foot racing yachts, including Dennis Connor's *Stars and Stripes* (the actual boat that won the America's Cup in 1987) and the *Canada II.* Anyone can help the crew grind winches, trim sails, and punch the stopwatch, or you can just sit back and watch everyone else work. The thrill of it is priceless, but book well in advance; this is the most popular shore excursion offered by cruise ships in the Caribbean. It's offered four times daily; the entire experience lasts about three hours. Only children over 12 are allowed. ⊠ *Bobby's Marina, Philipsburg* ☎ *721/542–0045* ⊕ *www.12metre.com.*

FRENCH SIDE

MP Yachting. You can rent boats here of all sizes, with or without a crew, for short trips and long, and it's located conveniently at Marina Port La Royale in Marigot. ⊠ *Marina Port La Royale, Marigot* ☎ *690/53–37–40* ⊕ *www.mpyachting.com.*

Sun Evasion. This charter company has locations all over the world, including St. Martin. You can take a half- or full-day charter to Tintamarre, St. Barth, or Ilet Pinel on a mono- or multihull powerboat, available with or without a skipper. ■ TIP→ **Book online for a 10% discount.** ⊠ *Marina Port La Royale, Marigot* ☎ *690/35–03–18* ⊕ *www.sun-evasion.com.*

FISHING

You can angle for yellowtail snapper, grouper, marlin, tuna, and wahoo on deep-sea excursions. Costs range from $150 per person for a half day to $250 for a full day. Prices usually include bait and tackle, instruction for novices, and refreshments. Ask about licensing and insurance.

DUTCH SIDE

Lee's Deepsea Fishing. Organize your excursion through Lee's Deepsea Fishing and when you return, Lee's Roadside Grill will cook your tuna, wahoo, or whatever else you catch and keep. Rates start at $200 per person for a half-day. ⊠ *84 Welfare Rd., Cole Bay* ☎ *721/544–4233* ⊕ *www.leesfish.com.*

Rudy's Deep Sea Fishing. One of the more experienced sport-angling outfits, Rudy's has been around for years. A private charter trip for four people starts at $525 for a half-day excursion. ■ TIP→ **Check the website for great tips on fishing around St. Maarten.** ⊠ *14 Airport Rd., Simpson Bay* ☎ *721/545–2177* ⊕ *www.rudysdeepseafishing.com.*

FRENCH SIDE

Private Yacht Charter. For deep-sea fishing, snorkeling trips, and catamaran trips including snacks and drinks, check out Private Yacht Charter. ⊠ *Oyster Pond Great House Marina, 14 Emerald Merit Rd., Oyster Pond, St. Maarten* ☎ *590/599–581–5305* ⊕ *www.privateyachtchartersxm.com.*

Big Sailfish Too. Your best bet for fishing excursions on the French side of the island operates out of the Radisson Blu Marina. ⊠ *Anse Marcel* ☎ *690/27–40–90.*

GOLF

DUTCH SIDE

Mullet Bay Golf Course. St. Maarten is not a golf destination. Nevertheless, there have been improvements to Mullet Bay Golf Course, on the Dutch side, which is now again an 18-hole course and the island's only choice. Although it seems to be improving, it's still not a major draw or a must-play. ⊠ *Airport Rd., north of airport, Mullet Bay* ☎ *721/545–3069.*

HORSEBACK RIDING

Island stables offer riding packages for everyone from novices to experts. A 90-minute ride along the beach costs $50 to $70 for group rides and $70 to $90 for private treks. Reservations are necessary. You can arrange rides directly or through most hotels.

DUTCH SIDE

Lucky Stables. These stables in Cay Bay offer two-hour rides three times a day and one-hour rides every hour on the hour all day long. For a romantic treat, book a sunset ride with champagne and a bonfire (complete with marshmallows) for $100 per person. All experience levels are welcome, but advanced riders can book private rides. ⊠ *64 Traybay Dr., Cay Bay* ☎ *721/544–5255* ⊕ *www.seasidenaturepark.com.*

KAYAKING

Kayaking is becoming very popular and is almost always offered at the many water-sports operations on both the Dutch and the French sides. Rental starts at about $15 per hour for a single and $19 for a double.

DUTCH SIDE

TriSports. This company organizes kayaking and snorkeling excursions in addition to its biking operation. ⊠ *Airport Rd. 14B, Simpson Bay* ☎ *721/545–4384* ⊕ *www.trisportsxm.com.*

FRENCH SIDE

Wind Adventures. Near Le Galion Beach, Wind Adventures offers rentals and instruction in kayaking, kitesurfing, windsurfing, Hobie cats, and stand-up paddle surfing. ⊠ *Baie Orientale* ☎ *590/29–41–57* ⊕ *www. wind-adventures.com.*

SCUBA DIVING

Diving in St. Maarten/St. Martin is mediocre at best, but those who want to dive will find a few positives. The water temperature here is rarely below 70°F (21°C) and visibility is often 60 to 100 feet. The island has more than 30 dive sites, from wrecks to rocky labyrinths. Right outside of Philipsburg, 55 feet under the water, is the HMS *Proselyte,* once explored by Jacques Cousteau. Although it sank in 1801, the boat's cannons and coral-encrusted anchors are still visible.

Off the north coast, in the protected and mostly current-free Grand Case Bay, is **Creole Rock.** The water here ranges in depth from 10 feet to 25 feet. Other sites off the north coast include **Ilet Pinel,** with its good shallow diving; **Green Key,** with its vibrant barrier reef; and **Tintamarre,** with its sheltered coves and geologic faults. On average, one-tank dives start at $55; two-tank dives are about $100. Certification courses start at about $400.

The Dutch side offers several full-service outfitters and SSI (Scuba Schools International) and/or PADI certification. There are no hyperbaric chambers on the island.

DUTCH SIDE

Dive Safaris. A shark-awareness dive occurs each Friday where participants can watch professional feeders give reef sharks a little nosh. The company also offers a full PADI training program and can tailor dive excursions and sophisticated instruction at any level. ⊠ *16 Airport Blvd., Simpson Bay* ☎ *721/545–2401* ⊕ *www.divestmaarten.com.*

Ocean Explorers Dive Shop. St. Maarten's oldest dive shop offers different types of certification courses. Serious divers like the six-person maximum policy, but this means you should reserve in advance. ⊠ *113 Welfare Rd., Simpson Bay* ☎ *721/544–5252* ⊕ *www.stmaartendiving.com.*

FRENCH SIDE

Octopus. Take advantage of PADI diving certification courses and all-inclusive dive packages, as well as private and group snorkel trips starting at $40, including all necessary equipment. The well-stocked dive shop also services regulators. ⊠ *15 bd. de Grand Case, Grand Case* ☎ *590/29–11–27* ⊕ *www.octopusdiving.com.*

SEA EXCURSIONS

DUTCH SIDE

Bluebeard II. This 60-foot custom-built daysail catamaran is specially designed for maximum safety and comfort. *Bluebeard II* sails around Anguilla's south and northwest coasts to Prickly Pear Cay, where there are excellent coral reefs for snorkeling and powdery white sands for sunning. ✉ *Simpson Bay* ☎ *721/587–5935* ⊕ *www. bluebeardcharters.com.*

Celine. For low-impact sunset and dinner cruises, try the catamaran *Celine.* ✉ *Skip Jack's Restaurant, Simpson Bay* ☎ *721/526–1170, 721/552–1335* ⊕ *www.sailstmaarten.com.*

FAMILY **Golden Eagle.** The sleek 76-foot catamaran *Golden Eagle* takes daysailors on ecofriendly excursions to outlying islets and reefs for snorkeling and partying. They can pick you up right from your hotel or condo. ✉ *Bobby's Marina, Philipsburg* ☎ *721/542–3323* ⊕ *www. sailingsxm.com.*

SNORKELING

Some of the best snorkeling on the Dutch side can be found around the rocks below Fort Amsterdam off Little Bay Beach, in the west end of Maho Bay, off Pelican Key, and around the reefs off Oyster Pond Beach. On the French side, the area around Orient Bay—including Caye Verte, Ilet Pinel, and Tintamarre—is especially lovely and is officially classified and protected as a regional underwater nature reserve. Sea creatures also congregate around Creole Rock at the point of Grand Case Bay. The average cost of an afternoon snorkeling trip is about $45 to $55 per person.

DUTCH SIDE

FAMILY **Aqua Mania Adventures.** This company offers a variety of snorkeling trips. The newest activity, called Rock 'n Roll Safaris, lets participants not only snorkel, but navigate their own motorized rafts. ✉ *Pelican Marina, Simpson Bay* ☎ *721/544–2640, 721/544–2631* ⊕ *www. stmaarten-activities.com.*

Eagle Tours. While Eagle Tours is geared more to cruise groups, anyone can sign on for the four-hour power rafting or sailing trips that include snorkeling, a beach break, and lunch. The sailing trips are done aboard a 76-foot catamaran. Some cruises stop in Grand Case or Marigot for a bit of shopping. ✉ *Bobby's Marina, Philipsburg* ☎ *721/542–3323* ⊕ *www.sailingsxm.com.*

FRENCH SIDE

Kontiki Watersports. Arrange equipment rentals and snorkeling trips through Kontiki Watersports. ✉ *Northern beach entrance, Parc de la Baie Orientale, Baie Orientale* ☎ *590/87–46–89.*

WATERSKIING

FRENCH SIDE

FlyBoard St. Maarten. In St. Martin, you can try out the latest trend in water sports: FlyBoarding. Water jets connect to a jet-ski turbine and allow you to fly above the waves to a height of up to 10 feet. For $150 you get 15 minutes of ground instruction on how to operate the Fly-Board® and approximately 30 minutes of flight time with a certified instructor. ■ TIP→ **You must download and complete an online train-ing program and sign a liability waiver beforehand.** ⊠ *Front de Mer, Marigot* ☎ *690/76–22–32* ⊕ *www.flyboardstmaarten.com.*

ST. VINCENT AND
THE GRENADINES

WELCOME TO ST. VINCENT AND THE GRENADINES

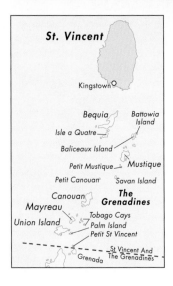

A STRING OF PEARLS

St. Vincent, which is 18 miles (29 km) long and 11 miles (18 km) wide, is the northernmost and largest of the chain of 32 islands that make up St. Vincent and the Grenadines and extend 45 miles (72 km) southwest toward Grenada. What these islands all have in common is a get-away-from-it-all atmosphere.

Restaurants	▼	Hotels	▼
Basil's Bar & Restaurant	**2**	Beachcombers Hotel	....**5**
Cobblestone Roof-Top	...**3**	Buccament Bay Resort	..**1**
The French Verandah	....**6**	Cobblestone Inn	.........**2**
High Tide	...............**7**	Grand View Beach Hotel	.............**4**
The Sapodilla Room	.....**5**	Grenadine House	........**3**
Vee Jay's Restaurant & Bar	........**4**	Mariners Hotel	...........**9**
Wallilabou Anchorage	..**1**	Paradise Beach Resort	.**10**
Young Island Resort	.....**8**	Rosewood Apartment Hotel	.........**8**
		Sunset Shores Beach Hotel	.............**6**
		Young Island Resort	.....**7**

KEY

⚓	*Beaches*
⚓	*Cruise Ship Terminal*
◥	*Dive Sites*
⛴	*Ferry*
1	*Restaurants*
①	*Hotels*

The 32 Grenadine islands and cays have some of the Caribbean's best anchorages and prettiest beaches.

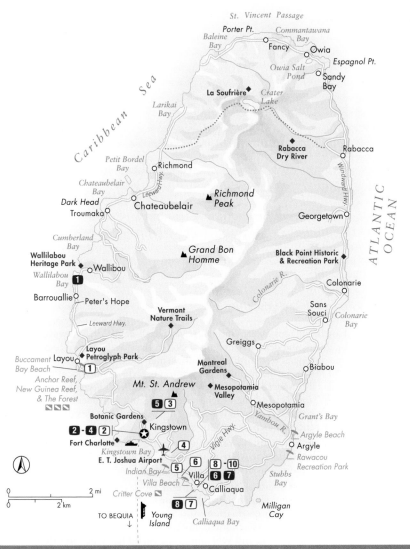

St. Vincent Passage

Porter Pt.
Commantawana Bay
Baleine Bay
Fancy
Owia
Espagnol Pt.
Owia Salt Pond
Sandy Bay
La Soufrière
Crater Lake
Larikai Bay

Caribbean Sea

Rabacca Dry River
Rabacca
Petit Bordel Bay
Richmond
Windward Hwy.
Chateaubelair Bay
Richmond Peak
Dark Head
Troumaka
Chateaubelair
Georgetown
Cumberland Bay
Grand Bon Homme
ATLANTIC OCEAN
Wallilabou Heritage Park
Wallibou
Black Point Historic & Recreation Park
Wallilabou Bay
1
Barrouallie
Peter's Hope
Colonarie
Colonarie R.
Sans Souci
Colonarie Bay
Leeward Hwy.
Vermont Nature Trails
Greiggs
Layou Petroglyph Park
Buccament Bay Beach
Layou
1
Biabou
Anchor Reef, New Guinea Reef, & The Forest
Mt. St. Andrew
Montreal Gardens
Mesopotamia Valley
Mesopotamia
Yambou R.
Grant's Bay
Botanic Gardens
5 **3**
2 - **4** **2**
Kingstown
Fort Charlotte
Vigie Hwy.
Argyle Beach
4
Argyle
Kingstown Bay
E. T. Joshua Airport
5
6
8 - **10**
Rawacou Recreation Park
Indian Bay
6 **7**
Villa Beach
Villa
Stubbs Bay
Critter Cove
Calliaqua
Milligan Cay
2 mi
8 **7**
2 km
TO BEQUIA
Young Island
Calliaqua Bay

ST. VINCENT AND THE GRENADINES

24

TOP REASONS TO VISIT ST. VINCENT AND THE GRENADINES

1 **Diverse Landscape:** St. Vincent offers a lush landscape, extraordinary hiking trails, remarkable botanical gardens, majestic waterfalls, and intriguing dive sites.

2 **Tranquility:** With few large resorts and no crowds, you're guaranteed peace and quiet.

3 **Sail Away:** Island-hopping sailing charters are the premier way to travel through the beautiful Grenadines.

4 **Beach Paradise:** Grenadine beaches have brilliant-white, powdery-soft sand washed by gentle waves in several shades of blue.

Updated by
Jane E. Zarem

A string of 32 islands and cays makes up the nation of St. Vincent and the Grenadines. St. Vincent is one of the least touristy islands in the Caribbean—an unpretentious and relatively quiet island, where fishermen get up at the crack of dawn to drop their nets into the sea, working people conduct business in town, and farmers work their crops in the countryside.

Hotels and inns on St. Vincent are almost all small, locally owned and operated, and definitely not glitzy. So far, there are only two resorts—one on a quiet bay north of Kingstown and another on a private island 600 feet from the mainland. Restaurants serve mainly local food—grilled fish, stewed or curried chicken, rice, and root vegetables (called "provisions"). And the beaches are either tiny crescents of black or brown sand on remote leeward bays or sweeping expanses of the same black sand pounded by Atlantic surf.

The Grenadines, on the other hand, dazzle vacationers with amazing inns and resorts, fine white-sand beaches, excellent sailing waters, and a get-away-from-it-all atmosphere.

Bequia, just south of St. Vincent and a pleasant hour's voyage by ferry, has many inns, hotels, restaurants, shops, and activities; it's a popular vacation destination in its own right. Its Admiralty Bay is one of the prettiest anchorages in the Caribbean. With superb views, snorkeling, hiking, and swimming, the island has much to offer the international mix of backpackers, landlubbers, and boaters who frequent its shores.

South of Bequia, on the exclusive and very private island of Mustique, elaborate villas are tucked into lush hillsides. Mustique does not encourage wholesale tourism, least of all to those hoping for a glimpse of the rich and famous who own or rent villas here. The appeal of Mustique is its seclusion.

Boot-shape Canouan, mostly quiet and unspoiled and with only 1,200 or so residents, is nevertheless a busy venue for chartering yachts. It also accommodates well-heeled guests of the posh resort and villa community that takes up the entire northern third of the island along with one of the Caribbean's most challenging and scenic golf courses.

Tiny Mayreau (fewer than 200 residents) has one of the area's most beautiful (and unusual) beaches. At Saltwhistle Bay, the Caribbean Sea is usually as calm as a mirror; just yards away, the rolling Atlantic surf washes the opposite shore. Otherwise, Mayreau has a single unnamed village, one road, rain-caught drinking water, and an inn—but no airport, no bank, and no problems!

Union Island, with its dramatic landscape punctuated by Mt. Taboi, is the transportation center of the southern Grenadines. Its small but busy airport serves landlubbers, and its yacht harbor and dive operators serve sailors and scuba divers. Clifton, the quaint main town, has shops, restaurants, and a few guesthouses. Ashton, the second significant town, is mainly residential.

Meanwhile, it took decades to turn the 100-acre, mosquito-infested mangrove swamp called Prune Island, a virtual stone's throw from Union Island, into the upscale private resort now known as Palm Island. Today, wealthy vacationers lounge on the island's five palm-fringed white-sand beaches.

Petit St. Vincent, another private, single-resort island, was reclaimed from the overgrowth by the late Hazen K. Richardson II. The luxury resort's cobblestone cottages are so private that, if you wish, you could spend your entire vacation completely undisturbed.

And finally, there are the Tobago Cays, five uninhabited islands south of Canouan and east of Mayreau that draw snorkelers, divers, and boaters. Surrounded by a shallow reef, the tiny islands have rustling palm trees, pristine beaches with powdery sand, the clearest water imaginable in varying shades of brilliant blue—and plenty of resident fish and sea turtles.

PLANNING

WHEN TO GO

High season runs from mid-December through mid-April; in the off-season, rates at larger resorts may be reduced by up to 40%. Seasonal discounts vary dramatically by resort and by island, with some of the luxury resorts offering specials periodically throughout the year; the most luxurious resorts, however, are always expensive. The small, less-expensive hotels and guesthouses have little or no seasonal variation in their rates.

GETTING HERE AND AROUND

AIR TRAVEL

Until Argyle International Airport opens (scheduled for late 2014), there are no nonstop flights between the United States and St. Vincent and the Grenadines. Instead, travelers from North America arrive at E.T. Joshua

International Airport (SVD) in St. Vincent or the airports in Bequia (BQU), Canouan (CIW), Mustique (MQS), or Union Island (UNI) via regional airlines that connect with major carriers serving Barbados, Grenada, Puerto Rico, or St. Lucia.

Airline Contacts Grenadine Air Alliance. Operating a shared-charter service via SVG Air and Mustique Airways, Grenadine Air Alliance links Barbados with St. Vincent and the four airports in the Grenadines. ☎ *246/418–1654 for shared-charter flights, 784/456–6793 for inter-Grenadine flights.* **LIAT.** LIAT flights connect St. Vincent and Canouan with Antigua, Barbados, Grenada, and St. Lucia, St. Maarten, Tortola, and Trinidad. ☎ *784/458–4841, 888/844–5428 throughout the Caribbean* ⊕ *www.liat.com.* **Mustique Airways.** This regional airline operates scheduled shared-charter service between Barbados and Mustique (with meet-and-greet service at the Barbados airport for in-transit passengers), as well as inter-Grenadine scheduled service and private charter flights to points around the Caribbean. ☎ *784/457–5777, 718/618–4492 in the U.S.* ⊕ *www.mustique. com.* **SVG Air.** SVG Air operates twice-daily shared-charter flights between St. Vincent and Barbados (through Grenadine Air Alliance) and between St. Vincent and St. Lucia's Hewanorra International, as well as frequent service between St. Vincent and the four airports in the Grenadines. ☎ *784/457–5124, 800/744–7285* ⊕ *www.svgair.com.* **SVG Air (Grenada).** SVG Air (Grenada) operates sched-uled flights between Grenada and Union Island, sometimes including Carriacou. ☎ *473/444–3549, 800/744–7285* ⊕ *www.svgair.com/grenada.*

Airport Contacts Grantley Adams International Airport (*BGI*). An official tourist information desk for St. Vincent and the Grenadines is at the Barba-dos airport, within the connecting-travelers area. ✉ *Christ Church, Barbados* ☎ *246/428–0961, 246/233–8746.*

Airports Canouan Airport (*CIW*). Commercial jets and private aircraft are able to use Canouan's airport. ✉ *Canouan* ☎ *784/458–8049.* **E.T. Joshua Airport** (*SVD*). This small, busy airport on St. Vincent, which accommodates only turbo-prop passenger aircraft or small private jets, will be replaced by Argyll Interna-tional Airport, scheduled for completion in late 2014. ✉ *Arnos Vale, St. Vincent* ☎ *784/458–4685.*

CAR TRAVEL

Car rental is available on St. Vincent, Bequia, or Mustique. Rental cars in St. Vincent and Bequia cost about $55 to $85 per day or $300 to $400 a week. Unless you already have an international driver's license, you'll need to buy a temporary driving permit for $24 (EC$65), valid for six months. To get one, present your valid driver's license at the police station on Bay Street or the Licensing Authority on Halifax Street, both in Kingstown, on St. Vincent, or at the Revenue Office in Port Elizabeth, Bequia.

Bequia Contacts Bequia Jeep Rentals ✉ *Friendship, Bequia* ☎ *784/458–3760* ⊕ *www.bequiajeeprentals.com.* **Challenger** ✉ *Belmont, Bequia* ☎ *784/458–3811.*

Mustique Contacts Mustique Mechanical Services ✉ *Mustique Company, Britannia Bay, Mustique* ☎ *784/488–8555.*

LOGISTICS

Getting to St. Vincent and the Grenadines: Until Argyle International Airport opens (scheduled for late 2014), there are no nonstop flights between the United States and St. Vincent and the Grenadines. Travelers from North America arrive at airports in St. Vincent, Bequia, Canouan, Mustique, or Union Island via regional airlines that connect to major airlines serving Barbados, Grenada, Puerto Rico, or St. Lucia. Some of the smaller Grenadines require both a flight and a boat transfer. Unless you're on a private jet, it's an exhausting, time-consuming trip (and fairly expensive), yet people still make the effort to reach some of the most wonderful, unspoiled islands in the Caribbean. Once you've landed on St. Vincent, it's also possible to hop to several different islands for a day or longer by air or by an interisland ferry.

Hassle Factor: High, but worth it.

On the Ground: St. Vincent's E.T. Joshua Airport is in Arnos Vale, about halfway between Kingstown and Villa Beach. It's a small but busy airport and accommodates turboprop passenger aircraft and small private jets. In the Grenadines, Canouan's modern airport has an extended runway that can accommodate jets. Bequia, Mustique, and Union islands each have an airstrip with frequent regional service. Taxis and buses are readily available at the airport on St. Vincent. The taxi fare to Kingstown or the Villa Beach area is $12 (or EC$30). Taxi service is available from the airports on Bequia, Mustique, Canouan, and Union islands.

St. Vincent Contacts Avis ✉ *E.T. Joshua International Airport, Arnos Vale, St. Vincent* ☎ *784/456–6861* ⊕ *www.avis.com.* **Ben's Auto Rental** ✉ *Sion Hill, St. Vincent* ☎ *784/456–2907* ⊕ *www.bensautorentals.com.* **David's Auto Clinic** ✉ *Upper Sion Hill, St. Vincent* ☎ *784/457–4026.* **Star Garage** ✉ *Grenville St., Kingstown, St. Vincent* ☎ *784/456–1743.*

FERRY TRAVEL

Traveling by ferry between St. Vincent and the Grenadine islands—particularly Bequia—is easy and relatively inexpensive. A fast ferry makes the trip between St. Vincent and Union in less than 90 minutes, stopping in Bequia and Canouan (and Mayreau, as needed) along the way. A one-way trip between St. Vincent and Bequia on the more conventional ferries takes 60 minutes and costs $9.50 (EC$25) each way or $17 (EC$45) round-trip with the same ferry company.

Contacts Admiralty Transport. This ferry makes several round-trips daily between Kingstown and Bequia. ✉ *Grenadines Wharf, Kingstown, St. Vincent* ☎ *784/458–3348* ⊕ *www.admiralty-transport.com.* **Jaden Sun.** This ferry's reliable, comfortable service goes between mainland St. Vincent and Bequia (25 minutes), Canouan (1½ hours), and Union islands (2 hours), with an "as needed" stop in Mayreau. There is no service on Tuesday, Wednesday afternoons, and Saturday—or on Thursday in the low season. The one-way fare between Kingstown and Bequia is $15; between Kingstown and Canouan, $34; between Kingstown and Union, $38. ✉ *Cruise Ship Terminal, Kingstown, St. Vincent* ☎ *784/451–2192* ⊕ *www.jadeninc.com.* **M/V Barracuda.** The interisland ferry M/V *Barracuda,* also known as "the mail boat," operates twice weekly. It leaves St. Vincent on Monday and Thursday mornings, stopping in Canouan, Mayreau, and Union Island. It makes the return trip Tuesday and Friday. On Saturday, it does a round-trip from St. Vincent to each island, returning the same day. ⊠ *Grenadines Wharf, Kingstown, St. Vincent* ☎ *784/456–5073.* **M/V *Bequia Express.*** This ferry runs several round-trips daily between Kingstown and Bequia. ⊠ *Grenadines Wharf, Kingstown, St. Vincent* ☎ *784/458–3472* ⊕ *www.bequiaexpress.net.* **M/V *Gem Star.*** This boat takes passengers from Kingstown to Canouan and Union on Tuesday and Friday mornings, returning early Wednesday and Saturday morning. ⊠ *Grenadines Wharf, Kingstown, St. Vincent* ☎ *784/526–1158.*

TAXI TRAVEL

Taxis are not metered. Settle on the price—and the currency—before entering the taxi. Taxis are always available at the airport in St. Vincent; the fare from the airport to Kingstown or Villa is $12 (EC$30). In Bequia, the taxis—usually pickup trucks with their beds fitted with benches accommodating four to six people under an awning—will take you to Port Elizabeth, to the various hotels, or on a day of sightseeing. On Canouan, resorts generally provide airport transfers, although taxis are available. On Mustique, transfers are usually provided, but taxis are available. On Union Island, it's a short walk or jitney ride from the airport to the Anchorage Yacht Club dock (a two-minute trip) or a taxi ride to the dock in Clifton, the main town, to meet the launch from Palm Island or Petit St. Vincent.

ESSENTIALS

Banks and Exchange Services ATMs are located at banks in Kingstown and their branches. U.S. dollars are accepted nearly everywhere, although you'll receive change in Eastern Caribbean currency (EC$). U.S. coins are not accepted anywhere. The exchange rate is fixed at EC$2.67 to US$1. Hotels, car-rental agencies, and most shops and restaurants also accept major credit cards and traveler's checks.

Dress Don't pack camouflage clothing. It is illegal to wear any form of camouflage clothing in St. Vincent and the Grenadines (as it is on most Caribbean islands), as that pattern is reserved for the local police. The law is strictly enforced, and the clothing may be confiscated.

Electricity Electric current is generally 220–240 volts, 50 cycles. Some large resorts, such as Petit St. Vincent, have 110 volts, 60 cycles (U.S. standard); many have 110-volt shaver outlets.

Passports Requirements You need a valid passport and an ongoing or return ticket to enter St. Vincent and the Grenadines.

Phones The area code is 784. If making a collect call to the United States, dial 800/CALLUSA (☎ *800/225–5872*). For international credit-card calling, dial 800/744–2000.

Taxes and Service Charges The departure tax from St. Vincent and the Grenadines is $18 (EC$50), payable at the airport in cash in either U.S. or EC currency; children under 12 are exempt. Increasingly, departure taxes are incorporated into the price paid for airfare, although St. Vincent and the Grenadines is currently an exception. A government tax of 10% is added to the room cost on hotel bills, a

ST. VINCENT DRIVING TIPS

About 360 miles (580 km) of paved roads wind around St. Vincent's perimeter—except for a section in the far north with no road at all, which precludes a circle tour of the island. A few roads jut into the interior a few miles, and a single east–west road (through the Mesopotamia Valley) bisects the island. Roads in the country are often not wide enough for two cars to pass, and people (including schoolchildren), dogs, goats, and chickens often share the roadway with cars, minibuses, and trucks. Outside populated areas, roads can be bumpy and potholed; be sure your rental car has tire-changing equipment and a spare. Drive on the left, and honk your horn before you enter blind curves out in the countryside, where you'll encounter plenty of steep hills and hairpin turns.

If you're planning an extended stay on St. Vincent and expect to travel frequently between Kingstown and, say, the Villa Beach area, a rental car might be useful, although both taxis and buses are inexpensive and readily available. On Bequia, a rental car will be handy if you're staying for several days in a remote location—that is, anywhere beyond Port Elizabeth. On Mustique, you'll get a kick out of driving around in a rented "mule" (beach buggy).

24

15% V.A.T. (value-added tax) is added to restaurant checks and other purchases, and a 10% service charge is often added to hotel bills and restaurant checks.

Tipping If a 10% service charge has not been added to your restaurant tab, a gratuity at that rate is appropriate. Otherwise, tipping is expected only for special service. For bellmen and porters, tip $1 per bag; housekeeping, $2 per day; taxi drivers and tour guides, 10% of the fare.

ACCOMMODATIONS

Mass tourism hasn't come to St. Vincent and the Grenadines, but that could change after the Argyle International Airport opens in 2014. With one or two exceptions, hotels and inns on St. Vincent are modest. Luxury and privacy can both be found in great abundance, however, at the exclusive resorts found throughout the Grenadines. If you have the time to island-hop by air or ferry, staying in simple guesthouses will maximize both your budget and experiences.

Luxury Resorts: On Young Island just a stone's throw from St. Vincent's shore, at Buccament Bay on St. Vincent, and scattered throughout the Grenadines, luxury resorts offer a laid-back vacation experience without sacrificing service, comfort, and privacy.

Simple Resorts and Guesthouses: Most lodgings in St. Vincent are simple, small, and relatively inexpensive. You'll also find small hotels and guesthouses with similarly attractive rates throughout the Grenadines—on Bequia and Union, in particular.

Villas: Luxurious villas, which make up the majority of accommodations on Mustique, offer every amenity you can imagine. Private villas are also available for rent on St. Vincent, Bequia, Palm Island, and Canouan.

HOTEL AND RESTAURANT PRICES

Prices in the restaurant reviews are the average cost of a main course at dinner or, if dinner is not served, at lunch; taxes and service charges are generally included. Prices in the hotel reviews are the lowest cost of a standard double room in high season, excluding taxes, service charges, and meal plans (except at all-inclusives). Prices for rentals are the lowest per-night cost for a one-bedroom unit in high season.

For expanded lodging reviews and current deals, visit Fodors.com.

VISITOR INFORMATION

Contacts St. Vincent and the Grenadines Tourism Authority ☎ *212/687–4981 in New York City, 800/729–1726* ⊕ *www.discoversvg.com.* **St. Vincent & the Grenadines Hotel & Tourism Association** ⊕ *www.svghotels.com.*

WEDDINGS

At least a 24-hour residency is required. A special governor-general's marriage license ($185 plus an $8 stamp fee) must be obtained in person from the Attorney General's office at the Ministry of Justice in Kingstown, St. Vincent. Bring valid passports, return or ongoing plane tickets, certified and notarized divorce decrees if applicable, and an appropriate death certificate if either party is widowed. An official marriage officer, priest, or minister registered in St. Vincent and the Grenadines must officiate at the ceremony, and two witnesses must be present.

ST. VINCENT

EXPLORING

Kingstown's shopping and business district, historic churches and cathedrals, and other points of interest can easily be seen in a half day, with another couple of hours for the Botanic Gardens. The coastal roads of St. Vincent offer spectacular panoramas and scenes of island life. The Leeward Highway follows the scenic Caribbean coastline; the Windward Highway follows the more dramatic Atlantic coast. A drive along the windward coast requires a full day. Exploring La Soufrière or the Vermont Nature Trails is also a major undertaking, requiring a very early start and a full day of strenuous hiking.

TOP ATTRACTIONS

FAMILY

Fodor'sChoice

★

Botanic Gardens. The oldest botanical garden in the Western Hemisphere is just north of downtown Kingstown—a few minutes by taxi. The garden was founded in 1765 after Captain Bligh—of *Bounty* fame—brought the first breadfruit tree to this island for landowners to propagate. The prolific bounty of the breadfruit trees was used to feed the slaves. You can see a direct descendant of the original tree among the specimen mahogany, rubber, teak, and other tropical trees and shrubs in the 20 acres of gardens. Two dozen rare St. Vincent parrots, confiscated from illegal collections, live in the small aviary. Guides explain all the medicinal and ornamental trees and shrubs; they also appreciate a tip (about $5 per person) at the end of the tour. ⊠ *Off Leeward*

Hwy., northeast of town, Montrose, Kingstown ☎ 784/453–1623 *Free ⊙ Daily 6–6.*

FAMILY
Fodor's Choice
★

Ft. Charlotte. Started by the French in 1786 and completed by the British in 1806, the fort was ultimately named for Britain's Queen Charlotte, wife of King George III. It sits on Berkshire Hill, a dramatic promontory 2 miles (3 km) north of Kingstown and 636 feet above sea level, affording a stunning view of the capital city and the Grenadines. Interestingly, its cannons face inland, as the fear of attack—by the French and their Carib allies—from the ridges above Kingstown was far greater than any threat approaching from the sea. In any case, the fort saw no action. Nowadays, it serves as a signal station for ships; the ancient cells house historical paintings of the island by Lindsay Prescott. ⊠ *Berkshire Hill, 2 miles north of town, Kingstown ⊙ Daily 6–6.*

> **DOLLAR BUSES**
>
> "Dollar buses" on St. Vincent are privately owned, brightly painted minivans; fares range from EC$1 to EC$6 (40¢ to $2.50). Routes are indicated on the windshield, and the bus will stop on demand. Just wave from the road or point your finger to the ground as a bus approaches. To get off, signal by tapping your knuckles twice above the window by your seat or ask the conductor, usually a young boy who rides along to open the door and collect fares; it's helpful to have the correct change in EC coins. In Kingstown, the central departure point is the bus terminal at the New Kingstown Fish Market.

24

WORTH NOTING

Barrouallie. Once an important whaling village, Barrouallie (*bar*-relly) today is home to anglers earning their livelihoods trawling for blackfish, which are actually small pilot whales. The one-hour drive north from Kingstown on the Leeward Highway takes you along ridges that drop to the sea, through small villages and lush valleys, and beside quiet bays with black-sand beaches and safe bathing. ⊠ *Barrouallie.*

FAMILY
Black Point Historic and Recreation Park. In 1815, under the supervision of British Colonel Thomas Browne, Carib and African slaves drilled a 360-foot tunnel through solid volcanic rock—an engineering marvel at the time—to facilitate the transportation of sugar from estates in the north to the port in Kingstown. Today, Jasper Rock Tunnel is the centerpiece of Black Point Historic and Recreation Park, which also has an interpretation center, children's playground, and washrooms. The tunnel, just off beautiful Black Point Beach between Georgetown and Colonarie (pronounced con-a-*ree*), links Grand Sable with Byrea Bay. The park is open daily 8 am to 6 pm. ⊠ *Windward Hwy., north of Colonarie, Black Point.*

Georgetown. St. Vincent's second-largest city (and former capital), halfway up the island's Atlantic coast and surrounded by acres and acres of coconut groves, is a convenient place to stop for a cool drink or snack or other essential shopping while traveling along the windward coast. It is also the site of the now-defunct Mount Bentinck sugar factory. A tiny, quiet town with a few small shops, a restaurant or two, and modest homes, Georgetown is completely unaffected by tourism. ⊠ *Georgetown.*

Kingstown. The capital of St. Vincent and the Grenadines, a city of 13,500 residents, wraps around Kingstown Bay on the island's southwestern coast; a ring of green hills and ridges studded with homes forms a backdrop for the city. This is very much a working city, with a busy harbor and few concessions to tourists. Kingstown Harbour is the only deepwater port on the island.

A few gift shops can be found on and around **Bay Street,** near the harbor. Upper Bay Street, which stretches along the bayfront, bustles with daytime activity—workers going about their business and housewives doing their shopping. Many of Kingstown's downtown buildings are built of stone or brick brought to the island as ballast in the holds of 18th-century ships (and replaced with sugar and spices for the return trip to Europe). The Georgian-style stone arches and second-floor overhangs on former warehouses—which provide shelter from midday sun and the brief, cooling showers common to the tropics—have earned Kingstown the nickname "City of Arches."

Grenadines Wharf, at the south end of Bay Street, is busy with schooners loading supplies and ferries loading people bound for the Grenadines. The **Cruise-Ship Complex,** just south of the commercial wharf, has a mall with a dozen or more shops, plus restaurants, a post office, communications facilities, and a taxi-minibus stand.

A huge selection of produce fills the **Kingstown Produce Market,** a three-story building that takes up a whole city block on Upper Bay, Hillsboro, and Bedford streets in the center of town. It's noisy, colorful, and open Monday through Saturday—but the busiest times (and the best times to go) are Friday and Saturday mornings. In the courtyard, vendors sell local arts and crafts. On the upper floors, merchants sell clothing, household items, gifts, and other products.

Little Tokyo, so called because funding for the project was a gift from Japan, is a waterfront shopping area with a bustling indoor fish market and dozens of stalls where you can buy inexpensive homemade meals, drinks, ice cream, bread and cookies, clothing, trinkets, and even get a haircut.

St. George's Cathedral, on Grenville Street, is a pristine, creamy-yellow Anglican church built in 1820. The dignified Georgian architecture includes simple wooden pews, an ornate chandelier, and beautiful stained-glass windows; one was a gift from Queen Victoria, who actually commissioned it for London's St. Paul's Cathedral in honor of her first grandson. When the artist created an angel with a red robe, she was horrified by the color and sent the window abroad. The markers in the cathedral's graveyard recount the history of the island. Across the street is **St. Mary's Roman Catholic Cathedral of the Assumption,** built in stages beginning in 1823. The strangely appealing design is a blend of Moorish, Georgian, and Romanesque styles applied to black brick. Nearby, freed slaves built the **Kingstown Methodist Church** in 1841. The exterior is brick, simply decorated with quoins (solid blocks that form the corners), and the roof is held together by metal straps, bolts, and wooden pins. **Scots Kirk** was built from 1839 to 1880 by and for Scottish settlers but became a Seventh-Day Adventist church in 1952. ⊠ *Kingstown.*

A waterfall near Wallilabou Bay, St. Vincent

La Soufrière. This towering volcano, which last erupted in 1979, is 4,048 feet high and so huge in area that its surrounding mountainside covers virtually the entire northern third of the island. The eastern trail to the rim of the crater, a two-hour ascent, begins at Rabacca Dry River. ⊠ *Rabacca Dry River, Rabacca.*

Layou Petroglyph Park. Just beyond the small fishing village of Layou, about 45 minutes north of Kingstown, petroglyphs (rock carvings) were carved into a giant boulder by pre-Columbian inhabitants in the 8th century. For about $2, you can be escorted along the nature trail to the site. ⊠ *Leeward Hwy., Layou* ☎ *784/454–8686* 🖃 *$2* ⊙ *Daily 8–5.*

Mesopotamia Valley. The rugged, ocean-lashed scenery along St. Vincent's windward coast is the perfect counterpoint to the lush, calm leeward coast. In between, the fertile Mesopotamia Valley (nicknamed Mespo) affords a view of dense rain forests, streams, and endless banana and coconut plantations. Breadfruit, sweet corn, peanuts, and arrowroot also grow in the rich soil here. Mountain ridges, including 3,181-foot Grand Bonhomme Mountain, surround the valley. ⊠ *Mesopotamia.*

Owia Salt Pond. Owia Salt Pond, in the village of Owia on the island's far northeastern coast and at least a two-hour drive from Kingstown, is a natural saltwater pond created by the pounding surf of the Atlantic Ocean overflowing a barrier reef of lava rocks and ridges. The village is the home of many descendants of the indigenous Carib people, as well as the home of the **Owia Arrowroot Processing Factory.** Long used to thicken sauces and flavor cookies, arrowroot is now also used in pharmaceutical products. St. Vincent produces 90% of the world's supply of arrowroot, but that is only a tiny fraction of the maximum levels exported in the 1960s. Take a pleasant swim in Owia Salt Pond and enjoy a picnic lunch on the adjacent grounds before the long return trip to Kingstown. ⊠ *Owia* ⊘ *Daily 9–6.*

Rabacca Dry River. This rocky gulch just north of Georgetown was carved from the earth by lava flow from the 1902 volcanic eruption of nearby **La Soufrière.** When it rains in the mountains, the riverbed changes from dry moonscape to a trickle of water to a gushing river—all within minutes—and then simply dries up again. Before the Rabacca Dry River Bridge opened in 2007, drivers would often get stranded on one side or the other whenever it rained. ⊠ *Rabacca.*

FAMILY   **Wallilabou Heritage Park.** The Wallilabou Estate, halfway up the island's leeward coast, once produced cocoa, cotton, and arrowroot. Today, it is Wallilabou Heritage Park, a recreational site with a river and small waterfall, which creates a small pool where you can take a freshwater plunge. You can also sunbathe, swim, picnic, or buy your lunch at Wallilabou Anchorage—a favorite stop for boaters staying overnight. The *Pirates of the Caribbean* movies left their mark on Wallilabou (pronounced wally-la-*boo*), a location used for filming the opening scenes of *The Curse of the Black Pearl* in 2003. Many of the buildings and docks built as stage sets remain, giving Wallilabou Bay (a port of entry for visiting yachts) an intriguingly historic (yet ersatz) appearance. ⊠ *Wallilabou.*

BEACHES

Aside from the beach on private Young Island, just offshore, all beaches on St. Vincent are public. Indian Bay is a popular swimming and snorkeling spot. Villa Beach, on the mainland opposite Young Island, is more of a waterfront area than a beach—except at the northern end, where the sand broadens considerably. The southern end of Villa Beach is sometimes so narrow that it becomes nonexistent; nevertheless, boats bob at anchor in the channel and dive shops, inns, and restaurants line the shore, making this an interesting place to be. At Buccament Bay, north of Kingstown, the owners of the huge villa community of the same name have covered the natural black beach with imported white sand. On the windward coast, dramatic swaths of broad black sand are strewn with huge black boulders, but the water is rough and unpredictable. Even on the leeward coast, swimming is recommended only in the lagoons, rivers, and bays.

Argyle Beach. Though this spectacular black-sand beach on St. Vincent's southeastern (windward) coast is not safe for swimming, you'll love to watch the surf crashing here. The new Argyle International Airport is very close to the beach. **Amenities:** none. **Best for:** solitude; walking. ⊠ *Argyle.*

Buccament Bay Beach. A long strand of (imported) white sand stretches in front of Buccament Bay Resort, about a half hour northwest of Kingstown. The water is calm, and snorkeling is very good. **Amenities:** food and drink; parking. **Best for:** snorkeling; sunset; swimming; walking. ⊠ *Buccament Bay.*

Indian Bay Beach. South of Kingstown and separated from Villa Beach by a rocky hill, Indian Bay has golden sand but is slightly rocky; it's very good for snorkeling. Grand View Hotel, high on a cliff overlooking Indian Bay Beach, operates a beach bar and grill. **Amenities:** food and drink. **Best for:** snorkeling; swimming. ⊠ *Villa.*

Rawacou Recreation Park. At Rawacou Bay, close to the new Argyle International Airport, two stunning black-sand, high-surf beaches are separated by a rocky headland with a trail down to a man-made lagoon—a swimming pool created by placing huge boulders in the sea to prevent the high surf from smashing against the shore. The water by the beaches isn't safe for swimming, but the lagoon pool is; however, be cautious when the surrounding water is particularly rough. The beautiful grounds of Rawacou Recreation Park, shaded by coconut and sea grape trees, include a performance venue and vendor huts. The park is a popular site for picnics, weekend parties, and special events. **Amenities:** food and drink; parking; showers; toilets. **Best for:** partiers; swimming; walking. ⊠ *8½ miles (13½ km) southeast of Kingstown, Argyle* ☼ *Daily 8–5.*

Villa Beach. The long stretch of sand in front of the row of hotels facing the Young Island Channel (Mariners, Paradise Beach, Sunset Shores, and Beachcombers hotels on the "mainland" and Young Island Resort across the channel) varies from 20 to 25 feet wide to practically nonexistent. The broadest, sandiest part is in front of Beachcombers Hotel, which is also the perfect spot for sunbathers to get lunch and liquid refreshments. It's a popular beach destination for cruise-ship passengers when a ship is in port. **Amenities:** food and drink; water sports. **Best for:** swimming. ⊠ *Villa.*

WHERE TO EAT

Nearly all restaurants in St. Vincent specialize in local West Indian cuisine, although you can find chefs with broad culinary experience at a few hotel restaurants. Local dishes to try include callaloo (similar to spinach) soup, curried goat or chicken, rotis (turnovers filled with curried meat or vegetables), fresh-caught seafood (lobster, kingfish, snapper, and mahimahi), local vegetables such as the squashlike christophene (also known as chayote) and pumpkin, "provisions" (roots such as yams and dasheen), and tropical fruit (including avocados, breadfruit, mangoes, soursop, pineapples, and papaya). Fried or baked chicken is available everywhere, often accompanied by "rice 'n' peas" or *pelau* (a stew made with rice, coconut milk, and either chicken or beef seared in caramelized sugar). At Campden Park, just north of Kingstown, the local beer, Hairoun, is brewed in accordance with a German recipe. Sunset is the local rum.

What to Wear. Restaurants are casual. You may want to dress up a little—long pants and collared shirts for gents, summer dresses or dress pants for the ladies—for an evening out at a pricey restaurant, *but none of the establishments listed below require men to wear a jacket or tie.* Beachwear, however, is never appropriate in restaurants.

$$$ CARIBBEAN
🍴 **Basil's Bar and Restaurant.** It's not just the air-conditioning that makes this restaurant cool. Basil's, at street level at the Cobblestone Inn, is owned by Basil Charles, whose Basil's Beach Bar on Mustique is a hangout for the vacationing rich and famous. This is the Kingstown power-lunch venue. Local businesspeople gather for the daily buffet (weekdays) or full menu of salads, sandwiches, barbecued chicken, or fresh seafood platters. Dinner entrées of pasta, local seafood, and chicken are served at candlelit tables. [$] *Average main: $24* ✉ *Upper Bay St., below Cobblestone Inn, Kingstown* ☎ *784/457–2713* 🌐 *www.basilsbar.com* 🕒 *Closed Sun.*

$$ CARIBBEAN
🍴 **Cobblestone Roof-Top Bar & Restaurant.** To reach what is perhaps the most pleasant, the breeziest, and the most satisfying breakfast and lunch spot in downtown Kingstown, diners must climb the equivalent of three flights of interior stone steps within the historic Cobblestone Inn. But getting to the open-air rooftop restaurant is half the fun, as en route diners get an up-close view of a 19th-century sugar (and later arrowroot) Georgian warehouse that's now a very appealing boutique inn. A full breakfast menu is available to hotel guests and the public alike. The luncheon menu ranges from homemade soups, salads (tuna, chicken, fruit, or tossed), sandwiches, or burgers and fries to full meals of roast beef, stewed chicken, or grilled fish served with rice, plantains, macaroni pie, and fresh local vegetables. [$] *Average main: $15* ✉ *Cobblestone Inn, Upper Bay St., Kingstown* ☎ *784/456–1937* 🕒 *No dinner.*

$$$ FRENCH Fodor's Choice ★
🍴 **The French Verandah.** Dining by candlelight on the waterfront terrace of Mariners Hotel means excellent French cuisine with Caribbean flair—and one of the best dining experiences on St. Vincent. Start with a rich soup (traditional French onion, fish with aioli, or callaloo and conch) or escargots, stuffed crab back, or conch salad. Main courses include fresh fish and shellfish grilled with fresh herbs, garlic butter and lime, or creole sauce. Landlubbers may prefer beef bourguignon, sautéed chicken paillard with cream sauce, grilled lamb chops, or beef tenderloin with béarnaise, Roquefort, or mushroom sauce. For dessert, there's the wonderful *mi-cuit*, a warm chocolate delicacy with vanilla ice cream. Lighter, equally delicious fare is served at lunch—and you can enjoy a full seaside breakfast. [$] *Average main: $28* ✉ *Mariners Hotel, Young Island Cut, Villa Beach, Villa* ☎ *784/453–1111* 🌐 *www.marinershotel.com* ✍ *Reservations essential.*

$$ ECLECTIC FAMILY
🍴 **High Tide Bar & Grill.** Enjoy simple, well-prepared fare dockside alongside the Young Island Cut, where you'll see boats maneuvering during the day and the twinkling lights of Young Island Resort in the evening. There's something on the menu that will appeal to everyone, kids included—burgers and fries, pizza, sandwiches, salads, or main courses of steak, chicken, or fresh fish. Dine inside or on the terrace. [$] *Average main: $18* ✉ *Young Island Cut, Villa Beach, Villa* ☎ *784/456–6700.*

$$$ EUROPEAN
🍴 **The Sapodilla Room.** The Sapodilla Room at the historic Grenadine House (1765) is a hidden gem. Whet your appetite with a fruity cocktail at the West Indies Bar—the actual bar is from an old English pub, and a gallery of classic black-and-white stills of movie stars graces the walls. Move inside to the stonewalled dining room and enjoy grilled fresh fish, creamy seafood risotto, or tasty beef, lamb, and chicken entrées that reflect

Caribbean flavors. Local people come here for special occasions and business dinners, as this is one of the few elegant dining spots on St. Vincent. They also enjoy the live jazz in the bar on Friday night. $ *Average main: $26 ⊠ Grenadine House, Kingstown Park, Kingstown* 🕾 *784/456–1800* ⊕ *www.grenadinehouse.com* ⌲ *Reservations essential* ⊗ *No lunch.*

$ ✕ **Vee Jay's Restaurant & Bar.** Come here for "authentic Vincy cuisine." Specials are chalked onto the blackboard: mutton or fish stew, chicken or vegetable rotis, curried goat, souse, and *buljol* (sautéed codfish, breadfruit, and vegetables). Not-so-Vincy sandwiches, fish-and-chips, and burgers can be authentically washed down with *mauby,* a bittersweet drink made from tree bark; linseed, peanut, passion-fruit, or sorrel punch; local Hairoun beer; or your choice of tropical cocktails. Lunch is buffet-style. $ *Average main: $12 ⊠ Lower Bay St., Kingstown* 🕾 *784/457–2845* ⊗ *Closed Sun.*

CARIBBEAN

$$$ ✕ **Wallilabou Anchorage.** Halfway up St. Vincent's Caribbean coast, this is a favorite lunch stop for boaters sailing the Grenadines and for landlubbers touring the leeward coast. The picturesque view of the bay is enhanced by the period stage sets left behind by the *Pirates of the Caribbean* filmmakers. Open all day from 8 am, the bar-and-restaurant serves snacks, sandwiches, tempting West Indian dishes, and lobster in season. Ice, telephones, business services, and shower facilities are available to boaters. $ *Average main: $24 ⊠ Leeward Hwy., Wallilabou* 🕾 *784/458–7270* ⊕ *www.wallilabou.com.*

CARIBBEAN

$$$$ ✕ **Young Island Resort Restaurant.** Take the little ferry (a two-minute ride from the dock at Villa Beach) to Young Island for a delightful lunch or a very special romantic evening. Stone paths lead to candlelit tables—some in breezy, thatch-roof kiosks— and gentle waves lap the shore. Five-course, prix-fixe dinners of grilled seafood, roast pork, succulent beef tenderloin, duck breast, and sautéed chicken are accompanied by local vegetables. Two or three choices are offered for each course, and freshly made breads (coconut, raisin, banana, country white, cinnamon, or whole-grain wheat) are sliced at your table. Lunch is à la carte—soups, salads, grilled meats, or fish—and served on the beachfront terrace. $ *Average main: $45 ⊠ Young Island Cut, Young Island* 🕾 *784/458–4826* ⊕ *www.youngisland.com* ⌲ *Reservations essential.*

CONTEMPORARY

Fodor'sChoice

★

WHERE TO STAY

With a few exceptions—most notably, Buccament Bay Resort northwest of the capital city—tourist accommodations and facilities on St. Vincent are in either Kingstown or the Villa Beach area. All guest rooms have air-conditioning, TV, and phone unless stated otherwise.

PRIVATE VILLAS AND CONDOS

Because the island's air service has been limited to small planes operated by regional carriers, huge villa communities and condo complexes have been late to arrive in St. Vincent—though the international airport set to open in late 2014 will likely change that. The island's first villa community at Buccament Bay opened in 2010; many of the one- and two-bedroom town houses are available for vacation rentals.

$ HOTEL 🏨 **Beachcombers Hotel & Spa.** Guests choose Beachcombers for its comfortable beachfront rooms, friendly service, and lively atmosphere both day and night. **Pros:** great value and location; best beachfront in the area, the place to be on weekends; complimentary Wi-Fi. **Cons:** popular with small groups, so book well ahead; standard rooms are very standard—deluxe or penthouse rooms cost only slightly more; the beachfront gets busy when a cruise ship is in port. [$] *Rooms from: $99* ✉ *Villa Beach, Villa* ☎ *784/458–4283* 🌐 *www.beachcombershotel.com* 🛏 *27 rooms, 4 suites* 🍴 *No meals.*

$$$$ RESORT FAMILY Fodor's Choice ★ 🏨 **Buccament Bay Resort.** This luxury villa community, by far the largest resort in St. Vincent, is on a pretty bay about a half-hour drive northwest of Kingstown. **Pros:** huge accommodations; lots of amenities and activities; eight restaurants serve a variety of cuisines; great spot for soccer-playing kids. **Cons:** very expensive; quite remote—a rental car is advised. [$] *Rooms from: $1070* ✉ *Buccament Bay, off Leeward Hwy., 5 miles north of Kingstown, Buccament* ☎ *784/457–4100* 🌐 *www.buccamentbay.com* 🛏 *102 villas* 🍴 *All-inclusive.*

$ B&B/INN 🏨 **Cobblestone Inn.** This boutique hotel is cozy, convenient, inexpensive, and loaded with historic charm—but it's nowhere near a beach. **Pros:** convenient for an overnight stay if you're taking an early ferry to the Grenadines; historical atmosphere; fascinating architecture, complimentary Wi-Fi. **Cons:** mostly tiny rooms; wandering around downtown streets at night is not recommended; not on the beach. [$] *Rooms from: $75* ✉ *Upper Bay St., Kingstown* ☎ *784/456–1937* 🌐 *www.thecobblestoneinn.com* 🛏 *20 rooms, 6 suites* 🍴 *No meals.*

$ HOTEL 🏨 **Grand View Beach Hotel.** The unobstructed view of the Grenadines from this stylish, family-run hotel perched on a very private promontory is very grand indeed. **Pros:** friendly, boutique vibe; beautiful (grand) sunset views; on-site amenities include a pool, squash court, gym, and yoga classes. **Cons:** hike down to the beach; a rental car would be handy. [$] *Rooms from: $154* ✉ *Villa Point, Villa* ☎ *784/458–4811* 🌐 *www.grandviewhotel.com* 🛏 *19 rooms, 2 suites* 🍴 *Multiple meal plans.*

$ B&B/INN 🏨 **Grenadine House.** Favored by business travelers, this Victorian-style boutique inn is also perfect for vacationers who want modern comforts in an elegant setting but don't require planned activities or beachfront resort features. **Pros:** attractive rooms; excellent dining; on-site spa and gym. **Cons:** quiet, residential area far from any beach and a $5 taxi ride to town. [$] *Rooms from: $170* ✉ *Kingstown Park, Kingstown* ☎ *784/458–1800, 866/659–8351* 🌐 *www.grenadinehouse.com* 🛏 *20 rooms* 🍴 *Breakfast.*

$ HOTEL 🏨 **Mariners Hotel.** This small, pleasant hotel on the Villa Beach waterfront, opposite Young Island, has large rooms with either a balcony or terrace facing the water or overlooking the small pool. **Pros:** the French restaurant here; the use of the lovely Young Island beach; many water sports available nearby; complimentary Wi-Fi. **Cons:** rooms are simply decorated; bathrooms have showers, no tubs; small pool (but definitely refreshing). [$] *Rooms from: $95* ✉ *Villa Beach, Villa* ☎ *784/457–4000* 🌐 *www.marinershotel.com* 🛏 *20 rooms* 🍴 *No meals.*

$ B&B/INN 🏨 **Paradise Beach Hotel.** Painted bright yellow with white gingerbread trim, the waterfront porches and balconies at Paradise Beach Hotel offer a million-dollar view of Young Island, the activity at Villa Beach, and an amazing sunset every evening. **Pros:** friendly, welcoming atmosphere; the view, particularly at sunset; the waterfront restaurant and bar; complimentary Wi-Fi. **Cons:** beach is narrow to nonexistent but gets broader nearby; no pool. ⓢ *Rooms from: $85* ✉ *Villa Beach, Villa* ☏ *784/457–4795, 784/570–0000* ⊕ *www.paradisesvg.com* ↪ *14 rooms, 4 apartments* ⑪ *Multiple meal plans.*

$
RENTAL ⛭ **Rosewood Apartment Hotel.** Perched high on a hillside overlooking Villa Beach and Young Island, every one of these self-contained apartments have mesmerizing views of the Grenadines from their patio or terrace—particularly at sunset. **Pros:** accommodating management, and what a view! **Cons:** not on the beach; very steep driveway and hillside location may complicate casual strolls. ⓢ *Rooms from: $78* ✉ *Rose Cottage, Villa* ☏ *784/457–5051* ⊕ *www.rosewoodsvg.com* ↪ *9 rooms, 1 suite* ⑪ *No meals.*

24

$
HOTEL
FAMILY ⛭ **Sunset Shores Beach Hotel.** Down a long, steep driveway off the main road, this lemon-yellow, low-rise, family-owned hotel faces a narrow curve of Villa beachfront. **Pros:** picturesque location opposite Young Island; pool–bar area lovely at sundown; the price is right. **Cons:** room decor is attractive but a bit bland; beach is slim. ⓢ *Rooms from: $150* ✉ *Villa Beach, Villa* ☏ *784/458–4411* ⊕ *www.sunsetshores.com* ↪ *32 rooms* ⑪ *Multiple meal plans.*

$$
RESORT
FAMILY
Fodor's Choice
★ ⛭ **Young Island Resort.** One of St. Vincent's two true resorts is actually 200 yards offshore on its own private 35-acre island ringed by powder-soft beaches, offering 29 airy, hillside cottages and a pool, spa, tennis court, and a superb alfresco restaurant. **Pros:** St. Vincent's best white-sand beach; casually elegant; romantic but also appropriate for families. **Cons:** Pricey, even though rates include breakfast and dinner; no a/c in some cottages; no phones or TVs in rooms (though this might be a plus for some). ⓢ *Rooms from: $532* ✉ *Young Island Cut, Young Island* ☏ *784/458–4826, 800/223–1108 in the U.S.* ⊕ *www.youngisland.com* ↪ *23 cottage rooms, 6 cottage suites* ⑪ *Multiple meal plans.*

NIGHTLIFE

Nightlife in St. Vincent consists mostly of once-a-week (in season) hotel barbecue buffets with a steel band or a local string band (usually older gents who play an assortment of string instruments). Jump-ups, so called because the lively calypso music makes listeners jump up and dance, happen around holidays, festivals, and Vincy Mas—St. Vincent's Carnival—which begins in June and is the biggest cultural event of the year.

SHOPPING

The 12 small blocks that hug the waterfront in **downtown Kingstown** make up St. Vincent's main shopping district. Among the shops that sell goods to fulfill household needs are a few that sell local crafts, gifts, and souvenirs. Bargaining is neither expected nor appreciated. The **cruise-ship complex,** on the waterfront in Kingstown, has a collection of a dozen or so boutiques, shops, and restaurants that cater primarily to cruise-ship passengers but welcome all shoppers. The best souvenirs of St. Vincent are intricately woven straw items, such as handbags, hats,

Young Island Resort

slippers, baskets, and grass mats that range in size from place mats to room-size floor mats. If you're inclined to bring home a floor mat, pack (or buy) a few heavy-duty plastic bags and some twine. The mats aren't heavy and roll or fold rather neatly; wrapped securely and tagged, they can be checked or carried on board as luggage for the flight home. Local artwork and carvings are available in galleries, from street vendors, and in shops at the cruise-ship complex. Hot sauce and other condiments, often produced in St. Vincent and sold in markets and gift shops, make tasty souvenirs to bring back home.

ANTIQUES AND FURNITURE

At Basil's. St. Vincent's only antiques and fine furniture store is near the Young Island ferry dock and the Mariners Hotel. Owned by Basil Charles, proprietor of Basil's Restaurant in Kingstown and Basil's Beach Bar in Mustique, it specializes in 200-year-old Asian pieces and the latest creations from Bali, India, and Africa. The merchandise here appeals to collectors, as well as to anyone seeking interesting, affordable items for either home or garden. Even if you're just looking, you might be attracted to the French wines, chocolates, and cheeses. ⊠ *Young Island Cut, Villa Beach, Villa* ☎ *784/456–2602.*

DUTY-FREE GOODS

Gonsalves Duty-Free Liquor. Duty-free prices for wine and liquor at this airport shop are discounted by up to 40%—among the best value in the region, although keep in mind airport regulations for liquids. If you have a connecting flight through, say, Barbados, you'll have to (carefully!) pack the bottle(s) in your checked luggage for your next flight. ⊠ *E.T. Joshua International Airport, Departure Lounge, Arnos Vale* ☎ *784/456–4781.*

Voyager. Among the few duty-free shops in St. Vincent, Voyager I has a small selection of cameras, electronics, watches, china, and jewelry. A second shop, Voyager II, is nearby on Bay St. ⊠ *R. C. Enterprises Ltd., Halifax St., Kingstown* ☎ *784/456–1686.*

FOOD

C. K. Greaves Supermarket. Whether you're putting together a picnic, stocking your kitchenette, provisioning a yacht, looking for locally made seasonings or sauces, or just want some snacks, C. K. Greaves Supermarket is the main supermarket and your best bet. **Sunrise Supermarket,** in Arnos Vale and across the road from the E.T. Joshua Airport, is owned by the same company. Both can be reached by the same phone number, and either store will deliver your order to the dock. ⊠ *Upper Bay St., Kingstown* ☎ *784/457–1074.*

Market Square. Don't miss visiting Market Square, a three-story enclosed building that really bustles on Friday and Saturday mornings, when vendors bring their produce, meats, and fish to market. ⊠ *Bay and Bedford Sts., Kingstown* ☉ *Closed Sun.*

LOCAL ART AND HANDICRAFTS

Little Art Gallery. The gallery's owner, Caroline Sardine, is an accomplished artist and the daughter of the owners of Grand View Beach Hotel. Many of her paintings are on display in the hotel; in the Little Art Gallery, she sells original art (her own and that of others), along with handcrafted items such as pottery, ceramics, coconut toys, handmade dolls, painted calabashes, goatskin drums, and mahogany carvings. The gallery is in the hotel's beachfront restaurant and is open every day but Monday after 2 pm. ⊠ *Grand View Grill, Indian Bay Beach, Villa* ☎ *784/458–4811.*

Nzimbu Browne. This self-taught craftsman, artist, musician, and drum maker is best known for his original banana art, which he creates from dried banana leaves, carefully selecting and snipping varicolored bits and arranging them on pieces of wood to depict intricate local scenes. Prices range from $15 or $20 for smaller items to several thousands of dollars for larger works sold in galleries. Browne has a kiosk in front of his house, but sometimes sets up shop on Bay Street, near the Cobblestone Inn. ⊠ *McKie's Hill, Kingstown* ☎ *784/457–1677* ⊕ *www.nzimbu-browne.com.*

St. Vincent Craftsmen's Centre. Locally made grass floor mats, place mats, and other straw articles, as well as batik cloth, handmade West Indian dolls, hand-painted calabashes, and framed artwork are all available at this store that's three blocks from the wharf. No credit cards are accepted. ⊠ *Frenches St., Kingstown* ☎ *784/457–2516.*

Wallilabou Craft Centre. Established in 1986, this local cooperative teaches villagers various techniques for weaving straw and other natural fibers. Workers create baskets, handbags, hats, toys, and other items that are sold in the Kingstown market; they make good souvenirs of a visit to St. Vincent. The workshop is on the leeward coast, about a half-hour's drive north of Kingstown. ⊠ *Leeward Hwy., Wallilabou* ☎ *784/456–0078.*

24

SPORTS AND ACTIVITIES

BICYCLING

Bicycles can be rented for about $25 per day, but roads aren't conducive to leisurely cycling. Serious cyclists, however, will enjoy mountain biking in wilderness areas.

Sailor's Wilderness Tours. Individuals or groups can head out for half-day or full-day guided bike tours through the Mesopotamia Valley, around Argyll and the Atlantic coast, or in and around Chateaubelair in the northwest. The price, which starts at about $50 per person, includes 21-speed mountain-bike rental and refreshments. ⊠ *Middle St., Kingstown* ☎ *784/457–1712, 784/457–9207 after hours* ⊕ *www. sailorswildernesstours.com.*

BOATING AND FISHING

Fodor's Choice   From St. Vincent you can charter a monohull or catamaran (bareboat or
★   complete with captain, crew, and cook) to weave you through the Grenadines for a day or a week of sailing or for a full- or half-day fishing trip. One of the most spectacular cruising areas in the world, particularly for sailing, the islands of the Grenadines are close enough to allow landfall at a different island nearly every day, yet some are far enough apart to allow for true blue-water sailing. Bequia and Union Island have excellent yacht services and waterfront activity. Mustique is a dream destination, as is Mayreau. Visitors on yachts can dine at the private Palm Island and Petit St. Vincent resorts. Canouan is a prime yacht-chartering locale, and many of its beaches are accessible only by boat. The nearby Tobago Cays are a don't-miss destination for snorkeling and diving.

Boats of all sizes and degrees of luxury are available for charter. Bareboat charter rates in high season start at about $350 and go up to $1,000 or more per day for monohull sailing yachts and $600-plus per day for catamarans; add $130 per day for a captain and $120 per day for a chef. Rates for a crewed luxury sailing yacht begin at about $7,500 per week for two guests and $18,500 or more per week for boats that accommodate eight guests. Fishing trips start at about $300 for a half day and $500 for a full day.

Barefoot Yacht Charters. Barefoot's fleet of catamarans and monohulls are in the 32- to 50-foot range. ⊠ *Blue Lagoon, Ratho Mill* ☎ *784/456–9526* ⊕ *www.barefootyachts.com.*

Crystal Blue Sportfishing Charters. Greg and Lisa Allen offer sportfishing charters on their 34-foot Bertram pirogue to both casual and serious fishermen. ⊠ *Villa* ☎ *784/457–4532.*

TMM Yacht Charters. The fully equipped yachts and catamarans here range from 38 to 51 feet and can come either bareboat or crewed. ⊠ *Blue Lagoon, Ratho Mill* ☎ *784/456–9608, 800/633–0155 in the U.S.* ⊕ *www.sailtmm.com.*

DIVING AND SNORKELING

Fodor's Choice   Novices and advanced divers alike will be impressed by the marine life in
★   the waters around St. Vincent—brilliant sponges, huge deepwater coral trees, and shallow reefs teeming with colorful fish. Many sites in the Grenadines are still virtually unexplored. It can't be emphasized enough, however, that the coral reef is extremely fragile; you must only look and never touch.

Most dive shops offer three-hour beginner "resort" courses, full certification courses, and day and night excursions to reefs, walls, and wrecks throughout the Grenadines. A single-tank dive costs $60 to $75; a two-tank, $100 to $135; a 10-dive package, $650. A half-day snorkel trip on a dive boat will cost $16 to $20. All prices include equipment.

St. Vincent, "the critter capital of the Caribbean," is ringed by one long, almost continuous reef. The best dive spots are in the small bays along the western coast between Kingstown and Layou; many are within 20 yards of shore and only 20 to 30 feet down. **Anchor Reef** has excellent visibility for viewing a deep-black coral garden, schools of squid, sea horses, and maybe a small octopus. **Critter Corner,** just 600 feet off Indian Bay Beach, is St. Vincent's hallmark "muck" dive site—a wealth of marine life lurks in and among the sand, silt, sea grass, and boulders. The **Forest,** although a shallow dive, is still dramatic with soft corals in pastel colors and schools of small fish. **New Guinea Reef** slopes to 90 feet and can't be matched for its quantity of corals and sponges. The pristine waters surrounding the **Tobago Cays,** in the southern Grenadines, provide a spectacular diving or snorkeling experience.

Dive Fantasea. Earl Habich takes guests on dive and snorkeling trips along the St. Vincent coast and to the Tobago Cays on his custom-built 42-foot snorkel/dive boat, *Get Wet.* ⌧ *Villa Beach, Villa* ☎ *784/457–4477* ⊕ *www.fantaseatours.com.*

Dive St. Vincent. Two PADI-certified dive masters offer beginner and certification courses for ages eight and up, advanced water excursions along the St. Vincent coast and to the southern Grenadines for diving connoisseurs, and an introductory scuba course for novices. ⌧ *Young Island Dock, Villa Beach, Villa* ☎ *784/457–4714, 784/457–4948* ⊕ *www.divestvincent.com.*

Indigo Dive. Indigo specializes in tailor-made dive experiences that match your experience level. PADI dive instructors offer a broad range of courses, from introductory through dive master. ⌧ *Buccament Bay Resort, Buccament* ☎ *784/493–9494* ⊕ *www.indigodive.com.*

GUIDED TOURS

Several operators on St. Vincent offer sightseeing tours on land or by sea. Per-person prices range from $30 for a two-hour tour to the Botanic Gardens to $150 for a day sail to the Grenadines. A full-day tour around Kingstown and either the leeward or windward coast, including lunch, will cost about $65 per person. You can arrange for informal land tours through taxi drivers, who double as knowledgeable guides. Expect to pay $30 per hour for up to four people.

Fantasea Tours. A fleet of four powerboats—ranging from a 28-foot Bowen to a 60-foot catamaran party boat—are ready to take you on a cruise to Bequia and Mustique, along the St. Vincent coast, whale- or dolphin-watching, or snorkeling in the Tobago Cays and Mayreau. Alternatively Fantasea offers land tours along the windward coast to Owia Salt Pond, along the leeward coast to Dark View Falls, or hikes along either the Vermont Nature Trail or up La Soufrière volcano. ⌧ *Villa Beach, Villa* ☎ *784/457–4477* ⊕ *www.fantaseatours.com.*

24

HazECO Tours. For bird-watchers, hikers, and ecotourists, Vincentians Clint and Millie Hazell offer wilderness tours, bird-watching expeditions, and hikes to explore the natural beauty and see historic sites throughout St. Vincent. ⊠ *Kingstown* ☎ *784/457–8634* ⊕ *www.hazecotours.com.*

Sailor's Wilderness Tours. Options from this company include a comfortable sightseeing drive (by day or by moonlight), mountain biking on remote trails, or a strenuous hike up La Soufrière volcano—and they're usually under the expert guidance of Trevor "Sailor" Bailey himself. ⊠ *Middle St., Kingstown* ☎ *784/457–1712* ⊕ *www.sailorswildernesstours.com.*

WORD OF MOUTH

"Bequia is a great island if you are seeking something small (only 7 square miles in area) and somewhat off the beaten path. The main village is located around Admiralty Bay, which is a popular spot for sailboaters. There's not a lot to do on the island, so…if you are looking to completely relax and 'get away from it all,' Bequia is the place to do it."

—RoamsAround

Sam's Taxi Tours. In addition to half- and full-day tours of St. Vincent, Sam's also offers hiking tours to La Soufrière and scenic walks along the Vermont Nature Trails. Also available: a day trip to Mustique and a tour on Bequia that includes snorkeling at Friendship Bay. ⊠ *Sion Hill, Cane Garden, Kingstown* ☎ *784/456–4338* ⊕ *www.samtaxiandtours.com.*

HIKING

St. Vincent offers hikers and trekkers a choice of experiences: easy, scenic walks near Kingstown; moderately difficult nature trails in the central valleys; and exhilarating climbs through a rain forest to the rim of an active volcano. Bring a hat, long pants, and insect repellent if you plan to hike in the bush.

Fodor's Choice ★ **La Soufrière.** La Soufrière, the queen of climbs, is St. Vincent's active volcano (it last erupted in 1979). Approachable from either the windward or leeward coast, this is *not* a casual excursion for the inexperienced—the massive mountain covers nearly the entire northern third of the island. Climbs take all day. You'll need stamina and sturdy shoes to reach the top (at just over 4,000 feet) to peek into the mile-wide (1½-km-wide) crater. Be sure to check the weather before you leave; hikers have been disappointed to find a cloud-obscured view at the summit. You can arrange for a guide ($25 to $30) through your hotel, the SVG Tourism Authority, or tour operators. The eastern approach is most popular. In a four-wheel-drive vehicle you pass through Rabacca Dry River, north of Georgetown, and the Bamboo Forest; then it's a two-hour, 3½-mile (5½-km) hike to the summit. If you're approaching from the west, near Châteaubelair, the climb is longer—6 miles (10 km)—and rougher, but even more scenic. If you hike up one side and down the other, you must arrange in advance to be picked up at the end. ⊠ *Rabacca.*

Vermont Nature Trails. These two hiking trails start near the top of the Buccament Valley, 5 miles (8 km) north of Kingstown. A network of 1½-mile (2½-km) loops passes through bamboo, evergreen forest, and rain forest. In the late afternoon you may be lucky enough to see the rare St. Vincent parrot, *Amazona guildingii.* ⊠ *Buccament.*

THE GRENADINES

The Grenadine Islands are known for great sailing, excellent scuba diving and snorkeling, magnificent beaches, and unlimited chances to relax with a picnic, watch the sailboats, and wait for the sun to set. Each island has a different appeal. Whether you like quiet relaxation, nonstop activity, or socializing (as long as you're not looking for wild nightlife), the Grenadines will hit the spot.

BEQUIA

Bequia (pronounced *beck*-way) is a Carib word meaning "island of the cloud." Hilly and green with several golden-sand beaches, Bequia is 9 miles (14½ km) south of St. Vincent's southwestern shore; with a population of 5,000, it's the largest of the Grenadines. Although boat-building, whaling, and fishing have been the predominant industries here for generations, sailing has now become almost synonymous with Bequia. Admiralty Bay is a favored anchorage for both privately owned and chartered yachts. Lodgings range from comfortable resorts and villas to cozy West Indian–style inns. Bequia's airport and the frequent ferry service from St. Vincent make this a favorite destination for day-trippers, as well. The ferry docks in Port Elizabeth, a tiny town with waterfront bars, restaurants, and shops where you can buy handmade souvenirs—including the exquisitely detailed model sailboats that are a famous Bequia export. The Easter Regatta is held during the four-day Easter weekend, when revelers gather to watch boat races and celebrate the island's seafaring traditions with food, music, dancing, and competitive games.

EXPLORING BEQUIA

To see the views, villages, beaches, and boatbuilding sites around Bequia, hire a taxi at the jetty in Port Elizabeth. Several usually line up under the almond trees to meet each ferry from St. Vincent. The driver will show you the sights in a couple of hours, point out a place for lunch, and (if you wish) drop you at a beach for swimming and snorkeling and pick you up later on. Negotiate the fare in advance, but expect to pay about $30 per hour for the tour. Water taxis are available for transportation between the jetty in Port Elizabeth and the beaches. The cost is $6 (EC$15) per person each way, but keep in mind that most of these operators are not regulated; ride at your own risk.

WORTH NOTING

Admiralty Bay. This huge sheltered bay on the leeward side of Bequia is a favorite yacht anchorage. Year-round it's filled with boats; in season they're moored or transom to bowsprit. It's the perfect spot for watching the sun dip over the horizon each evening—either from your boat or from the terrace bar at one of Port Elizabeth's waterfront hotels or restaurants. ⊠ *Port Elizabeth.*

Hamilton Battery/Ft. Hamilton. Just north of Port Elizabeth, high above Admiralty Bay, an 18th-century fort protected the harbor from marauders. Today it's simply a place to enjoy a magnificent view. ⊠ *Hamilton.*

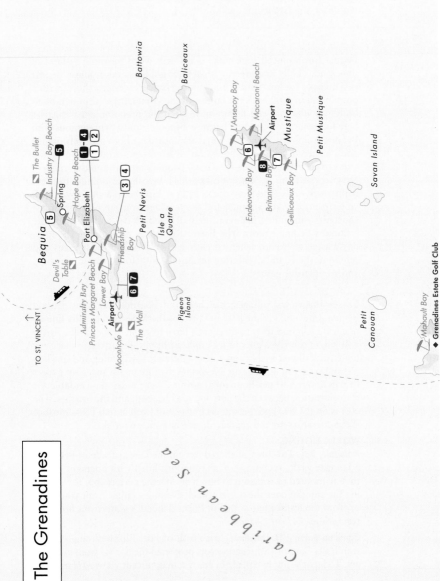

The Grenadines

ATLANTIC OCEAN

♦ Grenadines Estate Golf Club

Canouan

Godahl Beach

Charleston Bay

Grand Bay

South
Gibraltar
Glossy Bay

Friendship Bay

Airport

North Mayreau Channel

Sail Rock

○ Tobago Cays

Saltwhistle Bay Beach

Saline Bay
Beach

Mayreau

Bigsand

Clifton

Airport

Ashton

Palm Island

Chatham Bay

Union
Island

Martinique Channel

⑫ Petit St. Vincent

Carriacou

↓ TO CARRIACOU

KEY

◄━ Ferry
⤢ Beaches
⊿ Dive Sites
▮ Restaurants
① Hotels

0 ├─────┤ 4 miles
0 ├─────┤ 6 km

Restaurants

Anchorage Yacht Club	**10**
L'Auberge des Grenadines	**4**
Basil's Bar	**8**
Dawn's Creole	**5**
De Reef	**6**
Frangipani	**1**
Gingerbread	**2**
Jack's Bar	**7**
Lambi's	**9**
Mac's Pizzeria	**3**

Hotels

Bequia Beachfront Villas	**4**
Bequia Beach Hotel	**3**
Cotton House	**6**
Dennis' Hideaway	**9**
Firefly Mustique	**7**
Firefly Plantation, Bequia	**5**
Frangipani Hotel	**1**
Gingerbread Hotel	**2**
Kings Landing	**10**
Palm Island Resort	**11**
Petit St. Vincent	**12**
Tamarind Beach Hotel & Yacht Club	**8**

Mt. Pleasant. Bequia's highest point (at an elevation of 881 feet) is a reasonable goal for a hiking trek. Alternatively, it's a pleasant drive. The reward is a stunning view of the island and the surrounding Grenadines. ⊠ *Mt. Pleasant.*

FAMILY **Old Hegg Turtle Sanctuary.** In the far northeast of the island, Orton "Brother" King, a retired skin-diving fisherman, tends to more than 200 endangered hawksbill turtles until they can be released back into the sea. Call ahead, and he'll be glad to show you around and tell you how his project has increased the turtle population in Bequia. ⊠ *Park Beach, Industry* 🕿 *784/458–3245* ⊕ *www.turtles.bequia.net* 🖃 *$5 donation requested* ⊗ *By appointment only.*

Port Elizabeth. Bequia's capital and only town, referred to locally as "The Harbour," is on the northeastern side of Admiralty Bay. The ferry from St. Vincent docks at the jetty in the center of the tiny town, which is only a few blocks long and a couple of blocks deep. Walk north along Front Street (which faces the water) to the open-air market, where you can buy local fruits and vegetables and some handicrafts; farther along, you can find some of Bequia's famous model-boat shops. Walking south from the jetty, Belmont Walkway meanders along the bayfront past shops, cafés, restaurants, bars, and small hotels. ⊠ *Port Elizabeth.*

BEACHES

Bequia has clean, uncrowded, white-sand beaches. Some can be reached via a short water-taxi ride from the jetty at Port Elizabeth; others require land transportation.

FAMILY
Fodor's Choice
★
Friendship Bay Beach. This spectacular horseshoe-shape, mile-long (1½-km-long), protected beach on Bequia's midsouthern coast can be reached by land taxi. Refreshments are available at Bequia Beach Hotel's Bagatelle grill. **Amenities:** food and drink. **Best for:** snorkeling; swimming; walking. ⊠ *Friendship.*

Hope Bay Beach. Getting to this remote beach facing Bequia's windward side involves a long taxi ride across the island (about $10 from Port Elizabeth) and a mile-long (1½-km-long) walk downhill on a semipaved path. Your reward is a magnificent crescent of white sand, total seclusion, and—if you like—nude bathing. Be sure to ask your taxi driver to return at a prearranged time. Bring your own lunch and drinks, as there are no facilities. Even though the surf is fairly shallow, swimming may be dangerous because of the undertow. **Amenities:** none. **Best for:** solitude; nudists. ⊠ *Hope Bay, Hope Estate.*

Industry Bay Beach. This nearly secluded beach on the northeastern (windward) side of the island is fringed with towering palms; getting here requires transportation from Port Elizabeth. The beach is good for snorkelers who are strong swimmers, as there could be a strong undertow. Bring a picnic; the nearest facilities are at Firefly Bequia or Sugar Reef resorts, about a 10- to 15-minute walk. **Amenities:** none. **Best for:** solitude; snorkeling. ⊠ *Industry.*

FAMILY
Fodor's Choice
★
Lower Bay Beach. This broad, palm-fringed beach on the southern shore of Admiralty Bay, south of Port Elizabeth and Princess Margaret Beach, is reachable by land or water taxi or a healthy hike from town. It's an excellent beach for swimming and snorkeling. Refreshments are

Port Elizabeth, Bequia

available at beachfront restaurants, including Mango's Beach Bar and De Reef. **Amenities:** food and drink; toilets; water sports. **Best for:** snorkeling; swimming. ✉ *Lower Bay.*

FAMILY **Princess Margaret Beach.** Quiet and wide with a natural stone arch at one end, the beach is not far from Port Elizabeth's Belmont Walkway—but you still need to take a water or land taxi to get here. When you tire of the water, snoozing under the palm and sea grape trees is always an option. Plan to have lunch at Jack's Bar. **Amenities:** food and drink; toilets. **Best for:** snorkeling; swimming; walking. ✉ *Between Port Elizabeth and Lower Bay, Port Elizabeth.*

WHERE TO EAT

Dining on Bequia ranges from casual local-style meals to more elaborate cuisine, and both the food and the service are consistently good. Barbecues at Bequia's hotels mean spicy West Indian seafood, chicken, and beef, plus a buffet of side salads, vegetable dishes, and desserts.

$$$ CARIBBEAN ✗ **Dawn's Creole Beach Café.** It's worth the trip to Industry for the delicious West Indian food and the view. Call first, though, as this is really off the beaten path. Lunch options include callaloo soup, burgers, or barbecued chicken wings and fries, along with a lobster sandwich or the daily special such as "goat water" (a savory soup with bits of goat meat and root vegetables), fresh fish, and conch. At dinner (by reservation only), the five-course creole seafood, lobster, or vegetarian specials include the christophene (chayote) and breadfruit accompaniments that has made Dawn's so renowned. Barbecue is always available on request. There's live music at Sunday brunch; full-moon grill parties feature country music. [$] *Average main: $22* ✉ *Industry* ☎ *784/458–3400* ✍ *Reservations essential.*

$$
CARIBBEAN ✕ **De Reef.** This casual beach bar and restaurant on Lower Bay is the primary feeding station for long, lazy beach days. When the beach bar closes at dusk, the restaurant starts to fill up with those who have made reservations. For breakfast (from 7) or a light lunch, De Reef bakes its own breads, croissants, coconut cake, and cookies—and blends fresh juices to accompany them. For a full lunch or dinner, conch, lobster, whelk, and shrimp are treated the West Indian way; the curried conch and the lobster salad are favorites. Every other Saturday in season, there's a seafood buffet dinner accompanied by live music; on Sunday afternoon, a jam session. $ *Average main: $16* ⊠ *Lower Bay* ☎ *784/458–3958* ⌲ *Reservations essential* ▬ *No credit cards.*

$$$
CARIBBEAN ✕ **Frangipani.** By day, this is the perfect spot for a harborside breakfast or lunch; just before sunset, boaters comes ashore to what is arguably the most popular gathering place in Bequia—the Frangipani Hotel's open-air waterfront bar. After a drink and a chat, the mood turns romantic with candlelight and Caribbean cuisine in the open-air dining room. The à la carte menu emphasizes seafood and local dishes—and be sure to have a slice of Frangi's lime pie for dessert. On Monday night in high season, a local string band plays catchy tunes; on Friday night, folk-singers entertain. At the Thursday Jump-Up, the Frangi barbecue buffet (about $35) is accompanied by steel-band music. $ *Average main: $25* ⊠ *Frangipani Hotel, Belmont Walkway, Port Elizabeth* ☎ *784/458–3255* ⊕ *www.frangipanibequia.com* ⌲ *Reservations essential.*

$$$
CARIBBEAN ✕ **Gingerbread.** The airy dining verandah at the Gingerbread Hotel offers all-day dining and a panoramic view of Admiralty Bay and all the waterfront activity. The lunch crowd enjoys barbecued beef kebabs or chicken with fried potatoes or onions, grilled fish, homemade soups, salads, and sandwiches. In the evening, steaks, seafood, and curries are specialties of the house. Save room for warm, fresh gingerbread—served here with lemon sauce. In season, dinner is often accompanied by live music. $ *Average main: $22* ⊠ *Gingerbread Hotel, Belmont Walkway, Port Elizabeth* ☎ *784/458–3800* ⊕ *www.gingerbreadhotel.com* ⌲ *Reservations essential.*

$$
AMERICAN ✕ **Jack's Bar.** Jack's is a perfect spot for lunch when you're enjoying a day at Princess Margaret Beach or any day when you're on Bequia. The sandwiches, salads, burgers and fries, or the grilled catch of the day along with a refreshing cold drink will certainly satisfy. Dinner by the water is always a delight, but you'll have to maneuver some rough terrain (in your car or on foot) from the main road and then navigate a lot of stairs down to the restaurant—and back up, of course, after your meal. The Tuesday night barbecue is particularly popular. $ *Average main: $18* ⊠ *Princess Margaret Beach, between Port Elizabeth and Lower Bay, Port Elizabeth* ☎ *784/457–3160.*

$$
FRENCH ✕ **L'Auberge des Grenadines.** Owned by French-born Jacques Thevenot and his Vincentian wife, Eileen, this fine French restaurant is convenient for the yachting crowd, day-trippers, and anyone staying awhile. The extensive menu marries French and West Indian cuisines: seafood and local vegetables are prepared with a French twist. Lobster is the specialty; select yours from the live lobster pool. Light salads and sandwiches are available at lunch. Choose dinner from either the à la carte or prix-fixe menu. Delicious baguettes and delicate pastries round out any meal.

[$] *Average main: $22* ✉ *On north shore of Admiralty Bay, Hamilton* ☎ *784/458–3555* 🌐 *www.caribrestaurant.com* ✍ *Reservations essential.*

$$ PIZZA FAMILY 🍴 **Mac's Pizzeria.** Mac's has been serving brick-oven pizza in Bequia since 1980. Choose from 17 mouthwatering toppings (including lobster) or opt for homemade lasagne, quiche, conch fritters, pita sandwiches, or soup and salad. Mac's home-baked cookies, muffins, and banana bread (by the slice or the loaf) are great for dessert or a snack. Or top off your meal with a scoop or two of Maranne's homemade ice cream in tropical flavors. The outdoor terrace has water views. Take-out is also available. [$] *Average main: $20* ✉ *Belmont Walkway, Port Elizabeth* ☎ *784/458–3474* ✍ *Reservations essential* ⏲ *Closed Mon.*

WHERE TO STAY

In addition to several small hotels and inns in Port Elizabeth, Friendship Bay, and elsewhere on the island, a number of villas are available for vacation rental in Spring, Friendship Bay, Lower Bay, and other scenic areas of Bequia. The villas are suitable for two people or as many as a dozen, and the weekly rentals in high season run from as low as $560 a week for a "sweet and simple" villa to $9,000 or more for an elaborate villa with an Italian-style courtyard, gardens, and pool.

RENTAL CONTACT

Grenadine Island Villas ✉ *Belmont Walkway, Port Elizabeth* ☎ *784/457–3739, 784/529–8046 after hours* 🌐 *www.grenadinevillas.com.*

RECOMMENDED HOTELS AND RESORTS

$$ HOTEL FAMILY Fodor's Choice ★ 🏨 **Bequia Beach Hotel.** With an ideal location on pretty Friendship Bay, this sparkling boutique property is a great choice for a relaxing beach getaway or family vacation. **Pros:** expansive property, great for children; a beach lover's dream. **Cons:** lots of steps up to the restaurant from beachfront suites; Wi-Fi only in the main reception area and the restaurant; no TVs except in villas—is that a problem? [$] *Rooms from: $350* ✉ *On Friendship Bay, Friendship* ☎ *784/458–1600* 🌐 *www.bequiabeach.com* 🛏 *11 rooms, 30 suites, 7 villas* 🍽 *Multiple meal plans.*

$$$ B&B/INN Fodor's Choice ★ 🏨 **Firefly Plantation Bequia.** This small inn, under the same ownership as the Firefly in Mustique, is about 2 miles (3 km) north of Port Elizabeth on a 28-acre sugar plantation that dates back to the late 18th century. **Pros:** exquisite contemporary rooms with fabulous views; pool, books, and games available to amuse you; good restaurant and friendly bar; complimentary Wi-Fi. **Cons:** you'll want to rent a vehicle; five-minute walk to the beach and tennis court; negotiating the steep hillside and many steps to the upper-floor rooms can be daunting for the elderly or those with disabilities. [$] *Rooms from: $375* ✉ *Spring* ☎ *784/488–8414* 🌐 *www.fireflybequia.com* 🛏 *5 rooms* 🍽 *Breakfast.*

$$ RENTAL FAMILY 🏨 **Fort Recovery Bequia Beachfront Villa Hotel.** Perfectly situated on mile-long (1½-km-long) Friendship Bay beach, these self-catering suites are an excellent alternative for families and small groups. **Pros:** perfect for small groups; villas are 20 feet from the water; huge; all the comforts of home; complimentary Wi-Fi. **Cons:** far from town; rent a jeep to get around; steep climb up to the road might be difficult for those with disabilities. [$] *Rooms from: $311* ✉ *Friendship Bay, Friendship* ☎ *784/457–3423, 800/384–3355 in the U.S.* 🌐 *www.fortrecoverybequia.com* 🛏 *4 villas* 🍽 *No meals.*

$ HOTEL **Frangipani Hotel.** The venerable Frangipani, once a sea captain's home and also the birthplace of James Mitchell, the former prime minister of St. Vincent and the Grenadines, is known for its welcoming waterfront bar and restaurant. **Pros:** great waterfront location; beautiful harbor view from hillside rooms; lively bar and restaurant at night; complimentary Wi-Fi. **Cons:** steep hillside not easy for anyone with disabilities; no air-conditioning in most rooms; "original" rooms—and the cold-water bath—are really basic. [$] *Rooms from: $85* ✉ *Belmont Walkway, Port Elizabeth* ☎ *784/458–3255* 🌐 *www.frangipanibequia.com* 🛏 *15 rooms, 10 with bath* 🍴 *No meals.*

$ HOTEL FAMILY **Gingerbread Hotel.** Breezy waterfront suites—each suitable for up to three guests—are large and modern, with bedroom alcoves, adjoining salons, and full kitchens (but no air-conditioning). **Pros:** in the middle of all the action; lovely waterfront suites; good casual restaurant; discounted weekly rates available. **Cons:** you might miss air-conditioning if the breeze isn't brisk; no TV, if that matters. [$] *Rooms from: $230* ✉ *Belmont Walkway, Port Elizabeth* ☎ *784/458–3800* 🌐 *www.gingerbreadhotel.com* 🛏 *7 suites* 🍴 *No meals.*

SHOPPING

Long renowned for their boatbuilding skills, Bequians have translated that craftsmanship to building model boats. In their workshops in Port Elizabeth, you can watch as hair-thin lines are attached to delicate sails or individual strips of wood are glued together for decking. Other Bequian artisans create scrimshaw, carve wood, crochet, or work with fabric—designing or hand-painting it first, then creating clothing and gift items for sale. Bequia's shops are mostly on Front Street and Belmont Walkway, its waterfront extension, just steps from the jetty where the ferry arrives in Port Elizabeth. North of the jetty there's an open-air market; farther along that road, you'll find the model-boat workshops. Opposite the jetty, at Bayshore Mall, shops sell ice cream, baked goods, stationery, gifts, and clothing; there's also a grocery, liquor store, pharmacy, travel agent, and bank. On Belmont Walkway, south of the jetty, shops and studios showcase gifts and handmade articles. Shops are open weekdays from 8 to 5, Saturday 8 to noon.

Bequia Bookshop. Head here for Caribbean literature, cruising guides and charts, Caribbean flags, beach novels, souvenir maps, and exquisite scrimshaw and whalebone penknives carved by Bequian scrimshander Sam McDowell. ✉ *Belmont Walkway, Port Elizabeth* ☎ *784/458–3905.*

Claude Victorine. A small roadside sign marks the studio of French artist Claude Victorine. Stop by and admire her delicate, hand-painted, silk wall hangings and scarves—and the watercolors of her daughter, Louloune. ✉ *Lower Bay* ☎ *784/458–3150* 🕒 *Sat.–Thurs. noon–7.*

Local Color. This shops stocks an excellent and unusual selection of handmade jewelry, wood carvings, scrimshaw, and resort clothing. It's above the Porthole restaurant, near the jetty. Note that it's closed in October. ✉ *Belmont Walkway, Port Elizabeth* ☎ *784/458–3202.*

Fodor's Choice ★ **Mauvin's Model Boat Shop.** At this workshop, you can purchase a Bequia trademark—a handmade model "Bequia boat"—or special-order a replica of your own yacht. The models are incredibly detailed and quite expensive—priced from a few hundred to several thousand dollars. The simplest models take about a week to make. ⊠ *Front St., Port Elizabeth* ☎ *784/458–3669.*

Noah's Arkade. Gifts, souvenirs, and contemporary arts and crafts from around the Caribbean are available at this small shop. ⊠ *Frangipani Hotel, Belmont Walkway, Port Elizabeth* ☎ *784/458–3424.*

Fodor's Choice ★ **Sargeant Brothers Model Boat Shop.** In addition to handcrafted, expertly rigged, and authentically detailed model boats, the craftsmen at Sargeant Brothers also build custom models on commission. ⊠ *Front St., Port Elizabeth* ☎ *758/458–3344.*

SPORTS AND ACTIVITIES

BOATING AND SAILING

Fodor's Choice ★ With regular trade winds, visibility for 30 miles (48 km), and generally calm seas, Bequia is a big draw for those sailing the Grenadines—which easily rates among the best blue-water sailing anywhere in the world. At Port Elizabeth, you'll find all kinds of options: day sails or weekly charters, bareboat or fully crewed, monohulls or catamarans. Prices for day trips start at about $140 per person.

FAMILY

Fodor's Choice ★ *Friendship Rose.* This 80-foot schooner spent its first 25 years ferrying both passengers and mail between Bequia and neighboring islands. In the late 1960s it was refitted, and the *Friendship Rose* now takes passengers on day trips from Bequia to Mustique, Mayreau, and the Tobago Cays. Breakfast, lunch, snacks, drinks, and snorkeling gear are included in the price. One child per adult sails free. ⊠ *Waterfront, Port Elizabeth* ☎ *784/ 457–3888, 784/457–3739, 784/529–8046* ⊕ *www.friendshiprose.com.*

Nicola IV. Skippered by Bequian Nicki Hazell and his Spanish wife Cristina, this 44-foot C&C sailing yacht lets passengers participate. On a daysail to Mustique or a snorkeling trip to the nearby uninhabited island of Isle de Quatre, you can take the helm if you'd like or simply sit back and enjoy the view. Longer charters of a week or more are also available. ⊠ *Paget Farm* 🖷 *784/458–3093* ☎ *784/495–4229 cell* ⊕ *nicola.bequia.net.*

DIVING AND SNORKELING

About 35 dive sites around Bequia and nearby islands are accessible within 15 minutes by boat. The leeward side of the 7-mile (11-km) reef that fringes Bequia has been designated a marine park. The **Bullet**, off Bequia's northeast point, has limited access because of rough seas, but it's a good spot for spotting rays, barracuda, and the occasional nurse shark. **Devil's Table** is a shallow dive at the northern end of Admiralty Bay that's rich in fish and coral and has a sailboat wreck nearby at 90 feet. The **Wall** is a 90-foot drop off West Cay. Expect to pay dive operators $60 to $70 for a one-tank and $100 or so for a two-tank dive, including equipment. Dive boats welcome snorkelers for about $20 per person, but for the best snorkeling in Bequia, take a water taxi to the bay at Moonhole and arrange a pickup time.

Bequia Dive Adventures. This company offers PADI instruction courses and takes small groups on three dives daily. Rates include all equipment; harbor pickup and return is included for customers staying on yachts. ⊠ *Belmont Walkway, Port Elizabeth* ☎ *784/458–3826* ⊕ *www. bequiadiveadventures.com.*

24

Dive Bequia. Dive and snorkel tours, night dives, and full equipment rental is available from Dive Bequia. PADI instructors provide resort and certification courses—including several interactive e-learning courses. ⊠ *Gingerbread Hotel, Belmont Walkway, Port Elizabeth* ☎ *784/458–3504* ⊕ *www.divebequia.com.*

CANOUAN

Halfway down the Grenadines chain, this tiny boot-shape island—3½ miles (5½ km) long and 1¼ miles (2 km) wide—has only about 1,200 residents. But don't let its historically slow pace and quiet ways fool you. Canouan (pronounced *can*-o-wan), which is the Carib word for "turtle," has a modern airport with an extended runway suitable for small to midsize jets. The island has one of the region's largest and nicest villa communities, a championship golf course, a delightful small resort, and four of the most pristine beaches in the Caribbean. Canouan is also a busy port for yacht charters and diving expeditions to the Tobago Cays. Mt. Royal, the highest point on the island at 900 feet, offers panoramic 360-degree views of St. Vincent, all the Grenadines, and even St. Lucia on a clear day.

BEACHES

Canouan has four exquisite white-sand beaches, although land access to two of them is difficult because entry to the entire northern two-thirds of the island (where those two beaches are located) is controlled by a private resort and villa community. Canouan faces a mile-long (1½-km-long) coral reef—one of the longer barrier reefs in the Caribbean—that offers excellent diving and snorkeling opportunities. The island's proximity to several of the other Grenadines (Mayreau and the Tobago Cays, in particular) makes excursions to other beautiful beaches relatively easy.

Godahl Beach. This lovely stretch of white-sand beach (pronounced *Gud*-ul) at the southern end of Carenage Bay is surrounded by Canouan Resort and Grenadines Estate Villas, a private villa community. Those who are not resort guests or villa residents may access the beach only by boat. **Amenities:** none for nonguests/nonresidents. **Best for:** swimming; walking. ⊠ *Carenage Bay.*

Grand Bay Beach. In central Canouan on the leeward coast, Grand Bay is the island's longest beach and the site of Charlestown, the largest town, where ferries dock; it's alternatively called Charlestown Bay beach. **Amenities:** food and drink; toilets. **Best for:** swimming. ⊠ *Charlestown Bay.*

Mahault Bay Beach. This lovely but remote expanse of beach (pronounced *mah*-ho) is at the northern tip of the island, surrounded by Mt. Royal; the beach is accessible through Canouan Resort and Grenadines Estate Villas, a private villa community, or by sea. **Amenities:** none. **Best for:** solitude; swimming. ⊠ *Mahault Bay.*

South Glossy Bay Beach. This and other Glossy Bay beaches along the southwest (windward) coast of Canouan are absolutely spectacular. South Glossy Bay is within walking distance of the airport. **Amenities:** none. **Best for:** swimming; walking. ⊠ *Glossy Bay.*

Tamarind Beach Hotel

WHERE TO STAY

$$$$ RESORT FAMILY **Canouan Resort at Carenage Bay.** At this full-service beach resort, 13 roomy villas are sprinkled around 200 acres of the 1,200-acre property. **Pros:** beautiful accommodations; while a perfect setting for romance, there are lots of activities for the entire family; and ahh, the spa! **Cons:** madly expensive; everything is à la carte (except breakfast). [$] *Rooms from: $4160* ✉ *Carenage Bay* ☎ *784/458–8000* 🌐 *www.canouan.com* 🛏 *13 villas* 🍴 *Breakfast.*

$$ HOTEL FAMILY **Tamarind Beach Hotel & Yacht Club.** Thatched roofs are a trademark of this low-rise beachfront hotel. **Pros:** good value; excellent location for diving and boating enthusiasts; complimentary airport transfers; complimentary Wi-Fi. **Cons:** no pool; standard rooms are small. [$] *Rooms from: $295* ✉ *Charlestown* ☎ *784/458–8044* 🌐 *www.tamarindbeachhotel.com* 🛏 *32 rooms, 8 suites* 🕒 *Closed Sept. and Oct.* 🍴 *Multiple meal plans.*

SPORTS AND ACTIVITIES

BOATING

Fodor's Choice ★ The Grenadines have some of the most superb cruising waters in the world. Canouan is at the midpoint of the Grenadines, so it's an easy sail north to St. Vincent, Bequia, and Mustique or south to Mayreau, the Tobago Cays, and beyond.

Moorings. Adjacent to the Tamarind Beach Hotel & Yacht Club, Moorings has bareboat and crewed yacht charters of monohulls and catamarans ranging in size from 38 to 52 feet. ✉ *Tamarind Beach Hotel & Yacht Club, Charlestown* ☎ *784/482–0653* 🌐 *www.moorings.com.*

DIVING AND SNORKELING

The mile-long (1½-km-long) reef protecting Canouan offers excellent snorkeling, as well as spectacular sites for both novice and experienced divers. **Gibraltar,** a giant stone almost 30 feet down, is a popular site; plenty of colorful fish and corals are visible. **Windward Bay,** on Canouan's southeastern coast, is a large lagoon protected by a barrier reef, making it perfect for snorkeling. The crystalline waters surrounding the nearby **Tobago Cays** are filled with fish and sea turtles and offer marvelous diving and snorkeling.

One-tank dives cost $110 per dive; two-tank dives, $175 per dive; night dives, $130 per dive. A full range of PADI courses are offered; novices can take a Discover Scuba Diving course for $175. Three-hour snorkeling trips to the Tobago Cays cost $110 per person, including equipment.

Canouan Scuba Center. Specializing in taking small groups of divers, whether beginners or experts, to the Tobago Cays and other nearby sites, Canouan Scuba Center is a full-service PADI facility that also offers resort and certification courses. The dive center is located on the grounds of Tamarind Beach Hotel. ✉ *Tamarind Beach Hotel & Yacht Club, Charlestown* ☎ *784/532–8073, 917/796–1100 in the U.S.* ⊕ *www.canouandivecenter.com.*

GOLF

Grenadines Estate Golf Club. This 18-hole, par-72 championship course is spread over 60 acres within the Canouan Resort and Grenadines Estate Villas, a private villa community. It is open to residents staying at the resort and patrons purchasing a daily ticket. The first 9 holes of the Jim Fazio–designed course, along with holes 10 and 18, are in a pretty, green plain that slopes down to the sea. The rest have been carved into the mountainside, affording spectacular views of Canouan Island and the surrounding Grenadines. The 13th hole offers a wraparound view of the Grenadines; it's also the most challenging, because its unforgiving green is at the edge of a cliff. Greens fees for 18 holes are $195 for resort guests and $450 for nonresident patrons; rates include a golf cart. Golf instruction and rental clubs are available, and a pro shop and lounge are on-site. ✉ *Canouan Resort and Grenadine Estate Villas, at northern tip of island, Carenage Bay* ☎ *784/458–8000.*

MAYREAU

Mayreau (pronounced *my*-row) is minuscule—1½ square miles (4 square km). With the exception of 22 acres at its northern tip that was bought in 1977 by a German-Canadian family and 21 acres that comprise the island's single (unnamed) village and were acquired by St. Vincent and the Grenadines, Mayreau remains in the hands of heirs of the original French plantation owners. Only about 250 residents live in the little village on Station Hill, and there are no proper roads. Visitors enjoy these natural surroundings in one of the prettiest locations in the Grenadines—and a rather unique spot where the calm Caribbean is separated from the Atlantic surf by only a narrow strip of beach. It's a favorite stop for boaters, as well, who anchor in Saltwhistle Bay. Except for water sports and hiking, there's not much to do—but everyone prefers it that way. For a day's excursion, you can hike up Mayreau's only hill (wear sturdy shoes) for a stunning view of the Tobago Cays. Then stop for a drink at Dennis' Hideaway and enjoy a swim at Saline Bay beach, where you may be joined by a boatload of cruise-ship passengers. The only access to Mayreau is by boat (ferry, private, or hired), which you can arrange at Union Island.

BEACHES

Mayreau's primary beach, Saltwhistle Bay, is unique because the calm water of the Caribbean is on one side, and the more powerful Atlantic surf is on the other; a few yards of white-sand beach is all that separates them. Saline Bay Beach, also magnificent, is popular with small cruise ships that ply the waters of the Grenadines and anchor offshore for the day.

Saline Bay Beach. This beautiful 1-mile (1½-km) crescent of pure white sand on the southwestern coast of Mayreau has no facilities, but you can walk up the hill to Dennis' Hideaway for lunch or drinks. The adjacent dock is where the ferry that travels between St. Vincent and Union Island ties up, and small cruise ships occasionally anchor offshore to give passengers a beach break. **Amenities:** none. **Best for:** swimming. ✉ *Saline Bay.*

Saltwhistle Bay Beach. This beach at the northwestern tip of Mayreau takes top honors—it's an exquisite, 2.5-mile-long crescent of powdery white sand shaded by perfectly spaced palms, sea grape trees, and flowering bushes. It's a popular anchorage for the yachting crowd, as well as for day trips en route to or from the Tobago Cays. **Amenities:** none. **Best for:** snorkeling; swimming. ✉ *Saltwhistle Bay.*

WHERE TO STAY

$ B&B/INN 🏨 **Dennis' Hideaway.** Each room in this hilltop guesthouse has a private balcony with a perfect view of the sun as it sets over Saline Bay. **Pros:** great value; stunning views; excellent local food; good base for boaters and divers. **Cons:** no frills; little in the way of amenities; village life can get noisy at night (unless you're participating!). [$] *Rooms from: $93* ✉ *Above Saline Bay* ☎ *784/458–8594* 🌐 *www.dennis-hideaway.com* 🛏 *5 rooms* 🍴 *Breakfast.*

SPORTS AND ACTIVITIES

BOATING AND FISHING

Dennis' Hideaway charters. Yacht charters, drift-fishing trips, dive trips, and day sails can be arranged at Dennis' Hideaway. Expect to pay $40 per person for drift fishing for 1½ hours and $75–$100 per person (depending on the number of passengers) for a full day of sailing, swimming, and snorkeling—lunch included. ✉ *Near Saline Bay* ☎ *784/458–8594* 🌐 *www.dennis-hideaway.com.*

MUSTIQUE

This upscale haven, 18 miles (29 km) southeast of St. Vincent, is 3 miles (5 km) by 1¼ miles (2 km) at its widest point. The island is hilly and has several green valleys, each with a sparkling white-sand beach facing an aquamarine sea. The permanent population is about 300. Back in the 1960s, Britain's Princess Margaret put this small, private island on the map after the owner, the late Colin Tennant (Lord Glenconner), presented her with a 10-acre plot of land as a wedding gift. Tennant had bought the entire 1,400-acre island in 1958 for $67,500 (the equivalent of about $450,000 today). The Mustique Company—which Tennant formed in 1968 to develop the copra, sea-island cotton, and sugarcane estate into the glamorous hideaway it has become—now manages the privately owned villas, provides housing for all island employees, and operates Mustique Villa Rentals. Arrangements must be made about a year in advance to rent one of the luxury villas that now pepper the northern half of the island.

Sooner or later, stargazers see the resident glitterati at Basil's Bar, the island's social center. Proprietor Basil Charles also runs a boutique crammed with clothes and accessories from Bali. A pair of cotton-candy-color, gingerbread-style buildings, the centerpiece of the tiny village, house a gift shop and clothing boutique. There's also an antiques shop with fabulous objets d'art and a deli–grocery stocked with Brie and champagne.

The Mustique Blues Festival, held during the first two weeks of February, features artists from North America, Europe, and the Caribbean; shows occur nightly at Basil's Bar. The festival is quite a draw.

BEACHES

Mustique has a number of beautiful white-sand beaches at the foot of each of its lovely green valleys, one reason for its appeal to the rich and famous. Villas are strung out along the northern half of the island, but the best beach, the picture-perfect Macaroni Beach, is on the south side.

Britannia Bay Beach. This beach on Mustique's western coast is right next to the Brittania Bay jetty, and Basil's Bar is convenient for lunch. Firefly Mustique, on a steep hillside overlooking Britannia Bay, has steps leading down to the beach. **Amenities:** food and drink; toilets. **Best for:** swimming.

Endeavour Bay Beach. On the northwestern tip of Mustique, this is the main beach used by guests of the Cotton House. Swimming and snorkeling are ideal, and a dive shop with water-sports equipment rental is available on site. The resort's Beach Café restaurant and bar are convenient for lunch or snacks. **Amenities:** food and drink; toilets; water sports. **Best for:** snorkeling; swimming.

Gelliceaux Bay Beach. This rather remote beach on the southwestern coast, one of 10 marine conservation areas designated by St. Vincent and the Grenadines, provides the best snorkeling on Mustique. **Amenities:** none. **Best for:** snorkeling; swimming.

L'Ansecoy Bay Beach. At the island's very northern tip, adjacent to the Cotton House, this broad crescent of white sand fringes brilliant turquoise water. Just offshore, the French liner *Antilles* went aground in 1971. **Amenities:** none. **Best for:** snorkeling; swimming.

FAMILY
Fodor's Choice
★

Macaroni Beach. Macaroni is Mustique's most famous stretch of fine white sand—offering swimming (no lifeguards) in moderate surf that's several shades of blue, along with a few palm huts and picnic tables in a shady grove of trees. **Amenities:** parking. **Best for:** swimming.

WHERE TO EAT

$$$$
SEAFOOD
FAMILY

✕ **Basil's Bar.** Basil's is *the* place to be—only partly because it's just about the *only* place to be in Mustique. It's mainly a wooden deck perched on bamboo stilts over the waves; there's a thatched roof, a congenial bar, and a dance floor that's open to the stars—in every sense. You never know what celebrity may show up at the next table. The food is simple and good—mostly seafood, homemade ice cream, burgers, and salads, great French toast and banana pancakes, the usual cocktails, and unusual wines. Wednesday is Jump Up & Barbecue Night, with live music; Sunday is Locals Night, with a buffet of local dishes. $ *Average main: $34* ✉ *Britannia Bay* ☎ *784/488–8350* ⊕ *www.basilsmustique. com* ⚖ *Reservations essential.*

WHERE TO STAY

$$$$
RESORT
Fodor's Choice
★

Cotton House. Mustique's only full-service hotel allows travelers to enjoy the sun-kissed glam and idyllic beaches of this famous island in an intimate, island-chic setting that also shelters those in-the-know and the rich and famous (at least those without their own Mustique homes). **Pros:** direct beach access; beautiful rooms; personalized service with great attention to detail; excellent dining; a familial vibe. **Cons:** quite expensive; more sedate than, say, Firefly. $ *Rooms from: $1100* ✉ *Endeavor Bay* ☎ *784/456–4777* ⊕ *www.cottonhouse.net* ⚑ *5 rooms, 8 suites, 3 cottages, 1 villa* ⊘ *Closed Sept. and Oct.* ⦿ *Multiple meal plans.*

$$$$
ALL-INCLUSIVE

Firefly Mustique. Tiny and charming, this three-story hotel is wedged into dense tropical foliage on a steep hillside above Britannia Bay. **Pros:** relaxed and friendly spot; open-air ocean views from each amazing room; the bar—a hangout for guests and visiting celebrities—features martini and champagne menus. **Cons:** very expensive; house-party atmosphere at the bar can get noisy at night. $ *Rooms from: $1050* ☎ *784/488–8414* ⊕ *www.fireflymustique.com* ⚑ *5 rooms* ⦿ *All-inclusive.*

$$$$
RENTAL

Mustique Villa Rentals. Except for the Cotton House and the Firefly, Mustique is an island of privately owned villas—74 of them; rentals can be arranged through Mustique Villa Rentals. $ *Rooms from: $5000* ☎ *784/458–4621* ⊕ *www.mustique-island.com* ⚑ *74 villas* ⦿ *No meals.*

SPORTS AND ACTIVITIES

Water-sports facilities are available at Cotton House, and most villas include sports equipment. Four floodlighted tennis courts are near the airport for those whose villa lacks its own; there's a cricket field (matches on Sunday afternoon) and an equestrian center. Motorbikes or "mules" (beach buggies) to ride around the bumpy roads rent for $75 per day.

Cotton House

DIVING AND SNORKELING

FAMILY **Mustique Watersports.** Mustique is surrounded by coral reefs, and nearly 20 dive sites are nearby. Mustique Watersports, on Endeavour Bay Beach, offers PADI instruction and certification and has a 28-foot, fully equipped dive boat. Rates are $110 for an introductory course, $85 for a one-tank dive, and $350 for a five-dive package. A special "bubble maker" introduction-to-diving course is available for children ages 8–11. Snorkelers can rent a mask and fins for the day or join a snorkeling trip where equipment is provided. ⊠ *Cotton House, Endeavour Bay Beach* ☎ *784/456–3486* ⊕ *www.mustique-island.com.*

HORSEBACK RIDING

FAMILY **Mustique Equestrian Centre.** Mustique is the only island in the Grenadines where you can find a fine thoroughbred horse or pony to ride. Daily excursions leave from the Mustique Equestrian Centre, which is one block from the airport. Rates are $70 per hour for an island trek; private lessons begin at $60. All rides are accompanied, and children five years or older are allowed to ride. ☎ *784/488–8000* ⊕ *www. mustique-island.com.*

PALM ISLAND

A private speck of land (only 135 acres), exquisite Palm Island used to be an uninhabited, mosquito-infested swamp called Prune Island. One intrepid family put heart and soul—as well as muscle and brawn and lots of money—into taking the wrinkles out of the prune and rechristened it Palm Island. The Caldwell family cleaned up the five surrounding beaches, built bungalows, planted palm trees, and irrigated the swamp with seawater to kill the mosquitoes. The rustic getaway existed for 25 years before Palm Island's current owners, Elite Island Resorts, dolled up the property. Now it's one of the finest resorts in the Caribbean. Other than the resort, the island is populated only by a handful of privately owned villas. Access is via Union Island, 1 mile (1½ km) to the west and a 10-minute ride in the resort's launch.

WHERE TO STAY

$$$$

RESORT

Fodor'sChoice

★

☒ **Palm Island Resort.** Perfect for a honeymoon, rendezvous, or chic escape, this palm-studded resort island offers peace and tranquility, along with five dazzling white-sand beaches, a calm aquamarine sea for swimming and water sports, nature trails for quiet walks, a pool with waterfall, a "pitch-and-putt" golf course, sophisticated dining, impeccable service, and exquisite accommodations. **Pros:** private and romantic; fabulous beach; great snorkeling right outside beachfront cottages 15 and 16; free scuba resort course. **Cons:** quiet nights (early to bed and early to rise); fairly isolated; very expensive. $ *Rooms from: $645* ☎ *784/458–8824, 866/237–2157 in the U.S.* ⊕ *www.palmislandcaribbean.com* ⤶ *33 rooms, 8 suites, 2 villas* ⦵ *All-inclusive.*

PETIT ST. VINCENT

The southernmost of St. Vincent's Grenadines, tiny (115 acres), private Petit St. Vincent—pronounced "Petty" St. Vincent and affectionately called PSV—is ringed with white-sand beaches and covered with tropical foliage. The late Hazen Richardson created the resort in 1968. The current owners made extensive renovations (cottage upgrades, a casual beachside restaurant, an air-conditioned fitness and yoga center, an open-air spa, an air-conditioned library with a TV and Internet access, a new children's center, and landscaping upgrades), but have not changed the design or, more important, the nature of the property. To get to PSV, you fly from Barbados to Union Island, where the resort's motor launch meets you for the 20-minute voyage.

WHERE TO STAY

$$$$

RESORT

Fodor'sChoice

★

☒ **Petit St. Vincent.** The lack of phones, room TVs, outside interference, and even planned activities is particularly appealing when you can indulge your most luxurious, private-island fantasies. **Pros:** private island experience with secluded white-sand beaches; very accommodating service; spacious cottages; excellent cuisine (including the large jar of homemade cookies placed in your room upon arrival). **Cons:** you're pretty much a captive here, so bring a good, long book; some of the beaches adjacent to the cottages are rocky or have high surf; Wi-Fi and Internet available only in the front office; all this luxury and solitude is pricey. $ *Rooms from: $1400* ☎ *784/458–8801, 800/654–9326 in the U.S.* ⊕ *www.petitstvincent.com* ⤶ *22 cottages* ⦵ *Closed Aug.–Oct.* ⦵ *All-inclusive.*

24

TOBAGO CAYS

Fodor's Choice   Tobago Cays, a small group of five uninhabited islands (Petit Rameau,
★   Petit Bateau, Baradal, Petit Tabac, and Jamesby) just east of Mayreau in
the southern Grenadines, was declared a wildlife reserve—Tobago Cays
Marine Park—in 2006 by the St. Vincent and the Grenadines government to preserve the natural beauty and biodiversity of the cays and to
allow visitors to experience some of the best snorkeling in the world.
The sparkling-clear water within Horseshoe Reef, which surrounds
four of the islands, is studded with sponges and coral formations and
populated by countless colorful fish and sea turtles. All the major dive
operators and sailing and snorkeling day trips stop here, sometimes
making it a little overcrowded, but the Tobago Cays remain everyone's
version of a tropical paradise and one unforgettable place. All visitors to
the Tobago Cays Marine Park, including those on private or chartered
yachts and dive boats, are required to pay a user fee of $4 ($EC10) per
person; a yacht mooring costs $17 (EC$45) for 24 hours.

UNION ISLAND

Union Island is the commercial center of the southern Grenadines—a
popular anchorage for those sailing the Grenadines and a crossroads
for those heading to surrounding islands. Clifton, the main town and a
port of entry for yachts, is small, with a bustling harbor, a quaint town
square with a busy market, a few simple beachfront inns and restaurants, businesses that cater to yachts, and the regional airstrip—the
busiest in the Grenadines. Hugh Malzac Square, in the center of town,
honors a local islander, the first black man to captain a merchant-marine
ship. The ship was the *Booker T. Washington*; the time was 1942.

Taxis and minibuses are available to get around the island, and water
taxis go between islands—including Happy Island, a man-made islet
in the harbor where you can get a good stiff rum punch and even some
grilled lobster or fish. The Easterval Regatta occurs during the Easter
weekend with festivities that include boat races, sports and games, a
calypso competition, a beauty pageant, and a cultural show featuring
the Big Drum Dance (derived from French and African traditions).
Union Island has several small inns and hotels, some directly on the
waterfront and others inland.

BEACHES

Although it's an important hub for travelers heading to some of the
smaller islands in the Grenadines (especially the private retreats of Petit
St. Vincent and Palm Island and also Mayreau, which does not have an
airstrip), the hilly, volcanic island has few beaches that compare with
those on its closest neighbors. The best beach, Big Sands Beach, has
powdery white sand and is easily accessible from Clifton.

FAMILY   **Big Sands Beach.** Union has relatively few good beaches, but this one on
Belmont Bay—on the northern shore, a five-minute drive from Clifton—
is a pretty crescent of powdery white sand, protected by reefs, and with
lovely views of Mayreau and the Tobago Cays. **Amenities:** none. **Best
for:** solitude; snorkeling; swimming. ⊠ *Richmond Bay.*

Chatham Bay Beach. The desolate but lovely golden-sand beach at Chatham Bay offers good swimming. **Amenities:** none. **Best for:** solitude; swimming. ⊠ *Chatham Bay.*

WHERE TO EAT

$$$ ✕ **Anchorage Yacht Club.** You can't get much closer to waterfront dining
SEAFOOD than here at the AYC. This is the yachting crowd's favorite stop for
FAMILY land-side meals—breakfast, lunch, or dinner. Freshly baked croissants and other pastries, along with pitchers of fresh-squeezed juice and piping-hot coffee, present the perfect wake-up. At lunch, the sandwiches, salads, burgers, grilled fish, and more are served within striking distance (figuratively speaking) of the shark pool. And at dinner, the place comes alive with weekend entertainment (more often in season) as you enjoy fresh seafood cooked to order or, perhaps, a lobster prepared to your liking. $ *Average main: $22* ⊠ *Clifton* ☎ *784/458–8821* ⊕ *www. anchorage-union.com* ⬧ *Reservations essential.*

$$ ✕ **Lambi's.** Lambi's, which overlooks the waterfront in Clifton, offers
CARIBBEAN a daily buffet for all meals from November through May. The dinner buffet includes some 50 dishes, including the specialty: delicious conch creole. From June through October, dining is à la carte; you can choose from fish, chicken, conch, pork, lobster, shrimp, and beef dishes. Lambi is Creole patois for "conch," and the restaurant's walls are constructed from conch shells. Yachts and dinghies can tie up at the wharf, and there's steel-band music and limbo dancing every night in season. $ *Average main: $18* ⊠ *Clifton* ☎ *784/458–8549* ⊕ *www. lambisunion.weebly.com.*

WHERE TO STAY

$ 🏨 **Anchorage Yacht Club.** The popular AYC offers convenient, inexpen-
HOTEL sive land-side accommodations to boaters looking for a night or two on dry land, as well as to those beginning or ending a sailing vacation through the Grenadines. **Pros:** two minutes from airport via jitney; convenient for all boating activities; good restaurant; convivial atmosphere **Cons:** rooms are comfortable but definitely not luxurious; entrance into some beach cottages is through the bathroom! $ *Rooms from: $98* ⊠ *Clifton* ☎ *784/458–8221* ⊕ *www.anchorage-union.com* ⬧ *10 rooms, 3 cottages* 🍽 *No meals.*

$ 🏨 **Kings Landing Hotel.** Divers flock to Kings Landing, because Grena-
HOTEL dines Dive—the biggest operator in the region—is based here. **Pros:** great for divers; excellent waterfront location; good value. **Cons:** tiny beach; bathrooms have showers only. $ *Rooms from: $105* ⊠ *Clifton* ☎ *784/485–8823* ⊕ *www.kingslandinghotel.com* ⬧ *15 rooms, 2 cottages* 🍽 *Breakfast.*

SHOPPING

L'Atelier Turquoise. On the waterfront in Clifton, in the center of town next to Erika's Marine and adjacent to the main dock, this tiny shop sells a variety of Caribbean arts and crafts, colorful gifts and souvenirs, hats, T-shirts, and more. ⊠ *Clifton, Union* ☎ *784/458–8734.*

24

SPORTS AND ACTIVITIES

BOATING AND SAILING

Erika's Marine Services. At Erika's Marine Services on the waterfront in Clifton, you can arrange a day sail throughout the lower Grenadines: Palm Island, Mayreau, the Tobago Cays, Petit St. Vincent, and Carriacou. A full day of snorkeling, fishing, and swimming on a catamaran party boat costs about $75 per person for a scheduled sail or $750 for up to four passengers on a private charter—lunch and drinks included. ⊠ *Clifton* ☎ *784/485–8335, 416/848–7325 in the U.S.* ⊕ *www.erikamarine.com.*

Yannis Day Tours. Operated by nearby Palm Island Resort, Yannis catamaran trips depart from Clifton Harbour for day sails to Saltwhistle Bay on Mayreau and the Tobago Cays. Snorkeling gear, drinks, and a buffet lunch are included. ⊠ *Clifton* ☎ *784/458–8513.*

DIVING AND SNORKELING

Grenadines Dive. Glenroy Adams, a Bequia native who claims to know "every dive site in the Grenadines," is the dive master here. The company offers Tobago Cays snorkeling trips and wreck dives at the *Purina,* a sunken World War I English gunboat. Single-tank dives cost $65; multidive packages are discounted. Beginners can take a four-hour resort course, which includes a shallow dive. Certified divers can rent equipment by the day or week. ⊠ *Kings Landing Hotel, Clifton* ☎ *784/458–8138* ⊕ *www.grenadinesdive.com.*

TRINIDAD AND
TOBAGO

WELCOME TO TRINIDAD AND TOBAGO

Caribbean Sea

Blanchisseuse Bay

Cyril Bay
Tyrico Bay
Maracas Bay
La Vache Bay
Saddle Rd.

Chupara Pt. **11**

Las Cuevas Bay

Dragon's Mouth

Chaguaramas

9 **8**

El Tucuche **Asa Wright Nature Centre**

13 Tunapuna **Lopinot Complex**

Port of Spain ⭐

San Juan

1-12
1-7

Caroni Bird ◆ Sanctuary

Piarco International Airport **10**

Chaguaramas Military History & Aerospace ◆ Museum

Chaguanas

Dattareya ◆ Yoga Centre

Flanigin Town

California ○

Couva

Tabaquite

Gulf of Paria

San Fernando

Princes Town

New Grant

Oropuche Lagoon

Irois Bay La Brea

Penal

Pointe-a-Pierre

Cedros Bay Point Fortin

Basse Terre

Fullarton

San Francique

Moruga

Icacos Pt.

Islote Pt.

Erin Bay Erin Pt.

KEY

🚢 Ferry
🏖 Beaches
1 Restaurants
1 Hotels

0 ——— 10 mi
0 ——— 10 km

The most southerly of the Caribbean islands, Trinidad is also the most colorful. Islanders trace their roots to Africa, India, China, and Madeira, and they speak English, Spanish, Hindi, and French patois. On much quieter Tobago the most exciting event is often the palm trees swaying high above a gentle arc of a beach.

BUSINESS AND PLEASURE

The two-island republic is the southernmost link in the Antillean island chain, some 7 miles (11 km) off the coast of Venezuela, but Tobago's Main Ridge and Trinidad's Northern Range are believed to represent the farthest reaches of the Andes Mountains. Trinidad is a large petroleum and natural-gas producer. Tiny Tobago is known more for its quiet atmosphere and gorgeous, wild beaches.

TO TOBAGO

Grande Rivière

Madamas
Bay

Matelot

Toco

Sans
Souci

Salibea Bay

Galera Pt.

**♦ Galera Point
Lighthouse**

Mt. Oropuche

Redhead

Balandra Bay

El Cerro del Aripo

Matura
Main Rd.

Saline
Bay

Eastern

Arima

Valencia

Sangre Grande

Churchill-
Roosevelt
Hwy.

Matura
Bay

Manzanilla Beach

Cocos
Bay

Guataro Pt.

Tableland

Rio Claro

Pierreville

Mayaro
Bay

Guayaguayare

Galeota Pt.

Guayaguayare
Bay

ATLANTIC OCEAN

Tobago

Scarborough

25

Restaurants ▼		Hotels ▼	
Angelo's	5	Asa Wright Nature Centre Lodge	11
Apsara	6	The Carlton Savannah	7
Buzo Osteria	12	Coblentz Inn	3
Chaud	9	Courtyard by Marriott	8
Joseph's	4	Crews Inn	9
Mélange	8	Capital Plaza Hotel Trinidad	4
More Vino More Sushi	11	Hilton Trinidad	1
Prime Restaurant	1	Holiday Inn Express	10
Tiki Village	2	Hyatt Regency Trinidad	6
Trotters	10	Kapok Hotel	2
Veni Mangé	3	Le Grande Almandier	12
The Verandah	7	Monique's	5
Wings Restaurant	13		

TOP REASONS TO VISIT TRINIDAD AND TOBAGO

1 Carnival: Trinidad's Carnival is the Caribbean's biggest and best party, but nightlife is hopping the rest of the year, too.

2 Bird-Watching: Both Trinidad and Tobago are major bird-watching destinations; Trinidad itself has more resident species than any other Caribbean island.

3 Culture Sharing: A melding of many cultures means lively festivals year-round and a fabulous mix of cuisines.

4 Music: The steel pan was invented in Trinidad, and excellent bands play all over the island.

EATING WELL IN TRINIDAD AND TOBAGO

Food here blends indigenous, British, French, Spanish, African, South American, East Indian, Chinese, and Middle Eastern influences.

Referencing the national dish, acclaimed second-generation chef Debra Sardinha-Metivier notes, "We are a callaloo in people form. Maybe you had a Chinese grandmother or Indian grandfather who helped broaden, sophisticate your palate."

Today there's a growing awareness, pun intended, of returning to roots: "Everything comes full circle; organic-farm-to-table sustainability was always a necessity. More people then had a backyard garden . . . and shared. If I had a mango tree, and my neighbor had a coconut, we would barter. . . . Adapting to modern life while creatively meeting the needs of three square meals (including a rushed lunch for workers) began fusion cuisine." It's the fusion (particularly of Indian and Caribbean) that sets Trinidad apart.

STREET FOOD

Although much of what you'll find in restaurants and stalls here resembles variations on Caribbean standards, street food, which rules rushed Trini life, stands out. You'll find fresh rotis (akin to wraps) stuffed with curried meat, seafood, or chicken; chicken *geera* (an Indian dish heavily seasoned with cumin); pies—beef, cheese, fish, *aloo* (Hindi for potato); and *pows* (from the Cantonese *pao-tzu*, steamed wrapped buns with savory or sweet filling, typically pork).

CALLALOO

Reflecting the island's pronounced African influence, this hearty stew is the national dish (variants are found throughout the islands). Into the pot go the leaves of the dasheen, which resembles slightly bitter spinach and is also called taro or "callaloo bush," along with okra, chili peppers, coconut milk, *chadon bene* (an herb also known as culantro), garlic, onion, tubers, and sometimes crab. It's often served with macaroni pie (essentially pasta baked with cheese and eggs).

CRAB AND DUMPLING

Tobagonian cuisine mimics Trinidad's, for the most part, but its signature dish is messy, marvelous curried crab with dumpling. The sweet blue crabs and dumplings are simmered in a rich coconut sauce. Tobago is also celebrated for its sumptuously prepared "provisions" (often-starchy vegetables), soups, and stews.

PELAU

Pelau is another mainstay, its roots dating back to 5th-century-BC Mesopotamia and brought to Europe by Alexander the Great's army. International variations run from rice pilaf to Spain's paella; Trinidad's version borrows from several cultures. Chicken, beef, pork, or goat is cooked down with rice, pigeon peas, pumpkin, brown sugar, onions, garlic, and often the ubiquitous curry powder (which Trinis consider a metaphor for the spiciness of their lives).

ROTI

One of the great Indian contributions to Trinidad, this is unleavened flatbread cooked on an iron griddle called a *tawa/ tava* and stuffed with a variety of filling

fillings. *Sada* roti is the simplest kind, filled with curried lentils, fire-roasted tomato, eggplant, potato, and other vegetables. It's a popular breakfast option, along with *paratha* roti (aka "Buss-Up-Shut"), rubbed with clarified butter to enhance flavor and grilled until crisp, brown, and crumbly, and usually served with fried eggs. The classic roti, *dhalpuri*, is stuffed with ground yellow split peas, garlic, cumin, and pepper; meats are often added.

SWEETS

Guava paste, sticky-sweet but delectable candied tamarind or papaya balls, and Indian snacks like *gulab jamon* (creamy dough fried in sugar syrup scented with cardamom and rosewater) are common. Pone, which is similar to bread pudding, derives its consistency from ground provisions such as cassava (manioc), sweet potato, or pumpkin. Grated cinnamon, nutmeg, raisins, coconut, and sugar are added and baked in a casserole. Tobago chefs often add a pinch of black pepper to provide an edgy counterpoint.

—Jordan Simon

(Top left) Curried crab (Bottom right) Ingredients for a roti (Top right) Creole-style pelau

Updated
by Vernon
O'Reilly-
Ramesar

These lush islands lay claim to being the economic pow-
erhouse of the Caribbean. Vast oil and gas reserves have
led to a high standard of living, and tourism is not the
mainstay of the economy. Indeed, the word tourist is seldom used here; the preference is for the much friendlier
(and perhaps vaguer) visitor.

Trinidad's Northern Range is thought to be part of the Andes in South
America (it was connected to the mainland as recently as the last Ice
Age). This geological history helps explain why the range of flora and
fauna is much greater than on other Caribbean islands.

The two islands have very different histories, although both islands'
Amerindian populations were virtually wiped out by the arrival of Europeans. After Columbus landed in Trinidad in 1498, the island came
under Spanish rule. In an attempt to build the population and provide
greater numbers to fend off a potential British conquest, the government
at the time encouraged French Catholics from nearby islands to settle
in Trinidad. This migration can be seen in the large number of French
place-names scattered around the island. Despite this effort, the British
conquered the island in 1797.

Tobago had a much more turbulent history. Named after the tobacco
that was used by the native Amerindian population, it was settled by
the British in 1508. The island was to change hands at least 22 times
before eventually returning to Britain in 1814.

The two islands were merged into one crown colony in 1888, with
Tobago being made a ward of Trinidad. Independence was achieved in
1962 under the leadership of Dr. Eric Williams, who became the first
prime minister. The islands became an independent republic in 1976,
with a bicameral parliament and an appointed president.

Trinidad's capital city, Port of Spain, is home to some 300,000 of the
island's 1.3 million inhabitants. Downtown Port of Spain is a bustling
commercial center complete with high-rise office buildings and seemingly perpetual traffic. Happily, the northern mountain range rises just
behind the city and helps to take much of the edge off the urban clamor.

The majority of Trinidad's population is of either African or East Indian background—the descendants of African slaves and indentured East Indian laborers, who came to work the plantations in the 19th century. The island is always buzzing with a variety of celebrations and arts performances that might include African drumming and classical Indian dance. Although these two groups compose more than 80% of the population, other groups such as the French, Spanish, Chinese, and even Lebanese have left their mark.

Many of the art forms that are considered synonymous with the Caribbean were created on this relatively small island. Calypso was born here, as were soca, limbo, and the steel pan (steel drum). The island can also claim two winners of the Nobel Prize in Literature—V.S. Naipaul (2001), who was born in Trinidad and wrote several of his earlier books about the island, and Derek Walcott (1992), a St. Lucian who moved to Trinidad in 1953. Many tourists make a pilgrimage simply to trace the places mentioned in Naipaul's most famous novel, *A House for Mr. Biswas* (1961), which was partially based on his father's life.

Physically, the island offers an exact parallel to the rain forests of South America, which allows for interesting—and sometimes challenging— adventures. Beach lovers accustomed to the electric blue water and dazzling white sand of coral islands may be disappointed by the beaches on Trinidad. The best beaches are on the north coast, with peach sand, clean blue-green water, and the forest-covered Northern Range as a backdrop. Beaches are almost completely free of hotel development.

Tobago is 23 miles (37 km) northeast of Trinidad. The population here is much less ethnically diverse than that of Trinidad, with the majority being of African descent. Tobagonians have their own dialect and distinct culture. Tourism is much more a part of the island's economy, and you can find excellent resorts and facilities—along with pretty white-sand beaches.

PLANNING

WHEN TO GO

Trinidad is more of a business destination than a magnet for tourists, so hotel rates (particularly in Port of Spain) are fairly stable year-round; nevertheless, you can usually get a price break during the traditional Caribbean low season (from May to December). Carnival (in January, February, or March) brings the highest rates.

Tobago is much more of a tourist destination, but since the island is more popular with Europeans than Americans, its busy periods are sometimes different from those of islands with more of an American presence.

GETTING HERE AND AROUND

AIR TRAVEL

There are nonstops to Trinidad from Houston (United), Miami (American, Caribbean Airlines), New York–JFK (American, Caribbean Airlines), and New York–Newark (United). There are no nonstop flights to Tobago from the United States; to get to Tobago, you will have to fly from Trinidad to the A.N.R. Robinson International Airport on Caribbean Airlines or LIAT.

Airports A.N.R. Robinson International Airport (*Crown Point International Airport*). ✉ *TAB, Tobago* ☎ *868/639–0509* ⊕ *www.tntairports.com.* **Piarco International Airport.** Trinidad's airport is modern, with 14 air bridges. It's about 30 minutes east of Port of Spain. ✉ *POS, Trinidad* ☎ *868/669–4101* ⊕ *www.tntairports.com.*

Local Airline Contacts **American Airlines** ☎ *868/821–6000* ⊕ *www.aa.com.* **British Airways** ☎ *800/247–9297* ⊕ *www.ba.com.* **jetBlue** ☎ *800/538–2583 U.S., 801/449–2525 International.* **LIAT** ☎ *868/627–2982, 888/844–5428* ⊕ *www.liatairline.com.* **United Airlines** ☎ *800/461–2744* ⊕ *www.united.com.* **WestJet** ☎ *888/937–8538.*

FERRY TRAVEL

The seas between Trinidad and Tobago can be very rough, and flights are frequent and only 20 minutes long, so it's better to fly than take a ferry.

Contact **Port Authority of Trinidad and Tobago.** Trips between Trinidad and Tobago are made on one of the two high-speed CAT ferries and take 2½ hours. The ferries leave twice a day from the jetty at the foot of Independence Square in Port of Spain and three times a day from the cruise-ship complex in Scarborough. The round-trip fare is TT$100. There is also a water-taxi service that travels between Port of Spain and San Fernando in southern Trinidad for TT$15 each way. ☎ *868/625–2901 in Port of Spain, 868/639–2181 in Scarborough* ⊕ *www.patnt.com.*

CAR TRAVEL

Don't rent a car if you're staying in Port of Spain, but if you're planning to tour Trinidad, you'll need some wheels, as you will if you end up staying out on the island. In Tobago you're better off renting a four-wheel-drive vehicle than relying on expensive taxi service. On either island, driving is on the left, British-style. Be aware that Tobago has very few gas stations—the main ones are in Crown Point and Scarborough. Be cautious driving on either island, because despite the introduction of the Breathalyzer, many people still take their chances driving after drinking, and erratic driving is the norm rather than the exception.

Tobago Car Rentals **Baird's Rentals** ✉ *Crown Point Airport, Crown Point, Tobago* ☎ *868/639–7054.* **Rattan's Car Rentals** ✉ *Crown Point Airport, Crown Point, Tobago* ☎ *868/639–8271.* **Rollock's Car Rentals** ✉ *Crown Point Airport, Crown Point, Tobago* ☎ *868/639–0328.* **Thrifty** ✉ *Rex Turtle Beach Hotel, Great Courland Bay, Black Rock, Tobago* ☎ *868/639–8507.*

Trinidad Car Rentals **Auto Rentals** ✉ *Piarco International Airport, Piarco, Trinidad* ☎ *868/669–2277.* **Southern Sales Car Rentals** ✉ *Piarco International Airport, Piarco, Trinidad* ☎ *868/669–2424, 269 from courtesy phone in airport baggage area.* **Thrifty** ✉ *Piarco International Airport, Piarco, Trinidad* ☎ *868/669–0602.*

TAXI TRAVEL

In Trinidad, taxis are readily available at Piarco Airport; the fare to Port of Spain is set at $50 ($100 after 10 pm). In Tobago the fare from Crown Point Airport to Scarborough or Grafton Beach is about $65. Taxis in Trinidad and Tobago are easily identified by their license plates, which begin with the letter *H*. Passenger vans, called Maxi Taxis, pick up and drop off passengers as they travel (like a bus) and are color-coded

LOGISTICS

Getting to Trinidad and Tobago:
You can fly nonstop to Trinidad from several U.S. cities, but there are no nonstop flights to Tobago from the United States; to get to Tobago, you will have to take a short flight from Trinidad on LIAT or Caribbean Airlines. Trinidad's Piarco International Airport (POS), about 30 minutes east of Port of Spain (take Golden Grove Road north to the intersection with the Churchill-Roosevelt Highway and then follow it west for about 10 miles [16 km] to Port of Spain), is a modern facility with 16 air bridges. Tobago's small Crown Point Airport (TAB) is the gateway to the island.

Hassle Factor: Medium to high.

On the Ground: Few hotels provide airport transfers, but you can always ask when you make your reservations. If you've booked a package, sometimes transfers are included. In Trinidad, taxis are readily available at Piarco Airport; the fare to Port of Spain is set at $50 ($100 after 10 pm). In Tobago the fare from Crown Point Airport to Scarborough or Grafton Beach is about $65.

25

according to which of the six areas they cover. Rates are generally less than $1 per trip. (Yellow is for Port of Spain, red for eastern Trinidad, green for south Trinidad, and black for Princes Town. Brown operates from San Fernando to the southeast—Erin, Penal, Point Fortin. The only color for Tobago is blue.) They're easy to hail day or night along most of the main roads near Port of Spain. For longer trips you need to hire a private taxi. Cabs aren't metered, and hotel taxis can be expensive.

ESSENTIALS

Banks and Exchange Services At this writing, the exchange rate for the Trinidadian dollar (TT$) is about TT$6.40 to US$1. Most businesses on the islands will accept U.S. currency and credit cards, and ATM cards are almost universally accepted. Cash is necessary only in the smallest neighborhood convenience shops and roadside stalls. There are far fewer bank branches in Tobago than in Trinidad. Trinidad has ATMs in all but the most remote areas. In Tobago there are only a few in Scarborough and at the airport in Crown Point.

Electricity 110 volts/60 cycles (U.S. standard).

Emergency Services Ambulance and Fire ☎ 990. **Police** ☎ 999.

Passport Requirements Everyone coming into Trinidad and Tobago must have a valid passport.

Phones The area code for both islands is 868 ("TNT" if you forget). This is also the country code if you're calling to Trinidad and Tobago from another country. From the United States, just dial 1 plus the area code and number. To make a local call to any point in the country simply dial the seven-digit local number. Most hotels and guesthouses will allow you to dial a direct international call. To dial a number in North America or the Caribbean dial 1 and the U.S. or Canadian area code before the number you're calling, but watch out for the hefty surcharge for overseas calls that most hotels add.

Taxes The departure tax is TT$100, but is required by law to be included in the ticket price. All hotels add a 10% government tax. Prices for almost all goods and services include a 15% V.A.T. (value-added tax).

Tipping Almost all hotels will add a 10% to 15% service charge. Most restaurants include a 10% service charge, which is considered standard on these islands. If it isn't on the bill, tip according to service: 10% to 15% is fine. Tip taxi drivers 10%; housekeeping staff $1 to $2 per night.

ACCOMMODATIONS

Trinidad isn't a top tourist destination, so resorts are few and far between, and many are a long drive from Port of Spain and the airport. However, a few ecoconscious options are worth the hassle, particularly if you are a bird-watcher. Tobago has many lodging options, and it's a much smaller island with better beaches, so your choice of resort there is driven more by the amenities you want and your budget than by the resort's location.

Beach Resorts: Tobago has a nice mix of midsize resorts, including several offering a fair degree of luxury, but there are also many choices for budget-oriented tourists, as is the case in Trinidad, where fewer tourists mean better value at the small beach resorts that cater primarily to locals. Few hotels on either island offer anything but room-only rates, though there are now two all-inclusive resorts on Tobago.

Ecoresorts: An especially good option for nature lovers, particularly bird-watchers, is Trinidad's Asa Wright Nature Centre Lodge. Several of Tobago's small resorts are particularly green.

Hotels: Though they have nice pools and other resort-type amenities, Trinidad's hotels are geared more for business travelers. Options for beachgoers are more limited and farther removed from Port of Spain.

HOTEL AND RESTAURANT PRICES

Prices in the restaurant reviews are the average cost of a main course at dinner or, if dinner is not served, at lunch; taxes and service charges are generally included. Prices in the hotel reviews are the lowest cost of a standard double room in high season, excluding taxes, service charges, and meal plans (except at all-inclusives). Prices for rentals are the lowest per-night cost for a one-bedroom unit in high season.

For expanded lodging reviews and current deals, visit Fodors.com.

SAFETY

Travelers should exercise caution in Trinidad, especially in the highly populated east–west corridor and downtown Port of Spain, where walking on the streets at night is not recommended unless you're with a group. Trinidad has recorded more than 400 homicides annually for the past few years, but these do not generally involve tourists. As a general rule, Tobago is safer than its larger sister island. There is little visible police presence in most areas of Trinidad. Petty theft occurs on both islands, so don't leave cash or other easy-to-steal valuables in bags that you check at the airport, and use your hotel's safe.

VISITOR INFORMATION

Contacts TDC ✉ *Maritime Centre, Level 1, 9 10th Ave., Barataria* ☎ *868/638–7962* ⊕ *www.tdc.co.tt* ✉ *Piarco International Airport, Piarco* ☎ *868/669-5196.* **Tobago Division of Tourism** ✉ *N.I.B. Mall, Level 3, Wilson St., Scarborough* ☎ *868/639-2125* ⊕ *www.visittobago.gov.tt* ✉ *A.N.R. Robinson Airport, Crown Point, Tobago* ☎ *868/639-0509.*

WEDDINGS

There is a three-day residency requirement. A passport, airline ticket, and proof of divorce (if you've been married before) are all required, as is a $55 license fee.

Registrar General ✉ *Jerningham St., Scarborough, Tobago* ☎ *868/639–3210* ✉ *72–74 South Quay, Port of Spain, Trinidad* ☎ *868/624–1660.*

TRINIDAD

25

EXPLORING

The intensely urban atmosphere of Port of Spain belies the tropical beauty of the countryside surrounding it. You'll need a car and three to eight hours to see all there is to see. Begin by circling the Queen's Park Savannah to Saddle Road, in the residential district of Maraval. After a few miles the road begins to narrow and curve sharply as it climbs into the Northern Range and its undulating hills of dense foliage. Stop at the lookout on North Coast Road; a camera is a must-have here. You pass a series of lovely beaches, starting with Maracas. From the town of Blanchisseuse there's a winding route to the Asa Wright Nature Centre that takes you through canyons of towering palms, mossy grottoes, and imposing bamboo. In this rain forest keep an eye out for vultures, parakeets, hummingbirds, toucans, and, if you're lucky, maybe red-bellied, yellow-and-blue macaws. Trinidad also has more than 600 native species of butterflies and far more than 1,000 varieties of orchids.

PORT OF SPAIN

Most organized tours begin at the port. If you're planning to explore on foot, which will take two to four hours, start early in the day; by midday the port area can get very hot and crowded. It's best to end your tour on a bench in the Queen's Park Savannah, sipping a cool coconut water bought from one of the vendors operating out of flat-bed trucks. For about 75¢ he'll lop the top off a green coconut with a deft swing of the machete and, when you've finished drinking, lop again, making a bowl and spoon of coconut shell for you to eat the young pulp. Take extra care at night; women should not walk alone. Local police advise tourists and locals to avoid the neighborhoods just east of Port of Spain.

The town's main dock, **King's Wharf,** entertains a steady parade of cruise and cargo ships, a reminder that the city started from this strategic harbor. When hurricanes threaten other islands, it's not unusual to see as many as five large cruise ships taking advantage of the safety of the harbor. It's on Wrightson Road, the main street along the water on the southwest side of town. The previous national government embarked on a massive development plan to turn the area into a vibrant and attractive commercial and tourism zone. Many spanking-new high-rises have already been built, but the current government halted the project because of cost.

Across Wrightson Road and a few minutes' walk from the south side of King's Wharf, the busy **Independence Square** has been the focus of the downtown area's major gentrification. Flanked by government buildings and the familiar twin towers of the Financial Complex (they adorn all T&T dollar bills), the square (really a long rectangle) is a lovely park with trees, flagstone walkways, chess tables, and the Brian Lara Promenade (named after Trinidad's world-famous cricketer). On its south side is the International Waterfront Centre, with its gleaming skyscrapers and fast-ferry dock. On the eastern end of the square is the Cathedral of the Immaculate Conception; it was by the sea when it was built in 1832, but subsequent landfill around the port gave it an inland location. The imposing Roman Catholic structure is made of blue limestone from nearby Laventille.

Frederick Street, Port of Spain's main shopping drag, starting north from the midpoint of Independence Square, is a market street of scents and sounds—perfumed oils sold by sidewalk vendors and CDs (mostly pirated) being played from vending carts.

At Prince and Frederick streets, **Woodford Square** has served as the site of political meetings, speeches, public protests, and occasional violence. It's dominated by the magnificent Red House, a Renaissance-style building that takes up an entire city block. Trinidad's House of Parliament takes its name from a paint job done in anticipation of Queen Victoria's Diamond Jubilee in 1897. The original Red House was burned to the ground in a 1903 riot, and the present structure was built four years later. The building is undergoing a multiyear refurbishment, so the parliament is currently using one of the buildings at the International Waterfront Centre for sittings.

The view of the south side of the square is framed by the Gothic spires of Trinity, the city's Anglican cathedral, consecrated in 1823; its mahogany-beam roof is modeled after that of Westminster Hall in London. On the north are the impressive Public Library, the Hall of Justice, and City Hall.

QUEEN'S PARK SAVANNAH

If the downtown port area is the pulse of Port of Spain, the great green expanse of Queen's Park Savannah, roughly bounded by Maraval Road, Queen's Park West, Charlotte Street, and Saddle Road, is the city's soul. You can walk straight north on Frederick Street and get there within 20 minutes. Its 2-mile (3-km) circumference is a popular jogger's track. The northern end of the Savannah is devoted to plants. A rock garden, known as the Hollows, and a fishpond add to the rusticity. In the middle of the Savannah you will find a small graveyard where members of the Peschier family—who originally owned the land—are buried. The southern end near the National Academy for the Performing Arts turns into a massive food court every evening. Although the perimeter of the

CLOSE UP

East Indians in Trinidad

With the abolition of slavery in the British colonies in 1838, many plantation economies such as Trinidad were left looking for alternative sources of cheap labor. Trinidad tried to draw Europeans, but the heat made them ineffective. Attention finally turned to the Indian subcontinent, and in 1845 the first ship of Indian laborers arrived in Trinidad. These indentured workers came mainly from the poorer parts of Uttar Pradesh. They undertook the three-month journey to the New World with the understanding that after their five-year work stint was over, they could re-indenture themselves or return to India. The system stayed in place until 1917.

The Indians proved effective on the sugarcane and cocoa plantations, helping them return to prosperity. In an effort to discourage the Indians from returning home, the colony eventually offered a land grant as an incentive to stay. Many took up the offer and stayed to make new lives in their adopted homeland. Their descendants still maintain many traditions and, to some extent, language. East Indian culture is a vibrant component of T&T's national culture, and you can find Indian festivals and music sharing center stage at all national events. East Indians compose about half the islands' population.

25

Savannah is busy and safe, you should take care when walking across the park, as there have been occasional reports of muggings. The sheer size of the Savannah makes it difficult for local authorities to patrol, so it is best avoided altogether at night.

A series of astonishing buildings constructed in several 19th-century styles—known collectively as the **Magnificent Seven**—flanks the western side of the Savannah. Notable are Killarney, patterned (loosely) after Balmoral Castle in Scotland, with an Italian-marble gallery surrounding the ground floor; Whitehall, constructed in the style of a Venetian palace by a cacao-plantation magnate and, until recently, the office of the prime minister; Roomor (named for the Roodal and Morgan families—it's still occupied by the Morgans), a flamboyantly baroque colonial house with a preponderance of towers, pinnacles, and wrought-iron trim that suggests an elaborate French pastry; and the Queen's Royal College, in German Renaissance style, with a prominent tower clock that chimes on the hour. Sadly, several of these fine buildings have fallen into advanced decay.

Emperor Valley Zoo & Botanical Gardens. The cultivated expanse of parkland north of the Savannah is the site of the president's and prime minister's official residences and also the Emperor Valley Zoo & Botanical Gardens. A meticulous lattice of walkways and local flora, the parkland was first laid out in 1820 for Governor Ralph Woodford. In the midst of the serene wonderland is the 8-acre zoo, which exhibits mostly birds and animals of the region—including the brilliantly plumed scarlet ibis as well as slithering anacondas and pythons; you can also see (and hear) the wild parrots that breed in the surrounding foliage. Two African giraffes were added to the collection in late 2013 and have proven to be hugely attractive with locals. The zoo draws a quarter of a million visitors a year. Tours are free. ✉ *Northern side of Queen's Park Savannah, Port of Spain* ☎ *868/622–3530, 868/622–5343* 🖰 *Zoo TT$20 adults; TT$10 kids under 12, gardens free* ⏲ *Daily 9–6.*

National Academy for the Performing Arts. Head over to the southeast corner of the Savannah, which is dominated by the shiny National Academy for the Performing Arts. It opened in 2009 in time to host the opening ceremony for the Commonwealth Heads of Government Meeting. The Chinese-built structure looks something like a rounded glass-and-metal version of Sydney's famous opera house. ✉ *Queen's Park, Port of Spain.*

National Museum & Art Gallery. Be sure to see the National Museum & Art Gallery, especially its Carnival exhibitions, the Amerindian collection and historical re-creations, and the fine 19th-century paintings of Trinidadian artist Cazabon. Tours are free. ✉ *117 Upper Frederick St., Port of Spain* ☎ *868/623–5941* 🖰 *Free* ⏲ *Tues.–Sat. 10–6, Sun. 2–6.*

NEARBY PORT OF SPAIN

TOP ATTRACTIONS

Fodor's Choice ★   **Asa Wright Nature Centre.** Nearly 200 acres are covered with plants, trees, and multihued flowers, and the surrounding acreage is atwitter with more than 200 species of birds, including the gorgeous blue-crowned motmot and the rare (and protected) nocturnal oilbird. If you stay at the center's inn for two nights or more, take one of the guided hikes (included in your room price if you are staying here) to the oilbirds' breeding grounds in Dunston Cave (reservations for hikes are essential). Those who don't want to hike can relax on the inn's verandah and watch birds swoop about the porch feeders. You are also more than likely to see a variety of other animal species, including agoutis (similar to large guinea pigs) and alarmingly large golden tegu lizards. This stunning plantation house looks out onto the lush, untouched Arima Valley. Even if you're not staying over, book ahead for lunch (TT$160), offered Monday through Saturday, or for the noontime Sunday buffet (TT$240). The center is an hour outside Blanchisseuse. ✉ *Blanchisseuse Rd., Arima Valley* ☎ *868/667–4655* ⊕ *www.asawright.org* 🖰 *$10* ⏲ *Daily 9–5. Guided tours at 10:30 and 1:30.*

FAMILY   **Caroni Bird Sanctuary.** This large swamp with mazelike waterways is bordered by mangrove trees, some plumed with huge termite nests. If you're lucky, you may see lazy caimans idling in the water and large snakes hanging from branches on the banks, taking in the sun. In the middle of the sanctuary are several islets that are home to Trinidad's national bird, the scarlet ibis. Just before sunset the ibis arrive by the thousands, their richly colored feathers brilliant in the gathering dusk, and as more flocks alight, they turn the mangrove foliage a brilliant scarlet. Bring a sweater and insect repellent. The sanctuary's only official tour operator is Winston Nanan (⇨ *Bird-watching in Sports and Activities*). ✉ *Port of Spain* ⌖ *½ hr from Port of Spain; take Churchill Roosevelt Hwy. east to Uriah Butler south; turn right and in about 2 mins, after passing Caroni River Bridge, follow sign for sanctuary* ☎ *868/645–1305* 🖰 *$10* ⏲ *Daily dawn–dusk.*

Inside visitor center and lodge at Asa Wright Nature Centre, Trinidad

WORTH NOTING

Chaguaramas Military History & Aerospace Museum. Although this museum covers everything from Amerindian history to the Cold War, the emphasis is on the two World Wars, and it's a must-see for history buffs. The exhibits, on a former U.S. military base, are in a large hangarlike shed without air-conditioning, so dress appropriately. There's a decidedly charming and homemade feel to the place; in fact, most exhibits were made by the curator and founder, Commander Gaylord Kelshall of the T&T Coast Guard. The museum is set a bit off the main road but is easily spotted by the turquoise BWIA L1011 jet parked out front (Trinidad and Tobago's former national airline). ⊠ *Western Main Rd., Chaguaramas* ☎ *868/634–4391* ⊕ *www.militarymuseumtt. com* ⌨ *TT$30* ☉ *Mon.–Sat. 9–5.*

FAMILY **Dattatreya Yoga Centre.** This impressive temple site was constructed by artisans brought in from India. It is well worth a visit to admire the intricate architectural details of the main temple, learn about Trinidad Hinduism, and marvel at the towering 85-foot statue of the monkey deity, Hanuman. Krishna Ramsaran, the compound manager, is extremely helpful and proud to explain the history of the center and the significance of the various *murtis* (sacred statues). Kids are welcome, so this makes for a pleasant and educational family outing (kids seem especially interested in the giant elephant statues that guard the temple doors). This is a religious site, so appropriate clothing is required (no shorts), and shoes must be left outside the temple door. It's fine to take pictures of the statue and the temple exterior and grounds, but permission is required to take pictures inside, as it's an active place of worship. The temple is half an hour from Port of

Spain; take Churchill Roosevelt Highway east to Uriah Butler south; turn right until the Chase Village flyover (overpass); follow the signs south to Waterloo; then follow signs to the temple. ⌧ *Datta Dr. at Orangefield Rd., Carapichaima* ☎ *868/673–5328* ⌑ *Free* ☉ *Daily dawn–dusk, services daily.*

FAMILY **Galera Point Lighthouse.** This essential stop when touring the northeast was constructed in 1897 on a stunning cliff. It's still used to warn ships about the rough waters below, the point where the Atlantic Ocean and Caribbean Sea meet. You can walk out onto a nearby rocky outcropping that marks Trinidad's easternmost point. On most days Tobago is clearly visible from here. A local legend (unprovable) tells that a group of Arawaks jumped off this point to their deaths rather than be captured by the Spanish. You'll pass several beautiful beaches on the drive from Toco to the lighthouse. The journey from Port of Spain takes about two hours; take Churchill Roosevelt Highway east to Valencia Road; follow the road east to Toco Main Road sign; take this road all the way to Toco; from the Toco intersection, follow the sign to Galera Point. ⌧ *Galera Rd., 3 miles (5 km) from triangular Toco intersection* ⌑ *Free* ☉ *Daily dawn–dusk.*

Lopinot Complex. It's said that the ghost of the French count Charles Joseph de Lopinot prowls his former home on stormy nights. Lopinot came to Trinidad in 1800 and chose this magnificent site to plant cocoa. His restored estate house has been turned into a museum—a guide is available from 10 to 6—and a center for *parang*, the Venezuelan-derived folk music. Although worthwhile for those interested in the finer points of Trinidad history, this may not be worth the long and winding drive for most visitors. ⌧ *Lopinot Rd.* ⌖ *Take Eastern Main Rd. from Port of Spain to Arouca; look for sign that points north* ⌑ *Free* ☉ *Daily 6–6.*

BEACHES

Trinidad has some good beaches for swimming and sunning, particularly on the north coast, though none as picture perfect as those in Tobago. Although popular with some locals, the beaches of the western peninsula (such as Maqueripe) are not particularly attractive. All beaches on Trinidad are free and open to the public. Many locals are fond of playing loud music wherever they go, and even the most serene beach may suddenly turn into a seaside party.

Balandra Bay. On the northeast coast, this beige-sand beach—popular with locals on weekends—is sheltered by a rocky outcropping and is a favorite of bodysurfers. Much of the beach is suitable for swimming. It can be rather noisy on the weekends. Take the Toco Main Road from the Valencia Road, and turn off at the signs indicating Balandra (just after Salybia). **Amenities:** lifeguards. **Best for:** surfing; swimming. ⌧ *Off Valencia Rd. near Salybia.*

Blanchisseuse Bay. The facilities are nonexistent at this narrow, palm-fringed beach, but it's an ideal spot for a romantic picnic. A lagoon and river at the east end of the beach allow you to swim in fresh water, but beware of floating logs in the river, as they sometimes contain mites

CLOSE UP

The Steel Pan

25

The sound of a steel pan playing poolside has become emblematic of the Caribbean. What you may not know is that the fascinating instrument has an interesting and humble history that began in Trinidad.

In 1883 the British government banned the playing of drums on the island, fearful that they were being used to carry secret messages. Enterprising Afro-Trinidadians immediately found other means of creating music. Some turned to cut bamboo poles beaten rhythmically on the ground; these were called Tambu Bamboo bands, and they soon became a major musical force on the island. With the coming of industry, new materials such as hubcaps and biscuit tins were added as "instruments" in the bands. These metal additions were collectively known as "pan." Later, after the Americans established military bases on the islands during World War II, empty oil drums became available and were quickly put to musical use.

At some point it was discovered that these drums could be cut down, heated in a fire, and beaten into a

finely tuned instrument. The steel pan as we know it was thus born. Soon there were entire musical bands playing nothing but steel pans. For years the music gestated in the poorer districts of Port of Spain and was seen as being suitable only for the lower classes of society, a reputation not helped by the fact that the loyal followers of early steel bands sometimes clashed violently with their rivals. Eventually, the magical sound of the pan and its amazing ability to adapt to any type of music won it widespread acceptance.

Today the government recognizes the steel pan as the official musical instrument of Trinidad and Tobago. It's played year-round at official functions and social gatherings, but the true time for the steel pan is Carnival. In the annual Panorama festival, dozens of steel bands from around the country compete for the "Band of the Year" title. Some have fewer than a dozen steel pans, whereas others number in the hundreds. The performance of the larger bands creates a thunderous wall of sound.

that can cause a body rash (called *bete rouge* locally). You can haggle with local fishermen to take you out in their boats to explore the coast. This beach is about 14 miles (23 km) after Maracas; just keep driving along the road until you pass the Arima turnoff. The coastal and rain forest views here are spectacular. **Amenities:** none. **Best for:** swimming; walking. ⊠ *North Coast Rd. just beyond Arima turnoff.*

NEED A BREAK? **Kay's Pot.** On the long drive to Point Galera, be sure to stop at Kay's Pot for a great meal en route. Many consider it worth the drive all by itself. In a corner of the front parking lot of Arthur's Grocery and Bar, Kay serves an incredible array of local food such as souse (pickled pigs' feet in a lime-and-cucumber sauce), curried crab, and many kinds of grilled and jerk meats. The informal atmosphere, low prices, and music pouring out of the bar make for a fun and unusual dining experience. ⊠ *Toco Main Rd., Rampanalgas.*

Grande Riviere. On Trinidad's rugged northeast coast, Grande Riviere is well worth the drive. Swimming is good, and there are several guesthouses nearby for refreshments, but the main attractions here are turtles. Every year up to 500 giant leatherback turtles come onto the beach to lay their eggs. If you're here at night, run your hand through the black sand to make it glow—a phenomenon caused by plankton. **Amenities:** food and drink. **Best for:** swimming; walking. ⊠ *End of Toco Main Rd., Grande Riviere.*

Las Cuevas Bay. This narrow, picturesque strip on North Coast Road is named for the series of partially submerged and explorable caves that ring the beach. A food stand offers tasty snacks, and vendors hawk fresh fruit across the road. You can also buy fresh fish and lobster from the fishing depot near the beach. You have to park your car in the small parking lot and walk down a few steps to get to the beach, so be sure to take everything from the car (it will be out of sight once you are on the beach). There are basic changing and toilet facilities. It's less crowded here than at nearby Maracas Bay and seemingly serene, although, as at Maracas, the current can be treacherous. **Amenities:** food and drink; parking; toilets. **Best for:** swimming; walking. ⊠ *North Coast Rd., 7 miles (11 km) east of Maracas Bay.*

Manzanilla Beach. You can find picnic facilities and a pretty view of the Atlantic here, though the water is occasionally muddied by Venezuela's Orinoco River. The Cocal Road running the length of this beautiful beach is lined with stately palms. This is where many well-heeled Trinis have vacation houses. The Nariva River, which enters the sea just south of this beach and the surrounding Nariva Swamp, is home to the manatee and other rare species, including the much-maligned anaconda. To get here take the Mayaro turnoff at the town of Sangre Grande. Manzanilla is where this road first meets the coast. **Amenities:** food and drink; lifeguards. **Best for:** sunrise; walking. ⊠ *Southeast of Sangre Grande.*

Fodor'sChoice ★ **Maracas Bay.** This stretch of sand has a cove and a fishing village at one end. It's the local favorite, so it can get crowded on weekends. Lifeguards will guide you away from strong currents. Parking sites are ample, and there are snack bars selling the famous bake and shark, a must-try. Take the winding North Coast Road from Maraval (it intersects with

Long Circular Road right next to KFC Maraval) over the Northern Range; the beach is about 7 miles (11 km) from Maraval. **Amenities:** food and drink; lifeguards; parking; toilets. **Best for:** partiers; swimming; walking. ⊠ *North Coast Rd.*

Salibea Bay (Salybia Bay). This gentle beach has shallows and plenty of shade—perfect for swimming. Snack vendors abound in the vicinity. Like many of the beaches on the northeast coast, this one is packed with people and music trucks blaring soca and reggae on weekends. It's off the Toco Main Road, just after the town of Matura. **Amenities:** food and drink; parking; toilets. **Best for:** partiers; swimming; walking. ⊠ *Off Toco Main Rd. south of Toco.*

> ### BAKE AND SHARK
>
> Maracas Bay in Trinidad is famous for its bake and shark (about $5), a deep-fried piece of shark stuffed into fried bread. To this, you can add any of dozens of toppings, such as tamarind sauce and coleslaw. There are dozens of beach huts serving the specialty, as well as stands in the nearby parking lot. Richard's is by far the most popular.

25

WHERE TO EAT

The food on T&T is a delight to the senses and has a distinctively creole touch, though everyone has a different idea about what creole seasoning is (just ask around, and you'll see). Bountiful herbs and spices include bay leaf, chadon bene (aka culantro, and similar in taste to cilantro), nutmeg, turmeric, and different varieties of peppers. The cooking also involves a lot of brown sugar, rum, plantain, and local fish and meat. If there's fresh juice on the menu, be sure to try it. You can taste Asian, Indian, African, French, and Spanish influences, among others, often in a single meal. Indian-inspired food is a favorite: rotis (ample sandwiches of soft dough with a filling, similar to a wrap) are served as a fast food; a mélange of curried meat or fish and vegetables frequently makes an appearance, as do vindaloos (spicy meat, vegetable, and seafood dishes). Pelau (rice, peas, and meat stewed in coconut milk) is another local favorite. Crab lovers will find large bluebacks curried, peppered, or in callaloo (Trinidad's national dish), a stew made with green dasheen leaves, okra, and coconut milk. Shark and bake (lightly seasoned, fried shark meat) is the sandwich of choice at the beach.

What to Wear. Restaurants are informal: you won't find any jacket-and-tie requirements. Beachwear, however, is too casual for most places. A nice pair of shorts is appropriate for lunch, and pants or sundresses are probably a better choice for dinner.

$$$$ ✕ **Angelo's.** Calabrian chef Angelo Cofone married a Trinidadian and
ITALIAN soon found himself in the restaurant business. Popular with locals and visiting businesspeople alike, Angelo's has an innovative Italian menu that changes regularly, and there's always a daily special. The restaurant is on Ariapita Avenue, which locals now refer to as the restaurant strip or simply "the avenue." $ *Average main: $43* ⊠ *38 Ariapita Ave., Woodbrook, Port of Spain* ☎ *868/628–5551* ⊘ *Closed Sun. No lunch Sat.*

$$$$ INDIAN 🍴 **Apsara.** This upscale Indian eatery is one of the few in Trinidad that features genuine Indian cuisine and not the local (though equally tasty) version. The name means "celestial dancer," and the food here is indeed heavenly. The inviting terra-cotta interior is decorated with hand-painted interpretations of Moghul art. Choosing dishes from the comprehensive menu is a bit daunting, so don't be afraid to ask for help. The *Husseini boti kebab* (lamb marinated in poppy seeds and masala) is an excellent choice. Service can be a bit slow at times, and the prices are fairly high. [$] *Average main: $42* ✉ *13 Queen's Park E, Belmont, Port of Spain* ☎ *868/627–7364, 868/623–7659* 🕒 *Closed Sun.*

$$$ NORTHERN ITALIAN Fodor's Choice ★ 🍴 **Buzo Osteria Italiana.** This chic eatery and bar is tucked away on a side street in the Newtown area of uptown Port of Spain but every taxi driver in town will know where it is. Italian chef/patron Cristian Grini always has a selection of classic Italian favorites on offer—the authentic pizza is probably the best on the island and is surprisingly affordable. The bar attracts young professionals and local hipsters who come for the excellent cocktails and late-night desserts. This restaurant is associated with the even more upscale Prime Restaurant so the service is impeccable. [$] *Average main: $38* ✉ *6A Warner St., Port of Spain* ☎ *868/223–2896* ✍ *Reservations essential.*

$$$$ ECLECTIC Fodor's Choice ★ 🍴 **Chaud.** Style meets substance at veteran chef Khalid Mohammed's restaurant. Set in a restored house opposite the Queen's Park Savannah, the restaurant is adorned with local art work and offers expansive views of Port of Spain's largest park. Famous for his extravagance, Mohammed presents food that rises off the plate like a Manhattan skyscraper. There is an obsession with freshness here, and satisfaction is virtually guaranteed. Although the prices are high, it's well worth it for a special romantic evening. [$] *Average main: $43* ✉ *2 Queen's Park W, Port of Spain* ☎ *868/623–0375* 🌐 *www.chaudkm.com* ✍ *Reservations essential* 🕒 *Closed Sun. No lunch Sat.*

$$$ ECLECTIC Fodor's Choice ★ 🍴 **Joseph's.** Lebanese-born chef Joseph Habr has been serving fine cuisine at his Maraval location for over a decade, and has more than 25 years of experience under his belt. The restaurant is a lovely open affair with a dining room that looks out on a lush garden—complete with the sound of flowing water. Joseph visits every table and is always happy to offer helpful advice. The menu is comprehensive, and somehow there seems to be an Arabic element in even seemingly conventional dishes. If in doubt, it's impossible to go wrong with any of the lamb offerings. [$] *Average main: $35* ✉ *3A Rookery Nook, Maraval, Port of Spain* ✣ *Take Saddle Rd. into Maraval and follow it to RBTT Bank. Rookery Nook is on left* ☎ *868/622–5557* 🕒 *Closed Sun. No lunch Sat.*

$$$$ ECLECTIC 🍴 **Mélange.** Some of the most imaginative food on the island is to be found at this elegant establishment on restaurant row. Chef and owner Moses Ruben uses his years of experience as head chef at the Hilton to create delightfully balanced meals. His imaginative curried-crab-and-dumplings appetizer, which consists of delicately curried crabmeat served on a shell full of miniature dumplings, is exceptional. [$] *Average main: $45* ✉ *40 Ariapita Ave., Woodbrook, Port of Spain* ☎ *868/628–8687* 🕒 *Closed Sun. No lunch Sat. No dinner Mon.*

$$ JAPANESE 🍴 **More Vino More Sushi.** This popular after-work drinking and dining spot serves consistently excellent sushi. This was the first sushi establishment on the popular dining strip known to locals as "the avenue." Choose to dine on the wooden outdoor deck and take in the sights (and traffic sounds) of Ariapita Avenue or sit indoors for a cooler and more intimate experience with a view of the sushi masters at work. [$] *Average main: $31* ✉ *23 O'Connor St., at Ariapita Ave., Port of Spain* ☎ *868/622–8466* 🌐 *www.morevino.com* ⏲ *Closed Sun.*

$$$$ ECLECTIC 🍴 **Prime Restaurant.** Occupying the ground floor of the BHP Billiton tower, this upscale establishment caters to businesspeople armed with large expense accounts and demanding tastes. The subtle lighting, understated decor, and attentive staff also make this the ideal spot for a romantic dinner or a special-occasion splurge. Though a variety of options are available, most diners come for the excellent Angus steaks, and not without reason. The wine cellar is one of the best on the island, and a well-chosen vintage may help take some of the edge off the inevitably large bill. The restaurant is behind the Marriott and next door to the Movietowne complex. [$] *Average main: $55* ✉ *Ground fl., BHP Billiton Bldg., Invaders Bay* ☎ *868/624–6238* 🌐 *www.trentrestaurants.com/prime* ✍ *Reservations essential* ⏲ *Closed Sun.*

25

$$$$ ASIAN 🍴 **Tiki Village.** Port of Spainers in the know flock to the eighth floor of the Kapok Hotel, where the views of the city from this teak-lined dining room are simply spectacular, day and night. The solid menu includes the best of Polynesian and Asian fare. The Sunday dim sum—with tasting-size portions of dishes such as pepper squid and tofu-stuffed fish—is very popular. [$] *Average main: $32* ✉ *Kapok Hotel, 16–18 Cotton Hill, St. Clair, Port of Spain* ☎ *868/622–5765* ✍ *Reservations essential.*

$$$ AMERICAN 🍴 **Trotters.** Although Trinidad has many American sports-bar chain restaurants, this local version easily beats them at their own game. There is often a lively crowd watching the more than 20 giant screens featuring all the latest in soccer and international sports. The huge square bar in the middle of the restaurant is where folks gather. Dining areas branch off from the bar area, and though some are more isolated than others, it is virtually impossible to escape the cheers of the throng of sports enthusiasts. The food includes excellent burgers, hearty salads, and Italian favorites and steaks. The standard is consistently excellent, and the servers, bedecked in pins and wearing safari hats, are efficient and attentive. [$] *Average main: $18* ✉ *Corner of Maraval Rd. and Sweetbriar Rd., St. Clair* ☎ *868/627-8768* 🌐 *www.trotters.net.*

$$$ CARIBBEAN FAMILY Fodor's Choice ★ 🍴 **Veni Mangé.** The best lunches in town are served in this traditional West Indian house. The restaurant is the creation of Rosemary (Roses) Hezekiah and her late sister, Allyson Hennessy—a Cordon Bleu–trained chef who was a local television celebrity. The creative creole menu changes regularly, but there's always an unusual and delicious vegetarian entrée (Roses is vegetarian). Veni's version of Trinidad's national dish, callaloo, is considered one of the best on the island. The *chip chip* (a small local clam) cocktail is deliciously piquant and is a restaurant rarity. The restaurant's signature dish, stewed oxtail with dumplings, is not served every day but is worth ordering if it's available. The bar area is a popular hangout for local artists and sports celebrities.

[$] *Average main: $22* ✉ *67A Ariapita Ave., Woodbrook, Port of Spain* ☎ *868/624–4597* 🌐 *www.venimange.com* ⏲ *Closed weekends. No dinner Mon., Tues., or Thurs.*

$$$ CARIBBEAN Fodor's Choice ★ 🍴 **The Verandah.** Owner and hostess Phyllis Vieira has been running a restaurant since the 1980s; she prides herself on her "free-style Caribbean" dishes. The open verandah, interior, and courtyard of this beautiful gingerbread-style colonial house provide a suitable setting for the reasonably priced, consistently excellent menu, which changes weekly and is brought to you on a blackboard by the attentive, white-garbed staff. [$] *Average main: $35* ✉ *10 Rust St., St. Clair, Port of Spain* ☎ *868/622–6287* ✍ *Reservations essential* ⏲ *Closed Sun. No dinner Mon.–Wed. No lunch Sat.*

$ CARIBBEAN 🍴 **Wings Restaurant & Bar.** Rum shops and good food are an intrinsic part of Trinidad life, and both are combined in this colorful eatery, which is open from 10 to 6. Regulars from the nearby university and industrial park flock here at lunchtime to enjoy a wide selection of local Indian food. It can get a bit loud, but at least there are fans to keep the heat under control—just barely. To get here, turn off the Churchill Roosevelt Highway at the FedEx building (north side of the highway) in Tunapuna, and take the first left. [$] *Average main: $8* ✉ *16 Mohammed Terr., Tunapuna* ☎ *868/645–6607* 💳 *No credit cards* ⏲ *Closed Sun. No dinner.*

WHERE TO STAY

Because Trinidad is primarily a business destination, most accommodations are in or near Port of Spain. Standards are generally good, though not lavish. Port of Spain has a small downtown core—with a main shopping area along Frederick Street—and is surrounded by inner and outer suburbs. The inner areas include Belmont, Woodbrook, Newtown, St. Clair, St. Ann's, St. James, and Cascade. The nearest beach to most hotels is Maracas Bay, which is a half-hour drive over the mountains. Carnival visitors should book many months in advance and be prepared to pay top dollar for even the most modest hotel.

$$$ HOTEL 🏨 **Asa Wright Nature Centre Lodge.** This hotel, an hour's drive from the nearest beach or town, is designed for serious bird-watchers and is surrounded by 200 acres of wilderness, streams, waterfalls, and natural pools. **Pros:** best bird-watching on the island; main house has a wonderful colonial feel; peaceful setting. **Cons:** miles from anything else on the island; no dining choices; the lack of entertainment options at night can be unnerving; very expensive. [$] *Rooms from: $430* ✉ *Blanchisseuse Rd., Arima Valley* ☎ *868/667–4655, 800/426–7781* 🌐 *www.asawright.org* 🛏 *24 rooms* 🍽 *All meals.*

$ HOTEL 🏨 **Capital Plaza Hotel Trinidad.** Proximity to the port and Independence Square is both the draw and the drawback here: from any upper-floor room you have a lovely pastel panorama of the Old Town and of the gleaming waterfront, and you're within walking distance of the downtown sights and shops; but with proximity to the action come traffic and noise. **Pros:** close to downtown and the business core; much cheaper than the Hyatt for a similar downtown location. **Cons:** there's traffic noise by the pool area; renovations in progress as the hotel prepares to transform into a Radisson. $ *Rooms from: $170* ✉ *Wrightson Rd., Port of Spain* ☎ *868/625–3366* ⊕ *www.cplazatrinidad.com* ⤸ *243 rooms, 12 suites* ⦿ *Breakfast.*

$ ⌂ **The Carlton Savannah.** Those looking for a boutique hotel without
HOTEL compromising service and quality come to the Carlton, a chic and sleek hotel in the quiet Cascade area that has already attracted visiting dignitaries and discerning businessmen. **Pros:** convenient and quiet location; free Wi-Fi; stylish, modern feeling; excellent restaurants. **Cons:** not within walking distance of shopping; while staff are eager the service can sometimes be erratic $ *Rooms from: $135* ✉ *2–4 Coblentz Ave., Cascade* ☎ *868/621–5000* ⊕ *www.thecarltonsavannah.com* ⤸ *155 rooms, 10 suites* ⦿ *No meals.*

$$ ⌂ **Coblentz Inn.** Just a short drive from downtown in the quiet suburb
HOTEL of Cascade, this small boutique hotel offers peace, quiet, and style at a relatively affordable price. **Pros:** rooms have genuine charm; small but attentive staff; common areas are relaxing and great for catching up on reading. **Cons:** restaurant's food can be unreliable; small compound can feel cramped. $ *Rooms from: $175* ✉ *44 Coblentz Ave., Cascade, Port of Spain* ☎ *868/621–0541* ⊕ *www.coblentzinn.com* ⤸ *17 rooms* ⦿ *Breakfast.*

$ ⌂ **Courtyard by Marriott.** This large hotel in the capital offers excellent
HOTEL facilities and a great location. **Pros:** excellent location for shopping and dining; large and airy rooms; high service standards. **Cons:** just off busy highway; the many business travelers can make it feel a bit uncomfortable for leisure guests. $ *Rooms from: $259* ✉ *Invaders Bay, Audrey Jeffers Hwy., Port of Spain* ☎ *868/627–5555* ⊕ *www.marriott. com* ⤸ *116 rooms, 3 suites* ⦿ *No meals.*

$ ⌂ **Crews Inn Hotel & Yachting Centre.** On Trinidad's western peninsula,
HOTEL this hotel is in the middle of the island's most popular nightlife area, about 20 minutes from downtown. **Pros:** great view of marina; airy rooms are tastefully decorated; great for yachting enthusiasts. **Cons:** far from Port of Spain; limited shopping and dining nearby. $ *Rooms from: $224* ✉ *Point Gourde, Chaguaramas* ☎ *868/634–4384* ⊕ *www. crewsinn.com* ⤸ *42 rooms, 4 suites* ⦿ *Breakfast.*

$$ ⌂ **Hilton Trinidad & Conference Centre.** The Hilton was the most upscale
HOTEL hotel on the island before the arrival of the Hyatt Regency, and it still commands a loyal following. **Pros:** great view; contemporary rooms; full range of hotel services; reliable and consistent service; the thrill of saying you stayed at the hotel where the U.S. president stayed. **Cons:** pool area can be very noisy when parties are going on—especially at Carnival time. $ *Rooms from: $199* ✉ *Lady Young Rd., Port of Spain* ☎ *868/624–3211, 800/445–8667 in U.S.* ⊕ *www.hiltoncaribbean.com* ⤸ *385 rooms, 27 suites* ⦿ *No meals.*

$ ⌂ **Holiday Inn Express & Suites Trincity.** Just five minutes from the airport
HOTEL and with a complimentary shuttle service, this handy hotel is popular with short-stay travelers. **Pros:** convenient to the airport; close to Trincity Mall. **Cons:** not close to the major urban centers; nearby traffic can be horrendous; has that bland chain-hotel feeling. $ *Rooms from: $159* ✉ *1 Exposition Dr., Trincity* ☎ *868/669–6209* ⊕ *www.ichotelsgroup. com* ⤸ *62 rooms, 20 suites* ⦿ *Breakfast.*

25

Hyatt Regency Trinidad

$$$ HOTEL Fodor's Choice ★ 🏨 **Hyatt Regency Trinidad.** Trinidad's only full-service hotel on the waterfront is a striking high-rise structure and part of the government's dramatic makeover of the Port of Spain waterfront. **Pros:** easily the most upscale full-service hotel on the island; view from the rooftop pool is unbeatable; convenient to downtown and shopping. **Cons:** right on the city's busiest commuter road; waterfront area is usually teeming with people. [$] *Rooms from: $229* ✉ *1 Wrightson Rd., Port of Spain* ☎ *868/623–2222* 🌐 *trinidad.hyatt.com* 🛏 *418 rooms, 10 suites* 🍴 *No meals.*

$ HOTEL 🏨 **Kapok Hotel.** In a good neighborhood just off Queen's Park Savannah, the Kapok is a good all-around value if you want to stay in the city; it offers a high level of comfort and service. **Pros:** great location away from downtown noise; smaller alternative to Hilton and Hyatt; one of the best restaurants on the island. **Cons:** lacks some of the services of larger hotels; some rooms are much smaller than others; pool is a bit small. [$] *Rooms from: $138* ✉ *16–18 Cotton Hill, St. Clair, Port of Spain* ☎ *868/622–5765, 800/344–1212* 🌐 *www.kapokhotel.com* 🛏 *73 rooms, 12 suites, 9 studios* 🍴 *No meals.*

$ B&B/INN 🏨 **Le Grande Almandier.** This low-priced hotel is on Trinidad's remote and beautiful northeast coast in an area that is a popular weekend escape for locals seeking a lush rain-forest backdrop and expansive beach. **Pros:** right on the beach; great for turtle-watching in season; small, with a friendly-family vibe; Wi-Fi. **Cons:** far from the capital; no bar, and restaurant serves only wine; limited shopping and dining options; car is definitely required for any exploring. [$] *Rooms from: $151* ✉ *2 Hosang St., Grande Riviere* ☎ *868/670–1013* 🌐 *www.legrandealmandier.com* 🛏 *10 rooms* 🍴 *Breakfast.*

$ B&B/INN **Monique's.** Spacious but simple rooms and proximity to Port of Spain ensure the popularity of this guesthouse, which consists of two separate buildings. **Pros:** huge rooms; in a generally quiet area; family ownership shows in the concern for the comfort of guests; on the main road to Maracas Beach. **Cons:** room feel dated; no bar; not within walking distance of shopping or dining. [$] *Rooms from: $90* ✉ *114–116 Saddle Rd., Maraval, Port of Spain* ☎ *868/628–3334, 868/628–2351* 🌐 *www.moniquestrinidad.com* 🛏 *20 rooms* 🍴 *Breakfast.*

NIGHTLIFE AND THE ARTS

NIGHTLIFE

There's no lack of nightlife in Port of Spain, and spontaneity plays a big role—around Carnival time look for the handwritten signs announcing the "Panyard," where the next informal gathering of steel-drum bands is going to be. Gay and lesbian travelers can take advantage of an increasingly lively gay scene in Trinidad, with parties drawing upward of 200 people on most weekends.

51° Lounge. At this stylish club, there's entertainment on most nights, and Thursday is always packed to the rafters (go after 11 if you want to avoid the karaoke crowd). Don't even think about showing up in shorts, as there's a strict "elegant casual" dress code. Admission varies and sometimes requires an invitation be picked up ahead of time, so call ahead—and be prepared to stand in line for a bit. ✉ *51 Cipriani Blvd., Woodbrook, Port of Spain* ☎ *868/627–0051.*

Aria Lounge. Ariapita's newest hotspot for the well-heeled crowd on a weekend. Music goes on well into the night and the drink of choice is vintage champagne. There is a strict dress code in effect so no shorts, and tank tops are a definite no-no. ✉ *Corner Fitt St. and Ariapita Ave., Woodbrook, Port of Spain, Trinidad* ☎ *868/225–2742.*

Coco Lounge. This busy hangout on the popular Ariapita Avenue strip caters to upscale nightlifers who come to sip cocktails in the elegant, modern-plantation-style interior or watch the world go by from the huge verandah. ✉ *35 Carlos St., Woodbrook, Port of Spain* ☎ *868/622–6137.*

De Nu Pub (Mas Camp Pub). Port of Spain's most dependable nightspot for local entertainment and color features a large stage where a DJ or live band reigns, along with an ample bar and a kitchen that serves reasonably priced creole lunches. ✉ *Ariapita Ave. and French St., Woodbrook, Port of Spain* ☎ *868/627–4042.*

Drink! Wine Bar. A large and varied selection of wines and reasonably priced nibbles makes this cozy lounge popular with locals and visitors alike. There are snacks on offer and frequent performances from visiting DJs and musicians. It's a great place to meet members of the local arts community. ✉ *63 Rosalino St., Woodbrook, Port of Spain* ☎ *868/622–2895* ⏲ *Closed Mon.*

More Vino. Young professionals head here to network while sipping one of the more than 100 varieties of wine. Although most people choose to sit outside during the evening, seating is also available in the air-conditioned interior. Inside, you will also find an astonishing number of bottles on display for consumption on the premises or to take away. Cheeses and other items for nibbling are also available. ⊠ *23 O'Connor St., Woodbrook, Port of Spain* ☎ *868/622–8466.*

Trotters. An abundance of TV screens, as well as more than 30 varieties of beer from around the globe, await at this sports bar in a two-story atrium. It's incredibly popular on weekends—despite the pricey drinks. It's also one of the few establishments on the island that offers a free ride home for any patron who feels too intoxicated to drive. ⊠ *Maraval and Sweet Briar Rd., St. Clair, Port of Spain* ☎ *868/627–8768.*

Zen. What was once a movie theater now holds a very popular club with a stylish interior and a varied crowd. On the balcony is a VIP area (open to anyone who pays the extra admission charge) where the well-heeled keep track of the action on the dance floor below. The beat goes on until the sun comes up. ⊠ *9–11 Keate St., Port of Spain* ☎ *868/625–9936.*

CARNIVAL

Fodor's Choice
★

Trinidad always seems to be anticipating, celebrating, or recovering from a festival. Visitors are welcome at these events, which are a great way to explore the island's rich cultural traditions.

Trinidad's version of the pre-Lenten bacchanal may be the oldest in the Western Hemisphere; there are festivities all over the country, but the most lavish are in Port of Spain. Trinidad's Carnival has the warmth and character of a massive family reunion and is billed by locals (not unreasonably) as "The Greatest Show on Earth." The season begins right after Christmas, and the parties, called *fêtes,* don't stop until Ash Wednesday. Listen to a radio station or go online for five minutes, and you can find out where the action is. The Carnival event itself officially lasts only two days, from *J'ouvert* (2 am) on Monday to midnight the following day, Carnival Tuesday. But if you really want to *experience* Carnival, then you need to arrive in Trinidad a week or two early to enjoy the preliminary events. (Hotels fill up quickly, so be sure to make reservations months in advance, and be prepared to pay premium prices for a minimum five-night stay. Even bedrooms in private houses have been known to go for as much as $300 per night.) If you visit during Carnival, try to get tickets to one of the all-inclusive parties where thousands of people eat and drink to the sound of music all night long. And although the festivities are mostly of the adult variety, children can parade in a kiddie carnival that takes place on the Saturday morning the week before the official events.

Carnival is a showcase for performers of calypso, which mixes dance rhythms with social commentary—sung by characters with such evocative names as Shadow, the Mighty Sparrow, and Black Stalin—and soca, which fuses calypso with a driving dance beat. As Carnival approaches, many of these singers perform nightly in calypso tents around the city. Many hotels also have special concerts by popular local musicians. You can also visit the city's "panyards," where steel orchestras such as the Renegades, Desperadoes, Neal and Massy All-Stars, Invaders, and Phase II rehearse their musical arrangements (most can also be heard during the winter season).

From the Sunday before Lent until midnight on Carnival Tuesday, when Port of Spain's exhausted merrymakers finally go to bed, it's basically one big nonstop party. The next day, feet are sore, but spirits have been refreshed. Lent (and theoretical sobriety) takes over for a while.

SHOPPING

Good buys in Trinidad include Angostura bitters, Old Oak or Vat 19 rum, and leather goods, all widely available throughout the country. Thanks in large part to the costumes needed for Carnival, there's no shortage of fabric shops. The best bargains for Asian and East Indian silks and cottons can be found in downtown Port of Spain, on Frederick Street and around Independence Square. Recordings of local calypsonians and steel-pan performances as well as *chutney* (local East Indian music) are available throughout the islands and make great gifts. Note that duty-free goods are available only at the airport upon departure or arrival.

25

AREAS AND MALLS

Downtown Port of Spain, specifically **Frederick, Queen,** and **Henry streets,** is full of fabrics and shoes. **Ellerslie Plaza** is an attractive outdoor mall well worth a browse. **Excellent City Centre** is set in an old-style oasis under the lantern roofs of three of downtown's oldest commercial buildings. Look for cleverly designed keepsakes, trendy cotton clothes, and original artwork. The upstairs food court overlooks bustling Frederick Street. The **Falls at West Mall,** just west of Port of Spain, is a dazzling temple to upscale shopping that could hold its own anywhere in the world. **Long Circular Mall** has upscale boutiques that are great for window-shopping. The **Market at the Normandie Hotel** is a small collection of shops that specialize in indigenous fashions, crafts, jewelry, basketwork, and ceramics. You can also have afternoon tea in the elegant little café.

SPECIALTY ITEMS

CLOTHING

Meiling. Acclaimed local designer Meiling Esau showcases her classically detailed Caribbean resort clothing here. ⊠ *6 Carlos St., Woodbrook, Port of Spain* ☎ *868/627–6975* ⊕ *www.meilinginc.com.*

Radical. Radical is a good spot for T-shirts and original men's and women's casual clothing. ⊠ *The Falls at West Mall, Western Main Rd., Westmoorings* ☎ *868/632–5800.* ⊠ *Excellent City Centre, Independence Sq., Port of Spain* ☎ *868/627–6110.*

DUTY-FREE GOODS

De Lima's. All the traditional duty-free luxury goods are available from De Lima's. ⊠ *Piarco International Airport, Piarco* ☎ *868/669–4738.*

Stecher's. The branch at Ellerslie Plaza in Maraval carries only perfumes and cosmetics, but the Stecher's at the airport also carries china, crystal, handcrafted pieces, and jewelry. ⊠ *Piarco International Airport, Piarco* ☎ *868/669–4793.*

T-Wee Liquor Store. The deals on alcohol here would be hard to find in many other parts of the world. ⊠ *Piarco International Airport, Piarco* ☎ *868/669–4748.*

HANDICRAFTS

The tourism office can provide a list of local artisans who sell straw and cane work, miniature steel pans, and other crafts.

101 Art Gallery at Holder's Studio. Trinidad's foremost gallery showcases Jackie Hinkson (figurative watercolors), Peter Sheppard (stylized realist local landscapes in acrylic), Sundiata (semi-abstract watercolors), and other local artists. Openings are usually held Tuesday evenings; the gallery is closed Sunday and Monday. ⊠ *84 Woodford St., Newtown, Port of Spain* ☎ *868/628–4081.*

Cockey. For painted plates, ceramics, aromatic candles, wind chimes, and carved-wood pieces and instruments, check out Cockey. ⊠ *Level 3, Long Circular Mall, Long Circular Rd., St. James, Port of Spain* ☎ *868/628–6546.*

Rainy Days Gift Shop. Stylish handmade batik items, *Ajoupa* (an attractive, local terra-cotta pottery), CDs, local art, T-shirts and many other gift items are available here. ⊠ *Ellerslie Plaza, Long Circular Rd., Maraval, Port of Spain* ☎ *868/628–4387.*

MUSIC

Just CDs and Accessories. This shop carries a good selection of popular local musicians as well as other music genres. ⊠ *Long Circular Mall, Long Circular Rd., St. James, Port of Spain* ☎ *868/622–7516.*

Rhyner's. The soca and steel-pan recordings and other local music from this airport store (it's in duty-free) make great last-minute souvenirs. ⊠ *Piarco International Airport, Piarco* ☎ *868/669–3064.*

SPORTS AND ACTIVITIES

BIRD-WATCHING

Fodor's Choice ★ Trinidad and Tobago are among the top 10 spots in the world in terms of the number of species of birds per square mile—more than 430, many living within pristine rain forests, lowlands and savannas, and fresh- and saltwater swamps. If you're lucky, you might spot the collared trogon, Trinidad piping guan (known locally as the common pawi), or rare white-tailed Sabrewing hummingbird. Restaurants often hang feeders outside on their porches, as much to keep the birds away from your food as to provide a chance to see them. Both the Asa Wright Nature Centre and Caroni Bird Sanctuary *(⇨ Exploring Trinidad)* are major bird-watching destinations.

Point-a-Pierre Wildfowl Trust. This 26-acre haven for rare bird species is within the unlikely confines of a petrochemical complex; you must call in advance for a reservation. ⊠ *Petrotrin Complex, Point-a-Pierre* ☎ *868/658–4200.*

Winston Nanan. Nanan, a self-taught ornithologist, knows the local fauna as well as his own children. He will arrange personal tours in his own car anywhere on the island. His business is based at the Caroni Bird Sanctuary, but his expertise makes a trip with him to the Northern Range or the northeast a must for just about any true bird-watcher. It won't be cheap (figure on $400–$500 a day), but the personal attention and his willingness to try to find rare species are well worth the expense. ☎ *868/645–1305.*

FISHING

The islands off the northwest coast of Trinidad have excellent waters for deep-sea fishing; you may find wahoo, kingfish, and marlin, to name a few. The ocean here was a favorite angling spot of Franklin D. Roosevelt.

Bayshore Charters. Through Bayshore Charters you can fish for an afternoon or hire a boat for a weekend; the *Melissa Ann* is fully equipped for comfortable cruising, sleeps six, and has an air-conditioned cabin, a refrigerator, cooking facilities, and fishing equipment. Captain Sa Gomes is one of the most experienced charter captains on the islands. ⊠ *29 Sunset Dr., Bayshore, Westmoorings* ☎ *868/637–8711.*

GOLF

St. Andrew's Golf Club. The best course in Trinidad is just outside Port of Spain. Picture a valley setting adorned with beautiful mature tropical trees and you get an idea of St. Andrews. Established in 1892, it qualifies as one of the region's oldest layouts. As one might expect, this vintage course is not particularly long at 6,555 yards, but narrow tree-lined fairways and contoured putting surfaces place a premium upon accuracy and make it a sporting challenge. The most convenient tee times are available on weekdays. Golf shoes with soft spikes are required. ⊠ *Moka, Saddle Rd., Maraval, Port of Spain* ☎ *868/629–0066* ⊕ *golftrinidad.com* 🔖 *$40 for 9 holes, $75 for 18 holes.* ⅃ *18 holes, 6555 yards, par 72.*

GUIDED TOURS

Although any taxi driver in Trinidad or Tobago can take visitors to the major attractions, using a tour company often makes for a more leisurely and educational adventure. Tour operators are also more mindful of the sensitivities of tourists and are much less likely to subject passengers to breakneck speeds and "creative" driving.

Banwari Experience. Andrew Welch and his knowledgeable staff have numerous, customizable tour packages to serve your needs in T&T. They specialize in cultural experiences that immerse you in island customs, history, nature, and most of all food. A number of their tours reveal the best-kept secrets in Trinidad's dining scene. Mr. Welch has friends all over the island, and these friends are some of Trinidad's best chefs, artists, and adventurers. Individual and group tours as well as family packages are available, all at reasonable rates. ⊠ *Bourg Malatresse, Santa Cruz* ☎ *868/675–1619, 868/624–8687.*

Caribbean Discovery Tours Ltd. Stephen Broadbridge's tours are completely personalized and can include both on- and offshore activities. Tours can range from the strenuous to the leisurely, with prices based on the duration of the expedition and the number of participants. ⊠ *9B Fondes Amandes, St. Ann's, Port of Spain* ☎ *868/624–7281, 868/620–1989* ⊕ *www.caribbeandiscoverytours.com.*

Kalloo's. Tours from Kalloo's include a fascinating three-hour tour of Port of Spain as well as an overnight one devoted to turtle-watching. ⊠ *Piarco International Airport, Piarco* ☎ *868/669–5673, 868/622–9073* ⊕ *www.kalloos.com.*

Sensational Tours & Transport. One of the best choices for island tours. The affable owner Gerard Nicholas worked for the tourist board for many years and knows the island intimately. Tour prices are reasonable, too. ✉ *47 Reservoir Rd., La Pastora, Santa Cruz* ☎ *868/702–4129, 868/315–3652.*

TOBAGO

EXPLORING

A driving tour of Tobago, from Scarborough to Charlotteville and back, can be done in about four hours, but you'd never want to undertake this spectacular, and very hilly, ride in that time. The switchbacks can induce nausea as well as awe, so it's a good idea to take some motion-sickness pills along with you. Plan to spend at least one night at the Speyside end of the island, and give yourself a chance to enjoy this largely untouched country and seaside at leisure.

Charlotteville. This delightful fishing village in the northeast is within a series of steep hills. Fishermen here announce the day's catch by sounding their conch shells. A view of Man O' War Bay with Pigeon Peak (Tobago's highest mountain) behind it at sunset is an amazing sight.

Flagstaff Hill. One of the highest points on the island sits at the northern tip of Tobago. Surrounded by ocean on three sides and with a view of other hills, Charlotteville, and St. Giles Island, this was the site of an American military lookout and radio tower during World War II. It's an ideal spot for a sunset picnic. The turnoff to the hill is at the major bend in the road from Speyside to Charlotteville. It's largely unpaved, so the going may be a bit rough.

Ft. King George. On Mt. St. George, a short drive up the hill from Scarborough, Tobago's best-preserved historic monument clings to a cliff high above the ocean. Ft. King George was built in the 1770s and operated until 1854. It's hard to imagine that this lovely, tranquil spot commanding sweeping views of the bay and landscaped with lush tropical foliage was ever the site of any military action, but the prison, officers' mess, and several stabilized cannons attest otherwise. Just to the left of the tall wooden figures dancing a traditional Tobagonian jig is the former barrack guardhouse, now housing the small **Tobago Museum.** Exhibits include weapons and other pre-Columbian artifacts found in the area; the fertility figures are especially interesting. Upstairs are maps and photographs of Tobago's past. Be sure to check out the gift display cases for the perversely fascinating jewelry made from embalmed and painted lizards and sea creatures; you might find it hard to resist a pair of bright-yellow shrimp earrings. The **Fine Arts Centre** at the foot of the Ft. King George complex shows the work of local artists. ✉ *84 Fort St., Scarborough* ☎ *868/639–3970* 🖥 *Fort free, museum TT$5* ⊘ *Weekdays 9–5.*

Kimme Sculpture Museum. The diminutive and eccentric German-born sculptress Luise Kimme fell in love with the form of Tobagonians and devoted her life to capturing them in her sculptures. Her pieces can

A cannon at Ft. King George, Tobago

exceed 12 feet in height and are often wonderfully whimsical. Much of her work is done in wood (none of it local), but there are many bronze pieces as well. Ms Kimme passed away in 2013 but her work remains on permanent display at her former home. The museum itself is a turreted structure with a commanding view of the countryside. Most locals refer to it as "The Castle." There are numerous signs in Mt. Irvine directing visitors to the museum. ⊠ *Mt. Irvine* ☎ *868/639–0257* ⊕ *www. luisekimme.com* ✉ *TT$20* ⊙ *Sun. 10–2 or by appointment.*

Scarborough. Around Rockley Bay on the island's leeward hilly side, this town is both the capital of Tobago and a popular cruise-ship port, but it feels as if not much has changed since the area was settled two centuries ago. It may not be one of the delightful pastel-color cities of the Caribbean, but Scarborough does have its charms, including several interesting little shops. Whatever you do, be sure to check out the busy Scarborough Market, an indoor and outdoor affair with fresh vegetables, live chickens, and clothing. Note the red-and-yellow Methodist church on the hill, one of Tobago's oldest churches.

NEED A BREAK?

Ciao Café. With more than 20 flavors of gelato, Ciao Café is an essential stop on any visit to the capital. You can also get pizza slices and sandwiches if you're looking for a quick snack. There's seating in the air-conditioned interior and a lovely outdoor perch from which to absorb the downtown action sheltered from the blazing sun. In addition to the usual complement of coffees, cocktails are also available. ⊠ *20 Burnett St., Scarborough* ☎ *868/639–3001.*

Speyside. At the far reach of Tobago's windward coast, this small fishing village has a few lodgings and restaurants. Divers are drawn to the unspoiled reefs in the area and to the strong possibility of spotting giant manta rays. The approach to Speyside from the south affords one of the most spectacular vistas of the island. Glass-bottom boats operate between Speyside and **Little Tobago Island,** an important seabird sanctuary.

St. Giles Island. The underwater cliffs and canyons here off the northeastern tip of Tobago draw divers to this spot, where the Atlantic meets the Caribbean. ⊠ *Take Windward Rd. inland across mountains from Speyside.*

BEACHES

Tobago has many beautiful beaches ranging from the popular to the completely isolated. Store Bay near the airport is also a popular area for local food and entertainment. The beach most associated with Tobago—and certainly the most photographed—is Pigeon Point Beach, which is a beautiful stretch of white sand lined with palm trees and perfect for swimming. Because of the crime levels on both islands, exercise caution if planning to explore some of the more remote beaches.

Bacolet Beach. This dark-sand beach was the setting for the films *Swiss Family Robinson* and *Heaven Knows, Mr. Allison.* If you are not a guest at the Blue Haven Hotel, access is down a track next door to the hotel. The bathroom and changing facilities are for hotel guests only. **Amenities:** food and drink. **Best for:** swimming; walking. ⊠ *Windward Rd., east of Scarborough.*

Englishman's Bay. This mile-long crescent of sand looks like a frame ripped from a classic pirate movie. The somewhat steep sandy beach almost always has calm waters and backs onto unspoiled tropical rain forest. The beach is usually deserted but there are a few shacks offering food, drink, and souvenirs. **Amenities:** food and drink; toilets. **Best for:** snorkeling; solitude; walking. ⊠ *North Side Rd., east of Castara Bay.*

Great Courland Bay. This bay near Ft. Bennett has clear, tranquil waters. Along the sandy beach—one of Tobago's longest—you can find several glitzy hotels. A marina attracts the yachting crowd. **Amenities:** none. **Best for:** swimming; walking. ⊠ *Leeward Rd., northeast of Black Rock, Courland.*

King's Bay. Surrounded by steep green hills, this is the prettiest swimming site off the road from Scarborough to Speyside. The crescent beach is marked by a sign about halfway between the two towns. Just before you reach the bay, there's a bridge with an unmarked turnoff that leads to a parking lot; beyond that, a landscaped path leads to a waterfall with a rocky pool. Locals will likely offer to guide you to the top of the falls; however, you may find the climb not worth the effort. **Amenities:** food and drink; lifeguards; parking; showers. **Best for:** swimming; walking. ⊠ *Winward Rd., Delaford.*

Lovers Beach. You have to hire a local to bring you to this isolated retreat of pink sand. Ask one of the fishermen in Charlotteville to arrange a ride for you, but be sure to haggle. It should cost no more than TT$25 per person, round-trip. **Amenities:** none. **Best for:** solitude; snorkeling. ⊠ *North coast, reachable only by boat from Charlotteville.*

Mt. Irvine Beach. The beach across the street from the Mt. Irvine Bay Hotel has great surfing in July and August, and the snorkeling is excellent, too. It's also ideal for windsurfing in January and April. There are picnic tables surrounded by painted concrete pagodas and a snack bar. **Amenities:** food and drink; showers; toilets. **Best for:** snorkeling; surfing; swimming; windsurfing. ⊠ *Shirvan Rd., Mt. Irvine.*

Parlatuvier. On the north side of the island, the beach is best approached via the road from Roxborough. It's a classic Caribbean crescent, a scene peopled by villagers and fishermen. Local food and souvenir shops are literally steps from the sand, as the village fronts the beach. The local fishermen bringing in their catch is a photo opportunity not to be missed. **Amenities:** none. **Best for:** swimming. ⊠ *Parlatuvier.*

25

Pigeon Point Beach. This stunning locale is often displayed on Tobago travel brochures. The white-sand beach is lined with swaying coconut trees, and there are changing facilities and food stalls nearby. The beach is public but there is an admission fee (about TT$20). **Amenities:** food and drink; showers; toilets. **Best for:** partiers; swimming. ⊠ *Pigeon Point.*

Stone Haven Bay. This gorgeous stretch of sand is literally across the street (a small secondary road) from the Grafton Beach Resort and is great for tanning. There are strong currents and no lifeguards on duty so bear in mind that swimming poses risks. A better bet is to relax with a cocktail from the hotel beach bar and wait for one of the locals to come by offering handmade souvenirs. **Amenities:** food and drink. **Best for:** walking. ⊠ *Shirvan Rd., Black Rock.*

Store Bay. The beach, where boats depart for Buccoo Reef, is little more than a small sandy cove between two rocky breakwaters, but the food stands here are amazing: several huts licensed by the tourist board to local ladies who sell roti, pelau, and curried crab and dumplings. It's near the airport; just walk around the Crown Point Hotel to the beach entrance. **Amenities:** food and drink; showers; toilets. **Best for:** partiers; swimming. ⊠ *Crown Point.*

Turtle Beach. This beach is named for the leatherback turtles that lay their eggs here at night between February and June. (If you're very quiet, you can watch; the turtles don't seem to mind.) It's 8 miles (13 km) from the airport between Black Rock and Plymouth. **Amenities:** solitude. **Best for:** walking. ⊠ *Southern end of Great Courland Bay between Black Rock and Plymouth, Courland.*

WHERE TO EAT

Curried crab and dumplings is a Sunday-dinner favorite in Tobago. *Oil-down*—a local dish—tastes better than it sounds: it's a gently seasoned mixture of boiled breadfruit and salt beef or pork flavored with coconut milk. Mango ice cream or a sweet-and-sour tamarind ball makes a tasty finish. You may want to take home some hot-pepper sauce or chutney to a spice-loving friend or relative.

$$ TAPAS 🍴 **Azucar.** A new experience for Tobago, Azucar offers traditional tapas, a nice selection of main courses (many of which are Spanish), and a chance to salsa dance the night away. Reasonable prices and great cocktails keep everyone feeling good. You'll find the best (and probably only) paella on the island here. [$] *Average main: $25* ✉ *133 Shirvan Rd., Mt. Pleasant* ☎ *868/631–0121* 🌐 *www.azucartobago.com.*

$$ CARIBBEAN Fodor's Choice ★ 🍴 **Blue Crab Restaurant.** The Sardinha family has been serving the best local lunches at their home since the 1980s. The ebullient Alison entertains and hugs diners while her husband, Ken, does the cooking. The food is hearty and usually well seasoned in the creole style. The only bad news is that the restaurant is primarily a lunch spot—it's only open for dinner three days a week; the good news is that you may not have room for dinner after lunch here. [$] *Average main: $23* ✉ *Robinson and Main Sts., Scarborough* ☎ *868/639–2737* 🌐 *www.tobagobluecrab.com* ⏲ *Closed weekends. No dinner Tues. and Thurs.*

$$$ ECLECTIC 🍴 **Bonkers.** This restaurant at the Toucan Inn is atmospheric and excellent. Designed by expat British co-owner Chris James, the architecture is a blend of Kenyan and Caribbean styles, executed entirely in local teak and open on all sides. The menu is huge; Chris claims it pains him to remove any items, so he just keeps adding more. You can savor your lobster Rockefeller while enjoying the nightly entertainment. Open for breakfast, lunch, and dinner seven days a week, this is the busiest eatery on the island. [$] *Average main: $22* ✉ *Toucan Inn, Store Bay Local Rd., Crown Point* ☎ *868/639–7173* 🌐 *www.toucan-inn.com.*

$$$ ECLECTIC Fodor's Choice ★ 🍴 **Café Coco.** This stylish eatery seats 200, but it's divided into multiple levels, so there's still a sense of intimacy. Statuary is strewn about with carefree abandon, and the sound of flowing water permeates the room. The main courses vary widely and may include Cuban stewed beef as well as shrimp tempura. The restaurant is seldom full, so getting a table is usually not a problem. [$] *Average main: $25* ✉ *TTEC Substation Rd. off Crown Point Rd., Crown Point* ☎ *868/639–0996.*

$$$$ ECLECTIC 🍴 **Café Iguana.** This funky little restaurant and art gallery is a popular gathering place at night, as it serves some of the best cocktails on the island. The menu is eclectic, but there is a distinct Tobago touch to everything and an emphasis on local ingredients. The art on the walls is available for sale—you might want to exercise restraint with the cocktails before deciding to become an art investor. [$] *Average main: $35* ✉ *Store Bay Local Rd. at Milford Rd., Crown Point* ☎ *868/631–8205* ⏲ *Closed Wed.*

$$$$ CARIBBEAN 🍴 **Kariwak Village Restaurant.** Recorded steel-band music plays gently in the background at this romantic, candlelit spot in the Kariwak Village complex. In a bamboo pavilion that resembles an Amerindian round hut, Cynthia Clovis orchestrates a very original menu. Whatever the

dish, it will be full of herbs and vegetables picked from her organic garden. Be sure to try the delicious homemade ice cream and the reasonably priced but potent cocktails. Friday and Saturday buffets, with live jazz or calypso, are a Tobagonian highlight. $ *Average main: $34* ⊠ *Crown Point* ☎ *868/639–8442* ⊕ *www.kariwak.com.*

$
ITALIAN
✕ **La Tartaruga.** Milanese owner Gabriele de Gaetano has created the island's most prominent Italian eatery. Sitting on the large patio surrounded by lush foliage with Gabriele rushing from table to table chatting in Italian-laced English is all the entertainment you'll need. Cuisine ranges from basic but tasty pizzas to elaborate Northern Italian pasta dishes. The impressive cellar stocks only Italian wines. $ *Average main: $14* ⊠ *Buccoo Rd., Buccoo* ☎ *868/639–0940* ⊕ *www.latartarugatobago.com* ⟡ *Reservations essential* ⊗ *Closed Sun. No lunch.*

$
CAFÉ
Fodor'sChoice
★
✕ **Shore Things Café & Craft.** With a dramatic setting over the ocean on the Milford Road between Crown Point and Scarborough, this is a good spot to stop for lunch or a coffee break. Survey the view from the deck tables while enjoying a variety of freshly prepared juices (the tamarind is particularly refreshing) and nibbling on excellent sandwiches. The whole wheat pizza is great and owner Giselle Beaubrun takes special pride in her indulgent desserts. While waiting for your meal, you can shop for local crafts in the lovely and comprehensive gift shop. $ *Average main: $10* ⊠ *25 Old Milford Rd., Lambeau* ☎ *868/635–1072* ⊗ *Closed Sun. No dinner.*

$$$$
CARIBBEAN
✕ **Shutters on the Bay.** The warm-yellow dining area of this hotel restaurant is on the second floor of a colonial-style building and surrounded by white push-out shutters that frame a magical view of Bacolet Bay. The menu features a variety of dishes, all with a contemporary Caribbean twist. Fish dishes are a standout; don't be afraid to try some of the more exotic local offerings, such as callaloo soup, or some of the local starches (called "ground provisions"), such as dasheen (taro) or breadfruit. $ *Average main: $33* ⊠ *Blue Haven Hotel, Bacolet Bay, Scarborough* ☎ *868/660–7500* ⟡ *Reservations essential.*

$$$$
ECLECTIC
✕ **Tamara's.** At the elegant Coco Reef Resort you can dine on contemporary cuisine with an island twist. The peach walls and whitewashed wooden ceiling make the resort's restaurant feel airy and light, and island breezes waft through the palm-lined terrace. The prix-fixe menu changes seasonally, and the fish dishes are worth special attention. A full tropical buffet breakfast is served daily; dinner is served nightly. There is a prix-fixe choice of one, two, or three courses. A dress code is enforced but casual chic is fine and men are not required to wear jackets for dinner. $ *Average main: $40* ⊠ *Coco Reef Resort, Crown Point, Scarborough* ☎ *868/639–8571* ⟡ *Reservations essential* ⊗ *No lunch.*

25

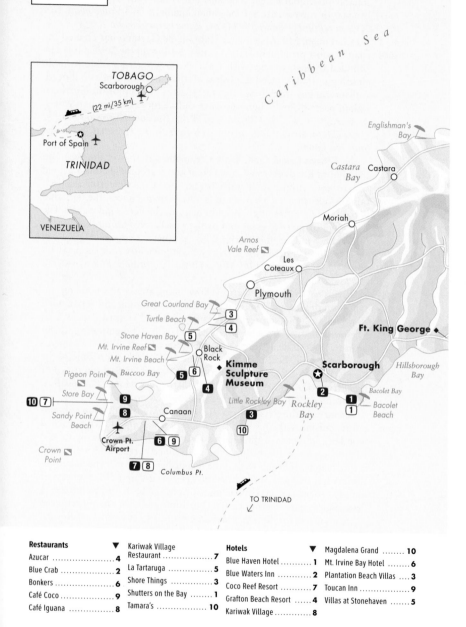

Tobago

Caribbean Sea

TOBAGO
Scarborough
(22 mi/35 km)
Port of Spain
TRINIDAD
VENEZUELA

Englishman's Bay

Castara Bay   Castara

Moriah

Arnos Vale Reef

Les Coteaux

Plymouth

Great Courland Bay

Turtle Beach   **3**

Stone Haven Bay   **4**

Mt. Irvine Reef   **5**

Mt. Irvine Beach   Black Rock

Pigeon Point   Buccoo Bay   **5**   **6**

Store Bay   **4**

Kimme Sculpture Museum

Ft. King George

Scarborough   *Hillsborough Bay*

Bacolet Bay

1   Bacolet Beach

2

1

10 **7**   **9**

8

Sandy Point Beach

Little Rockley Bay   *Rockley Bay*

3

Canaan

10

Crown Point

Crown Pt. Airport

6 **9**

7 **8**   Columbus Pt.

TO TRINIDAD

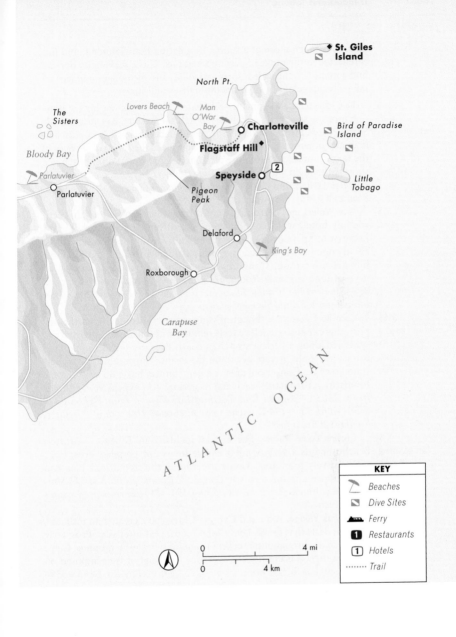

St. Giles
Island

North Pt.

Lovers Beach

Man
O'War
Bay

The
Sisters

Charlotteville

Bird of Paradise
Island

Flagstaff Hill

Bloody Bay

Parlatuvier

Speyside 2

Little
Tobago

Parlatuvier

Pigeon
Peak

Delaford

King's Bay

Roxborough

Carapuse
Bay

ATLANTIC OCEAN

ATLANTIC

KEY	
	Beaches
	Dive Sites
	Ferry
1	Restaurants
1	Hotels
....	Trail

0   4 mi

0   4 km

WHERE TO STAY

Tobago is much more of a tourist destination than Trinidad, and this is reflected in the range of accommodations. Those seeking luxury can find a number of upscale resorts and villas, and the budget-minded can take advantage of several more intimate establishments.

$
HOTEL
Fodor's Choice
★

Blue Haven Hotel. Justifiably celebrated, this 1940s-era luxury hotel overlooks a spectacular secluded beach on Bacolet Bay just outside Scarborough. **Pros:** historic charm; beautiful beach; more European flair than any other hotel on the island. **Cons:** lacks the range of services of the larger hotels; far from the attractions of Crown Point; beach is a short walk down a hillside. $ *Rooms from: $238* ⊠ *Bacolet Bay, Scarborough* ☎ *868/660–7400* ⊕ *www.bluehavenhotel.com* ⤵ *51 rooms, 8 suites* ⊚ *Multiple meal plans.*

$$$
HOTEL

Blue Waters Inn. A tropical rain forest creeps up behind this eco-friendly hotel, which sits on sheltered, turquoise Batteaux Bay; it's just east of Speyside and a 90-minute drive from Scarborough. **Pros:** rooms open onto the beach; enthusiastic and friendly staff; simple but delicious food. **Cons:** it's a long drive from Scarborough; in need of renovation. $ *Rooms from: $245* ⊠ *Batteaux Bay, Speyside* ☎ *868/660–4341* ⊕ *www.bluewatersinn.com* ⤵ *31 rooms, 3 suites, 4 bungalows* ⊚ *Multiple meal plans.*

$$$$
RESORT
FAMILY
Fodor's Choice
★

Coco Reef Resort. Although it's just a short distance from the airport, this expansive enclave feels remote, with pink buildings that are sprawled along a perfect stretch of coast. **Pros:** beautifully appointed rooms; the only private beach on the island; impeccable and understated service. **Cons:** pool area can get a bit too busy; no Wi-Fi; some rooms are far from the beach and reception; very expensive. $ *Rooms from: $283* ⊠ *Milford Rd., Coconut Bay, Crown Point* ☎ *868/639–8571, 800/221–1294* ⊕ *www.cocoreef.com* ⤵ *100 rooms, 27 suites, 8 villas* ⊚ *Breakfast.*

$
ALL-INCLUSIVE
FAMILY

Grafton Beach Resort. The first all-inclusive in Tobago —Grafton Beach remains a very popular choice for young couples. **Pros:** large rooms; lively pool area. **Cons:** so-so food; the free drinks plan sometimes make for a rowdy crowd. $ *Rooms from: $350* ⊠ *Shirvan Rd., Black Rock* ☎ *868/639–0191* ⤵ *102 rooms, 4 suites* ⊚ *All-inclusive.*

$
HOTEL

Kariwak Village. Alan and Cynthia Clovis have created an intimate, tranquil oasis that draws guests who return year after year. **Pros:** cozy and intimate throughout; excellent restaurant; beautiful grounds. **Cons:** the New Age concept not for everyone (although it isn't imposed on guests); no beach. $ *Rooms from: $225* ⊠ *Store Bay Rd.* ☎ *868/639–8442* ⊕ *www.kariwak.com* ⤵ *24 rooms* ⊚ *Breakfast.*

$$$
HOTEL

Magdalena Grand Beach & Golf Resort. This impressive seafront resort is located in a lovely gated residential area complete with golf course; the beach, however, is minuscule, requiring a complimentary shuttle to the much better Pigeon Point Beach. **Pros:** gorgeous ocean views; excellent restaurants and entertainment options. **Cons:** on-site beach is tiny; long walk from some rooms to reception. $ *Rooms from: $229* ⊠ *Milford Rd.* ☎ *868/660–8800* ⤵ *178 rooms, 22 suites* ⊚ *No meals.*

$ **Mt. Irvine Bay Hotel.** Although the hotel lacks some of the fancier ameni-
HOTEL   ties, there's still something magical about its 1970s shabby gentility that
can't be found at the flashy new resorts. **Pros:** beautiful grounds; perfect for the golf lover; access to one of the prettiest beaches. **Cons:** public
spaces feel dated; poor restaurant service; hotel frequently empty. $ *Rooms
from: $195* ⊠ *Shirvan Rd., Box 222, Mt. Irvine* ☎ *868/639–8871* ⊕ *www.
mtirvine.com* ⇝ *53 rooms, 6 suites, 46 cottages* ⧐ *No meals.*

$$ **Plantation Beach Villas.** If you're looking for luxury living in a well-
RENTAL   appointed Caribbean villa, you should be blissfully happy here. **Pros:**
FAMILY   an engaging alternative to a hotel room; on the beach; all the comforts
of home, along with maid service. **Cons:** no restaurant for dinner; lacks
the diversions of a large hotel. $ *Rooms from: $313* ⊠ *Stone Haven
Bay Rd., Black Rock* ☎ *868/639–9377* ⊕ *www.plantationbeachvillas.
com* ⇝ *6 3-bedroom villas* ⧐ *No meals.*

$ **Toucan Inn.** This budget hotel near the airport offers simple rooms and a
HOTEL   lively social scene. **Pros:** great value; good restaurant. **Cons:** pool and bar
area can be a bit raucous on weekends; rooms are serviceable but plain;
no beach. $ *Rooms from: $120* ⊠ *Store Bay Local Rd., Crown Point*
☎ *868/639–7173* ⊕ *www.toucan-inn.com* ⇝ *20 rooms* ⧐ *Breakfast.*

$$$$ **Villas at Stonehaven.** Perched on a hillside overlooking the ocean, this
RENTAL   villa complex sets the standard for luxury self-catering accommodations
Fodor'sChoice   on Tobago. **Pros:** as luxurious as Tobago gets; beautiful ocean views
★   from every villa; an infinity pool all to yourself. **Cons:** restaurant is
poor; not on the beach. $ *Rooms from: $520* ⊠ *Bon Accord, Grafton
Estate, Shirvan Rd., Box 1079, Black Rock* ☎ *868/639–0361* ⊕ *www.
stonehavenvillas.com* ⇝ *14 3-bedroom villas* ⧐ *No meals.*

25

NIGHTLIFE

Tobago is not that lively after dark, but there's usually some form of
nightlife to be found. Whatever you do the rest of the week, don't miss
the huge impromptu party, dubbed Sunday School, that gears up after
midnight on Saturday on all the street corners of Buccoo and breaks up
around dawn. Pick your band, hang out for a while, then move on. In
downtown Scarborough on weekend nights you can also find competing
sound systems blaring at informal parties that welcome extra guests. In
addition, "blockos" (spontaneous block parties) spring up all over the
island; look for the hand-painted signs. Tobago also has harvest parties
on Sunday throughout the year, when a particular village extends its
hospitality and opens its doors to visitors.

Bonkers. There's live entertainment every night except Sunday at this
usually busy club. ⊠ *Toucan Inn, Store Bay Local Rd., Crown Point*
☎ *868/639–7173.*

Grafton Beach Resort. Grafton Beach Resort has some kind of organized
cabaret-style event every night. Even if you hate that touristy stuff, check
out Les Couteaux Cultural Group, which does a high-octane dance ver-
sion of Tobagonian history. ⊠ *Shirvan Rd., Black Rock* ☎ *868/639–0191.*

Kariwak Village. As many locals as visitors frequent Kariwak Village on
Friday and Saturday nights, when one of the better local jazz-calypso
bands almost always plays. ⊠ *Crown Point* ☎ *868/639–8442.*

Shade. This sure bet for raucous late-night fun is open from 7 pm to 4 am Wednesday through Saturday. It's across the road from Crown Point's only gas station. ⊠ *Milford Rd. and Robert St., Crown Point* ☎ *868/639–9651.*

SHOPPING

Souvenir seekers will do better in Trinidad than in Tobago, but determined shoppers ought to be able to find a few things to take home. Scarborough has the largest collection of shops, and Burnett Street, which climbs sharply from the port to St. James Park, is a good place to browse.

FOOD

Forro's Homemade Delicacies. Eileen Forrester, wife of the Anglican archdeacon of Trinidad and Tobago, supervises a kitchen full of good cooks who boil and bottle the condiments sold here and pack them in little straw baskets—or even in bamboo. Most of the jars of tamarind chutney, lemon and lime marmalade, hot sauce, and guava and golden-apple jelly are small, easy to carry, and inexpensive. ⊠ *The Andrew's Rectory, Bacolet St., opposite fire station, Scarborough* ☎ *868/639–2485.*

HANDICRAFTS

Batiki Point. Tina Louis offers batik, imaginative local crafts, footwear, and clothing at this charming little store in Buccoo which is conveniently also open on Sunday during the area's raucous "Sunday School" evening party. ⊠ *Opposite Beach, Main Rd., Buccoo* ☎ *868/631–0111.*

Shore Things Café & Crafts. Masks and music are just two of the many kinds of souvenirs you can pick up at Shore Things Café & Crafts. ⊠ *25 Old Milford Rd., Lambeau* ☎ *868/635–1072.*

Store Bay. The stalls at Store Bay sell T-shirts, local handicrafts, and lots of other souvenirs. It's also convenient to the airport for any last-minute purchases. ⊠ *Store Bay, Crown Point.*

SPORTS AND ACTIVITIES

BIRD-WATCHING

Some 200 varieties of birds have been documented on Tobago: look for the yellow oriole, scarlet ibis, and the comical motmot—the male of the species clears sticks and stones from an area and then does a dance complete with snapping sounds to attract a mate. The flora is as vivid as the birds. Purple-and-yellow *poui* trees and spectacular orange immortelles splash color over the countryside, and something is blooming virtually every season.

Pioneer Journeys. Pat Turpin and Renson Jack at Pioneer Journeys can give you information about their bird-watching tours of Bloody Bay rain forest and Louis d'Or River valley wetlands. ☎ *868/660–4327* ✉ *pturpin@tstt.net.tt.*

Rooks Nature Tours. Naturalist and ornithologist David Rooks offers bird-watching walks inland and trips to offshore bird colonies. He's generally considered the best guide on the island. ⊠ *462 Moses Hill, Lambeau* ☎ *868/756–8594.*

Continued on page 1014

CARNIVAL IN TRINIDAD

Vernon O'Reilly Ramesar

The "Greatest Show on Earth" is also the best party in the Caribbean, and it's not brought to you by Barnum & Bailey but by the people of Trinidad. The island's pre-Lenten Carnival is rooted in Trinidad's African and French-Creole cultures and is more spontaneous than similar celebrations in Latin America; its influence reaches as far as Miami, Toronto, and London.

Trinidad's celebration has evolved through the years. What was once a two-day affair has turned into a lengthy party season starting in early January and lasting until Ash Wednesday. The biggest and best parties are held in and around Port of Spain, where locals max out their credit cards and even take out bank loans to finance their costumes and attend as many parties as possible.

On Carnival Monday and Tuesday the traffic lights of Port of Spain are turned off and the streets are turned over to a human traffic jam of costumed revelers. They jump and dance to the pounding sound of music trucks—featuring huge speakers and either live music or a DJ—and turn Port of Spain into a pulsing celebration of island life that they call the *mas*.

Mas bands—some with thousands of members, others with a mere handful—must follow a route and pass judging points to win a prize, but increasingly, they simply don't bother. They're in it for the fun. To grease the wheels, makeshift bars are set up along all the city's streets.

Children stiltwalkers in colorful Carnival costumes, Queens Park Savannah, Port of Spain

CARNIVAL 101

THE FETE

Huge outdoor parties (called *fetes*) are held in the months before Carnival; during the final week, there are usually several fetes every day. You can get tickets for many of them through the major hotels, but some exclusive fetes may require an invitation from a well-connected Trinidadian.

THE PANORAMA

While fetes are important to Carnival, the Panorama Steelpan Preliminaries and finals are essential. Two weeks before Carnival, the "Prelims" are held, when dozens of steel drum orchestras compete for a place in the finals held on Carnival Saturday. Music lovers go to hear the throbbing sound of hundreds of steelpans beating out a syncopated rhythm, and the rum-fueled party often rivals even the best fetes.

DIMANCHE GRAS

On Carnival Sunday, top calypsonians compete to be Calypso Monarch, and this offers you an especially good opportunity to experience Carnival in one easy shot. The show was once held in Queen's Park Savannah, but the location now varies.

THE COSTUMES

To be a true part of Carnival, you need a costume. Every mas band has its own costumes, which must be reserved months in advance (these days online). You pick up yours at the band's mas "camp" and find out where and when to meet your band. Then all you have to do is jump, walk, or wave in the Carnival procession as the spirit moves you. Drinks and food may be included.

(top) Trinidad Carnival celebrations during Junior Parade of the Bands, (bottom) masquerader in a colorful costume.

MUSIC

Carnival is powered by music, and though the steelpan still plays a big part, it is the *soca* performers who draw the biggest crowds. Some of the big names include Machel Montano, Shurwayne Winchester, and Allyson Hinds. You can hear the most popular performers at the bigger fetes and at the Soca Monarch competition held on Carnival Friday before the more prestigious Calypso Monarch contest.

THE MAS BANDS

Trinis are passionate about their favorite mas band. The most popular have costumes largely comprised of beaded bikinis and feathered headdresses and are called "pretty mas." Very large bands such as Tribe, Island People, and Hart's fall into this category. If you're not willing to show that much skin or want more theater, then choose a band like K2K & Associates, which offers more elaborate costumes with a thematic story. As has always been the case, women greatly outnumber men in the bands.

Carnival costumes are usually colorful—and skimpy.

TOP FETES

Safety is an increasing concern in Trinidad, especially at Carnival time. Fetes that attract a better heeled crowd offer more security and sufficient bars to cater to the thousands of revelers who attend. They usually command higher prices but are worth the cost.

Beach House. This fete attracts an upscale crowd at a different spot each year. The party runs till about 10 pm with catered food and premium drinks.

Eyes Wide Shut is held at The Oval (home of Trinidad cricket) and tends to attract a younger crowd.

Insomnia is an overnight fete held in Chaguaramas, just West of Port of Spain, on Carnival Saturday, and the partying doesn't stop till sunrise.

The Brian Lara and Moka all-inclusive fetes are both held on the afternoon of Carnival Sunday. Tickets for both are highly sought. Brian Lara is considered the most exclusive of all fetes and is the most expensive.

BOAT TOURS

Tobago offers many wonderful spots for snorkeling. Although the reefs around Speyside in the northeast are becoming better known, **Buccoo Reef,** off the island's southwest coast, is still the most popular—perhaps too popular. Over the years the reef has been badly damaged by the ceaseless boat traffic and by thoughtless visiting divers who take pieces of coral as souvenirs. Still, it's worth experiencing, particularly if you have children. Daily 2½-hour tours by glass-bottom boats let you snorkel at the reef, swim in a lagoon, and gaze at Coral Gardens—where fish and coral are as yet untouched. Most dive companies in the Black Rock area also arrange snorkeling tours. There's also good snorkeling near the **Arnos Vale Hotel** and the **Mt. Irvine Bay Hotel.**

Hew's Glass Bottom Boat Tours. These tours are perfect for those who want to see sealife but who neither snorkel nor dive. Boats leave daily at 11:30 am. ⊠ *Pigeon Point* ☎ *868/639–9058.*

DIVING

An abundance of fish and coral thrives on the nutrients of Venezuela's Orinoco River, which are brought to Tobago by the Guyana current. Off the west coast is **Arnos Vale Reef,** with a depth of 40 feet and several reefs that run parallel to the shore. Here you can spot French and queen angelfish, moray eels, southern stingrays, and even the Atlantic torpedo ray. Much of the diving is drift diving in the mostly gentle current. **Crown Point,** on the island's southwest tip, is a good place for exploring the Shallows—a plateau at 50 to 100 feet that's favored by turtles, dolphins, angelfish, and nurse sharks. Just north of Crown Point on the southwest coast, **Pigeon Point** is a good spot to submerge. North of Pigeon Point, long, sandy beaches line the calm western coast; it has a gradual offshore slope and the popular **Mt. Irvine Wall,** which goes down to about 60 feet.

A short trip from Charlotteville, off the northeast tip of the island, is **St. Giles Island.** Here are natural rock bridges—London Bridge, Marble Island, and Fishbowl—and underwater cliffs. The **waters off Speyside** on the east coast draw scuba divers who come for the many manta rays in the area. Exciting sites in this area include Batteaux Reef, Angel Reef, Bookends, Blackjack Hole, and Japanese Gardens—one of the loveliest reefs, with depths of 20 to 85 feet and lots of sponges.

Tobago is considered a prime diving destination, as the clear waters provide maximum visibility. Every species of hard coral and most soft corals can be found in the waters around the island. Tobago is also home to the largest-known brain coral. Generally, the best diving is around the Speyside area. Many hotels and guesthouses in this area cater to the diving crowd with basic accommodations and easy access to the water. You can usually get the best deals with these "dive-and-stay" packages.

AquaMarine Dive Ltd. On the northeast coast, AquaMarine is friendly, laid-back, and popular with casual divers. ⊠ *Blue Waters Inn, Batteaux Bay, Speyside* ☎ *868/639–4416* ⊕ *www.aquamarinedive.com.*

Tobago Dive Experience. Class sizes at Tobago Dive Experience are kept small to ensure that all divers get the attention they need. It has the most comprehensive range of courses, including PADI, NAUI, and BSAC, and

prices are very competitive. ⊠ *Manta Lodge, Speyside* ☎ *868/660-5268*
⊕ *www.tobagodiveexperience.com.*

FISHING

Dillon's Deep Sea Charters. This company is excellent for full- and half-day
trips for kingfish, barracuda, wahoo, mahimahi, blue marlin, and others. A full day on the sea with either a beach stop for lunch or a cruise
around the island runs about $750, including equipment. ⊠ *Crown
Point* ☎ *868/639–8765.*

Hard Play Fishing Charters. The colorful skipper at Hard Play, Gerard
"Frothy" De Silva, helps you bag your own marlin. ⊠ *13 The Evergreen, Old Grange, Mt. Irvine Bay* ☎ *868/639–7108.*

GOLF

Tobago Plantations Golf & Country Club. The 18-hole, par-72 course is set on
rolling greens. It offers some amazing views of the ocean as a bonus. Greens
fees are $100 for 18 holes, $50 for 9 holes. This is the newer of the two
main courses on the island and is by far the most popular. The course is well
maintained and contains areas of mangrove and forest that are home to
many bird species. The course and clubhouse were placed under the management of the Magdalena Grand Beach & Gold Resort in late 2013 and,
at this writing, are scheduled to undergo a $2 million upgrade in 2014 .
⊠ *Tobago Plantations Golf & Country Club, Lowlands* ☎ *868/387–0287.*

GUIDED TOURS

Frank's Glass Bottom Boat & Birdwatching Tours. In addition to glass-
bottom-boat and snorkeling tours of the shores of Speyside, Frank and
his son also conduct guided tours of the rain forest and Little Tobago.
As natives of Speyside, they are extremely knowledgeable about the
island's flora, fauna, and folklore. ⊠ *Speyside* ☎ *868/660–5438.*

Tobago Travel. The island's most experienced operator is almost certain
to have the perfect tour for you. ⊠ *TTEC Substation Rd off Crown
Point Rd., Crown Point* ☎ *868/639–8778.*

HIKING

Ecoconsciousness is strong on Tobago, where the rain forests of the
Main Ridge were set aside for protection in 1764, creating the first
such preserve in the Western Hemisphere. Natural areas include Little
Tobago and St. Giles islands, both major seabird sanctuaries. In addition, the endangered leatherback turtles maintain breeding grounds on
some of Tobago's leeward beaches.

Harris Jungle Tours. The knowledgeable Harris McDonald offers tours
that range from strenuous to laid-back. The more adventurous might
want to try the rain-forest-at-night tour, which promises the possibility
of encounters with some of Tobago's folklore characters, including La
Diablesse (a beautifully dressed she-devil with one cow's foot). ⊠ *Golden
Grove Rd., Canaan* ☎ *868/639–0513* ⊕ *www.harris-jungle-tours.com.*

Yes Tourism. Among the many tours from this company is an excellent
guided hike through the rain forest—the off-road jeep safari is hair-
raising but memorable. Sightseeing tours around Tobago as well as to
Trinidad are also possible. ⊠ *7 De Freitas Dr., Lowlands* ☎ *868/631–
0286* ⊕ *www.yes-tourism.com.*

25

TURKS AND CAICOS ISLANDS

WELCOME TO TURKS AND CAICOS ISLANDS

TO BAHAMAS

Caicos Passage

Three Mary's Cays

2 **4** **5** **7**
3 **6**

Parrot Cay

Fort George Cay

Football Fields ◢ Pine Cay

Little Water Cay

Northwest Point

Providenciales
Grace Bay

◆ Caicos Conch Farm

Cheshire Hall ◆

Sapodilla Hill ◆

Southwest Bluff

Juba Point

Spanish Point

Highas Cay

4 *Juniper Hole* Platico Point

North Caicos

◆ North Caicos

8 **3**

Middle Caicos

Middle Caicos ◆

Ocean Hole

Vine Point *Hole* Toll Crawl Point

Providenciales
see detail map

West Caicos

Southwest Reef

C A I C O S

I S L A N D S

◢ *Molasses Reef*

| 0 | | 14 miles |
| 0 | | 21 km |

C A I C O S   B A N K

Little Ambergris Cay

SEAL CAYS

White Cay

KEY	
◢	*Dive Sites*
1	*Restaurants*
1	*Hotels*

Only eight of these 40 islands between the Bahamas and Haiti are inhabited. Divers and snorkelers can explore one of the world's largest coral reefs. Land-based pursuits don't get much more taxing than teeing off at the Provo Golf and Country Club or sunset-watching from the seaside terrace of a laid-back resort.

GEOGRAPHICAL INFO

Though Providenciales is a major offshore banking center, sea creatures far outnumber humans in this archipelago of 40 islands, where the total population is a mere 45,000. From developed Provo to sleepy Grand Turk to sleepier South Caicos, the islands offer miles of undeveloped beaches, crystal clear water, and laid-back luxury resorts.

Restaurants	▼
Last Chance	4
Mudjin Bari	3
Pat's Place	2
Porter's Island Thyme Bistro	1

Hotels	▼
Blue Horizon Resort	8
Castaway	12
Couch Cottage	6
Datai Villa	4
Hollywood Beach Suites	5
Jodo Resort	3
Meridian Club	1
Parrot Cay Resort	2
Pelican Beach Hotel	7
Pirate's Hideaway	13
South Caicos Ocean & Beach Resort	9
Tradewinds Guest Suites	10
Villas of Salt Cay	11

26

TURKS AND CAICOS ISLANDS

ATLANTIC OCEAN

Haulover Point · Long Bay · Joe Grant Cay · Drum Point · East Caicos · Big Southern Bush · Big Cameron Cay · Middle Creek Cay · Sail Rock Island · South Caicos · Horse Cay · South Caicos · **9** High Point · Long Cay · Six Hill Cays · Fish Cays · Big Ambergris Cay · AMBERGRIS CAYS · Bush Cay · Shot Cay

Columbus Passage · Black Forest · The Library · **TURKS ISLANDS** · Cotton Cay · **1** **2** · **10**-**13** · Salt Cay · South Point · Big Sand Cay · Mouchoir Passage

Grand Turk see detail map · Grand Turk Island · Grand Turk · Gibb's Cay · Long Cay · East Cay · Toney Rock

TOP REASONS TO VISIT TURKS AND CAICOS ISLANDS

1 Beautiful Beaches: Even on Provo, there are miles of deserted beaches without any beach umbrellas in sight.

2 Excellent Diving: The third-largest coral-reef system in the world is among the world's top dive sites.

3 Easy Island-Hopping: Island-hopping beyond the beaten path will give you a feel for the islands.

4 The Jet Set: Destination spas, penthouse suites, and exclusive villas and resorts make celebrity-spotting a popular sport.

5 Exploring on the Sea: You'll find excellent fishing and boating among the uninhabited coves and cays.

Updated by
Ramona Settle

With water so turquoise that it glows, you may find it difficult to stray far from the beach in the Turks and Caicos. You may find no need for museums, and no desire to see ruins or even to read books. You may find yourself hypnotized by the water's many neon hues. And because the beaches are among the most incredible you will ever see, don't be surprised if you wake up on your last morning and realize that you didn't find a lot of time for anything else.

Although ivory-white, soft, sandy beaches and breathtaking turquoise waters are shared among all the islands, the landscapes are a series of contrasts, from the dry, arid bush and scrub on the flat, coral islands of Grand Turk, Salt Cay, South Caicos, and Providenciales to the greener, foliage-rich undulating landscapes of Middle Caicos, North Caicos, Parrot Cay, and Pine Cay.

A much-disputed legend has it that Columbus first discovered these islands in 1492. Despite being on the map for longer than most other island groups, the Turks and Caicos Islands (pronounced *kay*-kos) still remain part of the less-discovered Caribbean. More than 40 islands—only eight inhabited—make up this self-governing British overseas territory that lies just 575 miles (925 km) southeast of Miami on the third-largest coral-reef system in the world.

The political and historical capital island of the country is Grand Turk, but most of the tourism development, which consists primarily of boutique hotels and condo resorts, has occurred in Providenciales, thanks to Grace Bay, its 12-mile (18-km) stretch of ivory sand. Once home to a population of around 500 people plus a few donkey carts, Provo has become a hub of activity, resorts, spas, restaurants, and water sports. It's the temporary home for the majority of visitors who come to the Turks and Caicos.

LOGISTICS

Getting to the Turks and Caicos: Several major airlines fly nonstop to Providenciales from the United States. If you're going to one of the smaller islands, you'll usually need to make a connection in Provo. All international flights arrive at Providenciales International Airport (PLS), but you can hop over to the other islands from there.

Hassle Factor: Low–high, depending on the island and your home airport.

On the Ground: You can find taxis at the airports, and most resorts provide pickup service as well. Taxi fares are fairly reasonable on Provo and Grand Turk; on the smaller islands transfers can cost more since gas is much more expensive.

Getting Around the Islands: If you are staying on Provo, you'll probably want a car, at least for a couple of days. On Grand Turk, you can rent a car, but you probably won't need to.

Marks of the country's colonial past can be found in the wooden-and-stone, Bermudian-style clapboard houses—often wrapped in deep-red bougainvillea—that line the streets on the quiet islands of Grand Turk, Salt Cay, and South Caicos. Donkeys roam free in and around the salt ponds, which are a legacy from a time when residents of these island communities worked hard as both slaves and then laborers to rake salt (then known as "white gold") bound for the United States and Canada. In Salt Cay the remains of wooden windmills are now home to large osprey nests. In Grand Turk and South Caicos, the crystal-edge tidal ponds are regularly visited by flocks of rose-pink flamingos hungry for the shrimp to be found in the shallow, briny waters.

In all, only 45,000 people live in the Turks and Caicos Islands; more than half are "Belongers," the term for the native population, mainly descended from African and Bermudian slaves who settled here beginning in the 1600s. The majority of residents work in tourism, fishing, and offshore finance, as the country is a tax haven. Indeed, for residents and visitors, life in "TCI" is anything but taxing. But even though most visitors come to do nothing—a specialty in the islands—it does not mean there's nothing to do.

PLANNING

WHEN TO GO

High season in Turks and Caicos runs roughly from January through April, with the usual extra-high rates during the Christmas and New Year's holiday period. Several hotels on Provo offer shoulder-season rates at the end of April and May. During the off-season, rates are reduced substantially, as much as 40%. With bad world economies, you can find specials even during peak seasons or call resorts directly to negotiate.

GETTING HERE AND AROUND

AIR TRAVEL

You can fly nonstop from Atlanta (Delta), Boston (American and JetBlue), Charlotte (US Airways), Miami (American), New York–JFK (American and JetBlue), Newark–EWR (United), and Philadelphia (US Airways).

Although carriers and schedules can vary seasonally, there are many nonstop and connecting flights to Providenciales from several U.S. cities on American, Delta, JetBlue, and US Airways. There are also flights from other parts of the Caribbean on Air Turks & Caicos; this airline also flies to some of the smaller islands in the chain from Provo. There are also flights from Nassau on Bahamas Air, to Canadian cities on WestJet and Air Canada, and to London on British Airways.

Airports: The main gateways into the Turks and Caicos Islands are Providenciales International Airport (PLS) and Grand Turk International Airport (GDT). For private planes, Provo Air Center is a full-service FBO (Fixed Base Operator) offering refueling, maintenance, and short-term storage, as well as on-site customs and immigration clearance, a lounge, and concierge services. There are smaller airports on Grand Turk (GDT), North Caicos (NCS), South Caicos (XSC), and Salt Cay (SLX). Even if you are going on to other islands in the chain, you will probably stop in Provo first for customs, then take a domestic flight from there.

Airline Contacts Air Turks & Caicos ☎ 649/941–5481 ⊕ www. airturksandcaicos.com. **American Airlines** ☎ 649/946–4948, 800/433–7300 ⊕ www.aa.com. **Bahamas Air** ☎ 800/222–4262 ⊕ up.bahamasair.com. **Caicos Express** ☎ 649/941–5730 ⊕ caicosexpressairways.com. **Delta** ☎ 800/241–4141 ⊕ www.delta.com. **JetBlue** ☎ 800/538–2583 ⊕ www.jetblue.com. **United Airlines** ☎ 800/864–8331 ⊕ www.united.com. **US Airways** ☎ 800/438–4322 ⊕ usairways.com.

Airport Contacts Turks & Caicos Islands Airport Authority. The TCIAA website has a schedule of all flights coming into and out of the islands, along with real-time delay information. ⊕ www.tciairports.com.

BOAT AND FERRY TRAVEL

Despite the islands' relative proximity, ferry service is limited in the Turks and Caicos. You can take a ferry from Provo to North Caicos and South Caicos and from Grand Turk to Salt Cay and, if you're willing to spend the night, to South Caicos.

Contacts Caribbean Cruisin' ⊠ Walkin Marina, Leeward, Providenciales ☎ 649/946–5406, 649/231–4191 ⊕ www.tciferry.com; now offers daily service to South Caicos. **Salt Cay Ferry** ⊠ Salt Cay ☎ 649/244–1407 ⊕ www.turksandcaicoswhalewatching.com.

CAR TRAVEL

Driving here is on the left side of the road, British-style; when pulling out into traffic, remember to look to your right. Give way to anyone entering a roundabout, as roundabouts are still a relatively new concept in the Turks and Caicos; stop even if you are on what appears to be the primary road. The maximum speed is 40 mph (64 kph), 20 mph (30 kph) through settlements; speed limits, as well as the use of seat belts, are enforced.

If you are staying on Provo, you may find it useful to have a car since the island is so large and the resorts are so far-flung, if only for a few days of exploring or to get away from your hotel for dinner. On Grand Turk, you can rent a car, but you probably won't need to. Car- and jeep-rental rates average $39 to $80 per day on Provo, plus a $15 surcharge per rental as a government tax. Reserve well ahead of time during the peak winter season. Most agencies offer free mileage and airport pickup service. Avis and Budget have offices on the islands. You might also try local Provo agencies such as Grace Bay Car Rentals, Rent a Buggy, Tropical Auto Rentals, and Caicos Wheels—the latter rents scooters, colorful ATVs, cars, and even cell phones. Pelican Car Rentals is on North Caicos, as well as a number of other operators who meet the ferries when they arrive at Sandy Point.

Contacts Avis ⊠ *Airport, Providenciales* ☎ *649/946–4705, 649/941–7557, 649/946–8570* ⊕ *www.avis.tc.* **Budget** ⊠ *Airport, Providenciales* ☎ *649/946–4079* ⊕ *www.budget.com.* **Caicos Wheels** ⊠ *Grace Bay Court, Grace Bay Rd., Grace Bay, Providenciales* ☎ *649/242–6592, 649/946–8302* ⊕ *www.CaicosWheels.com.* **Grace Bay Car Rentals** ⊠ *Grace Bay Plaza, Grace Bay Rd., Grace Bay, Providenciales* ☎ *649/941–8500* ⊕ *www.gracebaycarrentals.com.* **Island Auto Rentals** ⊠ *Carnival Cruise Center, Grand Turk* ☎ *649/232–0933, 649/231–4214, 649/926–2042.* **Pelican Car Rentals** ⊠ *North Caicos* ☎ *649/241–8275.* **Rent a Buggy** ⊠ *1081 Leeward Hwy., Leeward, Providenciales* ☎ *649/946–4158, 649/231–6161* ⊕ *www.rentabuggy.tc* ☞ *Jeep rentals.* **Scooter Bob's** ⊠ *Turtle Cove, Providenciales* ☎ *649/946–4684* ⊕ *www.scooterbobstci.com.* **Tropical Auto Rentals** ⊠ *Tropicana Plaza, Leeward Hwy., Leeward, Providenciales* ☎ *649/946–5300* ⊕ *www.tropicalautorentaltci.com.*

TAXI TRAVEL

You can find taxis at the airports and the ferry dock on North Caicos, and most resorts have their own pickup service. A trip via taxi between Provo's airport and most major hotels runs about $12 per person. On Grand Turk a trip from the airport to Cockburn Town is about $8; it's $8 to $15 to hotels outside town on Grand Turk. Transfers usually cost more on the smaller islands, where gas is much more expensive. Taxis (actually large vans) in Providenciales are metered, and rates are regulated by the government at $2 per person per mile traveled. In the family islands, taxis may not be metered, so it's usually best to try to negotiate a cost for your trip in advance. On Grand Turk and South Caicos, it's useful to make advance arrangements with your hotel for an airport pickup.

ESSENTIALS

Banks and Exchange Services The official currency on the islands is U.S. dollars. On Provo, there are ATMs at all bank branches (Scotiabank and First Caribbean), at the Graceway IGA Supermarket Gourmet, and at Ports of Call shopping center. There are also Scotiabank and First Caribbean branches on Grand Turk. It's useful to have cash on hand when you visit the other islands because not everyone accepts credit cards.

Electricity Current is suitable for all U.S. appliances (120/240 volts, 60 Hz).

Guided Tours Big Blue Unlimited's educational ecotours include three-hour kayak trips and other guided journeys around the family islands. Its Coastal Ecology and Wildlife tour is a kayak adventure through red mangroves to bird habitats, rock iguana hideaways, and natural fish nurseries. The North Caicos Mountain Bike Eco Tour gets you on a bike to explore the island, the plantation ruins, the inland lakes, and a flamingo pond with a stop-off at Susan Butterfield's home for lunch. Package costs range from $85 to $225 per person. For an exciting overview of Provo, try an air tour with TCI Helicopters.

WHERE WHEN HOW

Check out ⊕ *www.wherewhenhow.com*, a terrific source with links to places to stay, restaurants, excursions, and transportation. You can pick up the printed version of the magazine all around the island.

Contacts **Big Blue Unlimited** ✉ *Leeward Marina, Leeward, Providenciales* ☎ *649/946–5034, 649/231–6455* ⊕ *www.bigblue.tc.* **TCI Helicopters.** Aerial tours of Providenciales are available for $195–$385 per person, depending on time in the air. ✉ *Provo Air Centre, Providenciales* ☎ *649/941–5079, 649/432–4354* ⊕ *www.tcihelicopters.tc.*

Passport Requirements A valid passport is required to fly to the Turks and Caicos. Everyone must have an ongoing or return ticket.

Phones The country code for the Turks and Caicos is 649. To call the Turks and Caicos from the United States, dial 1 plus the 10-digit number, which includes 649. Be aware that this is an international call. Calls from the islands are expensive, and many hotels add steep surcharges for long distance.

Taxes The departure tax is $60 and is usually included in the cost of your airline ticket. If not, it's payable only in cash or traveler's checks. Restaurants and hotels add an 11% government tax. Hotels also typically add 11% to 15% for service.

ACCOMMODATIONS

The Turks and Caicos can be a fairly expensive destination. Most hotels on Providenciales are pricey, but there are some moderately priced options; most accommodations are condo-style, but not all resorts are family-friendly. You'll find several upscale properties on the outer islands—including the famous Parrot Cay—but the majority of places are smaller inns. What you give up in luxury, however, you gain back tenfold in island charm. Though the smaller islands are relatively isolated, that's partly what makes them so attractive in the first place.

Resorts: Most of the resorts on Provo are upscale; many are condo-style, so at least you will have a well-furnished kitchen for breakfast and a few quick lunches. There are two all-inclusive resorts on Provo. A handful of other luxury resorts are on the smaller islands. Many resorts are closed from one to six weeks a year, depending on economics, the hurricane season, and employee vacations. Some resorts may also use slow periods (usually October) to refurbish, so ask questions when booking, particularly if you're booking in the fall.

Small Inns: Aside from the exclusive, luxury resorts, most of the places on the outlying islands are smaller, modest inns with relatively few amenities. Some are devoted to diving.

Villas and Condos: Villas and condos are plentiful, particularly on Provo, and usually represent a good value for families. However, you need to plan a few months in advance to get one of the better choices, unless you want to stay in a more developed condo complex.

HOTEL AND RESTAURANT PRICES

Prices in the restaurant reviews are the average cost of a main course at dinner or, if dinner is not served, at lunch; taxes and service charges are generally included. Prices in the hotel reviews are the lowest cost of a standard double room in high season, excluding taxes, service charges, and meal plans (except at all-inclusives). Prices for rentals are the lowest per-night cost for a one-bedroom unit in high season.

For expanded lodging reviews and current deals, visit Fodors.com.

VISITOR INFORMATION

The tourist offices on Grand Turk and Providenciales are open daily from 9 to 5.

Contacts Turks & Caicos Reservations. On-island service handles reservations for hotels, resorts, villas, restaurants, and more. Locals know. ⊠ *Providenciales* ☎ *877/302–4553, 649/941–8988* ⊕ *www.turksandcaicosreservations.tc.*

WEDDINGS

The residency requirement is 24 hours, after which you can apply for a marriage license to the registrar in Grand Turk. You must present a passport, original birth certificate, and proof of current marital status, as well as a letter stating both parties' occupations, ages, addresses, and fathers' full names. No blood tests are required. The license fee is $50.

Nila Destinations Wedding Planning ☎ *649/231–3986* ⊕ *www.niladestinations.com.*

PROVIDENCIALES

Passengers typically become silent when their plane starts its descent, mesmerized by the shallow, crystal clear turquoise waters of Chalk Sound National Park. This island, nicknamed Provo, was once called Blue Hills after the name of its first settlement. Just south of the airport and downtown area, Blue Hills is the closest thing you can get to a more typical Caicos island settlement on what's now the most developed of the islands in the chain. Most of the modern resorts, exquisite spas, water-sports operators, shops, business plazas, restaurants, bars, cafés, and the championship golf course are on or close by the 12-mile (18-km) stretch of Grace Bay beach. In spite of the ever-increasing number of taller and grander condominium resorts, it's still possible to find deserted stretches on the ivory-white shoreline. For guaranteed seclusion, rent a car and go explore the southern shores and western tip of the island, or set sail for a private island getaway on one of the many deserted cays nearby.

Progress and beauty come at a price: with plenty of new visitors arriving each year, the country's charms are no longer a secret, but don't worry—you'll still enjoy the gorgeous beaches and wonderful dinners. Although you may start to believe that every road leads to a big resort development, there are, happily, plenty of sections of beach where you can escape the din.

Although you may be kept quite content enjoying the beachscape and top-notch amenities of Provo itself, it's also a great starting point for island-hopping tours by sea or by air as well as fishing and diving trips. Resurfaced roads should help you get around and make the most of the main tourism and sightseeing spots.

EXPLORING

WORTH NOTING

FAMILY **Caicos Conch Farm.** More than 3 million conchs are farmed at this commercial operation on the northeast tip of Provo. It's a popular tourist attraction, too, with guided tours and a small gift shop selling conch-related souvenirs, jewelry, and freshwater pearls. You can even meet Jerry and Sally, the resident conchs that are brought out on demand. Fish farming is also part of the operation. ⊠ *Leeward-Going-Through, Leeward, Providenciales* ☏ *649/946–5330* ⊕ *www.caicosconchfarm. net/* 🎫 *$12* ⊙ *Weekdays 9–4, Sat. 9–2:30.*

Cheshire Hall. Standing eerily just west of downtown Provo are the remains of a circa-1700 cotton plantation owned by the Loyalist Thomas Stubbs. A trail weaves through the ruins, where a few interpretive signs tell the story of the island's doomed cotton industry, with little information about the plantation itself. A variety of local plants are also identified. The lack of context can be disappointing for history buffs; a visit to North Caicos Wades Green plantation or the Turks & Caicos National Museum could well prove a better fit. ⊠ *Leeward Hwy., behind Ace Hardware, Downtown, Providenciales* ☏ *649/941–5710 for National Trust* ⊕ *www.tcinationaltrust.com* 🎫 *$5* ⊙ *Weekdays 8:30–4:30, Sat. 9–1 (guided tour required).*

FAMILY **Sapodilla Hill.** On this cliff overlooking the secluded Sapodilla Bay, you can discover rocks carved with the names of shipwrecked sailors and dignitaries from TCI's maritime and colonial past. There are carvings on the rocks that some claim are secret codes and maps to hidden treasures; many have tried in vain to find these treasures. The hill is known by two other names, Osprey Rock and Splitting Rock. The less adventurous can see molds of the carvings at Provo's International Airport. It's best to go by boat with Captain Bill's Adventures, as cars in the parking area are occasionally broken into. ⊠ *Off South Dock Rd., west of South Dock, Chalk Sound, Providenciales.*

BEACHES

All the beaches of Turks and Caicos have bright white sand that's soft like baby powder. An added bonus is that no matter how hot the sun gets, your feet never burn. The sand is soft and clean, even in the water, so there is no fear of stepping on rocks or corals. Even the beach areas with corals for snorkeling have clear, clean sand for entry until you reach them.

Fodor's Choice ★ **Grace Bay.** The 12-mile (18-km) sweeping stretch of ivory-white, powder-soft sand on Provo's north coast is simply breathtaking. It's home to migrating starfish as well as shallow snorkeling trails. The majority of Provo's beachfront resorts are along this shore, and it's the primary reason the Turks and Caicos is a world-class destination. **Amenities:** food and drink; parking (free); water sports. **Best for:** sunset; swimming; walking. ⊠ *Grace Bay Rd., along north shore, Grace Bay, Providenciales.*

Fodor's Choice ★ **Half Moon Bay.** This natural ribbon of sand links two uninhabited cays; it's only inches above the sparkling turquoise waters and one of the most gorgeous beaches on the island. There are limestone cliffs to explore as well as small, sandy coves; there's even a small wreck offshore for snorkeling. It's only a short boat ride away from Provo, and most of the island's tour companies run excursions here or simply offer a beach drop-off. These companies include Silverdeep and Caicos Dream Tours (⇨ *Boating and Sailing, in Sports and Activities*). **Amenities:** none. **Best for:** solitude; snorkeling; swimming; walking. ⊠ *Between Pine Cay and Little Water Cay, Providenciales* ⊕ *Accessible only by boat, 15 min from Leeward Marina.*

Lower Bight Beach. Lower Bight Beach is often confused with Grace Bay Beach because it seems to blend right into it. Although the beach is gorgeous, it gets rocky here. It also has the best off-the-beach snorkeling—not just in Provo, but possibly the Caribbean. Thursday evening "fish fries" offer local food and music. **Amenities:** food and drink; parking (free). **Best for:** snorkeling; walking. ⊠ *Lower Bight Rd., The Bight, Providenciales.*

Sapodilla Bay. The best of the many secluded beaches and pristine sands around Provo can be found at this peaceful quarter-mile cove protected by Sapodilla Hill. The soft strand here is lapped by calm waves, and yachts and small boats move with the gentle tide. During low tide, little sandbar "islands" form—they're great for a beach chair. **Amenities:** parking (free). **Best for:** walking. ⊠ *End of South Dock Rd., North of South Dock, Chalk Sound, Providenciales* ✛ *From Leeward Hwy. take roundabout #6 toward Five Cays (there's no marking but there is a First Caribbean Bank in the corner). Follow until almost end, past small police station. Take right at Chalk Sound Rd. First dirt road on left leads to small parking area.*

26

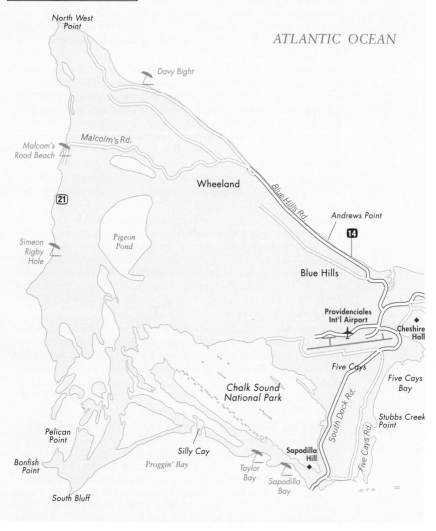

Providenciales

North West
Point

ATLANTIC OCEAN

Davy Bight

Malcom's Rd.

Malcom's
Road Beach

[21]

Wheeland

Blue Hills Rd.

Andrews Point

[14]

Simeon
Rigby
Hole

Pigeon
Pond

Blue Hills

Providenciales
Int'l Airport

Cheshire
Hall

Five Cays

Five Cays
Bay

Chalk Sound
National Park

South Dock Rd.

Stubbs Creek
Point

Pelican
Point

Silly Cay

Five Cays Rd.

Sapodilla
Hill

Bonfish
Point

Proggin' Bay

Taylor
Bay

Sapodilla
Bay

South Bluff

Water Cay

Little Water Cay

Donna Cay

Half Moon Bay

Mangrove Cay

Crist Point

13 **17** **18**

Leeward

Caicos
◆ Conch Farm

7 **16** **19**

Provo Golf & Country Club

Princess Alexandra National Marine Park

12 **13**

11 **15**

5 **10** **6** **12**

Leeward Hwy.

9 **14**

Stubbs Cove

Thompson Cove

Long Point

4 **5** **8**

The Bight

8

Long Bay

Grace Bay

6

9

Grace Bay

7

Long Bay Hills

1 **2** **1**

2 **4**

10

3

Leeward Hwy.

Richmond Hills

The Bight

Juba Point Salina

Turks Island Passage

3

Discovery Bay

Turtle Tail Dr.

Juba Point

Long Bay Hwy.

20

Cooper Jack Bight

Five Little Cays

Cooper Jack Point

0   2miles

0   2 km

WHERE TO EAT

Whichever Provo restaurant you eat at (and there are more than 50), you'll be able to spot the islands' own influence in fresh seafood specials, colorful presentations, and a tangy dose of spice. Some restaurants close during the slow season (late August through late October), with the exact dates fluctuating yearly.

Pick up a free copy of *Where When How's Dining Guide*, which you will find all over the island; it has menus, websites, and pictures of all the restaurants.

GRACE BAY

$$$$
MEDITERRANEAN

✕ **Anacaona.** At Grace Bay Club, this thatch-roofed restaurant has the best setting in the Turks and Caicos, and perhaps in the entire Caribbean. Despite its elite clientele and high prices, the restaurant continues to offer a memorable dining experience minus any formality and attitude (and minus the air-conditioning). That said, children under 12 are not allowed, and long pants and collared shirts are required for men. Oil lamps on the tables, gently revolving ceiling fans, and the murmur of the trade winds add to the Edenic environment. The entrancing ocean views and the careful service make this an ideal choice when you want to be pampered. The kitchen uses the island's bountiful seafood and fresh produce to craft healthy, Mediterranean-influenced cuisine. It's a good thing the setting is amazing, though; the portions are tiny for what you pay. $ *Average main: $40* ⊠ *Grace Bay Club, Grace Bay Circle Rd., Grace Bay, Providenciales* ☎ *649/946–5050* ⊕ *www.gracebayresorts.com/gracebayclub* ⚄ *Reservations essential* ⊘ *Closed Sept. No lunch.*

$$$$
INTERNATIONAL
FAMILY
Fodor'sChoice
★

✕ **Bay Bistro.** You simply can't eat any closer to the beach than here, the only restaurant in all of Provo to be built directly on the sand. You dine on a covered porch (or on one of three individual platforms) surrounded by palm trees and the sound of lapping waves. The spring-roll appetizer is delicious, and the oven-roasted chicken is the best on the island. At the very popular weekend brunch, which includes such favorites as eggs Benedict with mimosas (included), lines can be long if you don't have a reservation. Around the time of the full moon, ask about the memorable beach barbecue: all-you-can-eat ribs, pig roast, and bonfire on the sand. $ *Average main: $31* ⊠ *Sibonné Beach Hotel, Princess Dr., Grace Bay, Providenciales* ☎ *649/946–5396* ⊕ *sibonne. com/grace-bay-bistro* ⚄ *Reservations essential.*

$$$
ITALIAN

✕ **Caicos Café.** At what's probably the most popular restaurant with locals, the island dishes come with an Italian twist. The bruschetta that everyone gets at the start of the meal is delicious enough that you may ask for seconds, and the bread is baked fresh every day at the bakery next door. Blackened fish and jerk chicken on top of pasta are popular, but we think that ravioli with cream sauce is the tastiest dish. On windy nights, the inland setting offers protection from the breezes. Be sure to wear bug spray at night. $ *Average main: $30* ⊠ *Caicos Café Plaza, Grace Bay Rd., Grace Bay, Providenciales* ☎ *649/946–5278* ⚄ *caicoscafe@tciway.tc* ⊘ *Closed Sun.*

$$$$ INTERNATIONAL Fodor's Choice ★

🍴 **Coco Bistro.** With tables under palm trees, Coco Bistro has a divine setting, and the food is just as good. Though not directly on the beach, the location under the tropical tree grove still reminds you that you are on vacation. Main courses are complemented by both French flourishes (served au poivre, for example) and West Indian (such as with mango chutney) and are accompanied by fried plantains and mango slaw to maintain a Caribbean flair. Consider conch soup, soft-shell-crab tempura, and sun-dried tomato pasta from the internationally influenced menu. Do not miss this restaurant, it is the best of the best on the island. **TIP→ Make reservations at least 1 week ahead during nonpeak season, 2 to 3 weeks ahead in peak season, as this is the most popular restaurant on island.** [$] *Average main: $40* ✉ *Grace Bay Rd., Grace Bay, Providenciales* ☎ *649/946–5369* 🌐 *www.CocoBistro.tc* ✍ *Reservations essential* 🕒 *Closed Mon. No lunch.*

$$$$ INTERNATIONAL Fodor's Choice ★

🍴 **Coyaba Restaurant.** Directly behind Grace Bay Club at Caribbean Paradise Inn, this posh restaurant is in a palm-fringed setting. The nostalgic favorites here are served with tempting twists in conversation-piece crockery. Chef Paul Newman uses his culinary expertise for the daily-changing main courses, which include exquisitely presented dishes such as crispy, whole, yellow snapper fried in Thai spices. One standout is lobster Thermidor in a Dijon-mushroom cream sauce. You may want to try several different appetizers instead of an entrée for dinner; guava-and-tamarind barbecue ribs and coconut-shrimp tempura are two good choices if you go that route. If you enjoy creative menus, this is the place for you. Coyoba keeps the resident expat crowd happy with traditional favorites such as lemon meringue pie, albeit with his own tropical twist. Don't skip dessert; Paul makes incredible chocolate fondant. [$] *Average main: $34* ✉ *Caribbean Paradise Inn, Bonaventure Crescent, off Grace Bay Rd., Grace Bay, Providenciales* ☎ *649/946–5186* 🌐 *www.coyabarestaurant.com* ✍ *Reservations essential* 🕒 *Closed Tues. and Sept. and Oct.*

$$$ AMERICAN

🍴 **Fairways Bar & Grill.** New management at Fairways has transformed what once was a steak house into a more casual bar and grill that draws locals as well as golfers and tourists. Chef Paul Quinn was raised in Dublin, Ireland, and brings his international background to island fare. [$] *Average main: $15* ✉ *Provo Golf Club, Grace Bay* ☎ *649/946–5833* 🌐 *www.provogolfclub.com.*

$$$$ INTERNATIONAL

🍴 **Grace's Cottage.** At one of the prettiest dining settings on Provo, the tables are artfully set under wrought-iron cottage-style gazebos and around the wraparound verandah, which skirts the gingerbread-covered main building. The tangy and exciting entrées may include lobster lasagna with diced veggies or melt-in-your-mouth grilled beef tenderloin with truffle fries. The portions are small, but the quality is high. You might want to end with the mango-infused cheesecake, because after all you're at the beach. Service is impeccable (ladies are given a small stool so that their purses do not touch the ground). On Tuesday night, live music adds to the good vibes. [$] *Average main: $40* ✉ *Point Grace, off Grace Bay Rd., Grace Bay, Providenciales* ☎ *649/946–5096* 🌐 *www.pointgrace.com* ✍ *Reservations essential* 🕒 *No lunch.*

$$$ ✕**Hemingway's.** The casual and gorgeous setting, with a patio and deck
ECLECTIC   offering views of Grace Bay, makes this one of the most popular tourist
restaurants. At lunch don't miss the best fish tacos with mango chutney.
For dinner there is an excellent kids' menu and something for everyone,
including vegetarians. Order the popular "Old Man of the Sea," which
features the freshest fish of the day. It's known for great sauces such as
the wine reduction for the filet mignon, the creole for fish dishes, and
a delicious curry for chicken. If you're on a budget, go right before
6 pm, when you can still order the less expensive lunch menu items. On
Monday NaDa sings while you dine; Thursday and Friday night there's
additional live music that adds to the ambience. $ *Average main: $25*
✉ *The Sands at Grace Bay, Grace Bay Rd., Grace Bay, Providenciales*
☎ *649/946–8408* ⊕ *www.thesandstci.com.*

$$$$ ✕**Stelle.** At Stelle, Chef Matthew Doerner serves modern Mediterranean
MODERN ITALIAN   cuisine with island touches, including local conch, grouper, and spiny
lobster. You can choose either indoor dining or outdoor seating over-
looking the pool at Gansevoort resort. Side dishes cost extra for the
meat, poultry, and seafood entrées, but you can also get pasta dishes.
There are interesting items among the small plates, such as charcute-
rie, peppered beef carpaccio, and conch ceviche. $ *Average main: $37*
✉ *Gansevoort Resort, Grace Bay Beach, Providenciales* ☎ *649/941–*
7555 ⊕ *www.gansevoorttc.com.*

TURTLE COVE

$ ✕**Angela's Top o' the Cove New York Style Delicatessen.** Order deli sand-
DELI   wiches, salads, enticingly rich desserts, and freshly baked pastries at
this island institution on Leeward Highway, just south of Turtle Cove.
The location's not close to where most tourists stay, but it's worth
the drive. From the deli case you can buy the fixings for a picnic;
the shelves are stocked with a broad selection of fancy foodstuffs,
as well as beer and wine. It's open at 6:30 am for a busy trade in
coffees and cappuccinos. There's even a cheese steak comparable to
what you get in Philly. $ *Average main: $9* ✉ *Leeward Hwy., Turtle*
Cove, Providenciales ☎ *649/946–4694* ⊕ *www.provo.net/topothecove*
☽ *No dinner.*

$$$$ ✕**Magnolia Wine Bar and Restaurant.** The hands-on owners here, Gianni
ECLECTIC   and Tracey Caporuscio, make success seem simple. Expect well-prepared,
uncomplicated dishes from all over. You can construct an excellent meal
from the outstanding appetizers, which might include spring rolls and a
grilled-vegetable-and-fresh-mozzarella stack. Finish your meal with the
mouthwatering molten chocolate cake. The atmosphere is romantic,
the presentations are attractive, and the service is careful. It's easy to
see why the Caporuscios have a loyal following. The adjoining wine
bar includes a handpicked list of specialty wines, which can be ordered
by the glass. The marine setting is a great place to watch the sunset.
$ *Average main: $35* ✉ *Miramar Resort, Lower Bight Rd., Turtle Cove,*
Providenciales ☎ *649/941–5108* ⊕ *www.magnoliaprovo.com* ☽ *Closed*
Mon. No lunch.

$$$ ✕**Tiki Hut.** From a location overlooking the marina, the ever-popular
AMERICAN   Tiki Hut serves consistently tasty, value-priced meals in a fun atmo-
FAMILY   sphere. Locals take advantage of the Wednesday night chicken-and-rib

special, and the lively bar is a good place to sample local Turks Head brew. There's a special family-style menu (the best kids' menu in Provo) and kids' seating. Don't miss pizzas made with the signature white sauce, or the jerk wings, coated in a secret barbecue sauce and then grilled—they're out of this world. The restaurant can be busy, with long waits for a table, and you can reserve only with five people or more. $ *Average main: $20* ✉ *Turtle Cove Marina, Suzy Turn, Turtle Cove, Providenciales* ☎ *649/941–5341* ⊕ *tikihut.tc.*

ELSEWHERE ON PROVIDENCIALES

$$ ✕ **Da Conch Shack.** An institution in Provo for many years, this brightly
CARIBBEAN colored beach shack is justifiably famous for its conch and seafood. The conch is fished fresh out of the shallows and broiled, spiced, cracked, or fried to absolute perfection. This is the freshest conch anywhere on the island, as the staff dive for it only after you've placed your order, but if you don't like seafood, there's also chicken. Go on a Tuesday night, when jerk chicken, peas and rice, and slaw are only $10.99, or a Wednesday night when there's live music on the sand. $ *Average main: $15* ✉ *Blue Hills Rd., Blue Hills, Providenciales* ☎ *649/946–8877* ⊕ *www.conchshack.tc.*

26

WHERE TO STAY

Most of the resorts on Providenciales are on Grace Bay, but a few are more isolated or even off the beach.

PRIVATE VILLA RENTALS

On Provo you can rent a self-catering apartment or a private house. For the best villa selection, make your reservations three to six months in advance, or you may not get your first choice. Most villas can be rented on multiple villa-rental sites, which act as booking agents, and most have property managers or owners on-island to assist you.

Rental Contacts Coldwell Banker TCI. The agents at Coldwell Banker list some of the most beautiful vacation homes in Provo. ☎ *649/946–4969* ⊕ *www.coldwellbankertci.com.* **Prestigious Properties.** Modest to magnificent condos and houses in the Leeward, Grace Bay, and Turtle Cove areas of Providenciales are available from this company. ☎ *649/946–4379* ⊕ *www.prestigiousproperties.com.* **T.C. Safari.** This company manages numerous properties around Provo. ☎ *649/941–5043, 904/491–1415* ⊕ *www.tcsafari.tc.*

GRACE BAY

$$ 🏨 **The Alexandra Resort.** Situated on the most popular stretch of Grace
RESORT Bay Beach, the Alexandra is within walking distance of shops, Coral
FAMILY Garden's snorkeling, and excellent restaurants. **Pros:** luxury for (somewhat) less, with lots of good amenities. **Cons:** some rooms have only queen beds, not kings. $ *Rooms from: $325* ✉ *Princess Dr., Grace Bay, Providenciales* ☎ *649/946–5807, 800/704–9424* ⊕ *www.alexandraresort.com* ⇆ *88 rooms* ❍| *No meals.*

$$$$ ALL-INCLUSIVE FAMILY Fodor's Choice ★ 🏨 **Beaches Turks & Caicos Resort Villages & Spa.** The largest resort in the Turks and Caicos Islands can satisfy families who might be just as eager to spend some time apart as together, and a major renovation and expansion in fall 2013 has made it even better. **Pros:** great place for families; all-inclusive, gorgeous pools, kids love this place. **Cons:** with an all-inclusive plan you miss out on the island's other great restaurants; excursions such as catamaran trip can get crowded; very expensive. [$] *Rooms from: $884* ✉ *Lower Bight Rd., Grace Bay, Providenciales* ☎ *649/946–8000, 800/726–3257* 🌐 *www.beaches.com* 🛏 *359 rooms, 103 suites* 🍴 *All-inclusive.*

$$$$ ALL-INCLUSIVE 🏨 **Club Med Turkoise.** In contrast to the other, more tranquil Grace Bay resorts, this energetic property has a vibrant party atmosphere, nightly entertainment, and even a flying trapeze—it caters mainly to fun-loving singles and couples. **Pros:** all-inclusive; active; good value; adults only (of all ages, not just young); numerous languages spoken. **Cons:** even with some renovations, the rooms are dormlike and need updates and TLC; food just so-so. [$] *Rooms from: $554* ✉ *Grace Bay Rd., Grace Bay, Providenciales* ☎ *649/946–5500, 888/932–2582* 🌐 *www.clubmed.com* 🛏 *293 rooms* 🍴 *All-inclusive.*

$$$$ RESORT 🏨 **Gansevoort Turks + Caicos.** South Beach Miami chic meets island time at this gorgeous resort with modern, comfortable furnishings. **Pros:** service is pleasant and eager to please; gorgeous heated pool and beautiful rooms; great ambience. **Cons:** since this is one of Provo's few nightlife venues, Friday and Saturday nights can get a little lively; need transportation for shops and exploring. [$] *Rooms from: $750* ✉ *Lower Bight Rd., The Bight, Providenciales* ☎ *649/941–7555, 888/844–5986* 🌐 *www.gansevoortturksandcaicos.com* 🛏 *55 rooms, 32 suites, 4 penthouses* 🍴 *Breakfast.*

$$$$ RESORT FAMILY 🏨 **Grace Bay Club.** This stylish resort retains a loyal following because of its helpful, attentive staff and unpretentious elegance. **Pros:** gorgeous pool and restaurant lounge areas with outdoor couches, daybeds, and fire pits; all guests receive a cell phone to use on the island. **Cons:** no children allowed at Anacaona restaurant; have to stay in Estates section to get to its pool; expensive. [$] *Rooms from: $995* ✉ *Grace Bay Rd., behind Grace Bay Court, Grace Bay, Providenciales* ☎ *649/946–5050, 800/946–5757* 🌐 *www.gracebayclub.com* 🛏 *59 suites* 🍴 *Breakfast.*

$$ RENTAL 🏨 **Harbour Club Villas.** Although not on the beach, this small complex of villas is by the marina, making it a good base for scuba diving and bonefishing. **Pros:** nice value; great base for divers; personable and friendly hosts. **Cons:** need a car to get around island; not close to the better beaches; accommodations are a bit rustic. [$] *Rooms from: $255* ✉ *36 Turtle Tail Dr., Turtle Tail, Providenciales* ☎ *649/941–5748, 866/456–0210* 🌐 *www.harbourclubvillas.com* 🛏 *6 villas* 🍴 *No meals.*

$ RENTAL 🏨 **Island Club Townhouses.** If you're on a budget you won't find a place that gives you more for your money than this small condo complex. **Pros:** you can't get a better deal in Provo; centrally located so you can walk everywhere. **Cons:** the few condos for short-term rental go fast; no phones in the room; a block from the beach. [$] *Rooms from: $240* ✉ *Grace Bay Rd., Grace Bay, Providenciales* ☎ *649/946–5866, 877/211–3133* 🌐 *www.islandclubgracebay.com* 🛏 *12 2-bedroom apartments* 🍴 *No meals.*

$$$ RESORT FAMILY 🏨 **Ocean Club.** Enormous, locally painted pictures of hibiscus make a striking first impression as you enter the reception area at one of the island's most well-established condominium resorts. **Pros:** family-friendly resort with shuttles between the two shared properties; screened balconies and porches allow a respite from incessant air-conditioning. **Cons:** although clean, furniture is dated; if no car rental, you have to take the shuttle to get closer to the "hub." [$] *Rooms from: $309* ✉ *Grace Bay Rd., Grace Bay, Providenciales* ☎ *649/946–5880, 800/457–8787* 🌐 *www.oceanclubresorts.com* 🛏 *86 suites* 🍴 *No meals.*

$$$$ RESORT 🏨 **Point Grace.** Asian-influenced rooftop domes blend with Romanesque stone pillars and wide stairways in this plush resort, which offers spacious beachfront suites and romantic cottages surrounding the centerpiece: a turquoise infinity pool with perfect views of the beach. **Pros:** relaxing environment; beautiful pool. **Cons:** can be extremely quiet (there are signs reminding you around the pool). [$] *Rooms from: $656* ✉ *Grace Bay Rd., Grace Bay, Providenciales* ☎ *649/946–5096, 888/209–5582* 🌐 *www.pointgrace.com* 🛏 *23 suites, 9 cottage suites, 2 villas* ⏲ *Closed Sept.* 🍴 *Breakfast.*

$$$$ RESORT FAMILY 🏨 **Regent Palms.** High on luxury and glitz, this is a place where glamour meets the beach. **Pros:** great people-watching; lively; one of the best spas in the Caribbean, and lots of other amenities. **Cons:** in the summer, the pool bar can get hot in the sunken area; kind of formal around the pool; sky-high rates. [$] *Rooms from: $1250* ✉ *Princess Dr., Grace Bay, Providenciales* ☎ *649/946–8666, 866/630–5890* 🌐 *www.regenthotels.com* 🛏 *72 suites* 🍴 *Breakfast.*

26

$$ RESORT 🏨 **Royal West Indies Resort.** With a contemporary take on colonial architecture and the outdoor feel of a botanical garden, this unpretentious resort on Grace Bay Beach has plenty of garden-view and beachfront studios and suites for moderate self-catering budgets. **Pros:** the best bang for the buck on Provo; on one of the widest stretches of Grace Bay Beach. **Cons:** Club Med next door can be noisy. [$] *Rooms from: $310* ✉ *Bonaventure Crescent, Grace Bay, Providenciales* ☎ *649/946–5004, 800/332–4203* 🌐 *www.royalwestindies.com* 🛏 *99 suites* 🍴 *No meals.*

$$ RESORT FAMILY 🏨 **Sands at Grace Bay.** Spacious gardens and winding pools set the tone for one of Provo's most popular family resorts. **Pros:** one of the best places for families; central to shops and numerous restaurants; screened balconies and porches give an escape from incessant air-conditioning. **Cons:** the pool deck is dark wood, so keep your sandals or flip-flops handy; avoid courtyard rooms, which are not worth the price. [$] *Rooms from: $360* ✉ *Grace Bay Rd., Grace Bay, Providenciales* ☎ *649/941–5199, 877/777–2637* 🌐 *www.thesandstc.com* 🛏 *118 suites* 🍴 *No meals.*

$$$$ RESORT FAMILY Fodor's Choice ★ 🏨 **Seven Stars.** Fronting gorgeous Grace Bay beach, the tallest property on the island also sets a high mark for luxury with several buildings, an enormous heated pool, and huge in-room bathrooms—just about everything at Seven Stars is bigger and better than its competitors. **Pros:** beachside location; gorgeous inside and out; walking distance to everything in Grace Bay; terrific deck bar by the beach. **Cons:** some find the giant scale of the resort too big for the rest of the island. [$] *Rooms from: $618* ✉ *Grace Bay Rd., Grace Bay, Providenciales* ☎ *649/941–3777, 866/570–7777* 🌐 *www.sevenstarsgracebay.com* 🛏 *107 suites* 🍴 *Breakfast.*

West Bay Club

$ HOTEL 🏨 **Sibonné Beach Hotel.** Dwarfed by most of the nearby resorts, the smallest hotel on Grace Bay Beach has snug (by Provo's spacious standards) but pleasant rooms with Bermuda-style balconies and a tiny circular pool that's hardly used because the property is right on the beach. **Pros:** closest property to the beach; the island's best bargain directly on the beach. **Cons:** pool is small and dated. [$] *Rooms from: $175* ✉ *Princess Dr., Grace Bay, Providenciales* ☎ *649/946–5547, 800/528–1905* 🌐 *www.sibonne.com* 🛏 *29 rooms, 1 apartment* 🍴 *No meals.*

$$$$ RESORT 🏨 **The Somerset.** This luxury resort has the "wow" factor, starting with the architecture and ending in your luxuriously appointed suite. **Pros:** the most beautiful architecture on Provo; located in middle, so you can still walk to snorkel, still walk to shops. **Cons:** the cheapest lock-out rooms are not worth the cost—they can get noisy; service has suffered during management changes. [$] *Rooms from: $950* ✉ *Princess Dr., Grace Bay, Providenciales* ☎ *649/946–5900, 877/887–5722* 🌐 *www.thesomerset.com* 🛏 *53 suites* 🍴 *Breakfast.*

$$$$ RESORT 🏨 **The Tuscany.** This self-catering, quiet, upscale resort is the place for independent travelers to unwind around one of the prettiest pools on Provo. **Pros:** luxurious; all condos have ocean views; beautiful pool. **Cons:** no restaurant, and it's at the far end of the hub; very expensive for a self-catering resort. [$] *Rooms from: $950* ✉ *Grace Bay Rd., Grace Bay, Providenciales* ☎ *649/941–4667, 866/359–6466* 🌐 *www.thetuscanyresort.com* 🛏 *30 condos* 🍴 *No meals.*

$$$$ RENTAL 🏨 **Villa Renaissance.** Modeled after a Tuscan villa, this luxury property is self-catering and not really a full-service resort; nevertheless, you do get daily maid service, afternoon tea or coffee at the Pavilion Bar, and a weekly manager's cocktail reception. **Pros:** luxury for less; one of the

prettiest courtyards in Provo. **Cons:** the pool bar is not consistently manned; not a full-service resort. [$] *Rooms from: $760* ✉ *Ventura Dr., Grace Bay, Providenciales* ☎ *649/941–5300, 877/285–8764* 🌐 *www.villarenaissance.com* 🛏 *20 suites* 🍴 *No meals.*

$$ RESORT Fodor's Choice ★ 🏨 **West Bay Club.** One of Provo's newest resorts has a prime location on a pristine stretch of Grace Bay Beach just steps away from the best off-the-beach snorkeling. **Pros:** all rooms have a beach view; contemporary architecture makes it stand out from other resorts; amazing luxury for the price. **Cons:** you'll need transportation to go shopping and to get to the main hub. [$] *Rooms from: $365* ✉ *Lower Bight Rd., The Bight, Providenciales* ☎ *649/946–8550* 🌐 *www.thewestbayclub.com* 🛏 *46 suites* 🍴 *Breakfast.*

$$$ RESORT Fodor's Choice ★ 🏨 **Windsong Resort.** On a gorgeous beach lined with several appealing resorts, Windsong stands out for two reasons: the Sail Provo program and a magnificent pool. **Pros:** the pool is the coolest; Sail Provo; gorgeous huge bathrooms. **Cons:** studios only have a refrigerator and microwave; thinner stretch of beachfront here. [$] *Rooms from: $390* ✉ *Stubbs Rd., Lower Bight, Providenciales* ☎ *649/941–7700, 800/946–3766* 🌐 *www.windsongresort.com* 🛏 *16 studios, 30 suites* 🍴 *No meals.*

26

TURTLE COVE

$ B&B/INN 🏨 **Turtle Cove Inn.** This pleasant two-story inn is affordable and comfortable. **Pros:** very reasonable prices for Provo; nice marina views. **Cons:** not on the beach; requires a car to get around. [$] *Rooms from: $99* ✉ *Turtle Cove Marina, Turtle Cove* ☎ *649/946–4203, 800/887–0477* 🌐 *www.turtlecoveinn.com* 🛏 *28 rooms, 2 suites* 🍴 *No meals.*

ELSEWHERE ON PROVIDENCIALES

$$$$ RESORT Fodor's Choice ★ 🏨 **Amanyara.** If you seek seclusion, peace, and tranquillity in a Zen-like atmosphere—and you're ready to pay a lot for it—this is your place. **Pros:** on one of the best beaches on Provo; resort is quiet and secluded. **Cons:** isolated; far from restaurants, excursions, and other beaches; probably the most expensive place to stay in Provo. [$] *Rooms from: $1650* ✉ *Northwest Point, Providenciales* ☎ *649/941–8133* 🌐 *www.amanresorts.com* 🛏 *40 pavilions* 🍴 *No meals.*

NIGHTLIFE

Although Provo is not known for its nightlife, there are some live bands and bars worth checking out. Popular singers such as NaDa, Justice, Corey Forbes, and Quinton Dean perform at numerous restaurants and barbecue bonfires. Danny Buoy's, where you can always watch the latest game on big video screens, gets going late at night. Be sure to see if any ripsaw bands—aka rake-and-scrape—are playing while you're on island; this is one of the quintessential local music genres: it's popular at local restaurants in Blue Hills.

Late-night action can be found at Gansevoort Turks + Caicos (*see hotel review*), where DJs play until the wee hours on weekends, and Casablanca Casino, where everyone ends the night. The best time to come is wherever Daniel and Nadine are singing; this crowd-pleasing couple has developed a real following. And on Sunday, a barbecue bonfire at Seven Stars offers music while you dine on the sand.

Keep abreast of events and specials by checking **TCI eNews** (⊕ *www. tcienews.com*).

BARS AND CLUBS

Danny Buoy's. A popular Irish pub, Danny Buoy's has pool tables, darts, and big-screen TVs. It's a great place to watch sports broadcasts from all over. Different nights feature different nightlife; Tuesdays is karaoke, other nights have live music. It's open late every night. ⊠ *Grace Bay Rd., across from Carpe Diem Residences, Grace Bay, Providenciales* ☎ *649/946–5921* ⊕ *www.dannybuoys.com.*

SHOPS AND SPAS

Handwoven straw baskets and hats, polished conch-shell crafts, paintings, wood carvings, model sailboats, handmade dolls, and metalwork are crafts native to the islands and nearby Haiti. The natural surroundings have inspired local and international artists to paint, sculpt, print, craft, and photograph; most of their creations are on sale in Providenciales.

SHOPPING AREAS

There are several main shopping areas in Provo: Grace Bay has the newer **Saltmills** complex and **La Petite Place** retail plaza, the new **Regent Village**, and the original **Ports of Call** shopping village. Two markets on the beach near the Ocean Club and the Beaches Turks & Caicos Resort & Spa allow for barefoot shopping.

ART AND CRAFTS GALLERIES

ArtProvo. This is the island's largest gallery of designer wall art, but native crafts, jewelry, handblown glass, candles, and other gift items are also available. Featured artists include Trevor Morgan, from Salt Cay, and Dwight Outten. ⊠ *Regent Village, Regent St., Grace Bay, Providenciales* ☎ *649/941–4545* ⊕ *www.artprovo.tc.*

Making Waves Art Studio. At this gallery, Sara the proprietor paints turquoise scenes, often on wood that doesn't require framing—they're surprisingly affordable. She also gives group art lessons at the studio. ⊠ *Regent Village, Regent St., Grace Bay, Providenciales* ☎ *649/242–9588* ⊕ *www.makingwavesart.com.*

FOOD

After 5 Island Concierge. Sometimes you just need help before or during your trip. After 5 Island Concierge can do everything from find you a villa rental to provide grocery delivery or arrange a talented personal chef to cook during your condo or villa stay. Virtually any service you can think of is available from this company. ☎ *649/232–3483, 649/232–3370* ⊕ *www.islandconciergetc.com.*

Graceway IGA. With a large fresh-produce section, a bakery, gourmet deli, and extensive meat counter, the Provo's largest supermarket is likely to have what you're looking for. The most consistently well-stocked store on the island carries lots of known brands from the United Kingdom and North America, as well as a good selection of prepared foods, including rotisserie chicken, pizza, and potato salad. Expect prices to be much higher than at home. ⊠ *Leeward Hwy., Discovery Bay, Providenciales* ☎ *649/941–5000* ⊕ *www.gracewayiga.com.*

Island Pride. This often-overlooked supermarket carries lots of name brands, and it also has a Digicel phone store. ✉ *Town Centre Mall, Old Airport Rd., Downtown, Providenciales* ☎ 649/941–3329.

LIQUOR

Wine Cellar. Visit this store for its large selection of duty-free liquor, at very good prices. ✉ *Leeward Hwy., east of Suzie Turn Rd., Turtle Cove, Providenciales* ☎ 649/946–4536 ⊕ *www.winecellar.tc.*

SPAS

Except for Parrot Cay, Provo is the best destination in the Turks and Caicos if you are looking for a spa vacation. The spas here offer treatments with all the bells and whistles, and most get very good word of mouth. Most of Provo's high-end resorts have spas, but if you're staying at a villa, Spa Tropique will come to you.

Anani Spa at Grace Bay Club. Anani Spa at Grace Bay Club is on the Villas side of the complex; the six treatment rooms have alfresco showers, but treatments can also be performed on your balcony at Grace Bay Club facing the ocean. One of the most popular treatments is the Exotic Lime and Ginger Salt Glow; not only will it polish your skin, but the aroma it leaves on your skin is worth the treatment. ✉ *Villas at Grace Bay Club, Bonaventure Crescent, Grace Bay, Providenciales* ☎ 649/946–5050 ⊕ *www.gracebayresorts.com.*

26

Beaches Red Lane Spa. Open to nonresort guests, this spa has one hot plunge pool and one cold plunge pool to get the circulation going. During special hours, it offers kid's treatments, too. Although Beaches is an all-inclusive resort, spa treatments are an additional charge to guests. ✉ *Beaches Turks & Caicos Resort Villages & Spa, Lower Bight Rd., Grace Bay, Providenciales* ☎ 649/946–8000 ⊕ *www.beaches.com.*

Como Shambhala at Parrot Cay. Asian holistic treatments, yoga with the world's leading teachers in a stunning pavilion, and a signature health-conscious cuisine are all part of the program here. The infinity pool, Pilates studio, steam room, sauna, and outdoor Jacuzzi make you feel complete. If you're staying in Provo, you can call for reservations, but you have to pay for the boat ride to Parrot Cay. Some consider this one of the finest spas in the world, and you'd be hard-pressed to find a better one in the Turks and Caicos. ✉ *Parrot Cay Resort, Parrot Cay, Parrot Cay* ☎ 649/946–7788 ⊕ *www.comoshambhala.com.*

Regent Spa. Regent Spa is so gorgeous that it has been featured on several travel magazine covers. A reflecting pool with majestic date palms sets the scene. The signature treatment, a "Mother of Pearl Body Exfoliation," uses hand-crushed local conch shells to revitalize and soften skin. On an island with several terrific spas, the combination of a beautiful setting and treatments incorporating local ingredients makes this a standout. ✉ *Regent Palms, Princess Dr., Grace Bay, Providenciales* ☎ 649/946–8666 ⊕ *www.regenthotels.com.*

Spa Sanay. Spa Sanay recently moved into Alexandra resort, where it offers facials, massages, body treatments and nail services. There is also a line of men-only treatments. ✉ *Alexandra Resort, Grace Bay Beach, Grace Bay, Providenciales* ☎ 649/432–1092, 649/946–5807 ⊕ *www.spasanay.com.*

Spa Tropique. You pick the place, and this spa comes to you—an ideal option for those in more isolated villas who can't bear to leave their island paradise; the spa can also come to your hotel room (provided your hotel has no spa of its own). Have your treatment on your balcony, or on the beach or by the pool, which will make the treatments seem extra special. Spa Tropique's one-of-a-kind Turks Island Salt Glow incorporates local salts from Grand Turk and Salt Cay. The spa also has locations at Ocean Club West and the Sands Resort. ⊠ *Ports of Call Shopping Center, Grace Bay Rd., Grace Bay* ☎ *649/331–2400* ⊕ *www.spatropique.com.*

Teona Spa. Treatments here include the "Two Hot to Handle" couples massage, which includes a warming Boreh mask and Mediterranean hot-oil massage. Afterwards you can wind down with spice tea or a glass of wine. ⊠ *The Regent Grand Resort, Regent St., Grace Bay, Providenciales* ☎ *649/941–5051* ⊕ *www.theregentgrandresort.com.*

Thalasso Spa at Point Grace. Thalasso Spa at Point Grace has three white-washed open-air cabanas on the dunes looking out to the beach. French skin oils and the latest European techniques are incorporated in all skin treatments, along with elements of the ocean, including sea mud, seaweed, and sea salt. The setting alone, with the breezes and views of Grace Bay, is worth the stop. ⊠ *Point Grace Resort, Grace Bay Rd., Grace Bay, Providenciales* ☎ *649/946–5096* ⊕ *www.pointgrace.com.*

SPORTS AND ACTIVITIES

BOATING AND SAILING

Provo's calm, reef-protected seas combine with constant easterly trade winds for excellent sailing conditions. Several multihulled vessels offer charters with snorkeling stops, food and beverage service, and sunset vistas. Prices range from $89 per person for group trips (subject to passenger minimums) to $600 or more for private charters.

FAMILY

Fodor's Choice

★

Island Vibes. Shaun Dean makes these excursions stand out, since he grew up on these waters. If conditions are right, he'll have you snorkel the "abyss," where the reef drops 6000 feet. The sight is amazing. His boat is also the best on Provo, with a diving board on the roof as well as a bathroom. ⊠ *Turtle Cove Marina, Turtle Cove, Providenciales* ☎ *649/231–8423* ⊕ *www.islandvibestours.com.*

Sail Provo. Very popular for private charters, Sail Provo also runs 52-foot and 48-foot catamarans on scheduled half-day, full-day, sunset, and kid-friendly glow worm cruises (these are held in the first few days after full moons, when underwater creatures light up the sea's surface for several days). ⊠ *Windsong Resort, Stubbs Rd., The Bight, Providenciales* ☎ *649/946–4783* ⊕ *www.sailprovo.com.*

Silver Deep. Silverdeep sailing trips include time for snorkeling and beachcombing at a secluded beach. If you're thinking of fishing, keep in mind that Captain Arthur Dean here is said to be among the Caribbean's finest bonefishing guides. ⊠ *Ocean Club West Plaza, Grace Bay Rd., Grace Bay, Providenciales* ☎ *649/946–5612* ⊕ *www. silverdeep.com.*

Diving with stingrays

Sun Charters. The *Atabeyra*, operated by Sun Charters, is a retired rumrunner and the choice of residents for special events. Sunset rum punch parties and glow worm excursions are its specialty. There are also regularly scheduled sunset and half-day snorkeling cruises if you don't want to do a charter. ⊠ *Leeward Marina, Leeward, Providenciales* ☎ *649/231–0624* ⊕ *www.suncharters.tc.*

Undersea Explorer. For sightseeing below the waves, try a semi-submarine, the *Undersea Explorer*, operated by Caicos Tours out of the Turtle Cove Marina. You can stay dry within the small, lower observatory as it glides along on a one-hour tour of the reef, with large viewing windows on either side. The trip costs $60–$65, with child rates available. ⊠ *Turtle Cove Marina, Turtle Cove, Providenciales* ☎ *649/231–0006* ⊕ *www.caicostours.com.*

Water Play Provo. Right on the beach, they have windsurfing, stand-up paddleboards, and kayaks for multiple day or weekly rentals. ⊠ *Ocean Club, Grace Bay Rd., Grace Bay, Providenciales* ☎ *649/231–3122* ⊕ *www.waterplayprovo.com.*

DIVING AND SNORKELING

Fodor's Choice
★ The island's many shallow reefs offer excellent and exciting snorkeling relatively close to shore. Try **Smith's Reef,** over Bridge Road east of Turtle Cove.

Scuba diving in the crystalline waters surrounding the islands ranks among the best in the Caribbean. The reef and wall drop-offs thrive with bright, unbroken coral formations and lavish numbers of fish and marine life. Mimicking the idyllic climate, waters are warm all year, averaging 76°F to 78°F in winter and 82°F to 84°F in summer. With minimal rainfall and soil runoff, visibility is usually good and frequently superb, ranging from 60 feet to more than 150 feet. An extensive system of marine national parks and boat moorings, combined with an ecoconscious mind-set among dive operators, contributes to an uncommonly pristine underwater environment.

Dive operators in Provo regularly visit sites at **Grace Bay** and **Pine Cay** for spur-and-groove coral formations and bustling reef diving. They make the longer journey to the dramatic walls at **North West Point** and **West Caicos** depending on weather conditions. Instruction from the major diving agencies is available for all levels and certifications, including Technical diving. An average one-tank dive costs $45; a two-tank dive, $90. There are also two live-aboard dive boats available for charter working out of Provo.

Big Blue Unlimited. The educational ecotours from Big Blue include three-hour kayak trips and land-focused guided journeys around the family islands. Its Coastal Ecology and Wildlife tour is a kayak adventure through red mangroves to bird habitats, rock iguana hideaways, and natural fish nurseries. The Middle Caicos Bicycle Adventure gets you on a bike to explore the island, touring limestone caves in Conch Bar with a break for lunch with the Forbes family in the village of Bambarra. A new package explores South Caicos. Packages start at $255 for adults. No children under 12 are allowed. ☒ *Leeward Marina, Marina Rd., Leeward, Providenciales* ☎ *649/946–5034, 649/231–6455* ⊕ *www.bigblueunlimited.com.*

Caicos Adventures. Run by the friendly Frenchman Fifi Kuntz, Caicos Adventures offers daily trips to West Caicos, French Cay, and Molasses Reef. The company owns several boats, including the *Lady K*, a luxury motor boat available for private charters. ☒ *Regent Village, Grace Bay Rd., Grace Bay, Providenciales* ☎ *649/941–3346* ⊕ *www.tcidiving.com.*

Fodor's Choice ★ **Caicos Dream Tours.** Caicos Dream Tours offers several snorkeling trips, including one that has you diving for conch before lunch on a gorgeous beach. The company also offers private charters. ☒ *Alexandra Resort, Princess Dr., Grace Bay, Providenciales* ☎ *649/231–7274* ⊕ *www. caicosdreamtours.com.*

Dive Provo. Dive Provo is a PADI five-star operation that runs daily one- and two-tank dives to popular Grace Bay sites as well as West Caicos. ☒ *Ports of Call, Grace Bay Rd., Grace Bay, Providenciales* ☎ *649/946–5040, 800/234–7768* ⊕ *www.diveprovo.com.*

Provo Turtle Divers. Provo Turtle Divers, which also operates out of the Ocean Club and Ocean Club West, has been on Provo since the 1970s. The staff is friendly, knowledgeable, and unpretentious. ☒ *Turtle Cove Marina, Turtle Cove, Providenciales* ☎ *649/946–4232, 800/833–1341* ⊕ *www.provoturtledivers.com.*

FISHING

The islands' fertile waters are great for angling—anything from bottom- and reef-fishing (most likely to produce plenty of bites and a large catch) to bonefishing and deep-sea fishing (among the finest in the Caribbean). Each July the Caicos Classic Catch & Release Tournament attracts anglers from across the islands and the United States, who compete to catch the biggest Atlantic blue marlin, tuna, or wahoo. For any fishing activity, you are required to purchase a $15 visitor's fishing license; operators generally

CLOSE UP

Diving the Turks and Caicos Islands

Scuba diving was the original water sport to draw visitors to the Turks and Caicos Islands in the 1970s. Aficionados are still drawn by the abundant marine life, including humpback whales in winter, sparkling clean waters, warm and calm seas, and the coral walls and reefs around the islands. Diving in the Turks and Caicos—especially off Grand Turk, South Caicos, and Salt Cay—remains among the best in the world.

Off Providenciales, dive sites are along the north shore's barrier reef. Most sites can be reached in anywhere from 10 minutes to 1½ hours. Dive sites feature spur-and-groove coral formations atop a coral-covered slope. Popular stops such as **Aquarium, Pinnacles,** and **Grouper Hole** have large schools of fish, turtles, nurse

sharks, and gray reef sharks. From the south side, dive boats go to **French Cay, West Caicos, South West Reef,** and **Northwest Point.** Known for typically calm conditions and clear water, the West Caicos Marine National Park is a favorite stop. The area has dramatic walls and marine life, including sharks, eagle rays, and octopus, with large stands of pillar coral and huge barrel sponges.

Off Grand Turk, the 7,000-foot coral wall **drop-off** is actually within swimming distance of the beach. Buoyed sites along the wall have swim-through tunnels, cascading sand chutes, imposing coral pinnacles, dizzying vertical drops, and undercuts where the wall goes beyond the vertical and fades beneath the reef.

26

furnish all equipment, drinks, and snacks. Prices range from $100 to $375, depending on the length of trip and size of boat.

Grand Slam Fishing Charters. For deep-sea fishing trips in search of marlin, sailfish, wahoo, tuna, barracuda, and shark, look up this company. ⊠ *Turtle Cove Marina, Turtle Cove, Providenciales* ☎ *649/231–4420* ⊕ *www.gsfishing.com.*

GOLF

Fodor's Choice
★

Provo Golf and Country Club. The par-72, 18-hole championship course at Provo Golf and Country Club is a combination of lush greens and fairways, rugged limestone outcroppings, and freshwater lakes. Designed by Karl Litten, it is ranked among the Caribbean's top courses. Premium golf clubs are available ⊠ *Governor's Rd., Grace Bay, Providenciales* ☎ *649/946–5991* or *877/218–9124* ⊕ *www.provogolfclub.com* ⅃ *18 holes, 6705 yards, par 72* ☞ *$185 for 18 holes, $95 for 9 holes with shared cart.*

HORSEBACK RIDING

Provo Ponies. Provo Ponies offers morning and afternoon rides for all levels. A 60-minute ride costs $75; a 90-minute ride is $90. Reservations are required, and there is a 200-pound weight limit. You can get a pick-up at your Grace Bay hotel or villa (Grace Bay area only) for an additional $10 per person, which is a good deal if you don't have a rental car. It's closed on weekends. ⚠ **If you are staying at Beaches, make your own reservations; bookings through the excursion desk are not accepted.** ⊠ *Long Bay, Providenciales* ☎ *649/946–5252, 649/241–6350* ⊕ *www.provoponies.com.*

Parrot Cay Resort

PARROT CAY

Once said to be a hideout for Calico Jack Rackham and his fellow pirates Mary Read and Anne Bonny, the 1,000-acre cay, between Fort George Cay and North Caicos, is now the site of a luxury resort.

The only way to reach Parrot Cay is by private boat or the resort's private ferry from its own dock

WHERE TO STAY

$$$$ RESORT Fodor's Choice ★ **Parrot Cay Resort.** This private paradise, on its own island, pairs tranquility with the best service in Turks and Caicos. **Pros:** impeccable service; gorgeous, secluded beach; the spa is considered one of the best in the world. **Cons:** only two restaurants on the entire island; it's expensive to get back and forth to Provo for excursions, as there is only private ferry service. [$] *Rooms from: $750* ✉ *Parrot Cay, Parrot Cay* ☎ *649/946–7788, 877/754–0726* 🌐 *www.comohotels.com/parrotcay* 🛏 *42 rooms, 4 suites, 14 villas* 🍴 *Breakfast.*

PINE CAY

15 to 20 minutes by boat from Provo.

Pine Cay's 2½-mile-long (4-km-long) beach is among the most beautiful in the archipelago. The 800-acre private island, which is in the string of small cays between Provo and North Caicos, is home to a secluded resort and almost 40 private residences. The beach alone is reason to stay here: the sand seems a little whiter, the water a little brighter than beaches on the other cays. Nonguests of the Meridian Club can make reservations for lunch, which will include the private boat transfer. Expect to pay between $100 and $150 for the day; there are themed buffets on Sunday.

WHERE TO STAY

$$$$
RESORT
Fodor's Choice
★

Meridian Club. Feeling like a private club, this resort on the prettiest beach in Turks and Caicos is *the* place to de-stress, with no phones, no TVs, no a/c, no worries. **Pros:** the finest beach in Turks and Caicos; rates include some of the best food in the Turks and Caicos as well as snorkeling trips. **Cons:** no TVs or phones, so you are really unplugged here; expensive to get back to Provo for shopping or other Provo-based excursions or activities; all this simplicity costs a great deal. $ *Rooms from: $1060* ⊠ *Pine Cay, Pine Cay* ☎ *649/946–7758, 866/746–3229* ⊕ *www.meridianclub.com* ⇄ *12 rooms, 1 cottage, 7 villas* ⊗ *Closed Aug.–Oct.* ⦿ *All meals.*

NORTH CAICOS

Thanks to abundant rainfall, this 41-square-mile (106-square-km) island is the lushest in the Turks and Caicos chain. With an estimated population of only 1,500, the expansive island allows you to get away from it all. Bird lovers can see a large flock of flamingos here, anglers can find shallow creeks full of bonefish, and history buffs can visit the ruins of a Loyalist plantation. Although there's little traffic, almost all the roads are paved, so bicycling is an excellent way to sightsee. Even though it's a quiet place, you can find some small eateries around the settlements and in Whitby, giving you a chance to try local and seafood specialties, sometimes served with homegrown okra or corn. The beaches are more natural here, and they are sometimes covered with seaweed and pine needles, as there are no major resorts to rake them daily. Nevertheless, some of these secluded, less manicured strands are breathtaking.

North Caicos is definitely rustic, especially in comparison with shiny new Provo. Accommodations are clean but fairly basic. Locals are consistently friendly, and life always seems to move slowly.

EXPLORING NORTH CAICOS

WORTH NOTING

Flamingo Pond. This is a regular nesting place for the beautiful pink birds. They tend to wander out into the middle of the pond, so bring binoculars to get a better look. ⊠ *North Caicos.*

Kew. This settlement has a school, a church, and ruins of old plantations—all set among lush tropical trees bearing limes, papayas, and custard apples. Visiting Kew will give you a better understanding of the daily life of many islanders. ⊠ *North Caicos.*

Three Mary Cays. Three small rocks within swimming distance from Whitby Beach give you some of the best secluded snorkeling in all of the Turks and Caicos. You will often find ospreys nesting here, too. This is a protection area for wildlife, so do not fish or touch any of the corals. ✉ *Off Whitby Beach, North Caicos.*

FAMILY **Wades Green.** Visitors can view well-preserved ruins of the greathouse, overseer's house, and surrounding walls of one of the most successful plantations of the Loyalist era. A lookout tower provides views for miles. Contact the National Trust for tour details. ✉ *Kew, North Caicos* ☎ *649/941–5710 for National Trust* 🌐 *www.tcimall.tc/nationaltrust* 🎟 *$5* 🕒 *Daily, by appointment only.*

WHERE TO EAT

$ AMERICAN 🍴 **Last Chance Bar and Grill.** Overlooking the calm waters of Bottle Creek, this little place makes a great stop for day-trippers going to or from Middle Caicos. In addition to making smaller items such as conch fritters and burgers, owner Howard Gibbs provides four-course meals of grouper and local lobster at reasonable prices, with the desserts made by his wife, Cheryl. [$] *Average main: $30* ✉ *Bottle Creek, North Caicos* ☎ *649/232–4141* 🌐 *www.greatbonefishing.com* 💳 *No credit cards* 🕒 *Closed Sun.*

WHERE TO STAY

$$ RENTAL 🏨 **Hollywood Beach Suites.** With seven miles of secluded beaches and few others to share them with, this property with four self-contained units is completely relaxing. **Pros:** secluded; tranquil; upscale furnishings. **Cons:** might feel a little quiet if you're after a busy vacation or active social scene. [$] *Rooms from: $341* ✉ *Hollywood Beach Dr., Whitby, North Caicos* ☎ *649/231–1020, 800/551–2256* 🌐 *www.hollywoodbeachsuites.com* 🛏 *4 suites* 🍽 *No meals.*

$$ RENTAL 🏨 **Jodo Resort.** This new villa sits on 7 acres of the leeward side of the island, giving calm waters to its 400 feet of beachfront. [$] *Rooms from: $275* ✉ *Sandy Point, North Caicos* ☎ *609/513–6363* 🌐 *www.jodoresort.com* 🛏 *1 villa* 💳 *No credit cards* 🍽 *No meals.*

$ HOTEL 🏨 **Pelican Beach Hotel.** North Caicos islanders Susan and Clifford Gardiner built this small, palmetto-fringed hotel in the 1980s on the quiet, mostly deserted Whitby Beach. **Pros:** the beach is just outside your room, linens are crisp and clean. **Cons:** location may be too remote and sleepy for some people; beach is in a natural state, meaning seaweed and pine needles. [$] *Rooms from: $165* ✉ *Whitby, North Caicos* ☎ *649/946–7112, 877/774–5486* 🌐 *www.pelicanbeach.tc* 🛏 *14 rooms, 2 suites* 🕒 *Closed Aug. 15–Sept. 15* 🍽 *Some meals.*

Local Souvenirs

What should you bring home after a fabulous vacation in the Turks and Caicos Islands? Here are a few suggestions, some of which are free.

You can bring home up to three conch shells (shells only) between October 16 and July 14. No conch shells can be taken out of the country between July 15 and October 15, a new rule to prevent overfishing. The Middle Caicos Co-op shop, in addition to its Conch Bar location, sells its local crafts at a market in front of Gourmet IGA on Grace Bay the second Saturday of each month. You'll find locally made ceramics at Art Provo and at Turks & Caicos National Trust (at Town Center Mall or next to Island Scoop Ice Cream).

There are two cultural centers, one between Ocean Club East and Club Med, and the other in front of Beaches Resort. Here you'll find batik clothing and locally made jewelry. Custom-made pieces can be ordered.

The Conch Farm sells beautiful, affordable jewelry made from conch shells and freshwater pearls.

One of the best souvenirs is the hardcover coffee-table cookbook from the Red Cross. Not only is it gorgeous, featuring recipes from all the great chefs of the Turks and Caicos, but the proceeds help the Red Cross.

If you're a dog-lover, then maybe the best free souvenir would be to adopt a potcake puppy. Dogs come with a carrier, papers, and all their shots—and one will remind you year after year of your terrific vacation.

26

MIDDLE CAICOS

At 48 square miles (124 square km) and with fewer than 300 residents, this is the largest and least developed of the inhabited islands in the Turks and Caicos chain. A limestone ridge runs to about 125 feet above sea level, creating dramatic cliffs on the north shore and a cave system farther inland. Middle Caicos has rambling trails along the coast; the **Crossing Place Trail,** maintained by the National Trust, follows the path used by the early settlers to go between the islands. Inland are quiet settlements with friendly residents.

EXPLORING MIDDLE CAICOS

FAMILY **Conch Bar Caves.** These limestone caves have eerie underground lakes and milky-white stalactites and stalagmites. Archaeologists have discovered Lucayan artifacts in the caves and the surrounding area. The caves are now inhabited only by some harmless bats. If you visit, don't worry—they don't bother visitors. It's best to get a guide. If you tour the caves, be sure to wear sturdy shoes, not sandals. ⊠ *Middle Caicos.*

WHERE TO EAT

$$$ SEAFOOD 🍴 **Mudjin Bar and Grill.** After a long wait, this restaurant at Blue Horizon Resort is finally open. The view is wonderful, as it sits overlooking the spectacular Mudjin Harbor. Daily lunches concentrate on seafood items such as lobster bites, cracked conch, and fish and chips, although there are also burgers, chicken and ribs, and some vegetarian options (rare in these parts). Dinner is by reservation only and features a choice of several daily specials. [$] *Average main: $35* ✉ *Blue Horizon Resort, Mudjin Harbour, Middle Caicos* ☎ *649/946–6141* 🌐 *www.bhresort.com* ✍ *Reservations essential* 🕒 *Closed Sun. evening.*

WHERE TO STAY

$$ HOTEL Fodor's Choice ★ 🏨 **Blue Horizon Resort.** At this property, undulating cliffs skirt one of the most dramatic beaches in the Turks and Caicos. **Pros:** breathtaking views of Mudjin Harbour from the rooms; lack of development makes you feel like you're away from it all. **Cons:** need a car to explore; probably too isolated for some; three-night minimum. [$] *Rooms from: $290* ✉ *Mudjin Harbour, Middle Caicos* ☎ *649/946–6141* 🌐 *www.bhresort.com* 🛏 *5 cottages, 2 villas* 🍽 *No meals.*

SPORTS AND ACTIVITIES

CAVE TOURS

Cardinal Arthur. Although exploring Middle Caicos on your own can be fun, a guided tour with Cardinal can illuminate the island's secret spots, from caves to the spots where flamingos flock. He can also show you the sand bars that make vacationers giddy and that can't be found by car. By skiff he can show off all the hidden beaches reached only by water, too. ☎ *649/946–6107, 649/241–0730.*

SOUTH CAICOS

This 8½-square-mile (21-square-km) island was once an important salt producer; today it's the heart of the fishing industry. Nature prevails, with long, white beaches, jagged bluffs, quiet backwater bays, and salt flats. Diving and snorkeling on the pristine wall and reefs are a treat enjoyed by only a few.

In 2008 hurricanes Hanna and Ike gave South Caicos a one-two punch. Although the island has recovered, the few dive operators that were here disappeared. The best way to dive (other than independently) is through Sea Crystal Divers from Salt Cay, which requires spending the night at Salt Cay.

The major draw for South Caicos is its excellent diving and snorkeling on the wall and reefs (with an average visibility of 100 feet). It's practically the only thing to do on South Caicos other than to lie on the lovely beaches. Several local fishermen harvest spiny lobsters for the Turks and Caicos and for export. Making up the third-largest reef in the world, the coral walls surrounding South Caicos are dramatic, dropping dramatically from 50 feet to 6,000 feet in the blink of an eye.

EXPLORING SOUTH CAICOS

At the northern end of the island are fine white-sand beaches; the south coast is great for scuba diving along the drop-off, and there's excellent snorkeling off the windward (east) coast, where large stands of elkhorn and staghorn coral shelter several varieties of small tropical fish. A huge, sunken plane broken in pieces makes an excellent site. Spiny lobster and queen conch are found in the shallow Caicos Bank to the west and are harvested for export by local processing plants. The bonefishing here is some of the best in the West Indies.

Boiling Hole. Abandoned salinas (natural salt pans) make up the center of this island—the largest, across from the downtown ballpark, receives its water directly from an underground source connected to the ocean through this "boiling" hole. ⊠ *South Caicos.*

WHERE TO EAT

Restaurant choices on South Caicos are limited, and no one takes credit cards, so bring cash. Except for the Dolphin Pub at the South Caicos Ocean & Beach Resort, the best places are operated directly out of the owners' homes. **Love's** restaurant (on Airport Road) serves a daily menu of fresh seafood priced from $8 to $15. **Darryl's** (on Stubbs Road) is another casual restaurant that offers whatever is brought in for the day; expect to pay $10 to $20. Ask around to find out when (or if) these local favorites will be open; neither has a phone.

$$ ✕ **Dolphin Grill.** The only real restaurant on the island serves casual,
ECLECTIC crowd-pleasing food: you'll find burgers, chicken, and fish. There is some Asian influence in the sauces and rice, and there are certainly Caribbean influences in the jerk sauce on the fish. At night this turns into a gathering place for guests to tell their tales about the sea, the fish that they caught, or the sea eagle ray that they spotted while diving. If you are around for lunch (most visitors to South Caicos will be scuba diving), this is your only choice. $ *Average main: $15* ⊠ *South Caicos Ocean & Beach Resort, Tucker Hill, South Caicos* ☎ *649/946–3810.*

WHERE TO STAY

$ ⌂ **South Caicos Ocean & Beach Resort.** Rustic and basic—though perfectly
HOTEL acceptable—this is your only lodging option in South Caicos at this writing. **Pros:** each room has stunning views of the Caicos Banks; the best scuba diving off South Caicos is in front of the hotel; it has the only real restaurant on the island. **Cons:** you need cash for everything but your room; not on the beach; no dive shop at the resort. $ *Rooms from: $125* ⊠ *Tucker Hill, South Caicos* ☎ *649/946–3810* ⊕ *oceanandbeachresort. com* ⇄ *24 rooms, 6 apartments* ⊘ *No meals.*

GRAND TURK

Just 7 miles (11 km) long and a little more than 1 mile (1½ km) wide, this island, the capital and seat of the Turks and Caicos government, has been a longtime favorite destination for divers eager to explore the 7,000-foot-deep pristine coral walls that drop down only 300 yards out to sea. On shore, the tiny, quiet island is home to white-sand beaches, the National Museum, and a small population of wild horses and donkeys, which leisurely meander past the white-walled courtyards, pretty churches, and bougainvillea-covered colonial inns on their daily commute into town. But things aren't entirely sleepy: a cruise-ship complex at the southern end of the island brings about 600,000 visitors per year. That said, the dock is self-contained and is about 3 miles (5 km) from the tranquil, small hotels of Cockburn Town, Pillory Beach, and the Ridge and far from most of the western-shore dive sites.

EXPLORING GRAND TURK

Pristine beaches with vistas of turquoise waters, small local settlements, historic ruins, and native flora and fauna are among the sights on Grand Turk. Fewer than 4,000 people live on this 7½-square-mile (19-square-km) island, and it's hard to get lost, as there aren't many roads.

COCKBURN TOWN

WORTH NOTING

The buildings in the colony's capital and seat of government reflect a 19th-century Bermudian style. Narrow streets are lined with low stone walls and old street lamps. The once-vital *salinas* (natural salt pans, where the sea leaves a film of salt) have been restored, and covered benches along the sluices offer shady spots for observing wading birds, including flamingos that frequent the shallows. Be sure to pick up a copy of the tourist board's *Heritage Walk* guide to discover Grand Turk's rich architecture.

Her Majesty's Prison. This prison was built in the 19th century to house runaway slaves and slaves who survived the wreck of the *Trouvadore* in 1841. After the slaves were granted freedom, the prison housed criminals and even modern-day drug runners until it closed in the 1990s. The last hanging here was in 1960. Now you can see the cells, solitary-confinement area, and exercise patio. The prison is open only when there is a cruise ship at the port. ⊠ *Pond St., Cockburn Town, Grand Turk.*

FAMILY **Turks and Caicos National Museum.** In one of the oldest stone buildings on the islands, the national museum houses the Molasses Reef wreck, the earliest shipwreck—dating to the early 1500s—discovered in the Americas. The natural-history exhibits include artifacts left by Taíno, African, North American, Bermudian, French, and Latin American settlers. The museum has a 3-D coral reef exhibit, a walk-in Lucayan cave with wooden artifacts, and a gallery dedicated to Grand Turk's little-known involvement in the Space Race (John Glenn made landfall here after being the first American to orbit the Earth). An interactive children's gallery keeps knee-high visitors "edutained." The museum

All in the Family

Belongers, as local islanders are sometimes known, from the taxi driver meeting you to the chef feeding you, are often connected. "Oh, him?" you will hear. "He my cousin!" Development has been slow here, and as a result such family connections, as well as crafts, bush medicine, ripsaw music, storytelling, and even recipes, have remained constant. But where do such traditions come from? Recently, researchers came closer to finding out. Many Belongers had claimed that their great-great-grandparents told them their forebears came directly from Africa. For decades their stories were ignored. Indeed, most experts believed that Belongers were descendants of mostly second-generation Bermudian and Caribbean slaves.

In 2005, museum researchers continued their search for a lost slave ship called *Trouvadore.* The ship, which wrecked off East Caicos in 1841, carried a cargo of 193 Africans, captured to be sold into slavery, almost all of whom miraculously

survived the wreck. As slavery had been abolished in this British territory at the time, all the Africans were found and freed in the Turks and Caicos Islands. Since there were only a few thousand inhabitants in the islands at the time, these first-generation African survivors were a significant minority (about 7% of the population then). Researchers have concluded that all the existing Belongers may be linked by blood or marriage to this one incident.

During one expedition, divers found a wrecked ship of the right time period. If these remains are *Trouvadore,* the Belongers may finally have a physical link to their past to go with their more intangible cultural traditions. So while you're in the islands, look closely at the intricately woven baskets, and listen carefully to the African rhythms in the ripsaw music and the stories you hear. They may very well be the legacy of *Trouvadore* speaking to you from the past. For more information, check out the website ⊕ *www.trouvadore.org.*

26

also claims that Grand Turk was where Columbus first landed in the New World. The most original display is a collection of messages in bottles that have washed ashore from all over the world. ⊠ *Duke St., Cockburn Town, Grand Turk* ☎ *649/946–2160* ⊕ *www.tcmuseum. org* 🖃 *$7* ⊙ *Mon.–Wed. 9 am–1 pm, Thurs. 1–5 pm, plus all cruise ship days.*

BEYOND COCKBURN TOWN

Grand Turk Lighthouse. More than 150 years ago, the lighthouse, built in the United Kingdom and transported piece by piece to the island, protected ships from wrecking on the northern reefs. Use this panoramic landmark as a starting point for a breezy cliff-top walk by following the donkey trails to the deserted eastern beach. ⊠ *Lighthouse Rd., North Ridge, Grand Turk.*

BEACHES

Governor's Beach. A beautiful crescent of powder-soft sand and shallow, calm turquoise waters front the official British governor's residence, called Waterloo, framed by tall casuarina trees that provide plenty of natural shade. To have it all to yourself, go on a day when cruise ships are not in port (but bring your own water). On days when ships are in port, the beach is lined with lounge chairs, and bars and restaurants are open. **Amenities:** parking (free); toilets. **Best for:** swimming; walking. ⊠ *Cockburn Harbour, Grand Turk.*

WHERE TO EAT

Conch in every shape and form, fresh grouper, and lobster (in season) are the favorite dishes at the laid-back restaurants that line Duke Street. Away from these more touristy areas, smaller and less expensive eateries serve chicken and ribs, curried goat, peas and rice, and other native island specialties. Prices are more expensive than in the United States, as most of the produce has to be imported.

COCKBURN TOWN

$$$
CARIBBEAN
✕ **Birdcage Restaurant.** This has become the place to be on Sunday and Wednesday nights, when a sizzling barbecue of ribs, chicken, and lobster combines with live "rake-and-scrape" music from a local group called High Tide to draw an appreciative crowd. Arrive before 8 pm to secure beachside tables and an unrestricted view of the band; the location around the Osprey pool is lovely. The rest of the week, enjoy more elegant and eclectic fare accompanied by a well-chosen wine list. $ *Average main: $24* ⊠ *Osprey Beach Hotel, Duke St., Cockburn Town, Grand Turk* ☎ *649/946–2666* ⊕ *www.ospreybeachhotel.com/dining.*

$$
PIZZA
✕ **Mookie Pookie Pizza Palace.** Local husband-and-wife team "Mookie" and "Pookie" have created a wonderful backstreet restaurant that has gained well-deserved popularity over the years as much more than a pizza place. At lunchtime, the tiny eatery is packed with locals ordering specials such as steamed beef, curried chicken, and curried goat. You can also get burgers and omelets, but stick to the specials if you want fast service, and dine in if you want to get a true taste of island living. By night, the place becomes Grand Turk's only take-out pizza place. $ *Average main: $12* ⊠ *Hospital Rd., Cockburn Town, Grand Turk* ▭ *No credit cards* ⊘ *Closed Sun.*

$$
AMERICAN
✕ **Sand Bar.** Run by two Canadian sisters, this popular beachside bar is a good value; the menu is limited to fish-and-chips, quesadillas, and similarly basic bar fare. The tented wooden terrace jutting out onto the beach provides shade during the day, making it an ideal lunch spot, but it's also a great place to watch the sunset. The service is friendly, and the local crowd often spills into the street. $ *Average main: $14* ⊠ *Duke St., Cockburn Town, Grand Turk.*

$$
SEAFOOD
✕ **Secret Garden.** Simply prepared garlic shrimp or grilled grouper are among the more popular dishes at this local favorite. Located behind Salt Raker Inn in a pretty courtyard garden, it more than lives up to its name. Friday nights feature live music by rake-and-scrape bands. $ *Average main: $17* ⊠ *Cockburn Town, Grand Turk* ☎ *649/946–2260.*

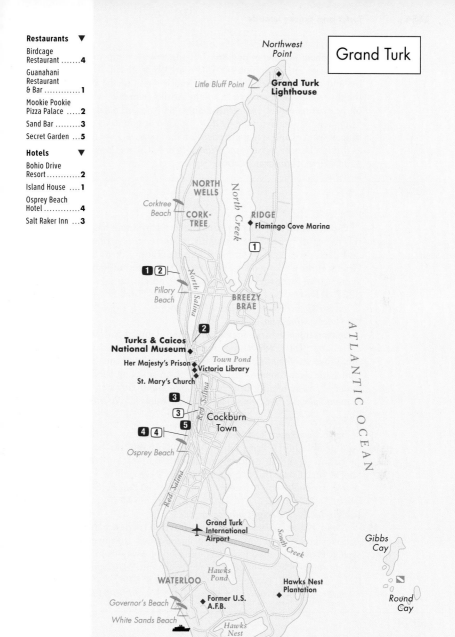

Grand Turk

Northwest
Point

Little Bluff Point

**Grand Turk
Lighthouse**

**NORTH
WELLS**

Corktree
Beach

**CORK-
TREE**

North Creek

RIDGE

Flamingo Cove Marina

1

1 2

Pillory
Beach

North Salina

**BREEZY
BRAE**

2

**Turks & Caicos
National Museum**

Her Majesty's Prison

Victoria Library

Town Pond

St. Mary's Church

Red Salina

3

3

**Cockburn
Town**

4 4

5

Osprey Beach

Red Salina

ATLANTIC OCEAN

Grand Turk
International
Airport

South Creek

Gibbs
Cay

WATERLOO

Hawks
Pond

Round
Cay

Governor's Beach

**Former U.S.
A.F.B.**

**Hawks Nest
Plantation**

White Sands Beach

Hawks
Nest
Salina

0   1/2 mi

0   1/2 km

Columbus' Landfall

KEY

⚓ *Cruise Ship Terminal*

Beaches

Dive Sites

1 *Restaurants*

1 *Hotels*

ELSEWHERE ON GRAND TURK

$$$ INTERNATIONAL 🍴 **Guanahani Restaurant and Bar.** Off the town's main drag, this restaurant sits on a stunning but quiet stretch of beach. The food goes beyond the usual Grand Turk fare and is some of the best in town, thanks to the talents of executive chef Jorika Mhende, who takes care of the evening meals. The menu changes daily, based partly on the fresh fish catch. Thursday nights feature a different country's cuisine every time, so sauces and spices are based on that pick. [$] *Average main: $26* ✉ *Bohio Dive Resort & Spa, Pillory Beach, Grand Turk* ☎ *649/946–2135* 🌐 *www.bohioresort.com.*

WHERE TO STAY

COCKBURN TOWN

$ HOTEL Fodor's Choice ★ 🏨 **Osprey Beach Hotel.** The veteran hotelier Jenny Smith has transformed this two-story oceanfront hotel with artistic touches: palms, frangipani, and deep-green azaleas frame it like a painting. **Pros:** best hotel on Grand Turk; walking distance to Front Street, restaurants, and excursions. **Cons:** three-night minimum; rocky beachfront. [$] *Rooms from: $225* ✉ *Duke St., Cockburn Town, Grand Turk* ☎ *649/946–2666* 🌐 *www.ospreybeachhotel.com* 🛏 *11 rooms, 16 suites* 🍽 *No meals* ☞ *3-night minimum.*

$ B&B/INN 🏨 **Salt Raker Inn.** A large anchor on the sun-dappled pathway marks the entrance to this 19th-century house, which is now an unpretentious inn. **Pros:** excellent location that is an easy walk to Front Street, restaurants, and excursions. **Cons:** the lack of no-smoking rooms. [$] *Rooms from: $115* ✉ *Duke St., Cockburn Town, Grand Turk* ☎ *649/946–2260* 🌐 *www.saltrakerinn.com* 🛏 *10 rooms, 3 suites* 🍽 *No meals.*

ELSEWHERE ON GRAND TURK

$ RESORT 🏨 **Bohio Dive Resort and Spa.** Divers are all drawn to this basic yet comfortable hotel. **Pros:** Guanahani is probably the best restaurant in Grand Turk; on a gorgeous beach; steps away from awesome snorkeling. **Cons:** three-night minimum doesn't allow for quick getaways from Provo. [$] *Rooms from: $195* ✉ *Pillory Beach, Grand Turk* ☎ *649/946–2135* 🌐 *www.bohioresort.com* 🛏 *12 rooms, 4 suites* 🍽 *No meals* ☞ *3-night minimum.*

$$ RENTAL FAMILY 🏨 **Island House.** Years of business-travel experience helped Colin Brooker create the comfortable, peaceful suites that overlook North Creek. **Pros:** full condo units feel like a home away from home. **Cons:** not on the beach; you need a car to get around. [$] *Rooms from: $150* ✉ *Lighthouse Rd., North Ridge, Grand Turk* ☎ *649/232–1439* 🌐 *www.islandhouse.tc* 🛏 *8 suites* 🍽 *No meals* ☞ *2-night minimum.*

NIGHTLIFE

Grand Turk is a quiet place where you come to relax and unwind, and most of the nightlife consists of little more than happy hour at sunset, so you have a chance to glimpse the elusive green flash. Most restaurants turn into gathering places where you can talk with the new friends you have made that day—for instance, every Wednesday and Sunday, there's

Cockburn Town, Grand Turk

lively rake-and-scrape music at the Osprey Beach Hotel, and similar bands visit the Salt Raker Inn on Friday. On some evenings, you'll be able to catch Mitch Rollings of Blue Water Divers; he often headlines the entertainment at the island's different restaurants.

SHOPPING

Shopping in Grand Turk is hard to come by—choices are slim. Let's just say that no true shopaholic would want to come here for vacation. You can get the usual T-shirts and dive trinkets at all the dive shops, but there are only a few options for more interesting shopping opportunities. When a ship is in port, the shops at the pier will be open, and these increase your options dramatically.

SPORTS AND ACTIVITIES

BICYCLING

Out of all the islands in Turks and Caicos, Grand Turk is the perfect island for biking: it's small enough that it is possible to tour it all that way. The island's mostly flat terrain isn't very taxing, and most roads have hard surfaces. Take water with you: there are few places to stop for refreshments. Most hotels have bicycles available, but you can also rent them for $10 to $15 a day from Oasis Divers. They also offer fun Segway tours.

DIVING AND SNORKELING

In these waters you can find undersea cathedrals, coral gardens, and countless tunnels, but note that you must carry and present a valid certificate card before you'll be allowed to dive. As its name suggests, the **Black Forest** offers staggering black-coral formations as well as the occasional black-tip shark. In the **Library** you can study fish galore, including large numbers of yellowtail snapper. At the Columbus Passage separating South Caicos from Grand Turk, each side of a 22-mile-wide (35-km-wide) channel drops more than 7,000 feet. From January through March, thousands of Atlantic humpback whales swim through en route to their winter breeding grounds. **Gibb's Cay,** a small cay a couple of miles off of Grand Turk, where you can swim with stingrays, makes for a great excursion.

Blue Water Divers. In operation on Grand Turk since 1983, Blue Water Divers is the only PADI Gold Palm five-star dive center on the island. The owner, Mitch, may put some of your underwater adventures to music in the evenings when he plays at the Osprey Beach Hotel or Salt Raker Inn. ⊠ *Duke St., Cockburn Town, Grand Turk* ☎ *649/946–2432* ⊕ *www.grandturkscuba.com.*

Grand Turk Diving. The outfitter offers full-service dives and trips to Gibbs Cay and Salt Cay. ⊠ *Cockburn Town, Grand Turk* ☎ *649/946–1559* ⊕ *www.gtdiving.com.*

Oasis Divers. Oasis Divers provides complete gear handling and pampering treatment. It also supplies Nitrox and rebreathers. The company also offers a wide variety of other tours, as well as renting bicycles and operating Segway tours. ⊠ *Duke St., Cockburn Town, Grand Turk* ☎ *649/946–1128* ⊕ *www.oasisdivers.com.*

SALT CAY

Fewer than 100 people live on this 2½-square-mile (6-square-km) dot of land, maintaining an unassuming lifestyle against a backdrop of stucco cottages, stone ruins, and weathered wooden windmills standing sentry in the abandoned salinas. The beautifully preserved island is bordered by beaches where weathered green and blue sea glass and pretty shells often wash ashore. Beneath the waves, 10 dive sites are minutes from shore.

EXPLORING SALT CAY

Salt sheds and salinas are silent reminders of the days when the island was a leading producer of salt. Now the salt ponds attract abundant birdlife. Island tours are often conducted by motorized golf cart. From January through April, humpback whales pass by on the way to their winter breeding grounds.

What little development there is on Salt Cay is found in its main community, Balfour Town. It's home to several small hotels and a few stores, as well as the main dock and the Coral Reef Bar & Grill, where locals hang out with tourists to watch the sunset and drink a beer.

White House. This grand stone house, which once belonged to a wealthy salt merchant, is testimony to the heyday of Salt Cay's eponymous industry. Still owned by the descendants of the original family, it's sometimes opened up for tours. Ask Tim Dunn, a descendant of the original owners, as he may give you a personal tour to see the still-intact, original furnishings, books, and medicine cabinet that date back to the early 1800s. ✉ *Victoria St., Balfour Town, Salt Cay* ☎ *649/243-9843* 🎟 *Free* 🕐 *By appointment only.*

WHERE TO EAT

$$$ CARIBBEAN 🍴 **Pat's Place.** Island native Pat Simmons can give you a lesson in the medicinal qualities of her garden plants and periwinkle flowers, as well as provide excellent native cuisine for a very reasonable price in her comforting Salt Cay home. Home cooking doesn't get any closer to home than this. Try conch fritters for lunch and steamed grouper with okra rice for dinner. Pat also has a small grocery shop selling staples. As with all places to eat in Salt Cay, put in your food order and tell them what time you want to eat in the morning. Pat only cooks when there's someone to cook for. [$] *Average main: $25* ✉ *South District, Salt Cay* ☎ *649/946-6919* ✍ *Reservations essential* 💳 *No credit cards.*

$$$ ECLECTIC Fodor's Choice ★ 🍴 **Porter's Island Thyme Bistro.** Owner Porter Williams serves potent alcoholic creations as well as fairly sophisticated local and international cuisine. Try steamed, freshly caught snapper in a pepper-wine sauce with peas and rice, or spicy-hot chicken curry served with tangy chutneys. Or you can order the "Porter" house steak. You can take cooking lessons from the chef, enjoy the nightly Filipino fusion tapas during happy hour, and join the gang for Friday-night pizza. This is a great place to make friends and the best place to catch up on island gossip. The airy, trellis-covered spot overlooks the salinas. There's a small shop with gifts and tourist information; you can also get a manicure or pedicure here. Reservations are essential here; put in your order for food in the morning and tell Porter what time you want to eat. Then explore, food will be waiting for you. [$] *Average main: $26* ✉ *Balfour Town, Salt Cay* ☎ *649/946-6977* 🌐 *www.islandthyme.tc* ✍ *Reservations essential* 🕐 *Closed Wed. mid-May–June and Sept.–late Oct.*

26

WHERE TO STAY

$$$ RENTAL Fodor's Choice ★ 🏨 **Castaway, Salt Cay.** This only lodging that sits directly on the stunning 3-mile (5-km) North Beach might just be what the doctor ordered if you're in need of total relaxation—it can be hard to fathom having one of the world's most beautiful beaches all to yourself. **Pros:** on a spectacular beach; truly a get away from it all, perfect for relaxing. **Cons:** it's a dark, secluded road into town at night. [$] *Rooms from: $299* ✉ *North Beach, Salt Cay* ☎ *649/946-6977* 🌐 *www.castawayonsaltcay.com* 🛏 *4 suites* 🍽 *Multiple meal plans.*

$$ RENTAL 🏨 **Pirates Hideaway and Blackbeard's Quarters.** Owner Candy Herwin—true to her self-proclaimed pirate status—has smuggled artistic treasures across the ocean and created her own masterpieces to deck out this lair. **Pros:** island personality throughout; great snorkeling off the beachfront.

Cons: the closest swimming beach a five-minute walk. $ *Rooms from: $175* ✉ *Victoria St., Balfour Town, Salt Cay* ☏ *649/244–1407* ⊕ *www.saltcay.tc* ⤳ *3 suites, 1 cottage* ⫯⊙⫯ *No meals.*

$$ 𝕋 **Tradewinds Guest Suites.** A grove of whispering casuarina trees sur-
RENTAL   rounds these five single-story, basic apartments, which offer a moder-
ate-budget option on Salt Cay with the option of dive packages. **Pros:**
walking distance to diving, fishing, dining. **Cons:** a/c costs extra; too
isolated for some people. $ *Rooms from: $161* ✉ *Victoria St., Salt Cay,
Balfour Town, Salt Cay* ☏ *649/241–1009* ⊕ *www.tradewinds.tc* ⤳ *5
apartments* ⫯⊙⫯ *No meals.*

$$ 𝕋 **Villas of Salt Cay.** One of the most convenient places to stay in Salt
RENTAL   Cay is centrally located on Victoria Street, in the middle of everything.
Pros: bedrooms are set up for extra privacy; on Victoria Street within
walking distance of everything; on a private stretch of beach. **Cons:** not
all rooms have a/c; cabanas don't have kitchens; shared pool. $ *Rooms
from: $225* ✉ *Victoria St., Balfour Town, Salt Cay* ☏ *649/343–2157*
⊕ *www.villasofsaltcay.tc* ⤳ *1 2-bedroom villa, 1 1-bedroom cottage,
3 cabanas* ⫯⊙⫯ *No meals.*

SPORTS AND ACTIVITIES

DIVING AND SNORKELING

Scuba divers can explore the wreck of the *Endymion*, a 140-foot wooden-
hull British warship that sank in 1790; you can swim through the hull
and spot cannons and anchors. It's off the southern point of Salt Cay.

Salt Cay Divers. Salt Cay Divers conducts daily dive trips and rents out
all the necessary equipment. In season, they run whale-watching trips.
They can also help get you to Salt Cay from Provo or Grand Turk, and
stock your villa with groceries. ☏ *649/241–1009* ⊕ *www.saltcaydivers.tc.*

WHALE-WATCHING

FAMILY   During the winter months (January through April), Salt Cay is a center
for whale-watching, when some 2,500 humpback whales pass close
to shore. Whale-watching trips can most easily be organized through
your inn or guesthouse.

Fodor'sChoice   **Crystal Seas Adventures.** Proprietor Tim Dunn, whose family descends
★   from the original owners of Salt Cay's historic White House, knows
these waters as well as anybody. His company offers a variety of excursions: diving with stingrays at Gibbs Cay, and trips to Grand Turk
and secluded beaches, such as Great Sand Cay. Whale-watching is
also very popular, and Dunn is the only outfitter with diving trips to
South Caicos, reputed to be one of the best places in the world for this.
☏ *649/431–9585* ⊕ *www.crystalseasadventures.com.*

UNITED STATES VIRGIN ISLANDS

WELCOME TO UNITED STATES VIRGIN ISLANDS

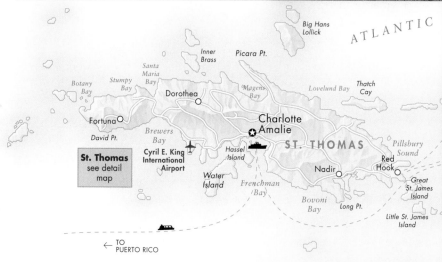

ATLANTIC

Big Hans
Lollick

Inner
Brass

Picara Pt.

Santa
Maria
Bay

Botany
Bay

Stumpy
Bay

Dorothea

Magens
Bay

Lovelund Bay

Thatch
Cay

Fortuna

David Pt.

Brewers
Bay

Cyril E. King
International
Airport

Hassel
Island

Charlotte
Amalie

ST. THOMAS

Pillsbury
Sound

Red
Hook

St. Thomas
see detail
map

Water
Island

Frenchman
Bay

Nadir

Great
St. James
Island

Bovoni
Bay

Long Pt.

Little St. James
Island

← TO
PUERTO RICO

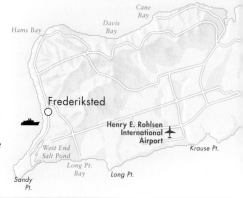

Cane
Bay

Hams Bay

Davis
Bay

Frederiksted

Henry E. Rohlsen
International Airport

West End
Salt Pond

Krause Pt.

Long Pt.
Bay

Long Pt.

Sandy
Pt.

AMERICA'S CARIBBEAN

About 1,000 miles (1,600 km) from the southern tip of Florida, the U.S. Virgin Islands were acquired from Denmark in 1917. St. Croix, at 84 square miles (218 square km), is the largest of the islands; St. John, at 20 square miles (52 square km), is the smallest. Together, they have a population of around 110,000, half of whom live on St. Thomas.

A perfect combination of the familiar and the exotic, the U.S. Virgin Islands are a little bit of home set in an azure sea. With hundreds of idyllic coves and splendid beaches, chances are that on one of the three islands you'll find your ideal Caribbean vacation spot.

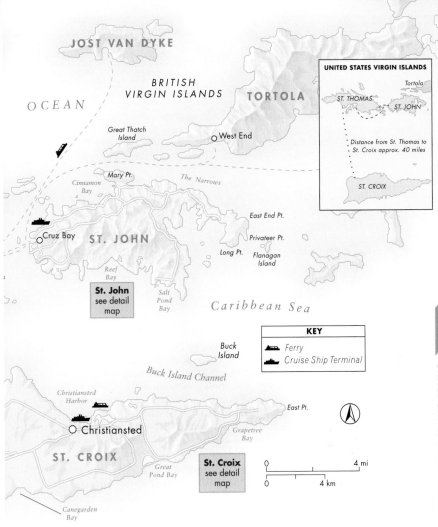

UNITED STATES VIRGIN ISLANDS

TOP REASONS TO VISIT UNITED STATES VIRGIN ISLANDS

1 Incomparable Sailing: St. Thomas is one of the Caribbean's major sailing centers.

2 Great Hiking: Two-thirds of St. John is a national park that's crisscrossed by excellent hiking trails.

3 Beaches: Though Magens Bay on St. Thomas and Trunk Bay on St. John are two of the most perfect beaches you'll ever find,

St. Croix's West End beaches are fetching in their own way.

4 Shopping: Shopping on both St. Thomas and St. Croix is stellar.

5 Deep-Sea Fishing: St. Thomas is one of the best places to catch Atlantic blue marlin between the months of June and October.

Updated by
Carol M.
Bareuther and
Lynda Lohr

The U.S. Virgin Islands—St. Thomas, St. John, and St. Croix—may fly the American flag, but "America's Paradise" is in reality a mix of the foreign and familiar that offers something for everyone to enjoy. The history, beautiful beaches, myriad activities, good food, and no-passport-required status make the Virgin Islands an inviting beach destination for many Americans.

With three islands to choose from, you're likely to find your piece of paradise. Check into a beachfront condo on the east end of St. Thomas; then eat burgers and watch football at a beachfront bar and grill. Or stay at an 18th-century plantation greathouse on St. Croix, go horseback riding at sunrise, and then dine that night on local seafood classics. Rent a tent or a cottage in the pristine national park on St. John; then take a hike, kayak off the coast, read a book, or just listen to the sounds of the forest. Or dive deep into "island time" and learn the art of limin' (hanging out, Caribbean-style) on all three islands.

History books give credit to Christopher Columbus for discovering the New World. In reality, the Virgin Islands, like the rest of the isles in the Caribbean chain, were populated as long ago as 2000 BC by nomadic waves of seagoing settlers as they migrated north from South America and eastward from Central America and the Yucatàn Peninsula.

Columbus met the descendants of these original inhabitants during his second voyage to the New World, in 1493. He anchored in Salt River, a natural bay west of what is now Christiansted, St. Croix, and sent his men ashore in search of fresh water. Hostile arrows rather than welcoming embraces made for a quick retreat, but Columbus did have time to name the island Santa Cruz (Holy Cross) before sailing north. He eventually claimed St. John, St. Thomas, and what are now the British Virgin Islands for Spain and at the same time named this shapely silhouette of 60-some islands Las Once Mil Virgenes, for the 11,000 legendary virgin followers of St. Ursula. Columbus believed the islands barren of the costly spices he sought, so he sailed off, leaving more than a century's gap in time before the next Europeans arrived.

Pioneers, planters, and pirates from throughout Europe ushered in the era of colonization. Great Britain and the Netherlands both claimed St. Croix in 1625. This peaceful coexistence ended abruptly when the Dutch governor killed his English counterpart, thus launching years of battles for possession that would see seven flags fly over this southernmost Virgin isle. Meanwhile, St. Thomas's sheltered harbor proved a magnet for pirates such as Blackbeard and Bluebeard. The Danes first colonized the island in 1666, naming their main settlement Taphus for its many beer halls. In 1691 the town received the more respectable name of Charlotte Amalie in honor of Danish king Christian V's wife. It wasn't until 1718 that a small group of Dutch planters raised their country's flag on St. John. As on the other Virgin Islands, a plantation economy soon developed.

Plantations depended on slave labor, and the Virgin Islands played a key role in the triangular route that connected the Caribbean, Africa, and Europe in the trade of sugar, rum, and human cargo. By the early 1800s a sharp decline in cane prices because of competing beet sugar and an increasing number of slave revolts motivated Governor-General Peter von Scholten to abolish slavery in the Danish colonies on July 3, 1848. This holiday is now celebrated as Emancipation Day.

After emancipation, the island's economy slumped. Islanders owed their existence to subsistence farming and fishing. Meanwhile, during the American Civil War the Union began negotiations with Denmark for the purchase of the Virgin Islands in order to establish a naval base. However, the sale didn't happen until World War I, when President Theodore Roosevelt paid the Danes $25 million for the three largest islands; an elaborate Transfer Day ceremony was held on the grounds of St. Thomas's Legislature Building on March 31, 1917. A decade later, Virgin Islanders were granted U.S. citizenship. Today the U.S. Virgin Islands is an unincorporated territory, meaning that citizens govern themselves and vote for their own governors, but cannot vote for president or congressional representation.

Nowadays, Virgin Islanders hail from more than 60 nations. The Danish influence is still strong in architecture and street names. Americana is everywhere, too, most notably in recognizable fast-food chains, familiar TV shows, and name-brand hotels. Between this diversity and the wealth that tourism brings, Virgin Islanders struggle to preserve their culture. Their rich, spicy West Indian–African heritage comes to full bloom at Carnival time, when celebrating and playing *mas* (with abandon) take precedence over everything else.

There's evidence, too, of growing pains. Traffic jams are common, a clandestine drug trade fuels crime, and there are few beaches left that aren't fronted by a high-rise hotel. Despite fairly heavy development, wildlife has found refuge here. The brown pelican is on the endangered list worldwide but is a common sight here. The endangered native boa tree is protected, as is the hawksbill turtle, whose females lumber onto the beaches to lay eggs.

PLANNING

WHEN TO GO

High season coincides with that on most other Caribbean islands, from December through April or May; before and after that time, rates can drop by as much as 25% to 50%, depending on the resort.

GETTING HERE AND AROUND

AIR TRAVEL

Fly nonstop to St. Thomas from Atlanta (Delta), Boston (American, seasonal; JetBlue via San Juan, seasonal), Charlotte (US Airways), Chicago (United), Fort Lauderdale (Spirit), Miami (American), New York–JFK (American), New York–Newark (Continental; United), Philadelphia (US Airways), or Washington, D.C.–Dulles (United). Fly nonstop to St. Croix from Miami (American). In the winter, US Airways flies nonstop from Charlotte, N.C.

If you can't fly nonstop, then you can connect in San Juan on Seaborne Airlines or Cape Air. You can also take a seaplane between St. Thomas and St. Croix. The only option for St. John is a ferry from either Red Hook or Charlotte Amalie in St. Thomas. Both Caneel Bay and the Westin have private ferries.

Airline Contacts American Airlines/Enjoy. On American, you can fly direct to St. Thomas from Miami and New York–JFK year-round and from Boston in winter. Envoy offers several daily nonstops between St. Thomas and San Juan, Puerto Rico, and other Caribbean islands. ☎ 800/474–4884 ⊕ www.aa.com. **Delta Airlines.** Delta flies direct from Atlanta. ☎ 800/221–1212 ⊕ www. delta.com. **JetBlue.** JetBlue flies direct from Boston five times a week, with a connection in San Juan. ☎ 800/538–2583 ⊕ www.jetblue.com. **Seaborne Airlines.** ☎ 340/773–6442, 866/359–8784 ⊕ www.seaborneairlines.com. **Spirit Airlines.** Spirit flies direct from Ft. Lauderdale. ☎ 800/772–7117 ⊕ www.spiritair.com. **United Airlines.** United flies direct from Chicago, Dulles, and Newark. ☎ 800/241–6522, 340/774–9190 in St. Thomas ⊕ www.united. com. **US Airways.** US Airways offers direct flights from Charlotte and Philadelphia. ☎ 800/622–1015 ⊕ www.usairways.com.

Airports Cyril E. King Airport (STT). ⊠ Rte. 30, Lindbergh Bay, St. Thomas ☎ 340/774–5100. **Henry Rohlsen Airport** (STX). ⊠ Airport Rd., Off Rte 66, Anguilla, St. Croix ☎ 340/778–1012.

BOAT AND FERRY TRAVEL

There's frequent service between St. Thomas and St. John and their neighbors, the BVI. Check with the ferry companies for the current schedules. These schedules are also printed in the free *St. Thomas + St. John This Week* magazine and on the website of the **Virgin Islands Vacation Guide & Community** (⊕ www.vinow.com).

There's frequent daily service from both Red Hook and Charlotte Amalie to Cruz Bay, St. John. About every hour there's a car ferry, which locals call the barge. You should arrive at least 15 minutes before departure.

Ferry Contacts Inter-Island Boat Service. Inter-Island has daily and weekly service between St. John and the British Virgin Islands of Jost Van Dyke, Tortola, Virgin Gorda, and Anegada. ☎ *340/776–6597 in St. John.* **Native Son.** Ferries operate daily between Charlotte Amalie and Red Hook, in St. Thomas, and West End and Road Town, in Tortola. ☎ *340/774–8685 in St. Thomas* ⊕ *www.nativesonferry.com.* **Smith's Ferry.** Smith's operates multiple trips daily between Charlotte Amalie and Red Hook in St. Thomas, and West End and Road Town, in Tortola. ☎ *340/775–7292 in St. Thomas* ⊕ *www.smithsferry. com.* **Speedy's.** Speedy's offers weekly ferry service to Virgin Gorda. The company also runs seasonal three-day weekend trips to Fajardo, Puerto Rico. ☎ *284/495–5235 in Tortola* ⊕ *www.speedysbvi.com.*

CAR TRAVEL

Driving is on the left, British-style. The law requires that *everyone* wear a seat belt. Traffic can be bad during rush hour on all three islands.

Car Rentals in St. Thomas: Avis, Budget, and Hertz all have counters at Cyril E. King Airport, but there are some other offices as well; in addition, there are local companies.

Car Rentals in St. John: All the car-rental companies in St. John are locally owned. Most companies are just a short walk from the ferry dock. Those a bit farther away will pick you up.

Car Rentals in St. Croix: There are both local and national companies on St. Croix; if your company doesn't have an airport location, you'll be picked up or a car will be delivered to you.

St. Thomas Car Rental Contacts Avis ⊠ *Cyril E. King Airport, 70 Lindbergh Bay, 4 miles west of Charlotte Amalie, Lindbergh Bay, St. Thomas* ☎ *340/774–1468* ⊕ *www.avis.com* ⊠ *Windward Passage Hotel, Seabourne Airlines, Charlotte Amalie, St. Thomas* ☎ *340/776–7329* ⊠ *Al Cohens Mall, Rte. 30, Havensight Cruise Ship Dock, Havensight, St. Thomas* ☎ *340/777– 8888.* **Budget** ⊠ *Cyril E. King Airport, 70 Lindbergh Bay, 4 miles west of Charlotte Amalie, Lindbergh Bay, St. Thomas* ☎ *340/776–5774* ⊕ *www. budgetstt.com* ⊠ *Sapphire Beach Resort, Rte. 38, Estate Smith Bay, St. Thomas* ☎ *340/774–2211* ⊠ *Havensight Cruise Ship Dock, Rte. 30, Havensight, St. Thomas* ☎ *340/776–5774.* **Dependable Car Rental** ⊠ *Estate Contant, 12 Lindbergh Bay, 1.5 miles east of Cyril E. King Airport off Rte. 308, turn north at Medical Arts Bldg., Lindbergh Bay, St. Thomas* ☎ *340/774–2253, 800/522–3076* ⊕ *www.dependablecar.com.* **Discount Car Rental.** The main office is in Lindbergh Bay, but they pick up at the Cyril E. King Airport and have small satellite locations with a desk at Bluebeard's Beach Club & Villas, Elysian Beach Resort, and Sugar Bay Resort & Spa. ⊠ *Cyril E. King Airport, 70 Lindbergh Bay, 4 miles west of Charlotte Amalie, car rental is adjacent to entrance road of airport, 1 min from terminal* ☎ *340/776–4858, 877/478– 2833* ⊕ *www.discountcar.vi.* **Hertz** ⊠ *Cyril E King Airport, Airport Rd., 4 miles west of Charlotte Amalie, Lindbergh Bay, St. Thomas* ☎ *340/774–1879* ⊕ *www.hertz.com.*

27

LOGISTICS

Getting to the USVI: There are many nonstop flights to St. Thomas from the United States, and there are a few nonstops to St. Croix; often, you'll have to change planes in Miami, San Juan, or St. Thomas to reach St. Croix. There are no flights at all to St. John; you have to take a ferry from St. Thomas.

Hassle Factor: Low to high, depending on your flight schedule.

On the Ground: Many travelers do just fine without a car in St. Thomas, but it's much harder if you are renting a villa; also be aware that taxis can be expensive when used every day. In St. John you must rent a car if you are staying in a villa or in Coral Bay, but you might be able to get by without one if you are staying elsewhere. A car is more of a necessity in St. Croix, regardless of where you stay.

Getting Around the Islands: Frequent, convenient ferries connect St. Thomas and St. John. St. Croix is farther removed, so a flight from St. Thomas is the most common mode of transport.

St. John Car Rental Contacts Best ⊠ *Near library, Cruz Bay, St. John* ☎ *340/693–8177.* **Cool Breeze** ⊠ *1 block east of passenger ferry dock, Cruz Bay, St. John* ☎ *340/776–6588* ⊕ *www.coolbreezecarrental.com.* **Courtesy** ⊠ *Near St. Ursula's Church, Cruz Bay, St. John* ☎ *340/776–6650* ⊕ *www. courtesycarrental.com.* **Delbert Hill Taxi & Jeep Rental Service** ⊠ *King St., Cruz Bay, St. John* ☎ *340/776–6637* ⊕ *www.delberthillcarrental.com.* **Denzil Clyne** ⊠ *North Shore Rd., across from Creek, Cruz Bay, St. John* ☎ *340/776–6715.* **O'Connor Car Rental** ⊠ *Rte. 104, near roundabout, Cruz Bay, St. John* ☎ *340/776–6343* ⊕ *www.oconnorcarrental.com.* **St. John Car Rental** ⊠ *Bay St., near Wharfside Village, Cruz Bay, St. John* ☎ *340/776–6103* ⊕ *www. stjohncarrental.com.* **Spencer's Jeep** ⊠ *Boulon Center Rd., near Creek, Cruz Bay, St. John* ☎ *340/693–8784, 888/776–6628* ⊕ *www.spencerjeeprentals.com.*

St. Croix Car Rental Contacts Avis ⊠ *Henry E. Rohlsen Airport, St. Croix* ☎ *340/778–9355, 800/331–1212* ⊕ *www.avis.com* ⊠ *Seaplane, Christiansted, St. Croix* ☎ *340/713–9355* ⊕ *www.avis.com.* **Budget** ⊠ *Henry E. Rohlsen Airport, St. Croix* ☎ *340/778–9636, 888/264–8894* ⊠ *Prince St., across from Seaplane, Christiansted, St. Croix* ☎ *340/713–9289* ⊕ *www.budgetstcroix.com.* **Hertz** ⊠ *Henry E. Rohlsen Airport, St. Croix* ☎ *340/778–1402, 888/248–4261* ⊕ *www.rentacarstcroix.com.* **Judi of Croix** ☎ *340/773–2123, 877/903–2123* ⊕ *www.judiofcroix.com.* **Midwest** ⊠ *Centerline Rd., Estate Carlton, Frederiksted, St. Croix* ☎ *340/772–0438, 877/772–0438* ⊕ *www.midwestautorental.com.* **Olympic** ⊠ *Rte. 70, Christiansted, St. Croix* ☎ *340/773–8000, 888/878–4227* ⊕ *www.olympicstcroix.com.*

TAXI TRAVEL

USVI taxis don't have meters; fares are per person, set by a schedule, and drivers usually take multiple fares, especially from the airport, ferry docks, and cruise-ship terminals. Many taxis are open safari vans, but some are air-conditioned vans.

St. Thomas East End Taxi ✉ *Urman Victor Fredericks Marine Terminal, 6117 Red Hook Quarters, off Rte. 38 in Red Hook, St. Thomas* ☎ *340/775–6974* ⊕ *www.eastendtaxi.cbt.cc.* **Islander Taxi and Tour Services** ✉ *Fortress Storage, Bldg. K, Suite 2025, at intersection of Rte. 313 and Rte. 38, Sugar Estate, St. Thomas* ☎ *340/774–4077* ⊕ *www.islandertaxiservice.com.* **V.I. Taxi Association** ✉ *68A Estate Contant, Charlotte Amalie, St. Thomas* ☎ *340/774–4550, 340/774–7457* ⊕ *www.vitaxi.com.*

St. Croix Antilles Taxi Service ✉ *St. Croix* ☎ *340/773–5020.* **St. Croix Taxi Association** ✉ *Henry E. Rohlsen Airport, St. Croix* ☎ *340/778–1088* ⊕ *www. stcroixtaxi.com.*

ESSENTIALS

Banks and Exchange Services The U.S. dollar is used throughout the U.S. Virgin Islands. All major credit cards are accepted by most hotels, restaurants, and shops. ATMs are common on St. Thomas. Banks on St. Thomas include Banco Popular, Scotia Bank, and First Bank. St. John has First Bank and Banco Popular in Cruz Bay and Scotia Bank at the Marketplace shopping center. St. Croix has branches of Banco Popular in the Orange Grove and Sunny Isle. V.I. Community Bank is in Sunny Isle, Frederiksted, Estate Diamond, Orange Grove, and Christiansted. Scotia Bank has branches in Sunny Isle, Frederiksted, Christiansted, and Sunshine Mall.

Electricity Electricity is the U.S. standard.

Safety Keep your hotel or vacation villa door locked at all times, and stick to well-lighted streets at night. Keep your rental car locked wherever you park, and lock possessions in the trunk. Don't leave valuables lying on the beach while you snorkel. Don't wander the streets of the main towns alone at night, whether you are in Charlotte Amalie, Cruz Bay, Christiansted, or Frederiksted.

Although crime is not as prevalent in St. John as it is on St. Thomas and St. Croix, it does exist. There are occasional burglaries at villas, even during daylight hours. Lock doors even when you're lounging by the pool. It's not a good idea to walk around Cruz Bay late at night. If you don't have a car, plan on taking a taxi. Because it can be hard to find a taxi in the wee hours of the morning, arrange in advance for a driver to pick you up.

ACCOMMODATIONS

St. Thomas is the most developed of the Virgin Islands; choose it if you want extensive shopping opportunities and a multitude of activities and restaurants. St. John, the least developed of the three, has a distinct following; it's the best choice if you want a small-island feel and easy access to great hiking. However, most villas there aren't directly on the beach. St. Croix is a sleeper. The diversity of the accommodations means that you can stay in everything from a simple inn to a luxury resort, but none of the beaches is as breathtaking as those on St. Thomas and St. John.

Resorts: Whether you are looking for a luxury retreat or a moderately priced vacation spot, there's going to be something for you in the USVI. St. Thomas has the most options. St. John has only two large resorts, both upscale; others are small, but it has two unique eco-oriented camping options. St. Croix's resorts are more midsize.

Small Inns: Particularly on St. Croix, you'll find a wide range of attractive and accommodating small inns; if you can live without being directly on the beach, these friendly, homey places are a good option. St. Thomas also has a few small inns in the historic district of Charlotte Amalie.

Villas: Villas are plentiful on all three islands, but they are especially popular on St. John, where they represent the majority of the available lodging. They're always a good bet for families who can do without a busy resort environment.

HOTEL AND RESTAURANT PRICES

Prices in the restaurant reviews are the average cost of a main course at dinner or, if dinner is not served, at lunch; taxes and service charges are generally included. Prices in the hotel reviews are the lowest cost of a standard double room in high season, excluding taxes, service charges, and meal plans (except at all-inclusives). Prices for rentals are the lowest per-night cost for a one-bedroom unit in high season.

For expanded lodging reviews and current deals, visit Fodors.com.

VISITOR INFORMATION

Contacts USVI Department of Tourism ☎ 340/774–8784, 800/372–8784 ⊕ *www.visitusvi.com.*

WEDDINGS

Apply for a marriage license at the Superior Court. There's a $100 application fee and $100 license fee. You have to wait eight days after the clerk receives the application to get married, and licenses must be picked up in person weekdays or on weekends for an additional $150, though you can apply by mail. A marriage ceremony at the Superior Court costs $400 in St. John and $200 in St. Thomas.

St. Croix Superior Court ☎ 340/778–9750.

St. Thomas Superior Court ☎ 340/774–6680.

ST. THOMAS

Updated by
Carol M.
Bareuther

If you fly to the 32-square-mile (83-square-km) island of St. Thomas, you land at its western end; if you arrive by cruise ship, you come into one of the world's most beautiful harbors. Either way, one of your first sights is the town of Charlotte Amalie. From the harbor you see an idyllic-looking village that spreads into the lower hills. If you were expecting a quiet hamlet with its inhabitants hanging out under palm trees, you've missed that era by about 300 years. Although other islands in the USVI developed plantation economies, St. Thomas cultivated its harbor, and it became a thriving seaport soon after it was settled by the Danish in the 1600s.

The success of the naturally perfect harbor was enhanced by the fact that the Danes—who ruled St. Thomas with only a couple of short interruptions from 1666 to 1917—avoided involvement in some 100 years' worth of European wars. Denmark was the only European country with colonies in the Caribbean to stay neutral during the War of the Spanish Succession in the early 1700s. Thus, products of the Dutch, English, and French islands—sugar, cotton, and indigo—were traded through Charlotte Amalie, along with the regular shipments of slaves. When the Spanish wars ended, trade fell off, but by the end of the 1700s Europe was at war again, Denmark again remained neutral, and St. Thomas continued to prosper. Even into the 1800s, while the economies of St. Croix and St. John foundered with the market for sugarcane, St. Thomas's economy remained vigorous. This prosperity led to the development of shipyards, a well-organized banking system, and a large merchant class. In 1845 Charlotte Amalie had 101 large importing houses owned by the English, French, Germans, Haitians, Spaniards, Americans, Sephardim, and Danes.

HOP ON THE BUS

On St. Thomas the island's large buses make public transportation a very comfortable—though slow—way to get from east and west to Charlotte Amalie and back (service to the north is limited). Buses run about every 30 minutes from stops that are clearly marked with "Vitran" signs. Fares are $1 between outlying areas and town and 75¢ in town. There are also safari taxis (open-air seats with a roof built on the back of a pickup truck) or "dollar buses" that run the same routes for $1 a ride.

Charlotte Amalie is still one of the world's most active cruise-ship ports. On almost any day at least one and sometimes as many as eight cruise ships are tied to the docks or anchored outside the harbor. Gently rocking in the shadows of these giant floating hotels are just about every other kind of vessel imaginable: sleek sailing catamarans that will take you on a sunset cruise complete with rum punch and a Jimmy Buffett soundtrack, private megayachts for billionaires, and barnacle-bottom sloops—with laundry draped over the lifelines—that are home to world-cruising gypsies. Huge container ships pull up in Sub Base, west of the harbor, bringing in everything from breakfast cereals to tires. Anchored right along the waterfront are down-island barges that ply the waters between the Greater Antilles and the Leeward Islands, transporting goods such as refrigerators, VCRs, and disposable diapers.

The waterfront road through Charlotte Amalie was once part of the harbor. Before it was filled in to build the highway, the beach came right up to the back door of the warehouses that now line the thoroughfare. Two hundred years ago those warehouses were filled with indigo, tobacco, and cotton. Today the stone buildings house silk, crystal, and diamonds. Exotic fragrances are still traded, but by island beauty queens in air-conditioned perfume palaces instead of through open market stalls. The pirates of old used St. Thomas as a base from which to raid merchant ships of every nation, though they were particularly fond of the gold- and silver-laden treasure ships heading to Spain. Pirates are still around, but today's versions use St. Thomas as a drop-off for their contraband: illegal immigrants and drugs.

27

Fort Christian (1672–80) is the oldest surviving structure in St. Thomas.

EXPLORING

To explore outside Charlotte Amalie, rent a car or hire a taxi. Your rental car should come with a good map; if not, pick up the pocket-size "St. Thomas–St. John Road Map" at a tourist information center. Roads are marked with route numbers, but they're confusing and seem to switch numbers suddenly. Roads are also identified by signs bearing the St. Thomas–St. John Hotel and Tourism Association's mascot, Tommy the Starfish. More than 100 of these color-coded signs line the island's main routes. Orange signs trace the route from the airport to Red Hook, green signs identify the road from town to Magens Bay, Tommy's face on a yellow background points from Mafolie to Crown Bay through the north side, red signs lead from Smith Bay to Four Corners via Skyline Drive, and blue signs mark the route from the cruise-ship dock at Haven-sight to Red Hook. These color-coded routes are not marked on most visitor maps, however. Allow yourself a day to explore, especially if you want to stop to take pictures or to enjoy a light bite or refreshing swim. Most gas stations are on the island's more populated eastern end, so fill up before heading to the north side. And remember to drive on the left!

CHARLOTTE AMALIE

Look beyond the pricey shops, T-shirt vendors, and bustling crowds for a glimpse of the island's history. The city served as the capital of Denmark's outpost in the Caribbean until 1917, an aspect of the island often lost in the glitz of the shopping district.

Emancipation Gardens, right next to the fort, is a good place to start a walking tour. Tackle the hilly part of town first: head north up Govern-ment Hill to the historic buildings that house government offices and have incredible views. Several regal churches line the route that runs west back to the town proper and the old-time market. Virtually all the alleyways that intersect Main Street lead to eateries serving frosty drinks, sandwiches, and West Indian fare. There are public restrooms in this area, too. Allow an hour for a quick view of the sights.

A note about the street names: In deference to the island's heritage, the streets downtown are labeled by their Danish names. Locals will use both the Danish name and the English name (such as Dronningens Gade and Norre Gade for Main Street), but most people refer to things by their location ("a block toward the waterfront off Main Street" or "next to the Little Switzerland Shop"). You may find it more useful if you ask for directions by shop names or landmarks.

99 Steps. This staircase "street," built by the Danes in the 1700s, leads to the residential area above Charlotte Amalie and to Blackbeard's Castle, a U.S. national historic landmark. If you count the stairs as you go up, you'll discover, as thousands have before you, that there are more than the name implies. ⊠ *Look for steps heading north from Government Hill.*

All Saints Episcopal Church. Built in 1848 from stone quarried on the island, the church has thick, arched window frames lined with the yellow brick that came to the islands as ballast aboard ships. Merchants left the brick on the waterfront when they filled their boats with molasses, sugar, mahogany, and rum for the return voyage. The church was built in celebration of the end of slavery in the USVI. ⊠ *13 Commandant Gade, near Emancipation Garden U.S. Post Office* ☎ *340/774–0217* ⊕ *www.episcopalvi.org* ⊙ *Mon.–Sat. 9–3.*

Cathedral of St. Peter & St. Paul. This building was consecrated as a parish church in 1848, and serves as the seat of the territory's Roman Catholic diocese. The ceiling and walls are covered with a dozen murals depicting biblical scenes; they were painted in 1899 by two Belgian artists, Father Leo Servais and Brother Ildephonsus. The marble altar and walls were added in the 1960s. ⊠ *22-AB Kronprindsens Gade, 1 block west of Market Square* ☎ *340/774–0201* ⊕ *cathedralvi.com* ⊙ *Mon.–Sat. 8–5.*

Danish Consulate Building. Built in 1830, this structure once housed the Danish Consulate. Although the Danish consul general, Søren Blak, has an office in Charlotte Amalie, the Danish Consulate is now in the Scandinavian Center in Havensight Mall. ⚠ **This building is not open to the public.** ⊠ *Take stairs north at corner of Bjerge Gade and Crystal Gade to Denmark Hill.*

Educators Park. A peaceful place amid the town's hustle and bustle, the park has memorials to three famous Virgin Islanders: educator Edith Williams, J. Antonio Jarvis (a founder of the *Daily News*), and educator and author Rothschild Francis. The last gave many speeches here. ⊠ *Main St., across from Emancipation Garden U.S. Post Office.*

FAMILY **Emancipation Garden.** A bronze bust of a freed slave blowing a conch shell commemorates slavery's end, in 1848—the garden was built to mark emancipation's 150th anniversary, in 1998. The gazebo here is used for official ceremonies. Two other monuments show the island's Danish-American connection—a bust of Denmark's King Christian and a scaled-down model of the U.S. Liberty Bell. ⊠ *Between Tolbod Gade and Ft. Christian, next to Vendor's Plaza.*

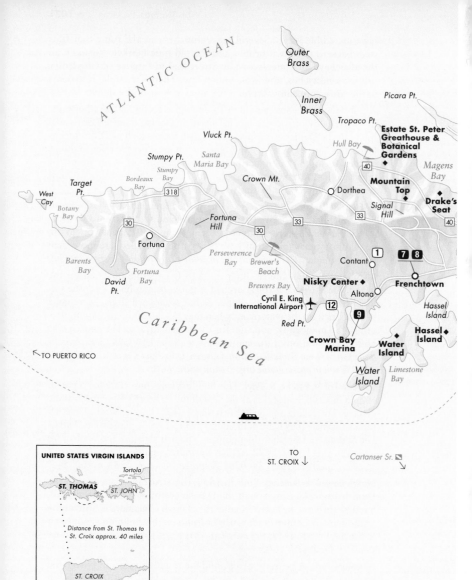

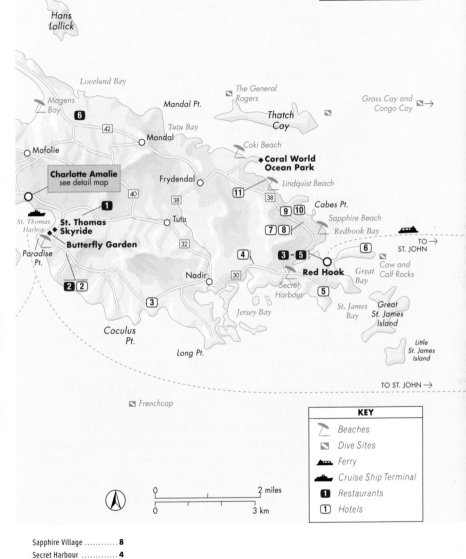

St. Thomas

Hans Lollick

Lovelund Bay

Magens Bay

6

Mandal Pt.

The General Rogers

Thatch Cay

Grass Cay and Congo Cay →

Mofolie

42

Tutu Bay

Mandal

Coki Beach

Coral World Ocean Park

Charlotte Amalie see detail map

Frydendal

Lindquist Beach

11

38

Cabes Pt.

40

38

9 **10**

Sapphire Beach

1

St. Thomas Harbor

St. Thomas Skyride

Tutu

7 **8**

Redhook Bay

TO → ST. JOHN

Butterfly Garden

32

4

3 - **5**

6

Paradise Pt.

Nadir

30

Red Hook

Great Bay

Cow and Calf Rocks

2 **2**

3

Secret Harbour

5

St. James Bay

Great St. James Island

Jersey Bay

Coculus Pt.

Long Pt.

Little St. James Island

TO ST. JOHN →

Frenchcap

KEY		
	Beaches	
	Dive Sites	
	Ferry	
	Cruise Ship Terminal	
1	Restaurants	
①	Hotels	

0 — 2 miles

0 — 3 km

Frederick Lutheran Church. This historic church has a massive mahogany altar, and its pews—each with its own door—were once rented to families of the congregation. Lutheranism is the state religion of Denmark, and when the territory was without a minister, the governor—who had his own elevated pew—filled in. ☒ *7 Norre Gade, across from Emancipation Garden and Grand Hotel* ☎ *340/776–1315* ⊕ *www.felc1666. org* ⊗ *Mon.–Sat. 9–4.*

FAMILY **Ft. Christian.** St. Thomas's oldest standing structure, this remarkable building was built between 1672 and 1680 and now has U.S. National Landmark status. Over the years, it was used as a jail, governor's residence, town hall, courthouse, and church. In 2005, a multimillion-dollar renovation project started to stabilize the structure and halt centuries of deterioration. The fort reopened for public tours in 2014. Inside you can visit the inner courtyard and rooms, and from the outside, you can see the four renovated faces of the famous 19th-century clock tower. ☒ *Waterfront Hwy., east of shopping district* ☎ *340/774–5541* ⊕ *stthomashistoricaltrust.org.*

Government House. Built in 1867, this neoclassical white brick-and-wood structure houses the offices of the governor of the Virgin Islands. Inside, the staircases are of native mahogany, as are the plaques, hand-lettered in gold with the names of the governors appointed and, since 1970, elected. Brochures detailing the history of the building are available, but you may have to ask for them. ☒ *Government Hill, 21–22 Kongens Gade, across from Emancipation Garden U.S. Post Office* ☎ *340/774–0001* ☒ *Free* ⊗ *Weekdays 8–5.*

Haagensen House. This lovingly restored house was built in the early 1800s by Danish entrepreneur Hans Haagensen. It's surrounded by an equally impressive cookhouse, outbuildings, and terraced gardens. A lower-level banquet hall showcases antique prints and photographs. Guided tours begin at the nearby Hotel 1829, then continue here. The tour includes stops at other restored 19th-century houses, a rum factory, amber museum, and finally, the lookout tour at Blackbeard's Castle. ☒ *Government Hill, 29–30 Kongens Gade, behind Hotel 1829* ☎ *340/776–1234* ☒ *Tours $10 adults, free children (under age 12)* ⊗ *Dec.–Apr., Tues.–Thurs. 9–3; May–Nov., Weekdays 9–2.*

Hassel Island. East of Water Island in Charlotte Amalie harbor, Hassel Island is part of the Virgin Islands National Park. On it are the ruins of a British military garrison (built during a brief British occupation of the USVI during the 1800s) and the remains of a marine railway (where ships were hoisted into dry dock for repairs). Daily guided kayak tours to the island are available from VI Ecotours. The St. Thomas Historical Trust also leads walking tours throughout the year. ☒ *Charlotte Amalie harbor* ☎ *340/776–6201 Virgin Islands National Park main office* ⊕ *www.nps.gov/viis.*

Hotel 1829. As its name implies, the hotel was built in 1829, but back then it was the private residence of a prominent merchant named Alexander Lavalette. The building's coral-color facade is accented with fancy wrought-iron railings, and the interior is paneled in dark wood, which makes it feel delightfully cool. From the terrace there's an exquisite view of the harbor framed by brilliant orange bougainvillea. You can combine a visit to this hotel with a walking tour of Haagensen House, Villa Notman, Britannia House, rum factory, amber museum, and the lookout tower at Blackbeard's Castle just above the hotel. The Castle, once reputed to be used by the notorious Edward Teach (aka Blackbeard), is surrounded by the largest collection of life-sized bronze and copper pirate statues in the world. ⊠ *Government Hill, 29–30 Kongens Gade, across from Emancipation Garden* ☎ *340/776–1829* ⊕ *www. hotel1829.com.*

Legislature Building. Its pastoral-looking lime-green exterior conceals the vociferous political wrangling of the Virgin Islands Senate. Constructed originally by the Danish as a police barracks, the building was later used to billet U.S. Marines, and much later it housed a public school. ■ TIP➔ You're welcome to sit in on sessions in the upstairs chambers. ⊠ *Waterfront Hwy. (aka Rte. 30), across from Ft. Christian* ☎ *340/774–0880* ⊕ *www.legvi.org* ⊙ *Daily 8–5.*

Memorial Moravian Church. Built in 1884, this church was named to commemorate the 150th anniversary of the Moravian Church in the Virgin Islands. ⊠ *17 Norre Gade, next to Roosevelt Park* ☎ *340/776–0066* ⊕ *www.memorialmoravianvi.org* ⊙ *Weekdays 8–5.*

Pissarro Building. Housing several shops and an art gallery, this was the birthplace and childhood home of the acclaimed 19th-century impressionist painter Camille Pissarro, who lived for most of his adult life in France. The art gallery on the second floor contains three original pages from Pissarro's sketchbook and two pastels by Pissarro's grandson, Claude. ⊠ *14 Dronningens Gade (aka Main St.), between Raadets Gade and Trompeter Gade.*

FAMILY **Roosevelt Park.** The former Coconut Park was renamed in honor of Franklin D. Roosevelt in 1945. It's a great place to put your feet up and people-watch. A 2007 renovation added five granite pedestals representing the five branches of the military, bronze urns that can be lighted to commemorate special events, and bronze plaques inscribed with the names of the territory's veterans who died defending the United States. There's also a children's playground. ⊠ *Intersection of Norre Gade and Rte. 35, adjacent to Memorial Moravian Church* ☎ *340/774–5541* ⊕ *www.stthomashistoricaltrust.org.*

Seven Arches Museum and Gallery. This restored 18th-century home is a striking example of classic Danish–West Indian architecture. There seem to be arches everywhere—seven to be exact—all supporting a "welcoming arms" staircase that leads to the second floor and the flower-framed front doorway. The Danish kitchen is a highlight: it's housed in a separate building away from the main house, as were all cooking facilities in the early days (for fire prevention). Inside the house you can see mahogany furnishings and gas lamps and colorful abstract canvases painted by the museum's curator, a local artist. ⊠ *Government Hill, 3 buildings east of Government House, 18A–B Dronningens Gade* ☎ *340/774–9295* ⊕ *www.sevenarchesmuseum.com* ⊠ *$5 donation* ⊙ *By appointment only.*

27

St. Thomas Historical Trust Museum. Tours of the museum take 30 minutes and include a wealth of pirate artifacts, as well as West Indian antique furniture and old-time postcards. ⊠ *West end of Roosevelt Park* ☎ *340/774–5541* ⊕ *www.stthomashistoricaltrust.org* ⊙ *Tues.–Thurs. 10:30–3:30.*

St. Thomas Reformed Church. This church has an austere loveliness that's amazing considering all it's been through. Founded in 1744, it's been rebuilt twice after fires and hurricanes. The unembellished cream-color hall is quite peaceful. The only other color is the forest green of the shutters and the carpet. Call ahead if you wish to visit at a particular time, as the doors are sometimes locked. Services are held at 9 am each Sunday. ⊠ *5 Crystal Gade at Nye Gade, 1½ blocks north of Main St.* ☎ *340/776–8255* ⊕ *www.stthomasreformedchurch.org* ⊙ *Weekdays 9–5.*

Synagogue of Beracha Veshalom Vegmiluth Hasidim. The synagogue's Hebrew name translates as the Congregation of Blessing, Peace, and Loving Deeds. The small building's white pillars contrast with rough stone walls, as does the rich mahogany of the pews and altar. The sand on the floor symbolizes the exodus from Egypt. Since the synagogue first opened its doors in 1833, it has held a weekly service, making it the oldest synagogue building in continuous use under the American flag and the second-oldest (after the one on Curaçao) in the Western Hemisphere. Guided tours can be arranged. Brochures detailing the key structures and history are also available. Next door the Weibel Museum showcases Jewish history on St. Thomas. ⊠ *Synagogue Hill, 15 Crystal Gade* ⟐ *From Main St., walk up Raadet's Gade (H. Stern is on corner) to top of hill, turn left and Synagogue is 2nd bldg. on right* ☎ *340/774–4312* ⊕ *www.onepaper.com/synagogue* ⊙ *Weekdays 9–4.*

FAMILY **Vendors Plaza.** Here merchants sell everything from T-shirts to African attire to leather goods. Look for local art among the ever-changing selections at this busy market. There are even a group of hair-braiders here, too. ⊠ *Waterfront, west of Ft. Christian* ⊙ *Weekdays 8–6, weekends 9–1.*

Weibel Museum. In this museum next to the synagogue, 300 years of Jewish history on St. Thomas are showcased. The small gift shop sells a commemorative silver coin celebrating the anniversary of the Hebrew congregation's establishment on the island in 1796. There are also tropically inspired items, such as menorahs painted to resemble palm trees. ⊠ *Synagogue Hill, 15 Crystal Gade* ⟐ *From Main Street, walk up Raadet's Gade (H. Stern is on corner) to top of hill, turn left and Synagogue is 2nd bldg. on right* ☎ *340/774–4312* ⊕ *www.onepaper.com/synagogue* ⊡ *Free* ⊙ *Weekdays 9–4.*

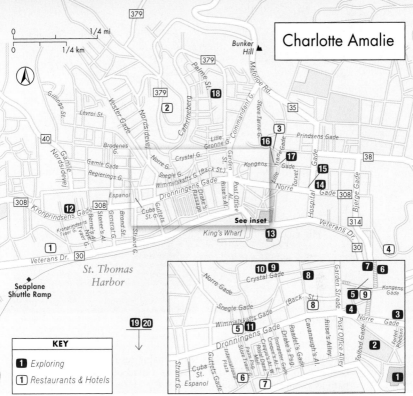

Charlotte Amalie

KEY

1 *Exploring*

1 *Restaurants & Hotels*

Coral World Ocean Park offers interactive sea-life encounters.

EAST END

Although the eastern end has many major resorts and spectacular beaches, don't be surprised if a cow or a herd of goats crosses your path as you drive through the relatively flat, dry terrain.

FAMILY
Fodor's Choice
★

Coral World Ocean Park. This interactive aquarium and water-sports center lets you experience a variety of sea life and other animals. There's a new 2-acre dolphin habitat, as well as several outdoor pools where you can pet baby sharks, feed stingrays, touch starfish, and view endangered sea turtles. During the Sea Trek Helmet Dive, you walk along an underwater trail wearing a helmet that provides a continuous supply of air. You can try "snuba," a cross between snorkeling and scuba diving. Swim with a sea lion and have a chance at playing ball or getting a big, wet, whistered kiss. You can also buy a cup of nectar and let the cheerful lorikeets perch on your hand and drink. The park also has an offshore underwater observatory, an 80,000-gallon coral reef exhibit (one of the largest in the world), and a nature trail with native ducks and tortoises. Daily feedings take place at most exhibits. ⊠ *Coki Point north of Rte. 38, 6450 Estate Smith Bay, Estate Frydendal* ☎ *340/775–1555* ⊕ *www.coralworldvi.com* ✉ *$19, Sea Lion Splash $126, Sea Lion Encounter $86, Sea Trek $79, Snuba $73, Shark and Turtle Encounters $53, Semi-Submarine $41* ⊗ *Daily 9–4. Off-season (May–Oct.) hrs may vary, so call to confirm.*

Red Hook. The IGY American Yacht Harbor marina here has fishing and sailing charter boats, a dive shop, and powerboat-rental agencies. There are also several bars and restaurants, including Molly Molone's, Duffy's Love Shack, and the Caribbean Saloon. Ferries depart from Red Hook en route to St. John and the British Virgin Islands. ⊠ *Red Hook, Intersection of Rtes. 38 and 32.*

SOUTH SHORE

FAMILY **Butterfly Garden.** Step into this 10,000-square-foot mesh enclosure and watch hundreds of colorful, exotic butterflies flutter all around you. A 25-minute tour takes you through their life cycle. Outside the enclosure, you can wander a garden of native plants designed to attract local butterflies and hummingbirds. The butterflies are most active in the morning. If you're a photographer, you'll probably prefer the afternoon, when the butterflies move more slowly and are more easily captured in a picture. ⊠ *Havensight Mall, 9016 Havensight Mall, adjacent to West Indian Company cruise-ship dock, Havensight* ☎ *340/715–3366* ⊕ *www.butterflygardenvi.com* ✆ *$15* ⊘ *Daily 8:30–4. Off-season (May–Oct.) hrs may vary, so call to confirm.*

Frenchtown. Popular for its bars and restaurants, Frenchtown is also the home of descendants of immigrants from St. Barthélemy (St. Barths). You can watch them pull up their brightly painted boats and display their equally colorful catch of the day along the waterfront. If you chat with them, you can hear speech patterns slightly different from those of other St. Thomians. Get a feel for the residential district of Frenchtown by walking west to some of the town's winding streets, where tiny wooden houses have been passed down from generation to generation. ⊠ *Turn south off Waterfront Hwy. (Rte. 30) at post office, Frenchtown.*

French Heritage Museum. Next to Joseph Aubain Ballpark, the museum houses fishing nets, accordions, tambourines, mahogany furniture, photographs, and other artifacts illustrating the lives of the French descendants during the 18th through 20th centuries. Admission is free, but donations are accepted. ⊠ *Rue de St. Anne and rue de St. Barthélemy, next to Joseph Aubain Ballpark, Frenchtown* ☎ *340/714–2583* ⊕ *www.frenchheritagemuseum.com* ✆ *Free* ⊘ *Mon.–Sat. 9–6.*

FAMILY **St. Thomas Skyride.** Fly skyward in a gondola to Paradise Point, an overlook with breathtaking views of Charlotte Amalie and the harbor. You'll find several shops, a bar, a restaurant, and a wedding gazebo. A ¼-mile (½-km) hiking trail leads to spectacular views of St. Croix. Wear sturdy shoes, as the trail is steep and rocky. You can also skip the $21 gondola ride and taxi to the top for $4 per person from the Havensight Dock. ⊠ *Rte. 30, across from Havensight Mall, Havensight* ☎ *340/774–9809* ✆ *$21* ⊘ *Thurs.–Tues. 9–5, Wed. 9–9.*

FAMILY **Water Island.** This island, the fourth-largest of the U.S. Virgin Islands, floats about ¼ mile (½ km) out in Charlotte Amalie harbor. A ferry between Crown Bay Marina and the island operates several times daily from 6:30 am to 6 pm Monday through Saturday, and from 8 am to 5 pm on Sunday and holidays at a cost of $10 round-trip. (On cruise-ship days, a ferry goes direct from the West India Company dock, but only for those passengers on the bike trip.) From the ferry dock, it's a hike of less than a half-mile to Honeymoon Beach (though you have to go up a big hill), where Brad Pitt and Cate Blanchett filmed a scene of the movie *The Curious Case of Benjamin Button*. Get lunch from a food truck that pulls up on weekends. ⊠ *Charlotte Amalie harbor, Charlotte Amalie* ☎ *340/690–4159 for ferry information.*

27

WEST END

Drake's Seat. Sir Francis Drake was supposed to have kept watch over his fleet and looked for enemy ships from this vantage point. The panorama is especially breathtaking (and romantic) at dusk, and if you arrive late in the day, you can miss the hordes of day-trippers on taxi tours who stop here to take a picture. ✉ *Rte. 40, ¼ mile west of intersection of Rte. 40 and 35, Estate Zufriedenheit.*

Estate St. Peter Greathouse and Botanical Gardens. This unusual spot is perched on a mountainside 1,000 feet above sea level, with views of more than 20 islands and islets. You can wander through a gallery displaying local art, sip a complimentary rum punch while looking out at the view, or follow a nature trail that leads you past nearly 70 varieties of tropical plants, including 17 varieties of orchids. ✉ *Rte. 40, directly across from Tree Limin' Extreme Zipline, Estate St. Peter* ☎ *340/774–4999* ⊕ *www.greathousevi.com* 💲 *$10.*

Magic Ice Gallery. This is one cool gallery! Life-size ice carvings feature sea life, a pirate ship, a chapel, a bar (a complimentary drink is included in the tour), a slide you can ride down, and much more. Insulated ponchos with hoods and mittens are provided, but you don't get to keep them. ✉ *Charlotte Amalie Waterfront, 21 Dronningens Gade, located next to Pizza Hut on Waterfront* ☎ *340/422–6000* ⊕ *www. magicice.vi* 💲 *$15* ☉ *Daily 10–5.*

FAMILY **Mountain Top.** Head out to the observation deck—more than 1,500 feet above sea level—to get a bird's-eye view that stretches from Puerto Rico's out-island of Culebra in the west all the way to the British Virgin Islands in the east. There's also a restaurant, restrooms, and duty-free shops that sell everything from Caribbean art to nautical antiques, ship models, and touristy T-shirts. Kids will like talking to the parrots—and hearing them answer back. ✉ *Head north off Rte. 33, look for signs, Mountain Top* ☎ *340/774–2400* ⊕ *www.mountaintopvi.com* 💲 *Free* ☉ *Daily 8–5.*

BEACHES

All 44 St. Thomas beaches are open to the public, although you can reach some of them only by walking through a resort. Hotel guests frequently have access to lounge chairs and floats that are off-limits to nonguests; for this reason you may feel more comfortable at one of the beaches not associated with a resort, such as Magens Bay (which charges an entrance fee to cover beach maintenance) or Coki Beach, the latter abutting Coral World Ocean Park and offering the island's best off-the-beach snorkeling. Remember to remove all your valuables from the car and keep them out of sight when you go swimming. Break-ins are possible on all three of the U.S. Virgin Islands; most locals recommend leaving your windows down and leaving absolutely nothing in your car.

EAST END

FAMILY **Coki Beach.** Funky beach huts selling local foods such as pâtés (fried
Fodor's Choice turnovers with a spicy ground-beef filling), quaint vendor kiosks, and
★ a brigade of hair braiders and taxi men make this beach overlooking picturesque Thatch Cay feel like an amusement park. But this is the best

place on the island to snorkel and scuba dive. Fish, including grunts, snappers, and wrasses, are like an effervescent cloud you can wave your hand through. **Amenities:** food and drink; lifeguards; parking; showers; restrooms; watersports. **Best for:** partiers; snorkeling. ⊠ *Rte. 388, next to Coral World Ocean Park, Estate Smith Bay.*

Lindquist Beach. The newest of the Virgin Islands' public beaches has a serene sense of wilderness that isn't found on the more crowded beaches. A lifeguard is on duty between 8 am and 5 pm. Picnic tables are available. Try snorkeling over the offshore reef. **Amenities:** lifeguards; parking; toilets. **Best for:** solitude; snorkeling. ⊠ *Rte. 38, at end of bumpy dirt road* 🕮 *$2 per person.*

FAMILY **Sapphire Beach.** A steady breeze makes this beach a boardsailor's paradise. The swimming is great, as is the snorkeling, especially at the reef near Pettyklip Point. Beach volleyball is big on the weekends. Sapphire Beach Resort and Marina has a snack shop, bar, and water-sports rentals. **Amenities:** food and drink; parking; restrooms; water sports. **Best for:** snorkeling; swimming; windsurfing. ⊠ *Rte. 38, ½ mile north of Red Hook, Sapphire Bay.*

Secret Harbour. Placid waters make it easy to stroke your way out to a swim platform offshore from the Secret Harbour Beach Resort & Villas. Nearby reefs give snorkelers a natural show. There's a bar and restaurant, as well as a dive shop. **Amenities:** food and drink; parking; restrooms; water sports. **Best for:** snorkeling; sunset; swimming. ⊠ *Rte. 322, take first right off Rte. 322, Red Hook.*

Vessup Beach. This wild, undeveloped beach is lined with sea grape trees and century plants. It's close to Red Hook harbor, so you can watch the ferries depart. The calm waters are excellent for swimming. West Indies Windsurfing is here, so you can rent Windsurfers, kayaks, and other water toys. It's popular with locals on weekends. **Amenities:** parking; water sports. **Best for:** swimming. ⊠ *Off Rte. 322, Vessup Bay.*

SOUTH SHORE

Brewer's Beach. Watch jets land at the Cyril E. King Airport as you dip into the usually calm seas. Rocks at either end of the shoreline, patches of grass poking randomly through the sand, and shady tamarind trees 30 feet from the water give this beach a wild, natural feel. Civilization has arrived, in the form of one or two mobile food vans park on the nearby road. Buy a fried-chicken leg and johnnycake or burgers and chips to munch on at the picnic tables. **Amenities:** food and drink; lifeguards; parking; restrooms. **Best for:** sunset; swimming. ⊠ *Rte. 30, west of University of the Virgin Islands.*

Morningstar Beach. Nature and nurture combine at this ¼-mile-long (½-km-long) beach between Marriott Frenchman's Reef and Morning Star Beach Resorts, where the amenities include beachside bar service. A concession rents floating mats, snorkeling equipment, sailboards, and Jet Skis. Swimming is excellent; there are good-size rolling waves year-round, but do watch the undertow. If you're feeling lazy, rent a lounge chair with umbrella and order a libation from one of two full-service beach bars. At 7 am and again at 5 pm, you can catch the cruise ships gliding majestically out to sea from the Charlotte Amalie harbor.

Amenities: food and drink; parking; restrooms; water sports. **Best for:** partiers; surfing; swimming. ⊠ *Rte. 315 ⊹ 2 miles (3 km) southeast of Charlotte Amalie, past Havensight Mall and cruise-ship dock.*

WEST END

FAMILY

Fodor's Choice

★

Magens Bay. Deeded to the island as a public park, this heart-shape stretch of white sand is considered one of the most beautiful in the world. The bottom of the bay is flat and sandy, so this is a place for sunning and swimming rather than snorkeling. On weekends and holidays the sounds of music from groups partying under the sheds fill the air. There's a bar, snack shack, and beachwear boutique; bathhouses with restrooms, changing rooms, and saltwater showers are close by. Sunfish, kayaks and paddleboards are the most popular rentals at the water-sports kiosk. East of the beach is Udder Delight, a one-room shop that serves a Virgin Islands tradition—a milk shake with a splash of Cruzan rum. (Kids can enjoy virgin versions, which have a touch of soursop, mango, or banana flavoring.) If you arrive between 8 am and 5 pm, you pay an entrance fee of $4 per person, $2 per vehicle; it's free for children under 12. **Amenities:** food and drink; lifeguards; parking (fee); showers; restrooms; water sports. **Best for:** partiers; swimming; walking. ⊠ *Magens Bay, Rte. 35, at end of road on north side of island* ☎ *340/777–6300.*

WHERE TO EAT

The beauty of St. Thomas and its sister islands has attracted a cadre of professionally trained chefs who know their way around fresh fish and local fruits. You can dine on terrific cheap local dishes such as goat water (a spicy stew) and fungi (a cornmeal side dish that's similar to polenta) as well as imports that include hot pastrami sandwiches and raspberries in crème fraîche.

Restaurants are spread all over the island, although fewer are found on the west and northwest parts of the island. Most restaurants out of town are easily accessible by taxi and have ample parking. If you dine in Charlotte Amalie, take a taxi. Parking close to restaurants can be difficult to find, and walking around after dark isn't always safe.

If your accommodations have a kitchen and you plan to cook, there's good variety in St. Thomas's mainland-style supermarkets. Just be prepared for grocery prices that are about 20% to 30% higher than those in the United States. As for drinking, a beer in a bar that's not part of a hotel will cost between $5 and $6 and a piña colada $8 or more.

What to Wear: Dining on St. Thomas is informal. Few restaurants require a jacket and tie. Still, at dinner in the snazzier places shorts and T-shirts are inappropriate; men would do well to wear slacks and a shirt with buttons. Dress codes on St. Thomas rarely require women to wear skirts, but you can never go wrong with something flowing.

CHARLOTTE AMALIE

$$$$

ECLECTIC

Fodor's Choice

★

✕ **Banana Tree Grille.** The eagle's-eye view of the Charlotte Amalie harbor from this breeze-cooled restaurant is as fantastic as the food. Linen tablecloths, china, and silver place settings combine with subdued lighting to make an elegant space. To start, try the flamed-grilled oysters or crispy calamari dipped in tangy lemon aioli. The signature dish here—and worthy of its fame—is a grass-fed pasture-raised filet mignon topped with plump shrimp and served with velvety Bearnaise sauce and fresh asparagus. Arrive before 6 pm to watch the cruise ships depart from the harbor while you enjoy a drink at the bar. [$] *Average main: $40* ✉ *Bluebeard's Castle, Bluebeard's Hill, 1331 Estate Taamburg* ☎ *340/776–4050* 🌐 *www.bananatreegrille.com* ✍ *Reservations essential* 🕑 *Closed Mon. No lunch.*

$$ CARIBBEAN 🍴 **Cuzzin's Caribbean Restaurant and Bar.** In a 19th-century livery stable on Back Street, this restaurant is hard to find but well worth it if you want to sample bona fide Virgin Islands cuisine. For lunch, order tender slivers of conch stewed in a rich onion-and-butter sauce, savory braised oxtail, or curried chicken. At dinner the island-style mutton, served in thick gravy and seasoned with locally grown herbs, offers a tasty treat that's deliciously different. Side dishes include peas and rice, boiled green bananas, fried plantains, and potato stuffing. [$] *Average main: $16* ✉ *7 Wimmelskafts Gade, also called Back St.* ☎ *340/777–4711.*

$$ CARIBBEAN Fodor's Choice ★ 🍴 **Gladys' Cafe.** Even if the local specialties—conch in butter sauce, jerk pork, panfried yellowtail snapper—didn't make this a recommended café, it would be worth coming for Gladys's smile. Her cozy alleyway restaurant is rich in atmosphere with its mahogany bar and native stone walls, making dining a double delight. While you're here, pick up a $5 or $10 bottle of her special hot sauce. There are mustard-, oil and vinegar–, and tomato-based versions; the tomato-based sauce is the hottest. **TIP→ Only Amex is accepted.** [$] *Average main: $14* ✉ *Waterfront, 28A Dronningens Gade, west side of Royal Dane Mall* ☎ *340/774–6604* 🌐 *www.gladyscafe.com* 🕑 *No dinner.*

$$ AMERICAN FAMILY 🍴 **Greenhouse Bar and Restaurant.** Fun-lovers come to this waterfront restaurant to eat, listen to music, and play games, both video and pool. Even the most finicky eater should find something to please on the eight-page menu that offers burgers, salads, and pizza served all day long, along with peel-and-eat shrimp, Maine lobster, Alaskan king crab, and Black Angus prime rib for dinner. This is generally a family-friendly place, though the Two-for-Tuesdays happy hour and Friday-night live reggae music that starts thumping at 10 pm draw an occasionally rambunctious young-adult crowd. [$] *Average main: $18* ✉ *Waterfront Hwy. at Storetvaer Gade* ☎ *340/774–7998* 🌐 *www.thegreenhouserestaurant.com.*

$$$$ ITALIAN 🍴 **Virgilio's.** For the island's best northern Italian cuisine, don't miss this intimate, elegant hideaway that's on a quiet side street. Eclectic art covers the two-story brick walls, and the sound of opera sets the stage for a memorable meal. Come here for more than 40 homemade pastas topped with superb sauces—capellini with fresh tomatoes and garlic or peasant-style spaghetti in a rich tomato sauce with mushrooms and prosciutto. House specialties include osso buco and tiramisu, which are expertly crafted by chef Ernesto Garrigos, who has prepared these two dishes on the Discovery Channel's *Great Chefs of the World* series. [$] *Average main: $32* ✉ *5150 Dronnigens Gade* ☎ *340/776–4920* 🌐 *www.virgiliosvi.com* ✍ *Reservations essential* 🕑 *Closed Sun.*

EAST END

$$$$ AMERICAN 🍴 **Caribbean Saloon.** Sports on wide-screen TVs and live music on weekends are two added attractions at this hip sports bar that's in the center of the action in Red Hook. The menu ranges from finger-licking barbecue ribs to more sophisticated fare, such as the signature filet mignon wrapped in bacon and smothered in melted Gorgonzola cheese. There's always a catch of the day; the fishing fleet is only steps away. A late-night menu is available from 10 pm until 4 am. [$] *Average main: $28* ✉ *American Yacht Harbor, Rte. 32, Bldg B., Red Hook* ☎ *340/775–7060* 🌐 *www.caribbeansaloon.com.*

$$ ECLECTIC 🍴 **Duffy's Love Shack.** If the floating bubbles don't attract you to this zany eatery, the lime-green shutters, loud rock music, and fun-loving waitstaff just might. It's billed as the "ultimate tropical drink shack," and the bartenders shake up such exotic concoctions as the Love Shack Volcano—a 50-ounce flaming extravaganza. The menu has a selection of burgers, tacos, burritos, and salads. Try the grilled mahimahi taco salad or jerk Caesar wrap. [$] *Average main: $15* ✉ *Red Hook Shopping Center, Rte. 32 and 6500 Red Hook Plaza, located in parking lot, Red Hook* ☎ *340/779–2080* 🌐 *www.duffysloveshack.com.*

$$$ IRISH FAMILY 🍴 **Molly Molone's.** This dockside eatery has a devoted following among local boaters, who swear by the traditional American and Irish fare. Opt for eggs Benedict or rashers of Irish sausages and eggs for breakfast, or fork into fish-and-chips, Irish stew, or bangers and mash (sausage and mashed potatoes) for lunch or dinner. ⚠ **Beware: the resident iguanas will beg for table scraps—bring your camera.** [$] *Average main: $24* ✉ *American Yacht Harbor, Bldg. D, Rte. 32, Red Hook* ☎ *340/775–1270* 🌐 *mollymalonesstthomas.com.*

$$$$ ECLECTIC Fodor's Choice ★ 🍴 **Old Stone Farmhouse.** Dine in the splendor of a beautifully restored plantation house. Come early and sidle up to the beautiful mahogany bar, where you can choose from an extensive wine list. Then, start with French onion soup, move on to osso buco with a lobster risotto; and finish with a house-made passion-fruit sorbet. Personalized attention makes dining here a delight. [$] *Average main: $36* ✉ *Rte. 42, 1 mile (1½ km) west of entrance to Mahogany Run Golf Course, Estate Lovenlund* ☎ *340/777–6277* 🌐 *www.oldstonefarmhouse.com* ✍ *Reservations essential* ⏲ *Closed Mon.*

SOUTH SHORE

$$$$ ECLECTIC Fodor's Choice ★ 🍴 **Havana Blue.** The cuisine here is described as Latin America meets Pacific Rim, but however you describe it, the dining experience is outstanding. A glowing wall of water meets you as you enter this beachfront eatery, and then you're seated at a table laid with linen and silver that's illuminated in a soft blue light radiating from above. Be sure to sample the mango mojito, made with fresh mango, crushed mint, and limes. Tapas-style entrées include slow-roasted pulled pork Cuban sliders, Szechuan peppercorn seared tuna, and shiitake spring rolls. Hand-rolled cigars and aged rums finish the night off in true Latin style. For something really special, request an exclusive table for two set on Morning Star Beach—you get a seven-course tasting menu, champagne, and your own personal waiter, all for $350 for two. [$] *Average main: $36* ✉ *Marriott Morningstar Beach Resort, Rte. 315, 2nd fl., above front desk, Estate Bakkeroe* ☎ *340/715–2583* 🌐 *www.havanaluerestaurant.com* ✍ *Reservations essential* ⏲ *No lunch.*

CLOSE UP

Where to Shop for Groceries

High food prices in Virgin Islands supermarkets are enough to dull anyone's appetite. Food is significantly more expensive than on the mainland.

Although you'll never match the prices back home, you can shop around for the best deals. If you're traveling with a group, it pays to stock up on the basics at warehouse-style stores such as Pricesmart (membership required) and Cost-U-Less. Even the nonbulk food items here are sold at lower prices than in the supermarkets or convenience stores. Good buys include beverages, meats, produce, and spirits.

After this, head to supermarkets such as Plaza Extra, Pueblo, and Food Center. Although the prices aren't as good as at the big-box stores, the selection is better.

Finally, if you want to splurge on top-quality meats, exotic produce, imported cheeses, exotic spices, and imported spirits, finish off your shopping at high-end shops such as Gourmet Gallery.

The Fruit Bowl is the place for fresh produce. The prices and selection are unbeatable.

For really fresh tropical fruits, vegetables, and seasoning herbs, visit the farmers' markets in Smith Bay (daily), at Market Square (daily), at Yacht Haven Grande (first and third Sunday of the month), and in Estate Bordeaux (second and last Sunday of every month).

$$$ ECLECTIC

🍴 **Randy's Bar and Bistro.** There's no view here—even though you're at the top of a hill—but the somewhat hidden location has helped to keep this one of the island's best dining secrets. This wine shop and deli caters to a local lunch crowd. At night, you forget you're tucked into a nearly windowless building. The tableside bread for starters is a thick, crusty focaccia flavored with nearly 10 different vegetables. Try the drunken shrimp sautéed in tequila or the veal parmigiana. After-dinner cigars and wine complete the experience. [$] *Average main: $23* ✉ *Al Cohen's Plaza, 4002 Raphune Hill, off Rte. 38, ½ mile (¾ km) east of Charlotte Amalie, Charlotte Amalie* ☎ *340/775–5001.*

WEST END

$$$ MEDITERRANEAN FAMILY

🍴 **Bella Blu.** In a quaint building in Frenchtown, this place has an ever-changing display of local art on the walls and delicious specials to match. The Austrian-inspired menu includes six varieties of schnitzel and boasts a Caribbean flair with fresh fish dishes such as snapper Provençal. Lunchtime attracts a business crowd that breaks bread and brokers deals at the same time. Fork into omelets, pancakes, or waffles during Saturday's Jazz Brunch from 10 am to 3 pm. [$] *Average main: $25* ✉ *Frenchtown Mall, 24-A Honduras St., across from ballpark, Frenchtown* ☎ *340/774–4349* 🌐 *www.bellabludining.com* ✍ *Reservations essential* 🕒 *Closed Sun.*

$$$ SEAFOOD FAMILY

🍴 **Hook, Line and Sinker.** Anchored on the breezy Frenchtown waterfront and close to the pastel-painted boats of the local fishing fleet, this harbor-view eatery serves high-quality fish dishes. The almond-crusted yellowtail snapper is a house specialty. Spicy jerk-seasoned swordfish and grilled tuna topped with a yummy mango-rum sauce are also good bets. This is one of the few independent restaurants serving Sunday brunch. [$] *Average main: $24* ✉ *Frenchtown Mall, 2 Honduras St., at head of Frenchtown Marina docks, Frenchtown* ☎ *340/776–9708* 🌐 *www.hooklineandsinkervi.com.*

$$ AMERICAN FAMILY 🍴 **Tickle's Dockside Pub.** Nautical types as well as the local working crowd come here for casual fare with homey appeal: chicken-fried steak, meat loaf with mashed potatoes, and baby back ribs. Hearty breakfasts feature eggs and pancakes, and lunch is a full array of burgers, salads, sandwiches, and soups. From November through April, the adjacent marina is full of enormous yachts, which make for some great eye candy while you dine. [$] *Average main: $17* ✉ *Crown Bay Marina, 8168 Crown Bay Marina, Suite 308, off Rte. 304, Estate Contant* ☎ *340/777–8792* 🌐 *ticklesdocksidepub.com.*

WHERE TO STAY

Of the USVI, St. Thomas has the most rooms and the greatest number and variety of resorts. You can let yourself be pampered at a luxurious resort—albeit at a price of $400 to more than $600 per night, not including meals. For much less, there are fine hotels (often with rooms that have a kitchen and a living area) in lovely settings throughout the island. There are also guesthouses and inns with great views and great service at about half the cost of what you'll pay at the beachfront pleasure palaces. Many of these are east and north of Charlotte Amalie or overlooking hills—ideal if you plan to get out and mingle with the locals. There are also inexpensive lodgings (most right in town) that are perfect if you just want a clean room to return to after a day of exploring or beach bumming.

East End condominium complexes are popular with families. Although condos are pricey (winter rates average $350 per night for a two-bedroom unit, which usually sleeps six), they have full kitchens, and you can definitely save money by cooking for yourself—especially if you bring some of your own nonperishable foodstuffs. (Virtually everything on St. Thomas is imported, and restaurants and shops pass shipping costs on to you.) Though you may spend some time laboring in the kitchen, many condos ease your burden with daily maid service and on-site restaurants; a few also have resort amenities, including pools and tennis courts. The East End is convenient to St. John, and it's a hub for the boating crowd, with some good restaurants. The prices *below* reflect rates in high season, which runs from December 15 to April 15. Rates are 25% to 50% lower the rest of the year.

PRIVATE VILLAS AND CONDOMINIUMS

St. Thomas has a wide range of private villas. Most will require that you book for seven nights during high season, five in low season. A minimum stay of up to two weeks is often required during the Christmas season. The agents who represent villa owners usually have websites and brochures that show photos of the properties they represent. Some villas are suitable for travelers with disabilities, but be sure to ask specific questions about your own needs.

RENTAL CONTACTS

Calypso Realty ☎ *340/774–1620, 800/747–4858* 🌐 *www.calypsorealty.com.*

McLaughlin-Anderson Luxury Caribbean Villas. Handling rental villas throughout the U.S. Virgin Islands, British Virgin Islands, and Grenada, McLaughlin-Anderson has a good selection in complexes on St. Thomas's East End. ☎ *340/776–0635, 800/537–6246* 🌐 *www.mclaughlinanderson.com.*

CHARLOTTE AMALIE

Accommodations in and near town mean that you're close to the airport, shopping, and a number of restaurants. The downside is that this is the most crowded and noisy area of the island. Crime can also be a problem. Don't go for a stroll at night in the heart of town. Use common sense and take the same precautions you would in any major city. Properties along the hillsides are less likely to have crime problems, and they also get a steady breeze from the cool trade winds. This is especially important if you're visiting in summer and early fall.

$ HOTEL 🏨 **The Green Iguana.** Atop Blackbeard's Hill, this value-priced small hotel offers the perfect mix of gorgeous harbor views, proximity to shopping (five-minute walk), and secluded privacy provided by the surrounding showy trees and bushy hibiscus. **Pros:** personalized service; near the center of town; laundry on premises. **Cons:** need a car to get around; town may be noisy at night depending on seasonal events. [$] *Rooms from: $140* ✉ *1002 Blackbeard's Hill* ☎ *340/776–7654, 855/473–4733* 🌐 *www.thegreeniguana.com* 🛏 *9 rooms* 🍴 *No meals.*

$ B&B/INN 🏨 **Hotel 1829.** Antique charm—though some may simply call it old—is readily apparent in this rambling 19th-century merchant's house, from the hand-painted Moroccan tiles to a Tiffany window. **Pros:** close to attractions; good prices; breakfast served on the verandah. **Cons:** some small rooms; tour groups during the day; neighborhood dicey at night. [$] *Rooms from: $125* ✉ *Government Hill, 29–30 Kongens Gade* ☎ *340/776–1829, 800/524–2002* 🌐 *www.hotel1829.com* 🛏 *15 rooms* 🍴 *Breakfast.*

$ HOTEL Fodor's Choice ★ 🏨 **Villa Santana.** Built by exiled General Antonio López Santa Anna of Mexico, this 1857 landmark provides a panoramic view of the harbor and plenty of West Indian charm, which will make you feel as if you're living in a charming slice of Virgin Islands history. **Pros:** historic charm; plenty of privacy. **Cons:** not on a beach; no restaurant; need a car to get around. [$] *Rooms from: $150* ✉ *2602 Bjerge Gade, 2D Denmark Hill* ☎ *340/776–1311* 🌐 *www.villasantana.com* 🛏 *6 rooms* 🍴 *No meals.*

$ HOTEL 🏨 **Windward Passage Hotel.** Business travelers, tourists on their way to the British Virgin Islands, and laid-back vacationers who want the convenience of being able to walk to duty-free shopping, sights, and restaurants, stay at this harborfront hotel. **Pros:** walking distance to Charlotte Amalie; nice harbor views; across from BVI ferry terminal. **Cons:** basic rooms; on a busy street; no water sports, but dive shop is on property. [$] *Rooms from: $220* ✉ *Waterfront Hwy.* ☎ *340/774–5200, 800/524–7389* 🌐 *www.windwardpassage.com* 🛏 *140 rooms, 11 suites* 🍴 *No meals.*

The Ritz-Carlton St. Thomas

EAST END

You can find most of the large, luxurious beachfront resorts on St. Thomas's East End. The downside is that these properties are about a 30-minute drive from town and a 45-minute drive from the airport (substantially longer during peak hours). On the upside, they tend to be self-contained, plus there are a number of good restaurants, shops, and water-sports operators in the area. Once you've settled in, you don't need a car to get around.

$$
RENTAL
FAMILY
The Anchorage Beach Resort. A beachfront setting and homey conveniences that include full kitchens and washer–dryer units are what attract families to these two- and three-bedroom suites on Cowpet Bay next to the St. Thomas Yacht Club. **Pros:** on the beach; good amenities. **Cons:** small pool; noisy neighbors; need a car to get around; petty theft is a problem in the neighborhood. $ *Rooms from: $375* ⊠ *Rte. 317, Estate Nazareth* ☎ *800/874–7897* ⊕ *www.antillesresorts.com* ⤶ *11 suites* ¶◯¶ *No meals.*

$
RENTAL
Pavilions and Pools Villa Hotel. Although the rates might lead you to believe you're buying resort ambience, the reality is that you get fairly basic accommodations here. **Pros:** intimate atmosphere; friendly host; private pools. **Cons:** some small rooms; on a busy road; long walk to beach. $ *Rooms from: $250* ⊠ *6400 Estate Smith Bay, off Rte. 38, Estate Smith Bay* ☎ *340/775–6110, 800/524–2001* ⊕ *www.pavilionsandpools.com* ⤶ *25 1-bedroom villas* ¶◯¶ *Breakfast.*

$$
RESORT
Point Pleasant Resort. Hilltop suites give you an eagle's-eye view of the East End and beyond, and those in a building adjacent to the reception area offer incredible sea views. **Pros:** lush setting; convenient

kitchens; pleasant pools. **Cons:** steep climb from beach; need a car to get around; some rooms need refurbishing. $ *Rooms from: $300* ✉ *6600 Estate Smith Bay, off Rte. 38, Estate Smith Bay* ☎ *340/775– 7200, 800/524–2300* ⊕ *www.pointpleasantresort.com* ☞ *128 suites* ❘○❘ *No meals.*

$$$$
RESORT
FAMILY
Fodor'sChoice
★

🏨 **Ritz-Carlton, St. Thomas.** Everything sparkles at the island's most luxurious resort, from the in-room furnishings and amenities to the infinity pool, white-sand beach, and turquoise sea beyond. **Pros:** gorgeous views; great water-sports facilities; beautiful beach; airport shuttle. **Cons:** service can sometimes be spotty for such an upscale (and pricey) hotel; food and drink can lack flair and are expensive ($19 hamburger, $12 piña colada); half-hour or more drive to town and airport. $ *Rooms from: $610* ✉ *6900 Estate Great Bay, off Rte. 317, Estate Great Bay* ☎ *340/775–3333, 800/241–3333* ⊕ *www.ritzcarlton.com* ☞ *255 rooms, 20 suites, 2 villas, 81 condos* ❘○❘ *No meals.*

$$$
RENTAL

🏨 **Sapphire Beach Condominium Resort.** A beautiful half-mile-long white-sand beach is the real ace here, because accommodations can be hit-or-miss, depending on whether you book with a private condo owner (hit) or the management company (miss). **Pros:** beachfront location; water sports abound; near ferries. **Cons:** some rooms need refurbishing; restaurant fare limited. $ *Rooms from: $435* ✉ *6720 Estate Smith Bay, Estate Smith Bay* ☎ *800/524–2090, 340/775–6100, 800/874– 7897* ⊕ *www.antillesresorts.com* ☞ *171 condos* ❘○❘ *No meals.*

$
RENTAL

🏨 **Sapphire Village Resort.** These high-rise towers feel more like apartment buildings than luxury resorts, so if you're looking for a home away from home, this might be the place. **Pros:** within walking distance of Red Hook; nice views; secluded feel. **Cons:** small rooms; limited dining options; noisy neighbors. $ *Rooms from: $210* ✉ *Rte. 38, ¼ mile northwest of Red Hook, Sapphire Bay* ☎ *340/779–1540, 800/874– 7897* ⊕ *antillesresorts.com* ☞ *15 condos* ❘○❘ *No meals.*

27

$$
RENTAL

🏨 **Secret Harbour Beach Resort.** There's not a bad view from these low-rise studios and one- and two-bedroom condos, which are either beachfront or perched on a hill overlooking an inviting cove. **Pros:** beautiful beach and great snorkeling; good restaurant; secluded location. **Cons:** car needed to get around; condo owners are territorial about beach chairs. $ *Rooms from: $355* ✉ *Rte. 317, Estate Nazareth* ☎ *340/775–6550, 800/524–2250* ⊕ *www.secretharbourvi.com* ☞ *73 suites* ❘○❘ *No meals.*

$$$$
ALL-INCLUSIVE
FAMILY

🏨 **Sugar Bay Resort & Spa.** The only completely all-inclusive resort on St. Thomas, this terra-cotta high-rise is surrounded by palm trees and lush greenery, but the rooms and the walkways between them feel a little generic. **Pros:** gorgeous pool area; full-service spa; on-site casino. **Cons:** some steps to climb; lawn by pool teems with iguanas; limited dining options. $ *Rooms from: $525* ✉ *6500 Estate Smith Bay, Estate Smith Bay* ☎ *340/777–7100, 800/927–7100* ⊕ *www.sugarbayresortandspa. com* ☞ *294 rooms, 7 suites* ❘○❘ *All-inclusive.*

SOUTH SHORE

The South Shore of St. Thomas connects town to the east end of the island via a beautiful road that rambles along the hillside with frequent peeks between the hills for a view of the ocean and, on a clear day, of St. Croix some 40 miles (64 km) to the south. The resorts here are on their own beaches. They offer several opportunities for water sports, as well as land-based activities, fine dining, and evening entertainment.

$$
RESORT
Bolongo Bay Beach Resort. All the rooms at this family-run resort tucked along a 1,000-foot-long palm-lined beach have balconies with ocean views; down the beach are 9 condos with full kitchens. **Pros:** family-run property; on the beach; water sports abound. **Cons:** a bit run-down; on a busy road; need a car to get around. $ *Rooms from: $385* ✉ *Rte. 30, Estate Bolongo* ☎ *340/775–1800, 800/524–4746* ⊕ *www.bolongobay. com* ⋑ *71 rooms, 9 condos* ⦿ *Multiple meal plans.*

$$$
RESORT
FAMILY
Frenchman's Reef & Morning Star Marriott Beach Resort. Set majestically on a promontory overlooking the east side of Charlotte Amalie's harbor, Frenchman's Reef is the high-rise full-service superhotel; Morning Star is the even more upscale boutique property that's closer to the fine white-sand beach. **Pros:** beachfront location; good dining options; plenty of activities. **Cons:** musty smell on lower levels; long walk between resorts; a crowded-cruise-ship feel. $ *Rooms from: $410* ✉ *Rte. 315, Estate Bakkeroe* ☎ *340/776–8500, 800/233–6388* ⊕ *www.marriott.com* ⋑ *479 rooms, 27 suites, 220 2- and 3-bedroom time-share units* ⦿ *No meals.*

WEST END

A few properties are in the hills overlooking Charlotte Amalie to the west or near French Town, which is otherwise primarily residential.

$
HOTEL
Best Western Emerald Beach Resort. You get beachfront ambience at this reasonably priced miniresort tucked beneath the palm trees, but the trade-off is that it's directly across from a noisy airport runway. **Pros:** beachfront location; good value; great Sunday brunch. **Cons:** airport noise until 10 pm; on a busy road; limited water sports. $ *Rooms from: $240* ✉ *8070 Lindberg Bay, Lindbergh Bay* ☎ *340/777–8800, 800/780–7234* ⊕ *www.emeraldbeach.com* ⋑ *90 rooms* ⦿ *Breakfast.*

$
B&B/INN
Island View Guesthouse. Perched 545 feet up the face of Crown Mountain, this small, homey inn has hands-on owners who can book tours or offer tips about the best sightseeing spots. **Pros:** spectacular views; friendly atmosphere; good value. **Cons:** small pool; need a car to get around. $ *Rooms from: $115* ✉ *Rte. 332, Estate Contant* ☎ *340/774–4270, 800/524–2023* ⊕ *www.islandviewstthomas.com* ⋑ *12 rooms, 10 with bath* ⦿ *Breakfast.*

NIGHTLIFE AND THE ARTS

On any given night, especially in season, you can find steel-pan bands, rock and roll, piano music, jazz, broken-bottle dancing (actual dancing atop broken glass), disco, and karaoke. Pick up a free copy of the bright yellow *St. Thomas–St. John This Week* magazine (⊕ *www.virginislandsthisweek. com*) when you arrive (it can be found at the airport, in stores, and in hotel lobbies). The back pages lists who's playing where. The Friday edition of the *Daily News* carries complete listings for the upcoming weekend.

NIGHTLIFE

CHARLOTTE AMALIE

Greenhouse Bar and Restaurant. Once this popular eatery puts away the salt-and-pepper shakers after 10 pm, it becomes a rock-and-roll club with a DJ or live reggae bands bringing the weary to their feet six nights a week. ⊠ *Waterfront Hwy. at Storetvaer Gade, Charlotte Amalie* ☎ *340/774–7998* ⊕ *www.thegreenhouserestaurant.com.*

EAST END

Duffy's Love Shack. At this island favorite, a live band and dancing under the stars are the big draws for locals and visitors alike. ⊠ *Red Hook Plaza, Rte. 32, Red Hook* ☎ *340/779–2080* ⊕ *www.duffysloveshack.com.*

SOUTH SHORE

Epernay Wine Bar & Bistro. Sometimes you need nothing more than small tables for easy chatting and wine and champagne by the glass. You can also mix and mingle with island celebrities here. The action at this intimate nightspot runs from 4 pm until the wee hours Monday through Saturday. ⊠ *Frenchtown Mall, 24-A Honduras St., Frenchtown* ☎ *340/774–5348.*

Iggies Beach Bar. Bolongo Bay's beachside bar offers karaoke on Saturday nights, so you can sing along to the sounds of the surf or the latest hits here. There are live bands on weekends, and you can dance inside or kick up your heels under the stars. Wednesday is Carnival Night, complete with steel-pan music, a limbo show and West Indian buffet. ⊠ *Bolongo Bay Beach Club & Villas, Rte. 30, Estate Bolongo* ☎ *340/775–1800* ⊕ *www.iggiesbeachbar.com.*

THE ARTS

SOUTH SHORE

Pistarkle Theater. This theater in the Tillett Gardens complex is air-conditioned and has more than 100 seats; it hosts a dozen or more productions annually, plus a children's summer drama camp. ⊠ *Tillett Gardens, Rte. 38, across from Tutu Park Shopping Mall, Estate Tutu* ☎ *340/775–7877* ⊕ *pistarckletheater.com.*

Reichhold Center for the Arts. St. Thomas's major performing arts center has an amphitheater, and its more expensive seats are covered by a roof. Throughout the year there's an entertaining mix of local plays, dance exhibitions, and music of all types. ⊠ *Rte. 30, across from Brewers Beach, Estate Lindberg Bay* ☎ *340/693–1559* ⊕ *www.reichholdcenter.com.*

SHOPPING

Fodor's Choice
★
St. Thomas lives up to its billing as a duty-free shopping destination. Even if shopping isn't your idea of how to spend a vacation, you still may want to slip in on a quiet day (check the cruise-ship listings—Monday and Sunday are usually the least crowded) to browse. Among the best buys are liquor, linens, china, crystal (most stores will ship), and jewelry. The amount of jewelry available makes this one of the few items for which comparison shopping is worth the effort. Local crafts include shell jewelry, carved calabash bowls, straw brooms, woven baskets, and dolls. The local doll maker Gwendolyn Harley makes

costumed West Indian market women and other creations who have become little goodwill ambassadors, bought by visitors from as far away as Asia. Spice mixes, hot sauces, and tropical jams and jellies are other native products.

On St. Thomas stores on Main Street in Charlotte Amalie are open weekdays and Saturday 9 to 5. The hours of the shops in the Havensight Mall (next to the cruise-ship dock) and the Crown Bay Commercial Center (next to the Crown Bay cruise-ship dock) are the same, though occasionally some stay open until 9 on Friday, depending on how many cruise ships are anchored nearby. You may also find some shops open on Sunday if cruise ships are in port. Hotel shops are usually open evenings as well.

There's no sales tax in the USVI, and you can take advantage of the $1,200 duty-free allowance per family member (remember to save your receipts). Although you can find the occasional salesclerk who will make a deal, bartering isn't the norm.

CHARLOTTE AMALIE

The prime shopping area in **Charlotte Amalie** is between Post Office and Market squares; it consists of two parallel streets that run east–west (Waterfront Highway and Main Street) and the alleyways that connect them. Particularly attractive are the historic **A.H. Riise Alley, Royal Dane Mall, Palm Passage,** and pastel-painted **International Plaza.**

Vendors Plaza, on the waterfront side of Emancipation Gardens in Charlotte Amalie, is a central location for vendors selling handmade earrings, necklaces, and bracelets; straw baskets and handbags; T-shirts; fabrics; African artifacts; and local fruits. Look for the many brightly colored umbrellas.

ART

Camille Pissarro Art Gallery. This second-floor gallery, at the birthplace of St. Thomas's famous artist, offers a fine collection of original paintings and prints by local and regional artists. ⊠ *14 Main St., Charlotte Amalie* ☎ *340/774–4621.*

Gallery St. Thomas. The gallery in this charming space has a nice collection of fine art and collectibles, including paintings, wood sculpture, glass, and jewelry that are from or inspired by the Virgin Islands. ⊠ *Palm Passage, Charlotte Amalie* ☎ *340/777–6363* ⊕ *gallerystthomas.com.*

CAMERAS AND ELECTRONICS

Boolchand's. This store sells brand-name cameras, audio and video equipment, and binoculars. ⊠ *31 Main St., Charlotte Amalie* ☎ *340/776–0794* ⊕ *www.boolchand.com.*

Royal Caribbean. The two branches of this shop are near each other; they stock a wide selection of cameras, camcorders, stereos, watches, and clocks. ⊠ *33 Main St., Charlotte Amalie* ☎ *340/776–5449* ⊕ *www.royalcaribbeanvi.com* ⊠ *33 Main St., Charlotte Amalie* ☎ *340/776–4110.*

Made in St. Thomas

Date-palm brooms, frangipani-scented perfume, historically clad dolls, sun-scorched hot sauces, aromatic mango candles: these are just a few of the handicrafts made in St. Thomas.

Justin Todman, aka the Broom Man, keeps the art of broom making alive. It's a skill he learned at the age of six from his father. From the fronds of the date palm, Todman cuts, strips, and dries the leaves. Then he weaves them into distinctively shaped brooms with birch-berry wood for handles. There are feather brooms, cane brooms, multicolor-yarn brooms, tiny brooms to fit into a child's hand, and tall, long-handled brooms to reach cobwebs on the ceiling. Some customers buy Todman's brooms—sold at the **Native Arts and Crafts Cooperative**—not for cleaning but rather for celebrating their nuptials. It's an old African custom for the bride and groom to jump over a horizontally laid broom to start their new life.

Gail Garrison puts the essence of local flowers, fruits, and leaves into perfumes, powders, and body splashes. Her Island Fragrances line includes frangipani-, white ginger–, and jasmine-scented perfumes; aromatic mango, lime, and coconut body splashes; and bay rum after-shave for men. Garrison compounds, mixes, and bottles the products herself in second-floor offices on

Charlotte Amalie's Main Street. Gwendolyn Harley preserves Virgin Islands culture in the personalities of her hand-sewn, softly sculptured historic dolls for sale at the Native Arts & Crafts Cooperative. There are quadrille dancers clad in long, colorful skirts; French women with their neat peaked bonnets; and farmers sporting handwoven straw hats. Each one-of-kind design is named using the last three letters of Harley's first name; the dolls have names like Joycelyn, Vitalyn, and Iselyn.

Cheryl Miller cooks up ingredients such as sun-sweetened papayas, fiery Scotch bonnet peppers, and aromatic basil leaves into the jams, jellies, and hot sauces she sells under her Cheryl's Taste of Paradise line. Five of Miller's products—Caribbean Mustango Sauce, Caribbean Sunburn, Mango Momma Jam, Mango Chutney, and Hot Green Pepper Jelly—have won awards at the National Fiery Foods Show in Albuquerque, New Mexico. You can buy her products at Cost-U-Less, the Native Arts and Crafts Cooperative, and the farmers' market at Yacht Haven Grande on the first and third Sunday of each month.

Jason Budsan traps the aromas of the islands, such as ripe mango and night jasmine, into sumptuous candles he sells at his **Tillett Gardens** workshop.

CHINA AND CRYSTAL

Little Switzerland. This popular Caribbean chain carries crystal from Baccarat, Waterford, and Orrefors; and china from Kosta Boda, Rosenthal, and Wedgwood. There's also an assortment of Swarovski cut-crystal animals, gemstone globes, and many other affordable collectibles. It also does a booming mail-order business. ⊠ *5 Dronningens Gade, across from Emancipation Garden, Charlotte Amalie* ☎ *340/776–2010* ⊕ *www.littleswitzerland.com* ⊠ *3B Main St., Charlotte Amalie* ☎ *340/776–2010.*

CLOTHING

FAMILY **Fresh Produce Sportswear.** This clothing store doesn't sell lime-green mangoes, peachy-pink guavas, or sunny-yellow bananas, but you will find these fun, casual colors on its clothing for children and adults. This is one of only 16 stores to stock all of the California-created, tropical-feel line of women's separates. The dresses, shirts, slacks, and skirts are in small to plus sizes, and bags and hats and other accessories are also available. ⊠ *Riise's Alley, 5189 Dronnigens Gade, across from Rolex store, Charlotte Amalie* 🕾 *340/774–0807* ⊕ *www.freshproduceclothes.com.*

FAMILY **Local Color.** This St. Thomas chain has clothes for men, women, and children among its brand names, which include Jams World, Fresh Produce, and Urban Safari. You can also find St. John artist Sloop Jones's colorful, hand-painted island designs on cool dresses, T-shirts, and sweaters. The tropically oriented accessories include big-brimmed straw hats, bold-color bags, and casual jewelry. ⊠ *Waterfront Hwy., at Raadets Gade, Charlotte Amalie* 🕾 *340/774–2280* ⊕ *www.usviweb. com/localcolor* ⊠ *Havensight Mall, Rte. 30, Bldg 7, 2 stores north of Post Office, Charlotte Amalie* 🕾 *340/774–3182.*

HANDICRAFTS

Native Arts and Crafts Cooperative. This crafts market is made up of a group of more than 40 local artists—including schoolchildren, senior citizens, and people with disabilities—who create the handcrafted items for sale here: African-style jewelry, quilts, calabash bowls, dolls, carved-wood figures, woven baskets, straw brooms, note cards, and cookbooks. ⊠ *48B Tolbod Gade, across from Emancipation Garden, Charlotte Amalie* 🕾 *340/777–1153.*

JEWELRY

Cardow Jewelry. You can get gold in several lengths, widths, sizes, and styles, along with jewelry made of diamonds, emeralds, and other precious gems from this small chain's main store. You're guaranteed 40% to 60% savings off U.S. retail prices, or your money will be refunded within 30 days of purchase. ⊠ *33 Main St., across from Emancipation Garden, Charlotte Amalie* 🕾 *340/776–1140* ⊕ *www.cardow.com* ⊠ *Marriott Frenchman's Reef Resort, Rte. 315, 00802, Estate Bakkeroe* 🕾 *340/774–0434.*

Diamonds International. At this large chain with several outlets on St. Thomas, just choose a diamond, emerald, or tanzanite gem and a mounting, and you can have your dream ring set in an hour. Famous for having the largest inventory of diamonds on the island, this shop welcomes trade-ins, has a U.S. service center, and includes diamond earrings with every purchase. ⊠ *31 Main St., Charlotte Amalie* 🕾 *340/774–3707* ⊕ *www.diamondsinternational.com* ⊠ *3 Drakes Passage, Charlotte Amalie* 🕾 *340/775–2010* ⊠ *7AB Drakes Passage, Charlotte Amalie* 🕾 *340/774–1516* ⊕ *www.diamondsinternational.com.*

H. Stern Jewelers. The World Collection of jewels set in modern, fashionable designs and an exclusive sapphire watch have earned this Brazilian jeweler a stellar reputation. There is another location in Havensight. ⊠ *8 Main St., Charlotte Amalie* 🕾 *340/776–1939* ⊕ *www.hstern.net* ⊠ *Marriott Frenchman's Reef Resort, Rte. 315, Estate Bakkeroe* 🕾 *340/776–3550.*

Jewels. This jewelry store sells name-brand jewelry and watches in abundance. Designer jewelry lines include David Yurman, Bulgari, Chopard, and Penny Preville. The selection of watches includes Jaeger le Coultre, Tag Heuer, Breitling, Movado, and Gucci. ⊠ *Main St. at Riise's Alley, Charlotte Amalie* ☎ *340/777–4222* ⊕ *www.jewelsonline.com* ⊠ *Waterfront at Hibiscus Alley, Charlotte Amalie* ☎ *340/777–4222* ⊕ *www. jewelsonline.com.*

Rolex Watches at A. H. Riise. A.H. Riise is the Virgin Islands' official Rolex retailer, and this shop offers one of the largest selections of these fine timepieces in the Caribbean. An After Sales Service Center helps you keep your Rolex ticking for a lifetime. ⊠ *37 Main St., at Riise's Alley, Charlotte Amalie* ☎ *340/776–2303* ⊕ *www.ahriise.com.*

LEATHER GOODS

Coach. This designer leather store has a full line of fine leather handbags, belts, gloves, and more for women, plus briefcases and wallets for men. Accessories for both sexes include organizers, travel bags, and cell-phone cases. ⊠ *Yacht Haven Grande, 5328 Yacht Haven Grande, Suite 104, Charlotte Amalie* ☎ *340/776–1930* ⊕ *www.coach.com.*

Zora's. This store specializes in fine, made-to-order leather sandals. There's also a selection of locally made backpacks, purses, and briefcases in durable, brightly colored canvas. ⊠ *34 Norre Gade, across from Roosevelt Park, Charlotte Amalie* ☎ *340/774–2559* ⊕ *www. zoraofstthomas.com.*

LINENS

Fabric in Motion. Fine Italian linens share space with Liberty London's silky cottons, colorful batiks, cotton prints, ribbons, and accessories in this small shop. ⊠ *7 Store Tvaer Gade, Charlotte Amalie* ☎ *340/ 774–2006.*

Mr. Tablecloth. This store has prices to please, and the friendly staff here will help you choose from the floor-to-ceiling selection of linens, which include Tuscan lace tablecloths and Irish linen pillowcases. ⊠ *6–7 Main St., Charlotte Amalie* ☎ *340/774–4343* ⊕ *mrtablecloth-vi.com.*

LIQUOR AND TOBACCO

A.H. Riise Liquors and Tobacco. This giant duty-free liquor outlet carries a large selection of tobacco (including imported cigars), as well as cordials, wines, and rare vintage Armagnacs, cognacs, ports, and Madeiras. It also stocks fruits in brandy and barware from England. Enjoy rum samples at the tasting bar. The prices are among the best in St. Thomas. ⊠ *37 Main St., at Riise's Alley, Charlotte Amalie* ☎ *340/776– 2303* ⊕ *www.ahriise.com.*

EAST END

Red Hook has **American Yacht Harbor,** a waterfront shopping area with a dive shop, a tackle store, clothing and jewelry boutiques, a bar, and a few restaurants.

ART

The Color of Joy Art & Framing. This gallery offers locally made arts and crafts, including pottery, batik, hand-painted linen-and-cotton clothing, glass plates and ornaments, and watercolors by owner Corinne Van

Rensselaer. There are also original prints by many local artists. Framing is available. ⊠ *Rte. 322, about 100 yards west of Ritz-Carlton, Red Hook* ☎ *340/775–4020* ⊕ *www.thecolorofjoyvi.com.*

FOODSTUFFS

Food Center. This supermarket sells fresh produce, meats, and seafood. There's also an on-site bakery and deli with hot and cold prepared foods, which are the big draw here, especially for those renting villas, condos, or charter boats in the East End area. ⊠ *Rte. 32, 1 mile west of Red Hook, Estate Frydenhoj* ☎ *340/777–8806* ⊕ *www.foodcentervi.com.*

JEWELRY

Diamonds International. As at others branches of this major jewelry chain, you can choose a diamond or other gem and a mounting and have your ring ready in an hour. The stores have the largest inventory of diamonds on St. Thomas. ⊠ *Wyndham Sugar Bay Beach Club & Resort, Rte. 38, Estate Smith Bay* ☎ *340/714–3248* ⊕ *www.diamondsinternational.com.*

Jewels. Designer jewelry available in this major chain include David Yurman, Bulgari, Chopard, and Penny Preville. The selection of watches is also extensive. ⊠ *Ritz-Carlton St. Thomas, Rte. 322, Estate Nazareth* ☎ *340/776–7850* ⊕ *www.jewelsonline.com.*

SOUTH SIDE

West of Charlotte Amalie, the pink-stucco **Nisky Center,** on Harwood Highway about ½ mile (1 km) east of the airport, is more of a hometown shopping center than a tourist area, but there's a bank, clothing store, and Radio Shack.

At the Crown Bay cruise-ship pier, the **Crown Bay Center,** off the Harwood Highway in Sub Base about ½ mile (1 km), has quite a few shops.

Havensight Mall, next to the cruise-ship dock, may not be as charming as downtown Charlotte Amalie, but it does have more than 60 shops. It also has a bank, a pharmacy, a gourmet grocery, and smaller branches of many downtown stores. The shops at **Port of $ale,** adjoining Havensight Mall (its buildings are pink instead of brown), sell discount goods. Next door to Port of $ale is the **Yacht Haven Grande** complex, a stunning megayacht marina with beautiful, safe walkways and many upscale shops.

East of Charlotte Amalie on Route 38, **Tillett Gardens** (⊕ *www.tillettgardens.com*) is an oasis of artistic endeavor. The late Jim and Rhoda Tillett converted this Danish farm into an artists' retreat in 1959. Today you can watch artisans produce silk-screen fabrics, candles, pottery, and other handicrafts. Something special is often happening in the gardens as well, including concerts and an arts-and-crafts fair, held in November and May.

Tutu Park Shopping Mall, across from Tillett Gardens, is the island's only enclosed mall. More than 50 stores and a food court are anchored by Kmart and the Plaza Extra grocery store. Archaeologists have discovered evidence that Arawak Indians once lived near the grounds.

ART

Mango Tango. This gallery sells and displays works by popular local artists—originals, prints, and note cards. There's a one-person show at least one weekend a month, and the store also has the island's largest humidor and a brand-name cigar gallery. ☒ *Al Cohen's Plaza, ½ mile (¾ km) east of Charlotte Amalie, Raphune Hill* ☎ *340/777–3060* ☒ *Yacht Haven Grande, Rte. 38, Crown Bay* ☎ *340/777–3060.*

CAMERAS AND ELECTRONICS

Boolchand's. This store sells brand-name cameras, audio and video equipment, and binoculars. There's also a location on Main Street, Charlotte Amalie. ☒ *Havensight Mall, Rte. 30, Bldg. II, Havensight* ☎ *340/776–0302* ⊕ *www.boolchand.com.*

CHINA AND CRYSTAL

Scandinavian Center. The Center carries the best of Scandinavia, including Royal Copenhagen, Georg Jensen, Kosta Boda, and Orrefors. Owners Søren and Grace Blak make regular buying trips to northern Europe and are a great source of information on crystal. Online ordering is available if you want to add to your collection once home. There's also a second store location at the Crown Bay Center. ☒ *Havensight Mall, Rte. 30, Bldg. III, last store closest to cruise ship dock, Havensight* ☎ *340/777– 8620, 877/454–8377* ⊕ *www.scandinaviancenter.com* ☒ *Crown Bay Commercial Center, Rte. 30, Crown Bay* ☎ *340/777–8620.*

FOODSTUFFS

Fruit Bowl. This grocery store is the best place on the island to go for fresh fruits and vegetables. There are many ethnic, vegetarian, and health-food items as well as a fresh meat, seafood department, and salad bar. ☒ *Wheatley Center, intersection of Rtes. 38 and 313, Charlotte Amalie* ☎ *340/774–8565* ⊕ *www.thefruitbowlvi.com.*

Gourmet Gallery. This is where visiting megayacht owners (or their staff) go to buy their caviar. There's also an excellent and reasonably priced wine selection, as well as specialty ingredients for everything from tacos to curries to chow mein. A full-service deli offers imported meats, cheeses, and in-store prepared foods that are perfect for a picnic. ☒ *Crown Bay Marina, Rte. 304, Estate Contant* ☎ *340/776–8555* ☒ *Havensight Mall, Bldg. VI, Rte. 30, Havensight* ☎ *340/774–4948.*

HANDICRAFTS

Caribbean Marketplace. This is a great place to buy handicrafts from the Caribbean and elsewhere. Also look for Sunny Caribee spices, teas from Tortola, and coffee from Trinidad. ☒ *Havensight Mall, Rte. 30, next to Deli Deck, Havensight* ☎ *340/776–5400.*

JEWELRY

H. Stern Jewelers. This Brazilian jeweler is known for the modern settings and designs of its offerings. The jewelry vault design center is located on Main Street, Charlotte Amalie. ☒ *Havensight Mall, Bldg. II, Rte. 30, Havensight* ☎ *340/776–1223* ⊕ *www.hstern.net.*

Jewels. Head here for name-brand jewelry and designer watches in abundance. Locations also at Havensight Mall, Crown Bay Center and the Ritz-Carlton, St. Thomas. ☒ *38 Dronnigans Gade (aka Main St.), Charlotte Amalie* ☎ *340/777–4222* ⊕ *www.jewelsonline.com.*

27

LIQUOR AND TOBACCO

Al Cohen's Discount Liquor. This warehouse of a store holds an extremely large wine and liquor selection. ⊠ *Rte. 30, across from main entrance to Havensight Mall, Havensight* ☎ *340/774–3690.*

Tobacco Discounters. This duty-free outlet carries a full line of discounted brand-name cigarettes, cigars, and tobacco accessories. ⊠ *9100 Port of $ale Mall, Rte. 30, next to Havensight Mall, Havensight* ☎ *340/ 774–2256.*

MUSIC

Music Shoppe II. This is a good place to buy CDs of the latest Caribbean releases—steel pan, reggae, and calypso, plus contemporary tunes in a broad range of genres. ⊠ *Havensight Mall, Bldg. III, Rte. 30, Suite D, Havensight* ☎ *340/774–1900.*

TOYS

FAMILY **Kmart.** This giant discount chain store has five aisles of toys for boys and girls: Barbie dolls, hula hoops, computer games, dollhouses, talking teddies, and more. ⊠ *Tutu Park Shopping Mall, Rte. 38, Estate Tutu* ☎ *340/714–5839* ⊠ *Lockhart Gardens, Rte. 38, Estate Long Bay* ☎ *340/774–4046.*

SPORTS AND ACTIVITIES

AIR TOURS

Caribbean Buzz Helicopters. On the Charlotte Amalie waterfront next to Tortola Wharf, Caribbean Buzz Helicopters offers a minimum 30-minute tour that includes St. Thomas, St. John, and Jost Van Dyke. It's a nice ride if you can afford the splurge (tours are $525 for up to three people), but in truth, you can see most of the aerial sights from Paradise Point, and there's no place you can't reach easily by car or boat. ⊠ *Jet Port, 8202 Lindbergh Bay, Charlotte Amalie* ☎ *340/775–7335* ⊕ *www.caribbean-buzz.com.*

BOATING AND SAILING

Calm seas, crystal waters, and nearby islands (perfect for picnicking, snorkeling, and exploring) make St. Thomas a favorite jumping-off spot for day- or weeklong sails or powerboat adventures. With more than 100 vessels from which to choose, St. Thomas is the charter-boat center of the U.S. Virgin Islands. You can go through a broker to book a sailing vessel with a crew or contact a charter company directly. Crewed charters start at approximately $3,100 per person per week, and bareboat charters can start at $2,000 per person for a 50- to 55-foot sailboat (not including provisioning), which can comfortably accommodate up to six people. If you want to rent your own boat, hire a captain. Most local captains are excellent tour guides.

Single-day charters are also a possibility. You can hire smaller boats for the day, including the services of a captain if you wish to have someone take you on a guided snorkeling trip around the islands.

Island Yachts. The sailboats and powerboats from Island Yachts are available for charter with or without crews. ⊠ *6100 Red Hook Quarter, 18B, Red Hook* ☎ *340/775–6666, 800/524–2019* ⊕ *www.iyc.vi.*

Continued on page 1108

BELOW THE WAVES By Lynda Lohr

Colorful reefs and wrecks rife with corals and tropical fish make the islands as interesting underwater as above. Brilliantly colored reef fish vie for your attention with corals in wondrous shapes. Scuba diving gets you up close and personal with the world below the waves.

Bright blue tangs and darting blue-headed wrasses. Corals in wondrous shapes—some look like brains, others like elk antlers. Colorful, bulbous sponges. All these and more can be spotted along the myriad reefs of the U.S. and British Virgin Islands. You might see a pink conch making its way along the ocean bottom in areas with seagrass beds. If you're really lucky, a turtle may swim into view, or a lobster may poke its antennae out of a hole in the reef or rocks. If you do a night dive, you might run into an octopus. But you may be surprised at how much you can see by simply hovering just below the surface, with nothing more than a mask and snorkel. It's a bird's-eye view, but an excellent one. Whether scuba diving or snorkeling, take along an underwater camera to capture memories of your exciting adventure. You can buy disposable ones at most dive shops or bring one from home.

DIVE AND SNORKELING SITES IN BRITISH VIRGIN ISLANDS

TORTOLA

Although a major base for dive operations in the BVI (due to its proximity to so many exceptional dive sites), Tortola itself doesn't have as much to offer divers. However, there are still some noteworthy destinations. The massive **Brewer's Bay Pinnacles** grow 70 feet high to within 30 feet of the surface; the rock mazes are only for advanced divers because of strong currents and they are not always acces-

sible. Abundant reefs close to shore make **Brewer's Bay** popular with snorkelers, as are **Frenchman's Cay** and **Long Bay Beef Island. Diamond Reef,** between Great Camanoe and Scrub Island, is a small wall about 200 yards long. **Shark Point,** off the northeast coast of Scrub Island, does have resident sharks. Though isolated in open ocean, the wreck of the **Chikuzen,** a Japanese refrigerator ship, is a popular site.

THE ISLANDS OF THE SIR FRANCIS DRAKE CHANNEL

Southeast of Tortola lie a string of islands with some of the BVI's finest dive sites, some world famous. The wreck of the royal mail ship **Rhone** is between Peter and Salt islands and is, perhaps, the most famous dive site in the BVI. **Wreck Alley,** consisting of three sunken modern ships, is between Salt and Cooper islands. At **Alice in Wonderland,** south of

Ginger Island, giant, mushroom-shaped corals shelter reef fish, moray eels, and crustaceans. **Alice's Backside,** off the northwestern tip of Ginger Island, is usually smooth enough for snorkeling and shallow enough so that beginner divers can get a good look at the myriad sealife and sponges.

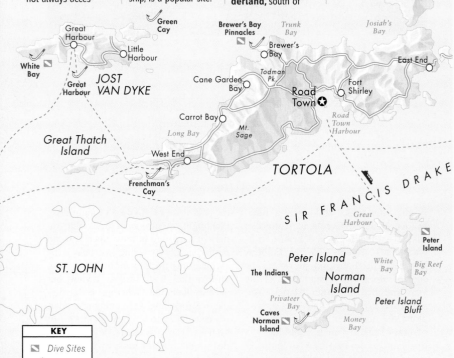

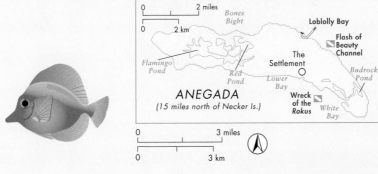

ANEGADA
(15 miles north of Necker Is.)

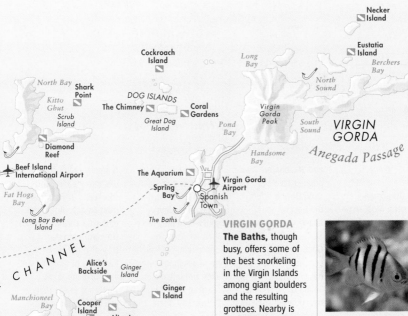

VIRGIN GORDA

The Baths, though busy, offers some of the best snorkeling in the Virgin Islands among giant boulders and the resulting grottoes. Nearby is **Spring Bay,** with fewer visitors and similar terrain. **The Aquarium,** close to Spanish Town and a good novice site, is so called because of the abundance of reef fish that swim around the submerged granite boulders that are similar to those of The Baths. Further west of Virgin Gorda, the Dog Islands have some in-

Virgin Gorda

teresting and popular sites, including **The Chimney,** a natural opening covered by sponges off Great Dog. South of Great Dog, **Coral Gardens** has a large coral reef with a submerged airplane wreck nearby. Fish are drawn to nearby **Cockroach Island.**

ANEGADA

Surrounded by the third-largest barrier reef in the world, Anegada has great snorkeling from virtually any beach on the island. But there are also some notable dive sites as well. The **Flash of**

Beauty Channel on the north shore is a great open-water dive, but only suitable for experienced divers. But even novices can enjoy diving at the **Wreck of the Rokus,** a Greek cargo ship off the island's southern shore.

DIVE AND SNORKELING SITES
IN U.S. VIRGIN ISLANDS

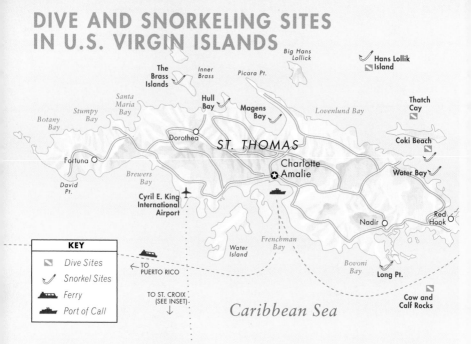

ST. THOMAS

St. Thomas has at least 40 popular dive sites, most shallow. Favorite reef dives off St. Thomas include **Cow and Calf Rocks,** which barely break water off the southeast coast of St. Thomas; the coral-covered pinnacles of **Frenchcap** south of St. Thomas; and tunnels where you can explore undersea from the Caribbean to the Atlantic at **Thatch Cay** (where the Coast Guard cutter *General Rogers* rests at 65 feet). **Grass Cay** and **Mingo Cay** between St. Thomas

and St. John are also popular dive sites. **Coki Beach** offers the best off-the-beach snorkeling in St. Thomas. Nearby Coral World offers a dive-helmet walk for the untrained, and Snuba of St. Thomas has tethered shallow dives for non-certified divers. **Magens Bay,** the most popular beach on St. Thomas, provides lovely snorkeling if you head along the edges. You're likely to see some colorful sponges, darting fish, and maybe even a turtle if you're lucky. This is a stop on every island tour.

ST. JOHN

St. John is particularly known for its myriad good snorkeling spots—certainly more than for its diving opportunities, though there are many dive sites within easy reach of Cruz Bay. **Trunk Bay** often receives the most attention because of its underwater snorkeling trail created by the National Park Service; signs let you know what you're seeing in terms of coral and other underwater features. And the beach is easy to reach since taxis leave on demand from Cruz Bay.

A patchy reef just offshore means good snorkeling at **Hawksnest Beach.** Additionally, **Cinnamon Bay** and **Leinster Bay** also get their fair share of praise as snorkeling spots. That's not to say that you can't find good dive sites near St. John. **Deaver's Bay** is a short boat ride around the point from Cruz Bay, where you can see angelfish, southern stingrays, and triggerfish feeding at 30 to 50 feet. **The Leaf** is a large coral reef off St. John's southern shore.

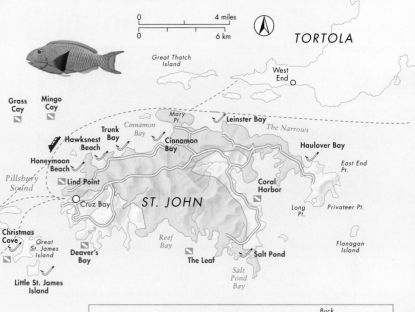

TORTOLA

Great Thatch Island

West End

Grass Cay

Mingo Cay

Cinnamon Bay

Mary Pt.

Leinster Bay

The Narrows

Hawksnest Beach

Trunk Bay

Cinnamon Bay

Haulover Bay

East End Pt.

Honeymoon Beach

Pillsbury Sound

Lind Point

Coral Harbor

Cruz Bay

ST. JOHN

Long Pt.

Privateer Pt.

Christmas Cove

Great St. James Island

Deaver's Bay

Reef Bay

Flanagan Island

Little St. James Island

The Leaf

Salt Pond

Salt Pond Bay

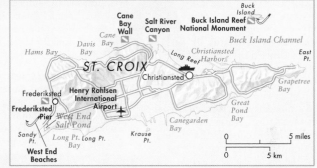

Buck Island

Cane Bay Wall

Salt River Canyon

Buck Island Reef National Monument

Cane Bay

Davis Bay

Buck Island Channel

Hams Bay

Christiansted Harbor

East Pt.

Long Reef

ST. CROIX

Christiansted

Grapetree Bay

Frederiksted

Henry Rohlsen International Airport

French Cap

Frederiksted Pier

West End Salt Pond

Great Pond Bay

Sandy Pt.

Long Pt. Bay

Long Pt. Pt.

Canegarden Bay

Krause Pt.

West End Beaches

0   5 miles

0   5 km

Coral near St. Croix

ST. CROIX

The largest of the U.S. Virgin Islands is a favorite of both divers and snorkelers and offers something for everyone. Snorkelers are often fascinated by the marked snorkeling trail at **Buck Island Reef,** which is a short boat ride from the island's east end; it's a U.S. national monument. Divers are drawn to the north shore, especially the **Cane Bay Wall,** a spectacular drop-off that's reachable from the beach, though usually reached by boat. Another north-shore site is the **Salt River Canyon,** where you can float downward through a canyon filled with colorful fish and coral. On the island's west end, **Frederiksted Pier** is home to a colony of sea horses, creatures seldom seen in the waters of the Virgin Islands. Casual snorkelers would also enjoy snorkeling at the **West End Beaches.**

SCUBA DIVING

St.Croix

If you've never been diving, start with an introductory lesson—often called a "resort course"—run by any one of the Virgin Islands' dive shops. All meet stringent safety standards. If they didn't, they'd soon be out of business. If you're staying at a hotel, you can often find the dive shop on-site; otherwise, your hotel probably has an arrangement with one nearby. If you're on a cruise, cruise-ship companies offer shore excursions that include transportation to and from the ship as well as the resort course. Certification requires much more study and practice, but it is required to rent air tanks, get air refills, and join others on guided dives virtually anywhere in the world.

The number one rule of diving is safety. The basic rules for safe diving are simple, and fools ignore them at their own peril. Serious diving accidents are becoming increasingly rare these days, thanks to the high level of diver training. However, they do still occur occasionally. Surfacing too rapidly without exhaling—or going too deep for too long—can result in an air embolism or a case of the bends. Schneider Regional Medical Center in St. Thomas has a decompression chamber that serves all the Virgin Islands. If you get the bends, you'll be whisked to the hospital for this necessary treatment.

Fauna is another concern. Though sharks, barracuda, and moray eels are on the most-feared list, more often it's sea urchins and fire coral that cause pain when you accidentally bump them. Part of any scuba-training program is a

Divers learn how to jump in from a boat

St.Croix

review of sea life and the importance of respecting the new world you're exploring. Dive professionals recognize the value of protecting fragile reefs and ecosystems in tropical waters, and instructors emphasize look-don't-touch diving (the unofficial motto is: take only pictures, leave only bubbles). Government control and protection of dive sites is increasing, especially in such heavily used areas as the Virgin Islands.

While you can scuba dive off a beach—and you can find shops renting scuba equipment and providing airfills at the most popular beaches—a trip aboard a dive boat provides a more extensive glimpse into this wonderful undersea world. Since the dive shops can provide all equipment, there's no need to lug heavy weights and a bulky BC in your luggage. For the most comfort, you might want to bring your own regulator if you have one. The dive-boat captains and guides know the best dive locations, can find alternatives when the seas are rough, and will help you deal with heavy tanks and cumbersome equipment. Trips are easy to organize. Dive shops on all islands make frequent excursions to a wide variety of diving spots, and your hotel, villa manager, or cruise-ship staff will help you make arrangements.

If you fly too soon after diving, you're at risk for decompression sickness, which occurs when nitrogen trapped in your bloodstream doesn't escape. This creates a painful and sometimes fatal condition called the bends, not a sickness you want to develop while you're winging your way home after a fun-filled beach vacation. Opinions vary, but as a rule of thumb, wait at least 12 hours after a single dive to fly. However, if you've made multiple dives or dived several days in a row, you should wait at least 18 hours. If you've made dives that required decompression stops, you should also wait at least 24 hours before flying. To be safe, consult with your physician.

The Virgin Islands offer a plethora of dive sites, and you'll be taken to some of the best if you sign on to a dive trip run by one of the many dive operations scattered around the islands.

DIVER TRAINING

Good to know: Divers can become certified through PADI *(www.padi.com)*, NAUI *(www.naui.org)*, or SSI *(www.divessi.com)*. The requirements for all three are similar, and if you do the classroom instruction and pool training with a dive shop associated with one organization, the referral for the open water dives will be honored by most dive shops. Note that you should not fly for at least 24 hours after a dive, because residual nitrogen in the body can pose health risks upon decompression. While there are no rigid rules on diving after flying, make sure you're well-hydrated before hitting the water.

Cost: The four-day cost for classroom dive training can range from $350 to $600, but be sure to ask if equipment, instruction manuals, and log books are extra. Some dive shops have relationships with hotels, so check for dive/stay packages. Referral dives (a collaborative effort among training agencies) run from $200 to $300 and discover scuba runs around $100 to $125.

SNUBA

Beyond snorkeling or the requirements of scuba, you also have the option of "Snuba." The word is a trademarked portmanteau or combo of snorkel and scuba. Marketed as easy-to-learn family fun, Snuba lets you breathe underwater via tubes from an air-supplied vessel above, with no prior diving or snorkel experience required.

NOT CERTIFIED?

Not sure if you want to commit the time and money to become certified? Not a problem. Most dive shops and many resorts will offer a discover scuba day-long course. In the morning, the instructor will teach you the basics of scuba diving: how to clear your mask, how to come to the surface in the unlikely event you lose your air supply, etc. In the afternoon, instructors will take you out for a dive in relatively shallow water—less than 30 feet. Be sure to ask where the dive will take place. Jumping into the water off a shallow beach may not be as fun as actually going out to the coral. If you decide that diving is something you want to pursue, the open dive may count toward your certification.

■TIP→ You can often book discover dives at the last minute. It may not be worth it to go out on a windy day when the currents are stronger. Also the underwater world looks a whole lot brighter on sunny days.

(top) Underwater shot of tropical reef, (bottom) Diver silhouette, Cane Bay, St Croix

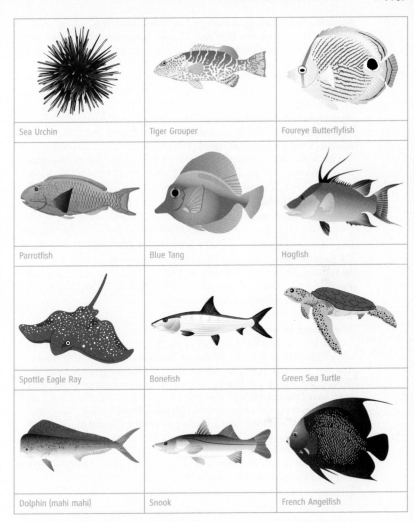

Sea Urchin	Tiger Grouper	Foureye Butterflyfish
Parrotfish	Blue Tang	Hogfish
Spottle Eagle Ray	Bonefish	Green Sea Turtle
Dolphin (mahi mahi)	Snook	French Angelfish

27

IN FOCUS BELOW THE WAVES

REEF CREATURES IN THE VIRGIN ISLANDS

From the striped sergeant majors to bright blue tangs, the reefs of the Virgin Islands are teeming with life, though not nearly as many as in eons past. Warming waters and pollution have taken their toll on both coral and fish species. But many reefs in the Virgin Islands still thrive; you'll also see sponges, crustaceans, perhaps a sea turtle or two, and bigger game fish like grouper and barracuda; sharks are seen but are rarely a problem for divers. Beware of fire corals, which are not really corals but rather a relative of the jellyfish and have a painful sting; if you brush up against a fire coral, spread vinegar on the wound as soon as possible to minimize the pain.

Magic Moments. *Luxury* is the word at Magic Moments, where crews aboard the 45-foot Sea Ray and 52-foot Sunseeker offer pampered island-hopping snorkeling cruises for $475 per person (children ages 2–10 are half price). Nice touches include a wine-and-lobster lunch and icy-cold eucalyptus-infused washcloths for freshening up. ⊠ *American Yacht Harbor, Docks B and C, Red Hook* ☎ *340/775–5066* ⊕ *www.yachtmagicmoments.com.*

Nauti Nymph. A large selection of 26- to 35-foot powerboats and power catamarans are available from this company. Rates, which vary from $560 to $945 a day, include snorkeling gear, water skis, and outriggers, but not fuel. You can hire a captain for $140 more per day. ⊠ *American Yacht Harbor Marina, Dock B and C, Red Hook* ☎ *540/775–5066, 800/734–7345* ⊕ *www.nautinymph.com.*

Stewart Yacht Charters. Run by longtime sailor Ellen Stewart, this company is skilled at matching clients with yachts and crews for week-long charter holidays. ⊠ *6501 Red Hook Plaza, Suite 20, Red Hook* ☎ *340/775–1358, 800/432–6118* ⊕ *www.stewartyachtcharters.com.*

VIP Yacht Charters. Bareboat sail- and powerboats, including a selection of stable trawlers, are available at VIP Yacht Charters. ⊠ *Compass Point Marina, south off Rte. 32, Estate Frydenhoj* ☎ *340/774–9224, 866/847–9224* ⊕ *www.vipyachts.com.*

BICYCLING

Water Island Adventures. In this company's fun biking trip, you first take a ferry ride from Crown Bay to Water Island and then jump on a Cannondale for 90 minutes of biking over rolling hills on dirt and paved roads. (On cruise-ship days, a direct ferry goes from the West India Company Docks, but this is only for cruise passengers who have booked the bike tour.) Explore the remains of the Sea Cliff Hotel, reputedly the inspiration for Herman Wouk's book *Don't Stop the Carnival,* and then take a cooling swim at beautiful Honeymoon Beach. Helmets, water, guides, and ferry fare are included in the $75 cost. Bike rentals are available on days when no tours are scheduled: call for details. ⊠ *Water Island* ☎ *340/626–9815, 340/690–4019* ⊕ *www.waterislandadventures.com.*

DIVING AND SNORKELING

Popular dive sites include such wrecks as the *Cartanser Sr.,* a beautifully encrusted World War II cargo ship sitting in 35 feet of water, and the *General Rogers,* a Coast Guard cutter resting at 65 feet. Here you can find a gigantic resident barracuda. Reef dives offer hidden caves and archways at **Cow and Calf Rocks,** coral-covered pinnacles at **French-cap,** and tunnels where you can explore undersea from the Caribbean to the Atlantic at **Thatch Cay, Grass Cay,** and **Congo Cay.** Many resorts and charter yachts offer dive packages. A one-tank dive starts at $110; two-tank dives are $130 and up. Call the USVI Department of Tourism to obtain a free eight-page guide to Virgin Islands dive sites. There are plenty of snorkeling possibilities, too.

Admiralty Dive Center. Boat dives, rental equipment, and a retail store are available from this dive center. You can also get multiple-tank packages if you want to dive over several days. ⊠ *Windward Passage Resort,*

Waterfront Hwy. (aka Rte. 30), Charlotte Amalie ☎ 340/777–9802, 888/900–3483 ⊕ www.admiraltydive.com.

Blue Island Divers. This full-service dive shop offers both day and night dives to wrecks and reefs and specializes in custom dive charters. ⊠ *Crown Bay Marina, Rte. 304, Estate Contant ☎ 340/774–2001 ⊕ www.blueislanddivers.com.*

B.O.S.S. Underwater Adventure. As an alternative to traditional diving, try an underwater motor scooter called BOSS, or Breathing Observation Submersible Scooter. A 3½-hour tour, including snorkel equipment, rum punch, and towels, is $120 per person. ⊠ *Crown Bay Marina, Rte. 304, Charlotte Amalie ☎ 340/777–3549 ⊕ www.bossusvi.com.*

FAMILY **Coki Dive Center.** Snorkeling and dive tours in the fish-filled reefs off Coki Beach are available from this PADI Five Star outfit, as are classes, including one on underwater photography. It's run by the avid diver Peter Jackson. ⊠ *Rte. 388, at Coki Point, Estate Frydendal ☎ 340/775–4220 ⊕ www.cokidive.com.*

Snuba of St. Thomas. In snuba, a snorkeling and scuba-diving hybrid, a 20-foot air hose connects you to the surface. The cost is $74. Children must be eight or older to participate. ⊠ *Rte. 388, at Coki Point, Estate Smith Bay ☎ 340/693–8063 ⊕ www.visnuba.com.*

St. Thomas Diving Club. This PADI Five Star center offers boat dives to the reefs around Buck Island and nearby offshore wrecks as well as multiday dive packages. ⊠ *Bolongo Bay Beach Resort, Rte. 30, Estate Bolongo ☎ 340/776–2381 ⊕ www.stthomasdivingclub.com.*

FISHING

Fishing here is synonymous with blue marlin angling—especially from June through October. Four 1,000-pound-plus blues, including three world records, have been caught on the famous North Drop, about 20 miles (32 km) north of St. Thomas. A day charter for marlin with up to six anglers costs $1,800 for the day. If you're not into marlin fishing, try hooking sailfish in winter, dolphinfish (the fish that's also known as mahimahi, not the mammal) in spring, and wahoo in fall. Inshore trips for four hours start at $600. To find the trip that will best suit you, walk down the docks at either American Yacht Harbor or Sapphire Beach Marina in the late afternoon and chat with the captains and crews.

Abigail III. Captain Red Bailey's *Abigail III* specializes in marlin fishing. It operates out of the Sapphire Condominium Resort's marina. ⊠ *Estate Smith Bay, Rte. 38, 1/4 mile northwest of Red Hook, Sapphire Bay ☎ 340/775–6024 ⊕ www.visportfish.com.*

Charter Boat Center. This is a major source for sail and powerboat as well as sportfishing charters. Sportfishing charters offered include full-day trips for marlin as well as full, three-quarter, and half days for offshore and inshore species such as tuna, wahoo, dolphin (mahi-mahi), snapper, and kingfish. ⊠ *American Yacht Harbor, 6300 Smith Bay 16-3, Red Hook ☎ 340/775–7990 ⊕ www.charterboat.vi.*

27

FAMILY **Double Header Sportfishing.** This company offers trips out to the North Drop on its 40-foot sportfisher and half-day reef and bay trips aboard its two speedy 35-foot center consoles. ✉ *Sapphire Bay Marina, Rte. 38, Sapphire Bay* ☎ *340/777–7317* ⊕ *www.doubleheadersportfishing.net.*

Marlin Prince. Captain Eddie Morrison, one of the most experienced charter operators in St. Thomas, specializes in fly-fishing for blue marlin from his 45-foot Viking boat. ✉ *American Yacht Harbor, 6100 Red Hook Quarters #2, slip A-16, Red Hook* ☎ *340/693–5929* ⊕ *www.marlinprince.com.*

GOLF

Mahogany Run Golf Course. The Mahogany Run Golf Course is the only course in St. Thomas and it attracts golfers who are drawn by its spectacular view of the British Virgin Islands and the challenging three-hole Devil's Triangle of holes 13–15. At this Tom and George Fazio–designed course, is not particularly long, but in addition to the scenery, you will experience lots of natural flora and fauna. There's a fully stocked pro shop, snack bar, and open-air clubhouse. Walking is not permitted and the course enforces a dress code. Open daily, and there are frequently informal weekend tournaments. ✉ *Rte. 42, Estate Lovenlund* ☎ *340/777–6006, 800/253–7103* ⊕ *www.mahoganyrungolf.com* ⚑ *$165 for 18 holes; $115 for 9 holes during peak winter season* ⚐ *18 holes, par 70.*

GUIDED TOURS

VI Taxi Association Tropical Paradise St. Thomas Island Tour. Aimed at cruise-ship passengers, this two-hour tour for two people is done in an open-air safari bus or enclosed van. The $29 tour includes stops at Drake's Seat and Mountain Top. Other tours include a three-hour trip to Coki Beach with a shopping stop in downtown Charlotte Amalie for $35 per person, a three-hour trip to the Coral World Ocean Park for $45 per person, and a five-hour beach tour to St. John for $75 per person. For $35 to $40 for two, you can hire a taxi for a customized three-hour drive around the island. Make sure to see Mountain Top, as the view is wonderful. ☎ *340/774–4550* ⊕ *www.vitaxi.com.*

SEA EXCURSIONS

Landlubbers and seafarers alike can experience wind in their hair and salt spray in the air while exploring the waters surrounding St. Thomas. Several businesses can book you on a snorkel-and-sail to a deserted cay for a half day that starts at $95 per person or a full day (at least $130 per person). An excursion over to the British Virgin Islands starts at $150 per person, not including customs fees. A luxury daylong motor-yacht cruise complete with lunch is $475 or more per person.

Adventure Center. For a soup-to-nuts choice of sea tours including a Stand-Up Paddleboard (SUP) safari, full- and half-day sails and sunset cruises contact the Adventure Center. ✉ *Marriott's Frenchman's Reef Hotel, Rte. 315, Estate Bakkeroe* ☎ *340/774–2992, 866/868–7784* ⊕ *www.adventurecenters.net.*

Charter Boat Center. The specialty here is day trips to the British Virgin Islands aboard 42-foot 12-passenger motoryachts *Stormy Petrel* and *Pirate's Penny.* There's also day- or weeklong sailing charters. ✉ *American Yacht Harbor, 6300 Smith Bay 16-3, Red Hook* ☎ *340/775–7990* ⊕ *www.charterboat.vi.*

Treasure Isle Cruises. Jimmy Loveland at Treasure Isle Cruises can set you up with everything from a half-day sail to a seven-day Caribbean cruise. ✉ *Rte. 32, Estate Nadir* ☎ *340/775–9500* ⊕ *www.treasureislecruises.com.*

SEA KAYAKING

FAMILY Fish dart, birds sing, and iguanas lounge on the limbs of dense mangrove trees deep within a marine sanctuary on St. Thomas's southeast shore.

FAMILY

Fodor's Choice

★

Virgin Islands Ecotours. Virgin Islands Ecotours offer three- and five-hour guided kayak tours to St. Thomas' Mangrove Lagoon, Hassel Island, Henley Cay and St. John's Caneel Bay. All trips include free snorkel instruction with snacks on three-hour and lunch on five-hour trips. The historic Hassel Island tour includes a visit to some of the historic forts and military structures on the island, a short hike to a breathtaking vista, and swim off a deserted beach. Costs range from $79 to $143 per person, depending on length and location. In addition, many resorts on St. Thomas's East End also rent kayaks. ✉ *Mangrove Lagoon, Rte. 32, 2 miles (3 km) east of intersection of Rte. 32 and 30, Estate Nadir* ☎ *340/779–2155, 877/845–2925* ⊕ *www.viecotours.com.*

WINDSURFING

FAMILY Expect some spills, anticipate the thrills, and try your luck clipping through the seas. Most beachfront resorts rent Windsurfers and offer one-hour lessons for about $120.

Island Sol. If you want to learn to windsurf, try Paul Stoeken's Island Sol. The two-time Olympic athlete charges $85 per hour for a private lesson. There's a free clinic every Tuesday at 9:30 am. There are also private kite-boarding lessons for $385 for three hours, and kayak and stand-up paddleboard (SUP) rentals for $25 per hour. ✉ *Ritz-Carlton St. Thomas, Rte. 317, on Great Bay Beach, Estate Nazareth* ☎ *340/643–2251* ⊕ *www.islandsol.vi.*

West Indies Windsurfing. At West Indies, one of the island's best-known independent windsurfing companies, a private kiteboarding lesson costs $125 per hour for the land portion and $250 for a two-hour private lesson on the water. The company also rents stand-up paddleboards (SUP) for $40 per hour, or $200 to $225 per day based on the quality of the board. There's usually calm water—perfect for SUPs—right off Vessup Beach or around the peninsula in Great Bay. ✉ *Vessup Beach, No. 9, next to Latitude 18 restaurant, Estate Nazareth* ☎ *340/775–6530.*

27

ST. JOHN

Updated by
Lynda Lohr

St. John's heart is Virgin Islands National Park, a treasure that takes up a full two-thirds of St. John's 20 square miles (53 square km). The park helps keep the island's interior in its pristine and undisturbed state, but if you go at midday, you'll probably have to share your stretch of beach with others, particularly at Trunk Bay.

The island is booming (its population of 5,000 is joined by more than 800,000 visitors each year), and it can get crowded at the ever-popular Trunk Bay Beach during the busy winter season; parking woes plague the island's main town of Cruz Bay, but you won't find traffic jams or pollution. It's easy to escape from the fray, however: just head off on a hike or go early or late to the beach. The sun won't be as strong, and you may have that perfect crescent of white sand all to yourself.

St. John doesn't have a major agrarian past like her sister island, St. Croix, but if you're hiking in the dry season, you can probably stumble upon the stone ruins of old plantations. The less adventuresome can visit the repaired ruins at the park's Annaberg Plantation and Caneel Bay Resort.

In 1675 Jorgen Iverson claimed the unsettled island for Denmark. By 1733 there were more than 1,000 slaves working more than 100 plantations. In that year the island was hit by a drought, hurricanes, and a plague of insects that destroyed the summer crops. With famine a real threat and the planters keeping them under tight rein, the slaves revolted on November 23, 1733. They captured the fort at Coral Bay, took control of the island, and held it for six months. During this period, about 20% of the island's total population was killed, the tragedy affecting both black and white residents in equal percentages. The rebellion was eventually put down with the help of French troops from Martinique. Slavery continued until 1848, when slaves in St. Croix marched on Frederiksted to demand their freedom from the Danish government. This time it was granted. After emancipation, St. John fell into decline, with its inhabitants eking out a living on small farms. Life continued in much the same way until the national park opened in 1956 and tourism became an industry.

Of the three U.S. Virgin Islands, St. John has the strongest sense of community, which is primarily rooted in a desire to protect the island's natural beauty. Despite the growth, there are still many pockets of tranquility. Here you can truly escape the pressures of modern life for a day, a week—perhaps forever.

EXPLORING

St. John is an easy place to explore. One road runs along the northern shore, another across the center of the mountains. There are a few roads that branch off here and there, but it's hard to get lost. Pick up a map at the visitor center before you start out and you'll have no problems. Few residents remember the route numbers, so have your map in hand if you stop to ask for directions. Bring along a swimsuit for stops at some of the most beautiful beaches in the world. You can spend all day or just a couple of hours exploring, but be advised that the roads are narrow and wind up and down steep hills, so don't expect to get anywhere in a hurry. There are lunch spots at Cinnamon Bay and in Coral Bay, or you can do what the locals do—find a secluded spot for a picnic. The grocery stores in Cruz Bay sell Styrofoam coolers just for this purpose.

If you plan to do a lot of touring, renting a car will be cheaper and will give you much more freedom than relying on taxis; on St. John taxis are shared safari vans, and drivers are reluctant to go anywhere until they have a full load of passengers. Although you may be tempted by an open-air Suzuki or Jeep, a conventional car will let you lock up your valuables. You can get just about everywhere on the paved roads

Sugar mill ruins at Annaberg Plantation

without four-wheel drive unless it rains. Then four-wheel drive will help you get up the wet, hilly roads. You may be able to share a van or open-air vehicle (called a safari bus) with other passengers on a tour of scenic mountain trails, secret coves, and eerie bush-covered ruins.

CRUZ BAY

St. John's main town may be compact (it consists of only several blocks), but it's definitely a hub: the ferries from St. Thomas and the British Virgin Islands pull in here, and it's where you can get a taxi or rent a car to travel around the island. There are plenty of shops, a number of watering holes and restaurants, and a grassy square with benches where you can sit back and take everything in. Look for the current edition of the handy, amusing "St. John Map," featuring Max the Mongoose.

Elaine Ione Sprauve Library. On the hill just above Cruz Bay is the Enighed Estate great house, built in 1757. *Enighed* is Danish for "concord" (unity or peace). The greathouse and its outbuildings (a sugar factory and horse-driven mill) were destroyed by fire and hurricanes, and the house sat in ruins until 1982. The library offers Internet access for $2 an hour. ⊠ *Rte. 104, make right past St. Ursula's Church* ☎ *340/776–6359* 🖃 *Free* ☉ *Weekdays 9–5.*

V.I. National Park Visitors Center. To pick up a useful guide to St. John's hiking trails, see various large maps of the island, and find out about current Park Service programs, including guided walks and cultural demonstrations, stop by the park visitor center. ⊠ *North Shore Rd., near Creek* ☎ *340/776–6201* ⊕ *www.nps.gov/viis* ☉ *Daily 8–4:30.*

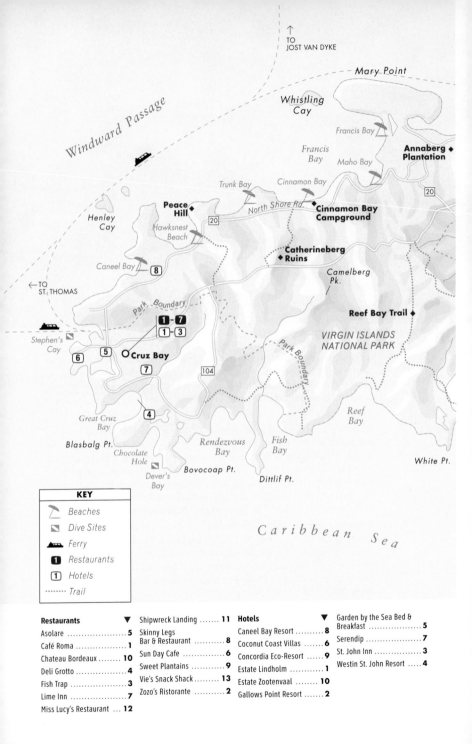

↑
TO
JOST VAN DYKE

Mary Point

Whistling Cay

Windward Passage

Francis Bay

Annaberg ◆ Plantation

Francis Bay

Maho Bay

Trunk Bay

Cinnamon Bay

Peace Hill ◆

Henley Cay

Hawksnest Beach

North Shore Rd.

Cinnamon Bay Campground

20

Catherineberg ◆ Ruins

Caneel Bay

8

Camelberg Pk.

←TO
ST. THOMAS

Park Boundary

Reef Bay Trail ◆

VIRGIN ISLANDS NATIONAL PARK

1 - 7
1 - 3

Stephen's Cay

6   5

7

Cruz Bay

104

Park Boundary

4

Great Cruz Bay

Blasbalg Pt.

Chocolate Hole

Dever's Bay

Rendezvous Bay

Bovocoap Pt.

Fish Bay

Dittlif Pt.

Reef Bay

White Pt.

Caribbean Sea

KEY

⌒	Beaches
◺	Dive Sites
⛴	Ferry
1	Restaurants
1	Hotels
·······	Trail

St. John

The Narrows

TO TORTOLA

Leinster Bay

Brown Bay

TO TORTOLA →

VIRGIN ISLANDS NATIONAL PARK

Centerline Rd.

Park Boundary

10

Sir Francis Drake Channel

Coral Bay

10

8 - 10

Palestina

Haulover Bay

King Hill Rd.

Coral Harbor

Hurricane Hole

Newfound Bay

13

East End Pt.

Park Boundary

EAST END

East End Bay

Bordeaux Mountain

Sanders Bay

107

Round Bay

Privateer Pt.

Privateer Bay

Coral Bay

Long Pt.

11

Lagoon Pt.

Calabash

12

Lameshur Bay

John's Folly Bay

Leduck Island

9

Drunk Bay

Salt Pond Bay

Salt Pond Peninsula

Ram Head

UNITED STATES VIRGIN ISLANDS

Tortola

ST. THOMAS

ST. JOHN

Distance from St. Thomas to St. Croix approx. 40 miles

ST. CROIX

0   1 mile

0   1 km

NORTH SHORE

Fodor's Choice ★ **Annaberg Plantation.** In the 18th century, sugar plantations dotted the steep hills of this island. Slaves and free Danes and Dutchmen toiled to harvest the cane that was used to create sugar, molasses, and rum for export. Built in the 1780s, the partially restored plantation at Leinster Bay was once an important sugar mill. Although there are no official visiting hours, the National Park Service has regular tours, and some well-informed taxi drivers will show you around. Occasionally you may see a living-history demonstration—someone making johnnycake or weaving baskets. For information on tours and cultural events, contact the V.I. National Park Visitors Center. ⊠ *Leinster Bay Rd., Annaberg* ☎ *340/776–6201* ⊕ *www.nps.gov/viis* ⊠ *Free* ☉ *Daily dawn–dusk.*

Peace Hill. It's worth stopping here, just past the Hawksnest Bay overlook, for great views of St. John, St. Thomas, and the BVI. On the flat promontory is an old sugar mill. ⊠ *Off Rte. 20, Denis Bay.*

MID ISLAND

Catherineberg Ruins. At this fine example of an 18th-century sugar and rum factory, there's a storage vault beneath the windmill. Across the road, look for the round mill, which was later used to hold water. In the 1733 slave revolt Catherineberg served as headquarters for the Amina warriors, a tribe of Africans captured into slavery. ⊠ *Catherineberg Rd., off Rte. 10, Catherineberg.*

Fodor's Choice ★ **Reef Bay Trail.** This is one of the most interesting hikes on St. John, but unless you're a rugged individualist who wants a physical challenge (and that describes a lot of people who stay on St. John), you can probably get the most out of the trip if you join a hike led by a park service ranger. A ranger can identify the trees and plants on the hike down, fill you in on the history of the Reef Bay Plantation, and tell you about the petroglyphs on the rocks at the bottom of the trail. A side trail takes you to the plantation's greathouse, a gutted but mostly intact structure with vestiges of its former beauty. Take the safari bus from the park's visitor center. A boat takes you from the beach at Reef Bay back to the visitor center, saving you the uphill climb. It's a good idea to make reservations for this trip, especially during the winter season. They can be made at the Friends of the Park store, in Mongoose Junction. ⊠ *Rte. 10, Reef Bay* ☎ *340/779–8700 for reservations* ⊕ *www.nps.gov/viis* ⊠ *$30 includes safari bus ride to trailhead, guided tour, and boat ride back to visitor center* ☉ *Tours at 9:30 am; days change seasonally.*

CORAL BAY AND ENVIRONS

Coral Bay. This laid-back community at the island's dry, eastern end is named for its shape rather than for its underwater life—the word *coral* comes from *krawl,* Dutch for "corral." Coral Bay is growing fast, but it's still a small, neighborly place. You'll probably need a four-wheel-drive vehicle if you plan to stay at this end of the island, as some of the rental houses are up unpaved roads that wind around the mountain. If you come just for lunch, a regular car will be fine. ⊠ *Coral Bay.*

CLOSE UP

St. John Archaeology

Archaeologists continue to unravel St. John's past through excavations at Trunk Bay and Cinnamon Bay, both prime tourist destinations within Virgin Islands National Park.

Work began back in the early 1990s, when the park wanted to build new bathhouses at the popular Trunk Bay. In preparation for that project, the archaeologists began to dig, turning up artifacts and the remains of structures that date to AD 900. The site was once a village occupied by the Taíno, a group that lived in the area until AD 1500. A similar but slightly more recent village was discovered at Cinnamon Bay.

By the time the Taíno got to Cinnamon Bay, roughly a century later, their society had developed to include chiefs, commoners, workers, and slaves. The location of the national park's busy Cinnamon Bay campground was once a Taíno temple that belonged to a king or chief. When archaeologists began digging in 1998, they uncovered several dozen *zemis*, which are small clay gods used in ceremonial activities, as well as beads, pots, and many other artifacts.

Near the end of the Cinnamon Bay dig archaeologists turned up another less ancient but still surprising discovery. A burned layer indicated that a plantation slave village had also stood near Cinnamon Bay campground; it was torched during the 1733 revolt because its slave inhabitants had been loyal to the planters. Since the 1970s, bones from slaves buried in the area have been uncovered at the water's edge by beach erosion.

27

BEACHES

St. John is blessed with many beaches, and all of them fall into the good, great, and don't-tell-anyone-else-about-this-place categories. Some are more developed than others—and many are crowded on weekends, holidays, and in high season—but by and large they're still pristine. Beaches along the south and eastern shores are quiet and isolated. Break-ins occur on all the U.S. Virgin Islands; most locals recommend leaving your windows down and leaving absolutely nothing in your car, rather than locking it up and risking a broken window.

NORTH SHORE

Cinnamon Bay Beach. This long, sandy beach faces beautiful cays and abuts the national park campground. You can rent water-sports equipment here—a good thing, because there's excellent snorkeling off the point to the right; look for the big angelfish and large schools of purple triggerfish. Afternoons on Cinnamon Bay can be windy—a boon for windsurfers but an annoyance for sunbathers—so arrive early to beat the gusts. The Cinnamon Bay hiking trail begins across the road from the beach parking lot; ruins mark the trailhead. There are actually two paths here: a level nature trail (signs along it identify the flora) that loops through the woods and passes an old Danish cemetery, and a steep trail that starts where the road bends past the ruins and heads straight up to Route 10. Restrooms are on the main path from the commissary to the beach and scattered around the campground.

Amenities: food and drink; parking; showers; toilets; water sports. **Best for:** snorkeling; swimming, walking; windsurfing. ⊠ *North Shore Rd., Rte. 20, about 4 miles (6 km) east of Cruz Bay, Cinnamon Bay* ⊕ *www.nps.gov/viis.*

Francis Bay Beach. Because there's little shade, this beach gets toasty warm in the afternoon when the sun comes around to the west, but the rest of the day it's a delightful stretch of white sand. The only facilities are a few picnic tables tucked among the trees and a portable restroom, but folks come here to watch the birds that live in the swampy area behind the beach. The park offers bird-watching hikes here on Friday morning; sign up at the visitor center in Cruz Bay. To get here, turn left at the Annaberg intersection. **Amenities:** parking; toilets. **Best for:** snorkeling, swimming, walking. ⊠ *North Shore Rd., Rte. 20, ¼ mile (½ km) from Annaberg intersection, Francis Bay* ⊕ *www.nps.gov/viis.*

Hawksnest Beach. Sea grape and waving palm trees line this narrow beach, and there are restrooms, cooking grills, and a covered shed for picnicking. A patchy reef just offshore means snorkeling is an easy swim away, but the best underwater views are reserved for ambitious snorkelers who head farther to the east along the bay's fringes. Watch out for boat traffic—a channel guides dinghies to the beach, but the occasional boater strays into the swim area. It's the closest drivable beach to Cruz Bay, so it's often crowded with locals and visitors. **Amenities:** parking; toilets. **Best for:** snorkeling; swimming. ⊠ *North Shore Rd., Rte. 20, about 2 miles (3 km) east of Cruz Bay, Hawksnest Bay* ⊕ *www.nps.gov/viis.*

Maho Bay Beach. Maho Bay Beach is a gorgeous strip of sand that sits right along the North Shore Road. It's a popular place, particularly on weekends, when locals come out in droves to party at the picnic tables at the south end of the beach. Snorkeling along the rocky edges is good, but the center is mostly sea grass. If you're lucky, you'll cross paths with turtles. **Amenities:** parking; toilets. **Best for:** snorkeling; swimming. ⊠ *North Shore Rd., Rte. 20, Maho Bay* ⊕ *www.nps.gov/viis.*

Fodor'sChoice
★

Trunk Bay Beach. St. John's most-photographed beach is also the preferred spot for beginning snorkelers because of its underwater trail. (Cruise-ship passengers interested in snorkeling for a day flock here, so if you're looking for seclusion, arrive early or later in the day.) Crowded or not, this stunning beach is one of the island's most beautiful. There are changing rooms with showers, bathrooms, a snack bar, picnic tables, a gift shop, phones, lockers, and snorkeling-equipment rentals. The parking lot often overflows, but you can park along the road as long as the tires are off the pavement. **Amenities:** food and drink; lifeguards; parking; toilets; water sports. **Best for:** snorkeling; swimming; windsurfing ⊠ *North Shore Rd., Rte. 20, about 2½ miles (4 km) east of Cruz Bay, Trunk Bay* ⊕ *www.nps.gov/viis* ⌫ *$4.*

CORAL BAY AND ENVIRONS

Lameshur Bay Beach. This sea grape–fringed beach is toward the end of a partially paved road on the southeast coast. The reward for your long drive is solitude, good snorkeling, and a chance to spy on some pelicans.

The beach has a couple of picnic tables, rusting barbecue grills, and a portable restroom. The ruins of the old plantation are a five-minute walk down the road past the beach. The area has good hiking trails, including a trek (more than a mile) up Bordeaux Mountain before an easy walk to Yawzi Point. **Amenities:** parking; toilets. **Best for:** solitude; snorkeling; swimming; walking. ✉ *Off Rte. 107, about 1½ miles (2½ km) from Salt Pond, Lameshur Bay* 🌐 *www.nps.gov/viis.*

Salt Pond Bay Beach. If you're adventurous, this rocky beach on the scenic southeastern coast—next to Coral Bay and rugged Drunk Bay—is worth exploring. It's a short hike down a hill from the parking lot, and the only facilities are an outhouse and a few picnic tables scattered about. Tide pools are filled with all sorts of marine creatures, and the snorkeling is good, particularly along the bay's edges. A short walk takes you to a pond where salt crystals collect around the edges. Hike farther uphill past cactus gardens to Ram Head for see-forever views. Leave nothing valuable in your car, as thefts are common. **Amenities:** parking; toilets. **Best for:** snorkeling; swimming; walking. ✉ *Rte. 107, about 3 miles (5 km) south of Coral Bay, Salt Pond Bay* 🌐 *www.nps.gov/viis.*

WHERE TO EAT

27

The cuisine on St. John seems to get better every year, with chefs vying to see who can come up with the most imaginative dishes, whether you're at one of the elegant establishments at Caneel Bay Resort (where men may be required to wear a jacket at dinner) or a casual joint near Cruz Bay. For quick lunches, try the West Indian food stands in Cruz Bay Park and across from the post office. The cooks prepare fried chicken legs, pâtés (meat- and fish-filled pastries), and callaloo.

Some restaurants close for vacation in September and even October. If you have your heart set on a special place, call ahead to make sure it's open during these months.

CRUZ BAY AND ENVIRONS

$$$ ASIAN 🍴 **Asolare.** Contemporary Asian cuisine dominates the menu at this elegant open-air eatery in an old St. John house. Come early and relax over drinks while you enjoy the sunset lighting up the harbor. Start with an appetizer such as tempora fried oysters, then move on to entrées such as sesame crusted tuna with cilantro aioli or smoked pork tenderloin lamb loin. If you still have room for dessert, try the mimosa-poached pears with honey. [$] *Average main: $28* ✉ *Rte. 20 on Caneel Hill, Estate Lindholm* ☎ *340/779–4747* 🌐 *www.asolarestjohn.com* 🕒 *No lunch.*

$$$ ITALIAN FAMILY 🍴 **Café Roma.** This second-floor restaurant in the heart of Cruz Bay is *the* place for traditional Italian cuisine: lasagna, spaghetti and meatballs, and three-cheese manicotti. Small pizzas are available at the table, but larger ones are for takeout or at the bar. Tiramisu is a dessert specialty. This casual place can get crowded in winter, so show up early. [$] *Average main: $24* ✉ *Vesta Gade* ☎ *340/776–6524* 🌐 *www.stjohncaferoma.com* 🕒 *No lunch.*

$ ECLECTIC 🍴 **Deli Grotto.** At this air-conditioned (but no-frills) sandwich shop you place your order at the counter and wait for it to be delivered to your table or for takeout. The portobello panini with savory sautéed onions is a favorite, but the other sandwiches, such as the smoked turkey and artichoke, also get rave reviews. Order a brownie or cookie for dessert. [$] *Average main: $9* ✉ *Mongoose Junction Shopping Center, North Shore Rd.* ☎ *340/777–3061* 💳 *No credit cards* 🕒 *No dinner.*

$$$$ AMERICAN FAMILY 🍴 **Fish Trap Restaurant and Seafood Market.** The main dining room here is open to the breezes and buzzes with a mix of locals and visitors, but the back room has air-conditioning. Start with a tasty appetizer such as conch fritters or fish chowder (a creamy combination of snapper, white wine, paprika, and spices). You can always find steak and chicken dishes, as well as the interesting fish of the day. [$] *Average main: $36* ✉ *Bay and Strand Sts., next to Our Lady of Mount Carmel Church* ☎ *340/693–9994* 🌐 *www.thefishtrap.com* 🕒 *Closed Mon. No lunch.*

$$$ ECLECTIC 🍴 **Lime Inn.** The vacationers and mainland transplants who call St. John home like to flock to this alfresco spot for the congenial hospitality and good food, including all-you-can-eat shrimp on Wednesday night. Fresh lobster is the specialty, and the menu also includes shrimp-and-steak dishes and rotating chicken and pasta specials. [$] *Average main: $28* ✉ *Lemon Tree Mall, King St.* ☎ *340/776–6425* 🌐 *www.limeinn.com* 🕒 *No lunch Sat. Closed Sun.*

$ DELI Fodor's Choice ★ 🍴 **Sam and Jack's Deli.** The sandwiches are scrumptious, but this deli also dishes up wonderful to-go meals that just need heating. If the truffle–wild mushroom ravioli is on the menu, don't hesitate to order it—it's a winner. There are a few seats inside, but most folks opt to eat at the tables in front of the deli. [$] *Average main: $12* ✉ *Marketplace Shopping Center, Rte. 104* ☎ *340/714–3354* 🌐 *www.samandjacksdeli.com* 🕒 *Closed Sun. No dinner.*

NORTH SHORE

$$ ECLECTIC 🍴 **Sun Dog Café.** There's an unusual assortment of dishes at this charming alfresco restaurant, which you'll find tucked into a courtyard in the upper reaches of the Mongoose Junction shopping center. Kudos to the white pizza with artichoke hearts, roasted garlic, mozzarella cheese, and capers. The Jamaican jerk chicken salad and the black-bean quesadilla are also good choices. [$] *Average main: $18* ✉ *Mongoose Junction Shopping Center, North Shore Rd.* ☎ *340/693–8340* 🌐 *www.sundogcafe.com* 🕒 *No dinner Sun.*

$$$$ ITALIAN Fodor's Choice ★ 🍴 **Zozo's at the Sugar Mill.** Creative takes on old standards coupled with lovely presentations draw the crowds to this restaurant at Caneel Bay Resort. Start with crispy fried calamari served with a pesto mayonnaise. The chef dresses up roasted mahimahi with a pistachio crust and serves it with a warm goat cheese–and–arugula salad. The slow-simmered osso buco comes with prosciutto-wrapped asparagus and saffron risotto. The sunset views will take your breath away. [$] *Average main: $40* ✉ *Caneel Bay Resort, Rte. 20, Caneel Bay* ☎ *340/693–9200* 🌐 *www.zozos.net* 🕒 *No lunch.*

MID ISLAND

$$ ECLECTIC 🍴 **Chateau Bordeaux.** Your hamburgers and sweet potato fries come with a side of fabulous views of Coral Bay and the British Virgin Islands. Located at the popular Bordeaux overlook, this restaurant also serves salads made with local greens, and fish sandwiches. The adjacent ice-cream shop blends up some delicious fruit smoothies, and you can stop by for breakfast too. [$] *Average main: $18* ✉ *Rte. 10, Bordeaux* ☎ *340/776–6611* 🌐 *www.chateaubordeaux.net* ⏲ *No dinner Fri.–Mon.*

CORAL BAY AND ENVIRONS

$$$ CARIBBEAN 🍴 **Miss Lucy's Restaurant.** Sitting seaside at remote Friis Bay, Miss Lucy's dishes up Caribbean food with a contemporary flair. Dishes such as tender conch fritters, a spicy West Indian stew called callaloo, and fried fish make up most of the menu, but you also find a generous paella filled with seafood, sausage, and chicken on the menu. Sunday brunches are legendary, and if you're around when the moon is full, stop by for the monthly full-moon party. The handful of small tables near the water is the nicest, but if they're taken or the mosquitoes are swarming, the indoor tables do nicely. [$] *Average main: $29* ✉ *Rte. 107, Friis Bay* ☎ *340/693–5244* 🌐 *www.misslucysrestaurant.com* ⏲ *Closed Mon. No dinner Sun.*

$$$ AMERICAN 🍴 **Shipwreck Landing.** A favorite with locals and visitors, this alfresco restaurant serves up tasty food in a casual setting. Opt for the tables closest to the road for the best breezes and water views. The menu includes lots of seafood, but the chicken and beef dishes ensure that everyone's satisfied. If it's a day when the chef made homemade soup, try at least a cup. For lunch, the grilled mahimahi sandwich is always a good bet. [$] *Average main: $23* ✉ *Rte. 107, Freeman's Ground* ☎ *340/693–5640* 🌐 *www.shipwrecklanding.net.*

$ AMERICAN 🍴 **Skinny Legs Bar and Restaurant.** Sailors who live aboard boats anchored offshore and an eclectic coterie of residents gather for lunch and dinner at this funky spot in the middle of a boatyard and shopping complex. If owner Moe Chabuz is around, take a gander at his gams; you'll see where the restaurant got its name. It's a great place for burgers, fish sandwiches, and whatever sports are on the satellite TV. [$] *Average main: $11* ✉ *Rte. 10* ☎ *340/779–4982* 🌐 *www.skinnylegs.com.*

$$$ CARIBBEAN FAMILY 🍴 **Sweet Plaintains.** The food here is a sophisticated take on Caribbean cuisine. The fish of the day—it could be mahimahi or swordfish—is always especially good. Or try one of the curries if you don't want seafood. For a real local taste, start with the saltfish cakes served with shredded cabbage and mango puree. The coconut flan for dessert is another Caribbean favorite. [$] *Average main: $27* ✉ *Rte. 107* ☎ *340/777–4653* 🌐 *www.sweetplantains-stjohn.com* ⏲ *Closed Sun. and Tues. No lunch.*

$ CARIBBEAN 🍴 **Vie's Snack Shack.** Stop by Vie's when you're out exploring the island. Although it's just a shack by the side of the road, Vie's serves up some great cooking. The garlic chicken legs are crisp and tasty, and the conch fritters are really something to write home about. Plump and filled with fresh herbs, a plateful will keep you going for the rest of the afternoon. Save room for a wedge of coconut pie—called a tart in this neck of the woods. When you're finished eating, a spectacular white-sand beach down the road beckons. [$] *Average main: $10* ✉ *Rte. 10, Hansen Bay* ☎ *340/693–5033* 🌐 *www.hansenbaycampground.com* 💳 *No credit cards* ⏲ *Closed Sun. and Mon. No dinner.*

WHERE TO STAY

St. John doesn't have many beachfront hotels, but that's a small price to pay for all the pristine sand. However, the island's two excellent resorts—Caneel Bay Resort and the Westin St. John Resort & Villas—*are* on the beach. Sandy, white beaches string out along the north coast, which is popular with sunbathers and snorkelers and is where you can find the Caneel Bay Resort and Cinnamon and Maho Bay campgrounds. Most villas are in the residential south-shore area, a 15-minute drive from the north-shore beaches. If you head east, you come to the laid-back community of Coral Bay, where there are growing numbers of villas and cottages. Bands sometimes play at a couple of Coral Bay's nightspots, so if you're renting a villa in the hills above the village, you may hear music later than you'd like. A stay outside of Coral Bay will be peaceful and quiet.

If you're looking for West Indian village charm, there are a few inns in Cruz Bay. Keep in mind that when bands play at any of the town's bars (some of which stay open until the wee hours), the noise can be a problem. Your choice of accommodations also includes condominiums and cottages near town; two campgrounds, one at the edge of a beautiful beach (bring bug repellent); ecoresorts; and luxurious villas, often with a pool or a hot tub (sometimes both) and a stunning view.

If your lodging comes with a fully equipped kitchen, you'll be happy to know that St. John's handful of grocery stores sell everything you're likely to need—though the prices will take your breath away. If you're on a budget, consider bringing some staples (pasta, canned goods, paper products) from home. Hotel rates throughout the island are fairly expensive, but they do include endless privacy and access to most water sports.

Many of the island's condos are just minutes from the hustle and bustle of Cruz Bay, but you can find more scattered around the island. St. John also has a handful of camping spots ranging from the basic Cinnamon Bay Campground to the more comfortable Maho Bay Camps. They appeal to those who don't mind bringing their own beach towels from home or busing their own tables at dinner. If you want your piña colada delivered beachside by a smiling waiter, you'd be better off elsewhere—and ready to pay for the privilege.

PRIVATE CONDOS AND VILLAS

Here and there between Cruz Bay and Coral Bay are about 500 private villas and condos (prices range from $ to $$$$). With pools or hot tubs, full kitchens, and living areas, these lodgings provide a fully functional home away from home. They're perfect for couples and extended groups of family or friends. You need a car, since most lodgings are in the hills and very few are at the beach. Villa managers usually pick you up at the dock, arrange for your rental car, and answer questions on arrival as well as during your stay. Prices drop in the summer season, which is generally after April 15. Some companies begin off-season pricing a week or two later, so be sure to ask.

If you want to be close to Cruz Bay's restaurants and boutiques, a villa in the Chocolate Hole and Great Cruz Bay areas will put you a few minutes away. The Coral Bay area has a growing number of villas, but you'll be about 20 minutes from Cruz Bay. Beaches lie out along the North Shore, so you won't be more than 15 minutes from the water no matter where you stay.

RENTAL CONTACTS

Carefree Get-Aways. This company manages vacation villas on the island's southern and western edges. ☎ *340/779–4070, 888/643–6002* ⊕ *www.carefreegetaways.com.*

Caribbean Villas & Resorts. Caribbean Villas handles condo rentals for Cruz Views and Gallow's Point Resort, as well as for many private villas. ☎ *340/776–6152, 800/338–0987* ⊕ *www.caribbeanvilla.com.*

Caribe Havens. Specializing in the budget market, Caribe Havens has properties scattered around the island. ⊠ *Box 455, Cruz Bay* ☎ *340/776–6518* ⊕ *www.caribehavens.com.*

Catered to Vacation Homes. Specializing in luxury villas, this company has listings mainly in the middle of the island and on the western edge. ⊠ *Marketplace Suite 206, 5206 Enighed, Cruz Bay* ☎ *340/776–6641, 800/424–6641* ⊕ *www.cateredto.com.*

Cloud 9 Villas. Most of Cloud 9 Villas' offerings are in the Gifft Hill and Chocolate Hole area. ☎ *340/774–9633* ⊕ *www.cloud9villas.com.*

Island Getaways. Options from Island Getaways are mainly villas in the Rendezvous, Chocolate Hole, and Coral Bay areas. ☎ *340/693–7676, 888/693–7676* ⊕ *www.islandgetawaysinc.com.*

On-Line Vacations. On-Line Vacations books villas for most management companies and is based on St. John. ☎ *340/776–6036, 888/842–6632* ⊕ *www.onlinevacations.com.*

Private Homes for Private Vacations. This company handles villa rentals across the island. ⊠ *7605 Mamey Peak Rd., Coral Bay* ☎ *340/776–6876* ⊕ *www.privatehomesvi.com.*

Seaview Vacation Homes. As the name implies, this company's specialty are houses with views of the ocean: they are in the Chocolate Hole, Great Cruz Bay, and Fish Bay areas. ☎ *340/776–6805, 888/625–2963* ⊕ *www.seaviewhomes.com.*

Star Villas. Star has cozy villas just outside Cruz Bay. ☎ *340/776–6704* ⊕ *www.starvillas.com.*

St. John Properties. This firm handles villas mainly in the Cruz Bay area but has a couple mid-island properties as well. ⊠ *Cruz Bay* ☎ *800/283–1746, 340/693–8485* ⊕ *www.stjohnproperties.com.*

St. John Ultimate Villas. ☎ *340/776–4703, 888/851–7588* ⊕ *www.stjohnultimatevillas.com.*

Vacation Vistas. This company's villas are mainly in the Chocolate Hole, Great Cruz Bay, and Rendezvous areas. ☎ *340/776–6462* ⊕ *www.vacationvistas.com.*

Windspree. Windspree's stock is mainly in and around Coral Bay. ⊠ *7924 Emmaus, Coral Bay* ☎ *340/693–5423, 888/742–0357* ⊕ *www.windspree.com.*

27

CRUZ BAY AND ENVIRONS

$$ RENTAL 🏨 **Coconut Coast Villas.** This small condominium complex with studio, two-, and three-bedroom apartments is a 10-minute walk from Cruz Bay, but is insulated from the town's noise in a sleepy suburban neighborhood. **Pros:** good snorkeling; full kitchens; walk to Cruz Bay. **Cons:** small beach; some uphill walks; nearby utility plant can be noisy. [$] *Rooms from: $289* ✉ *Near pond, Turner Bay* ☎ *340/693–9100, 800/858–7989* 🌐 *www.coconutcoast.com* 🛏 *9 units* 🍴 *No meals.*

$$ B&B/INN 🏨 **Estate Lindholm Bed and Breakfast.** Built among old stone ruins on a lushly planted hill overlooking Cruz Bay, Estate Lindholm has an enchanting setting. **Pros:** lush landscaping; gracious host; pleasant decor. **Cons:** can be noisy; some uphill walks; on a busy road. [$] *Rooms from: $340* ✉ *Rte. 20, at Caneel Hill, Cruz Bay* ☎ *340/776–6121, 800/322–6335* 🌐 *www.estatelindholm.com* 🛏 *14 rooms* 🍴 *Breakfast.*

$$$$ RENTAL 🏨 **Gallows Point Resort.** You're a short walk from restaurants and shops at this waterfront location just outside Cruz Bay, but once you step into your condo, the hustle and bustle are left behind. **Pros:** walk to shopping; excellent restaurant; comfortably furnished rooms. **Cons:** some rooms can be noisy; mediocre beach; insufficient parking. [$] *Rooms from: $545* ✉ *Bay St., Cruz Bay* ☎ *340/776–6434, 800/323–7229* 🌐 *www.gallowspointresort.com* 🛏 *60 units* 🍴 *No meals.*

$ B&B/INN 🏨 **Garden by the Sea Bed and Breakfast.** Located in a middle-class residential neighborhood, this cozy bed-and-breakfast is an easy walk from Cruz Bay. **Pros:** homey atmosphere; great breakfasts; breathtaking view from deck; near a bird-filled salt pond. **Cons:** noise from nearby power substation; some uphill walks; basic amenities. [$] *Rooms from: $250* ✉ *Near pond, Enighed* ☎ *340/779–4731* 🌐 *www.gardenbythesea.com* 🛏 *3 rooms* 💳 *No credit cards* 🍴 *Breakfast.*

$$$ RENTAL 🏨 **Grande Bay Resort.** Located just a few minutes' walk from Cruz Bay's restaurants and shops, this modern condominium complex puts you close to the town's hustle and bustle. **Pros:** close to restaurants and shops; modern decor; walking distance to the ferry. **Cons:** need car or taxi to reach island attractions and the best beaches; beach across the street is minimal. [$] *Rooms from: $405* ✉ *Bay St., Cruz Bay* ☎ *340/693–4668* 🌐 *www.grandebayresortusvi.com* 🛏 *64 condos* 🍴 *Breakfast.*

$$$$ RENTAL 🏨 **Sea Shore Allure.** Located at the water's edge in a residential neighborhood, Sea Shore Allure combines attractive and modern decor with an easy, and safe, walk to Cruz Bay's restaurants and shops. **Pros:** lovely decor; waterfront location; close to town. **Cons:** need car or taxi to get to beach; road passes through modest but safe local neighborhood. [$] *Rooms from: $485* ✉ *Pond Mouth Rd., Turner Bay* ☎ *340/779–2880, 855/779–2880* 🌐 *www.seashoreallure.com* 🛏 *8 units* 🍴 *No meals.*

$ RENTAL 🏨 **Serendip.** This complex offers modern apartments on lush grounds with lovely views and makes a great pick for a budget stay in a residential locale. **Pros:** comfortable accommodations; good views; nice neighborhood. **Cons:** no beach; need car to get around; nearby construction. [$] *Rooms from: $240* ✉ *Off Rte. 104, Enighed* ☎ *340/776–6646, 888/800–6445* 🌐 *www.serendipstjohn.com* 🛏 *10 apartments* 🍴 *No meals.*

Caneel Bay Resort

$ **B&B/INN** **St. John Inn.** A stay here gives you a bit of style at what passes for budget prices in St. John. **Pros:** walk to restaurants and shops; convivial atmosphere; pretty pool. **Cons:** need a car to get around; noisy location; insufficient parking. [$] *Rooms from: $200* ✉ *Off Rte. 104, Cruz Bay* ☎ *340/693–8688, 800/666–7688* 🌐 *www.stjohninn.com* 🛏 *11 units* 🍴 *Breakfast.*

$$$$ **RESORT** **Westin St. John Resort and Villas.** The island's largest resort provides a nice beachfront location and enough activities to keep you busy. **Pros:** entertaining children's programs; pretty pool area; many activities. **Cons:** mediocre beach; long walk to some parts of the resort; need car to get around. [$] *Rooms from: $539* ✉ *Rte. 104, Great Cruz Bay* ☎ *340/693–8000, 800/808–5020* 🌐 *www.westinresortstjohn.com* 🛏 *174 rooms, 194 villas* 🍴 *No meals.*

NORTH SHORE

$$$$ **RESORT** Fodor's Choice ★ **Caneel Bay Resort.** If you dream of spending your days on gorgeous beaches, paddling kayaks to and fro, and enjoying languorous dinners with your feet in the sand, there's no finer laid-back-luxury resort on St. John. **Pros:** seven lovely beaches; gorgeous rooms; lots of amenities. **Cons:** staff can be chilly; isolated location; pricey; no TVs or phones (just a warning for tech-junkies). [$] *Rooms from: $539* ✉ *Rte. 20, Caneel Bay* ☎ *340/776–6111, 855/226–3358* 🌐 *www.caneelbay.com* 🛏 *166 rooms* 🍴 *Breakfast.*

CORAL BAY AND ENVIRONS

$ RENTAL Fodor's Choice ★ **Concordia Eco-Resort.** This off-the-beaten-path resort is on the remote Salt Pond peninsula. **Pros:** good views; ecofriendly environment; beach nearby. **Cons:** need car to get around; lots of stairs. [$] *Rooms from: $175* ✉ *Off Rte. 107, Concordia* ☎ *340/693–5855, 800/392–9004* 🌐 *www.concordiaeco-resort.com* 🛏 *5 condos, 17 studios, 25 tents* 🍴 *No meals.*

$$ RENTAL **Estate Zootenvaal.** Comfortable and casual, this small cottage colony gives you the perfect place to relax. **Pros:** quiet beach; private; near restaurants. **Cons:** some traffic noise; no air-conditioning in some units. [$] *Rooms from: $290* ✉ *Rte. 10, Hurricane Hole, Zootenvaal* ☎ *340/776-6321* 🌐 *www.estatezootenvaal.com* 🛏 *4 units* 🍴 *No meals.*

NIGHTLIFE

St. John isn't the place to go for glitter and all-night partying. Still, after-hours Cruz Bay can be a lively little town in which to dine, drink, dance, chat, or flirt. Notices posted on the bulletin board outside the Connections telephone center—up the street from the ferry dock in Cruz Bay—or listings in *Tradewinds* (🌐 *www.stjohntradewindsnews.com*), will keep you apprised of special events, comedy nights, movies, and the like.

CRUZ BAY

Motu Bar. Drinks made with freshly squeezed juices, frequent theme parties, and stellar views of Cruz Bay create a comfortable ambience for happy hour and beyond. ✉ *1 Bay St., Cruz Bay* ☎ *407/758–6924* 🌐 *www.motubar.com.*

Tap Room. A rotating selection of distinctive brews make the Tap Room popular with locals and visitors. ✉ *Mongoose Junction Shopping Center, Mongoose Junction, Cruz Bay* ☎ *340/715–7775* 🌐 *www.stjohnbrewers.com.*

Woody's. Young folks like to gather here, where the sidewalk tables provide a close-up view of Cruz Bay action. ✉ *Near First Bank, Cruz Bay* ☎ *340/779–4625* 🌐 *www.woodysseafood.com.*

CORAL BAY AND ENVIRONS

Shipwreck Landing. Live rock, bluegrass, and more are on tap several nights a week at this restaurant. ✉ *Rte. 107, Freemans Ground, Coral Bay* ☎ *340/693–5640.*

Skinny Legs Bar and Restaurant. Landlubbers and old salts listen to music and swap stories at this popular casual restaurant and bar on the far side of the island. ✉ *Rte. 10, Coral Bay* ☎ *340/779–4982* 🌐 *www.skinnylegs.com.*

FREE PARKING

Cruz Bay's parking problem is maddening. Your best bet is to rent a car from a company that allows you to park in its lot. Make sure you ask before you sign on the dotted line if you plan to spend time in Cruz Bay.

Yoga is a morning ritual at Concordia Eco-Resort.

SHOPPING

CRUZ BAY

Luxury goods and handicrafts can be found on St. John. Most shops carry a little of this and a bit of that, so it pays to poke around. The Cruz Bay shopping district runs from **Wharfside Village,** just around the corner from the ferry dock, to **Mongoose Junction,** an inviting shopping center on North Shore Road. (The name of this upscale shopping mall, by the way, is a holdover from a time when those furry island creatures gathered at a nearby garbage bin.) Out on Route 104, stop in at the **Marketplace** to explore its gift and crafts shops. On St. John, store hours run from 9 or 10 to 5 or 6. Wharfside Village and Mongoose Junction shops in Cruz Bay are often open into the evening.

ART

Fodor'sChoice
★
Bajo el Sol. This gallery sells works by owner Livy Hitchcock, plus pieces from a roster of the island's best artists. You can also shop for oils, pastels, watercolors, and turned wood pieces. ⊠ *Mongoose Junction Shopping Center, North Shore Rd., Cruz Bay* ☎ *340/693–7070* ⊕ *www. bajoelsolgallery.net.*

Caravan Gallery. Caravan sells unusual jewelry that its owner, Radha Speer, has traveled the world to find. The more you look, the more you see—Caribbean larimar jewelry and unusual sterling pieces, tribal art, and masks for sale cover the walls and tables, making this a great place to browse. ⊠ *Mongoose Junction Shopping Center, North Shore Rd., Cruz Bay* ☎ *340/779–4566* ⊕ *www.caravangallery.com.*

Coconut Coast Studios. This waterside shop, a five-minute walk from the center of Cruz Bay, showcases the work of Elaine Estern. She specializes in undersea scenes. ⊠ *Frank Bay, Cruz Bay* ☎ *340/776–6944* ⊕ *www. coconutcoaststudios.com.*

BOOKS

National Park Headquarters Bookstore. The bookshop at Virgin Islands National Park Headquarters sells several good histories of St. John, including *St. John Backtime: Eyewitness Accounts From 1718 to 1956*, by Ruth Hull Low and Rafael Lito Valls, and, for intrepid explorers, longtime resident Pam Gaffin's *St. John Feet, Fins and Four-Wheel Drive*, a "complete guide to all of the islands beaches, trails, and roads." ⊠ *Rte. 20, Cruz Bay* ☎ *340/776–6201* ⊕ *www.nps.gov/viis.*

CLOTHING

Big Planet Adventure Outfitters. You knew when you arrived that someplace on St. John would cater to the outdoor enthusiasts who hike up and down the island's trails. This store sells flip-flops and Reef footwear, along with colorful and durable cotton clothing and accessories by Billabong. The store also sells children's clothes. ⊠ *Mongoose Junction Shopping Center, North Shore Rd., Cruz Bay* ☎ *340/776–6638* ⊕ *www.big-planet.com.*

Bougainvillea Boutique. This store is your destination if you want to look as if you've stepped out of the pages of the resort-wear spread in an upscale travel magazine. Owner Susan Stair carries very chic men's and women's clothes, straw hats, leather handbags, and fine gifts. ⊠ *Mongoose Junction Shopping Center, North Shore Rd., Cruz Bay* ☎ *340/693–7190* ⊕ *www.shoppingstjohn.com.*

FOOD

If you're renting a villa, condo, or cottage and doing your own cooking, there are several good places to shop for food; just be aware that prices are much higher than those at home.

Starfish Market. The island's largest store usually has the best selection of meat, fish, and produce. ⊠ *The Marketplace, Rte. 104, Cruz Bay* ☎ *340/779–4949* ⊕ *www.starfishmarket.com.*

GIFTS

Bamboula. This multicultural boutique carries unusual housewares, rugs, bedspreads, accessories, and men's and women's clothes and shoes that owner Jo Sterling has found on her world travels. ⊠ *Mongoose Junction Shopping Center, North Shore Rd., Cruz Bay* ☎ *340/693–8699* ⊕ *www. bamboulastjohn.com.*

Best of Both Worlds. Pricey metal sculptures and attractive artworks hang from the walls of this gallery; the nicest are small glass decorations shaped like mermaids and sea horses. ⊠ *Mongoose Junction Shopping Center, North Shore Rd., Cruz Bay* ☎ *340/693–7005* ⊕ *www. thebestofstjohn.com.*

Donald Schnell Studio. You'll find distinctive clay pieces, unusual hand-blown glass, wind chimes, kaleidoscopes, fanciful fountains, and pottery bowls here. Your purchases can be shipped worldwide. ⊠ *Amore Center, Rte. 104, near roundabout, Cruz Bay* ☎ *340/776–6420* ⊕ *www. donaldschnellstudio.com.*

Fabric Mill. There's a good selection of women's clothing in tropical brights, as well as lingerie, sandals, and batik wraps here. Or take home several yards of colorful batik fabric to make your own dress. ⊠ *Mongoose Junction Shopping Center, North Shore Rd., Cruz Bay* ☎ *340/776–6194.*

Gallows Point Gift and Gourmet. The store at Gallows Point Resort has a bit of this and a bit of that. Shop for Caribbean books and CDs, picture frames decorated with shells, and T-shirts with tropical motifs. Residents and visitors also drop by for a cup of coffee. ⊠ *Gallows Point Resort, Bay St., Cruz Bay* ☎ *340/693–7730* ⊕ *www.stjohnadventures.com.*

Nest and Company. This small shop carries perfect take-home gifts in colors that reflect the sea. Shop here for soaps in tropical scents, dinnerware, and much more. ⊠ *Mongoose Junction Shopping Center, North Shore Rd., Cruz Bay* ☎ *340/715–2552* ⊕ *www.nestvi.com.*

Pink Papaya. Head to this shop and art gallery for the work of long-time Virgin Islands resident Lisa Etre. There's also huge collection of one-of-a-kind gifts, including bright tableware, trays, and tropical jewelry. ⊠ *Lemon Tree Mall, King St., Cruz Bay* ☎ *340/693–8535* ⊕ *www.pinkpapaya.com.*

JEWELRY

Free Bird Creations. This is your on-island destination for special handcrafted jewelry—earrings, bracelets, pendants, chains—as well as a good selection of water-resistant watches. ⊠ *Dockside Mall, next to ferry dock, Cruz Bay* ☎ *340/693–8625* ⊕ *www.freebirdcreations.com.*

Little Switzerland. A branch of the St. Thomas store, Little Switzerland carries emeralds, diamonds, and other jewels in attractive yellow- and white-gold settings, as well as strings of creamy pearls, watches, and other designer jewelry. ⊠ *Mongoose Junction Shopping Center, North Shore Rd., Cruz Bay* ☎ *340/776–6007* ⊕ *www.littleswitzerland.com.*

R&I Patton goldsmithing. This store is owned by Rudy and Irene Patton, who design most of the lovely silver and gold jewelry on display. The rest comes from various designer friends. Sea fans (those large, lacy plants that sway with the ocean's currents) in filigreed silver, starfish and hibiscus pendants in silver or gold, and gold sand-dollar-shape charms and earrings are choice selections. ⊠ *Mongoose Junction Shopping Center, North Shore Rd., Cruz Bay* ☎ *340/776–6548* ⊕ *www.pattongold.com.*

St. Johnimals. Pampered pets are the ultimate consumers for the goods in this cozy store. The shelves are stocked with carriers made of buttery soft leather, leashes and collars made with crystals, hand-painted pet bowls, and toys of all sorts. ⊠ *Wharfside Village shopping center, Cruz Bay* ☎ *340/777–9588* ⊕ *www.stjohnimals.com.*

Verace. This store is filled with jewelry from such well-known designers as Toby Pomeroy and Patrick Murphy. Murphy's stunning gold sailboats with gems for hulls will catch your eye. ⊠ *Wharfside Village, Strand St., Cruz Bay* ☎ *340/693–7599* ⊕ *www.verace.com.*

27

CORAL BAY AND ENVIRONS
CLOTHING

Jolly Dog. Head here for the stuff you forgot to pack. Sarongs in cotton and rayon, beach towels with tropical motifs, and hats and T-shirts sporting the "Jolly Dog" logo fill the shelves. ⊠ *Skinny Legs Shopping Complex, Rte. 10, Coral Bay* ☏ *340/693–5900.*

Sloop Jones. This store's worth the trip all the way out to the island's east end to shop for made-on-the-premises clothing and pillows, in fabrics splashed with tropical colors. Fabrics are in cotton, gauze, and modal and are supremely comfortable. ⊠ *Off Rte. 10, East End* ☏ *340/779–4001* ⊕ *www.sloopjones.com.*

FOOD

Lily's Gourmet Market. This small store in Coral Bay carries the meat, fish, produce, and staples. ⊠ *Cocoloba Shopping Center, Rte. 107, Coral Bay* ☏ *340/777–3335.*

Love City Mini Mart. The store may not look like much from the road, but it's one of the very few places to shop in Coral Bay and has a surprising selection. ⊠ *Off Rte. 107, Coral Bay* ☏ *340/693–5790.*

GIFTS

Mumbo Jumbo. With what may be the best prices in St. John, Mumbo Jumbo carries tropical clothing, stuffed sea creatures, and other gifty items in a cozy little shop. ⊠ *Skinny Legs Shopping Complex, Rte. 10, Coral Bay* ☏ *340/779–4277.*

SPORTS AND ACTIVITIES

BOATING AND SAILING

If you're staying at a hotel or campground, your activities desk will usually be able to help you arrange a sailing excursion aboard a nearby boat. Most day sails leaving Cruz Bay head out along St. John's north coast. Those that depart from Coral Bay might drop anchor at some remote cay off the island's east end or even in the nearby British Virgin Islands. Your trip usually includes lunch, beverages, and at least one snorkeling stop. Keep in mind that inclement weather could interfere with your plans, though most boats will still go out if rain isn't too heavy.

Ocean Runner. For a speedier trip to the cays and remote beaches off St. John, you can rent a powerboat with a captain from Ocean Runner. The company rents two-engine boats for $580 to $690 per day. Gas and oil will run you $100 to $300 a day extra, depending on how far you're going. ⊠ *Wharfside Village, Waterfront, Cruz Bay* ☏ *340/693–8809* ⊕ *www.oceanrunnerusvi.com.*

Sail Safaris. Even novice sailors can take off in a small sailboat from Cruz Bay Beach with Sail Safaris to one of the small islands off St. John. Guided half-day tours on small or large boats start at $75 per person. Rentals run $50 per hour. ⊠ *Bay St., Cruz Bay* ☏ *340/626–8181* ⊕ *www.sailsafaris.net.*

St. John Concierge Service. The capable staff can find a charter sail or power boat that fits your style and budget. The company also books fishing and scuba trips. ⊠ *Henry Samuel St., across from post office, Cruz Bay* ☏ *340/514–5262* ⊕ *www.stjohnconciergeservice.com.*

DIVING AND SNORKELING

Although just about every beach has nice snorkeling—Trunk Bay, Cinnamon Bay, and Waterlemon Cay at Leinster Bay get the most praise—you need a boat to head out to the more remote snorkeling locations and the best scuba spots. Sign on with any of the island's water-sports operators to get to spots farther from St. John. If you use the one at your hotel, just stroll down to the dock to hop aboard. Their boats will take you to hot spots between St. John and St. Thomas, including the tunnels at **Thatch Cay**, the ledges at **Congo Cay**, and the wreck of the *General Rogers*. Dive off St. John at **Stephens Cay**, a short boat ride out of Cruz Bay, where fish swim around the reefs as you float downward. At **Devers Bay**, on St. John's south shore, fish dart about in colorful schools. **Carval Rock**, shaped like an old-time ship, has gorgeous rock formations, coral gardens, and lots of fish. It can be too rough here in winter, though. Count on paying $75 for a one-tank dive and $90 for a two-tank dive. Rates include equipment and a tour. If you've never dived before, try an introductory course, called a resort course. Or if certification is in your vacation plans, the island's dive shops can help you get your card.

Cruz Bay Watersports. The owners of Cruz Bay, Marcus and Patty Johnston, offer regular reef, wreck, and night dives and USVI and BVI snorkel tours. The company holds both PADI Five Star and NAUI-Dream-Resort status. ⊠ *Lumberyard Shopping Complex, Boulon Center Rd., Cruz Bay* ☎ *340/776–6234* ⊕ *www.divestjohn.com* ⊠ *Westin St. John, Rte. 104, Great Cruz Bay* ☎ *340/776–6234.*

Low Key Watersports. Low Key Watersports offers two-tank dives and specialty courses. It's certified as a PADI Five Star training facility. ⊠ *1 Bay St., Cruz Bay* ☎ *340/693–8999, 800/835–7718* ⊕ *www.divelowkey.com.*

FISHING

Well-kept charter boats—approved by the U.S. Coast Guard—head out to the north and south drops or troll along the inshore reefs, depending on the season and what's biting. The captains usually provide bait, drinks, and lunch, but you need to bring your own hat and sunscreen. Fishing charters run about $1,100 for the full-day trip.

FAMILY **Offshore Adventures.** An excellent choice for fishing charters, Captain Rob Richards is patient with beginners—especially kids—but also enjoys going out with more experienced anglers. He runs the 40-foot center console *Mixed Bag I* and 32-foot *Mixed Bag II*. Although he's based in St. John, he will pick up parties in St. Thomas. ⊠ *Westin St. John, 3008 Chocolate Hole Rd., Great Cruz Bay* ☎ *340/513–0389* ⊕ *www.sportfishingstjohn.com.*

GUIDED TOURS

In St. John, taxi drivers provide tours of the island, making stops at various sites, including Trunk Bay and Annaberg Plantation. Prices run around $15 a person. The taxi drivers congregate near the ferry in Cruz Bay. The dispatcher will find you a driver for your tour.

27

V.I. National Park Visitors Center. Along with providing trail maps and brochures about Virgin Islands National Park, the park service gives several guided tours, both on- and offshore. Some are offered only during particular times of the year, and some require reservations. ⊠ *Cruz Bay* ☎ *340/776–6201* ⊕ *www.nps.gov/viis.*

HIKING

Although it's fun to go hiking with a Virgin Islands National Park guide, don't be afraid to head out on your own. To find a hike that suits your ability, stop by the park's visitor center in Cruz Bay and pick up the free trail guide; it details points of interest, trail lengths, and estimated hiking times, as well as any dangers you might encounter. Although the park staff recommends long pants to protect against thorns and insects, most people hike in shorts because it can get very hot. Wear sturdy shoes or hiking boots even if you're hiking to the beach. Don't forget to bring water and insect repellent.

Fodor's Choice ★ **Virgin Islands National Park.** Head to the park for more than 20 trails on the north and south shores, with guided hikes along the most popular routes. A full-day trip to Reef Bay is a must; it's an easy hike through lush and dry forest, past the ruins of an old plantation, and to a sugar factory adjacent to the beach. It can be a bit arduous for young kids, however. The park runs a $30 guided tour to Reef Bay that includes a safari bus ride to the trailhead and a boat ride back to the Visitors Center. The schedule changes from season to season; call for times and to make reservations, which are essential. ⊠ *North Shore Rd., near Creek, Cruz Bay* ☎ *340/776–6201* ⊕ *www.nps.gov/viis.*

HORSEBACK RIDING

Carolina Corral. Clip-clop along the island's byways for a slower-pace tour of St. John. Carolina Corral offers horseback trips and wagon rides down scenic roads with owner Dana Barlett. She has a way with horses and calms even the most novice riders. Rates start at $75 for a one-hour ride. ⊠ *Off Rte. 10, Coral Bay* ☎ *340/693–5778* ⊕ *www.carolinacorral.com.*

SEA KAYAKING

Poke around the clear bays here and explore undersea life from a sea kayak. Rates run about $70 for a full day in a double kayak. Tours start at $65 for a half day.

Arawak Expeditions. This company's guides use traditional and sit-on-top kayaks for exploring Cruz Bay's waters. The company also rents single and double kayaks as well as standup paddleboards, so you can head independently to nearby islands such as Stephen's Cay. ⊠ *Mongoose Juction Shopping Center, North Shore Rd., Cruz Bay* ☎ *340/693–8312, 800/238–8687* ⊕ *www.arawakexp.com.*

Crabby's Watersports. Explore Coral Bay Harbor and Hurricane Hole on the eastern end of the island in a sea kayak or a standup paddleboard from Crabby's Watersports. If you don't want to paddle into the wind to get out of Coral Bay Harbor, the staff will drop you off in Hurricane Hole so you can paddle downwind back to Coral Bay. Crabby's also rents snorkel gear, beach chairs, umbrellas, coolers, and floats. ⊠ *Rte. 107, next to Cocoloba shopping center, Coral Bay* ☎ *340/714–2415* ⊕ *www.crabbyswatersports.com.*

Hidden Reef EcoTours. Coral reefs, mangroves, and lush sea-grass beds filled with marine life are what you can see on Hidden Reef's two- and three-hour, full-day and full-moon kayak tours through Coral Reef National Monument and its environs. ⊠ *Rte. 10, Round Bay* ☎ *340/513–9613, 877/529–2575* ⊕ *www.kayaksj.com.*

WINDSURFING

Cinnamon Bay Campground. Steady breezes and expert instruction make learning to windsurf a snap. Try Cinnamon Bay Campground, where rentals are $40 to $100 per hour. Lessons are available right at the waterfront; just look for the Windsurfers stacked up on the beach. The cost for a one-hour lesson starts at $60, plus the cost of the board rental. You can also rent kayaks, stand-up paddle boards, Boogie boards, small sailboats, and surfboards. ⊠ *Rte. 20, Cinnamon Bay* ☎ *340/693–5902, 340/626–4769* ⊕ *www.windnsurfingadventures.com.*

ST. CROIX

Updated by
Lynda Lohr

History is a big draw in St. Croix: planes are filled with Danish visitors who come mainly to explore the island's colonial history. Of course, like the rest of us, they also make sure to spend some time sunning at the island's powdery beaches, getting pampered at the hotels, and dining at interesting restaurants.

Until 1917 Denmark owned St. Croix and her sister Virgin Islands, a fact reflected in street names in the main towns of Christiansted and Frederiksted as well as the surnames of many island residents. In the 18th and 19th centuries, some of those early Danish settlers, as well as other Europeans, owned plantations, all of them worked by African slaves and white indentured servants lured to St. Croix to pay off their debt to society. Some of the plantation ruins—such as the Christiansted National Historic Site, Whim Plantation, the ruins at St. George Village Botanical Garden, and those at Estate Mount Washington and Judith's Fancy—are open for easy exploration. Others are on private land, but a drive around the island reveals the ruins of 100 plantations here and there on St. Croix's 84 square miles (218 square km). Their windmills, greathouses, and factories are all that's left of the 224 plantations that once grew sugarcane, tobacco, and other crops at the island's height.

The downturn began in 1801, when the British occupied the island. The end of the slave trade in 1803, an additional British occupation (from 1807 to 1815), droughts, the development of the sugar-beet industry in Europe, political upheaval, and an economic depression all sent the island into a downward spiral.

St. Croix never recovered. The end of slavery in 1848, followed by labor riots, fires, hurricanes, and an earthquake during the last half of the 19th century, brought what was left of the island's economy to its knees. In the 1920s, the start of prohibition in the United States ended the island's rum industry, further crippling the economy. The situation remained dire—so bad that President Herbert Hoover called the territory an "effective poorhouse" during a 1931 visit—until the rise

St. Croix

TO
ST. THOMAS

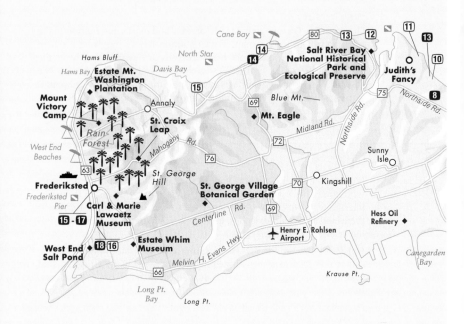

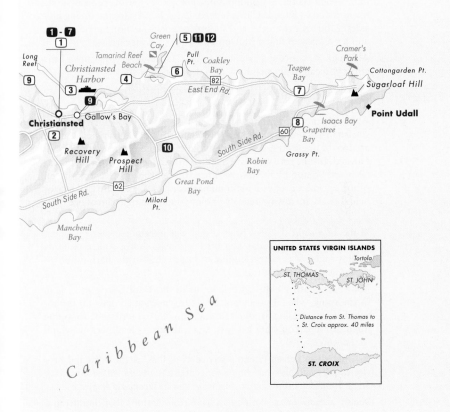

Buck Island

Buck Island Reef
National Monument

1 - **7**
1

Long
Reef

9

Christiansted
Harbor

3

9

Christiansted

2

Gallow's Bay

Recovery
Hill

Prospect
Hill

South Side Rd.

62

Tamarind Reef
Beach

4

Green
Cay

6

5 **11** **12**

Pull
Pt.

Coakley
Bay

East End Rd.

82

10

Great Pond
Bay

Milord
Pt.

Manchenil
Bay

Teague
Bay

7

Cramer's
Park

Cottongarden Pt.

Sugarloaf Hill

Point Udall

Isaacs Bay

8

Grapetree
Bay

60

Grassy Pt.

Robin
Bay

South Side Rd.

Caribbean Sea

UNITED STATES VIRGIN ISLANDS

Tortola

ST. THOMAS

ST. JOHN

Distance from St. Thomas to
St. Croix approx. 40 miles

ST. CROIX

0   2 miles

0   3 km

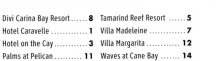

of tourism in the late 1950s and 1960s. With tourism came economic improvements coupled with an influx of residents from other Caribbean islands and the mainland: St. Croix also depends on industries such as the huge oil refinery outside Frederiksted to provide employment.

Today suburban subdivisions fill the fields where sugarcane once waved in the tropical breeze. Condominium complexes line the beaches along the north coast outside Christiansted. Large houses dot the rolling hillsides. Modern strip malls and shopping centers sit along major roads, and it's as easy to find a McDonald's as it is Caribbean fare.

Although St. Croix sits definitely in the 21st century, with only a little effort you can easily step back into the island's past.

EXPLORING

Although there are things to see and do in St. Croix's two towns, Christiansted and Frederiksted (both named after Danish kings), there are lots of interesting spots in between them and to the east of Christiansted. Just be sure you have a map in hand (pick one up at rental-car agencies, or stop by the tourist office for an excellent one that's free). Many secondary roads remain unmarked; if you get confused, ask for help. Locals are always ready to point you in the right direction.

CHRISTIANSTED

In the 1700s and 1800s Christiansted was a trading center for sugar, rum, and molasses. Today law offices, tourist shops, and restaurants occupy many of the same buildings, which start at the harbor and go up the gently sloped hillsides.

Your best bet to see the historic sights in this Danish-style town is in the morning, when it's still cool. Break for lunch at an open-air restaurant before spending as much time as you like exploring the shopping opportunities. You can't get lost, since all streets lead back downhill to the water.

St. Croix Visitor Center. Friendly advice as well as useful maps and brochures are available from the visitor center. ⊠ *Government House, King St.* ☎ *340/773–1404* ⊕ *www.visitusvi.com* ☉ *Weekdays 8–5.*

Danish Customs House. Built in 1830 on foundations that date from a century earlier, the historic building, which is near Ft. Christiansvaern, originally served as both a customs house and a post office. In 1926 it became the Christiansted Library, and it's been a national park facility since 1972. It's closed to the public, but the sweeping front steps make a nice place to take a break. ⊠ *King St.* ☎ *340/773–1460* ⊕ *www.nps.gov/chri.*

D. Hamilton Jackson Park. When you're tired of sightseeing, stop at this shady park on the street side of Fort Christiansvaern for a rest. It's named for a famed labor leader, judge, and journalist who started the first newspaper not under the thumb of the Danish crown (his birthday, November 1, is a territorial holiday celebrated with much fanfare in St. Croix). ⚠ There are no facilities. ⊠ *Between Fort Christiansvaern and Danish Customs House.*

Fort Christiansvaern is a National Historic Site.

Point Udall. This rocky promontory, the easternmost point in the United States, is about a half-hour drive from Christiansted. A paved road takes you to an overlook with glorious views. More adventurous folks can hike down to the pristine beach below. On the way back, look for the Castle Aura, an enormous Moorish-style mansion. It was built by Nadia Farber, the former Contessa de Navarro, who's an extravagant local character. ⚠ **Point Udall is sometimes a popular spot for thieves, so don't leave anything valuable in your car, and leave it unlocked.** ✉ *Rte. 82, Et Stykkeland.*

MID ISLAND

A drive through the countryside between these two towns takes you past ruins of old plantations, many bearing whimsical names (Morningstar, Solitude, Upper Love). The traffic moves quickly—by island standards—on the main roads, but you can pause and poke around if you head down some side lanes. It's easy to find your way west, but driving from north to south requires good navigation. Don't leave your hotel without a map. Allow an entire day for this trip, so you'll have enough time for a swim at a north-shore beach. Although you can find lots of casual eateries on the main roads, pick up a picnic lunch if you plan to head off the beaten path.

Captain Morgan Distillery. The base for Captain Morgan brand rum is made from molasses at this distillery. The tour includes exhibits on island and rum history; a movie about the process; and a tram tour of the distillery. In keeping with the company's responsible-drinking policy, the drink samples at the end of the tour are limited to two. ✉ *Melvin Evans Hwy. and Rte. 663, Annaberg and Shannon Grove* ☎ *340/713–5654* ⊕ *www.captainmorgan.com* ✉ *$10* ⊙ *Weekdays 9–5.*

Ft. Christiansvaern. The large yellow fortress dominates the waterfront. Because it's so easy to spot, it makes a good place to begin a walking tour. In 1749 the Danish built the fort to protect the harbor, but the structure was repeatedly damaged by hurricane-force winds and had to be partially rebuilt in 1771. It's now a national historic site, the best preserved of the few remaining Danish-built forts in the Virgin Islands. The park's visitor center is here. Rangers are on hand to answer questions. ■TIP→ **Your paid admission also includes the Steeple Building.** ⊠ *Hospital St.* ☎ *340/773–1460* ⊕ *www.nps.gov/chri* 🖻 *$3* ⊙ *Weekdays 8–4:30, weekends 9–4:30.*

Government House. One of the town's most elegant structures was built as a home for a Danish merchant in 1747. Today it houses offices. If you're here weekdays from 8 to 4:30, slip into the peaceful inner courtyard to admire the still pools and gardens. A sweeping staircase leads you to a second-story ballroom, still used for official government functions. ⊠ *King St.* ☎ *340/773–1404.*

Post Office Building. Built in 1749, Christiansted's former post office was once the Danish West India & Guinea Company warehouse. It now serves as the park's administrative building. ⊠ *Church St.*

Scale House. Constructed in 1856, this was once the spot where goods passing through the port were weighed and inspected. The park staffers here have on offer a good selection of books about St. Croix history and its flora and fauna. ⊠ *King St.* ☎ *340/773–1460* ⊕ *www.nps.gov/chri* ⊙ *Weekdays 8–4:30, weekends 9–4:30.*

Steeple Building. The first Danish Lutheran church on the island when it was built in 1753, the Steeple Building is now used as a museum. It's worth the short walk to see the archaeological artifacts and exhibits on plantation life, the architectural development of Christiansted, the island's Indian inhabitants, and Alexander Hamilton, who grew up in St. Croix. Hours are irregular, so ask at the visitor center. ■TIP→ **Your paid admission includes Ft. Christiansvaern, too.** ⊠ *Church St.* ☎ *340/773–1460* 🖻 *$3.*

EAST END

An easy drive along flat, well-marked roads to St. Croix's eastern end takes you through some choice real estate. Ruins of old sugar estates dot the landscape. You can make the entire loop on the road that circles the island in about an hour, a good way to end the day. If you want to spend a full day exploring, you can find some nice beaches and easy walks with places to stop for lunch.

Buck Island Reef National Monument. Buck Island has pristine beaches that are just right for sunbathing, but there's also some shade for those who don't want to fry. The snorkeling trail set in the reef allows close-up study of coral formations and tropical fish. Overly warm seawater temperatures have led to a condition called coral bleaching that has killed some of the coral. The reefs are starting to recover, but how long it will take is anyone's guess. There's an easy hiking trail to the island's highest point, where you can be rewarded for your efforts by spectacular views of St. John. Charter-boat trips leave daily from the Christiansted waterfront or from Green Cay Marina, about 2 miles (3 km) east of Christiansted. Check with your hotel for recommendations. ⊠ *Off North Shore of St. Croix* ☎ *340/773–1460* ⊕ *www.nps.gov/buis.*

27

Cruzan Rum Distillery. A tour of the company's factory, which was established in 1760, culminates in a tasting of its products, all sold here at good prices. It's worth a stop to look at the distillery's charming old buildings even if you're not a rum connoisseur. ⊠ *West Airport Rd., Estate Diamond* ☎ *340/692–2280* ⊕ *www.cruzanrum.com* ☎ *$5* ⊘ *Weekdays 9–4.*

FAMILY

Fodor's Choice

★

Estate Whim Museum. The lovingly restored estate, with a windmill, cook house, and other buildings, gives a sense of what life was like on St. Croix's sugar plantations in the 1800s. The oval-shape greathouse has high ceilings and antique furniture and utensils. Notice its fresh, airy atmosphere—the waterless stone moat around the great house was used not for defense but for gathering cooling air. If you have kids, the grounds are the perfect place for them to run around, perhaps while you browse in the museum gift shop. It's just outside of Frederiksted. ⊠ *Rte. 70, Estate Whim* ☎ *340/772–0598* ⊕ *www.stcroixlandmarks.com* ☎ *$10* ⊘ *Wed.–Sat. 10–4 and cruise-ship days.*

Fodor's Choice

★

St. George Village Botanical Garden. At this 17-acre estate, fragrant flora grows amid the ruins of a 19th-century sugarcane plantation. There are miniature versions of each ecosystem on St. Croix, from a semiarid cactus grove to a verdant rain forest. The small museum is also well worth a visit. ⊠ *Rte. 70, turn north at sign, St. George* ☎ *340/692–2874* ⊕ *www.sgvbg.org* ☎ *$8* ⊘ *Daily 9–5.*

FREDERIKSTED AND ENVIRONS

St. Croix's second-largest town, Frederiksted, was founded in 1751. Just as Christiansted is famed for its Danish buildings, Frederiksted is known for its Victorian architecture. A stroll around its historic sights will take you no more than an hour. Allow a little more time if you want to duck into the few small shops. One long cruise-ship pier juts into the sparkling sea. It's the perfect place to start a tour of this quaint city.

Caribbean Museum Center for the Arts. Sitting across from the waterfront in a historic building, this small museum hosts an always-changing roster of exhibits. Many are cutting-edge multimedia efforts that you might be surprised to find in such an out-of-the-way location. The openings are popular events. ⊠ *10 Strand St.* ☎ *340/772–2622* ⊕ *www.cmcarts.org* ☎ *Free* ⊘ *Thurs.–Sat. (and any cruise-ship day) 10–5.*

Estate Mount Washington Plantation. Several years ago, while surveying the property, the owners discovered the ruins of a sugar plantation beneath the rain-forest brush. The grounds have since been cleared and opened to the public. You can take a self-guided walking tour of the mill, the rum factory, and other ruins. ⊠ *Rte. 63, Mt. Washington* ⊘ *Daily dawn–dusk.*

FAMILY

Fort Frederik. On July 3, 1848, 8,000 slaves marched on this fort to demand their freedom. Danish governor Peter von Scholten, fearing they would burn the town to the ground, stood up in his carriage parked in front of the fort and granted their wish. The fort, completed in 1760, houses an art gallery and a number of interesting historical exhibits, including some focusing on the 1848 Emancipation and the 1917 transfer of the Virgin Islands from Denmark to the United States. It's within earshot of the Frederiksted Visitor Center. ⊠ *Waterfront* ☎ *340/772–2021* ☎ *$3* ⊘ *Weekdays (and any cruise-ship day) 8:30–4.*

27

Turtles on St. Croix

Green, leatherback, and hawksbill turtles crawl ashore during their annual April-to-November nesting season to lay their eggs. They return from their life at sea every two to seven years to the beach where they were born. Since turtles can live for up to 100 years, they may return many times to nest in St. Croix.

The leatherbacks like Sandy Point National Wildlife Refuge and other spots on St. Croix's western end, but the hawksbills prefer Buck Island and the East End. Green turtles are also found primarily on the East End.

All are endangered species that face numerous predators, some natural, some the result of the human presence. Particularly in the Frederiksted area, dogs and cats prey on the nests and eat the hatchlings.

Occasionally a dog will attack a turtle about to lay its eggs, and cats train their kittens to hunt at turtle nests, creating successive generations of turtle-egg hunters. In addition, turtles have often been hit by fast-moving boats that leave large slices in their shells if they don't kill them outright.

The leatherbacks are the subject of a project by the Earthwatch conservation group. Each summer, teams arrive at Sandy Point National Wildlife Refuge to ensure that poachers, both natural and human, don't attack the turtles as they crawl up the beach. The teams also relocate nests that are laid in areas prone to erosion. When the eggs hatch, teams stand by to make sure the turtles make it safely to the sea, and scientists tag them so they can monitor their return to St. Croix.

Frederiksted Visitor Center. Head here for brochures from numerous St. Croix businesses, as well as a few exhibits about the island. ⊠ *Pier* ☎ *340/773–0495* ☉ *Weekdays 8–5.*

West End Salt Pond. A bird-watcher's delight, this salt pond attracts a large number of winged creatures, including flamingos. ⊠ *Veteran's Shore Dr., Hesselberg.*

NORTH SHORE

Judith's Fancy. In this upscale neighborhood are the ruins of an old greathouse and tower of the same name, both remnants of a circa-1750 Danish sugar plantation. The "Judith" comes from the first name of a woman buried on the property. From the guardhouse at the neighborhood entrance, follow Hamilton Drive past some of St. Croix's loveliest houses. At the end of Hamilton Drive the road overlooks Salt River Bay, where Christopher Columbus anchored in 1493. On the way back, make a detour left off Hamilton Drive onto Caribe Road for a close look at the ruins. The million-dollar villas are something to behold, too. ⊠ *Turn north onto Rte. 751, off Rte. 75, Judith's Fancy.*

Mt. Eagle. At 1,165 feet, this is St. Croix's highest peak. Leaving Cane Bay and passing North Star Beach, follow the coastal road that dips briefly into a forest; then turn left on Route 69. Just after you make the turn, the pavement is marked with the words "The Beast" and a set of giant paw prints. The hill you're about to climb is the famous

Beast of the St. Croix Half Ironman Triathlon, an annual event during which participants must cycle up this intimidating slope. ⊠ *Rte. 69, Davis Bay.*

Salt River Bay National Historical Park and Ecological Preserve. This joint national and local park commemorates the area where Christopher Columbus's men skirmished with the Carib Indians in 1493 on his second visit to the New World. The peninsula on the bay's east side is named for the event: Cabo de las Flechas (Cape of the Arrows). Although the park is still developing, it has several sights with cultural significance. A ball court, used by the Caribs in religious ceremonies, was discovered at the spot where the taxis park. Take a short hike up the dirt road to the ruins of an old earthen fort for great views of Salt River Bay. The area also encompasses a coastal estuary with the region's largest remaining mangrove forest, a submarine canyon, and several endangered species, including the hawksbill turtle and the roseate tern. A visitor center, open winter only, sits just uphill to the west. The water at the beach can be on the rough side, but it's a nice place for sunning. ⊠ *Rte. 75 to Rte. 80, Salt River* ☎ *340/773–1460* ⊕ *www.nps.gov/sari* ☽ *Nov.–June, Tues.–Thurs. 9–4.*

BEACHES

St. Croix's beaches aren't as spectacular as those on St. John or St. Thomas. But that's not to say you won't find some good places to spread out for a day on the water. The best beach is on nearby Buck Island, a national monument where a marked snorkeling trail leads you through an extensive coral reef while a soft, sandy beach beckons a few yards away. Other great beaches are the unnamed west end beaches both south and north of Frederiksted. You can park yourself at any of the handful of restaurants north of Frederiksted. Some rent loungers, and you can get food and drinks right on the beach. Remember to remove all your valuables from the car and keep them out of sight when you go swimming. Break-ins happen on all three of the U.S. Virgin Islands, and most locals recommend leaving your windows down and leaving nothing in your car.

27

EAST END

Fodor's Choice ★ **Buck Island.** Part of Buck Island Reef National Monument, this is a must-see for anyone in St. Croix. The beach is beautiful, but its finest treasures are those you can see when you plop off the boat and adjust your mask, snorkel, and fins to swim over colorful coral and darting fish. Don't know how to snorkel? No problem—the boat crew will have you outfitted and in the water in no time. Take care not to step on those black-pointed spiny sea urchins or touch the mustard-color fire coral, which can cause a nasty burn. Most charter-boat trips start with a snorkel over the lovely reef before a stop at the island's beach. An easy 20-minute hike leads uphill to an overlook for a bird's-eye view of the reef below. Find restrooms at the beach. **Amenities:** toilets. **Best for:** snorkeling; swimming. ⊠ *5 miles (8 km) north of St. Croix* ☎ *340/773–1460* ⊕ *www.nps.gov/buis.*

NORTH SHORE

Cane Bay. On the island's breezy North Shore, Cane Bay does not always have gentle waters, but there are seldom many people around, and the scuba diving and snorkeling are wondrous. You can see elkhorn and brain corals, and less than 200 yards out is the drop-off called Cane Bay Wall. Cane Bay can be an all-day destination. You can rent kayaks and snorkeling and scuba gear at water-sports shops across the road, and a couple of casual restaurants beckon when the sun gets too hot. **Amenities:** food and drink; water sports. **Best for:** solitude; snorkeling; swimming. ✉ *Rte. 80, about 4 miles (6 km) west of Salt River, Cane Bay.*

FREDERIKSTED

West End beaches. There are several unnamed beaches along the coast road north of Frederiksted, but it's best if you don't stray too far from civilization. For safety's sake, most vacationers plop down their towel near one of the casual restaurants spread out along Route 63. The beach at the Rainbow Beach Club, a five-minute drive outside Frederiksted, has a bar, a casual restaurant, water sports, and volleyball. If you want to be close to the cruise-ship pier, just stroll on over to the adjacent sandy beach in front of Ft. Frederik. On the way south out of Frederiksted, the stretch near Sandcastle on the Beach hotel is also lovely. **Amenities:** food and drink; water sports. **Best for:** snorkeling; swimming; walking. ✉ *Rte. 63, north and south of Frederiksted, Frederiksted.*

WHERE TO EAT

Seven flags have flown over St. Croix, and each has left its legacy in the island's cuisine. Fresh local seafood is plentiful and always good; wahoo, mahimahi, and conch are most popular. Island chefs often add Caribbean twists to familiar dishes. For a true island experience, stop at a local restaurant for goat stew, curried chicken, or fried pork chops. Regardless of where you eat, your meal will be an informal affair. As is the case everywhere in the Caribbean, prices are higher than you'd pay on the mainland. Some restaurants may close for a week or two in September or October, so if you're traveling during these months, it's best to call ahead.

CHRISTIANSTED

$$ ECLECTIC 🍴 **Angry Nates.** Serving breakfast, lunch, and dinner, Angry Nates has something for everyone on its extensive menu. Dinner can be as fancy as tilapia and garlic shrimp with mushrooms, white white, and garlic butter, or as basic as a burger or chicken sandwich. If your taste buds run to hot, try the shrimp pistolette—a hollowed-out baguette filled with shrimp and laced with really hot sauce. [$] *Average main: $22* ✉ *King Cross St., at Boardwalk* ☎ *340/692–6283.*

$ ECLECTIC 🍴 **Avocado Pitt.** Locals gather at this Christiansted waterfront spot for the breakfast and lunch specials as well as for a bit of gossip. Breakfast runs to stick-to-the-ribs dishes like oatmeal and pancakes. Lunches include such basics as a crispy chicken-breast sandwich. The yellowfin tuna sandwich is made from fresh fish and gives a new taste to a standard lunchtime favorite. [$] *Average main: $12* ✉ *King Christian Hotel, 59 Kings Wharf* ☎ *340/773–9843* 🕒 *No dinner.*

Some of St. Croix's best beaches are on the west end of the island around Frederiksted.

$$ FRENCH 🍴 **Café Christine.** At this favorite with the professionals who work in downtown Christiansted the presentations are as dazzling as the food. The small menu changes daily, but look for dishes such as shrimp-and-asparagus salad drizzled with a lovely vinaigrette or a vegetarian plate with quiche, salad, and lentils. Desserts are perfection. If the pear pie topped with chocolate is on the menu, don't hesitate. This tiny restaurant has tables in both the air-conditioned dining room and on the outside porch that overlooks historic buildings. [$] *Average main: $14* ✉ *Apothecary Hall Courtyard, 4 Company St.* ☎ *340/713–1500* 💳 *No credit cards* 🕒 *Closed weekends and July–mid-Nov. No dinner.*

$ CARIBBEAN 🍴 **Harvey's.** The dining room is plain, even dowdy, and plastic lace tablecloths constitute the sole attempt at decor—but who cares? The food is delicious. Daily specials, such as mouthwatering goat stew and tender conch in butter, served with big helpings of rice and vegetables, are listed on the blackboard. Genial owner Sarah Harvey takes great pride in her kitchen, bustling out from behind the stove to chat and urge you to eat up. [$] *Average main: $11* ✉ *11B Company St.* ☎ *340/773–3433* 🕒 *No dinner. Closed Sun.*

$$$ INTERNATIONAL 🍴 **Kendricks.** The chef at this elegant open-air restaurant—a longtime favorite among locals—conjures up creative contemporary cuisine. To start, try the Alaskan snow-crab cakes with habanero aioli or the warm chipotle pepper with a garlic and onion soup. Move on to the house specialty: herb-crusted rack of lamb with roasted garlic and fresh thyme sauce. [$] *Average main: $30* ✉ *Company St. and King Cross St.* ☎ *340/773–9199* 🕒 *No lunch. Closed Sun.*

$$$ ECLECTIC FAMILY Fodor's Choice ★ 🍴 **Rum Runners.** The view is as stellar as the food at this highly popular local standby. Sitting right on the Christiansted boardwalk, Rum Runners serves a little bit of everything, including a to-die-for salad of crispy romaine lettuce and tender grilled lobster drizzled with lemongrass vinaigrette. More hearty fare includes baby back ribs cooked with the restaurant's special spice blend and Guinness stout. [$] *Average main: $25* ✉ *Hotel Caravelle, 44A Queen Cross St.* ☎ *340/773–6585* 🌐 *www.rumrunnersstcroix.com.*

$$$ ECLECTIC 🍴 **Savant.** Savant is one of those small but special spots that locals love. The cuisine is a fusion of Mexican, Thai, and Caribbean—an unusual combination that works surprisingly well. You can find anything from fresh fish to Thai curry with chicken to stuffed filet with portobello mushrooms and goat cheese coming out of the kitchen. With 20 tables crammed into the indoor dining room and small courtyard, this little place can get crowded. Call early for reservations. [$] *Average main: $27* ✉ *4C Hospital St.* ☎ *340/713–8666* 🌐 *www.savantstx.com* 🕒 *No lunch. Closed Sun.*

$$$ ITALIAN 🍴 **Tutto Bene.** With murals on the walls, brightly striped cushions, and painted trompe-l'oeil tables, Tutto Bene looks more like a sophisticated Mexican cantina than an Italian *cucina*. One bite of the food, however, will clear up any confusion. The menu includes such specialties as veal saltimbocca and medallions of veal with prosciutto and sage. Among the desserts are a decadent tiramisu. [$] *Average main: $24* ✉ *Boardwalk Shopping Center, Hospital St., Gallows Bay* ☎ *340/773–5229* 🌐 *www.tuttobenerestaurant.com* 🕒 *Closed Mon. and Tues.*

WEST OF CHRISTIANSTED

$$$ ECLECTIC FAMILY 🍴 **Breezez.** This aptly named restaurant is poolside at the Club St. Croix condominiums. Visitors and locals are drawn by its reasonable prices and good food. This is *the* place on the island to be for Sunday brunch. Locals gather for lunch, when the menu includes everything from burgers to blackened prime rib with a horseradish sauce. For dessert, try the Amaretto cheesecake with either chocolate or fruit topping. [$] *Average main: $25* ✉ *Club St. Croix, 3220 Golden Rock, off Rte. 752, Golden Rock* ☎ *340/718–7077.*

$$$ ITALIAN 🍴 **Salud Bistro.** This eatery's imaginative menu takes its cue from the fresh flavors of the Mediterranean. Start with the savory cheese plate served with homemade bread and crostini before moving on to fresh fish or the grilled duck with a hibiscus confit. [$] *Average main: $27* ✉ *Princess Shopping Center, Rte. 75, La Grande Princess* ☎ *340/718–7900* 🌐 *www.saludbistro.com* 🕒 *Closed Sun. No lunch.*

EAST END

$$$ ECLECTIC 🍴 **The Deep End.** A favorite with locals and vacationers, this poolside restaurant serves up terrific chicken sandwiches, steak, seafood, and delicious pasta dishes. To get here from Christiansted, take Route 82 and turn left at the sign for Green Cay Marina. [$] *Average main: $23* ✉ *Tamarind Reef Hotel, Rte. 82, Annas Hope* ☎ *340/773–4455.*

$$$ ECLECTIC 🍴 **The Galleon.** This popular dockside restaurant is always busy. Start with the Caesar salad or perhaps a duck-liver pâté with cherry compote and arugula. The chef's signature dish is a tender filet mignon topped with fresh local lobster. Fish lovers should try the pan-seared sea scallops

with roasted tomatoes and a kalamata olive risotto. Take Route 82 out of Christiansted, and then turn left at the sign for Green Cay Marina. [$] *Average main: $30* ✉ *Green Cay Marina, off Rte. 82, Annas Hope* ☎ *340/718–9948* 🌐 *www.galleonrestaurant.com* ⏲ *No lunch Mon.–Sat.*

NORTH SHORE

$$ AMERICAN Fodor's Choice ★ 🍴 **Eat @ Cane Bay.** The fabulous food matches the view of Cane Bay at this casual spot in the heart of Cane Bay. The lunch menu includes a build-your-own beef, veggie, or grilled chicken burger that gives you a choice of toppings, dressings, and cheese. If you opt for, say, a roasted turkey club sandwich, the onion rings that come with it are terrific. Dinner offerings include pasta, fish, steak, and sandwiches. [$] *Average main: $18* ✉ *Rte. 80, Cane Bay* ☎ *340/718–0360* 🌐 *www.eatatcanebay.com* ⏲ *Closed Tues.*

$$ AMERICAN 🍴 **Off the Wall.** Divers fresh from a plunge at the North Shore's popular Cane Bay Wall gather at this breezy spot on the beach. If you want to sit a spell before you order, a hammock beckons. Deli sandwiches, served with delicious chips, make up most of the menu. Pizza and salads are also available. [$] *Average main: $14* ✉ *Rte. 80, Cane Bay* ☎ *340/778–4771* 🌐 *www.otwstx.com.*

FREDERIKSTED

$$$ ECLECTIC 🍴 **Beach Side Café.** Sunday brunch is big, but locals and visitors also flock to this oceanfront bistro at Sandcastle on the Beach resort for lunch and dinner. Both menus include burgers and salads, but at dinner the crispy half duck with berry sauce shines. For lunch, the hummus plate is a good bet. [$] *Average main: $29* ✉ *Sandcastle on the Beach, 127 Smithfield* ☎ *340/772–1266* 🌐 *www.sandcastleonthebeach.com* ⏲ *Closed Tues. and Wed.*

$$$ AMERICAN Fodor's Choice ★ 🍴 **Blue Moon.** This terrific little bistro, which has a loyal local following, offers a changing menu that draws on Cajun and Caribbean flavors. Try the spicy gumbo with andouille sausage or crab cakes with a spicy aioli for your appetizer. A grilled chicken breast served with spinach and artichoke hearts and topped with Parmesan and cheddar cheeses makes a good entrée. The Almond Joy sundae should be your choice for dessert. There's live jazz on Wednesday and Friday. [$] *Average main: $23* ✉ *7 Strand St.* ☎ *340/772–2222* ⏲ *Closed Mon.*

$$ ECLECTIC 🍴 **Polly's at the Pier.** With an emphasis on fresh ingredients, this very casual spot right on the waterfront serves delicious fare. The gourmet grilled cheese sandwich comes with your choice of three cheeses as well as delicious additions like basil, fresh Bosc pears, and avocado. Salads are a specialty, and many are made with local bibb lettuce and organic mixed greens. [$] *Average main: $13* ✉ *3 Strand St.* ☎ *340/719–9434* ⏲ *No dinner.*

$ DELI FAMILY 🍴 **Turtles Deli.** You can eat outside at this tiny spot just as you enter downtown Frederiksted. Lunches are as basic as a corned beef on rye or as imaginative as the Raven (turkey breast with bacon, tomato, and melted cheddar cheese on French bread). Also good is the Beast, named after the grueling hill that challenges bikers in the annual triathlon. It's piled high with hot roast beef, raw onion, and melted Swiss cheese with horseradish and mayonnaise. Early risers stop by for cinnamon buns and espresso. [$] *Average main: $12* ✉ *38 Strand St., at Prince Passage* ☎ *340/772–3676* 🌐 *www.turtlesdeli.com* 💳 *No credit cards* ⏲ *No dinner. Closed Sun.*

WHERE TO STAY

If you sleep in either the Christiansted or Frederiksted area, you'll be closest to shopping, restaurants, and nightlife. Most of the island's other hotels will put you just steps from the beach. St. Croix has several small but special properties that offer personalized service. If you like all the comforts of home, you may prefer to stay in a condominium or villa. Room rates on St. Croix are competitive with those on other islands, and if you travel off-season, you can find substantially reduced prices. Many properties offer money-saving honeymoon and dive packages. Whether you stay in a hotel, a condominium, or a villa, you'll enjoy up-to-date amenities. Most properties have room TVs, but at some bed-and-breakfasts there might be only one, in the common room.

Although a stay right in historic Christiansted may mean putting up with a little urban noise, you probably won't have trouble sleeping. Christiansted rolls up the sidewalks fairly early, and humming air conditioners drown out any noise. Solitude is guaranteed at hotels and inns outside Christiansted and those on the outskirts of sleepy Frederiksted.

PRIVATE CONDOMINIUMS AND VILLAS

Most of the villas in St. Croix are in the center or on the East End. Renting a villa gives you the convenience of home as well as top-notch amenities. Many have pools, hot tubs, and deluxe furnishings. Most companies meet you at the airport, arrange for a rental car, and provide helpful information about the island.

If you want to be close to the island's restaurants and shopping, look for a condominium or villa in the hills above Christiansted or on either side of the town. An East End location gets you out of Christiansted's hustle and bustle, but you're still only 15 minutes from town. North Shore locations are lovely, with gorgeous sea views and lots of peace and quiet.

RENTAL CONTACTS

Vacation St. Croix ✉ *400 La Grande Princess, Christiansted* ☎ *340/718–0361, 877/788–0361* 🌐 *www.vacationstcroix.com.*

CHRISTIANSTED

$ HOTEL 🏨 **Hotel Caravelle.** A stay at the Caravelle, which is near the harbor, puts you at the waterfront end of a pleasant shopping arcade and steps from shops and restaurants. **Pros:** good restaurant; convenient location; convenient parking. **Cons:** no beach; busy in-town neighborhood. [$] *Rooms from: $150* ✉ *44A Queen Cross St.* ☎ *340/773–0687, 800/524–0410* 🌐 *www.hotelcaravelle.com* 🛏 *43 rooms, 1 suite* 🍴 *No meals.*

$ RESORT 🏨 **Hotel on the Cay.** Hop on the free ferry to reach this peaceful lodging in the middle of Christiansted Harbor. **Pros:** quiet; convenient location; lovely beach. **Cons:** accessible only by ferry; no parking available. [$] *Rooms from: $259* ✉ *Protestant Cay* ☎ *340/773–2035, 855/654–0301* 🌐 *www.hotelonthecay.com* 🛏 *53 rooms* 🍴 *No meals.*

WEST OF CHRISTIANSTED

$ B&B/INN Fodor's Choice ★ 🏨 **Carringtons Inn.** Local flavor, personalized service, and individual style make this intimate inn a welcome respite from the realm of cookie-cutter resorts, with its location in a former private home that offers a lovely pool and unbeatable ocean views. **Pros:** feels like a private home;

welcoming host; tasteful rooms; great breakfasts. **Cons:** no beach; need car to get around. [$] *Rooms from: $150* ✉ *4001 Estate Hermon Hill, Christiansted* ☎ *340/713–0508, 877/658–0508* 🌐 *www.carringtonsinn.com* 🛏 *5 rooms* 🍴 *Breakfast.*

$ RENTAL FAMILY 🏨 **Club St. Croix.** Sitting beachfront just outside Christiansted, this modern condominium complex faces a lovely sandy beach. **Pros:** beachfront location; good restaurant; full kitchens. **Cons:** need car to get around; sketchy neighborhood. [$] *Rooms from: $195* ✉ *Rte. 752, Estate Golden Rock* ☎ *340/718–9150, 800/524–2025* 🌐 *www.antillesresorts.com* 🛏 *53 apartments* 🍴 *No meals.*

$ RENTAL FAMILY 🏨 **Colony Cove.** In a string of condominium complexes, Colony Cove lets you experience comfortable beachfront living. **Pros:** beachfront location; comfortable units; good views. **Cons:** sketchy neighborhood; need car to get around. [$] *Rooms from: $235* ✉ *Rte. 752, Estate Golden Rock* ☎ *340/718–1965, 800/524–2025* 🌐 *www.antillesresorts.com* 🛏 *62 apartments* 🍴 *No meals.*

$ RESORT 🏨 **The Palms at Pelican Cove.** A 10-minute drive from Christiansted's interesting shopping and restaurants, this resort, with its mixed-bag of guests, has a gorgeous strand of white sand at its doorstep. **Pros:** nice beach; good dining options; friendly staff. **Cons:** need car to get out and about; neighborhood not the best. [$] *Rooms from: $239* ✉ *Off Rte. 752, La Grande Princesse* ☎ *340/718–8920, 800/548–4460* 🌐 *www.palmspelicancove.com* 🛏 *41 rooms* 🍴 *No meals.*

EAST END

$$ RESORT FAMILY 🏨 **The Buccaneer.** Aimed at travelers who want everything at their fingertips, this resort has sandy beaches, swimming pools, and extensive sports facilities. **Pros:** beachfront location; numerous activities; nice golf course. **Cons:** pricey rates; insular environment; need car to get around. [$] *Rooms from: $360* ✉ *Rte. 82, Box 25200, Shoys* ☎ *340/712–2100, 800/255–3881* 🌐 *www.thebuccaneer.com* 🛏 *138 rooms, 1 villa* 🍴 *Breakfast.*

$ RESORT FAMILY 🏨 **Chenay Bay Beach Resort.** The seaside setting and complimentary tennis and water-sports equipment make this resort a real find, particularly for families with active kids. **Pros:** beachfront location; good children's program; wide array of water sports. **Cons:** need car to get around; lacks pizzazz. [$] *Rooms from: $165* ✉ *Rte. 82, Green Cay* ☎ *340/773–2918, 866/357–2970* 🌐 *www.chenaybay.com* 🛏 *50 rooms* 🍴 *No meals.*

$ ALL-INCLUSIVE 🏨 **Divi Carina Bay Resort.** An oceanfront location, the island's only casino, and plenty of activities make this resort a good bet. **Pros:** spacious beach; good restaurant; on-site casino. **Cons:** need car to get around; many stairs to climb; staff can seem chilly. [$] *Rooms from: $249* ✉ *25 Rte. 60, Estate Turner Hole* ☎ *340/773–9700, 877/773–9700* 🌐 *www.divicarina.com* 🛏 *174 rooms, 2 suites, 20 villas* 🍴 *All-inclusive.*

$ HOTEL 🏨 **Tamarind Reef Resort.** Spread out along a sandy beach, these low-slung buildings offer casual comfort. **Pros:** good snorkeling; tasty restaurant; rooms have kitchenettes. **Cons:** need car to get around; motel-style rooms. [$] *Rooms from: $275* ✉ *5001 Tamarind Reef, off Rte. 82, Annas Hope* ☎ *340/773–4455, 800/619–0014* 🌐 *www.tamarindreefresort.com* 🛏 *39 rooms* 🍴 *No meals.*

27

The Buccaneer is still a family-owned resort.

$$ **Villa Madeleine.** If you like privacy and your own private pool,
RENTAL you'll like Villa Madeleine. **Pros:** pleasant decor; full kitchens; private pools. **Cons:** lower units sometimes lack views; need car to get around; no beachfront. $ *Rooms from: $285* ✉ *Off Rte. 82, Teague Bay* ☎ *340/718–0361, 877/788–0361* ⊕ *www.vacationstcroix.com* ⮑ *43 villas* ⦿ *No meals.*

FREDERIKSTED

$ **Sandcastle on the Beach.** Right on a gorgeous stretch of white beach,
RESORT Sandcastle has a tropical charm that harks back to a simpler time in the Caribbean; its nearness to Frederiksted's interesting dining scene is also a plus. **Pros:** lovely beach; close to restaurants; gay-friendly vibe. **Cons:** neighborhood sketchy at night; need car to get around; no children's activities. $ *Rooms from: $179* ✉ *127 Smithfield, Rte. 71* ☎ *340/772–1205, 800/524–2018* ⊕ *www.sandcastleonthebeach.com* ⮑ *12 rooms, 8 suites, 3 villas* ⦿ *No meals.*

NORTH SHORE

$ **Arawak Bay: The Inn at Salt River.** With stellar views of St. Croix's North
B&B/INN Shore and an affable host, this small inn allows you to settle into island life at a price that doesn't break the bank. **Pros:** 20 minutes from Christiansted; good prices. **Cons:** no beach nearby; can be some road noise. $ *Rooms from: $179* ✉ *Rte. 80, Salt River* ☎ *340/772–1684* ⊕ *www. arawakbaysaltriver.co.vi* ⮑ *12 rooms* ⦿ *Breakfast.*

$$ **Renaissance St. Croix Carambola Beach Resort and Spa.** We like this
RESORT resort's stellar beachfront setting and peaceful ambience. **Pros:** lovely beach; relaxing atmosphere; close to golf. **Cons:** isolated location; need car to get around. $ *Rooms from: $329* ✉ *Rte. 80, Davis Bay*

☎ *340/778–3800, 888/503–8760* 🌐 *www.carambolabeachresort.com* 🛏 *151 rooms* 🍴 *No meals.*

$ B&B/INN 🏨 **Villa Margarita.** This quiet retreat provides a particularly good base if you want to admire the dramatic views of the windswept coast. **Pros:** friendly host; great views; snorkeling nearby. **Cons:** isolated location; need car to get around; limited amenities. [$] *Rooms from: $175* ✉ *Off Rte. 80, Salt River* ☎ *340/713–1930* 🌐 *www.villamargarita.com* 🛏 *3 units* 🍴 *No meals.*

$ HOTEL 🏨 **Waves at Cane Bay.** St. Croix's famed Cane Bay Wall is just offshore from this hotel, giving it an enviable location. **Pros:** great diving; restaurants nearby; beaches nearby. **Cons:** need car to get around; on main road; bland decor. [$] *Rooms from: $120* ✉ *Rte. 80, Cane Bay* ☎ *340/718–1815* 🌐 *www.canebaystcroix.com* 🛏 *10 rooms* 🍴 *No meals.*

NIGHTLIFE AND THE ARTS

Christiansted has a lively and eminently casual club scene near the waterfront. Frederiksted has a couple of restaurants and clubs offering weekend entertainment. To find out what's happening in St. Croix's ever-changing nightlife and eclectic arts scene, check out the local newspapers—*V.I. Daily News* (🌐 *virginislandsdailynews.com*) and *St. Croix Avis*.

CHRISTIANSTED

Fort Christian Brew Pub. Locals and visitors come here to listen to live music several nights a week. ✉ *Boardwalk at end of Kings Alley, Christiansted* ☎ *340/713–9820* 🌐 *www.fortchristianbrewpub.com.*

Hotel on the Cay. This off-shore resort hosts a West Indian buffet on Tuesday night in the winter season, when you can watch a broken-bottle dancer (a dancer who braves a carpet of shattered glass) and mocko jumbie (stilt-dancing) characters. ✉ *Protestant Cay, Christiansted* ☎ *340/773–2035* 🌐 *www.hotelonthecay.com.*

EAST END

Divi Carina Bay Resort. Although you can gamble at the island's only casino, it's really the nightly music that draws big crowds to this resort. ✉ *25 Rte. 60, Estate Turner Hole* ☎ *340/773–7529* 🌐 *www.divicarina.com.*

MID ISLAND

Whim Plantation Museum. The museum outside Frederiksted hosts classical music concerts in winter. ✉ *Rte. 70, Estate Whim* ☎ *340/772–0598* 🌐 *www.stcroixlandmarks.com.*

FREDERIKSTED

Fodor's Choice ★ **Blue Moon.** Blue Moon is a popular waterfront restaurant in Frederiksted, and it's the place to be for live jazz on Wednesday and Friday, one of the few nightlife options on this end of the island. ✉ *7 Strand St., Frederiksted* ☎ *340/772–2222* 🌐 *www.bluemoonstcroix.com.*

Fodor's Choice ★ **Sunset Jazz.** This outdoor event is a hot ticket in Frederiksted, drawing crowds of visitors and locals at 5:30 pm on the third Friday of every month to watch the sun go down and hear good music. ✉ *Waterfront, Frederiksted* ☎ *340/690–1741.*

SHOPPING

Although the shopping on St. Croix isn't as varied or extensive as that on St. Thomas, the island does have several small stores with unusual merchandise. St. Croix shop hours are usually Monday through Saturday 9 to 5, but there are some shops in Christiansted open in the evening. Stores are often closed on Sunday.

CHRISTIANSTED

In Christiansted the best shopping areas are the **Pan Am Pavilion** and **Caravelle Arcade**, off Strand Street, and along **King** and **Company streets.** These streets give way to arcades filled with boutiques. **Gallows Bay** has a blossoming shopping area in a quiet neighborhood.

BOOKS

Undercover Books. This well-stocked independent bookseller sells Caribbean-themed books as well as the latest good reads. The store is in the Gallows Bay shopping area. ⊠ *5030 Anchor Way, across from post office, Gallows Bay* ☎ *340/719–1567* ⊕ *www.undercoverbooksvi.com.*

CLOTHING

From the Gecko. This store sells the hippest island-style clothes on St. Croix, as well as other items. ⊠ *2106 Company St., Christiansted* ☎ *340/778–9433* ⊕ *www.fromthegecko.com.*

Hot Heads. This small store sells hats, hats, and more hats, which are often perched on top of cotton shifts, comfortable shirts, and other tropical wear. If you forgot your bathing suit, this store has a good selection. ⊠ *1244 Queen Cross St., Christiansted* ☎ *340/773–7888.*

Island Tribe. Colorful batik dresses, shirts, shifts, and scarves in soft rayon and cotton round out your tropical wardrobe. Sizes range from small to 4X. The clothing, and an interesting array of jewelry, comes from Bali. ⊠ *57 Company St., Christiansted* ☎ *340/719–0936.*

GIFTS

The Blue Mutt. Shop for a good cause at this small shop that benefits the St. Croix Animal Welfare Center. The shelves are filled with local art, T-shirts, cards, soaps, candles, and much more—all with a pet theme. ⊠ *55 Company St., Christiansted* ☎ *340/690–4624.*

Cache of the Day. This tiny store sells whatever its sea theme has tossed up. Mermaid dolls recline on shelves next to dishtowels printed with shapes of the sea. The sea-themed books make for good beach reads and the cards are perfect for take home gifts. ⊠ *55 Company St., Christiansted* ☎ *340/773–3648.*

Gone Tropical. On her travels about the world, Margot Meacham keeps an eye out for special delights for her shop—items include island-style furnishings, gifts, and accessories as well as unique jewelry. ⊠ *5 Company St., Christiansted* ☎ *340/773–4696* ⊕ *www.gonetropical.com.*

Many Hands. This shop sells pottery in bright colors, paintings of St. Croix and the Caribbean, prints, and maps. They are all made by local artists, and they all make for perfect take-home gifts. ■ **TIP➔ The owners ship all over the world.** ⊠ *21 Pan Am Pavilion, Strand St., Christiansted* ☎ *340/773–1990.*

Mitchell-Larsen Studio. This glass gallery offers an interesting amalgam of carefully crafted glass plates, sun-catchers, and more. The pieces, all made on-site by a St. Croix glassmaker, are often whimsically adorned with tropical fish, flora, and fauna. ⊠ *58 Company St., Christiansted* ☎ *340/719–1000* ⊕ *www.mitchelllarsenstudio.com.*

FodorsChoice   **Royal Poinciana.** The attractive Royal Poinciana is filled with island sea-
★   sonings and hot sauces, West Indian crafts, bath gels, and herbal teas. Shop here for tablecloths and paper goods in tropical brights. ⊠ *1113 Strand St., Christiansted* ☎ *340/773–9892.*

Tesoro. Among the colorful and bold merchandise here are metal sculptures made from retired steel pans, mahogany bowls, and hand-painted place mats in bright tropical colors. ⊠ *3A Queen Cross St., Christiansted* ☎ *340/773–1212* ⊕ *www.tesorostcroix.com.*

HOUSEWARES

Designworks. This store and gallery carries furniture as well as one of the largest selections of local art, along with Caribbean-inspired bric-a-brac and jewelry in all price ranges. If a mahogany armoire or cane-back rocker catches your fancy, the staff can have it shipped to your home at no charge from its mainland warehouse. ⊠ *6 Company St., Christiansted* ☎ *340/713–8102.*

JEWELRY

Crucian Gold. St. Croix native Brian Bishop's trademark piece is the Turk's Head ring (a knot of interwoven gold strands), but his jewelry made of shards of plantation-era china set in gold are just lovely. ⊠ *1112 Strand St., Christiansted* ☎ *340/773–5241* ⊕ *www.cruciangold.com.*

Gold Worker. This shop specializes in handcrafted jewelry in silver and gold that will remind you of the Caribbean. Hummingbirds dangle from silver chains, and sand dollars adorn gold necklaces. The sugar mills in silver and gold speak of St. Croix's past. ⊠ *3 Company St., Christiansted* ☎ *340/514–6042.*

ib designs. This small shop showcases the handcrafted jewelry of local craftsman Whealan Massicott. Whether in silver or gold, the designs are simply elegant. ⊠ *Company St. at Queen Cross St., Christiansted* ☎ *340/773–4322* ⊕ *www.islandboydesigns.com.*

Nelthropp and Low. The jewelers at Nelthropp and Low can create one-of-a-kind pieces to your design. The shop specializes in gold jewelry but also carries diamonds, emeralds, rubies, and sapphires. ⊠ *1102 Strand St., Christiansted* ☎ *340/773–0365, 800/416–9078* ⊕ *www.nelthropp-low.com.*

Sonya's. This store is owned and operated by Sonya Hough, who invented the popular hook bracelet. She has added an interesting decoration to these bracelets: the swirling symbol used in weather forecasts to indicate hurricanes. ⊠ *1 Company St., Christiansted* ☎ *340/778–8605* ⊕ *www.sonyaltd.com.*

27

LIQUOR AND TOBACCO

Baci Duty Free. The walk-in humidor here has a good selection of Arturo Fuente, Partagas, and Macanudo cigars. Baci also carries sleek Swiss-made watches and fine jewelry. ✉ *1235 Queen Cross St., Christiansted* ☎ *340/773–5040* ⊕ *www.bacidutyfree.com.*

WEST OF CHRISTIANSED

FOOD

Pueblo. This market is similar to those stores back in the mainland. ✉ *Golden Rock Shopping Center, Rte. 75, Christiansted* ☎ *340/773–0118.*

EAST END

FOOD

Schooner Bay Market. Although it's on the smallish side, this market has good-quality deli items. ✉ *Rte. 82, Mount Welcome* ☎ *340/773–3232* ⊕ *www.schoonerbaymarket.com.*

MID ISLAND

FOOD

Cost-U-Less. This warehouse-type store is great for visitors because it doesn't charge a membership fee. It's in the busy Sunny Isle area. ✉ *Rte. 70, Sunny Isle* ☎ *340/719–4442* ⊕ *www.costuless.com.*

Plaza Extra. This supermarket chain has a good selection of Middle Eastern foods in addition to the usual grocery-store items. ✉ *United Shopping Plaza, Rte. 70, Sion Farm* ☎ *340/778–6240* ⊕ *www.plazaextra. com* ✉ *Rte. 70, Sion Farm* ☎ *340/719–1870* ⊕ *www.plazaextra.com.*

Pueblo. This stateside-style market has another branch west of Christiansed. ✉ *Villa La Reine Shopping Center, Rte. 75, La Reine* ☎ *340/ 778–1272.*

LIQUOR AND TOBACCO

Kmart. The U.S. discount chain has two branches on St. Croix, both of which carry a huge line of deep discounted, duty-free liquor, among many other items. ✉ *Sunshine Mall, Rte. 70, Frederiksted* ☎ *340/ 692–5848* ✉ *Sunny Isle Shopping Center, Rte. 70, Sunny Isle* ☎ *340/ 719–9190.*

FREDERIKSTED

The best shopping in Frederiksted is along **Strand Street** and in the side streets and alleyways that connect it with **King Street.** Most stores close on Sunday, except when a cruise ship is in port. Keep in mind that Frederiksted has a reputation for muggings, so it's best to stick to populated areas of Strand and King streets, where there are few—if any—problems.

SPORTS AND ACTIVITIES

BOAT TOURS

Almost everyone takes a day trip to Buck Island aboard a charter boat. Most leave from the Christiansted waterfront or from Green Cay Marina and stop for a snorkel at the island's eastern end before dropping anchor off a gorgeous sandy beach for a swim, a hike, and lunch. Sailboats can often stop right at the beach; a larger boat might have

Deep-sea fishing in St. Croix's coastal waters

to anchor a bit farther offshore. A full-day sail runs about $100, with lunch included on most trips. A half-day sail costs about $68.

Big Beard's Adventure Tours. From catamarans that depart from the Christiansted waterfront you'll head to Buck Island for snorkeling before dropping anchor at a private beach for a barbecue lunch. ⊠ *Waterfront, Christiansted* ☎ *340/773–4482* ⊕ *www.bigbeards.com.*

Buck Island Charters. These charters are on two trimarans, *Teroro II* and *Dragonfly,* which leave Green Cay Marina for full- or half-day sails. Bring your own lunch. ⊠ *Green Cay Marina, Annas Hope* ☎ *340/773–3161* ⊕ *www.gotostcroix.com/heinz/index.php.*

Caribbean Sea Adventures. With craft leaving from the Christiansted waterfront, Caribbean Sea Adventures has both half- and full-day trips. ⊠ *Waterfront, Christiansted* ☎ *340/773–2628* ⊕ *www. caribbeanseaadventures.com.*

DIVING AND SNORKELING

At **Buck Island,** a short boat ride from Christiansted or Green Cay Marina, the reef is so nice that it's been named a national monument. You can dive right off the beach at **Cane Bay,** which has a spectacular drop-off called the Cane Bay Wall. Dive operators also do boat trips along the Wall, usually leaving from Salt River or Christiansted. **Frederiksted Pier** is home to a colony of sea horses, creatures seldom seen in the waters of the Virgin Islands. At **Green Cay,** just outside Green Cay Marina in the east end, you can see colorful fish swimming around the reefs and rocks. Two exceptional North Shore sites are **North Star** and **Salt River,** which you can reach only by boat. At Salt River you can float downward through a canyon filled with colorful fish and coral.

The island's dive shops take you out for one- or two-tank dives. Plan to pay about $65 for a one-tank dive and $100 for a two-tank dive, including equipment and an underwater tour. All companies offer certification and introductory courses called resort dives for novices.

Which dive outfit you pick usually depends on where you're staying. Your hotel may have one on-site. If so, you're just a short stroll away from the dock. If not, other companies are close by. Where the dive boat goes on a particular day depends on the weather, but in any case, all St. Croix dive sites are special. All shops are affiliated with PADI, the Professional Association of Diving Instructors.

Cane Bay Dive Shop. This is the place if you want to do a beach dive or boat dive along the North Shore. The famed Cane Bay Wall is 200 yards from the PADI Five Star facility. This company also has shops at Pan Am Pavilion in Christiansted, on Strand Street in Frederiksted, and at the Divi Carina Bay Resort. ⊠ *Rte. 80, Cane Bay* ☎ *340/718–9913, 800/338–3843* ⊕ *www.canebayscuba.com.*

Dive Experience. Handy for those staying in Christiansted, Dive Experience runs trips to the North Shore walls and reefs in addition to offering the usual certification and introductory classes. It's a PADI Five Star facility. ⊠ *1111 Strand St., Christiansted* ☎ *340/773–3307, 800/235–9047* ⊕ *www.divexp.com.*

N2 the Blue. N2 takes divers right off the beach near the Frederiksted Pier, on night dives off the Frederiksted Pier, or on boat trips to the Salt River Wall. ⊠ *Customs House St., Frederiksted* ☎ *340/772–3483, 877/579–0572* ⊕ *www.n2theblue.com.*

St. Croix Ultimate Bluewater Adventures. This company can take you to your choice of more than 75 sites; it also offers a variety of packages that include hotel stays. ⊠ *Queen Cross St., Christiansted* ☎ *340/773–5994, 877/567–1367* ⊕ *www.stcroixscuba.com.*

FISHING

Since the early 1980s, some 20 world records—many for blue marlin—have been set in these waters. Sailfish, skipjack, bonito, tuna (allison, blackfin, and yellowfin), and wahoo are abundant. A charter runs about $500 for a half day (for up to six people), with most boats going out for four-, six-, or eight-hour trips.

Captain Festus. Captain Festus takes you to spots all around St. Croix on his 55-foot boat *Sea Hunter* and 35-foot *Triton.* ⊠ *Kings Wharf, Christiansted* ☎ *340/277–1751.*

Gone Ketchin'. Captain Grizz, a true old salt, heads these trips. ⊠ *Salt River Marina, Rte. 80, Salt River* ☎ *340/713–1175* ⊕ *www.goneketchin.com.*

GOLF

Fodor's Choice ★   **Buccaneer Golf Course.** This 18-hole course is close to Christiansted and features views of the Caribbean from 13 of its holes. Golf lessons and club rentals are available. ⊠ *Rte. 82, Shoys* ☎ *340/712–2144* ⊕ *www. thebuccaneer.com* ⊡ *$110 for 18 holes; $70 for 9 holes; additional $20 for cart rental* ⚑ *18 holes, 5688 yards, par 70.*

Horseback riding in the island's rain forest

Carambola Golf Club. This spectacular 18-hole course in the northwest valley was designed by Robert Trent Jones Sr. Fees include the use of a golf cart. ✉ *Rte. 69, River* ☎ *340/778–5638* ⊕ *www.golfcarambola. com* 🎫 *$125.*

GUIDED TOURS

St. Croix Transit. Departing from Renaissance Carambola Beach Resort, St. Croix Transit's three-hour van tours cost from $65 per person, which includes the admission fees to all attractions. ✉ *Renaissance Carambola Beach Resort, Rte. 80, Davis Bay* ☎ *340/772–3333.*

Sweeny's St. Croix Safari Tours. These van tours of St. Croix depart from Christiansted and last about five hours. Costs run from $70 per person, including admission fees to attractions. ✉ *Christiansted* ☎ *340/773–6700* ⊕ *www.gotostcroix.com/guided-island-tours.*

HIKING

Although you can set off by yourself on a hike through a rain forest or along a shore, a guide will be able to point out what's important and tell you why.

Ay-Ay Eco Hike and Tours. Ras Lumumba Corriette takes hikers up hill and down dale in some of St. Croix's most remote places, including the rain forest and Mt. Victory. Some hikes include stops at old ruins. The cost is $60 per person for a three- or four-hour hike. There's a three-person minimum. ☎ *340/772–4079* ⊕ *www.chantvi.org.*

HORSEBACK RIDING

Paul and Jill's Equestrian Stables. From Sprat Hall, just north of Frederiksted, co-owner Jill Hurd will take you through the rain forest, across the pastures, along the beaches, and through valleys—explaining the flora, fauna, and ruins on the way. A 1½-hour ride costs $100. ⊠ *Rte. 58, Frederiksted* ☎ *340/772–2880, 340/772–2627* ⊕ *www.paulandjills.com.*

KAYAKING

Caribbean Adventure Tours. These kayak tours take you on trips through Salt River Bay National Historical Park and Ecological Preserve, one of the island's most pristine areas. All tours run $45. ⊠ *Salt River Marina, Rte. 80, Salt River* ☎ *340/778–1522* ⊕ *www.stcroixkayak.com.*

Virgin Kayak Tours. Virgin runs guided kayak trips on the Salt River and rents kayaks so you can tour around the Cane Bay area by yourself. Tours start at $50, and kayak rentals are $40 for the entire day. ⊠ *Rte. 80, Cane Bay* ☎ *340/778–0071* ⊕ *www.virginkayaktours.com.*

WATER SPORTS

St. Croix Watersports. St. Croix Watersports rents WaveRunners, standup paddleboards, kayaks, windsurfers, and snorkel gear. The half-hour guided WaveRunner tour allows you to zip around Christiansted's harbor in style for $60. ⊠ *Hotel on Cay, Protestant Cay, Christiansted* ☎ *340/773–7060* ⊕ *www.stcroixwatersports.com.*

INDEX

PHOTO CREDITS

Front cover: Lorne Resnick/The Image Bank/Getty Images [Description: Jumby Bay, Antigua]. Back cover (from left to right): BlueOrange Studio/Shutterstock; Blacqbook/Shutterstock; Raffles Hotels and Resorts. Spine: Natchapon L./Shutterstock. 1, Timothy O'Keefe / age fotostock. 2, Alvaro Leiva / age footstock. 5,Carlos Villoch-MagicSea.com / Alamy. Chapter 1 Experience the Caribbean: 10–11, Christian Goupi / age fotostock. 20, Peter Phipp/Peter Phipp/age fotostock. 21 (left), Philip Coblentz/ Medioimages. 21 (right), TIDCO. 26 and 27 (right), Fabrice RAMBERT/Hostal Nicolas de Ovando. 27 (left), Tatiana Popova/Shutterstock. 28 (left), John A. Anderson/iStockphoto. 28 (top center), John A. Anderson/iStockphoto. 28 (bottom center), Michael DeFreitas / age fotostock. 28 (top right), Durden-Images/ iStockphoto. 28 (bottom right), MeegsC/wikipedia.org. 29 (top left), The Dominican Republic Ministry of Tourism. 29 (bottom left), St Vincent & The Grenadines Tourist Office. 29 (center), Alvaro Leiva / age fotostock. 29 (right), Franz Marc Frei / age fotostock. 30, Grenada Board of Tourism. 31 (left and right), Casa de Campo. 32, St. Maarten Tourist Bureau. 33 (left), Denis Jr. Tangney/iStock-photo. 33 (right), Dominican Republic Ministry of Tourism. 34, Ramona Settle. 35, Jim Lopes/Shutterstock. 36, Olga Bogatyrenko/Shutterstock. 37, Christian Wheatley/Shutterstock. 40, Aruba Tourism Authority. 41 (left), Brenda S and R Duncan Kirby. 41 (right), Coral World Ocean Park, St. Thomas. 42, Heeb Christian / age fotostock. 43 (top), Nico Tondini / age fotostock. 43 (bottom left and right), Dom/Shutterstock. 44 (top), Kobako/wikipedia.org. 44 (bottom), Rohit Seth/Shutterstock. 45 (top left), Karen Wunderman/Shutterstock. 45 (center left), Mulling it Over/Flickr. 45 (top right), Midori/wikipedia.org. 45 (center right), stu_spivack/Flickr. 45 (bottom), PL.Viel / age fotostock. 46 (top left), Arkady/ Shutterstock. 46 (bottom left), Mlvalentin/wikipedia.org. 46 (top right), ahnhuynh/Shutterstock. 46 (bottom right), Sakurai Midori/wikipedia.org. 47 (top left), HLPhoto/Shutterstock. 47 (bottom left), Elena Elisseeva/Shutterstock. 47 (bottom right), Only Fabrizio/Shutterstock. 47 (top right), cck/Flickr. 48 (left), Ingolf Pompe / age fotostock. 48, (left center) yosoynuts/Flickr. 48 (right center), Charles Tobias. 48 (right), Knut.C/wikipedia.org. 49 (left), cogdogblog/Flickr. 49 (left center), NorthJoe/Flickr. 49 (top right), Robert S. Donovan/Flickr. 49 (right center), Granstrom/wikipedia.org. 49 (bottom right), pocketwiley/Flickr. 50, Gavin Hellier / age fotostock. Chapter 2 Anguilla: 51, Chris Caldicott / age fotostock. 52 (bottom), aturkus/Flickr. 52 (top), Philip Coblentz/Digital Vision. 54, Ku. 57, Rick Strange / age fotostock. 66, Straw Hat. 71, The Leading Hotels of the World. 73, Viceroy Hotel Group. Chapter 3 Antigua and Barbuda: 79, Philip Coblentz/Medioimages. 80 (top and bottom), Philip Coblentz/Digital Vision. 81, Philip Coblentz/Digital Vision. 82, Geoff Howes/Antigua & Barbuda Tourist Office. 84, Alvaro Leiva / age fotostock. 89, Steve Geer/iStockphoto. 99, nik wheeler / Alamy. Chapter 4 Aruba: 113, Aruba Tourism Authority. 114 (bottom), Philip Coblentz/Medioimages. 114 (top), Aruba Tourism Authority. 116, Famke Backx/iStockphoto. 135, Amsterdam Manor Beach Resort Aruba. 145, Aruba Tourism Authority. Chapter 5 Barbados: 149, John Miller / age fotostock.150, Doug Scott/age fotostock. 152, Barbados Tourism Authority/Andrew Hulsmeier. 161, Walter Bibikow / age fotostock. 165, St. Nicholas Abbey. 181, Fairmont Hotels & Resorts. 183, Coral Reef Club. 185, Roy Riley / Alamy. 191, Christian Goupi / age fotostock. 194 (left), Jose Gil/iStockphoto. 194 (right), Conway Bowman. 195, Nataliya Hora/Shutterstock. Chapter 6 Bonaire: 199, Philip Coblentz/Medioimages. 200 (top), Tourism Corporation Bonaire. 200 (bottom), Suzi Swygert for the Bonaire Tourist Office. 201, Harry Thomas/istock. 202, Harbour Village Beach Club. 215, Harbour Village Beach Club. 221, Kees Opstal/ istockphoto. Chapter 7 British Virgin Islands: 225, Alvaro Leiva / age fotostock. 226 (bottom), Joel Blit/ Shutterstock. 226 (top), lidian neeleman/iStockphoto. 228, Ramunas Bruzas/Shutterstock. 237, Walter Bibikow / age fotostock. 247, Charles Krallman/Surfsong Villa Resort. 251, Alvaro Leiva / age fotostock. 253, Eric Sanford / age fotostock. 254 (top), Randy Lincks / Alamy. 254 (bottom), iStockphoto. 255 (top), Doug Scott / age fotostock. 255 (bottom), Slavoljub Pantelic/iStockphoto. 256, Doug Scott / age fotostock. 258, Giovanni Rinaldi/iStockphoto. 259, Walter Bibikow / age fotostock. 263, FB-Fischer/imagebroker.net/photolibrary.com. 272, Bitter End Yacht Club International, LLC. 275, Andre Jenny / Alamy. 280, Paul Zizka/Shutterstock. Chapter 8 Cayman Islands: 283, Peter Heiss/iStockphoto. 284 (top and bottom), Cayman Islands Department of Tourism. 285, Kevin Panizza/istockphoto. 286, Cayman Islands Department of Tourism. 291, Cayman Islands Department of Tourism. 313, Don McDougall/Cayman Islands Department of Tourism. 324, Corbis. 331, DurdenImages/iStockphoto. Chapter 9 Curaçao: 343, Philip Coblentz/Digital Vision. 344 (bottom), Fotoconcept Inc./ age fotostock. 344 (top), Curaçao Tourism. 346, Curaçao Tourism. 349, Walter Bibikow / age fotostock. 355, Curacao Tourist Board. 358, Walter Bibikow / age fotostock. Chapter 10 Dominica: 375, Xavier Font/age fotostock. 376, Dominica Tourist Office. 377 (top), John Anderson/istockphoto. 377 (bottom), Dominica Tourist Office. 378, Buddy Mays / Alamy. 379 (left), John Gabriel Stedman/wikipedia.org. 379 (right), J.E. (Julius Eduard) Muller/Tropenmuseum (Creative Commons Attribution-Share Alike 3.0

NOTES